PHILOSOPHY
OF LAW

PHILOSOPHY OF LAW

FIFTH EDITION

Edited by

Joel Feinberg

and

Hyman Gross

Wadsworth Publishing Company

I T P™ An International Thomson Publishing Company

Belmont • Albany • Bonn • Boston • Cincinnati • Detroit • London • Madrid • Melbourne
Mexico City • New York • Paris • San Francisco • Singapore • Tokyo • Toronto • Washington

Philosophy Editor: Tammy Goldfeld
Editorial Assistant: Kelly Zavislak
Production Editor: Robin Lockwood
Designer: Merle Sanderson
Print Buyer: Karen Hunt
Permissions Editor: Bob Kauser
Copy Editor: Toni Murray
Cover: Paula Goldstein
Compositor: Thompson Type
Printer: R. R. Donnelley & Sons

Printed in the United States of America

For more information, contact:

Wadsworth Publishing Company
10 Davis Drive
Belmont, California 94002

International Thomson Publishing
Berkshire House 168-173
High Holborn
London, WC1V7AA
England

Thomas Nelson Australia
102 Dodds Street
South Melbourne 3205
Victoria, Australia

Nelson Canada
1120 Birchmount Road
Scarborough, Ontario
Canada M1K 5G4

International Thomson Publishing GmbH
Königwinterer Strasse 418
53227 Bonn
Germany

International Thomson Publishing Asia
221 Henderson Road #05-10
Singapore 0315

International Thomson Publishing–Japan
Hirakawacho-cho Kyowa Building, 3F
2-2-1 Hirakawacho-cho
Chiyoda-ku, 102 Tokyo
Japan

1 2 3 4 5 6 7 8 9 10—01 00 99 98 97 96 95

Library of Congress Cataloging-in-Publication Data

Philosophy of law / edited by Joel Feinberg and Hyman Gross.—5th ed.
    p.   cm.
    Includes bibliographical references.
    ISBN 0-534-23988-9
    1. Law—Philosophy. 2. Law and ethics. 3. Law—United States.
I. Feinberg, Joel, 1926–   . II. Gross, Hyman.
K231.P47   1995
340'.1—dc20   94-13770
                                                        CIP

CONTENTS

PREFACE

There is currently a widespread and truly philosophical perplexity about law. That perplexity is occasioned by the events of the day and the legal proceedings to which they give rise. Increasing numbers of students have been attracted to courses in philosophy of law and social philosophy offered by philosophy departments, and law students, constantly challenged by the theoretical dimensions of law school subjects, are prompted more than ever to enroll in jurisprudence courses. These students often are disappointed by what seems to them an excessively abstract approach. Portentous terms such as *law, morality,* and *justice* are manipulated like counters in an uncertain game, and hoary figures from the past are marched by, each with a distinctive dogmatic pronouncement and curious technical vocabulary. No wonder traditional jurisprudence often seems among the driest and most remote of academic subjects.

We have tried in this volume to relate the traditional themes of legal philosophy to the live concerns of modern society in a way that invigorates one and illuminates the other. The volume begins with essays by classic and contemporary figures on the essential nature of law and on the relation of law to morality or other sources of principle outside the legal system. No attempt is made to give contending doctrines equal time or even to give them all a day in court. We have passed over much excellent material that might have been included, though this is sure to cause some displeasure in an area of jurisprudential concern that is so marked by

doctrinal partisanship. Our endeavor is not to represent all important points of view, nor to represent any in a truly comprehensive way, but instead to offer a series of selections that raise sharply the most important issues. Many of these philosophical issues debated in the first part recur later in the book, where authors take up specific problems about liberty, justice, responsibility, and punishment.

This fifth edition is the most thorough revision to date. Of a total of eighty-eight selections, over half are new. Some of the new selections are in wholly new subsections devoted to topics and problems not covered before except, at most, in single articles.

The new subsections include one devoted entirely to the updating and clarifying of traditional natural law theory and its problems, including two new and little-known articles by well-known scholars (Norman Kretzmann and Anthony D'Amato) and one by one of the editors (Joel Feinberg), written specifically for this edition. (To prevent confusion about chronology, that essay is placed at the end of the subsection devoted to the debate between natural law theory and legal positivism.) Another altogether new heading occurs in Part Two, after a long sequence of United States Supreme Court opinions in famous (though recent) First Amendment cases. Fittingly, the new subsection has the title Principles of Constitutional Interpretation.

In Part Three is another new heading that introduces a topic that was conspicuously absent from previous editions; the heading is Legal Injustices to Women. This entirely new division contains seven articles dealing with some of the vexatious problems raised by rape law; the nature and relevance of consent, reasonable but false beliefs about the existence of consent, and sincere but unreasonable beliefs about consent; battered women and their rights; the "battered woman syndrome" as a defense to homicide and the relation of the syndrome to the traditional self-defense justification; sexual harassment; and even the sort of gender discrimination that could work unfairly against males (for example, some statutory rape laws). Part Three also presents a subsection about justice in contract law. That section contains three new articles directly or indirectly about surrogate motherhood, another issue of very special, though not exclusive, interest to women.

The new subsection in Part Four, Responsibility for Results, merges two topics treated separately in earlier editions: legal causation; negligence; and the moral significance, if there truly is any, of *results* in the moral appraisal of actors and their acts, particularly when the sole difference between two similar criminal acts is one determined by external causal factors over which neither actor had any control. These questions then lead in a very natural way to consideration of the role of good or bad luck both in criminal and tort law.

The fifth new subsection, Victims' Rights: Restitution or Vengeance? is found in Part Five. The articles in this subsection discuss closely related questions about punishment. The victims' rights movement has now attracted a considerable following in the United States, creating a new interest both in restitution as a kind of replacement for punishment and in vengeance as a legitimate response to cruel lawbreaking.

The new selections consist of a balance between articles about current practical problems and controversies and theoretical articles. Among the contemporary issues discussed are the obligations of judges interpreting "immoral" laws, the grounds for the criminalization of bigamy, flag desecration and political speech, hate speech, the rights of homosexuals, the relevance of "original meaning" of the founding fathers for the contemporary interpretation of constitutional hard cases, jury nullification, criminal entrapment as a defense, surrogate motherhood, date and/or acquaintance rape, rules for understanding "consent" in rape law, the battered woman defense, sexual harassment, mistake as to fact, the necessity defense, the impossibility defense to charges of attempted crime, the so-called psychopathic personality disorder, diminished responsibility, moral judgment and emotion, restitution of victims as a new major aim of criminal law (rather than punishment), the distinction between desert and vengeance, the moral status of vengeance, the Supreme Court's use of victim impact statements, and the morality of punishing criminals by putting them to death.

We have benefited from the advice of many professors who used some or all of the earlier editions of this book. We especially wish to thank those who agreed to write formal reviews: Jerome Balmuth, Colgate University; Kenneth Baynes, SUNY—Stony Brook; Susan J. Brison, Dartmouth College; Douglas Husak, Rutgers University; William C. Starr, Marquette University; Burleigh T. Wilkins, UC Santa Barbara.

Finally, Hyman Gross wishes to thank Joel Feinberg for assuming the full burden of choosing the readings for this fifth edition and for discharging all the other editorial responsibilities involved in its preparation. Professor Feinberg acknowledges in turn the many solid and important selections contributed by Hyman Gross to the first four editions, most of which remain in this edition. Professor Feinberg looks forward to Professor Gross's collaboration in the preparation of future editions.

We appreciate also the extremely helpful work of research assistants Michele Svatos, Linda Radzik, and Christi Favor, who gathered candidate materials for us and typed, photocopied, and prepared the manuscript.

Joel Feinberg
Hyman Gross

PART ONE

Law

The question "What is law?" seems at first glance hardly to deserve a philosopher's attention. Ask a lawyer about the law: if he or she is unable to give an answer on the spot, such a professional knows where to look it up, or at least where to get the ingredients for a reliable opinion. Statutes, judicial opinions, administrative regulations, constitutional provisions are all official pronouncements of law. When these texts leave the matter ambiguous, a lawyer knows the appropriate techniques to resolve the ambiguity, and in aid of that consults scholarly works of interpretation and other sources of authoritative opinion. The question "What is law?" then seems simply a request for a general definition that covers all those, and only those, items of official pronouncement that lawyers finally treat as law. It is true that even the best dictionary may leave us unsatisfied, for something more informative than a mere guide for word use is wanted. Still, at first sight nothing in the question appears to need the fine grinding of the philosopher's mill, and we conclude that we are adequately acquainted with the notion of something as familiar as law, with only the details remaining to be filled in.

Our simple belief is shattered not only by philosophical reflection, but also by the common experience of those who use and are subject to the law. The late Professor H.L.A. Hart, whose work has dominated Anglo-American legal philosophy, has described this illusion of understanding with these words:[1]

> The same predicament was expressed by some famous words of St. Augustine about the notion of time. "What then is time? If no one asks me I know: if I wish to explain it to one that asks I know not." It is in this way that even skilled lawyers have felt that, though they know

> the law, there is much about law and its relations to other things that they cannot explain and do not fully understand. Like a person who can get from one point to another in a familiar town but cannot explain or show others how to do it, those who press for a definition need a map exhibiting clearly the relationships dimly felt to exist between the law they know and other things.

The articles in Part One present important theories about the nature of law. The articles are arranged in four sections:

Natural Law Theory
Legal Positivism's Challenge to Natural Law Theory
The Moral Obligation to Obey the Law
Other Leading Theories of the Nature of Law

This introduction to Part One will acquaint you with the subject matter of each section and, in many cases, discuss how particular articles have influenced the theory and practice of law.

Natural Law Theory

Any philosopher who constructs a theory about the nature of law is likely to express that theory in the form of a definition of the word *law* or, when that definition seems ambiguous, a definition of each important sense. In the long history of this subject there have been two main types of definition. The first, chronologically speaking, goes with the natural law theory that prevailed from the time of the ancient Stoic philosophers and Roman lawyers, through the age of the medieval schoolmen, to the seventeenth- and

eighteenth-century revolutionaries. The formal definition of *law* proposed by St. Thomas Aquinas in the
thirteenth century is typical of definitions of this class:
"Law is, by its very nature, an ordinance of reason for
the promotion of the common good (Law's function,
what it is *for*) promulgated by him (or those) who has
(have) the care of the community, either by the whole
people acting collectively or by an agent of the whole
people, some one or some group delegated to act in
their name." The second type of definition is that associated with the theory called legal positivism, of
which John Austin's definition in the nineteenth century is typical:

> *A valid law [that is, one that exists and is in
> effect in a given legal jurisdiction] is a* com-
> mand, *that is (1) an expression of a general
> desire that others act or forbear in certain
> ways (2) together with a threat of evil for non-
> compliance (a sanction), (3) together with the
> power to enforce compliance, (4) emanating
> from a person (or group of persons) who alone
> is (or are) habitually obeyed by the bulk of the
> society and who habitually obey no one else
> (that person or persons is the* sovereign *in that
> society).*

There are several important differences between these classes of definitions: The natural law
definitions are *normative*. They do not attempt to
eliminate such terms as *rational, common good,* and
properly possessing authority. Instead they employ
these terms, using their own standards of application.
The positivists, on the other hand, think of themselves
as more "scientific." They are sympathetic to efforts to
eliminate normative terms by defining them in turn in
non-normative terms. The positivists' key terms are
words like *command, threat, power, habit,* and *obedience,* which they regard as empirical notions capable of empirical apprehension, confirmation, and
even measurement. The positivists' account of law is
intended to be entirely neutral in respect to moral-
political controversies. The natural law theory denies
that a conceptual analysis of law *can* be neutral, since
some minimal principles, at least, of morality and justice are built in to the very concept of law. Moreover,
the natural law theorists' definition is avowedly of the
kind called functional or teleological. Like definitions
of organs that function within larger organisms; and
component parts of machines; and tools and instruments, jobs and professions, so-called functional
terms must be defined by reference to their *telos:* what

they are *for*. Legal positivists, on the other hand,
would prefer to define *law* in terms that describe its
actual functioning and structure. They will insist that
as "analytic jurisprudents," they are more interested in
what law *is* than in what law *ought to be*. Positivists
reject the natural law theorists' claim that reference to
morality (or to that part of morality called justice) is an
essential part of any account of what law *is*. But positivists insist that their theory does not preclude them
from advocating changes in an existing legal code that
will make it more like what it ought to be—more just,
reasonable, and humane—or from evaluating existing
laws and systems as good or bad, better or worse, fair
or unfair, etc.

Legal positivists, moreover, are likely to distinguish two senses of morality: (1) the conventional morality of a given community at some particular time
and place (there are better and worse moralities in this
sense, and some moralities that are actually immoral!)
and (2) rational, critical, or "true" morality, which can
be used as a standard for judging conventional moralities. The most important of the questions that divide
the schools of natural law and legal positivism is the
following: "Is reference to critical, rational, or true morality—as opposed to merely conventional morality—
an essential part of any adequate account of what
law is?"

Legal positivism answers this question categorically and negatively. It holds that law is one thing and
morality another, and that neither can be reduced to
the other. Positivists happily concede that it is a good
idea for law to conform to morality—that is, to be fair
and humane—but an unfair rule is still a valid law
provided only that it is made in accordance with the
accepted lawmaking rules of an existing legal system.
As the positivist H.L.A. Hart was wont to say, there
is a content-neutral test for determining (a) whether
a legal system exists in a given community and
(b) whether a given rule is a valid law within that
system. The validity of a particular rule is determined
by its *pedigree* (how it was made), not by its *content*
(what it says).

Natural law theorists, as we have already seen,
give an affirmative answer to our question. Morality
is not simply a desirable feature to import into law,
but rather an essential part of law as it really is. No
adequate test of the validity of a legal rule, or the existence of a legal system, could possibly be content-
neutral, since it is usually the content of a rule that
determines whether it is fair or unfair, reasonable or
unreasonable. That is, simply to pronounce the obvi-

ous truth of whether or not a given rule is (say) *fair,* depends at least in part on what sort of conduct it requires, permits, or prohibits, or in other words on its *content*.

St. Thomas Aquinas—like Plato, Aristotle, Cicero, and Augustine before him—formulated the doctrine in the language of a famous slogan of the natural law school: *Lex iniusta non est lex.* In the first article in this section of Part One, Norman Kretzmann, the Cornell scholar in the area of medieval and Renaissance philosophy, examines both Aquinas's arguments and his motives for endorsing that doctrine. As a result, Kretzmann comes up with some surprising conjectures concerning the dispensability of the classic slogan, and a critical theory explaining Aquinas's apparent reluctance to embrace it. Two other articles are meant to enable the student to appreciate the attractiveness of the natural law theory and the sources of the traditional dissatisfaction with it among the American judiciary. Anthony D'Amato, of the Northwestern University College of Law, invents an ingenious fictional tale of an "unjust law" in the course of his effort to persuade us that justice is indeed a part of the very structure of law, as the old natural law theorists claimed all along. Joel Feinberg, in "The Dilemmas of Judges Who Must Interpret 'Immoral Laws'," considers the consequences of the positivism–natural law debate for conflicts in the political arena. He uses, as his chief example, the conflict among American abolitionist judges over the Fugitive Slave Acts of 1793 and 1850—unjust enactments if ever there were any. (This article is placed after the Hart–Fuller debate, in the second section of Part One, because it contains some discussion of Hart and Fuller—discussion that would be confusing to the reader who had not yet read those writers' materials.)

Legal Positivism's Challenge to Natural Law Theory

John Austin's *The Province of Jurisprudence Determined* was published in England in 1832, and it has long been regarded in the Anglo-American tradition as the leading work in opposition to natural law theory. It is an exceedingly careful work of great range and refinement. The portions reprinted here set forth only the essentials of Austin's views about the nature of law. His theory has been one of the first to be stud-

ied by English-speaking students for over a century and a half now, so it is no wonder that it has called forth more abundant criticism than any other.

A consensus has formed over the difficulties encountered by Austin's sort of positivism, the most authoritative statement of which is that of the leading twentieth-century positivist, H.L.A. Hart, in his seminal work, *The Concept of Law,* published in 1961. In our selection from that work, Hart analyzes the concept of a legal system as a union of two kinds of rules. The first, like an ordinary criminal statute, prohibits, requires, or permits specific kinds of conduct. The second type of rule confers powers on persons to create, to revise, or to terminate specific legal relationships (for example, creditor-debtor, husband-wife, seller-buyer). The full statement of a power-conferring rule will function in a way similar to that of a recipe: The rule is a set of directions for changing our legal status in some respects, and doing so voluntarily. Such rules tell us how to get married, how to get divorced, how to make out a will, etc. Of prime interest among these secondary rules, as Hart calls them, are the rules telling us how to make, revise, or revoke primary rules. Late in the selection, Hart addresses the concept of legal validity and develops a much more subtle account than Austin's of a "rule of recognition" that enables judges to distinguish legitimate from spurious claims of legality, and to do so in a "content-neutral" way.

Various kinds of controversy are possible over the truth of theories about the nature and validity of law, but most of them are of the kind we have already anticipated: They regard the relationship between two sets of norms for regulating conduct, law, and morality. Those who are spoken of as positivists tend to view a legal system as having its *own* criteria for valid laws, and so tend to regard moral judgments about laws as important in deciding what the law should be (a question for legislators and voters), yet not relevant in deciding what the law is. Hart's famous Holmes Lecture at the Harvard Law School, "Positivism and the Separation of Law and Morals," was published in the *Harvard Law Review* about three years before Hart's book. We publish it here for the new light it shed at the time on its subject, and partly because a reply to it was published in the next issue of the *Harvard Law Review* by America's most distinguished legal philosopher at the time, Lon L. Fuller, of Harvard. (Hart spent almost thirty years as Professor of Jurisprudence at Oxford.) In "Positivism and Fidelity to Law," Fuller found much to admire in Hart's lecture, but as a kind of natural law theorist himself, he was in basic disagreement with Hart's position. Fuller's natural law theory was as imaginative and original a departure from the more traditional natural law theories as Hart's theory was from the earlier forms of positivism. The debate between these towering figures was a great event in the history of legal philosophy in the twentieth century.

Among the more interesting of Fuller's innovations were his effort to construct a natural law theory without a theological foundation and his argument that morality provides criteria for the (continued) existence of a whole system of rules, not criteria for the validity of a single rule or statute. It is possible then, according to Fuller, for an unjust law to be a valid law, but if the whole network of rules and rule-making powers, or a substantial subsection thereof, is antithetical to morality (as in Nazi Germany, where a genuine legal system was corrupted and undermined), then it is no longer a functioning legal system but, at best, another method of social control—one based on arbitrary power.

Another innovation in Fuller's theory was his novel insistence that the morality that is essential to law is what he called "the internal morality of law" or "the morality that makes law possible," not the more usual prohibition of immoral *content* in rules. The internal morality of law is summed up in a handful of procedural rules requiring promulgation and understandability, and invalidating retroactivity, contradiction, and constant change. He discusses eight of these "ways" in "Eight Ways to Fail to Make Law," a chapter of his book *The Morality of Law*. That chapter is reprinted here.

The Moral Obligation to Obey the Law

Most positivists agree with their natural law rivals that citizens in a democracy have a *moral* obligation—parallel to their moral obligations to keep promises, tell the truth, oppose injustice, and so on—to obey the valid laws of their country. (But see Feinberg's essay on civil disobedience for a dissenting opinion.) One might similarly affirm that any individual judge in a functioning democracy whose institutions are more or less just, has a moral obligation of fidelity to the law that the judge is sworn to apply impartially to others.

Each standard theory then must give some account of the basis for this moral obligation (if there is one), and some explanation of how it can fail to apply—as when, for example, *disobedience* (or judicial nullification) is morally justified.

There are two articles in this section of Part One. The powerfully eloquent "Letter from Birmingham Jail," by Martin Luther King, Jr., is a classic in the history of political action and theory, philosophy, and legal theory. King justifies his resistance even to "legal" racial segregation, by appealing to a "higher law" version of natural law theory. His description of deliberately disobedient acts against a background of general respect for law (otherwise), must have had considerable influence on John Rawls, inspiring him to write in his *A Theory of Justice,* the clearest and most complete account in the literature of the distinction between civil disobedience and other forms of deliberate infringement of law. King is the model civil disobedient.

Finally this section presents "Civil Disobedience in the Modern World." In it, Joel Feinberg denies one of the presuppositions common to natural law theory and legal positivism alike in their approaches to the problem of disobedience—namely, that there is some moral obligation in a democracy to obey the law of the land even when a powerful case can be made for the injustice of the content of the law.

Other Leading Theories of the Nature of Law

With the retirement of Professor Hart, the person who has had the greatest impact on the philosophy of law in our time is probably Hart's successor at University College, Oxford: Ronald Dworkin, an American. (Dworkin has also been a regular faculty member for many years at the college of Law of New York University.) Even when legal positivism was riding high at Oxford, partly because of Hart's influence, Dworkin was publishing articles meant to expose its defects. In "The Model of Rules," reprinted here, he argues that there is much more to a system of law than mere rules, even when primary rules are supplemented by secondary ones. Any full-fledged system of law will also contain what Dworkin calls principles, a miscellany that includes in its precise and narrow sense such moral precepts as "No man may profit by his own wrong." The latter principle was a part of the law, Dworkin argues, that was violated when a trial court permitted Elmer Palmer to inherit money from the will of Elmer's grandfather, even though Elmer had been convicted of murdering the testator (before he could change his mind). Needless to say, the will was invalidated through a civil suit brought by two daughters of the testator, even though no rule (in Hart's sense) seemed to be violated. Even the dissenting opinion in this case seemed to invoke a Dworkinian principle—namely, that courts have no warrant, in the absence of explicit legislative authorization, to "add to the respondent's penalties by depriving him of property." The formerly obscure case of *Riggs* v. *Palmer,* since Dworkin's article, has become quite famous. *Riggs* v. *Palmer* is summarized in an article in this section.

The other selection from Dworkin, "'Natural' Law Revisited," develops in outline Dworkin's full theory of the nature of law and answers, among other questions, a query about its relation to traditional natural law theory. His answer to the latter question is brief and simple enough to quote: If a natural law theory is "any theory which makes the content of law sometimes depend on the correct answer to some moral question, then I am guilty of natural law. . . . Suppose this is natural law. What in the world is wrong with it?" There follows, in this useful summary of Professor Dworkin's work, a recommendation, to judges, of a way to decide so-called hard cases, those occasions for judgment in which the usual resources of a judge—statutes, precedents, and so on—are insufficient to dictate a decision one way or another. What Dworkin requires for a full justification of a decision in such circumstances is such a heavy burden of learning that no actual flesh-and-blood judge could possibly discharge it. So, for that reason, Dworkin invents a superhuman judge called Hercules to help illustrate what a full justification would be like. The rest of the theory is too complex to summarize further in this introduction. Suffice it only to point out how much more inclusive and subtle Dworkin's theory is than those of typical (pre-Hart) positivists (one must also exclude Hart's brilliant student Joseph Raz) and how much less vague than the typical natural law theorist at least before Fuller and, more recently, John Finnis (*Natural Law and Natural Rights,* 1980).

But if Dworkin's theory isn't exactly like traditional natural law and positivist theories, then J. L. Mackie was entirely justified in baptizing it "the third theory of law," giving it its own precise set of defining arguments, and then formulating his own distinctive

polemical arguments to match them. In philosophy, the more original a given set of arguments are, the more original an inevitable set of counterarguments are likely to be. In "The Third Theory of Law," Mackie effectively voices his doubts that Herculean judicial labor would produce the decision that Dworkin would prefer at least in one class of cases, the Fugitive Slave Acts cases discussed by Feinberg in his earlier essay in Part One. Mackie also concludes his discussions with some important observations about the likely effects of Dworkin's theory if it were adopted explicitly as a guide to adjudication in hard cases.

A disproportionate number of the contributors to Part One of this collection are British. But Americans too have made important contributions to the philosophy of law. No single essay in Anglo-American jurisprudence has received more attention than Oliver Wendell Holmes's "The Path of the Law," first published in 1897. His famous declaration that "The prophecies of what the courts will do in fact, and nothing more pretentious, are what I mean by the law" became the cornerstone of legal realism in America. How such prophecies are best made is a matter that occupies much of Holmes's attention in the selection that is included here.

The brief selection that follows next is from the writings of another distinguished American judge, Jerome Frank. Here one sees how the law appears to those who wish to use it and not simply make it the subject of a body of theory. A legal saga unfolds as the affairs of the Joneses and the Williamses are put in the hands of their lawyers, and the conception of law that emerges gives weight to Holmes's opening remark: "When we study law we are not studying a mystery but a well known profession." Read together, these two selections concentrate our minds on the question that perhaps must precede all others in this branch of the philosophy of law: "What, exactly, is its proper subject matter?"

Andrew Altman's "Legal Realism, Critical Legal Studies, and Dworkin" represents a far more radical critique of Dworkin's position, and indeed is a critique of the entire mainstream of Anglo-American jurisprudence. The movement known as critical legal studies (CLS), for which Altman is here both spokesman and critic, does not share the assumption that judges are free to decide cases according to one or another theory of judicial decision. Judges are inevitably under the influence of ideological forces, though certainly they do not see themselves as acting under such constraints. Legal realism (some of whose themes appear in this volume in the selections from Holmes and Frank) serves in part as a foundation for CLS, particularly the realist account of the random processes and the personal factors that can generate and resolve legal disputes. CLS goes beyond these skeptical observations, and views legal issues as implicating ideological conflicts that even Dworkin's Judge Hercules could not resolve in a neutral way.

---

1 *H.L.A. Hart,* The Concept of Law *(Oxford University Press, 1961),* pp. 13–14.

Natural Law Theory

LEX INIUSTA NON EST LEX:
Laws on Trial in Aquinas' Court of Conscience

Norman Kretzmann

1. Introduction

The laws of a state are understandably described as the state's system of justice, but there is nothing unusual about a citizen's deciding that some law of the state is unjust. As Hart puts it, "We think and talk of 'justice *according to* law' and yet also of the justice or injustice *of* laws."[1] Of course people disagree over their individual assessments of laws as just or unjust, at least in part because they are applying different moral standards. But disagreement among individuals over the moral assessment of laws is something I want to ignore in order to focus on the underlying disagreement between a moral system and a legal system; so I'm going to proceed on the basis of a single set of moral standards. And since I'm primarily concerned with Aquinas' treatment of disagreements between morality and law, I'll adopt his moral system for purposes of this investigation.

From Aquinas' point of view, morality has an essential connection with Christian theology, and civil legislation is a prerogative of the state. For those reasons, in the questions with which I'll begin this investigation the individual citizen could be thought of as a Christian, and the questions could be seen as raising issues of Church and State as well as of morality and law. But for purposes of this investigation Aquinas' theologically based moral and legal philosophy can be almost entirely secularized, as we'll see.

Is an individual citizen entitled or obliged to decide whether a law of the state is unjust? If so, on what grounds is he or she supposed to make the decision? And if an individual citizen has decided on appropriate grounds that a law of the state is unjust, what is he or she entitled or obliged to do about it?

2. The Dismissive Judgment Regarding Unjust Laws

Several familiar issues are apparent in those questions. There is bound to be controversy over an individual's right to take action against laws he or she considers unjust, or even to pass judgment on the laws of the state. But the issue I'm concerned with now is less apparent, obscured by its association with the undoubted fact that people are sometimes convinced that a law under which they live is unjust and are particularly angry that their system of justice itself should be flawed in that way.

*Kretzmann, Norman. "*Lex Iniusta Non Est Lex:*—Interpreting St. Thomas Aquinas ("Laws on Trial in Aquinas' Court of Conscience"), *The American Journal of Jurisprudence* (1988), pp. 99–122. Reprinted with permission from *The American Journal of Jurisprudence.*

This issue arises because people with such convictions sometimes express them in a radically negative judgment, dismissive of morally bad legislation. Plato provides what is probably the oldest instance of this dismissive judgment when he declares, in the *Laws,* that "enactments, so far as they are not for the common interest of the whole community, are *no true laws*" (IV 715B). In other words, laws that fail to fulfill a certain moral condition are not full-fledged laws even if they are on the books. (Plato says things like this elsewhere about laws—e.g., *Hippias major* 284D—and about constitutions—e.g., *Laws* IV 712E–713A and *Statesman* 293D–E—but the passage I've quoted is the clearest and most appropriate for my purposes.) Aristotle, too, expresses the dismissive judgment about certain forms of government or constitutions—e.g., in *Politics* IV 4, 1292a31–34: "it would seem to be a reasonable criticism to say that such a democracy is *not a constitution at all*"; and he links this judgment with an assessment of individual laws when he says that laws in conformity with perverted constitutions are necessarily unjust (III 6, 1282/b12–13). And Cicero, in his treatise on laws, provides what may be the fullest pre-Christian statement of the dismissive judgment: "those who formulated wicked and unjust statutes for nations, thereby breaking their promises and agreements, put into effect *anything but laws*. It may thus be clear that in the very definition of the term 'law' there inheres the idea and principle of choosing what is just and true."[2]

But for my purpose in this investigation of Aquinas' philosophy of law the only relevant instance of the dismissive judgment earlier than Aquinas' is Augustine's, the only one Aquinas explicitly cites (with approval). Augustine's famous expression of the dismissive judgment occurs in a speech of his own in his dialogue with Evodius on freedom of choice: "A soldier is even ordered by law to kill the enemy, and if he hangs back from the slaughter, he is punished by his commander. Shall we dare to say that those laws are unjust—or, rather, no laws at all? For *that which is not just does not seem to me to be a law"* ("*lex mihi esse non videtur, quae iusta non fuerit" De libero arbitrio* I v 11).[3] Aquinas, who did at least as much as anyone else to make this Augustinian passage famous, quotes only the last sentence of it and omits the words "to me."[4] Without the context and without those words Augustine's expression of the dismissive judgment sounds more general and more confident than it originally was, and it is Aquinas' stronger version of it that has attracted most critical attention in recent legal philosophy.

The immediate target of that attention is the form of words typically used to express the dismissive judgment, and the issue I'm concerned with has most often been generated around an expression of the judgment even less tentative than Aquinas' version of Augustine, in the slogan "An unjust law is not a law," quoted by British and American writers almost as often in Latin: "*Lex iniusta non est lex.*" I haven't seen this *non-est-lex* slogan in Augustine or Aquinas in just those words, and I don't know who coined it.[5] But the tradition of the controversy makes it convenient to adopt *non est lex* as the standard expression of the dismissive judgment regarding a law. Setting fine points aside temporarily, I think Plato, Aristotle, Cicero, Augustine, and Aquinas are among those who would apply *non est lex* to morally bad laws.[6] As for the issue that has grown up around the slogan, it can be effectively introduced as Hart presents it: "the assertion that 'an unjust law is not a law' has the same ring of exaggeration and paradox, if not falsity, as '*statutes* are not laws' or '*constitutional* law is not law'."[7]

3. *Non Est Lex:* The Slogan and the Issue

But there is something wrong with the way an issue has been generated around the *non-est-lex* slogan. Its form of words has been exploited, because the expression of the judgment (in Aquinas' predecessors, in the slogan, and to a great extent even in Aquinas himself) seems to be genuinely uncontroversial, no more than a familiar device for expressing emphatic rejection in cases of a sort I think I can pick out, at least roughly.

Many kinds of things have inclusion conditions that are entirely non-evaluative. For instance, it seems reasonable to suppose that no natural kinds have evaluative conditions among their standard inclusion conditions. There are also non-natural, conventional kinds whose inclusion conditions are entirely non-evaluative—e.g., iambic pentameter, or employee. On the other hand, some conventional kinds have evaluative as well as non-evaluative conditions of inclusion. Among these kinds some are overtly and invariably evaluative kinds—e.g., literary masterpiece, or child prodigy. But the cases important for my purposes are cases of conventional kinds that have both non-evaluative and evaluative inclusion conditions *without* being overtly and invariably evaluative kinds—e.g., sonnet, or archeologist. It is only in connection with such kinds, I think, that the dismissive judgment is appropriate. It might be expressed simply as "*That's* no sonnet," "*He's* no archeologist." But such sentences will express the dismissive judgment I'm concerned with only if they are applied to instances that *fulfill* the *non*-evaluative conditions for inclusion in those kinds, only if they can be backed up in such ways as these: "A banal sonnet is not really a sonnet, despite the fact that it has the prescribed meter, rhyme scheme, and number of lines"; "An imprecise archeologist is not really an archeologist, despite the fact that he is a professor of archeology and regularly publishes the results of his excavations." It would of course be absurd to infer that someone who says that an imprecise archeologist is not really an archeologist means to deny the possibility or even the existence of imprecise archeologists. One way of bringing out the absurdity is to notice that the same kind of emphatic rejection could have been expressed by saying that an imprecise archeologist is worse than no archeologist at all. The stereotypical rejection speech "You're no son of mine!" would lose its dramatic point if the furious father weren't sure the young man *was* indeed his son in all non-evaluative respects.[8]

Dismissive judgments of these familiar sorts are, I think, not even exaggerations, much less paradoxes. If I'm right in thinking that the conditions of being included in certain kinds involve implicit evaluative conditions, then a dismissive judgment applied to a technically certifiable instance of one of those kinds can and should be interpreted straightforwardly as emphatically denying that *x* is really *ϕ* just because *x* is *ϕ* only technically, just because *x* is not a *true, genuine, paradigmatic ϕ,* not *ϕ simpliciter,* in virtue of lacking one or more of the evaluative inclusion conditions that supplement the non-evaluative conditions. It seems that evaluative inclusion conditions may be associated primarily with kinds of things that have a recognized function of a sort that directly affects human beings, and that the dismissive judgment is likely to be expressed by someone who believes that the thing being dismissed does not perform that function.[9]

But whatever the explanation of these differences among kinds may turn out to be, I think that law is a kind just like sonnet and archeologist in the relevant respects, a kind that has both non-evaluative and evaluative inclusion conditions without being overtly and invariably an evaluative kind, a kind that has

a humanly important function, a kind in connection with which the dismissive judgment is therefore appropriate. And I think it is even clearer that the point of applying the dismissive judgment to a law is to provide moral people with a basis for disobeying that law in good conscience.

But philosophers confronting *non est lex* tend to react to it as if that dismissive judgment were the only one they'd ever encountered, and as if it gave rise to absurd conclusions such as no one would think of drawing from other dismissive judgments except facetiously. Arthur Danto, for instance, sets out to embarrass "the Thomistic defenders of natural law" over "their dictum 'there cannot be an unjust law'."[10] Since he identifies no other source for this alleged dictum, he is presumably taking the *non-est-lex* slogan to imply that there *cannot be* an unjust law. But of course it doesn't. In fact, as we've seen, the dismissive judgment presupposes that the dismissed instance technically *is* a thing of the kind in question.[11]

Hart, on the other hand, points to the *non-est-lex* slogan as evidence that "the Thomist tradition" is committed to "a *refusal,* made once and for all, to recognize evil laws as valid for *any* purpose. This is too crude a way with delicate and complex moral issues."[12] Although this inference of Hart's is less rash than Danto's, in allowing that the tradition can identify the objects of its dismissive judgment as evil *laws,* we will see that Hart's inference, too, is quite unjustified, at least as regards Aquinas himself.[13]

We can learn more about the generation of the *non-est-lex* issue around the *non-est-lex* slogan by looking at the way it is carried out by David Lyons. Lyons expresses himself more cautiously than either Danto or Hart does, beginning with what seems to me to be just the right line: "The idea that law and morality are *essentially* connected is expressed by the claim that 'an unjust law is no law at all.' This claim is associated with traditional ideas of 'natural law,' and . . . is suggested by Aquinas. The claim appears paradoxical, for it seems to say that something which *is* law (unjust law) is *not* law. But that is misleading. It may be like the claim that a counterfeit dollar is not a real dollar: an unjust law is so much a perversion of the idea of law that it cannot be counted as a law at all. That would dissolve the paradox." I think Lyons is right to reject the idea that there is anything paradoxical in the *non-est-lex* slogan. But his counterfeit dollar example gives him unnecessary trouble just because a counterfeit dollar is not a dollar in *any* respect, any more than a female impersonator is a female. It is a *counterfeit,* and *not* a perversion. Perverted instances of a kind—

such as plagiarized term papers, corrupt judges, or fair-weather friends—instances that satisfy the non-evaluative but not the evaluative inclusion conditions, will turn out to be more appropriate than counterfeit dollars as analogues to unjust laws as assessed by the *non-est-lex* slogan.

The unnecessary trouble Lyons' example leads him into appears in the continuation of the passage I'm quoting, where, having dismissed the notion that the slogan is *paradoxical,* he suggests that it must, nevertheless, be obviously *false:* "But can the claim be true? It seems difficult to deny that laws can intelligibly be judged good or bad, wise or foolish, just or unjust. If there *are* moral standards by which laws may properly be judged, then it would seem that laws can *be* good or bad, just or unjust. . . . Aquinas' apparent endorsement of this traditional natural law claim is itself misleading, since he agrees that laws framed by humans are either just or unjust."[14] It seems to me that when Lyons noticed that Aquinas does indeed recognize the existence of unjust laws, he ought to have considered that Aquinas' interpretation of the slogan must have been different from his, rather than inferring that Aquinas' endorsement of the slogan was misleading. But I think I'll be able to show how the *non-est-lex* slogan can after all be true, and that Aquinas' endorsement of it is not misleading when considered in more detail.

The way contemporary philosophers have generated the *non-est-lex* issue out of the *non-est-lex* slogan expresses the spirit of legal positivism, which can be traced back at least as far as the English jurist John Austin (1790–1859), who sums up its leading idea in these words: "The existence of law is one thing; its merit or demerit is another. Whether it be or be not is one enquiry; whether it be or be not conformable to an assumed standard, is a different enquiry."[15] Here is Austin's own diatribe against *non est lex* as he discerned it to Blackstone: "Now, to say that human laws which conflict with the divine law are not binding, that is to say, are *not laws,* is to talk *stark nonsense.* The most pernicious laws, and therefore those which are most opposed to the will of God, have been and are continually enforced as laws by judicial tribunals. Suppose an act innocuous, or positively beneficial, be prohibited by the sovereign under the penalty of death; if I commit this act, I shall be tried and condemned, and if I object to the sentence, that it is contrary to the law of God, who has commanded that human lawgivers shall not prohibit acts which have no evil consequences, the Court of Justice will demonstrate the inconclusiveness of my reasoning by

hanging me up, in pursuance of the law of which I have impugned the validity."[16] Like Danto in our time, Austin reads the *non-est-lex* slogan as if it entailed the absurd claim that unjust laws are never promulgated or enforced, and then takes himself to have refuted the slogan by pointing out in patronizing detail the undoubted fact that they sometimes are. Austin's attempted refutation of *non est lex* is as silly as it would be to try to contradict the dismissive judgment that a plagiarized term paper is not really a term paper by pointing out that plagiarized papers do get turned in as term papers and are sometimes accepted as term papers.

To call the claim that unjust laws are never promulgated or enforced absurd is of course not yet to show that Aquinas didn't make that claim or say things that imply it. But even in our necessarily brief investigation of Aquinas' treatment of the questions regarding a citizen's appraisal of the laws of the state we'll see that his philosophy of law is not guilty as charged. Correctly understood, the *non-est-lex* slogan is neither absurd nor even inflammatory, but commonsensical and useful. The fervor and frequency of the attacks on it by philosophers of law is explained to some extent by its association with the concepts of natural law or even of divine law, which are of course anathema to legal positivism and unfashionable to boot. We have seen some of the attackers suggesting such an association, and what they were suggesting certainly is at the heart of Aquinas' philosophy of law, to which we can now turn.

4. The Four Types of Law and the Interrelations

Everything Aquinas has to say about law rests on his classification of law into four types and his understanding of the relationships among those types.

Eternal law is the foundation of the other three types and can be thought of as God's plan, God's providence, God's intellect, or simply God himself conceived of as the ruler of the universe. The laws of physics as well as the principles of morality are completely included within the eternal law, which human beings know only very incompletely and often uncertainly. Absolutely every sort of rational law or principle derives more or less directly from the eternal law, whether or not it is recognized as having that source.[17]

Natural law occurs only in human beings, in the form of innate principles of rational action, and is explained as a (very limited) participation in the eternal law, appropriate for a rational creature since "it is itself a participant in providence, providing both for itself and for others."[18]

Human law, broadly speaking, is just what you'd expect it to be: the legislation devised by human beings for their organization and governance. To the extent to which human laws are rational, they depend on principles of natural law either as conclusions inferred from premises (as in legislation against murder) or as particular determinations of general principles of rational action (as in legislation regulating traffic).[19]

Divine law, the fourth and last of these basic types, consists in the moral and legal contents of Scripture, expressly revealed elements of the eternal law intended as aids to human life and as indispensable guides to what Aquinas sees as the ultimate, supernatural goal of human existence and action.[20]

My investigation from now on will be concerned almost exclusively with natural law and human law, especially human law. The role of eternal law in this scheme will not concern me much and can for present purposes be understood in terms of the universal applicability of general principles of rationality. Divine law will play only a very small part in the rest of this investigation.

5. Aquinas' Conception of Natural Law

It is human nature to which natural law is natural, and human nature, or rational animality, is a set of essential potentialities associated with inclinations to actualize those potentialities. We all recognize in ourselves inclinations that we have in common with other living things, as well as natural but distinctively human inclinations. Because we naturally have such inclinations, we naturally recognize the objects of those inclinations as good to get and as bad to be deprived of. The innate precepts of natural law can be thought of as more or less articulate injunctions corresponding to such natural recognitions. As such, they are the fundamental directives of human action, founded directly on the principles of practical reason.

Here is how Aquinas introduces the most fundamental of those principles and precepts: "The first thing that comes to the attention of the practical reason, which is oriented toward action, is what is good; for every agent acts for an end which has the nature

of a good. And so the first principle in practical reason is the one that is founded on the nature of the good: *The good is what all things seek.* Therefore, the first precept of law is this: *What is good is to be done and pursued; what is bad is to be avoided.* All the other precepts of natural law are founded on this, so that *all* the things that practical reason naturally recognizes as human goods pertain to precepts of natural law as things to be done (or to be avoided)."[21] And here is his account of the connection of the precepts with the inclinations, in which we can also see at least suggestions of some less general, secondary precepts: "The order of the precepts of natural law follows the order of natural inclinations. For in a human being there is, first of all, an inclination toward a natural good which he shares with all substances, insofar as every substance seeks the preservation of its being according to its own nature. In keeping with this inclination, conditions in which a human being's life is preserved and its contrary is prevented pertain to natural law. Second, there is in a human being an inclination toward certain more specific [goods], an inclination he shares with other animals. In this connection those things that nature has taught to all animals are said to belong to natural law, such as the mating of male and female and the raising of offspring. Third, there is in a human being an inclination to what is good according to the nature of reason, an inclination that is his alone—e.g., a person has a natural inclination to find out the truth about God, and to live in society. In this connection things that have to do with an inclination of that sort pertain to natural law—e.g., that a person avoid ignorance, that he not offend others with whom he has to live, and the like."[22] Our unhesitating recognition of the unjustness of the Nazis' laws regarding Jews or of nineteenth-century America's laws regarding blacks could, therefore, be explained in terms of our natural adherence to precepts of natural law innate in us.

Since we're heading toward a consideration of issues raised regarding a conscientious individual's assessment of his community's laws, and since Aquinas, like most of us, thinks of that assessment as carried out at least initially in an individual's conscience, it is important to note the essential connection between natural law and conscience in Aquinas' view: "Conscience is called the law of our intellect insofar as it is a dispositional state containing the precepts of natural law, which are the first principles of human actions."[23]

As principles of human action, the precepts of natural law are the fundamental moral rules. And since we've already noted that Aquinas takes human laws to depend on precepts of natural law, it may look more and more as if he must conceive of human laws as no more than derived moral rules. If he does conceive of them in that way, the *non-est-lex* issue will get a new lease on life, since an unjust moral rule is not merely a perversion, like an unjust law, but a counterfeit, a contradiction in terms. But Aquinas does *not* conceive of human laws as no more than moral rules, as can be seen from the following passage, in which he is discussing the relationship between natural and human law: "It is on the basis of the precepts of natural law, as from general and indemonstrable principles of a certain sort, that human reason must proceed to certain matters that must be dealt with in more detail. And those detailed dispositions, arrived at in accordance with human reason, are called human laws, *provided that the other conditions that pertain to the essence of law have been met.*"[24] Appropriate derivation from the precepts of natural law— i.e., the fundamental moral rules—is not by itself a sufficient condition for inclusion in human law; and so it is already apparent that Aquinas does not identify human laws with moral rules.

6. Definition and Evaluation in Aquinas' Treatise on Law

A philosopher who, like Aquinas, seriously invokes anything like *non est lex* in assessing a law must be basing his assessment on a putatively complete list of inclusion conditions for law. Aquinas develops such a list in his "Treatise on Law," which occupies Questions 90–108 of *Summa theologiae* IaIIae. The last part of the Treatise, Questions 98–108, deals specifically with divine law and has very little to contribute to the issues we are concerned with now. Definitional and evaluative passages occur together throughout Questions 90–97, but Questions 95–97 deal with human laws in general (q. 95), with the power of human laws (q. 96), and with their alterability (q. 97); and so the greatest concentration of evaluative claims occurs there. But by that stage of the Treatise, Aquinas has already conducted an investigation of law's essential characteristics, and so the most important definitional passages are naturally clustered in Questions 90 (the essence of law), 91 (the kinds of law), and 92 (the effects of law). (Questions 93 and 94 deal with the eternal law and the natural law, respectively.) Nowhere in the Treatise do we get a unified, complete list of inclusion conditions, however. We have to assemble such a list ourselves out of conditions Aquinas lists in various definitional passages or appeals to in evaluative passages.

7. Inclusion Conditions for Law

At the end of the Question on the essence of law, Aquinas announces that from the four articles of the Question we can put together "a definition of law: *Law is nothing other than an ordinance of reason directed toward the common good, promulgated by one who has responsibility for the community.*"[25] Near the beginning of the next Question, on the kinds of law, he invokes that definition in these words: "*Law is nothing other than a dictate of practical reason in a sovereign (princeps) who governs a complete community.*"[26] Although the phrase "nothing other than" in both of these definitional passages appears to guarantee completeness, each of them contains at least one inclusion condition the other omits.[27] Drawing on both of them, we can extract the following inclusion conditions for law:

(A) a directive of reason,
(B) aimed at the common good,
(C) promulgated by the government,
(D) pertaining to a complete community.

These four conditions did get mentioned in the four articles of Question 90,[28] but so did at least two others, which were not included in either of the definitional passages:

(E) leading people to or restraining them from certain actions,[29]
(F) having coercive power.[30]

I suppose that (E) could be thought to be entailed in the notion of an ordinance, a dictate, or a directive in (A), and I'm not sure it isn't. But (F) strikes me as clearly not entailed in that notion or in the notion of the government (the sovereign, the one responsible for the community) in (C), and those are the only likely places to look for it in the first four conditions. So to be on the safe side it seems right to say that by the end of the Question expressly devoted to the essence of law Aquinas has provided us with these six inclusion conditions. The fact that each of them appears again in later Questions is strong confirmation for including all six in the list.[31]

A seventh inclusion condition is employed more than once after those two definitional passages and should probably be added to the list at once:

(G) intended to be obeyed.[32]

Characteristic (G) is obviously closely related to (F), but it seems clearly distinguishable from (F) since a law might fulfill (G) without fulfilling (F), although presumably not (F) without (G). (There is at least one more interesting candidate for inclusion among the essential characteristics, but it raises problems that aren't relevant to our present concerns, and so I'm leaving it out of account.[33]) We now have a list that is at least nearly complete and certainly full enough to support some general observations about the conditions and some investigation of the ways Aquinas uses them in evaluating laws.

8. Non-Evaluative and Evaluative Conditions

Conditions (A) and (B) are fundamentally different from conditions (C)–(G), although Aquinas' initial presentation of these conditions obscures the difference. (A) and (B) are evaluative (moral) conditions of inclusion among full-fledged laws; (C)–(G), on the other hand, set out non-evaluative (formal) conditions that must be met by anything that is to count as a law at all. To take one of Aquinas' examples of a failure to satisfy a formal condition, the head of a household may make rules that fulfill conditions (A)–(C) and (E)–(G), but because a household is not a complete community (a political unit with some degree of sovereignty) those rules do not satisfy condition (D). In failing to meet one of the formal conditions, those household rules fail to count as laws even technically. If they were put forward as laws, they would be to laws as counterfeit dollars are to dollars: "A person who governs a family can of course make rules or regulations, but not such as have the nature of law strictly speaking."[34] A so-called law that failed to meet any one of the formal conditions would simply be a non-starter in the process of assessment that interests me now. It seems clear that conditions (A) and (B) are at issue only in case conditions (C)–(G) have been met. Aquinas indicates as much when he says that the derivability of a human law from a precept of natural law (or at least its compatibility with those precepts) becomes crucial to its status *provided that the other* [i.e., the formal] conditions that pertain to the essence of law *have been met.* The status of a law that meets those formal conditions and fails to meet either of the moral conditions remains to be seen, but it should

already be clear that Aquinas will not declare it to be no law *at all*.

Aquinas' discussion of law is an extension of his moral philosophy, in which conformity to reason is the principal moral criterion; and so it comes as no surprise to find that his first inclusion condition for law [condition (A)] is that it be a directive of reason. As for condition (B), it can hardly be surprising to find *any* writer on jurisprudence maintaining that being aimed at the common good is an evaluative inclusion condition of law. On the basis of (A) and (B) we expect to find Aquinas dismissing irrational laws or laws that run contrary to the common good, and we won't be disappointed.

But in view of my having begun this investigation by focusing on the slogan "An *unjust* law is not a law" and listing Aquinas as a subscriber to it, it might well be surprising that the *justness* of a law is not explicitly cited among these evaluative conditions. And the surprise would only be heightened by finding out that one of the definitions of law propounded by Aquinas' respected predecessor, Isidore of Seville (ca. 560–636), began with the words: "A law will be virtuous, *just,* naturally possible, ..."[35] But the reason Aquinas doesn't explicitly include justness among the evaluative inclusion conditions of laws is that he takes it to be involved in both (A) and (B) in different ways.[36] In commenting on Isidore's definition, he says "Human discipline of course gives primary consideration to the order of *reason,* and that order is implied in Isidore's using the word 'just' ".[37] Likewise, in one of Aquinas' evaluations of laws he says that "in order for [someone's] willing of things that are commanded [by that person] to have the nature of law, they must be regulated by some reason. That is how we understand the claim that the sovereign's will has the force of law; otherwise the sovereign's will would be *injustice (iniquitas)* rather than law."[38] In other words, justness as a moral condition of laws is implicit in rationality as a condition.

That he considers it to be implicit also in the notion of the common good is apparent when he says, drawing on Aristotle, that "justice is counted as a virtue, whether it is particular justice, which directs a person's action rightly relative to another individual human being, or legal justice, which directs a person's action rightly *relative to the common good of society.*"[39] In the same vein he says that "the acts of all the virtues can pertain to justice in the sense in which it directs a person to the common good. . . . And since it pertains to law to direct people to the common good (as was maintained above), justice of that sort . . . is called *legal justice,* because through it a person comes to agree with the law directing the acts of all the virtues toward the common good."[40] So when Aquinas dismisses a law as lacking either of the explicit moral conditions, (A) or (B), he can also be understood to be dismissing it as unjust.

9. Aquinas' Assessments of Laws

Aquinas' assessment of certain actual laws as unjust is not always merely implicit. More importantly (in view of the controversy over the *non-est-lex* slogan), not even an explicit assessment of that sort is always explicitly dismissive, as in this remark of his, which simply acknowledges the existence of unjust laws: "some lawgivers have made statutes contrary to secondary precepts of natural law, statutes which are unjust (*iniqua*)."[41]

But what happens when he does offer the kind of dismissive judgment the *non-est-lex* slogan leads us to expect? Not what its critics lead us to expect. Here is the first full-fledged instance of that sort in the Treatise on Law: "A tyrannical law, since it is not in accord with reason,"—i.e., since it fails to meet condition (A)—"is *not unconditionally* a law but is, rather, a *perversion* of law. And yet, insofar as it *does have something of the nature of law,* it aims at the citizens' being good. For it has the nature of law only in the sense that it is a dictate of someone who presides over subjects"—condition (C)—"and that it aims at the subjects' being properly obedient to the law"—condition (G). "Their being properly obedient *is* their being good—not unconditionally, but in relation to such a government."[42] Two of the five formal conditions we have identified are expressly mentioned here, and they are said to be the only respects in which a tyrannical law is law, but there is every reason to suppose that the other three formal conditions—(D), (E), and (F)—would also apply to such a case. At least one of the two moral conditions—rationality—is said to be unfulfilled and, as a consequence, Aquinas says (in effect), "An irrational law is not a law." But in this passage he has spelled out what he means by the dismissive judgment. An irrational law is not a law unconditionally because it falls short of at least one of the moral conditions essential to full-fledged law, but it is a law in a certain respect because it satisfies the formal conditions sufficient to establish it technically as a law. It is not a counterfeit but, like the plagiarized paper, a perversion. No "dictum" that "there *cannot*

be an unjust law," such as Danto thought he had identified, could stem from this dismissive judgment regarding tyrannical law, a judgment which also contains *the contrary* of what Hart called "a refusal . . . to recognize evil laws as valid for any purpose."

A second example of a dismissive judgment, this one more emphatic than the first, should help to confirm the impression that the critics of the *non-est-lex* slogan have misinterpreted it. "A human law has the nature of law to the extent to which it is in accord with right reason, and it is clear that in that respect it derives from the eternal law. But to the extent to which it falls short of reason, it is called an unjust law. In that case it does not have the nature of law but, rather, of a kind of violence. And yet, an unjust law itself also derives from the eternal law to the extent to which something of the image of law is preserved in it because the power belonging to the one who administers the law has an ordered relationship [to other power]; for all power is from the Lord God, as is said in Romans 13:1."[43] The same lessons are to be learned from this second example, I think, but I want especially to call attention to the fact that while it expressly says that an unjust law "does *not* have the nature of law," it also labors to bring out a respect in which it *is* law, emphasizing with its recurrent use of "to the extent to which" (*inquantum*) that the dismissive judgment admits of degrees. Austin, Danto, Hart, and even Lyons are barking up trees Aquinas never considered climbing.[44]

10. Laws on Trial in the Court of Conscience

We have now seen something of Aquinas' conception and classification of law, of the evaluative and non-evaluative conditions he considers essential to genuine law, and of the way he applies those conditions as criteria in dismissing unjust laws. Against that background we can understand and evaluate his answers to the questions with which I began. First, is an individual citizen entitled or obliged to decide whether a law of the state is unjust? Second, if so, on what grounds is he or she supposed to make the decision? And third, if an individual citizen has decided on appropriate grounds that a law of the state is unjust, what is he or she entitled or obliged to do about it?

By far the most important source for Aquinas' answers to such questions is his reply to Question 96, article 4, "Does human law impose necessity on a person in the court of conscience?"

> *Laws laid down by human beings are either just or unjust. It they are* just, *they do of course have the force of obligating a person in the court of conscience, [a force they acquire] from the eternal law, from which they derive (in accordance with Proverbs 8:15: "Through me kings reign and lawgivers decree just things"). Now laws are said to be just [1] on the basis of their* end—*i.e., when they are directed toward the common good; [2] on the basis of their* source or authority—*i.e., when the law that is decreed does not exceed the power of the one who decrees it; and [3] on the basis of their* form—*i.e., when burdens for the sake of the common good are imposed on those subject to them in accord with proportional equality. . . . Laws of that sort, which impose burdens proportionally, are just, they do obligate a person in the court of conscience, and they are legal laws.*
>
> *On the other hand, laws are* unjust (iniustae) *in two ways. In the first way [I], by being* contrary to human good *because of opposition to the conditions mentioned above. Either [I.1] with reference to the* end—*e.g., when someone in authority imposes on people subject to his authority burdensome laws that pertain not to the common good but, rather, to his own greed or glorification; or [I.2] with reference to the* source or authority—*e.g., when someone decrees a law that goes beyond the power entrusted to him; or [I.3] with reference to the* form—*e.g., when burdens are unequally distributed in the community, even if they are directed toward the common good. Occurrences of that sort are instances of violence rather than laws; for, as Augustine says, "that which is not just does not seem to be a law." Therefore,* such laws do not obligate a person in the court of conscience, except, perhaps, for the sake of avoiding a scandal or disruption, for which a person should even give up his right *(in accordance with Matthew 4:40–41: "If someone compels you to go a mile, go with him another two miles; and if someone takes away your coat, give him your shirt as well"*[45]*).*
>
> *Laws can be unjust in a second way [II] by being* contrary to divine good—*e.g., tyrants' laws leading people to idolatry or to anything else that is contrary to the divine law.* Such laws must not be observed in any way *because, as is said in Acts 5:29, "We ought to obey God rather than men."*

Aquinas' reply offers answers to all three of my questions, but it can be understood and evaluated only in the light of the question it explicitly addresses. If that question had been merely "Does human law impose necessity on a person?," John Austin's line regarding the probable fate of the conscientious objector to a law of the state would constitute an appropriate answer after all. The fact that the question is about the effect of human laws only *in the court of conscience (in foro conscientiae)* shows that the primary interest is not in what the community should do about laws of one sort or another, but in what the individual should think about them (and, secondarily, in what the individual should do on the basis of those thoughts). And in fact that the question is whether they impose necessity *in the court of conscience* shows that the primary concern is not whether they create *legal* obligations—we should assume they do—but whether they create *moral* obligations. Finally, although the question itself does not show this, Aquinas' citations of Scriptural authority indicate that in his view it is pre-eminently the conscience of the morally upright, Christian citizen in which these laws are on trial.

Since every citizen, Christian or not, is a rational creature, every citizen has a conscience and, as we have seen, a conscience is at least potentially furnished with the precepts of natural law, morality's innate Constitution, against which every human law is measurable—somewhat as laws promulgated in this country are measurable against its Constitution. With just these observations my first question can already be answered affirmatively: Every individual citizen is at least entitled to decide in the court of conscience whether a law of the state is unjust.

But *three* verdicts are available. A law of the state may be judged just, unjust-I, or unjust-II. Beginning with the third and easiest of them, we can see that the grounds on which to hand down the verdict "unjust-II" is that the law on trial is contrary to some precept of *divine* law, which is taken to be publicly accessible (in Scripture), and which the Christian citizen is obliged to employ in the court of conscience as a criterion of human law. That answers my second question, about the grounds on which the decision that the law is unjust-II is to be made. And the answer to my third question is plain in this case, too. If an individual Christian has decided on those divinely established, objectively accessible grounds that a law of the state is unjust-II, then he or she is *obliged not to obey it:* such "human laws are directed against a commandment of God, which is outside the range of the power of those laws; and so in such cases the human law must not be obeyed."[46] The reliance on divine law rather than unaided natural law for the verdict "unjust-II" seems to indicate that only a Christian's conscience could render that verdict, but I think that a secular version of "unjust-II" is and ought to be available for any conscience confronted with a law that is blatantly and grossly—i.e., intolerably—unjust.

The verdict "just" is not hard to understand, especially given Aquinas' three explicit criteria for it, evidently intended to be separately necessary and jointly sufficient. (Notice that criterion [1]—"when they are directed toward the common good"—is identical with condition (B), and that condition (A) seems implicit in criteria [2] and [3].) It is also easy to see the answer to my third question in this case: just laws do obligate a person in the court of conscience. In a sense the answer to my second question is easy as well: the grounds for the decision are spelled out in the three conditions. But there is a subsidiary empirical question that is not easy to answer: How can a person be sure that the three criteria have been met? Naturally there can be no standard, universally applicable answer to that question, but the guiding principle in the court of conscience must be "just unless proven unjust." The likelihood of subjective error is one pragmatic consideration supporting that principle, but not the only one, as we'll see.

Obviously, the most interesting and difficult cases are those for which the verdict "unjust-I" is appropriate. Since the three criteria for the justness of a law are separately necessary, the failure of any one of them is sufficient to render a law unjust-I; but the disjunction of I.1, I.2, or I.3 is only a superficial complication. And it is easy to think of laws of each of those three varieties which would be assessed as unjust by any disinterested person. The difficulty in answering my second question regarding cases of this sort is only the unavoidable empirical difficulty we already noticed in connection with handing down the verdict "just."[47] It is Aquinas' answer to my third question that is interestingly difficult, and apparently worrisome.

His answer comes in two parts. First, "such laws *do not obligate* a person in the court of conscience"— i.e., if an individual has decided on appropriate grounds that a law of the state is unjust-I, he or she is not morally obliged to obey that law—i.e., he or she

has a moral right not to obey that law—and is *not* morally *obliged* not to obey that law (as in the case of a law that is unjust-II). If I am right in my reading of this first part, it strikes me as eminently sensible. It is the second part that looks worrisome, claiming that one might after all *be* obliged by such a law in the court of conscience "for the sake of *avoiding a scandal or disruption,* for which a person should even *give up his right.*"

Of course the suggestion that we should not exercise a moral right we have often turns out to be wise and not worrisome; but it is seldom a suggestion to be taken lightly. And when the reason provided for our giving up our moral right is the avoidance of scandal or disruption, we should of course suspect that we are being offered a counsel of moral cowardice. On the plausible hypothesis that Aquinas is not suggesting moral cowardice as a morally allowable and sometimes obligatory alternative to civil disobedience, what are we to make of this part of his answer?[48]

The first thing to notice is that this alternative, whatever it turns out to be, is mentioned only in connection with laws that are unjust-I. Laws that are unjust-II *must not* be obeyed, whether or not scandal and disruption ensue. A law that sanctions the abuse of children, for example, *must* be disobeyed. So part of what makes the alternative of giving up one's right appropriate in the case of laws that are unjust-I is, presumably, that the stakes are lower in that case. The good to which *those* unjust laws are contrary is human only, not also divine.

A second bit of help is available further on in this same article, where Aquinas in replying to an objection says that a person is not obliged to obey a law that inflicts unjust oppression on those subject to it "*if* he can resist it without [causing] a scandal or *a greater harm.*"[49] Aquinas confronting a law that is unjust-I would clearly not countenance the bravado of the sixteenth-century maxim "*Fiat iustitia, et ruant coeli.*"[50] He takes the cautious approach of weighing the potential harm of resisting an unjust law against the potential harm the law is likely to cause if left unchallenged. In another context he offers an illuminating example from the history of the conflict between Church and State: "At that time, the Church in its infancy did not yet have the power of restraining earthly sovereigns, and so it permitted the faithful to obey [the emperor] Julian the Apostate in matters that were not contrary to the faith *in order to avoid a greater danger* to the faith."[51] But in every case of comparing particular potential harms to provide a basis for deciding whether or not to engage in civil disobedience—even a case as dramatically clear as Aquinas' example—there would or should remain the worry that moral cowardice would be a covert make-weight on the side of doing nothing.

I think there is good evidence, however, that for *all* cases of this sort Aquinas had a single sort of scandal or disruption in mind, one the consideration of which should take precedence over all others. I also think that he fosters a responsible moral decision-procedure in cases of this sort by prescribing a remedy for the unavoidable and most important sort of harm caused by civil disobedience. For a person engaging in disobeying a law for the purpose of proclaiming his or her conscientious objection to it is thereby indicating that the law ought to be changed—repealed or amended. But, as Aquinas observes in reply to the question "Should human law be changed whenever something better comes along?",[52] "The mere change of law, considered just in itself, *involves a kind of harm to the common good;* for custom contributes a great deal to the observance of laws, so that things that are done contrary to custom are seen as serious even if they are slight in themselves. For that reason, whenever a law is changed, *the binding power of law is weakened* to the extent to which custom is violated.

And so human law ought never to be changed *unless the common good is compensated in some way to the extent to which it was weakened in that respect.*"[53]

On the basis of his recognition of the fragility of the fabric of law Aquinas may be seen as advocating *conscientious* conscientious objection. Of course every rebel with a cause could heartily agree that the harm inflicted on the common good as a consequence of his or her morally motivated unlawful act must and will be compensated for—*eventually:* once the revolution has succeeded, or apartheid has been abolished, or the university has provided enough parking spaces for the faculty. If Aquinas had insisted on *immediate* compensation, his policy would have a tendency to stifle dissent. I think he would see the conscientious objector's deficit as having a time-limit on it, however, and would insist on *prompt* compensation, at the earliest possible opportunity.[54] He seems to have understood that moral people do occasionally need to operate under a long-term debt to the common good, to have been, like thoughtful people in any age, concerned about the concomitant threat to the fabric of law, and consequently to have tried to provide a rational formula of compensation acceptable in the court of conscience.[55]

---

1. H.L.A. Hart, The Concept of Law *(Oxford: The Clarendon Press, 1961), p. 7.*

2. De legibus *II v 11, cited by John Finnis in his* Natural Law and Natural Rights *(Oxford: The Clarendon Press, 1980), p. 363. Finnis also cited relevant passages from Plato and Aristotle, but my choices (based on a cursory survey) are in some respects different from his. The opening sections of my paper owe something to Finnis's Ch. XII, "Unjust Laws," the thesis of which strikes me as largely correct.*

3. Finnis, *op cit., p. 363: "St. Augustine in his early dialogue on* Free Will *makes one of his characters say, rather breezily, 'a law that was unjust wouldn't seem to be law'." Finnis misquotes the Latin, omitting the "mihi" between "lex" and "esse" (as Aquinas regularly does also). Notice that his translation is debatable, that the character into whose mouth the speech is put is also the author of the dialogue, and that "rather breezily" is an exaggeration.*

4. See, e.g., *ST IaIIae q. 96, a. 4.*

5. I have seen it attributed to Augustine, but without a specific reference—e.g., " '. . . saying with Augustine, 'Lex inuista [sic] non est lex,'" Kai Nielsen, "The Myth of Natural Law," in Sidney Hook, ed., Law and Philosophy *(New York: New York University Press, 1964), p. 139; see also n. 9 below. When Hart first introduces "An unjust law is not a law" in* The Concept of Law, *his reference is* " 'Non videtur esse lex quae justa non fuerit': *St. Augustine I,*' De Libero Arbitrio, 5; Aquinas, Summa Theologica Qu. xcv, Arts. 2, 4." (p. 8, n. 1). The Latin is a misquotation and Aquinas does not use the Augustine passage in ST IaIIae q. 95, a. 4. But what's worth noting is that Hart evidently knows of no better source than the Augustine passage for "An unjust law is not a law" (which he cites in Latin—"Lex iniusta non est lex"—on p. 152).

6. Not everyone would agree that Augustine and Aquinas belong in this list. In his article "The Essence of Law According to Thomas Aquinas," The American Journal of Jurisprudence 30 [1985], pp. 79–96, Edward J. Damich observes that "Positivists criticize naturalists for maintaining that an unjust law is not a law at all. But not all naturalists assert the truth of this statement. Thomas Aquinas . . . maintains that unjust laws seem not to be laws at all" (p. 79). And since the word "seems," the cornerstone of Damich's thesis, comes into Aquinas' Treatise on Law via his quotation of the passage from Augustine's De libero arbitrio, Damich would presumably exclude Augustine as well from among the adherents of non est lex. But it is a mistake to rest such a thesis on an emphasized English word that picks up only one ordinary sense of the Latin word "videtur," which can (and in the Augustine passage pretty clearly does) also have the sense of the English phrase "is evidently." Damich goes even further, claiming that "if we examine the writings of Thomas Aquinas . . . we cannot find a single passage in which he declares without qualification that unjust law is not a law at all" (p. 80). But in discussing unjust laws in the Treatise on Law itself Aquinas says, for example, that they "are instances of violence rather than laws" and, again, "an unjust law . . . does not have the nature of law, but, rather, of a kind of violence." I came across Damich's article only after I had written mine; while he and I agree in thinking that Aquinas' position can and should be defended against some of the criticism leveled against it in recent legal philosophy, our tactics are quite different.

7. Op. Cit., p. 8; emphasis added.

8. Cf. J. R. Pennock, Democratic Political Theory, *(Princeton, N.J.: Princeton University Press, 1979), p. 11: "The practice of having both an ideal and a practical or technical definition, the first of which tends to be substantive and the second formal or procedural, is by no means uncommon. For instance, we might say of a university properly incorporated and authorized to grant degrees by the appropriate authority (in the United States, a state or the*

federal legislature), that even though it is technically a university, it is not 'really' a university, because it has no graduate schools, or those it has are so poor that they are not worthy of the name, or for some like reason." (I am grateful to David Lyons for calling this passage to my attention.)

9. *It should be noted that natural (or other) kinds that would ordinarily lack a humanly important function can easily be assigned one. In ordinary circumstances a maple leaf's function is not humanly important, and so the dismissive judgment does not ordinarily apply to damaged maple leaves on maple trees. But if the leaves are being considered as specimens for an exhibit, they have been assigned a humanly important function, in which case a damaged maple leaf might very well be dismissed with the judgment "That's no maple leaf!" (I'm grateful to Sydney Shoemaker and Robert Stalnaker for helpful suggestions about these classifications of kinds.)*

10. *"Human Nature and Natural Law," in Hook, op. cit., pp. 187–199; p. 187 (quoted in Finnis, op cit., p. 364).*

11. *In his "Letter from Birmingham City Jail," (April 16, 1963), Martin Luther King clearly employed the non-est-lex slogan as an expression of the dismissive attitude in a context which shows that it is not only compatible with but really entails the acceptance of the existence of unjust laws: "There are just laws and there are unjust laws. I would be the first to advocate obeying just laws. One has not only a legal but moral responsibility to obey just laws. Conversely, one has a moral responsibility to disobey unjust laws. I would agree with Saint Augustine that 'An unjust law is no law at all'." Quoted in Wolfgang Friedmann, "An Analysis of [H. A. Rommen's] 'In Defense of Natural Law'," in Hook, op cit., pp. 144–160; p. 152.*

12. *Op. Cit., pp. 152 and 206–07; emphasis added.*

13. *Hart has, however, often drawn inferences as rash as Danto's. See Finnis's collection of them, op cit., p. 364.*

14. Ethics and the Rule of Law *(Cambridge: Cambridge University Press, 1984), pp. 62–63.*

15. The Province of Jurisprudence Determined *(first published 1832; reprinted, with Introduction by H.L.A. Hart, London, 1954), p. 184.*

16. *Op. cit., p. 185; quoted by Finnis, op. cit., pp. 354–355; emphasis added.*

17. *See esp. ST IaIIae q. 91, a. 1, and q. 93.*

18. *ST IaIIae q. 91, a. 2; see also esp. q. 94.*

19. *See esp. ST IaIIae q. 91, a. 3, and qq. 95–97.*

20. *See esp. ST IaIIae q. 91, aa. 4 & 5, and qq. 98–108.*

21. *ST IaIIae q. 94, a. 2.*

22. *Ibid.*

23. *ST IaIIae q. 94, a. 1, ad 2. The word I have translated "conscience" here is actually "synderesis," not "conscientia." Aquinas draws a technical distinction between synderesis and conscience (ST Ia, q. 79, aa. 12 & 13), but it is irrelevant in this context.*

24. *Q. 91, a. 3.*

25. *Q. 90, a. 4.*

26. *Q. 91, a. 1.*

27. *The facts that there are discrepancies between these two occurrences of the "definition" and that some inclusion conditions frequently employed by Aquinas are entirely omitted from the "definition" suggest that it is only a loose summation. His applications of the inclusion conditions, both before and after the introduction of the "definition," give us a much more reliable understanding of his concept of law than we can get from the "definition."*

28. *For (A), see q. 90, a. 1, ad 2; ad 3; a. 2, ad 3. For (B), see q. 90, a. 2c; ad 3. For (C), see q. 90, a. 3; a. 4. For (D), see q. 90, a. 3, ad 3.*

29. *Q. 90, a. 1.*

30. *Q. 90, a. 3, ad 2.*

31. *Some later occurrences—(A): q. 91, a. 1; a. 3; q. 92, a. 1c; ad 4; q. 93, a. 1; a. 3c; ad 2; q. 94, a. 2, obj. 3; ad 3; q. 97, a. 1c; a. 3c. (B): q. 91, a. 5; q. 93, a. 1, ad 1; q. 94, a. 3, obj. 1; ad 1; q. 95, a. 3c; a. 4c; q. 96, a. 1c; a. 3, obj. 3; a. 3c; a. 4c; a. 6c; q. 97, a. 2c. (C): q. 91, a. 1c(?); ad 3(?); a. 6(?); q. 92, a. 1, ad 4; q. 93, a. 1; q. 93, a. 3, ad 2; q. 93, a. 5; q. 95, a. 4c; q. 97, a. 3c; a. 4c. (D): q. 91,*

a. 1 [the universe as the paradigm of the complete community]; q. 92, a. 1, and 4(?). (E): q. 91, a. 4; q. 92, a. 1, ad 1; a. 2; q. 93, a. 1c; ad 1; a. 3; a. 4, s.c.; a. 5c; ad 1; q. 95, a. 1, obj. 3; a. 1c; a. 4c; q. 96, a. 1, obj. 2; a. 2c; a. 5c; q. 97, a. 1c. (F): q. 93, a. 3, ad 2; q. 95, a. 1c; q. 96, a. 5c; q. 97, a. 2c.

32. *Q. 91, a. 5; q. 92, a. 1c; ad 4.*

33. *Aquinas sometimes writes as if it were an essential characteristic of law to contribute to an individual's achieving of his ultimate end—perfect happiness in the beatific vision. See, e.g., q. 91, a. 4: "By law a human being is directed to actions that are appropriate in connection with his ordered relationship toward his ultimate end." But an individual's ultimate end can't be included in the common good (except accidentally), and Aquinas surely does not think that any law other than the divine law can make a direct contribution to an individual's destiny. Elsewhere in the Treatise Aquinas writes in a way that heightens the impression that the suggestion in q. 91, a. 4, is unintentional. See esp. q. 96, a. 1: "Now the end of law is the common good, because, as Isidore says* (Etymologiae II, 10; V, 21), *'A law must be framed for no private advantage but for the common benefit of the citizens.' That is why human laws must be adapted to the common good."*

34. *The head-of-the-household example is discussed in q. 90, a. 3, obj. 3 and ad 3.*

35. Etymologiae *V, 21; quoted in the introduction to q. 95, a. 3.*

36. *In at least one passage in the Treatise on Law he does come very close to making justness an explicit criterion, however, apart from any consideration of Isidore's definition: "it pertains to law to direct human actions in accord with the order of justice" (q. 91, a. 5).*

37. *Q. 95, a. 3.*

38. *Q. 90, a. 1, ad 3.*

39. *ST IaIIae q. 113, a. 1; cf. q. 100, a. 2, and q. 96, a. 3.*

40. *ST IIaIIae q. 58, a. 5; cf. q. 58 passim.*

41. *ST IaIIae q. 94, a. 6, ad 3.*

42. *Q. 92, a. 1, and 4.*

43. *Q. 93, a. 3, ad 2.*

44. *The dismissive judgment that comes closest to looking like what the critics say it is may be this one: "As Augustine says in* De libero arbitrio, *Bk. I, 'that which is not just does not seem to be a law.' Thus it has the force of law to the extent to which it has justice. Now in human affairs something is called just because it is right according to a rule of reason, but the first rule of reason is natural law (as is clear from things said earlier). Therefore, every law laid down by human beings has the nature of law to the extent to which it derives from natural law; but if it is inconsistent with natural law in some respect, it will no longer be law but a corruption of law" (q. 95, a. 3). But here, too, it seems to me there is evidence of flexibility, which is strengthened by the fact that this passage comes after the two evaluative passages we have just been looking at.*

45. *Aquinas is obviously quoting (paraphrasing) from memory here.*

46. *Q. 96, a. 4, ad 2.*

47. *In ST IIaIIae q. 147, a. 4, Aquinas offers practical advice relevant to the quandary of the individual faced with difficulties formally similar to one above.*

48. *As John Boler pointed out to me, Aquinas' detailed discussion of scandal should be taken into account here (ST IIaIIae q. 43). Scandal as Aquinas conceives of it has two components. It is something said or done with less than perfect moral justification (dictum vel factum minus rectum), and it provides an occasion for someone's spiritual downfall (praebens occasionem ruinae). If the avoidance of scandal in this technical sense were the only reason Aquinas gave for giving up one's moral right, my discussion of this issue in the remainder of the paper would be simpler and would draw heavily on IIaIIae q. 43, a. 7, "Should temporal [goods] be given up for the sake of [avoiding] scandal?" But the fact that Aquinas here speaks of the avoidance of "scandal or disruption" calls for a broader treatment.*

49. *Q. 96, a. 4, ad 3.*

50. The Oxford Dictionary of Quotations *attributes the maxim to the Emperor Ferdinand I (1503–1564) in the form "Fiat iustitia, et pereat*

mundus," and to William Watson (1559?–1603) in the more familiar form in which I quote it here.

51. *ST IIaIIae q. 12, a. 2, ad 1.*

52. *Q. 97, a. 2.*

53. *Cf. Aristotle,* Politics *II 5, 1268b23–1269a28.*

54. *ST IIaIIae q. 62 has to do with restitution, and although it is concerned primarily with restitution by one individual to another, I think it can be applied, cautiously, to cases of the sort at issue here. Q. 63, a. 8, asks whether a person "is bound to make restitution immediately or can legitimately defer it." The heart of Aquinas' position is that "everyone is bound to make restitution immediately or to request a postponement from the person who can grant him the use of the thing" that does not rightfully belong to him. And in his rejoinder to the objection that "sometimes a person cannot make restitution immediately" (obj. 2) Aquinas says, "When someone cannot make restitution immediately, that inability itself excuses him from making instant restitution (just as a person who is entirely unable to make restitution is entirely excused from it). He is, however, obliged to request forgiveness or postponement, either in his own right or through someone else, from the person to whom he owes it."*

55. *For comments and criticisms I'm indebted to the members of my Aquinas seminar at Cornell in the spring term of 1986, to philosophical audiences at several institutions, to Barbara Ensign Kretzmann, to John Bennett, to John Boler, and especially to Eleonore Stump. But the largest debt of gratitude by far I owe to David Lyons, who wrote three extremely helpful sets of comments on various drafts and who was, as always, unfailingly generous in his advice and counsel.*

ON THE CONNECTION BETWEEN LAW AND JUSTICE*

Anthony D'Amato

Introduction

Legal and political theorists since the time of Plato have wrestled with the problem of whether justice is part of law or is simply a moral judgment about law. An example of the latter is when we speak of an "unjust law." Nearly every writer on the subject has either concluded that justice is only a judgment about law or has offered no reason to support a conclusion that justice is somehow part of law. This Essay attempts to reason toward such a conclusion, arguing that justice is an inherent component of the law and not separate or distinct from it. Given the history of the topic, I start with a disclaimer. The issues involved in these questions are as vast as they are fundamental. I do not pretend to have a definitive solution. I do, however, attempt a suggestive solution based on an extended hypothetical case. If you, the reader, are not persuaded by it, I hope at least that it will have heuristic value for you. . . .

Let me start by mentioning my current project on justice. For the past decade or so I've been on something of a crusade to persuade law schools to teach justice. Justice, I argue, is what law is for; justice is what lawyers should do; justice is what judges should render.[1] "Law" is nothing but a set of tools—admittedly complex and intellectually engaging. But we should not get so caught up in the intellectual interest of law that we forget that law in itself cannot solve human problems. Like any other tool, law may facilitate the solution of a given problem. But we cannot expect law to tell us how the problem ought to be resolved. Although I would never challenge the proposition that the training of lawyers requires familiarization with the tools of the trade,[2] I contend that simply teaching students how to find and use the tools of the trade—including verbal and rhetorical skills—is hardly ennobling, is hardly why we can call law a "profession," is hardly the reason students should study law or why the best students come to law school in the first place. Nor can we cop a plea by saying that our duty is only to serve our clients, because some desires of some clients (such as planning a crime) are and should be excluded from a lawyer's professional

*D'Amato, Anthony. "On the Connection Between Law and Justice," University of California, Davis Law Review. vol. 26, 1993. Reprinted with permission of the author.

responsibility. If serving a client is a lawyer's highest aspiration, then that lawyer is just a hired gun. To the contrary, the reason law is properly called a profession is because our job is to help achieve justice—justice for our clients, to be sure, but justice nevertheless. By achieving justice for our clients, we simultaneously add a measure of justice to society.[3]

Yet when audiences ask me for a purely instrumental reason why law schools should teach justice—something that will play well at the next meeting of the curriculum committee—I respond that justice *arguments* are the ones that are likely to win negotiations and litigations. Since our job is to train our students to be effective in negotiations and litigations, we must have courses on justice and the role it plays in legal advocacy.

The reason I give for contending that justice arguments are winners is worth summarizing here because it will tie in at several places to the theme of this Essay. I start by saying that good lawyers on either side of a negotiation or litigation will probably succeed in checkmating each other with their legal arguments. Our law schools do an admirable job in training students to come up with plausible legal arguments on any side of any controversy. After they graduate, our students will meet other equally well-trained attorneys who will come up with plausible arguments on the other side of any given controversy. Once all the legal arguments are ventilated, justice often tips the scale at the end because the decision-maker[4] will likely be swayed by what is, under the circumstances, fair.[5] Faced with opposing briefs that are equally, or just about equally,[6] persuasive, the decision-maker in the end will likely be guided by his or her sense of justice. This is especially true if the decision-maker is a judge, partly because it is an ancient tradition and belief that the role of the judge is to do justice to the parties. . . .

To be sure, it's hard for a professor or lawyer to be opposed to justice. Like motherhood and apple pie, there's not much controversy about the desirability of justice. Indeed, the danger is that justice may become an honorific term that sweeps through law-school classrooms, touching everything and influencing nothing.

But it's easy enough to make "justice" quite controversial. All you have to do is assert that judges should decide cases according to justice and not according to law. Even though judges may in fact do this, as soon as you assert that they *should* do it you can rock the foundations of the academic legal establishment.

That question, accordingly, has considerable value in organizing our thoughts about justice. What does it mean to assert that judges should decide cases according to justice and not according to the law? Is there something incoherent in the question itself? That question will serve as our springboard in examining what is—or should be—the connection between justice and law. . . .

Justice Is Part of the Law: A Hypothetical Case

A. *Case and Criteria*

The argumentative use of hypothetical cases not only characterizes good classroom teaching in law schools, but is found in questions judges ask from the bench during oral argument and in many other areas of law study and practice. My intention here is to use a single, extended hypothetical case to prove the proposition that justice is an integral part of law. Immediately you will object that this is far too heavy a load to place on any one example. If I can pull it off, the hypothetical case has to be well selected.

The most important criterion is that it must be general. If there is any element of idiosyncracy, the hypothetical case will not work as a general argument. Thus it should be set in any jurisdiction, and not a particular jurisdiction (such as the United States). It should also be an ordinary, even humdrum, example, to avoid charges that I have reached for something unusual and hence inapplicable to ordinary circumstances.

I will choose a motor vehicle regulation that, as far as I know, is fairly standard throughout the world: the parallel (double) white lines down the center of a road. I will focus on the parallel lines and *not* the statutory regulation behind it, because once we look at a particular statute, we have an interpretive problem that could vary from country to country or from language to language. The parallel lines therefore offer a purely semantic and generalizable legal rule, meaning, in effect, "don't cross me." The driver of a car understands the parallel lines as a legal prohibition, barring vehicles from driving over and hence crossing the parallel lines. It is this *meaning* that I will focus upon, rather than any particular set of statutory words that purports to express the meaning. Nevertheless, in order to make the example realistic, I will invent a back-up example of a regulation that gives legal effect to the white lines.

Since this example will involve justice, I must make the justice element in itself completely uncontroversial. For no purpose will be served by getting into an extended discussion of whether an act related to this example is itself just or unjust, and then having to *assume* its injustice in order to get on with the project. Hence, the act that is uncontrovertibly unjust is running over and killing a child. The child is an "innocent child" in the sense that she has not committed a crime such that her execution is an appropriate penalty. But it is a "darting child"—one who runs out in front of a moving automobile at the last minute. If the driver of the car wants to avoid killing the child, the driver's only option (as I construct this hypothetical case) is to drive across the parallel lines.

Before I sketch in the details of this imagined case, let me comment on the phrase that I have placed in quotation marks: "innocent child." A person could argue that a child who darts out into the street at the last minute in front of a moving car is hardly "innocent." The child is at least guilty of an error in judgment, and perhaps guilty of disobeying her parents' instructions. Nevertheless, I suppose that no one would argue that killing the child is an appropriate penalty for the child's error in judgment or her disobedience of parents. To be sure, we might imagine a society—H.G. Wells imagined one in his famous short story, *The Time Machine*—where killing pedestrians is a routine aspect of driving a car.[7] (In Wells' future society there is a severe overpopulation problem, so no one objects to the bizarre practice of killing pedestrians.) But I don't think that any reasonable person would maintain, in today's world, that justice is served by running over the darting child.

Let us now sketch in a few details. The darting child runs out into the street from behind a car parked at the curb. No driver of an oncoming car could have seen the child because the child was small in size and completely hidden by the parked car; only when the child darted out into the street was the child visible. Hence we completely rule out any possible negligence on the part of the driver of the car. Moreover, let us stipulate that it is physically possible, without risk of personal injury, for the driver to avoid hitting the child by crossing the parallel white lines. There is no car coming in the opposite direction in the other lane that would hit the driver's car head-on if the driver crossed the lines. Moreover, the driver cannot steer to the right because there are parked cars along the curb and he would hit those cars—and even possibly glance off them and run over the child in any event. Hence, what we have is a road with two lanes, one going in each direction, with parallel white lines down the middle, a driver proceeding in one of those lanes, a child who darts in front of the driver at the last minute, and the opportunity for the driver to avoid hitting the child by crossing the parallel lines and driving (temporarily) in the other lane. There is no car or other vehicle in the other lane at the moment when this event occurs.

Now let us split this hypothetical case into two similar cases. In the first one, driver *A* sees the child at the last minute, drives across the parallel lines, avoiding the child, and then drives back into the proper lane after the child is passed. In the second case, driver *B* sees the child at the last minute, refrains from crossing the parallel lines (though physically able to do so), and runs over and kills the child. In both cases, a police officer is present at the scene, observing everything that occurred. In neither case is there any factual dispute or conflicting testimony. I will mostly discuss the first case of driver *A* (Alice); driver *B* (Bruce) will serve primarily as a reference point.

B. The Arrest

In the first case, right after Alice has succeeded in avoiding the darting child, the police officer on the scene flags her down and gives her a ticket:

ALICE: Why are you giving me a ticket? I avoided killing that child.

OFFICER: I know. I'm glad you did. But you still committed a traffic violation.

ALICE: Are you saying that I should have stayed in my lane and run over the child?

OFFICER: You have to realize that by saving the child's life you violated the law. I'm sure you felt it was the right thing to do.

ALICE: Yes, I did. And didn't you?

OFFICER: Yes. It was the right thing to do. I'm sure the judge in traffic court will agree, and say that the violation was only a technical one.

ALICE: Then why give me a ticket?

OFFICER: Well, it was a violation. Technical or not, you violated the law. My job is to arrest anyone who violates the law. It's not my job to make a judgment on why you did what you did, even though, as I said, I think you did the right thing in this case.

ALICE: But this means I have to show up in traffic court. And already your stopping me has delayed me from my business appointment.

OFFICER: I'm sorry. The judge will be sympathetic, take my word for it.

C. Traffic Court

The next scene is in traffic court, where the judge listens patiently to the police officer and to Alice. There is no conflicting testimony.

JUDGE: I find the defendant guilty of crossing the parallel lines. Please pay the clerk fifty dollars. This will be entered on your driving record as a moving traffic infraction. A third conviction for such an offense within a two-year period means suspension of your driver's license.

ALICE: Wait a minute. Are you saying I should have run over the child?

JUDGE: This court will not give legal advice. The duty of this court is to pass judgment on past events, not to advise you about what you should have done or what you should do in the future. But having said this, let me add a personal observation. I am frankly surprised at your behavior here this morning. You are taking the attitude that the law should somehow grant you a personal exception for crossing the parallel lines, something which the law does not do for any other driver. We are all subject to the law: you, myself, and everyone else.

ALICE: But judge, I did the right thing. I avoided killing an innocent child.

JUDGE: Do you really believe that you did the morally right thing?

ALICE: Yes, I do.

JUDGE: Then why are you complaining about paying the fine? Surely fifty dollars is a trivial price to pay for saving the life of an innocent child! If you are as morally secure in your convictions as you say you are, then you should pay the fine cheerfully, and go home with the feeling that you saved a life and did the right thing. Next case!

ALICE: Well, I want to appeal your decision.

JUDGE: That's your privilege. You have thirty days to file an appeal. But you have to pay the fine on your way out this morning.

D. The Appeal

Alice's friends try to dissuade her from proceeding with the appeal. They point out that she has lost the time spent in court already, plus fifty dollars, plus the time when she was arrested in the first place. They tell her that an appeal will be expensive, far more expensive than the fifty dollars she might get back if she wins. But they don't know Adamant Alice. She has no intention of accepting the status of a lawbreaker when she did nothing wrong, even though it was only a relatively minor infraction of a traffic regulation.

She looks up the jurisdiction's traffic regulations. Since this is a "generic" hypothetical, let us assume that the following is found in the state's traffic code:

> Section 205. Streets shall be clearly marked for the purpose of traffic regulation.
>
> (a) If a roadway is marked by a broken white line which traverses its length, motorists may cross the broken white line if it is safe to do so and only after first signalling their intention to do so.
>
> (b) If a roadway is marked by a solid white line which traverses its length, motorists may not cross the line except: in an emergency, and then only if safe to do so.
>
> (c) If a roadway is marked by double white lines (parallel lines) which traverse its length, motorists may not cross the lines.
>
> Section 206. The penalty for violating any provision of section 205 shall be fifty dollars. The defendant shall be charged with a moving vehicle traffic violation.

In her brief before the Intermediate Appellate Court, Alice argues that the parallel line rule, while reasonable in the vast majority of cases, worked an injustice in her case. The court should carve out an exception for "darting-child cases" in the name of justice.

Here are some excerpts from the appellate court's majority opinion:

> Normally we would affirm without opinion a case such as this one. However, because of the philosophical issues involved, we have decided to append a brief written opinion to our judgment of affirmance.
>
> The appellant argues that section 205, as applied, works an injustice. It is unjust to penalize her, she argues, for temporarily and technically violating the parallel-line rule when her purpose was to save the life of an innocent child.
>
> The law, however, is plain and admits of no exceptions. There is nothing in section 205 that

can fairly be read as providing an exception in cases where, in the driver's judgment, there is an important need to violate the rule.

Our interpretation of section 205 is based on the section as a whole, not simply on subsection (c) (the parallel lines paragraph). The statutory scheme is comprehensive and admits of no exceptions. In particular, if the legislature had wanted to allow the appellant to cross a dividing line under the facts of her particular case, it would have provided for a single *white line under subsection (b). But in fact the traffic department, on the roadway the appellant used, painted parallel lines as provided in subsection (c). This may be taken as a deliberate legislative decision to bar the crossing of the dividing lines even in the event of an emergency.*

We are not unmindful of the appellant's courageous decision to violate the law in order to save a child's life. But the fact is that she violated the law. The law's penalty is, as the trial judge said, a small price to pay for saving the life of a child.

This court does not have the power to change the law. That power is reserved to the legislature. A court has a far more limited role: to apply the law as written. To be sure, if we were persuaded that if a court were ever to depart from the plain meaning of a statute, then the instant case is the most justifiable case for such a departure. Nevertheless, there is a vast hidden cost in such a departure. We would thereby erode the public's confidence in the plain meaning of statutes. Further, we would undermine the legislature's confidence in the judiciary. We would be setting up the courts as the ultimate, unelected, undemocratic arbiter of the law.

Courts must respect the plain meaning of statutes. As the Supreme Court of the United States said in United States *v.* Locke,[8] *even if the legislative rule is* arbitrary, *it must be accorded its plain meaning.[9] If that was true in* Locke, *it is certainly true in the present case. The parallel-line rule is not arbitrary. It is the rule selected by the legislature. If on occasion its application appears to work an injustice, a court may not invoke the concept of injustice to overrule the law itself. We have no constitutional mandate to invalidate laws, or write exceptions into laws when their plain language*

admits of no exceptions, all in the name of justice. The history of constitutional democracy argues to the contrary. It is only the legislature, representing the will of the people, that is entitled to create laws and create exceptions to laws. If a court were to take on a legislative role, the court would eventually imperil its own existence. The ensuing uncertainty would far outweigh the occasional injustice felt by some persons when a law is applied exactly according to its terms.

The appellant in her brief virtually concedes that the parallel-line rule was correctly applied in her case. She asks this court to create an "exception" to the rule. But our job is simply to apply the law as written. We would suggest that the appellant expend her energies in petitioning the legislature to amend the parallel-line rule, instead of asking this court to act as a legislature.

If the preceding opinion strikes you as eminently reasonable and persuasive, it is because I have deliberately used concepts and phrases that are hallowed in judicial history. These concepts are familiar to all lawyers. They "resonate" in some of our deepest conceptions of the limited role of the judiciary. But although I have made the argument as persuasive as I can, I want to show that it is really constructed on a bed of sand, that it is ultimately unconvincing, that it is rhetoric and not sound analysis.

To begin the process of chipping away at the majority's opinion, here is an invented excerpt from the dissent in Alice's case:

Assume for a moment that the parallel divider lines had no legal significance. Suppose they were simply painted on the roadway as a guide for motorists. Indeed, in the early days of automobile travel, road signs were placed simply to help traffic flow more easily. The early traffic signal light was invented simply to reduce the confusion at intersections when drivers at right angles to each other misinterpreted each other's signals as to who should proceed first. It was only after traffic signals were installed and working that some state legislatures began making the signals legally compulsory.

Under our temporary assumption that the parallel lines in the present case are without legal significance, no one would seriously maintain that the appellant should run over a child when she had the clear alternative of running over the white lines. In fact, if the appellant did kill the child instead of observing the (legally insignificant) parallel lines, she could be prosecuted for manslaughter or even murder. There is hardly a clearer case of injustice than one in which a temporary and safe deviation from a given route is not taken when the cost of not taking it is the life of an innocent child.

The only difference between our assumed case and the actual instant case is that the parallel lines are backed by a statute. But why should that make a difference where a child's life is concerned? For in the present case, the appellant made a temporary and safe deviation from a prescribed *route in order to save a child's life. It would have been morally monstrous of her to run over the child in such circumstances.*

Yet the majority is penalizing her for not killing the child. I'm afraid that Charles Dickens' observation in Oliver Twist *will be applied by commentators to the holding in the present case: "The law is a[n] ass—a[n] idiot." When the law itself is the only difference between saving or not saving the life of a child, how can my colleagues vote to penalize the appellant for what she did?*

The appellant's obligation in driving her car was not to drive blindly. Our obligation is not to apply the law blindly. The decision below should have been reversed.

The dissenting judge has made an emotional appeal. But the judge has not been articulate as to exactly how the appellant's conduct comes within the law. The connection between justice and the law, in other words, is not explicit in the dissenting judge's opinion.

E. The Television Special

Let us develop the hypothetical case further. Suppose soon after Alice's case, Bruce's case occurs. Bruce ran over the darting child. The officer on the scene assisted in calling the ambulance (useless, the child was dead), but otherwise did not give Bruce a ticket.

Shortly thereafter, there was a TV special on the darting child. Alice and Bruce were interviewed. Here are some excerpts from Bruce's interview:

BRUCE: It was horrible. Tragic. I saw the child dart out in front of my car.

TV REPORTER: Did you think of crossing the double white lines so as to avoid hitting the child?

BRUCE: I don't know. I did and I didn't. I'm just not a person who breaks the law. I've never been arrested. Even for a traffic violation. I've tried and tried to think about that moment, the poor child, but some voice was telling me not to cross the double lines. I mean, I've never crossed the double lines. Even if I was going to be injured myself, like by hitting something solid in front of me, I still wouldn't have crossed the lines.

TV REPORTER: If you had it to do over again, would you cross the white lines to avoid hitting the child?

BRUCE: Well, sure. But it's easy to say that now. If you're a law abiding citizen, and you've ever been in that kind of situation, your instinct is to obey the law. I can't be sure that I would have acted differently, knowing what I know now. Although I hope I can act differently if, God forbid, it should ever happen again.

The parents of the dead child are interviewed, followed by an interview with a member of the state legislature:

TV REPORTER: Do you think that the driver, Bruce, did the wrong thing?

MOTHER: Of course. He's a monster. I can't believe he would deliberately run over my child. He should be prosecuted for murder.

FATHER: It's more the law's fault than Bruce's fault. Alice, you've interviewed her on this program, did the right thing. She avoided hitting a darting child. But some dumb judges found her guilty of violating the traffic regulation!

TV REPORTER: So the really guilty parties are the judges?

FATHER: Right. How can they penalize Alice for saving a child, and do nothing about Bruce, who ran over our own daughter?

MOTHER: For shame.

VOICEOVER: But the traffic rules say you can't cross double white lines. Aren't the legislators who passed the law in the first place the real murderers here?

LEGISLATOR: My committee is going to hold hearings on this white line business.

TV REPORTER: Did you ever intend that the white line law should stop people from crossing it even to save the life of a child?

LEGISLATOR: We never thought of that contingency. But the answer to your question is no. Certainly, if someone had asked us whether the law prohibited a driver from crossing the white lines to avoid hitting a child, every legislator, myself included, would say that saving the child's life comes first.

TV REPORTER: Would you have ever expected that a court would fine Alice for crossing the white lines to save a child?

LEGISLATOR: Of course not. Those judges were out to lunch.

TV REPORTER: But you passed a statute with no exceptions.

LEGISLATOR: True. But we passed the statute in the expectation that human beings, people who are called judges, would apply the statute in a sensible way. The so-called judges in Alice's case acted like robots, like computers. If the legislature wanted computers to apply the law, then we might save a lot of money. But we have judges to apply the law so that they can apply it in light of the requirements of justice.

TV REPORTER: And a computer can't do that?

LEGISLATOR: Right. The one thing we can't program into a computer is a sense of justice. So that's why we pay judges their high salaries, and give them lifetime tenure. We legislators expect the judges to act like sensible human beings. And here they do dumb things, like fining Alice for saving a child's life.

TV REPORTER: So you think it was unfair for the court to fine Alice fifty dollars?

LEGISLATOR: It's not the fifty dollars that bothers me. I don't think it's the fifty dollars that bothers Alice, judging from what she said on this program.

TV REPORTER: Well, then what does bother you?

LEGISLATOR: The precedent of it. The outcome in Alice's case sends a message to the public—to people like Bruce. It says, "it's always illegal to cross the parallel white lines, no matter what." And some

people out there absorb the message, people like Bruce. They decide that if a court tells them something is illegal, then they won't do it. Period. It builds up an instinctive reaction in people: never cross the double lines. Even if you have to run over a child. That's what troubles me about what the court did in Alice's case.

F. The Legislative Hearings

The TV program generated intense public disapproval of the Intermediate Appellate Court's holding in Alice's case. Alice asked the state's Supreme Court to review her case. The next event to occur was the legislative hearing on revision of the traffic code.

It was soon apparent to any impartial observer of the legislative hearings that reforming the traffic code was an enormously complex problem. Testimony was first heard from people who sympathized with Alice and who asked the legislative committee to add a final clause to section 205(c) so that the provision would read in full as follows:

> (c) If a roadway is marked by double white lines (parallel lines) which traverse its length, motorists may not cross the line except if it is safe to do so and if it is absolutely necessary to save the life of a darting child.

But later witnesses said "absolutely necessary" replicates all the previous problems because drivers like Bruce will be wondering whether it really is "absolutely necessary" and their hesitation might be fatal for the darting child. Others pointed out that the phrase "darting child" is underinclusive; what if a child is suddenly seen by the driver as simply standing in the road, instead of "darting"? A legislator suggested omitting the phrases "absolutely necessary" and "darting." But another legislator said that then the phrase "save the life of a child" might apply to a child inside the driver's car, as would be the case if the driver were hurrying to get the child to the emergency room of a nearby hospital. Others pointed out that "save the life" was underinclusive; a driver should not be required to hit the child, instead of crossing the white lines, if the driver reasonably believes that the child will only be seriously injured by the collision but not actually killed.

Then came the senior citizens lobby. Why "child" at all? Why not just "person"? After all, a senior citizen might wander out into the middle of the street at the wrong time. What if someone fell out of the trunk of a car, or the back of a truck, in front of the driver? Suppose that person had jumped out of a car of kidnappers. The person would, through no personal fault, suddenly be sitting, standing, or lying directly in front of the motorist. Therefore the statute should specifically exclude all persons who, for whatever reason, find themselves in the street in front of an oncoming car which has the choice of averting them by crossing the dividing lines. As a result of this onslaught of citizen testimony, some legislators suggested that the word "child" be changed to "person."

But then the animal-rights lobbyists showed up. Why shouldn't it be right to cross the double white lines to save the life of a darting squirrel? Or cat? A legislator replied that it is preferable to run over the squirrel than to allow drivers to cross the double white lines because crossing the double white lines creates a significant risk of accident to human life; after all, that's why the double white lines are there in the first place. But the lobbyist replied that the language "if safe to do so" solves this problem; it means that a motorist certainly cannot cross the double lines if it is unsafe to do so, even if the purpose is to save the life of a dog or cat or other beautiful animal.

After several days, a legislator proposed cutting through the morass simply by using the general term "emergency." Double white lines could be crossed, if safe to do so, in any emergency.

For a few moments it seemed as if this was the most reasonable way out of the difficulty. But then one legislator pointed out that the new change would render the double white divider lines exactly the same as the single white divider lines. In other words, section 205(c) would read the same as section 205(b). Someone pointed out that this was the simplest and most elegant solution; by simplifying the traffic code instead of adding to it, it would solve everyone's problems. But another legislator suggested that there must have been a legislative reason in the first place to have double white lines, and we shouldn't do away with them before considering what that reason was.

Some research revealed that, in the beginning, there were only single white divider lines on roadways. It was permissible to cross those lines when safe to do so in the event of an emergency. But it was soon found in practice that motorists got into the habit of crossing the single white line too often. The concept of "emergency" became attenuated in the minds of motorists. When stopped by police officers, the motorists would argue vehemently that there was indeed an emergency. "Emergencies" included the following:

a need to get to the airport in time to catch a plane; a need to get to an important business meeting on time; a need to avoid hitting a darting squirrel; a need to "save a marriage" by getting home for dinner in time; and so forth. So the legislature, in its wisdom, decided to use double white lines to eliminate all these "excuses" that motorists were concocting.

So, it seemed to the committee that the double white lines served a useful function. Nevertheless, Alice's case was troubling. How could an exception be written to solve Alice's case and yet not be as broad as "emergency," which would open the door to all the problems formerly connected with the single white line?

No matter how they struggled with the statute, the legislators could not come up with a form of words that would solve Alice's problem (and related problems, such as darting persons who are not children), and yet keep the double-lines [law] "tight" so that motorists would not, over time, disregard them by concocting excuses.

An expert in psychological linguistics was called to the legislative hearings. She told the committee that words, symbols, and signs, such as double white lines down a highway, only make sense to the human mind in the context in which they occur and with the history that they have in the mind of the observer. For example, a "stop" sign on a street corner would be unintelligible to a visitor from outer space. Assuming the extraterrestrial visitor could read English, what is it that should stop? Should the visitor stop breathing? Stop every internal organ from functioning? How long should they stay stopped? By observing traffic patterns, the visitor would conclude that "stop" means "stop, then go," and appears to apply only to motor-driven vehicles and not pedestrians, and so forth. In other words, the extraterrestrial visitor would begin to fill in the context and begin to make sense out of the "stop" sign.[10]

Any law is necessarily general, the expert continued. Even if the law contains an exception, the exception itself is a generalization. Laws, like words and signals and signs, can only have a general signification. But real people working in the real world can only use these generalizations as guides to their behavior in the context in which they (necessarily) interpret the generalizations. For example, Alice interpreted the double white lines as a general prohibition on her driving behavior. But she regarded that general prohibition as trumped in the unforeseen case of a darting child. Why did she "interpret" the double white lines as not constraining her to run over the child? Simply because, in the situation she confronted, it struck her as absurd that a traffic regulation should require her to deliberately kill a child. And therefore, she interpreted that traffic regulation as *not* requiring her to kill the child.

We use general words, signs, and symbols, and enact general rules, because they are the most efficient ways of communicating to people in general about situations in general. But general efficiency should not equal general compulsion. The double white lines, the expert summed up, are efficient just the way they are in conveying a message to drivers. That message may amount to: "don't cross the dividing lines unless there is an objectively compelling reason rooted in justice that overrides the lines." But the important point, she concluded, "is that you don't want to put into the statute what I've just said, because if you did, you would simply erode and undermine the very message that the dividing lines are meant to convey. You will open the door to self-serving excuses from drivers about what constitute objectively compelling reasons. My opinion is that the dividing lines already contain this very message if they are reasonably interpreted by reasonable drivers and reasonable judges."

G. The Supreme Court

Alice's petition for certiorari is accepted by the Supreme Court of the jurisdiction in which she resides. The justices of the Court are aware of the developments and arguments as I have recounted them above, but of course do not refer to them. (Courts want the public to think that their judgments are based on existing law, and not on the twists and turns of political arguments and media coverage.)

The Supreme Court unanimously decides to overrule the Intermediate Appellate Court and enter a judgment in Alice's favor. (How do I know this? Because I'm making it all up.)

Let us assume that the Court in its opinion restates and revisits all the arguments that we have examined so far. I will only present a few excerpts from the Court's opinion that either make new arguments or present the old ones with a different slant:

Difficulties arise in statutory interpretation when a statute is viewed as a computer program. A computer lacks human reason, human judgment, and human sensitivity. It will literally do what the programmer wants it to do. (Parenthetically, it is interesting to note

that in this age of computerization, we can see more clearly than ever the difference between people and machines. In the nineteenth century's age of industrialization, a machine was regarded as the height of efficiency and rationality. Perhaps the leading legal positivists of that era were attracted to a mechanical jurisprudence because of the general fascination with machines. Today, because computers can do so much, we see more clearly than ever that which they cannot do.)

The police officer who arrested Alice acted in the manner of a computer. He found that Alice had crossed the double white lines and he believed that the traffic regulations prohibited such crossing. There was no thought involved; the actions could have been handled by a computerized robot wearing a police uniform.[11]

The traffic court similarly acted in computerized fashion in finding Alice guilty of a traffic infraction. To be sure, the presiding judge indicated by his remarks that he realized the moral ramifications of the situation. But since these moral considerations had no bearing on his decision—indeed, he explicitly disavowed any bearing that they might have on his decision—he acted, for all intents and purposes, as a computer.

What is worse, both the arresting officer and the traffic court judge treated Alice as if she were also a computer. A robot that is programmed to drive a car, if given the instruction never to cross a double line divider, would never cross those lines. Even if the car were to run over ten schoolchildren crossing the street, the car would not cross the white lines.

We cannot imagine that the legislature intended the result in Alice's case when it enacted section 205 of the Motor Vehicle Act. As representatives of the people, we must give the legislators the interpretive courtesy of regarding their statutes as addressed to human beings and not computers. And we must attribute to them their own interpretive expectation that their statutes will be enforced by human police officers and human judges, and not by computers.

But we do not rest our opinion on any assumptions of interpretive courtesy to the legislature. Let us consider what the legislature would have enacted if the legislators had thought of the possibility of a case such as the darting child. The legislature could have taken two paths. First, it might have written an exception for the darting-child case into the statute. Second, it might have written an exception for the darting-child case out of the statute, that is, by deliberately excluding such an exception. These are the only two possibilities. Let us consider each of them.

First, let us assume that the legislature wrote into the double white lines provision an exception for avoiding darting children. [Here, the Supreme Court recounts the arguments given above in the discussion of the legislative hearings. The court concludes by agreeing with the expert in psycholinguistics.]

For these reasons, we conclude that the best "exception" provision the legislature could have written into the law would have been an exception "if justice so requires." But the problem is that if the exception were written exactly like that, drivers would construe it too broadly. So we must assume that the "justice" exception is to be construed ultimately by courts as a part of this regulation. The regulation in the present case is no different from any statute in any case. The only reasonable way for a court to interpret a statute is to interpret it in light of the context of justice in which it is designed to play a part. In particular, courts should not interpret statutes literally if literal interpretation would do violence to the dictates of justice. For it is only a humane concession to the public interest to assume that rational adults are entitled to interpret statutes as if they are written against a societal background of justice, and not as if they are disengaged from all social and human considerations (like a computer program).

The justice considerations we have just mentioned will of course vary depending upon the situation and context to which the statute applies. This is not a weakness, but a strength. Courts must interpret statutes not mechanically, but as people faced with new situations (many of which the legislature never contemplated) and who will reasonably interpret them.

In the particular case of a traffic regulation, the broad context is that of traffic safety and efficiency. Traffic regulations are designed to allow drivers of motor vehicles to proceed efficiently to their destinations with due regard

to their own safety, the safety of other drivers, and the safety of pedestrians. Each regulation is a legislative attempt to balance these considerations. Thus, for example, the double white divider lines are intended to keep drivers in their own lanes and prohibit them, in general, from crossing the lines. Crossing the lines might endanger their lives and the lives of drivers of oncoming vehicles. But the "safety" aspect of the double white lines is contradicted if they are interpreted in such a way as to endanger pedestrians. To interpret the double white lines as requiring a motorist to run over a darting child, when the motorist could have safely crossed the lines, is to contradict the broad purpose of the legislature in enacting traffic regulations. If the "plain meaning" rule as enunciated by the appellate court below is given unbridled priority, then such a contradiction would indeed be expected to occur. The "plain meaning" rule, as the court below interpreted it, would mean that in the name of safety, innocent children should be run over. The inconsistency is manifest. No so-called rule of interpretation, whether "plain meaning" or any other, should hinder a court from interpreting a statute according to the fundamental dictates of justice that underlie the legislature's broad purpose.

Second, let us assume that the darting-child exception is explicitly excluded from the statute. For example, section 205 might read:

(c) If a roadway is marked by double white lines (parallel lines) which traverse its length, motorists may not cross the lines, even to save the life of a darting child.

This latter clause, as we have imagined it, seems outrageous. It seems unlike any bill that any legislature would enact. Yet we must note that it constitutes the exact interpretation that the police officer and the traffic court gave to the existing section 205(c). For both the police officer and the traffic court judge found the petitioner to have violated section 205(c) by crossing the lines, even though it was an uncontroverted fact that the petitioner crossed the lines to save the life of a darting child.

The fact that the clause we have imagined seems outrageous, is just another way of concluding that it is outrageous for any court to assume that the legislature intended that section 205(c) be interpreted as if such a clause were contained in the statute. As we said above, we cannot imagine that the legislature intended that a motorist should not cross the white lines, when safe to do so, even if not crossing the lines means running over an innocent child.

But we can extend the analysis farther than that. Suppose the legislature did propose the clause we have just imagined. Surely there would have been a public outcry—indeed, the same kind of public outcry that we take judicial notice has occurred in recent weeks in connection with such "darting child" cases. The public surely would have found it outrageous for a legislature to contemplate the death of innocent children in a legislative provision that was deliberately intended to bring about such a horrible result. Indeed, any legislator who is at all attuned to public concerns would reasonably expect such a public outcry to attend any attempt to pass a bill containing the clause we have just imagined. And therefore, such a clause simply would not have been proposed, much less enacted.

If such a clause would neither have been proposed nor enacted, then a court, interpreting the provision that was enacted, should not read into it such a clause. To do so is to do interpretive violence to the provision that was in fact enacted.

Finally, let us imagine the outrageous. Let us consider the effect of a legislature actually enacting section 205(c) as we have imagined it, with the clause that motorists may not cross the lines even to save the life of a darting child. If there were such a statute, which after all is the clearest possible case from the viewpoint of the police officer who arrested the petitioner in the present case, would a traffic court be entitled to find the petitioner guilty of a traffic offense?

We think not— even in that clearest of cases. A court should instead hold such a statutory provision invalid as contrary to the elementary considerations of justice that underlie the legal system as a whole.[12] When the state sentences someone to death, the accused person is entitled to a fair and public trial. The accused person must be found guilty beyond a reasonable doubt of a capital offense. These hallowed procedural safeguards are required in all cases where the legal system enforces the ultimate penalty of death against any individual. Ac-

cordingly, any traffic regulation that condemns to death an innocent child, when the child's death could have been safely averted by the driver, violates these societal considerations of elementary justice. A court simply will not give effect to a statute, even a lowly statute such as a traffic regulation, if it contains a provision that requires a motorist to run over a child or other person. That person cannot be sentenced to death by a traffic regulation.

For all these reasons, therefore, we conclude that it makes no sense to interpret section 205 the way it was interpreted by the courts below. The real meaning of section 205—the meaning as exactly enacted by the legislature—is not contained in the words of section 205 apart from the societal context in which those words were intended to apply. Rather, the real meaning is contained in the way the legal system as a whole impacts the social system, namely, to help deliver justice to that social system. To omit considerations of fairness and justice in interpreting statutes is to fail to do justice to the reason for the existence of statutes.

Conclusion

If the preceding hypothetical case strikes you as a generic one—applicable, with modifications, to any real-life situation where a statute impacts human behavior—then I hope I have proved that it is legally impermissible to omit "justice" considerations from the interpretation and application of statutes. For the "justice" considerations are built in to the very enterprise of affecting human behavior through law.

I have said little about the common law. If I have proven that justice is an inherent part of what statutes mean, then in the absence of statutes—when a court is simply engaging in common-law adjudication—justice considerations are just as compelling if not more compelling. If a court must interpret statutes in light of a justice context, then surely they must interpret their own previous decisions in the same light.

The most important factor in the entire legal equation is that of a court made up of human (not robotic) judges. These judges are called upon to decide cases and controversies: to apply "the law" to human conflicts. The point of this Essay has been to show that "the law" *includes* considerations of justice. More precisely, the legal system is a system of the application of justice to human conflicts. As I hope to have shown, a court cannot simply apply "justice" without law, because the law—the full panoply of rules, statutes, and precedents—is part of the *facts* of the parties' situation. No decision can be based on justice if relevant facts are unknown to the decision-maker. Since law is part of the facts of any case, the law must be made known to the decision-maker (as it is, through the services of counsel) and must be taken into account by the decision-maker in order to render full justice to the parties.

Thus, what I presented above as "Proposition (1)"* should now be reformulated as follows:

> PROPOSITION (2). *Judges should decide cases according to justice. The law is a fact that is as relevant as any other material fact in the determination of what is just under the circumstances.*

---

*In a section of D'Amato's article that is not included in this reprint, he formulated what he called Proposition (1), which consisted of these words: "Judges should decide cases according to justice and not according to law."

---

1. *My usual opening salvo: Law schools don't teach justice for the same reason that medical schools don't teach health; namely, if there were perfect justice and health in the world, we might not need lawyers or doctors. Nevertheless (I add), the lawyers' professional responsibility is to promote justice, and the professional responsibility of doctors is to promote health. It's just a matter of bringing the teaching institutions in line with our professions' goals.*

2. *See Anthony D'Amato, The Decline and Fall of Law Teaching in the Age of Student Consumerism, 37 J. Legal Educ. 461 (1987).*

3. *Clearly, the more justice is done to individuals, the more just is the society as a whole.*

4. *Including, if it's a negotiation, the person you're trying to persuade.*

5. *I assume throughout that the decision-maker is not bribed, is not corrupt, and does not have a conflict of interest. These can surely be more powerful motivating forces than "justice." But if they exist, then you're whistling in the dark. Neither legal arguments nor justice arguments will work.*

6. *If we had infinite time and resources, a heroic judge, like Ronald Dworkin's mythical Judge Hercules, might ultimately come up with a better legal-political rationale for one side in a given case. See Ronald Dworkin, Taking Rights Seriously 81–130 (1977). My*

guess is that even then, another equally talented and infinitely patient judge, Judge Apollo, could very well be persuaded of the opposite result!

7. *Herbert G. Wells, The Time Machine (1895).*

8. *471 U.S. 84 (1985). For a critical analysis of the Court's reasoning, see Anthony D'Amato,* Counterintuitive Consequences of "Plain Meaning," *33 Ariz. L. Rev. 529, 535–39 (1991).*

9. *471 U.S. at 93–96.*

10. *For a discussion of related interpretive problems with "stop" signs, see Anthony D'Amato, Judicial Legislation, 1 Cardozo L. Rev. 63, 74–75 (1979).*

11. *For an early discussion on the limits of computerized justice, see Anthony D'Amato, Can/Should Computers Replace Judges? 11 Ga. L. Rev. 1277 (1977).*

12. *I am purposefully keeping this language in abstract terms. If the court is in the United States, then the Due Process Clause can be invoked as a specific constitutional provision invalidating such a statute. See U.S. Const. amend. V. In addition, the Bill of Attainder Clause might be invoked, as well as the more generalized notion of "implicit in the concept of ordered liberty." See U.S. Const. art. I, § 9, cl. 3;* Palko v. Connecticut, *302 U.S. 319, 325 (1937).*

Legal Positivism's Challenge to Natural Law Theory

A Positivist Conception of Law*

John Austin

Lecture I

The matter of jurisprudence is positive law: law, simply and strictly so called: or law set by political superiors to political inferiors. But positive law (or law, simply and strictly so called) is often confounded with objects to which it is related by *resemblance,* and with objects to which it is related in the way of *analogy:* with objects which are *also* signified, *properly* and *improperly,* by the large and vague expression *law.* To obviate the difficulties springing from that confusion, I begin my projected Course with determining the province of jurisprudence, or with distinguishing the matter of jurisprudence from those various related objects: trying to define the subject of which I intend to treat, before I endeavour to analyse its numerous and complicated parts.

A law, in the most general and comprehensive acceptation in which the term, in its literal meaning, is employed, may be said to be a rule laid down for the guidance of an intelligent being by an intelligent being having power over him. Under this definition are concluded, and without impropriety, several species. It is necessary to define accurately the line of demarcation which separates these species from one another, as much mistiness and intricacy has been infused into the science of jurisprudence by their being confounded or not clearly distinguished. In the comprehensive sense above indicated, or in the largest meaning which it has, without extension by metaphor or analogy, the term *law* embraces the following objects:—Laws set by God to his human creatures, and laws set by men to men.

The whole or a portion of the laws set by God to men is frequently styled the law of nature, or natural law: being, in truth, the only natural law of which it is possible to speak without a metaphor, or without a blending of objects which ought to be distinguished broadly. But, rejecting the appellation Law of Nature as ambiguous and misleading, I name those laws or rules, as considered collectively or in a mass, the *Divine law,* or the *law of God.*

Laws set by men to men are of two leading or principal classes: classes which are often blended, although they differ extremely; and which, for that reason, should be severed precisely, and opposed distinctly and conspicuously.

Of the laws or rules set by men to men, some are established by *political* superiors, sovereign and subject: by persons exercising supreme and subordinate *government,* in independent nations, or independent political societies. The aggregate of the rules thus established, or some aggregate forming a portion of that aggregate, is the appropriate matter of jurispru-

*From *The Province of Jurisprudence Determined,* Selections from Lectures I and VI. First published in 1832.

dence, general or particular. To the aggregate of the rules thus established, or to some aggregate forming a portion of that aggregate, the term *law,* as used simply and strictly, is exclusively applied. But, as contradistinguished to *natural* law, or to the law of *nature* (meaning, by those expressions, the law of God), the aggregate of the rules, established by political superiors, is frequently styled *positive* law, or law existing *by position.* As contradistinguished to the rules which I style *positive morality,* and on which I shall touch immediately, the aggregate of the rules, established by political superiors, may also be marked commodiously with the name of *positive law.* For the sake, then, of getting a name brief and distinctive at once, and agreeable to frequent usage, I style that aggregate of rules, or any portion of that aggregate, *positive law:* though rules, which are *not* established by political superiors are also *positive,* or exist *by position,* if they be rules or laws, in the proper signification of the term.

Though *some* of the laws or rules, which are set by men to men, are established by political superiors, *others* are *not* established by political superiors, or are *not* established by political superiors, in that capacity or character.

Closely analogous to human laws of this second class, are a set of objects frequently but *improperly* termed *laws,* being rules set and enforced by *mere opinion,* that is, by the opinions or sentiments held or felt by an indeterminate body of men in regard to human conduct. Instances of such a use of the term *law* are the expressions—"The law of honour"; "The law set by fashion"; and rules of this species constitute much of what is usually termed "International law."

The aggregate of human laws properly so called belonging to the second of the classes above mentioned, with the aggregate of objects *improperly* but by *close analogy* termed laws, I place together in a common class, and denote them by the term *positive morality.* The name *morality* severs them from *positive law,* while the epithet *positive* disjoins them from the *law of God.* And to the end of obviating confusion, it is necessary or expedient that they *should* be disjoined from the latter by that distinguishing epithet. For the name *morality* (or *morals*), when standing unqualified or alone, denotes indifferently either of the following objects: namely, positive morality *as it is,* or without regard to its merits; and positive morality *as it would be,* if it conformed to the law of God, and were, therefore, deserving of *approbation.*

Besides the various sorts of rules which are included in the literal acceptation of the term law, and those which are by a close and striking analogy,

though improperly, termed laws, there are numerous applications of the term law, which rest upon a slender analogy and are merely metaphorical or figurative. Such is the case when we talk of *laws* observed by the lower animals; of *laws* regulating the growth or decay of vegetables; of *laws* determining the movements of inanimate bodies or masses. For where *intelligence* is not, or where it is too bounded to take the name of *reason,* and, therefore, is too bounded to conceive the purpose of a law, there is not the *will* which law can work on, or which duty can incite or restrain. Yet through these misapplications of a *name,* flagrant as the metaphor is, has the field of jurisprudence and morals been deluged with muddy speculation.

Having suggested the *purpose* of my attempt to determine the province of jurisprudence: to distinguish positive law, the appropriate matter of jurisprudence, from the various objects to which it is related by resemblance, and to which it is related, nearly or remotely, by a strong or slender analogy: I shall now state the essentials of a *law* or *rule* (taken with the largest signification which can be given to the term *properly*).

Every *law* or *rule* (taken with the largest signification which can be given to the term *properly*) is a *command.* Or, rather, laws or rules, properly so called, are a *species* of commands.

Now, since the term *command* comprises the term *law,* the first is the simpler as well as the larger of the two. But, simple as it is, it admits of explanation. And, since it is the *key* to the sciences of jurisprudence and morals, its meaning should be analysed with precision.

Accordingly, I shall endeavour, in the first instance, to analyse the meaning of *'command':* an analysis which I fear, will task the patience of my hearers, but which they will bear with cheerfulness, or, at least, with resignation, if they consider the difficulty of performing it. The elements of a science are precisely the parts of it which are explained least easily. Terms that are the largest, and, therefore, the simplest of a series, are without equivalent expressions into which we can resolve them *concisely.* And when we endeavour to *define* them, or to translate them into terms which we suppose are better understood, we are forced upon awkward and tedious circumlocutions.

If you express or intimate a wish that I shall do or forbear from some act, and if you will visit me with an evil in case I comply not with your wish, the *expression* or *intimation* of your wish is a *command.* A command is distinguished from other significations of desire, not by the style in which the desire is signified, but by the power and the purpose of the party commanding to inflict an evil or pain in case the desire be disregarded. If you cannot or will not harm me in case I comply not with your wish, the expression of your wish is not a command, although you utter your wish in imperative phrase. If you are able and willing to harm me in case I comply not with your wish, the expression of your wish amounts to a command, although you are prompted by a spirit of courtesy to utter it in the shape of a request. *"Preces* erant, sed *quibus contradici non posset."* Such is the language of Tacitus, when speaking of a petition by the soldiery to a son and lieutenant of Vespasian.

A command, then, is a signification of desire. But a command is distinguished from other significations of desire by this peculiarity: that the party to whom it is directed is liable to evil from the other, in case he comply not with the desire.

Being liable to evil from you if I comply not with a wish which you signify, I am *bound* or *obliged* by your command, or I lie under a *duty* to obey it. If, in spite of that evil in prospect, I comply not with the wish which you signify, I am said to disobey your command, or to violate the duty which it imposes.

Command and duty are, therefore, correlative terms: the meaning denoted by each being implied or supposed by the other. Or (changing the expression) wherever a duty lies, a command has been signified; and whenever a command is signified, a duty is imposed.

Concisely expressed, the meaning of the correlative expressions is this: He who will inflict an evil in case his desire be disregarded, utters a command by expressing or intimating his desire. He who is liable to the evil in case he disregard the desire, is bound or obliged by the command.

The evil which will probably be incurred in case a command be disobeyed or (to use an equivalent expression) in case a duty be broken, is frequently called a *sanction,* or an *enforcement of obedience.* Or (varying the phrase) the command or the duty is said to be *sanctioned* or *enforced* by the chance of incurring the evil.

Considered as thus abstracted from the command and the duty which it enforces, the evil to be incurred by disobedience is frequently styled a *punishment*. But, as punishments, strictly so called, are only a *class* of sanctions, the term is too narrow to express the meaning adequately.

I observe that Dr. Paley, in his analysis of the term *obligation,* lays much stress upon the *violence* of the motive to compliance. In so far as I can gather a

meaning from his loose and inconsistent statement, his meaning appears to be this: that unless the motive to compliance be *violent* or *intense,* the expression or intimation of a wish is not a *command,* nor does the party to whom it is directed lie under a *duty* to regard it.

If he means, by a *violent* motive, a motive operating with certainty, his proposition is manifestly false. The greater the evil to be incurred in case the wish be disregarded, and the greater the chance of incurring it on that same event, the greater, no doubt, is the *chance* that the wish will *not* be disregarded. But no conceivable motive will *certainly* determine to compliance, or no conceivable motive will render obedience inevitable. If Paley's proposition be true, in the sense which I have now ascribed to it, commands and duties are simply impossible. Or, reducing his proposition to absurdity by a consequence as manifestly false, commands and duties are possible, but are never disobeyed or broken.

If he means by a *violent* motive, an evil which inspires fear, his meaning is simply this: that the party bound by a command is bound by the prospect of an evil. For that which is not feared is not apprehended as an evil: or (changing the shape of the expression) is not an evil in prospect.

The truth is, that the magnitude of the eventual evil, and the magnitude of the chance of incurring it, are foreign to the matter in question. The greater the eventual evil, and the greater the chance of incurring it, the greater is the efficacy of the command, and the greater is the strength of the obligation: Or (substituting expressions exactly equivalent), the greater is the *chance* that the command will be obeyed, and that the duty will not be broken. But where there is the smallest chance of incurring the smallest evil, the expression of a wish amounts to a command, and, therefore, imposes a duty. The sanction, if you will, is feeble or insufficient; but still there *is* a sanction, and, therefore, a duty and a command.

By some celebrated writers (by Locke, Bentham, and I think, Paley), the term *sanction,* or *enforcement of obedience,* is applied to conditional good as well as to conditional evil: to reward as to punishment. But, with all my habitual veneration for the names of Locke and Bentham, I think that this extension of the term is pregnant with confusion and perplexity.

Rewards are, indisputably, *motives* to comply with the wishes of others. But to talk of commands and duties as *sanctioned* or *enforced* by rewards, or to talk of rewards as *obliging* or *constraining* to obedience, is surely a wide departure from the established meaning of the terms.

If *you* expressed a desire that *I* should render a service, and if you proffered a reward as the motive or inducement to render it, *you* would scarcely be said to *command* the service, nor should *I*, in ordinary language, be *obliged* to render it. In ordinary language, *you* would *promise* me a reward, on condition of my rendering the service, whilst *I* might be *incited* or *persuaded* to render it by the hope of obtaining the reward.

Again: If a law holds out a *reward* as an inducement to do some act, an eventual *right* is conferred, and not an *obligation* imposed, upon those who shall act accordingly: The *imperative* part of the law being addressed or directed to the party whom it requires to *render* the reward.

In short, I am determined or inclined to comply with the wish of another, by the fear of disadvantage or evil. I am also determined or inclined to comply with the wish of another, by the hope of advantage or good. But it is only by the chance of incurring *evil,* that I am *bound* or *obliged* to compliance. It is only by conditional *evil,* that duties are *sanctioned* or *enforced*. It is the power and the purpose of inflicting eventual *evil,* and *not* the power and the purpose of imparting eventual *good,* which gives to the expression of a wish the name of a *command*.

If we put *reward* into the import of the term *sanction,* we must engage in a toilsome struggle with the current of ordinary speech; and shall often slide unconsciously, notwithstanding our efforts to the contrary, into the narrower and customary meaning.

It appears, then, from what has been premised, that the ideas or notions comprehended by the term *command* are the following. 1. A wish or desire conceived by a rational being, that another rational being shall do or forbear. 2. An evil to proceed from the former, and to be incurred by the latter, in case the latter comply not with the wish. 3. An expression or intimation of the wish by words or other signs.

It also appears from what has been premised, that *command, duty,* and *sanction* are inseparably connected terms: that each embraces the same ideas as the others, though each denotes those ideas in a peculiar order or series.

"A wish conceived by one, and expressed or intimated to another, with an evil to be inflicted and incurred in case the wish be disregarded," are signified directly and indirectly by each of the three expressions. Each is the name of the same complex notion.

But when I am talking *directly* of the expression or intimation of the wish, I employ the term *command:* The expression or intimation of the wish being presented *prominently* to my hearer; whilst the evil to be incurred, with the chance of incurring it, are kept (if I may so express myself) in the background of my picture.

When I am talking *directly* of the chance of incurring the evil, or (changing the expression) of the liability or obnoxiousness to the evil, I employ the term *duty,* or the term *obligation:* The liability or obnoxiousness to the evil being put foremost, and the rest of the complex notion being signified implicitly.

When I am talking *immediately* of the evil itself, I employ the term *sanction,* or a term of the like import: The evil to be incurred being signified directly; whilst the obnoxiousness to that evil, with the expression or intimation of the wish, are indicated indirectly or obliquely.

To those who are familiar with the language of logicians (language unrivalled for brevity, distinctness, and precision), I can express my meaning accurately in a breath:—Each of the three terms *signifies* the same notion; but each *denotes* a different part of that notion, and *connotes* the residue.

Commands are of two species. Some are *laws* or *rules*. The others have not acquired an appropriate name, nor does language afford an expression which will mark them briefly and precisely. I must, therefore, note them as well as I can by the ambiguous and inexpressive name of "*occasional* or *particular* commands."

The term *laws* or *rules* being not unfrequently applied to occasional or particular commands, it is hardly possible to describe a line of separation which shall consist in every respect with established forms of speech. But the distinction between laws and particular commands may, I think, be stated in the following manner.

By every command, the party to whom it is directed is obliged to do or to forbear.

Now where it obliges *generally* to acts or forbearances of a *class,* a command is a law or rule. But where it obliges to a *specific* act or forbearance, or to acts or forbearances which it determines *specifically* or *individually,* a command is occasional or particular. In other words, a class or description of acts is determined by a law or rule, and acts of that class or description are enjoined or forbidden generally. But where a command is occasional or particular, the act or acts, which the command enjoins or forbids, are assigned or determined by their specific or individual natures as well as by the class or description to which they belong.

The statement which I have given in abstract expressions I will now endeavour to illustrate by apt examples.

If you command your servant to go on a given errand, or *not* to leave your house on a given evening, or to rise at such an hour on such a morning, or to rise at that hour during the next week or month, the command is occasional or particular. For the act or acts enjoined or forbidden are specially determined or assigned.

But if you command him *simply* to rise at that hour, or to rise at that hour *always,* or to rise at that hour *till further orders,* it may be said, with propriety, that you lay down a *rule* for the guidance of your servant's conduct. For no specific act is assigned by the command, but the command obliges him generally to acts of a determined class.

If a regiment be ordered to attack or defend a post, or to quell a riot, or to march from their present quarters, the command is occasional or particular. But an order to exercise daily till further orders shall be given would be called a *general* order, and *might* be called a *rule.*

If Parliament prohibited simply the exportation of corn, either for a given period or indefinitely, it would establish a law or rule: a *kind* or *sort* of acts being determined by the command, and acts of that kind or sort being *generally* forbidden. But an order issued by Parliament to meet an impending scarcity, and stopping the exportation of corn *then shipped and in port,* would not be a law or rule, though issued by the sovereign legislature. The order regarding exclusively a specified quantity of corn, the negative acts or forbearances, enjoined by the command, would be determined specifically or individually by the determinate nature of their subject.

As issued by a sovereign legislature, and as wearing the form of a law, the order which I have now imagined would probably be *called* a law. And hence the difficulty of drawing a distinct boundary between laws and occasional commands.

Again: An act which is not an offence, according to the existing law, moves the sovereign to displeasure: and, though the authors of the act are legally innocent or unoffending, the sovereign commands that they shall be punished. As enjoining a specific punishment in that specific case, and as not enjoining generally acts or forbearances of a class, the order uttered by the sovereign is not a law or rule.

Whether such an order would be *called* a law, seems to depend upon circumstances which are purely immaterial: immaterial, that is, with reference to the present purpose, though material with reference to others. If made by a sovereign assembly deliberately, and with the forms of legislation, it would probably be called a law. If uttered by an absolute monarch, without deliberation or ceremony, it would scarcely be confounded with acts of legislation, and would be styled an arbitrary command. Yet, on either of these suppositions, its nature would be the same. It would not be a law or rule, but an occasional or particular command of the sovereign One or Number.

To conclude with an example which best illustrates the distinction, and which shows the importance of the distinction most conspicuously, *judicial commands* are commonly occasional or particular, although the commands which they are calculated to enforce are commonly laws or rules.

For instance, the lawgiver commands that thieves shall be hanged. A specific theft and a specified thief being given, the judge commands that the thief shall be hanged, agreeably to the command of the lawgiver.

Now the lawgiver determines a class or description of acts; prohibits acts of the class generally and indefinitely; and commands, with the like generality, that punishment shall follow transgression. The command of the lawgiver is, therefore, a law or rule. But the command of the judge is occasional or particular. For he orders a specific punishment, as the consequence of a specific offence.

According to the line of separation which I have now attempted to describe, a law and a particular command are distinguished thus:—Acts of forbearances of a *class* are enjoined *generally* by the former. Acts *determined specifically* are enjoined or forbidden by the latter.

A different line of separation has been drawn by Blackstone and others. According to Blackstone and others, a law and a particular command are distinguished in the following manner:—A law obliges *generally* the members of the given community, or a law obliges *generally* persons of a given class. A particular command obliges a *single* person, or persons whom it determines *individually.*

That laws and particular commands are not to be distinguished thus, will appear on a moment's reflection.

For, *first,* commands which oblige generally the members of the given community, or commands which oblige generally persons of given classes, are not always laws or rules.

Thus, in the case already supposed; that in which the sovereign commands that all corn actually shipped for exportation be stopped and detained; the command is obligatory upon the whole community, but as it obliges them only to a set of acts individually assigned, it is not a law. Again, suppose the sovereign to issue an order, enforced by penalties, for a general mourning, on occasion of a public calamity. Now, though it is addressed to the community at large, the order is scarcely a rule, in the usual acceptation of the term. For, though it obliges generally the members of the entire community, it obliges to acts which it assigns specifically, instead of obliging generally to acts or forbearances of a class. If the sovereign commanded that *black* should be the dress of his subjects, his command would amount to a law. But if he commanded them to wear it on a specified occasion, his command would be merely particular.

And, *secondly,* a command which obliges exclusively persons individually determined, may amount, notwithstanding, to a law or a rule.

For example, A father may set a *rule* to his child or children: a guardian, to his ward: a master, to his slave or servant. And certain of God's *laws* were as binding on the first man, as they are binding at this hour on the millions who have sprung from his loins.

Most, indeed, of the laws which are established by political superiors, or most of the laws which are simply and strictly so called, oblige generally the members of the political community, or oblige generally persons of a class. To frame a system of duties for every individual of the community, were simply impossible: and if it were possible, it were utterly useless. Most of the laws established by political superiors are, therefore, *general* in a twofold manner: as enjoining or forbidding generally acts of kinds or sorts; and as binding the whole community, or, at least, whole classes of its members.

But if we suppose that Parliament creates and grants an office, and that Parliament binds the grantee to services of a given description, we suppose a law established by political superiors, and yet exclusively binding a specified or determinate person.

Laws established by political superiors, and exclusively binding specified or determinate persons, are styled, in the language of the Roman jurists, *privilegia.* Though that, indeed, is a name which will hardly denote them distinctly: for, like most of the leading terms in actual systems of law, it is not the name of a definite class of objects, but a heap of heterogeneous objects.[1]

It appears, from what has been premised, that a law, properly so called, may be defined in the following manner.

A law is a command which obliges a person or persons.

But, as contradistinguished or opposed to an occasional or particular command, a law is a command which obliges a person or persons, and obliges *generally* to acts or forbearances of a class.

In language more popular but less distinct and precise, a law is a command which obliges a person or persons to a *course* of conduct.

Laws and other commands are said to proceed from *superiors,* and to bind or oblige *inferiors.* I will, therefore, analyse the meaning of those correlative expressions; and will try to strip them of a certain mystery, by which that simple meaning appears to be obscured.

Superiority is often synonymous with *precedence* or *excellence.* We talk of superiors in rank; of superiors in wealth; of superiors in virtue: comparing certain persons with certain other persons; and meaning that the former precede or excel the latter in rank, in wealth, or in virtue.

But, taken with the meaning wherein I here understand it, the term *superiority* signifies *might:* the power of affecting others with evil or pain, and of forcing them, through fear of that evil, to fashion their conduct to one's wishes.

For example, God is emphatically the *superior* of Man. For his power of affecting us with pain, and of forcing us to comply with his will, is unbounded and resistless.

To a limited extent, the sovereign One or Number is the superior of the subject or citizen: the master, of the slave or servant: the father, of the child.

In short, whoever can *oblige* another to comply with his wishes, is the *superior* of that other, so far as the ability reaches: The party who is obnoxious to the impending evil, being, to that same extent, the *inferior.*

The might or superiority of God, is simple or absolute. But in all or most cases of human superiority, the relation of superior and inferior, and the relation of inferior and superior, are reciprocal. Or (changing the expression) the party who is the superior as viewed from one aspect, is the inferior as viewed from another.

For example, To an indefinite, though limited extent, the monarch is the superior of the governed: his power being commonly sufficient to enforce compliance with his will. But the governed, collectively or in mass, are also the superior of the monarch: who is checked in the abuse of his might by his fear of exciting their anger; and of rousing to active resistance the might which slumbers in the multitude.

A member of a sovereign assembly is the superior of the judge: the judge being bound by the law which proceeds from that sovereign body. But, in his character of citizen or subject, he is the inferior of the judge: the judge being the minister of the law, and armed with the power of enforcing it.

It appears, then, that the term *superiority* (like the terms *duty* and *sanction*) is implied by the term *command*. For superiority is the power of enforcing compliance with a wish: and the expression or intimation of a wish, with the power and the purpose of enforcing it, are the constituent elements of a command.

"That *laws* emanate from *superiors*" is, therefore, an identical proposition. For the meaning which it affects to impart is contained in its subject.

If I mark the peculiar source of a given law, or if I mark the peculiar source of laws of a given class, it is possible that I am saying something which may instruct the hearer. But to affirm of laws universally "that they flow from *superiors*," or to affirm of laws universally "that *inferiors* are bound to obey them," is the merest tautology and trifling.

Like most of the leading terms in the sciences of jurisprudence and morals, the term *laws* is extremely ambiguous. Taken with the largest signification which can be given to the term properly, *laws* are a species of *commands*. But the term is improperly applied to various objects which have nothing of the imperative character: to objects which are *not* commands; and which, therefore, are *not* laws, properly so called.

Accordingly, the proposition "that laws are commands" must be taken with limitations. Or, rather, we must distinguish the various meanings of the term *laws;* and must restrict the proposition to that class of objects which is embraced by the largest signification that can be given to the term properly.

I have already indicated, and shall hereafter more fully describe, the objects improperly termed laws, which are *not* within the province of jurisprudence (being either rules enforced by opinion and closely analogous to laws properly so called, or being laws so called by a metaphorical application of the term merely). There are other objects improperly termed laws (not being commands) which yet may properly be included within the province of jurisprudence. These I shall endeavour to particularise:—

1. Acts on the part of legislatures to *explain* positive law, can scarcely be called laws, in the proper signification of the term. Working no change in the actual duties of the governed, but simply declaring what those duties *are,* they properly are acts of *interpretation* by legislative authority. Or, to borrow an expression from the writers on the Roman Law, they are acts of *authentic* interpretation.

But, this notwithstanding, they are frequently styled laws; *declaratory* laws, or declaratory statutes. They must, therefore, be noted as forming an exception to the proposition "that laws are a species of commands."

It often, indeed, happens (as I shall show in the proper place), that laws declaratory in name are imperative in effect: Legislative, like judicial interpretation, being frequently deceptive; and establishing new law, under guise of expounding the old.

2. Laws to repeal laws, and to release from existing duties, must also be excepted from the proposition "that laws are a species of commands." In so far as they release from duties imposed by existing laws, they are not commands, but revocations of commands. They authorise or permit the parties, to whom the repeal extends, to do or to forbear from acts which they were commanded to forbear from or to do. And, considered with regard to *this,* their immediate or direct purpose, they are often named *permissive laws,* or, more briefly and more properly, *permissions.*

Remotely and indirectly, indeed, permissive laws are often or always imperative. For the parties released from duties are restored to liberties or rights: and duties answering those rights are, therefore, created or revived.

But this is a matter which I shall examine with exactness, when I analyse the expressions "legal right", "permission by the sovereign or state," and "civil or political liberty."

3. Imperfect laws, or laws of imperfect obligation, must also be excepted from the proposition "that laws are a species of commands."

An imperfect law (with the sense wherein the term is used by the Roman jurists) is a law which wants a sanction, and which, therefore, is not binding. A law declaring that certain acts are crimes, but annexing no punishment to the commission of acts of the class, is the simplest and most obvious example.

Though the author of an imperfect law signifies a desire, he manifests no purpose of enforcing compliance with the desire. But where there is not a purpose of enforcing compliance with the desire, the expression of a desire is not a command. Consequently, an imperfect law is not so properly a law, as counsel, or exhortation, addressed by a superior to inferiors.

Examples of imperfect laws are cited by the Roman jurists. But with us in England, laws professedly imperative are always (I believe) perfect or obligatory. Where the English legislature affects to command, the English tribunals not unreasonably presume that the legislature exacts obedience. And, if no specific sanction be annexed to a given law, a sanction is supplied by the courts of justice, agreeably to a general maxim which obtains in cases of the kind.

The imperfect laws, of which I am now speaking, are laws which are imperfect, in the sense of *the Roman jurists:* that is to say, laws which speak the desires of political superiors, but which their authors (by oversight or design) have not provided with sanctions. Many of the writers on *morals,* and on the so called *law of nature,* have annexed a different meaning to the term *imperfect.* Speaking of imperfect obligations, they commonly mean duties which are *not legal:* duties imposed by commands of God, or duties imposed by positive morality, as contradistinguished to duties imposed by positive law. An imperfect obligation, in the sense of the Roman jurists, is exactly equivalent to no obligation at all. For the term *imperfect* denotes simply, that the law wants the sanction appropriate to laws of the kind. An imperfect obligation, in the other meaning of the expression, is a religious or a moral obligation. The term *imperfect* does not denote that the law imposing the duty wants the appropriate sanction. It denotes that the law imposing the duty is *not* a law established by a political superior: that it wants that *perfect,* or that surer or more cogent sanction, which is imparted by the sovereign or state.

I believe that I have now reviewed all the classes of objects, to which the term *laws* is improperly applied. The laws (improperly so called) which I have here lastly enumerated, are (I think) the only laws which are not commands, and which yet may be properly included within the province of jurisprudence. But though these, with the so called laws set by opinion and the objects metaphorically termed laws, are the only laws which *really* are not commands, there are certain laws (properly so called) which may *seem* not imperative. Accordingly, I will subjoin a few remarks upon laws of this dubious character.

1. There are laws, it may be said, which *merely* create *rights:* And, seeing that every command imposes a *duty,* laws of this nature are not imperative.

But, as I have intimated already, and shall show completely hereafter, there are no laws *merely* creating *rights.* There are laws, it is true, which *merely* create *duties:* duties not correlating with correlating rights, and which, therefore may be styled *absolute.* But every law, really conferring a right, imposes expressly or tacitly a *relative* duty, or a duty correlating with the right. If it specify the remedy to be given, in case the right shall be infringed, it imposes the relative duty expressly. If the remedy to be given be not specified, it refers tacitly to pre-existing law, and clothes the right which it purports to create with a remedy provided by that law. Every law, really conferring a right is, therefore, imperative: as imperative, as if its only purpose were the creation of a duty, or as if the relative duty, which it inevitably imposes, were merely absolute.

The meanings of the term *right,* are various and perplexed; taken with its proper meaning, it comprises ideas which are numerous and complicated; and the searching and extensive analysis, which the term, therefore, requires, would occupy more room than could be given to it in the present lecture. It is not, however, necessary, that the analysis should be performed here. I purpose, in my earlier lectures, to determine the province of jurisprudence; or to distinguish the laws established by political superiors, from the various laws, proper and improper, with which they are frequently confounded. And this I may accomplish exactly enough, without a nice inquiry into the import of the term *right.*

2. According to an opinion which I must notice *incidentally* here, though the subject to which it relates will be treated *directly* hereafter, *customary laws* must be excepted from the proposition "that laws are a species of command."

By many of the admirers of customary laws (and, especially, of their German admirers), they are thought to oblige legally (independently of the sovereign or state), *because* the citizens or subjects have observed or kept them. Agreeably to this opinion, they are not the *creatures* of the sovereign or state, although the sovereign or state may abolish them at pleasure. Agreeably to this opinion, they are positive law (or law, strictly so called), inasmuch as they are enforced by the courts of justice: But, that notwithstanding, they exist as *positive law* by the spontaneous adoption of the governed, and not by position or establishment on the part of political superiors. Consequently, customary laws, considered as positive law, are not commands. And, consequently, customary laws, considered as positive law, are not laws or rules properly so called.

An opinion less mysterious, but somewhat allied to this, is not uncommonly held by the adverse party: by the party which is strongly opposed to customary law; and to all law made judicially, or in the way of judicial legislation. According to the latter opinion, all judge-made law, or all judge-made law established by *subject* judges, is purely the creature of the judges by whom it is established immediately. To impute it to the sovereign legislature, or to suppose that it speaks the will of the sovereign legislature, is one of the foolish or knavish *fictions* with which lawyers, in every age and nation, have perplexed and darkened the simplest and clearest truths.

I think it will appear, on a moment's reflection, that each of these opinions is groundless: that customary law is *imperative,* in the proper signification of the term; and that all judge-made law is the creature of the sovereign or state.

At its origin, a custom is a rule of conduct which the governed observe spontaneously, or not in pursuance of a law set by a political superior. The custom is transmuted into positive law, when it is adopted as such by the courts of justice, and when the judicial decisions fashioned upon it are enforced by the power of the state. But before it is adopted by the courts, and clothed with the legal sanction, it is merely a rule of positive morality: a rule generally observed by the citizens or subjects; but deriving the only force, which it can be said to possess, from the general disapprobation falling on those who transgress it.

Now when judges transmute a custom into a legal rule (or make a legal rule not suggested by a custom), the legal rule which they establish is established by the sovereign legislature. A subordinate or subject judge is merely a minister. The portion of the sovereign power which lies at his disposition is merely delegated. The rules which he makes derive their legal force from authority given by the state: an authority which the state may confer expressly, but which it commonly imparts in the way of acquiescence. For, since the state may reverse the rules which he makes, and yet permits him to enforce them by the power of the political community, its sovereign will "that his rules shall obtain as law" is clearly evinced by its conduct, though not by its express declaration.

The admirers of customary law love to trick out their idol with mysterious and imposing attributes. But to those who can see the difference between positive law and morality, there is nothing of mystery about it. Considered as rules of positive morality, customary laws arise from the consent of the governed, and not from the position or establishment of political superiors. But, considered as moral rules turned into positive laws, customary laws are established by the state: established by the state directly, when the customs are promulgated in its statutes; established by the state circuitously, when the customs are adopted by its tribunals.

The opinion of the party which abhors judge-made laws, springs from their inadequate conception of the nature of commands.

Like other significations of desire, a command is express or tacit. If the desire be signified by *words* (written or spoken), the command is express. If the desire be signified by conduct (or by any signs of desire which are *not* words), the command is tacit.

Now when customs are turned into legal rules by decisions of subject judges, the legal rules which emerge from the customs are *tacit* commands of the sovereign legislature. The state, which is able to abolish, permits its ministers to enforce them: and it, therefore, signifies its pleasure, by that its voluntary acquiescence, "that they shall serve as a law to the governed."

My present purpose is merely this: to prove that the positive law styled *customary* (and all positive law made judicially) is established by the state directly or circuitously, and, therefore, is *imperative*. I am far from disputing, that law made judicially (or in the way of improper legislation) and law made by statute (or in the properly legislative manner) are distinguished by weighty differences. I shall inquire, in future lectures, what those differences are; and why subject judges, who are properly ministers of the law, have commonly shared with the sovereign in the business of making it.

I assume, then, that the only laws which are not imperative, and which belong to the subject-matter of jurisprudence, are the following:—1. Declaratory laws, or laws explaining the import of existing positive law. 2. Laws abrogating or repealing existing positive law. 3. Imperfect laws, or laws of imperfect obligation (with the sense wherein the expression is used by the Roman jurists).

But the space occupied in the science by these improper laws is comparatively narrow and insignificant. Accordingly, although I shall take them into account so often as I refer to them directly, I shall throw them out of account on other occasions. Or (changing the expression) I shall limit the term *law* to laws which are imperative, unless I extend it expressly to laws which are not.

Lecture VI

. . . The superiority which is styled sovereignty, and the independent political society which sovereignty implies, is distinguished from other superiority, and from other society, by the following marks or characters:—1. The *bulk* of the given society are in a *habit* of obedience or submission to a *determinate* and *common* superior: let that common superior be a certain individual person or a certain body or aggregate of individual persons. 2. That certain individual, or that certain body of individuals, is *not* in a habit of obedience to a determinate human superior. Laws (improperly so called) which opinion sets or imposes, may permanently affect the conduct of that certain individual or body. To express or tacit commands of other determinate parties, that certain individual or body may yield occasional submission. But there is no . determinate person, or determinate aggregate of persons, to whose commands, express or tacit, that certain individual or body renders habitual obedience.

Or the notions of sovereignty and independent political society may be expressed concisely thus.—If a *determinate* human superior, *not* in a habit of obedience to a like superior, receive *habitual* obedience from the *bulk* of a given society, that determinate superior is sovereign in that society, and the society (including the superior) is a society political and independent.

To that determinate superior, the other members of the society are *subject:* or on that determinate superior, to other members of the society are *dependent*. The position of its other members towards that determinate superior, is *a state of subjection,* or *a state of dependence*. The mutual relation which subsists between that superior and them, may be styled *the relation of sovereign and subject, or the relation of sovereignty and subjection.*

Hence it follows, that it is only through an ellipsis, or an abridged form of expression, that the *society* is styled *independent*. The party truly independent (independent, that is to say, of a determinate human superior), is not the society, but the sovereign portion of the society: that a certain member of the society, or that certain body of its members, to whose com-

mands, expressed or intimated, the generality or bulk of its members render habitual obedience. Upon that certain person, or certain body of persons, the other members of the society are *dependent:* or to that certain person, or certain body of persons, the other members of the society are *subject*. By "an independent political society," or "an independent and sovereign nation," we mean a political society consisting of a sovereign and subjects, as opposed to a political society which is merely subordinate: that is to say, which is merely a limb or member of another political society, and which therefore consists entirely of persons in a state of subjection.

In order that a given society may form a society political and independent, the two distinguishing marks which I have mentioned above must unite. The *generality* of the given society must be in the *habit* of obedience to a *determinate* and *common* superior: whilst that determinate persons, or determinate body of persons must *not* be habitually obedient to a determinate person or body. It is the union of that positive, with this negative mark, which renders that given society (including that certain superior) a society political and independent.

To show that the union of those marks renders a given society a society political and independent, I call your attention to the following positions and examples.

1. In order that a given society may form a society political, the generality or bulk of its members must be in a *habit* of obedience to a determinate and common superior.

In case the generality of its members obey a determinate superior, but the obedience be rare or transient and not habitual or permanent, the relation of sovereignty and subjection is not created thereby between that certain superior and the members of that given society. In other words, that determinate superior and the members of that given society do not become thereby an independent political society. Whether that given society be political and independent or not, it is not an independent political society whereof that certain superior is the sovereign portion.

For example: In 1815 the allied armies occupied France; and so long as the allied armies occupied France, the commands of the allied sovereigns were obeyed by the French government, and, through the French government, by the French people generally. But since the commands and the obedience were comparatively rare and transient, they were not sufficient to constitute the relation of sovereignty and subjection between the allied sovereigns and the members of the invaded nation. In spite of those commands, and in spite of that obedience, the French government was sovereign or independent. Or in spite of those commands, and in spite of that obedience, the French government and its subjects were an independent political society whereof the allied sovereigns were not the sovereign portion.

Now if the French nation, before the obedience to those sovereigns, had been an independent society in a state of nature or anarchy, it would not have been changed by the obedience into a society political. And it would not have been changed by the obedience into a society political, because the obedience was not habitual. For, inasmuch as the obedience was not habitual, it was not changed by the obedience from a society political and independent, into a society political but subordinate.—A given society, therefore, is not a society political, unless the generality of its members be in a *habit* of obedience to a determinate and common superior.

Again: A feeble state holds its independence precariously, or at the will of the powerful states to whose aggressions it is obnoxious. And since it is obnoxious to their aggressions, it and the bulk of its subjects render obedience to commands which they occasionally express or intimate. Such, for instance, is the position of the Saxon government and its subjects in respect of the conspiring sovereigns who form the Holy Alliance. But since the commands and the obedience are comparatively few and rare, they are not sufficient to constitute the relation of sovereignty and subjection between the powerful states and the feeble state with its subjects. In spite of those commands, and in spite of that obedience, the feeble state is sovereign or independent. Or in spite of those commands, and in spite of that obedience, the feeble state and its subjects are an independent political society whereof the powerful states are not the sovereign portion. Although the powerful states are permanently *superior,* and although the feeble state is permanently *inferior,* there is neither a *habit* of command on the part of the former, nor a *habit* of obedience on the part of the latter. Although the latter is unable to defend and maintain its independence, the latter is independent of the former in fact or practice.

From the example now adduced, as from the example adduced before, we may draw the following inference: that a given society is not a society political, unless the generality of its members be in a *habit* of obedience to a determinate and common superior.— By the obedience to the powerful states, the feeble

state and its subjects are not changed from an independent, into a subordinate political society. And they are not changed by the obedience into a subordinate political society, because the obedience is not habitual. Consequently, if they were a natural society (setting that obedience aside), they would not be changed by that obedience into a society political.

2. In order that a given society may form a society political, habitual obedience must be rendered, by the *generality* or *bulk* of its members, to a determinate and *common* superior. In other words, habitual obedience must be rendered, by the *generality* or *bulk* of its members, to *one and the same* determinate person, or determinate body of persons.

Unless habitual obedience be rendered by the *bulk* of its members, and be rendered by the bulk of its members to *one and the same* superior, the given society is either in a state of nature, or is split into two or more independent political societies.

For example: In case a given society be torn by intestine war, and in case the conflicting parties be nearly balanced, the given society is in one of the two positions which I have now supposed.—As there is no common superior to which the bulk of its members render habitual obedience, it is not a political society single or undivided.—If the bulk of each of the parties be in a habit of obedience to its head, the given society is broken into two or more societies, which, perhaps, may be styled independent political societies.— If the bulk of each of the parties be not in that habit of obedience, the given society is simply or absolutely in a state of nature or anarchy. It is either resolved or broken into its individual elements, or into numerous societies of an extremely limited size: of a size so extremely limited, that they could hardly be styled societies independent and *political*. For, as I shall show hereafter, a given independent society would hardly be styled *political,* in case it fell short of a *number* which cannot be fixed with precision, but which may be called considerable, or not extremely minute.

3. In order that a given society may form a society political, the generality or bulk of its members must habitually obey a superior *determinate* as well as common.

On this position I shall not insist here. For I have shown sufficiently in my fifth lecture, that no indeterminate party can command expressly or tacitly, or can receive obedience or submission: that no indeterminate body is capable of corporate conduct, or is capable, as a body, of positive or negative deportment.

4. It appears from what has preceded, that, in order that a given society may form a society political, the bulk of its members must be in a habit of obedience to a certain and common superior. But, in order that the given society may form a society political and independent, that certain superior must *not* be habitually obedient to a determinate human superior.

The given society may form a society political and independent, although that certain superior be habitually affected by laws which opinion sets or imposes. The given society may form a society political and independent, although that certain superior render occasional submission to commands of determinate parties. But the society is not independent, although it may be political, in case that certain superior habitually obey the commands of a certain person or body.

Let us suppose, for example, that a viceroy obeys habitually the author of his delegated powers. And, to render the example complete, let us suppose that the viceroy receives habitual obedience from the generality or bulk of the persons who inhabit his province.—Now though he commands habitually within the limits of his province, and receives habitual obedience from the generality or bulk of its inhabitants, the viceroy is not sovereign within the limits of his province, nor are he and its inhabitants an independent political society. The viceroy, and (through the viceroy) the generality or bulk of its inhabitants, are habitually obedient or submissive to the sovereign of a larger society. He and the inhabitants of his province are therefore in a state of subjection to the sovereign of that larger society. He and the inhabitants of his province are a society political but subordinate, or form a political society which is merely a limb of another.

---

1. *Where a* privilegium *merely imposes a duty, it exclusively obliges a determinate person or persons. But where a* privilegium *confers a right, and the right conferred* avails against the world at large, *the law* is privilegium *as viewed from a certain aspect, but is also* a general law *as viewed from another aspect. In respect of the right conferred, the law exclusively regards a determinate person,* and, therefore, is privilegium. In respect of the duty imposed, and corresponding to the right conferred, the law regards generally the members of the entire community.

This I shall explain particularly at a subsequent point of my Course, when I consider the peculiar nature of so-called privilegia, or of so-called private laws.

A More Recent Positivist Conception of Law*

H. L. A. Hart

Law as the Union of Primary and Secondary Rules

A Fresh Start

[As I have discussed elsewhere] at various crucial points, the simple model of law as the sovereign's coercive orders failed to reproduce some of the salient features of a legal system. To demonstrate this, we did not find it necessary to invoke (as earlier critics have done) international law or primitive law which some may regard as disputable or borderline examples of law; instead we pointed to certain familiar features of municipal law in a modern state, and showed that

---

these were either distorted or altogether unrepresented in this over-simple theory.

The main ways in which the theory failed are instructive enough to merit a second summary. First, it became clear that though of all the varieties of law, a criminal statute, forbidding or enjoining certain actions under penalty, most resembles orders backed by threats given by one person to others, such a statute nonetheless differs from such orders in the important respect that it commonly applies to those who enact it and not merely to others. Secondly, there are other varieties of law, notably those conferring legal powers to adjudicate or legislate (public powers) or to create or vary legal relations (private powers) which cannot, without absurdity, be construed as orders backed by threats. Thirdly, there are legal rules which differ from orders in their mode of origin, because they are not brought into being by anything analogous to explicit prescription. Finally, the analysis of law in terms of the sovereign, habitually obeyed and necessarily exempt from all legal limitation, failed to account for the continuity of legislative authority characteristic of a modern legal system, and the sovereign, person or persons could not be identified with either the electorate or the legislature of a modern state.

It will be recalled that in thus criticizing the conception of law as the sovereign's coercive orders we considered also a number of ancillary devices which were brought in at the cost of corrupting the primitive simplicity of the theory to rescue it from its difficulties. But these too failed. One device, the notion of a *tacit* order, seemed to have no application to the complex actualities of a modern legal system, but only to very much simpler situations like that of a general who deliberately refrains from interfering with orders given by his subordinates. Other devices, such as that of treating power-conferring rules as mere fragments of rules imposing duties, or treating all rules as directed only to officials, distort the ways in which these are spoken of, thought of, and actually used in social life. This had no better claim to our assent than the theory that all the rules of a game are "really" directions to the umpire and the scorer. The device, designed to reconcile the self-binding character of legislation with the theory that a statute is an order given to *others*, was to distinguish the legislators acting in their official capacity, as *one* person ordering *others* who include themselves in their private capacities. This device, impeccable in itself, involved supplementing the theory with something it does not contain: this is the notion of a rule defining what must be done to legislate; for it is only in conforming with such a rule that legislators

have an official capacity and a separate personality to be contrasted with themselves as private individuals.

[My previous discussions] are therefore the record of a failure and there is plainly need for a fresh start. Yet the failure is an instructive one, worth the detailed consideration we have given it, because at each point where the theory failed to fit the facts it was possible to see at least in outline why it was bound to fail and what is required for a better account. The root cause of failure is that the elements out of which the theory was constructed, viz. the ideas of orders, obedience, habits, and threats, do not include, and cannot by their combination yield, the idea of a rule, without which we cannot hope to elucidate even the most elementary forms of law. It is true that the idea of a rule is by no means a simple one: we have already seen in [a previous discussion] the need, if we are to do justice to the complexity of a legal system, to discriminate between two different though related types. Under rules of the one type, which may well be considered the basic or primary type, human beings are required to do or abstain from certain actions, whether they wish to or not. Rules of the other type are in a sense parasitic upon or secondary to the first; for they provide that human beings may be doing or saying certain things introduce new rules of the primary type, extinguish or modify old ones, or in various ways determine their incidence or control their operations. Rules of the first type impose duties; rules of the second type confer powers, public or private. Rules of the first type concern actions involving physical movement or changes; rules of the second type provide for operations which lead not merely to physical movement or change, but to the creation or variation of duties or obligations.

We have already given some preliminary analysis of what is involved in the assertion that rules of these two types exist among a given social group, and in this chapter we shall not only carry this analysis a little farther but we shall make the general claim that in the combination of these two types of rule there lies what Austin wrongly claimed to have found in the notion of coercive orders, namely, "the key to the science of jurisprudence." We shall not indeed claim that wherever the word "law" is "properly" used this combination of primary and secondary rules is to be found; for it is clear that the diverse range of cases of which the word "law" is used are not linked by any such simple uniformity, but by less direct relations — often of analogy of either form or content to a central case. What we shall attempt to show, in this and the succeeding chapters, is that most of the features of law which have proved most perplexing and have both provoked and eluded the search for definition can best be rendered clear, if these two types of rule and the interplay between them are understood. We accord this union of elements a central place because of their explanatory power in elucidating the concepts that constitute the framework of legal thought. The justification for the use of the word "law" for a range of apparently heterogeneous cases is a secondary matter which can be undertaken when the central elements have been grasped.

The Idea of Obligation

It will be recalled that the theory of law as coercive orders, notwithstanding its errors, started from the perfectly correct appreciation of the fact that where there is law, there human conduct is made in some sense non-optional or obligatory. In choosing this starting-point the theory was well inspired, and in building up a new account of law in terms of the interplay of primary and secondary rules we too shall start from the same idea. It is, however, here, at this crucial first step, that we have perhaps most to learn from the theory's errors.

Let us recall the gunman situation. A orders B to hand over his money and threatens to shoot him if he does not comply. According to the theory of coercive orders this situation illustrates the notion of obligation or duty in general. Legal obligation is to be found in this situation writ large; A must be the sovereign habitually obeyed and the orders must be general, prescribing courses of conduct not single actions. The plausibility of the claim that the gunman situation displays the meaning of obligation lies in the fact that it is certainly one in which we would say that B, if he obeyed, was "obliged" to hand over his money. It is, however, equally certain that we should misdescribe the situation if we said, on these facts, that B "had an obligation" or a "duty" to hand over the money. So from the start it is clear that we need something else for an understanding of the idea of obligation. There is a difference, yet to be explained, between the assertion that someone *was obliged* to do something and the assertion that he *had an obligation* to do it. The first is often a statement about the beliefs and motives with which an action is done: B was obliged to hand over his money may simply mean, as it does in the gunman case, that he believed that some harm or other unpleasant consequences would befall him if he did not hand it over and he handed it over to avoid those consequences. In such cases the prospect of

what would happen to the agent if he disobeyed has rendered something he would otherwise have preferred to have done (keep the money) less eligible.

Two further elements slightly complicate the elucidation of the notion of being obliged to do something. It seems clear that we should not think of B as obliged to hand over the money if the threatened harm was, according to common judgments, trivial in comparison with the disadvantage or serious consequences, either for B or for others, of complying with the orders, as it would be, for example, if A merely threatened to pinch B. Nor perhaps should we say that B was obliged, if there were no reasonable grounds for thinking that A could or would probably implement his threat of relatively serious harm. Yet, though such references to common judgments of comparative harm and reasonable estimates of likelihood, are implicit in this notion, the statement that a person was obliged to obey someone is, in the main, a psychological one referring to the beliefs and motives with which an action was done. But the statement that someone *had an obligation* to do something is of a very different type and there are many signs of this difference. Thus not only is it the case that the facts about B's action and his beliefs and motives in the gunman case, though sufficient to warrant the statement that B was obliged to hand over his purse, are *not sufficient* to warrant the statement that he had an obligation to do this; it is also the case that facts of this sort, i.e. facts about beliefs and motives, are *not necessary* for the truth of a statement that a person had an obligation to do something. Thus the statement that a person had an obligation, e.g. to tell the truth or report for military service, remains true even if he believed (reasonably or unreasonably) that he would never be found out and had nothing to fear from disobedience. Moreover, whereas the statement that he had this obligation is quite independent of the question whether or not he in fact reported for service, the statement that someone was obliged to do something, normally carries the implication that he actually did it.

Some theorists, Austin among them, seeing perhaps the general irrelevance of the person's beliefs, fears, and motives to the question whether he had an obligation to do something, have defined this notion not in terms of these subjective facts, but in terms of the *chance* or *likelihood* that the person having the obligation will suffer a punishment or "evil" at the hands of others in the event of disobedience. This, in effect, treats statements of obligation not as psychological statements but as predictions or assessments of chances of incurring punishment or "evil." To many later theorists this has appeared as a revelation, bringing down to earth an elusive notion and restating it in the same clear, hard, empirical terms as are used in science. It has, indeed, been accepted sometimes as the only alternative to metaphysical conceptions of obligation or duty as invisible objects mysteriously existing "above" or "behind" the world of ordinary, observable facts. But there are many reasons for rejecting this interpretation of statements of obligation as predictions, and it is not, in fact, the only alternative to obscure metaphysics.

The fundamental objection is that the predictive interpretation obscures the fact that, where rules exist, deviations from them are not merely grounds for a prediction that hostile reactions will follow or that a court will apply sanctions to those who break them, but are also a reason or justification for such reaction and for applying the sanctions. We have already drawn attention in [a previous discussion] to this neglect of the internal aspect of rules and we shall elaborate it later in this chapter.

There is, however, a second, simpler, objection to the predictive interpretation of obligation. If it were true that the statement that a person had an obligation meant that *he* was likely to suffer in the event of disobedience, it would be a contradiction to say that he had an obligation, e.g. to report for military service but that, owing to the fact that he had escaped from the jurisdiction, or had successfully bribed the police or the court, there was not the slightest chance of his being caught or made to suffer. In fact, there is no contradiction in saying this, and such statements are often made and understood.

It is, of course, true that in a normal legal system, where sanctions are exacted for a high proportion of offences, an offender usually runs a risk of punishment; so, usually the statement that a person has an obligation and the statement that he is likely to suffer for disobedience will both be true together. Indeed, the connexion between these two statements is somewhat stronger than this: at least in a municipal system it may well be true that, unless *in general* sanctions were likely to be exacted from offenders, there would be little or no point in making particular statements about a person's obligations. In this sense, such statements may be said to presuppose belief in the continued normal operation of the system of sanctions much as the statement "he is out" in cricket presupposes, though it does not assert, that players, umpire, and scorer will probably take the usual steps. Nonetheless, it is crucial for the understanding of the idea of obligation to see that in individual cases the state-ment that a person has an obligation under some rule and the prediction that he is likely to suffer for disobedience may diverge.

It is clear that obligation is not to be found in the gunman situation, though the simpler notion of being obliged to do something may well be defined in the elements present there. To understand the general idea of obligation as a necessary preliminary to understanding it in its legal form, we must turn to a different social situation which, unlike the gunman situation, includes the existence of social rules; for this situation contributes to the meaning of the statement that a person has an obligation in two ways. First, the existence of such rules, making certain types of behaviour a standard, is the normal, though unstated, background or proper context for such a statement; and, secondly, the distinctive function of such statement is to apply such a general rule to a particular person by calling attention to the fact that his case falls under it. We have already seen in [a previous discussion] that there is involved in the existence of any social rules a combination of regular conduct with a distinctive attitude to that conduct as a standard. We have also seen the main ways in which these differ from mere social habits, and how the varied normative vocabulary ("ought," "must," "should") is used to draw attention to the standard and to deviations from it, and to formulate the demands, criticisms, or acknowledgments which may be based on it. Of this class of normative words the words "obligation" and "duty" form an important sub-class, carrying with them certain implications not usually present in the others. Hence, though a grasp of the elements generally differentiating social rules from mere habits is certainly indispensable for understanding the notion of obligation or duty, it is not sufficient by itself.

The statement that someone has or is under an obligation does indeed imply the existence of a rule; yet it is not always the case that where rules exist the standard of behaviour required by them is conceived of in terms of obligation. "He ought to have" and "He had an obligation to" are not always interchangeable expressions, even though they are alike in carrying an implicit reference to existing standards of conduct or are used in drawing conclusions in particular cases from a general rule. Rules of etiquette or correct speech are certainly rules: they are more than convergent habits or regularities of behaviour; they are taught and efforts are made to maintain them; they are used in criticizing our own and other people's behaviour in the characteristic normative vocabulary. "You ought to take your hat off," "It is wrong to say 'you was.'" But to use in connexion with rules of this kind the words "obligation" or "duty" would be misleading and not merely stylistically odd. It would misdescribe a social situation; for though the line separating rules of obligation from others is at points a vague one, yet the main rationale of the distinction is fairly clear.

Rules are conceived and spoken of as imposing obligations when the general demand for conformity is insistent and the social pressure brought to bear upon those who deviate or threaten to deviate is great. Such rules may be wholly customary in origin: there may be no centrally organized system of punishments for breach of the rules; the social pressure may take only the form of a general diffused hostile or critical reaction which may stop short of physical sanctions. It may be limited to verbal manifestations of disapproval or of appeals to the individuals' respect for the rule violated; it may depend heavily on the operation of feelings of shame, remorse, and guilt. When the pressure is of this last-mentioned kind we may be inclined to classify the rules as part of the morality of the social group and the obligation under the rules as moral obligation. Conversely, when physical sanctions are prominent or usual among the forms of pressure, even though these are neither closely defined nor administered by officials but are left to the community at large, we shall be inclined to classify the rules as a primitive or rudimentary form of law. We may, of course, find both these types of serious social pressure behind what is, in an obvious sense, the same rule of conduct; sometimes this may occur with no indication that one of them is peculiarly appropriate as primary and the other secondary, and then the question whether we are confronted with a rule of morality or rudimentary law may not be susceptible of an answer. But for the moment the possibility of drawing the line between law and morals need not detain us. What is important is that the insistence on importance or *seriousness* of social pressure behind the rules is the primary factor determining whether they are thought of as giving rise to obligations.

Two other characteristics of obligation go naturally together with this primary one. The rules supported by this serious pressure are thought important because they are believed to be necessary to the maintenance of social life or some highly prized feature of it. Characteristically, rules so obviously essential as those which restrict the free use of violence are thought of in terms of obligation. So too rules which require honesty or truth or require the keeping of promises, or specify what is to be done by one who performs a distinctive role or function in the social

group are thought of in terms of either "obligation" or perhaps more often "duty." Secondly, it is generally recognized that the conduct required by these rules may, while benefitting others, conflict with what the person who owes the duty may wish to do. Hence obligations and duties are thought of as characteristically involving sacrifice or renunciation, and the standing possibility of conflict between obligation or duty and interest is, in all societies, among the truisms of both the lawyer and the moralist.

The figure of a *bond* binding the person obligated, which is buried in the word "obligation," and the similar notion of a debt latent in the word "duty" are explicable in terms of these three factors, which distinguish rules of obligation or duty from other rules. In this figure, which haunts much legal thought, the social pressure appears as a chain binding those who have obligations so that they are not free to do what they want. The other end of the chain is sometimes held by the group or their official representatives, who insist on performance or exact the penalty: sometimes it is entrusted by the group to a private individual who may choose whether or not to insist on performance or its equivalent in value to him. The first situation typifies the duties or obligations of criminal law and the second those of civil law where we think of private individuals having rights correlative to the obligations.

Natural and perhaps illuminating though these figures or metaphors are, we must not allow them to trap us into a misleading conception of obligation as essentially consisting in some feeling of pressure or compulsion experienced by those who have obligations. The fact that rules of obligation are generally supported by serious social pressure does not entail that to have an obligation under the rules is to experience feelings of compulsion or pressure. Hence there is no contradiction in saying of some hardened swindler, and it may often be true, that he had an obligation to pay the rent but felt no pressure to pay when he made off without doing so. To *feel* obliged and to have an obligation are different though frequently concomitant things. To identify them would be one way of misinterpreting, in terms of psychological feelings, the important internal aspect of rules to which we drew attention in [a previous discussion].

Indeed, the internal aspect of rules is something to which we must again refer before we can dispose finally of the claims of the predictive theory. For an advocate of that theory may well ask why, if social pressure is so important a feature of rules of obligation, we are yet so concerned to stress the inadequacies of the predictive theory; for it gives this very feature a central place by defining obligation in terms of the likelihood that threatened punishment or hostile reaction will follow deviation from certain lines of conduct. The difference may seem slight between the analysis of a statement of obligation as a prediction, or assessment of the chances, of hostile reaction to deviation, and our own contention that though this statement presupposes a background in which deviations from rules are generally met by hostile reactions, yet its characteristic use is not to predict this but to say that a person's case falls under such a rule. In fact, however, this difference is not a slight one. Indeed, until its importance is grasped, we cannot properly understand the whole distinctive style of human thought, speech, and action which is involved in the existence of rules and which constitutes the normative structure of society.

The following contrast again in terms of the "internal" and "external" aspect of rules may serve to mark what gives this distinction its great importance for the understanding not only of law but of the structure of any society. When a social group has certain rules of conduct, this fact affords an opportunity for many closely related yet different kinds of assertion; for it is possible to be concerned with the rules, either merely as an observer who does not himself accept them, or as a member of the group which accepts and uses them as guides to conduct. We may call these respectively the "external" and the "internal points of view." Statements made from the external point of view may themselves be of different kinds. For the observer may, without accepting the rules himself, assert that the group accepts the rules, and thus may from outside refer to the way in which *they* are concerned with them from the internal point of view. But whatever the rules are, whether they are those of games, like chess or cricket, or moral or legal rules, we can if we choose occupy the position of an observer who does not even refer in this way to the internal point of view of the group. Such an observer is content merely to record the regularities of observable behaviour in which conformity with the rules partly consists and those further regularities, in the form of the hostile reaction, reproofs, or punishments, with which deviations from the rules are met. After a time the external observer may, on the basis of the regularities observed, correlate deviation with hostile reaction, and be able to predict with a fair measure of success, and to assess the chances that a deviation from the group's normal behaviour will meet with hostile reaction or punishment. Such knowledge may

not only reveal much about the group, but might enable him to live among them without unpleasant consequences which would attend one who attempted to do so without such knowledge.

If, however, the observer really keeps austerely to this extreme external point of view and does not give any account of the manner in which members of the group who accept the rules view their own regular behaviour, his description of their life cannot be in terms of rules at all, and so not in the terms of the rule-dependent notions of obligation or duty. Instead, it will be in terms of observable regularities of conduct, predictions, probabilities, and signs. For such an observer, deviations by a member of the group from normal conduct will be a sign that hostile reaction is likely to follow, and nothing more. His view will be like the view of one who, having observed the working of a traffic signal in a busy street for some time, limits himself to saying that when the light turns red there is a high probability that the traffic will stop. He treats the light merely as a natural *sign that* people will behave in certain ways, as clouds are a *sign that* rain will come. In so doing he will miss out on a whole dimension of the social life of those whom he is watching, since for them the red light is not merely a sign that others will stop: they look upon it as a *signal for* them to stop, and so a reason for stopping in conformity to rules which make stopping when the light is red a standard of behaviour and an obligation. To mention this is to bring into account the way in which the group regards its own behaviour. It is to refer to the internal aspect of rules seen from their internal point of view.

The external point of view may very nearly reproduce the way in which the rules function in the lives of certain members of the group, namely those who reject its rules and are only concerned with them when and because they judge that unpleasant consequences are likely to follow violation. Their point of view will need for its expression, "I was obliged to do it," "I am likely to suffer for it if . . . ," "You will probably suffer for it if . . . ," "They will do that to you if. . . . " But they will not need forms of expression like "I had an obligation" or "You have an obligation" for these are required only by those who see their own and other persons' conduct from the internal point of view. What the external point of view, which limits itself to the observable regularities of behaviour, cannot reproduce is the way in which the rules function as rules in the lives of those who normally are the majority of society. These are the officials, lawyers, or private persons who use them, in one situation after another, as guides to the conduct of social life, as the basis for claims, demands, admissions, criticism, or punishment, viz., in all the familiar transactions of life according to rules. For them the violation of a rule is not merely a basis for the prediction that a hostile reaction will follow but a *reason* for hostility.

At any given moment the life of any society which lives by rules, legal or not, is likely to consist in a tension between those who, on the one hand, accept and voluntarily co-operate in maintaining the rules, and so see their own and other persons' behaviour in terms of the rules, and those who, on the other hand, reject the rules and attend to them only from the external point of view as a sign of possible punishment. One of the difficulties facing any legal theory anxious to do justice to the complexity of the facts is to remember the presence of both these points of view and not to define one of them out of existence. Perhaps all our criticisms of the predictive theory of obligation may be best summarized as the accusation that this is what it does to the internal aspect of obligatory rules.

The Elements of Law

It is, of course, possible to imagine a society without a legislature, courts or officials of any kind. Indeed, there are many studies of primitive communities which not only claim that this possibility is realized but depict in detail the life of a society where the only means of social control is that general attitude of the group towards its own standard modes of behaviour in terms of which we have characterized rules of obligation. A social structure of this kind is often referred to as one of "custom"; but we shall not use this term, because it often implies that the customary rules are very old and supported with less social pressure than other rules. To avoid these implications we shall refer to such a social structure as one of primary rules of obligation. If a society is to live by such primary rules alone, there are certain conditions which, granted a few of the most obvious truisms about human nature and the world we live in, must clearly be satisfied. The first of these conditions is that the rules must contain in some form restrictions on the free use of violence, theft, and deception to which human beings are tempted but which they must, in general, repress, if they are to coexist in close proximity to each other. Such rules are in fact always found in the primitive societies of which we have knowledge, together with a variety of others imposing on individuals various positive duties to perform services or make contribu-

tions to the common life. Secondly, though such a society may exhibit the tension, already described, between those who accept the rules and those who reject the rules except where fear of social pressure induces them to conform, it is plain that the latter cannot be more than a minority, if so loosely organized a society of persons, approximately equal in physical strength, is to endure: for otherwise those who reject the rules would have too little social pressure to fear. This too is confirmed by what we know of primitive communities where, though there are dissidents and malefactors, the majority live by the rules seen from the internal point of view.

More important for our present purpose is the following consideration. It is plain that only a small community closely knit by ties of kinship, common sentiment, and belief, and placed in a stable environment, could live successfully by such a régime of unofficial rules. In any other conditions such a simple form of social control must prove defective and will require supplementation in different ways. In the first place, the rules by which the group lives will not form a system, but will simply be a set of separate standards, without any identifying or common mark, except of course that they are the rules which a particular group of human beings accepts. They will in this respect resemble our own rules of etiquette. Hence if doubts arise as to what the rules are or as to the precise scope of some given rule, there will be no procedure for settling this doubt, either by reference to an authoritative text or to an official whose declarations on this point are authoritative. For, plainly, such a procedure and the acknowledgement of either authoritative text or persons involve the existence of rules of a type different from the rules of obligation or duty which *ex hypothesi* are all that the group has. This defect in the simple social structure of primary rules we may call its *uncertainty*.

A second defect is the *static* character of the rules. The only mode of change in the rules known to such a society will be the slow process of growth, whereby courses of conduct once thought optional become first habitual or usual, and then obligatory, and the converse process of decay, when deviations, once severely dealt with, are first tolerated and then pass unnoticed. There will be no means, in such a society, of deliberately adapting the rules to changing circumstances, either by eliminating old rules or introducing new ones: for, again, the possibility of doing this presupposes the existence of rules of a different type from the primary rules of obligation by which alone the society lives. In an extreme case the rules may be static in a more drastic sense. This, though never perhaps fully realized in any actual community, is worth considering because the remedy for it is something very characteristic of law. In this extreme case, not only would there be no way of deliberately changing the general rules, but the obligations which arise under the rules in particular cases could not be varied or modified by the deliberate choice of any individual. Each individual would simply have fixed obligations or duties to do or abstain from doing certain things. It might indeed very often be the case that others would benefit from the performance of these obligations; yet if there are only primary rules of obligation they would have no power to release those bound from performance or to transfer to others the benefits which would accrue from performance. For such operations of release or transfer create changes in the initial positions of individuals under the primary rules of obligation, and for these operations to be possible there must be rules of a sort different from the primary rules.

The third defect of this simple form of social life is the *inefficiency* of the diffuse social pressure by which the rules are maintained. Disputes as to whether an admitted rule has or has not been violated will always occur and will, in any but the smallest societies, continue interminably, if there is no agency specially empowered to ascertain finally, and authoritatively, the fact of violation. Lack of such final and authoritative determinations is to be distinguished from another weakness associated with it. This is the fact that punishments for violations of the rules, and other forms of social pressure involving physical effort or the use of force, are not administered by a special agency but are left to the individuals affected or to the group at large. It is obvious that the waste of time involved in the group's unorganized efforts to catch and punish offenders, and the smouldering vendettas which may result from self help in the absence of an official monopoly of "sanctions," may be serious. The history of law does, however, strongly suggest that the lack of official agencies to determine authoritatively the fact of violation of the rules is a much more serious defect; for many societies have remedies for this defect long before the other.

The remedy for each of these three main defects in this simplest form of social structure consists in supplementing the *primary* rules of obligation with *secondary* rules which are rules of a different kind. The introduction of the remedy for each defect might, in itself, be considered a step from the pre-legal into the legal world; since each remedy brings with it many elements that permeate law: certainly all three remedies together are enough to convert the régime of primary rules into what is indisputably a legal system. We shall consider in turn each of these remedies and show why law may most illuminatingly be characterized as a union of primary rules of obligation with such secondary rules. Before we do this, however, the following general points should be noted. Though the remedies consist in the introduction of rules which are certainly different from each other, as well as from the primary rules of obligation which they supplement, they have important features in common and are connected in various ways. Thus they may all be said to be on a different level from the primary rules, for they are all *about* such rules; in the sense that while primary rules are concerned with the actions that individuals must or must not do, these secondary rules are all concerned with the primary rules themselves. They specify the ways in which the primary rules may be conclusively ascertained, introduced, eliminated, varied, and the fact of their violation conclusively determined.

The simplest form of remedy for the *uncertainty* of the régime of primary rules is the introduction of what we shall call a "rule of recognition." This will specify some feature or features possession of which by a suggested rule is taken as a conclusive affirmative indication that it is a rule of the group to be supported by the social pressure it exerts. The existence of such a rule of recognition may take any of a huge variety of forms, simple or complex. It may, as in the early law of many societies, be no more than that an authoritative list or text of the rules is to be found in a written document or carved on some public monument. No doubt as a matter of history this step from the pre-legal to the legal may be accomplished in distinguishable stages, of which the first is the mere reduction to writing of hitherto unwritten rules. This is not itself the crucial step, though it is a very important one: what is crucial is the acknowledgement of reference to the writing or inscription as *authoritative,* i.e. as the *proper* way of disposing of doubts as to the existence of the rule. Where there is such an acknowledgement there is a very simple form of secondary rule: a rule for conclusive identification of the primary rules of obligation.

In a developed legal system the rules of recognition are of course more complex; instead of identifying rules exclusively by reference to a text or list they do so by reference to some general characteristic possessed by the primary rules. This may be the fact of their having been enacted by a specific body, or their long customary practice, or their relation to judicial decisions. Moreover, where more than one of such general characteristics are treated as identifying criteria, provision may be made for their possible conflict by their arrangement in an order of superiority, as by the common subordination of custom or precedent to statute, the latter being a "superior source" of law. Such complexity may make the rules of recognition in a modern legal system seem very different from the simple acceptance of an authoritative text: yet even in this simplest form, such a rule brings with it many elements distinctive of law. By providing an authoritative mark it introduces, although in embryonic form, the idea of a legal system: for the rules are now not just a discrete unconnected set but are, in a simple way, unified. Further, in the simple operation of identifying a given rule as possessing the required feature of being an item on an authoritative list of rules we have the germ of the idea of legal validity.

The remedy for the *static* quality of the régime of primary rules consists in the introduction of what we shall call "rules of change." The simplest form of such a rule is that which empowers an individual or body of persons to introduce new primary rules for the conduct of the life of the group, or of some class within it, and to eliminate old rules. As we have already argued in [a previous discussion] it is in terms of such a rule, and not in terms of orders backed by threats, that the ideas of legislative enactment and repeal are to be understood. Such rules of change may be very simple or very complex: the powers conferred may be unrestricted or limited in various ways: and the rules may, besides specifying the persons who are to legislate, define in more or less rigid terms the procedure to be followed in legislation. Plainly, there will be a very close connexion between the rules of change and the rules of recognition: for where the former exists the latter will necessarily incorporate a reference to legislation as an identifying feature of the rules, though it need not refer to all the details of procedure involved in legislation. Usually some official certificate or official copy will, under the rules of recognition, be taken as a sufficient proof of due enactment. Of course if there is a social structure so simple that the only "source of law" is legislation, the rule of recognition will simply specify enactment as the unique identifying mark or criterion of validity of the rules. This will be the case for example in the imaginary kingdom of Rex I depicted in [a previous discussion]: there the rule of recognition would simply be that whatever Rex I enacts is law.

We have already described in some detail the rules which confer on individuals power to vary their initial positions under the primary rules. Without such private power-conferring rules society would lack some of the chief amenities which law confers upon it. For the operations which these rules make possible are the making of wills, contracts, transfers of property, and many other voluntarily created structures of rights and duties which typify life under law, though of course an elementary form of power-conferring rule also underlies the moral institution of a promise. The kinship of these rules with the rules of change involved in the notion of legislation is clear, and as recent theory such as Kelsen's has shown, many of the features which puzzle us in the institutions of contract or property are clarified by thinking of the operations of making a contract or transferring property as the exercise of limited legislative powers by individuals.

The third supplement to the simple régime of primary rules, intended to remedy the *inefficiency* of its diffused social pressure, consists of secondary rules empowering individuals to make authoritative determinations of the question whether, on a particular occasion, a primary rule has been broken. The minimal form of adjudication consists in such determinations, and we shall call the secondary rules which confer the power to make them "rules of adjudication." Besides identifying the individuals who are to adjudicate, such rules will also define the procedure to be followed. Like the other secondary rules these are on a different level from the primary rules: though they may be reinforced by further rules imposing duties on judges to adjudicate, they do not impose duties but confer judicial powers and a special status on judicial declarations about the breach of obligations. Again these rules, like the other secondary rules, define a group of important legal concepts: in this case the concepts of judge or court, jurisdiction and judgment. Besides these resemblances to the other secondary rules, rules of adjudication have intimate connexions with them. Indeed, a system which has rules of adjudication is necessarily also committed to a rule of recognition of an elementary and imperfect sort. This is so because, if courts are empowered to make authoritative determinations of the fact that a rule has been broken, these cannot avoid being taken as authoritative determinations of what the rules are. So the rule which confers jurisdiction will also be a rule of recognition, identifying the primary rules through the judgments of the courts and these judgments will become a "source" of law. It is true that this form of rule of recognition, inseparable from the minimum form of jurisdiction, will be very imperfect. Unlike an authoritative text or a statute book, judgments may not be couched in general terms and their use as authoritative guides to the rules depends on a somewhat shaky inference from particular decisions, and the reliability of this must fluctuate both with the skill of the interpreter and the consistency of the judges.

It need hardly be said that in few legal systems are judicial powers confined to authoritative determinations of the fact of violation of the primary rules. Most systems have, after some delay, seen the advantages of further centralization of social pressure; and have partially prohibited the use of physical punishments or violent self help by private individuals. Instead they have supplemented the primary rules of obligation by further secondary rules, specifying or at least limiting the penalties for violation, and have conferred upon judges, where they have ascertained the fact of violation, the exclusive power to direct the application of penalties by other officials. These secondary rules provide the centralized official "sanctions" of the system.

If we stand back and consider the structure which has resulted from the combination of primary rules of obligation with the secondary rules of recognition, change and adjudication, it is plain that we have here not only the heart of a legal system, but a most powerful tool for the analysis of much that has puzzled both the jurist and the political theorist.

Not only are the specifically legal concepts with which the lawyer is professionally concerned, such as those of obligation and rights, validity and source of law, legislation and jurisdiction, and sanction, best elucidated in terms of this combination of elements. The concepts (which bestride both law and political theory) of the state, of authority, and of an official require a similar analysis if the obscurity which still lingers about them is to be dissipated. The reason why an analysis in these terms of primary and secondary rules has this explanatory power is not far to seek. Most of the obscurities and distortions surrounding legal and political concepts arise from the fact that these essentially involve reference to what we have called the internal point of view: the view of those who do not merely record and predict behaviour conforming to rules, but *use* the rules as standards for the appraisal of their own and others' behaviour. This requires more detailed attention in the analysis of legal and political concepts then it has usually received. Under the simple régime of primary rules the internal

point of view is manifested in its simplest form, in the use of those rules as the basis of criticism, and as the justification of demands for conformity, social pressure, and punishment. Reference to this most elementary manifestation of the internal point of view is required for the analysis of the basic concepts of obligation and duty. With the addition to the system of secondary rules, the range of what is said and done from the internal point of view is much extended and diversified. With this extension comes a whole set of new concepts and they demand a reference to the internal point of view for their analysis. These include the notions of legislation, jurisdiction, validity and, generally, of legal powers, private and public. There is a constant pull towards an analysis of these in the terms of ordinary or "scientific," fact-stating or predictive discourse. But this can only reproduce their external aspect: to do justice to their distinctive, internal aspect we need to see the different ways in which the law-making operations of the legislator, the adjudication of a court, the exercise of private or official powers, and other "acts-in-the-law" are related to secondary rules.

In [a subsequent discussion] we shall show how the ideas of the validity of law and sources of law, and the truths latent among the errors of the doctrines of sovereignty may be rephrased and clarified in terms of rules of recognition. But we shall conclude this chapter with a warning: though the combination of primary and secondary rules merits, because it explains many aspects of law, the central place assigned to it, this cannot by itself illuminate every problem. The union of primary and secondary rules is at the centre of a legal system; but it is not the whole, and as we move away from the centre we shall have to accommodate, in ways indicated in later chapters, elements of a different character.

The Foundations of a Legal System

Rule of Recognition and Legal Validity

According to the theory criticized in [a previous discussion] the foundations of a legal system consist of the situation in which the majority of a social group habitually obey the orders backed by threats of the sovereign person or persons, who themselves habitually obey no one. This social situation is, for this theory, both a necessary and a sufficient condition of the existence of law. We have already exhibited in some detail the incapacity of this theory to account for some of the salient features of a modern municipal legal system: yet nonetheless, as its hold over the minds of many thinkers suggests, it does contain, though in a blurred and misleading form, certain truths about certain important aspects of law. These truths can, however, only be clearly presented, and their importance rightly assessed, in terms of the more complex social situation where a secondary rule of recognition is accepted and used for the identification of primary rules of obligation. It is this situation which deserves, if anything does, to be called the foundations of a legal system. In this chapter we shall discuss various elements of this situation which have received only partial or misleading expression in the theory of sovereignty and elsewhere.

Wherever such a rule of recognition is accepted, both private persons and officials are provided with authoritative criteria for identifying primary rules of obligation. The criteria so provided may, as we have seen, take any one or more of a variety of forms: these include reference to an authoritative text; to legislative enactment; to customary practice; to general declarations of specified persons, or to past judicial decisions in particular cases. In a very simple system like the world of Rex I depicted in [a previous discussion], where only what he enacts is law and no legal limitations upon his legislative power are imposed by customary rule or constitutional document, the sole criterion for identifying the law will be a simple reference to fact of enactment by Rex I. The existence of this simple form of rule of recognition will be manifest in the general practice, on the part of officials or private persons, of identifying the rules by this criterion. In a modern legal system where there are a variety of "sources" of law, the rule of recognition is correspondingly more complex: the criteria for identifying the law are multiple and commonly include a written constitution, enactment by a legislature, and judicial precedents. In most cases, provision is made for possible conflict by ranking these criteria in an order of relative subordination and primacy. It is in this way that in our system "common law" is subordinate to "statute."

It is important to distinguish this relative *subordination* of one criterion to another from *derivation,* since some spurious support for the view that all law is essentially or "really" (even if only "tacitly") the product of legislation, has been gained from confusion of these two ideas. In our own system, custom and precedent are subordinate to legislation since customary and common law rules may be deprived of their status as law by statute. Yet they owe their status of law, precarious as this may be, not to a "tacit" exercise of legislative power but to the acceptance of a rule of recognition which accords them this independent though subordinate place. Again, as in the simple case, the existence of such a complex rule of recognition with this hierarchical ordering of distinct criteria is manifested in the general practice of identifying the rules by such criteria.

In the day-to-day life of a legal system its rule of recognition is very seldom expressly formulated as a rule; though occasionally, courts in England may announce in general terms the relative place of one criterion of law in relation to another, as when they assert the supremacy of Acts of Parliament over other sources or suggested sources of law. For the most part the rule of recognition is not stated, but its existence is *shown* in the way in which particular rules are identified, either by courts or other officials or private persons or their advisers. There is, of course, a difference in the use made by courts of the criteria provided by the rule and the use of them by others: for when courts reach a particular conclusion on the footing that a particular rule has been correctly identified as law, what they say has a special authoritative status conferred on it by other rules. In this respect, as in many others, the rule of recognition of a legal system is like the scoring rule of a game. In the course of the game the general rule defining the activities which constitute scoring (runs, goals, &c.) is seldom formulated; instead it is *used* by officials and players in identifying the particular phases which count towards winning. Here too, the declarations of officials (umpire or scorer) have a special authoritative status attributed to them by other rules. Further, in both cases there is the possibility of a conflict between these authoritative applications of the rule and the general understanding of what the rule plainly requires according to its terms. This, as we shall see later, is a complication which must be catered for in any account of what it is for a system of rules of this sort to exist.

The use of unstated rules of recognition, by courts and others, in identifying particular rules of the system is characteristic of the internal point of view. Those who use them in this way thereby manifest their own acceptance of them as guiding rules and with this attitude there goes a characteristic vocabulary different from the natural expressions of the external point of view. Perhaps the simplest of these is the expression, "It is the law that . . . ," which we may find on the lips not only of judges, but of ordinary men living under a legal system, when they identify a given rule of the system. This, like the expression "Out" or "Goal," is the language of one assessing a situation by reference to rules which he in common with others acknowledges as appropriate for this purpose. This attitude of shared acceptance of rules is to be contrasted with that of an observer who records *ab extra* the fact that a social group accepts such rules but does not himself accept them. The natural expression of this external point of view is not "It is the law that . . ." but "In England they recognize as law . . . whatever the Queen in Parliament enacts. . . ." The first of these forms of expression we shall call an *internal statement* because it manifests the internal point of view and is naturally used by one who, accepting the rule of recognition and without stating the fact that it is accepted, applies the rule in recognizing some particular rule of the system as valid. The second form of expression we shall call an *external statement* because it is the natural language of an external observer of the system who, without himself accepting its rule of recognition, states the fact that others accept it.

If this use of an accepted rule of recognition in making internal statements is understood and carefully distinguished from an external statement of fact that the rule is accepted, many obscurities concerning the notion of legal "validity" disappear. For the word "valid" is most frequently, though not always, used, in just such internal statements, applying to a particular rule of a legal system, an unstated but accepted rule of recognition. To say that a given rule is valid is to recognize it as passing all the tests provided by the rule of recognition and so as a rule of the system. We can indeed simply say that the statement that a particular rule is valid means that it satisfies all the criteria provided by the rule of recognition. This is incorrect only to the extent that it might obscure the internal character of such statements; for, like the cricketers' "Out," these statements of validity normally apply to a particular case a rule of recognition accepted by the speaker and others, rather than expressly state that the rule is satisfied.

Some of the puzzles connected with the idea of legal validity are said to concern the relation between the validity and the "efficacy" of law. If by "efficacy" is meant that the fact that a rule of law which requires certain behaviour is obeyed more often than not, it is plain that there is no necessary connexion between the validity of any particular rule and *its* efficacy, unless the rule of recognition of the system includes among its criteria, as some do, the provision (some-

times referred to as a rule of obsolescence) that no rule is to count as a rule of the system if it has long ceased to be efficacious.

From the inefficacy of a particular rule, which may or may not count against its validity, we must distinguish a general disregard of the rules of the system. This may be so complete in character and so protracted that we should say, in the case of a new system, that it had never established itself as the legal system of a given group, or, in the case of a once-established system, that it had ceased to be the legal system of the group. In either case, the normal context or background for making any internal statement in terms of the rules of the system is absent. In such cases it would be generally *pointless* either to assess the rights and duties of particular persons by reference to the primary rules of a system or to access the validity of any of its rules by reference to its rules of recognition. To insist on applying a system of rules which had either never actually been effective or had been discarded would, except in special circumstances mentioned below, be as futile as to assess the progress of a game by reference to a scoring rule which had never been accepted or had been discarded.

One who makes an internal statement concerning the validity of a particular rule of a system may be said to *presuppose* the truth of the external statement of fact that the system is generally efficacious. For the normal use of internal statements is in such a context of general efficacy. It would however be wrong to say that statements of validity "mean" that the system is generally efficacious. For though it is normally pointless or idle to talk of the validity of a rule of a system which has never established itself or has been discarded, none the less it is not meaningless nor is it always pointless. One vivid way of teaching Roman Law is to speak *as if* the system were efficacious still and to discuss the validity of particular rules and solve problems in their terms; and one way of nursing hopes for the restoration of an old social order destroyed by revolution, and rejecting the new, is to cling to the criteria of legal validity of the old régime. This is implicitly done by the White Russian who still claims property under some rule of descent which was a valid rule of Tsarist Russia.

A grasp of the normal contextual connexion between the internal statement that a given rule of a system is valid and the external statement of fact that the system is generally efficacious, will help us see in its proper perspective the common theory that to assert the validity of a rule is to predict that it will be enforced by courts or some other official action taken.

In many ways this theory is similar to the predictive analysis of obligation which we considered and rejected in [a previous discussion]. In both cases alike the motive for advancing this predictive theory is the conviction that only thus can metaphysical interpretations be avoided: that either a statement that a rule is valid must ascribe some mysterious property which cannot be detected by empirical means or it must be a prediction of future behaviour of officials. In both cases also the plausibility of the theory is due to the same important fact: that the truth of the external statement of fact, which an observer might record, that the system is generally efficacious and likely to continue so, is normally presupposed by anyone who accepts the rules and makes an internal statement of obligation or validity. The two are certainly very closely associated. Finally, in both cases alike the mistake of the theory is the same: it consists in neglecting the special character of the internal statement and treating it as an external statement about official action.

This mistake becomes immediately apparent when we consider how the judge's own statement that a particular rule is valid functions in judicial decision; for, though here too, in making such a statement, the judge presupposes but does not state the general efficacy of the system, he plainly is not concerned to predict his own or others' official action. His statement that a rule is valid is an internal statement recognizing that the rule satisfies the tests for identifying what is to count as law in his court, and constitutes not a prophecy of but part of the *reason* for his decision. There is indeed a more plausible case for saying that a statement that a rule is valid is a prediction when such a statement is made by a private person; for in the case of conflict between unofficial statements of validity or invalidity and that of a court in deciding a case, there is often good sense in saying that the former must then be withdrawn. Yet even here, as we shall see when we come . . . to investigate the significance of such conflicts between official declarations and the plain requirements of the rules, it may be dogmatic to assume that it is withdrawn as a statement now shown to be *wrong,* because it has falsely *predicted* what a court would say. For there are more reasons for withdrawing statements than the fact that they are wrong, and also more ways of being wrong than this allows.

The rule of recognition providing the criteria by which the validity of other rules of the system is assessed is in an important sense, which we shall try to clarify, an *ultimate* rule: and where, as is usual, there are several criteria ranked in order of relative subor-

dination and primacy one of them is *supreme.* These ideas of the ultimacy of the rule of recognition and the supremacy of one of its criteria merit some attention. It is important to disentangle them from the theory, which we have rejected, that somewhere in every legal system, even though it lurks behind legal forms, there must be a sovereign legislative power which is legally unlimited.

Of these two ideas, supreme criterion and ultimate rule, the first is the easiest to define. We may say that a criterion of legal validity or source of law is supreme if rules identified by reference to it are still recognized as rules of the system, even if they conflict with rules identified by reference to the other criteria, whereas rules identified by reference to the latter are not so recognized if they conflict with the rules identified by reference to the supreme criterion. A similar explanation in comparative terms can be given of the notions of "superior" and "subordinate" criteria which we have already used. It is plain that the notions of a superior and a supreme criterion merely refer to a *relative* place on a scale and do not import any notion of legally *unlimited* legislative power. Yet "supreme" and "unlimited" are easy to confuse—at least in legal theory. One reason for this is that in the simpler forms of legal system the ideas of ultimate rule of recognition, supreme criterion, and legally unlimited legislature seem to converge. For where there is a legislature subject to no constitutional limitations and competent by its enactment to deprive all other rules of law emanating from other sources of their status as law, it is part of the rule of recognition in such a system that enactment by that legislature is the supreme criterion of validity. This is, according to constitutional theory, the position in the United Kingdom. But even systems like that of the United States in which there is no such legally unlimited legislature may perfectly well contain an ultimate rule of recognition which provides a set of criteria of validity, one of which is supreme. This will be so, where the legislative competence of the ordinary legislature is limited by a constitution which contains no amending power, or places some clauses outside the scope of that power. Here there is no legally unlimited legislature, even in the widest interpretation of "legislature"; but the system of course contains an ultimate rule of recognition and, in the clauses of its constitution, a supreme criterion of validity.

The sense in which the rule of recognition is the *ultimate* rule of a system is best understood if we pursue a very familiar chain of legal reasoning. If the question is raised whether some suggested rule is legally valid, we must, in order to answer the question, use a criterion of validity provided by some other rule. Is this purported by-law of the Oxfordshire County Council valid? Yes: because it was made in exercise of the powers conferred, and in accordance with the procedure specified, by a statutory order made by the Minister of Health. At this first stage the statutory order provides the criteria in terms of which the validity of the by-law is assessed. There may be no practical need to go farther; but there is a standing possibility of doing so. We may query the validity of the statutory order and assess its validity in terms of the statute empowering the minister to make such orders. Finally when the validity of the statute has been queried and assessed by reference to the rule that what the Queen in Parliament enacts is law, we are brought to a stop in inquiries concerning validity: for we have reached a rule which, like the intermediate statutory order and statute, provides criteria for the assessment of the validity of other rules; but it is also unlike them in that there is no rule providing criteria for the assessment of its own legal validity.

There are, indeed, many questions which we can raise about this ultimate rule. We can ask whether it is the practice of courts, legislatures, officials, or private citizens in England actually to use this rule as an ultimate rule of recognition. Or has our process of legal reasoning been an idle game with the criteria of validity of a system now discarded? We can ask whether it is a satisfactory form of legal system which has such a rule at its root. Does it produce more good than evil? Are there prudential reasons for supporting it? Is there a moral obligation to do so? These are plainly very important questions; but, equally plainly, when we ask them about the rule of recognition, we are no longer attempting to answer the same kind of question about it as those which we answered about other rules with its aid. When we move from saying that a particular enactment is valid, because it satisfies the rule that what the Queen in Parliament enacts is law, to saying that in England this last rule is used by courts, officials, and private persons as the ultimate rule of recognition, we have moved from an internal statement of law asserting the validity of a rule of the system to an external statement of fact which an observer of the system might make even if he did not accept it. So too when we move from the statement that a particular enactment is valid, to the statement that the rule of recognition of the system is an excellent one and the system based on it is one worthy of support, we have moved from a statement of legal validity to a statement of value.

Some writers, who have emphasized the legal ultimacy of the rule of recognition, have expressed this by saying that, whereas the legal validity of other rules of the system can be demonstrated by reference to it, its own validity cannot be demonstrated but is "assumed" or "postulated" or is a "hypothesis." This may, however, be seriously misleading. Statements of legal validity made about particular rules in the day-to-day life of a legal system whether by judges, lawyers, or ordinary citizens do indeed carry with them certain presuppositions. They are internal statements of law expressing the point of view of those who accept the rule of recognition of the system and, as such, leave unstated much that could be stated in external statements of fact about the system. What is thus left unstated forms the normal background or context of statements of legal validity and is thus said to be "presupposed" by them. But it is important to see precisely what these presupposed matters are, and not to obscure their character. They consist of two things. First, a person who seriously asserts the validity of some given rule of law, say a particular statute, himself makes use of a rule of recognition which he accepts as appropriate for identifying the law. Secondly, it is the case that this rule of recognition, in terms of which he assesses the validity of a particular statute, is not only accepted by him but is the rule of recognition actually accepted and employed in the general operation of the system. If the truth of this presupposition were doubted, it could be established by reference to actual practice: to the way in which courts identify what is to count as law, and to the general acceptance of or acquiescence in these identifications.

Neither of these two presuppositions are well described as "assumptions" of a "validity" which cannot be demonstrated. We only need the word "validity," and commonly only use it, to answer questions which arise *within* a system of rules where the status of a rule as a member of the system depends on its satisfying certain criteria provided by the rule of recognition. No such question can arise as to the validity of the very rule of recognition which provides the criteria; it can neither be valid nor invalid but is simply accepted as appropriate for use in this way. To express this simple fact by saying darkly that its validity is "assumed but cannot be demonstrated," is like saying that we assume, but can never demonstrate, that the standard metre bar in Paris which is the ultimate test of the correctness of all measurement in metres, is itself correct.

A more serious objection is that talk of the "assumption" that the ultimate rule of recognition is valid conceals the essentially factual character of the second presupposition which lies behind the lawyers' statements of validity. No doubt the practice of judges, officials, and others, in which the actual existence of a rule of recognition consists, is a complex matter. As we shall see later, there are certainly situations in which questions as to the precise content and scope of this kind of rule, and even as to its existence, may not admit of a clear or determinate answer. None the less it is important to distinguish "assuming the validity" from "presupposing the existence" of such a rule; if only because failure to do this obscures what is meant by the assertion that such a rule *exists*.

In the simple system of primary rules of obligation sketched in the last chapter, the assertion that a given rule existed could only be an external statement of fact such as an observer who did not accept the rules might make and verify by ascertaining whether or not, as a matter of fact, a given mode of behaviour was generally accepted as a standard and was accompanied by those features which, as we have seen, distinguish a social rule from mere convergent habits. It is in this way also that we should now interpret and verify the assertion that in England a rule—though not a legal one—exists that we must bare the head on entering a church. If such rules as these are found to exist in the actual practice of a social group, there is no separate question of their validity to be discussed, though of course their value or desirability is open to question. Once their existence has been established as a fact we should only confuse matters by affirming or denying that they were valid or by saying that "we assumed" but could not show their validity. Where, on the other hand, as in a mature legal system, we have a system of rules which includes a rule of recognition so that the status of a rule as a member of the system now depends on whether it satisfies certain criteria provided by the rule of recognition, this brings with it a new application of the word "exist." The statement that a rule exists may now no longer be what it was in the simple case of customary rules—an external statement of the *fact* that a certain mode of behaviour was generally accepted as a standard in practice. It may now be an internal statement applying an accepted but unstated rule of recognition and meaning (roughly) no more than "valid given the systems criteria of validity." In this respect, however, as in others a rule of recognition is unlike other rules of the system. The assertion that it exists can only be an external statement of fact. For whereas a subordinate rule of a system may be valid and in that sense "exist" even if it is generally disregarded, the rule of recognition exists only as a complex, but normally concordant, practice of the courts, officials, and private persons in identifying the law by reference to certain criteria. Its existence is a matter of fact.

POSITIVISM AND THE SEPARATION OF LAW AND MORALS*

H. L. A. Hart

In this article I shall discuss and attempt to defend a view which Mr. Justice Holmes, among others, held and for which he and they have been much criticized. But I wish first to say why I think that Holmes, whatever the vicissitudes of his American reputation may be, will always remain for Englishmen a heroic figure in jurisprudence. This will be so because he magically combined two qualities: One of them is imaginative power, which English legal

*From 71 *Harvard Law Review* 593 (1958). Copyright © 1958 by The Harvard Law Review Association. Reprinted by permission of the author and the publisher. Footnotes edited and renumbered.

thinking has often lacked; the other is clarity, which English legal thinking usually possesses. The English lawyer who turns to read Holmes is made to see that what he had taken to be settled and stable is really always on the move. To make this discovery with Holmes is to be with a guide whose words may leave you unconvinced, sometimes even repelled, but never mystified. Like our own Austin, with whom Holmes shared many ideals and thoughts, Holmes was sometimes clearly wrong; but again like Austin, when this was so he was always wrong clearly. This surely is a sovereign virtue in jurisprudence. Clarity I know is said not to be enough; this may be true, but there are still questions in jurisprudence where the issues are confused because they are discussed in a style which Holmes would have spurned for its obscurity. Perhaps this is inevitable: Jurisprudence trembles so uncertainly on the margin of many subjects that there will always be need for someone, in Bentham's phrase, "to pluck the mask of Mystery" from its face. This is true, to a preeminent degree, of the subject of this article. Contemporary voices tell us we must recognize something obscured by the legal "positivists" whose day is now over: that there is a "point of intersection between law and morals," or that what is and what ought to be are somehow indissolubly fused or inseparable, though the positivists denied it. What do these phrases mean? Or rather which of the many things that they could mean, do they mean? Which of them do "positivists" deny and why is it wrong to do so?

I

I shall present the subject as part of the history of an idea. At the close of the eighteenth century and the beginning of the nineteenth the most earnest thinkers in England about legal and social problems and the architects of great reforms were the great utilitarians. Two of them, Bentham and Austin, constantly insisted on the need to distinguish, firmly and with the maximum of clarity, law as it is from law as it ought to be. This theme haunts their work, and they condemned the natural-law thinkers precisely because they had blurred this apparently simple but vital distinction. By contrast, at the present time in this country and to a lesser extent in England, this separation between law and morals is held to be superficial and wrong. Some critics have thought that it blinds men to the true nature of law and its roots in social life. Others have thought it not only intellectually misleading but corrupting in practice, at its worst apt to weaken resistance to state tyranny or absolutism, and at its best apt to bring law into disrespect. The nonpejorative name "legal positivism," like most terms which are used as missiles in intellectual battles, has come to stand for a baffling multitude of different sins. One of them is the sin, real or alleged, of insisting, as Austin and Bentham did, on the separation of law as it is and law as it ought to be.

How then has this reversal of the wheel come about? What are the theoretical errors in this distinction? Have the practical consequences of stressing the distinction as Bentham and Austin did been bad? Should we now reject it or keep it? In considering these questions we should recall the social philosophy which went along with the utilitarians' insistence on this distinction. They stood firmly but on their own utilitarian ground for all the principles of liberalism in law and government. No one has ever combined, with such even-minded sanity as the utilitarians, the passion for reform with respect for law together with a due recognition of the need to control the abuse of power even when power is in the hands of reformers. One by one in Bentham's works you can identify the elements of the *Rechtstaat* and all the principles for the defense of which the terminology of natural law has in our day been revived. Here are liberty of speech, and of press, the right of association, the need that laws should be published and made widely known before they are enforced, the need to control administrative agencies, the insistence that there should be no criminal liability without fault, and the importance of the principle of legality, *nulla poena sine lege*. Some, I know, find the political and moral insight of the utilitarians a very simple one, but we should not mistake this simplicity for superficiality nor forget how favorably their simplicities compare with the profundities of other thinkers. Take only one example: Bentham on slavery. He says the question at issue is not whether those who are held as slaves can reason, but simply whether they suffer. Does this not compare well with the discussion of the question in terms of whether or not there are some men whom Nature has fitted only to be the living instruments of others? We owe it to Bentham more than anyone else that we have stopped discussing this and similar questions of social policy in that form.

So Bentham and Austin were not dry analysts fiddling with verbal distinctions while cities burned, but were the vanguard of a movement which laboured with passionate intensity and much success to bring about a better society and better laws. Why then did they insist on the separation of law as it is and law as it ought to be? What did they mean? Let us first see what they said. Austin formulated the doctrine:

> *The existence of law is one thing; its merit or demerit is another. Whether it be or be not is one enquiry; whether it be or be not conformable to an assumed standard, is a different enquiry. A law, which actually exists, is a law, though we happen to dislike it, or though it vary from the text, by which we regulate our approbation and disapprobation. This truth, when formally announced as an abstract proposition, is so simple and glaring that it seems idle to insist upon it. But simple and glaring as it is, when enunciated in abstract expressions the enumeration of the instances in which it has been forgotten would fill a volume.*
>
> *Sir William Blackstone, for example, says in his "Commentaries," that the laws of God are superior in obligation to all other laws; that no human laws should be suffered to contradict them; that human laws are of no validity if contrary to them; and that all valid laws derive their force from that Divine original.*
>
> *Now he* may *mean that all human laws ought to conform to the Divine laws. If this be his meaning, I assent to it without hesitation. . . . Perhaps, again, he means that human lawgivers are themselves obliged by the Divine laws to fashion the laws which they impose by that ultimate standard, because if they do not, God will punish them. To this also I entirely assent. . . .*
>
> *But the meaning of this passage of Blackstone, if it has a meaning, seems rather to be this: that no human law which conflicts with the Divine law is obligatory or binding; in other words, that no human law which conflicts with the Divine law* is *a law. . . .*

Austin's protest against blurring the distinction between what law is and what it ought to be is quite general: it is a mistake, whatever our standard of what

ought to be, whatever "the text by which we regulate our approbation or disapprobation." His examples, however, are always a confusion between law as it is and law as morality would require it to be. For him, it must be remembered, the fundamental principles of morality were God's commands, to which utility was an "index": besides this there was the actual accepted morality of a social group or "positive" morality.

Bentham insisted on this distinction without characterizing morality by reference to God but only, of course, by reference to the principles of utility. Both thinkers' prime reason for this insistence was to enable men to see steadily the precise issues posed by the existence of morally bad laws, and to understand the specific character of the authority of a legal order. Bentham's general recipe for life under the government of laws was simple: it was *"to obey punctually; to censure freely."* But Bentham was especially aware, as an anxious spectator of the French revolution, that this was not enough: the time might come in any society when the law's commands were so evil that the question of resistance had to be faced, and it was then essential that the issues at stake at this point should neither be oversimplified nor obscured.[1] Yet, this was precisely what the confusion between law and morals had done and Bentham found that the confusion had spread symmetrically in two different directions. On the one hand Bentham had in mind the anarchist who argues thus: "This ought not to be the law, therefore it is not and I am free not merely to censure but to disregard it." On the other hand he thought of the reactionary who argues: "This is the law, therefore it is what it ought to be," and thus stifles criticism at its birth. Both errors, Bentham thought, were to be found in Blackstone: there was his incautious statement that human laws were invalid if contrary to the law of God,[2] and "that spirit of obsequious *quietism* that seems constitutional in our Author" which "will scarce ever let him recognise a difference" between what is and what ought to be. This indeed was for Bentham the occupational disease of lawyers: "[I]n the eyes of lawyers—not to speak of their dupes—that is to say, as yet, the generality of non-lawyers—the *is* and *ought to be* . . . were one and indivisible." There are therefore two dangers between which insistence on this distinction will help us to steer: the danger that law and its authority may be dissolved in man's conceptions of what law ought to be and the danger that the existing law may supplant morality as a final test of conduct and so escape criticism.

In view of later criticisms it is also important to distinguish several things that the utilitarians did not mean by insisting on their separation of law and morals. They certainly accepted many of the things that might be called "the intersection of law and morals." First, they never denied that, as a matter of historical fact, the development of legal systems had been powerfully influenced by moral opinion, and, conversely, that moral standards had been profoundly influenced by law, so that the content of many legal rules mirrored moral rules or principles. It is not in fact always easy to trace this historical causal connection, but Bentham was certainly ready to admit its existence; so too Austin spoke of the "frequent coincidence" of positive law and morality and attributed the confusion of what law is with what law ought to be to this very fact.

Secondly, neither Bentham nor his followers denied that by explicit legal provisions moral principles might at different points be brought into a legal system and form part of its rules, or that courts might be legally bound to decide in accordance with what they thought just or best. Bentham indeed recognized, as Austin did not, that even the supreme legislative power might be subjected to legal restraints by a constitution and would not have denied that moral principles, like those of the Fifth Amendment, might form the content of such legal constitutional restraints. Austin differed in thinking that restraints on the supreme legislative power could not have the force of law, but would remain merely political or moral checks; but of course he would have recognized that a statute, for example, might confer a delegated legislative power and restrict the area of its exercise by reference to moral principles.

What both Bentham and Austin were anxious to assert were the following two simple things: first, in the absence of an expressed constitutional or legal provision, it could not follow from the mere fact that a rule violated standards of morality that it was not a rule of law; and, conversely, it could not follow from the mere fact that a rule was morally desirable that it was a rule of law.

The history of this simple doctrine in the nineteenth century is too long and too intricate to trace here. Let me summarize it by saying that after it was propounded to the world by Austin it dominated English jurisprudence and constitutes part of the framework of most of those curiously English and perhaps unsatisfactory productions—the omnibus surveys of the whole field of jurisprudence. A succession of these were published after a full text of Austin's lectures finally appeared in 1863. In each of them the utilitarian separation of law and morals is treated as something

that enables lawyers to attain a new clarity. Austin was said by one of his English successors, Amos, "to have delivered the law from the dead body of morality that still clung to it"; and even Maine, who was critical of Austin at many points, did not question this part of his doctrine. In the United States men like N. St. John Green, Gray, and Holmes considered that insistence on this distinction had enabled the understanding of law as a means of social control to get off to a fruitful new start; they welcomed it both as self-evident and as illuminating—as a revealing tautology. This distinction is, of course, one of the main themes of Holmes' most famous essay "The Path of the Law," but the place it had in the estimation of these American writers is best seen in what Gray wrote at the turn of the century in *The Nature and Sources of the Law*. He said:

> *The great gain in its fundamental conceptions which Jurisprudence made during the last century was the recognition of the truth that the Law of a State . . . is not an ideal, but something which actually exists. . . . [I]t is not that which ought to be, but that which is. To fix this definitely in the Jurisprudence of the Common Law, is the feat that Austin accomplished.*

II

So much for the doctrine in the heyday of its success. Let us turn now to some of the criticisms. Undoubtedly, when Bentham and Austin insisted on the distinction between law as it is and as it ought to be, they had in mind *particular* laws the meanings of which were clear and so not in dispute, and they were concerned to argue that such laws, even if morally outrageous, were still laws. It is, however, necessary, in considering the criticisms which later developed, to consider more than those criticisms which were directed to this particular point if we are to get at the root of the dissatisfaction felt; we must also take account of the objection that, even if what the utilitarians said on this particular point were true, their insistence on it, in a terminology suggesting a general cleavage between what is and ought to be law, obscured the fact that at other points there is an essential point of contact between the two. So in what follows I shall consider not only criticisms of the particular point which the utilitarians had in mind, but also the claim that an essential connection between law and morals emerges if we examine how laws, the meanings of which are in dispute, are interpreted and applied in concrete cases; and that this connection emerges again if we widen our point of view and ask, not whether every particular rule of law must satisfy a moral minimum in order to be a law, but whether a system of rules which altogether failed to do this could be a legal system.

There is, however, one major initial complexity by which criticism has been much confused. We must remember that the utilitarians combined with their insistence on the separation of law and morals two other equally famous but distinct doctrines. One was the important truth that a purely analytical study of legal concepts, a study of the meaning of the distinctive vocabulary of the law, was as vital to our understanding of the nature of law as historical or sociological studies, though of course it could not supplant them. The other doctrine was the famous imperative theory of law—that law is essentially a command.

These three doctrines constitute the utilitarian tradition in jurisprudence; yet they are distinct doctrines. It is possible to endorse the separation between law and morals and to value analytical inquiries into the meaning of legal concepts and yet think it wrong to conceive of law as essentially a command. One source of great confusion in the criticism of the separation of law and morals was the belief that the falsity of any one of these three doctrines in the utilitarian tradition showed the other two to be false; what was worse was the failure to see that there were three quite separate doctrines in this tradition. The indiscriminate use of the label "positivism" to designate ambiguously each one of these three separate doctrines (together with some others which the utilitarians never professed) has perhaps confused the issue more than any other single factor.[3] Some of the early American critics of the Austinian doctrine were, however, admirably clear on just this matter. Gray, for example, added at the end of the tribute to Austin, which I have already quoted, the words, "He may have been wrong in treating the Law of the State as being the command of the sovereign" and he touched shrewdly on many points where the command theory is defective. But other critics have been less clearheaded and have thought that the inadequacies of the command theory which gradually came to light were sufficient to demonstrate the falsity of the separation of law and morals.

This was a mistake, but a natural one. To see how natural it was we must look a little more closely at the command idea. The famous theory that law is a command was a part of a wider and more ambitious

claim. Austin said that the notion of a command was "the *key* to the sciences of jurisprudence and morals," and contemporary attempts to elucidate moral judgments in terms of "imperative" or "prescriptive" utterances echo this ambitious claim. But the command theory, viewed as an effort to identify even the quintessence of law, let alone the quintessence of morals, seems breathtaking in its simplicity and quite inadequate. There is much, even in the simplest legal system, that is distorted if presented as a command. Yet the utilitarians thought that the essence of a legal system could be conveyed if the notion of a command were supplemented by that of a habit of obedience. The simple scheme was this: What is a command? It is simply an expression by one person of the desire that another person should do or abstain from some action, accompanied by a threat of punishment which is likely to follow disobedience. Commands are laws if two conditions are satisfied: First, they must be general; second, they must be commanded by what (as both Bentham and Austin claimed) exists in every political society whatever its constitutional form, namely, a person or a group of persons who are in receipt of habitual obedience from most of the society but pay no such obedience to others. These persons are its sovereign. Thus law is the command of the uncommanded commanders of society—the creation of the legally untrammelled will of the sovereign who is by definition outside the law.

It is easy to see that this account of a legal system is threadbare. One can also see why it might seem that its inadequacy is due to the omission of some essential connection with morality. The situation which the simple trilogy of command, sanction, and sovereign avails to describe, if you take these notions at all precisely, is like that of a gunman saying to his victim, "Give me your money or your life." The only difference is that in the case of a legal system the gunman says it to a large number of people who are accustomed to the racket and habitually surrender to it. Law surely is not the gunman situation writ large, and legal order is surely not to be thus simply identified with compulsion.

This scheme, despite the points of obvious analogy between a statute and a command, omits some of the most characteristic elements of law. Let me cite a few. It is wrong to think of a legislature (and a fortiori an electorate) with a changing membership, as a group of persons habitually obeyed: this simple idea is suited only to a monarch sufficiently long-lived for a "habit" to grow up. Even if we waive this point, nothing which legislators do makes law unless they comply with fundamental accepted rules specifying the essential lawmaking procedures. This is true even in a system having a simple unitary constitution like the British. These fundamental accepted rules specifying what the legislature must do to legislate are not commands habitually obeyed, nor can they be expressed as habits of obedience to persons. They lie at the root of a legal system, and what is most missing in the utilitarian scheme is an analysis of what it is for a social group and its officials to accept such rules. This notion, not that of a command as Austin claimed, is the "key to the science of jurisprudence," or at least one of the keys.

Again, Austin, in the case of a democracy, looked past the legislators to the electorate as "the sovereign" (or in England as part of it). He thought that in the United States the mass of the electors to the state and federal legislatures were the sovereign whose commands, given by their "agents" in the legislatures, were law. But on this footing the whole notion of the sovereign outside the law being "habitually obeyed" by the "bulk" of the population must go: for in this case the "bulk" obeys the bulk, that is, it obeys itself. Plainly the general acceptance of the authority of a lawmaking procedure, irrespective of the changing individuals who operate it from time to time, can be only distorted by an analysis in terms of mass habitual obedience to certain persons who are by definition outside the law, just as the cognate but much simpler phenomenon of the general social acceptance of a rule, say of taking off the hat when entering a church, would be distorted if represented as habitual obedience by the mass to specific persons.

Other critics dimly sensed a further and more important defect in the command theory, yet blurred the edge of an important criticism by assuming that the defect was due to the failure to insist upon some important connection between law and morals. This more radical defect is as follows. The picture that the command theory draws of life under law is essentially a simple relationship of the commander to the commanded, of superior to inferior, of top to bottom; the relationship is vertical between the commanders or authors of the law conceived of as essentially outside the law and those who are commanded and subject to the law. In this picture no place, or only an accidental or subordinate place, is afforded for a distinction between types of legal rules which are in fact radically different. Some laws require men to act in certain ways or to abstain from acting whether they wish to or not. The criminal law consists largely of rules of this sort: like commands they are simply "obeyed" or "dis-

obeyed." But other legal rules are presented to society in quite different ways and have quite different functions. They provide facilities more or less elaborate for individuals to create structures of rights and duties for the conduct of life within the coercive framework of the law. Such are the rules enabling individuals to make contracts, wills, and trusts, and generally to mould their legal relations with others. Such rules, unlike the criminal law, are not factors designed to obstruct wishes and choices of an antisocial sort. On the contrary, these rules provide facilities for the realization of wishes and choices. They do not say (like commands) "do this whether you wish it or not," but rather "if you wish to do this, here is the way to do it." Under these rules we exercise powers, make claims, and assert rights. These phrases mark off characteristic features of laws that confer rights and powers; they are laws which are, so to speak, put at the disposition of individuals in a way in which the criminal law is not. Much ingenuity has gone into the task of "reducing" laws of this second sort to some complex variant of laws of the first sort. The effort to show that laws conferring rights are "really" only conditional stipulations of sanctions to be exacted from the person ultimately under a legal duty characterizes much of Kelsen's work. Yet to urge this is really just to exhibit dogmatic determination to suppress one aspect of the legal system in order to maintain the theory that the stipulation of a sanction, like Austin's command, represents the quintessence of law. One might as well urge that the rules of baseball were "really" only complex conditional directions to the scorer and that this showed their real or "essential" nature.

One of the first jurists in England to break with the Austinian tradition, Salmond, complained that the analysis in terms of commands left the notion of a right unprovided with a place. But he confused the point. He argued first, and correctly, that if laws are merely commands it is inexplicable that we should have come to speak of legal rights and powers as conferred or arising under them, but then wrongly concluded that the rules of a legal system must necessarily be connected with moral rules or principles of justice and that only on this footing could the phenomenon of legal rights be explained. Otherwise, Salmond thought, we would have to say that a mere "verbal coincidence" connects the concepts of legal and moral right. Similarly, continental critics of the utilitarians, always alive to the complexity of the notion of a subjective right, insisted that the command theory gave it no place. Hägerström insisted that if laws were merely commands the notion of an individual's right was really inexplicable, for commands are, as he said, something which we either obey or we do not obey; they do not confer rights. But he, too, concluded that moral, or, as he put it, commonsense, notions of justice must therefore be necessarily involved in the analysis of any legal structure elaborate enough to confer rights.

Yet, surely these arguments are confused. Rules that confer rights, though distinct from commands, need not be moral rules or coincide with them. Rights, after all, exist under the rules of ceremonies, games, and in many other spheres regulated by rules which are irrelevant to the question of justice or what the law ought to be. Nor need rules which confer rights be just or morally good rules. The rights of a master over his slaves show us that. "Their merit or demerit," as Austin termed it, depends on how rights are distributed in society and over whom or what they are exercised. These critics indeed revealed the inadequacy of the simple notions of command and habit for the analysis of law; at many points it is apparent that the social acceptance of a rule or standard of authority (even if it is motivated only by fear or superstition or rests on inertia) must be brought into the analysis and cannot itself be reduced to the two simple terms. Yet nothing in this showed the utilitarian insistence on the distinction between the existence of law and its "merits" to be wrong.

III

I now turn to a distinctively American criticism of the separation of the law that is from the law that ought to be. It emerged from the critical study of the judicial process with which American jurisprudence has been on the whole so beneficially occupied. The most skeptical of these critics—the loosely named "Realists" of the 1930s—perhaps too naïvely accepted the conceptual framework of the natural sciences as adequate for the characterization of law and for the analysis of rule-guided action of which a living system of law at least partly consists. But they opened men's eyes to what actually goes on when courts decide cases, and the contrast they drew between the actual facts of judicial decision and the traditional terminology for describing it as if it were a wholly logical operation was usually illuminating; for in spite of some exaggeration the "Realists" made us acutely conscious of one cardinal feature of human language and human thought, emphasis on which is vital not only for the

understanding of law but in areas of philosophy far beyond the confines of jurisprudence. The insight of this school may be presented in the following example. A legal rule forbids you to take a vehicle into the public park. Plainly this forbids an automobile, but what about bicycles, roller skates, toy automobiles? What about airplanes? Are these, as we say, to be called "vehicles" for the purpose of the rule or not? If we are to communicate with each other at all, and if, as in the most elementary form of law, we are to express our intentions that a certain type of behavior be regulated by rules, then the general words we use— like "vehicle" in the case I consider—must have some standard instance in which no doubts are felt about its application. There must be a core of settled meaning, but there will be, as well, a penumbra of debatable cases in which words are neither obviously applicable nor obviously ruled out. These cases will each have some features in common with the standard case; they will lack others or be accompanied by features not present in the standard case. Human invention and natural processes continually throw up such variants on the familiar, and if we are to say that these ranges of facts do or do not fall under existing rules, then the classifier must make a decision which is not dictated to him, for the facts and phenomena to which we fit our words and apply our rules are as it were *dumb*. The toy automobile cannot speak up and say, "I am a vehicle for the purpose of this legal rule," nor can the roller skates chorus, "We are not a vehicle." Fact situations do not await us neatly labeled, creased, and folded, nor is their legal classification written on them to be simply read off by the judge. Instead, in applying legal rules, someone must take the responsibility of deciding that words do or do not cover some case in hand with all the practical consequences involved in this decision.

We may call the problems which arise outside the hard core of standard instances or settled meaning "problems of the penumbra"; they are always with us whether in relation to such trivial things as the regulation of the use of the public park or in relation to the multidimensional generalities of a constitution. If a penumbra of uncertainty must surround all legal rules, then their application to specific cases in the penumbral area cannot be a matter of logical deduction, and so deductive reasoning, which for generations has been cherished as the very perfection of human reasoning, cannot serve as a model for what judges, or indeed anyone, should do in bringing particular cases under general rules. In this area men cannot live by deduction alone. And it follows that if legal arguments and legal decisions of penumbral questions are to be rational, their rationality must lie in something other than a logical relation to premises. So if it is rational or "sound" to argue and to decide that for the purposes of this rule an airplane is not a vehicle, this argument must be sound or rational without being logically conclusive. What is it then that makes such decisions correct or at least better than alternative decisions? Again, it seems true to say that the criterion which makes a decision sound in such cases is some concept of what the law ought to be; it is easy to slide from that into saying that it must be a moral judgment about what law ought to be. So here we touch upon a point of necessary "intersection between law and morals" which demonstrates the falsity or, at any rate, the misleading character of the utilitarians' emphatic insistence on the separation of law as it is and ought to be. Surely, Bentham and Austin could only have written as they did because they misunderstood or neglected this aspect of the judicial process, because they ignored the problems of the penumbra.

The misconception of the judicial process which ignores the problems of the penumbra and which views the process as consisting preeminently in deductive reasoning is often stigmatized as the error of "formalism" or "literalism." My question now is, how and to what extent does the demonstration of this error show the utilitarian distinction to be wrong or misleading? Here there are many issues which have been confused, but I can only disentangle some. The charge of formalism has been leveled both at the "positivist" legal theorist and at the courts, but of course it must be a very different charge in each case. Leveled at the legal theorist, the charge means that he has made a theoretical mistake about the character of legal decision; he has thought of the reasoning involved as consisting in deduction from premises in which the judges' practical choices or decision play no part. It would be easy to show that Austin was guiltless of this error; only an entire misconception of what analytical jurisprudence is and why he thought it important has led to the view that he, or any other analyst, believed that the law was a closed logical system in which judges deduced their decisions from premises. On the contrary, he was very much alive to the character of language, to its vagueness or open character; he thought that in the penumbral situation judges must necessarily legislate, and, in accents that sometimes recall those of the late Judge Jerome Frank, he berated the common-law judges for legislating feebly and timidly and for blindly relying on real or fancied analogies with past cases instead of adapting their decisions

to the growing needs of society as revealed by the moral standard of utility. The villains of this piece, responsible for the conception of the judge as an automaton, are not the utilitarian thinkers. The responsibility, if it is to be laid at the door of any theorist, is with thinkers like Blackstone and, at an earlier stage, Montesquieu. The root of this evil is preoccupation with the separation of powers and Blackstone's "childish fiction" (as Austin termed it) that judges only "find," never "make," law.

But we are concerned with "formalism" as a vice not of jurists but of judges. What precisely is it for a judge to commit this error, to be a "formalist," "automatic," a "slot machine"? Curiously enough the literature which is full of the denunciation of these vices never makes this clear in concrete terms; instead we have only descriptions which cannot mean what they appear to say: it is said that in the formalist error courts make an excessive use of logic, take a thing to "a dryly logical extreme," or make an excessive use of analytical methods. But just how in being a formalist does a judge make an excessive use of logic? It is clear that the essence of his error is to give some general term an interpretation which is blind to social values and consequences (or which is in some other way stupid or perhaps merely disliked by critics). But logic does not prescribe interpretation of terms; it dictates neither the stupid nor intelligent interpretation of any expression. Logic only tells you hypothetically that *if* you give a certain term a certain interpretation then a certain conclusion follows. Logic is silent on how to classify particulars—and this is the heart of a judicial decision. So this reference to logic and to logical extremes is a misnomer for something else, which must be this. A judge has to apply a rule to a concrete case—perhaps the rule that one may not take a stolen "vehicle" across state lines, and in this case an airplane has been taken. He either does not see or pretends not to see that the general terms of this rule are susceptible of different interpretations and that he has a choice left open uncontrolled by linguistic conventions. He ignores, or is blind to, the fact that he is in the area of the penumbra and is not dealing with a standard case. Instead of choosing in the light of social aims, the judge fixes the meaning in a different way. He either takes the meaning that the word most obviously suggests in its ordinary nonlegal context to ordinary men, or one which the word has been given in some other legal context, or, still worse, he thinks of a standard case and then arbitrarily identifies certain features in it—for example, in the case of a vehicle, (1) normally used on land, (2) capable of carrying a human person, (3) capable of being self-propelled—and treats these three as always necessary and always sufficient conditions for the use in all contexts of the word "vehicle," irrespective of the social consequences of giving it this interpretation. This choice, not "logic," would force the judge to include a toy motor car (if electrically propelled) and to exclude bicycles and the airplane. In all this there is possibly great stupidity but no more "logic," and no less, than in cases in which the interpretation given to a general term and the consequent application of some general rule to a particular case is consciously controlled by some identified social aim.

Decisions made in a fashion as blind as this would scarcely deserve the name of decisions; we might as well toss a penny in applying a rule of law. But it is at least doubtful whether any judicial decisions (even in England) have been quite as automatic as this. Rather either the interpretations stigmatized as automatic have resulted from the conviction that it is fairer in a criminal statute to take a meaning which would jump to the mind of the ordinary man at the cost even of defeating other values, and this itself is a social policy (though possibly a bad one); or much more frequently, what is stigmatized as "mechanical" and "automatic" is a determined choice made indeed in the light of a social aim but of a conservative social aim. Certainly many of the Supreme Court decisions at the turn of the century which have been so stigmatized represent clear choices in the penumbral area to give effect to a policy of a conservative type. This is peculiarly true of Mr. Justice Peckham's opinions defining the spheres of police power and due process.

But how does the wrongness of deciding cases in an automatic and mechanical way and the rightness of deciding cases by reference to social purposes show that the utilitarian insistence on the distinction between what the law is and what it ought to be is wrong? I take it that no one who wished to use these vices of formalism as proof that the distinction between what is and what ought to be is mistaken would deny that the decisions stigmatized as automatic are law; nor would he deny that the system in which such automatic decisions are made is a legal system. Surely he would say that they are law, but they are bad law, they ought not to be law. But this would be to use the distinction, not to refute it; and of course both Bentham and Austin used it to attack judges for failing to decide penumbral cases in accordance with the growing needs of society.

Clearly, if the demonstration of the errors of formalism is to show the utilitarian distinction to be

wrong, the point must be drastically restated. The point must be not merely that a judicial decision to be rational must be made in the light of some conception of what ought to be, but that the aims, the social policies and purposes to which judges should appeal if their decisions are to be rational, are themselves to be considered as part of the law in some suitably wide sense of "law" which is held to be more illuminating than that used by the utilitarians. This restatement of the point would have the following consequence: Instead of saying that the recurrence of penumbral questions shows us that legal rules are essentially incomplete, and that, when they fail to determine decisions, judges must legislate and so exercise a creative choice between alternatives, we shall say that the social policies which guide the judges' choice are in a sense there for them to discover; the judges are only "drawing out" of the rule what, if it is properly understood, is "latent" within it. To call this judicial legislation is to obscure some essential continuity between the clear cases of the rule's application and the penumbral decisions. I shall question later whether this way of talking is salutary, but I wish at this time to point out something obvious, but likely, if not stated, to tangle the issues. It does not follow that, because the opposite of a decision reached blindly in the formalist or literalist manner is a decision intelligently reached by reference to some conception of what ought to be, we have a junction of law and morals. We must, I think, beware of thinking in a too simple-minded fashion about the word "ought." This is not because there is no distinction to be made between law as it is and ought to be. Far from it. It is because the distinction should be between what is and what from many different points of view ought to be. The word "ought" merely reflects the presence of some standard of criticism; one of these standards is a moral standard but not all standards are moral. We say to our neighbour, "You ought not to lie," and that may certainly be a moral judgment, but we should remember that the baffled poisoner may say, "I ought to have given her a second dose." The point here is that intelligent decisions which we oppose to mechanical or formal decisions are not necessarily identical with decisions defensible on moral grounds. We may say of many a decision: "Yes, that is right; that is as it ought to be," and we may mean only that some accepted purpose or policy has been thereby advanced; we may not mean to endorse the moral propriety of the policy or the decision. So the contrast between the mechanical decision and the intelligent one can be reproduced inside a system dedicated to the pursuit of the most evil aims. It does not exist as a contrast to be found only in legal systems which, like our own, widely recognize principles of justice and moral claims of individuals.

An example may make this point plainer. With us the task of sentencing in criminal cases is the one that seems most obviously to demand from the judge the exercise of moral judgment. Here the factors to be weighed seem clearly to be moral factors: society must not be exposed to wanton attack; too much misery must not be inflicted on either the victim or his dependents; efforts must be made to enable him to lead a better life and regain a position in the society whose laws he has violated. To a judge striking the balance among these claims, with all the discretion and perplexities involved, his task seems as plain an example of the exercise of moral judgment as could be; and it seems to be the polar opposite of some mechanical application of a tariff of penalties fixing a sentence careless of the moral claims which in our system have to be weighed. So here intelligent and rational decision is guided however uncertainly by moral aims. But we have only to vary the example to see that this need not necessarily be so and surely, if it need not necessarily be so, the utilitarian point remains unshaken. Under the Nazi regime men were sentenced by courts for criticism of the regime. Here the choice of sentence might be guided exclusively by consideration of what was needed to maintain the state's tyranny effectively. What sentence would both terrorize the public at large and keep the friends and family of the prisoner in suspense so that both hope and fear would cooperate as factors making for subservience? The prisoner of such a system would be regarded simply as an object to be used in pursuit of these aims. Yet, in contrast with a mechanical decision, decision on these grounds would be intelligent and purposive, and from one point of view the decision would be as it ought to be. Of course, I am not unaware that a whole philosophical tradition has sought to demonstrate the fact that we cannot correctly call decisions or behavior truly rational unless they are in conformity with moral aims and principles. But the example I have used seems to me to serve at least as a warning that we cannot use the errors of formalism as something which per se demonstrates the falsity of the utilitarian insistence on the distinction between law as it is and law as *morally* it ought to be.

We can now return to the main point. If it is true that the intelligent decision of penumbral questions is one made not mechanically but in the light of aims, purposes, and policies, though not necessarily in the light of anything we would call moral principles, is it wise to express this important fact by saying that the firm utilitarian distinction between what the law is and what it ought to be should be dropped? Perhaps the claim that it is wise cannot be theoretically refuted for it is, in effect, an *invitation* to revise our conception of what a legal rule is. We are invited to include in the "rule" the various aims and policies in the light of which its penumbral cases are decided on the ground that these aims have, because of their importance, as much right to be called law as the core of legal rules whose meaning is settled. But though an invitation cannot be refuted, it may be refused and I would proffer two reasons for refusing this invitation. First, everything we have learned about the judicial process can be expressed in other less mysterious ways. We can say laws are incurably incomplete and we must decide the penumbral cases rationally by reference to social aims. I think Holmes, who had such a vivid appreciation of the fact that "general propositions do not decide concrete cases," would have put it that way. Second, to insist on the utilitarian distinction is to emphasize that the hard core of settled meaning is law in some centrally important sense and that even if there are borderlines, there must first be lines. If this were not so the notion of rules controlling courts' decisions would be senseless as some of the "Realists"—in their most extreme moods, and, I think, on bad grounds—claimed.

By contrast, to soften the distinction, to assert mysteriously that there is some fused identity between law as it is and as it ought to be, is to suggest that all legal questions are fundamentally like those of the penumbra. It is to assert that there is no central element of actual law to be seen in the core of central meaning which rules have, that there is nothing in the nature of a legal rule inconsistent with *all* questions being open to reconsideration in the light of social policy. Of course, it is good to be occupied with the penumbra. Its problems are rightly the daily diet of the law schools. But to be occupied with the penumbra is one thing, to be preoccupied with it another. And preoccupation with the penumbra is, if I may say so, as rich a source of confusion in the American legal tradition as formalism in the English. Of course we might abandon the notion that rules have authority; we might cease to attach force or even meaning to an argument that a case falls clearly within a rule and the scope of a precedent. We might call all such reasoning "automatic" or "mechanical," which is already the routine invective of the courts. But until we decide that this *is* what we want; we should not encourage it by obliterating the utilitarian distinction.

IV

The third criticism of the separation of law and morals is of a very different character; it certainly is less an intellectual argument against the utilitarian distinction than a passionate appeal supported not by detailed reasoning but by reminders of a terrible experience. For it consists of the testimony of those who have descended into Hell, and, like Ulysses or Dante, brought back a message for human beings. Only in this case the Hell was not beneath or beyond earth, but on it; it was a Hell created on earth by men for other men.

This appeal comes from those German thinkers who lived through the Nazi regime and reflected upon its evil manifestations in the legal system. One of these thinkers, Gustav Radbruch, had himself shared the "positivist" doctrine until the Nazi tyranny, but he was converted by this experience and so his appeal to other men to discard the doctrine of the separation of law and morals has the special poignancy of a recantation. What is important about this criticism is that it really does confront the particular point which Bentham and Austin had in mind in urging the separation of law as it is and as it ought to be. These German thinkers put their insistence on the need to join together what the utilitarians separated just where this separation was of most importance in the eyes of the utilitarians; for they were concerned with the problem posed by the existence of morally evil laws.

Before his conversion Radbruch held that resistance to law was a matter for the personal conscience, to be thought out by the individual as a moral problem, and the validity of a law could not be disproved by showing that the effect of compliance with the law would be more evil than the effect of disobedience. Austin, it may be recalled, was emphatic in condemning those who said that if human laws conflicted with the fundamental principles of morality then they cease to be [laws. He said they were] talking "stark nonsense."

> *The most pernicious laws, and therefore those which are most opposed to the will of God, have been and are continually enforced as laws by judicial tribunals. Suppose an act innocuous, or positively beneficial, be prohibited by the sovereign under the penalty of death; if I commit this act, I shall be tried and condemned, and if I object to the sentence, that it is contrary to the law of God . . . the court of justice will demonstrate the inconclusiveness of my reasoning by hanging me up, in pursuance of the law of which I have impugned the validity. An exception, demurrer, or plea, founded on the law of God was never heard in a Court of Justice, from the creation of the world down to the present moment.*

These are strong, indeed brutal words, but we must remember that they went along—in the case of Austin and, of course, Bentham—with the conviction that if laws reached a certain degree of iniquity then there would be a plain moral obligation to resist them and to withhold obedience. We shall see, when we consider the alternatives, that this simple presentation of the human dilemma which may arise has much to be said for it.

Radbruch, however, had concluded from the ease with which the Nazi regime had exploited subservience to mere law—or expressed, as he thought, in the "positivist" slogan "law is law" *(Gesetz als Gesetz)*—and from the failure of the German legal profession to protest against the enormities which they were required to perpetrate in the name of law, that "positivism" (meaning here the insistence on the separation of law as it is from law as it ought to be) had powerfully contributed to the horrors. His considered reflections led him to the doctrine that the fundamental principles of humanitarian morality were part of the very concept of *Recht* or Legality and that no positive enactment or statute, however clearly it was expressed and however clearly it conformed with the formal criteria of validity of a given legal system, could be valid if it contravened basic principles of morality. This doctrine can be appreciated fully only if the nuances imported by the German word *Recht* are grasped. But it is clear that the doctrine meant that every lawyer and judge should denounce statutes that transgressed the fundamental principles not as merely immoral or wrong but as having no legal character, and enactments which on this ground lack the quality of law should not be taken into account in working out the legal position of any given individual in particular circumstances. The striking recantation of his previous doctrine is unfortunately omitted from the translation of his works, but it should be read by all who wish to think afresh on the question of the interconnection of law and morals.

It is impossible to read without sympathy Radbruch's passionate demand that the German legal conscience should be open to the demands of morality and his complaint that this has been too little the case in the German tradition. On the other hand there is an extraordinary naïveté in the view that insensitiveness to the demands of morality and subservience to state power in a people like the Germans should have arisen from the belief that law might be law though it failed to conform with the minimum requirements of morality. Rather this terrible history prompts inquiry into why emphasis on the slogan "law is law," and the distinction between law and morals, acquired a sinister character in Germany, but elsewhere, as with the utilitarians themselves, went along with the most enlightened liberal attitudes. But something more disturbing than naïveté is latent in Radbruch's whole presentation of the issues to which the existence of morally iniquitous laws give rise. It is not, I think, uncharitable to say that we can see in his argument that he has only half digested the spiritual message of liberalism which he is seeking to convey to the legal profession. For everything that he says is really dependent upon an enormous overvaluation of the importance of the bare fact that a rule may be said to be a valid rule of law, as if this, once declared, was conclusive of the final moral question: "Ought this rule of law to be obeyed?" Surely the truly liberal answer to any sinister use of the slogan "law is law" or of the distinction between law and morals is, "Very well, but that does not conclude the question. Law is not morality; do not let it supplant morality."

However, we are not left to a mere academic discussion in order to evaluate the plea which Radbruch made for the revision of the distinction between law and morals. After the war Radbruch's conception of law as containing in itself the essential moral principle of humanitarianism was applied in practice by German courts in certain cases in which local war criminals, spies, and informers under the Nazi regime were punished. The special importance of these cases is that the persons accused of these crimes claimed that what they had done was not illegal under the laws of the regime in force at the time these actions were performed. This plea was met with the reply that the laws upon which they relied were invalid as contravening the fundamental principles of morality. Let me cite briefly one of these cases.

In 1944 a woman, wishing to be rid of her husband, denounced him to the authorities for insulting remarks he had made about Hitler while home on leave from the German army. The wife was under no legal duty to report his acts, though what he had said was apparently in violation of statutes making it illegal to make statements detrimental to the government of the Third Reich or to impair by any means the military

defense of the German people. The husband was arrested and sentenced to death, apparently pursuant to these statutes, though he was not executed but was sent to the front. In 1949 the wife was prosecuted in a West German court for an offense which we would describe as illegally depriving a person of his freedom (*rechtswidrige Freiheitsberaubung*). This was punishable as a crime under the German Criminal Code of 1871 which had remained in force continuously since its enactment. The wife pleaded that her husband's imprisonment was pursuant to the Nazi statutes and hence that she had committed no crime. The court of appeal to which the case ultimately came held that the wife was guilty of procuring the deprivation of her husband's liberty by denouncing him to the German courts, even though he had been sentenced by a court for having violated a statute, since, to quote the words of the court, the statute "was contrary to the sound conscience and sense of justice of all decent human beings." This reasoning was followed in many cases which have been hailed as a triumph of the doctrines of natural law and as signaling the overthrow of positivism. The unqualified satisfaction with this result seems to me to be hysteria. Many of us might applaud the objective—that of punishing a woman for an outrageously immoral act—but this was secured only by declaring a statute established since 1934 not to have the force of law, and at least the wisdom of this course must be doubted. There were, of course, two other choices. One was to let the woman go unpunished; one can sympathize with and endorse the view that this might have been a bad thing to do. The other was to face the fact that if the woman were to be punished it must be pursuant to the introduction of a frankly retrospective law and with a full consciousness of what was sacrificed in securing her punishment in this way. Odious as retrospective criminal legislation and punishment may be, to have pursued it openly in this case would at least have had the merits of candour. It would have made plain that in punishing the woman a choice had to be made between two evils, that of leaving her unpunished and that of sacrificing a very precious principle of morality endorsed by most legal systems. Surely if we have learned anything from the history of morals it is that the thing to do with a moral quandary is not to hide it. Like nettles, the occasions when life forces us to choose between the lesser of two evils must be grasped with the consciousness that they are what they are. The vice of this use of the principle that, at certain limiting points, what is utterly immoral cannot be law or lawful is that it will serve to cloak the true nature of the problems with which we are faced and will encourage the romantic optimism that all the values we cherish ultimately will fit into a single system, that no one of them has to be sacrificed or compromised to accommodate another.

> *All Discord Harmony not Understood*
> *All Partial Evil Universal Good*

This is surely untrue and there is an insincerity in any formulation of our problem which allows us to describe the treatment of the dilemma as if it were the disposition of the ordinary case.

It may seem perhaps to make too much of forms, even perhaps of words, to emphasize one way of disposing of this difficult case as compared with another which might have led, so far as the woman was concerned, to exactly the same result. Why should we dramatize the difference between them? We might punish the woman under a new retrospective law and declare overtly that we were doing something inconsistent with our principles as the lesser of two evils; or we might allow the case to pass as one in which we do not point out precisely where we sacrifice such a principle. But candour is not just one among many minor virtues of the administration of law, just as it is not merely a minor virtue of morality. For if we adopt Radbruch's view, and with him the German courts make our protest against evil law in the form of an assertion that certain rules cannot be law because of their moral iniquity, we confuse one of the most powerful, because it is the simplest, forms of moral criticism. If with the utilitarians we speak plainly, we say that laws may be law but too evil to be obeyed. This is a moral condemnation which everyone can understand and it makes an immediate and obvious claim to moral attention. If, on the other hand, we formulate our objection as an assertion that these evil things are not law, here is an assertion which many people do not believe, and if they are disposed to consider it at all, it would seem to raise a whole host of philosophical issues before it can be accepted. So perhaps the most important single lesson to be learned from this form of the denial of the utilitarian distinction is the one that the utilitarians were most concerned to teach: when we have the ample resources of plain speech we must not present the moral criticism of institutions as propositions of a disputable philosophy.

V

I have endeavored to show that, in spite of all that has been learned and experienced since the utilitarians wrote, and in spite of the defects of other parts of their doctrine, their protest against the confusion of what is and what ought to be law has a moral as well as an intellectual value. Yet it may well be said that, though this distinction is valid and important if applied to any particular law of a system, it is at least misleading if we attempt to apply it to "law," that is, to the notion of a legal system, and that if we insist, as I have, on the narrower truth (or truism), we obscure a wider (or deeper) truth. After all, it may be urged, we have learned that there are many things which are untrue of laws taken separately, but which are true and important in a legal system considered as a whole. For example, the connection between law and sanctions and between the existence of law and its "efficacy" must be understood in this more general way. It is surely not arguable (without some desperate extension of the word "sanction" or artificial narrowing of the word "law") that every law in a municipal legal system must have a sanction, yet it is at least plausible to argue that a legal system must, to be a legal system, provide sanctions for certain of its rules. So too, a rule of law may be said to exist though enforced or obeyed in only a minority of cases, but this could not be said of a legal system as a whole. Perhaps the differences with respect to laws taken separately and a legal system as a whole are also true of the connection between moral (or some other) conceptions of what law ought to be and law in this wider sense.

This line of argument, found (at least in embryo form) in Austin, where he draws attention to the fact that every developed legal system contains certain fundamental notions which are "necessary" and "bottomed in the common nature of man," is worth pursuing—up to a point—and I shall say briefly why and how far this is so.

We must avoid, if we can, the arid wastes of inappropriate definition, for, in relation to a concept as many-sided and vague as that of a legal system, disputes about the "essential" character, or necessity to the whole, of any single element soon begin to look like disputes about whether chess could be "chess" if played with pawns. There is a wish, which may be understandable, to cut straight through the question whether a legal system, to be a legal system, must measure up to some moral or other standard with simple statements of fact: for example, that no system which utterly failed in this respect has ever existed or could endure; that the normally fulfilled assumption that a legal system aims at some form of justice colours the whole way in which we interpret specific rules in particular cases, and if this normally fulfilled assumption were not fulfilled no one would have any reason to obey except fear (and probably not that) and still less, of course, any moral obligation to obey. The connection between law and moral standards and principles of justice is therefore as little arbitrary and as "necessary" as the connection between law and sanctions, and the pursuit of the question whether this necessity is logical (part of the "meaning" of law) or merely factual or causal can safely be left as an innocent pastime for philosophers.

Yet in two respects I should wish to go further (even though this involves the use of a philosophical fantasy) and show what could intelligibly be meant by the claim that certain provisions in a legal system are "necessary." The world in which we live, and we who live in it, may one day change in many different ways; and if this change were radical enough not only would certain statements of fact now true be false and vice versa, but whole ways of thinking and talking which constitute our present conceptual apparatus, through which we see the world and each other, would lapse. We have only to consider how the whole of our social, moral, and legal life, as we understand it now, depends on the contingent fact that though our bodies do change in shape, size, and other physical properties they do not do this so drastically nor with such quicksilver rapidity and irregularity that we cannot identify each other as the same persistent individual over considerable spans of time. Though this is but a contingent fact which may one day be different, on it at present rest huge structures of our thought and principles of action and social life. Similarly, consider the following possibility (not because it is more than a possibility but because it reveals why we think certain things necessary in a legal system and what we mean by this): suppose that men were to become invulnerable to attack by each other, were clad perhaps like giant land crabs with an impenetrable carapace, and could extract the food they needed from the air by some internal chemical process. In such circumstances (the details of which can be left to science fiction) rules forbidding the free use of violence and rules constituting the minimum form of property—with its rights and duties sufficient to enable food to grow and be retained until eaten—would not have the necessary nonarbitrary status which they have for us, constituted as we are in a world like ours. At present, and until such radical changes supervene, such rules are so fundamental that if a legal system did not have them there would be no point in having any other rules at all. Such rules overlap with basic moral principles vetoing murder, violence, and theft; and so we

can add to the factual statement that all legal systems in fact coincide with morality at such vital points, the statement that this is, in this sense, necessarily so. And why not call it a "natural" necessity?

Of course even this much depends on the fact that in asking what content a legal system must have we take this question to be worth asking only if we who consider it cherish the humble aim of survival in close proximity to our fellows. Natural-law theory, however, in all its protean guises, attempts to push the argument much further and to assert that human beings are equally devoted to and united in their conception of aims (the pursuit of knowledge, justice to their fellow men) other than that of survival, and these dictate a further necessary content to a legal system (over and above my humble minimum) without which it would be pointless. Of course we must be careful not to exaggerate the differences among human beings, but it seems to me that above this minimum the purposes men have for living in society are too conflicting and varying to make possible much extension of the argument that some fuller overlap of legal rules and moral standards is "necessary" in this sense.

Another aspect of the matter deserves attention. If we attach to a legal system the minimum meaning that it must consist of general rules—general both in the sense that they refer to courses of action, not single actions, and to multiplicities of men, not single individuals—this meaning connotes the principle of treating like cases alike, though the criteria of when cases are alike will be, so far, only the general elements specified in the rules. It is, however, true that *one* essential element of the concept of justice is the principle of treating like cases alike. This is justice in the administration of the law, not justice of the law. So there is, in the very notion of law consisting of general rules, something which prevents us from treating it as if morally it is utterly neutral, without any necessary contact with moral principles. Natural procedural justice consists therefore of those principles of objectivity and impartiality in the administration of the law which implement just this aspect of law and which are designed to ensure that rules are applied only to what are genuinely cases of the rule or at least to minimize the risks of inequalities in this sense.

These two reasons (or excuses) for talking of a certain overlap between legal and moral standards as necessary and natural, of course, should not satisfy anyone who is really disturbed by the utilitarian or "positivist" insistence that law and morality are distinct. This is so because a legal system that satisfied these minimum requirements might apply, with the

most pedantic impartiality as between the persons affected, laws which were hideously oppressive, and
might deny to a vast rightless slave population the
minimum benefits of protection from violence and
theft. The stink of such societies is, after all, still in our
nostrils and to argue that they have (or had) no legal
system would only involve the repetition of the argument. Only if the rules failed to provide these essential
benefits and protection for anyone—even for a slave-
owning group—would the minimum be unsatisfied
and the system sink to the status of a set of meaningless taboos. Of course no one denied those benefits
would have any reason to obey except fear and would
have every moral reason to revolt.

VI

I should be less than candid if I did not, in conclusion,
consider something which, I suspect, most troubles
those who react strongly against "legal positivism."
Emphasis on the distinction between law as it is and
law as it ought to be may be taken to depend upon
and to entail what are called "subjectivist" and "relativist" or "noncognitive" theories concerning the very
nature of moral judgments, moral distinctions, or "values." Of course the utilitarians themselves (as distinct
from later positivists like Kelsen) did not countenance
any such theories, however unsatisfactory their moral
philosophy may appear to us now. Austin thought ultimate moral principles were the commands of God,
known to us by revelation or through the "index" of
utility, and Bentham thought they were verifiable
propositions about utility. Nonetheless I think (though
I cannot prove) that insistence upon the distinction
between law as it is and ought to be has been, under
the general head of "positivism," confused with a
moral theory according to which statements of what is
the case ("statements of fact") belong to a category or
type radically different from statements of what ought
to be ("value statements"). It may therefore be well to
dispel this source of confusion.

There are many contemporary variants of this
type of moral theory: according to some, judgments of
what ought to be, or ought to be done, either are or
include as essential elements expression of "feeling,"
"emotion," or "attitudes" or "subjective preferences";
in others such judgments both express feelings or
emotions or attitudes and enjoin others to share them.
In other variants such judgments indicate that a particular case falls under a general principle or policy of

action which the speaker has "chosen" or to which he
is "committed" and which is itself not a recognition of
what is the case but analogous to a general "imperative" or command addressed to all including the
speaker himself. Common to all these variants is the
insistence that judgments of what ought to be done,
because they contain such "non-cognitive" elements,
cannot be argued for or established by rational methods as statements of fact can be, and cannot be shown
to follow from any statement of fact but only from
other judgments of what ought to be done in conjunction with some statement of fact. We cannot, on such
a theory, demonstrate, for example, that an action was
wrong, ought not to have been done, merely by showing that it consisted of the deliberate infliction of pain
solely for the gratification of the agent. We only show
it to be wrong if we add to those verifiable "cognitive"
statements of fact a general principle not itself verifiable or "cognitive" that the infliction of pain in such
circumstances is wrong, ought not to be done. Together with this general distinction between statements of what is and what ought to be go sharp
parallel distinctions between statements about means
and statements of moral ends. We can rationally discover and debate what are appropriate means to
given ends, but ends are not rationally discoverable or
debatable; they are "fiats of the will," expression of
"emotions," "preferences," or "attitudes."

Against all such views (which are of course far
subtler than this crude survey can convey) others urge
that all these sharp distinctions between is and ought,
fact and value, means and ends, cognitive and noncognitive, are wrong. In acknowledging ultimate ends
or moral values we are recognizing something as
much imposed upon us by the character of the world
in which we live, as little a matter of choice, attitude,
feeling, emotion as the truth of factual judgments
about what is the case. The characteristic moral argument is not one in which the parties are reduced to
expressing or kindling feelings or emotions or issuing
exhortations or commands to each other but one by
which parties come to acknowledge after closer examination and reflection that an initially disputed case
falls within the ambit of a vaguely apprehended principle (itself no more "subjective," no more a "fiat of
our will" than any other principle of classification) and
this has as much title to be called "cognitive" or "rational" as any other initially disputed classification of
particulars.

Let us now suppose that we accept this rejection of "noncognitive" theories of morality and this
denial of the drastic distinction in type between state-

ments of what is and what ought to be, and that moral judgments are as rationally defensible as any other kind of judgments. What would follow from this as to the nature of the connection between law as it is and law as it ought to be? Surely, from this alone, nothing. Laws, however morally iniquitous, would still (so far as this point is concerned) be laws. The only difference which the acceptance of this view of the nature of moral judgments would make would be that the moral iniquity of such laws would be something that could be demonstrated; it would surely follow merely from a statement of what the rule required to be done that the rule was morally wrong and so ought not to be law or conversely that it was morally desirable and ought to be law. But the demonstration of this would not show the rule not to be (or to be) law. Proof that the principles by which we evaluate or condemn laws are rationally discoverable, and not mere "fiats of the will," leaves untouched the fact that there are laws which may have any degree of iniquity or stupidity and still be laws. And conversely there are rules that have every moral qualification to be laws and yet are not laws.

Surely something further or more specific must be said if disproof of "noncognitivism" or kindred theories in ethics is to be relevant to the distinction between law as it is and law as it ought to be, and to lead to the abandonment at some point or some softening of this distinction. No one has done more than Professor Lon Fuller of the Harvard Law School in his various writings to make clear such a line of argument and I will end by criticising what I take to be its central point. It is a point which again emerges when we consider not those legal rules or parts of legal rules the meanings of which are clear and excite no debate but the interpretation of rules in concrete cases where doubts are initially felt and argument develops about their meaning. In no legal system is the scope of legal rules restricted to the range of concrete instances which were present or are believed to have been present in the minds of legislators; this indeed is one of the important differences between a legal rule and a command. Yet, when rules are recognized as applying to instances beyond any that legislators did or could have considered, their extension to such new cases often presents itself not as a deliberate choice or fiat on the part of those who so interpret the rule. It appears neither as a decision to give the rule a new or extended meaning nor as a guess as to what legislators, dead perhaps in the eighteenth century, would have said had they been alive in the twentieth century. Rather, the inclusion of the new case under the rule

takes its place as a natural elaboration of the rule, as something implementing a "purpose" which it seems natural to attribute (in some sense) to the rule itself rather than to any particular person dead or alive. The utilitarian description of such interpretative extension of old rules to new cases as judicial legislation fails to do justice to this phenomenon; it gives no hint of the differences between a deliberate fiat or decision to treat the new case in the same way as past cases and a recognition (in which there is little that is deliberate or even voluntary) that inclusion of the new case under the rule will implement or articulate a continuing and identical purpose, hitherto less specifically apprehended.

Perhaps many lawyers and judges will see in this language something that precisely fits their experience; others may think it a romantic gloss on facts better stated in the utilitarian language of judicial "legislation" or in the modern American terminology of "creative choice."

To make the point clear Professor Fuller uses a nonlegal example from the philosopher Wittgenstein which is, I think, illuminating.[4]

> Someone says to me: "Show the children a game." I teach them gaming with dice and the other says "I did not mean that sort of game." Must the exclusion of the game with dice have come before his mind when he gave me the order?

Something important does seem to me to be touched on in this example. Perhaps there are the following (distinguishable) points. First, we normally do interpret not only what people are trying to do but what they say in the light of assumed common human objectives so that unless the contrary were expressly indicated we would not interpret an instruction to show a young child a game as a mandate to introduce him to gambling even though in other contexts the word "game" would be naturally so interpreted. Second, very often, the speaker whose words are thus interpreted might say: "Yes, that's what I mean [or "that's what I meant all along"] though I never thought of it until you put this particular case to me." Third, when we thus recognize, perhaps after argument or consultation with others, a particular case not specifically envisaged beforehand as falling within the ambit of some vaguely expressed instruction, we may find this experience falsified by description of it as a mere decision on our part so to treat the particular case, and that we can only describe this faithfully as coming to realize and to articulate what we "really" want or our "true purpose"—phrases which Professor Fuller uses later in the same article.[5]

I am sure that many philosophical discussions of the character of moral argument would benefit from attention to cases of the sort instanced by Professor Fuller. Such attention would help to provide a corrective to the view that there is a sharp separation between "ends" and "means" and that in debating "ends" we can only work on each other nonrationally, and that rational argument is reserved for discussion of "means." But I think the relevance of his point to the issue whether it is correct or wise to insist on the distinction between law as it is and law as it ought to be is very small indeed. Its net effect is that in interpreting legal rules there are some cases which we find after reflection to be so natural an elaboration or articulation of the rule that to think of and refer to this as "legislation," "making law," or a "fiat" on our part would be misleading. So, the argument must be, it would be misleading to distinguish in such cases between what the rule is and what it ought to be—at least in some sense of ought. We think it ought to include the new case and come to see after reflection that it really does. But even if this way of presenting a recognizable experience as an example of a fusion between is and ought to be is admitted, two caveats must be borne in mind. The first is that "ought" in this case need have nothing to do with morals for the reasons explained already in section III: there may be just the same sense that a new case will implement and articulate the purpose of a rule in interpreting the rules

of a game or some hideously immoral code of oppression whose immorality is appreciated by those called in to interpret it. They too can see what the "spirit" of the game they are playing requires in previously unenvisaged cases. More important is this: After all is said and done we must remember how rare in the law is the phenomenon held to justify this way of talking, how exceptional is this feeling that one way of deciding a case is imposed upon us as the only natural or rational elaboration of some rule. Surely it cannot be doubted that, for most cases of interpretation, the language of choice between alternatives, "judicial legislation" or even "fiat" (though not arbitrary fiat), better conveys the realities of the situation.

Within the framework of relatively well-settled law there jostle too many alternatives too nearly equal in attraction between which judge and lawyer must uncertainly pick their way to make appropriate here language which may well describe those experiences which we have in interpreting our own or others' principles of conduct, intention, or wishes, when we are not conscious of exercising a deliberate choice, but rather of recognizing something awaiting recognition. To use in the description of the interpretation of laws the suggested terminology of a fusion of inability to separate what is law and ought to be will serve (like earlier stories that judges only find, never make, law) only to conceal the facts, that here if anywhere we live among uncertainties between which we have to choose, and that the existing law imposes only limits on our choice and not the choice itself.

1. See Bentham, Principles of Legislation, in The Theory of Legislation 1, 65 n.* (Ogden ed. 1931) (c. XII, 2d para. n.*).
Here we touch upon the most difficult of questions. If the law is not what it ought to be; if it openly combats the principle of utility; ought we to obey it? Ought we to violate it? Ought we to remain neuter between the law which commands an evil, and morality which forbids it? See also Bentham, A Fragment on Government, in 1 Works 221, 287–88 (Bowring ed. 1859) (c. IV, 20th–25th paras.).
2. 1 Blackstone, Commentaries *41. Bentham criticized "this dangerous maxim," saying "the natural tendency of such a doctrine is to impel a man, by the force of conscience, to rise up in arms against any law whatever that he happens not to like." Bentham, A Fragment on Government, in 1 Works 221, 287 (Bowring ed. 1859) (c. IV, 19th para.). See also Bentham, A Comment on the Commentaries 49 (1928) (c. III). For an expression of a fear lest anarchy result from such a doctrine, combined with a recognition that resistance may be justified on grounds of utility, see Austin, The Province of Jurisprudence Determined, 186 (Library of Ideas ed. 1954).
3. It may help to identify five (there may be more) meanings of "positivism" bandied about in contemporary jurisprudence:
(1) the contention that laws are commands of human beings.

(2) the contention that there is no necessary connection between law and morals or law as it is and ought to be.
(3) the contention that the analysis (or study of the meaning of legal concepts) is (a) worth pursuing and (b) to be distinguished from historical inquiries into the causes or origins of laws, from sociological inquiries into the relation of law and other social phenomena, and from the criticism or appraisal of law whether in terms of morals, social aims, "functions," or otherwise.
(4) the contention that a legal system is a "closed logical system" in which correct legal decisions can be deduced by logical means from predetermined legal rules without reference to social aims, policies, moral standards.
(5) the contention that moral judgments cannot be established or defended, as statements of facts can, by rational argument, evidence, or proof ("noncognitivism" in ethics).
Bentham and Austin held the views described in (1), (2), and (3) but not those in (4) and (5). Opinion (4) is often ascribed to analytical jurists, but I know of no "analyst" who held this view.
4. Fuller, Human Purpose and Natural Law, 53 J. Philos. 697, 700 (1956).
5. Id. at 701, 702.

Positivism and Fidelity to Law—A Reply to Professor Hart*

Lon L. Fuller

. . .

I. The Definition of Law

Throughout his essay Professor Hart aligns himself with a general position which he associates with the names of Bentham, Austin, Gray, and Holmes. He recognizes, of course, that the conceptions of these men as to "what law is" vary considerably, but this diversity he apparently considers irrelevant in his defense of their general school of thought.

If the only issue were that of stipulating a meaning for the word "law" that would be conducive to intellectual clarity, there might be much justification for treating all of these men as working in the same direction. Austin, for example, defines law as the command of the highest legislative power, called the sovereign. For Gray, on the other hand, law consists in the rules laid down by judges. A statute is, for Gray, not a law, but only a source of law, which becomes law only after it has been interpreted and applied by a court. Now if our only object were to obtain that clarity which comes from making our definitions explicit and then adhering strictly to those definitions, one could argue plausibly that either conception of the meaning of "law" will do. Both conceptions appear to avoid a confusion of morals and law, and both writers let the reader know what meaning they propose to attribute to the word "law."

The matter assumes a very different aspect, however, if our interest lies in the ideal of fidelity to law, for then it may become a matter of capital importance what position is assigned to the judiciary in the general frame of government. Confirmation for this observation may be found in the slight rumbling of constitutional crisis to be heard in this country today. During the past year readers of newspapers have been writing to their editors urging solemnly, and even apparently with sincerity, that we should abolish the Supreme Court as a first step toward a restoration of the rule of law. It is unlikely that this remedy for our governmental ills derives from any deep study of Austin or Gray, but surely those who propose it could hardly be expected to view with indifference the divergent definitions of law offered by those two jurists. If it be said that it is a perversion of Gray's meaning to extract from his writings any moral for present controversies about the role of the Supreme Court, then it seems to me there is equal reason for treating what he wrote as irrelevant to the issue of fidelity of law generally.

Another difference of opinion among the writers defended by Professor Hart concerns Bentham and Austin and their views on constitutional limitations on the power of the sovereign. Bentham considered that a constitution might preclude the highest legislative power from issuing certain kinds of laws. For Austin, on the other hand, any legal limit on the highest lawmaking power was an absurdity and an impossibility. What guide to conscience would be offered by these two writers in a crisis that might some day arise out of the provision of our constitution to the effect that the amending power can never be used to deprive any state without its consent of its equal representation in the Senate? Surely it is not only in the affairs of everyday life that we need clarity about the obligation of fidelity to law, but most particularly and urgently in times of trouble. If all the positivist school has to offer in such times is the observation that, however you may choose to define law, it is always something different from morals, its teachings are not of much use to us.

I suggest, then, that Professor Hart's thesis as it now stands is essentially incomplete and that before he can attain the goals he seeks he will have to concern himself more closely with a definition of law that will make meaningful the obligation of fidelity to law.

II. The Definition of Morality

It is characteristic of those sharing the point of view of Professor Hart that their primary concern is to preserve the integrity of the concept of law. Accordingly, they have generally sought a precise definition of law, but have not been at pains to state just what it is they mean to exclude by their definitions. They are like men building a wall for the defense of a village, who must know what it is they wish to protect, but who need not, and indeed cannot, know what invading forces those walls may have to turn back.

When Austin and Gray distinguish law from morality, the word "morality" stands indiscriminately for almost every conceivable standard by which human conduct may be judged that is not itself law. The inner voice of conscience, notions of right and wrong based on religious belief, common conceptions of decency and fair play, culturally conditioned prejudices—all of these are grouped together under the heading of "morality" and are excluded from the domain of law. For the most part Professor Hart follows in the tradition of his predecessors. When he speaks of morality he seems generally to have in mind all sorts of extra-legal notions about "what ought to be," regardless of their sources, pretensions, or intrinsic worth. This is particularly apparent in his treatment of the problem of interpretation, where uncodified notions of what ought to be are viewed as affecting only the penumbra of law, leaving its hard core untouched.

Toward the end of the essay, however, Professor Hart's argument takes a turn that seems to depart from the prevailing tenor of his thought. This consists in reminding us that there is such a thing as an immoral morality and that there are many standards of "what ought to be" that can hardly be called moral. Let us grant, he says, that the judge may properly and inevitably legislate in the penumbra of a legal enactment, and that this legislation (in default of any other standard) must be guided by the judge's notions of what ought to be. Still, this would be true even in a society devoted to the most evil ends, where the judge would supply the insufficiencies of the statute with the iniquity that seemed to him most apt for the occasion. Let us also grant, says Professor Hart toward the end of his essay, that there is at times even something that looks like discovery in the judicial process, when a judge by restating a principle seems to bring more clearly to light what was really sought from the beginning. Again, he reminds us, this could happen in a society devoted to the highest refinements of sin, where the implicit demands of an evil rule might be a matter for discovery when the rule was applied to a situation not consciously considered when it was formulated.

I take it that this is to be a warning addressed to those who wish "to infuse more morality into the law." Professor Hart is reminding them that if their program is adopted the morality that actually gets infused may not be to their liking. If this is his point it is certainly a valid one, though one wishes it had been made more explicitly, for it raises much the most fundamental issue of his whole argument. Since the point is made obliquely, and I may have misinterpreted it, in commenting I shall have to content myself with a few summary observations and questions.

First, Professor Hart seems to assume that evil aims may have as much coherence and inner logic as good ones. I, for one, refuse to accept that assumption. I realize that I am here raising, or perhaps dodging, questions that lead into the most difficult problems of the epistemology of ethics. Even if I were competent to undertake an excursus in that direction, this is not the place for it. I shall have to rest on the assertion of a belief that may seem naïve, namely, that coherence and goodness have more affinity than coherence and evil. Accepting this belief, I also believe that when men are compelled to explain and justify their decisions, the effect will generally be to pull those decisions toward goodness, by whatever standards of ultimate goodness there are. Accepting these beliefs, I find a considerable incongruity in any conception that envisages a possible future in which the common law would "work itself pure from case to case" toward a more perfect realization of iniquity.

Second, if there is a serious danger in our society that a weakening of the partition between law and morality would permit an infusion of "immoral morality," the question remains, what is the most effective protection against this danger? I cannot myself believe it is to be found in the positivist position espoused by Austin, Gray, Holmes, and Hart. For those writers seem to me to falsify the problem into a specious simplicity which leaves untouched the difficult issues where real dangers lie.

Third, let us suppose a judge bent on realizing through his decisions an objective that most ordinary citizens would regard as mistaken or evil. Would such a judge be likely to suspend the letter of the statute by openly invoking a "higher law"? Or would he be more likely to take refuge behind the maxim that "law is law" and explain his decision in such a way that it would appear to be demanded by the law itself?

Fourth, neither Professor Hart nor I belong to anything that could be said in a significant sense to be a "minority group" in our respective countries. This has its advantages and disadvantages to one aspiring to a philosophic view of law and government. But suppose we were both transported to a country where our beliefs were anathemas, and where we, in turn, regarded the prevailing morality as thoroughly evil. No doubt in this situation we would have reason to fear that the law might be covertly manipulated to our disadvantage; I doubt if either of us would be apprehensive that its injunctions would be set aside by an appeal to a morality higher than law. If we felt that the law itself was our safest refuge, would it not be because even in the most perverted regimes there is a certain hesitancy about writing cruelties, intolerances, and inhumanities into law? And is it not clear that this hesitancy itself derives, not from a separation of law and morals, but precisely from an identification of law with those demands of morality that are the most urgent and the most obviously justifiable, which no man need be ashamed to profess?

Fifth, over great areas where the judicial process functions, the danger of an infusion of immoral, or at least unwelcome, morality does not, I suggest, present a real issue. Here the danger is precisely the opposite. For example, in the field of commercial law the British courts in recent years have, if I may say so, fallen into a "law-is-law" formalism that constitutes a kind of belated counterrevolution against all that was accomplished by Mansfield. The matter has reached a stage approaching crisis as commercial cases are increasingly being taken to arbitration. The chief reason for this development is that arbitrators are willing to take into account the needs of commerce and ordinary standards of commercial fairness. I realize that Professor Hart repudiates "formalism," but I shall try to show later why I think his theory necessarily leads in that direction.

Sixth, in the thinking of many there is one question that predominates in any discussion of the relation of law and morals, to the point of coloring everything that is said or heard on the subject. I refer to the kind of question raised by the Pope's pronouncement concerning the duty of Catholic judges in divorce actions. This pronouncement does indeed raise grave issues. But it does not present a problem of the relation between law, on the one hand, and, on the other, generally shared views of right conduct that have grown spontaneously through experience and discussion. The issue is rather that of a conflict between two pronouncements, both of which claim to be authoritative; if you will, it is one kind of law against another. When this kind of issue is taken as the key to the whole problem of law and morality, the discussion is so denatured and distorted that profitable exchange becomes impossible. In mentioning this last aspect of the dispute about "positivism," I do not mean to intimate that Professor Hart's own discussion is dominated by any *arriére-pensée;* I know it is not. At the same time I am quite sure that I have indicated accurately the issue that will be uppermost in the minds of many as they read his essay.

In resting content with these scant remarks, I do not want to seem to simplify the problem in a direction opposite to that taken by Professor Hart. The questions raised by "immoral morality" deserve a more careful exploration than either Professor Hart or I have offered in these pages.

III. The Moral Foundations of a Legal Order

Professor Hart emphatically rejects "the command theory of law," according to which law is simply a command backed by a force sufficient to make it effective. He observes that such a command can be given by a man with a loaded gun, and "law surely is not the gunman situation writ large." There is no need to dwell here on the inadequacies of the command theory, since Professor Hart has already revealed its defects more clearly and succinctly than I could. His conclusion is that the foundation of a legal system is not coercive power, but certain "fundamental accepted rules specifying the essential lawmaking procedures."

When I reached this point in his essay, I felt certain that Professor Hart was about to acknowledge an important qualification on his thesis. I confidently expected that he would go on to say something like this: I have insisted throughout on the importance of keeping sharp the distinction between law and morality. The question may now be raised, therefore, as to the nature of these fundamental rules that furnish the framework within which the making of law takes place. On the one hand, they seem to be rules, not of law, but of morality. They derive their efficacy from a general acceptance, which in turn rests ultimately on a perception that they are right and necessary. They can hardly be said to be law in the sense of an authoritative pronouncement, since their function is to state when a pronouncement is authoritative. On the other hand, in the daily functioning of the legal system they are often treated and applied much as ordinary rules of law are. Here, then, we must confess there is something that can be called a "merger" of law and morality, and to which the term "intersection" is scarcely appropriate.

Instead of pursuing some such course of thought, to my surprise I found Professor Hart leaving completely untouched the nature of the fundamental rules that make law itself possible, and turning his attention instead to what he considers a confusion of thought on the part of the critics of positivism. Leaving out of account his discussion of analytical jurisprudence, his argument runs something as follows: Two views are associated with the names of Bentham and Austin. One is the command theory of law, the other is an insistence on the separation of law and morality. Critics of these writers came in time to perceive—"dimly," Professor Hart says—that the command theory is untenable. By a loose association of ideas they wrongly supposed that in advancing reasons for rejecting the command theory they had also refuted the view that law and morality must be sharply separated. This was a "natural mistake," but plainly a mistake just the same.

I do not think any mistake is committed in believing that Bentham and Austin's error in formulating improperly and too simply the problem of the relation of law and morals was part of a larger error that led to the command theory of law. I think the connection between these two errors can be made clear if we ask ourselves what would have happened to Austin's system of thought if he had abandoned the command theory.

One who reads Austin's Lectures V and VI cannot help being impressed by the way he hangs doggedly to the command theory, in spite of the fact that every pull of his own keen mind was toward abandoning it. In the case of a sovereign monarch, law is what the monarch commands. But what shall we say of the "laws" of succession which tell who the "lawful" monarch is? It is of the essence of a command that it be addressed by a superior to an inferior, yet in the case of a "sovereign many," say, a parliament, the sovereign seems to command itself since a member of parliament may be convicted under a law he himself drafted and voted for. The sovereign must be unlimited in legal power, for who could adjudicate the legal bounds of a supreme lawmaking power? Yet a "sovereign many" must accept the limitation of rules before it can make law at all. Such a body can gain the power to issue commands only by acting in a "corporate capacity"; this it can do only by proceeding "agreeably to the modes and forms" established and accepted for the making of law. Judges exercise a power delegated to them by the supreme lawmaking power, and are commissioned to carry out its "direct or circuitous commands." Yet in a federal system it is the courts which must resolve conflicts of competence between the federation and its components.

All of these problems Austin sees with varying degrees of explicitness, and he struggles mightily with them. Over and over again he teeters on the edge of an abandonment of the command theory in favor of what Professor Hart has described as a view that discerns the foundations of a legal order in "certain fundamental accepted rules specifying the essential lawmaking procedures." Yet he never takes the plunge. He does not take it because he had a sure insight that it would forfeit the black-and-white distinction between law and morality that was the whole object of his Lectures—indeed, one may say, the enduring object of a dedicated life. For if law is made possible by "fundamental accepted rules"—which for Austin must be rules, not of law, but of positive morality—what are we to say of the rules that the lawmaking power enacts to regulate its own lawmaking? We have election laws, laws allocating legislative representation to specific geographic areas, rules of parliamentary procedure, rules for the qualification of voters, and many other laws and rules of similar nature. These do not remain fixed, and all of them shape in varying degrees the lawmaking process. Yet how are we to distinguish between those basic rules that owe their validity to acceptance, and those which are properly rules of law, valid even when men generally consider them to be evil or ill-advised? In other words, how are we to define the words "fundamental" and "essential" in Professor Hart's own formulation: "certain fundamental accepted rules specifying the essential lawmaking procedure"?

The solution for this problem in Kelsen's theory is instructive. Kelsen does in fact take the plunge over which Austin hesitated too long. Kelsen realizes that before we can distinguish between what is law and what is not, there must be an acceptance of some basic procedure by which law is made. In any legal system there must be some fundamental rule that points unambiguously to the source from which laws must come in order to be laws. This rule Kelsen called "the basic norm." In his own words,

> *The basic norm is not valid because it has been created in a certain way, but its validity is assumed by virtue of its content. It is valid, then, like a norm of natural law. . . . The idea of a pure positive law, like that of natural law, has its limitations.*

It will be noted that Kelsen speaks, not as Professor Hart does, of "fundamental rules" that regulate the making of law, but of a single rule or norm. Of course, there is no such single rule in any modern society. The notion of the basic norm is admittedly a symbol, not a fact. It is a symbol that embodies the positivist quest for some clear and unambiguous test of law, for some clean, sharp line that will divide the rules which owe their validity to acceptance and intrinsic appeal. The difficulties Austin avoided by sticking with the command theory, Kelsen avoids by a fiction which simplifies reality into a form that can be absorbed by positivism.

A full exploration of all the problems that result when we recognize that law becomes possible only by virtue of rules that are not law, would require drawing into consideration the effect of the presence or absence of a written constitution. Such a constitution in some ways simplifies the problems I have been discussing, and in some ways complicates them. In so far as a written constitution defines basic lawmaking procedure, it may remove the perplexities that arise when a parliament in effect defines itself. At the same time, a legislature operating under a written constitution may enact statutes that profoundly affect the lawmaking procedure and its predictable outcome. If these statutes are drafted with sufficient cunning, they may remain within the frame of the constitution and yet undermine the institutions it was intended to establish. If the "court-packing" proposal of the thirties does not illustrate this danger unequivocally, it at least suggests that the fear of it is not fanciful. No written constitution can be self-executing. To be effective it requires not merely the respectful deference we show for ordinary legal enactments, but that willing convergence of effort we give to moral principles in which we have an active belief. One may properly work to

amend a constitution, but so long as it remains unamended one must work with it, not against it or around it. All this amounts to saying that to be effective a written constitution must be accepted, at least provisionally, not just as law, but as good law.

What have these considerations to do with the ideal of fidelity to law? I think they have a great deal to do with it, and that they reveal the essential incapacity of the positivistic view to serve that ideal effectively. For I believe that a realization of this ideal is something for which we must plan, and that is precisely what positivism refuses to do.

Let me illustrate what I mean by planning for a realization of the ideal of fidelity to law. Suppose we are drafting a written constitution for a country just emerging from a period of violence and disorder in which any thread of legal continuity with previous governments has been broken. Obviously such a constitution cannot lift itself unaided into legality; it cannot be law simply because it says it is. We should keep in mind that the efficacy of our work will depend upon general acceptance and that to make this acceptance secure there must be a general belief that the constitution itself is necessary, right, and good. The provisions of the constitution should, therefore, be kept simple and understandable, not only in language, but also in purpose. Preambles and other explanations of what is being sought, which would be objectionable in an ordinary statute, may find an appropriate place in our constitution. We should think of our constitution as establishing a basic procedural framework for future governmental action in the enactment and administration of laws. Substantive limitations on the power of government should be kept to a minimum and should generally be confined to those for which a need can be generally appreciated. In so far as possible, substantive aims should be achieved procedurally, on the principle that if men are compelled to act in the right way, they will generally do the right things.

These considerations seem to have been widely ignored in the constitutions that have come into existence since World War II. Not uncommonly these constitutions incorporate a host of economic and political measures of the type one would ordinarily associate with statutory law. It is hardly likely that these measures have been written into the constitution because they represent aims that are generally shared. One suspects that the reason for their inclusion is precisely the opposite, namely, a fear that they would not be able to survive the vicissitudes of an ordinary exercise of parliamentary power. Thus, the divisions of opinion that are a normal accompaniment of lawmaking are written into the document that makes law itself possible. This is obviously a procedure that contains serious dangers for a future realization of the ideal of fidelity to law.

I have ventured these remarks on the making of constitutions not because I think they can claim any special profundity, but because I wished to illustrate what I mean by planning the conditions that will make it possible to realize the ideal of fidelity to law. Even within the limits of my modest purpose, what I have said may be clearly wrong. If so, it would not be for me to say whether I am also wrong clearly. I will, however, venture to assert that if I am wrong, I am wrong significantly. What disturbs me about the school of legal positivism is that it not only refuses to deal with problems of the sort I have just discussed, but bans them on principle from the province of legal philosophy. In its concern to assign the right labels to the things men do, this school seems to lose all interest in asking whether men are doing the right things.

IV. The Morality of Law Itself

Most of the issues raised by Professor Hart's essay can be restated in terms of the distinction between order and good order. Law may be said to represent order *simpliciter.* Good order is law that corresponds to the demands of justice, or morality, or men's notions of what ought to be. This rephrasing of the issue is useful in bringing to light the ambitious nature of Professor Hart's undertaking, for surely we would all agree that it is no easy thing to distinguish order from good order. When it is said, for example, that law simply represents that public order which obtains under all governments—democratic, Fascist, or Communist— the order intended is certainly not that of a morgue or cemetery. We must mean a functioning order, and such an order has to be at least good enough to be considered as functioning by some standard or other. A reminder that workable order usually requires some play in the joints, and therefore cannot be too orderly, is enough to suggest some of the complexities that would be involved in any attempt to draw a sharp distinction between order and good order.

For the time being, however, let us suppose we can in fact clearly separate the concept of order from that of good order. Even in this unreal and abstract form the notion of order itself contains what may be called a moral element. Let me illustrate this "morality of order" in its crudest and most elementary form. Let us suppose an absolute monarch, whose word is the only law known to his subjects. We may further suppose him to be utterly selfish and to seek in his relations with his subjects solely his own advantage. This monarch from time to time issues commands, promising rewards for compliance and threatening punishment for disobedience. He is, however, a dissolute and forgetful fellow, who never makes the slightest attempt to ascertain who have in fact followed his directions and who have not. As a result he habitually punishes loyalty and rewards disobedience. It is apparent that this monarch will never achieve even his own selfish aims until he is ready to accept that minimum self-restraint that will create a meaningful connection between his words and his actions.

Let us now suppose that our monarch undergoes a change of heart and begins to pay some attention to what he said yesterday when, today, he has occasion to distribute bounty or to order the chopping off of heads. Under the strain of this new responsibility, however, our monarch relaxes his attention in other directions and becomes hopelessly slothful in the phrasing of his commands. His orders become so ambiguous and are uttered in so inaudible a tone that his subjects never have any clear idea what he wants them to do. Here, again, it is apparent that if our monarch for his own selfish advantage wants to create in his realm anything like a system of law he will have to pull himself together and assume still another responsibility. Law, considered merely as order, contains, then, its own implicit morality. This morality of order must be respected if we are to create anything that can be called law, even bad law. Law by itself is powerless to bring this morality into existence. Until our monarch is really ready to face the responsibilities of his position, it will do no good for him to issue still another futile command, this time self-addressed and threatening himself with punishment if he does not mend his ways.

There is a twofold sense in which it is true that law cannot be built on law. First of all, the authority to make law must be supported by moral attitudes that accord to it the competency it claims. Here we are dealing with a morality external to law, which makes law possible. But this alone is not enough. We may stipulate that in our monarchy the accepted "basic norm" designates the monarch himself as the only possible source of law. We still cannot have law until our monarch is ready to accept the internal morality of law itself.

In the life of a nation these external and internal moralities of law reciprocally influence one another; a deterioration of the one will almost inevitably produce a deterioration in the other. So closely related are they that when the anthropologist Lowie speaks of "the generally accepted ethical postulates underlying our . . . legal institutions as their ultimate sanction and guaranteeing their smooth functioning," he may be presumed to have both of them in mind.

What I have called "the internal morality of law" seems to be almost completely neglected by Professor Hart. He does make brief mention of "justice in the administration of the law," which consists in the like treatment of like cases, by whatever elevated or perverted standards the word "like" may be defined. But he quickly dismisses this aspect of law as having no special relevance to his main enterprise.

In this I believe he is profoundly mistaken. It is his neglect to analyze the demands of a morality of order that leads him throughout his essay to treat law as a datum projecting itself into human striving. When we realize that order itself is something that must be worked for, it becomes apparent that the existence of a legal system, even a bad or evil legal system, is always a matter of degree. When we recognize this simple fact of everyday legal experience, it becomes impossible to dismiss the problems presented by the Nazi regime with a simple assertion: "Under the Nazis there was law, even if it was bad law." We have instead to inquire how much of a legal system survived the general debasement and perversion of all forms of social order that occurred under the Nazi rule, and what moral implications this mutilated system had for the conscientious citizen forced to live under it.

It is not necessary, however, to dwell on such moral upheavals as the Nazi regime to see how completely incapable the positivistic philosophy is of serving the one high moral ideal it professes, that of fidelity to law. Its default in serving this ideal actually becomes most apparent, I believe, in the everyday problems that confront those who are earnestly desirous of meeting the moral demands of a legal order, but who have responsible functions to discharge in the very order toward which loyalty is due.

Let us suppose the case of a trial judge who has had an extensive experience in commercial matters and before whom a great many commercial disputes are tried. As a subordinate in a judicial hierarchy, our judge has of course the duty to follow the law laid down by his supreme court. Our imaginary Scrutton has the misfortune, however, to live under a supreme court which he considers woefully ignorant of the ways and needs of commerce. To his mind, many of this court's decisions in the field of commercial law simply do not make sense. If a conscientious judge caught in this dilemma were to turn to the positivistic philosophy what succor could he expect? It will certainly do no good to remind him that he has an obligation of fidelity to law. He is aware of this already and painfully so, since it is the source of his predicament. Nor will it help to say that if he legislates, it must be "interstitially," or that his contributions must be "confined from molar to molecular motions." This mode of statement may be congenial to those who like to think of law, not as a purposive thing, but as an expression of the dimensions and directions of state power. But I cannot believe that the essentially trite idea behind this advice can be lifted by literary eloquence to the point where it will offer any real help to our judge; for one thing, it may be impossible for him to know whether his supreme court would regard any particular contribution of his as being wide or narrow.

Nor is it likely that a distinction between core and penumbra would be helpful. The predicament of our judge may well derive, not from particular precedents, but from a mistaken conception of the nature of commerce which extends over many decisions and penetrates them in varying degrees. So far as his problem arises from the use of particular words, he may well find that the supreme court often uses the ordinary terms of commerce in senses foreign to actual business dealings. If he interprets those words as a business executive or accountant would, he may well reduce the precedents he is bound to apply to a logical shambles. On the other hand, he may find great difficulty in discerning the exact sense in which the supreme court used those words, since in his mind that sense is itself the product of a confusion.

It is not clear that it is precisely positivism's insistence on a rigid separation of law as it is from law as it ought to be that renders the positivistic philosophy incapable of aiding our judge? Is it not also clear that our judge can never achieve a satisfactory resolution of his dilemma unless he views his duty of fidelity to law in a context which also embraces his responsibility for making law what it ought to be?

The case I have supposed may seem extreme, but the problem it suggests pervades our whole legal system. If the divergence of views between our judge and his supreme court were less drastic, it would be more difficult to present his predicament graphically, but the perplexity of his position might actually increase. Perplexities of this sort are a normal accompaniment of the discharge of any adjudicative function; they perhaps reach their most poignant intensity in the field of administrative law.

One can imagine a case—surely not likely in Professor Hart's country or mine—where a judge might hold profound moral convictions that were exactly the opposite of those held, with equal attachment, by his supreme court. He might also be convinced that the precedents he was bound to apply were the direct product of a morality he considered abhorrent. If such a judge did not find the solution for his dilemma in surrendering his office, he might well be driven to a wooden and literal application of precedents which he could not otherwise apply because he was incapable of understanding the philosophy that animated them. But I doubt that a judge in this situation would need the help of legal positivism to find these melancholy escapes from his predicament. Nor do I think that such a predicament is likely to arise within a nation where both law and good law are regarded as collaborative human achievements in need of constant renewal, and where lawyers are still at least as interested in asking "What is good law?" as they are in asking "What is law?"

V. The Problem of Restoring Respect for Law and Justice After the Collapse of a Regime That Respected Neither

After the collapse of the Nazi regime the German courts were faced with a truly frightful predicament. It was impossible for them to declare the whole dictatorship illegal or to treat as void every decision and legal enactment that had emanated from Hitler's government. Intolerable dislocations would have resulted from any such wholesale outlawing of all that occurred over a span of twelve years. On the other hand, it was equally impossible to carry forward into the new government the effects of every Nazi perversity that had been committed in the name of law; any such course would have tainted an indefinite future with the poisons of Nazism.

This predicament—which was, indeed, a pervasive one, affecting all branches of law—came to a dramatic head in a series of cases involving informers who had taken advantage of the Nazi terror to get rid of personal enemies or unwanted spouses. If all Nazi statutes and judicial decisions were indiscriminately

"law," then these despicable creatures were guiltless, since they had turned their victims over to processes which the Nazis themselves knew by the name of law. Yet it was intolerable, especially for the surviving relatives and friends of the victims, that these people should go about unpunished, while the objects of their spite were dead, or were just being released after years of imprisonment, or, more painful still, simply remained unaccounted for.

The urgency of this situation does not by any means escape Professor Hart. Indeed, he is moved to recommend an expedient that is surely not lacking itself in a certain air of desperation. He suggests that a retroactive criminal statute would have been the least objectionable solution to the problem. This statute would have punished the informer, and branded him as a criminal, for an act which Professor Hart regards as having been perfectly legal when he committed it.

On the other hand, Professor Hart condemns without qualification those judicial decisions in which the courts themselves undertook to declare void certain of the Nazi statutes under which the informer's victims had been convicted. One cannot help raising at this point the question whether the issue as presented by Professor Hart himself is truly that of fidelity to law. Surely it would be a necessary implication of a retroactive criminal statute against informers that, for purposes of that statute at least, the Nazi laws as applied to the informers or their victims were to be regarded as void. With this turn the question seems no longer to be whether what was once law can now be declared not to have been law, but rather who should do the dirty work, the courts or the legislature.

But, as Professor Hart himself suggests, the issues at stake are much too serious to risk losing them in a semantic tangle. Even if the whole question were one of words, we should remind ourselves that we are in an area where words have a powerful effect on human attitudes. I should like, therefore, to undertake a defense of the German courts, and to advance reasons why, in my opinion, their decisions do not represent the abandonment of legal principle that Professor Hart sees in them. In order to understand the background of those decisions we shall have to move a little closer, within smelling distance of the witches' caldron, than we have been brought so far by Professor Hart. We shall have also to consider an aspect of the problem ignored in his essay, namely, the degree to which the Nazis observed what I have called the inner morality of law itself.

Throughout his discussion Professor Hart seems to assume that the only difference between Nazi law and, say, English law is that the Nazis used their laws to achieve ends that are odious to an Englishman. This assumption is, I think, seriously mistaken, and Professor Hart's acceptance of it seems to me to render his discussion unresponsive to the problem it purports to address.

Throughout their period of control the Nazis took generous advantage of a device not wholly unknown to American legislatures, the retroactive statute curing past legal irregularities. The most dramatic use of the curative powers of such a statute occurred on July 3, 1934, after the "Roehm purge." When this intraparty shooting affair was over and more than seventy Nazis had been—one can hardly avoid saying— "rubbed out," Hitler returned to Berlin and procured from his cabinet a law ratifying and confirming the measures taken between June 30, and July 1, 1934, without mentioning the names of those who were now considered to have been lawfully executed. Some time later Hitler declared that during the Roehm purge "the supreme court of the German people . . . consisted of myself," surely not an overstatement of the capacity in which he acted if one takes seriously the enactment conferring retroactive legality on "the measures taken."

Now in England and America it would never occur to anyone to say that "it is in the nature of law that it cannot be retroactive," although, of course, constitutional inhibitions may prohibit certain kinds of retroactivity. We would say it is normal for a law to operate prospectively, and that it may be arguable that it ought never operate otherwise, but there would be a certain occult unpersuasiveness in any assertion that retroactivity violates the very nature of law itself. Yet we have only to imagine a country in which all laws are retroactive in order to see that retroactivity presents a real problem for the internal morality of law. If we suppose an absolute monarch who allows his realm to exist in a constant state of anarchy, we would hardly say that he could create a regime of law simply by enacting a curative statute conferring legality on everything that had happened up to its date and by announcing an intention to enact similar statutes every six months in the future.

A general increase in the resort to statutes curative of past legal irregularities represents a deterioration in that form of legal morality without which law itself cannot exist. The threat of such statutes hangs over the whole legal system, and robs every law on the books of some of its significance. And surely a general threat of this sort is implied when a government is willing to use such a statute to transform into lawful execution what was simple murder when it happened.

During the Nazi regime there were repeated rumors of "secret laws." In the article criticized by Professor Hart, Radbruch mentions a report that the wholesale killings in concentration camps were made "lawful" by a secret enactment. Now surely there can be no greater legal monstrosity than a secret statute. Would anyone seriously recommend that following the war the German courts should have searched for unpublished laws among the files left by Hitler's government so that citizens' rights could be determined by a reference to these laws?

The extent of the legislator's obligation to make his laws known to his subjects is, of course, a problem of legal morality that has been under active discussion at least since the Secession of the Plebs. There is probably no modern state that has not been plagued by this problem in one form or another. It is most likely to arise in modern societies with respect to unpublished administrative directions. Often these are regarded in quite good faith by those who issue them as affecting only matters of internal organization. But since the procedures followed by an administrative agency, even in its "internal" actions, may seriously affect the rights and interests of the citizen, these unpublished, or "secret," regulations are often a subject for complaint.

But as with retroactivity, what in most societies is kept under control by the tacit restraints of legal decency broke out in monstrous form under Hitler. Indeed, so loose was the whole Nazi morality of law that it is not easy to know just what should be regarded as an unpublished or secret law. Since unpublished instructions to those administering the law could destroy the letter of any published law by imposing on it an outrageous interpretation, there was a sense in which the meaning of every law was "secret." Even a verbal order from Hitler that a thousand prisoners in concentration camps be put to death was at once an administrative direction and a validation of everything done under it as being "lawful."

But the most important affronts to the morality of law by Hitler's government took no such subtle forms as those exemplified in the bizarre outcroppings I have just discussed. In the first place, when legal forms became inconvenient, it was always possible for the Nazis to bypass them entirely and "to act through the party in the streets." There was no one who dared bring them to account for whatever outrages might thus be committed. In the second place, the Nazi-dominated courts were always ready to disregard any statute, even those enacted by the Nazis themselves, if this suited their convenience or if they feared that a lawyer-like interpretation might incur displeasure "above."

This complete willingness of the Nazis to disregard even their own enactments was an important factor leading Radbruch to take the position he did in the articles so severely criticized by Professor Hart. I do not believe that any fair appraisal of the action of the postwar German courts is possible unless we take this factor into account, as Professor Hart fails completely to do.

These remarks may seem inconclusive in their generality and to rest more on assertion than evidentiary fact. Let us turn at once, then, to the actual case discussed by Professor Hart.

In 1944 a German soldier paid a short visit to his wife while under travel orders on a reassignment. During the single day he was home, he conveyed privately to his wife something of his opinion of the Hitler government. He expressed disapproval of *(sich abf ßllig geäussert über)* Hitler and other leading personalities of the Nazi party. He also said it was too bad Hitler had not met his end in the assassination attempt that had occurred on July 20th of that year. Shortly after his departure, his wife, who during his long absence on military duty "had turned to other men" and who wished to get rid of him reported his remarks to the local leader of the Nazi party, observing that "a man who would say a thing like that does not deserve to live." The result was a trial of the husband by a military tribunal and a sentence of death. After a short period of imprisonment, instead of being executed, he was sent to the front again. After the collapse of the Nazi regime, the wife was brought to trial for having procured the imprisonment of her husband. Her defense rested on the ground that her husband's statements to her about Hitler and the Nazis constituted a crime under the laws then in force. Accordingly, when she informed on her husband she was simply bringing a criminal to justice.

This defense rested on two statutes, one passed in 1934, the other in 1938. Let us first consider the second of these enactments, which was part of a more comprehensive legislation creating a whole series of special wartime criminal offenses. I reproduce below a translation of the only pertinent section:

The following persons are guilty of destroying the national power of resistance and shall be punished by death: Whoever publicly solicits or incites a refusal to fulfill the obligations of ser-

vice in the armed forces of Germany, or in armed forces allied with Germany, or who otherwise publicly seeks to injure or destroy the will of the German people or an allied people to assert themselves stalwartly against their enemies.

It is almost inconceivable that a court of present-day Germany would hold the husband's remarks to his wife, who was barred from military duty by her sex, to be a violation of the final catch-all provision of this statute, particularly when it is recalled that the test reproduced above was part of a more comprehensive enactment dealing with such things as harboring deserters, escaping military duty by self-inflicted injuries, and the like. The question arises, then, as to the extent to which the interpretive principles applied by the courts of Hitler's government should be accepted in determining whether the husband's remarks were indeed unlawful.

This question becomes acute when we note that the act applies only to *public* acts or utterances, whereas the husband's remarks were in the privacy of his own home. Now it appears that the Nazi courts (and it should be noted we are dealing with a special military court) quite generally disregarded this limitation and extended the act to all utterances, private or public. Is Professor Hart prepared to say that the legal meaning of this statute is to be determined in the light of this apparently uniform principle of judicial interpretation?

Let us turn now to the other statute upon which Professor Hart relies in assuming that the husband's utterance was unlawful. This is the act of 1934, the relevant portions of which are translated below:

(1) Whoever publicly makes spiteful or provocative statements directed against, or statements which disclose a base disposition toward, the leading personalities of the nation or of the National Socialist German Workers' Party, or toward measures taken or institutions established by them, and of such a nature as to undermine the people's confidence in their political leadership, shall be punished by imprisonment.

(2) Malicious utterances not made in public shall be treated in the same manner as public utterances when the person making them realized or should have realized they would reach the public.

(3) Prosecution for such utterances shall be only on the order of the National Minister of

Justice; in case the utterance was directed against a leading personality of the National Socialist German Workers' Party, the Minister of Justice shall order prosecution only with the advice and consent of the Representative of the Leader.

(4) The National Minister of Justice shall, with the advice and consent of the Representative of the Leader, determine who shall belong to the class of leading personalities for purposes of Section 1 above.

Extended comment on this legislative monstrosity is scarcely called for, overlarded and undermined as it is by uncontrolled administrative discretion. We may note only: first, that it offers no justification whatever for the death penalty actually imposed on the husband, though never carried out; second, that if the wife's act in informing on her husband made his remarks "public," there is no such thing as a private utterance under this statute. I should like to ask the reader whether he can actually share Professor Hart's indignation that, in the perplexities of the postwar reconstruction, the German courts saw fit to declare this thing not a law. Can it be argued seriously that it would have been more beseeming to the judicial process if the postwar courts had undertaken a study of "the interpretative principles" in force during Hitler's rule and had than solemnly applied those "principles" to ascertain the meaning of this statute? On the other hand, would the courts really have been showing respect for Nazi law if they had construed the Nazi statutes by their own, quite different, standards of interpretation? Professor Hart castigates the German courts and Radbruch, not so much for what they believed had to be done, but because they failed to see that they were confronted by a moral dilemma of a sort that would have been immediately apparent to Bentham and Austin. By the simple dodge of saying, "When a statute is sufficiently evil it ceases to be law," they ran away from the problem they should have faced.

This criticism is, I believe, without justification. So far as the courts are concerned, matters certainly would not have been helped if, instead of saying, "This is not law," they had said, "This is law but it is so evil we will refuse to apply it." Surely moral confusion reaches its height when a court refuses to apply something it admits to be law, and Professor Hart does not recommend any such "facing of the true issue" by the courts themselves. He would have preferred a retroactive statute. Curiously, this was also the prefer-

ence of Radbruch. But unlike Professor Hart, the German courts and Gustav Radbruch were living participants in a situation of drastic emergency. The informer problem was a pressing one, and if legal institutions were to be rehabilitated in Germany it would not do to allow the people to begin taking the law into their own hands, as might have occurred while the courts were waiting for a statute.

As for Gustav Radbruch, it is, I believe, wholly unjust to say that he did not know he was faced with a moral dilemma. His postwar writings repeatedly stress the antinomies confronted in the effort to rebuild decent and orderly government in Germany. As for the ideal of fidelity to law, I shall let Radbruch's own words state his position:

> We must not conceal from ourselves—especially not in the light of our experiences during the twelve-year dictatorship—what frightful dangers for the rule of law can be contained in the notion of "statutory lawlessness" and in refusing the quality of law to duly enacted statutes.

The situation is not that legal positivism enables a man to know when he faces a difficult problem of choice, while Radbruch's beliefs deceive him into thinking there is no problem to face. The real issue dividing Professor Hart and Radbruch is: How shall we state the problem? What is the nature of the dilemma in which we are caught?

I hope I am not being unjust to Professor Hart when I say that I can find no way of describing the dilemma as he sees it but to use some such words as the following: On the one hand, we have an amoral datum called law, which has the peculiar quality of creating a moral duty to obey it. On the other hand, we have a moral duty to do what we think is right and decent. When we are confronted by a statute we believe to be thoroughly evil, we have to choose between those two duties.

If this is the positivist position, then I have no hesitancy in rejecting it. The "dilemma" it states has the verbal formulation of a problem, but the problem it states makes no sense. It is like saying I have to choose between giving food to a starving man and being mimsy with the borogoves. I do not think it is unfair to the positivistic philosophy to say that it never gives any coherent meaning to the moral obligation of fidelity to law. This obligation seems to be conceived as sui generis, wholly unrelated to any of the ordinary, extralegal ends of human life. The fundamental postulate of positivism—that law must be strictly severed from morality—seems to deny the possibility of any bridge between the obligation to obey law and other moral obligations. No mediating principle can measure their respective demands on conscience, for they exist in wholly separate worlds.

While I would not subscribe to all of Radbruch's postwar views—especially those relating to "higher law"—I think he saw, much more clearly than does Professor Hart, the true nature of the dilemma confronted by Germany in seeking to rebuild her shattered legal institutions. Germany had to restore both respect for law and respect for justice. Though neither of these could be restored without the other, painful antinomies were encountered in attempting to restore both at once, as Radbruch saw all too clearly. Essentially Radbruch saw the dilemma as that of meeting the demands of order, on the one hand, and those of good order, on the other. Of course no pat formula can be derived from this phrasing of the problem. But, unlike legal positivism, it does not present us with opposing demands that have no living contact with one another, that simply shout their contradictions across a vacuum. As we seek order, we can meaningfully remind ourselves that order itself will do us no good unless it is good for something. As we seek to make our order good, we can remind ourselves that justice itself is impossible without order, and that we must not lose order itself in the attempt to make it good.

VI. The Moral Implications of Legal Positivism

We now reach the question whether there is any ground for Gustav Radbruch's belief that a general acceptance of the positivistic philosophy in pre-Nazi Germany made smoother the route to dictatorship. Understandably, Professor Hart regards this as the most outrageous of all charges against positivism.

Here indeed we enter upon a hazardous area of controversy, where ugly words and ugly charges have become commonplace. During the last half century in this country no issue of legal philosophy has caused more spilling of ink and adrenalin than the assertion that there are "totalitarian" implications in the views of Oliver Wendell Holmes, Jr. Even the most cautiously phrased criticisms of that grand old figure from the age of Darwin, Huxley, and Haeckel seem to stir the reader's mind with the memory of past acerbities.

It does no good to suggest that perhaps Holmes did not perceive all the implications of his own philosophy, for this is merely to substitute one insult for another. Nor does it help much to recall the dictum of one of the closest companions of Holmes' youth— surely no imperceptive observer—that Holmes was "composed of at least two and a half different people rolled into one, and the way he keeps them together in one tight skin, without quarreling any more than they do, is remarkable."

In the venturing upon these roughest of all jurisprudential waters, one is not reassured to see even so moderate a man as Professor Hart indulging in some pretty broad stokes of the oar. Radbruch disclosed "an extraordinary naïveté" in assessing the temper of his own profession in Germany and in supposing that its adherence to positivism helped the Nazis to power. His judgment on this and other matters shows that he had "only half-digested the spiritual message of liberalism he mistakenly thought he was conveying to his countrymen. A state of "hysteria" is revealed by those who see a wholesome reorientation of German legal thinking in such judicial decisions as were rendered in the informer cases.

Let us put aside at least the blunter tools of invective and address ourselves as calmly as we can to the question whether legal positivism, as practiced and preached in Germany, had, or could have had, any causal connection with Hitler's ascent to power. It should be recalled that in the seventy-five years before the Nazi regime the positivistic philosophy had achieved in Germany a standing such as it enjoyed in no other country. Austin praised a German scholar for bringing international law within the clarity-producing restraints of positivism. Gray reported with pleasure that the "abler" German jurists of his time were "abjuring all '*nicht positivisches Recht*,'" and cited Bergbohm as an example. This is an illuminating example, for Bergbohm was a scholar whose ambition was to make German positivism live up to its own pretensions. He was distressed to encounter vestigial traces of natural law thinking in writings claiming to be positivistic. In particular, he was disturbed by the frequent recurrence of such notions as that law owes its efficacy to a perceived moral need for order, or that it is in the nature of man that he requires a legal order, etc. Bergbohm announced a program, never realized, to drive from positivistic thinking these last miasmas from the swamp of natural law. German jurists generally tended to regard the Anglo-American common law as a messy and unprincipled conglomerate of law and morals. Positivism was the only theory of law that could claim to be "scientific" in an Age of Science. Dissenters from this view were characterized by positivists with that epithet modern man fears above all others: "naïve." The result was that it could be reported by 1927 that "to be found guilty of adherence to natural law theories is a kind of social disgrace."

To this background we must add the observation that the Germans seem never to have achieved that curious ability possessed by the British, and to some extent by the Americans, of holding their logic on short leash. When a German defines law, he means his definition to be taken seriously. If a German writer had hit upon the slogan of American legal realism, "Law is simply the behavior patterns of judges and other state officials," he would not have regarded this as an interesting little conversation-starter. He would have believed it and acted on it.

German legal positivism not only banned from legal science any consideration of the moral ends of law, but it was also indifferent to what I have called the inner morality of law itself. The German lawyer was therefore peculiarly prepared to accept as "law" anything that called itself by that name, was printed at government expense, and seemed to come *"von oben herab."*

In the light of these considerations I cannot see either absurdity or perversity in the suggestion that the attitudes prevailing in the German legal profession were helpful to the Nazis. Hitler did not come to power by a violent revolution. He was Chancellor before he became the Leader. The exploitation of legal forms started cautiously and became bolder as power was consolidated. The first attacks on the established order were on ramparts which, if they were manned by anyone, were manned by lawyers and judges. These ramparts fell almost without a struggle.

Professor Hart and others have been understandably distressed by references to a "higher law" in some of the decisions concerning informers and in Radbruch's postwar writings. I suggest that if German jurisprudence had concerned itself more with the inner morality of law, it would not have been necessary to invoke any notion of this sort in declaring void the more outrageous Nazi statutes.

To me there is nothing shocking in saying that a dictatorship which clothes itself with a tinsel of legal form can so far depart from the morality of order, from the inner morality of law itself, that it ceases to be a legal system. When a system calling itself law is predicated upon a general disregard by judges of the terms of the laws they purport to enforce, when this system habitually cures its legal irregularities, even the grossest, by retroactive statutes, when it has only to resort to forays of terror in the streets, which no one dares challenge, in order to escape even those scant restraints imposed by the pretence of legality—when all these things have become true of a dictatorship, it is not hard for me, at least, to deny to it the name of law.

I believe that the invalidity of the statutes involved in the informer cases could have been grounded on considerations such as I have just outlined. But if you were raised with a generation that said "law is law" and meant it, you may feel the only way you can escape one law is to set another off against it, and this perforce must be a "higher law." Hence these notions of "higher law," which are a justifiable cause for alarm, may themselves be a belated fruit of German legal positivism.

It should be remarked at this point that it is chiefly in Roman Catholic writings that the theory of natural law is considered, not simply as a search for those principles that will enable men to live together successfully, but as a quest for something that can be called "a higher law." This identification of natural law with a law that is above human laws seems in fact to be demanded by any doctrine that asserts the possibility of an authoritative pronouncement of the demands of natural law. In those areas affected by such pronouncements as have so far been issued, the conflict between Roman Catholic doctrine and opposing views seems to me to be a conflict between two forms of positivism. Fortunately, over most of the area with which lawyers are concerned, no such pronouncements exist. In these areas I think those of us who are not adherents of its faith can be grateful to the Catholic Church for having kept alive the rationalistic tradition in ethics.

I do not assert that the solution I have suggested for the informer cases would not have entailed its own difficulties, particularly the familiar one of knowing where to stop. But I think it demonstrable that the most serious deterioration in legal morality under Hitler took place in branches of the law like those involved in the informer cases; no comparable deterioration was to be observed in the ordinary branches of private law. It was in those areas where the ends of law were most odious by ordinary standards of decency that the morality of law itself was most flagrantly disregarded. In other words, where one would have been most tempted to say, "This is so evil it cannot be a law," one could usually have said instead, "This thing is the product of a system so oblivious to the morality of law that it is not entitled to be called a law." I think there is something more than accident here, for the overlapping suggests that legal morality cannot live when it is severed from a striving toward justice and decency.

But as an actual solution for the informer cases, I, like Professors Hart and Radbruch, would have preferred a retroactive statute. My reason for this preference is not that this is the most nearly lawful way of making unlawful what was once law. Rather I would see such a statute as a way of symbolizing a sharp break with the past, as a means of isolating a kind of cleanup operation from the normal functioning of the judicial process. By this isolation it would become possible for the judiciary to return more rapidly to a condition in which the demands of legal morality could be given proper respect. In other words, it would make it possible to plan more effectively to regain for the ideal of fidelity to law its normal meaning.

VII. The Problem of Interpretation: The Core and the Penumbra

It is essential that we be just as clear as we can be about the meaning of Professor Hart's doctrine of "the core and the penumbra," because I believe the casual reader is likely to misinterpret what he has to say. Such a reader is apt to suppose that Professor Hart is merely describing something that is a matter of everyday experience for the lawyer, namely, that in the interpretation of legal rules it is typically the case (though not universally so) that there are some situations which will seem to fall rather clearly within the rule, while others will be more doubtful. Professor Hart's thesis takes no such jejune form. His extended discussion of the core and the penumbra is not just a complicated way of recognizing that some cases are hard, while others are easy. Instead, on the basis of a theory about language meaning generally, he is proposing a theory of judicial interpretation which is, I believe, wholly novel. Certainly it has never been put forward in so uncompromising a form before.

As I understand Professor Hart's thesis (if we add some tacit assumptions implied by it, as well as some qualifications he would no doubt wish his readers to supply) a full statement would run something as follows: The task of interpretation is commonly that of determining the meaning of the individual words of a legal rule, like "vehicle" in a rule excluding vehicles from a park. More particularly, the task of interpretation is to determine the range of reference of such a word, or the aggregate of things to which it points. Communication is possible only because words have a "standard instance," or a "core of meaning" that remains relatively constant, whatever the context in which the word may appear. Except in unusual circumstances, it will always be proper to regard a word like "vehicle" as embracing its "standard instance," that is, that aggregate of things it would include in all ordinary contexts, within or without the law. This meaning the word will have in any legal rule, whatever its purpose. In applying the word to its "standard instance," no creative role is assumed by the judge. He is simply applying the law "as it is."

In addition to a constant core, however, words also have a penumbra of meaning which, unlike the core, will vary from context to context. When the object in question (say, a tricycle) falls within this penumbral area, the judge is forced to assume a more creative role. He must now undertake, for the first time, an interpretation of the rule in the light of its purpose or aim. Having in mind what was sought by the regulation concerning parks, ought it to be considered as barring tricycles? When questions of this sort are decided there is at least an "intersection" of "is" and "ought," since the judge, in deciding what the rule "is," does so in the light of his notions of what "it ought to be" in order to carry out its purpose.

If I have properly interpreted Professor Hart's theory as it affects the "hard core," then I think it is quite untenable. The most obvious defect of his theory lies in its assumption that problems of interpretation typically turn on the meaning of individual words. Surely no judge applying a rule of the common law ever followed any such procedure as that described (and, I take it, prescribed) by Professor Hart; indeed, we do not normally even think of his problem as being one of "interpretation." Even in the case of statutes, we commonly have to assign meaning, not to a single word, but to a sentence, a paragraph, or a whole page or more of text. Surely a paragraph does not have a "standard instance" that remains constant whatever the context in which it appears. If a statute seems to have a kind of "core meaning" that we can apply without a too precise inquiry into its exact purpose, this is because we can see that, however one might formulate the precise objective of the statute, *this* case would still come within it.

Even in situations where our interpretive difficulties seem to head up in a single word, Professor Hart's analysis seems to me to give no real account of what does or should happen. In his illustration of the "vehicle," although he tells us this word has a core of meaning that in all contexts defines unequivocally a range of objects embraced by it, he never tells us what these objects might be. If the rule excluding vehicles from parks seems easy to apply in some cases, I submit this is because we can see clearly enough what the rule "is aiming at in general" so that we know there is no need to worry about the difference between Fords and Cadillacs. If in some cases we seem to be able to apply the rule without asking what its purpose is, this is not because we can treat a directive arrangement as if it had no purpose. It is rather because, for example, whether the rule be intended to preserve quiet in the park, or to save carefree strollers from injury, we know, "without thinking," that a noisy automobile must be excluded.

What would Professor Hart say if some local patriots wanted to mount on a pedestal in the park a truck used in World War II, while other citizens, regarding the proposed memorial as an eyesore, support their stand by the "no vehicle" rule? Does this truck, in perfect working order, fall within the core or the penumbra?

Professor Hart seems to assert that unless words have "standard instances" that remain constant regardless of context, effective communication would break down and it would become impossible to construct a system of "rules which have authority." If in every context words took on a unique meaning, peculiar to that context, the whole process of interpretation would become so uncertain and subjective that the ideal of a rule of law would lose its meaning. In other words, Professor Hart seems to be saying that unless we are prepared to accept his analysis of interpretation, we must surrender all hope of giving an effective meaning to the ideal of fidelity to law. This presents a very dark prospect indeed, if one believes, as I do, that we cannot accept his theory of interpre-

tation. I do not take so gloomy a view of the future of the ideal of fidelity to law.

An illustration will help to test, not only Professor Hart's theory of the core and the penumbra, but its relevance to the ideal of fidelity to law as well. Let us suppose that in leafing through the statutes, we come upon the following enactment: "It shall be a misdemeanor, punishable by a fine of five dollars, to sleep in any railway station." We have no trouble in perceiving the general nature of the target toward which this state is aimed. Indeed, we are likely at once to call to mind the picture of a disheveled tramp, spread out in an ungainly fashion on one of the benches of the station, keeping weary passengers on their feet and filling their ears with raucous and alcoholic snores. This vision may fairly be said to represent the "obvious instance" contemplated by the statute, though certainly it is far from being the "standard instance" of the physiological state called "sleep."

Now let us see how this example bears on the ideal of fidelity to law. Suppose I am a judge, and that two men are brought before me for violating this statute. This first is a passenger who was waiting at 3 A.M. for a delayed train. When he was arrested he was sitting upright in an orderly fashion, but was heard by the arresting officer to be gently snoring. The second is a man who had brought a blanket and pillow to the station and had obviously settled himself down for the night. He was arrested, however, before he had a chance to go to sleep. Which of these cases presents the "standard instance" of the word "sleep"? If I disregard that question, and decide to fine the second man and set free the first, have I violated a duty of fidelity to law? Have I violated that duty if I interpret the word "sleep" as used in this statute to mean something like "to spread oneself out on a bench or floor to spend the night, or as if to spend the night"?

. . .

Eight Ways to Fail to Make Law*

Lon L. Fuller

This chapter will begin with a fairly lengthy allegory. It concerns the unhappy reign of a monarch who bore the convenient, but not very imaginative and not even very regal sounding name of Rex. . . .

Rex came to the throne filled with the zeal of a reformer. He considered that the greatest failure of his predecessors had been in the field of law. For generations the legal system had known nothing like a basic reform. Procedures of trial were cumbersome, the rules of law spoke in the archaic tongue of another age, justice was expensive, the judges were slovenly and sometimes corrupt. Rex was resolved to remedy all this and to make his name in history as a great lawgiver. It was his unhappy fate to fail in this ambition. Indeed, he failed spectacularly, since not only did he not succeed in introducing the needed reforms, but he never even succeeded in creating any law at all, good or bad.

His first official act was, however, dramatic and propitious. Since he needed a clean slate on which to write, he announced to his subjects the immediate repeal of all existing law, of whatever kind. He then set about drafting a new code. Unfortunately, trained as a lonely prince, his education had been very defective. In particular he found himself incapable of making even the simplest generalizations. Though not lacking in confidence when it came to deciding specific controversies, the effort to give articulate reasons for any conclusion strained his capacities to the breaking point.

Becoming aware of his limitations, Rex gave up the project of a code and announced to his subjects that henceforth he would act as a judge in any disputes that might arise among them. In this way under the stimulus of a variety of cases he hoped that his latent powers of generalization might develop and, proceeding case by case, he would gradually work out a system of rules that could be incorporated in a code. Unfortunately the defects in his education were more deep-seated than he had supposed. The venture failed completely. After he had handed down literally hundreds of decisions neither he nor his subjects could detect in those decisions any pattern whatsoever. Such tentatives toward generalization as were to be found in his opinions only compounded the confusion, for they gave false leads to his subjects and threw his own meager powers of judgment off balance in the decision of later cases.

After this fiasco Rex realized it was necessary to take a fresh start. His first move was to subscribe to a course of lessons in generalization. With his intellectual powers thus fortified, he resumed the project of a code and, after many hours of solitary labor, succeeded in preparing a fairly lengthy document. He was still not confident, however, that he had fully overcome his previous defects. Accordingly, he announced to his subjects that he had written out a code and would henceforth be governed by it in deciding cases, but that for an indefinite future the contents of the code would remain an official state secret, known only to him and his scrivener. To Rex's surprise this sensible plan was deeply resented by his subjects. They declared it was very unpleasant to have one's case decided by rules when there was no way of knowing what those rules were.

Stunned by this rejection Rex undertook an earnest inventory of his personal strengths and weaknesses. He decided that life had taught him one clear lesson, namely, that it is easier to decide things with the aid of hindsight than it is to attempt to foresee and control the future. Not only did hindsight make it easier to decide cases, but—and this was of supreme importance to Rex—it made it easier to give reasons. Deciding to capitalize on this insight, Rex hit on the following plan. At the beginning of each calendar year he would decide all the controversies that had arisen

---

among his subjects during the preceding year. He would accompany his decisions with a full statement of reasons. Naturally, the reasons thus given would be understood as not controlling decisions in future years, for that would be to defeat the whole purpose of the new arrangement, which was to gain the advantages of hindsight. Rex confidently announced the new plan to his subjects, observing that he was going to publish the full text of his judgments with the rules applied by him, thus meeting the chief objection to the old plan. Rex's subjects received this announcement in silence, then quietly explained through their leaders that when they said they needed to know the rules, they meant they needed to know them *in advance* so they could act on them. Rex muttered something to the effect that they might have made that point a little clearer, but said he would see what could be done.

Rex now realized that there was no escape from a published code declaring the rules to be applied in future disputes. Continuing his lessons in generalization, Rex worked diligently on a revised code, and finally announced that it would shortly be published. This announcement was received with universal gratification. The dismay of Rex's subjects was all the more intense, therefore, when his code became available and it was discovered that it was truly a masterpiece of obscurity. Legal experts who studied it declared that there was not a single sentence in it that could be understood either by an ordinary citizen or by a trained lawyer. Indignation became general and soon a picket appeared before the royal palace carrying a sign that read, "How can anybody follow a rule that nobody can understand?"

The code was quickly withdrawn. Recognizing for the first time that he needed assistance, Rex put a staff of experts to work on a revision. He instructed them to leave the substance untouched, but to clarify the expression throughout. The resulting code was a model of clarity, but as it was studied it became apparent that its new clarity had merely brought to light that it was honeycombed with contradictions. It was reliably reported that there was not a single provision in the code that was not nullified by another provision inconsistent with it. A picket again appeared before the royal residence carrying a sign that read, "This time the king made himself clear—in both directions."

Once again the code was withdrawn for revision. By now, however, Rex had lost his patience with his subjects and the negative attitude they seemed to adopt toward everything he tried to do for them. He decided to teach them a lesson and put an end to their carping. He instructed his experts to purge the code of contradictions, but at the same time to stiffen drastically every requirement contained in it and to add a long list of new crimes. Thus, where before the citizen summoned to the throne was given ten days in which to report, in the revision the time was cut to ten seconds. It was made a crime, punishable by ten years' imprisonment, to cough, sneeze, hiccough, faint or fall down in the presence of the king. It was made treason not to understand, believe in, and correctly profess the doctrine of evolutionary, democratic redemption.

When the new code was published a near revolution resulted. Leading citizens declared their intention to flout its provisions. Someone discovered in an ancient author a passage that seemed apt: "To command what cannot be done is not to make law; it is to unmake law, for a command that cannot be obeyed serves no end but confusion, fear and chaos." Soon this passage was being quoted in a hundred petitions to the king.

The code was again withdrawn and a staff of experts charged with the task of revision. Rex's instructions to the experts were that whenever they encountered a rule requiring an impossibility, it should be revised to make compliance possible. It turned out that to accomplish this result every provision in the code had to be substantially rewritten. The final result was, however, a triumph of draftsmanship. It was clear, consistent with itself, and demanded nothing of the subject that did not lie easily within his powers. It was printed and distributed free of charge on every street corner.

However, before the effective date for the new code had arrived, it was discovered that so much time had been spent in successive revisions of Rex's original draft, that the substance of the code had been seriously overtaken by events. Ever since Rex assumed the throne there had been a suspension of ordinary legal processes and this had brought about important economic and institutional changes within the country. Accommodation to these altered conditions required many changes of substance in the law. Accordingly as soon as the new code became legally effective, it was subjected to a daily stream of amendments. Again popular discontent mounted; an anonymous pamphlet appeared on the streets carrying scurrilous cartoons of the king and a leading article with the title: "A law that changes every day is worse than no law at all."

Within a short time this source of discontent began to cure itself as the pace of amendment gradually slackened. Before this had occurred to any noticeable degree, however, Rex announced an important decision. Reflecting on the misadventures of his reign, he concluded that much of the trouble lay in bad advice he had received from experts. He accordingly declared he was reassuming the judicial power in his own person. In this way he could directly control the application of the new code and insure his country against another crisis. He began to spend practically all of his time hearing and deciding cases arising under the new code.

As the king proceeded with this task, it seemed to bring to a belated blossoming his long dormant powers of generalization. His opinions began, indeed, to reveal a confident and almost exuberant virtuosity as he deftly distinguished his own previous decisions, exposed the principles on which he acted, and laid down guide lines for the disposition of future controversies. For Rex's subjects a new day seemed about to dawn when they could finally conform their conduct to a coherent body of rules.

This hope was, however, soon shattered. As the bound volumes of Rex's judgments became available and were subjected to closer study, his subjects were appalled to discover that there existed no discernible relation between those judgments and the code they purported to apply. Insofar as it found expression in the actual disposition of controversies, the new code might just as well not have existed at all. Yet in virtually every one of his decisions Rex declared and redeclared the code to be the basic law of his kingdom.

Leading citizens began to hold private meetings to discuss what measures, short of open revolt, could be taken to get the king away from the bench and back on the throne. While these discussions were going on Rex suddenly died, old before his time and deeply disillusioned with his subjects.

The first act of his successor, Rex II, was to announce that he was taking the powers of government away from the lawyers and placing them in the hands of psychiatrists and experts in public relations. This way, he explained, people could be made happy without rules.

The Consequences of Failure

Rex's bungling career as legislator and judge illustrates that the attempt to create and maintain a system of legal rules may miscarry in at least eight ways; there are in this enterprise, if you will, eight distinct routes to disaster. The first and most obvious lies in a failure to achieve rules at all, so that every issue must be decided on an ad hoc basis. The other routes are: (2) a failure to publicize, or at least to make available to the affected party, the rules he is expected to observe; (3) the abuse of retroactive legislation, which not only cannot itself guide action, but undercuts the integrity of rules prospective in effect, since it puts them under the threat of retrospective change; (4) a failure to make rules understandable; (5) the enactment of contradictory rules or (6) rules that require conduct beyond the powers of the affected party; (7) introducing such frequent changes in the rules that the subject cannot orient his action by them; and, finally, (8) a failure of congruence between the rules as announced and their actual administration.

A total failure in any one of these eight directions does not simply result in a bad system of law; it results in something that is not properly called a legal system at all, except perhaps in the Pickwickian sense in which a void contract can still be said to be one kind of contract. Certainly there can be no rational ground for asserting that a man can have a moral obligation to obey a legal rule that does not exist, or is kept secret from him, or that came into existence only after he had acted, or was unintelligible, or was contradicted by another rule of the same system, or commanded the impossible, or changed every minute. It may not be impossible for a man to obey a rule that is disregarded by those charged with its administration, but at some point obedience becomes futile—as futile, in fact, as casting a vote that will never be counted. As the sociologist Simmel has observed, there is a kind of reciprocity between government and the citizen with respect to the observance of rules.[1] Government says to the citizen in effect, "These are the rules we expect you to follow. If you follow them, you have our assurance that they are the rules that will be applied to your conduct." When this bond of reciprocity is finally and completely ruptured by government, nothing is left on which to ground the citizen's duty to observe the rules.

The citizen's predicament becomes more difficult when, though there is no total failure in any direction, there is a general and drastic deterioration in legality, such as occurred in Germany under Hitler.[2] A situation begins to develop, for example, in which though some laws are published, others, including the most important, are not. Though most laws are prospective in effect, so free a use is made of retrospective legislation that no law is immune to change ex post facto if it suits the convenience of those in power. For the trial of criminal cases concerned with loyalty to the regime, special military tribunals are established and these tribunals disregard, whenever it suits their convenience, the rules that are supposed to control their decisions. Increasingly the principal object of government seems to be, not that of giving the citizen rules by which to shape his conduct, but to frighten him into impotence. As such a situation develops, the problem faced by the citizen is not so simple as that of a voter who knows with certainty that his ballot will not be counted. It is more like that of the voter who knows that the odds are against his ballot being counted at all, and that if it is counted, there is a good chance that it will be counted for the side against which he actually voted. A citizen in this predicament has to decide for himself whether to stay with the system and cast his ballot as a kind of symbolic act expressing the hope of a better day. So it was with the German citizen under Hitler faced with deciding whether he had an obligation to obey such portions of the laws as the Nazi terror had left intact.

In situations like these there can be no simple principle by which to test the citizen's obligation of fidelity to law, any more than there can be such a principle for testing his right to engage in a general revolution. One thing is, however, clear. A mere respect for constituted authority must not be confused with fidelity to law. Rex's subjects, for example, remained faithful to him as king throughout his long and inept reign. They were not faithful to his law, for he never made any.

---

1. The Sociology of Georg Simmel *(1950)*, trans. Wolff, §4, "Interaction in the Idea of 'Law,'" pp. 186–89; see also Chapter 4, "Subordination under a Principle," pp. 250–67. Simmel's discussion is worthy of study by those concerned with defining the conditions under which the ideal of "the rule of law" can be realized.
2. I have discussed some of the features of this deterioration in my article. "Positivism and Fidelity to Law," 71 Harvard Law Review 630, 648–57 (1958). This article makes no attempt at a comprehensive survey of all the postwar judicial decisions in Germany concerned with events occurring during the Hitler regime. Some of the later decisions rested the nullity of judgments rendered by the courts under Hitler not on the ground that the statutes applied were void, but on the ground that the Nazi judges misinterpreted the statutes of their own government. See Pappe, "On the Validity of Judicial Decisions in the Nazi Era," 23 Modern Law Review 260–74 (1960). Dr. Pappe makes more of this distinction than seems to me appropriate. After all, the meaning of a statute depends in part on accepted modes of interpretation. Can it be said that the postwar German courts gave full effect to Nazi laws when they interpreted them by their own standards instead of the quite different standards current during the Nazi regime? Moreover, with statutes of the kind involved, filled as they were with vague phrases and unrestricted delegations of power, it seems a little out of place to strain over questions of their proper interpretation.

THE DILEMMAS OF JUDGES WHO MUST INTERPRET "IMMORAL LAWS"*

Joel Feinberg

Filling in the Gaps in Human Law with Precepts of the Natural Law

Perhaps the most distinctive tenet of natural law theory is that morality—or some sector of morality, notably justice—is not simply a useful criterion for evaluating any given system of human law, and not simply a desirable feature to import into law. In natural law theory, morality is an essential part of law as it is. Some reference to morality (that is, to critical, objective, natural morality, not simply to the conven-

---

*Written specifically for this volume. Not previously published.

tional morality that happens to prevail in one place or another) must be made as part of the very analysis of what human law is as well as what substantive rules it contains. According to natural law theorists, this connection is a necessary one, derived from conceptual analysis, or definition, of the terms involved. It is not, therefore, a merely contingent connection that could vanish in time as human institutions change.

Legal positivists have been especially puzzled by this claim. What are the ways, they ask, in which human law could be thought to connect with a moral law that is only discovered by human beings, not invented or created by them? One natural law reply is that judges must appeal to natural justice in those "hard cases," as they are called, where the law seems somehow incomplete or indeterminate, yet judgment is required anyway. There are at least three types of hard case. First, the case before the court may be one in which a statute's wording is vague and the court must decide, by eliminating the linguistic indeterminacy, whether a defendant is properly convicted of violating it. Suppose a person is charged with violating a local ordinance against "reckless" or "drunk driving," because while drunk he was discovered riding a horse along the side of a public road. Suppose the facts are not contested. He was drunk; he was on horseback; he was moving along a public road. What is at issue is whether horseback riding is a form of driving. Suppose that because of vagueness the legal issue cannot be settled on linguistic grounds alone. Suppose further that conscientious efforts by the judge to determine the intentions of the original legislators one hundred years earlier are totally frustrated. It is commonly said that, in circumstances like this, where there is a gap in the positive law, the judge is free to legislate on her own and decide the culpability of the horseman on grounds of public policy, including effects on the economic interests of local businesses. At this point, a somewhat cautious natural law theorist might agree, though his misgivings might lead him to add that, if any principle of natural justice is applicable to the issues in the gap of the positive law, they take instant priority over considerations of any other kind. In fact, insofar as justice does apply in the gap, it is no real gap at all, because natural justice brings with itself a kind of automatic legal relevance. This is especially true when the judge's reasonings "in the gap" lead to results that conflict with principles of fairness that are only implicit in the written part of the law or that can be presumed to apply in the gap simply because it goes without saying that at least some minimal reasonableness is an essential element of law.

Minimal reasonableness is, after all, part of the very concept of law, whether put explicitly in the language of a statute or not.

In other words, a vaguely written statute might leave out any mention of fairness or unfairness, in which case, natural justice, though unstated, must be assumed to cover the omission. Or the statute might, in a way, be overwritten, making explicit judgments of fairness that are incorrect, since they conflict with the models of fairness that are a part of natural law. One principle of justice thought to derive from natural law, for example, maintains that justice consists in the exclusion of arbitrary inequalities in the allocation of the benefits or burdens of citizenship. As Aristotle put it, relevantly similar cases are to be treated in similar ways and relevantly dissimilar cases, in dissimilar ways and in direct proportion to the degree of dissimilarity between them.[1] Interpreting relevance can be a difficult matter, but some of the irrelevant dissimilarities, at least, can be easily spotted. In deciding which of two persons, A or B, is to be taxed more heavily, conscripted into military service, awarded the starring role in a stage play,[2] or appointed to an appellate court, skin color, as such, is self-evidently irrelevant. So any rule for settling such matters that treats skin color as relevant, has not excluded the arbitrary. There may or may not exist some cases in which gender *is* relevant. But that there exist *any* such cases at all is controversial and a reason for reserving special scrutiny (as our constitutional tradition puts it) for claims that the dissimilarities between men and women are *ever* relevant. Perhaps women's relative muscular weakness renders them less suitable for heavy physical labor than men, or more vulnerable to harm, say, in military combat. Or perhaps their greater biological fitness for the care of infants gives them a priority for work in maternity wards, etc. The point is that some such *reason* must be offered, defended, and then examined with very careful scrutiny if discriminatory treatment based on gender is to pass the test of natural justice. This test is presumed to be implicit in all substantive legal rules, but should be especially visible where there is an interstice (gap) in the written law.

Natural law theorists are especially persuasive when they point to examples of a kind of unreasonableness that undermines fairness in a perfectly transparent fashion. In these cases the unreasonable claims are in a statute's language when that language is interpreted with almost childish literalness; natural justice, on the other hand, lingers in the interstices, unspoken.

A specimen example is *People* v. *Johnson*,[3] a New York case from 1967.[4]

The defendant was charged with the violation of a statute designed to regulate the resale of theatre tickets, in that she did sell two tickets to an opera for $40 each, which tickets were originally priced at $20 each. The court found the defendant not guilty. It appeared that the defendant had purchased the tickets for $20 each in the hope of making them the key to a reunion with her estranged husband. When her husband refused to accompany her, she decided not to attend the opera, and placed an ad in a local newspaper inviting offers to purchase the tickets. In response to the ad a city police inspector telephoned the defendant. He and a policewoman went to the defendant's apartment, agreed upon a price of $40 a ticket, and after the exchange was made the officers disclosed their identity and placed the defendant under arrest, charged with the resale of tickets of admission. . . . The court could not believe that it was the legislative intent to embrace a case such as the one at bar within the ambit of the statute. Rather, the court said, the statute was designed to apply to those engaged in the business *of reselling tickets, and the court observed that "business" has been described as a word of large import, rather than a mere isolated transaction. . . . The court found that the prosecution's contention that any sale, even to a relative or friend, of a ticket . . . with or without profit, constituted a violation of the law, was unacceptable, and a* reductio ad absurdum *[of the prosecution's case].*

There was not even an apparent gap in this case. The conflict with justice was located entirely in what was said in the statute and its interpretation by the prosecution. Here the prosecution provided its own interpretation of the imprecise words in the statute in such a way that the words applying to the case at bar were utterly unreasonable and unfair. No statute could be that arbitrary and still be valid law! So, if this statute *is* valid law, it must be interpreted in such a way that it does not conflict with the minimal rationality and fairness that natural law contributes to all valid human law.

The judge in *People* v. *Johnson* never mentions natural justice or natural law, but it is not far off the mark to take his case for acquittal to be an appeal to natural justice. Its main argument is not a survey of relevant precedents nor does it depend on the exact

language or plain meaning of a statute. There is no insistence on the fact that explicit exceptions do not appear in the wording of the statute. Rather, the judge relies on the conviction that neither valid law nor legislative intent could be as crazy as this statute is when it is not understood to contain tacit exceptions. And when the exceptions are made explicit by sensible judicial interpretation, the statute is seen to be reasonable.

I trust that it is not too misleading to characterize an argument as an appeal to "natural justice" if it appeals to a fairness or reasonableness that is based upon considerations other than or in addition to "the letter of the law." Some will appeal to standard rational principles of justice, like the Aristotelian exclusion of arbitrary inequalities or the principle of fair opportunity. Tacit appeals to natural justice then can be used to support an interpretation of a legal judgment or rule, on the one hand, or a declaration of its validity or invalidity, on the other. Typically, such appeals are used, as in *People* v. *Johnson,* both to support an interpretation and in an intertwined fashion, a judgment of validity or invalidity. The interpretation of this statute must be so and so because, otherwise, the statute would be laughably unreasonable and cryably unfair, hence invalid, even though we didn't think of it as invalid in the beginning. That is one way the argument might go. Alternatively, it might concede that the statute is properly interpreted as such and such and then judge it invalid because it leads to extreme unfairness, as properly interpreted, and valid law cannot be that unjust.

How severely unfair must a statute be if it is properly to be declared invalid on the ground of conflict with natural justice? The difficulty of this question is perhaps the chief impediment in the way of accepting the natural law doctrine as a theory of legal validity. Cicero, Augustine, and Aquinas all espoused the doctrine (or at least gave lip service to it) that *lex iniusta non est lex* (an unjust law is no law at all). When we think of cases like *People* v. *Johnson*—or, better, those actual or hypothetical cases like *People* v. *Johnson* except that interpretations like the prosecution's in that case are explicitly endorsed in the statute itself—we can be very easily tempted by the *"non est lex"* position. But it is a sobering thought that many or most statutes accepted as valid by the courts, partly because of the legitimacy of their origins (the procedures by which they were enacted) are at least to some degree unfair to someone or other. Some are extremely unfair to whole classes of people. Sales taxes, for example, since they are regressive, hurt the poor more than the wealthy. As a result, they are unfair, but even the thousands of citizens who share that opinion recognize, nevertheless, that the statutes imposing the taxes are valid laws creating moral obligations to comply. It is almost impossible to imagine the chaos that would result if everyone honestly believed that unjust laws are not laws at all, but only acts of force obliging compliance without morally obligating anyone to comply.

In addition to statutes whose key words (like "drive") are vague, there are at least two other types of situation that can seem to present judges with gaps, or interstices, in the law. A second type of hard case results from another class of words used in the formulation of legal rules and principles, those that express what have come to be known as essentially contested concepts. In an example of Ronald Dworkin's,[5] a statute may render void all "sacrilegious" contracts, requiring a judge to decide in a particular case whether a contract signed on a Sunday is truly sacrilegious. Similarly, a court may have to decide whether a lower judge's sentencing of a convicted criminal is truly "cruel"; or whether a given price is "just compensation"; or whether some behavior was "due," "reasonable," or "appropriate" in the circumstances. According to some theories at least, the judge is on her own in these cases too; she must apply her own moral standards—that is, what she honestly believes are the objectively correct moral standards—to the case at issue. Insofar as the law requires the judge to speak first as a moralist and only then as a jurist, these are hard cases too.

Finally there are cases that are hard because they are "cases of first impression" with no binding precedent nor even a close analogy to any prior cases in the judge's jurisdiction. The lack of precedent may be because the facts are novel or it may be because, though the facts are familiar, the bringing of a suit under those facts is unprecedented. In the former category are recent suits for the custody of frozen embryos or for the removal of feeding tubes from a patient in a persistent vegetative state. In the second category, to select just one example, was the first tort suit for emotional damage to a relative of the direct victim of a negligently caused accident.

In both types of hard case described in the preceding two paragraphs, the judge appears to be required not only to legislate, but to legislate in a special way, not by appealing to general policy considerations as a genuine legislature might do, or to a guess about "legislative intentions," or a dictionary's description of the common usage of words like *drive,*

death (in the feeding tubes case), or *damage.* Rather, the judge is called upon to decide the case—if it is to be decided at all—by affirming and defending a substantive moral judgment and thus engaging in a type of reasoning for which the written law provides very little guidance. Is it *fair* to make a negligent motorist pay for a purely psychological kind of suffering, with no physical basis, of the direct victim's aunt who learns in a telephone call of injury to her nephew? Is it fair, to a husband filing for divorce from his wife, for the wife to preserve, over his protest, the embryo that they had earlier agreed to create by the fertilization in vitro of her ovum by his sperm, for implantation in her womb? Which is the more important interest here: the wife's interest at the age of forty in bearing a child of her own (this may be her last chance) or her ex-husband's desire not to have a child of his raised by a biological mother he despises? Is a contract signed on the sabbath truly sacrilegious? All of these questions are issues some judge had once to decide, with clear guidance neither from statute nor precedent, but only by the application of some commonly acknowledged or rationally certified principle of natural justice to an unusual-fact situation. Critics of "judicial activism"[6] often say that this construal of the situation suffers the fatal flaw of permitting the judge to apply *her own* values or appeal to *her own* moral convictions as if it would be better if she appealed to someone else's moral principles that she does not personally share. Of course the principles she uses must be "her own"—that is, principles that she genuinely believes in. Otherwise, her opinion in the case would lack conviction and she would lack sincerity and integrity. Those principles, however, are relevant and proper not because they are hers. Rather, they are hers because she thinks they are cogent for quite independent reasons, because the reasoning that leads her to them is sound, and because the principle of natural justice that she invokes is correct. There can be no certainty about that, of course, but practical certainty is hard to come by even in those complex legal decisions that confront no gap, involve no purely moral reasoning, and require no leap across the chasm to natural justice.

Natural Law as a Handful of Partly Uninterpreted Abstract Principles

If any of the propositions of the natural law are in some sense a part of the human law too, it must be the more abstract ones. The natural law itself should be thought of as more like a constitution than a municipal code and not at all like the complete set of particularized rules both procedural and substantive—that is, statutes, judgments, and judicial precedents. Some book collections of rules require whole buildings for their storage. The natural law may be a collection of principles, precepts, and very general rules; if so, it is a collection of only the most general of them, before they are actually applied to fact situations. The result of their application will be particularized rules about safety precautions in boiler factories; hours in which the drivers of ice cream trucks are permitted to ring bells; the maximal percentage of alcohol permitted in the blood of car drivers, but perhaps not horse and mule drivers; distinctions between grades of burglary; etc. (I deliberately make this list as miscellaneous as possible. I don't think that Aquinas, for example, conceived of the natural law as even mentioning alcohol, ice cream, gasoline combustion vehicles, boiler factories, and so on. It is more likely, I think, that the natural law resembles the Ten Commandments, or perhaps a small, very small, list of maxims of justice, all put in the abstract, like Aristotle's formulae for distinguishing between genuine equality of treatment and invidious discrimination. The United States Constitution, with its Bill of Rights and its Fourteenth Amendment, come to think of it, might make a better model than even the Ten Commandments and the conclusions of Aristotle's theory of distributive justice. In short, if we wrote down the "natural law," it might appear as a list of ten or twelve moral judgments of a very abstract kind and the whole printed document might be no more than two or three pages long. Perhaps there could be a single ultimate principle, or two or three. Indeed, John Rawls sums everything up in two principles of justice; his utilitarian opponents, in one.[7] Blackstone wrote that we should live honestly, should hurt nobody, and should render to everybody his due, "to which three general precepts Justinian has reduced the whole doctrine of law."[8]) Less abstract but more thorough philosophers might formulate the requirements of equal justice; several more principles of liberty; and still a few others, spelling out the principles of autonomy (what is now misleadingly called "privacy."[9]) Absolute orders of priority among the principles, to guide judges to decisions in cases where principles seem to conflict, would probably be impossible. No mechanical decision procedure in these cases could substitute for moral sensibility, analogical reasoning, and Solomonic wisdom.[10] A statement of the full content of natural law would not only contain the principles that protect citizens from their governments, but also the principles that protect them from each other. Those principles might include the most general—responsibility, justification, and excuse—as well as the first principles of tort and contract liability, child custodianship, and property rights. Perhaps our full statement of the natural law at this point would come to seven or eight printed pages, a statement longer than the Ten Commandments but approximately the same length as the Constitution with its amendments. In fact, a system of human law that consisted of no more than that brief statement of natural law would be very much like one that could lead judges to leap to the constitutional level immediately in every case, a system that could cut the rest of the law adrift.

We can think of the abstract natural law precepts, in this model, as related in one or both of two ways to the more particular judgments and rules of the human law with which they exist. Natural law functions both as a progenitor of human law rules or a standard of legitimacy by which the complex and particularized rules are judged valid or not. Typically, I should think, the general (natural) and particular (positive) rules are not allowed to conflict because the natural rules have themselves been used to produce the positive ones, by application to ever more complex factual circumstances and ever more refined restatements of the generating rules themselves as they spin off exceptive clauses and the like. If a generating rule seems to conflict with some of its offspring, it is understandable that, other things being equal, the more concrete derived judgments should be the ones that are invalidated, since they are inconsistent with the rational precepts that were to have produced them in the first place.

Consequently, a town ordinance that permits blacks to sit only in the back row of a public bus is flatly inconsistent with a precept of natural law requiring that law not be used to enforce arbitrary inequalities. In that case the ordinance, in contradicting a principle of justice, is itself shown to be unjust and, therefore (the difficult step), legally invalid. As Cicero and Augustine would have said, it is as if there were no law (governing the distribution of bus seats by race) at all. It is instead just a blunt and forcible way of putting blacks in their place, as guns or clubs might do. The American Supreme Court came to the same result (*non est lex*) *not explicitly via natural law,* but in virtue of the supreme authority of the *U.S. Constitution,* whose Fourteenth Amendment is itself subject to a kind of natural law interpretation, especially when it invites its judicial interpreters to apply moral standards of what is fitting, appropriate, due, reasonable, unreasonable, cruel, excessive, impartial, equal, private, and so on. Where can the judge turn to find answers to subtle moral questions if not to the objective moral judgments discovered by reason rather than merely invented to serve one's pleasure? That zone, the argument concludes, is the realm of natural law.

Some natural law theorists, of whom Blackstone is perhaps the most typical example, give more than a routine respectful nod to positive law. They believe that positive law rightfully prevails *except* where it contains "flat absurdity or injustice."[11] Only when it is extremely unfair and downright irrational is an otherwise legitimate positive law invalidated by its content. This seems to be simply another way of saying that positive law is to prevail except where it contains a gap but that, within the gap and until it is closed by the enactment of new positive law, natural law is to prevail. If the natural law in the gap conflicts with the positive law that surrounds the gap, then positive law wins out. In these respects, this intersticial theory of natural law is the very opposite of the "higher law" version of the natural law theory associated with Ghandi and Martin Luther King, Jr.

From examples like this we can see that positivists often differ only in degree and emphasis from other positivists, just as natural law partisans often differ only in such ways from other natural law advocates. Each group of philosophers contains people who respect both established law and its duties of fidelity and obedience, on the one hand, and precepts of justice with their duties of reasonable fairness, on the other. Given the conflicting claims to superior authority of these positive and natural rules, it is not surprising that some nominal positivists bend over backward to accommodate natural justice,[12] and some natural law theorists in their writings make at least a respectful nod to such positivist precepts as that expressed by *stare decisis*.[13]

Even pure positivists who insist that law is one thing and morality another, and never shall the one concept be reduced to the other, are likely, as we have seen, to interpret what their rivals call natural law as a set of objective criteria for evaluating a given statute or a given set of established positive rules as good or bad, just or unjust, efficient or cumbersome. They agree with their natural law friends that positive law *ought* to be just and that the criteria of justice are themselves objective truths accessible to reason, denying only that these standards of evaluation are themselves actually part of the law. The positivist writ-

ers, on the other hand, who are most respectful of natural law are those described above who would let enacted or judicially established law prevail except where there are gaps in the positive law itself. These gaps are a consequence of the open texture of language, the unavoidability of essentially contested concepts in the wording of statutes and constitutions, and the legal vacuums produced by unprecedented factual circumstances. Such vacuums are often the consequence of new technology or sometimes simply a reflection of the fact that every precedent in the law is a link in a chain of cases that goes back to an original precedent that was itself decided in the absence of still earlier relevant precedent. Some otherwise positivist judges would insist that courts always decide these cases of first impression on moral grounds, by appealing directly to natural justice, for example. Anti-slavery judges in the nineteenth century, torn apart by the conflict between their anti-slavery consciences and their sworn duty as judges to uphold the established law, tried hard to reinterpret some laws regarded by their colleagues as established. These judges tried to show that the laws were not really established, because gaps existed in them. In some of these instances it was difficult to know whether to classify the judge as a positivist or a natural law theorist, since he tried so hard to find gaps in the positive law into which he could cram as much natural law as possible.

Most of the theories about how morality or natural law is related to positive or human law are, in one of the ways discussed, compromises between two distinct and often conflicting kinds of value. At one extreme, we have the higher law version of natural law theory, which pays little respect to positive law as such. (The fact that segregation statutes in the South were properly enacted by legitimate rule-making bodies had very little weight with them.) At the other extreme, pure positivism, even when sympathetic to the goal of suffusing more justice into the law, had no sympathy for the view that *lex iniusta non est lex,* that unjust requirements are already excluded from law by definition. Apart from these groups, the other theories can be understood as efforts somehow to have it both ways, to be a natural law theorist who respects the moral importance of established law or a positivist with a very tender sense of justice, particularly pertaining to the operations of his or her country's legal system. These matters may seem at first to be merely problems for scholars and philosophers trying to achieve consistency, but when we turn to the moral obligation of obedience to law, we soon discover that they mask conflicts of practical commitment, sometimes with matters of life or death riding on their outcome.

Fuller, Radbruch, and Hart: The German Experience with Nazism

Perhaps the most influential of the non-Thomist natural law theories in the twentieth century was that of Lon Fuller. Fuller insisted on the essential connection between law and morality, but his secularized version of legal naturalism had no theological grounding. Moreover, morality provides criteria, in Fuller's view, for the existence of a *legal system,* not criteria for the validity of a single rule or statute. It is possible then, according to Fuller, for an unjust law to be a valid law. But if the whole network of rules and rule-making powers, or a substantial subsection thereof, is antithetical to morality, then it is no longer a functioning legal system; it is, at best, another method of social control based on arbitrary power.

The morality that Fuller held essential to the existence of a legal system is wholly procedural and does not apply directly to the substantive content of regulations and statutes. Fuller denied that there is some higher law, external to established law, to which the latter must correspond if it is to exist. The morality that is essential to law Fuller calls "the internal morality of law" or "the morality that makes law possible." In his book *The Morality of Law* he sketches the principles of this internal morality:[14]

1. The rules must be general and not mere ad hoc commands.
2. There can be no secret (unpromulgated) rules.
3. There can be no retroactive rules.
4. The rules must be understandable by those to whom they apply.
5. The rules must not be either self-contradictory or contradictory as a group.
6. The rules must not demand actions that are beyond their subjects' powers to perform.
7. The rules must not be constantly changing.
8. There must be some minimal correspondence between what the rules say and how they are administered or interpreted by the courts.

A total failure in respect to any one of these principles, or a partial failure in respect to most or all of them, implies not simply that there is a bad legal system, but that there is not a legal system at all.

One consequence of Fuller's conception is that the existence of a legal system is always a matter of degree, since the degree of conformity to the internal morality of law can itself be a matter of degree. Some critics of Fuller found degrees of existence to be an odd notion. Other critics, including even some who could make sense of it, objected to Fuller's use of the word "morality" for the principles of order that make a legal system, whether just or not, workable. "Why not call them the conditions for effective lawmaking, or the maxims of legal craftsmanship?" they asked. A traditional legal naturalist might say of some particular positive law of the Nazi era, "This is so evil, it cannot be a law." In most of these cases, Fuller claims, one could usually have said instead: "This thing is a product of a system so oblivious to the (inner) morality of law that it is not entitled to be called a law."

In their famous debate in *The Harvard Law Review* in 1958 and 1959, Fuller and H.L.A. Hart differed over the legal consequences in the postwar period of actions performed under the laws (pseudo-laws?) of the Nazi regime. Fuller staunchly defended, and Hart respectfully criticized, the position of Gustav Radbruch. Radbruch, once a leading German legal positivist, had converted to a traditional natural law theory in his efforts to deal with the claims of German citizens in response to moral outrages against them in the Nazi era by acts that were considered perfectly legal at the time committed. Despite their philosophical differences over the relations between law and morality, Radbruch, Hart, and Fuller came to similar practical conclusions. German citizens had been under no overriding moral obligation to obey the Nazi statutes, they all concluded. Fuller held this view because the statutes were the product of a system that could not claim to be a legal system; Radbruch, because the individual statutes were too evil to be legally valid; and Hart, because the statutes, though legally valid, were too morally evil to be obeyed, since there are moral obligations that can, in given cases, outweigh the moral obligation to obey valid law.

These differences were so subtle that some commentators suspected that they were theoretically insignificant. Lloyd L. Weinreb, for example, asked "Can it possibly make so much difference whether we say, 'This enactment is too immoral to obligate us; therefore it is not law' or 'This law is too immoral to obligate us; therefore it ought not to be obeyed?'"[15] It is easy to sympathize with Weinreb's complaint, but in what space remains, I shall try to clarify the controversy and reformulate the obedience problem in a way that recaptures its importance and its poignancy.

Most but by no means all writers believe that there is a moral obligation to obey the valid laws of one's community, especially in a country that is genuinely democratic and by and large just.[16] In the past I have had some difficulty accepting the arguments usually made in support of this belief, but I must admit that it has almost a common-sense status for the great majority of people who hold it, so I am more than willing to assume it here for the sake of argument. To affirm it, after all, is very much like saying that there is a moral obligation to keep one's promises or to tell the truth. Notoriously, life is capable of creating circumstances in which these "moral obligations" conflict so that, whatever one does, one will be violating at least one of them. So, for example, there may be circumstances such that, if I tell the truth, I will be breaking a promise and, if I keep my promise, I will be telling a lie. Instead of concluding that whatever we do in those circumstances will be wrong, philosophers have reinterpreted the moral principles, imposing the duties as conditional. We have a general moral obligation to tell the truth, for example, except when we are under another moral obligation that is even more stringent in the circumstances, and there may indeed be such a conflicting obligation. Moral obligations, then, do differ in degrees of stringency, or weight, and vary in such a way that it is impossible in the abstract to formulate a hierarchy of weightiness on the moral scales, a hierarchy that will hold whatever the circumstances are like. In some circumstances the duty to tell the truth takes priority; in others, the duty to keep a promise. It all depends on the circumstances.

According to H.L.A. Hart, we do have a moral obligation to obey any valid law, even an unjust or evil one. But we also have a moral obligation to oppose injustice and, when a valid law reaches a certain degree of evil, the obligation to obey is outweighed by an even more stringent moral obligation to resist. Insofar as the statute in question is a valid one, we are tugged one way; insofar as it is immoral, it tugs in the other—sometimes it tugs even harder. The moral obligation to obey the law is an example, therefore, of what some writers call a prima facie obligation (abbreviated henceforth as PFO).[17]

Not in every case is a PFO a decisive moral reason, but it is always a relevant supporting reason and one that would be conclusive if no other relevant reason of greater strength applied to the situation. Hart's account is "candid," he says, because it allows us to say both of these things: that the validity of an applicable rule is always a reason, and a powerful one, for obeying it (or if one is a judge, for applying it), but that it is not necessarily a decisive reason when it comes into conflict with moral PFOs of other kinds. This account, Hart maintains, explains exactly and truly what we are doing when we conscientiously disobey the law. We are acting illegally and we know it. Fidelity to enacted law is morally required of us, but it is not the whole of what is morally required of us. Some things, at some times, may be even more important morally, and it is disingenuous to label these things as law too. That would be to disguise even from ourselves what we are really doing—namely, deliberately disobeying the law for the sake of something we deem more important.

Duty Versus Conscience: The American Experience with Slavery

Some of the moral duties generally believed to be created by laws are private duties—for example, the negative duties not to harm others or to be rude or tactless to them, and the positive duties to be sociable and cooperative. Some of the private duties can be interpreted as the duties of a *citizen:* to stay informed, to vote, to pay one's bills and taxes. Still others are the duties of a *neighbor:* to maintain the exterior appearances of one's property and to be prepared to help one's neighbors in emergencies and, at any time, to do minor favors, like taking in a neighbor's mail when she is on vacation. Examples of these kinds might tempt us to the view that all duties are in a sense public—that is, derived from one's occupancy of an office in some institution. The temptation is reinforced by our ability, usually, to add the words *as an office holder* to our description of our own duties. I have duties not only as a citizen and as a neighbor, but also as a father and as a husband, and some of my duties are as a teacher or policeman (or whatever my job happens to be). A family is a relatively private sort of institution—compared, say, to a corporation or a jury—but it is some sort of institution. And there are still other duties that are more private still, deriving from no institutional office at all, public or private, but rather from my status as a human being among other mostly unrelated human beings. Our duties to strangers encountered in lonely places (our duties not to beat and rob them, for example) are duties we have simply as human beings, not as institutional office holders of any kind—not private, like the family, not more public, like the employer-corporation.

On the other hand, many of our more important and determinate duties are near the public end of the spectrum. A so-called public official is a person with a very specific set of duties derived from his or her job. These public duties are added to those moral duties that the official shares with everyone. Some public officials, like tenured judges, hold their offices for extended periods of time. Others occupy temporary offices created for specific tasks. A good example of the latter would be the office of juror in a public trial in a criminal court. To understand what it is to be a judge or a juror is just to know what the duties are that define the job. Those duties then descend on a person when he or she is actually sworn in as a judge or juror. What creates the special duties of the job is often an oath in which the designate swears to discharge the job-defining duties to the best of personal ability.

The juror solemnly promises to obey the judge's instructions, chief among which is to base one's verdict strictly on the evidence and find the defendant guilty only if the presented evidence establishes guilt beyond a reasonable doubt. It is also the juror's duty to vote for the defendant's acquittal if and only if the evidence leaves a reasonable doubt of guilt. From a solemn promise, sworn in a public oath, derives the juror's clear duty not to acquit unless the evidence does leave the required residue of doubt. And yet the court, in a number of ways, seems almost to encourage juries to cheat! The jury members, for example, have both a *moral duty* to honor their oath and (let us imagine) to convict the accused thereby, and a *legal power* to acquit without answering to anyone. Jury deliberations are secret, they are not subject to review after the trial; jurors may not be subjected to any penalty for bad judgment or for dereliction of official duty; and acquittal verdicts may not be appealed or overturned because of the constitutional protection against double jeopardy. It is evident that there is no way to prevent a jury from acquitting a clearly guilty defendant when conviction would offend their consciences—when, for example, the jurors must pass judgment on a clearly guilty eight-year-old child charged with stealing a turnip during the early Victorian period, when such a petty theft was a capital crime. In such cases the jury knows that it can set the child free by "voting its conscience" instead of doing its duty. And yet juries are instructed that they have, individually and collectively, an unqualified duty to fol-

low the judge's instructions and put their consciences aside as they decide on guilt or innocence according to the evidence alone. Each juror takes a solemn oath to do just that. So it appears that the law, in a perfectly explicit way, confers a power on juries to do what they have an equally explicit duty not to do.

As things now stand, conscientious jurors in morally difficult cases are in an unenviable position. From the purely legal standpoint, their position is not so difficult. Their duty is to decide according to the evidence only. If the evidence leaves no reasonable doubt of guilt, their duty is to convict. But human beings are more than the sum of the duties of their stations, and the morally right way to act may violate any given one of their official duties or even the sum total of their duties on balance. What morality requires of a person, in morally difficult circumstances, is not something to be mechanically determined by an examination of the person's office or role-centered duties. An individual must on rare occasions have the courage to rise above all that and obey the dictates of conscience. One's conscience may be wholly convincing, considered only on its own terms. But its conflict with duty will nevertheless make the occasion for decision morally complex and difficult. It is no laughing matter, morally speaking, deliberately to violate one's own privately acknowledged duties, and our public institutions would be gravely endangered if their officials as a matter of routine were prepared to do that. The circumstances must be extreme, and the emphasis on duty strong and unremitting, if an official is even to consider such a drastic course. A juror has no moral right to violate the solemn oath on the ground that there would probably be some unfairness in punishing the defendant, even though he or she is plainly guilty, or because the juror disapproves of the statute the defendant is charged with breaking. Rather, the jurors must place a substantial surcharge[18] on departures from their official obligations. Conviction must seem more than unfair; it must seem unconscionable, a gross injustice given the defendant's undeniable moral right to do what he or she did. A single juror who makes these moral judgments can nullify the judge's instructions quite surreptitiously, so that no one will ever know what has happened. Sometimes, in morally desperate circumstances, that is what a juror should do, since secret nullification does less damage to a just institution (jury trials as currently instituted) than open and clear nullification would do. But departures from duty—any duty—should never be taken lightly.

The Moral Duties of Judges

When we discuss disobedience of ordinary citizens, either to the validly enacted statutes of their communities or to the rules defining their own official roles, if any, in their community's legal system, the quarrels between positivists and natural law theorists are likely to seem arid and picky. What difference does it make, we might ask in our impatience, whether this extremely unjust statute is too wicked really to be a statute at all (despite its impeccable pedigree), as the natural law theorist might maintain, or that it is a legal statute all right, but one that is too wicked to obey, as the positivist would have it? The positivist would admit that, insofar as it is a valid statute, he or she has a moral obligation to obey it, but argue that that prima facie obligation (PFO) has little weight when placed on the scales against stronger PFOs that will outweigh it in these circumstances. In any event, the positivist and the natural law theorist will be allies against any wicked dictatorship that tries to disguise its unjust commands by representing them as valid law (as they may or may not be). Neither will have any respect for the egregiously unjust content of the law, or pseudo-law, that they disobey. So what practical difference can there be between them, and between the legal philosophies they espouse?

The conscientious judge's situation is quite different, especially when he or she is a judge in the nation's highest appellate court. This judge will have a conscience that could on occasion be in conflict with the duties of office, duties the judge has solemnly sworn to discharge. But the judge does not have legal power of the same degree of effectiveness as that of the ordinary citizen or the juror. Paradoxically, the higher we climb in the court system, the less effective power to breach official duties do we find. I suspect that is because the duties themselves, at that level, are regarded with awe and thought to be of maximal or supreme stringency. After all, the Supreme Court justice has solemnly, and with great publicity, sworn to uphold the highest source of law in the land, the Constitution itself. No justice can take *that* duty lightly. Moreover, the Supreme Court judge is not protected by the same degree of secrecy as the mere juror. Nor can he or she so easily escape sanctions afterward. The Supreme Court justice is subject to impeachment, and subject to great social pressure to give an accounting of each judicial decision and mode of argument. Such a judge is not truly free to be candid and confess that he or she knowingly violated a most sacred prom-

ise to the public and did so in order to satisfy personal conscience. Very likely the critics will respond that a willingness to break so important a promise betrays not so much a sensitive conscience as a conscience insensitive to the moral bindingness of voluntary commitments.

It is puzzling to know how to exercise our terminological options in this situation. Most of us, I think, would be made uncomfortable by talk of a conflict between duty and conscience. After all, our ordinary role- or job-connected duties also have a voice in the chorus that is conscience. Moreover, a person could say without being incoherent that conscience forbids him or her from being derelict in (other) duties, or that he or she has a duty to obey conscience. And yet there *is* an intuitive distinction between, say, my duty as a teacher and all or most of my other duties combined. The collective voice of the other duties may have the timbre and tone that we attribute to conscience.

The best historical example of an intractable struggle within the forum of a judge's mind between the duties of public office and the duties of private conscience is that which tormented large sections of the American judiciary in the decades preceding the Civil War. A number of distinguished judges of profound and genuine abolitionist convictions, men who hated slavery with an intense moral passion, struggled to reconcile their consciences with what looked like their plain constitutional duty: the duty to order the return of escaped slaves to their southern masters. On one side of these intrapersonal conflicts was a role-duty as stringent and weighty on the moral scales as role-duties ever are, partly because it derived from the most basic source of law in our legal system, the Constitution itself, and partly because it was so undeniably explicit, precise, and unambiguous. On the other side was a moral consensus against human slavery. This consensus dated back to the early Christians, Stoic philosophers, and even Roman jurists and included the leading political philosophers of the seventeenth and eighteenth centuries—Locke, Puffendorf, Montesquieu—and the ideological fathers of the French and American Revolutions. Every schoolchild could recite passages from the Declaration of Independence; the Constitutional Preamble; and the speeches of Patrick Henry, Madison, and Jefferson (ironically, all from the southern slave-holding state of Virginia). These works affirmed the natural rights of *all* people, whatever the positive laws of their governments might say or leave unsaid, to the contrary. Moreover, these rights were said to be noncontroversial because their existence was *self-evident*. Taken together, all this authority constituted as powerful a display of intellectual reinforcement for a consensus of conscience that anyone could ever hope for, even though much of its support under pressure turned out to be mere lip service and political rhetoric.

By 1850, most of the American judiciary joined most of the educated public in thinking of the Constitution, in critical part, as a compromise over slavery.[19] The compromise consisted of the agreement of the slave-holding states to join the union, provided that the new nation's Constitution recognized and promised to preserve the legal legitimacy of slavery in those states that wanted to keep the practice. Those who were impressed by this interpretation could point to five provisions in the original Articles that were evidence for it, chief of which was "the bloody clause," as Wendell Phillips called it.[20] This clause was the original fugitive slave provision, the price paid by the free states, according to the Great Compromise theory, for having the benefits of an enlarged union from the beginning of national independence. The fugitive slave clause in the original federal Constitution (superseded after the Civil War by the Thirteenth Amendment) declared that

> No person held to service or labor in one state, under the law thereof, escaping into another, shall, in consequence of any law or regulation therein, be discharged from such service or labor, but shall be delivered up on claim of the party to whom such service or labor may be due.

Thus, if Massachusetts enacted a statute requiring that fugitive slaves be fully liberated upon crossing their borders and permitted to stay on, as free persons in permanent residence there, the statute would be clearly unconstitutional; it would be void ab initio in virtue of this clause. Slave owners from the escaped slave's state could then dispatch slave hunters to Massachusetts to capture the escapee; certify with the local authorities that the hunter was reclaiming his employer's property; and return the wretched slave, in shackles, to servitude. Periodically, the slave would be intercepted by local citizens and rescued, at least for a time. Often these conflicts got into the courts, as would-be rescuers and their aiders and abettors appealed convictions for interfering with property, or the slave owners petitioned for return of their property. Almost invariably the slavers triumphed in court, in virtue of that inescapable barrier to justice and humanity, the bloody clause. It cannot have been a pleasant experience for the judges, particularly those of abolitionist conviction and natural law philosophy.

In his penetrating history of the legal struggles against slavery in the first half of the nineteenth century, Robert Cover distinguishes five possible responses of a judge caught in the grip of a duty-versus-conscience struggle.[21] (Actually he mentions only four choices, but a fifth is a clearly implicit in his discussion.)

> *[1] He may apply the law against his conscience. [2] He may apply conscience and be faithless to the law. [3] He may resign. [4] Or he may cheat, [and] state that the law is not what he believes it to be, and thus preserve an appearance (to others) of the conformity to law and morality.*

Finally, there is a fifth possibility. The judge may adopt an ameliorist solution. He "may introduce his own sense of what 'ought to be' interstitially, where no hard law yet exists.' "[22]

All five of these choices were actually made and/or advocated by otherwise abolitionist judges. Most of them stopped resisting the clear language of the bloody clause. There it was in plain English, a clear constitutional recognition of slavery. Clearly, a given judge's duty as a judge was to obey the explicit dictates of a Constitution that could no longer be respected and morally embraced. It was of course a literal bloody shame that thousands of human beings were oppressed and, at best, treated as animals. But it must be remembered that such results are not the personal responsibility of the judge but, rather, commands of the impersonal voice of the law. The judge's job is to discover the law and then be its voice, totally uninfluenced by his personal opinions, even by his moral convictions. He can say "Not I, directly or indirectly . . . but the law, which is given to me and is my master, says thus."[23]

At first that kind of political eloquence functioned primarily as a line of defense for the judge. As such, it was an argument from humility, more a self-minimizing kind of apology than a full-blooded justification. But the fuller justification, usually forthcoming, was simply to opt for legal positivism, except perhaps in respect to those gaps in the positive law, where one can hope to introduce natural law interstitially in virtue of "a sort of bend-over-backward principle . . . an obligation to achieve a profreedom [anti-slavery] result unless there is a very specific, concrete positive law that prevents it."[24] Perhaps it was possible at the time of the Constitutional Convention to deny that the fugitive slave clause was specific or concrete. But the fugitive slave clause was a kind of invitation to Congress and to state legislatures to provide their own detailed implementation language. The Fugitive Slave Acts of 1793 and 1850 enjoined very specific procedures to be used in capturing and returning fugitive slaves—none of which were at all advantageous to the fugitive. Northern abolitionists loudly accused Congress of interfering with (more irony) states' rights, in particular the Constitutional rights of the states to establish their own rules providing more due process for the prisoner and his rescuers both (including a jury trial guaranteed elsewhere in the Constitution). By 1850 very few interstices were left in those statutes that further restricted the rights of the escaped slave. By then the bend-over-backward principle was rarely used and, in fact, often explicitly rejected. Ameliorist natural law theories intended only for that diminishing interstitial area of the positive law tended to be absorbed by the "legal duty" option and the legal positivism that was its foundation.

The second option was for the judge to abandon the very law he was sworn to apply and to apply instead the dictates of his own conscience. It is difficult to understand, of course, how such reasonings could be explained by the judge in presenting his conclusions to the public. Could he write an opinion affirming his conscientious conviction that slavery is monumental injustice and cruelty, rejected almost everywhere as contrary to the laws of nature (morality) and therefore impossible for a right-thinking person to promote? Could he continue by pointing out that his clear legal duty would require that he contribute to the strengthening of slavery and that, therefore, he had decided to reject his legal duty (his duty as a judge) and vote instead for the position recommended by his conscience? It would be acceptable to the public if he affirmed those premises but drew a different conclusion from them—namely, that he must resign his appointment as a judge immediately and not take part at all in the legal proceedings that are already under way. That is the third option, resignation, a choice that was very popular with abolitionist judges. But that is altogether different from saying "I know my duty but I am not going to do it. I will do what is contrary to my duty instead." I can imagine that universal condemnation and impeachment would await the judge at the end of that line. And his colleagues would hector him repeatedly about what the legal system would be like if every judge felt free to renounce his duty whenever it conflicted with one of his own moral beliefs.

The resignation option was chosen by Wendell Phillips, who not only resigned his own judgeship, but wrote a book advocating resignation by public officials and the organizing of a political party encouraging withdrawal and noncooperation. In his book[25] Phillips quotes from the letter of resignation of one Francis Jackson, who wrote that

> *"The oath to support the Constitution of the United States is a solemn promise to do that which is a violation of the natural rights of man, and a sin in the sight of God. . . . I withdraw all profession of allegiance to it [The Constitution] and all my voluntary efforts to sustain it." . . . More and more, it appeared the question ought not to be put, "How should a judge of integrity decide these cases?" but rather "How can a man of integrity judge these cases [at all]?"*

The making of dramatic resignations conjures up pictures of heroic resistance, but in some instances there is a suspicion that *self-indulgence* might be the better term. If a judge's resignation is motivated entirely by his desire to preserve his own moral purity, so that his hands will not be soiled with the blood of others, then he makes a poor hero, though his conduct on his own behalf might have required considerable courage. But wouldn't a more fruitful use of his courage and a craftier use of the power of his office, if any, be more commendable? What help does he give the suffering slaves by concentrating his efforts on his own integrity? I suspect that efforts to preserve integrity in situations like these will inevitably be self-defeating, because true integrity requires more effective resistance and less narcissistic self-concern. "It is a waste to refuse to use accessible power for a good purpose. . . ."[26]

Few did, and few would now, embrace the fourth choice, requiring the conscientious but frustrated judge to cheat. That can hardly be the kind of advice that one would expect to find in a law manual, a text, or casebook. The advice to violate legal norms in order to avoid morally unacceptable results cannot itself be a legal norm; an enumeration of the duties of a judge can hardly include the duty to cheat when there is no other way to produce a just result. Still, we should note that the moral situation of an abolitionist judge at a hearing concerning the fate of an escaped slave is basically no different from that of a juror in a trial of an eight-year-old child for the capital offense of stealing a turnip from a neighbor's fields. The main relevant differences are that the juror's cheating is secret and may never be known; the judge's opportunities are not as great. Moreover, the judge speaks officially on behalf of the nation's legal system; the juror speaks only to a question of fact. The juror's "cheating" consists simply in lying about those facts in order to prevent suffering and injustice. Both the juror and the judge must pay a price for the nullification they achieve by their untruthfulness. But we are all threatened more by the judge, who because of greater visibility and greater impact generally, has a greater potential for harming the system if the scheme goes awry. In both cases great emphasis must be put on the importance of legal duty, and its strict bindingness, if we are to ensure that misrepresentation happen only rarely, in the most extreme cases, and not as a general rule.

The chief opponent of the resignation school, Lysander Spooner, was also the chief spokesman for the cheating alternative. He did not convince many judges, so far as we know, but one cannot but smile at his ingenuity.[27]

> *Spooner was willing to treat the problem* arguendo *as one of a judge who had sworn to uphold an unjust constitution (even though he, Spooner, believed that the U.S. Constitution is properly interpreted as a just nonslavery instrument). Spooner acknowledged that the dominant position seemed to be that such a judge should resign. But he thought that the proper analogy was one of a man given a weapon on condition that he kill an innocent and helpless victim. In such a situation, Spooner argued, it is proper to make the promise, keep the weapon, and use it to defend rather than attack the victim. To give up the sword, to resign the judicial office, is "only a specimen of the honor that is said to prevail among thieves."*

In both cases, that of the judge torn between morality (conscience) and law (duty) and that of the party who accepts his neighbor's weapon, the cheating consists of breaking a promise to uphold the law even when it conflicts with morality or, in Spooner's example, to kill the innocent third party. The receiver of his friend's weapon could certainly not ever justify *keeping* his promise to his neighbor to kill the third party. Suppose, nevertheless, that he does keep his promise and shoots the third party dead with the weapon given him for that purpose by his neighbor. "I hated having to kill him," he might say, "but if I had saved him instead, that would have been to break my promise,

and I couldn't do *that!*" The abiding message of this analogy is that duties to keep one's promises don't *always and necessarily* take precedence over the prima facie duties with which they may conflict.

In Closing: A Friendly Philosophical Dialogue

Do we need a conception of natural law to do justice to the claims that morality makes on legislators and judges? William James once wrote that "Every difference must make a difference."[28] That is to say that, if two theories are distinct in meaning, it must be because there is at least some conceivable difference it would make to our experience if one, but not the other, were true. Alternatively, if some single theory has a sense to it, that sense must be the difference we can imagine for our experience if the theory happened to be true. Whether that pragmatic theory of meaning is correct is a technical question well beyond the scope of this paper. But its full adequacy aside, the theory can provide useful assistance to our understanding of a philosophical proposition. It advises us simply to look for the difference it would make in our lives if the proposition were true and creates a presumption at least that, if its truth would make no practical difference, then there is really no theoretical difference either, between its being true and its being false.

More precisely, our questions are these: "Does morality have to pretend to be literally a part of law in order for it to perform its function as protector of human interests and ground of political obligations?" "Does it really matter to any of our practical purposes and values whether we think of morality as inside, or outside, or both inside and outside our legal codes?" We saw earlier that we expect jural laws of a variety of kinds to impose moral obligations on the citizens who are subject to them. The criminal code, for example, imposes obligations of obedience on everybody, whereas the rules defining public offices–– either relatively permanent, like the office of judge, or relatively temporary, like the office of juror—impose moral obligations only on their occupants. In addition, the making of promises and the swearing of oaths are legal mechanisms for generating official duties. In the same way, ordinary promises between citizens generate ordinary moral obligations between them, whether enforceable by the state or not. Likewise, social roles, both when filled voluntarily (like that of husband or wife) and even when filled involuntarily (like that of daughter or son), are recognized generators of moral obligation. Our classification approaches completeness when we add mention of informal social roles (like that of neighbor) and private institutional roles, offices, or jobs (like that defined by the duties of a janitor or the duties of a chief executive officer in a private corporation). All of these duties are or can be moral duties—both those generated by private rules and procedures, informal or institutional, and those derived from legal rules, both those that apply to all citizens alike and those that impose the moral obligations of public officials and are peculiar to them.

Earlier I discussed the moral obligations normally imposed by a legal system, at least in a democratic, more or less just country, on all citizens. Sometimes particular statutes in such a system are extremely unjust or even irrational ("crazy," as we say), and questions arise whether our normal obligation to obey *any* valid law is weakened or even dissolved in this case. For a judge presiding over a trial of a citizen for violating such a "law," the problem to be dealt with is one of judicial *duty*. Does the normal duty as a judge, to apply the law as it is written, get weakened or suspended in the case at bar because of the immoral content of the governing statute? For the defendant, a private citizen occupying no judicial office, the problem is, or was, one of private conscience. The statute the defendant deliberately violated was so utterly wicked, she didn't think it could possibly have any obligatory force. Moreover, she could not act as the law seemed to enjoin her to act, without a severe crisis of conscience.

Suppose, for example, that the statute defines a capital offense—perhaps not an act so utterly trivial as stealing a turnip, but close. It forbids any derogatory oral statement about the country's political leader, on pain of death, and requires the persons overhearing such a statement to inform the police. If they fail to do so, they are subject to life imprisonment at hard labor. Moreover, the conscience-stricken citizen has learned that the law was not debated in her country's parliament but only given a unanimous rubber-stamp approval ordered secretly by the country's leader. The parliamentary approval was intended to place an ex post facto veneer of legality over the punishment of a dissident, which had occurred a few days earlier. The legal system is now obviously breaking down and has reached the point where Lon Fuller is prepared to pronounce it nearly dead.

The positivistic H.L.A. Hart concluded about this only partly fictitious case that the law deliberately broken by the conscientious citizen was indeed a valid statute in the legal system (if that system still existed), having been duly enacted by an elected legislature in accordance with the procedure prescribed by the country's unamended ancient constitution. Nevertheless, he found it so extremely wicked that his conscience too would forbid him from obeying it. As a legal philosopher, he would admit that the offending law was valid; as a moral philosopher, he would deny that he was under a moral obligation, all things considered, to obey it, since the moral obligation of obedience normally generated by a valid law was not produced in this case.

On the other side, Lon Fuller, in the position of the conscientious citizen, would also have disobeyed, but he would have denied that he had broken a valid law in any operative legal system. When the content of a rule is that wicked, cruel, and unjust and the methods of generating it so corrupt, then it is no legal rule at all, but only a pretender to legal status. And since it was not a valid legal rule and/or the legal system of which it might have been a part hardly exists any more, of course it does not generate a duty derived from the general capacity of valid law to generate moral obligations of obedience. Ergo, Fuller would conclude, he was under no obligation to obey.

And so Hart and Fuller, for all their philosophical quarreling, would be allies in the political arena and perhaps cell mates in the same prison. Is there really any actual difference between their philosophies, then? Do we have an answer to Lloyd Weinreb, who wonders what possible difference it makes whether we describe the moral situation in Nazi Germany as Fuller did (no legal system, no obligation of obedience) or as Hart did (a valid law but too evil to obey)?

I think we can say that, if there is an important theoretical difference between these two positions, it is not because of any important practical difference they yield. The ruthless dictator, after all, would have them both butchered. As we have seen, Hart did claim a small advantage for his position in what he called the merit of candor. As he reconstructs the practical reasoning of two dissidents, one a legal positivist and the other a natural law theorist, the positivist would tally up the score in such a way that disobedience would have a huge balance over obedience but not a complete shutout. The score might be 9 to 1 (these numbers, of course, are not to be taken seriously), but that one point would register on any sensitive conscience, since it is the minimal force that comes from the recognition of a valid law. For the positivist there is a conflict of prima facie obligations: the PFO of obedience to valid law (here represented as weakly as possible) versus the PFOs (all of them here at maximal strength) to oppose injustice, to prevent suffering, to speak truth, and more. It is a one-sided conflict, Hart would say, but a conflict for all that, and to characterize it in that fashion is to exercise the virtue of candor. Fuller, on the other side, would tally the score as 10 to 0 against obedience. For him there was no conflict at all, since all the relevant PFOs spoke with one voice, and there was no valid law involved that might bring the moral duty of fidelity to law into play.

I conclude, then, that the famous differences between the positivist and the natural law theorist on the question of the private citizen's moral obligation to obey the law do not amount to much. But I am reluctant to draw the further inference, without some caution, that the difference between legal positivism and natural law theory, as *general* accounts of the relation between law and morality, don't come to much. I don't wish to be hasty and skeptical about that, not after studying the way those called positivists and those called natural law theorists divided over the vital political issue of fugitive slave laws that, in the end, split the country and exploded into a bloody conflagration.

There is at least one possibly significant way in which the Hart–Fuller problem, inspired by the historical record of the Nazi government of Germany and the fugitive slave issue of the shaky American union between the Revolution and Civil War, can be shown to make a difference. In our example from Fuller and Hart, we are concerned with the moral obligations people had *as private citizens* to obey the law. In the example from the Civil War period, we are dealing with the moral obligations that one class of public officials (appellate judges) had to interpret and apply laws that others had written. Let us explore, then, how the *judge's* moral obligations might be importantly different depending on whether he is a positivist or a natural law theorist.

This time let us consider how a fictitious Supreme Court judge, who happens to be a theorist of natural law (NL), might have debated that matter with a time-traveling judge from the twentieth century, who happens to be a legal positivist (LP).

LP: Surely it is as clear as it ever is in law that the Fugitive Slave Acts are valid law, whatever reservations we have about their content. The question of legal validity in America is settled by reference to the Constitution, and that document, our ultimate "rule of recognition," goes out of its way, in Article IV, to recognize the legitimacy of human slavery, and it very explicitly requires that escaped slaves "shall be delivered up" on claim of their masters.

NL: We both know that the reason why this statement was included in the Constitution is that it was part of the original bargain that induced the slave states to join the Union in the first place. But, in any complete and accurate consideration of a judge's moral obligations when an appeal of the fugitive or his rescuer comes before him, that can hardly be the end of the matter. You and your colleagues have within your collective power the fate not just of this one wretched human being— sick, undernourished, and devastated psychologically, and subject to who knows how many fierce beatings upon return—but also, in virtue of precedents, thousands more who will follow.

LP: I sincerely and deeply regret that my actions may have those terrible results. You know that I hate the institution of human chattel slavery just as much as you do, and I have opposed it just as long, and just as strenuously, as you have. But I don't see how I have any choice in the matter. I didn't make that loathsome law nor do I have the power to change it. My job is simply to apply the law as it is, indeed, as others have written it. I may have political convictions *as a private citizen* about the moral merits or demerits of the laws I am to apply, but my duty *as a judge* is to determine what the law is, not what it ought to be. In short, I am here to make strictly legal judgments. Moral judgments are for others, and I am sworn to put them aside.

NL: But I insist that you cannot separate law and morality in that facile and complacent fashion. Certain minimal conditions of reasonableness and fairness must be presumed to be a part, usually an unwritten implicit part, of any valid law. Cicero said that and so did Augustine, Aquinas, and the leading writers of our own revolutionary period. And surely our own Constitution is full of testimony to the natural rights of man and the moral foundation of all legitimate government. The fugitive slave clause flies in the teeth of all that. Its presence in the Constitution renders that document incoherent and contradictory. There cannot be an ultimate source of positive law, as our Constitution claims to be, whose parts are mutually contradictory. When all but one part of the document affirms human rights to freedom, equality, autonomy, and the means to happiness, and one specific part explicitly denies those rights, then clearly the only reasonable way to restore coherence is to invalidate that one clashing part.

LP: Good heavens, look at what you are saying! You say that the fugitive slave clause conflicts with morality, human rights, and justice. But even if that were so, it would not follow that it is not valid law! Are you suggesting that a part of the Constitution itself could be unconstitutional? Look who is talking about inconsistency and contradiction!

NL: No, it makes no sense to say that the Constitution, or one of its parts, could be unconstitutional. But the Constitution could suffer a kind of disability analogous to unconstitutionality. It could conflict sharply with a basic principle of morality—a principle of justice, or equality, or humaneness, or autonomy.

LP: I agree that there are certain abstract principles of morality that, despite their appearance as vacuous and imprecise—or perhaps because of it—are objective truths endorsed by a large and confident consensus. Justice, for example, excludes arbitrary inequalities. We can all agree on *that* precept, provided it is kept abstract. There will be more disagreements when we try to decide whether a given inequality *is* arbitrary or when a dissimilarity—say, in skin color—is relevant as a ground for dissimilar or unequal treatment. I concede further that there is some reason to be optimistic about the possibility of strong consensus even about those more determinate derivative moral judgments. But my main point is that my duty as a judge, to which I was solemnly sworn, is to interpret and apply only what is internal to the law. We both have the highest respect for morality, even perhaps as much as for law. But morality is something outside of law, and I am only to consider what is inside law, so to speak.

NL: Well that seems to be the nub of the disagreement between us. I am strongly inclined to say that the basic principles of justice, for example, have a home within every actual legal system, or a kind of implicit presence in the interstices of every legal statute, in effect putting a limit on how far that statute can drift away from justice without losing the character of legality. The Fugitive Slave Acts, I should say, are about as far from conformity with that internal justice requirement as it is possible to get. You need not fear violating your judicial duty

by declaring them, because of their extreme immorality, null and void as law.

LP: Would that it were that simple! What can it mean for a moral principle to be "part" of a legal rule? Or for morality to be "implicit in the interstices" of law? This smacks of obscurantism. Normally, law and morality are understood as contrasting. Law is law and morality is morality. You would convert a generic distinction into one between a genus and one of its own species. Instead of morality having a character different enough from law's to disqualify it as something properly called law, you juggle the terms about so that morality suddenly becomes a species of law rather than a contrasting genus. And not only is morality itself a kind of law, even a part of a system of positive law, it now becomes a *higher* kind of law, or a test of what else can be or not be law. Why don't we simply say, with Bishop Butler,[29] that "a thing is what it is and not another thing" and add that a system of law that fails to measure up to the standards of morality is a pretty lousy system of law?

NL: But still law?

LP: Yes, still law.

NL: Would you then have decided cases in 1850 in such a way that certain northern states would be prevented from declaring a fugitive slave to be a free citizen and welcoming him or her to permanent residence?

LP: I couldn't say now. Your question is too hypothetical.

NL: But can you think of *any* circumstances in which your legal philosophy would permit you to decide a case in accordance with the abstract principles of justice instead of the plain meaning of the terms in which the governing rule is stated?

LP: Maybe my legal philosophy is not where we should turn. Try my moral philosophy instead. I might have no doubt at all what my duty as a judge requires of me. But as a full human being, not just a judge, I may be so appalled morally at what my legal duty requires that my conscience will tell me not to do my judicial duty.

NL: Give me an example other than the fugitive slave example.

LP: Well, this is a bit fanciful, but suppose that back in the days before women had the franchise (back in your time) somebody introduced a bill, in the usual way, on the floor of a state legislature. Imagine that a quorum of legislators were in attendance, in accordance with the state's constitutional requirement for valid lawmaking, and they astonish the world by passing the bill into law. The bill legalizes rape in that state. I would not hesitate to judge that a valid law had just been created, but I would be prepared, as the morally sensitive human being I am, to throttle personally any young scoundrel I would see who was attempting a legal rape. I wouldn't care that his behavior was legal. I would beat the hell out of him anyway.

NL: But judge, you are now talking about your duties, liberties, and liabilities as an ordinary private citizen. What I want to know is whether you would discharge your judicial duty (as you see it) to uphold this law the first time the question of its constitutionality arises or whether, in the same spirit as that manifested in your attack on the scoundrel in the other example, you would vote to invalidate the statute because of its conflict with justice and morality?

LP: Well, maybe I would declare it invalid for the reason you mention, but if I did that I might want to conceal what my real reason was. I don't want the world to think that I would shrink from my duty for the wrong kind of reason. There would probably be something in the state constitution I could cite as conflicting with the statute, thus entailing its unconstitutionality. Its injustice and immorality needn't be mentioned.

NL: If you *were* to refer to the statute's injustice or inhumanity, would you be going outside of the law for your justification?

LP: Yes, I would. I think the conceptual distinction between law and morality is too useful to undermine as you keep trying to do. But as I said before, I might nevertheless choose to go outside the law in violation of my legal duty, because when I take into account all the prima facie obligations (PFOs) that I am subject to as a human being, my judicial duty (which is also one of my moral duties) may be outbalanced by the other PFOs that have a bearing in those circumstances on my decision.

NL: Your reasoning, then, is precisely parallel to that of H.L.A. Hart in his discussion of the moral duties of ordinary citizens when confronted with extremely unjust laws that they know, in addition, to be the work of thoroughly corrupt legislatures. In both examples, we are dealing with the problem of determining our resultant bottom-line duties as human beings when there is conflict among the various PFOs to which we are subject, including

the very special and stringent PFOs of a public official generated in part by the solemn promises of office. Does the fact that the deliberating individual in the second example is a *judge,* with an additional kind of duty to throw on the deliberative scales, make no difference then? Or is there no real difference between the positions of the natural law theorist and the legal positivist in respect to their judgments about the duties of judges?

LP: I would say that there is some difference but perhaps not as much as I thought before this discussion. What confuses or troubles me most is the abundance of distinctions among types of duty that this discussion generates. Assume that we are discussing purely moral philosophy and our question is of quite the same kind as if we asked whether in some hypothetical case a person should do his or her moral duty (PFO) to tell the truth and thereby violate in those unusual circumstances the duty (PFO) to keep a promise. In that event, we may be talking about moral duties that do not come from the definition of some role, station, or office. The conflicting PFOs are PFOs to which the person is subject simply as a human being. In deciding, he will have to weigh, so to speak, these PFOs against one another and then be moved in the direction of the weightier one. One PFO may outweigh (or "outscore," to use our earlier sports metaphor) the other by an overwhelming amount (a score of 10 to 1 or 9 to 1, as in the earlier example) or the score may be close—perhaps 5 to 4 or 4 to 5, as in the fugitive slave dilemma.

Perhaps, in the majority of cases where the decision to be made has this form, at least one of the contending PFOs will derive from the definition of a social role or a job assignment or office occupied by the decision maker, but even then the role or office duty will be just one among the several that have relevance to the decision. Some PFOs will derive from very general and ill-defined roles we all have, for example, the role of citizen. In the Nazi example debated by Fuller and Hart, these two eminent legal philosophers agreed that the PFOs they had *as citizens* to obey the law were outweighed by far by other PFOs they had, perhaps also as citizens, to oppose social injustice. The bottom-line duty,[30] as you called it, is by definition the PFO that carries the day. Adjusting this terminology to fit our moral priorities is a very difficult and even dangerous thing. It is dangerous because it may lead us to overlook the way our terminology can commit us to positions that we do not hold, positions whose truth or falsity, before argument, should be open questions. Thus we can think of the duty that "carries the day" as being identical by definition with a duty we have as human beings, not merely as role players or job or office holders. But that begs the question in favor of a controversial substantive position—namely, that when role and office duties clash with more general nonrole and nonoffice duties, the latter must *always* win out. A person's duty as a judge, for example, can never be as weighty as a clashing duty that he or she has quite apart from any role, relation, or job, or any promise already made. More confusion can result if we think of the winning duty as the one we will *call* our duty as human beings. Then, if on argumentative or intuitive grounds, we find that a competing PFO, which we have as role or office occupants, seems weightier, we will have to call *that* duty the duty we have as human beings. This result undermines our original distinction.

  We also have available, as a way of referring to the bottom-line duty, the term *conscientious duty*. That is a term commonly reserved, I suspect, for the bottom-line winner, because it seems odd that a lesser PFO could outweigh a PFO of conscience. After all, it is conscience that "sits on the throne." But if in fact a role duty *can* outweigh a stringent nonrole duty in certain circumstances, and that is at least a genuine possibility, then, I suppose, we should have to say "Ignore your conscience and do your role duty instead." But that sounds so cynical, even if inadvertently so, that we should probably avoid that usage. But suppose we define *conscientious duty* as the duty that is the weightiest of the competing duties before us. Then, when the duty that seems intuitively to win out is a role duty, we would have to call *it* the voice of conscience, and the distinction between conscientious duties and role duties is undermined. It would be better in advance of argument not to identify the bottom-line duty (the one that carries the day), by definition, with any other category.

  [Pausing for breath] Wow, these things are complicated! Am I still on the right track?

NL: Yes, I think so. You have already made enough distinctions to cover the Hart–Fuller case. There the personal moral decision of the citizen was to

overrule the individual's PFO to obey the valid laws of the community, and do instead the PFO (also as a citizen? more likely, simply as a human being) to oppose injustice, particularly political injustice. Now what further distinction must we make, I wonder, to apply to the PFOs of the *judge* in our two examples? Consider (1) the historical example of the fugitive slave cases and (2) your strange example of the legalization of rape.

LP: In the judicial cases, we simply have the possibility of new PFOs that are present only when the moral deliberator is a judge. The judge must deliberate on two levels. The first is entirely legal. He or she must look inside the law for rules, statutes, precedents, and the other appropriate legal data that might enable a judicial decision. But the judge is not a mere computer. First of all, before a judge is ever a judge, he or she is a human being made of flesh and blood, not merely of computer chips, and subject to many more PFOs than simply that of the job of judge. Normally his or her PFOs as judge are extremely stringent and the opposing PFOs on the scale are greatly outweighed, so that deliberation is quick and easy. But normally the judge doesn't have to put the evil of human slavery or of rape on the scales at all. But in this case the comparative "weight measurement" is extremely close. After hours of weighing and reweighing, the judge sees that the more stringent PFO is not the duty as a judge but instead the duty as a human being.

NL: Now we are precisely at the point where a difference will appear, if it is to appear at all. What should the human being–judge do at this point, and how can he do it? His counterpart in the private citizen example at this point omits legal duty—the legal duty, say, to inform on a neighbor or a spouse. The private citizen leaves town without an exit permit. He or she writes a farewell letter that condemns the country's political leader, then sends a copy to a newspaper for publication as a letter to the editor. The citizen fires shots at policemen when they are trying to arrest a known dissident; joins the underground resistance; and renounces once and for all, as in a declaration of war, the PFO to obey the laws of the government. The judge could well be a natural law theorist (like me or Lon Fuller) who denies that the citizen is breaking a law at all through all these rebellious activities, since there are no laws to break. That makes it extremely easy. But a colleague of this judge could just as well be a legal positivist like you or H.L.A. Hart, in disagreement with the judge over whether the citizen is breaking a law but morally bound to behavior no different from that of the other judge. So far, their philosophical differences make no difference to their conduct.

When the human being–judge decides that his PFOs to resist injustice, which he has as a human being, outweigh the PFO that derives from the definition of his job, even when the latter is reinforced by his PFO to keep his promises and honor his oaths, what does he do? Here the parallel with the case of the private citizen begins to break down. The judge can overrule the actions of a lower court in judging the appeal before him, even though the opposite course appeared clearly to be the legally correct one. But the judge cannot do that secretly, so that nobody notices it, and then sneak out of town like a common criminal. He must stand up in a public forum and declare his conclusion and the legal reasons supporting it. In effect, he will be either presenting arguments that support a conclusion other than the one he declares to be correct or (equivalently) arguing, not really for the course that it is his duty as judge to certify, but rather for the course that it is his moral duty as citizen perhaps, but more likely *as* human being, to do. After that, he can avoid the hubbub by resigning his judgeship, but that would probably be a self-defeating thing to do, since he would be replaced by a more reliably "dutiful" judge, who in time would find a way to undo whatever he had achieved.

Now if the judge were a legal positivist, he would find it impossible to give a straightforward legal argument for the conclusion his conscience would have him declare. He would have to admit that a judge can only refer to matters internal to the law in arguing for a legal conclusion and that, by his lights, questions about justice and injustice are external to the law and therefore may not be considered. That leaves him only the option of giving all the arguments that support his bottom-line duty as a human being and violating his duty as a judge. If he is candid, then, he must in effect tell the world that he did not reach the judgment that it was his duty as a judge to reach, but rather the judgment imposed on him by his conscience. That would be almost as shocking as a confession of a crime. Your fellow legal positivists would lead the chase, denouncing as usurpation any judge's claim that he has discretion to appeal to wider considerations to settle a question of law. In the period before the American Civil War, Great Britain's Lord Camden was often quoted: "The discretion of a judge is the law of tyrants. . . . [At] its best it is often-times caprice—[at] its worst, it is every vice, folly, and passion to which human nature is liable." I think that, if the positivists knew more people like *you,* they would be less unwilling to confer on a judge the discretion to appeal to natural justice in arguments. But as this quotation shows, it was not that most of them disparaged justice. It was rather that most of them distrusted *people,* especially people in positions of power, like judges.

LP: Perhaps the only legitimate course for the judge in hard cases of the sort we have been considering, in effect, is to *cheat,* paradoxical though that would be. If I were a judge in one of the fugitive slave appeals, I could try to present as plausible an argument as I could find for invalidating the bloody clause without once mentioning such external factors as its natural injustice, arbitrariness, inhumanity, and so on. I could say that the recognition of slavery was at odds with the whole drift of the Constitution and the other foundational documents of our government. I could show the banner of states rights (a huge irony in 1860) and deny the power of the federal government to prevent individual (northern) states from holding fugitives until their lot could be determined by the state's own rules of due process, including the trial by jury guaranteed by the federal Constitution. I could try all those gambits, but it would be a heroic, uphill, losing fight. After all, good friend, the damned bloody clause in Article IV came right out and said that fugitive slaves must be "delivered up" as soon as an authenticated representative of their owner made claim to them. There is simply no way around that, even for so wily a lawyer as me.

Anyway, even if my cleverness enabled me to make some sort of standard argument for the morally preferable outcome, albeit a hopelessly unpersuasive one, that would simply help to gum up the law and create tricky precedents of the kind that any self-respecting positivist would abhor. So the position of the morally conscientious legal positivist judge in these examples is an unenviable one. Would the morally conscientious judge who is an advocate of natural law theory be in any better a position?

NL: Well, I for one, would be much better off. In my theory, when I appeal to natural justice, I am appealing to something internal to the law. I do not have to concede, as you would, that contrary to my oath I am going outside the law for considerations that will support my legal conclusions. And in response to those who will accuse me of substituting merely my own opinions about morality and justice, subjective and ungrounded as they are thought to be, for the straightforward and objective dictates of the law, I can cite a dazzling array of authorities—from Cicero, Aquinas, and Blackstone, down to Jefferson, and in our own time Lincoln—for the proposition that the principles of justice are objective and rooted securely in the nature of things, independent of anyone's mere opinion. It would be hard to pin the label *moral crackpot* on me or my mere opinions, so long as I am in *that* company.

LP: There is a subtle point, I think, about a source of discomfort that would apply as well to the natural law theorist as to the positivist in their roles as judges. There is something essentially *public* about the judge's reasons for acting. The judge's reasons, even those that he might give for what is essentially an act of judicial nullification, become a part of the official record, where they remain forever in a position to influence the future course of the law. The judge is an official spokesman for the state; there is something impersonal about that arrangement that makes it peculiarly jolting for a judge to introduce predominately autobiographical materials into his reasonings about the validity of laws, for example. And that is just what is done by the judge, whether he be a positivist or a natural law partisan, when he states and defends a position about his own duties, not as a judge, but as a human being.

In this respect the judge's dilemmas that we have been considering differ from both the moral dilemmas of the ordinary citizen as citizen or as human being, on the one hand, and that of other officials, like jurors, on the other. The juror, for example, makes nothing public but her verdict. She is not required to give her reasons even for that. Her defiant act of jury nullification, if any, is done in secret, and its reasons and supporting argument become part of no record. Moreover, the juror, in theory, decides only about the facts. She is in no position, therefore, to influence the future course of law. And in no sense does she speak for the state.

I must admit at this point that the only place where one's stand on the positivism–natural law

controversy seems to have practical effects is the situation in which the philosophers are also judges and they have good reason to find their personal, moral duties as human beings even more stringent than their sworn duties as judges when those duties are weighed on the scales of conscience, all things considered. The main practical difference made in these circumstances by one's philosophical stance seems to be to the disadvantage of my allies, the legal positivists. Their position, as we said, is more uncomfortable than that of their natural law counterparts. Comfort, to be sure, is much to be preferred to discomfort. But isn't there a limit to the relevance of such a consideration when we come to evaluate theories as true or false? Is there not even a limit to the relevance of discomfort to a determination of whether the two theories really have *differences* in their morally important consequences?

I am glad that we had this chat, even though we are a long way from resolution of the problems that engage us. I must confess that you have made natural law theory a good deal more plausible than I ever believed it was. But I can hardly accept it at this stage of our discussions, for I must first be led to understand one of the tenets that is both obscure and central to natural law theory: namely, the notion that moral principles are a part of, or identical with, or essentially connected to, legal rules or are themselves legal rules of a special implicit kind; or that as "higher law" they are part and parcel of every legal system, capable of invalidating any other legal rules whose content conflicts with their own; or that they fill the interstices of all legal systems, and similar claims. If you could explain how morality got into the law in the first place or what it can mean to say that its necessary presence within every legal system is conceptually entailed by the very idea of law, I would be more friendly to your view. The consequences of natural law theory in courts of law have often been benign, but until these notions are clarified, I am unwilling to accept the theory as true.

NL: I too enjoyed our philosophic exchange, but we must get together again soon to continue our discussion right where you left it. In the meantime, permit me also a moment of politeness. You have succeeded in puzzling me about my own theory, and if only to that extent, leading me to have more respect for legal positivism. But if I too am a bit uncertain what it means to assert that deep and fundamental moral principles are implicitly a part of every legal system, simply as a definitional truth like "All true laws are promulgated" or "Secret laws are not true laws," I am much less puzzled about what it means to *advocate* or *recommend* that some moral precepts be acknowledged as part of *our* legal system, not because of some alleged conceptual truth that ties *all* legal systems to certain moral precepts necessarily, but rather because such a measure would promote both justice and efficiency, and that is reason enough. You ask how morality got into the law. Part of the answer to that question, especially in respect to the minimal requirements of fairness and reasonableness, is that *we put it there*. If it seems not to be there at all in our legal system, then our legislators ought to put it there.

LP: But I'm not sure that our suspicious legislators would be very enthusiastic about that suggestion! They are happy to give lip service to such glittering ideas as justice and morality, but when it comes to practical action, they would probably let us down.

NL: We would have a better chance if we emphasized that it is only a bare minimal morality that we would put into law. We ask only that they agree that there is (or should be) a limit to how crazy, mean, cruel, or senseless a law (or legal interpretation) can be. To my mind, the natural law theory, which assures us that morality is already in law, is most persuasive when it is the relatively noncontroversial minimal morality we are talking about. Then I can say something that strikes your ear as obscure and rhapsodical—that morality is just naturally there growing like flowers on a bed of law—and say this while confident that I can get even good legal positivists like yourself to join our efforts to *make* this true, even if it is not already true by nature.

LP: What, then, do you propose, you compromised former natural law theorist?

NL: It's very simple. I would have moral principles (at first very abstract and not very controversial ones) made quite explicit, perhaps in an asterisked endnote at the bottom of the page on which every bill of legislation and every enacted statute is printed, just as the words "We are an equal opportunity employer," or words to that effect, now appear on the official stationery of many universities. At first, the explicit statement should be quite minimal, ruling out only extremely unjust and irrational rules, judgments, verdicts, and sentences. Once it is understood that there *is* such a super-rule or higher law, in our system, the way is open for courts to find some laws to be invalid for no other reason than their conflict with (those) principles of justice. It would have to be heavily emphasized, of course, that simple unfairness and commonplace unreasonableness are not enough, that only transparently flawed legislation could be invalidated in this fashion: flagrant, gross, and outrageous injustice, and utterly crazy pointless unreasonableness. Anyone who has made even a casual perusal of casebooks knows, however, that such flagrant flaws are frequently found in the arguments of prosecutors, judges, and others. And to the objection that this procedure would give too much power to judges, who in turn would use their new discretion in capricious ways, I would reply by pointing to the other places in the law where judges are invited to apply their own standards to determine what is substantial, reasonable, excessive, cruel, fitting, appropriate, due, and other such predicates. A legal system in the modern world could hardly get along without such open-textured and essentially contested terms and the discretion they bring with them. My proposal would only empower courts to filter out the most extreme unreasonableness and unfairness from our laws, without giving discretion to judges to enter into the deeper questions of justice on their own, without controls. And legal philosophers need no longer be puzzled about what it means to say that moral precepts are a part of our legal system (if not all other legal systems). They need only look at the printed message at the bottom of the page.

---

1. Aristotle, Nicomachean Ethics, *1131 a 32–3 (paraphrased)*.

2. *Some purists might insist that Shakespeare's* Othello *requires that Desdemona be white and Othello black and that a black actress and a white actor in those roles would distract an audience into missing a good deal of the dramatic clash that Shakespeare was trying to exploit. A more reasonable view now, however, is that audiences can be expected not to be distracted by so very irrelevant a thing as skin color and therefore can be relied upon to provide their own appropriate projection of historic setting. One must admit, however, that a switch in gender might overtax an audience's imaginative resources.*

3. People v. Johnson *(1967) 52 Misc 2d 1087, 278 NYS 2d 80.*

4. *The quotation is from Lynn C. Cobb, "Annotation, Validity of State or Local Regulation Dealing with Resale of Tickets to Theat*

rical or Sporting Events," American Law Reports, 3d, Cases and Annotations, *vol. 81 (1977), p. 672.4.*

5. *Ronald Dworkin, "Hard Cases" in* Taking Rights Seriously *(Cambridge, Mass.: Harvard University Press, 1971).*

6. *For a critique of judicial activism, see Robert H. Bork,* The Tempting of America *(New York: Free Press, 1990).*

7. *Compare John Rawls,* A Theory of Justice *(Cambridge, Mass.: Harvard University Press, 1971), pp. 54–117, and J. S. Mill,* Utilitarianism *(1861), chap. 1.*

8. *Sir William Blackstone,* Commentaries on the Laws of England, *vol. 1 (Chicago: University of Chicago Press, 1979), p. 40.*

9. *See Joel Feinberg,* Harm to Self *(New York: Oxford University Press, 1986), pp. 87–94, on the differences between privacy, in the ordinary sense, and autonomy, or self-determination.*

10. *That occasions for "Solomonic wisdom" still exist is shown by recent well-publicized cases in the United States of hospital-switched babies later suing for "divorce" from their biological parents.*

11. *Blackstone,* op. cit. *(see note 8), 1:70.*

12. *See Robert M. Cover,* Justice Accused: Antislavery and the Judicial Process *(New Haven, Conn.: Yale University Press, 1975), p. 62: "The court can assert a sort of bend-over-backward principle by which there is an obligation to achieve a profreedom (antislavery) result unless there is a very specific, concrete positive law that prevents it."*

13. *R. Dworkin, "The Model of Rules" in* Taking Rights Seriously *(Cambridge, Mass.: Harvard University Press, 1977). In his interesting discussion of the distinction between legal rules and legal principles, Dworkin treats* stare decisis *as an example of a conservative principle.*

14. *Lon L. Fuller,* The Morality of Law *(New Haven, Conn.: Yale University Press, 1964), pp. 33–38.*

15. *Lloyd L. Weinreb,* Natural Law and Justice *(Cambridge, Mass.: Harvard University Press, 1987), p. 4.*

16. *Exceptions to this consensus include Rolf Sartorius,* Individual Conduct and Social Norms *(Belmont, Calif.: Wadsworth, 1975); A. John Simmons,* Moral Principles and Political Obligations *(Princeton: Princeton University Press, 1979); M.B.E. Smith, "Is There a Prima Facie Obligation to Obey the Law?"* Yale Law Journal *82 (1973); and Joel Feinberg, "Civil Disobedience in the Modern World," this book, pp. 000–000.*

17. *PFOs are explained and discussed in greater detail in Feinberg, supra, pp. 000–000.*

18. *Mortimer and Sanford Kadish,* Discretion to Disobey *(Palo Alto, California: Stanford University Press, 1973), pp. 27–28.*

19. *Cover,* op. cit. *(see note 12), pp. 151 ff.*

20. *Cover,* Ibid., *p. 171.*

21. *Ibid., p. 6.*

22. *Loc. Cit.*

23. *Francis Lieber,* Political Ethics, *2nd ed. (Philadelphia: Lippincott, 1875), I: 344, as quoted by Cover,* op. cit., *p. 147.*

24. *Cover, see note 12.*

25. *Wendell Phillips,* The Constitution: A Pro-Slavery Compact, *quoted by Cover,* op. cit., *pp. 153, 178.*

26. *Cover,* op. cit., *p. 158.*

27. *Lysander Spooner,* The Unconstitutionality of Slavery, *quoted by Cover,* loc. cit.

28. *William James, "What Pragmatism Means" in* Essays in Pragmatism *(New York: Hafner Publishing, 1948), p. 144.*

29. *Joseph Butler, Bishop of Durham, 1662–1752. I do not know the exact source.*

30. *There are at least six phrases we can use to give definition to the PFO that wins out in the competition, in some specific set of circumstances, with other PFOs that are less weighty in those circumstances. We can refer to (1) a resultant (as opposed to a component) duty; (2) a bottom-line duty; (3) an "all things considered" duty; (4) (the term used by W. P. Ross) the duty sans phrase, or the duty without the qualifying phrase* prima facie; *(5) the duty that trumps; or (6) the duty that carries the day.*

The Moral Obligation to Obey the Law

LETTER FROM BIRMINGHAM JAIL*

Martin Luther King, Jr.

April 16, 1963

My Dear Fellow Clergymen:

While confined here in the Birmingham city jail, I came across your recent statement calling my present activities "unwise and untimely." Seldom do I pause to answer criticism of my work and ideas. If I sought to answer all the criticisms that cross my desk, my secretaries would have little time for anything other than such correspondence in the course of the day, and I would have no time for constructive work. But since I feel that you are men of genuine good will and that your criticisms are sincerely set forth, I want to try to answer your statement in what I hope will be patient and reasonable terms.

I think I should indicate why I am here in Birmingham, since you have been influenced by the view which argues against "outsiders coming in." I have the honor of serving as president of the Southern Christian Leadership Conference, an organization operating in every southern state, with headquarters in Atlanta, Georgia. We have some eighty-five affiliated organizations across the South, and one of them is the Alabama Christian Movement for Human Rights. Frequently we share staff, educational and financial resources with our affiliates. Several months ago the affiliate here in Birmingham asked us to be on call to engage in a nonviolent direct-action program if such were deemed necessary. We readily consented, and when the hour came we lived up to our promise. So I, along with several members of my staff, am here because I was invited here. I am here because I have organizational ties here.

But more basically, I am in Birmingham because injustice is here. Just as the prophets of the eighth century B.C. left their villages and carried their "thus saith the Lord" far beyond the boundaries of their home towns, and just as the Apostle Paul left his village of Tarsus and carried the gospel of Jesus Christ to the far corners of the Greco-Roman world, so am I compelled to carry the gospel of freedom beyond my own home town. Like Paul, I must constantly respond to the Macedonian call for aid.

Moreover, I am cognizant of the interrelatedness of all communities and states. I cannot sit idly by in Atlanta and not be concerned about what happens in Birmingham. Injustice anywhere is a threat to justice everywhere. We are caught in an inescapable network of mutuality, tied in a single garment of destiny. Whatever affects one directly, affects all indirectly. Never again can we afford to live with the narrow,

*Reprinted by arrangement with The heirs to the estate of Martin Luther King, Jr., c/o Joan Daves Agency as agent for the proprietor.

provincial "outside agitator" idea. Anyone who lives inside the United States can never be considered an outsider anywhere within its bounds.

You deplore the demonstrations taking place in Birmingham. But your statement, I am sorry to say, fails to express a similar concern for the conditions that brought about the demonstrations. I am sure that none of you would want to rest content with the superficial kind of social analysis that deals merely with effects and does not grapple with underlying causes. It is unfortunate that demonstrations are taking place in Birmingham, but it is even more unfortunate that the city's white power structure left the Negro community with no alternative.

In any nonviolent campaign there are four basic steps: collection of the facts to determine whether injustices exist; negotiation; self-purification; and direct action. We have gone through all these steps in Birmingham. There can be no gainsaying the fact that racial injustice engulfs this community. Birmingham is probably the most thoroughly segregated city in the United States. Its ugly record of brutality is widely known. Negroes have experienced grossly unjust treatment in the courts. There have been more unsolved bombings of Negro homes and churches in Birmingham than in any other city in the nation. These are the hard, brutal facts of the case. On the basis of these conditions, Negro leaders sought to negotiate with the city fathers. But the latter consistently refused to engage in good-faith negotiation.

Then, last September, came the opportunity to talk with leaders of Birmingham's economic community. In the course of the negotiations, certain promises were made by the merchants—for example, to remove the stores' humiliating racial signs. On the basis of these promises, the Reverend Fred Shuttlesworth and the leaders of the Alabama Christian Movement for Human Rights agreed to a moratorium on all demonstrations. As the weeks and months went by, we realized that we were the victims of a broken promise. A few signs, briefly removed, returned; the others remained.

As in so many past experiences, our hopes had been blasted, and the shadow of deep disappointment settled upon us. We had no alternative except to prepare for direct action, whereby we would present our very bodies as a means of laying our case before the conscience of the local and the national community. Mindful of the difficulties involved, we decided to undertake a process of self-purification. We began a series of workshops on nonviolence, and we repeatedly asked ourselves: "Are you able to accept blows without retaliating?" "Are you able to endure the ordeal of jail?" We decided to schedule our direct-action program for the Easter season, realizing that except for Christmas, this is the main shopping period of the year. Knowing that a strong economic-withdrawal program would be the by-product of direct action, we felt that this would be the best time to bring pressure to bear on the merchants for the needed change.

Then it occurred to us that Birmingham's mayoral election was coming up in March, and we speedily decided to postpone action until after election day. When we discovered that the Commissioner of Public Safety, Eugene "Bull" Connor, had piled up enough votes to be in the run-off, we decided again to postpone action until the day after the run-off so that the demonstrations could not be used to cloud the issues. Like many others, we waited to see Mr. Connor defeated, and to this end we endured postponement after postponement. Having aided in this community need, we felt that our direct-action program could be delayed no longer.

You may well ask: "Why direct action? Why sit-ins, marches and so forth? Isn't negotiation a better path?" You are quite right in calling for negotiation. Indeed, this is the very purpose of direct action. Nonviolent direct action seeks to create such a crisis and foster such a tension that a community which has constantly refused to negotiate is forced to confront the issue. It seeks so to dramatize the issue that it can no longer be ignored. My citing the creation of tension as part of the work of the nonviolent-resister may sound rather shocking. But I must confess that I am not afraid of the word "tension." I have earnestly opposed violent tension, but there is a type of constructive, nonviolent tension which is necessary for growth. Just as Socrates felt that it was necessary to create a tension in the mind so that individuals could rise from the bondage of myths and half-truths to the unfettered realm of creative analysis and objective appraisal, so must we see the need for nonviolent gadflies to create the kind of tension in society that will help men rise from the dark depths of prejudice and racism to the majestic heights of understanding and brotherhood.

The purpose of our direct-action program is to create a situation so crisis-packed that it will inevitably open the door to negotiation. I therefore concur with you in your call for negotiation. Too long has our beloved Southland been bogged down in a tragic effort to live in monologue rather than dialogue.

One of the basic points in your statement is that the action that I and my associates have taken in Birmingham is untimely. Some have asked: "Why didn't you give the new city administration time to act?" The only answer that I can give to this query is that the new Birmingham administration must be prodded about as much as the outgoing one, before it will act. We are sadly mistaken if we feel that the election of Albert Boutwell as mayor will bring the millennium to Birmingham. While Mr. Boutwell is a much more gentle person than Mr. Connor, they are both segregationists, dedicated to maintenance of the status quo. I have hope that Mr. Boutwell will be reasonable enough to see the futility of massive resistance to desegregation. But he will not see this without pressure from devotees of civil rights. My friends, I must say to you that we have not made a single gain in civil rights without determined legal and nonviolent pressure. Lamentably, it is an historical fact that privileged groups seldom give up their privileges voluntarily. Individuals may see the moral light and voluntarily give up their unjust posture; but, as Reinhold Niebuhr has reminded us, groups tend to be more immoral than individuals.

We know through painful experience that freedom is never voluntarily given by the oppressor; it must be demanded by the oppressed. Frankly, I have yet to engage in a direct-action campaign that was "well timed" in the view of those who have not suffered unduly from the disease of segregation. For years now I have heard the word "Wait!" It rings in the ear of every Negro with piercing familiarity. This "Wait" has almost always meant "Never." We must come to see, with one of our distinguished jurists, that "justice too long delayed is justice denied."

We have waited for more than 340 years for our constitutional and God-given rights. The nations of Asia and Africa are moving with jetlike speed toward gaining political independence, but we still creep at horse-and-buggy pace toward gaining a cup of coffee at a lunch counter. Perhaps it is easy for those who have never felt the stinging darts of segregation to say, "Wait." But when you have seen vicious mobs lynch your mothers and fathers at will and drown your sisters and brothers at whim; when you have seen hate-filled policemen curse, kick and even kill your black brothers and sisters; when you see the vast majority of your twenty million Negro brothers smothering in an airtight cage of poverty in the midst of an affluent society; when you suddenly find your tongue twisted and your speech stammering as you seek to explain to your six-year-old daughter why she can't go to the public amusement park that has just been advertised on television, and see tears welling up in her eyes when she is told that Funtown is closed to colored children, and see ominous clouds of inferiority beginning to form in her little mental sky, and see her beginning to distort her personality by developing an unconscious bitterness toward white people; when you have to concoct an answer for a five-year-old son who is asking: "Daddy, why do white people treat colored people so mean?"; when you take a cross-country drive and find it necessary to sleep night after night in the uncomfortable corners of your automobile because no motel will accept you; when you are humiliated day in and day out by nagging signs reading "white" and "colored"; when your first name becomes "nigger," your middle name becomes "boy" (however old you are) and your last name becomes "John," and your wife and mother are never given the respected title "Mrs."; when you are harried by day and haunted by night by the fact that you are a Negro, living constantly at tiptoe stance, never quite knowing what to expect next, and are plagued with inner fears and outer resentments; when you are forever fighting a degenerating sense of "nobodiness"—then you will understand why we find it difficult to wait. There comes a time when the cup of endurance runs over, and men are no longer willing to be plunged into the abyss of despair. I hope, sirs, you can understand our legitimate and unavoidable impatience.

You express a great deal of anxiety over our willingness to break laws. This is certainly a legitimate concern. Since we so diligently urge people to obey the Supreme Court's decision of 1954 outlawing segregation in the public schools, at first glance it may seem rather paradoxical for us consciously to break laws. One may well ask: "How can you advocate breaking some laws and obeying others?" The answer lies in the fact that there are two types of laws: just and unjust. I would be the first to advocate obeying just laws. One has not only a legal but a moral responsibility to obey just laws. Conversely, one has a moral responsibility to disobey unjust laws. I would agree with St. Augustine that "an unjust law is no law at all."

Now, what is the difference between the two? How does one determine whether a law is just or unjust? A just law is a man-made code that squares with the moral law or the law of God. An unjust law is a code that is out of harmony with the moral law. To put it in the terms of St. Thomas Aquinas: An unjust law is a human law that is not rooted in eternal and natural law. Any law that uplifts human personality is just. Any law that degrades human personality is unjust. All segregation statutes are unjust because segregation distorts the soul and damages the personality.

It gives the segregator a false sense of superiority and the segregated a false sense of inferiority. Segregation, to use the terminology of the Jewish philosopher Martin Buber, substitutes an "I-it" relationship for an "I-thou" relationship and ends up relegating persons to the status of things. Hence segregation is not only politically, economically and sociologically unsound, it is morally wrong and sinful. Paul Tillich has said that sin is separation. Is not segregation an existential expression of man's tragic separation, his awful estrangement, his terrible sinfulness? Thus it is that I can urge men to obey the 1954 decision of the Supreme Court, for it is morally right; and I can urge them to disobey segregation ordinances, for they are morally wrong.

Let us consider a more concrete example of just and unjust laws. An unjust law is a code that a numerical or power majority group compels a minority group to obey but does not make binding on itself. This is *difference* made legal. By the same token, a just law is a code that a majority compels a minority to follow and that it is willing to follow itself. This is *sameness* made legal.

Let me give another explanation. A law is unjust if it is inflicted on a minority that, as a result of being denied the right to vote, had no part in enacting or devising the law. Who can say that the legislature of Alabama which set up that state's segregation laws was democratically elected? Throughout Alabama all sorts of devious methods are used to prevent Negroes from becoming registered voters, and there are some counties in which, even though Negroes constitute a majority of the population, not a single Negro is registered. Can any law enacted under such circumstances be considered democratically structured?

Sometimes a law is just on its face and unjust in its application. For instance, I have been arrested on a charge of parading without a permit. Now, there is nothing wrong in having an ordinance which requires a permit for a parade. But such an ordinance becomes unjust when it is used to maintain segregation and to deny citizens the First-Amendment privilege of peaceful assembly and protest.

I hope you are able to see the distinction I am trying to point out. In no sense do I advocate evading or defying the law, as would the rabid segregationist. That would lead to anarchy. One who breaks an unjust law must do so openly, lovingly, and with a willingness to accept the penalty. I submit that an individual who breaks a law that conscience tells him is unjust, and who willingly accepts the penalty of imprisonment in order to arouse the conscience of the community over its injustice, is in reality expressing the highest respect for law.

Of course, there is nothing new about this kind of civil disobedience. It was evidenced sublimely in the refusal of Shadrach, Meshach and Abednego to obey the laws of Nebuchadnezzar, on the ground that a higher moral law was at stake. It was practiced superbly by the early Christians, who were willing to face hungry lions and the excruciating pain of chopping blocks rather than submit to certain unjust laws of the Roman Empire. To a degree, academic freedom is a reality today because Socrates practiced civil disobedience. In our own nation, the Boston Tea Party represented a massive act of civil disobedience.

We should never forget that everything Adolf Hitler did in Germany was "legal" and everything the Hungarian freedom fighters did in Hungary was "illegal." It was "illegal" to aid and comfort a Jew in Hitler's Germany. Even so, I am sure that, had I lived in Germany at the time, I would have aided and comforted my Jewish brothers. If today I lived in a Communist country where certain principles dear to the Christian faith are suppressed, I would openly advocate disobeying that country's antireligious laws.

I must make two honest confessions to you, my Christian and Jewish brothers. First, I must confess that over the past few years I have been gravely disappointed with the white moderate. I have almost reached the regrettable conclusion that the Negro's great stumbling block in his stride toward freedom is not the White Citizen's Counciler or the Ku Klux Klanner, but the white moderate, who is more devoted to "order" than to justice; who prefers a negative peace which is the absence of tension to a positive peace which is the presence of justice; who constantly says: "I agree with you in the goal you seek, but I cannot agree with your methods of direct action"; who paternalistically believes he can set the timetable for another man's freedom; who lives by a mythical concept of time and who constantly advises the Negro to wait for a "more convenient season." Shallow understanding from people of good will is more frustrating than absolute misunderstanding from people of ill will. Lukewarm acceptance is much more bewildering than outright rejection.

I had hoped that the white moderate would understand that law and order exist for the purpose of establishing justice and that when they fail in this purpose they become the dangerously structured dams that block the flow of social progress. I had hoped that the white moderate would understand that the present tension in the South is a necessary phase of the transition from an obnoxious negative peace, in which the Negro passively accepted his unjust plight, to a substantive and positive peace, in which all men will respect the dignity and worth of human personality. Actually, we who engage in nonviolent direct action are not the creators of tension. We merely bring to the surface the hidden tension that is already alive. We bring it out in the open, where it can be seen and dealt with. Like a boil that can never be cured so long as it is covered up but must be opened with all its ugliness to the natural medicines of air and light, injustice must be exposed, with all the tension its exposure creates, to the light of human conscience and the air of national opinion before it can be cured.

In your statement you assert that our actions, even though peaceful, must be condemned because they precipitate violence. But is this a logical assertion? Isn't this like condemning a robbed man because his possession of money precipitated the evil act of robbery? Isn't this like condemning Socrates because his unswerving commitment to truth and his philosophical inquiries precipitated the act by the misguided populace in which they made him drink hemlock? Isn't this like condemning Jesus because his unique God-consciousness and never-ceasing devotion to God's will precipitated the evil act of crucifixion? We must come to see that, as the federal courts have consistently affirmed, it is wrong to urge an individual to cease his efforts to gain his basic constitutional rights because the quest may precipitate violence. Society must protect the robbed and punish the robber.

I had also hoped that the white moderate would reject the myth concerning time in relation to the struggle for freedom. I have just received a letter from a white brother in Texas. He writes: "All Christians know that the colored people will receive equal rights eventually, but it is possible that you are in too great a religious hurry. It has taken Christianity almost two thousand years to accomplish what it has. The teachings of Christ take time to come to earth." Such an attitude stems from a tragic misconception of time, from the strangely irrational notion that there is something in the very flow of time that will inevitably cure all ills. Actually, time itself is neutral; it can be used either destructively or constructively. More and more I feel that the people of ill will have used time much more effectively than have the people of good will. We will have to repent in this generation not merely for the hateful words and actions of the bad people

but for the appalling silence of the good people. Human progress never rolls in on wheels of inevitability; it comes through the tireless efforts of men willing to be co-workers with God, and without this hard work, time itself becomes an ally of the forces of social stagnation. We must use time creatively, in the knowledge that the time is always ripe to do right. Now is the time to make real the promise of democracy and transform our pending national elegy into a creative psalm of brotherhood. Now is the time to lift our national policy from the quicksand of racial injustice to the solid rock of human dignity.

You speak of our activity in Birmingham as extreme. At first I was rather disappointed that fellow clergymen would see my nonviolent efforts as those of an extremist. I began thinking about the fact that I stand in the middle of two opposing forces in the Negro community. One is a force of complacency, made up in part of Negroes who, as a result of long years of oppression, are so drained of self-respect and a sense of "somebodiness" that they have adjusted to segregation; and in part of a few middle-class Negroes who, because of a degree of academic and economic security and because in some ways they profit by segregation, have become insensitive to the problems of the masses. The other force is one of bitterness and hatred, and it comes perilously close to advocating violence. It is expressed in the various black nationalist groups that are springing up across the nation, the largest and best-known being Elijah Muhammad's Muslim movement. Nourished by the Negro's frustration over the continued existence of racial discrimination, this movement is made up of people who have lost faith in America, who have absolutely repudiated Christianity, and who have concluded that the white man is an incorrigible "devil."

I have tried to stand between these two forces, saying that we need emulate neither the "do-nothingism" of the complacent nor the hatred and despair of the black nationalist. For there is the more excellent way of love and nonviolent protest. I am grateful to God that, through the influence of the Negro church, the way of nonviolence became an integral part of our struggle.

If this philosophy had not emerged, by now many streets of the South would, I am convinced, be flowing with blood. And I am further convinced that if our white brothers dismiss as "rabble-rousers" and "outside agitators" those of us who employ nonviolent direct action, and if they refuse to support our nonviolent efforts, millions of Negroes will, out of frustration and despair, seek solace and security in black-nationalist ideologies—a development that would inevitably lead to a frightening racial nightmare.

Oppressed people cannot remain oppressed forever. The yearning for freedom eventually manifests itself, and that is what has happened to the American Negro. Something within has reminded him of his birthright of freedom, and something without has reminded him that it can be gained. Consciously or unconsciously, he has been caught up by the *Zeitgeist,* and with his black brothers of Africa and his brown and yellow brothers of Asia, South America and the Caribbean, the United States Negro is moving with a sense of great urgency toward the promised land of racial justice. If one recognizes this vital urge that has engulfed the Negro community, one should readily understand why public demonstrations are taking place. The Negro has many pent-up resentments and latent frustrations, and he must release them. So let him march; let him make prayer pilgrimages to the city hall; let him go on freedom rides—and try to understand why he must do so. If his repressed emotions are not released in nonviolent ways, they will seek expression through violence; this is not a threat but a fact of history. So I have not said to my people: "Get rid of your discontent." Rather, I have tried to say that this normal and healthy discontent can be channeled into the creative outlet of nonviolent direct action. And now this approach is being termed extremist.

But though I was initially disappointed at being categorized as an extremist, as I continued to think about the matter I gradually gained a measure of satisfaction from the label. Was not Jesus an extremist for love: "Love your enemies, bless them that curse you, do good to them that hate you, and pray for them which despitefully use you, and persecute you." Was not Amos an extremist for justice: "Let justice roll down like waters and righteousness like an everflowing stream." Was not Paul an extremist for the Christian gospel: "I bear in my body the marks of the Lord Jesus." Was not Martin Luther an extremist: "Here I stand; I cannot do otherwise, so help me God." And John Bunyan: "I will stay in jail to the end of my days before I make a butchery of my conscience." And Abraham Lincoln: "This nation cannot survive half slaves and half free." And Thomas Jefferson: "We hold these truths to be self-evident, that all men are created equal. . . . " So the question is not whether we will be extremists, but what kind of extremists we will be. Will we be extremists for hate or for love? Will we be extremists for the preservation of injustice or for the extension of justice? In that dramatic scene on Calvary's hill three men were crucified. We must never forget that all three were crucified for the same crime—the crime of extremism. Two were extremists for immorality, and thus fell below their environment. The other, Jesus Christ, was an extremist for love, truth and goodness, and thereby rose above his environment. Perhaps the South, the nation and the world are in dire need of creative extremists.

I had hoped that the white moderate would see this need. Perhaps I was too optimistic; perhaps I expected too much. I suppose I should have realized that few members of the oppressor race can understand the deep groans and passionate yearnings of the oppressed race, and still fewer have the vision to see that injustice must be rooted out by strong, persistent and determined action. I am thankful, however, that some of our white brothers in the South have grasped the meaning of this social revolution and committed themselves to it. They are still all too few in quantity, but they are big in quality. Some—such as Ralph McGill, Lillian Smith, Harry Golden, James McBride Dabbs, Ann Braden and Sarah Patton Boyle—have written about our struggle in eloquent and prophetic terms. Others have marched with us down nameless streets of the South. They have languished in filthy, roach-infested jails, suffering the abuse and brutality of policemen who view them as "dirty nigger-lovers." Unlike so many of their moderate brothers and sisters, they have recognized the urgency of the moment and sensed the need for powerful "action" antidotes to combat the disease of segregation.

Let me take note of my other major disappointment. I have been so greatly disappointed with the white church and its leadership. Of course, there are some notable exceptions. I am not unmindful of the fact that each of you has taken some significant stands on this issue. I commend you, Reverend Stallings, for your Christian stand on this past Sunday, in welcoming Negroes to your worship service on a nonsegregated basis. I commend the Catholic leaders of this state for integrating Spring Hill College several years ago.

But despite these notable exceptions. I must honestly reiterate that I have been disappointed with the church. I do not say this as one of those negative critics who can always find something wrong with the church. I say this as a minister of the gospel, who loves the church; who was nurtured in its bosom; who has been sustained by its spiritual blessings and who will remain true to it as long as the cord of life shall lengthen.

When I was suddenly catapulted into the leadership of the bus protest in Montgomery, Alabama, a few years ago, I felt we would be supported by the white church. I felt that the white ministers, priests and rabbis of the South would be among our strongest allies. Instead, some have been outright opponents, refusing to understand the freedom movement and misrepresenting its leaders; all too many others have been more cautious than courageous and have remained silent behind the anesthetizing security of stained-glass windows.

In spite of my shattered dreams, I came to Birmingham with the hope that the white religious leadership of this community would see the justice of our cause and, with deep moral concern, would serve as the channel through which our just grievances could reach the power structure. I had hoped that each of you would understand. But again I have been disappointed.

I have heard numerous southern religious leaders admonish their worshippers to comply with a desegregation decision because it is the law, but I have longed to hear white ministers declare: "Follow this decree because integration is morally right and because the Negro is your brother." In the midst of blatant injustices inflicted upon the Negro, I have watched white churchmen stand on the sidelines and mouth pious irrelevancies and sanctimonious trivialities. In the midst of a mighty struggle to rid our nation of racial and economic injustice, I have heard many ministers say: "Those are social issues, with which the gospel has no real concern." And I have watched many churches commit themselves to a completely otherworldly religion which makes a strange, un-Biblical distinction between body and soul, between the sacred and the secular.

I have traveled the length and breadth of Alabama, Mississippi and all the other southern states. On sweltering summer days and crisp autumn mornings I have looked at the South's beautiful churches with their lofty spires pointing heavenward. I have beheld the impressive outlines of her massive religious-education buildings. Over and over I have found myself asking: "What kind of people worship here? Who is their God? Where were their voices when the lips of Governor Barnett dripped with words of interposition and nullification? Where were they when Governor Wallace gave a clarion call for defiance and hatred? Where were their voices of support when bruised and weary Negro men and women decided to rise from the dark dungeons of complacency to the bright hills of creative protest?"

Yes, these questions are still in my mind. In deep disappointment I have wept over the laxity of the church. But be assured that my tears have been tears of love. There can be no deep disappointment where there is not deep love. Yes, I love the church. How could I do otherwise? I am in the rather unique position of being the son, the grandson and the great-grandson of preachers. Yes, I see the church as the body of Christ. But, oh! How we have blemished and scarred that body through social neglect and through fear of being nonconformists.

There was a time when the church was very powerful—in the time when the early Christians rejoiced at being deemed worthy to suffer for what they believed. In those days the church was not merely a thermometer that recorded the ideas and principles of popular opinion; it was a thermostat that transformed the mores of society. Whenever the early Christians entered a town, the people in power became disturbed and immediately sought to convict the Christians for being "disturbers of the peace" and "outside agitators." But the Christians pressed on, in the conviction that they were "a colony of heaven," called to obey God rather than man. Small in number, they were big in commitment. They were too God-intoxicated to be "astronomically intimidated." By their effort and example they brought an end to such ancient evils as infanticide and gladiatorial contests.

Things are different now. So often the contemporary church is a weak, ineffectual voice with an uncertain sound. So often it is an archdefender of the status quo. Far from being disturbed by the presence of the church, the power structure of the average community is consoled by the church's silent—and often even vocal—sanction of things as they are.

But the judgment of God is upon the church as never before. If today's church does not recapture the sacrificial spirit of the early church, it will lose its authenticity, forfeit the loyalty of millions, and be dismissed as an irrelevant social club with no meaning for the twentieth century. Every day I meet young people whose disappointment with the church has turned into outright disgust.

Perhaps I have once again been too optimistic. Is organized religion too inextricably bound to the status quo to save our nation and the world? Perhaps I must turn my faith to the inner spiritual church, the church within the church, as the true *ekklesia* and the hope of the world. But again I am thankful to God that some noble souls from the ranks of organized religion have broken loose from the paralyzing chains of conformity and joined us as active partners in the struggle for freedom. They have left their secure congregations and walked the streets of Albany, Georgia, with us. They have gone down the highways of the South on tortuous rides for freedom. Yes, they have gone to jail with us. Some have been dismissed from their churches, have lost the support of their bishops and fellow ministers. But they have acted in the faith that right defeated is stronger than evil triumphant. Their witness has been the spiritual salt that has preserved the true meaning of the gospel in these troubled times. They have carved a tunnel of hope through the dark mountain of disappointment.

I hope the church as a whole will meet the challenge of this decisive hour. But even if the church does not come to the aid of justice, I have no despair about the future. I have no fear about the outcome of our struggle in Birmingham, even if our motives are at present misunderstood. We will reach the goal of freedom in Birmingham and all over the nation, because the goal of America is freedom. Abused and scorned though we may be, our destiny is tied up with America's destiny. Before the pilgrims landed at Plymouth, we were here. Before the pen of Jefferson etched the majestic words of the Declaration of Independence across the pages of history, we were here. For more than two centuries our forebears labored in this country without wages; they made cotton king; they built the homes of their masters while suffering gross injustice and shameful humiliation—and yet out of a bottomless vitality they continued to thrive and develop. If the inexpressible cruelties of slavery could not stop us, the opposition we now face will surely fail. We will win our freedom because the sacred heritage of our nation and the eternal will of God are embodied in our echoing demands.

Before closing I feel impelled to mention one other point in your statement that has troubled me profoundly. You warmly commended the Birmingham police force for keeping "order" and "preventing violence." I doubt you would have so warmly commended the police force if you had seen its dogs sinking their teeth into unarmed, nonviolent Negroes. I doubt that you would so quickly commend the policemen if you were to observe their ugly and inhumane treatment of Negroes here in the city jail; if you were to watch them push and curse old Negro women and young Negro girls; if you were to see them slap and kick old Negro men and young boys; if you were to observe them, as they did on two occasions, refuse to give us food because we wanted to sing our grace together. I cannot join you in your praise of the Birmingham police department.

It is true that the police have exercised a degree of discipline in handling the demonstrators. In this sense they have conducted themselves rather "nonviolently" in public. But for what purpose? To preserve the evil system of segregation. Over the past few years I have consistently preached that nonviolence demands that the means we use must be as pure as the ends we seek. I have tried to make clear that it is wrong to use immoral means to attain moral ends. But now I must affirm that it is just as wrong, or perhaps even more so, to use moral means to preserve immoral ends. Perhaps Mr. Connor and his policemen have been rather nonviolent in public, as was Chief Pritchett in Albany, Georgia, but they have used the moral means of nonviolence to maintain the immoral end of racial injustice. As T. S. Eliot has said: "The last temptation is the greatest treason: To do the right deed for the wrong reason."

I wish you had commended the Negro sitinners and demonstrators of Birmingham for their sublime courage, their willingness to suffer and their amazing discipline in the midst of great provocation. One day the South will recognize its real heroes. They will be the James Merediths, with the noble sense of purpose that enables them to face jeering and hostile mobs, and with the agonizing loneliness that characterizes the life of the pioneer. They will be old, oppressed, battered Negro women, symbolized in a seventy-two-year-old woman in Montgomery, Alabama, who rose up with a sense of dignity and with her people decided not to ride segregated buses, and who responded with ungrammatical profundity to one who inquired about her weariness: "My feets is tired, but my soul is at rest." They will be the young high school and college students, the young ministers of the gospel and a host of their elders, courageously and nonviolently sitting in at lunch counters and willingly going to jail for conscience' sake. One day the South will know that when these disinherited children of God sat down at lunch counters, they were in reality standing up for what is best in the American dream and for the most sacred values in our Judaeo-Christian heritage, thereby bringing our nation back to those great wells of democracy which were dug deep by the founding fathers in their formulation of the Constitution and the Declaration of Independence.

Never before have I written so long a letter. I'm afraid it is much too long to take your precious time. I can assure you that it would have been much shorter if I had been writing from a comfortable desk, but what else can one do when he is alone in a narrow jail cell, other than write long letters, think long thoughts and pray long prayers?

If I have said anything in this letter that overstates the truth and indicates an unreasonable impatience, I beg you to forgive me. If I have said anything that understates the truth and indicates my having a patience that allows me to settle for anything less than brotherhood, I beg God to forgive me.

I hope this letter finds you strong in the faith. I also hope that circumstances will soon make it possible for me to meet each of you, not as an integrationist or a civil-rights leader but as a fellow clergyman and a Christian brother. Let us all hope that the dark clouds of racial prejudice will soon pass away and the deep fog of misunderstanding will be lifted from our fear-drenched communities, and in some not too distant tomorrow the radiant stars of love and brotherhood will shine over our great nation with all their scintillating beauty.

Yours for the cause of Peace and Brotherhood,
Martin Luther King, Jr.

CIVIL DISOBEDIENCE IN THE MODERN WORLD*

Joel Feinberg

The common element among the various kinds of actions that have been called "civilly disobedient" is, as Professor Daube puts it, "an offense against human authority, committed openly in a higher cause, or a cause thought to be higher."[1] The focus of the modern discussion of civil disobedience, however, is somewhat narrower, since it is restricted to disobedience of political authority, usually by acts that violate the law of the state and thereby incur criminal sanctions. In Western countries in the nineteenth and twentieth centuries the focus is narrower still. Civilly disobedient acts do not aim to overthrow whole régimes thought to be illegitimate; nor do they reject an accepted principle of legitimacy itself, like that of "the divine right of kings" or "the consent of the governed." They occur in post-revolutionary countries against a background of acknowledged just constitutions, democratic parliaments, and valid laws; and their purpose is not to undermine authority but to protest its misuse.

Closely related to civil disobedience but properly distinguishable from it are rule departures by state officials, those of policemen who do not arrest lawbreakers, prosecutors who don't prosecute them, jurors who acquit obviously guilty defendants, judges who depart from judicial rules—in general, deliberate failures, often for conscientious reasons, to discharge the duties of one's office. Such official derelictions resemble civil disobedience in important ways, but they do not normally render officials liable to criminal punishment, so I won't consider them to be civilly disobedient, even though when their intended beneficiary is himself an avowed civil disobedient, refusal to arrest, prosecute, or convict him form part of the complete treatment of our subject. In this article I shall not discuss the official's problem but shall concentrate on civil disobedience as a moral problem for the private citizen. My question will be, When, if ever, is there a moral right to commit civil disobedience? and not the closely related derivative question, What are the moral duties of legal officials toward the civilly disobedient lawbreakers?

Civil disobedience, however, is not just *any* kind of deliberate infraction of valid penal law; so it will be useful, at the outset, to distinguish it from other sorts of lawbreaking with which it can be confused.

*From *Humanities in Society,* vol. 2, no. 1, Winter 1979, pp. 37–60. Reprinted by permission of the publisher.

First of all, the common crimes of robbers, muggers, burglars, killers, rapists, and con artists, though they are instances of deliberate lawbreaking, have no other resemblance to the acts with which we are concerned. Civil disobedience is lawbreaking from certain motives only and in certain circumstances only. The common crimes are committed from such familiar motives as personal gain, malice, and hate; their specific intent is to harm the interests of others; and they are accompanied either by a desire to escape apprehension or an emotionally induced indifference to the risk of apprehension. In all of these ways they differ from civil disobedience. In other respects civil disobedience contrasts with acts of "warfare against the state"—assassination, sabotage, terrorism, riot, insurrection, avowed revolution—since civil disobedience is a kind of resistance within the accepted political structure, a violation of the law without loss of respect for law and the other basic political institutions, which are acknowledged to be, by and large, fair.

When the only alternative in the circumstances to the evil of lawbreaking is to permit an evil that is greater still, a desperate choice of the illegal "lesser evil" may often look like civil disobedience, but since most modern legal systems accept the defense of "necessity" as a complete justification, it is not really "disobedience" at all. I have in mind such examples as borrowing a stranger's car without his permission in order to get a heart attack victim quickly to the hospital, destroying another's property to prevent the spread of a raging fire, violating the speed limit in pursuit of an escaping criminal, and so on. The traditional attitude of the Anglo-American law toward such actions is well expressed in the words of the judge in the sixteenth-century criminal case: "An act may break the words of the law and yet not break the law itself." The defense of necessity is a generalized justification based on two judgments, first, that when the evil produced by breaking a rule is likely to be substantially less than the evil that would result in a given case from complying with it, then it is reasonable to breach it and, second, that it is unfair to impose criminal liability on objectively reasonable conduct. Rule departures resulting from such forced choices of a lesser evil, then, are not examples of civil disobedience. But if our legal system did not recognize the defense of necessity and remained rigidly and stupidly literalistic, then exceeding the speed limit to get a wife in labor to the maternity ward might well count as civilly disobedient, dissimilar though it may be to the acts of disinterested political protest that are the most familiar examples, in our time, of that broad genre.

Even closer to civil disobedience, but probably still worth distinguishing from it, are deliberately created test cases for statutes of doubtful validity. These phenomena are a peculiar feature of the American system, in which private citizens can get constitutionally suspect laws overthrown by the tactic of getting themselves convicted for disobeying them and then launching an appeal upward through the courts. "You pays your money and you takes your chances," as carnival barkers used to say. You violate the explicit prohibitions of the suspect law; you are found guilty; you get an expensive constitutional lawyer, and proceed through the appellate system perhaps even to the Supreme Court, arguing always that the reason why you are innocent is not that you didn't do what the prosecution alleges that you did, but rather that the statute you violated was not a valid law in the first place. If you win, then you are a public benefactor, for you have effectively employed what is virtually the only way in our system to get rid of popular but unconstitutional pseudo-laws, and you have paid a price in money, time, and anxiety in order to do that public service. But if you lose, and the Supreme Court does not accept your arguments, you are as unlucky as any losing gambler, and the law may treat you no differently from any common criminal. In addition to all the previously mentioned personal costs, you may be sent to prison for a while as a reward for your public service. Such test cases raise moral issues similar to those we shall be considering, but I still wish to distinguish them from genuine civil disobedience because the "lawbreaker" is not intentionally violating a law. He thinks that what he is doing is entirely within his legal rights, an opinion that happens to disagree with that of the local police, the prosecutor, and the courts. He wants the appellate courts to settle the disagreement, and "disobedience" is the only way *he* can get them to do so, since he must have "standing" if he is to use the courts for that purpose, and one cannot acquire standing by complying with the law in question. Of course, he may want to repeat his behavior even after the Supreme Court has declared it illegal once and for all, as an act of public protest against an unfair law, and that would begin to look like civil disobedience proper.

Three types of lawbreaking remain to be discussed: conscientious evasion, conscientious refusal, and disobedience as moral protest. Many writers, following John Rawls, speak of the third of these (moral protests) as civil disobedience proper and contrast it with acts of conscientious evasion and refusal. There are differences, of course, among these three forms of disobedience, and clarity is always served by a recognition of dissimilarities among classes otherwise easily confused. But since the three types of conduct raise importantly similar moral questions, we can lump them together, along with forced choices of the lesser evil in a system that does not recognize the necessity defense, under the generic label "civil disobedience in the wide sense" and reserve the label "civil disobedience in the narrow sense" for moral protests, those acts of lawbreaking that Rawls thinks of as "civil disobedience proper." Our concern in the second half of this essay will be with the moral justification of civil disobedience in the broad sense.

Acts of conscientious evasion might be thought of as borderline cases of civil disobedience since they share with covert crimes the hope of escaping apprehension and arrest. Their impelling motives, however, are strikingly different from those of most ordinary crimes. The conscientious evader genuinely believes that the law he violates is morally wrong, even though validly enacted, and personal gain is not a large element—if it is present at all—in his motivation for violating it. He thinks that he can do more good for the cause of justice by remaining free to violate the iniquitous law some more than by making a martyr of himself. The clearest historical examples of what I have in mind were the covert infractions by white northerners of the fugitive slave laws before the Civil War.

"Conscientious refusal" is the term Rawls uses to describe deliberate "noncompliance with a more or less direct legal injunction or administrative order,"[2] where one's action is assumed to be known to the authorities, however much one might wish, in some cases, to conceal it. Among the examples cited by Rawls are the refusal of Jehovah's Witnesses to salute the flag, the refusal of pacifists to serve in the armed forces, and Thoreau's famous refusal to pay his taxes during the Mexican War on the ground that payment would make him a participant in a great evil. Conscientious refusal resembles civil disobedience in the narrow sense in that its motives are conscientious. It is not done from the desire for personal gain, but there is little hope of escaping apprehension. But neither is it impelled by a desire to act as a form of public protest. Rather one acts either to avert an evil close at hand or else simply to keep one's own hands, morally speaking, clean. (Thoreau had no hope of stopping the Mexican War, but at least he could avoid having guilt on *his* hands.)

Civil disobedience (in what I call the "narrow sense") is defined by Rawls as "a public, nonviolent, conscientious yet political act contrary to law usually done with the aim of bringing about a change in the law or policies of the government."[3] Rawls here describes a kind of conduct that was frequently engaged in by moral protestors in the 1960s, first against racial discrimination and then against the Vietnamese War. Let us briefly consider the defining elements of this form of protest, one by one.

Civil disobedience is *public*—engaged in openly, often even with prior notice, since the protestor wants as much publicity and attention as possible for his tactical purposes. Civil disobedience is *nonviolent* for the simple tactical reason that injury to others, harm to property, and extreme inconvenience to others, are likely to be self-defeating, since they can obscure one's message, cause bitter resentment, and distract public attention from what is vital. The main reason, in short, why the civil disobedient wants his act to be nonviolent is the same as his reason for wanting it to be public—so that he can convince the majority of his fellow citizens that the act is indeed conscientious and sincere and intended to address the public's sense of justice. Indeed it is absolutely essential to civil disobedience as Rawls conceives it that it is a form of address, a symbolic way of making a statement, in his words "an expression of profound and conscientious political conviction . . . in the public forum."[4] As such it can be valued on the one hand as an end in itself, either a kind of "bearing witness" to a moral truth for its own sake, or a disavowal of responsibility, or on the other hand (what is more likely) as a *tactic*. When it is meant to be a method for producing reform, it must be distinguished from *intimidation*. It is in essential contrast to such tactics as disruption of traffic, strikes, boycotts, and political pressure. It does not say "Give us our way or else." That sort of threat often backfires. The only pressure involved is "moral pressure"—dramatically sincere appeal to the public's sense of justice.

The third defining characteristic in Rawls's account is *deliberate unlawfulness*. Under this heading two types of civil disobedience must be distinguished. *Direct* civil disobedience violates the very law that is the target of the protest, whereas *indirect* civil disobedience violates some other law whose reasonableness is not in question. As Rawls points out, civil disobedience cannot always be direct: "If the government enacts a vague and harsh statute against treason, it would not be appropriate to commit treason as a way of objecting to it."[5] To which Carl Cohen adds the observation that one doesn't protest capital punishment for rape by committing rape. In fact it is surprisingly difficult to protest the most likely sorts of unjust laws and policies by direct civil disobedience. White men sitting in the black sections of segregated buses in the 1950s and war protestors burning their draft cards are good examples, but more characteristically, acts of civil disobedience in recent years have been indirect, the most familiar being those that violate local trespass ordinances, for example, "sitting in" at an atomic energy site until one must be forcibly carried away by the police in order to protest, not trespass laws, but rather the policy of building atomic power plants.

Finally, civilly disobedient acts in Rawls's conception must be *conscientious*. The main point of this part of the definition presumably is to rule out the motives of private or personal gain or malicious emotion as primary and immediate. Insofar as those motives, which are characteristic of ordinary crimes, are present at all, we should hesitate to classify an infraction as "civil disobedience." Rawls reminds us that the civil disobedient suffers inconvenience, expense, taunts, threats, real danger, and eventually punishment. His willingness, in the typical case, to suffer these consequences helps to demonstrate that his purpose is to protest an injustice or a wrong—not to achieve some *immediate* gain for himself. He suffers for a *cause,* some larger goal or principle for whose sake he breaks the law publicly and thereby sacrifices at least his short-run interests. While all of this is true, the word "conscientious," as we shall see, may be a misleading way of expressing it.

What does it mean to act conscientiously? I shall want to qualify the following answer shortly, but let me begin by giving what might be called "the strongest account of conscientiousness," namely that to act conscientiously is to act because of one's honest and sincere conviction that what one is doing is right, not merely in the sense of "all right," but rather in the sense of "morally mandatory"—the uniquely correct thing to do, whatever the cost. "Here I stand; I can do no other," said Luther. "Here I sit; I can do no other" might have been said during the Southern sit-ins of the early 1960s. There are two important, though obvious, things to say about conscientiousness so construed: (1) people can be wrong in their conscientious convictions as in any other ones; but (2) insofar as convictions are genuinely conscientious, in this strong sense, they deserve respect from everyone and respectful treatment, insofar as that is consistent with other goals, from the law. Conscientious motives have a very special kind of moral value.

There is no denying that the motives of many acts of civil disobedience fit the above description, but if the strong account of conscientiousness is included in our definition, then many apparent examples of civil disobedience are not civil disobedience at all, because they are *not* "conscientious." I have in mind not acts done from a sense of duty, but rather acts done because the actor wishes to stand on his *rights*—to affirm them, vindicate them, and demand their recognition and enforcement. These are acts done *in* a clear conscience, but not *from* conscientiousness (in the strong sense). Publicly drinking beer during Prohibition and attending a marijuana smoke-in are examples. The drinker may well have been affirming thereby his moral right to drink beer, but he was not doing what he did because his conscience required beer drinking. One can hardly compare him with Luther! When one is prepared to sacrifice one's short-run interests in order to secure one's rights and acts out of genuine conviction that moral principle does indeed confer those rights, then there is a sense in which one's action is disinterested, at least more so than actions that demand, in the absence of moral deliberation or conviction of any kind, that others simply "gimme, gimme, gimme, gimme, what I cry for." We can even call them "conscientious" in a weaker sense of that term. It is important, however, to understand that civil disobedience (in the wide sense that includes principled protest, evasion, and refusal) need not be conscientious in the usual strong sense. To persist in the contrary view may be to fall into a serious muddle about the very concept of a *conscience.*

It is essential to the idea of a person's conscience that it is a faculty of self-address concerned only with the duties of its possessor. My conscience tells *me* what it is right for *me* to do, what I must do, what it is my duty to do, and not merely what I may do if I wish. If we say, on the contrary, that my conscience tells me what my *rights* are, then we are committed logically to the view that one person's conscience can tell him what other people's duties are, which is not only conceptually odd, but politically dangerous as well.

The modern discussion among philosophers of the justifiability of civil disobedience has at least a dual source, partly in democratic political theory and partly in philosophical jurisprudence. On the one hand, the problem civil disobedience raises for our moral judgments derives from the almost universal belief that every citizen in a constitutional democracy with at least approximately just institutions has a general obligation to obey the valid laws and lawful commands of his government. Civil disobedience by definition is a violation of those laws or commands. How then can it be justified? Duties of course can be overridden in particular cases by a "higher duty," or in a "higher cause." What then must these higher principles be like, and when are they strong enough, to override the general moral obligation to be law abiding? That in turn depends, at least in part, on the grounds, strength, and limits of the latter obligation. In this way the question of civil disobedience draws philosophers into the venerable problem of the nature of political obligation.

There is also a path through the philosophy of law to the same destination. The period during which civil disobedience began to challenge modern thinkers largely corresponded with the rise of the doctrine called "legal positivism" and the decline of the traditional doctrines of natural law. According to the natural law theory, the validity of humanly made coercive laws depends in part on their *content,* that is, on what they require or prohibit. If they are, in the appropriate way, arbitrary, unjust, cruel, pointless, or immoral, then they have no authority or force of law whatever, in which case there is no more moral obligation to obey them than there is to comply with any pseudo-law or mere masquerade as law. To the legal positivists that view was intolerably paradoxical. The validity of law, they insisted, is one thing; its justice or morality is another; so there can be no contradiction in characterizing a statute as an unjust valid law. The validity of law, on their view, stems from its proper *enactment.* All valid law is enacted law. So-called laws of nature may be standards for distinguishing good from bad law, but law is law, whether good or bad. It is the pedigree of a law (where it comes from) rather than its content (what it commands) that determines its validity.

The positivist account of legal validity obviously gains much support from common sense, but historically the legal positivists have often held another doctrine that is hard to reconcile with the first, namely that valid law as such, no matter what its content, deserves our respect and our general fidelity. Even if valid law is bad law, we have some obligation to obey it simply because it is law. But how can this be so if a law's validity has nothing to do with its content? Why should I have *any* respect or duty of fidelity toward a statute with a wicked or stupid content just because it was passed into law by a bunch of men (possibly very wicked men like the Nazi legislators) according to the accepted recipes for making law? Thus Lon Fuller, the leading American critic of legal positivism, triumphantly springs his trap: the positivist cannot explain

how "laws, even bad laws, have a claim to our respect."[6] The two doctrines of validity by pedigree and respect for law as such yield in combination an unstable conception of law as "an amoral datum" that has a kind of magical capacity to generate moral obligations. One easy way out for the positivist, and I think the only way, is to abandon the second doctrine and admit that there is no moral duty whatever to obey law simply because it is valid law. To support that startlingly radical proposition the positivist must cast his skeptical eye on the variously alleged grounds for "the moral obligation to obey the law as such," and soon he is likely to encounter the political theorist exploring the possible grounds for a perfectly general moral obligation to obey the democratic state and the moralist puzzled about the moral justifiability of civil disobedience.

The standard way of characterizing the individual citizen's moral problem concerning civil disobedience is as a conflict of reasons of basically different types. According to this conception, the question, Is it ever right to disobey a law, and if so, under what conditions? is exactly the same in form as the question(s), Is it ever right to break a promise, tell a lie, inflict pain on others . . . etc., and if so, under what conditions? This approach to the problem assumes that there is (to use philosophical jargon that I don't altogether like) a "*prima facie* obligation" to obey the law that can in principle conflict with, override, or be overridden by "*prima facie* obligations" of other kinds. I would prefer to speak of "reasons for" and "reasons against," but since the term *prima facie obligation* has become fixed by a strong convention, it will be well to come to terms with it. So for the moment let us see what philosophers have meant by *prima facie* obligation, or PFO, as I shall abbreviate it.

In explaining what they mean by a PFO, some philosophers resort to an analogy with the idea of a vector of forces that is used in physics. The analogy is useful up to a point. We do feel "pulled in both ways," as we say, when we are in situations like that which Plato describes in the *Republic,* in which we have promised a neighbor to keep a weapon for him and return it when he requests and he then comes back in a furious homicidal rage against another party and demands that we return his property to him. Thinking no doubt of cases of this sort, Carl Cohen writes:

> *One's ultimate or actual obligation in any morally complex situation will require the careful weighing of several, even many,* prima facie *obligations, some of which may conflict*

head-on with others. We may think of such
prima facie *obligations as components, or vec-*
tors, pushing us in different directions with dif-
fering degrees of force, the morally correct
outcome of the set being our resultant
obligation.[7]

Despite the intuitively familiar points of resemblance between PFOs and physical forces, this analogy is more misleading than helpful. In physics, a resultant force compounded out of component forces is always a kind of splitting of the difference, not always right down the middle of course, but a result determined in some measure by each of its components. When two forces act on a body, the resultant direction and velocity of that object will be a kind of "compromise." Its resultant direction, if the two forces are equal and at right angles to one another, will be at a 45° angle, splitting the difference between where it would have gone if only the one force were acting on it and where it would have gone if only the other force were acting on it. But in morals there is often no way of splitting the difference, in which case one must do the one duty or the other, rather than do a part of each. Plato's householder could hardly solve his problem by means of a compromise between the moral demand that he keep his promise to return another's lethal weapon and the moral demand that he protect a third party from harm. It would not do, for example, to substitute a less lethal weapon—say a somewhat brittle wooden club—for the original sword.

I think that we can avoid this difficulty and achieve greater clarity by thinking of PFOs and resultant obligations simply in terms of supporting and conclusive reasons. Then we can say that one's having promised to do an act A (say) is always a reason of direct relevance and at least some cogency in favor of doing A and one's promise not to do B is a reason against doing B, and in the absence of other reasons having a bearing on the situation, either would be a conclusive reason. Further, a PFO (general type of supporting reason) is not in every case a decisive reason, but it is always a relevant one and one which would be conclusive if no other relevant reason of greater strength applied to the situation. Thus if Jones has a PFO to do A, then he has a moral reason to do A which is such that unless he has a moral reason *not* to do A that is at least as strong, then not doing A is wrong, and he has an actual obligation to do A.[8]

Philosophers have differed over the question of how many general kinds of PFOs there are and over which are basic and which derivative. The following list of basic PFOs is, I think, representative and plausible, though I can make no stronger claim for it here:

1. The PFO of fidelity: to keep promises.
2. The PFO of veracity: to tell the truth (or better—not to tell lies).
3. The PFO of fair play: not to exploit, cheat, or "free load" on others.
4. The PFO of gratitude: to return favors.
5. The PFO of nonmaleficence: not to cause pain or suffering to others.
6. The PFO of beneficence: to help others in distress when this involves no great danger to oneself or third parties.
7. The PFO of reparation: to repair harms to others that are one's own fault.
8. The PFO not to kill others (except in self-defense).
9. The PFO not to deprive others of their property.
10. The PFO to oppose injustices when this involves no great cost to oneself.
11. The PFO to promote just institutions and to work toward their establishment, maintenance, and improvement.

Insofar as a given act is an instance of one of the above eleven kinds, that is a moral reason in favor of doing it, and if it is not, at the same time, a negative instance of one of the other categories on the list, then it is a decisive reason. If it is a positive instance of one type and a negative instance of another, say a promise that can only be kept by telling a lie, then one's actual duty will be to perform the PFO which is the more stringent in the circumstances. That is all that a moralist can say in the abstract with any degree of certainty.

In addition to the list of eleven PFOs, is there also a PFO to obey the law? Is the fact that a contemplated act would be illegal a reason against doing it? Of course it might always be a prudential reason of some weight against doing it. You might get caught, and the risk is always a consideration to be weighed carefully by any reasonable person. But that is not what we are concerned about. We wish to know whether illegality is also a type of *moral reason,* a consideration that tends to bind us morally to refrain from the act and will ground an actual obligation to refrain if no other conflicting PFOs are pulling us even harder in the opposite direction. Philosophers have differed sharply over this question. Few are tempted these days to hold the view, so effectively demolished by Richard Wasserstrom,[9] that it can *never* be right to disobey a law, that "X is illegal" is always a decisive moral reason against doing X. But a growing number of philosophers hold the very opposite and surprisingly plausible view that "*X* is illegal" is no kind of reason at all, that there isn't even a PFO to obey the law. (We do, of course, have a PFO not to do many of the things prohibited by law—not to kill, steal, etc.—but because these things are *mala in se,* not because they are illegal.) These philosophers usually argue that there is no sort of reason why anyone ought to obey a rotten rule created in a rotten system under an authoritarian régime or a thoroughly iniquitous constitution. Nazi rules against helping Jews were "valid laws" in Germany, all right, and duly enacted by Nazi legislatures. Their ruthless enforcement, moreover, gave every German citizen a prudential reason for obeying them. But the fact that helping Jews was illegal was itself morally irrelevant, neither here nor there in the moral universe, utterly beside the point. Surely, these philosophers conclude, not just *any* legal obligation in *any* legal system imposes a moral PFO, giving us a moral reason of any strength at all for obedience.

Philosophers on the other side usually grant the point and make a small strategic retreat. If there is a PFO to obey the law as such, they concede, it can only be in a reasonably just society, under a reasonably just constitution, with fair (presumably democratic) procedures for making and changing laws. But in such a state, they insist, the fact that *X* is illegal is always a moral reason, of some discernible weight at least, against doing *X*. But even that reasonably modified position no longer gains unanimous assent, and more and more philosophers, myself included, are coming to question it.

There is a dilemma for adherents of even the weakest version of the doctrine that there is a moral PFO to obey the law. (I refer to the version that restricts the PFO to valid laws in the citizen's own legal system when that system is democratic and by and large just.) Either this alleged PFO is one of the basic ones, on the same level as the eleven on our list, or it is derivative from some one or combination of them. If basic, it can only be defended by an appeal to self-evidence, for *ex hypothesi* there is no more basic ethical principle from which it follows. But whereas that kind of appeal is plausible in the other eleven cases (who could deny, for example, that "you promised" is always *a* reason, at the very least, for doing what was promised?), it seems much less so in this case. In any event when so many astute philosophers[10] are saying "I don't see it," it certainly lacks argumentative force to rest one's case on the insistence that it is just obviously so. But if, on the other hand, the PFO to obey

the law is derivative from one or more of the basic ones, one must be able to show how it is derived, and that is a notoriously difficult undertaking, not yet successfully done.[11]

Almost all of the basic PFOs on our list have been thought by one philosopher or another to be the ground, or part of the ground, for a derivative PFO to obey the law, but the most interesting attempts to derive such a PFO, and the most popular, invoke numbers 4 (gratitude), 1 (fidelity), 3 (fair play), and 10-11 (justice). Let us examine each of these attempts briefly but critically.

The argument from gratitude proceeds as follows. In general, by accepting benefits from others we incur "debts of gratitude." Many moralists derive the PFO to help one's parents from this basic one, and indeed Socrates, in Plato's dialogue the *Crito,* likens his own relation to the Athenian state to that of a son to his parents and declines to resist even a fatally unjust application of its laws on that ground. We do accept the protection of the police, the armed forces, and the Public Health Service, and the benefits of the money system, the postal service, public schools, and so on; therefore we are said to have a debt of gratitude to the state and a PFO to obey its laws. Not to do so would be ungrateful.

What are we to make of this curious argument? In the first place, it should be observed that debts of gratitude don't have anything to do with gratitude in the usual sense, which is a certain motive, attitude, or feeling. There can be no duty to have a particular feeling or to act from a certain motive, for the pinpoint control over our emotions that would be required by such a duty is beyond our powers of self-manipulation. Our only plausible duties are to do, or to omit doing, certain things (from whatever motive). A duty to repay services is less paradoxically called a "duty of reciprocation" than a duty of gratitude. Indeed, so separate are the ideas of reciprocation and gratitude that sometimes the former is taken as a sign of the *absence* of the latter, as was noted by St. Thomas Aquinas, who quotes with approval a passage from Seneca that "a person who wants to repay a gift too quickly with a gift in return is an unwilling debtor and an ungrateful person."[12] Nevertheless a duty of reciprocation is fully discharged by appropriate payment even when done in a grudging spirit of ungrateful resentment, and gratitude without suitable repayment, however commendable for its own sake, cannot discharge a duty of reciprocation.

A stronger and more relevant point is also yielded by the example of the gift. Unlike formal loans and contractual performances, a gift is not the sort of thing that one has a duty to "repay." Gratitude may be appropriate though it is not the sort of thing that can be exacted, but repayment is not the sort of concept that has any application at all to the gift situation. There can no more be a duty of reciprocation than a duty of gratitude to return gratuitous gifts and favors. Suppose that the Joneses, obscure acquaintances of yours, invite you to dinner, and you accept, to your later regret. Do you have a PFO to reciprocate by inviting them to dinner? Would you be blamably "ungrateful" if you did not? Would a cash payment sent later through the mails be an acceptable mode of repayment? Suppose that Jones is a rich man or the president of your university, someone who entertains others constantly and lavishly and is more than occupied by his own busy social schedule. Are you torn over your duty to reciprocate? Or, to take examples of another kind, suppose that a young woman receives flowers from an admirer, then candy, then dresses, then electrical appliances, despite her continued efforts to discourage him. Finally she begins to "doubt his motives." Is there even a trace of a moral reason here for reciprocation? cooperation? obedience? Or suppose that a college teacher gives a pretty coed a good grade when the student knows that her work is poor. She might well wonder "What is he up to anyway?" but certainly not "What should I do for him?" In the latter two cases not only is a duty of reciprocation out of the question; it is also the case that one of the psychologically necessary conditions for the emergence of the feeling of gratitude itself is absent, namely, the belief that the gratuitous gift or favor was offered from genuinely disinterested friendship or benevolence, with no "ulterior motive." In any event, even if we are grateful—let us suppose for a good dinner given us by well-meaning but very boring persons who wished only to please us—it does not follow that we have a moral PFO to reciprocate, but at most that we may feel some trace of a desire or inclination to do so. (If only they weren't so boring!)

The case for deriving a PFO to obey the laws of the state from a basic PFO of "gratitude" collapses completely in the light of the above observations. If the argument is meant only to establish a ground for the feeling of gratitude, then it needs to be supplemented by a showing that the state's undoubted services and protections are genuine gifts rather than contractual performances and, further, that its motive was personal benevolence or disinterested friendship (an unenviable task); and even if there is a ground for gratitude, there can be no duty to *feel* grateful; and

even if there were such a duty, it could not in turn ground a duty of reciprocation. Finally, and most conclusively, even if there is some sort of duty of repayment (which is most implausible), it could not take the form required by the argument, namely faithful obedience to commands, for as M. B. E. Smith puts it, "The mere fact that a person has conferred benefits on me, even the most momentous benefits conferred from genuinely benevolent motives, doesn't establish his right to dictate all my behavior."[13] The benefits are no reason at all in support of *that* PFO. A fifty-year-old son may have numerous duties toward his eighty-year-old parents, but they will all be duties to help them, not to obey them. No matter how grateful he is to them for their past services, he can have no duty to let them determine, for example, what hour he must come home at night or what foods he may eat.

Like any theory that has been defended by great philosophers in the past, the gratitude theory does have a grain of truth. There is a more plausible interpretation of something that can be called a duty of gratitude, and no doubt such a duty can yield, under very special circumstances, something like a PFO to comply with the laws of a state and even to perform certain positive services for it. If there is such a thing in ordinary interpersonal relations as a PFO of gratitude, it is not an obligation to reciprocate favor for favor, service for service, benefit for benefit, but rather an obligation to stand ready, in case one's benefactor should ever falter, to help him too. If a wealthy friend of his father gives a young person enough money to pay for his whole college education, he will appropriately feel grateful, especially if he believes that the gift was a genuine expression of benevolence or friendship without ulterior motive. But insofar as the payment was a genuine gift and not a loan, the young person will have no burdensome duty to repay a like sum during his postgraduate years. Presumably if the benefactor had intended to impose such a burden, he would have explicitly described his transfer of funds as a *loan,* not a gift. Suppose, however, that years later it comes to the attention of the younger man, now middle-aged and comfortable, that the elderly benefactor has come upon hard times, having lost all his money through unlucky investments, and now is suffering from bad health. Not to help him *now,* if he can, would indeed be ungrateful and a violation of a moral duty to reciprocate the old man's earlier favors. Similarly, an expatriate living happily abroad, though with warm feelings toward his native land and "gratitude" for having learned its language and culture and for having been shaped by its institutions, might feel morally impelled to come to the aid of his country in its time of dire need and pay taxes and bear arms in its defense. On the other hand, an Englishman at the start of World War II or an Israeli at the outset of the Yom Kippur War who takes all of his goods and flees to Geneva or Cuernavaca would rightly be thought a morally derelict ingrate by his countrymen. In such cases one has a moral duty to come to the aid of one's country, a duty derived perhaps in part from having benefited from its laws and services in the past. But that is quite another thing than a general duty in good or hard times to obey each and every law or order.

The second way of deriving a moral PFO of obedience to law bases it on a deliberate undertaking of the citizen, a kind of formal promise to comply with laws, or at least a voluntary granting of one's consent to the lawmaker's authority, which amounts to the same thing. Thus the PFO of obedience is like the obligation to discharge one's part of a bargain; the state provides its benefits *in exchange for which* the citizen provides his constant fidelity to law. (State benefits, on this view, are more like loans than gifts.) The argument can be stated simply: (1) a person can have no obligation to obey or support the state unless he has personally granted his consent to its authority, but once that consent is granted or promise made, a duty of obedience has been assumed; (2) we all have granted that consent; therefore, (3) we all have the standing duty (like all general duties, a PFO) to obey the law of the state.

The most doubtful part of the argument, of course, is its second premise. The reader might well claim that he (for one) never granted consent of the sort required by the argument. In fact, no representative of the state ever asked him to do so. His friend Angelo did so at the naturalization ceremony as part of a solemn oath with his hand on a Bible. But most of us native-born citizens never did anything of the kind. It won't do to say in reply to this that the reader's ancestors took the oath, either at the time of "the original contract" or at later naturalization proceedings, for there is no way to explain how a person can be bound morally by a promise made by another person at a time before he even came into existence.

A more plausible rejoinder than the "inherited obligation" ploy is that for which John Locke is famous: Of course the reader gave no explicit statement of consent; rather he granted a "tacit consent," not in language but in conduct from which the consent can be inferred. A. John Simmons, in an important article, has given a definitive refutation of this claim.[14] He points out first that there *is* a kind of behavior that

can be called "tacit consent," but that it is not "unexpressed consent deduced from conduct," but rather "consent expressed in a certain way—by silence."[15] For an example he has us imagine a board meeting at which the chairman announces: "We will meet again next Thursday unless there are objections to that date. Does anyone have objections?" There is silence for one full minute, at the conclusion of which the chairman notes that all have agreed (consented) to his proposal. The reader will recognize this familiar notion of consent by silence but strenuously resist its application to his own case. How could anyone think that he consented to the authority of his government simply by being silent? No one in authority ever asked him if he consented. He was never presented with options and alternatives and asked to decide. He was no more aware that his silence on this question constituted consent than he is that his silence about network TV scheduling constitutes an agreement to watch all the shows.

Simmons pointed out, however, that Locke surely did not mean by "tacit consent" the familiar notion of consent by silence. Rather he argued in two other ways, first, that our consent is implied by our acceptance of government benefits and, second, by our continued residence in the country of our citizenship. The odd thing about these closely interrelated arguments is that they imply that we can give our binding consent by accident, so to speak, unknowingly and unintentionally. Perhaps if I had known that I was assuming a lifelong obligation of fidelity I would at least have hesitated before accepting benefits. As it is, Locke puts me in the position that would be occupied by the lady in our earlier example if she learned belatedly that her acceptance of gifts from her suitor was a way of getting married and that he is now her husband come what may, for better or worse.

Elsewhere Locke writes that a sure sign of consent to governmental authority (whatever the consenter's actual intentions) is one's continued residence in a country. But in the absence of a clearly presented choice and a formal convention for indicating consent (like the board meeting described above), this too would be an "unknowing or unintentional consent," which is to say an absurdity. In modern nations at the present time, at least, there is no such general procedure; no genuine choice is ever made available to most of us. The reader might complain that he did not know that he was incurring a permanent obligation of obedience when he chose to settle down in his native land until he read Locke, and by then it was too late!

Perhaps it is possible in principle, however, though not presently the case, to design a political procedure that would make residence a sign of "tacit consent" to a country's laws. Simmons reminds us that Socrates in the *Crito* claimed that such formal procedures *were* available to every Athenian on attaining the "age of manhood." The Athenian state in effect told every young man that he could take all his property and "go wherever you wish with our blessing, if you don't like it here. Your silence will be taken as an acknowledgment of a lifelong obligation to obey our laws." Assuming that this was an accurate account of things in at least one ancient Greek city-state and that young Athenians were able to make a *truly voluntary choice* of political allegiance, we must now ask whether it is possible to design such a procedure for the modern state.

Surely the difficulties would be formidable. Perhaps it was not very difficult, economically or psychologically, for free Hellenic Greeks to change their residence from one city-state to another. All moves are disruptive, of course, but in total impact on the lives of the movers, a change from Athens to Corinth was probably no harder than a change from New York to California today. But now, the "option" for a twenty-one-year-old American youth to say good-bye to his family and friends, pack his bags, change his money, and board a jet plane for a new life in whatever alien land would deign to receive him is hardly a genuine "choice" at all. Simmons is hardly less scathing than David Hume had been in his eighteenth-century reply to Locke[16] when he (Simmons) writes that "our most precious 'possessions' are not movable property that can be put on the boat with one's books and TV set."[17] The legal opportunity to emigrate then hardly provides a procedure for voluntarily expressing one's consent by silence. Simmons's example of the opportunity at the board meeting to express an objection, freely and knowingly, by the easy and conventionally understood device of raising one's arm in response to a question bears little analogy to the forced and dangerous expedient of emigrating. The latter, Simmons tells us, is more like the case of the boss at the board meeting inviting all those who object to so signify by lopping off their right arms or implying by his manner that objection however expressed carries a high risk of demotion or firing.[18]

The third way of basing a PFO to obey the law is to derive it from the PFO of fair play. This argument was well formulated (and first named) in an influential article of John Rawls, which was later severely qualified and even renamed in Rawls's book.[19] A PFO of

fair play comes into existence not only in sports and competitive games (as its name suggests) but also in a large variety of social settings. Its principal home, in fact, is in cooperative rather than competitive joint undertakings, in voluntary rule-structured associations like clubs, teams, partnerships, political parties, and the like, and in more informal joint enterprises, like voluntary clean-up of repair work among a group of friends who possess a car in common. Each person has his own share to do if all are to gain, but it is possible for a given person to *cheat,* not do his share, and thus take his benefit as "free" only because the others are doing *their* shares. The "free rider" doesn't "play fair." He may not harm anybody directly, but by cheating he *exploits* the others' cooperativeness to his own benefit. He "takes advantage of them," as we say. A paradigmatic example is not paying one's fare on a railroad train. The others pay in full confidence that everyone will, and the free rider takes advantage of that trust. So he gains at their expense. It is not that he *harms* them; that is not the gravamen of their grievance. Their share of the costs of the railroad (reflected in the owners' adjusted prices) may go up only a tiny fraction of a penny because of his nonpayment. But they have voluntarily foregone the benefits he got in expectation that he would forego them too. Their grievance is that he took advantage of them.

That complaint can just as well be expressed in the language of rights and duties. Adapting one of Simmons's examples, we can consider a community scheme to preserve water pressure during a dry spell by prohibiting the watering of lawns in the evening, although the facts are such that if as many as five percent of the homeowners watered their lawns, there would be no lowering of the pressure. Jones waters his lawn in the evening. He causes no harm to anyone because noncompliance has not passed the five percent threshold. Nevertheless, his neighbors are understandably indignant. They see that Jones profits *only because they forbear*. They cooperated and discharged their duties of fair play, and they had a right that Jones do so too.

Perhaps the most apt and familiar example is drawn from one of the largest of all the collective activities of our time, the cooperative movement of automobiles in all directions through a modern nation's highway system. Suppose that there is a restricted lane reserved for emergency vehicles on the right shoulder of a multilaned road. We are creeping along bumper to bumper in heavy traffic returning from a well-attended football game. You look in your rearview mirror and see a car pull into that forbidden lane and accelerate rapidly by the line of cars jammed in the permitted lanes. Generously you infer that there is some extreme emergency that has impelled this motorist to so desperate a course. But as he passes on your right you note that his car is packed with spirited revelers; there are pennants flying from all the windows, and lusty voices are singing the college fight song. The rest of us have stayed out of the restricted lane and because—only because—of our obedience, the disobedient motorist profits. He has exploited our good faith for his own benefit.

If a general PFO to obey the law can be derived from the basic PFO of fair play, then each individual citizen's duty of obedience is owed ultimately, not to the state, but to the other citizens, for it is essentially a duty not to take advantage of them even in "harmless" ways. There are indeed many examples of legal disobedience that do exploit unfairly the law-abidingness of others. Traffic infractions of course provide one class of examples. Income tax evasion provides another. But there are too many counterexamples for there to be a perfectly general PFO of obedience derived from the basic PFO of fair play. There are many types of cases where violating the law doesn't take advantage of anyone, and since the element of exploitation is not involved *necessarily* in every instance of law breaking, "fair play" is by no means a perfect model. In those cases where exploitation of other citizens is involved (and indeed they are common), we have a PFO to obey the law not simply because it *is* the law, but rather because it would be unfair exploitation not to, just as in other cases, we may have a duty to obey the law, not because it is the law, but because it would harm someone, or break a promise to someone, or so on, not to.

Examples of nonexploitative lawbreaking may not be typical instances of crimes in a democracy, but they are not so rare as to seem exotic. Most traffic violations either endanger or take advantage of others, but particular instances even of generally dangerous or exploitative types do neither—running a red light on empty streets late at night under perfect conditions of visibility, for example, or exceeding the speed limit on an empty stretch of highway when it is perfectly safe (except for the possibility of apprehension by a traffic cop) to do so. Whatever the reasons for avoiding such conduct, there is surely no one who can complain that he has been taken advantage of by it. Such lawbreaking is neither harmful nor dangerous nor exploitative. When then could be the basis of a moral PFO to abstain from it? Then there are examples of so-called victimless crimes like smoking marijuana

or cohabitation which abound in almost all penal codes. Not only do they not harm (or at least not *wrong*) anyone; they don't take advantage of anyone either. Surely the models of driving in a restricted lane and cheating on one's income tax do not apply to them.

Most deliberate lawbreaking is obviously harmful to someone, namely, its victims. But even much wrongful lawbreaking of that class cannot be thought of as exploitative of other parties who are *not* its victims. When A rapes B may all of the rest of us males complain that A took unfair advantage of our compliance with the rape law to benefit at our expense? When B murders her husband in a fit of wrathful jealousy, may all the other married people complain that she was able to get her way only because of their forbearance, that it is unfair to *them* that she acted on her wrath when they must repress theirs? Not very likely.

It is *prima facie* more plausible, however, to claim that civil disobedience in the narrow sense (political protest) does invariably have the characteristic of unfair play and that exploitation is at least one of its inevitable moral costs even when it is justified on balance. If that is so, then there is always *some* reason against that kind of disobedience (a PFO to refrain from it) even when counterbalanced by reasons on the other side. When you sit in at the atomic energy site, for example, your fellow citizens might all be entitled to say: "You are able to violate the trespass laws to further your favorite moral cause *only* because we don't do the same every time we think we have a higher moral cause. If all our moral causes were promoted in your fashion, the costs to our democratic institutions, our public civility, and our domestic tranquility would be disastrous." This is often a quite proper thing to say to the rash civil disobedient whose political anger is more like self-righteousness than genuinely disinterested indignation. Civil disobedience is often *not* justified precisely on the ground that it is not fair play and is made possible only by the self-sacrificial forbearance of others. There is in fact a moral PFO of fair play, and when civil disobedience violates that PFO, it is usually unjustified. But some disobedience does not violate that PFO, and if it also does not violate any other basic and obvious PFO, there can be no grounds for calling it unjustified, except perhaps its contravention of an alleged PFO to obey the law as such. Civil disobedience in the narrow sense can be justified, as Rawls has insisted all along,[20] only when (1) it is done sincerely for a "higher moral cause," (2) when there are no other legal means available (when all democratic remedies have been exhausted), and (3) when civil disobedience is not yet so widespread as to be self-defeating and dangerous to the survival of mutually beneficial institutions. When it is done under these conditions, it retains its character as an unusual and extreme step and is not "exploitative" of anyone. To the question, What if everyone did it? the justified civil disobedient can answer that if everyone did it (where by "it" we mean disobedience that satisfies the above condition), the results would not be bad at all.

There is one further respect in which some lawbreaking departs from the unfair play models, and this too has been emphasized by Rawls, especially in his book, in which he severely qualifies his earlier view of the importance of the fair play analogy. The benefits of government and the rule of law are not as equally distributed among the citizens of a modern industrial state as the benefits of traffic laws, for example, are distributed among motorists. So long as there is economic deprivation, social discrimination, and unequal access to powerful offices, society is not a "mutually advantageous" cooperative venture. If there is a PFO of obedience derived from the basic PFO of fair play, therefore, it could apply at most to the more favored members of society.

The final argument for a PFO of obedience to law derives it from what Rawls in his more mature work called the "natural duty to uphold just institutions."[21] This argument has the advantage over his earlier reliance on "fair play" in that the basic PFO in question is one we *all* share, regardless of our position in society and the degree to which we share the benefits of common undertakings. Rawls begins by distinguishing technical senses of *obligation* and *duty* (terms which I have treated here, for reasons of convenience, as synonyms). Obligations are incurred only by one's own voluntary acts, for example the obligations to keep one's promises, pay one's debts, and honor one's agreements. Duties typically attach to special stations, offices, or roles, whether or not we voluntarily occupy them; but our "natural duties" are those that everyone has, regardless of his jobs or roles—for example, duties to be generally friendly, helpful to those in need, and not to be cruel. Among our other natural duties, Rawls reports, is a duty to work toward the establishment of just institutions and to strengthen and support them once they are established.

Rawls's account of these matters has much to recommend it. I think that there clearly is a "natural duty," in his sense, to uphold just institutions, and that

it is one of the basic PFOs in our sense. Individual justice is much less likely to be done in general in the absence of strong and reliable just institutions that are constituted by clear and reasonable rules. I have in mind especially such political institutions and constitutive rules as the jury system, the universal franchise, free speech, majority rule in legislatures, and courts organized on the principle of due process. Insofar as one damages these institutional practices, one harms the cause of justice generally. That we are morally bound not to do such harm is as self-evident, I think, as that we are bound not to harm the cause of human happiness in general. Nevertheless, I doubt that a general PFO to obey valid laws can be derived from the basic PFO to support just institutions. Much lawbreaking does damage or threaten just institutions, but equally certainly much lawbreaking (including much unjustified lawbreaking) has no damaging effect on them whatever—for example, running a red light at three in the morning, cohabiting, playing poker at home with friends (where this is illegal). These examples are of actions that do not generate "disrespect for law," because they are unwitnessed or done in private. Perhaps many open and public acts of civil disobedience do damage just institutions, but there is no necessity that this be so. Rawls himself writes that civil disobedience, when it satisfies certain minimal conditions of reasonableness (including the circumstantial condition that such acts have not already become so common as to threaten to poison public discourse and lower standards of civility), actually functions as "a final device to maintain the stability of a just constitution,"[22] because it is an escape valve for pent-up indignations and is "disobedience to law within the framework of fidelity to law, although at the outer edge thereof."[23] Warfare against the state, covert subversion, disruption, violent intimidation, and the like do always carry the high risk of weakening just institutions, but civil disobedience, paradoxically, can actually strengthen them.

There could be a derivative moral PFO to obey the law only if, of necessity, every individual instance of deliberate disobedience were a violation of some basic PFO, but that seems to be no more true of the PFO to uphold just institutions than of the PFOs of gratitude, promise keeping, and fair play. The fact that an act would be illegal then, we may conclude, has no tendency whatever to make that act wrong. Why, in that case, does our conclusion seem, at first sight, so startling? That may be because in our legal system, as well as in many others that we can imagine, most of the actions that are legally prohibited also happen to be wrong on other grounds. The typical crimes of fraud and violence are wrong because they harm or endanger other people; they would be no less wrong if they were perfectly legal. Other prohibited acts, like driving in restricted lanes, are wrong even when harmless in the given case because they unfairly take advantage of the forbearance of others. If we knew that ninety percent of all illegal acts in our country are in similar ways wrong on grounds independent of their illegality and all we knew of a given act is that it is illegal, then we would be entitled to infer, with a degree of confidence proportioned to the evidence, that the given act is wrong too. That is to say that illegal acts are *"prima facie* wrong" in a sense different from the one we have been considering, namely, that there is a *statistical presumption* that they are, in any given case, wrong. But that is not to say that it is their character as illegal that makes them wrong or contributes in any degree to their wrongness. Rather their illegality is a characteristic contingently linked to the other properties that truly make them wrong; so that its presence may be a more or less reliable index or clue to the presence of wrongness, not its ground or basis.

The conclusions of this essay can now be stated tersely:

1. There is no general moral PFO to obey valid law, even in a democratic state with a just constitution.
2. The individual's moral problem in civil disobedi-

ence is not that of choosing between his higher moral cause and the PFO of obedience to law, but rather it is either
a) no problem at all since his civil disobedience will not violate any PFOs but *only* break the law; or
b) the problem of choosing between his higher moral cause and prudence (for example, personal safety), or
c) the moral problem of choosing between conflicting PFOs, one which supports his loyalty to the higher moral cause and another basic PFO (such as the PFO of fair play or the PFO to support just institutions) that may in this particular case be in conflict with it.

In case (*c*) no *general* advice from a moral philosopher is possible except to weigh sensitively the two conflicting PFOs and act in accordance with the one that seems weightier in the present circumstances.

3. Legal positivists should drop their assumption that even bad laws deserve respect simply because they are laws and that they impose some small obligation, at least, of obedience. Then, having no more problem of reconciliation, they can hold to their primary contention that all properly enacted law is valid law.
4. The ancient quest for a perfectly general ground of political obligation can be abandoned.

---

1. *David Daube,* Civil Disobedience in Antiquity *(Edinburgh, 1972), p. 1.*
2. *John Rawls,* A Theory of Justice *(Cambridge, Mass., 1971), p. 368.*
3. *Ibid., p. 364.*
4. *Ibid., p. 366.*
5. *Ibid., p. 365.*
6. *Lon L. Fuller, "Positivism and Fidelity to Law: A Reply to Professor Hart,"* Harvard Law Review *71 (1958): 630.*
7. *Carl Cohen,* Civil Disobedience: Conscience, Tactics, and the Law *(New York, 1971), p. 6.*
8. *Compare M. B. E. Smith, "Is There a Prima Facie Obligation to Obey the Law?,"* The Yale Law Journal *82 (1973): 950.*
9. *Richard Wasserstrom, "The Obligation to Obey the Law,"* UCLA Law Review *10 (1963).*
10. *For example, Rolf Sartorius,* Individual Conduct and Social Norms *(Belmont, Calif., 1975), chap. 6; A. John Simmons,* Moral Principles and Political Obligations *(Princeton, N.J., 1979), chap. 8; Smith, "Prima Facie Obligation." I have found Simmons's brilliant new book especially useful.*
11. *One early sketchy attempt was that of W. D. Ross,* The Right and the Good *(Oxford, 1930), pp. 27–28, who derived the PFO to obey laws of one's country "partly (as Socrates contends in the* Crito*) from the duty of gratitude for the benefits one has received from it, partly from the implicit promise to obey which seems to be*

involved in permanent residence in a country whose laws we know we are expected to obey, and still more clearly involved when we ourselves invoke the protection of its law . . . ; and partly (if we are fortunate in our country) from the fact that its laws are potent instruments for the general good."
12. *As quoted by Josef Pieper,* Justice *(London, 1957), p. 107.*
13. *Smith, "Prima Facie Obligation," p. 952.*
14. *A. John Simmons, "Tacit Consent and Political Obligation,"* Philosophy and Public Affairs *5 (1976).*
15. *Ibid., p. 279.*
16. *David Hume, "Of the Original Contract," first published in his* Essays Moral and Political *(1748).*
17. *Simmons,* Moral Principles, *p. 99.*
18. *Ibid.*
19. *The earlier formulation is in John Rawls's, "Legal Obligation and the Duty of Fair Play" in* Law and Philosophy, *edited by Sidney Hook (New York, 1964), pp. 3–18. Rawls's second thoughts are found in his* Theory of Justice, *pp. 342–49 et passim. In the book Rawls refers to "the principle of fairness" rather than "the principle of fair play," in part, apparently, to avoid the suggestion that all life is a game.*
20. *Theory of Justice, pp. 371–77.*
21. *Ibid., 333–41.*
22. *Ibid., p. 384.*
23. *Ibid., p. 366.*

Other Leading Theories of the Nature of Law

THE MODEL OF RULES*

Ronald M. Dworkin

Embarrassing Questions

Lawyers lean heavily on the connected concepts of legal right and legal obligation. We say that someone has a legal right or duty, and we take that statement as a sound basis for making claims and demands, and for criticizing the acts of public officials. But our understanding of these concepts is remarkably fragile, and we fall into trouble when we try to say what legal rights and obligations are. We say glibly that whether someone has a legal obligation is determined by applying "the law" to the particular facts of this case, but this is not a helpful answer, because we have the same difficulties with the concept of law.

We are used to summing up our troubles in the classic questions of jurisprudence: What is "the law"? When two sides disagree, as often happens, about a proposition "of law," what are they disagreeing about, and how shall we decide which side is right? Why do we call what "the law" says a matter of legal "obligation"? Is "obligation" here just a term of art, meaning only "what the law says"? Or does legal obligation have something to do with moral obligation? Can we say that we have, in principle at least, the same reasons for meeting our legal obligations that we have for meeting our moral obligations?

These are not puzzles for the cupboard, to be taken down on rainy days for fun. They are sources of continuing embarrassment, and they nag at our attention. They embarrass us in dealing with particular problems that we must solve, one way or another. Suppose a novel right-of-privacy case comes to court, and there is no statute or precedent either granting or denying the particular right of anonymity claimed by the plaintiff. What role in the court's decision should be played by the fact that most people in the community think that private individuals are "morally" entitled to that particular privacy? Suppose the Supreme Court orders some prisoner freed because the police used procedures that the Court now says are constitutionally forbidden, although the Court's earlier decisions upheld these procedures. Must the Court, to be consistent, free all other prisoners previously convicted through these same procedures?[1] Conceptual puzzles about "the law" and "legal obligation" become acute when a court is confronted with a problem like this.

These eruptions signal a chronic disease. Day in and day out we send people to jail, or take money away from them, or make them do things they do not want to do, under coercion of force, and we justify all of this by speaking of such persons as having broken

---

*From 35 *University of Chicago Law Review* 14 (1967). Reprinted by permission of the author and the publisher.

the law or having failed to meet their legal obligations, or having interfered with other people's legal rights. Even in clear cases (a bank robber or a willful breach of contract), when we are confident that someone had a legal obligation and broke it, we are not able to give a satisfactory account of what that means, or why that entitles the state to punish or coerce him. We may feel confident that what we are doing is proper, but until we can identify the principles we are following we cannot be sure that they are sufficient, or whether we are applying them consistently. In less clear cases, when the issue of whether an obligation has been broken is for some reason controversial, the pitch of these nagging questions rises, and our responsibility to find answers deepens.

Certain lawyers (we may call them "nominalists") urge that we solve these problems by ignoring them. In their view the concepts of "legal obligation" and "the law" are myths, invented and sustained by lawyers for a dismal mix of conscious and subconscious motives. The puzzles we find in these concepts are merely symptoms that they are myths. They are unsolvable because unreal, and our concern with them is just one feature of our enslavement. We would do better to flush away the puzzles and the concepts altogether, and pursue our important social objectives without this excess baggage.

This is a tempting suggestion, but it has fatal drawbacks. Before we can decide that our concepts of law and of legal obligation are myths, we must decide what they are. We must be able to state, at least roughly, what it is we all believe that is wrong. But the nerve of our problem is that we have great difficulty in doing just that. Indeed, when we ask what law is and what legal obligations are, we are asking for a theory of how we use these concepts and of the conceptual commitments our use entails. We cannot conclude, before we have such a general theory, that our practices are stupid or superstitious.

Of course, the nominalists think they know how the rest of us use these concepts. They think that when we speak of "the law," we mean a set of timeless rules stocked in some conceptual warehouse awaiting discovery by judges, and that when we speak of legal obligation we mean the invisible chains these mysterious rules somehow drape around us. The theory that there are such rules and chains they call "mechanical jurisprudence," and they are right in ridiculing its practitioners. Their difficulty, however, lies in finding practitioners to ridicule. So far they have had little luck in caging and exhibiting mechanical

jurisprudence (all specimens captured—even Blackstone and Joseph Beale—have had to be released after careful reading of their texts).

In any event, it is clear that most lawyers have nothing like this in mind when they speak of the law and of legal obligation. A superficial examination of our practices is enough to show this, for we speak of laws changing and evolving, and of legal obligation sometimes being problematical. In these and other ways we show that we are not addicted to mechanical jurisprudence.

Nevertheless, we do use the concepts of law and legal obligation, and we do suppose that society's warrant to punish and coerce is written in that currency. It may be that when the details of this practice are laid bare, the concepts we do use will be shown to be as silly and as thick with illusion as those the nominalists invented. If so, then we shall have to find other ways to describe what we do, and either provide other justifications or change our practices. But until we have discovered this and made these adjustments, we cannot accept the nominalists' premature invitation to turn our backs on the problems our present concepts provide.

Of course the suggestion that we stop talking about "the law" and "legal obligation" is mostly bluff. These concepts are too deeply cemented into the structure of our political practices—they cannot be given up like cigarettes or hats. Some of the nominalists have half-admitted this and said that the myths they condemn should be thought of as Platonic myths and retained to seduce the masses into order. This is perhaps not so cynical a suggestion as it seems; perhaps it is a covert hedging of a dubious bet.

If we boil away the bluff, the nominalist attack reduces to an attack on mechanical jurisprudence. Through the lines of the attack, and in spite of the heroic calls for the death of law, the nominalists themselves have offered an analysis of how the terms "law" and "legal obligation" should be used which is not very different from that of more classical philosophers. Nominalists present their analysis as a model of how legal institutions (particularly courts) "really operate." But their model differs mainly in emphasis from the theory first made popular by the nineteenth century philosopher John Austin, and now accepted in one form or another by most working and academic lawyers who hold views on jurisprudence. I shall call this theory, with some historical looseness, "positivism." I want to examine the soundness of positivism, particularly in the powerful form that Professor

H. L. A. Hart of Oxford has given to it. I choose to focus on his position, not only because of its clarity and elegance, but because here, as almost everywhere else in legal philosophy, constructive thought must start with a consideration of his views.

Positivism

Positivism has a few central and organizing propositions as its skeleton, and though not every philosopher who is called a positivist would subscribe to these in the way I present them, they do define the general position I want to examine. These key tenets may be stated as follows:

(a) The law of a community is a set of special rules used by the community directly or indirectly for the purpose of determining which behavior will be punished or coerced by the public power. These special rules can be identified and distinguished by specific criteria, by tests having to do not with their content but with their *pedigree* or the manner in which they were adopted or developed. These tests of pedigree can be used to distinguish valid legal rules from spurious legal rules (rules which lawyers and litigants wrongly argue are rules of law) and also from other sorts of social rules (generally lumped together as "moral rules") that the community follows but does not enforce through public power.

(b) The set of these valid legal rules is exhaustive of "the law," so that if someone's case is not clearly covered by such a rule (because there is none that seems appropriate, or those that seem appropriate are vague, or for some other reason) then that case cannot be decided by "applying the law." It must be decided by some official, like a judge, "exercising his discretion," which means reaching beyond the law for some other sort of standard to guide him in manufacturing a fresh legal rule or supplementing an old one.

(c) To say that someone has a "legal obligation" is to say that his case falls under a valid legal rule that requires him to do or to forbear from doing something. (To say he has a legal right, or has a legal power of some sort, or a legal privilege or immunity, is to assert, in a shorthand way, that others have actual or hypothetical legal obligations to act or not to act in certain ways touching him.) In the absence of such a valid legal rule there is no legal obligation; it follows that when the judge decides an issue by exercising his discretion, he is not enforcing a legal obligation as to that issue.

This is only the skeleton of positivism. The flesh is arranged differently by different positivists, and some even tinker with the bones. Different versions differ chiefly in their description of the fundamental test of pedigree a rule must meet to count as a rule of law.

Austin, for example, framed his version of the fundamental test as a series of interlocking definitions and distinctions.[2] He defined having an obligation as lying under a rule, a rule as a general command, and a command as an expression of desire that others behave in a particular way, backed by the power and will to enforce that expression in the event of disobedience. He distinguished classes of rules (legal, moral or religious) according to which person or group is the author of the general command the rule represents. In each political community, he thought, one will find a sovereign—a person or a determinate group whom the rest obey habitually, but who is not in the habit of obeying anyone else. The legal rules of a community are the general commands its sovereign has deployed. Austin's definition of legal obligation followed from this definition of law. One has a legal obligation, he thought, if one is among the addressees of some general order of the sovereign, and is in danger of suffering a sanction unless he obeys that order.

Of course, the sovereign cannot provide for all contingencies through any scheme of orders, and some of his orders will inevitably be vague or have furry edges. Therefore (according to Austin) the sovereign grants those who enforce the law (judges) discretion to make fresh orders when novel or troublesome cases are presented. The judges then make new rules or adapt old rules, and the sovereign either overturns their creations, or tacitly confirms them by failing to do so.

Austin's model is quite beautiful in its simplicity. It asserts the first tenet of positivism, that the law is a set of rules specially selected to govern public order, and offers a simple factual test—what has the sovereign commanded?—as the sole criterion for identifying those special rules. In time, however, those who studied and tried to apply Austin's model found it too simple. Many objections were raised, among which were two that seemed fundamental. First, Austin's key assumption that in each community a determinate group or institution can be found, which is in ultimate control of all other groups, seemed not to hold in a complex society. Political control in a modern nation is pluralistic and shifting, a matter of more or less, of compromise and cooperation and alliance, so that it is often impossible to say that any person or group has that dramatic control necessary to qualify as an Austinian sovereign. One wants to say, in the United States for example, that the "people" are sovereign. But this means almost nothing, and in itself provides no test for determining what the "people" have commanded, or distinguishing their legal from their social or moral commands.

Second, critics began to realize that Austin's analysis fails entirely to account for, even to recognize, certain striking facts about the attitudes we take toward "the law." We make an important distinction between law and even the general orders of a gangster. We feel that the law's strictures—and its sanctions—are different in that they are obligatory in a way that the outlaw's commands are not. Austin's analysis has no place for any such distinction, because it defines an obligation as subjection to the threat of force, and so founds the authority of law entirely on the sovereign's ability and will to harm those who disobey. Perhaps the distinction we make is illusory—perhaps our feelings of some special authority attaching to the law is based on religious hangover or another sort of mass self-deception. But Austin does not demonstrate this, and we are entitled to insist that an analysis of our concept of law either acknowledge and explain our attitudes, or show why they are mistaken.

H. L. A. Hart's version of positivism is more complex than Austin's, in two ways. First, he recognizes, as Austin did not, the rules are of different logical kinds (Hart distinguishes two kinds, which he calls "primary" and "secondary" rules). Second, he rejects Austin's theory that a rule is a kind of command, and substitutes a more elaborate general analysis of what rules are. We must pause over each of these points, and then note how they merge in Hart's concept of law.

Hart's distinction between primary and secondary rules is of great importance.[3] Primary rules are those that grant rights or impose obligations upon members of the community. The rules of the criminal law that forbid us to rob, murder or drive too fast are good examples of primary rules. Secondary rules are those that stipulate how, and by whom, such primary rules may be formed, recognized, modified or extinguished. The rules that stipulate how Congress is composed, and how it enacts legislation, are examples of secondary rules. Rules about forming contracts and executing wills are also secondary rules because they stipulate how very particular rules governing particular legal obligations (that is, the terms of a contract or the provisions of a will) come into existence and are changed.

His general analysis of rules is also of great importance.[4] Austin had said that every rule is a general command, and that a person is obligated under a rule if he is liable to be hurt should he disobey it. Hart points out that this obliterates the distinction between being *obliged* to do something and being *obligated* to do it. If one is bound by a rule he is obligated, not merely obliged, to do what it provides, and therefore being bound by a rule must be different from being subject to an injury if one disobeys an order. A rule differs from an order, among other ways, by being *normative,* by setting a standard of behavior that has a call on its subject beyond the threat that may enforce it. A rule can never be binding just because some person with physical power wants it to be so. He must have *authority* to issue the rule or it is no rule, and such authority can only come from another rule which is already binding on those to whom he speaks. That is the difference between a valid law and the orders of a gunman.

So Hart offers a general theory of rules that does not make their authority depend upon the physical power of their authors. If we examine the way different rules come into being, he tells us, and attend to the distinction between primary and secondary rules, we see that there are two possible sources of a rule's authority.[5]

(a) A rule may become binding upon a group of people because that group through its practices *accepts* the rule as a standard for its conduct. It is not enough that the group simply conforms to a pattern of behavior: even though most Englishmen may go to the movies on Saturday evening, they have not accepted a rule requiring that they do so. A practice constitutes the acceptance of a rule only when those who follow the practice regard the rule as binding, and recognize the rule as a reason or justification for their own behavior and as a reason for criticizing the behavior of others who do not obey it.

(b) A rule may also become binding in quite a different way, namely by being enacted in conformity with some *secondary* rule that stipulates that rules so enacted shall be binding. If the constitution of a club stipulates, for example, that by-laws may be adopted by a majority of the members, then particular by-laws so voted are binding upon all the members, not because of any practice of acceptance of these particular by-laws, but because the constitution says so. We use the concept of *validity* in this connection: rules binding because they have been created in a manner stipulated by some secondary rule are called "valid" rules. Thus we can record Hart's fundamental distinction this way: a rule may be binding (a) because it is accepted or (b) because it is valid.

Hart's concept of law is a construction of these various distinctions.[6] Primitive communities have only primary rules, and these are binding entirely because of practices of acceptance. Such communities cannot be said to have "law," because there is no way to distinguish a set of legal rules from amongst other social rules, as the first tenet of positivism requires. But when a particular community has developed a fundamental secondary rule that stipulates how legal rules are to be identified, the idea of a distinct set of legal rules, and thus of law, is born.

Hart calls such a fundamental secondary rule a "rule of recognition." The rule of recognition of a given community may be relatively simple ("What the king enacts is law") or it may be very complex (the United States Constitution, with all its difficulties of interpretation, may be considered a single rule of recognition). The demonstration that a particular rule is valid may therefore require tracing a complicated chain of validity back from that particular rule ultimately to the fundamental rule. Thus a parking ordinance of the city of New Haven is valid because it is adopted by a city council, pursuant to the procedures and within the competence specified by the municipal law adopted by the state of Connecticut, in conformity with the procedures and within the competence specified by the constitution of the state of Connecticut, which was in turn adopted consistently with the requirements of the United States Constitution.

Of course, a rule of recognition cannot itself be valid, because by hypothesis it is ultimate, and so cannot meet tests stipulated by a more fundamental rule. The rule of recognition is the sole rule in a legal system whose binding force depends upon its acceptance. If we wish to know what rule of recognition a particular community has adopted or follows, we must observe how its citizens, and particularly its officials, behave. We must observe what ultimate arguments they accept as showing the validity of a particular rule, and what ultimate arguments they use to criticize other officials or institutions. We can apply no mechanical test, but there is no danger of our confusing the rule of recognition of a community with its rules of morality. The rule of recognition is identified by the fact that its province is the operation of the governmental apparatus of legislatures, courts, agencies, policemen, and the rest.

In this way Hart rescues the fundamentals of positivism from Austin's mistakes. Hart agrees with Austin that valid rules of law may be created through the acts of officials and public institutions. But Austin thought that the authority of these institutions lay only in their monopoly of power. Hart finds their authority in the background of constitutional standards against which they act, constitutional standards that have been accepted, in the form of a fundamental rule of recognition, by the community which they govern. This background legitimates the decisions of government and gives them the cast and call of obligation that the naked commands of Austin's sovereign lacked. Hart's theory differs from Austin's also, in recognizing that different communities use different ultimate tests of law, and that some allow other means of creating law than the deliberate act of a legislative institution. Hart mentions "long customary practice" and "the relation [of a rule] to judicial decisions" as other criteria that are often used, though generally along with and subordinate to the test of legislation.

So Hart's version of positivism is more complex than Austin's, and his test for valid rules of law is more sophisticated. In one respect, however, the two models are very similar. Hart, like Austin, recognizes that legal rules have fuzzy edges (he speaks of them as having "open texture") and, again like Austin, he accounts for troublesome cases by saying that judges have had to exercise discretion to decide these cases by fresh legislation.[7] (I shall later try to show why one who thinks of law as a special set of rules is almost inevitably drawn to account for difficult cases in terms of someone's exercise of discretion.)

Rules, Principles, and Policies

I want to make a general attack on positivism, and I shall use H. L. A. Hart's version as a target, when a particular target is needed. My strategy will be organized around the fact that when lawyers reason or dispute about legal rights and obligations, particularly in those hard cases when our problems with these concepts seem most acute, they make use of standards that do not function as rules, but operate differently as principles, policies, and other sorts of standards. Positivism, I shall argue, is a model of and for a system of rules, and its central notion of a single fundamental test for law forces us to miss the important roles of these standards that are not rules.

I just spoke of "principles, policies, and other sorts of standards." Most often I shall use the term "principle" generically, to refer to the whole set of these standards other than rules; occasionally, however, I shall be more precise, and distinguish between principles and policies. Although nothing in the present argument will turn on the distinction, I should state how I draw it. I call a "policy" that kind of standard that sets out a goal to be reached, generally an improvement in some economic, political, or social feature of the community (though some goals are negative, in that they stipulate that some present feature is to be protected from adverse change). I call a "principle" a standard that is to be observed, not because it will advance or secure an economic, political, or social situation deemed desirable, but because it is a requirement of justice or fairness or some other dimension of morality. Thus the standard that automobile accidents are to be decreased is a policy, and the standard that no man may profit by his own wrong a principle. The distinction can be collapsed by construing a principle as stating a social goal (that is, the goal of a society in which no man profits by his own wrong), or by construing a policy as stating a principle (that is, the principle that the goal the policy embraces is a worthy one) or by adopting the utilitarian thesis that principles of justice are disguised statements of goals (securing the greatest happiness of the greatest number). In some contexts the distinction has uses which are lost if it is thus collapsed.[8]

My immediate purpose, however, is to distinguish principles in the generic sense from rules, and I shall start by collecting some examples of the former. The examples I offer are chosen haphazardly; almost any case in a law school casebook would provide examples that would serve as well. In 1889 a New York court, in the famous case of *Riggs* v. *Palmer*,[9] had to decide whether an heir named in the will of his grandfather could inherit under that will, even though he had murdered his grandfather to do so. The court began its reasoning with this admission: "It is quite true that statutes regulating the making, proof and effect of wills, and the devolution of property, if literally construed, and if their force and effect can in no way and under no circumstances be controlled or modified, give this property to the murderer."[10] But the court continued to note that "all laws as well as all contracts may be controlled in their operation and effect by general, fundamental maxims of the common law. No one shall be permitted to profit by his own fraud, or to take advantage of his own wrong, or to found any claim upon his own iniquity, or to acquire property by his own crime."[11] The murderer did not receive his inheritance.

In 1960, a New Jersey court was faced, in *Henningsen* v. *Bloomfield Motors, Inc.*,[12] with the impor-

tant question of whether (or how much) an automobile manufacturer may limit his liability in case the automobile is defective. Henningsen had bought a car, and signed a contract which said that the manufacturer's liability for defects was limited to "making good" defective parts—"this warranty being expressly in lieu of all other warranties, obligations or liabilities." Henningsen argued that, at least in the circumstances of his case, the manufacturer ought not to be protected by this limitation, and ought to be liable for the medical and other expenses of persons injured in a crash. He was not able to point to any statute, or to any established rule of law, that prevented the manufacturer from standing on the contract. The court nevertheless agreed with Henningsen. At various points in the court's argument the following appeals to standards are made: (a) "[W]e must keep in mind the general principle that, in the absence of fraud, one who does not choose to read a contract before signing it cannot later relieve himself of its burdens."[13] (b) "In applying that principle, the basic tenet of freedom of competent parties to contract is a factor of importance."[14] (c) "Freedom of contract is not such an immutable doctrine as to admit of no qualification in the area in which we are concerned."[15] (d) "In a society such as ours where the automobile is a common and necessary adjunct of daily life, and where its use is so fraught with danger to the driver, passengers and the public, the manufacturer is under a special obligation in connection with the construction, promotion and sale of his cars. Consequently, the courts must examine purchase agreements closely to see if consumer and public interests are treated fairly."[16] (e) " '[I]s there any principle which is more familiar or more firmly embedded in the history of Anglo-American law than the basic doctrine that the courts will not permit themselves to be used as instruments of inequity and injustice?' "[17] (f) " 'More specifically, the courts generally refuse to lend themselves to the enforcement of a "bargain" in which one party has unjustly taken advantage of the economic necessities of another. . . . ' "[18]

The standards set out in these quotations are not the sort we think of as legal rules. They seem very different from propositions like "The maximum legal speed on the turnpike is sixty miles an hour" or "A will is invalid unless signed by three witnesses." They are different because they are legal principles rather than legal rules.

The difference between legal principles and legal rules is a logical distinction. Both sets of standards point to particular decisions about legal obligation in particular circumstances, but they differ in the character of the direction they give. Rules are applicable in an all-or-nothing fashion. If the facts a rule stipulates are given, then either the rule is valid, in which case the answer it supplies must be accepted, or it is not, in which case it contributes nothing to the decision.

This all-or-nothing is seen most plainly if we look at the way rules operate, not in law, but in some enterprise they dominate—a game, for example. In baseball a rule provides that if the batter has had three strikes, he is out. An official cannot consistently acknowledge that this is an accurate statement of a baseball rule, and decide that a batter who has had three strikes is not out. Of course, a rule may have exceptions (the batter who has taken three strikes is not out if the catcher drops the third strike). However, an accurate statement of the rule would take this exception into account, and any that did not would be incomplete. If the list of exceptions is very large, it would be too clumsy to repeat them each time the rule is cited; there is, however, no reason in theory why they could not all be added on, and the more that are, the more accurate is the statement of the rule.

If we take baseball rules as a model, we find that rules of law, like the rule that a will is invalid unless signed by three witnesses, fit the model well. If the requirement of three witnesses is a valid legal rule, then it cannot be that a will has been signed by only two witnesses and is valid. The rule might have exceptions, but if it does then it is inaccurate and incomplete to state the rule so simply, without enumerating the exceptions. In theory, at least, the exceptions could all be listed, and the more of them that are, the more complete is the statement of the rule.

But this is not the way the sample principles in the quotations operate. Even those which look most like rules do not set out legal consequences that follow automatically when the conditions provided are met. We say that our law respects the principle that no man may profit from his own wrong, but we do not mean that the law never permits a man to profit from wrongs he commits. In fact, people often profit, perfectly legally, from their legal wrongs. The most notorious case is adverse possession—if I trespass on your land long enough, some day I will gain a right to cross your land whenever I please. There are many less dramatic examples. If a man leaves one job, breaking a contract, to take a much higher paying job, he may have to pay damages to his first employer, but he is usually entitled to keep his new salary. If a man jumps bail and crosses state lines to make a brilliant investment in another state, he may be sent back to jail, but he will keep his profits.

We do not treat these—and countless other counter-instances that can easily be imagined—as showing that the principle about profiting from one's wrongs is not a principle of our legal system, or that it is incomplete and needs qualifying exceptions. We do not treat counter-instances as exceptions (at least not exceptions in the way in which a catcher's dropping the third strike is an exception) because we could not hope to capture these counter-instances simply by a more extended statement of the principle. They are not, even in theory, subject to enumeration, because we would have to include not only these cases (like adverse possession) in which some institution has already provided that profit can be gained through a wrong, but also those numberless imaginary cases in which we know in advance that the principle would not hold. Listing some of these might sharpen our sense of the principle's weight (I shall mention that dimension in a moment), but it would not make for a more accurate or complete statement of the principle.

A principle like "No man may profit from his own wrong" does not even purport to set out conditions that make its application necessary. Rather, it states a reason that argues in one direction, but does not necessitate a particular decision. If a man has or is about to receive something, as a direct result of something illegal he did to get it, then that is a reason which the law will take into account in deciding whether he should keep it. There may be other principles or policies arguing in the other direction—a policy of securing title, for example, or a principle limiting punishment to what the legislature has stipulated. If so, our principle may not prevail, but that does not mean that it is not a principle of our legal system, because in the next case, when these contravening considerations are absent or less weighty, the principle may be decisive. All that is meant, when we say that a particular principle is a principle of our law, is that the principle is one which officials must take into account, if it is relevant, as a consideration inclining in one direction or another.

The logical distinction between rules and principles appears more clearly when we consider principles that do not even look like rules. Consider the proposition, set out under "(d)" in the excerpts from the *Henningsen* opinion, that "the manufacturer is under a special obligation in connection with the construction, promotion and sale of his cars." This does not even purport to define the specific duties such a special obligation entails, or to tell us what rights automobile consumers acquire as a result. It merely states—and this is an essential link in the *Henningsen* argument—that automobile manufacturers must be held to higher standards than other manufacturers, and are less entitled to rely on the competing principle of freedom of contract. It does not mean that they may never rely on that principle, or that courts may rewrite automobile purchase contracts at will; it means only that if a particular clause seems unfair or burdensome, courts have less reason to enforce the clause than if it were for the purchase of neckties. The "special obligation" counts in favor, but does not in itself necessitate, a decision refusing to enforce the terms of an automobile purchase contract.

This first difference between rules and principles entails another. Principles have a dimension that rules do not—the dimension of weight or importance. When principles intersect (the policy of protecting automobile consumers intersecting with principles of freedom of contract, for example), one who must resolve the conflict has to take into account the relative weight of each. This cannot be, of course, an exact measurement, and the judgment that a particular principle or policy is more important than another will often be a controversial one. Nevertheless, it is an integral part of the concept of a principle that it has this dimension, that it makes sense to ask how important or how weighty it is.

Rules do not have this dimension. We can speak of rules as being *functionally* important or unimportant (the baseball rule that three strikes are out is more important than the rule that runners may advance on a balk, because the game would be much more changed with the first rule altered than the second). In this sense, one legal rule may be more important than another because it has a greater or more important role in regulating behavior. But we cannot say that one rule is more important than another within the system of rules, so that when two rules conflict one supersedes the other by virtue of its greater weight. If two rules conflict, one of them cannot be a valid rule. The decision as to which is valid, and which must be abandoned or recast, must be made by appealing to considerations beyond the rules themselves. A legal system might regulate such conflicts by other rules, which prefer the rule enacted by the higher authority, or the rule enacted later, or the more specific rule, or something of that sort. A legal system may also prefer the rule supported by the more important principles. (Our own legal system uses both of these techniques.)

It is not always clear from the form of a standard whether it is a rule or a principle. "A will is invalid unless signed by three witnesses" is not very different in form from "A man may not profit from his own

wrong," but one who knows something of American laws knows that he must take the first as stating a rule and the second as stating a principle. In many cases the distinction is difficult to make—it may not have been settled how the standard should operate, and this issue may itself be a focus of controversy. The First Amendment to the United States Constitution contains the provision that Congress shall not abridge freedom of speech. Is this a rule, so that if a particular law does abridge freedom of speech, it follows that it is unconstitutional? Those who claim that the first amendment is "an absolute" say that it must be taken in this way, that is, as a rule. Or does it merely state a principle, so that when an abridgement of speech is discovered, it is unconstitutional unless the context presents some other policy or principle which in the circumstances is weighty enough to permit the abridgement? That is the position of those who argue for what is called the "clear and present danger" test or some other form of "balancing."

Sometimes a rule and a principle can play much the same role, and the difference between them is almost a matter of form alone. The first section of the Sherman Act states that every contract in restraint of trade shall be void. The Supreme Court had to make the decision whether this provision should be treated as a rule in its own terms (striking down every contract "which restrains trade," which almost any contract does) or as a principle, providing a reason for striking down a contract in the absence of effective contrary policies. The Court construed the provision as a rule, but treated that rule as containing the word "unreasonable," and as prohibiting only "unreasonable" restraints of trade.[19] This allowed the provision to function logically as a rule (whenever a court finds that the restraint is "unreasonable" it is bound to hold the contract invalid) and substantially as a principle (a court must take into account a variety of other principles and policies in determining whether a particular restraint in particular economic circumstances is "unreasonable").

Words like "reasonable," "negligent," "unjust," and "significant" often perform just this function. Each of these terms makes the application of the rule which contains it depend to some extent upon principles or policies lying beyond the rule, and in this way makes that rule itself more like a principle. But they do not quite turn the rule into a principle, because even the least confining of these terms restricts the *kind* of other principles and policies on which the rule depends. If we are bound by a rule that says that "unreasonable" contracts are void, or that grossly "unfair" contracts will not be enforced, much more judgment is required than if the quoted terms were omitted. But suppose a case in which some consideration of policy or principle suggests that a contract should be enforced even though its restraint is not reasonable, or even though it is grossly unfair. Enforcing these contracts would be forbidden by our rules, and thus permitted only if these rules were abandoned or modified. If we were dealing, however, not with a rule but with a policy against enforcing unreasonable contracts, or a principle that unfair contracts ought not to be enforced, the contracts could be enforced without alteration of the law.

Principles and the Concept of Law

Once we identify legal principles as separate sorts of standards, different from legal rules, we are suddenly aware of them all around us. Law teachers teach them, lawbooks cite them, legal historians celebrate them. But they seem most energetically at work, carrying most weight, in difficult lawsuits like *Riggs* and *Henningsen*. In cases like these principles play an essential part in arguments supporting judgments about particular legal rights and obligations. After the case is decided, we may say that the case stands for a particular rule (that is, the rule that one who murders is not eligible to take under the will of his victim). But the rule does not exist before the case is decided; the court cites principles as its justification for adopting and applying a new rule. In *Riggs,* the court cited the principle that no man may profit from his own wrong as a background standard against which to read the statute of wills and in this way justified a new interpretation of that statute. In *Henningsen,* the court cited a variety of intersecting principles and policies as authority for a new rule respecting manufacturer's liability for automobile defects.

An analysis of the concept of legal obligation must therefore account for the important role of principles in reaching particular decisions of law. There are two very different tacks we might take.

(a) We might treat legal principles the way we treat legal rules and say that some principles are binding as law and must be taken into account by judges and lawyers who make decisions of legal obligation. If we took this tack, we should say that in the United States, at least, the "law" includes principles as well as rules.

(b) We might, on the other hand, deny that principles can be binding the way some rules are. We would say, instead, that in cases like *Riggs* or *Henningsen* the judge reaches beyond the rules that he is bound to apply (reaches, that is, beyond the "law") for extralegal principles he is free to follow if he wishes.

One might think that there is not much difference between these two lines of attack, that it is only a verbal question of how one wants to use the word "law." But that is a mistake, because the choice between these two accounts has the greatest consequences for an analysis of legal obligation. It is a choice between two *concepts* of a legal principle, a choice we can clarify by comparing it to a choice we might make between two concepts of a legal rule. We sometimes say of someone that he "makes it a rule" to do something, when we mean that he has chosen to follow a certain practice. We might say that someone has made it a rule, for example, to run a mile before breakfast because he wants to be healthy and believes in a regimen. We do not mean, when we say this, that he is *bound* by the rule that he must run a mile before breakfast, or even that he regards it as binding upon him. Accepting a rule as binding is something different from making it a rule to do something. If we use Hart's example again, there is a difference between saying that Englishmen make it a rule to see a movie once a week, and saying that the English have a rule that one must see a movie once a week. The second implies that if an Englishman does not follow the rule, he is subject to criticism or censure, but the first does not. The first does not exclude the possibility of a *sort* of criticism—we can say that one who does not see movies is neglecting his education—but we do not suggest that he is doing something wrong *just* in not following the rule.[20]

If we think of the judges of a community as a group, we could describe the rules of law they follow in these two different ways. We could say, for instance, that in a certain state the judges make it a rule not to enforce wills unless there are three witnesses. This would not imply that the rare judge who enforces such a will is doing anything wrong just for that reason. On the other hand we can say that in that state a rule of law requires judges not to enforce such wills; this does imply that a judge who enforces them is doing something wrong. Hart, Austin and other positivists, of course, would insist on this latter account of legal rules; they would not at all be satisfied with the "make it a rule" account. It is not a verbal question of which account is right. It is a question of which describes the social situation more accurately. Other important issues turn on which description we accept. If judges simply "make it a rule" not to enforce certain contracts, for example, then we cannot say, before the decision, that anyone is "entitled" to that result, and that proposition cannot enter into any justification we might offer for the decision.

The two lines of attack on principles parallel these two accounts of rules. The first tack treats principles as binding upon judges, so that they are wrong not to apply the principles when they are pertinent. The second tack treats principles as summaries of what most judges "make it a principle" to do when forced to go beyond the standards that bind them. The choice between these approaches will affect, perhaps even determine, the answer we can give to the question whether the judge in a hard case like *Riggs* or *Henningsen* is attempting to enforce preexisting legal rights and obligations. If we take the first tack, we are still free to argue that because such judges are applying binding legal standards they are enforcing legal rights and obligations. But if we take the second, we are out of court on that issue, and we must acknowledge that the murderer's family in *Riggs* and the manufacturer in *Henningsen* were deprived of their property by an act of judicial discretion applied *ex post facto*. This may not shock many readers—the notion of judicial discretion has percolated through the legal community—but it does illustrate one of the most nettlesome of the puzzles that drive philosophers to worry about legal obligation. If taking property away in cases like these cannot be justified by appealing to an established obligation, yet another justification must be found, and nothing satisfactory has yet been supplied.

In my skeleton diagram of positivism, previously set out, I listed the doctrine of judicial discretion as the second tenet. Positivists hold that when a case is not covered by a clear rule, a judge must exercise his discretion to decide that case by what amounts to a fresh piece of legislation. There may be an important connection between this doctrine and the question of which of the two approaches to legal principles we must take. We shall therefore want to ask whether the doctrine is correct, and whether it implies the second approach, as it seems on its face to do. En route to these issues, however, we shall have to polish our understanding of the concept of discretion. I shall try to show how certain confusions about that concept, and in particular a failure to discriminate different

senses in which it is used, account for the popularity of the doctrine of discretion. I shall argue that in the sense in which the doctrine does have a bearing on our treatment of principles, it is entirely unsupported by the arguments the positivists use to defend it.

Discretion

The concept of discretion was lifted by the positivists from ordinary language, and to understand it we must put it back *in habitat* for a moment. What does it mean, in ordinary life, to say that someone "has discretion"? The first thing to notice is that the concept is out of place in all but very special contexts. For example, you would not say that I either do or do not have discretion to choose a house for my family. It is not true that I have "no discretion" in making that choice, and yet it would be almost equally misleading to say that I do have discretion. The concept of discretion is at home in only one sort of context: when someone is in general charged with making decisions subject to standards set by a particular authority. It makes sense to speak of the discretion of a sergeant who is subject to orders of superiors, or the discretion of a sports official or contest judge who is governed by a rule book or the terms of the contest. Discretion, like the hole in a doughnut, does not exist except as an area left open by a surrounding belt of restriction. It is therefore a relative concept. It always makes sense to ask, "Discretion under which standards?" or "Discretion as to which authority?" Generally the context will make the answer to this plain, but in some cases the official may have discretion from one standpoint though not from another.

Like almost all terms, the precise meaning of "discretion" is affected by features of the context. The term is always colored by the background of understood information against which it is used. Although the shadings are many, it will be helpful for us to recognize some gross distinctions.

Sometimes we use "discretion" in a weak sense, simply to say that for some reason the standards an official must apply cannot be applied mechanically but demand the use of judgment. We use this weak sense when the context does not already make that clear, when the background our audience assumes does not contain that piece of information. Thus we might say, "The sergeant's orders left him a great deal of discretion." To those who do not know what the sergeant's orders were or who do not know something that made those orders vague or hard to carry out. It would make perfect sense to add, by way of amplification, that the lieutenant had ordered the sergeant to take his five most experienced men on patrol but that it was hard to determine which were the most experienced.

Sometimes we use the term in a different weak sense, to say only that some official has final authority to make a decision and cannot be reviewed and reversed by any other official. We speak this way when the official is part of a hierarchy of officials structured so that some have higher authority but in which the patterns of authority are different for different classes of decision. Thus we might say that in baseball certain decisions, like the decision whether the ball or the runner reached second base first, are left to the discretion of the second base umpire, if we mean that on this issue the head umpire has no power to substitute his own judgment if he disagrees.

I call both of these senses weak to distinguish them from a stronger sense. We use "discretion" sometimes not merely to say that an official must use judgment in applying the standards set for him by authority, or that no one will review that exercise of judgment, but to say that on some issue he is simply not bound by standards set by the authority in question. In this sense we say that a sergeant has discretion who has been told to pick any five men for patrol he chooses or that a judge in a dog show has discretion to judge airedales before boxers if the rules do not stipulate an order of events. We use this sense not to comment on the vagueness or difficulty of the standards, or on who has the final word in applying them, but on their range and the decisions they purport to control. If the sergeant is told to take the five most experienced men, he does not have discretion in this strong sense because that order purports to govern his decision. The boxing referee who must decide which fighter has been the more aggressive does not have discretion, in the strong sense, for the same reason.[21]

If anyone said that the sergeant or the referee had discretion in these cases, we should have to understand him, if the context permitted, as using the term in one of the weak senses. Suppose, for example, the lieutenant ordered the sergeant to select the five men he deemed most experienced, and then added that the sergeant had discretion to choose them. Or the rules provided that the referee should award the round to the more aggressive fighter, with discretion in selecting him. We should have to understand these

statements in the second weak sense, as speaking to the question of review of the decision. The first weak sense—that the decisions take judgment—would be otiose, and the third, strong sense is excluded by the statements themselves.

We must avoid one tempting confusion. The strong sense of discretion is not tantamount to license, and does not exclude criticism. Almost any situation in which a person acts (including those in which there is no question of decision under special authority, and so no question of discretion) makes relevant certain standards of rationality, fairness and effectiveness. We criticize each other's acts in terms of these standards, and there is no reason not to do so when the acts are within the center rather than beyond the perimeter of the doughnut of special authority. So we can say that the sergeant who was given discretion (in the strong sense) to pick a patrol did so stupidly or maliciously or carelessly, or that the judge who had discretion in the order of viewing dogs made a mistake because he took boxers first although there were only three airedales and many more boxers. An official's discretion means not that he is free to decide without recourse to standards of sense and fairness, but only that his decision is not controlled by a standard furnished by the particular authority we have in mind when we raise the question of discretion. Of course this latter sort of freedom is important; that is why we have the strong sense of discretion. Someone who has discretion in this third sense can be criticized, but not for being disobedient, as in the case of the soldier. He can be said to have made a mistake, but not to have deprived a participant of a decision to which he was entitled, as in the case of a sports official or contest judge.

We may now return, with these observations in hand, to the positivists' doctrine of judicial discretion. That doctrine argues that if a case is not controlled by an established rule, the judge must decide it by exercising discretion. We want to examine this doctrine and to test its bearing on our treatment of principles; but first we must ask in which sense of discretion we are to understand it.

Some nominalists argue that judges always have discretion, even when a clear rule is in point, because judges are ultimately the final arbiters of the law. This doctrine of discretion uses the second weak sense of that term, because it makes the point that no higher authority reviews the decisions of the highest court. It therefore has no bearing on the issue of how we account for principles, any more than it bears on how we account for rules.

The positivists do not mean their doctrine this way, because they say that a judge has no discretion when a clear and established rule is available. If we attend to the positivists' arguments for the doctrine, we may suspect that they use discretion in the first weak sense to mean only that judges must sometimes exercise judgment in applying legal standards. Their arguments call attention to the fact that some rules of law are vague (Professor Hart, for example, says that all rules of law have "open texture"), and that some cases arise (like *Henningsen*) in which no established rule seems to be suitable. They emphasize that judges must sometimes agonize over points of law, and that two equally trained and intelligent judges will often disagree.

These points are easily made; they are commonplace to anyone who has any familiarity with law. Indeed, that is the difficulty with assuming that positivists mean to use "discretion" in this weak sense. The proposition that, when no clear rule is available discretion in the sense of judgment must be used, is a tautology. It has no bearing, moreover, on the problem of how to account for legal principles. It is perfectly consistent to say that the judge in *Riggs,* for example, had to use judgment, and that he was bound to follow the principle that no man may profit from his own wrong. The positivists speak as if their doctrine of judicial discretion is an insight rather than a tautology, and as if it does have a bearing on the treatment of principles. Hart, for example, says that when the judge's discretion is in play, we can no longer speak of his being bound by standards, but must speak rather of what standards he "characteristically uses."[22] Hart thinks that when judges have discretion, the principles they cite must be treated on our second approach, as what courts "make it a principle" to do.

It therefore seems that positivists, at least sometimes, take their doctrine in the third, strong sense of discretion. In that sense it does bear on the treatment of principles; indeed, in that sense it is nothing less than a restatement of our second approach. It is the same thing to say that when a judge runs out of rules he has discretion, in the sense that he is not bound by any standards from the authority of law, as to say that the legal standards judges cite other than rules are not binding on them.

So we must examine the doctrine of judicial discretion in the strong sense. (I shall henceforth use the term "discretion" in that sense.) Do the principles judges cite in cases like *Riggs* or *Henningsen* control their decisions, as the sergeant's orders to take the most experienced men or the referee's duty to choose the more aggressive fighter control the decisions of these officials? What arguments could a positivist supply to show that they do not?

(1) A positivist might argue that principles cannot be binding or obligatory. That would be a mistake. It is always a question, of course, whether any particular principle is *in fact* binding upon some legal official. But there is nothing in the logical character of a principle that renders it incapable of binding him. Suppose that the judge in *Henningsen* had failed to take any account of the principle that automobile manufacturers have a special obligation to their consumers, or the principle that the courts seek to protect those whose bargaining position is weak, but had simply decided for the defendant by citing the principle of freedom of contract without more. His critics would not have been content to point out that he had not taken account of considerations that other judges have been attending to for some time. Most would have said that it was his duty to take the measure of these principles and that the plaintiff was entitled to have him do so. We mean no more, when we say that a *rule* is binding upon a judge, than that he must follow it if it applies, and that if he does not he will on that account have made a mistake.

It will not do to say that in a case like *Henningsen* the court is only "morally" obligated to take particular principles into account, or that it is "institutionally" obligated, or obligated as a matter of judicial "craft," or something of that sort. The question will still remain why this type of obligation (whatever we call it) is different from the obligation that rules impose upon judges, and why it entitles us to say that principles and policies are not part of the law but are merely extralegal standards "courts characteristically use."

(2) A positivist might argue that even though some principles are binding, in the sense that the judge must take them into account, they cannot determine a particular result. This is a harder argument to assess because it is not clear what it means for a standard to "determine" a result. Perhaps it means that the standard *dictates* the result whenever it applies so that nothing else counts. If so, then it is certainly true that individual principles do not determine results, but that is only another way of saying that principles are not rules. Only rules dictate results, come what may. When a contrary result has been reached, the rule has been abandoned or changed. Principles do not work that way; they incline a decision one way, though not conclusively, and they survive intact when they do not prevail. This seems no reason for

concluding that judges who must reckon with principles have discretion because a set of principles *can* dictate a result. If a judge believes that principles he is bound to recognize point in one direction and that principles pointing in the other direction, if any, are not of equal weight, then he must decide accordingly, just as he must follow what he believes to be a binding rule. He may, of course, be wrong in his assessment of the principles, but he may also be wrong in his judgment that the rule is binding. The sergeant and the referee, we might add, are often in the same boat. No one factor dictates which soldiers are the most experienced or which fighter the more aggressive. These officials must make judgments of the relative weights of these various factors; they do not on that account have discretion.

(3) A positivist might argue that principles cannot count as law because their authority, and even more so their weight, are congenitally *controversial*. It is true that generally we cannot *demonstrate* the authority or weight of a particular principle as we can sometimes demonstrate the validity of a rule by locating it in an act of Congress or in the opinion of an authoritative court. Instead, we make a case for a principle, and for its weight, by appealing to an amalgam of practice and other principles in which the implications of legislative and judicial history figure along with appeals to community practices and understandings. There is no litmus paper for testing the soundness of such a case—it is a matter of judgment, and reasonable men may disagree. But again this does not distinguish the judge from other officials who do not have discretion. The sergeant has no litmus paper for experience, the referee none for aggressiveness. Neither of these has discretion, because he is bound to reach an understanding, controversial or not, of what his orders or the rules require, and to act on that understanding. That is the judge's duty as well.

Of course, if the positivists are right in another of the doctrines—the theory that in each legal system there is an ultimate *test* for binding law like Professor Hart's rule of recognition—it follows that principles are not binding law. But the incompatibility of principles with the positivists' theory can hardly be taken as an argument that principles must be treated any particular way. That begs the question; we are interested in the status of principles because we want to evaluate the positivists' model. The positivist cannot defend his theory of a rule of recognition by fiat; if principles are not amenable to a test he must show some other reason why they cannot count as law. Since principles seem to play a role in arguments about legal obligation (witness, again *Riggs* and *Henningsen*), a model that provides for that role has some initial advantage over one that excludes it, and the latter cannot properly be inveighed in its own support.

These are the most obvious of the arguments a positivist might use for the doctrine of discretion in the strong sense, and for the second approach to principles. I shall mention one strong counterargument against that doctrine and in favor of the first approach. Unless at least some principles are acknowledged to be binding upon judges, requiring them as a set to reach particular decisions, then no rules, or very few rules, can be said to be binding upon them either.

In most American jurisdictions, and now in England also, the higher courts not infrequently reject established rules. Common law rules—those developed by earlier court decisions—are sometimes overruled directly, and sometimes radically altered by further development. Statutory rules are subjected to interpretation and reinterpretation, sometimes even when the result is not to carry out what is called the "legislative intent."[23] If courts had discretion to change established rules, then these rules would of course not be binding upon them, and so would not be law on the positivists' model. The positivist must therefore argue that there are standards, themselves binding upon judges, that determine when a judge may overrule or alter an established rule, and when he may not.

When, then, is a judge permitted to change an existing rule of law? Principles figure in the answer in two ways. First, it is necessary, though not sufficient, that the judge find that the change would advance some policy or serve some principle, which policy or principle thus justifies the change. In *Riggs* the change (a new interpretation of the statute of wills) was justified by the principle that no man should profit from his own wrong; in *Henningsen* certain rules about automobile manufacturers' liability were altered on the basis of the principles and policies I quoted from the opinion of the court.

But not any principle will do to justify a change, or no rule would ever be safe. There must be some principles that count and others that do not, and there must be some principles that count for more than others. It could not depend on the judge's own preferences amongst a sea of respectable extralegal standards, any one in principle eligible, because if that were the case we could not say that any rules were binding. We could always imagine a judge whose preferences amongst extralegal standards were such as would justify a shift or radical reinterpretation of even the most entrenched rule.

Second, any judge who proposes to change existing doctrine must take account of some important standards that argue against departures from established doctrine, and these standards are also for the most part principles. They include the doctrine of "legislative supremacy," a set of principles and policies that require the courts to pay a qualified deference to the acts of the legislature. They also include the doctrine of precedent, another set of principles and policies reflecting the equities and efficiencies of consistency. The doctrines of legislative supremacy and precedent incline toward the *status quo,* each within its sphere, but they do not command it. Judges are not free, however, to pick and choose amongst the principles and policies that make up these doctrines—if they were, again, no rule could be said to be binding.

Consider, therefore, what someone implies who says that a particular rule is binding. He may imply that the rule is affirmatively supported by principles the court is not free to disregard, and which are collectively more weighty than other principles that argue for a change. If not, he implies that any change would be condemned by a combination of conservative principles of legislative supremacy and precedent that the court is not free to ignore. Very often, he will imply both, for the conservative principles, being principles and not rules, are usually not powerful enough to save a common law rule or an aging statute that is entirely unsupported by substantive principles the court is bound to respect. Either of these implications, of course, treats a body of principles and policies as law in the sense that rules are; it treats them as standards binding upon the officials of a community, controlling their decisions of legal right and obligation.

We are left with this issue. If the positivists' theory of judicial discretion is either trivial because it uses "discretion" in a weak sense, or unsupported because the various arguments we can supply in its defense fall short, why have so many careful and intelligent lawyers embraced it? We can have no confidence in our treatment of that theory unless we can deal with that question. It is not enough to note (although perhaps it contributes to the explanation) that "discretion" has different senses that may be confused. We do not confuse these senses when we are not thinking about law.

Part of the explanation, at least, lies in a lawyer's natural tendency to associate laws and rules, and to think of "the law" as a collection or system of rules. Roscoe Pound, who diagnosed this tendency long ago, thought that English-speaking lawyers were tricked into it by the fact that English uses the same word, changing only the article, for "a law" and "the law."[24] (Other languages, on the contrary, use two words: "loi" and "droit," for example, and "Gesetz" and "Recht.") This may have had its effect, with the English-speaking positivists, because the expression "a law" certainly does suggest a rule. But the principal reason for associating law with rules runs deeper, and lies, I think, in the fact that legal education has for a long time consisted of teaching and examining those established rules that form the cutting edge of law.

In any event, if a lawyer thinks of law as a system of rules, and yet recognizes, as he must, that judges change old rules and introduce new ones, he will come naturally to the theory of judicial discretion in the strong sense. In those other systems of rules with which he has experience (like games), the rules are the only special authority that govern official decisions, so that if an umpire could change a rule, he would have discretion as to the subject matter of that rule. Any principles umpires might mention when changing the rules would represent only their "characteristic" preferences. Positivists treat law like baseball revised in this way.

There is another, more subtle consequence of this initial assumption that law is a system of rules. When the positivists do attend to principles and policies, they treat them as rules *manqué*. They assume that *if* they are standards of law they must be rules, and so they read them as standards that are trying to be rules. When a positivist hears someone argue that legal principles are part of the law, he understands this to be an argument for what he calls the "higher law" theory, that these principles are the rules of a law above the law.[25] He refutes this theory by pointing out that these "rules" are sometimes followed and sometimes not, that for every "rule" like "no man shall profit from his own wrong" there is another competing "rule" like "the law favors security of title," and that there is no way to test the validity of "rules" like these. He concludes that these principles and policies are not valid rules of a law above the law, which is true, because they are not rules at all. He also concludes that they are extralegal standards which each judge selects according to his own rights in the exercise of his discretion, which is false. It is as if a zoologist had proved that fish are not mammals, and then concluded that they are really only plants.

The Rule of Recognition

This discussion was provoked by our two competing accounts of legal principles. We have been exploring the second account, which the positivists seem to adopt through their doctrine of judicial discretion, and we have discovered grave difficulties. It is time to return to the fork in the road. What if we adopt the first approach? What would the consequences of this be for the skeletal structure of positivism? Of course we should have to drop the second tenet, the doctrine of judicial discretion (or, in the alternative, to make plain that the doctrine is to be read merely to say that judges must often exercise judgment). Would we also have to abandon or modify the first tenet, the proposition that law is distinguished by tests of the sort that can be set out in a master rule like Professor Hart's rule of recognition? If principles of the *Riggs* and *Henningsen* sort are to count as law, and we are nevertheless to preserve the notion of a master rule for law, then we must be able to deploy some test that all (and only) the principles that do count as law meet. Let us begin with the test Hart suggests for identifying valid *rules* of law, to see whether these can be made to work for principles as well.

Most rules of law, according to Hart, are valid because some competent institution enacted them. Some were created by a legislature, in the form of statutory enactments. Others were created by judges who formulated them to decide particular cases, and thus established them as precedents for the future. But this test of pedigree will not work for the *Riggs* and *Henningsen* principles. The origin of these as legal principles lies not in a particular decision of some legislature or court, but in a sense of appropriateness developed in the profession and the public over time. Their continued power depends upon this sense of appropriateness being sustained. If it no longer seemed unfair to allow people to profit by their wrongs, or fair to place special burdens upon oligopolies that manufacture potentially dangerous machines, these principles would no longer play much of a role in new cases, even if they had never been overruled or repealed. (Indeed, it hardly makes sense to speak of principles like these as being "overruled" or "repealed." When they decline they are eroded, not torpedoed.)

True, if we were challenged to back up our claim that some principle is a principle of law, we would mention any prior cases in which that principle was cited, or figured in the argument. We would also mention any statute that seemed to exemplify that principle (even better if the principle was cited in the preamble of the statute, or in the committee reports or other legislative documents that accompanied it). Unless we could find some such institutional support, we would probably fail to make out our case, and the more support we found, the more weight we could claim for the principle.

Yet we could not devise any formula for testing how much and what kind of institutional support is necessary to make a principle a legal principle, still less to fix its weight at a particular order of magnitude. We argue for a particular principle by grappling with a whole set of shifting, developing and interacting standards (themselves principles rather than rules) about institutional responsibility, statutory interpretation, the persuasive force of various sorts of precedent, the relation of all these to contemporary moral practices, and hosts of other such standards. We could not bolt all of these together into a single "rule," even a complex one, and if we could the result would bear little relation to Hart's picture of a rule of recognition, which is the picture of a fairly stable master rule specifying "some feature or features possession of which by a suggested rule is taken as a conclusive affirmative indicating that it is a rule. . . ."[26]

Moreover, the techniques we apply in arguing for another principle do not stand (as Hart's rule of recognition is designed to) on an entirely different level from the principles they support. Hart's sharp distinction between acceptance and validity does not hold. If we are arguing for the principle that a man should not profit from his own wrong, we could cite the acts of courts and legislatures that exemplify it, but this speaks as much to the principle's acceptance as its validity. (It seems odd to speak of a principle as being valid at all, perhaps because validity is an all-or-nothing concept, appropriate for rules, but inconsistent with a principle's dimension of weight.) If we are asked (as we might well be) to defend the particular doctrine of precedent, or the particular technique of statutory interpretation, that we used in this argument, we should certainly cite the practice of others in using that doctrine or technique. But we should also cite other general principles that we believe support that practice, and this introduces a note of validity into the chord of acceptance. We might argue, for example, that the use we make of earlier cases and statutes is supported by a particular analysis of the point of practice of legislation or the doctrine of precedent, or by the principles of democratic theory, or by a particular position on the proper division of authority between national and local institutions, or something else of that sort. Nor is this path of support a one-way street leading to some ultimate principle resting on acceptance alone. Our principles of legislation, precedent, democracy, or federalism might be challenged too; and if they were we should argue for them, not only in terms of practice, but in terms of each other and in terms of the implications of trends of judicial and legislative decisions, even though this last would involve appealing to those same doctrines of interpretation we justified through the principles we are now trying to support. At this level of abstraction, in other words, principles rather hang together than link together.

So even though principles draw support from the official acts of legal institutions, they do not have a simple or direct enough connection with these acts to frame that connection in terms of criteria specified by some ultimate master rule of recognition. Is there any other route by which principles might be brought under such a rule?

Hart does say that a master rule might designate as law not only rules enacted by particular legal institutions, but rules established by *custom* as well. He has in mind a problem that bothered other positivists, including Austin. Many of our most ancient legal rules were never explicitly created by a legislature or a court. When they made their first appearance in legal opinions and texts, they were treated as already being part of the law because they represented the customary practice of the community, or some specialized part of it, like the business community. (The examples ordinarily given are rules of mercantile practice, like the rules governing what rights arise under a standard form of commercial paper.[27]) Since Austin thought that all law was the command of a determinate sovereign, he held that these customary practices were not law until the courts (as agents of the sovereign) recognized them, and that the courts were indulging in a fiction in pretending otherwise. But that seemed arbitrary. If everyone thought custom might in itself be law, the fact that Austin's theory said otherwise was not persuasive.

Hart reversed Austin on this point. The master rule, he says, might stipulate that some custom counts as law even before the courts recognize it. But he does not face the difficulty this raises for this general theory, because he does not attempt to set out the criteria a master rule might use for this purpose. It cannot use, as its only criterion, the provision that the community regard the practice as *morally* binding, for this would not distinguish legal customary rules from moral customary rules, and of course not all of the community's long-standing customary moral obligations are enforced as law. If, on the other hand, the test is whether the community regards the customary practice as *legally* binding, the whole point of the master rule is undercut, at least for this class of legal rules. The master rule, says Hart, marks the transformation from a primitive society to one with law, because it provides a test for determining social rules of law other than by measuring their acceptance. But if the master rule says merely that whatever other rules the community accepts as legally binding are legally binding, then it provides no such test at all, beyond the test we should use were there no master rule. The master rule becomes (for these cases) a nonrule of recognition; we might as well say that every primitive society has a secondary rule of recognition, namely the rule that whatever is accepted as binding is binding. Hart himself, in discussing international law, ridicules the idea that such a rule could be a rule of recognition, by describing the proposed rule as "an empty repetition of the mere fact that the society concerned . . . observes certain standards of conduct as obligatory rules."[28]

Hart's treatment of custom amounts, indeed, to a confession that there are at least some rules of law that are not binding because they are valid under standards laid down by a master rule but are binding—like the master rule—because they are accepted as binding by the community. This chips at the neat pyramidal architecture we admired in Hart's theory: we can no longer say that only the master rule is binding because of its acceptance, all other rules being valid under its terms.

This is perhaps only a chip, because the customary rules Hart has in mind are no longer a very significant part of the law. But it does suggest that Hart would be reluctant to widen the damage by bringing under the head of "custom" all those crucial principles and policies we have been discussing. If he were to call these part of the law and yet admit that the only test of their force lies in the degree to which they are accepted as law by the community or some part thereof, he would very sharply reduce that area of the law over which his master rule held any dominion. It is not just that all the principles and policies would escape its sway, though that would be bad enough. Once these principles and policies are accepted as law, and thus as standards judges must follow in determining legal obligations, it would follow that *rules* like those announced for the first time in *Riggs* and *Henningsen* owe their force at least in part to the authority of principles and policies, and so not entirely to the master rule of recognition.

So we cannot adapt Hart's version of positivism by modifying his rule of recognition to embrace principles. No tests of pedigree, relating principles to acts of legislation, can be formulated, nor can his concept of customary law, itself an exception to the first tenet of positivism, be made to serve without abandoning that tenet altogether. One more possibility must be considered, however. If no rule of recognition can provide a test for identifying principles, why not say that principles are ultimate, and *form* the rule of recognition of our law? The answer to the general question "What is valid law in an American jurisdiction?" would then require us to state all the principles (as well as ultimate constitutional rules) in force in that jurisdiction at the time, together with appropriate assignments of weight. A positivist might then regard the complete set of these standards as the rule of recognition of the jurisdiction. This solution has the attraction of paradox, but of course it is an unconditional surrender. If we simply designate our rule of recognition by the phrase "the complete set of principles in force," we achieve only the tautology that law is law. If, instead, we tried actually to list all the principles in force we would fail. They are controversial, their weight is all important, they are numberless, and they shift and change so fast that the start of our list would be obsolete before we reached the middle. Even if we succeeded, we would not have a key for law because there would be nothing left for our key to unlock.

I conclude that if we treat principles as law we must reject the positivists' first tenet, that the law of a community is distinguished from other social standards by some test in the form of a master rule. We have already decided that we must then abandon the second tenet—the doctrine of judicial discretion—or clarify it into triviality. What of the third tenet, the positivists' theory of legal obligation?

This theory holds that a legal obligation exists when (and only when) an established rule of law imposes such an obligation. It follows from this that in a hard case—when no such established rule can be found—there is no legal obligation until the judge creates a new rule for the future. The judge may apply that new rule to the parties in the case, but this is *ex post facto* legislation, not the enforcement of an existing obligation.

The positivists' doctrine of discretion (in the strong sense) required this view of legal obligation, because if a judge has discretion there can be no legal right or obligation—no entitlement—that he must enforce. Once we abandon that doctrine, however, and treat principles as law, we raise the possibility that a legal obligation might be imposed by a constellation of principles as well as by an established rule. We might want to say that a legal obligation exists whenever the case supporting such an obligation, in terms of binding legal principles of different sorts, is stronger than the case against it.

Of course, many questions would have to be answered before we could accept that view of legal obligation. If there is no rule of recognition, no test for law in that sense, how do we decide which principles are to count, and how much, in making such a case? How do we decide whether one case is better than another? If legal obligation rests on an undemonstrable judgment of that sort, how can it provide a justification for a judicial decision that one party had a legal obligation? Does this view of obligation square with the way lawyers, judges and laymen speak, and is it consistent with our attitudes about moral obligation? Does this analysis help us to deal with the classical jurisprudential puzzles about the nature of law?

These questions must be faced, but even the questions promise more than positivism provides. Positivism, on its own thesis, stops short of just those puzzling, hard cases that send us to look for theories of law. When we reach these cases, the positivist remits us to a doctrine of discretion that leads nowhere and tells nothing. His picture of law as a system of rules has exercised a tenacious hold on our imagination, perhaps through its very simplicity. If we shake ourselves loose from this model of rules, we may be able to build a model truer to the complexity and sophistication of our own practices.

---

1. *See* Linkletter *v. Walker, 381 U.S. 618 (1965).*
2. *J. Austin, The Province of Jurisprudence Determined (1832).*
3. See *H. L. A. Hart, The Concept of Law 89–96 (1961).*
4. Id. *at 79–88.*
5. Id. *at 97–107.*
6. Id. passim, *particularly ch. VI.*

7. Id., ch. VII.

8. See *Dworkin, Wasserstrom: The Judicial Decision, 75 Ethics 47 (1964), reprinted as* Does Law Have a Function?, *74 Yale L. J. 640 (1965).*

9. *115 N.Y. 506, 22 N.E. at 188 (1889).*

10. Id. *at 509, 22 N.E. at 189.*

11. Id. *at 511, 22 N.E. at 190.*

12. *32 N.J. 358, 161 A.2d 69 (1960).*

13. Id. *at 386, 161 A.2d at 84.*

14. Id.

15. Id. *at 388, 161 A.2d at 86.*

16. Id. *at 387, 161 A.2d at 85.*

17. Id. *at 389, 161 A.2d at 86 quoting Frankfurter, J., in* United States v. Bethlehem Steel, *315 U.S. 289, 326 (1942).*

18. Id.

19. *Standard Oil v. United States, 221 U.S. 1, 60 (1911); United States v. American Tobacco Co., 221 U.S. 106, 180 (1911).*

20. *The distinction is in substance the same as that made by Rawls,* Two Concepts of Rules, *64 Philosophical Rev. 3 (1955).*

21. *I have not spoken of that jurisprudential favorite, "limited" discretion, because that concept presents no special difficulties if we remember the relativity of discretion. Suppose the sergeant is told* to choose from "amongst" experienced men, or to "take experience into account." We might say either that he has (limited) discretion in picking his patrol, or (full) discretion to either pick amongst experienced men or decide what else to take into account.

22. *H. L. A. Hart, The Concept of Law 144 (1961).*

23. See *Wellington & Albert,* Statutory Interpretation and the Political Process: A Comment on Sinclair v. Atkinson, *72 Yale L. J. 1547 (1963).*

24. *R. Pound, An Introduction to the Philosophy of Law 56 (rev. ed. 1954).*

25. See, e.g., *Dickinson,* The Law Behind Law *(pts. 1 & 2), 29 Colum. L. Rev. 112, 254 (1929).*

26. *H. L. A. Hart, The Concept of Law 92 (1961).*

27. See *Note,* Custom and Trade Usage: Its Application to Commercial Dealings and the Common Law, *55 Colum. L. Rev. 1192 (1955), and materials cited therein at 1193 n.1. As that note makes plain, the actual practices of courts in recognizing trade customs follow the pattern of applying a set of general principles and policies rather than a test that could be captured as part of a rule of recognition.*

28. *H. L. A. Hart, The Concept of Law 230 (1961).*

---

*RIGGS V. PALMER**

Court of Appeals of New York, 1889

Rights of Legatees—Murder of Testator

The law of New York relating to the probate of wills and the distributions of estates will not be construed so as to secure the benefit of a will to a legatee who has killed the testator in order to prevent a revocation of the will. GRAY and DANFORTH, JJ., dissenting.

Appeal from supreme court, general term, third department.

Leslie W. Russell, for appellants. *W. M. Hawkins,* for respondents.

EARL, J. on the 13th day of August 1880, Francis B. Palmer made his last will and testament, in which he gave small legacies to his two daughters, Mrs. Riggs and Mrs. Preston, the plaintiffs in this action, and the remainder of his estate to his grandson, the defendant Elmer E. Palmer, subject to the support of Susan Palmer, his mother, with a gift over to the two daughters, subject to the support of Mrs. Palmer in case Elmer should survive him and die under age, unmarried, and without any issue. The testator, at the date of his will, owned a farm, and considerable personal property. He was a widower, and thereafter, in March, 1882, he was married to Mrs. Bresee, with whom, before his marriage, he entered into an antenuptial contract, in which it was agreed that in lieu of dower and all other claims upon his estate in case she survived him she should have her support upon his farm during her life, and such support was expressly charged upon the farm. At the date of the will, and subsequently to the death of the testator, Elmer lived with him as a member of his family, and at his death was 16 years old. He knew of the provisions made in his favor in the will, and, that he might prevent his grandfather from revoking such provisions, which he had manifested some

---

intention to do, and to obtain the speedy enjoyment and immediate possession of his property, he willfully murdered him by poisoning him. He now claims the property, and the sole question for our determination is, can he have it?

The defendants say that the testator is dead; that his will was made in due form, and has been admitted to probate; and that therefore it must have effect according to the letter of the law. It is quite true that statutes regulating the making, proof, and effect of wills and the devolution of property, if literally construed, and if their force and effect can in no way and under no circumstances be controlled or modified, give this property to the murderer. The purpose of those statutes was to enable testators to dispose of their estates to the objects of their bounty at death, and to carry into effect their final wishes legally expressed; and in considering and giving effect to them this purpose must be kept in view. It was the intention of the law-makers that the donees in a will should have the property given to them. But it never could have been their intention that a donee who murdered the testator to make the will operative should have any benefit under it. If such a case had been present to their minds, and it had been supposed necessary to make some provision of law to meet it, it cannot be doubted that they would have provided for it. It is a familiar canon of construction that a thing which is within the intention of the makers of a statute is as much within the statute as if it were within the letter; and a thing which is within the letter of the statute is not within the statute unless it be within the intention of the makers. The writers of laws do not always express their intention perfectly, but either exceed it or fall short of it, so that judges are to collect it from probable or rational conjectures only, and this is called "rational interpretation;" and Rutherford, in his Institutes, (page 420) says: "Where we make use of rational interpretation, sometimes we restrain the meaning of the writer so as to take in less, and sometimes we extend or enlarge his meaning so as to take in more, than his words express." Such a construction ought to be put upon a statute as will best answer the intention which the makers had in view.... Many cases are mentioned where it was held that matters embraced in the general words of statutes nevertheless were not within the statutes, because it could not have been the intention of the law-makers that they should be included. They were taken out of the statutes by an equitable construction; and it is said in Bacon: "By an equitable construction a case not within the letter of a statute is sometimes holden to be within

the meaning, because it is within the mischief for which a remedy is provided. The reason for such construction is that the law-makers could not set down every case in express terms. In order to form a right judgment whether a case be within the equity of a statute, it is a good way to suppose the law-maker present, and that you have asked him this question: Did you intend to comprehend this case? Then you must give yourself such answer as you imagine he, being an upright and reasonable man, would have given. If this be that he did mean to comprehend it, you may safely hold the case to be within the equity of the statute; for while you do no more than he would have done, you do not act contrary to the statute, but in conformity thereto." 9 Bac. Abr. 248. In some cases the letter of a legislative act is restrained by an equitable construction; in others, it is enlarged; in others, the construction is contrary to the letter. . . . If the law-makers could, as to this case, be consulted, would they say that they intended by their general language that the property of a testator or of an ancestor should pass to one who had taken his life for the express purpose of getting his property? In 1 Bl. Comm. 91, the learned author, speaking of the construction of statutes, says: "If there arise out of them collaterally any absurd consequences manifestly contradictory to common reason, they are with regard to those collateral consequences void. Where some collateral matter arises out of the general words, and happens to be unreasonable, there the judges are in decency to conclude that this consequence was not foreseen by the parliament, and therefore they are at liberty to expound the statute by equity, and only *quoad hoc* disregard it;" and he gives as an illustration, if an act of parliament gives a man power to try all causes that arise within his manor of Dale, yet, if a cause should arise in which he himself is party, the act is construed not to extend to that, because it is unreasonable that any man should determine his own quarrel. There was a statute in Bologna that whoever drew blood in the streets should be severely punished, and yet it was held not to apply to the case of a barber who opened a vein in the street. It is commanded in the decalogue that no work shall be done upon the Sabbath, and yet giving the command a rational interpretation founded upon its design the Infallible Judge held that it did not prohibit works of necessity, charity, or benevolence on that day.

What could be more unreasonable than to suppose that it was the legislative intention in the general laws passed for the orderly peaceable, and just devolution of property that they should have operation in favor of one who murdered his ancestor that he might speedily come into the possession of his estate? Such an intention is inconceivable. We need not, therefore, be much troubled by the general language contained in the laws. Besides, all laws, as well as all contracts, may be controlled in their operation and effect by general, fundamental maxims of the common law. No one shall be permitted to profit by his own fraud, or to take advantage of his own wrong, or to found any claim upon his own iniquity, or to acquire property by his own crime. These maxims are dictated by public policy, have their foundation in universal law administered in all civilized countries, and have nowhere been superseded by statutes. They were applied in the decision of the case of *Insurance Co.* v. *Armstrong*, 117 U. S. 599, 6 Sup. Ct. Rep. 877. There it was held that the person who procured a policy upon the life of another, payable at his death, and then murdered the assured to make the policy payable, could not recover thereon. Mr. Justice FIELD, writing the opinion, said: "Independently of any proof of the motives of Hunter in obtaining the policy, and even assuming that they were just and proper, he forfeited all rights under it when, to secure its immediate payment, he murdered the assured. It would be a reproach to the jurisprudence of the country if one could recover insurance money payable on the death of a party whose life he had feloniously taken. As well might he recover insurance money upon a building that he had willfully fired." These maxims, without any statute giving them force or operation, frequently control the effect and nullify the language of wills. A will procured by fraud and deception, like any other instrument, may be decreed void, and set aside; and so a particular portion of a will may be excluded from probate, or held inoperative, if induced by the fraud or undue influence of the person in whose favor it is. . . . So a will may contain provisions which are immoral, irreligious, or against public policy, and they will be held void.

Here there was no certainty that this murderer would survive the testator, or that the testator would not change his will, and there was no certainty that he would get this property if nature was allowed to take its course. He therefore murdered the testator expressly to vest himself with an estate. Under such circumstances, what law, human or divine, will allow him to take the estate and enjoy the fruits of his crime? The will spoke and became operative at the death of the testator. He caused that death, and thus by his crime made it speak and have operation. Shall it speak and operate in his favor? If he had met the testator, and taken his property by force, he would have had

no title to it. Shall he acquire title by murdering him? If he had gone to the testator's house, and by force compelled him, or by fraud or undue influence had induced him, to will him his property, the law would not allow him to hold it. But can he give effect and operation to a will by murder, and yet take the property? To answer these questions in the affirmative it seems to me would be a reproach to the jurisprudence of our state, and an offense against public policy. Under the civil law, evolved from the general principles of natural law and justice by many generations of jurisconsults, philosophers, and statesmen, one cannot take property by inheritance or will from an ancestor or benefactor whom he has murdered. . . . In the Civil Code of Lower Canada the provisions on the subject in the Code Napoleon have been substantially copied. But, so far as I can find, in no country where the common law prevails has it been deemed important to enact a law to provide for such a case. Our revisers and law-makers were familiar with the civil law, and they did not deem it important to incorporate into our statutes its provisions upon this subject. This is not a *casus omissus*. It was evidently supposed that the maxims of the common law were sufficient to regulate such a case, and that a specific enactment for that purpose was not needed. For the same reasons the defendant Palmer cannot take any of this property as heir. Just before the murder he was not an heir, and it was not certain that he ever would be. He might have died before his grandfather, or might have been disinherited by him. He made himself an heir by the murder, and he seeks to take property as the fruit of his crime. What has before been said to him as legatee applies to him with equal force as an heir. He cannot vest himself with title by crime. My view of this case does not inflict upon Elmer any greater or other punishment for his crime than the law specifies. It takes from him no property, but simply holds that he shall not acquire property by his crime, and thus be rewarded for its commission.

Our attention is called to *Owens* v. *Owens*, 100 N. C. 240, 6 S. E. Rep. 794, as a case quite like this. There a wife had been convicted of being an accessory before the fact to the murder of her husband, and it was held that she was nevertheless entitled to dower. I am unwilling to assent to the doctrine of that case. The statutes provide dower for a wife who has the misfortune to survive her husband, and thus lose his support and protection. It is clear beyond their purpose to make provision for a wife who by her own crime makes herself a widow, and willfully and intentionally deprives herself of the support and protection of her husband. As she might have died before him, and thus never have been his widow, she cannot by her crime vest herself with an estate. The principle which lies at the bottom of the maxim *volenti non fit injuria* should be applied to such a case, and a widow should not, for the purpose of acquiring, as such, property rights, be permitted to allege a widowhood which she has wickedly and intentionally created.

The facts found entitled the plaintiffs to the relief they sought. The error of the referee was in his conclusion of law. Instead of granting a new trial, therefore, I think the proper judgment upon the facts found should be ordered here. The facts have been passed upon twice with the same result,—first upon the trial of Palmer for murder, and then by the referee in this action. We are therefore of opinion that the ends of justice do not require that they should again come in question. The judgment of the general term and that entered upon the report of the referee should therefore be reversed, and judgment should be entered as follows: That Elmer E. Palmer and the administrator be enjoined from using any of the personalty or real estate left by the testator for Elmer's benefit; that the devise and bequest in the will to Elmer be declared ineffective to pass the title to him; that by reason of the crime of murder committed upon the grandfather he is deprived of any interest in the estate left by him; that the plaintiffs are the true owners of the real and personal estate left by the testator, subject to the charge in favor of Elmer's mother and the widow of the testator, under the antenuptial agreement, and that the plaintiffs have costs in all the courts against Elmer. All concur, except GRAY, J., who reads dissenting opinion, and DANFORTH, J., concurs.

GRAY, J., (*dissenting.*) This appeal represents an extraordinary state of facts, and the case, in respect to them, I believe, is without precedent in this state. The respondent, a lad of 16 years of age, being aware of the provisions in his grandfather's will, which constituted him the residuary legatee of the testator's estate, caused his death by poison, in 1882. For this crime he was tried, and was convicted of murder in the second degree, and at the time of the commencement of this action he was serving out his sentence in the state reformatory. This action was brought by two of the children of the testator for the purpose of having those provisions of the will in the respondent's favor canceled and annulled. The appellants' argument for a reversal of the judgment, which dismissed their complaint, is that the respondent unlawfully prevented a

revocation of the existing will, or a new will from being made, by his crime; and that he terminated the enjoyment by the testator of his property, and effected his own succession to it, by the same crime. They say that to permit the respondent to take the property willed to him would be to permit him to take advantage of his own wrong. To sustain their position the appellants' counsel has submitted an able and elaborate brief, and, if I believed that the decision of the question could be effected by considerations of an equitable nature, I should not hesitate to assent to views which commend themselves to the conscience. But the matter does not lie within the domain of conscience. We are bound by the rigid rules of law, which have been established by the legislature, and within the limits of which the determination of this question is confined. The question we are dealing with is whether a testamentary disposition can be altered, or a will revoked, after the testator's death, through an appeal to the courts, when the legislature has by its enactments prescribed exactly when and how wills may be made, altered, and revoked, and apparently, as it seems to me, when they have been fully complied with, has left no room for the exercise of an equitable jurisdiction by courts over such matters. Modern jurisprudence, in recognizing the right of the individual, under more or less restrictions, to dispose of his property after his death, subjects it to legislative control, both as to extent and as to mode of exercise. Complete freedom of testamentary disposition of one's property has not been and is not the universal rule, as we see from the provisions of the Napoleonic Code, from the systems of jurisprudence in countries which are modeled upon the Roman law, and from the statutes of many of our states. To the statutory restraints which are imposed upon the disposition of one's property by will are added strict and systematic statutory rules for the execution, alteration, and revocation of the will, which must be, at least substantially, if not exactly, followed to insure validity and performance. The reason for the establishment of such rules, we may naturally assume, consists in the purpose to create those safeguards about these grave and important acts which experience has demonstrated to be the wisest and surest. That freedom which is permitted to be exercised in the testamentary disposition of one's estate by the laws of the state is subject to its being exercised in conformity with the regulations of the statutes. The capacity and the power of the individual to dispose of his property after death, and the mode by which that power can be exercised, are matters of which the legislature has assumed the entire control, and has undertaken to regulate with comprehensive particularity.

The appellants' argument is not helped by reference to those rules of the civil law, or to those laws of other governments, by which the heir, or legatee, is excluded from benefit under the testament if he has been convicted of killing, or attempting to kill, the testator. In the absence of such legislation here, the courts are not empowered to institute such a system of remedial justice. The deprivation of the heir of his testamentary succession by the Roman law, when guilty of such a crime, plainly was intended to be in the nature of a punishment imposed upon him. The succession, in such a case of guilt, escheated to the exchequer. . . . I concede that rules of law which annul testamentary provisions made for the benefit of those who have become unworthy of them may be based on principles of equity and of natural justice. It is quite reasonable to suppose that a testator would revoke or alter his will, where his mind has been so angered and changed as to make him unwilling to have his will executed as it stood. But these principles only suggest sufficient reasons for the enactment of laws to meet such cases.

The statutes of this state have prescribed various ways in which a will may be altered or revoked; but the very provision defining the modes of alterations and revocation implies a prohibition of alteration or revocation in any other way. The words of the section of the statute are: "No will in writing, except in the cases hereinafter mentioned, nor any part thereof, shall be revoked or altered otherwise," etc. Where, therefore, none of the cases mentioned are met by the facts, and the revocation is not in the way described in the section, the will of the testator is unalterable. I think that a valid will must continue as a will always, unless revoked in the manner provided by the statutes. Mere intention to revoke a will does not have the effect of revocation. The intention to revoke is necessary to constitute the effective revocation of a will, but it must be demonstrated by one of the acts contemplated by the statute. As WOODWORTH, J., said in *Dan v. Brown,* 4 Cow. 490; "Revocation is an act of the mind, which must be demonstrated by some outward and visible sign of revocation." The same learned judge said in that case: "The rule is that if the testator lets the will stand until he dies, it is his will; if he does not suffer it to do so, it is not his will.". . . The finding of fact of the referee that presumably the testator would have altered his will had he known of his

grandson's murderous intent cannot affect the question. We may concede it to the fullest extent; but still the cardinal objection is undisposed of,—that the making and the revocation of a will are purely matters of statutory regulation, by which the court is bound in the determination of questions relating to these acts.

Two cases,—in this state and in Kentucky,—at an early day, seem to me to be much in point. *Gains v. Gains,* 2 A. K. Marsh. 190, was decided by the Kentucky court of appeals in 1820. It was there urged that the testator intended to have destroyed his will, and that he was forcibly prevented from doing so by the defendant in error or devisee; and it was insisted that the will, though not expressly, was thereby virtually, revoked. The court held, as the act concerning wills prescribed that manner in which a will might be revoked, that, as none of the acts evidencing revocation were done, the intention could not be substituted for the act. In that case the will was snatched away, and forcibly retained. In 1854, Surrogate BRADFORD, whose opinions are entitled to the highest consideration, decided the case of *Leaycraft* v. *Simmons,* 3 Bradf. Sur. 35. In that case the testator, a man of 89 years of age, desired to make a codicil to his will, in order to enlarge the provisions for his daughter. His son, having custody of the instrument, and the one to be prejudiced by the change, refused to produce the will at the testator's request, for the purpose of alteration. The learned surrogate refers to the provisions of the civil law for such and other cases of unworthy conduct in the heir or legatee, and says: "Our statute has undertaken to prescribe the mode in which wills can be revoked [citing the statutory provision]. This is the law by which I am governed in passing upon questions touching the revocation of wills. The whole of this subject is now regulated by statute; and a mere intention to revoke, however well authenticated, or however defeated, is not sufficient." And he held that the will must be admitted to probate. I may refer also to a case in the Pennsylvania courts. In that state the statute prescribed the mode for repealing or altering a will, and in *Clingan* v. *Micheltree,* 31 Pa. St. 25, the supreme court of the state held, where a will was kept from destruction by the fraud and misrepresentation of the devisee, that to declare it canceled as against the fraudulent party would be to enlarge the statute.

I cannot find any support for the argument that the respondent's succession to the property should be avoided because of his criminal act, when the laws are silent. Public policy does not demand it; for the demands of public policy are satisfied by the proper execution of the laws and the punishment of the crime. There has been no convention between the testator and his legatee; nor is there any such contractual element, in such a disposition of property by a testator, as to impose or imply conditions in the legatee. The appellants' argument practically amounts to this: that, as the legatee has been guilty of a crime, by the commission of which he is placed in a position to sooner receive the benefits of the testamentary provision, his rights to the property should be forfeited, and he should be divested of his estate. To allow their argument to prevail would involve the diversion by the court of the testator's estate into the hands of persons whom, possibly enough, for all we know, the testator might not have chosen or desired as its recipients. Practically the court is asked to make another will for the testator. The laws do not warrant this judicial action, and mere presumption would not be strong enough to sustain it. But, more than this, to concede the appellants' views would involve the imposition of an additional punishment or penalty upon the respondent. What power or warrant have the courts to add to the respondent's penalties by depriving him of property? The law has punished him for his crime, and we may not say that it was an insufficient punishment. In the trial and punishment of the respondent the law has vindicated itself for the outrage which he committed, and further judicial utterance upon the subject of punishment or deprivation of rights is barred. We may not, in the language of the court in *People* v. *Thornton,* 25 Hun. 456, "enhance the pains, penalties, and forfeitures provided by law for the punishment of crime." The judgment should be affirmed, with costs.

DANFORTH, J., concurs.

NATURAL LAW REVISITED*

Ronald M. Dworkin

1. What Is Naturalism?

Everyone likes categories, and legal philosophers like them very much. So we spend a good deal of time, not all of it profitably, labeling ourselves and the theories of law we defend. One label, however, is particularly dreaded: no one wants to be called a natural lawyer. Natural law insists that what the law is depends in some way on what the law should be. This seems metaphysical or at least vaguely religious. In any case it seems plainly wrong. If some theory of law is shown to be a natural law theory, therefore, people can be excused if they do not attend to it much further.

In the past several years, I have tried to defend a theory about how judges should decide cases that some critics (though not all) say is a natural law theory and should be rejected for that reason. I have of course made the pious and familiar objection to this charge, that it is better to look at theories than labels. But since labels are so much a part of our common intellectual life it is almost as silly to flee as to hurl them. If the crude description of natural law I just gave is correct, that any theory which makes the content of law sometimes depend on the correct answer to some moral question is a natural law theory, then I am guilty of natural law. I am not now interested, I should add, in whether this crude characterization is historically correct, or whether it succeeds in distinguishing natural law from positivist theories of law. My present concern is rather this. Suppose this is natural law. What in the world is wrong with it?

*Ronald Dworkin, "Natural Law Revisited," *University of Florida Law Review.* v. 34 (1982) pp. 165–88. Reprinted here by permission of the University of Florida Law School.

A. Naturalism

I shall start by giving the picture of adjudication I want to defend a name, and it is a name which accepts the crude characterization. I shall call this picture naturalism. According to naturalism, judges should decide hard cases by interpreting the political structure of their community in the following, perhaps special way: by trying to find the best *justification* they can find, in principles of political morality, for the structure as a whole, from the most profound constitutional rules and arrangements to the details of, for example, the private law of tort or contract. Suppose the question arises for the first time, for example, whether and in what circumstances careless drivers are liable, not only for physical injuries to those whom they run down, but also for any emotional damage suffered by relatives of the victim who are watching. According to naturalism, judges should then ask the following questions of the history (including the contemporary history) of their political structure. Does the best possible justification of that history suppose a principle according to which people who are injured emotionally in this way have a right to recover damages in court? If so, what, more precisely, is that principle? Does it entail, for example, that only immediate relatives of the person physically injured have that right? Or only relatives on the scene of the accident, who might themselves have suffered physical damage?

Of course a judge who is faced with these questions in an actual case cannot undertake anything like a full justification of all parts of the constitutional arrangement, statutory system and judicial precedents that make up his "law." I had to invent a mythical judge, called Hercules, with superhuman powers in order even to contemplate what a full justification of the entire system would be like. Real judges can attempt only what we might call a partial justification of the law. They can try to justify, under some set of principles, those parts of the legal background which seem to them immediately relevant, like, for example, the prior judicial decisions about recovery for various sorts of damage in automobile accidents. Nevertheless it is useful to describe this as a partial justification—as a part of what Hercules himself would do—in order to emphasize that, according to this picture, a judge should regard the law he minds and studies as embedded in a much larger system, so that it is always relevant for him to expand his investigation by asking whether the conclusions he reaches are consistent with what he would have discovered had his study been wider.

It is obvious why this theory of adjudication invites the charge of natural law. It makes each judge's decision about the burden of past law depend on his judgment about the best political justification of that law, and this is of course a matter of political morality. Before I consider whether this provides a fatal defect in the theory, however, I must try to show how the theory might work in practice. It may help to look beyond law to other enterprises in which participants extend a discipline into the future by re-examining its past. This process is in fact characteristic of the general activity we call interpretation, which has a large place in literary criticism, history, philosophy and many other activities. Indeed, the picture of adjudication I have just sketched draws on a sense of what interpretation is like in these various activities, and I shall try to explicate the picture through an analogy to literary interpretation. I shall, however, pursue that analogy in a special context designed to minimize some of the evident differences between law and literature, and so make the comparison more illuminating.

B. The Chain Novel

Imagine, then, that a group of novelists is engaged for a particular project. They draw lots to determine the order of play. The lowest number writes the opening chapter of a novel, which he then sends to the next number who is given the following assignment. He must add a chapter to that novel, which he must write so as to make the novel being constructed the best novel it can be. When he completes his chapter, he then sends the two chapters to the next novelist, who has the same assignment, and so forth. Now every novelist but the first has the responsibility of interpreting what has gone before in the sense of interpretation I described for a naturalist judge. Each novelist must decide what the characters are "really" like; what motives in fact guide them; what the point or theme of the developing novel is; how far some literary device or figure consciously or unconsciously used can be said to contribute to these, and therefore should be extended, refined, trimmed or dropped. He must decide all this in order to send the novel further in one direction rather than another. But all these decisions must be made, in accordance with the directions given, by asking which decisions make the continuing novel better as a novel.

Some novels have in fact been written in this way (including the soft-core pornographic novel NAKED CAME THE STRANGER) though for a debunking purpose, and certain parlor games, for rainy week-ends in English country houses, have something of the same structure. But in this case the novelists are expected to take their responsibilities seriously, and to recognize the duty to create, so far as they can, a single unified novel rather than, for example, a series of independent short stories with characters bearing the same names. Perhaps this is an impossible assignment; perhaps the project is doomed to produce, not simply an impossibly bad novel, but no novel at all, because the best theory of art requires a single creator, or if more than one, that each have some control over the whole. (But what about legends and jokes? What about the Old Testament, or, on some theories, the ILIAD?) I need not push that question further, because I am interested only in the fact that the assignment makes sense, that each of the novelists in the chain can have some sense of what he or she is asked to do, whatever misgivings each might have about the value or character of what will then be produced.

The crucial question each must face is this. What is the difference between continuing the novel in the best possible way, by writing plot and development that can be seen to flow from what has gone before, and starting a fresh novel with characters having the same names? Suppose you are a novelist well down the chain, and are handed several chapters which are, in fact, the first sections of the Dickens short novel, A CHRISTMAS CAROL. You consider these two interpretations of the central character: that Scrooge is irredeemably, inherently evil, and so an example of the degradation of which human nature is intrinsically capable, or that Scrooge is inherently good, but progressively corrupted by the false values and perverse demands of high capitalist society. The interpretation you adopt will obviously make an enormous difference in the way you continue the story. You aim, in accordance with your instructions, to make the continuing novel the best novel it can be; but you must nevertheless choose an interpretation that makes the novel a single work of art. So you will have to respect the text you have been given, and not choose an interpretation that you believe the text rules out. The picture that text gives of Scrooge's early life, for example, might be incompatible with the claim that he is inherently wicked. In that case you have no choice. If, on the other hand, the text is equally consistent with both interpretations, then you do have a choice. You will choose the interpretation that you believe makes the work more significant or otherwise better, and this will probably (though not inevitably) depend on whether you think people like Scrooge are

in fact, in the real world, born bad or corrupted by capitalism.

Now consider a more complex case. Suppose the text does not absolutely rule out either interpretation, but is marginally less consistent with one, which is, however, the interpretation you would pick if they both fit equally well. Suppose you believe that the original sin interpretation (as we might call it) is much the more accurate depiction of human nature. But if you choose that interpretation you will have to regard certain incidents and attributions established in the text you were given as "mistakes." You must then ask yourself which interpretation makes the work of art better *on the whole,* recognizing, as you will, that a novel whose plot is inconsistent or otherwise lacks integrity is thereby flawed. You must ask whether the novel is still better as a novel, read as a study of original sin, even though it must now be regarded as containing some "mistakes" in plot, than it would be with fewer "mistakes" but a less revealing picture of human nature. You may never have reflected on that question before, but that is no reason why you may not do so now, and once you make up your mind you will believe that the correct interpretation of Scrooge's character is the interpretation that makes the novel better on the whole.

C. The Chain of Law

Naturalism is a theory of adjudication not of the interpretation of novels. But naturalism supposes that common law adjudication is a chain enterprise sharing many of the features of the story we invented. According to naturalism, a judge should decide fresh cases in the spirit of a novelist in the chain writing a fresh chapter. The judge must make creative decisions, but must try to make these decisions "going on as before" rather than by starting in a new direction as if writing on a clean slate. He must read through (or have some good idea through his legal training and experience) what other judges in the past have written, not simply to discover what these other judges have said, or their state of mind when they said it, but to reach an opinion about what they have collectively *done,* in the way that each of our novelists formed an opinion about the collective novel so far written. Of course, the best interpretation of past judicial decisions is the interpretation that shows these in the best light, not aesthetically but politically, as coming as close to the correct ideals of a just legal system as possible. Judges in the chain of law share with the chain novelists the imperative of interpretation, but they bring different standards of success—political rather than aesthetic—to bear on that enterprise.

The analogy shows, I hope, how far naturalism allows a judge's beliefs about the personal and political rights people have "naturally"—that is, apart from the law—to enter his judgments about what the law requires. It does not instruct him to regard these beliefs as the only test of law. A judge's background and moral convictions will influence his decisions about what legal rights people have under the law. But the brute facts of legal history will nevertheless limit the role these convictions can play in those decisions. The same distinction we found in literary interpretation, between interpretation and ideal, holds here as well. An Agatha Christie mystery thriller cannot be interpreted as a philosophical novel about the meaning of death even by someone who believes that a successful philosophical novel would be a greater literary achievement than a successful mystery. It cannot be interpreted that way because, if it is, too much of the book must be seen as accidental, and too little as integrated, in plot, style and trope, with its alleged genre or point. Interpreted that way it becomes a shambles and so a failure rather than a success at anything at all. In the same way, a judge cannot plausibly discover, in a long and unbroken string of prior judicial decisions in favor of the manufacturers of defective products, any principle establishing strong consumers' rights. For that discovery would not show the history of judicial practice in a better light; on the contrary it would show it as the history of cynicism and inconsistency, perhaps of incoherence. A naturalist judge must show the facts of history in the best light he can, and this means that he must not show that history as unprincipled chaos.

Of course this responsibility, for judges as well as novelists, may best be fulfilled by a dramatic reinterpretation that both unifies what has gone before and gives it new meaning or point. This explains why a naturalist decision, though it is in this way tied to the past, may yet seem radical. A naturalist judge might find, in some principle that has not yet been recognized in judicial argument, a brilliantly unifying account of past decisions that shows them in a better light than ever before. American legal education celebrates dozens of such events in our own history. In the most famous single common law decision in American jurisprudence, for example, Cardozo reinterpreted a variety of cases to find, in these cases, the principle on which the modern law of negligence was built.

Nevertheless the constraint, that a judge must continue the past and not invent a better past, will often have the consequence that a naturalist judge cannot reach decisions that he would otherwise, given his own political theory, want to reach. A judge who, as a matter of political conviction, believes in consumers' rights may nevertheless have to concede that the law of his jurisdiction has rejected this idea. It is in one way misleading to say, however, that he will be then forced to make decisions *at variance with* his political convictions. The principle that judges should decide consistently with principle, and that law should be coherent, is part of his convictions, and it is this principle that makes the decision he otherwise opposes necessary.

D. Interpretation in Practice

In this section I shall try to show how a self-conscious naturalist judge might construct a working approach to adjudication, and the role his background moral and political convictions would play in that working approach. When we imagined you to be a novelist in the chain novel, several pages ago, we considered how you would continue the first few chapters of A CHRISTMAS CAROL. We distinguished two dimensions of a successful interpretation. An interpretation must "fit" the data it interprets, in order not to show the novel as sloppy or incoherent, and it must also show that data in its best light, as serving as well as can be some proper ambition of novels. Just now, in noticing how a naturalist judge who believed in consumers' rights might nevertheless have to abandon the claim that consumers' rights are embedded in legal history, [sic] the same distinction between these two dimensions was relied upon. A naturalist judge would be forced to reject a politically attractive interpretation, we supposed, simply because he did not believe it fit the record well enough. If fit is indeed an independent dimension of success in interpretation, then any judge's working approach would include some tacit conception of what "fit" is, and of how well a particular interpretation must fit the record of judicial and other legal decisions in order to count as acceptable.

This helps us to explain why two naturalist judges might reach different interpretations of past judicial decisions about accidents, for example. They might hold different conceptions of "fit" or "best fit," so that, for instance, one thinks that an interpretation provides an acceptable fit only if it is supported by the opinions of judges in prior cases, while the other thinks it is sufficient, to satisfy the dimension of fit, that an interpretation fit the actual decisions these judges reached even if it finds no echo in their opinions. This difference might be enough to explain, for example, why one judge could accept an "economic" interpretation of the accident cases—that the point of negligence law is to reduce the overall social costs of accidents—while another judge, who also found that interpretation politically congenial, would feel bound by his beliefs about the requirement of fit to reject it.

At some point, however, this explanation of differences between two judges' theories of the same body of law would become strained and artificial. Suppose Judge X believes, for example, that pedestrians ought to look out for themselves, and have no business walking in areas in which drivers are known normally to exceed the legal speed limit. He might rely on this opinion in deciding that "our law recognizes no general right to recover whenever someone is injured by a speeding driver while walking on a highway where most drivers speed." If Judge Y reaches a different judgment about what the law is, because he believes that pedestrians should be entitled to assume that people will obey the law even when there is good evidence that they will not, then it would strain language to explain this difference by saying that these judges disagree about the way or the degree in which an interpretation of the law must fit past decisions. We would do better to say that these judges interpret the law differently, in this instance, because they bring different background theories of political morality to their interpretations, just as two art critics might disagree about the correct interpretation of impressionism because they bring different theories about the value of art to that exercise.

Any naturalist judge's working approach to interpretation will recognize this distinction between two "dimensions" of interpretations of the prior law, and so we might think of such a theory as falling into two parts. One part refines and develops the idea that an interpretation must fit the data it interprets. This part takes up positions on questions like the following. How many decisions (roughly) can an interpretation set aside as mistakes, and still count as an interpretation of the string of decisions that includes those "mistakes"? How far is an interpretation better if it is more consistent with later rather than earlier past decisions? How far and in what way must a good interpretation fit the opinions judges write as well as the decisions they make? How far must it take account of popular morality contemporary with the decisions it offers to interpret? A second part of any judge's tacit theory of interpretation, however, will be quite independent of these "formal" issues. It will contain the

substantive ideals of political morality on which he relies in deciding whether any putative interpretation is to be preferred because it shows legal practice to be better as a matter of substantive justice. Of course, if any working approach to interpretation has these two parts, then it must also have principles that combine or adjudicate between them.

This account of the main structure of a working theory of interpretation has heuristic appeal. It provides judges, and others who interpret the law, with a model they might use in identifying the approach they have been using, and self-consciously to inspect and improve that model. A thoughtful judge might establish for himself, for example, a rough "threshold" of fit which any interpretation of data must meet in order to be "acceptable" on the dimension of fit, and then suppose that if more than one interpretation of some part of the law meets this threshold, the choice among these should be made, not through further and more precise comparisons between the two along that dimension, but by choosing the interpretation which is "substantively" better, that is, which better promotes the political ideals he thinks correct. Such a judge might say, for example, that since both the foreseeability and the area-of-physical-risk interpretations rise above the threshold of fit with the emotional damages cases I mentioned earlier, foreseeability is better *as an interpretation* because it better accords with the "natural" rights of people injured in accidents.

The practical advantages of adopting such a threshold of fit are plain enough. A working theory need specify that threshold in only a rough and impressionistic way. If two interpretations both satisfy the threshold, then, as I said, a judge who uses such a theory need make no further comparisons along that dimension in order to establish which of them in fact supplies the "better" fit, and he may therefore avoid many of the difficult and perhaps arbitrary decisions about better fit that a theory without this feature might require him to make. But there are nevertheless evident dangers in taking the device too seriously, as other than a rule-of-thumb practical approach. A judge might be tricked into thinking that these two dimensions of interpretations are in some way deeply competitive with one another, that they represent the influence of two different and sometimes contradictory ambitions of adjudication.

He will then worry about those inevitable cases in which it is unclear whether some substantively attractive interpretation does indeed meet the threshold of fit. He will think that in such cases he must define that threshold, not impressionistically, as calling for a "decent" fit, but precisely, perhaps everything will then turn on whether that interpretation in fact just meets or just fails the crucial test. This rigid attitude toward the heuristic distinction would miss the point that any plausible theory of interpretation, in law as in literature, will call for some cross influence between the level of fit at which the threshold is fixed and the substantive issues involved. If an interpretation of some string of cases is far superior "substantively" it may be given the benefit of a less stringent test of fit for that reason.

For once again the underlying issue is simply one of comparing two pictures of the judicial past to see which offers a more attractive picture, from the standpoint of political morality, overall. The distinction between the dimensions of fit and substance is a rough distinction in service of that issue. The idea of a threshold of fit, and therefore of a lexical ordering between the two dimensions, is simply a working hypothesis, valuable so far as the impressionistic characterization of fit on which it depends is adequate, but which must be abandoned in favor of a more sophisticated and piecemeal analysis when the occasion demands.

Of course the moment when more sophisticated analysis becomes necessary, because the impressionistic distinction of the working theory no longer serves, is a moment of difficulty calling for fresh political judgments that may be hard to make. Suppose a judge faces, for the first time, the possibility of overruling a narrow rule followed for some time in his jurisdiction. Suppose, for example, that the courts have consistently held, since the issue was first raised, that lawyers may not be sued in negligence. Our judge believes that this rule is wrong and unjust, and that it is inconsistent in principle with the general rule allowing actions in negligence against other professional people like doctors and accountants. Suppose he can nevertheless find some putative principle, in which others find though he does not, which would justify the distinction the law has drawn. Like the principle, for example, that lawyers owe obligations to the courts or to abstract justice, it would be unfair to impose on the many legal obligation of due care to their clients. He must ask whether the best interpretation of the past includes *that* principle in spite of the fact that he himself would reject it.

Neither answer to this question will seem wholly attractive to him. If he holds that the law does include this putative principle, then this argument would present the law, including the past decisions about suits against lawyers as coherent; but he would then ex-

pose what he would believe to be a flaw in the substantive law. He would be supposing that the law includes a principle he believes is wrong, and therefore has no place in a just and wise system. If he decides that the law does not include the putative principle, on the other hand, then he can properly regard this entire line of cases about actions against lawyers as mistakes, and ignore or overrule them; but he then exposes a flaw in the record of a different sort, namely that past judges have acted in an unprincipled way, and a demerit in his own decision, that it treats the lawyer who loses the present case differently from how judges have treated other lawyers in the past. He must ask which is, in the end, the greater of these flaws; which way of reading the record shows it, in the last analysis, in the better and which in the worse light.

It would be absurd to suppose that all the lawyers and judges of any common law community share some set of convictions from which a single answer to that question could be deduced. Or even that many lawyers or judges would have ready at hand some convictions of their own which could supply an answer without further ado. But it is nevertheless possible for any judge to confront issues like these in a principled way, and this is what naturalism demands of him. He must accept that in deciding one way rather than another about the force of a line of precedents, for example, he is developing a working theory of legal interpretation in one rather than another direction, and this must seem to him the right direction as a matter of political principle, not simply an appealing direction for the moment because he likes the answer it recommends in the immediate case before him. Of course there is, in this counsel, much room for deception, including self-deception. But in most cases it will be possible for judges to recognize when they have submitted some issue to the discipline this description requires and also to recognize when some other judge has not.

Let me recapitulate. Interpretation is not a mechanical process. Nevertheless, judges can form working styles of interpretation, adequate for routine cases, and ready for refinement when cases are not routine. These working styles will include what I called formal features. They will set out, impressionistically, an account of fit, and may characterize a threshold of fit an interpretation must achieve in order to be eligible. But they will also contain a substantive part, formed from the judge's background political morality, or rather that part of his background morality which has become articulate in the course of his career. Sometimes this heuristic distinction between fit and substantive justice, as dimensions of a successful interpretation, will itself seem problematic, and a judge will be forced to elaborate that distinction by reflecting further on the full set of the substantive and procedural political rights of citizens a just legal system must respect and serve. In this way any truly hard case develops as well as engages a judge's style of adjudication. . . .

THE THIRD THEORY OF LAW*

J. L. Mackie

I have resisted the temptation to entitle this paper "Taking Rights Seriously and Playing Fast and Loose with the Law." But it will become plain, as I go on, why I was tempted.

Professor Dworkin's theory of law is now well known, especially since the publication of his book, *Taking Rights Seriously.*[1] But it may be as well to review it, and show how some of his main theses fit together.

I call it the third theory of law because it contrasts both with legal positivism and with the doctrine of natural law, and is in some ways intermediate between the two. The natural law doctrine is well summarized by Blackstone: "This law of nature being coeval with mankind and dictated by God himself is of course superior in obligation to any other. It is binding over the whole globe, in all countries and at all times. No human laws are of any validity if contrary to this, and such of them as are valid derive their force and all their authority, mediately or immediately, from this original."[2] This entails that a judge, relying on his rational knowledge of natural law, may overrule even what appears to be the settled law of the land— unambiguous and regularly enacted statutes or clearly relevant and unopposed precedents—and declare that the apparently settled law is not the law. Against this, I think that Professor Dworkin would concede that all law is made somehow by human beings, and that the (detailed) question, What is the law? makes sense only if construed as asking, What is at a certain time the law of England, or of France, or of the United States, or of South Dakota? The validity of a law is wholly relative to the legal system to which it belongs. Consequently the finding out of what is the law is an empirical task, not a matter of *a priori* reasoning. But, this being conceded, Professor Dworkin stresses a series of contrasts between his view and legal positivism, even such a cautious form of positivism as Professor Hart's.

First, he holds that the law consists not only of rules but also of principles, the distinction between these being logical: "Rules are applicable in an all-or-nothing fashion," whereas principles have the extra dimension of weight (*TRS*, pp. 22–28).

Secondly, he rejects the positivist notion of a single ultimate or fundamental test for law, such as Professor Hart's "rule of recognition." In its place he puts the sort of reasoning that he ascribes, in "Hard Cases," to his imaginary judge, Hercules. Some parts of the law in a certain jurisdiction are settled and relatively uncontroversial, in the constitution or statutes or precedents. Hercules uses these as data, seeking the theory, in terms of further rights and principles, which best explains and justifies this settled law. Having developed this theory, he then applies it to the hard case (*TRS*, pp. 105–123).

Thirdly, and as a result of this method, Professor Dworkin holds that in any sufficiently rich legal system (notably in that of England no less than in that of the United States) the question, What is the law on this issue? always has a right answer, discoverable in principle, and it is the duty of the judge to try to discover it. One of the parties will always have a right to a decision in his favor. "Judicial decisions enforce existing political rights." There is a theoretical possibility of a tie, a dead heat, between competing sets of principles when all relevant considerations have been taken into account, but this is so unlikely that it may in practice be ignored. (See *TRS*, pp. 81, 279–290, esp. 286–287.)

Consequently, and fourthly, though judges in hard or controversial cases have discretion in the weak sense that they are called upon to exercise judgment—they are not supplied with any cut and dried decision procedure—they never have discretion in the strong sense which would exclude a duty to decide the case one way rather than the other (*TRS*, pp. 31–35, 68–71).

Fifthly, though it is really only another way of making the same point, Professor Dworkin holds that even in a hard case one does not reach a stage where the law has run out before it has yielded a decision, and the judge has to make some new law to deal with a new problem. Judges never need to act, even surreptitiously, as legislators, though he has allowed that they may in fact do so as they sometimes do when they make a mistake or when they prospectively overrule a clear precedent.[3]

A sixth point is a further consequence of this. If judges were in effect legislating, it would be appropriate for them to do so in the light of considerations of policy—in particular, of utility or the general welfare of the community or the known will of the majority of the people. But if they are not legislating but still discovering an already existing law, they must confine themselves to considerations of principle; if they let policy outweigh principle, they will be sacrificing someone's rights in order to benefit or satisfy others, and this is unjust. There is, however, an exception to this point. It holds uniformly in civil cases, Professor Dworkin says, but only asymmetrically in criminal cases. The accused may have a right to be acquitted, but the prosecution never has a right to a conviction. So a court may sometimes justly acquit, for reasons of policy, someone who is in fact guilty (*TRS*, pp. 82–100).

Seventhly, Professor Dworkin rejects the traditional positivist separation of law from morality. However, this is a tricky issue. The legal positivism he has explicitly taken as his main target is that of Professor Hart, and Professor Hart recognizes many ways in which law and morality are closely linked. For example, he says, "In some systems, as in the United States, the ultimate criteria of legal validity explicitly incorporate principles of justice or substantive moral values . . ." ". . . statutes may be a mere legal shell and demand by their express terms to be filled out with the aid of moral principles; the range of enforceable contracts may be limited by reference to conceptions of morality and fairness . . ." and "Judicial decision, especially on matters of high constitutional import, often involves a choice between moral values. . . ." But one point on which Professor Hart stands firm is that we can sometimes say, "This is law but too iniquitous to obey or apply," rather than, "Because this is iniquitous it is not law." He argues (against supporters of natural law) that it is both more clearheaded and morally better to allow that something can be valid law and yet evil.[4] It is not clear to me whether Professor Dworkin would deny this. But he makes the following important point. The task which he assigns to Hercules in "Hard Cases" is to find the theory that best explains and justifies the settled law, and to use this theory to decide otherwise unsettled issues. He construes the phrase "best explains and justifies" as including a moral dimension; Hercules has to find the morally best justification of the constitution, statutes, practices, and so on which are not in dispute. In doing this, Hercules must himself make substantive moral judgments, and not merely take account of conventional morality, of widely accepted social rules (*TRS*, pp. 123–128; cf. pp. 206–222).

This third theory of law combines descriptive with prescriptive elements. On the one hand, Professor Dworkin is claiming that it gives the best theoretical understanding of legal procedures and legal reasoning actually at work in such systems as those of England and the United States. But on the other, he wants it to be more explicitly accepted and more consciously followed. He wants it to become a truer description than it yet is, whereas some views that might count as interpretations of the positivist model—for example, the "strict constructionist" view favored by ex-President Nixon—would, he thinks, have deplorable results (*TRS*, pp. 131–149).

It follows that discussion of this theory must also be on more than one level. We are concerned with both its truth as a description and its merit as a recommendation. Let us consider it first as a description. Professor Dworkin argues that courts do, in fact, appeal to principles as distinct from rules and that no coherent description of their procedures can be given by a theory which recognizes only rules as constituting the law. This must, I think, be conceded. But he further maintains that the way in which judges reason in hard cases is some approximation to that which he ascribes to his "superhuman judge, Hercules; and such a view is much more controversial. Along with other aspects of his descriptive theory it needs to be checked empirically and in detail. But some general preliminary comments can be made.

First, there is a distinction—and there may be a divergence—between what judges say they are doing, what they think they are doing, and the most accurate objective description of what they actually are doing. They may say and even believe that they are discovering and applying an already existing law, they may be following procedures which assume this as their aim, and yet they may in fact be making new law. Such a divergence is not even improbable, because even where new law is being made, it will seem fairer if this fact is concealed and the decision is believed to enforce only presently existing rights; and because the making of new law will usually mean only that existing rules or principles are extended somewhat beyond their previous field of application.

Secondly, even though legal reasoning in hard cases involves appeals to principles and rights and is affected by "the gravitational force of precedents," it does not follow that it does or must or even should work in terms of a complete theory of the underlying law for the jurisdiction in question. The superhuman Hercules is, as his name indicates, a mythical figure, and human judges will always operate in a more limited way. However, the practical force of Professor Dworkin's account is that it allows and encourages judges to bring to bear upon a controversial case general considerations and notions about rights which are supported by elements in the settled law that are remote from the case in hand. We may or may not want this; but I would stress that this holistic treatment of the law is in no way required by the admission that legal reasoning appeals to principles as well as to rules. That admission allows such remote control, but does not require it.

Thirdly, though legal reasoning in hard cases refers to rights, this does not entail that it can take no account of interests. Admittedly, to take rights seriously is to see them as having some resistance to interests; in particular, it is to recognize that the rights of an individual will often justify a decision in his favor which is against the interests of the community as a whole. However, Professor Dworkin himself does not regard all rights as absolute, but admits that they may sometimes be overruled by community interest. And when rights conflict with one another, interests may help to determine which right is the stronger in the particular circumstances.

There is no doubt that judges sometimes argue in this way, as in *Miller* v. *Jackson and Another,* heard in the British Court of Appeal—reported in *The Times,* 7 April 1977. The plaintiff lived in a house built in 1972 near a village cricket ground which had been used for over seventy years. He sought an injunction to prevent the club members from playing cricket unless they took adequate steps to prevent stray balls from hitting his house and garden. There is a conflict of rights here: *prima facie* the club has a right to go on playing cricket and the plaintiff has a right to enjoy his home and garden in safety. The court refused, by two to one, to grant the injunction. The judges on the majority side spoke of the public interest and also stressed that the injunction sought was a discretionary remedy. Lord Denning said that the public interest lay in protecting the environment by preserving playing fields in the face of mounting development and enabling our youth to enjoy the benefits of outdoor games, in contrast to the private interest, which lay in securing the privacy of a home and garden without intrusion or interference. Lord Justice Cumming-Bruce said that in considering whether to exercise a judicial discretion to grant an injunction the court was under a duty to consider the interests of the public. That is, they seemed to think that while each party had a *prima facie* right, when these rights came into conflict the importance of the public interest made the cricket club's right the stronger. Professor Dworkin may deplore such reasoning, but he can hardly deny that it occurs, nor can he argue that it should not occur merely because in a hard case there are appeals to principles and rights.

Fourthly, it would be a mere fallacy (which I want to guard against, but do not accuse Professor Dworkin of committing) to argue from the premise that hard cases should be reasoned (partly) in terms of rights—including *prima facie,* non-absolute rights—to the conclusion that in such a case one party must have a (final or resultant) right to a decision in his favor.

Fifthly, there is a weakness in the argument that an exactly equal balance between the considerations on either side is so unlikely that it is almost certain that one party will have an antecedent right to win (*TRS,* pp. 286–287). This argument assumes too simple a metric for the strength of considerations, that such strengths are always commensurable on a linear scale, so that the strength of the case for one side must be either greater than that of the case for the other side, or less, or else they must be equal in the sense of being so finely balanced that even the slightest additional force on either side would make it the stronger. But in fact considerations may be imperfectly commensurable, so that neither of the opposing cases is stronger than the other, and yet they are not finely balanced. Consider the analogous question about three brothers: Is Peter more like James than he is like John? There may be an objectively right and determinable answer to this question, but again there may not. It may be that the only correct reply is that Peter is more like James in some ways and more like John in others, and that there is no objective reason for putting more weight on the former points of resemblance than on the latter or vice versa. While we might say that Peter's likeness to James is equal to his likeness to John (because neither is determinately the greater), this does not mean that any slight additional resemblance to either would decide the issue; hence, it does not mean that this equality expresses an improbably exact balance.

Sixthly, we must note an implication of Professor Dworkin's inclusion of a moral dimension in the reasoning he assigns to Hercules. Hercules' judgment about what the law is on some specific issue depends on what he finds to be the best explanatory and justificatory theory of the settled law. So what the law is, on Professor Dworkin's view, may crucially depend on what is morally best—what is best, not what is conventionally regarded as best in that society. Now I would argue, though I cannot do so here, that moral judgments of this kind have an irreducibly subjective element.[5] If so, then Professor Dworkin's theory automatically injects a corresponding subjectivity into statements about what the law is. Of course, Professor Dworkin is right in arguing that the moral judgments people make—and this may also be true for those that Hercules can be presumed to make—are not, in general, reports of socially established rules or even such reports conjoined with the speaker's acceptance or endorsement of those rules (*TRS*, pp. 45–58). Moral judgments typically include what I call a claim to objectivity and to the objectivity precisely of their prescriptive authority. But these claims, I maintain, are always false. Prescriptive moral judgments are really subjective, though those who make them commonly think that they are objectively valid and mean them to be objectively valid. Suppose Hercules and another judge in the same jurisdiction, both following Professor Dworkin's methods, reach different conclusions about what the law on some issue is because each has reasoned coherently in the light of his own moral

views. Though each of them will sincerely and consistently believe that the law already is as he determines it, I maintain that they will both be wrong. The grounds on which they rely fail to determine an objective preexisting law. Whichever judge's opinion wins the day in the final court of appeal will become the law and will then be the law. The judges who finally decide the case will have been legislating, though they will sincerely, consistently, and rationally believe that they have not. By making a choice determined by their subjective moral judgments for which they honestly but mistakenly claim objective validity, they will have been making law on an issue on which there was previously no determinate law, on which they had no antecedent duty to decide one way rather than the other, and on which neither party had a right to a decision in his favor.

These six general points cast doubt on some parts of Professor Dworkin's descriptive theory, but they should be tested along with the theory, against actual examples of hard cases. I now want to leave the question of description and consider the merits of the third theory as a recommendation. I can do this best by going straight to a concrete example, taken from the legal history of the United States. Professor Dworkin, in a review of Robert M. Cover's book *Justice Accused*, applies his theory to cases which arose before the American Civil War under the Fugitive Slave Acts.[6]

He finds it puzzling that such judges as Joseph Story and Lemuel Shaw, though themselves strongly opposed to slavery, enforced these acts, sending alleged runaway slaves back from states in which slavery was not permitted to states where it still existed and from which they were alleged to have escaped. But why is there a puzzle? Were these judges not, as they themselves said, simply doing their legal duty of enforcing what was then the law of the land, despite the fact that it conflicted with their own moral views? Professor Dworkin argues that it is not so simple. The relevant law was not settled: these cases were controversial. Though the judges in question explicitly denied this, in their deeper thinking they admitted it. But then, being legal positivists, they concluded that they had to legislate, to make new law by their findings. But why, then, did they not make the law in accordance with their moral convictions and their sense of justice? Because, says Professor Dworkin, following Cover, they saw themselves as subordinate legislators only, bound to make the law in harmony with the discoverable intentions of the superior legislators in Congress and, earlier, in the Constitutional Con-

vention. These legislators had, in their several enactments, created and maintained a compromise
between the slave states and the nonslave states;
therefore, sending an alleged slave back to the state
from which he had come was the natural fulfillment
of that compromise.

According to Professor Dworkin, the reasoning
of these judges was a "failure of jurisprudence." If
they had been adherents, not of positivism, but of the
third theory, they could have found in the general
structure of the American Constitution "a conception
of individual freedom antagonistic to slavery, a conception of procedural justice that condemned the procedures established by the Fugitive Slave Acts, and a
conception of federalism inconsistent with the idea
that the State of Massachusetts had no power to supervise the capture of men and women within its territory." These principles were "more central to the law
than were the particular and transitory policies of the
slavery compromise."

It is not in dispute that if these judges had been
adherents of the natural law doctrine—as evidently
they were not—they might have refused to enforce
the Fugitive Slave Acts. Then the judges would have
held that even if the Acts were settled law in the sense
of being unambiguous and regularly enacted statutes,
they were not genuine law because they violated principles of justice and natural right which were prior to
any man-made system of law. The problem is whether
the third theory would have yielded the same result.

First, was the law really not settled? Professor
Dworkin says that the (federal) Fugitive Slave Acts
"left open many questions of procedure, particularly
about the power of the free states themselves to impose restrictions on the process in the interests of the
alleged slave." And Massachusetts had enacted such
restrictions. However, the judges held that these restrictions were overruled by the federal laws, and this
seems to follow from a straightforward interpretation
of Article VI of the United States Constitution: "This
Constitution, and the laws of the United States which
shall be made in pursuance thereof, . . . shall be the
supreme law of the land; and the judges in every State
shall be bound thereby, anything in the constitution
or laws of any State notwithstanding." Professor
Dworkin refers also to "narrowly legalistic and verbal
arguments" on behalf of the alleged slaves, but arguments of that description, too easily produced, will not
show that the law was not, for all that, settled. The
only ground on which he can claim, in a way that is
even initially plausible, that the law was not settled, is
that the procedures laid down in these acts "offended

ordinary notions of due process." The federal official
who returned the alleged slave to his purported master was "a mere commissioner who received a higher
fee if the alleged slave was sent back than if he was
not, there was no question of a jury trial, and the defendant was not allowed to contest whether he was in
fact a slave, that issue being left to be decided in the
slave state after his return."

But it is far from clear that these provisions offend against due process. They would be defended
on the ground that these proceedings were only preliminary: the legal issue about the fugitive's status was
still to be decided in the state from which he had
come, and that, surely, was where witnesses to his
identity and status would be available. He was not
being deprived of liberty without due process of law;
the due process would take place in, say, Virginia.
This argument could be rebutted only by casting
doubt on the legal respectability of the Virginia courts,
and whatever private doubts the Massachusetts judges
may have had about this, it was an essential part of
the federal compromise that they should not be
guided by such doubts in their legal decisions. Article
IV, Section 1, of the Constitution says that "full faith
and credit shall be given in each State to the public
acts, records, and judicial proceedings of any other
State." The Virginia slave-owner could have argued
that if he were not allowed to get his slave back without bringing a large number of witnesses five hundred
miles so as to have his claim heard before a Massachusetts jury which was likely to be hostile to the very
institution of slavery on which his claim was based, he
would be, in effect, being deprived of his property,
namely the slave, without due process of law. Article
IV, Section 2, of the Constitution is quite explicit: "No
person held to service or labor in one State, under the
laws thereof, escaping into another, shall, in consequence of any law or regulation therein, be discharged from such service or labor, but shall be
delivered up on claim of the party to whom such service or labor may be due."

That, in the face of all this, Professor Dworkin
can hold that the law was not settled brings out an
important characteristic of his theory, highly relevant
to the assessment of its merits as a recommendation:
the third theory often takes as unsettled issues which
on a legal positivist view belong clearly to the realm
of settled law.

But suppose that the law was not settled, and
that a judge at the time had tried to decide these cases
by Professor Dworkin's method. What conclusion
would he have reached? Hercules, being a product of

Professor Dworkin's imagination, would no doubt have argued as Professor Dworkin does. But let us invent another mythical judge, say Rhadamanthus.[7] He might have argued as follows:

> *What principles that are relevant to this case are implicit in the settled law? The fundamental fact is the Union itself, which arose out of an alliance, against Britain, of thirteen separate and very different colonies. It was recognized from the start that these colonies, and the states which they have become, have diverse institutions and ways of life. The Union exists and can survive only through compromises on issues where these differing institutions and ways of life come into conflict. One salient principle, then, enshrined as clearly as anything could be in the federal Constitution and in various statutes, is that the rights which individuals have by virtue of the institutions of the states in which they live are to be protected throughout the Union. A Virginian slave-owner's property in his slaves is one of these rights; the clear intention of Article IV, Section 2, of the Constitution and of the Fugitive Slave Acts is to protect this right. Therefore, whatever merely technical defects may be found in them the law of the land, as determined by the third theory of law which I hold, is that the alleged slave should be returned from Massachusetts to Virginia, where it can be properly decided, by the evidence of many witnesses, whether he is in fact the slave of the man who claims him.*
>
> *The contrary view, that the Constitution presupposes a conception of freedom antagonistic to slavery, cannot be upheld. Jefferson, who actually wrote the Declaration of Independence, and who later was mainly responsible for the amendments which most strongly assert individual rights, was himself a slave-owner. The individual freedom which the Constitution presupposes was never intended to apply to slaves. Nor will the requirements of procedural justice, which can indeed be seen as principles enshrined in the settled law, support a finding in favor of the alleged slave. On the presumption that slave-owners have legally valid property rights in their slaves, procedural justice will best be secured by sending the alleged slave back. The conception of federalism does no doubt give the state of Massachusetts the power to supervise the capture of men and women in its territory, but this power must be exercised in ways that respect the institutions of Virginia and the rights of citizens of Virginia, especially as these are further protected by federal law.*

Even if Joseph Story and Lemuel Shaw had shared Professor Dworkin's theory of jurisprudence, they might still have followed Rhadamanthus rather than Hercules and, without for a moment abandoning their reliance on principles on their concern for rights, might have reached just those decisions they did reach by a more positivistic route. This brings out a second characteristic of the third theory, highly relevant to the assessment of its merits as a recommendation: the rights thesis, like the natural law doctrine that it in some ways resembles, is a two-edged weapon. It is particularly risky for an opponent of slavery and of racial discrimination to appeal to states' rights within a federal system. The special importance which Professor Dworkin, in his essays on applied jurisprudence (*TRS*, pp. 206–258), gives to the right to equality is not a necessary consequence of the rights thesis as such.

A third important characteristic of Professor Dworkin's theory is that its adoption would tend to make the law not only less certain but also less determinate than it would be on the rival positivist view. Of course, it is never completely determinate. Reasonable judges may well disagree on hard cases, whatever theory of jurisprudence they hold. But the third theory introduces a further source of indeterminacy. It is well known that the inference from a precedent to a general rule supposed to be implicit in it is not watertight; but a much larger degree of freedom is introduced if the judge has to frame hypotheses, not merely about rules which apply directly to cases, but also about far more general and abstract principles of justice and their implications.

Professor Dworkin would deny this. He would say that it is legal positivism that would make the law in hard cases indeterminate, since it envisages situations in which the law as a whole, not merely the settled law, has run out. Judges are then called upon to legislate, bringing in consideration of policy as well as morality, and it tells judges that they thus have discretion in the strong sense. His theory, on the other hand, holds that there is on every issue a determinate and, in principle, discoverable, though perhaps not settled or certain, law.

This is why I am tempted to speak of professor Dworkin playing fast and loose with the law.[8] The alleged determinacy of the law in hard cases is a myth, and the practical effect of the acceptance of this myth would be to give, in three ways, a larger scope for what is in reality judicial legislation. First, it would shift the boundary between the settled and the unsettled law, it would make what on another view would be easy cases into hard ones. Secondly, this approach would encourage a holistic treatment of the law, letting very general principles and remote parts of the law bear upon each specific issue. Thirdly, it would encourage judges, in this holistic treatment, to rely upon their necessarily subjective views about a supposedly objective morality.

The third theory of law is thus a plea for a more speculative and enterprising handling by judges of their traditional materials and data. Like the natural law doctrine, this theory allows the consciences and the speculations of judges to intervene more significantly between what the legislative and executive branches try to do—or, for whatever reason, leave un-

done—and the law as it actually operates. We know well that people's prejudices, training, and social position—the movements in which they are caught up and the ideologies linked with these—strongly influence their consciences and their speculations. Whether we consider this a merit or a demerit depends upon our judgment of the judges, and particularly upon comparative judgments we make between them, the legislators, and the holders of executive office. Which of these three, with their characteristic methods and the influences to which they are exposed or from which they are sheltered, are the more to be trusted with the opportunity for partly independent decision in the making and remaking of the law? Should we give up some certainty and determinacy about what the law is, and some freedom for legislators to decide what it shall be, in order to give greater weight to what judges will see as people's rights or just claims? I do not know what answer to give, but I want it to be clear that this is the choice.

---

1. *Ronald Dworkin,* Taking Rights Seriously *(London, 1977).*
2. Commentaries, *quoted by Julius Stone,* The Providence and Function of Law *(Sydney, 1946), p. 227.*
3. TRS, *pp. 82–84. Professor Dworkin gave this clarification in reply to a question from Professor Sir Rupert Cross at a seminar on Hard Cases in Oxford, 12 May 1976.*
4. *H. L. A. Hart,* The Concept of Law *(Oxford, 1961), pp. 181–207, esp. 199–200 and 205–207.*
5. *I have argued for this view in Chapter 1 of my* Ethics: Inventing Right and Wrong *(Harmondsworth, 1977).*

6. The Times Literary Supplement, *5 December 1975.*
7. *Cf. Plato,* The Apology of Socrates *40ᶜ–41ᵃ: "Would it be such a bad journey if one arrived in Hades, having got rid of the self-styled judges here, and found the true judges who are said to have jurisdiction there, Minos and Rhadamanthus and Aeacus and Triptolemus and such other demigods as were just during their lives?"*
8. *Cf.* Oxford English Dictionary: *"Fast and loose: A cheating game played with a stick and a belt or string, so arranged that a spectator would think he could make the latter fast by placing a stick through its intricate folds, whereas the operator could detach it at once."*

THE PATH OF THE LAW*

O. W. Holmes, Jr.

When we study law we are not studying a mystery but a well known profession. We are studying what we shall want in order to appear before judges, or to advise people in such a way as to keep them out of court. The reasons why it is a profession, why people will pay lawyers to argue for them or to advise them

is that in societies like ours the command of the public force is intrusted to the judges in certain cases, and the whole power of the state will be put forth, if necessary, to carry out their judgments and decrees. People want to know under what circumstances and how far they will run the risk of coming against what is so

---

*Oliver Wendell Holmes, "The Path of the Law," *Harvard Law Review,* vol. 10 (1897), pp. 457–68.

much stronger than themselves, and hence it becomes a business to find out when this danger is to be feared. The object of our study, then, is prediction, the prediction of the incidence of the public force through the instrumentality of the courts.

The means of the study are a body of reports, of treatises, and of statutes, in this country and in England, extending back for six hundred years, and now increasing annually by hundreds. In these sibylline leaves are gathered the scattered prophecies of the past upon the cases in which the axe will fall. These are what properly have been called the oracles of the law. Far the most important and pretty nearly the whole meaning of every new effort of legal thought is to make these prophecies more precise, and to generalize them into a thoroughly connected system. The process is one, from a lawyer's statement of a case, eliminating as it does all the dramatic elements with which his client's story has clothed it, and retaining only the facts of legal import, up to the final analyses and abstract universals of theoretic jurisprudence. The reason why a lawyer does not mention that his client wore a white hat when he made a contract, while Mrs. Quickly would be sure to dwell upon it along with the parcel gilt goblet and the sea-coal fire, is that he foresees that the public force will act in the same way whatever his client had upon his head. It is to make the prophecies easier to be remembered and to be understood that the teachings of the decisions of the past are put into general propositions and gathered into text-books, or that statutes are passed in a general form. The primary rights and duties with which jurisprudence busies itself again are nothing but prophecies. One of the many evil effects of the confusion between legal and moral ideas, about which I shall have something to say in a moment, is that theory is apt to get the cart before the horse, and to consider the right or the duty as something existing apart from and independent of the consequences of its breach, to which certain sanctions are added afterward. But, as I shall try to show, a legal duty so called is nothing but a prediction that if a man does or omits certain things he will be made to suffer in this or that way by judgment of the court;—and so of a legal right.

The number of our predictions when generalized and reduced to a system is not unmanageably large. They present themselves as a finite body of dogma which may be mastered within a reasonable time. It is a great mistake to be frightened by the ever increasing number of reports. The reports of a given jurisdiction in the course of a generation take up pretty much the whole body of the law, and restate it from the present point of view. We could reconstruct the corpus from them if all that went before were burned. The use of the earlier reports is mainly historical, a use about which I shall have something to say before I have finished.

I wish, if I can, to lay down some first principles for the study of this body of dogma or systematized prediction which we call the law, for men who want to use it as the instrument of their business to enable them to prophesy in their turn, and, as bearing upon the study, I wish to point out an ideal which as yet our law has not attained.

The first thing for a business-like understanding of the matter is to understand its limits, and therefore I think it desirable at once to point out and dispel a confusion between morality and law, which sometimes rises to the height of conscious theory, and more often and indeed constantly is making trouble in detail without reaching the point of consciousness. You can see very plainly that a bad man has as much reason as a good one for wishing to avoid an encounter with the public force, and therefore you can see the practical importance of the distinction between morality and law. A man who cares nothing for an ethical rule which is believed and practised by his neighbors is likely nevertheless to care a good deal to avoid being made to pay money, and will want to keep out of jail if he can.

I take it for granted that no hearer of mine will misinterpret what I have to say as the language of cynicism. The law is the witness and external deposit of our moral life. Its history is the history of the moral development of the race. The practice of it, in spite of popular jests, tends to make good citizens and good men. When I emphasize the difference between law and morals I do so with reference to a single end, that of learning and understanding the law. For that purpose you must definitely master its specific marks, and it is for that that I ask you for the moment to imagine yourselves indifferent to other and greater things.

I do not say that there is not a wider point of view from which the distinction between law and morals becomes of secondary or no importance, as all mathematical distinctions vanish in presence of the infinite. But I do say that that distinction is of the first importance for the object which we are here to consider,—a right study and mastery of the law as a business with well understood limits, a body of dogma enclosed within definite lines. I have just shown the practical reason for saying so. If you want to know the law and nothing else, you must look at it as a bad man, who cares only for the material consequences which such knowledge enables him to predict, not as a good one, who finds his reasons for conduct, whether inside the law or outside of it, in the vaguer sanctions of conscience. The theoretical importance of the distinction is no less, if you would reason on your subject aright. The law is full of phraseology drawn from morals, and by the mere force of language continually invites us to pass from one domain to the other without perceiving it, as we are sure to do unless we have the boundary constantly before our minds. The law talks about rights, and duties, and malice, and intent, and negligence, and so forth, and nothing is easier, or, I may say, more common in legal reasoning, than to take these words in their moral sense, at some stage of the argument, and so to drop into fallacy. For instance, when we speak of the rights of man in a moral sense, we mean to mark the limits of interference with individual freedom which we think are prescribed by conscience, or by our ideal, however reached. Yet it is certain that many laws have been enforced in the past, and it is likely that some are enforced now, which are condemned by the most enlightened opinion of the time, or which at all events pass the limit of interference as many consciences would draw it. Manifestly, therefore, nothing but confusion of thought can result from assuming that the rights of man in a moral sense are equally rights in the sense of the Constitution and the law. No doubt simple and extreme cases can be put of imaginable laws which the statute-making power would not dare to enact, even in the absence of written constitutional prohibitions, because the community would rise in rebellion and fight; and this gives some plausibility to the proposition that the law, if not a part of morality, is limited by it. But this limit of power is not coextensive with any system of morals. For the most part it falls far within the lines of any such system, and in some cases may extend beyond them, for reasons drawn from the habits of a particular people at a particular time. I once heard the late Professor Agassiz say that a German population would rise if you added two cents to the price of a glass of beer. A statute in such a case would be empty words, not because it was wrong, but because it could not be enforced. No one will deny that wrong statutes can be and are enforced, and we should not all agree as to which were the wrong ones.

The confusion with which I am dealing besets confessedly legal conceptions. Take the fundamental question, What constitutes the law? You will find some text writers telling you that it is something different from what is decided by the courts of Massachusetts or England, that it is a system of reason, that it is a deduction from principles of ethics or admitted axioms or what not, which may or may not coincide with the decisions. But if we take the view of our friend the bad man we shall find that he does not care two straws for the axioms or deductions, but that he does want to know what the Massachusetts or English courts are likely to do in fact. I am much of his mind. The prophecies of what the courts will do in fact, and nothing more pretentious, are what I mean by the law.

Take again a notion which as popularly understood is the widest conception which the law contains;—the notion of legal duty, to which already I have referred. We fill the word with all the content which we draw from morals. But what does it mean to a bad man? Mainly, and in the first place, a prophecy that if he does certain things he will be subjected to disagreeable consequences by way of imprisonment or compulsory payment of money. But from his point of view, what is the difference between being fined and being taxed a certain sum for doing a certain thing? That his point of view is the test of legal principles is shown by the many discussions which have arisen in the courts on the very question whether a given statutory liability is a penalty or a tax. On the answer to this question depends the decision whether conduct is legally wrong or right, and also whether a man is under compulsion or free. Leaving the criminal law on one side, what is the difference between the liability under the mill acts or statutes authorizing a taking by eminent domain and the liability for what we call a wrongful conversion of property where restoration is out of the question? In both cases the party taking another man's property has to pay its fair value as assessed by a jury, and no more. What significance is there in calling one taking right and another wrong from the point of view of the law? It does not matter, so far as the given consequence, the compulsory payment, is concerned, whether the act to which it is attached is described in terms of praise or in terms of blame, or whether the law purports to prohibit it or allow it. If it matters at all, still speaking from the bad man's point of view, it must be because in one case and not in the other some further disadvantages, or at least some further consequences, are attached to the act by the law. The only other disadvantages thus attached to it which I ever have been able to think of are to be found in two somewhat insignificant legal doctrines, both of which might be abolished without much disturbance. One is, that a contract to do a prohibited act is unlawful, and the other, that, if one of two or more joint wrongdoers has to pay all the damages, he cannot recover contribution from his fellows.

And that I believe is all. You see how the vague circumference of the notion of duty shrinks and at the same time grows more precise when we wash it with cynical acid and expel everything except the object of our study, the operations of the law.

Nowhere is the confusion between legal and moral ideas more manifest than in the law of contract. Among other things, here again the so called primary rights and duties are invested with a mystic significance beyond what can be assigned and explained. The duty to keep a contract at common law means a prediction that you must pay damages if you do not keep it,—and nothing else. If you commit a tort, you are liable to pay a compensatory sum. If you commit a contract, you are liable to pay a compensatory sum unless the promised event comes to pass, and that is all the difference. But such a mode of looking at the matter stinks in the nostrils of those who think it advantageous to get as much ethics into the law as they can. It was good enough for Lord Coke, however, and here, as in many other cases, I am content to abide with him. In *Bromage* v. *Genning*,[1] a prohibition was sought in the King's Beach against a suit in the marches of Wales for the specific performance of a covenant to grant a lease, and Coke said that it would subvert the intention of the covenantor, since he intends it to be at his election either to lose the damages or to make the lease. Sergeant Harris for the plaintiff confessed that he moved the matter against his conscience, and a prohibition was granted. This goes further than we should go now, but it shows what I venture to say has been the common law point of view from the beginning, although Mr. Harriman, in his very able little book upon Contracts has been misled, as I humbly think, to a different conclusion.

I have spoken only of the common law, because there are some cases in which a logical justification can be found for speaking of civil liabilities as imposing duties in an intelligible sense. These are the relatively few in which equity will grant an injunction, and will enforce it by putting the defendant in prison or otherwise punishing him unless he complies with the order of the court. But I hardly think it advisable to shape general theory from the exception, and I think it would be better to cease troubling ourselves about primary rights and sanctions altogether, than to describe our prophecies concerning the liabilities commonly imposed by the law in those inappropriate terms.

I mentioned, as other examples of the use by the law of words drawn from morals, malice, intent, and negligence. It is enough to take malice as it is used

in the law of civil liability for wrongs,—what we lawyers call the law of torts,—to show you that it means something different in law from what it means in morals, and also to show how the difference has been obscured by giving to principles which have little or nothing to do with each other the same name. Three hundred years ago a parson preached a sermon and told a story out of Fox's Book of Martyrs of a man who had assisted at the torture of one of the saints, and afterward died, suffering compensatory inward torment. It happened that Fox was wrong. The man was alive and chanced to hear the sermon, and thereupon he sued the parson. Chief Justice Wray instructed the jury that the defendant was not liable, because the story was told innocently, without malice. He took malice in the moral sense, as importing a malevolent motive. But nowadays no one doubts that a man may be liable, without any malevolent motive at all, for false statements manifestly calculated to inflict temporal damage. In stating the case in pleading, we still should call the defendant's conduct malicious; but, in my opinion at least, the word means nothing about motives, or even about the defendant's attitude toward the future, but only signifies that the tendency of his conduct under the known circumstances was very plainly to cause the plaintiff temporal harm.[2]

In the law of contract the use of moral phraseology has led to equal confusion, as I have shown in part already, but only in part. Morals deal with the actual internal state of the individual's mind, what he actually intends. From the time of the Romans down to now, this mode of dealing has affected the language of the law as to contract, and the language used has reacted upon the thought. We talk about a contract as a meeting of the minds of the parties, and thence it is inferred in various cases that there is no contract because their minds have not met; that is, because they have intended different things or because one party has not known of the assent of the other. Yet nothing is more certain than that parties may be bound by a contract to things which neither of them intended, and when one does not know of the other's assent. Suppose a contract is executed in due form and in writing to deliver a lecture, mentioning no time. One of the parties thinks that the promise will be construed to mean at once, within a week. The other thinks that it means when he is ready. The court says that it means within a reasonable time. The parties are bound by the contract as it is interpreted by the court, yet neither of them meant what the court declares that they have said. In my opinion no one will understand the true theory of contract or be able even to discuss some fundamental questions intelligently until he has understood that all contracts are formal, that the making of a contract depends not on the agreement of two minds in one intention, but on the agreement of two sets of external signs,—not on the parties' having *meant* the same thing but on their having *said* the same thing. Furthermore, as the signs may be addressed to one sense or another,—to sight or to hearing,—on the nature of the sign will depend the moment when the contract is made. If the sign is tangible, for instance, a letter, the contract is made when the letter of acceptance is delivered. If it is necessary that the minds of the parties meet, there will be no contract until the acceptance can be read,—none, for example, if the acceptance be snatched from the hand of the offerer by a third person.

This is not the time to work out a theory in detail, or to answer many obvious doubts and questions which are suggested by these general views. I know of none which are not easy to answer, but what I am trying to do now is only by a series of hints to throw some light on the narrow path of legal doctrine, and upon two pitfalls which, as it seems to me, lie perilously near to it. Of the first of these I have said enough. I hope that my illustrations have shown the danger, both to speculation and to practice, of confounding morality with law, and the trap which legal language lays for us on that side of our way. For my own part, I often doubt whether it would not be a gain if every word of moral significance could be banished from the law altogether, and other words adopted which should convey legal ideas uncolored by anything outside the law. We should lose the fossil records of a good deal of history and the majesty got from ethical associations, but by ridding ourselves of an unnecessary confusion we should gain very much in the clearness of our thought.

So much for the limits of the law. The next thing which I wish to consider is what are the forces which determine its content and its growth. You may assume, with Hobbes and Bentham and Austin, that all law emanates from the sovereign, even when the first human beings to enunciate it are the judges, or you may think that law is the voice of the Zeitgeist, or what you like. It is all one to my present purpose. Even if every decision required the sanction of an emperor with despotic power and a whimsical turn of mind, we should be interested nonetheless, still with a view to prediction, in discovering some order, some rational explanation, and some principle of growth for the rules which he laid down. In every system there are such explanations and principles to be found. It is

with regard to them that a second fallacy comes in, which I think it important to expose.

The fallacy to which I refer is the notion that the only force at work in the development of the law is logic. In the broadest sense, indeed, that notion would be true. The postulate on which we think about the universe is that there is a fixed quantitative relation between every phenomenon and its antecedents and consequents. If there is such a thing as a phenomenon without these fixed quantitative relations, it is a miracle. It is outside the law of cause and effect, and as such transcends our power of thought, or at least is something to or from which we cannot reason. The condition of our thinking about the universe is that it is capable of being thought about rationally, or, in other words, that every part of it is effect and cause in the same sense in which those parts are with which we are most familiar. So in the broadest sense it is true that the law is a logical development, like everything else. The danger of which I speak is not the admission that the principles governing other phenomena also govern the law, but the notion that a given system, ours, for instance, can be worked out like mathematics from some general axioms of conduct. This is the natural error of the schools, but it is not confined to them. I once heard a very eminent judge say that he never let a decision go until he was absolutely sure that it was right. So judicial dissent often is blamed, as if it meant simply that one side or the other were not doing their sums right, and, if they would take more trouble, agreement inevitably would come.

This mode of thinking is entirely natural. The training of lawyers is a training in logic. The processes of analogy, discrimination, and deduction are those in which they are most at home. The language of judicial decision is mainly the language of logic. And the logical method and form flatter that longing for certainty and for repose which is in every human mind. But certainly generally is illusion, and repose is not the destiny of man. Behind the logical form lies a judgment as to the relative worth and importance of competing legislative grounds, often an inarticulate and unconscious judgment, it is true, and yet the very root and nerve of the whole proceeding. You can give any conclusion a logical form. You always can imply a condition in a contract. But why do you imply it? It is because of some belief as to the practice of the community or of a class, or because of some opinion as to policy, or, in short, because of some attitude of yours upon a matter not capable of exact quantitative measurement, and therefore not capable of founding exact logical conclusions. Such matters really are battle grounds where the means do not exist for determinations that shall be good for all time, and where the decision can do no more than embody the preference of a given body in a given time and place. We do not realize how large a part of our law is open to reconsideration upon a slight change in the habit of the public mind. No concrete proposition is self-evident, no matter how ready we may be to accept it, not even Mr. Herbert Spencer's, Every man has a right to do what he wills, provided he interferes not with a like right on the part of his neighbors.

Why is a false and injurious statement privileged, if it is made honestly in giving information about a servant? It is because it has been thought more important that information should be given freely, than that a man should be protected from what under other circumstances would be an actionable wrong. Why is a man at liberty to set up a business which he knows will ruin his neighbor? It is because the public good is supposed to be best subserved by free competition. Obviously such judgments of relative importance may vary in different times and places. Why does a judge instruct a jury that an employer is not liable to an employee for an injury received in the course of his employment unless he is negligent, and why do the jury generally find for the plaintiff if the case is allowed to go to them? It is because the traditional policy of our law is to confine liability to cases where a prudent man might have foreseen the injury, or at least the danger, while the inclination of a very large part of the community is to make certain classes of persons insure the safety of those with whom they deal. Since the last words were written, I have seen the requirement of such insurance put forth as part of the programme of one of the best known labor organizations. There is a concealed, half conscious battle on the question of legislative policy, and if any one thinks that it can be settled deductively, or once for all, I only can say that I think he is theoretically wrong, and that I am certain that his conclusion will not be accepted in practice *semper ubique et ab omnibus.*

Indeed, I think that even now our theory upon this matter is open to reconsideration, although I am not prepared to say how I should decide if a reconsideration were proposed. Our law of torts comes from the old days of isolated, ungeneralized wrongs, assaults, slanders, and the like, where the damages might be taken to lie where they fell by legal judgment. But the torts with which our courts are kept busy today are mainly the incidents of certain well known businesses. They are injuries to person or property by railroads, factories, and the like. The liability for them is estimated, and sooner or later goes into the price paid by the public. The public really pays the damages, and the question of liability, if pressed far enough, is really the question how far it is desirable that the public should insure the safety of those whose work it uses. It might be said that in such cases the chance of a jury finding for the defendant is merely a chance, once in a while rather arbitrarily interrupting the regular course of recovery, most likely in the case of an unusually conscientious plaintiff, and therefore better done away with. On the other hand, the economic value even of a life to the community can be estimated, and no recovery, it may be said, ought to go beyond that amount. It is conceivable that some day in certain cases we may find ourselves imitating, on a higher plane, the tariff for life and limb which we see in the Leges Barbarorum.

I think that the judges themselves have failed adequately to recognize their duty of weighing considerations of social advantage. The duty is inevitable, and the result of the often proclaimed judicial aversion to deal with such considerations is simply to leave the very ground and foundation of judgments inarticulate, and often unconscious, as I have said. When socialism first began to be talked about, the comfortable classes of the community were a good deal frightened. I suspect that this fear has influenced judicial action both here and in England, yet it is certain that it is not a conscious factor in the decisions to which I refer. I think that something similar has led people who no longer hope to control the legislatures to look to the courts as expounders of the Constitutions, and that in some courts new principles have been discovered outside the bodies of those instruments, which may be generalized into acceptance of the economic doctrines which prevailed about fifty years ago, and a wholesale prohibition of what a tribunal of lawyers does not think about right. I cannot but believe that if the training of lawyers led them habitually to consider more definitely and explicitly the social advantage on which the rule they lay down must be justified, they sometimes would hesitate where now they are confident, and see that really they were taking sides upon debatable and often burning questions.

---

1. *I Roll. Rep. 368.*

2. *See* Hanson v. Globe Newspaper Co., *159 Mass. 293, 302.*

LEGAL REALISM*

Jerome Frank

We have talked much of the law. But what is "the law"? A complete definition would be impossible and even a working definition would exhaust the patience of the reader. But it may not be amiss to inquire what, in a rough sense, the law means to the average man of our times when he consults his lawyer.

The Jones family owned the Blue & Gray Taxi Company, a corporation incorporated in Kentucky. That company made a contract with the A. & B. Railroad Company, also a Kentucky corporation, by which it was agreed that the Blue & Gray Taxi Company was to have the exclusive privilege of soliciting taxicab business on and adjacent to the railroad company's depot.

A rival taxicab company, owned by the Williams family, the Purple Taxi Company, began to ignore this contract; it solicited business and parked its taxicabs in places assigned by the railroad company to the Blue & Gray Company and sought in other ways to deprive the Blue & Gray Company of the benefits conferred on it by the agreement with the railroad.

The Jones family were angered; their profits derived from the Blue & Gray stock, which they owned, were threatened. They consulted their lawyer, a Louisville practitioner, and this, we may conjecture, is about what he told them: "I'm afraid your contract is not legally valid. I've examined several decisions of the highest court of Kentucky and they pretty clearly indicate that you can't get away with that kind of an agreement in this state. The Kentucky court holds such a contract to be bad as creating an unlawful monopoly. But I'll think the matter over. You come back tomorrow and I'll try meanwhile to find some way out."

So, next day, the Joneses returned. And this time their lawyer said he thought he had discovered how to get the contract sustained: "You see, it's this way. In most courts, except those of Kentucky and of a few other states, an agreement like this is perfectly good. But, unfortunately, as things now stand, you'll have to go into the Kentucky courts.

"If we can manage to get our case tried in the federal court, there's a fair chance that we'll get a different result, because I think the federal court will follow the majority rule and not the Kentucky rule. I'm not sure of that, but it's worth trying.

"So this is what we'll do. We'll form a new Blue & Gray Company in Tennessee. And your Kentucky Blue & Gray Company will transfer all its assets to the new Tennessee Blue & Gray Company. Then we'll have the railroad company execute a new contract with the new Tennessee Blue & Gray Company, and at the same time cancel the old contract and, soon after, dissolve the old Kentucky Blue & Gray Company."

"But," interrupted one of the Joneses, "what good will all that monkey-business do?"

The lawyer smiled broadly. "Just this," he replied with pride in his cleverness: "The A. & B. Railroad Company is organized in Kentucky. So is the Purple Taxi which we want to get at. The federal court will treat these companies as if they were citizens of Kentucky. Now, a corporation which is a citizen of Kentucky can't bring this kind of suit in the federal court against other corporations which are also citizens of Kentucky. But if your company becomes a Tennessee corporation, it will be considered as if it were a citizen of Tennessee. Then your new Tennessee company can sue the other two in the federal court, because the suit will be held to be one between citizens of different states. And that kind of suit, based on what we lawyers call 'diversity of citizenship,' can

*Jerome Frank, "Legal Realism," from *Law and the Modern Mind* (New York: Doubleday and Co. Anchor edition, 1963), 46–52. Originally published by Brentanos, Inc. in 1930. Copyright 1930, 1933, 1949 by Coward McCann, Inc. Copyright reviewed in 1958 by Florence K. Frank. Copyright © 1930 by Brentanos, Inc. Reprinted by arrangement with Barbara Kiastern and Peter Smith Publisher, Inc.

be brought in the federal court by a corporation which organized in Tennessee against corporations which are citizens of another state, Kentucky. And the federal court, as I said, ought to sustain your contract."

"That sounds pretty slick," said one of the Joneses admiringly. "Are you sure it will work?"

"No," answered the lawyer. "You can't ever be absolutely sure about such a plan. I can't find any case completely holding our way on all these facts. But I'm satisfied that's the law and that that's the way the federal court ought to decide. I won't guarantee success. But I recommend trying out my suggestion."

His advise was followed. Shortly after the new Tennessee Blue & Gray Company was organized and had entered into the new contract, suit was brought by the Joneses' new Blue & Gray Corporation of Tennessee in the Federal District Court against the competing Purple Company and the railroad company. In this suit, the Blue & Gray Taxi Company of Tennessee asked the court to prevent interference with the carrying out of its railroad contract.

As the Joneses' lawyer had hoped, the federal court held, against the protest of the Purple Company's lawyer, first, that such a suit could be brought in the federal court and, second, that the contract was valid. Accordingly the court enjoined the Purple Company from interfering with the depot business of the Joneses' Blue & Gray Company. The Joneses were elated, for now their profits seemed once more assured.

But not for long. The other side appealed the case to the Federal Circuit Court of Appeals. And the Joneses' lawyer was somewhat worried that that court might reverse the lower federal court. But it didn't, and the Joneses again were happy.

Still the Purple Company persisted. It took the case to the Supreme Court of the United States. That Court consists of nine judges. And the Joneses' lawyer couldn't be certain just how those judges would line up on all the questions involved. "Some new men on the bench, and you never can tell about Holmes and Brandeis. They're very erratic," was his comment.

When the United States Supreme Court gave its decision, it was found that six of the nine judges agreed with counsel for the Joneses. Three justices (Homes, Brandeis, and Stone) were of the contrary opinion. But the majority governs in the United States Supreme Court, and the Joneses' prosperity was at last firmly established.

Now, what was "the law" for the Joneses, who owned the Blue & Gray Company, and the Williamses, who owned the Purple Company? The answer will depend on the date of the question. If asked before the new Tennessee Company acquired this contract, it might have been said that it was almost surely "the law" that the Joneses would lose; for any suit involving the validity of that contract could then have been brought only in the Kentucky state court and the prior decisions of that court seemed adverse to such an agreement.

After the suggestion of the Joneses' lawyer was carried out and the new Tennessee corporation owned the contract, "the law" was more doubtful. Many lawyers would have agreed with the Joneses' lawyer that there was a good chance that the Jones family would be victorious if suit were brought in the federal courts. But probably an equal number would have disagreed: they would have said that the formation of the new Tennessee company was a trick used to get out of the Kentucky courts and into the federal court, a trick of which the federal court would not approve. Or that, regardless of that question, the federal court would follow the well-settled Kentucky rule as to the invalidity of such contracts as creating unlawful monopolies (especially because the use of Kentucky real estate was involved) and that therefore the federal court would decide against the Joneses. "The law," at any time before the decision of the United States Supreme Court, was indeed unsettled. (That is, it was unsettled whether the Williamses had the energy, patience, and money to push an appeal. If not, then the decision of the lower federal court was the actual settled law for the Jones and Williams families.) No one could know what the court would decide. Would it follow the Kentucky cases? If so, the law was that no "rights" were conferred by the contract. Would it refuse to follow the Kentucky cases? If so, rights were conferred by the contract. To speak of settled law governing that controversy, or of the fixed legal rights of those parties, as antedating the decision of the Supreme Court, is mere verbiage. If two more judges on that bench had agreed with Justices Holmes, Brandeis, and Stone, the law and the rights of the parties would have been of a directly opposite kind.

After the decision, "the law" was fixed. There were no other courts to which an appeal could be directed. The judgment of the United States Supreme Court could not be disturbed and the legal "rights" of the Joneses and the Williamses were everlastingly established.

We may now venture a rough definition of law from the point of view of the average man: For any particular lay person, the law, with respect to any particular set of facts, is a decision of a court with respect to those facts so far as that decision affects that particular person. Until a court has passed on those facts no law on that subject is yet in existence. Prior to such a decision, the only law available is the opinion of lawyers as to the law relating to that person and to those facts. Such opinion is not actually law but only a guess as to what a court will decide. (The United States Supreme Court has wittily been called the "court of ultimate conjecture.")

Law, then, as to any given situation is either (*a*) actual law, that is, a specific past decision, as to that situation, or (*b*) probable law, that is, a guess as to a specific future decision.

Usually when a client consults his lawyer about "the law," his purpose is to ascertain not what the courts have actually decided in the past but what the courts will probably decide in the future. He asks,

"Have I a right, as a stockholder of the American Taffy Company of Indiana, to look at the corporate books?" Or, "Do I have to pay an inheritance tax to the State of New York on bonds left me by my deceased wife, if our residence was in Ohio, but the bonds, at the time of her death, were in a safety-deposit box in New York?" Or, "Is there a right of 'peaceful' picketing in a strike in the State of California?" Or, "If Jones sells me his Chicago shoe business and agrees not to compete for ten years, will the agreement be binding?" The answers (although they may run "There is such a right," "The law is that the property is not taxable," "Such picketing is unlawful," "The agreement is not legally binding") are in fact prophecies or predictions of judicial action. It is from this point of view that the practice of law has been aptly termed an art of prediction. . . .

LEGAL REALISM, CRITICAL LEGAL STUDIES, AND DWORKIN*

Andrew Altman

I

In contemporary Anglo-American legal philosophy, little attention has been paid to the work in legal theory carried out in this country during the first half of the century. Indeed, it would be only a slight exaggeration to say that legal theory prior to the publication of H. L. A. Hart's classic *The Concept of Law*, is generally treated as belonging to a kind of prehistorical legal philosophy.[1] Contemporary authors feel it unnecessary to grapple with the theories belonging to this prehistory, as it is widely viewed that such theories have been transcended by the work of Hart and those who followed in his wake.

Nowhere is this attitude toward the legal theories of the first half of the century more evident than in the contemporary treatment of American legal realism. Attention to the realist movement is, to say the least, scanty. Ronald Dworkin devotes approximately one page to the movement in the more than three hundred pages of *Taking Rights Seriously*.[2] Theodore Benditt is more generous in the space he devotes to discussing realism: two chapters of his *Law as Rule and Principle*. Yet, Benditt treats realism as little more than a historical relic.[3] To be sure, realism is regarded as having had its insights, but they are thought of as having been long ago recognized and absorbed into mainstream legal philosophy, while the deficiencies have been presumably identified and repudiated.

Such is the dominant message about realism transmitted by most current work in legal philosophy.[4]

A principal part of the explanation for why most current legal philosophers seem to accept this message lies, I believe, in the apparently cogent critique of realism offered by Hart in *The Concept of Law*. Hart's theory absorbed many of the claims associated with the realist movement. At the same time, he repudiated what were called the "excesses" of realism by invoking a well worked out conception of law as a system of rules. Among those so-called excesses was the idea that the law was shot through with indeterminacy, so that in almost any dispute which reached the stage of litigation the law failed to dictate any specific outcome. Hart's theoretical strategy was to admit that there was a significant amount of indeterminacy in the law, but to argue that such indeterminacy necessarily occupied a peripheral zone in the work of the legal system. Hart thus domesticated the realist indeterminacy thesis. Subsequently, under the influence of Ronald Dworkin, mainstream legal philosophy became preoccupied with the issue of whether or not Hart had himself exaggerated the zone of legal indeterminacy. The more radical indeterminacy of the realist was consigned to the category of realist excesses which everyone now recognized and repudiated.

In this article, I shall begin by examining the realist indeterminacy thesis. Hart's criticisms of realism, I argue, do not come to grips with the most radical source of legal indeterminacy posited by realism. The same may be said for the extensive set of criticisms offered by Benditt. Dworkin's jurisprudence will then be analyzed as an effort to provide a superior response to realism than that offered by Hart. In assessing the Dworkinian approach, I shall be especially concerned to explore its relations to the only contemporary school of legal thought which has tried to utilize and expand upon the realist indeterminacy analysis, namely, the Critical Legal Studies movement (hereafter referred to as CLS). Although it will prove impossible to resolve the basic disagreements between Dworkin and CLS in the context of this article, I shall try to show that CLS does raise some very serious and unanswered questions about the soundness of Dworkinian jurisprudence and of mainstream legal philosophy in general.

II

One of the now familiar theses defended by Hart in *The Concept of Law* is that there are some cases in which the rules of a legal system do not clearly specify the correct legal outcome.[5] Hart claims that such cases arise because of the ineliminable open-texture of natural language: all general terms have a penumbral range in which it is unclear and irresolvably controversial as to whether the term applies to some particular. Yet, this penumbral range of extensional indeterminacy is necessarily much smaller than the core extension in which the term's application is clear and uncontroversial. For Hart, then, the indeterminacy of law is a peripheral phenomenon in a system of rules which, by and large, does provide specific outcomes to cases.

The realist analysis of indeterminacy sees it as both more pervasive and deeper than the indeterminacy Hart attributes to the legal order. For the realist, there is no way to confine indeterminacy to some peripheral region of the law. For my purposes here, I shall be concerned mainly with the realist analysis of common-law adjudication. It should not be forgotten, however, that the realists could and did extend their analysis to all types of adjudication found in our legal system, including those involving statutory and constitutional issues.[6]

The realist analysis of indeterminacy can be presented in two stages.[7] The first stage proceeded from the idea that there was always a cluster of rules relevant to the decision in any litigated case. Thus, deciding whether an uncle's promise to pay his nephew a handsome sum of money if he refrained from smoking, drinking, and playing pool was enforceable brought into play a number of rules, for example, rules regarding offer, acceptance, consideration, revocation, and so on.[8] The realists understood that the vagueness of any one of these rules could affect the outcome of the case. In any single case, then, there were multiple potential points of indeterminacy due to rule vagueness, not a single point as Hart's account sometimes seems to suggest.

The second stage of the realist analysis began with the rejection of a distinction central to the doctrine of precedent, namely, that between holding and dictum.[9] The holding in a case referred to the essential grounds of the decision and thus what subsequent judges were bound by. The dicta were everything in an opinion not essential to the decision, for example, comments about points of law not treated as the basis of the outcome. The realists argued that in its actual operation the common-law system treated the distinction as a vague and shifting one. Even when the judge writing an opinion characterized part of it as "the holding," judges writing subsequent opinions were not bound by the original judge's perception of what was essential for the decision. Subsequent judges were indeed bound by the decision itself, that is, by the finding for or against the plaintiff, and very rarely was the decision in a precedent labeled as mistaken. But this apparently strict obligation to follow precedent was highly misleading, according to the realists. For later judges had tremendous leeway in being able to redefine the holding and the dictum in the precedential cases. This leeway enabled judges, in effect, to rewrite the rules of law on which earlier cases had been decided. The upshot was that in almost any case which reached the state of litigation, a judge could find opinions which read relevant precedents as stating a contrary rule. The common-law judge thus faced an indeterminate legal situation in which he had to render a decision by choosing which of the competing rules was to govern the case. In other words, while the realists claimed that all cases implicated a cluster of rules, they also contended that in any cluster there were competing rules leading to opposing outcomes.[10]

It is this second form of indeterminacy which the realist saw as the deepest and most pervasive. Depending upon how a judge would read the holdings in the cases deemed to be precedents, she would extract different rules of law capable of generating conflicting outcomes in the case before her. In the common-law system, it was left undetermined as to which rules, of a number of incompatible rules, were to govern a case. This type of indeterminacy cuts a much deeper and wider path than the kind Hart was willing to acknowledge. For Hart, the cases afflicted with indeterminacy are the ones in which we know which rule applies but are uncertain over the outcome because the rule contains some vague general term. This second type of realist indeterminacy stems from the fact that the choice of which rules to apply in the first place is not dictated by the law and that competing rules will be available in almost any case which reaches the stage of litigation.

In discussing realism, Hart makes three concessions to realist indeterminacy claims, while at the same time coupling each claim with a major qualification designed to show that actual indeterminacy is far less radical than realism suggests. First, Hart concedes that "there is no single method of determining the rule for which a given authoritative precedent is an authority." But he quickly adds: "Notwithstanding this, in the vast majority of decided cases, there is very little doubt. The headnote is usually correct enough."[11] It is simply question begging, though, for Hart to assert that the headnote usually provides a sufficiently

accurate statement of the correct rule. The realist point is that there is nothing that can be thought of as "the correct rule" for which a precedent stands, and so there is no standard against which one can say that a given rule is "correct enough." On the realist analysis, the headnote, or indeed a later opinion, states only one of any number of competing rules which may, with equal legitimacy, be said to constitute the holding of a case. Hart's assertions do nothing to show that this analysis is wrong: they merely presuppose that it is wrong.

Hart's second concession to realism is that "there is no authoritative or uniquely correct formulation of any rule to be extracted from cases." But then he adds that "there is often very general agreement, when the bearing of a precedent on a later case is in issue, that a given formulation is adequate."[12] Hart seems to be saying here that lawyers may disagree on the precise formulation of a rule but still agree on the correct outcome of a case and so be able to accept, for the purposes of the case, a formulation which, in the given instance, straddles the different versions of the rule. This claim may very well be accurate, but it fails to defeat the realist indeterminacy claims for two reasons. It assumes that the problem of being able to extract conflicting rules from the same line of precedents has been resolved, and, as I argued in connection with Hart's first pair of points, that assumption is question begging. Second, even if there is general agreement on the outcome of a case and on some rough statement of the governing rule (and this, of course, ignores the disagreement which will always be found between the attorneys for the litigants), it does not follow that they agree on the outcome because they agree (roughly) on the legal rule which is said to govern the case. In other words, it does not follow that the law determines the outcome. Agreement on the outcome and on the rough statement of the rule used to justify the outcome may both be the result of some more fundamental political value choice which is agreed upon. Indeed, this is exactly what the realist analysis would suggest by way of explaining board agreement on outcomes and rules. Realism is not committed to denying broad agreement. It is simply committed to the view that the agreement cannot be explained by the determinacy of the law. Thus, Hart's invocation of agreement here does nothing to defeat the realist's indeterminacy thesis.

Hart's third concession to realism is that courts invariably engage in narrowing and widening the rules which precedents lay down. Yet he says that, despite this, the doctrine of precedent has produced "a body of rules of which a vast number, of both major and minor importance, are as determinate as any statutory rule."[13] The problem with this claim, though, is that it misses the crucial realist point regarding the availability of competing rules: let each legal rule be as precise as is humanly possible, the realists insist that the legal system contains competing rules which will be available for a judge to choose in almost any litigated case. The claims made by Hart in his effort to domesticate the realist notion of legal indeterminacy all systematically fail to deal with this crucial realist point.

Benditt's arguments against realism are similarly flawed: none of them directly attack the problem of competing rules.[14] Indeed, this is not surprising, since Benditt's entire account of realism is distorted by his insistence on interpreting realism as denying the existence of authoritative legal rules.[15] While such "rule nihilism" may be suggested in some of the remarks of some realists, the more influential members and allies of the movement were clear that it is precisely the existence of competing *authoritative* rules which creates the radical indeterminacy problem. Llewellyn, perhaps the principal spokesperson for realism during its heyday, characterizes the problem as due to the fact that there are opposing "authoritative premises" for any case.[16] And Dewey's highly influential piece, "Logical Method and Law," stresses the problem of choice among competing rules, rather than denying the existence of authoritative rules.[17] Realists were undoubtedly a very heterogeneous group, at least when measured by their ideas about law, and some of the criticisms made by Hart and Benditt against some realist claims are persuasive.[18] But the standard criticisms do not touch the realist thesis that there is a pervasive indeterminacy in the legal system owing to the existence of competing rules of law.

III

To this point, I have portrayed the realists as focusing upon the choice of competing legal rules which judges in common-law cases must make. This may seem to leave the realist open to one of the principal criticisms which Dworkinians have made of Hart: the law is more than just legal rules. It is also the ethical principles and ideals of which the rules are an (albeit imperfect) expression, and it is these principles and ideals which help to guide judges to a determinate outcome.[19] Indeed, the Dworkinian might try to use

the realist indeterminacy analysis to his advantage: if the law were simply a collection of rules, as Hart thinks, it would be afflicted by exactly the kind of deep and pervasive indeterminacy which the realist posits. Yet, if the law were indeterminate to the degree suggested by the realist analysis, it would not be much more than a pious fraud: judges would be "legislating" not only in penumbral cases, but in all cases. Judges would always be creating law, in flagrant violation of their institutional duty to apply preexisting law. The Dworkinian may conclude that we face this choice: either include principles and ideals as part of the law in order to contain (and, perhaps, eliminate) the indeterminacy it would have were it simply a collection of rules or admit that common-law adjudication is a fraud. Although the latter choice is logically possible, assumptions shared by both Dworkin and his positivist critics make it an entirely implausible one from their point of view. The only plausible alternative may thus seem to be the acceptance of Dworkin's important idea that ethical principles be understood as part of the law even when they are not explicitly formulated in some authoritative legal text or clearly identifiable by the application of some noncontroversial, positivist rule for specifying authoritative legal norms in terms of their source. Thus, Dworkin argues that adjudication requires the invocation of principles which take judges "well past the point where it would be accurate to say that any 'test' of pedigree exists. . . ."[20] Moreover, such principles are, on Dworkin's view, binding on judges and so we must realize that "legal obligation . . . [is] . . . imposed by a constellation of principles as well as by an established rule."[21] Indeed, it is this constellation of principles which must guide the judge to a determinate outcome when the relevant legal rules are in competition with one another. For instance, the principles could indicate to the judge the proper scope of application of each of the competing rules and thus resolve any apparent conflict by showing that just one of the rules was properly applicable in the case at hand.

Yet, which principles are legally binding? Dworkin's answer is that they are those which belong to the "soundest theory of the settled law."[22] The settled law consists of those legal rules and doctrines which would be accepted as authoritative by the consensus of the legal community. The soundest theory is the most defensible ethical and political theory which coheres with and justifies those legal rules and doctrines. The coherence does not have to be perfect, for Dworkin allows that the soundest theory may characterize some rules and legal outcomes as mistakes, but coherence with most of the settled law is demanded. In principle, the soundest theory is to encompass every area of law: every branch of the common law, all statutes, the whole body of administrative law, and the entire range of constitutional law. Of course, Dworkin recognizes that no merely human judge could ever formulate and defend such a theory. But his character, Hercules, is intended to show us that, in principle, such a theory could be formulated and defended by a sufficiently great intelligence.[23] Even though the fictional, judicial Hercules has powers far beyond those of mortal judges, Dworkin tells us that mortal judges are committed both to the logical possibility of such a character and to the task of trying to arrive at the outcome he would arrive at were he to be hearing their cases. Mortal judges thus can and do appeal to principles in reaching determinate outcomes, and, in doing so, they are giving force to pre-existing legal obligations, and not simply making a political choice among competing legal rules.

It should be noted that the realists were not blind to seeing legal rules as expressions of ethical principles. Nonetheless, there are tremendous differences between the way in which a realist such as Thurman Arnold viewed these principles and the way in which Dworkin and his followers see them. Arnold was thoroughly cynical about the ethical ideals in terms of which the law was understood: they were high-sounding phrases which appealed to people's emotions and satisfied their need to think of the legal order as more than just some arbitrary and contingent setup. But they had no meaning other than this emotive one and could not be the subject of any rational discussion or defense.[24] Other realists, such as Felix Cohen, were not at all cynical and believed that ethical principles were amenable to rational discussion. Yet they did little to analyze carefully the ethical principles embedded in law or to examine the implications of the existence of such principles for the problem of indeterminacy.[25]

In this section, I have raised the possibility that Dworkin's jurisprudential project succeeds where Hart failed in defeating the radical realist indeterminacy thesis. However, it would be premature to make a judgment regarding the success of Dworkin's project in this respect, for scholars in the Critical Legal Studies movement have picked up and elaborated realist ideas in a way that seriously threatens the foundations of Dworkinian jurisprudence. It is to CLS that I shall turn presently. One important point should be made before I do that, however. For the most part, proponents of CLS and Dworkinians have ignored one another's positions. There are some passing references to CLS in some pieces by avowed Dworkinians, such as Charles Fried.[26] And there is some treatment of Dworkin in the CLS literature.[27] Yet, neither side seems to do anything more than make very superficial, highly polemical points against the other. The interchange of ideas between Dworkinians and CLSers is one which I have constructed with the deliberate aim of avoiding the superficial polemics which have thus far characterized the few occasions on which the one side has deigned in print to deal with the position of the other.

IV

CLS scholars accept the Dworkinian idea that legal rules are infused with ethical principles and ideals.[28] Moreover, they take such principles as seriously as Dworkinians in that they conceive of the articulation and examination of such principles to be one of the major tasks of legal theory.[29] Thus, Duncan Kennedy has analyzed the role in the form and content of legal doctrine of what he characterizes as "individualist" and "altruist" ethical conceptions. And Roberto Unger has examined the normative principles which he takes to be embodied in the common law of contracts.[30] Yet, one of the main themes of CLS work is that the incorporation of ethical principles and ideals into the law cuts against Dworkinian efforts to rescue legal determinacy. The operative claim in CLS analysis is that the law is infused with irresolvably opposed principles and ideals. Kennedy writes that the opposing ethical conceptions which inform legal doctrine "reflect a deeper level of contradiction. At this deeper level, we are divided, among ourselves and also within ourselves, between irreconcilable visions of humanity and society, and between radically different aspirations for our common future."[31] While the realists stress competing rules, CLSers stress competing, and indeed irreconcilable, principles and ideals. Yet, the basic theme is the same: the judge must make a choice which is not dictated by the law. In the CLS analysis, the choice is one of several competing principles or ideals to be used in guiding her to a decision. Different choices lead to different outcomes. Thus, from the CLS perspective, the jurisprudential invocation of principles only serves to push back to another stage the point at which legal indeterminacy enters and judicial choice takes place.

The Dworkinian response would be to deny that legal indeterminacy follows from the fact that the law contains principles which pull in opposing directions. One of Dworkin's major points in his account of principles is that they have differing weights.[32] Thus, even if we have a case in which two competing principles appear applicable, for example, "A person should not be held liable unless she was at fault" versus "As between two innocents, the one who caused the harm should pay," Dworkin will argue that, in all likelihood, one of those principles will carry greater weight in the case at hand and it is that principle which determines the correct legal outcome. Dworkin does allow for the possibility that there may be a case in which the weights of all applicable principles are exactly equal, leaving the legal outcome truly indeterminate, but goes on to claim that such cases will be extremely rare in any developed legal system.

It must be noted here that Dworkin's conception of the soundest theory of the settled law assumes that there is some metalevel principle for determining the appropriate weights to be assigned to the different principles which may be applicable in a given case. This assumption becomes clear once we see that Dworkin's conception of the soundest theory rejects intuitionism, according to which relative weights are intuited in each case without there being any higher order standard in virtue of which each principle has its particular weight. Dworkin's position is that there is a legal fact of the matter regarding the weight of a given principle in a given case, and this fact is determined by the weight that principle receives according to the standards of the soundest theory of the settled law. Moreover, this rejection of intuitionism is firmly rooted in a commitment to the rule of law ideal.[33] That ideal requires that legal decisions be the outcome of reasoning that can be reconstructed according to principles which can be articulated and understood. To use a term which has been popular among legal theorists, judicial decision must be "principled."[34] This means that the judge cannot simply appeal to his inarticulate sense that a particular principle is weightier than some competing principle in the case before him. He must believe that there is some higher order principle which makes the one weightier than the other, and he must at least try to figure out and articulate what that higher order principle is.

Now, one line of CLS attack against Dworkin is to argue that there is no discoverable metaprinciple for assigning weights. Duncan Kennedy suggests this line in discussing the possibility of using moral theory to justify legal doctrine. Kennedy admits that, in the context of the fact situation of a particular case, opposing principles do not necessarily carry the same

weight: "we are able to distinguish particular fact situations in which one side is more plausible than the other. The difficulty, the mystery, is that there are no available metaprinciples to explain just what it is about these particular situations that make them ripe for resolution."[35] Actually, Kennedy's point should be put in a less sweeping way: no one has come up with such metaprinciples, and it is implausible to think that it can be done. When put in these terms, the CLS position becomes an essentially reactive one which awaits Dworkinian efforts and then reacts against them: Dworkinians put forth their rational/ethical reconstructions of the law (or some portion of it), complete with metaprinciples for assigning weights to principles, and then CLSers and others attempt to show that the reconstruction is inadequate and incoherent. The burden of production thus seems to be on the Dworkinians. What have they produced?

The closest thing we have from them of a Dworkinian reconstruction of a portion of the settled law is Charles Fried's effort to reconstruct contract law on the basis of the principle that one ought to keep one's promises and related conceptions from a liberal individualist philosophy.[36] Yet, Fried sought to avoid the problem of developing metaprinciples by narrowly defining the body of law which he attempted to reconstruct. Thus, he did not attempt to incorporate collective bargaining law with its decidedly greater collectivist orientation than the common law of contracts, and he even banished to other fields of law doctrines which are standardly treated as part of the common law of contracts but which do not fit neatly with the individualist principles animating his reconstruction.[37] This is not to imply any assessment regarding the success or failure of Fried's effort to reconstruct his highly streamlined body of contract law. For now my point is the modest one that by gerrymandering doctrine, he attempted, in effect, to evade the difficulty of developing higher order standards to harmonize the competing principles which infuse the law of contracts, and so he simply delayed tackling one of the principal obstacles in the path of constructing the kind of theory which Dworkinian jurisprudence presumes we can and should build.

It is important to recognize here that I am not talking about the theory which Dworkin's Hercules would try to construct, one encompassing the entire body of the law. Rather, what is at issue is a theory for some connected but limited portion of the law, such as the law of contracts. Both CLS and I assume that Dworkinians are committed to the notion that such limited theories can be built by humans, not merely by gods. For if humans cannot construct even such modest theories, the problem of legal indeterminacy will be irresolvable from a human point of view, no matter what may be true from a divine point of view. If the rule of law is to be a guiding ideal for humans, and not just gods, then the problem of legal indeterminacy must be resolvable from a human point of view. Moreover, Dworkinian jurisprudence itself prohibits evasion of the problem of competing principles by so gerrymandering doctrine that one never has to harmonize such principles. Dworkin is clear that different parts of the law have to be understood in terms of each other, for example, a statute affecting tort liability will properly play a role in a judge's decision in a common-law tort action.[38] The judge cannot ignore the statute on the ground that it embodies principles in some tension with common-law principles and thus is difficult to reconcile with them. The judge is supposed to (try to) reconcile the tension and not avoid facing it.

CLS scholars would clearly go further than I have so far and reject as wrongheaded even the relatively modest project Fried has undertaken to reconstruct common-law contract doctrine from the promise principle. In addition, CLSers would judge as totally implausible the belief that any coherent Dworkinian theory, complete with metaprinciples, can be developed for any significant portion of the settled law. Yet, the CLS claims in this regard are unpersuasive, given the argument that has been adduced in their behalf to this point. Even if it is admitted that there are difficulties in the way of constructing a Dworkinian theory for any significant portion of the settled law because such a portion will invariably embody principles in tension with one another, surely no argument has yet been given that makes it implausible to believe that such a theory can be constructed. Nonetheless, the points made so far do not by any means exhaust the potential CLS critique of Dworkinian jurisprudence. While CLS rhetoric often does make the invalid leap from the premise that there are competing principles which infuse settled doctrine to the conclusion that there must be pervasive legal indeterminacy, there are within CLS distinct and more powerful lines of reasoning against the viability of the Dworkinian project.

The additional lines of reasoning are premised on the idea that the settled law is the transitory and contingent outcome of ideological struggles among social factions in which conflicting conceptions of justice, goodness, and social and political life get compromised, truncated, vitiated, and adjusted.[39] The point here is not simply that there are competing principles embodied in settled doctrine, although that is a starting point for the statement of the problem. More fundamentally, the point is that these principles have their weight and scope of application in the settled law determined, not by some metalevel philosophical principle which imposes order and harmony, but by an ideological power struggle in which coherent theories become compromised and truncated as they fit themselves into the body of law. The settled law as a whole, and each field within it, represents the (temporary) outcome of such an ideological conflict. This is, to be sure, a causal claim about the genesis of legal doctrines and principles, rather than a logical one regarding the lack of amenability of such doctrines and principles to rational reconstruction. But the CLS positions can be interpreted as linking the logical claim to the causal one. The position is that it is implausible to believe that any system of norms generated by such a process of struggle and compromise will be capable of an ethically principled reconstruction. Unger summarizes the CLS view this way:

> . . . it would be strange if the results of a coherent, richly developed normative theory were to coincide with a major portion of any extended branch of law. The many conflicts of interest and vision that lawmaking involves, fought out by countless minds and wills working at cross purposes, would have to be the vehicle of an immanent moral rationality whose message could be articulated by a single cohesive theory. This daring and implausible sanctification of the actual is in fact undertaken by the dominant legal theories. . . .[40]

This idea that the law is a patchwork quilt, as it were, of irreconcilably opposed ideologies is tied to CLS's version of the repudiation of the distinction between law (adjudication) and politics. Sometimes CLS scholars suggest that the distinction unravels principally because of the fact that controversial normative and descriptive judgments are just as much an ineliminable part of adjudication as they are of politics. Yet, I think that there is a more important, though related, way in which the distinction is thought to unravel. The idea is this: all of those ideological controversies which play a significant part in the public debate of our political culture are replicated in the argument of judicial decision. In other words, the spectrum of ideological controversy in politics is reproduced in the law. Of course, CLS recognizes that in legal argument the controversies will often be masked or hidden by talk of the intent of the framers, the requirements of *stare decisis,* and so on. The point is that the same ideological debates which fragment political discourse are replicated in one form or another in a legal argument. As a patchwork quilt of irreconcilable ideologies, the law is a mirror which faithfully reflects the fragmentation of our political culture. Such, as least, is a principal CLS theme.

How is it possible to parlay these CLS ideas regarding the patchwork-quilt character of doctrine and the unraveling of the law/politics distinction into a cogent argument against Dworkinian jurisprudence? I think there are two principal lines of argument. The first seeks to show that it makes no sense to think there is any soundest theory of the settled law. The second seeks to show that the Dworkinian theory fails on its own terms to provide a satisfactory account of the legitimacy of judicial decision making. Let us explore each of these lines of argument in turn.

V

One possible line of CLS argument is that legal doctrine is so internally inconsistent that it is implausible to believe that there is any single, coherent theory capable of justifying enough of it to satisfy the Dworkinian fit requirement. Consistently applying any of the theories embodied in some significant portion of the law across the entire body of doctrine would, the argument goes, involve such substantial doctrinal reconstruction that it would violate the Dworkinian mandate that any theory invoked to decide cases fit or cohere with the bulk of the settled law. Thus, ethically principled reconstruction of any substantial portion of doctrine is ruled out by the law's internal contradictions, such contradictions being symptomatic of the law's conception in ideological compromise and struggle and of its tendency to reflect the range of political conflict present in the culture. This means that there simply is no soundest theory of the settled law, and so the Dworkinian efforts to rescue legal determinacy by appealing to such a notion fail.

It may be helpful in clarifying this CLS argument to show how Dworkin's responses to more conventional criticisms of his jurisprudence completely fail to come to grips with the central claim of this argument. A typical conventional criticism will claim that legal indeterminacy survives the Dworkinian efforts to erase it because there are multiple, conflicting theories no one of which can be cogently established as pro-

viding an account of the settled law which is superior to that of any of the other theories. In other words, the concept of the soundest theory really has more than one referent, and they provide different answers to questions regarding who should win cases.[41]

Dworkin's response to this type of criticism is in two stages. First, he argues that, although there may be several theories which fit the settled law well enough when one is talking about the settled law of a simple, undeveloped legal system, the probability of that happening in a complex and developed system such as we have is very small. Second, he claims that even if there were several theories which fit well enough, that would not defeat his claims since the soundest theory would be the one from those several which is most defensible on the grounds of political and ethical philosophy. Thus, he concludes that two claims must be sustained in order to defeat his position: that there are multiple theories which fit the settled law well enough, and that political and ethical philosophy suffer from an indeterminacy (or an irremediable subjectivity) which makes it impossible to choose just one of those theories as the most defensible.[42]

However convincing this Dworkinian argument may be against conventional legal philosophers, it does not even begin to join the issue with CLS. For the CLS patchwork-quilt argument is not that there is legal indeterminacy due to the fact that there are several "soundest theories"; rather the argument is that there is indeterminacy because there are none. Or, more accurately, the argument is that there is indeterminacy because of what excludes the possibility of any soundest theory, namely, the internally incoherent character of legal doctrine. This argument makes it completely beside the point whether ethical and political philosophy is indeterminate or subjective. If doctrine is as internally contradictory as CLS claims, then Dworkinian jurisprudence fails to rescue legal determinacy even if there is a uniquely and objectively true ethical and political philosophy.

Dworkin's replies to conventional critics of his jurisprudence are essentially irrelevant here because those critics share Dworkin's assumption that doctrine is by and large coherent. More generally, the conventional critics share Dworkin's assumption that legal doctrine and argument are largely in good logical order, though they believe that indeterminacy has a somewhat broader toehold in the law than Dworkin is willing to admit. CLS dissents from these assumptions. In this respect the CLS position may be usefully analogized with Alasdair MacIntyre's diagnosis of the ethical thought of modern culture.[43] MacIntyre argues that such thought is internally incoherent. This state of incoherence is due to the fact that modern ethical thought amounts to an amalgam of fragments of irreconcilable ethical views. Conventional philosophers not only fail to perceive the utter incoherence of modern ethical thought, but operate on the assumption that it is largely in good order. For them the issue is the best way to systematize that thought, not whether it is so self-contradictory that systematization is impossible. The result is that the debates fought out among conventional ethical philosophers, such as Rawls and Nozick, do not join the issue with MacIntyre's position. He repudiates the assumptions which the conventional antagonists share. In a very similar way, the debate between Dworkin and his conventional critics fails to join the issue with CLS. They assume a doctrinal coherence which CLS repudiates, and so the conventional debate takes place in terms which are largely irrelevant to the CLS position.

Duncan Kennedy makes the CLS position on doctrinal incoherence plain in his description of a private law field which he takes to be representative of doctrine in general:

> In contract law, for example, there are two principles: there is a reliance, solidarity, joint enterprise concept, and there is a hands-off, arms length, expectancy-oriented, "no flexibility and no excuses" orientation. They can be developed very coherently, but only if one accepts that they are inconsistent. There are fifteen or twenty contract doctrines about which there is a conflict. . . . That is the structure of contract doctrine, and it's typical. Doctrine is not consistent or coherent. The outcomes of these conflicts form a patchwork, rather than following straight lines.[44]

Given the terms in which the CLS position has been stated, it is clear what the Dworkinian reply must be in order to join the issue: that doctrine is not as internally contradictory as CLS claims. The main argument would have to be that any internal inconsistencies in legal doctrine are merely marginal, capable of characterization as "mistakes" without any substantial rupture to the fabric of doctrine. This argument would be supplemented, I think, by one to the effect that CLS exaggerates the degree to which theory must fit the settled law in order to be said to fit well enough. To make out these arguments would not be at all easy. CLS analyses have sought to exhibit the deep and pervasive incoherence of doctrine in such areas as constitutional law, labor law, contract law, administrative law, and criminal law, to name only a few.[45] Indeed, I think it is accurate to say that CLS has, through these analyses, made a much more thorough and stronger case for the incoherence of legal doctrine than MacIntyre has made for the incoherence of ethical thought. Meanwhile, Dworkinians have done little to respond to these CLS analyses. Moreover, Dworkin's most recent efforts to clarify the character of the fit test provide little ammunition against the CLS argument. Let us briefly examine those efforts in order to see why this is so.

Dworkin's recent writing indicates that the fit test is more sophisticated than some of his critics have taken it to be.[46] He tells us that the degree of fit is not just a matter of adding up the number of precedents and rules for which a given theory accounts. One must also take into consideration such factors as the trend of recent decisions. Two theories may account for the same number of precedents and rules, but, if one accounts for more of the recent decisions and the other for more of the older decisions, then the former has a better fit, according to Dworkin.

Dworkin does not indicate how much weight should be given to the capacity to account for recent trends. Nor does he explain why accounting for a trend in new decisions makes for a better fit than accounting for the pre-trend pattern of old ones. Moreover, he ignores the point that the question of what counts as a significant trend and what counts as an insignificant blip or anomaly is not a theory-neutral one. What counts as a trend from the perspective of one theory may count as an anomaly to be ignored from the perspective of another. It does no good to be told here that the soundest theory of the law determines what is a trend and what is an anomaly, since the fit test is supposed to help us figure out which theory is the soundest one. But, more to the point for the doctrinal incoherence issue, the CLS contention is that the patchwork character of law is manifested within the body of recent decisions and not just between recent ones and old ones. There may be trends but there are countertrends as well. Some decisions may introduce or expand new lines of doctrine, but other recent decisions will continue the older lines. By characterizing the former as "trends" and giving their line of doctrine greater weight, Dworkin is merely picking out one line of doctrine for favored status from among several conflicting lines. His aim does seem to be to reduce doctrinal dissonance, but he provides no argument for giving greater importance to trends than countertrends and so he does not succeed.

Even if Dworkin were able to provide some convincing argument for according greater importance to trends, it is not at all obvious that he would thereby solve the problem of doctrinal incoherence. His recent writing explicitly states that there is some threshold level of fit which any theory must satisfy in order to be the soundest theory of the law.[47] Presumably, this threshold would require a theory to account for most, but not all, of the doctrinal materials. However, CLS analyses suggest that doctrinal incoherence is so deep and pervasive that, even if one grants that accounting for certain doctrinal lines (the trends) gives somewhat better fit than accounting for others (the countertrends), any coherent theory will prove incompatible with such a broad range of doctrine as to make implausible the notion that it has satisfied the threshold. These analyses do not conclusively establish the point, but they do raise a strong prima facie case to which there has been only the most meager response by conventional legal philosophers of any stripe, Dworkinian or otherwise.

It seems to me, then, that the patchwork-quilt line of argument presents unmet and serious challenges to the viability of the Dworkinian jurisprudential project, as well as to other conventional legal philosophies. Even if this CLS argument is met by some cogent conventional response, however, there is an independent line of CLS argument against another key Dworkinian position. Let us now turn to that position.

VI

Dworkin is concerned to defend the legitimacy of judicial decision making that invokes controversial principles of ethical or political philosophy. The Dworkinian judge is licensed to rely on such principles because, as Dworkin well realizes, it is inevitable that a judge who, in a hard case, seeks to enunciate and invoke the principles embodied in the settled law will fail to find principles on which everyone can agree. If the judge is to guide her decision by the principles she thinks are embodied in the law, then the reliance of adjudication on controversial principles is inescapable, at least for many cases. In this sense, Dworkin is willing to acknowledge that adjudication

is "political."[48] Yet, he thinks that such an acknowledgment does nothing to impugn the legitimacy of the adjudication.

Dworkin's arguments in favor of the legitimacy of such admittedly "political adjudication" are not entirely clear. Let me suggest the following as the principal Dworkinian argument on this point. The invocation of controversial ethical or political principles in adjudication is constrained by the judicial duty to decide a hard case according to the dictates of the soundest theory of the settled law. Thus, the "political" reasoning and choice of the judge take place within much narrower confines than if she were a legislator deciding what sort of legislative enactment was best. As Dworkin says in his discussion of a judge deciding an abortion case, it is one thing for her to decide whether political philosophy dictates that government should acknowledge a right to an abortion, and it is quite another for her to decide whether the settled law of our legal/political system is best accounted for by a theory incorporating a conception of dignity which entails such a right.[49] The former decision is of course, appropriate for a legislature, not a court. Yet, it is the latter decision, not the former, which the Dworkinian judge is under a duty to make, and it is a decision which is made within much narrower confines than the former. Thus, it is misguided to think that the kind of "political adjudication" endorsed by Dworkinian jurisprudence constitutes an illegitimately broad exercise of judicial power and is tantamount to judicial legislation. Such adjudication is inevitably controversial, but it is substantially constrained by the duty under which judges, but not legislators, act.

Certain CLS claims regarding the law/politics distinction can be parlayed into an argument against this Dworkinian defense of the legitimacy of adjudication in hard cases. What makes this CLS argument particularly interesting for current purposes is that it does not hinge on the adequacy of the patchwork-quilt argument examined in the preceding section. Indeed, it can be construed as granting, *arguendo,* that there is a unique soundest theory of the law which does dictate the correct legal outcomes in hard cases. Let us set the stage for such a CLS argument.

In trying to undo the law/politics distinction, CLS claims that the spectrum of ideological controversy in the political arena is replicated in the legal forum. The claim means that all of the arguments and ideologies which are a significant part of political debate in our culture are to be found, in one form or another, in legal argument and doctrine. It is undoubtedly true that certain ideological viewpoints are foreclosed from the legal arena. Thus, the ideology of Islamic theocracy is to be found embodied nowhere in our legal doctrine. But such ideologies also play no significant role in the internal political debates of our polity.

It is also undeniable that the canons of legal argument place certain formal constraints on the ideological controversies which manifest themselves within judicial decision making. Judges cannot ignore the authoritative texts of the legal culture: the Constitution, statutes, case law, and so on. And legal argument is constrained by the need to phrase itself in terms of the framer's intent, *stare decisis,* and so on. Controversy in the political arena is not bound as strongly by such formal constraints, even though the language of legal opinion does often spill over into the political arena. CLS does not deny any of these distinctive, formal marks of legal argument. What they do claim is that beneath these legal forms one can find all of the significant ideological controversies of the political culture. The substance of the political debates is replicated in judicial argument, even if the form of the debates is distinctive. Legal form fails to screen out or significantly reduce the range of ideological conflict present within the general political culture.

CLS supports these contentions regarding the range of ideological conflict within legal doctrine and argument by analyses of doctrinal principles and the kinds of arguments found in judicial decisions. Consider again Kennedy's description of the structure of contract law. Doctrines from the "solidarity" side of contract law, for example, those of duress, unconscionability, and reasonable reliance, are taken to embody the principles of the political left: welfare-state liberals and, to some extent, left-wing egalitarians. Doctrines from the "individualist" side, such as those of consideration, the revocability of an offer until there is acceptance, and the demand that acceptance be a mirror image of the offer, are taken to embody the principles of the political right: free-marketeers and libertarians. The political middle is represented by attempts to mix the two sides of doctrine in varying proportions (attempts which, in CLS eyes, are doomed to logical incoherence for reasons made clear in the patchwork-quilt argument). A hard case emerges when the two sides of doctrine collide in a single fact situation: there was no consideration, but there was reliance; or there was consideration, but it was quite disproportionate in value to what was received in exchange. The CLS view is that such cases implicate

doctrinal materials and arguments representing the spectrum of conflicting political viewpoints.

The CLS claim that the range of ideological conflict in the political arena is replicated in legal doctrine and argument can be viewed in two ways. On the first, it is taken as reinforcing the patchwork-quilt argument against Dworkin. To the extent that one documents the claim, one lends support to the idea that doctrine is a patchwork quilt of inconsistent political ideologies of which no single, coherent political theory could ever capture very much. Take Kennedy's account of contract law. The CLS argument can be put this way: to the extent that we have no reason to believe that the political philosophy of a welfare-state liberal can be reconciled with that of a libertarian, we have no reason to think that the opposing doctrines of contract law can be logically reconciled with one another, for those doctrines are the legal embodiment of just those opposing political philosophies (or something close to them). The position is then generalized to cover all fields of law. This way of setting up the CLS argument is, at bottom, another effort to show that the law is too internally incoherent for there to be any soundest theory of it and thereby to discredit Dworkin's attempts to defend judicial legitimacy by invoking a judicial duty to decide according to the dictates of the soundest theory.

There is, however, another way to view the CLS claim about the range of ideological conflict embodied in legal doctrine. This alternate reading leads to a line of argument whose key contention is that, even if there were a Dworkinian soundest theory, it would impose no practical constraint on judges whose favored political ideology is in conflict with the one embodied in that theory. The theory would exert no effective pull or tug on the decisions of judges who fail to share its ideology. This is because judges who conscientiously attempt to carry out their Dworkinian duty to decide a hard case according to the soundest theory of the law will read their favored ideology into the settled and see it as the soundest theory. This would happen, the argument goes, because the authoritative legal materials, in replicating the ideological conflicts of the political arena, contain a sufficient number of doctrines, rules, and arguments representing any politically significant ideology that a judge who conscientiously consults the materials would find his favored ideology in some substantial portion of the settled law and conclude that it was the soundest theory of the law.

Of course, no one expects that the true soundest theory of law will have the power to persuade all conscientious judges of its status. However, the Dworkinian argument for the legitimacy of adjudication in hard cases does presuppose that the theory imposes some practical constraint on judicial decision making by exerting a kind of gravitational pull on those judges who recognize their abstract duty to decide according to the soundest theory but who are in fact in ideological disagreement with the principles of the true theory. (Keep in mind that this judicial duty is abstract in the sense that the statement of the duty contains no specification of the particular theory which is the soundest one, and so recognition of the duty, by itself, does nothing to insure that a judge's decisions will be pulled in any particular direction.) The pull of the true soundest theory doesn't have to be an irresistible one, but, for the Dworkinian legitimacy argument to work, it must be substantial enough to make a difference to the decisions of conscientious judges who in fact hold to an ideology which conflicts with the soundest theory. Many of the decisions of these judges would have to be different from what they would be if there were no soundest theory, and the difference has to be explainable in terms of the pull of the theory. If the soundest theory were to lack any such pull, then the constraint imposed by the duty to decide according to the soundest theory would be illusory, and the Dworkinian defense of judicial legitimacy would fall apart. The CLS argument is that the constraint is an illusion. Judges holding to virtually any ideology which is of significance in the American political arena will simply read their favored ideology into the settled law as its soundest theory. This can be and is done, even by the most conscientious judge, because each view on the political spectrum is embodied in some substantial portion of the authoritative materials.

It should be noted that the CLS view on this point is not the same as a view often expressed by mainstream critics of Dworkin and against which Dworkin has directed several arguments. That view consists of the idea that in a hard case, the law "runs out" and the judge makes her decision in a kind of legal vacuum. Dworkin has argued quite forcefully that this gives us a false picture of how judges should and characteristically do go about deciding hard cases.[50] It leads us to think that judges first consult the authoritative materials, find that there is no unambiguous answer there, and then proceed to forget the legal materials and decide by some wholly extralegal criterion. Dworkin counters with a picture of judges who search for the most cogent principles and theories which can be thought of as embodied in the relevant authoritative materials and who decide according

to such principles and theories. This is, in Dworkin's eyes, the search for (the relevant portion of) the soundest theory of the settled law.

CLS can agree with Dworkin's important point that judges do not leave the authoritative materials behind when they make a decision in a case where those materials fail to dictate unambiguously an answer to the case. It can also agree with Dworkin that in such cases judges look for the most convincing principles and theories embodied in the materials.[51] The point of the present CLS argument is that, even though judges typically do decide in such Dworkinian fashion and even if there happens to be a soundest theory dictating the correct legal outcome, the existence of such a theory makes no practical difference because a judge will typically see her favored ideology as constituting that theory. The soundest theory is not some brooding omnipresence in the sky, but rather a brooding irrelevance in the sky (assuming it is anywhere at all).

There are two potential lines of response for the Dworkinian to this CLS argument. The first is to deny that the full spectrum of ideological controversy in politics is to be found in legal doctrine and decision and so to hold on to the idea that legal form, particularly the fit requirement, does screen out a significant range of political controversy. This line of response does not appear to me to be very promising. There are a host of CLS analyses of both private and public law, making quite persuasive its contention regarding the extent of ideological controversy within legal doctrine and argument.

A second line of response is to deny that the legitimacy of "political adjudication" in hard cases hinges on whether or not ideological controversy within the law is as wide as it is in the political arena. The idea is that Dworkin's defense of adjudication works, even if the law/politics distinction unravels in precisely the way CLS asserts. In fact, we can find in Dworkin's work two arguments which can be construed in this way. They concern the issue of whether courts have correctly held that there is a legal right to an abortion under our constitutional arrangements. Dworkin imagines the issue turning on the question of whether the concept of dignity implicit in our legal and political institutions implies the existence of such a right.[52] He then examines the suggestion that legislatures, which reflect the will and ideas of the ordinary person, rather than courts, are the most appropriate forum in which to find the answer to such a question. In other words, the suggestion is the positivist one that in hard cases courts should act as legislatures would.

Dworkin claims that there are two arguments

against such a suggestion and, by implication, in favor of the judge deciding the issue by what she thinks the (soundest theory of the) law dictates, and not by what (she thinks) the legislature thinks it ought to be.[53] The first argument is that judges think more carefully about the meaning our institutions give to the idea of dignity when they decide cases than ordinary folks do when they cast their ballots (or politicians do when they vote on legislation). Judges are thus thought to have greater competence in handling such hard cases than legislatures do. The second argument is that a Dworkinian judge will legitimately refuse to defer to legislative judgment, even if she thinks that it does reflect the considered opinion of the ordinary person, when she thinks that the opinion is inconsistent with the soundest theory of the law. This is legitimate because such a judge believes that the law really does have a determinate answer to the hard case before her and that it is her duty to discover and announce it, whatever anyone else thinks. By doing so she is acting no differently from a positivist judge in an easy case, who would certainly refrain from a decision contrary to his legal judgment, no matter what the ordinary person/legislature may think.

Neither one of these arguments provides a convincing response to the CLS position. The first would justify the most far-reaching judicial usurpations on the grounds that judges have thought more carefully about the issue in question than did the electorate or their representatives. There is virtually no legislative enactment or policy which is safe from such reasoning. The second argument clearly begs the whole question of whether the law is determinate in hard cases. The Dworkinian judge may believe that it is, but, if that belief is incorrect or even unjustified, it can hardly be claimed that her refusal to defer to legislative judgment in a hard case is analogous to the positivist judge's refusal to do so in an easy case. Yet, even granting the law's determinacy, Dworkin's argument presumes that the soundest theory of the law does impose some effective constraints on judicial decision making. For otherwise there will be no practical difference between a legal regime in which judges have no duty to decide hard cases according to the dictates of (the soundest theory of) the law but may decide such cases on the basis of their favored ideology, and one in which they do have such a duty. Dworkin's views commit him to the claim that there is not only a difference between the two regimes, but that the latter sort of regime alone can be legitimated in terms of the principles of liberal democracy.

Let me hasten to add that CLS does not accept an important assumption shared by both Dworkinians and their positivist critics, namely, that the exercise of judicial power, even in hard cases, is largely legitimate and that the issue is over how to account for that legitimacy. For CLSers, the legitimacy of the exercise of judicial power is not something that can be assumed but is deeply problematic. Thus, they are no more persuaded by the positivist's efforts to wrap judicial decision in the cloak of legislative legitimacy than they are by Dworkin's invocation of the duty to decide by the soundest theory of law. From the CLS perspective, the positivist injunction to decide according to the will of the legislature leaves as much room for judges to make their favored ideology the basis of decision as does the Dworkinian injunction to decide according to the soundest theory. My principal point here, though, concerns Dworkinian jurisprudence. Dworkinians must show that the soundest theory of law is not only a logical possibility, given the tensions existing within doctrine, but that it can exert an effective practical constraint on judges who hold conflicting ideological views. CLS's law/politics argument raises serious doubts about whether the theory, even conceding its existence, would exert any such constraint, and thus far Dworkinians have done little to assuage such doubts.

VII

In this article, I have not aimed at providing the last word on the points of contention between CLS and Dworkinian jurisprudence. I have tried to locate some of the more important issues within a frame that recognizes the influence of legal realism on contemporary legal thought. CLS has picked up and elaborated upon the realist contention that the law largely fails to determine the outcome in cases which are brought to litigation. Among the important advances of the CLS analysis over that of their realist forerunners are: the effort to take seriously and to analyze the conflicting ethical visions and principles which infuse legal doctrine; the painstaking attempts to display doctrinal inconsistencies and incoherencies; and the effort to show how debates in the political arena are replicated in unsuspected corners of private-law doctrine. I believe that these are substantial advances on the realist position and that they can be parlayed into powerful arguments which are thus far unmet by Dworkinians or indeed by conventional legal philosophers of any stripe. It is well past the time when legal philosophers can justifiably ignore the body of work associated with the Critical Legal Studies movement.

For illuminating discussions of many of the issues treated in this article, I would like to thank Lewis Sargentich, Duncan Kennedy, Morton Horwitz, and John Fellas. Comments and suggestions made by the Editors of Philosophy & Public Affairs helped me improve my arguments at several points. The article was conceived and written while I was a liberal arts fellow at Harvard Law School, 1984–5. I am greatly indebted to the John Dewey Foundation for its generous financial support during that time.

1. H. L. A. Hart, The Concept of Law (Oxford: Oxford University Press, 1961).

2. Ronald Dworkin, Taking Rights Seriously (Cambridge, MA: Harvard University Press, 1977), pp. 3–4; also see pp. 15–16.

3. Theodore Benditt, Law as Rule and Principle (Stanford: Stanford University Press, 1978), chaps. 1–2. In his preface, Benditt says that his reason for such an extended treatment of realism is that "students find [it] interesting and persuasive" (p. vii). It is difficult for me to interpret the remark as anything but a put-down of both realism and any contemporary theorists who find it both interesting and persuasive.

4. A principal exception to the general failure to treat realism as having contemporary significance is R. S. Summers, Instrumentalism and American Legal Theory (Ithaca, NY: Cornell University Press, 1982). Also see the articles in the "Symposium on American Legal Theory," Cornell Law Review 66 (1981): 860. It is useful to think of the realist movement as constituted by six distinct themes. First, there is the instrumentalist theme, according to which law should be understood and evaluated as animated by social purposes and policies. This theme has been absorbed into much mainstream legal thinking. Second, there is the behaviorist theme, which reduces the meaning of legal concepts and doctrines to the particular actions of legal officials. Such a theory of meaning stands repudiated by virtually all contemporary theorists. (See footnote 18 below.) The third theme is that of legal indeterminacy, which is the focus of this article. Fourth, there is the anticonceptualist theme, according to which legal thinking should always take place at a very low level of abstraction and should never stray very far from the particular fact pattern presented by a case. (See footnote 28 below.) Fifth, there is the realist idea that private law concepts and doctrines ought to be reconceptualized so that they are understood as instruments of state imposed regulatory policies. This theme, which is clearly related to the instrumentalist one, has been a major influence on contemporary legal scholars working in the area of contract law. See Patrick Atiyah, The Rise and Fall of Freedom of Contract (Oxford: Oxford University Press, 1979), pp. 405–419, and Grant Gilmore, The Death of Contract (Columbus, Ohio: Ohio State University Press, 1974). Finally, there is the master theme of legal realism, that of the breakdown of any sharp distinction between law (adjudication) and politics. Each of the five previous themes can be understood as various ways in which the realists tried to unravel that distinction.

5. Hart, The Concept of Law, pp. 119, 123–25.

6. A provocative realist analysis of constitutional adjudication is found in George Braden, "The Search for Objectivity in Constitutional Law," Yale Law Journal 57 (1948): 571. The classic realist statement of the indeterminacy of statutory interpretation is found in Appendix C of Karl Llewellyn, The Common Law Tradition (Boston: Little, Brown, 1960), pp. 521–35. Also see his The Bramble Bush (New York: Oceana, 1960), pp. 88–90.

7. On the indeterminacy of the common-law system, see Llewellyn, The Bramble Bush, pp. 61–77; also see the chapter, "The Leeways of Precedent," in The Common Law Tradition.

8. The facts in this example are from Hamer v. Sidway 124 NY 538 (1891).

9. For a general historical discussion of stare decisis, see Harold J. Berman and William R. Greiner, The Nature and Functions of Law, 4th ed. (Mineola, NY: Foundation Press, 1980), pp. 587–88. For a realist critique of the distinction between holding and dictum, see Felix Cohen, "The Ethical Basis of Legal Criticism," Yale Law Journal 41 (1931): 201.

10. Llewellyn, "Some Realism About Realism," Harvard Law Review 44 (1931): 1222, 1252.

11. Hart, The Concept of Law, p. 131.

12. Ibid.

13. Ibid., p. 132.

14. Benditt, Law as Rule and Principle, pp. 25–42.

15. Ibid., pp. 10–11, 22.

16. Llewellyn, "Some Realism About Realism," p. 1252. Llewellyn takes fellow realist Jerome Frank to task for suggesting that rules and precedents lack authoritative status; see his contribution to "Law and the Modern Mind: A Symposium," Columbia Law Review 31 (1931): 82, 90.

17. John Dewey, "Logical Method and Law," Cornell Law Quarterly 10 (1924): 17.

18. For example, the criticism Hart and Benditt make of the theory of the meaning endorsed by realists is extremely persuasive. The theory is asserted in Felix Cohen, "Transcendental Nonsense and the Functional Approach," Columbia Law Review 35 (1935): 809. The seminal statement of the position is in Oliver Wendell Holmes, The Path of the Law, Collected Papers (New York: Harcourt, Brace, 1921), p. 173. For the criticisms, see Hart, The Concept of Law, pp. 39, 88; Benditt, Law as Rule and Principle, pp. 46–50.

19. Dworkin, Taking Rights Seriously, pp. 25–26, 36, 44–45, 67–68, 71–80, 82–90, 96–97, 105ff.

20. Ibid., p. 67.

21. Ibid., p. 44.

22. Ibid., pp. 67–68, 79, 283, and 340.

23. Ibid., pp. 105ff.

24. Thurman Arnold, "Law Enforcement: An Attempt at Social Dissection," Yale Law Journal 42 (1932); 1, 12–13, 23. Symbols of Government (New Haven: Yale University Press, 1935), pp. 71, 125, 248–249.

25. Felix Cohen was the realist most concerned with ethical issues in the law. See almost any of his essays in Lucy K. Cohen, ed., The Legal Conscience: Selected Papers of Felix S. Cohen (New Haven: Yale University Press, 1960). There was, however, a considerable tension between Cohen's highly reductionist theory of the meaning of legal concepts, on the one hand, and his efforts to see the law as infused with cognitively meaningful ethical ideals, on the other. That kind of theory makes it very difficult to explain how ideals can impose any cognitively meaningful, normative constraints on the operation of the legal system and leads quite readily to Arnold's kind of cynical emotivism. For a closely related criticism of Cohen, see Martin Godling, "Realism and Functionalism in the Legal Thought of Felix S. Cohen," Cornell Law Review 66 (1981): 1032, 1054.

26. Charles Fried, "The Laws of Change: The Cunning of Reason in Moral and Legal History," Journal of Legal Studies 9 (1980): 335, and Contract as Promise (Cambridge, MA: Harvard University Press, 1981), pp. 2–3, 90–91, and 149. It is interesting that Fried gives endorsement to Dworkin's jurisprudence even though his political commitments are decidedly less liberal than those of Dworkin. I characterize Fried as a Dworkinian on account of his endorsement of Dworkin's ideas that legal doctrine is animated by and derivable from moral principles, that judges are obligated to resolve cases in the light of such principles, that the law has a determinate answer for all cases which come before it, and that it

is only because the law is animated by moral principles that it has determinate answers for such disputes. See Contract as Promise, pp. 67–69.

27. See Elizabeth Mensch, "The History of Mainstream Legal Thought," In David Kairys, ed., The Politics of Law (New York: Pantheon, 1982), p. 19, and Peter Gabel, "Review of Taking Rights Seriously," Harvard Law Review 91 (1977): 302. Mensch dismissed Dworkin's theory in six lines of a footnote, characterizing his contribution to jurisprudence as "vastly overrated." Gabel's treatment is more extended, and yet he never really joins the issue with Dworkin. He simply assumes that judges pervasively exercise political choice in a way that is inconsistent with Dworkin's theory. Instead of meeting Dworkin on his own terms, Gabel takes for granted the truth of an orthodox version of historical materialism and seeks to expose Dworkin's jurisprudence as just the latest in a series of theoretical efforts to justify capitalism.

It is important to realize that Critical Legal Studies embraces a substantial variety of conflicting theoretical approaches, many of them quite hostile to anything similar to orthodox Marxist theory. (See footnote 39 below.) In this article, I shall be able to touch upon only a few of the more important themes developed in the literature. Among the important themes which will be left untreated are the critique of social hierarchy and the rather vigorous "left-wing" egalitarianism which accompany many CLS writings. It is often pointed out, correctly I believe, that there is no necessary connection between CLS claims regarding legal indeterminacy and its egalitarian political vision. But this simply means that the one does not logically stand or fall with the other. There is, however, a kind of strategic connection: CLS's political vision requires that one see the current legal order as essentially illegitimate. CLS's claims regarding legal indeterminacy serve to delegitimate that order by undercutting that order's own conception of why it is legitimate. See Duncan Kennedy, "The Political Significance of the Structure of the Law School Curriculum," Seton Hall Law Review 14 (1983): 1, 14. For an extensive bibliography of CLS writings, see Yale Law Journal 94 (1984): 464.

28. A seminal CLS text on this theme is Duncan Kennedy: "Form and Substance in Private Law Adjudication," Harvard Law Review 89 (1976): 1685. This text and other CLS writings exhibit an important difference with legal realism on the so-called issue of "conceptualism." Several realists argued that legal thinking should take place at a very low level of abstraction. Abstractions, especially those purporting to represent ethical ideals, were rejected as useless or worse in the conduct of legal thinking. CLS scholars have not followed these realists on the point. It is true that some, such as Kennedy, have suggested that judicial decisions rest on an appreciation of the peculiar fact pattern of the case at bar, rather than any effort to see the result as following from highly abstract principles which transcend that fact pattern. This is because Kennedy believes that ascending to higher levels of abstraction does not add to the cogency of arguments made in terms of the case's particular fact pattern. Disagreements which arise at the lower levels of abstraction will, in his view, simply be replicated at the higher level. And yet much of Kennedy's work, as well as that of other CLS theorists, is premised on the assumption that very high level abstractions have tremendous heuristic value in thinking about the law. Kennedy's "Form and Substance in Private Law Adjudication" is an extended examination of two abstractions which he calls "individualism" and "altruism." The premise is that the abstractions, each representing a competing ideal for human social life, will help us better grasp the terrain of legal doctrine, even if it will not help us in the end make a clinching legal argument. Moreover, some CLS writers clearly believe that such systematic thinking can be of far more than heuristic importance and teach us something crucial about the historical development of legal doctrine and its connection to social transformation generally. See Morton Horwitz, "Review of G. Gilmore, The Ages of American Law," Buffalo Law Review 27 (1977): 47, and The Transformation of American Law, 1780–1860 (Cambridge, MA: Harvard University Press, 1977).

29. There is some disagreement within CLS regarding the task of constructing a defensible ethical theory. Roberto Unger considers it desirable to undertake the task and thinks there is no good reason to believe that it will never succeed. His most recent steps in carrying out the task are in Passion: An Essay on Personality (New York: Free Press, 1984). Duncan Kennedy is skeptical about the value, and prospects for success, of any such ethical theorizing. See his Legal Education and the Reproduction of Hierarchy (Cambridge: Afar, 1983), pp. 82–83. It would be a mistake, however, to infer from this that Kennedy is an ethical subjectivist of some sort. See "Form and Substance in Private Law Adjudication," pp. 1771–72.

30. Kennedy, "Form and Substance in Private Law Adjudication"; Unger, "Critical Legal Studies Movement," Harvard Law Review 96 (1983): 561, 616–46. Also see Kennedy, "The Structure of Blackstone's Commentaries," Buffalo Law Review 28 (1978): 205. Morton Horwitz, The Transformation of American Law: 1780–1860 (Cambridge, MA: Harvard University Press, 1977); and Mark Kelman, "Interpretive Construction in the Substantive Criminal Law," Stanford Law Review 33 (1981): 591.

31. Kennedy, "Form and Substance in Private Law Adjudication," p. 1685.

32. Dworkin, Taking Rights Seriously, p. 26.

33. Dworkin, "A Reply by Ronald Dworkin," in M. Cohen, ed., Ronald Dworkin and Contemporary Jurisprudence (Totowa, NJ: Rowman and Allanheld, 1984), pp. 278–79.

34. Articulating the dominant view of his time, and one which is still widely held, Herbert Wechsler wrote that "the main constituent of the judicial process is that it must be genuinely principled, resting on analyses and reasons quite transcending the immediate result that is achieved." "Toward Neutral Principles of Constitutional Law," Harvard Law Review 73 (1959): 1, 15. Dworkin is clearly a direct heir of this view, although I believe that his effort to draw a sharp distinction between principle and policy for the purpose of distinguishing the legal from the legislative process goes beyond what the main legal theorists of the 1950s would have endorsed. See Taking Rights Seriously, pp. 82–84 and contrast with Henry Hart and Albert Sacks, The Legal Process (tent. ed. 1958), pp. 158–71.

35. Kennedy, "Form and Substance in Private Law Adjudication," p. 1724.

36. Fried, Contract as Promise.

37. Among the best CLS analyses of labor law are Karl Klare, "Judicial Deradicalization of the Wagner Act and the Origins of Modern Legal Consciousness, 1937–1941," Minnesota Law Review 62 (1978): 265, and "Critical Legal Theory and Labor Relations Law," in Kairys, ed., The Politics of Law, pp. 65–88. In Contract as Promise, Fried does not discuss labor law or collective bargaining at all, except to mention that they do not fit his model of obligations willed by the individual upon himself (p. 2). For Fried's discussion of the doctrines which he expels from contract law, see his remarks on unjust enrichment and reasonable reliance, pp. 23–26.

38. Dworkin, Taking Rights Seriously, pp. 119–20.

39. Unger, "The Critical Legal Studies Movement," p. 571. This line of CLS argument presumes the falsity of the thesis of orthodox Marxism that law is a superstructural phenomenon which merely reinforces the existing relations of production by giving expression to the ideology of the dominant economic class. Many CLS writers repudiate this Marxist position. They see law and ideology generally as much more complex than can be captured by notions such as "capitalist," and they see causation in social life as much more complex than theories regarding superstructure and base can suggest. See, for example, Kennedy, "The Structure of Blackstone's Commentaries," pp. 362–63, fn. 56, and Klare, "Critical Theory and Labor Relations Law." For a CLS description of modern Western society as more complicated than that portrayed in the class analysis of orthodox Marxism, see Unger, Knowledge and Politics (New York: Free Press, 1975), pp. 151–85, and Law in Modern Society (New York: Free Press, 1976), pp. 66–76, 171.

40. Unger, "The Critical Legal Studies Movement," p. 571.

41. For such a conventional criticism of Dworkin, see Neil MacCormick, "Dworkin as Pre-Benthamite," in Cohen, ed., Ronald Dworkin and Contemporary Jurisprudence, pp. 184–85, 192.

42. *Dworkin, "No Right Answer?"* New York University Law Review *53 (1978): 1, 31–33; also see "A Reply by Ronald Dworkin," in* Cohen, ed., Ronald Dworkin and Contemporary Jurisprudence, *pp. 278–79.*

43. *Alasdair MacIntyre,* After Virtue *(Notre Dame, IN: University of Notre Dame Press, 1981), see esp. pp. 2–4, 227–37.*

44. *Kennedy, "The Political Significance of the Structure of the Law School Curriculum," p. 15.*

45. *See, e.g., Mark Tushnet, "Critical Legal Studies and Constitutional Law: An Essay in Deconstruction,"* Stanford Law Review *36 (1984): 623; Paul Brest, "State Action and Liberal Theory: A Casenote on* Flagg Brothers v. Brooks," *University of Pennsylvania Law Review 130 (1982): 130; Richard Parker, "The Past of Constitutional Theory—And Its Future,"* Ohio State Law Journal *42 (1981): 223; Karl Klare, "The Public/Private Distinction in Labor Law,"* University of Pennsylvania Law Review *130 (1982): 1358; Gerald Frug, "The Ideology of Bureaucracy in American Law,"* Harvard Law Review *97 (1984): 1276; Unger, "The Critical Legal Studies Movement," pp. 602–47, and Kelman, "Interpretive Construction in the Substantive Criminal Law."*

46. *Dworkin, "A Reply by Ronald Dworkin," p. 272.*

47. *Ibid.*

48. *Dworkin,* Taking Rights Seriously, *p. 127.*

49. *Ibid.*

50. *Ibid., pp. 35–45, 81–130.*

51. *CLS would naturally add that, to the extent that judges think that there is a soundest theory of the law, they are victims of legal false-consciousness.*

52. *Dworkin,* Taking Rights Seriously, *pp. 127–29.*

53. *Ibid., p. 129.*

PART TWO

Liberty

Under what conditions, and for what reasons, can the presumption in favor of political liberty be overridden? This is not merely an abstract question addressed to philosophers, but an unavoidable practical question to be faced by every democratic legislator. In effect, it is a question of the limits beyond which restrictive lawmaking is morally illegitimate.

The Case for Self-Determination

John Stuart Mill, the first essayist presented in this part, gives the classic liberal answer to the question. Restriction of the liberty of one citizen, he argues, can be justified only to prevent harm to others. We can refer to Mill's position as the "harm to others principle," or, more succinctly, the harm principle. Several things should be noted about this principle at the outset. First, by *harm,* Mill means not only direct personal injury such as broken bones or the loss of money, but also more diffuse social harms such as air pollution or the impairment of public institutions. Second, the principle does not propose a sufficient condition for the restriction of liberty, because some harms to others are too slight to outbalance the very real harm or danger involved in the restriction of liberty. Thus, in close cases, legislators must balance the value of the interests to be restricted by proposed coercive legislation *and* the collateral costs of enforcing any coercive law, on the one hand, against the value of the interests to be protected by the proposed legislation, on the other. It is only when the probable harms prevented by the statute are greater than those that it will cause that the legislation is justified. Finally, the harm principle should be interpreted as a claim about *rea-*

sons: Only one kind of consideration is ever morally relevant to the justification of coercion, namely, that it is necessary to prevent harm to others. It is never a relevant reason that the conduct to be restricted is merely offensive (as opposed to harmful) or even that it is intrinsically immoral, nor is it relevant that coercion is necessary to prevent a person from harming himself or herself (as opposed to others).

Challenges to Self-Determination: Legal Paternalism and Legal Moralism

No one would disagree that prevention of harm to others is always a relevant reason for coercion, but many disagree with Mill's contention that it is the *only* relevant consideration. Thus, no one will seriously suggest that laws against battery, larceny, and homicide are unjustified, but many maintain that the state is also justified, at least in some circumstances, in prohibiting (1) actions that hurt or endanger the actor (the principle of legal paternalism), (2) "immoralities" even when they harm no one but their perpetrators (the principle of legal moralism), and (3) conduct that is offensive though not harmful to others (the offense principle).[1] These rival doctrines cannot easily be proved or refuted in the abstract. Rather, they are best judged by how faithfully they reflect, and how systematically they organize, our considered judgments in particular cases; for such principles, after all, purport to be explicit renderings of the axioms to which we are committed by the most confident judgments we make in everyday discourse about problems of liberty.

The main areas of controversy in which such problems arise are those concerning unorthodox expressions of opinion, "morals offenses" in the criminal law (especially when committed in private by solitary individuals or among consenting adults), pornography and obscenity (when offered or displayed to the public or to nonconsenting individuals), activities that are harmful or dangerous to those who voluntarily engage in them (voluntary suicide and euthanasia), otherwise harmless invasions of the privacy of others, and conscientious acts of civil disobedience. The cautious theorist will begin with Mill's harm principle as an account of at least one set of reasons that is always relevant in such controversies, and then apply it to the various problem areas to determine the extent, if any, to which it must be supplemented to provide solutions that are both plausible and consistent. In particular, we must decide, in each area, whether we need have recourse to the offense principle, legal moralism, or legal paternalism.

Under most of the problem area headings, there is still another kind of controversy to be settled, namely, whether even the unsupplemented harm principle can justify *too much* coercion, and whether, therefore, doing justice to our considered judgments requires also a doctrine of *natural rights,* which limits the applicability of the harm principle (or any of the other liberty-limiting principles that might apply at all). Perhaps this kind of question arises most prominently in the area of free expression of opinion. There is no doubt that expressions of opinion, in speech or writing, do often cause vast amounts of harm. Politicians sometimes advocate policies that would lead to disastrous consequences if adopted, and scientists sometimes defend theories that are false and detrimental to scientific progress. If we apply the harm principle in a straightforward, unqualified way—by prohibiting all particular expressions which seem, on the best evidence, likely to cause more harm than good—we might very well justify widespread invasions of what we should naturally take to be a moral right of free speech. To avoid this embarrassing consequence, the partisan of the harm principle will have to propose subtle refinements and mediating norms for the application of this principle, weighing such matters as the balancing of rival interests and social costs, and the measurements of probabilities, dangers, and risks.

In a broader analysis of paternalism, Gerald Dworkin considers, in a comprehensive and systematic way, the question of whether paternalistic statutes (defined roughly as those interfering with a person's liberty "for his own good") are ever justified. He treats Mill's absolutistic position with respect, but points out how widespread paternalistic restrictions are and how drastic their total elimination would be. Laws requiring hunters to wear red caps, and motorcyclists to wear helmets, or those requiring medical prescriptions for certain therapeutic drugs, for example, seem innocuous to most of us. Even more so are laws that actually protect children and incompetents from their own folly, and those which persons regard as "social insurance" against their own future decisions that might be not only dangerous but irreversible. Dworkin then attempts to find criteria that can be used to separate unjustified paternalistic restrictions from those he thinks any rational person would welcome. Dworkin's "Paternalism: Some Second Thoughts," written fifteen years after the original essay, is also included.

The liberalism of John Stuart Mill has come under attack not only from adherents of legal paternalism, but from those loosely grouped under the rubric legal moralism. Patrick Devlin, not the purest example of a legal moralist, argues for the enforcement of a society's moral code, but not as an end in itself. He identifies the conventions of one time and place not as commandments of true morality, but rather as means of preventing the social and personal harms that would result from the weakening of social cohesion. "An established morality," he insists, "is as necessary as good government to the welfare of society." On that ground, Devlin would justify the legal enforcement even of those parts of the established morality that forbid actions that are not in themselves directly harmful to anyone, for example, homosexual sex acts performed by consenting adults in private.

In his second essay included here, Devlin goes on the attack against his liberal critics, by arguing that it is their liberalism, not his legal moralism, that is out of step with "contemporary social reality." He finds two fundamental principles and eight specific crimes that seem inconsistent with Mill's harm principle. Devlin's argument will force the liberal to offer more explicit and plausible rationales for a number of traditional legal practices and rules—from the refusal to accept consent as a defense to battery and homicide, to the criminalization of bigamy.

The Model Penal Code[2] recommendations about so-called "morals offenses" were the work of a special group of enlightened would-be lawmakers who were very much opposed to legal moralism but unwilling, if only on grounds of political realism, to urge extremely radical departures from the past ways of the law. Sexual behavior that is immoral by conventional standards should not be made criminal, according to the code, unless it involves violence or exploitation of children and other incompetents; the traditional crimes of fornication, adultery, and sodomy are to be wiped from the books. In the absence of unconsented-to harm to others, the sexual behavior of individuals is no one else's business. Open lewdness, on the other hand, like other flagrant affronts to the sensibilities of others, is another matter. Not only conventionally "immoral" sexual acts but even perfectly "normal" ones can be criminally proscribed if done in *public,* not because public sex acts harm anyone, but because they cause offense (quite another thing) to the unwilling observer.[3] Thus, the Model Penal Code, while rejecting legal moralism, seems to endorse the offense principle.

The idea of privacy made a major new entry into American constitutional law through the celebrated case of *Griswold* v. *Connecticut,* decided by the United States Supreme Court in 1965. (See also the contribution of Robert Bork to Part Two of this book.) The opinions in that case raise a variety of genuinely philosophical issues and might well have been included with equal relevance in any of the first three sections in Part One. The decision overturned a Connecticut statute making the use of contraceptives by any person a criminal offense. That statute was unconstitutional, Mr. Justice Douglas wrote, because it violated a right of marital privacy "older than the Bill of Rights" but included in the "penumbra" of the First, Fourth, Fifth, Eighth, Ninth, and Fourteenth Amendments. A penumbra of a right is a set of further rights not specifically guaranteed in so many words, but properly inferable from the primary right either as necessary means for its fulfillment or as implied by it in certain factual circumstances not necessarily foreseen by those who formulated it. Thus the right to read whatever one wishes is in the penumbra of the right of free expression if only because the latter, which is mentioned in the Constitution, would have little point if it existed without the former, which is not mentioned in the Constitution.

Similarly, the Constitution does not specifically spell out a right of marital privacy. The dissenters on the Court (Justices Stewart and Black) were suspicious of the technique of finding anything a judge thinks just and reasonable in the penumbra of a specific guarantee. Justice Goldberg in his concurring opinion had rested his case for a constitutional right of marital privacy on the Ninth Amendment's reference to fundamental rights "retained by the people," and Justices Harlan and White in their concurring opinions (not reprinted here) derived the unconstitutionality of the anti-contraception statute from its capriciousness, irrationality, and offensiveness to a "sense of fairness and justice." A careful reader of Part One of this book will recognize here the overtones of the natural law tradition, whereas in Justice Black's dissenting opinion, a skeptical stricture on the catchwords of natural justice, there is the powerful echo of the tradition of legal positivism.

The doctrine of privacy applied by the majority opinions in *Griswold* affirms that there is a domain in which the individual's own choice must reign supreme. *Eisenstadt* v. *Baird* (1972) extended the right of marital privacy to individuals, married or single, allowing them to use contraceptives if they so choose and freeing them of governmental intrusion in an area that is their business alone. In *Loving* v. *Virginia* (1967), privacy was made the basis of a person's right freely to decide to marry a person of another race. In *Stanley* v. *Georgia* (1969), a right to view porno films or tapes in one's own home was also said to be implied by the fundamental right to privacy, and in 1973 in *Roe* v. *Wade,* a right to choose an abortion was similarly derived. Throughout this period, there were both controversy and confusion. The latter was caused, according to some critics, by a misnaming of the constitutional right in question—a misnaming that conferred on all individuals *autonomy* (self-government) in some fundamental areas of life, not *privacy,* which is quite another thing.

The most controversial of the "privacy" decisions has been the famous abortion case of 1973, which extended the right of privacy to a woman's autonomous choice of whether to terminate her pregnancy during the first two trimesters. Here a woman's autonomy had to be balanced against the state's growing interest in the potentiality of human life, which can become dominant in the third trimester. Abortion is unique among other privacy issues in requiring courts and critics to consider not only moral principles and constitutional precedents, but also conceptual or metaphysical questions such as "What is a person?" In the *Casey* case (1992) the court settled twenty years of intense controversy by explicitly upholding *Roe* v. *Wade.* In so doing, however, it kindled new quarrels by permitting more grounds for state regulation of abortions—even to the point of placing a substantial obstacle in the path of a woman seeking an abortion during the first two trimesters. Thus another constitutional criterion was born: the "undue burden standard," which permit legislatures to regulate up to a point but not beyond. Beyond that point, according to the standard, the burden placed on a woman bent on exercising her constitutional privacy right becomes an undue burden.

By 1986, the year in which *Bowers* v. *Hardwick* was decided, the positivist position was that of the court's new majority. The new majority challenged the new minority to find, in the explicit language of the Constitution itself, a right to practice sodomy—or at least to find a general constitutional principle, with impeccable credentials from which that specific right follows logically. This Supreme Court case probably presents the clearest confrontation yet between legal moralists, who would restrict "immoral" behavior even when discreet and harmless, and the intellectual descendants of Mill, who find legitimate only those restrictions of liberty that protect people from harms or risks of harm to which they have not voluntarily consented.

Freedom of Expression and Its Limits

In the first essay in this section, Joel Feinberg considers further how the harm principle must be qualified if it is to guarantee free expression of opinion in a morally satisfactory way. He examines first the relatively noncontroversial limits on free speech imposed by Anglo-American law: civil liability for defamatory utterances and for nondefamatory statements that reveal information that is properly private, criminal liability for irresponsible statements that cause panics or riots, laws against incitements to crime, and (more controversially) sedition. They are considered in part because each raises its own questions of interest for the philosophy of law and in part because each provides a challenge for the harm principle to provide a rationale for sensible restrictions on liberty that will not at the same time justify restrictions on free speech unacceptable to Mill and other liberals. Feinberg then attempts to provide a philosophical rationale for Justice Holmes's "clear and present danger" test, and concludes with comments on the inevitable balancing of interests so central to the harm principle approach to problems of liberty.

One kind of case that has caused some difficulty for liberal advocates of free speech is the public use of "obscene" language—even when that language is used to express political opinion. This sort of problem

for the free-speech advocate was dramatically illustrated in the United States Supreme Court case of *Cohen* v. *California,* in 1971. Cohen was convicted by a Los Angeles municipal Court for lingering in the corridors of a public building while wearing a jacket emblazoned with the words "Fuck the Draft." In his appeal to the Supreme Court of California and later to the United States Supreme Court, Cohen claimed that his right to free speech, guaranteed by the First and Fourteenth Amendments, had been violated. The California authorities argued that they had properly applied against him a valid statute forbidding "willfully . . . offensive conduct." Now there are two ways in which a written or spoken statement can be offensive: It can express an opinion that some auditors might find offensive, or it can express an opinion in language that is itself offensive, independent of the substantive message it conveys. Neither the United States Constitution nor the libertarian principles of free expression of opinion espoused by Mill and Feinberg would permit legal interference with free speech in order to prevent the expression of an "offensive" opinion. However, restrictions on obscene, scurrilous, and incitive words, quite apart from their role in the expression of unpopular opinion, might well be justified by the offense principle, and indeed by the Constitution itself insofar as it tacitly employs the offense principle to mark out a class of exceptions to the free speech guarantee. Justice Harlan, however, rejected this approach to the case. He argued that the free expression of opinion, protected by the Constitution, extends not merely to the proposition declared by a statement, but also to the speaker's (or writer's) emotions or the intensity of his or her attitudes—in the case at hand, "the depths of his feelings against the Vietnam War and the draft." Harlan's distinction points to an important function of what are ordinarily called obscene words: Unseemly epithets can shock and jolt and, in virtue of their very character as socially unacceptable, give expression to intense feelings more accurately than any other words in the language.

In *Village of Skokie* v. *National Socialist Party of America,* the Supreme Court of Illinois carried out the mandate of a previous United States Supreme Court decision. The decision allowed a march by the American Nazi Party through a predominantly Jewish suburb of Chicago. The focal issue was whether the use of swastikas by the marchers was protected by the First Amendment's protection of free speech. The Court regarded the swastika as a form of protected symbolic expression that cannot be banned because of the offense it may cause or even because of the violence it may provoke. The Court held that the "fighting words" exception to First Amendment protection did not apply here. In addition, the Court maintained that the fact that those who would be upset by the sight of swastikas could avoid it without great inconvenience distinguished this case from other cases involving intrusion into the home or a captive audience. (On the other side it was argued that severe psychic hurt can be produced without actual physical confrontation.) Following *Cohen, Skokie* naturally invites comparison of the nature and degree of the offense in the two cases: on the one hand, hearing or seeing the obscene word *fuck* in a public place, and, on the other, witnessing the proud and threatening display of the symbol of the political party under whose sponsorship unspeakably brutal and genocidal slaughterings took place.

In *Texas* v. *Johnson* a third type of offensiveness is described for comparison with the other two: that which follows the witnessing of a wanton (one is almost tempted to say sacrilegious) destruction of a politically sacred symbol. For the philosopher as well as the judge, the three types of offensiveness and the cases to which they give rise require consistency of treatment. In turn this requirement for consistency may require that apparently similar cases nevertheless be distinguished in some morally relevant way or that dissimilar results, despite their various differences, be reconciled—that is, shown to be similar in some crucially relevant respect.

In recent years another class of odious expressions has led to fresh legislative efforts to delimit free speech. Public humiliation of groups—such as racial and ethnic minorities, political dissenters, and homosexuals—and sexual harassment, usually of women, has seemed to increase. Extremely insulting signs or utterances referring to these and other groups occurred in such circumstances as to be clearly within the law—both the criminal law and the civil law of nuisance and defamation. These uses of language came to be called hate speech, and legislatures in a number of states tried to draft statutes stating the conditions under which it is prohibited. To the consternation of most students and faculty members, a large number of cases of alleged hate speech occurred on university campuses, where free speech and free inquiry have always been especially treasured. No sooner were new rules formulated than hard cases for their application stimulated new controversy. Thomas Grey, Professor of Law at Stanford University, was one of the earliest to draft rules governing student conduct in this area. His lucid article highlights the pitfalls

threatening all new codes. In particular, his account of the conflict between civil rights and civil liberties explains how traditional liberal values can lead not only to disagreements among liberals on specific issues, but also to conflicts within the minds or hearts of particular liberal individuals who may, as a result, be too confused to take a stand. In regard to resolving dilemmas of this kind, Grey's article shows the value of careful philosophical methods.

Principles of Constitutional Interpretation

"Congress shall make no law . . . abridging the freedom of speech, or of the press." Those are the words, and the only words, contained in the U.S. Constitution—all in the First Amendment—to guide courts in deciding so-called free speech cases. Fourteen words by the grammarian's measure, but only four that actually breed the notorious perplexity that free speech cases engender: namely, the words "abridging," "freedom," "speech," and "press." Never in the history of political institutions have so many scholars poured so many words into the interpretation of so few. The original words are few, without question, but the value attached to those words by political figures and legal scholars has been almost beyond measure. Their constant reinterpretation has been a labor of love.

The more philosophical a judge or scholarly commentator is, the more likely he or she is to pause frequently to ask just what the rules are in the game of interpretation. What makes an authoritative interpretation of a short and cryptic constitutional passage? Does the interpreter find all the clues inside the text itself? Or are there principles of justice outside the text to which he or she can legitimately refer in order to make better sense of the few clues provided by the text itself? Is evidence of the founding fathers' intentions ever relevant? Is it ever not relevant? Is anything apart from such evidence ever relevant?

Disagreement about the answers to these questions has created the leading current controversies over the limits of law, or the boundaries of liberty. It is perhaps accurate (though too simple) to say that the chief focus of these controversies in the status of the so-called right of privacy, as spelled out in *Griswold* v. *Connecticut* and several dozen other Supreme Court cases that followed in *Griswold's* wake.[4] The problem is that the Constitution nowhere explicitly confers a right of that name on all citizens, so the Court must explain where a basic right can come from if not from the Constitution. Alternatively, if the right *is* in the Constitution, but only tacitly expressed or sketchily suggested, that needs explanation too. For either of these purposes, a full and detailed legal philosophy is required.

Part Two concludes, therefore, with the work of representatives of three currently competing schools of thought on interpretive questions. Robert Bork heaps scorn on the alleged natural right to privacy and

the uses to which it has been put. John Ely casts his skeptical eye on the multitude of allegedly implicit moral principles that have been said by some philosophers to be in the Constitution. Activist judges, he maintains, project their own personal fundamental values into the Constitution. Ely wonders why, if anybody's personal values should play this role, it should be those of judges rather than those, for example, of legislators. Finally, David Lyons, in defending liberal orthodoxy, attacks the "original intent" theory so vigrously defended by Bork, and to a lesser degree the skepticism of Professor Ely.

---

1. *Some liberal writers who would normally follow Mill do not go quite so far as Mill does on the issue of offensiveness. These writers would allow that offense to others can be an acceptable reason for prohibitory statutes usually, but a good or decisive reason only rarely, when a complex of other conditions are satisfied. See Joel Feinberg,* Offense to Others *(New York: Oxford University Press, 1986), chapter 1. Feinberg and the authors of the* Model Penal Code *are among those who would restrict penal statutes to harmful and (in some cases) offensive behavior.*
2. *The Modern Penal Code is published by the American Law Institute (Philadelphia, 1962).*
3. *See note 1.*

4. *In* Griswold, *Justice Douglas's passionate tribute to the institution of marriage made it seem as though a main part of the point of* Griswold *was to protect marriage and restrict the right to use contraceptives to married couples. But seven years later, in* Eisenstadt v. Baird, *405 U.S. 438 (1972), the Supreme Court clearly indicated that the right of privacy recognized in* Griswold *could not be limited to married couples: "If the right of privacy means anything, it is the right of the individual, married or single, to be free from unwarranted governmental intrusion into matters so fundamentally affecting a person as the decision whether to bear or beget a child" [emphasis added].*

The Case for Self-Determination

ON LIBERTY*

John Stuart Mill

The object of this Essay is to assert one very simple principle, as entitled to govern absolutely the dealings of society with the individual in the way of compulsion and control, whether the means used be physical force in the form of legal penalties, or the moral coercion of public opinion. That principle is, that the sole end for which mankind are warranted, individually or collectively, in interfering with the liberty of action of any of their number, is self-protection. That the only purpose for which power can be rightfully exercised over any member of a civilized community, against his will, is to prevent harm to others. His own good, either physical or moral, is not a sufficient warrant. He cannot rightfully be compelled to do or forbear because it will be better for him to do so, because it will make him happier, because, in the opinions of others, to do so would be wise, or even right. These are good reasons for remonstrating with him, or reasoning with him, or persuading him, or entreating him, but not for compelling him, or visiting him with any evil, in case he do otherwise. To justify that, the conduct from which it is desired to deter him must be calculated to produce evil to some one else. The only part of the conduct of any one, for which he is amenable to society, is that which concerns others. In the part which merely concerns himself, his independence is, of right, absolute. Over himself, over his own body and mind, the individual is sovereign.

It is, perhaps, hardly necessary to say that this doctrine is meant to apply only to human beings in the maturity of their faculties. We are not speaking of children, or of young persons below the age which the law may fix as that of manhood or womanhood. Those who are still in a state to require being taken care of by others, must be protected against their own actions as well as against external injury. For the same reason, we may leave out of consideration those backward states of society in which the race itself may be considered as in its nonage. The early difficulties in the way of spontaneous progress are so great, that there is seldom any choice of means for overcoming them; and a ruler full of the spirit of improvement is warranted in the use of any expedients that will attain an end, perhaps otherwise unattainable. Despotism is a legitimate mode of government in dealing with barbarians, provided the end be their improvement, and the means justified by actually effecting that end. Liberty, as a principle, has no application to any state of things anterior to the time when mankind have become capable of being improved by free and equal discussion. Until then, there is nothing for them but implicit obedience to an Akbar or a Charlemagne, if they are so fortunate as to find one. But as soon as mankind have attained the capacity of being guided to their own improvement by conviction or persuasion (a period long since reached in all nations with whom we need here concern ourselves), compulsion, either in the direct form or in that of pains and penalties for non-compliance, is no longer admissible as a means

*From *On Liberty*, excerpts from Chapters I and II, and all of Chapter IV. First published in 1859.

to their own good, and justifiable only for the security of others.

It is proper to state that I forego any advantage which could be derived to my argument from the idea of abstract right, as a thing independent of utility. I regard utility as the ultimate appeal on all ethical questions; but it must be utility in the largest sense, grounded on the permanent interests of man as a progressive being. Those interests, I contend, authorize the subjection of individual spontaneity to external control, only in respect to those actions of each, which concern the interest of other people. If any one does an act hurtful to others, there is a *prima facie* case for punishing him, by law, or, where legal penalties are not safely applicable, by general disapprobation. There are also many positive acts for the benefit of others, which he may rightfully be compelled to perform; such as, to give evidence in a court of justice; to bear his fair share in the common defence, or in any other joint work necessary to the interest of the society of which he enjoys the protection; and to perform certain acts of individual beneficence, such as saving a fellow creature's life, or interposing to protect the defenceless against ill-usage, things which whenever it is obviously a man's duty to do, he may rightfully be made responsible to society for not doing. A person may cause evil to others not only by his actions but by his inaction, and in either case he is justly accountable to them for the injury. The latter case, it is true, requires a much more cautious exercise of compulsion than the former. To make any one answerable for doing evil to others, is the rule; to make him answerable for not preventing evil, is, comparatively speaking, the exception. Yet there are many cases clear enough and grave enough to justify that exception. In all things which regard the external relations of the individual, he is *de jure* amenable to those whose interests are concerned, and if need be, to society as their protector. There are often good reasons for not holding him to the responsibility; but these reasons must arise from the special expediencies of the case: either because it is a kind of case in which he is on the whole likely to act better, when left to his own discretion, than when controlled in any way in which society have it in their power to control him; or because the attempt to exercise control would produce other evils, greater than those which it would prevent. When such reasons as these preclude the enforcement of responsibility, the conscience of the agent himself should step into the vacant judgment-seat, and protect those interests of others which have no external protection; judging himself all the more rigidly, because the case does not admit of his being made accountable to the judgment of his fellow-creatures.

But there is a sphere of action in which society, as distinguished from the individual, has, if any, only an indirect interest; comprehending all that portion of a person's life and conduct which affects only himself, or, if it also affects others, only with their free, voluntary, and undeceived consent and participation. When I say only himself, I mean directly, and in the first instance: for whatever affects himself, may affect others *through* himself; and the objection which may be grounded on this contingency, will receive consideration in the sequel. This, then, is the appropriate region of human liberty. It comprises, first, the inward domain of consciousness; demanding liberty of conscience, in the most comprehensive sense; liberty of thought and feeling; absolute freedom of opinion and sentiment on all subjects, practical or speculative, scientific, moral, or theological. The liberty of expressing and publishing opinions may seem to fall under a different principle, since it belongs to that part of the conduct of an individual which concerns other people; but, being almost of as much importance as the liberty of thought itself, and resting in great part on the same reasons, is practically inseparable from it. Secondly, the principle requires liberty of tastes and pursuits; of framing the plan of our life to suit our own character; of doing as we like, subject to such consequences as may follow; without impediment from our fellow-creatures, so long as what we do does not harm them, even though they should think our conduct foolish, perverse, or wrong. Thirdly, from this liberty of each individual, follows the liberty, within the same limits, of combination among individuals; freedom to unite, for any purpose not involving harm to others: the persons combining being supposed to be of full age, and not forced or deceived.

No society on which these liberties are not, on the whole, respected, is free, whatever may be its form of government; and none is completely free in which they do not exist absolute and unqualified. The only freedom which deserves the name, is that of pursuing our own good in our own way, so long as we do not attempt to deprive others of theirs, or impede their efforts to obtain it. Each is the proper guardian of his own health, whether bodily, or mental and spiritual. Mankind are greater gainers by suffering each other to live as seems good to themselves, than by compelling each to live as seems good to the rest. . . .

We have now recognized the necessity to the mental well-being of mankind (on which all their other well-being depends) of freedom of opinion, and freedom of the expression of opinion, on four distinct grounds; which we will now briefly recapitulate.

First, if any opinion is compelled to silence that opinion may, for aught we can certainly know, be true. To deny this is to assume our own infallibility.

Secondly, though the silenced opinion be an error, it may, and very commonly does, contain a portion of truth; and since the general or prevailing opinion on any subject is rarely or never the whole truth, it is only by the collision of adverse opinions that the remainder of the truth has any chance of being supplied.

Thirdly, even if the received opinion be not only true, but the whole truth; unless it is suffered to be, and actually is vigorously and earnestly contested, it will, by most of those who receive it, be held in the manner of a prejudice, with little comprehension or feeling of its rational grounds. And not only this, but, fourthly, the meaning of the doctrine itself will be in danger of being lost, or enfeebled, and deprived of its vital effect on the character and conduct: the dogma becoming a mere formal profession, inefficacious for good, but cumbering the ground, and preventing the growth of any real and heartfelt conviction from reason or personal experience. . . .

Of the Limits to the Authority of Society over the Individual

What, then, is the rightful limit to the sovereignty of the individual over himself? Where does the authority of society begin? How much of human life should be assigned to individuality, and how much to society?

Each will receive its proper share, if each has that which more particularly concerns it. To individuality should belong the part of life in which it is chiefly the individual that is interested; to society, the part which chiefly interests society.

Though society is not founded on a contract, and though no good purpose is answered by inventing a contract in order to deduce social obligations from it, every one who receives the protection of society owes a return for the benefit, and the fact of living in society renders it indispensable that each should be bound to observe a certain line of conduct towards the rest. This conduct consists, first, in not injuring the interests of one another; or rather certain interests, which, either by express legal provision or by tacit understanding, ought to be considered as rights; and secondly, in each person's bearing his share (to be fixed on some equitable principle) of the labors and sacrifices incurred for defending the society or its members from injury and molestation. These conditions society is justified in enforcing, at all costs to those who endeavor to withhold fulfillment. Nor is this all that society may do. The acts of an individual may be hurtful to others, or wanting in due consideration for their welfare, without going the length of violating any of their constituted rights. The offender may then be justly punished by opinion, though not by law. As soon as any part of a person's conduct affects prejudicially the interests of others, society has jurisdiction over it, and the question whether the general welfare will or will not be promoted by interfering with it, becomes open to discussion. But there is no room for entertaining any such question when a person's conduct affects the interests of no persons besides himself, or needs not affect them unless they like (all the persons concerned being of full age, and the ordinary amount of understanding). In all such cases there should be perfect freedom, legal and social, to do the action and stand the consequences.

It would be a great misunderstanding of this doctrine, to suppose that it is one of selfish indifference, which pretends that human beings have no business with each other's conduct in life, and that they should not concern themselves about the well-doing or well-being of one another, unless their own interest is involved. Instead of any diminution, there is need of a great increase of disinterested exertion to promote the good of others. But disinterested benevolence can find other instruments to persuade people to their good, than whips and scourges, either of the literal or the metaphorical sort. I am the last person to undervalue the self-regarding virtues; they are only second in importance, if even second, to the social. It is equally the business of education to cultivate both. But even education works by conviction and persuasion as well as by compulsion, and it is by the former only that, when the period of education is past, the self-regarding virtues should be inculcated. Human beings owe to each other help to distinguish the better from the worse, and encouragement to choose the former and avoid the latter. They should be forever stimulating each other to increased exercise of their higher faculties, and increased direction of their feelings and aims towards wise instead of foolish, elevating instead of degrading, objects and contemplations. But neither one person, nor any number of persons, is warranted in saying to another human creature of ripe years, that he shall not do with his life for his own benefit what he chooses to do with it. He is the person most interested in his own well-being: the interest which any other person, except in cases of strong personal attachment, can have in it, is trifling, compared with that which he himself has; the interest which society has in him individually (except as to his conduct to others) is fractional, and altogether indirect: while, with respect to his own feelings and circumstances, the most ordinary man or woman has means of knowledge immeasurably surpassing those that can be possessed by anyone else. The interference of society to overrule his judgment and purposes in what only regards himself, must be grounded on general presumptions; which may be altogether wrong, and even if right, are as likely as not to be misapplied to individual cases, by persons no better acquainted with the circumstances of such cases than those are who look at them merely from without. In this department, therefore, of human affairs, individuality has its proper field of action. In the conduct of human beings towards one another, it is necessary that general rules should for the most part be observed, in order that people may know what they have to expect; but in each person's own concerns, his individual spontaneity is entitled to free exercise. Considerations to aid his judgment, exhortations to strengthen his will, may be offered to him, even obtruded on him, by others; but he, himself, is the final judge. All errors which he is likely to commit against advice and warning, are far outweighed by the evil of allowing others to constrain him to what they deem his good.

I do not mean that the feelings with which a person is regarded by others, ought not to be in any way affected by his self-regarding qualities or deficiencies. This is neither possible nor desirable. If he is eminent in any of the qualities which conduce to his own good, he is, so far, a proper object of admiration. He is so much the nearer to the ideal perfection of human nature. If he is grossly deficient in those qualities, a sentiment the opposite of admiration will follow. There is a degree of folly, and a degree of what may be called (though the phrase is not unobjectionable) lowness or depravation of taste, which, though it cannot justify doing harm to the person who manifests it, renders him necessarily and properly a subject of distaste, or, in extreme cases, even of contempt: a person would not have the opposite qualities in due strength without entertaining these feelings. Though doing no wrong to anyone, a person may so act as to compel us to judge him, and feel to him, as a fool, or as a being of an inferior order: and since this judgment

and feeling are a fact which he would prefer to avoid, it is doing him a service to warn him of it beforehand, as of any other disagreeable consequence to which he exposes himself. It would be well, indeed, if this good office were much more freely rendered than the common notions of politeness at present permit, and if one person could honestly point out to another that he thinks him in fault, without being considered unmannerly or presuming. We have a right, also, in various ways, to act upon our unfavorable opinion of any one, not to the oppression of his individuality, but in the exercise of ours. We are not bound, for example, to seek his society; we have a right to avoid it (though not to parade the avoidance), for we have a right to choose the society most acceptable to us. We have a right, and it may be our duty to caution others against him, if we think his example or conversation likely to have a pernicious effect on those with whom he associates. We may give others a preference over him in optional good offices, except those which tend to his improvement. In these various modes a person may suffer very severe penalties at the hands of others, for faults which directly concern only himself; but he suffers these penalties only in so far as they are the natural, and, as it were, the spontaneous consequences of the faults themselves, not because they are purposely inflicted on him for the sake of punishment. A person who shows rashness, obstinacy, self-conceit—who cannot live within moderate means—who cannot restrain himself from hurtful indulgences—who pursues animal pleasures at the expense of those of feelings and intellect—must expect to be lowered in the opinion of others, and to have a less share of their favorable sentiments, but of this he has no right to complain, unless he has merited their favor by special excellence in his social relations and has thus established a title to their good offices, which is not affected by his demerits towards himself.

What I contend for is, that the inconveniences which are strictly inseparable from the unfavorable judgment of others, are the only ones to which a person should ever be subjected for that portion of his conduct and character which concerns his own good, but which does not affect the interests of others in their relations with him. Acts injurious to others require a totally different treatment. Encroachment on their rights; infliction on them of any loss or damage not justified by his own rights; falsehood or duplicity in dealing with them; unfair or ungenerous use of advantages over them; even selfish abstinence from defending them against injury—these are fit objects of moral reprobation, and, in grave cases, of moral retribution and punishment. And not only these acts, but the dispositions which lead to them, are properly immoral, and fit subjects of disapprobation which may rise to abhorrence. Cruelty of disposition; malice and ill-nature; that most anti-social and odious of all passions, envy; dissimulation and insincerity; irascibility on insufficient cause, and resentment disproportioned to the provocation; the love of domineering over others; the desire to engross more than one's share of advantages (the πλεονεξία of the Greeks); the pride which derives gratification from the abasement of others; the egotism which thinks self and its concerns more important than everything else, and decides all doubtful questions in his own favor—these are moral vices, and constitute a bad and odious moral character: unlike the self-regarding faults previously mentioned, which are not properly immoralities, and to whatever pitch they may be carried, do not constitute wickedness. They may be proofs of any amount of folly, or want of personal dignity and self-respect; but they are only a subject of moral reprobation when they involve a breach of duty to others, for whose sake the individual is bound to have care for himself. What are called duties to ourselves are not socially obligatory, unless circumstances render them at the same time duties to others. The term duty to oneself, when it means anything more than prudence, means self-respect or self-development; and for none of these is any one accountable to his fellow-creatures, because for none of them is it for the good of mankind that he be held accountable to them.

The distinction between the loss of consideration which a person may rightly incur by defect of prudence or of personal dignity, and the reprobation which is due to him for an offence against the rights of others, is not a merely nominal distinction. It makes a vast difference both in our feelings and in our conduct towards him, whether he displeases us in things in which we think we have a right to control him, or in things in which we know that we have not. If he displeases us, we may express our distaste, and we may stand aloof from a person as well as from a thing that displeases us; but we shall not therefore feel called on to make his life uncomfortable. We shall reflect that he already bears, or will bear, the whole penalty of his error; if he spoils his life by mismanagement, we shall not, for that reason, desire to spoil it still further: instead of wishing to punish him, we shall rather endeavor to alleviate his punishment, by showing him how he may avoid or cure the evils his conduct tends to bring upon him. He may be to us an object of pity, perhaps of dislike, but not of anger or resentment; we shall not treat him like an enemy of society: the worst we shall think ourselves justified in doing is leaving him to himself, if we do not interfere benevolently by showing interest or concern for him. It is far otherwise if he has infringed the rules necessary for the protection of his fellow-creatures, individually or collectively. The evil consequences of his acts do not then fall on himself, but on others; and society, as the protector of all its members, must retaliate on him; must inflict pain on him for the express purpose of punishment, and must take care that it be sufficiently severe. In the one case, he is an offender at our bar, and we are called on not only to sit in judgment on him, but, in one shape or another, to execute our own sentence: in the other case, it is not our part to inflict any suffering on him, except what may incidentally follow from our using the same liberty in the regulation of our own affairs, which we allow to him in his.

The distinction here pointed out between the part of a person's life which concerns only himself, and that which concerns others, many persons will refuse to admit. How (it may be asked) can any part of the conduct of a member of society be a matter of indifference to the other members? No person is an entirely isolated being; it is impossible for a person to do anything seriously or permanently hurtful to himself, without mischief reaching at least to his near connections, and often far beyond them. If he injures his property, he does harm to those who directly or indirectly derived support from it, and usually diminishes, by a greater or less amount, the general resources of the community. If he deteriorates his bodily or mental faculties, he not only brings evil upon all who depended on him for any portion of their happiness, but disqualifies himself for rendering the services which he owes to his fellow-creatures generally; perhaps becomes a burden on their affection or benevolence; and if such conduct were very frequent, hardly any offence that is committed would detract more from the general sum of good. Finally, if by his vices or follies a person does no direct harm to others, he is nevertheless (it may be said) injurious by his example; and ought to be compelled to control himself, for the sake of those whom the sight or knowledge of his conduct might corrupt or mislead.

And even (it will be added) if the consequences of misconduct could be confined to the vicious or thoughtless individual, ought society to abandon to their own guidance those who are manifestly unfit for it? If protection against themselves is confessedly due to children and persons under age, is not society equally bound to afford it to persons of mature years who are equally incapable of self-government? If gambling, or drunkenness, or incontinence, or idleness, or uncleanliness, are as injurious to happiness, and as great a hindrance to improvement, as many or most of the acts prohibited by law, why (it may be asked) should not law, so far as is consistent with practicability and social convenience, endeavor to repress these also? And as a supplement to the unavoidable imperfections of law, ought not opinion at least to organize a powerful police against these vices, and visit rigidly with social penalties those who are known to practise them? There is no question here (it may be said) about restricting individuality, or impeding the trial of new and original experiments in living. The only things it is sought to prevent are things which have been tried and condemned from the beginning of the world until now; things which experience has shown not to be useful or suitable to any person's individuality. There must be some length of time and amount of experience, after which a moral or prudential truth may be regarded as established: and it is merely desired to prevent generation after generation from falling over the same precipice which has been fatal to their predecessors.

I fully admit that the mischief which a person does to himself, may seriously affect, both through their sympathies and their interests, those nearly connected with him, and in a minor degree, society at large. When, by conduct of this sort, a person is led to violate a distinct and assignable obligation to any other person or persons, the case is taken out of the self-regarding class, and becomes amenable to moral disapprobation in the proper sense of the term. If, for example, a man, through intemperance or extravagance, becomes unable to pay his debts, or, having undertaken the moral responsibility of a family, becomes from the same cause incapable of supporting or educating them, he is deservedly reprobated, and might be justly punished; but it is for the breach of duty to his family or creditors, not for the extravagance. If the resources which ought to have been devoted to them, had been diverted from them for the most prudent investment, the moral culpability would have been the same. George Barnwell murdered his uncle to get money for his mistress, but if he had done it to set himself up in business, he would equally have been hanged. Again, in the frequent case of a man who causes grief to his family by addiction to bad habits, he deserves reproach for his unkindness or ingratitude; but so he may for cultivating habits not in themselves vicious, if they are painful to those with whom he passes his life, or who from personal ties are dependent on him for their comfort. Whoever fails in the consideration generally due to the interests and feelings of others, not being compelled by some more imperative duty, or justified by allowable self-preference, is a subject of moral disapprobation for that failure, but not for the cause of it, nor for the errors, merely personal to himself, which may have remotely led to it. In like manner; when a person disables himself, by conduct purely self-regarding, from the performance of some definite duty incumbent on him to the public, he is guilty of a social offence. No person ought to be punished simply for being drunk; but a soldier or a policeman should be punished for being drunk on duty. Whenever, in short, there is a definite damage, or a definite risk of damage, either to an individual or to the public, the case is taken out of the province of liberty, and placed in that of morality or law.

But with regard to the merely contingent, or, as it may be called, constructive injury which a person causes to society, by conduct which neither violates any specific duty to the public, nor occasions perceptible hurt to any assignable individual except himself; the inconvenience is one which society can afford to bear, for the sake of the greater good of human freedom. If grown persons are to be punished for not taking proper care of themselves, I would rather it were for their own sake, than under pretence of preventing them from impairing their capacity of rendering to society benefits which society does not pretend it has a right to exact. But I cannot consent to argue the point as if society had no means of bringing its weaker members up to its ordinary standard of rational conduct, except waiting till they do something irrational, and then punishing them, legally or morally, for it. Society has had absolute power over them during all the early portion of their existence: it has had the whole period of childhood and nonage in which to try whether it could make them capable of rational conduct in life. The existing generation is master both of the training and the entire circumstances of the generation to come; it cannot indeed make them perfectly wise and good, because it is itself so lamentably deficient in goodness and wisdom; and its best efforts are not always, in individual cases, its most successful ones; but it is perfectly well able to make the rising generation, as a whole, as good as, and a little better than, itself. If society lets any considerable number of its members grow up mere children, incapable of being acted on by rational consideration of distant motives, society has itself to blame for the consequences.

Armed not only with all the powers of education, but with the ascendency which the authority of a received opinion always exercises over the minds who are least fitted to judge for themselves; and aided by the *natural* penalties which cannot be prevented from falling on those who incur the distaste or the contempt of those who know them; let not society pretend that it needs, besides all this, the power to issue commands and enforce obedience in the personal concerns of individuals, in which, on all principles of justice and policy, the decision ought to rest with those who are to abide the consequences. Nor is there anything which tends more to discredit and frustrate the better means of influencing conduct, than a resort to the worse. If there be among those whom it is attempted to coerce into prudence or temperance, any of the material of which vigorous and independent characters are made, they will infallibly rebel against the yoke. No such person will ever feel that others have a right to control him in his concerns, such as they have to prevent him from injuring them in theirs; and it easily comes to be considered a mark of spirit and courage to fly in the face of such usurped authority, and do with ostentation the exact opposite of what it enjoins; as in the fashion of grossness which succeeded, in the time of Charles II, to the fanatical moral intolerance of the Puritans. With respect to what is said of the necessity of protecting society from the bad example set to others by the vicious or the self-indulgent; it is true that bad example may have a pernicious effect, especially the example of doing wrong to others with impunity to the wrongdoer. But we are now speaking of conduct which, while it does no wrong to others, is supposed to do great harm to the agent himself: and I do not see how those who believe this, can think otherwise than that the example, on the whole, must be more salutary than hurtful, since, if it displays the misconduct, it displays also the painful or degrading consequences which, if the conduct is justly censured, must be supposed to be in all or most cases attendant on it.

But the strongest of all the arguments against the interference of the public with purely personal conduct, is that when it does interfere, the odds are that it interferes wrongly, and in the wrong place. On questions of social morality, of duty to others, the opinion of the public, that is, of an overruling majority, though often wrong, is likely to be still oftener right; because on such questions they are only required to judge of their own interests; of the manner in which some mode of conduct, if allowed to be practised, would affect themselves. But the opinion of a similar majority, imposed as a law on the minority, on questions of self-regarding conduct, is quite as likely to be wrong as right; for in these cases public opinion means, at the best, some people's opinion of what is good or bad for other people; while very often it does not even mean that; the public, with the most perfect indifference, passing over the pleasure or convenience of those whose conduct they censure, and considering only their own preference. There are many who consider as an injury to themselves any conduct which they have a distaste for, and resent it as an outrage to their feelings; as a religious bigot, when charged with disregarding the religious feelings of others, has been known to retort that they disregard his feelings, by persisting in their abominable worship or creed. But there is no parity between the feeling of a person for his own opinion, and the feeling of another who is offended at his holding it; no more than between the desire of a thief to take a purse, and the desire of the right owner to keep it. And a person's taste is as much his own peculiar concern as his opinion or his purse. It is easy for any one to imagine an ideal public, which leaves the freedom and choice of individuals in all uncertain matters undisturbed, and only requires them to abstain from modes of conduct which universal experience has condemned. But where has there been seen a public which set any such limit to its censorship? or when does the public trouble itself about universal experience? In its interferences with personal conduct it is seldom thinking of anything but the enormity of acting or feeling differently from itself; and this standard of judgment, thinly disguised, is held up to mankind as the dictate of religion and philosophy, by nine tenths of all moralists and speculative writers. These teach that things are right because they are right; because we feel them to be so. They tell us to search in our own minds and hearts for laws of conduct binding on ourselves and on all others. What can the poor public do but apply these instructions, and make their own personal feelings of good and evil, if they are tolerably unanimous in them, obligatory on all the world?

The evil here pointed out is not one which exists only in theory; and it may perhaps be expected that I should specify the instances in which the public of this age and country improperly invests its own preferences with the character of moral laws. I am not writing an essay on the aberrations of existing moral feeling. That is too weighty a subject to be discussed parenthetically, and by way of illustration. Yet examples are necessary, to show that the principle I maintain is of serious and practical moment, and that I am not endeavoring to erect a barrier against imaginary evils. And it is not difficult to show, by abundant instances, that to extend the bounds of what may be called moral police, until it encroaches on the most unquestionably legitimate liberty of the individual, is one of the most universal of all human propensities.

As a first instance, consider the antipathies which men cherish on no better grounds than that persons whose religious opinions are different from theirs, do not practise their religious observances, especially their religious abstinences. To cite a rather trivial example, nothing in the creed or practice of Christians does more to envenom the hatred of Mahomedans against them, than the fact of their eating pork. There are few acts which Christians and Europeans regard with more unaffected disgust, than Mussulmans regard this particular mode of satisfying hunger. It is, in the first place, an offence against their religion; but this circumstance by no means explains either the degree or the kind of their repugnance; for wine also is forbidden by their religion, and to partake of it is by all Mussulmans accounted wrong, but not disgusting. Their aversion to the flesh of the "unclean beast" is, on the contrary, of that peculiar character, resembling an instinctive antipathy, which the idea of uncleanness, when once it thoroughly sinks into the feelings, seems always to excite even in those whose personal habits are anything but scrupulously cleanly, and of which the sentiment of religious impurity, so intense in the Hindoos, is a remarkable example. Suppose now that in a people, of whom the majority were Mussulmans, that majority should insist upon not permitting pork to be eaten within the limits of the country. This would be nothing new in Mahomedan countries.[1] Would it be a legitimate exercise of the moral authority of public opinion? and if not, why not? The practice is really revolting to such a public. They also sincerely think that it is forbidden and abhorred by the Deity. Neither could the prohibition be censured as religious persecution. It might be religious in its origin, but it would not be persecution for religion, since nobody's religion makes it a duty to eat pork. The only tenable ground of condemnation would be, that with the personal tastes and self-regarding concerns of individuals the public has no business to interfere.

To come somewhat nearer home: the majority of Spaniards consider it a gross impiety, offensive in the highest degree to the Supreme Being, to worship him in any other manner than the Roman Catholic; and no other public worship is lawful on Spanish soil. The people of all Southern Europe look upon a married clergy as not only irreligious, but unchaste, indecent, gross, disgusting. What do Protestants think of these perfectly sincere feelings, and of the attempt to enforce them against non-Catholics? Yet, if mankind are justified in interfering with each other's liberty in things which do not concern the interests of others, on what principle is it possible consistently to exclude these cases? or who can blame people for desiring to suppress what they regard as a scandal in the sight of God and man? No stronger case can be shown for prohibiting anything which is regarded as a personal immorality, than is made out for suppressing these practices in the eyes of those who regard them as impieties; and unless we are willing to adopt the logic of persecutors, and to say that we may persecute others because we are right, and that they must not persecute us because they are wrong, we must beware of admitting a principle of which we should resent as a gross injustice the application to ourselves.

The preceding instances may be objected to, although unreasonably, as drawn from contingencies impossible among us: opinion, in this country, not being likely to enforce abstinence from meats, or to interfere with people for worshipping, and for either marrying or not marrying, according to their creed or inclination. The next example, however, shall be taken from an interference with liberty which we have by no means passed all danger of. Wherever the puritans have been sufficiently powerful, as in New England, and in Great Britain at the time of the Commonwealth, they have endeavored, with considerable success, to put down all public, and nearly all private, amusements: especially music, dancing, public games, or other assemblages for purposes of diversion, and the theatre. There are still in this country large bodies of persons by whose notions of morality and religion these recreations are condemned; and those persons belonging chiefly to the middle class, who are the ascendant power in the present social and political condition of the kingdom, it is by no means impossible that persons of these sentiments may at some time or other command a majority in Parliament. How will the remaining portion of the community like to have the amusements that shall be permitted to them regulated by the religious and moral sentiments of the stricter Calvinists and Methodists? Would they not, with considerable peremptoriness, desire these intrusively pious members of society to mind their own business? This is precisely what should be said to every government and every public, who have the pretension that no person shall enjoy any pleasure which they think wrong. But if the principle of the pretension be admitted, no one can reasonably object to its being acted on in the sense of the majority, or other preponderating power in the country; and all persons must be ready to conform to the idea of a Christian commonwealth, as understood by the early settlers in New England, if a religious profession similar to theirs should ever succeed in regaining its lost ground, as religions supposed to be declining have so often been known to do.

To imagine other contingency, perhaps more likely to be realized than the one last mentioned. There is confessedly a strong tendency in the modern world towards a democratic constitution of society, accompanied or not by popular political institutions. It is affirmed that in the country where this tendency is most completely realized—where both society and the government are most democratic—the United States—the feeling of the majority, to whom any appearance of a more showy or costly style of living than they can hope to rival is disagreeable, operates as a tolerably effectual sumptuary law, and that in many parts of the Union it is really difficult for a person possessing a very large income, to find any mode of spending it, which will not incur popular disapprobation. Though such statements as these are doubtless much exaggerated as a representation of existing facts, the state of things they describe is not only a conceivable and possible, but a probable result of democratic feeling, combined with the notion that the public has a right to a veto on the manner in which individuals shall spend their incomes. We have only further to suppose a considerable diffusion of Socialist opinions, and it may become infamous in the eyes of the majority to possess more property than some very small amount, or any income not earned by manual labor. Opinions similar in principle to these, already prevail widely among the artisan class, and weigh oppressively on those who are amenable to the opinion chiefly of that class, namely, its own members. It is known that the bad workmen who form the majority of the operatives in many branches of industry, are decidedly of opinion that bad workmen ought to receive the same wages as good, and that no one ought to be allowed, through piecework or otherwise, to earn by superior skill or industry more than others can without it. And they employ a moral police, which occasionally becomes a physical one, to deter skilful workmen from receiving, and employers from giving, a larger remuneration for a more useful service. If the public have any jurisdiction over private concerns, I cannot see that these people are in fault, or that any individual's particular public can be blamed for as-

serting the same authority over his individual conduct, which the general public asserts over people in general.

But, without dwelling upon suppositious cases, there are, in our own day, gross usurpations upon the liberty of private life actually practised, and still greater ones threatened with some expectation of success, and opinions proposed which assert an unlimited right in the public not only to prohibit by law everything which it thinks wrong, but in order to get at what it thinks wrong, to prohibit any number of things which it admits to be innocent.

Under the name of preventing intemperance, the people of one English colony, and of nearly half the United States, have been interdicted by law from making any use whatever of fermented drinks, except for medical purposes: for prohibition of their sale is in fact, as it is intended to be, prohibition of their use. And though the impracticability of executing the law has caused its repeal in several of the States which had adopted it, including the one from which it derives its name, an attempt has notwithstanding been commenced, and is prosecuted with considerable zeal by many of the professed philanthropists, to agitate for a similar law in this country. The association, or "Alliance" as it terms itself, which has been formed for this purpose, has acquired some notoriety through the publicity given to a correspondence between its Secretary and one of the very few English public men who hold that a politicians's opinions ought to be founded on principles. Lord Stanley's share in this correspondence is calculated to strengthen the hopes already built on him, by those who know how rare such qualities as are manifested in some of his public appearances, unhappily are among those who figure in political life. The organ of the Alliance, who would "deeply deplore the recognition of any principle which could be wrested to justify bigotry and persecution," undertakes to point out the "broad and impassable barrier" which divides such principles from those of the association. "All matters relating to thought, opinion, conscience, appear to me," he says, "to be without the sphere of legislation; all pertaining to social act, habit, relation, subject only to a discretionary power vested in the State itself, and not in the individual, to be within it." No mention is made of a third class, different from either of these, viz., acts and habits which are not social, but individual; although it is to this class, surely, that the act of drinking fermented liquors belongs. Selling fermented liquors, however, is trading, and trading is a social act. But the infringement complained of is not on the liberty of the seller, but on that of the buyer and consumer; since the State might just as well forbid him to drink wine, as purposely make it impossible for him to obtain it. The Secretary, however, says, "I claim, as a citizen, a right to legislate whenever my social rights are invaded by the social act of another." And now for the definition of these "social rights." "If anything invades my social rights, certainly the traffic in strong drink does. It destroys my primary right of security, by constantly creating and stimulating social disorder. It invades my right of equality, by deriving a profit from the creation of a misery, I am taxed to support. It impedes my right to free moral and intellectual development, by surrounding my path with dangers, and by weakening and demoralizing society, from which I have a right to claim mutual aid and intercourse." A theory of "social rights," the like of which probably never before found its way into distinct language—being nothing short of this—that it is the absolute social right of every individual, that every other individual shall act in every respect exactly as he ought; that whosoever fails thereof in the smallest particular, violates my social right, and entitles me to demand from the legislature the removal of the grievance. So monstrous a principle is far more dangerous than any single interference with liberty; there is no violation of liberty which it would not justify; it acknowledges no right to any freedom whatever, except perhaps to that of holding opinions in secret, without ever disclosing them: for the moment an opinion which I consider noxious, passes any one's lips, it invades all the "social rights" attributed to me by the Alliance. The doctrine ascribes to all mankind a vested interest in each other's moral, intellectual, and even physical perfection, to be defined by each claimant according to his own standard.

Another important example of illegitimate interference with the rightful liberty of the individual, not simply threatened, but long since carried into triumphant effect, is Sabbatarian legislation. Without doubt, abstinence on one day in the week, so far as the exigencies of life permit, from the usual daily occupation, though in no respect religiously binding on any except Jews, it is a highly beneficial custom. And inasmuch as this custom cannot be observed without a general consent to that effect among the industrious classes, therefore, in so far as some persons by working may impose the same necessity on others, it may be allowable and right that the law should guarantee to each, the observance by others of the custom, by suspending the greater operations of industry on a particular day. But this justification, grounded on the direct interest which others have in each individual's observance of the practice, does not apply to the self-chosen occupations in which a person may think fit to employ his leisure; nor does it hold good, in the smallest degree, for legal restrictions on amusements. It is true that the amusement of some is the day's work of others; but the pleasure, not to say the useful recreation, of many, is worth the labor of a few, provided the occupation is freely chosen, and can be freely resigned. The operatives are perfectly right in thinking that if all worked on Sunday seven days' work would have to be given for six days' wages: but so long as the great mass of employments are suspended, the small number who for the enjoyment of others must still work, obtain a proportional increase of earnings; and they are not obliged to follow those occupations, if they prefer leisure to emolument. If a further remedy is sought, it might be found in the establishment by custom of a holiday on some other day of the week for those particular classes of persons. The only ground, therefore, on which restrictions on Sunday amusements can be defended, must be that they are religiously wrong; a motive of legislation which never can be too earnestly protested again. "Deorum injuriae Diis curae." It remains to be proved that society or any of its officers holds a commission from on high to avenge any supposed offence to Omnipotence, which is not also a wrong to our fellow-creatures. The notion that it is one man's duty that another should be religious, was the foundation of all the religious persecutions ever perpetrated, and if admitted, would fully justify them. Though the feeling which breaks out in the repeated attempts to stop railway travelling on Sunday, in the resistance to the opening of Museums, and the like, has not the cruelty of the old persecutors, the state of mind indicated by it is fundamentally the same. It is a determination not to tolerate others in doing what is permitted by their religion, because it is not permitted by the persecutor's religion. It is a belief that God not only abominates the act of the misbeliever, but will not hold us guiltless if we leave him unmolested.

I cannot refrain from adding to these examples of the little account commonly made of human liberty, the language of downright persecution which breaks out from the press of this country, whenever it feels called on to notice the remarkable phenomenon of Mormonism. Much might be said on the unexpected and instructive fact, that an alleged new revelation, and a religion founded on it, the product of palpable imposture, not even supported by the *prestige* of extraordinary qualities in its founder, is believed by hundreds of thousands, and has been made the foundation of a society, in the age of newspapers, railways, and the electric telegraph. What here concerns us is, that this religion, like other and better religions, has its martyrs; that its prophet and founder was, for his teaching, put to death by a mob; that others of its adherents lost their lives by the same lawless violence; that they were forcibly expelled, in a body, from the country in which they first grew up; while, now that they have been chased into a solitary recess in the midst of a desert, many of this country openly declare that it would be right (only that it is not convenient) to send an expedition against them, and compel them by force to conform to the opinion of other people. The article of the Mormonite doctrine which is the chief provocative to the antipathy which thus breaks through the ordinary restraints of religious tolerance, is its sanction of polygamy; which, though permitted to Mahomedans, and Hindoos, and Chinese, seems to excite unquenchable animosity when practised by persons who speak English, and profess to be a kind of Christians. No one has a deeper disapprobation than I have of the Mormon institution; both for other reasons, and because, far from being in any way countenanced by the principle of liberty, it is a direct infraction of that principle, being a mere riveting of the chains of one half of the community, and an emancipation of the other from reciprocity of obligation towards them. Still, it must be remembered that this relation is as much voluntary on the part of the women concerned in it, and who may be deemed the sufferers by it, as is the case with any other form of the marriage institution; and however surprising this fact may appear, it has its explanation in the common ideas and customs of the world, which teaching women to think marriage the one thing needful, make it intelligible that many a woman should prefer being one of several wives, to not being a wife at all. Other countries are not asked to recognize such unions, or release any portion of their inhabitants from their own laws on the score of Mormonite opinions. But when the dissen-

tients have conceded to the hostile sentiments of others, far more than could justly be demanded; when they have left the countries to which their doctrines were unacceptable, and established themselves in a remote corner of the earth, which they have been the first to render habitable to human beings; it is difficult to see on what principles but those of tyranny they can be prevented from living there under what laws they please, provided they commit no aggression on other nations, and allow perfect freedom of departure to those who are dissatisfied with their ways. A recent writer, in some respects of considerable merit, proposes (to use his own words) not a crusade, but a *civilizade,* against this polygamous community, to put an end to what seems to him a retrograde step in civilization. It also appears so to me, but I am not aware that any community has a right to force another to be civilized. So long as the sufferers by the bad law do not invoke assistance from other communities, I cannot admit that persons entirely unconnected with them ought to step in and require that a condition of things with which all who are directly interested appear to be satisfied, should be put an end to because it is a scandal to persons some thousands of miles distant, who have no part or concern in it. Let them send missionaries, if they please, to preach against it; and let them, by any fair means (of which silencing the teachers is not one), oppose the progress of similar doctrines among their own people. If civilization has got the better of barbarism when barbarism had the world to itself, it is too much to profess to be afraid lest barbarism, after having been fairly got under, should revive and conquer civilization. A civilization that can thus succumb to its vanquished enemy must first have become so degenerate, that neither its appointed priests and teachers, nor anybody else, has the capacity, or will take the trouble, to stand up for it. If this be so, the sooner such a civilization receives notice to quit, the better. It can only go on from bad to worse, until destroyed and regenerated (like the Western Empire) by energetic barbarians.

---

1. *The case of the Bombay Parsees is a curious instance in point. When this industrious and enterprising tribe, the descendants of the Persian fire-worshippers, flying from their native country before the Caliphs, arrived in Western India, they were admitted to toleration by the Hindoo sovereigns, on condition of not eating beef. When those regions afterwards fell under the dominion of Maho-* *medan conquerors, the Parsees obtained from them a continuance of indulgence, on condition of refraining from pork. What was at first obedience to authority became a second nature, and the Parsees to this day abstain both from beef and pork. Though not required by their religion, the double abstinence has had time to grow into a custom of their tribe; and custom, in the East, is a religion.*

Challenges to Self-Determination: Legal Paternalism and Legal Moralism

PATERNALISM*

Gerald Dworkin

Neither one person, nor any number of persons, is warranted in saying to another human creature of ripe years, that he shall not do with his life for his own benefit what he chooses to do with it. [Mill]

I do not want to go along with a volunteer basis. I think a fellow should be compelled to become better and not let him use his discretion whether he wants to get smarter, more healthy or more honest. [General Hershey]

I take as my starting point the "one very simple principle" proclaimed by Mill *On Liberty* . . .

That principle is, that the sole end for which mankind are warranted, individually or collectively, in interfering with the liberty of action of any of their number, is self-protection. That the only purpose for which power can be rightfully exercised over any member of a civilized community, against his will, is to prevent harm to others. He cannot rightfully be compelled to do or forbear because it will be better

for him to do so, because it will make him happier, because, in the opinion of others, to do so would be wise, or even right.

This principle is neither "one" nor "very simple." It is at least two principles; one asserting that self-protection or the prevention of harm to others is sometimes a sufficient warrant and the other claiming that the individual's own good is *never* a sufficient warrant for the exercise of compulsion either by the society as a whole or by its individual members. I assume that no one, with the possible exception of extreme pacifists or anarchists, questions the correctness of the first half of the principle. This essay is an examination of the negative claim embodied in Mill's principle—the objection to paternalistic interferences with a man's liberty.

I

By paternalism I shall understand roughly the interference with a person's liberty of action justified by reasons referring exclusively to the welfare, good, happiness, needs, interests or values of the person being coerced. One is always well-advised to illustrate one's definitions by examples but it is not easy to find "pure" examples of paternalistic interferences. For almost any piece of legislation is justified by several different kinds of reasons and even if historically a piece of legislation can be shown to have been introduced for purely paternalistic motives, it may be that advocates of the legislation with an antipaternalistic outlook can find sufficient reasons justifying the legislation without appealing to the reasons which were originally adduced to support it. Thus, for example, it may be that the original legislation requiring motorcyclists to wear safety helmets was introduced for purely paternalistic reasons. But the Rhode Island Supreme Court recently upheld such legislation on the grounds that it was "not persuaded that the legislature is powerless to prohibit individuals from pursuing a course of conduct which could conceivably result in their becoming public charges," thus clearly introducing reasons of a quite different kind. Now I regard this decision as being based on reasoning of a very dubious nature but it illustrates the kind of problem one has in finding examples. The following is a list of the kinds of interferences I have in mind as being paternalistic.

II

1. Laws requiring motorcyclists to wear safety helmets when operating their machines.
2. Laws forbidding persons from swimming at a public beach when lifeguards are not on duty.
3. Laws making suicide a criminal offense.
4. Laws making it illegal for women and children to work at certain types of jobs.
5. Laws regulating certain kinds of sexual conduct, for example, homosexuality among consenting adults in private.
6. Laws regulating the use of certain drugs which may have harmful consequences to the user but do not lead to antisocial conduct.
7. Laws requiring a license to engage in certain professions with those not receiving a license subject to fine or jail sentence if they do engage in the practice.
8. Laws compelling people to spend a specified fraction of their income on the purchase of retirement annuities (Social Security).
9. Laws forbidding various forms of gambling (often justified on the grounds that the poor are more likely to throw away their money on such activities than the rich who can afford to).
10. Laws regulating the maximum rates of interest for loans.
11. Laws against duelling.

In addition to laws which attach criminal or civil penalties to certain kinds of action there are laws, rules, regulations, decrees which make it either difficult or impossible for people to carry out their plans and which are also justified on paternalistic grounds. Examples of this are:

1. Laws regulating the types of contracts which will be upheld as valid by the courts, for example, (an example of Mill's to which I shall return) no man may make a valid contract for perpetual involuntary servitude.
2. Not allowing assumption of risk as a defense to an action based on the violation of a safety statute.
3. Not allowing as a defense to a charge of murder or assault the consent of the victim.
4. Requiring members of certain religious sects to have compulsory blood transfusions. This is made possible by not allowing the patient to have recourse to civil suits for assault and battery and by means of injunctions.
5. Civil commitment procedures when these are specifically justified on the basis of preventing the person being committed from harming himself. The D. C. Hospitalization of the Mentally Ill Act provides for involuntary hospitalization of a person who "is mentally ill, and because of that illness, is likely to injure himself or others if allowed to remain at liberty." The term injure in this context applies to unintentional as well as intentional injuries.

All of my examples are of existing restrictions on the liberty of individuals. Obviously one can think of interferences which have not yet been imposed. Thus one might ban the sale of cigarettes, or require that people wear safety belts in automobiles (as opposed to merely having them installed), enforcing this by not allowing a motorist to sue for injuries even when caused by other drivers if the motorist was not wearing a seat belt at the time of the accident.

I shall not be concerned with activities which though defended on paternalistic grounds are not interferences with the liberty of persons, for example, the giving of subsidies in kind rather than in cash on the grounds that the recipients would not spend the money on the goods which they really need, or not including a $1,000 deductible provision in a basic protection automobile insurance plan on the ground that the people who would elect it could least afford it. Nor shall I be concerned with measures such as "truth-in-advertising" acts and Pure Food and Drug legislation which are often attacked as paternalistic but which should not be considered so. In these cases all that is provided—it is true by the use of compulsion—is information which it is presumed that rational persons are interested in having in order to make wise decisions. There is no interference with the liberty of the consumer unless one wants to stretch a point beyond good sense and say that his liberty to apply for a loan without knowing the true rate of interest is diminished. It is true that sometimes there is sentiment for going further than providing information, for example when laws against usurious interest are passed preventing those who might wish to contract loans at high rates of interest from doing so, and these measures may correctly be considered paternalistic.

III

Bearing these examples in mind, let me return to a characterization of paternalism. I said earlier that I meant by the term, roughly, interference with a person's liberty for his own good. But, as some of the examples show, the class of persons whose good is involved is not always identical with the class of persons whose freedom is restricted. Thus, in the case of professional licensing it is the practitioner who is directly interfered with but it is the would-be patient whose interests are presumably being served. Not allowing the consent of the victim to be a defense to certain types of crime primarily affects the would-be aggressor but it is the interests of the willing victim that we are trying to protect. Sometimes a person may fall into both classes as would be the case if we banned the manufacture and sale of cigarettes and a given manufacturer happened to be a smoker as well.

Thus we may first divide paternalistic interferences into "pure" and "impure" cases. In "pure" paternalism the class of persons whose freedom is restricted is identical with the class of persons whose benefit is intended to be promoted by such restrictions. Examples: the making of suicide a crime, requir-

ing passengers in automobiles to wear seat belts, requiring a Christian Scientist to receive a blood transfusion. In the case of "impure" paternalism in trying to protect the welfare of a class of persons we find that the only way to do so will involve restricting the freedom of other persons besides those who are benefitted. Now it might be thought that there are no cases of "impure" paternalism since any such case could always be justified on nonpaternalistic grounds, that is, in terms of preventing harm to others. Thus we might ban cigarette manufacturers from continuing to manufacture their product on the grounds that we are preventing them from causing illness to others in the same way that we prevent other manufacturers from releasing pollutants into the atmosphere, thereby causing danger to the members of the community. The difference is, however, that in the former but not the latter case the harm is of such a nature that it could be avoided by those individuals affected if they so chose. The incurring of the harm requires, so to speak, the active cooperation of the victim. It would be mistaken theoretically and hypocritical in practice to assert that our interference in such cases is just like our interference in standard cases of protecting others from harm. At the very least someone interfered with in this way can reply that no one is complaining about his activities. It may be that impure paternalism requires arguments or reasons of a stronger kind in order to be justified, since there are persons who are losing a portion of their liberty and they do not even have the solace of having it be done "in their own interest." Of course in some sense, if paternalistic justifications are ever correct, then we are protecting others, we are preventing some from injuring others, but it is important to see the differences between this and the standard case.

Paternalism then will always involve limitations on the liberty of some individuals in their own interest but it may also extend to interferences with the liberty of parties whose interests are not in question.

IV

Finally, by way of some more preliminary analysis, I want to distinguish paternalistic interference with liberty from a related type with which it is often confused. Consider, for example, legislation which forbids employees to work more than, say, forty hours per week. It is sometimes argued that such legislation is paternalistic for if employees desired such a restriction on their hours of work they could agree among themselves to impose it voluntarily. But because they do not the society imposes its own conception of their best interests upon them by the use of coercion. Hence this is paternalism.

Now it may be that some legislation of this nature is, in fact, paternalistically motivated. I am not denying that. All I want to point out is that there is another possible way of justifying such measures which is not paternalistic in nature. It is not paternalistic because, as Mill puts it in a similar context, such measures are "required not to overrule the judgment of individuals respecting their own interest, but to give effect to that judgment: they being unable to give effect to it except by concert, which concert again cannot be effectual unless it receives validity and sanction from the law" (*Principles of Political Economy*).

The line of reasoning here is a familiar one first found in Hobbes and developed with great sophistication by contemporary economists in the last decade or so. There are restrictions which are in the interests of a class of persons taken collectively but are such that the immediate interest of each individual is furthered by his violating the rule when others adhere to it. In such cases the individuals involved may need the use of compulsion to give effect to their collective judgment of their own interest by guaranteeing each individual compliance by the others. In these cases compulsion is not used to achieve some benefit which is not recognized to be a benefit by those concerned, but rather because it is the only feasible means of achieving some benefit which *is* recognized as such by all concerned. This way of viewing matters provides us with another characterization of paternalism in general. Paternalism might be thought of as the use of coercion to achieve a good which is not recognized as such by those persons for whom the good is intended. Again while this formulation captures the heart of the matter—it is surely what Mill is objecting to in *On Liberty*—the matter is not always quite like that. For example, when we force motorcyclists to wear helmets we are trying to promote a good—the protection of the person from injury—which is surely recognized by most of the individuals concerned. It is not that a cyclist doesn't value his bodily integrity; rather, as a supporter of such legislation would put it, he either places, perhaps irrationally, another value or good (freedom from wearing a helmet) above that of physical well-being or, perhaps, while recognizing the danger in the abstract, he either does not fully appreciate it or he underestimates the likelihood of its oc-

curring. But now we are approaching the question of possible justifications of paternalistic measures and the rest of this essay will be devoted to that question.

V

I shall begin for dialectical purposes by discussing Mill's objections to paternalism and then go on to discuss more positive proposals.

An initial feature that strikes one is the absolute nature of Mill's prohibitions against paternalism. It is so unlike the carefully qualified admonitions of Mill and his fellow utilitarians on other moral issues. He speaks of self-protection as the *sole* end warranting coercion, of the individual's own goals as *never* being a sufficient warrant. Contrast this with his discussion of the prohibition against lying in *Utilitarianism*:

> Yet that even this rule, sacred as it is, admits of possible exception, is acknowledged by all moralists, the chief of which is where the withholding of some fact . . . would save an individual . . . from great and unmerited evil.

The same tentativeness is present when he deals with justice:

> It is confessedly unjust to break faith with any one: to violate an engagement, either express or implied, or disappoint expectations raised by our own conduct, at least if we have raised these expectations knowingly and voluntarily. Like all the other obligations of justice already spoken of, this one is not regarded as absolute, but as capable of being overruled by a stronger obligation of justice on the other side.

This anomaly calls for some explanation. The structure of Mill's argument is as follows:

1. Since restraint is an evil the burden of proof is on those who propose such restraint.
2. Since the conduct which is being considered is purely self-regarding, the normal appeal to the protection of the interests of others is not available.
3. Therefore we have to consider whether reasons involving reference to the individual's own good, happiness, welfare, or interests are sufficient to overcome the burden of justification.
4. We either cannot advance the interests of the individual by compulsion, or the attempt to do so involves evils which outweigh the good done.
5. Hence the promotion of the individual's own inter-

ests does not provide a sufficient warrant for the use of compulsion.

Clearly the operative premise here is (4), and it is bolstered by claims about the status of the individual as judge and appraiser of his welfare, interests, needs, et cetera:

> *With respect to his own feelings and circumstances, the most ordinary man or woman has means of knowledge immeasurably surpassing those that can be possessed by any one else.*

> *He is the man most interested in his own well-being: the interest which any other person, except in cases of strong personal attachment, can have in it is trifling, compared to that which he himself has.*

> *These claims are used to support the following generalizations concerning the utility of compulsion for paternalistic purposes.*

> *The interferences of society to overrule his judgment and purposes in what only regards himself must be grounded on general presumptions; which may be altogether wrong, and even if right, are as likely as not to be misapplied to individual cases.*

> *But the strongest of all the arguments against the interference of the public with purely personal conduct is that when it does interfere, the odds are that it interferes wrongly and in the wrong place.*

> *All errors which the individual is likely to commit against advice and warning are far outweighed by the evil of allowing others to constrain him to what they deem his good.*

Performing the utilitarian calculations by balancing the advantages and disadvantages, we find that: "Mankind are greater gainers by suffering each other to live as seems good to themselves, than by compelling each other to live as seems good to the rest." Ergo, (4).

This classical case of a utilitarian argument with all the premises spelled out is not the only line of reasoning present in Mill's discussion. There are asides, and more than asides, which look quite different and I shall deal with them later. But this is clearly the main channel of Mill's thought and it is one which

has been subjected to vigorous attack from the moment it appeared—most often by fellow utilitarians. The link that they have usually seized on is, as Fitzjames Stephen put it in *Liberty, Equality, Fraternity,* the absence of proof that the "mass of adults are so well acquainted with their own interests and so much disposed to pursue them that no compulsion or restraint put upon them by any others for the purpose of promoting their interest can really promote them." Even so sympathetic a critic as H. L. A. Hart is forced to the conclusion that:

> *In Chapter 5 of his essay [On Liberty] Mill carried his protests against paternalism to lengths that may now appear to us as fantastic. . . . No doubt if we no longer sympathise with his criticism this is due, in part, to a general decline in the belief that individuals know their own interest best.*
>
> *Mill endows the average individual with "too much of the psychology of a middle-aged man whose desires are relatively fixed; not liable to be artificially stimulated by external influences; who knows what he wants and what gives him satisfaction or happiness; and who pursues these things when he can."*

Now it is interesting to note that Mill himself was aware of some of the limitations on the doctrine that the individual is the best judge of his own interests. In his discussion of government intervention in general (even where the intervention does not interfere with liberty but provides alternative institutions to those of the market) after making claims which are parallel to those just discussed, for example, "People understand their own business and their own interests better, and care for them more, than the government does, or can be expected to do," he goes on to an intelligent discussion of the "very large and conspicuous exceptions" to the maxim that:

> *Most persons take a juster and more intelligent view of their own interest, and of the means of promoting it than can either be prescribed to them by a general enactment of the legislature, or pointed out in the particular case by a public functionary.*

Thus there are things

> *of which the utility does not consist in ministering to inclinations, nor in serving the daily uses of life, and the want of which is least felt where the need is greatest. This is peculiarly*

true of those things which are chiefly useful as
tending to raise the character of human be-
ings. The uncultivated cannot be competent
judges of cultivation. Those who most need to
be made wiser and better, usually desire it
least, and, if they desire it, would be incapable
of finding the way to it by their own lights.

. . . A second exception to the doctrine that in-
dividuals are the best judges of their own inter-
est, is when an individual attempts to decide
irrevocably now what will be best for his inter-
est at some future and distant time. The pre-
sumption in favor of individual judgment
is only legitimate, where the judgment is
grounded on actual, and especially on present,
personal experience; not where it is formed
antecedently to experience, and not suffered
to be reversed even after experience has con-
demned it.

The upshot of these exceptions is that Mill does not
declare that there should never be government interference with the economy but rather that

. . . in every instance, the burden of making
out a strong case should be thrown not on
those who resist but those who recommend gov-
ernment interference. Letting alone, in short,
should be the general practice: every departure
from it, unless required by some great good, is
a certain evil.

In short, we get a presumption, not an absolute prohibition. The question is why doesn't the argument
against paternalism go the same way?

I suggest that the answer lies in seeing that in
addition to a purely utilitarian argument Mill uses another as well. As a utilitarian, Mill has to show, in Fitzjames Stephen's words, that: "Self-protection apart, no
good object can be attained by any compulsion which
is not in itself a greater evil than the absence of the
object which the compulsion obtains." To show this is
impossible, one reason being that it isn't true. Preventing a man from selling himself into slavery (a
paternalistic measure which Mill himself accepts as
legitimate), or from taking heroin, or from driving a
car without wearing seat belts may constitute a lesser
evil than allowing him to do any of these things. A
consistent utilitarian can only argue against paternalism on the grounds that it (as a matter of fact) does not
maximize the good. It is always a contingent question
that may be returned by the evidence. But there is also

a noncontingent argument which runs through *On
Liberty.* When Mill states that "there is a part of the life
of every person who has come to years of discretion,
within which the individuality of that person ought to
reign uncontrolled either by any other person or by
the public collectively," he is saying something about
what it means to be a person, an autonomous agent.
It is because coercing a person for his own good denies this status as an independent entity that Mill objects to it so strongly and in such absolute terms. To
be able to choose is a good that is independent of the
wisdom of what is chosen. A man's "mode of laying
out his existence is the best, not because it is the best
in itself, but because it is his own mode." It is the
privilege and proper condition of a human being, arrived at the maturity of his faculties, to use and interpret experience in his own way.

As further evidence of this line of reasoning in
Mill, consider the one exception to his prohibition
against paternalism.

In this and most civilised countries, for exam-
ple, an engagement by which a person should
sell himself, or allow himself to be sold, as a
slave, would be null and void; neither enforced
by law nor by opinion. The ground for thus
limiting his power of voluntarily disposing of
his own lot in life, is apparent, and is very
clearly seen in this extreme case. The reason
for not interfering, unless for the sake of others,
with a person's voluntary acts, is consideration
for his liberty. His voluntary choice is evidence
that what he so chooses is desirable, or at least
endurable, to him, and his good is on the
whole best provided for by allowing him to take
his own means of pursuing it. But by selling
himself for a slave, he abdicates his liberty; he
foregoes any future use of it beyond that single
act. He therefore defeats, in his own case, the
very purpose which is the justification of allow-
ing him to dispose of himself. He is no longer
free; but is thenceforth in a position which has
no longer the presumption in its favour, that
would be afforded by his voluntarily remain-
ing in it. The principle of freedom cannot re-
quire that he should be free not to be free. It
is not freedom to be allowed to alienate his
freedom.

Now leaving aside the fudging on the meaning of freedom in the last line, it is clear that part of this argument
is incorrect. While it is true that *future* choices of
the slave are not reasons for thinking that what he

chooses then is desirable for him, what is at issue is limiting his immediate choice; and since this choice is made freely, the individual may be correct in thinking that his interests are best provided for by entering such a contract. But the main consideration for not allowing such a contract is the need to preserve the liberty of the person to make future choices. This gives us a principle—a very narrow one—by which to justify some paternalistic interferences. Paternalism is justified only to preserve a wider range of freedom for the individual in question. How far this principle could be extended, whether it can justify all the cases in which we are inclined upon reflection to think paternalistic measures justified, remains to be discussed. What I have tried to show so far is that there are two strains of argument in Mill—one a straight-forward utilitarian mode of reasoning and one which relies not on the goods which free choice leads to but on the absolute value of the choice itself. The first cannot establish any absolute prohibition but at most a presumption and indeed a fairly weak one given some fairly plausible assumptions about human psychology; the second, while a stronger line of argument, seems to me to allow on its own grounds a wider range of paternalism than might be suspected. I turn now to a consideration of these matters.

VI

We might begin looking for principles governing the acceptable use of paternalistic power in cases where it is generally agreed that it is legitimate. Even Mill intends his principles to be applicable only to mature individuals, not those in what he calls "non-age." What is it that justifies us in interfering with children? The fact that they lack some of the emotional and cognitive capacities required in order to make fully rational decisions. It is an empirical question to just what extent children have an adequate conception of their own present and future interests but there is not much doubt that there are many deficiencies. For example, it is very difficult for a child to defer gratification for any considerable period of time. Given these deficiencies and given the very real and permanent dangers that may befall the child, it becomes not only permissible but even a duty of the parent to restrict the child's freedom in various ways. There is however an important moral limitation on the exercise of such parental power which is provided by the notion of the child eventually coming to see the correctness of his par-

ent's interventions. Parental paternalism may be thought of as a wager by the parent on the child's subsequent recognition of the wisdom of the restrictions. There is an emphasis on what could be called future-oriented consent—on what the child will come to welcome, rather than on what he does welcome.

The essence of this idea has been incorporated by idealist philosophers into various types of "real-will" theory as applied to fully adult persons. Extensions of paternalism are argued for by claiming that in various respects, chronologically mature individuals share the same deficiencies in knowledge, capacity to think rationally, and the ability to carry out decisions that children possess. Hence in interfering with such people we are in effect doing what they would do if they were fully rational. Hence we are not really opposing their will, hence we are not really interfering with their freedom. The dangers of this move have been sufficiently exposed by Berlin in his Two Concepts of Liberty. I see no gain in theoretical clarity nor in practical advantage in trying to pass over the real nature of the interferences with liberty that we impose on others. Still the basic notion of consent is important and seems to me the only acceptable way of trying to delimit an area of justified paternalism.

Let me start by considering a case where the consent is not hypothetical in nature. Under certain conditions it is rational for an individual to agree that others should force him to act in ways which, at the time of action, the individual may not see as desirable. If, for example, a man knows that he is subject to breaking his resolves when temptation is present, he may ask a friend to refuse to entertain his requests at some later stage.

A classical example is given in the Odyssey when Odysseus commands his men to tie him to the mast and refuse all future orders to be set free, because he knows the power of the Sirens to enchant men with their songs. Here we are on relatively sound ground in later refusing Odysseus' request to be set free. He may even claim to have changed his mind but, since it is *just* such changes that he wished to guard against, we are entitled to ignore them.

A process analogous to this may take place on a social rather than individual basis. An electorate may mandate its representatives to pass legislation which when it comes time to "pay the price" may be unpalatable. I may believe that a tax increase is necessary to halt inflation though I may resent the lower pay check each month. However in both this case and that of Odysseus, the measure to be enforced is specifically requested by the party involved and at some point in time there is genuine consent and agreement on the part of those persons whose liberty is infringed. Such is not the case for the paternalistic measures we have been speaking about. What must be involved here is not consent to specific measures but rather consent to a system of government, run by elected representatives, with an understanding that they may act to safeguard our interests in certain limited ways.

I suggest that since we are all aware of our irrational propensities, deficiencies in cognitive and emotional capacities, and avoidable and unavoidable ignorance, it is rational and prudent for us to in effect take out "social insurance policies." We may argue for and against proposed paternalistic measures in terms of what fully rational individuals would accept as forms of protection. Now clearly, since the initial agreement is not about specific measures we are dealing with a more-or-less blank check and therefore there have to be carefully defined limits. What I am looking for are certain kinds of conditions which make it plausible to suppose that rational men could reach agreement to limit their liberty even when other men's interest are not affected.

Of course as in any kind of agreement schema there are great difficulties in deciding what rational individuals would or would not accept. Particularly in sensitive areas of personal liberty, there is always a danger of the dispute over agreement and rationality being a disguised version of evaluative and normative disagreement.

Let me suggest types of situations in which it seems plausible to suppose that fully rational individuals would agree to having paternalistic restrictions imposed upon them. It is reasonable to suppose that there are "goods" such as health which any person would want to have in order to pursue his own good—no matter how that good is conceived. This is an argument used in connection with compulsory education for children but it seems to me that it can be extended to other goods which have this character. Then one could agree that the attainment of such goods should be promoted even when not recognized to be such, at the moment, by the individuals concerned.

An immediate difficulty arises from the fact that men are always faced with competing goods and that there may be reasons why even a value such as health—or indeed life—may be overridden by competing values. Thus the problem with the Christian Scientist and blood transfusions. It may be more important for him to reject "impure substances" than

to go on living. The difficult problem that must be faced is whether one can give sense to the notion of a person irrationally attaching weights to competing values.

Consider a person who knows the statistical data on the probability of being injured when not wearing seat belts in an automobile and knows the types of gravity of the various injuries. He also insists that the inconvenience attached to fastening the belt every time he gets in and out of the car outweighs for him the possible risks to himself. I am inclined in this case to think that such a weighing is irrational. Given his life plans, which we are assuming are those of the average person, his interests and commitments already undertaken, I think it is safe to predict that we can find inconsistencies in his calculations at some point. I am assuming that this is not a man who for some conscious or unconscious reasons is trying to injure himself nor is he a man who just likes to "live dangerously." I am assuming that he is like us in all the relevant respects but just puts an enormously high negative value on inconvenience—one which does not seem comprehensible or reasonable.

It is always possible, of course, to assimilate this person to creatures like myself. I, also, neglect to fasten my seat belt and I concede such behavior is not rational but not because I weigh the inconvenience differently from those who fasten the belts. It is just that having made (roughly) the same calculation as everybody else, I ignore it in my actions. [Note: a much better case of weakness of the will than those usually given in ethics tests.] A plausible explanation for this deplorable habit is that although I know in some intellectual sense what the probabilities and risks are I do not fully appreciate them in an emotionally genuine manner.

We have two distinct types of situation in which a man acts in a nonrational fashion. In one case he attaches incorrect weights to some of his values; in the other he neglects to act in accordance with his actual preferences and desires. Clearly there is a stronger and more persuasive argument for paternalism in the latter situation. Here we are really not—by assumption—imposing a good on another person. But why may we not extend our interference to what we might call evaluative delusions? After all, in the case of cognitive delusions we are prepared, often, to act against the expressed will of the person involved. If a man believes that when he jumps out the window he will float upwards—Robert Nozick's example—would not we detain him, forcibly if necessary? The reply will be that this man doesn't wish to be injured and if we could convince him that he is mistaken as to the consequences of his action, he would not wish to perform the action. But part of what is involved in claiming that the man who doesn't fasten his seatbelts is attaching an incorrect weight to the inconvenience of fastening them is that if he were to be involved in an accident and severely injured he would look back and admit that the inconvenience wasn't as bad as all that. So there is a sense in which, if I could convince him of the consequences of his action, he also would not wish to continue his present course of action. Now the notion of consequences being used here is covering a lot of ground. In one case it's being used to indicate what will or can happen as a result of a course of action and in the other it's making a prediction about the future evaluation of the consequences—in the first sense—of a course of action. And whatever the difference between facts and values—whether it be hard and fast or soft and slow—we are genuinely more reluctant to consent to interferences where evaluative differences are the issue. Let me now consider another factor which comes into play in some of these situations which may make an important difference in our willingness to consent to paternalistic restrictions.

Some of the decisions we make are of such a character that they produce changes which are in one or another way irreversible. Situations are created in which it is difficult or impossible to return to anything like the initial stage at which the decision was made. In particular, some of these changes will make it impossible to continue to make reasoned choices in the future. I am thinking specifically of decisions which involve taking drugs that are physically or psychologically addictive and those which are destructive of one's mental and physical capacities.

I suggest we think of the imposition of paternalistic interferences in situations of this kind as being a kind of insurance policy which we take out against making decisions which are far-reaching, potentially dangerous and irreversible. Each of these factors is important. Clearly there are many decisions we make that are relatively irreversible. In deciding to learn to play chess, I could predict in view of my general interest in games that some portion of my free time was going to be preempted and that it would not be easy to give up the game once I acquired a certain competence. But my whole life style was not going to be jeopardized in an extreme manner. Further it might be argued that even with addictive drugs such as heroin one's normal life plans would not be seriously interfered with if an inexpensive and adequate supply were readily available. So this type of argument might have a much narrower scope than appears to be the case at first.

A second class of cases concerns decisions which are made under extreme psychological and sociological pressures. I am not thinking here of the making of the decision as being something one is pressured into—for example, a good reason for making duelling illegal is that unless this is done many people might have to manifest their courage and integrity in ways in which they would rather not do so—but rather of decisions, such as that to commit suicide, which are usually made at a point where the individual is not thinking clearly and calmly about the nature of his decision. In addition, of course, this comes under the previous heading of all-too-irrevocable decisions. Now there are practical steps which a society could take if it wanted to decrease the possibility of suicide—for example not paying social security benefits to the survivors or, as religious institutions do, not allowing persons to be buried with the same status as natural deaths. I think we may count these as interferences with the liberty of persons to attempt suicide and the question is whether they are justifiable.

Using my argument schema the question is whether rational individuals would consent to such limitations. I see no reason for them to consent to an absolute prohibition but I do think it is reasonable for them to agree to some kind of enforced waiting period. Since we are all aware of the possibility of temporary states, such as great fear or depression, that are inimical to the making of well-informed and rational decisions, it would be prudent for all of us if there were some kind of institutional arrangement whereby we were restrained from making a decision which is so irreversible. What this would be like in practice is difficult to envisage and it may be that if no practical arrangements were feasible we would have to conclude that there should be no restriction at all on this kind of action. But we might have a "cooling off" period, in much the same way that we now require couples who file for divorce to go through a waiting period. Or, more far-fetched, we might imagine a Suicide Board composed of a psychologist and another member picked up by applicant. The Board would be required to meet and talk with the person proposing to take his life, though its approval would not be required.

A third class of decisions—these classes are not supposed to be disjoint—involves dangers which are either not sufficiently understood or appreciated correctly by the persons involved. Let me illustrate, using the example of cigarette smoking, a number of possible cases.

1. A man may not know the facts—for example, smoking between one and two packs a day shortens life expectancy 6.2 years, the costs and pain of the illness caused by smoking, et cetera.
2. A man may know the facts, wish to stop smoking, but not have the requisite willpower.
3. A man may know the facts but not have them play the correct role in his calculation because, say, he discounts the danger psychologically since it is remote in time and/or inflates the attractiveness of other consequences of his decision which he regards as beneficial.

In case 1 what is called for is education, the posting of warnings, et cetera. In case 2 there is no theoretical problem. We are not imposing a good on someone who rejects it. We are simply using coercion to enable people to carry out their own goals. (Note: There obviously is a difficulty in that only a subclass of the individuals affected wish to be prevented from doing what they are doing.) In case 3 there is a sense in which we are imposing a good on someone in that given his current appraisal of the facts he doesn't wish to be restricted. But in another sense we are not imposing a good since what is being claimed—and what must be shown or at least argued for—is that an accurate accounting on his part would lead him to reject his current course of action. Now we all know that such cases exist, that we are prone to disregarding dangers that are only possibilities, that immediate pleasures are often magnified and distorted.

If in addition the dangers are severe and far-reaching, we could agree to allow the state a certain degree of power to intervene in such situations. The difficulty is in specifying in advance, even vaguely, the class of cases in which intervention will be legitimate.

A related difficulty is that of drawing a line so that it is not the case that all ultra-hazardous activities are ruled out, for example, mountain-climbing, bull-fighting, sports-car racing, et cetera. There are some risks—even very great ones—which a person is entitled to take with his life.

A good deal depends on the nature of the deprivation—for example, does it prevent the person from engaging in the activity completely or merely limit his participation—and how important to the nature of the activity is the absence of restriction when this is weighed against the role that the activity plays in the life of the person. In the case of automobile seat belts, for example, the restriction is trivial in nature, interferes not at all with the use or enjoyment of the activity, and does, I am assuming, considerably reduce a high risk of serious injury. Whereas, for example, making mountain-climbing illegal completely prevents a person from engaging in an activity which may play an important role in his life and his conception of the person he is.

In general, the easiest cases to handle are those which can be argued about in the terms which Mill thought to be so important—a concern not just for the happiness or welfare, in some broad sense, of the individual but rather a concern for the autonomy and freedom of the person. I suggest that we would be most likely to consent to paternalism in those instances in which it preserves and enhances for the individual his ability to rationally consider and carry out his own decisions.

I have suggested in this essay a number of types of situations in which it seems plausible that rational men would agree to granting the legislative powers of a society the right to impose restrictions on what Mill calls "self-regarding" conduct. However, rational men knowing something about the resources of ignorance, ill-will and stupidity available to the lawmakers of a society—a good case in point is the history of drug legislation in the United States—will be concerned to limit such intervention to a minimum. I suggest in closing two principles designed to achieve this end.

In all cases of paternalistic legislation there must be a heavy and clear burden of proof placed on the authorities to demonstrate the exact nature of the harmful effects (or beneficial consequences) to be avoided (or achieved) and the probability of their occurrence. The burden of proof here is twofold—what lawyers distinguish as the burden of going forward and the burden of persuasion. That the authorities have the burden of going forward means that it is up to them to raise the question and bring forward evidence of the evils to be avoided. Unlike the case of new drugs, where the manufacturer must produce some evidence that the drug has been tested and found not harmful, no citizen has to show with respect to self-regarding conduct that it is not harmful or promotes his best interest. In addition the nature and cogency of the evidence for the harmfulness of the course of action must be set at a high level. To paraphrase a formulation of the burden of proof for criminal proceedings—better two men ruin themselves than one man be unjustly deprived of liberty.

Finally I suggest a principle of the least restrictive alternative. If there is an alternative way of accomplishing the desired end without restricting liberty although it may involve great expense, inconvenience, et cetera, the society must adopt it.

PATERNALISM: SOME SECOND THOUGHTS*

Gerald Dworkin

"I changed my mind."
"Oh, yeah? Does it work any better?"
　　　　　　　—FROM A MAE WEST MOVIE

I

As seems appropriate for second thoughts, I shall begin at the beginning—the definition of paternalism. Earlier, I defined the concept as

> *Interference with a person's liberty of action justified by reasons referring exclusively to the welfare, good, happiness, needs, interests, or values of the person being coerced.*[1]

A number of critics have objected that confining the concept to interferences with liberty is too restrictive in scope.[2] Given the problem I was interested in, i.e., the proper limits of state coercion, this restriction was reasonable, although even here one ought to be aware that the state has other ways of influencing people's behavior. It may refuse to enforce contracts, give in-kind rather than cash aid, set up licensing boards, require manufacturers to install seat-belts as original equipment, and so forth.

If, however, one wishes to consider the issue of paternalism in other contexts, for example, in the professions, one will need a broader definition. Not all paternalistic acts are acts of the state. Not all paternalistic acts involve interference with liberty. The doctor who lies to her terminally ill patients, the parent who stipulates in her will that a child may not inherit an estate before the age of thirty, the psychiatrist who tells his adolescent patient that he must inform her parents of her drug usage, the professor who refuses to recommend her Ph.D. student to a certain university because he will be "out of his league"—these are all cases of paternalism that do not involve the use of coercion or force and, therefore, on standard views of liberty do not involve restrictions on liberty.

How should one broaden the definition? One way is to include such specific elements as deception. Buchanan, for example, characterizes paternalism as

> *interference with a person's freedom of action or freedom of information, or the deliberate dissemination of misinformation.*[3]

Given a suitably broad notion of freedom of information, this definition will include not only the case of a doctor acting paternalistically toward a patient by misinforming him or by not revealing information, but also the case of a doctor telling a patient more than he wants to know. A patient may make it quite clear that he does not want to know something about his condition and a doctor may insist on telling him the whole truth for his own good.

Still this definition seems too restrictive in scope. There are other ways to paternalize besides coercing or manipulating one's information set. Suppose, for example, we play tennis together and I realize that you are getting upset about the frequency with

---

*From *Paternalism,* ed. by Rolf Sartorius (Minneapolis: University of Minnesota Press, 1983), pp. 105–12. Reprinted by permission of the publisher.

which you lose to me. So, for your own good and against your wishes, I refuse to play with you. My refusal to engage in a form of social cooperation does not seem to me an infringement of your liberty. But it also seems to me a case of paternalism.

On the other hand, the attempt to broaden the notion by including any violation of a moral rule is too restrictive because it will not cover cases such as the following.[4] A husband who knows his wife is suicidal hides his sleeping pills. He violates no moral rule. They are his pills and he can put them wherever he wishes.

This example, as well as that of the doctor who tells the patient the truth against his wishes, also works against defining paternalism in terms of acts that violate the rights of the person in question. The wife does not have a right to those pills, nor does the patient have a right not to be told the truth.

It begins to look as if the only condition that will work is one that depends upon the fact that the person who is being treated paternalistically does not wish to be treated that way. The wife has no right to the pills, but she does not want her husband to hide them. The patient has no right to not be told the truth, but he doesn't want to hear it. But something more must be present in order to include a case like the following:

Consider a father (a lawyer) who wants his daughter to become a lawyer. The daughter believes that she would make a very good lawyer. Indeed, she believes it likely that she would be more successful professionally than her father, who has managed to survive only on a marginal basis. Because she believes that such success would make her father very unhappy, the daughter decides to become a doctor instead. Here is a decision made against the wishes of another person for that person's own good. Yet, I think that this is not a case of paternalism. The daughter does nothing to interfere with the self-determination of the father. She does not act in accordance with her father's judgment, but neither does she act in such a fashion as to substitute her judgment for that of her father.

There must be a violation of a person's autonomy (which I conceive as a distinct notion from that of liberty) for one to treat another paternalistically. There must be a usurpation of decision-making, either by preventing people from doing what they have decided or by interfering with the way in which they arrive at their decisions.

An implication of this view is that there are no methods of influencing people that are necessarily immune to being used paternalistically. It is not as if rational argument cannot be paternalistic while brute force must be. Some people may want to make their decisions impulsively, without rational deliberation; insisting that they hear arguments (for their own good) is paternalism. On the other hand, brute force used to prevent someone from crossing a washed-out bridge need not be paternalism.

What we must ascertain in each case is whether the act in question constitutes an attempt to substitute one person's judgment for another's, to promote the latter's benefit.

It is because of the violation of the autonomy of others that normative questions about the justification of paternalism arise. The denial of autonomy is inconsistent with having others share the ends of one's actions—for if they would share the end, it would not be necessary to usurp their decision-making powers. At one level, therefore, paternalism seems to treat others as means (with the important difference that it is a means to their ends, not ours). But, at the same time, because we know that the relation between the good of a person and what that person wants is not a simple one, because what is in a person's interests is not always what satisfies his or her current desires, and because we can conceive of situations in which we would want to have our autonomy denied, the possibility of justifying some paternalistic intervention emerges.

One useful heuristic to guide our judgments about the justifiability of such interventions is to ask under what conditions does A's attempt to substitute his or her judgment for B's consitute treating B as less than a moral equal.

II

It is useful to distinguish between "hard" and "soft" paternalism. By soft paternalism, I mean the view that (1) paternalism is sometimes justified, and (2) it is a necessary condition for such justification that the person for whom we are acting paternalistically is in some way not competent. This is the view defended by Feinberg in his article "Legal Paternalism."[5] More precisely, his view is slightly stronger since the necessary condition is either that the conduct in question be substantially nonvoluntary, or that we need time to determine whether the conduct is voluntary or not. By hard paternalism, I mean the view that paternalism is sometimes justified even if the action is fully voluntary.

In arguing for a "hypothetical consent" scheme for justifying paternalism, I did not make clear whether I regarded the argument as *always* resting upon some deficiency in competence against which we wished to protect ourselves. I spoke of "irrational propensities, deficiencies in cognition and emotional capacities, and avoidable and unavoidable ignorance[6] as being rational reasons for agreeing (hypothetically) to limitations of our conduct, even when others' interest are not affected. I also spoke of insuring ourselves against making decisions which are "far-reaching, potentially dangerous, and irreversible." One set of considerations focuses on the agent; the other on the character of the decision. The former raises questions of rationality and competence; the latter of danger and harm.

The example of forcing people to wear seat-belts illustrates the difficulty I felt both about the correctness of paternalistic intervention and about the proper basis for its justification in such cases. Since I felt that intervention was legitimate, I sought to show that persons who do not fasten their seat-belts (at least most of them) are in some way failing in rationality. They either put an unreasonably high negative weight on what is at most an inconvenience, or discount unreasonably the probability or seriousness of future injury.

I think now that the issue must be faced more squarely. While it is possible to relate such cases to the soft paternalist thesis by claiming ignorance or weakness of the will, the strategy seems too ad hoc to be convincing. In any case, there will be other situations (for example, not allowing individuals to become slaves) in which this approach seems implausible. I propose, therefore, to consider three cases which are difficult for the soft paternalist, and to examine the strategies for dealing with them.

The first set of cases I shall call "safety cases." These include requiring motorcyclists to wear helmets, hunters to wear brightly colored jackets, sailors to carry life-preservers, and drivers to wear seat-belts. These are all instances of making people buy and use various items. They also include cases of preventing people from buying and using various things—bans on Red Dye No. 2, firecrackers, heroin.

The second set of cases is illustrated by the issue of putting fluoride in the community water supply. These cases differ from safety cases since, for example, we do not *require* anybody to drink fluoridated water. We just make it easy for those who wish to receive fluoride to do so and we make it correspondingly more difficult for those who do not wish to do so to avoid it. Since the argument for such measures involves a claim that there are certain actions that should be done collectively, I shall refer to these cases as "collective decisions."

The third set of cases are those forbidding people to sell themselves into slavery or to sell body parts to others. I shall refer to such cases as "slavery cases."

For all three types of cases I shall be making the assumption that there is no convincing reason for regarding the actions of the parties (not to wear helmets, not to be fluoridated, to enter into slavery) as necessarily less than voluntary.

Therefore, if one believes that the restrictive actions are justified, and if one believes that the justification is at least in part paternalistic, we have test cases for soft paternalism.

Of course, one can reject these as counter-examples by claiming that it would be wrong or unjustifiable to prevent people from becoming slaves or to force sailors to carry life-preservers. I confess that I do not see how to progress further with the argument if this is the point of disagreement. These judgments (that it is wrong to prevent people from becoming slaves, etc.) are part of a perfectly consistent position and one that is not in any way crazy. Of course, those who accept this consequence may do so because they are convinced on independent grounds that hard paternalism is unjustifiable. If so, one may be able to show that their arguments are not sound. But if the disagreement centers on these intuitions, I find it hard to see how it can be resolved.

The first strategy is to argue that the assumption I made about these cases is not valid. Anybody who would agree to become a slave or who would object to carrying a life-preserver must be in some way distracted, misinformed, impetuous, weak-willed, self-destructive, or so forth. In effect, this move denies that these are test-cases for soft paternalism. The contention seems implausible. One cannot argue *a priori* that persons who do such things are acting nonvoluntarily. Nothing in the concept of becoming a slave prohibits one doing this freely.

While there might be empirical evidence for the nonvoluntary character of many such actions, it is unlikely that all such acts will be nonvoluntary. I do not see how one can rule out the possibility that hard paternalism may be the only position which can justify restrictions on such actions.

The most likely response is that while interference may be justified in such cases, it may be for non-paternalistic reasons. The justification is based on the interests of third parties who are affected in ways that they have a right to be protected against.

The argument in the "safety" cases is that persons who are injured or killed because of their risky behavior impose costs on the rest of us. When the costs are economic, such as the costs of medical care, the obvious reply is that this might show that we can require such individuals to purchase medical insurance, but it does not show that we can require them to actually wear safety helmets.

Note that in purely economic terms it is quite likely that the effect of requiring motorcycle helmets is to cause badly injured persons to survive (requiring costly medical care) who otherwise might have died from head injuries!

If the costs result from the efforts involved in rescue operations and so forth, one could again require compensation for such effort as a matter of contract or tort law. But there will be certain individuals who intentionally or otherwise will not insure themselves and who may not be in a position to make financial compensation.

What do we do in the case of such individuals? The libertarian answer is that we announce ahead of time that such individuals will not be aided by us. But surely this imposes a psychic cost on us—that of ignoring or abandoning people in distress. There does seem to be an argument for interference here, because the rest of us do not want to be put in such a position.

In the case of hunters who are shot by other hunters because they do not wear brightly-colored clothing, there is another kind of cost. People have to bear the knowledge that they have caused harm (perhaps death) to another.

Ultimately I am left with the feeling that these arguments either are not relevant to justifying restrictions on behavior (although they may justify compulsory insurance) or, if they are relevant, do not seem strong enough to tip the scale by themselves. In the final analysis, I think we are justified in requiring sailors to take along life-preservers because it minimizes the risk of harm to them at the cost of a trivial interference with their freedom.

The second set of cases, those of "collective decisions," create difficulties for any consent scheme that requires unanimous consent; it is implausible to suppose that one can argue for the rationality of such consent without making various ad hoc assumptions about the extent to which we share common values, religious outlooks, and risk-taking preferences.

We are faced with the following problem. Suppose that most people in a community would consent to a certain practice, but that a minority would not. Although the best solution would be to exempt the minority, considerations of administrative and economic efficiency may make this solution very expensive. It is both more effective and cheaper to put fluoride in the community water supply than it is to distribute fluoride pills to those who want them or to supply nonfluoridated water to those who do not want fluoride.

If justice takes precedence over efficiency, the solution is clear. But this is not a question of determining the basic structure of society. It is more a constitutional question of deciding what powers to give the legislature. I am inclined to think that some balancing of interests is appropriate here. Knowing that we will be in the minority on some issues, and in the majority on others, it is reasonable not to demand unanimity for certain issues.

The relevant conditions are: (1) that the majority interest must be important (such as health); (2) that the imposition on the minority must be relatively minor (they have to buy their own water); and (3) that the administrative and economic costs of not imposing on the minority would be very high. However, fairness requires that if there are economic costs to the minority (such as purchasing nonfluoridated water), they should be borne by those who gain.

In this analysis, the restriction on the minority is not motivated by paternalistic considerations, but by the interests of a majority who wish to promote their own welfare. Hence, these are not paternalistic decisions, and do not count against soft paternalism.

Finally, we come to "slavery cases" in which people are not allowed to enter into certain voluntary agreements that would result in great loss of liberty or serious risk of bodily injury. While there may be a presumption in light of what we know about human nature that such choices are usually not fully voluntary, this is a presumption that may be rebutted in particular cases. These are also difficult cases for soft paternalism.

In these cases, however, there is a different line of argument open to the soft paternalist. Since the issue is whether a certain contract will be enforced rather than whether there will be a first-order restriction on the conduct itself, one might argue that different principles apply. Refusal to enforce such agreements may frustrate desires, but it is not a direct interference with liberty.

Again, one may look for third-party considerations. Most of us do not want to live in a society in which, for example, we are legally obligated to return runaway slaves to their owners. Such considerations underlie the general doctrine in contract law which does not require specific performance for the breach of a personal-service contract.

In my original paper, I argued that our objection to allowing voluntary slavery was linked to the promotion of the very value against which paternalism offends—autonomy. If we conceive of autonomy as the capacity of individuals to critically reflect on and take responsibility for the kind of persons they want to be, then we stop people from becoming slaves in order to preserve their future ability to define the kind of lives they want to lead. While I still find this argument plausible, my more recent reflections on autonomy raise the following theoretical problem. There is nothing in the idea of autonomy which precludes a person from saying:

I want to be the kind of person who acts at the command of others. I define myself as a slave and endorse those attitudes and preferences. My autonomy consists in being a slave.

If this is coherent, and I think it is, one cannot argue against such slavery on grounds of autonomy. The argument will have to appeal to some idea of what is a fitting life for a person and, thus, be a direct attempt to impose a conception of what is "good" on another person.

If, as I suspect, any person who adopted the above attitude would argue for it on grounds of maximizing some other good, the case may reduce to a safety-case as one of mistaken calculation about the best way of securing a person's good as conceived by her or him. The hard theoretical position may never be reached.

---

1. *Gerald Dworkin, "Paternalism,"* The Monist *56, no. 1, January 1972, p. 65.*
2. *See, for example, Bernard Gert and Charles Culver, "Paternalistic Behavior,"* Philosophy and Public Affairs *6, no. 1 (Fall, 1976), pp. 45–57.*
3. *Allen Buchanan, "Medical Paternalism,"* Philosophy and Public Affairs *7, no. 4 (Summer, 1978), p. 372.*

4. *This condition is Gert and Culver's.*
5. *Joel Feinberg, "Legal Paternalism,"* Canadian Journal of Philosophy *1, no. 1, pp. 106–24.*
6. *I would like to thank Daniel Brock, Leslie Francis, and Eric Mack for helpful comments on an earlier draft.*

MORALS AND THE CRIMINAL LAW*

Patrick Devlin

I think it is clear that the criminal law as we know it is based upon moral principle. In a number of crimes its function is simply to enforce a moral principle and nothing else. The law, both criminal and civil, claims to be able to speak about morality and immorality generally. Where does it get its authority to do this and how does it settle the moral principles which it en-

forces? Undoubtedly, as a matter of history, it derived both from Christian teaching. But I think that the strict logician is right when he says that the law can no longer rely on doctrines in which citizens are entitled to disbelieve. It is necessary therefore to look for some other source.

In jurisprudence . . . everything is thrown open

---

*From Patrick Devlin, *The Enforcement of Morals* (1965). Reprinted by permission of Oxford University Press.

to discussion and, in the belief that they cover the whole field, I have framed three interrogatories addressed to myself to answer:

1. Has society the right to pass judgement at all on matters of morals? Ought there, in other words, to be a public morality, or are morals always a matter for private judgement?
2. If society has the right to pass judgement, has it also the right to use the weapon of the law to enforce it?
3. If so, ought it to use that weapon in all cases or only in some; and if only in some, on what principles should it distinguish?

[1] I shall begin with the first interrogatory and consider what is meant by the right of society to pass a moral judgement, that is, a judgement about what is good and what is evil. The fact that a majority of people may disapprove of a practice does not of itself make it a matter for society as a whole. Nine men out of ten may disapprove of what the tenth man is doing and still say that it is not their business. There is a case for a collective judgement (as distinct from a large number of individual opinions which sensible people may even refrain from pronouncing at all if it is upon somebody else's private affairs) only if society is affected. Without a collective judgement there can be no case at all for intervention. Let me take as an illustration the Englishman's attitude to religion as it is now and as it has been in the past. His attitude now is that a man's religion is his private affair; he may think of another man's religion that it is right or wrong, true or untrue, but not that it is good or bad. In earlier times that was not so; a man was denied the right to practise what was thought of as heresy, and heresy was thought of as destructive of society.

The language [in] the Wolfenden Report suggests the view that there ought not to be a collective judgement about immorality *per se*. Is this what is meant by "private morality" and "individual freedom of choice and action"? Some people sincerely believe that homosexuality is neither immoral nor unnatural. Is the "freedom of choice and action" that is offered to the individual, freedom to decide for himself what is moral or immoral, society remaining neutral; or is it freedom to be immoral if he wants to be? The language of the Report may be open to question, but the conclusions at which the Committee arrive answer this question unambiguously. If society is not prepared to say that homosexuality is morally wrong, there would be no basis for a law protecting youth from "corruption" or punishing a man for living on the "immoral"

earnings of a homosexual prostitute, as the Report recommends.[1] This attitude the Committee makes even clearer when they come to deal with prostitution. In truth, the Report takes it for granted that there is in existence a public morality which condemns homosexuality and prostitution. What the Report seems to mean by private morality might perhaps be better described as private behaviour in matters of morals.

This view—that there is such a thing as public morality—can also be justified by *a priori* argument. What makes a society of any sort is community of ideas, not only political ideas but also ideas about the way its members should behave and govern their lives; these latter ideas are its morals. Every society has a moral structure as well as a political one: or rather, since that might suggest two independent systems, I should say that the structure of every society is made up both of politics and morals. Take, for example, the institution of marriage. Whether a man should be allowed to take more than one wife is something about which every society has to make up its mind one way or the other. In England we believe in the Christian idea of marriage and therefore adopt monogamy as a moral principle. Consequently the Christian institution of marriage has become the basis of family life and so part of the structure of our society. It is there not because it is Christian. It has got there because it is Christian, but it remains there because it is built into the house in which we live and could not be removed without bringing it down. The great majority of those who live in this country accept it because it is the Christian idea of marriage and for them the only true one. But a non-Christian is bound by it, not because it is part of Christianity but because, rightly or wrongly, it has been adopted by the society in which he lives. It would be useless for him to stage a debate designed to prove that polygamy was theologically more correct and socially preferable; if he wants to live in the house, he must accept it as built in the way in which it is.

We see this more clearly if we think of ideas or institutions that are purely political. Society cannot tolerate rebellion; it will not allow argument about the rightness of the cause. Historians a century later may say that the rebels were right and the Government was wrong and a percipient and conscientious subject of the State may think so at the time. But it is not a matter which can be left to individual judgement.

The institution of marriage is a good example for my purpose because it bridges the division, if there is one, between politics and morals. Marriage is part of the structure of our society and it is also the basis of a moral code which condemns fornication and adultery. The institution of marriage would be gravely threatened if individual judgements were permitted about the morality of adultery; on these points there must be a public morality. But public morality is not to be confined to those moral principles which support institutions such as marriage. People do not think of monogamy as something which has to be supported because our society has chosen to organize itself upon it; they think of it as something that is good in itself and offering a good way of life and that it is for that reason that our society has adopted it. I return to the statement that I have already made, that society means a community of ideas; without shared ideas on politics, morals, and ethics no society can exist. Each one of us has ideas about what is good and what is evil; they cannot be kept private from the society in which we live. If men and women try to create a society in which there is no fundamental agreement about good and evil they will fail; if, having based it on common agreement, the agreement goes, the society will disintegrate. For society is not something that is kept together physically; it is held by the invisible bonds of common thought. If the bonds were too far relaxed the members would drift apart. A common morality is part of the bondage. The bondage is part of the price of society; and mankind, which needs society, must pay its price. . . .

[2] You may think that I have taken far too long in contending that there is such a thing as public morality, a proposition which most people would readily accept, and may have left myself too little time to discuss the next question which to many minds may cause greater difficulty: to what extent should society use the law to enforce its moral judgements? But I believe that the answer to the first question determines the way in which the second should be approached and may indeed very nearly dictate the answer to the second question. If society has no right to make judgements on morals, the law must find some special justification for entering the field of morality: if homosexuality and prostitution are not in themselves wrong, then the onus is very clearly on the lawgiver who wants to frame a law against certain aspects of them to justify the exceptional treatment. But if society has the right to make a judgement and has it on the basis that a recognized morality is as necessary to society as, say, a recognized government, then society may use the law to preserve morality in the same way as it uses it to safeguard anything else that is essential to its existence. If therefore the first proposition is securely established with all its impli-

cations, society has a *prima facie* right to legislate against immorality as such.

The Wolfenden Report, notwithstanding that it seems to admit the right of society to condemn homosexuality and prostitution as immoral, requires special circumstances to be shown to justify the intervention of the law. I think that this is wrong in principle and that any attempt to approach my second interrogatory on these lines is bound to break down. I think that the attempt by the Committee does break down and that this is shown by the fact that it has to define or describe its special circumstances so widely that they can be supported only if it is accepted that the law is concerned with immorality as such.

The widest of the special circumstances are described as the provision of "sufficient safeguards against exploitation and corruption of others, particularly those who are specially vulnerable because they are young, weak in body or mind, inexperienced, or in a state of special physical, official or economic dependence."[2] The corruption of youth is a well-recognized ground for intervention by the State and for the purpose of any legislation the young can easily be defined. But if similar protection were to be extended to every other citizen, there would be no limit to the reach of the law. The "corruption and exploitation of others" is so wide that it could be used to cover any sort of immorality which involves, as most do, the co-operation of another person. Even if the phrase is taken as limited to the categories that are particularized as "specially vulnerable," it is so elastic as to be practically no restriction. This is not merely a matter of words. For if the words used are stretched almost beyond breaking-point, they still are not wide enough to cover the recommendations which the Committee makes about prostitution.

Prostitution is not in itself illegal and the Committee does not think that it ought to be made so.[3] If prostitution is private immorality and not the law's business, what concern has the law with the ponce or the brothel-keeper or the householder who permits habitual prostitution? The Report recommends that the laws which make these activities criminal offences should be maintained or strengthened and brings them (so far as it goes into principle; with regard to brothels it says simply that the law rightly frowns on them) under the head of exploitation.[4] There may be cases of exploitation in this trade, as there are or used to be in many others, but in general a ponce exploits a prostitute no more than an impresario exploits an actress. The Report finds that "the great majority of prostitutes are women whose psychological makeup is such that they choose this life because they find in it a style of living which is to them easier, freer and more profitable than would be provided by any other occupation. . . ." In the main the association between prostitute and ponce is voluntary and operates to mutual advantage.[5] The Committee would agree that this could not be called exploitation in the ordinary sense. They say: "It is in our view an oversimplification to think that those who live on the earnings of prostitution are exploiting the prostitute as such. What they are really exploiting is the whole complex of the relationship between prostitute and customer; they are, in effect, exploiting the human weaknesses which cause the customer to seek the prostitute to meet the demand."[6]

All sexual immorality involves the exploitation of human weaknesses. The prostitute exploits the lust of her customers and the customer the moral weakness of the prostitute. If the exploitation of human weaknesses is considered to create a special circumstance, there is virtually no field of morality which can be defined in such a way as to exclude the law.

I think, therefore, that it is not possible to set theoretical limits to the power of the State to legislate against immorality. It is not possible to settle in advance exceptions to the general rule or to define inflexibly areas of morality into which the law is in no circumstances to be allowed to enter. Society is entitled by means of its laws to protect itself from dangers, whether from within or without. Here again I think that the political parallel is legitimate. The law of treason is directed against aiding the king's enemies and against sedition from within. The justification for this is that established government is necessary for the existence of society and therefore its safety against violent overthrow must be secured. But an established morality is as necessary as good government to the welfare of society. Societies disintegrate from within more frequently than they are broken up by external pressures. There is disintegration when no common morality is observed and history shows that the loosening of moral bonds is often the first stage of disintegration, so that society is justified in taking the same steps to preserve its moral code as it does to preserve its government and other essential institutions.[7] The suppression of vice is as much the law's business as the suppression of subversive activities; it is no more possible to define a sphere of private morality than it is to define one of private subversive activity. It is wrong to talk of private morality or of the law not being concerned with immorality as such or to try to set rigid bounds to the part which the law may play in the suppression of vice. There are no theoretical limits to the power of the State to legislate treason and sedition, and likewise I think there can be no theoretical limits to legislation against immorality. You may argue that if a man's sins affect only himself it cannot be the concern of society. If he chooses to get drunk every night in the privacy of his own home, is any one except himself the worse for it? But suppose a quarter or a half of the population got drunk every night, what sort of society would it be? You cannot set a theoretical limit to the number of people who can get drunk before society is entitled to legislate against drunkenness. The same may be said of gambling. The Royal Commission on Betting, Lotteries, and Gaming took as their test the character of the citizen as a member of society. They said: "Our concern with the ethical significance of gambling is confined to the effect which it may have on the character of the gambler as a member of society. If we were convinced that whatever the degree of gambling, this effect must be harmful, we should be inclined to think that it was the duty of the state to restrict gambling to the greatest extent practicable."[8]

[3] In what circumstances the State should exercise its power is the third of the interrogatories I have framed. But before I get to it I must raise a point which might have been brought up in any one of the three. How are the moral judgements of society to be ascertained? By leaving it until now, I can ask it in the more limited form that is now sufficient for my purpose. How is the law-maker to ascertain the moral judgements of society? It is surely not enough that they should be reached by the opinion of the majority; it would be too much to require the individual assent of every citizen. English law has evolved and regularly uses a standard which does not depend on the counting of heads. It is that of the reasonable man. He is not to be confused with the rational man. He is not expected to reason about anything and his judgement may be largely a matter of feeling. It is the viewpoint of the man in the street—or to use an archaism familiar to all lawyers—the man in the Clapham omnibus. He might also be called the right-minded man. For my purpose I should like to call him the man in the jury box, for the moral judgement of society must be something about which any twelve men or women drawn at random might after discussion be expected to be unanimous. This was the standard the judges applied in the days before Parliament was as active as it is now and when they laid down rules of public policy. They did not think of themselves as making law but simply as stating principles which every right-minded person

would accept as valid. It is what Pollock called "practical morality," which is based not on theological or philosophical foundations but "in the mass of continuous experience half-consciously or unconsciously accumulated and embodied in the morality of common sense." He called it also "a certain way of thinking on questions of morality which we expect to find in a reasonable civilized man or a reasonable Englishman, taken at random."[9]

Immorality then, for the purpose of the law, is what every right-minded person is presumed to consider to be immoral. Any immorality is capable of affecting society injuriously and in effect to a greater or lesser extent it usually does; this is what gives the law its *locus standi*. It cannot be shut out. But—and this brings me to the third question—the individual has a *locus standi* too; he cannot be expected to surrender to the judgement of society the whole conduct of his life. It is the old and familiar question of striking a balance between the rights and interests of society and those of the individual. . . .

. . . It is possible to make general statements of principle which it may be thought the legislature should bear in mind when it is considering the enactment of laws enforcing morals.

I believe that most people would agree upon the chief of these elastic principles. There must be toleration of the maximum individual freedom that is consistent with the integrity of society. It cannot be said that this is a principle that runs all through the criminal law. Much of the criminal law that is regulatory in character—the part of it that deals with *malum prohibitum* rather than *malum in se*—is based upon the opposite principle, that is, that the choice of the individual must give way to the convenience of the many. But in all matters of conscience the principle I have stated is generally held to prevail. It is not confined to thought and speech; it extends to action, as is shown by the recognition of the right to conscientious objection in war-time; this example shows also that conscience will be respected even in times of national danger. The principle appears to me to be peculiarly appropriate to all questions of morals. Nothing should be punished by the law that does not lie beyond the limits of toleration. It is not nearly enough to say that a majority dislike a practice; there must be a real feeling of reprobation. Those who are dissatisfied with the present law on homosexuality often say that the opponents of reform are swayed simply by disgust. If that were so it would be wrong, but I do not think one can ignore disgust if it is deeply felt and not manufactured. Its presence is a good indication that the

bounds of toleration are being reached. Not everything is to be tolerated. No society can do without intolerance, indignation, and disgust [citation omitted]; they are the forces behind the moral law, and indeed it can be argued that if they or something like them are not present, the feelings of society cannot be weighty enough to deprive the individuals of freedom of choice. I suppose that there is hardly anyone nowadays who would not be disgusted by the thought of deliberate cruelty to animals. No one proposes to relegate that or any other form of sadism to the realm of private morality or to allow it to be practised in public or in private. It would be possible no doubt to point out that until a comparatively short while ago nobody thought very much of cruelty to animals and also that pity and kindliness and the unwillingness to inflict pain are virtues more generally esteemed now than they have ever been in the past. But matters of this sort are not determined by rational argument. Every moral judgement, unless it claims a divine source, is simply a feeling that no right-minded man could behave in any other way without admitting that he was doing wrong. It is the power of a common sense and not the power of reason that is behind the judgements of society. But before a society can put a practice beyond the limits of tolerance there must be a deliberate judgement that the practice is injurious to society. There is, for example, a general abhorrence of homosexuality. We should ask ourselves in the first instance whether, looking at it calmly and dispassionately, we regard it as a vice so abominable that its mere presence is an offence. If that is the genuine feeling of the society in which we live, I do not see how society can be denied the right to eradicate it. Our feeling may not be so intense as that. We may feel about it that, if confined, it is tolerable, but that if it spread it might be gravely injurious; it is in this way that most societies look upon fornication, seeing it as a natural weakness which must be kept within bounds but which cannot be rooted out. It becomes then a question of balance, the danger to society in one scale and the extent of the restriction in the other. On this sort of point the value of an investigation by such a body as the Wolfenden Committee and of its conclusions is manifest.

The limits of tolerance shift. This is supplementary to what I have been saying but of sufficient importance in itself to deserve statement as a separate principle which lawmakers have to bear in mind. I suppose that moral standards do not shift; so far as they come from divine revelation they do not, and I am willing to assume that the moral judgements made by a society always remain good for that society. But the extent to which society will tolerate—I mean tolerate, not approve—departures from moral standards varies from generation to generation. It may be that over-all tolerance is always increasing. The pressure of the human mind, always seeking greater freedom of thought, is outwards against the bonds of society forcing their gradual relaxation. It may be that history is a tale of contraction and expansion and that all developed societies are on their way to dissolution. I must not speak of things I do not know; and anyway as a practical matter no society is willing to make provision for its own decay. I return therefore to the simple and observable fact that in matters of morals the limits of tolerance shift. Laws, especially those which are based on morals, are less easily moved. It follows as another good working principle that in any new matter of morals the law should be slow to act. By the next generation the swell of indignation may have abated and the law be left without the strong backing which it needs. But it is then difficult to alter the law without giving the impression that moral judgement is being weakened. This is now one of the factors that is strongly militating against any alteration to the law on homosexuality.

A third elastic principle must be advanced more tentatively. It is that as far as possible privacy should be respected. This is not an idea that has ever been made explicit in the criminal law. Acts or words done or said in public or in private are all brought within its scope without distinction in principle. But there goes with this a strong reluctance on the part of judges and legislators to sanction invasions of privacy in the detection of crime. The police have no more right to trespass than the ordinary citizen has; there is no general right of search; to this extent an Englishman's home is still his castle. The Government is extremely careful in the exercise even of those powers which it claims to be undisputed. Telephone tapping and interference with the mails afford a good illustration of this. . . .

This indicates a general sentiment that the right to privacy is something to be put in the balance against the enforcement of the law. Ought the same sort of consideration to play any part in the formation of the law? Clearly only in a very limited number of cases. When the help of the law is invoked by an injured citizen, privacy must be irrelevant; the individual cannot ask that his right to privacy should be measured against injury criminally done to another. But when all who are involved in the deed are consenting parties and the injury is done to morals, the public interest in the moral order can be balanced against the claims of privacy. The restriction on police powers of investigation goes further than the affording of a parallel; it means that the detection of crime committed in private and when there is no complaint is bound to be rather haphazard and this is an additional reason for moderation. These considerations do not justify the exclusion of all private immorality from the scope of the law. I think that, as I have already suggested, the test of "private behaviour" should be substituted for "private morality" and the influence of the factor should be reduced from that of a definite limitation to that of a matter to be taken into account. Since the gravity of the crime is also a proper consideration, a distinction might well be made in the case of homosexuality between the lesser acts of indecency and the full offence, which on the principle of the Wolfenden Report it would be illogical to do.

---

1. *The Wolfenden Report* (New York: Stein and Day, 1963), Para. 76.

2. *The Wolfenden Report* (New York: Stein and Day, 1963), Para. 13.

3. *The Wolfenden Report* (New York: Stein and Day 1963), Paras. 224, 285, and 318.

4. *The Wolfenden Report* (New York: Stein and Day, 1963), Paras. 302 and 320.

5. *The Wolfenden Report* (New York: Stein and Day, 1963), Para. 223.

6. *The Wolfenden Report* (New York: Stein and Day, 1963), Para. 306.

7. *It is somewhere about this point in the argument that Professor Hart in Law, Liberty and Morality discerns a proposition which he describes as central to my thought. He states the proposition and his objection to it as follows (p. 51). "He appears to move from the acceptable proposition that some shared morality is essential to the existence of any society . . . to the unacceptable proposition that a society is identical with its morality as that is at any given moment of its history, so that a change in its morality is tantamount to the destruction of a society. The former proposition might be even accepted as a necessary rather than an empirical truth depending on a quite plausible definition of society as a body of men who hold certain moral views in common. But the latter proposition is absurd. Taken strictly, it would prevent us saying that the morality of a given society had changed, and would compel us instead to say that one society had disappeared and another one taken its place. But it is only on this absurd criterion of what it is for the same society to continue to exist that it could be asserted without evidence that any deviation from a society's shared morality threatens its existence." In conclusion (p. 82) Professor Hart condemns the whole thesis in the lecture as based on "a confused definition of what a society is."*

I do not assert that any deviation from a society's shared morality threatens its existence any more than I assert that any subversive activity threatens its existence. I assert that they are both activities which are capable in their nature of threatening the existence of society so that neither can be put beyond the law.

For the rest, the objection appears to me to be all a matter of words. I would venture to assert, for example, that you cannot have a game without rules and that if there were no rules there would be no game. If I am asked whether that means that the game is "identical" with the rules, I would be willing for the question to be answered either way in the belief that the answer would lead to nowhere. If I am asked whether a change in the rules means that one game has disappeared and another has taken its place, I would reply probably not, but that it would depend on the extent of the change.

Likewise I should venture to assert that there cannot be a contract without terms. Does this mean that an "amended" contract is a "new" contract in the eyes of the law? I once listened to an argument by an ingenious counsel that a contract, because of the substitution of one clause for another, had "ceased to have effect" within the meaning of a statutory provision. The judge did not ac-

cept the argument; but if most of the fundamental terms had been changed, I dare say he would have done.

The proposition that I make in the text is that if (as I understand Professor Hart to agree, at any rate for the purposes of the argument) you cannot have a society without morality, the law can be used to enforce morality as something that is essential to a society. I cannot see why this proposition (whether it is right or wrong) should mean that morality can never be changed without the destruction of society. If morality is changed, the law can be changed. Professor Hart refers (p. 72) to the proposition as "the use of legal punishment to freeze into immobility the morality dominant at a particular time in a society's existence." One might as well say that the inclusion of a penal section into a statute prohibiting certain acts freezes the whole statute into immobility and prevents the prohibitions from ever being modified.

8. (1951) Cmd. 8190, para. 159.
9. Essays in Jurisprudence and Ethics (1882), Macmillan, pp. 278 and 353.

MORALS AND CONTEMPORARY SOCIAL REALITY*

Patrick Devlin

Those who have followed the current controversy about the relationship between law and morals have now a number of doctrines to choose from. First and foremost, there is Mill's doctrine of liberty enunciated in 1859. Then there is the doctrine of Mr. Justice Stephen contained in his work *Liberty, Equality, Fraternity,* published in 1873, in which interest has recently been revived because of Professor Hart's detailed study of it in his book *Law, Liberty and Morality.* Then there is the statement of principle in the Wolfenden Committee's Report that "there must remain a realm of private morality and immorality which is, in brief and crude terms, not the law's business."[1] . . . Mr. Justice Stephen and myself can hardly claim doctrinal status; but we have been noticed because, as Professor Hart puts it, "though their arguments are at points confused, they certainly still deserve the compliment of rational opposition."[2] Then there are other modern statements of principle, notably by Dr. St. John-Stevas.

It is not therefore premature to inquire what is the doctrine held by Professor Hart.

There are at present four things to be said about that. The first is that it is not the doctrine enunciated by Mill, though Professor Hart still gives pride of place to "the famous sentence"[3] which is the core of Mill on liberty. Secondly, it has not yet been stated with that power of clarity and definition which Mill used so persuasively and which, I can say without flattery, Professor Hart is generally recognized also to possess. Thirdly, its nature has so far been revealed only accidentally in the course of Professor Hart's attempts to bring Mill's doctrine into contact with "contemporary social reality." Fourthly, it will, when it is stated, probably be well grounded on *terra firma* because it is one of Professor Hart's general objections to the views of Stephen and myself that they are not. "Stephen's doctrine, and much of Lord Devlin's," Professor Hart writes, "may seem to hover in the air above the *terra firma* of contemporary social reality; it may be a well-articulated construction, interesting because it reveals the outlook of the English judiciary but lacking application to contemporary society."[4]

I do not know that this is the outlook of the

*From Patrick Devlin, *The Enforcement of Morals* (1965). Reprinted by permission of Oxford University Press.

English judiciary. Certainly they are more often accused by their academic critics of crawling about on *terra firma* with their noses on the ground than of hovering above it. But in this case, and pursuing as I was an extra-judicial activity, I must at once admit the charge. I did not think that the argument had anything to do with contemporary social reality. I thought that it was completely doctrinaire. After all, Mill's doctrine has existed for over a century and no one has ever attempted to put it into practice. The vast majority of people in this country still believe that certain practices are morally wrong and are content that they should be forbidden by the law as such. There are groups of active and intelligent people who propose legal reforms which are thought to involve some impairment of moral principle, for example, about abortion and euthanasia. But no one goes so far as to suggest that abortions and killings of consenting adults are not part of the law's business. The recommendation of the Wolfenden Committee that homosexuality between consenting adults should no longer be criminal, in spite of the fact that it was backed by the overwhelming majority of its members, has not gained popular approval. On a free vote in the House of Commons in 1960 it was turned down by a large majority. If ever a bill of reform is introduced to give effect to it, it will, I venture to think, be supported only on the practical grounds which are so powerfully set out in the Report; and any ardent theorist who tries to tell the assembled legislators that their duty is without further ado to repeal a law that it was never their business to enact, is likely to be pulled down by the coat-tails by the contemporary realists behind him.

The pressure of opinion that in the end makes and unmakes laws is not to be found in the mouths of those who talk most about morality and reform, but in the hearts of those who continue without much reflection to believe most of what they learnt from their fathers and to teach their children likewise. What they believe may be quite wrong: but it is quite contemporary and quite real. So in a democracy the existing laws contain the best and most comprehensive statement of contemporary social reality. They are not a perfect statement. There is always some unrepealed junk that nobody will make the effort to get rid of. Moreover, of its nature the law cannot be immediately responsive to new developments and may need as a corrective the observation of the man up aloft who gauges the strength and direction of the winds of change. It is, for example, an arguable statement that the exaction of the death penalty is an antiquated idea on its way out. I dare say that the majority still favours its retention but probably with a declining belief in its value; and the House of Commons has actually voted in favour of its abolition. But at least until the point is reached when there is strong pressure against a particular law, the ideas of reformers, however well and articulately expressed, are not contemporary social reality but wishful thinking about the sort of society they would like to see; and if and when they become contemporary, it is improbable that they will take the exact form of the wishful thoughts. At present there is no real pressure whatever—the sort of pressure that governments have to take account of sooner or later—for any reform of the law based on the extrusion of moral principle. Mill's doctrine of liberty has made no conquests on *terra firma*.

I have not said any of this so as to decry the value of advanced thinking. I protest only against the notion that everyone who does not assent to the immediate colonization of all the territory that has been reconnoitred and skirmished over is lacking in a sense of contemporary reality. Nor did I use the word "doctrinaire" contemptuously. I believe that arguments about doctrine are useful as well as interesting. I do not suppose that a doctrine, such as Mill's on liberty, will ever be adopted or that law will ever be made in accordance with the principles he laid down. Examination over the years has revealed too many impracticabilities and possibly also, as Professor Hart suggests, "theoretical deficiencies."[5] But there is in it a vein of truth that has influenced immensely those who have studied it and will continue to do so. Undoubtedly, Professor Hart would agree with that, though he and I would differ profoundly about what is truth and what is error. That is a battle worth fighting but it has nothing whatever to do with contemporary social reality.

For these reasons I doubt whether it is now profitable to consider Mill's doctrine, except perhaps incidentally, in terms of its applicability to social reality. Certainly, it is not for the opponents of the doctrine, such as Mr. Justice Stephen and myself in matters of morals, to determine how it is to be applied. The most that we can do—and perhaps as much as it is legitimate to do—is to draw the attention of Mill's disciples to the fact that there is in England, as in all countries there always has been, a great deal of law that is inconsistent with the doctrine and to inquire what, if anything, they propose should be done about it. In fact, both Stephen and I made this inquiry, introducing it with what Professor Hart has called some "not very perspicuous remarks."[6]

Mill left the answer to Stephen's inquiry to his disciple, John Morley, who dismissed as "bustling ponderosity" this appeal to contemporary social reality. It was, he said, wholly irrelevant. The question was not what the laws were but what they ought to be. The controversy has, I think, remained at this high theoretical level until Professor Hart brought a practical mind to bear on it. Incidentally, Morley had opportunities rarely obtained by a rationalist philosopher of putting his theories into practice. He was a Member of Parliament for a great many years and one of the four men who formed the dominant group in Mr. Gladstone's last Cabinet. But he does not appear to have made any use of them.

Professor Hart does not take the high line. He acknowledges "the innocuous conservative principle that there is a presumption that common and long established institutions are likely to have merits not apparent to the rationalist philosopher."[7] I do not want here to assess the weight that should be given to the conservative principle. I think, if I may say so, that Professor Hart is right in thinking that with many minds its persuasive force would be very considerable; and that it is, so to speak, well worth his while to tackle the point and to clear up, if he can, what he says is the "confused and confusing"[8] use made by Stephen and others, including myself, of examples taken from the existing law. These include two fundamental principles and eight specific crimes which prima facie are inconsistent with the doctrine and the criminal law should be used only to protect others from harm to which they do not consent. Professor Hart would retain the two principles as clarified by himself, and two out of the eight specific crimes, namely, bigamy and cruelty to animals. One of the crimes, homosexuality, he would abolish. (I am of course considering these crimes only in so far as they relate to acts done in private between consenting adults.) There are five other crimes, namely, abortion, buggery in the form of bestiality, incest, obscenity, e.g. the sale of pornography, and offences connected with prostitution, such as pimping, poncing, and brothel keeping which can conveniently be categorized as the commercialization of vice. Professor Hart is silent about all of these, although there are indications that he would grant neither to abortion nor to the commercialization of vice the full protection afforded by the private realm. Undoubtedly, protection was denied to the latter by the recommendations of the Wolfenden Committee on prostitution.

It would, I hope, not be too uncharitable to suppose that Professor Hart has selected those examples which he finds it most convenient to deal with; but it would also be churlish not to acknowledge that he is, I believe, the first high authority to condescend so far. It is a curious thing that a century after the statement of the doctrine it is still not possible to say what amendments to the criminal law would flow from it; and that there is only one crime, that of homosexuality, that is known with certainty to lie within the private realm.

I should like to review Professor Hart's treatment of these matters. My purpose is not to see how far Professor Hart has succeeded in his object, though inevitably my opinion will emerge that within the framework of Mill's statement of his doctrine he has failed. My purpose is to see what happens to Mill's doctrine in the process. It seems to me that it is bumped so severely on *terra firma* as to be battered out of all recognition; and that what Professor Hart is prepared to put in its place can be glimpsed only through a glass darkly.

The first clash of principle arises over the part played by morality in the assessment of punishment. Mill would not allow morality to play any part in the making of the law. The bulk of the criminal law is taken up with offences which have the two characteristics of being offences against the moral law and of causing physical harm to the persons or property of other individuals. It is the second characteristic only which in the eyes of Mill and his disciples justifies the existence of the law. But if what justifies the making of the law is simply the prevention of harm, the offender must be punished accordingly. He must be punished for theft as he would be, for example, for a parking offence; the penalty must be calculated to prevent the repetition of the offence by him and to deter others from committing it. The offender's moral guilt is not a matter with which the law is concerned.[9]

This is not how in fact the law is administered. The degree of moral guilt is not the only determinant of the severity of the sentence but it is universally regarded as a very important one. It manifests itself in two ways. Firstly, in the gradation of offences in the criminal calendar: in order of gravity they are not arranged simply according to the harm done. Secondly, by taking into account the wickedness in the way the crime is committed: sentences for theft are not graded simply according to the amount of money stolen nor even according to more refined methods of estimating the harm done.

Professor Hart does not, as one might think he would, advocate the extrusion of morality from the assessment of punishment. Instead, he distinguishes between the system of punishment, whereunder only harmful conduct should be punished, and the quantum of punishment. He describes Stephen's failure to perceive the distinction between system and quantum as "an illuminating error."[10] I have a strong predisposition to think that there must be something in anything that is said by Professor Hart; but here I must admit failing to perceive either the error or what it illuminates. It is a doctrine firmly embedded in English law that power which is given for one purpose, whether to a minister or to a judge, must not be used for another purpose. That is abuse of power: and its prevention is essential to the existence of a free society. Under the law as it is now administered it would be an abuse of power to punish for immorality that is outside the law. It sometimes happens that an act which is a breach of the criminal law is also a breach of that part of the moral law that is not included in the criminal. Thus a course of deception might include an adultery. In such a case it would be wrong for the judge to increase the sentence appropriate to the crime because of the adultery. A judge may proportion his sentence according to the degree of immorality involved in the act itself but not according to extraneous immorality. On Mill's doctrine all immorality is extraneous. The moral content, if any, of an enactment is accidental and its presence or absence should make no difference.

Let me illustrate this by a comparison of morality with religion. The enactment of a law designed simply to enforce a religious belief would rightly be regarded as objectionable. Does this mean that we should now repeal a law which prohibits Sunday trading? Not necessarily, because it is desirable that there should be a universal day of rest and it might as well be Sunday as any other day; it can be justified on that ground. But would it then be proper, in the case of a breach by a practising Jew, to double the sentence on the ground that he was offending against a religious principle as well as against a social regulation? That would at once be condemned as bringing religion into the law. Why then is it permissible in the area of punishment to bring morality into the law?

Stephen's error, according to Professor Hart, lies in his "failure to see that the questions 'What sort of conduct may justifiably be punished?' and 'How severely should we punish different offences?' are distinct and independent questions."[11] I do not think that they are independent questions. They are a division, made for the sake of convenience, of the single question which is: "What justifies the sentence of punish-

ment?" The justification must be found in the law and there cannot be a law which is not concerned with a man's morals and yet which permits him to be punished for his immorality. If one can imagine a judge dividing a sentence into parts and sentencing a man to three months for the harm he has done to his victim and six months for his wickedness in doing it, the result would be just the same as if he had been separately charged under two separate sections of a statute, one which made the act an offence if done without any intent and another which made it a graver offence if done with a wicked intent. Consider a more plausible example of that sort given by Stephen. A judge says to the prisoner: "This is your first offence and a petty theft. In ordinary circumstances I would have given you another chance. But this particular theft was a despicable one, the stealing of money from someone who had trusted and befriended you. I cannot overlook that and shall sentence you to three months imprisonment." That is punishment for moral depravity and for nothing else.

I do not quarrel with the reasons which Professor Hart gives for allowing moral considerations to enter into the assessment of punishment. He points out[12] that if the scale of punishments for crimes conflicted with common estimates of their comparative wickedness, moral judgements might be confused and the law brought into disrepute. Principles of justice or fairness between different offenders, he says, require morally distinguishable offences to be treated differently and morally similar offences to be treated alike. I agree with this. But it seems to me to force his withdrawal from the firm line that the law is not concerned with morality as such. He says: " . . . in the theory of punishment, what is in the end morally tolerable is apt to be more complex than our theories initially suggest. We cannot usually in social life pursue a single value or a single moral aim, untroubled by the need to compromise with others."[13] This, if I may say so, is excellent sense. But why only "in the theory of punishment"? These are considerations which apply with equal force to the making of the law—to the question whether there should, for example, be a law against homosexuality at all. If the statutes in question were to be repealed, moral judgements might be confused and the law brought into disrepute because people would see moral wickedness going unpunished. That is one of the arguments against repeal. Against that there are the arguments of the misery caused to individuals and so on. The answer may be a compromise. But Professor Hart will not compromise on this because he says homosexuality is within the realm into which the law has no claim to enter; he cannot therefore discuss terms of entry. This is a theoretical proposition and must be defended as such.

Neither can there be any compromise in the theory of punishment. If by any chance Mill's doctrine had become the law and what we were discussing was how to make an impracticable piece of theory work in a way which would give as little dissatisfaction as possible to sensible people, then what Professor Hart says would be very much in point. But what we are discussing is quite different. It is whether the theory that the law may not be used to enforce morality as such is consistent with the theory that punishment under law may be adjusted according to the moral gravity of the act done. To my mind it clearly is not; and it seems to me to be an emasculation of Mill's doctrine to say that it is to apply only to the making of the law and not to the administration of it.

The second fundamental principle has to do with the function of consent in the criminal law. Mill's doctrine should make it always a good defence because the law should be concerned only with harming another against his will. But in general, consent is no defence, though there are crimes, such as rape and larceny, in which the absence of consent is an ingredient of the offence and has to be proved by the prosecution accordingly. One example of the ordinary crimes to which consent is no defence is murder in cases of euthanasia, duelling, and suicide pacts. Another is assault; some form of masochism would perhaps today be the most likely case of a willing submission to an assault.

The conclusion which I drew from this in my first lecture was that a breach of the criminal law was regarded as an offence not merely against the person injured but against society as a whole; and that an act done by consent, such as euthanasia, could be prohibited only as the breach of a moral principle which society required to be observed. Professor Hart says roundly that this "is simply not true."[14] The emphasis suggests that I have overlooked the obvious. What, alas, I did not foresee was that some of the crew who sail under Mill's flag of liberty would mutiny and run paternalism up the mast. Professor Hart considers that it is paternalism and not moral principle that is the justification of the law in these matters and he is thereby enabled to accept the second principle. "The rules excluding the victim's consent as a defence to charges of murder or assault may perfectly well be explained as a piece of paternalism, designed to protect individuals against themselves."[15]

"Mill no doubt might have protested," Professor Hart goes on in a meiosis which deserves to be commemorated. This tears the heart out of his doctrine. "His own good either physical or moral is not a sufficient warrant. He cannot rightfully be compelled to do or forbear because it will be better for him to do so, because it will make him happier, because in the opinions of others, to do so would be wise or even right."[16]

Professor Hart suggests that Mill might have objected not quite as much to paternalism as to the enforcement of moral principle.[17] He bases this on Mill's particularization of the three grounds on which compulsion would be wrongful. These, he says, are separate, the first two as I understand it, referring to paternalism, and the third to enforcement of morality. This seems to me a forced reading. Mill states his reasons cumulatively and not alternatively. If a man does what is wise and right, surely in Mill's view it would make him better and happier; he would not have distinguished between them. But anyway Professor Hart makes it quite plain that if the doctrine is divisible he abandons at least half of it.

I think, if I may say so without impertinence, that Professor Hart's argument might have been clearer if he had left Mill out of it. He gains no advantage by citing Mill as an authority. If Mill was obviously wrong about paternalism, why should he be right about enforcement of morals? Freed from the incubus of Mill, Professor Hart would doubtless have stated in his own words and with his customary precision how he defined the boundaries of the private realm. As it is, he does it by means of what he describes without overstatement as a "modification"[18] of Mill. I for one am left in genuine doubt about what the modification is.

Clearly it must be one that will accommodate paternalism at least to some extent. But will that be complete paternalism, i.e., in respect of all that makes a man better and happier? Or is a distinction being drawn between a man's physical good and his moral good? Is Professor Hart, so to speak, a physical paternalist and a moral individualist? I believe that one would have the answer to this if only one knew exactly what the distinction was between paternalism and legal moralism. The neglect of this distinction is, Professor Hart says, "a form of a more general error."[19] But what is legal moralism? It occurs when judges go "out of their way to express the view that the enforcement of sexual morality is a proper part of the law's business."[20] That is all the Professor Hart says about it.

But what exactly is it? If it is only a reprehensible judicial habit of moralizing *obiter,* it cannot be contrasted with paternalism so as to produce an illuminating distinction. Is it perhaps only another way of describing paternalism in matters of morality, which I shall call for short moral paternalism? This makes the whole argument readily comprehensible, provided only that it is possible to draw a line (which, for reasons I shall give, I think that it is not) between physical and moral paternalism.

If that is not the distinction, then it must lie between legal moralism and complete paternalism, that is, presumably, between the use of the law to enforce morals and its use to force a man to do what is for his own moral good. This is undoubtedly the distinction that fits in best with the language used by Professor Hart; he never expressly qualifies the use of the paternalism he advocates and there are passages in the text that suggest it to be of the widest kind. But then would not complete paternalism justify laws against immorality? (When talking of immorality in this part of the argument I had better restrict it to homosexuality because that is, as I have said, the only immorality which we know for certain is in Professor Hart's view both covered by the existing criminal law and included within the private realm as not the law's business.) Surely paternalism would make homosexuality the law's business if it is morally harmful to the man who is being paternalized. Yet if there is one thing that is clear, it is that Professor Hart wholeheartedly supports the Wolfenden Committee's recommendation that the law against homosexuality should be repealed on the ground that it is not the law's business.

Let me consider how "the famous sentence" in Mill would have to be restated so as to cover these alternative hypotheses.

Firstly, on the assumption that it has to cover only physical paternalism. Then it could read as follows. "The only purposes for which power can rightfully be exercised over any member of a civilized community against his will are to prevent harm to others or for his own physical good. His own moral good is not a sufficient warrant. He can rightfully be compelled to do or forbear because it will be physically better for him to do so or because it will make him [?physically] happier, but not because in the opinions of others, to do so would be wise or even right."

Secondly, on the assumption that it has to cover complete paternalism, physical and moral. Then it would have to read as follows. "The only purposes for which power can rightfully be exercised over any member of a civilized community against his will are to prevent harm to others or for his own physical or moral good. His own good either physical or moral is therefore a sufficient warrant. He can rightfully be compelled to do or forbear because it will be better for him to do so or because it will make him happier, but not because in the opinions of others, to do so would be wise or even right."

Clearly, the first restatement is less unattractive than the second. Its apologists who are prepared to believe that the doctrine is divisible can claim for this version that the amendment does not annihilate much more than half the doctrine and so might be described as an act of modification. The second restatement, I think it would have to be admitted, injures the whole doctrine almost to the point of destruction by direct contradiction and adds to the injury the insult of reducing it to nonsense. If the law will not let a man judge for himself whether an act will make him better and happier, how can it be judged except by the opinions of others? And if in the opinions of others the act is unwise or wrong, how could it in their opinion make him better and happier?

I shall now examine the distinction between physical and moral paternalism on which the first restatement is based. When dealing with the exclusion of consent as a defence to murder or assault, Professor Hart uses a phrase which suggests that he might be drawing a distinction between physical and moral paternalism. He refers to "using the law to protect even a consenting victim from *bodily* harm."[21] But I do not think that—at least in this connexion—he can mean the word "bodily" to be distinctive. It would be quite unrealistic to treat the crimes with which Professor Hart is dealing as offences against the body of the consenting party and not against morals. The most common case of a man willingly submitting to assault would, as I have suggested, be a case of masochism. To say that the law should intervene there not because of the vice but to protect the man in his own best interests from getting bodily hurt hardly seems sense. So in euthanasia. It cannot seriously be suggested that, if there were no moral principle involved, the law in a free country would tell a man when he was and when he was not to die, obtaining its mandate from its paternal interest in his body and not in his soul. Or that in euthanasia the crime lies not in the moral decision to seek death but purely in the physical and no doubt painless act that causes it.

If however there is an element of physical paternalism in the law that forbids masochism and euthanasia these crimes seem to me as good examples as any that could be selected to illustrate the difficulty in practice of distinguishing between physical and moral paternalism. Neither in principle nor in practice can a line be drawn between legislation controlling the individual's physical welfare and legislation controlling his moral welfare. If paternalism be the principle, no father of a family would content himself with looking after his children's welfare and leaving their morals to themselves. If society has an interest which permits it to legislate in the one case, why not in the other? If, on the other hand, we are grown up enough to look after our own morals, why not after our own bodies?

The terms in which Professor Hart justifies the sort of paternalism he advocates lead to the same conclusion. There is, he says, "a general decline in the belief that individuals know their own interests best."[22] There can be no reason to believe that if unable to perceive their own physical good unaided, they can judge of their own moral good. He continues: "Choices may be made or consent given without adequate reflection or appreciation of the consequences; or in pursuit of merely transitory desires; or in various predicaments when the judgment is likely to be clouded; or under inner psychological compulsion; or under pressure by others of a kind too subtle to be susceptible of proof in a law court."[23] These words, it seems to me, might almost have been written with homosexuals in mind. It is moral weakness rather than physical that leads to predicaments when the judgement is likely to be clouded and is the cause of inner psychological compulsion.

These considerations drive one to the conclusion that a distinction between moral and physical paternalism is not what Professor Hart has in mind. But the alternative hypothesis seems even more unacceptable. If it is difficult to draw a line between moral and physical paternalism, it is impossible to draw one of any significance between moral paternalism and the enforcement of the moral law. A moral law, that is, a public morality, is a necessity for paternalism, otherwise it would be impossible to arrive at a common judgement about what would be for a man's moral good. If then society compels a man to act for his own moral good, society is enforcing the moral law; and it is a distinction without a difference to say that society is acting for a man's own good and not for the enforcement of the law. Does the avoidance of legal moralism mean no more than that a judge ought not, when passing sentence, to mention that he is enforcing the law but only that he is acting for a man's own good?

Even this distinction vanishes if, as Professor Hart holds, a judge is entitled when passing sentence

to take into account the breach of the moral law. In such circumstances a sentence that avoided legal moralism would have to be framed on the following lines. "John Doe and Richard Roe, you have pleaded guilty to an act of gross indecency. In this country we regard such acts as morally wrong, but you are not standing in the dock because of that. You are in the dock because you have broken a law that was passed for your own moral good and because it is my duty to prevent you from breaking it again. If I were considering only your own good, I should bind you over on condition that you submitted to psychiatric treatment. But the law says that in order not to confuse moral judgements or to bring the law itself into disrepute, I am when passing sentence to have regard to the moral wickedness of your act. I shall therefore sentence you each to three months' imprisonment."

Finally, if it is possible, which I doubt, to draw a theoretical distinction between moral paternalism and the enforcement of morality, it is not one that is relevant to the present argument. The issue is whether there is a realm of private morality and immorality that is not the law's business. Paternalism, unless it is limited in some way as yet unstated, must, as I have pointed out, make all morality the law's business.

So both the restatements I have been considering lead to untenable, if not absurd, positions. Whatever modification Professor Hart contemplates is hardly likely to lead to absurdity. He must have in mind some substitution which he has yet to formulate.

In addition to the necessity for accommodating paternalism, a restatement or new statement will have to allow for other modifications which Professor Hart is prepared to admit. The offence of cruelty to animals can be accommodated if protection from harm is extended beyond humanity to all sentient beings. Some such thought may well have been in Mill's mind; for in his definition of the standard of morality in his *Utilitarianism* he refers not only to "all mankind" but also "so far as the nature of things admits, to the whole sentient creation."[24] Yet he did not go beyond mankind in "the famous sentence." It is not at once apparent how the modification would fit in with it, for if (apart from an obligation to refrain from cruelty as morally harmful to the perpetrator) a duty towards animals is admitted, it is not of the same kind as a duty towards other members of the same society.

Bigamy is also a crime which Professor Hart is prepared to accept on the ground that it is a public act offensive to religious feelings.[25] He thinks it doubtful whether Mill would have allowed the punishment of bigamy on this ground. Mill's own exception in respect of public acts was expressed as covering those which "are a violation of good manners" in which category he placed "offences against decency."[26]

Bigamy violates neither good manners nor decency. It is therefore a difficult crime for Mill's disciples to deal with. When it is committed without deception it harms no one; yet in these days of easy divorce bigamists do not arouse sympathy as homosexuals do and no one is very enthusiastic about altering the law in their favour. A variety of reasons for leaving the law as it is have been put forward, but the one selected by Professor Hart seems to me to wound Mill's doctrine more sharply than any other. A marriage in a registry office is only in form a public act. Mill's exception is grounded not upon a formal distinction between public and private but upon the right of society not to have obnoxious conduct forced on its attention. No one with deep religious feelings is likely to attend in the registry office; and the chance of the happy couple as they leave the office running into a man who happens to combine deep religious feelings with the knowledge that one of the parties has been married before is remote.

We have now reached a position in which the exceptions to Mill's doctrine must be expanded to cover the whole field of criminal punishment, some form of paternalism and offences against religious susceptibilities; and we are still left with five crimes about which Professor Hart says nothing. They are a diverse lot. It would be futile for me to try to anticipate the further series of modifications that would be necessary to accommodate them. I venture to think that Professor Hart's treatment of Mill has already proceeded far beyond the permissible limits of exegesis or even of amendment.

That completes the survey of the so-called modifications of Mill. It is not, I think, pedantic to insist that if they are to win any degree of acceptance, or even of understanding, they must be stated with a much higher degree of exactness. After all, Mill's doctrine of liberty, be it right or wrong, was formulated carefully and comprehensively and with exemplary clarity. It deserves the compliment of more precise treatment than it has received at the hands of Professor Hart. Until there has been a satisfactory restatement of it or a replacement of it by some other statement of comparable merit, there appears to me to be no room for any further discussion at the theoretical level.

At the practical level I think also with respect that Professor Hart's treatment of the subject is defective. At this level I assume that the purpose is to further the sort of reforms of the criminal law which Professor Hart mentions in the preface to his book. I do not doubt that a strong case can be made out for each of them taken by itself and on its own merits. There can be no practical reason for invoking some general principle of liberty in moral behaviour unless it is to cover a group of reforms which thus united in principle have an appeal which taken singly each would lack. If the statement that "there must remain a realm of private morality and immorality, which is, in brief and crude terms, not the law's business" is meant only as a slogan to draw attention in a dramatic way to the fact that homosexual offences are usually committed in private and without direct injury except to the participants, it is not worth further comment whether at the practical or theoretical level. If it is really meant as a statement of principle to include other immoralities besides the homosexual, every practical reformer before he makes use of it will want to be told what else it embraces. To do as Professor Hart does and to pick out one or two offences which it excludes will win no adherents. What those interested in reform will want to know is whether, if the principle is conceded in the case of homosexuality, some other and what parts of the existing criminal law will be carried away as well. Incest? Abortion? Bestiality? Does the principle cover legislation against brothels and pornography; and if not, why not? These are not questions that can be shirked indefinitely by anyone who regards the principle as relevant to contemporary social reality.

---

1. *The Wolfenden Report, para. 61.*
2. *H. L. A. Hart,* Law, Liberty and Morality *(Stanford University Press, 1964), p. 17.*
3. *Ibid., p. 4. The famous sentence is quoted at p. 103,* supra.
4. *Hart, op. cit., p. 63.*
5. *Ibid., p. 16.*
6. *Ibid., p. 29.*
7. *Loc. cit.*
8. *Ibid.*
9. *This is the view adopted by Lady Wooton when* Crime and the Criminal Law, *pp. 41ff. It would involve an upheaval of the criminal law that evidently does not commend itself to Professor Hart.*
10. *Hart, op cit., p. 34.*
11. *Ibid., p. 36.*
12. *Ibid., pp. 36—37.*
13. *Ibid., p. 38.*

14. Ibid., *p. 31.*
15. Loc. cit.
16. *Mill,* On Liberty, *chap. 4.*
17. *I confess that there is no real distinction between the two.*
18. *Hart, op. cit., p. 33.*
19. Ibid., *p. 34.*
20. Ibid., *p. 6.*

21. Ibid., *p. 31. Emphasis added.*
22. Ibid., *p. 32.*
23. Ibid., *p. 33.*
24. *Mill,* op. cit., *chap. 1.*
25. *Hart,* op. cit., *p. 42.*
26. *Mill,* op cit., *chap. 3.*

Constitutional Privacy

*GRISWOLD V. CONNECTICUT**

United States Supreme Court, 1965

Mr. Justice Douglas delivered the opinion of the Court.

Appellant Griswold is Executive Director of the Planned Parenthood League of Connecticut. Appellant Buxton is a licensed physician and a professor at the Yale Medical School who served as Medical Director for the League at its Center in New Haven—a center open and operating from November 1 to November 10, 1961, when appellants were arrested.

They gave information, instruction, and medical advice to *married persons* as to the means of preventing conception. They examined the wife and prescribed the best contraceptive device or material for her use. Fees were usually charged, although some couples were serviced free.

The statutes whose constitutionality is involved in this appeal are §§ 53-32 and 54-196 of the General Statutes of Connecticut (1958 rev.). The former provides:

> *"Any person who uses any drug, medicinal article or instrument for the purpose of preventing conception shall be fined not less than fifty dollars or imprisoned not less than sixty days nor more than one year or be both fined and imprisoned."*

Section 54-196 provides:

> *"Any person who assists, abets, counsels, causes, hires or commands another to commit any offense may be prosecuted and punished as if he were the principal offender."*

The appellants were found guilty as accessories and fined $100 each, against the claim that the accessory statute as so applied violated the Fourteenth Amendment. The Appellate Division of the Circuit Court affirmed. The Supreme Court of Errors affirmed that judgment.

We think that appellants have standing to raise the constitutional rights of the married people with whom they had a professional relationship. . . . Certainly the accessory should have standing to assert that the offense which he is charged with assisting is not, or cannot constitutionally be, a crime. . . .

Coming to the merits, we are met with a wide range of questions that implicate the Due Process Clause of the Fourteenth Amendment. Overtones of some arguments suggest that *Lochner* v. *New York,* 198 U.S. 45, should be our guide. But we decline that invitation. We do not sit as a super-legislature to determine the wisdom, need, and propriety of laws that touch economic problems, business affairs, or social conditions. This law, however, operates directly on an intimate relation of husband and wife and their physician's role in one aspect of that relation.

The association of people is not mentioned in the Constitution nor in the Bill of Rights. The right to educate a child in a school of the parents' choice—

*381 U.S. 479 (1965). Excerpts only. Footnotes renumbered. Citations omitted.

whether public or private or parochial—is also not mentioned. Nor is the right to study any particular subject or any foreign language. Yet the First Amendment has been construed to include certain of those rights.

By *Pierce* v. *Society of Sisters,* the right to educate one's children as one chooses is made applicable to the States by the force of the First and Fourteenth Amendments. By *Meyer* v. *Nebraska,* the same dignity is given the right to study the German language in a private school. In other words, the State may not, consistently with the spirit of the First Amendment, contract the spectrum of available knowledge. The right of freedom of speech and press includes not only the right to utter or to print, but the right to distribute, the right to receive, the right to read and freedom of inquiry, freedom of thought, and freedom to teach—indeed the freedom of the entire university community. Without those peripheral rights the specific rights would be less secure. . . .

In *NAACP* v. *Alabama,* 357 U.S. 449, 462, we protected the "freedom to associate and privacy in one's associations," noting that freedom of association was a peripheral First Amendment right. Disclosure of membership lists of a constitutionally valid association, we held, was invalid "as entailing the likelihood of a substantial restraint upon the exercise by petitioner's members of their right to freedom of association." *Ibid.* In other words, the First Amendment has a penumbra where privacy is protected from governmental intrusion. In like context, we have protected forms of "association" that are not political in the customary sense but pertain to the social, legal, and economic benefit of the members. In *Schware* v. *Board of Bar Examiners,* 353 U.S. 232, we held it not permissible to bar a lawyer from practice, because he had once been a member of the Communist Party. The man's "association with that Party" was not shown to be "anything more than a political faith in a political party" and was not action of a kind proving bad moral character.

Those cases involved more than the "right of assembly"—a right that extends to all irrespective of their race or ideology. The right of "association," like the right of belief, is more than the right to attend a meeting; it includes the right to express one's attitudes or philosophies by membership in a group or by affiliation with it or by other lawful means. Association in that context is a form of expression of opinion; and while it is not expressly included in the First Amendment its existence is necessary in making the express guarantees fully meaningful.

The foregoing cases suggest that specific guarantees in the Bill of Rights have penumbras, formed by emanations from those guarantees that help give them life and substance. Various guarantees create zones of privacy. The right of association contained in the penumbra of the First Amendment is one, as we have seen. The Third Amendment in its prohibition against the quartering of soldiers "in any house" in time of peace without the consent of the owner is another facet of that privacy. The Fourth Amendment explicitly affirms the "right of the people to be secure in their persons, houses, papers, and effects, against unreasonable searches and seizures." The Fifth Amendment in its Self-Incrimination Clause enables the citizen to create a zone of privacy which government may not force him to surrender to his detriment. The Ninth Amendment provides: "The enumeration in the Constitution, of certain rights, shall not be construed to deny or disparage others retained by the people."

The Fourth and Fifth Amendments were described in *Boyd* v. *United States,* 116 U.S. 616, 630, as protection against all governmental invasions "of the sanctity of a man's home and the privacies of life." We recently referred in *Mapp* v. *Ohio,* 367 U.S. 643, 656, to the Fourth Amendment as creating a "right to privacy, no less important than any other right carefully and particularly reserved to the people." These cases bear witness that the right of privacy which presses for recognition here is a legitimate one.

The present case, then, concerns a relationship lying within the zone of privacy created by several fundamental constitutional guarantees. And it concerns a law which, in forbidding the *use* of contraceptives rather than regulating their manufacture or sale, seeks to achieve its goals by means having a maximum destructive impact upon that relationship. Such a law cannot stand in light of the familiar principle, so often applied by this Court, that a "governmental purpose to control or prevent activities constitutionally subject to state regulation may not be achieved by means which sweep unnecessarily broadly and thereby invade the area of protected freedoms." *NAACP* v. *Alabama,* 377 U.S. 288, 307. Would we allow the police to search the sacred precincts of marital bedrooms for telltale signs of the use of contraceptives? The very idea is repulsive to the notions of privacy surrounding the marriage relationship.

We deal with a right of privacy older than the Bill of Rights—older than our political parties, older than our school system. Marriage is a coming together for better or for worse, hopefully enduring, and intimate to the degree of being sacred. It is an association that promotes a way of life, not causes; a harmony in living, not political faiths; a bilateral loyalty, not commercial or social projects. Yet it is an association for as noble a purpose as any involved in our prior decisions.

Reversed.

Mr. Justice Goldberg, whom The Chief Justice and Mr. Justice Brennan join, concurring. . . . My Brother Stewart dissents on the ground that he "can find no . . . general right of privacy in the Bill of Rights, in any other part of the Constitution, or in any case ever before decided by this Court." He would require a more explicit guarantee than the one which the Court derives from several constitutional amendments. This Court, however, has never held that the Bill of Rights or the Fourteenth Amendment protects only those rights that the Constitution specifically mentions by name. . . .

My Brother Stewart, while characterizing the Connecticut birth control law as "an uncommonly silly law," would nevertheless let it stand on the ground that it is not for the courts to "'substitute their social and economic beliefs for the judgment of legislative bodies, who are elected to pass laws.'" Elsewhere, I have stated that "[w]hile I quite agree with Mr. Justice Brandeis that . . . 'a . . . State may . . . serve as a laboratory; and try novel social and economic experiments,' I do not believe that this includes the power to experiment with the fundamental liberties of citizens. . . ." The vice of the dissenters' views is that it would permit such experimentation by the States in the area of the fundamental personal rights of its citizens. I cannot agree that the Constitution grants such either to the States or to the Federal Government.

The logic of the dissents would sanction federal or state legislation that seems to me even more plainly unconstitutional than the statute before us. Surely the Government, absent a showing of a compelling subordinating state interest, could not decree that all husbands and wives must be sterilized after two children have been born to them. Yet by their reasoning such an invasion of marital privacy would not be subject to constitutional challenge because, while it might be "silly," no provision of the Constitution specifically prevents the Government from curtailing the marital right to bear children and raise a family. While it may shock some of my Brethren that the Court today holds that the Constitution protects the right of marital privacy in my view it is far more shocking to believe that the personal liberty guaranteed by the Constitution does not include protection against such totalitarian

limitation of family size, which is at complete variance with our constitutional concepts. Yet, if upon a showing of a slender basis of rationality, a law outlawing voluntary birth control by married persons is valid, then, by the same reasoning a law requiring compulsory birth control also would seem to be valid. In my view, however, both types of law would unjustifiably intrude upon rights of marital privacy which are constitutionally protected.

In a long series of cases this Court has held that where fundamental personal liberties are involved, they may not be abridged by the States simply on a showing that a regulatory statute has some rational relationship to the effectuation of a proper state purpose. "Where there is a significant encroachment upon personal liberty, the State may prevail only upon showing a subordinating interest which is compelling," *Bates* v. *Little Rock,* 361 U.S. 516, 524. The law must be shown "necessary, and not merely rationally related, to the accomplishment of a permissible state policy." *McLaughlin* v. *Florida,* 379 U.S. 184, 196.

Although the Connecticut birth-control law obviously encroaches upon a fundamental personal liberty, the State does not show that the law serves any "subordinating [state] interest which is compelling" or that it is "necessary . . . to the accomplishment of a permissible state policy." The State, at most, argues that there is some rational relation between this statute and what is admittedly a legitimate subject of state concern—the discouraging of extra-marital relations. It says that preventing the use of birth-control devices by married persons helps prevent the indulgence by some in such extra-marital relations. The rationality of this justification is dubious, particularly in light of the admitted widespread availability to all persons in the State of Connecticut, unmarried as well as married, of birth-control devices for the prevention of disease, as distinguished from the prevention of conception. But, in any event, it is clear that the state interest in safeguarding marital fidelity can be served by a more discriminately tailored statute, which does not, like the present one, sweep unnecessarily broadly, reaching far beyond the evil sought to be dealt with and intruding upon the privacy of all married couples. Here, as elsewhere, "[p]recision of regulation must be the touchstone in an area so closely touching our most precious freedoms." *NAACP* v. *Button,* 371 U.S. 415, 438. The State of Connecticut does have statutes, the constitutionality of which is beyond doubt, which prohibit adultery and fornication. These statutes demonstrate that means for achieving the same basic purpose of protecting marital fidelity are available to Connecticut without the need to "invade the area of protected freedoms." *NAACP* v. *Alabama, supra,* at 307.

Finally, it should be said of the Court's holding today that it in no way interferes with a State's proper regulation of sexual promiscuity or misconduct. As my Brother Harlan so well stated in his dissenting opinion in *Poe* v. *Ullman,*

> *"Adultery, homosexuality and the like are sexual intimacies which the State forbids . . . but the intimacy of husband and wife is necessarily an essential and accepted feature of the institution of marriage, an institution which the State not only must allow, but which always and in every age it has fostered and protected. It is one thing when the State exerts its power either to forbid extra-marital sexuality . . . or to say who may marry, but it is quite another when, having acknowledged a marriage and the intimacies inherent in it, it undertakes to regulate by means of the criminal law the details of that intimacy."*

In sum, I believe that the right of privacy in the marital relation is fundamental and basic—a personal right "retained by the people" within the meaning of the Ninth Amendment. Connecticut cannot constitutionally abridge this fundamental right, which is protected by the Fourteenth Amendment from infringement by the States. I agree with the Court that petitioners' convictions must therefore be reversed. . . .

Mr. Justice Black, with whom Mr. Justice Stewart joins, dissenting.

I agree with my Brother Stewart's dissenting opinion. And like him I do not to any extent whatever base my view that this Connecticut law is constitutional on a belief that the law is wise or that its policy is a good one. In order that there may be no room at all to doubt why I vote as I do, I feel constrained to add that the law is every bit as offensive to me as it is to my Brethren of the majority and my Brothers Harlan, White and Goldberg who, reciting reasons why it is offensive to them, hold it unconstitutional. There is no single one of the graphic and eloquent strictures and criticisms fired at the policy of this Connecticut law either by the Court's opinion or by those of my concurring Brethren to which I cannot subscribe—except their conclusion that the evil qualities they see in the law make it unconstitutional. . . .

The Court talks about a constitutional "right of privacy" as though there is some constitutional provision or provisions forbidding any law ever to be passed which might abridge the "privacy" of individ-

uals. But there is not. There are, of course, guarantees in certain specific constitutional provisions which are designed in part to protect privacy at certain times and places with respect to certain activities. Such, for example, is the Fourth Amendment's guarantee against "unreasonable searches and seizures." But I think it belittles that Amendment to talk about it as though it protects nothing but "privacy." To treat it that way is to give it a niggardly interpretation, not the kind of liberal reading I think any Bill of Rights provision should be given. The average man would very likely not have his feelings soothed any more by having his property seized openly than by having it seized privately and by stealth. He simply wants his property left alone. And a person can be just as much, if not more, irritated, annoyed and injured by an unceremonious public arrest by a policeman as he is by a seizure in the privacy of his office or home.

One of the most effective ways of diluting or expanding a constitutionally guaranteed right is to substitute for the crucial word or words of a constitutional guarantee another word or words, more or less flexible and more or less restricted in meaning. This fact is well illustrated by the use of the term "right of privacy" as a comprehensive substitute for the Fourth Amendment's guarantee against "unreasonable searches and seizures." "Privacy" is a broad, abstract and ambiguous concept which can easily be shrunken in meaning but which can also, on the other hand, easily be interpreted as a constitutional ban against many things other than searches and seizures. I have expressed the view many times that First Amendment freedoms, for example, have suffered from a failure of the courts to stick to the simple language of the First Amendment in construing it, instead of invoking multitudes of words substituted for those the Framers used. For these reasons I get nowhere in this case by talk about a constitutional "right of privacy" as an emanation from one or more constitutional provisions. I like my privacy as well as the next one, but I am nevertheless compelled to admit that government has a right to invade it unless prohibited by some specific constitutional provision. For these reasons I cannot agree with the Court's judgment and the reasons it gives for holding this Connecticut law unconstitutional. . . .

The due process argument which my Brothers Harlan and White adopt here is based, as their opinions indicate, on the premise that this Court is vested with power to invalidate all state laws that it considers to be arbitrary, capricious, unreasonable, or oppressive, or on this Court's belief that a particular state law under scrutiny has no "rational or justifying" purpose, or is offensive to a "sense of fairness and justice." If these formulas based on "natural justice," or others which mean the same thing,[1] are to prevail, they require judges to determine what is or is not constitutional on the basis of their own appraisal of what laws are unwise or unnecessary. The power to make such decisions is of course that of a legislative body. Surely it has to be admitted that no provision of the Constitution specifically gives such blanket power to courts to exercise such a supervisory veto over the wisdom and value of legislative policies and to hold unconstitutional those laws which they believe unwise or dangerous. I readily admit that no legislative body, state or national, should pass laws that can justly be given any of the invidious labels invoked as constitutional excuses to strike down state laws. But perhaps it is not too much to say that no legislative body ever does pass laws without believing that they will accomplish a sane, rational, wise and justifiable purpose. While I completely subscribe to the holding of *Marbury* v. *Madison,* and subsequent cases, that our Court has constitutional power to strike down statutes, state or federal, that violate commands of the Federal Constitution, I do not believe that we are granted power by the Due Process Clause or any other constitutional provision or provisions to measure constitutionality by our belief that legislation is arbitrary, capricious or unreasonable, or accomplishes no justifiable purpose, or is offensive to our own notions of "civilized standards of conduct."[2] Such an appraisal of the wisdom of legislation is an attribute of the power to make laws, not of the power to interpret them. The use by federal courts of such a formula or doctrine or whatnot to veto federal or state laws simply takes away from Congress and States the power to make laws based on their own judgment of fairness and wisdom and transfers that power to this Court for ultimate determination—a power which was specifically denied to federal courts by the convention that framed the Constitution. . . .

My Brother Goldberg has adopted the recent discovery[3] that the Ninth Amendment as well as the Due Process Clause can be used by this Court as authority to strike down all state legislation which this Court thinks violates "fundamental principles of liberty and justice," or is contrary to the "traditions and [collective] conscience of our people." He also states,

without proof satisfactory to me, that in making decisions on this basis judges will not consider "their personal and private notions." One may ask how they can avoid considering them. Our Court certainly has no machinery with which to take a Gallup Poll.[4] And the scientific miracles of this age have not yet produced a gadget which the Court can use to determine what traditions are rooted in the "[collective] conscience of our people." Moreover, one would certainly have to look far beyond the language of the Ninth Amendment[5] to find that the Framers vested in this Court any such awesome veto powers over lawmaking, either by the States or by the Congress. Nor does anything in the history of the Amendment offer any support for such a shocking doctrine. The whole history of the adoption of the Constitution and Bill of Rights points the other way, and the very material quoted by my Brother Goldberg shows that the Ninth Amendment was intended to protect against the idea that "by enumerating particular exceptions to the grant of power" to the Federal Government, "those rights which were not singled out, were intended to be assigned into the hands of the General Government [the United States], and were consequently insecure."[6] That Amendment was passed, not to broaden the powers of this Court or any other department of "the General Government," but, as every student of history knows, to assure the people that the Constitution in all its provisions was intended to limit the Federal Government to the powers granted expressly or by necessary implication. If any broad, unlimited power to hold laws unconstitutional because they offend what this Court conceives to be the "[collective] conscience of our people" is vested in this Court by the Ninth Amendment, the Fourteenth Amendment, or any other provision of the Constitution, it was not given by the Framers, but rather has been bestowed on the Court by the Court. This fact is perhaps responsible for the peculiar phenomenon that for a period of a century and a half no serious suggestion was ever made that the Ninth Amendment, enacted to protect state powers against federal invasion, could be used as a weapon of federal power to prevent state legislatures from passing laws they consider appropriate to govern local affairs. Use of any such broad, unbounded judicial authority would make of this Court's members a day-to-day constitutional convention.

---

1. *A collection of the catchwords and catch phrases invoked by judges who would strike down under the Fourteenth Amendment* *laws which offend their notions of natural justice would fill many pages. Thus it has been said that this Court can forbid state action*

which "shocks the conscience," Rochin v. California, *342 U.S. 165, 172*, sufficiently to "shock itself into the protective arms of the Constitution," Irvine v. California, *347 U.S. 128, 138 (concurring opinion)*. It has been urged that States may not run counter to the "decencies of civilized conduct," Rochin, supra, at *173*, or "some principle of justice so rooted in the traditions, and conscience of our people as to be ranked as fundamental," Snyder v. Massachusetts, *291 U.S. 97, 105*, or to "those canons of decency and fairness which express the notions of justice of English-speaking peoples," Malinski v. New York, *324 U.S. 401, 417 (concurring opinion)*, or to "the community's sense of fair play and decency," Rochin, supra, at *173*. It has been said that we must decide whether a state law is "fair, reasonable and appropriate," or is rather "an unreasonable, unnecessary and arbitrary interference with the right of the individual to his personal liberty or to enter into . . . contracts," Lochner v. New York, *198 U.S. 45, 56*. States, under this philosophy, cannot act in conflict with "deeply rooted feelings of the community," Haley v. Ohio, *332 U.S. 596, 604 (separate opinion)*, or with "fundamental notions of fairness and justice," id., *607*. See also, e.g., Wolf v. Colorado, *338 U.S. 25, 27* ("rights . . . basic to our free society"); Hebert v. Louisiana, *272 U.S. 312, 316* ("fundamental principles of liberty and justice"); Adkins v. Children's Hospital, *261 U.S. 525, 561* ("arbitrary restraint of . . . liberties"); Betts v. Brady, *316 U.S. 455, 462* ("denial of fundamental fairness, shocking to the universal sense of justice"); Poe v. Ullman, *367 U.S. 497, 539 (dissenting opinion)* ("intolerable and unjustifiable"). Perhaps the clearest, frankest and briefest explanation of how this due process approach works is the statement in another case handed down today that this Court is to invoke the Due Process Clause to strike down state procedures or laws which it can "not tolerate." Linkletter v. Walker, post, p. 618, at 631.

2. See Hand, The Bill of Rights (1958) 70: "[J]udges are seldom content merely to annul the particular solution before them; they do not, indeed they may not, say that taking all things into consideration, the legislators' solution is too strong for the judicial stomach. On the contrary they wrap up their veto in a protective veil of adjectives such as 'arbitrary,' 'artificial,' 'normal,' 'reasonable,' 'inherent,' 'fundamental,' or 'essential,' whose office usually, though quite innocently, is to disguise what they are doing and impute to it a derivation far more impressive than their personal preferences, which are all that in fact lie behind the decision." [Citations omitted—Eds.]

3. See Patterson, The Forgotten Ninth Amendment (1955). Mr. Patterson urges that the Ninth Amendment be used to protect unspecified "natural and inalienable rights." P. 4. The Introduction by Roscoe Pound states that "there is a marked revival of natural law ideas throughout the world. Interest in the Ninth Amendment is a symptom of that revival." P. iii.

4. Of course one cannot be oblivious to the fact that Mr. Gallup has already published the results of a poll which he says show that 46% of the people in this country believe schools should teach about birth control. Washington Post, May 21, 1965, p. 2, col. 1. I can hardly believe, however, that Brother Goldberg would view 46% of the persons polled as so overwhelming a proportion that this Court may now rely on it to declare that the Connecticut law infringes "fundamental" rights, and overrule the long-standing view of the people of Connecticut expressed through their elected representatives.

5. U.S. Const., Amend. IX, provides: "The enumeration in the Constitution, of certain rights, shall not be construed to deny or disparage others retained by the people."

6. Annuals of Congress 439.

*ROE V. WADE**

United States Supreme Court, 1973

In decisions handed down on January 22, 1973, the U.S. Supreme Court declared unconstitutional the Texas and Georgia abortion laws. The Texas case, *Roe* v. *Wade,* concerned a statute which restricted legal abortions to those deemed necessary to save the woman's life. The Georgia case, *Doe* v. *Bolton,* dealt with a state law permitting abortions only when required by the woman's health, or to prevent birth of a deformed child, or when pregnancy resulted from rape. The court's invalidation of these laws impliied that similarly restrictive laws in most other states are also unconstitutional.

Majority Opinion by Justice Harry A. Blackmun (Concurred in by Six Others)

. . . A recent review of the common law precedents argues . . . that even post-quickening abortion was never established as a common law crime. This is of some importance because while most American courts ruled, in holding or dictum, that abortion of an unquickened fetus was not criminal under their

---

received common law, others followed Coke in stating that abortion of a quick fetus was a "misprison," a term they translated to mean "misdemeanor." That their reliance on Coke on this aspect of the law was uncritical and, apparently in all the reported cases, dictum (due probably to the paucity of common law prosecutions for post-quickening abortion), makes it now appear doubtful that abortion was ever firmly established as a common law crime even with respect to the destruction of a quick fetus. . . .

It is thus apparent that at common law, at the time of the adoption of our Constitution, and throughout the major portion of the 19th century, abortion was viewed with less disfavor than under most American statutes currently in effect. Phrasing it another way, a woman enjoyed a substantially broader right to terminate a pregnancy than she does in most States today. At least with respect to the early stage of pregnancy, and very possibly without such a limitation, the opportunity to make this choice was present in this country well into the 19th century. Even later, the law continued for some time to treat less punitively an abortion procured in early pregnancy. . . .

Three reasons have been advanced to explain historically the enactment of criminal abortion laws in the 19th century and to justify their continued existence.

It has been argued occasionally that these laws were the product of a Victorian social concern to discourage illicit sexual conduct. Texas, however, does not advance this justification in the present case, and it appears that no court or commentator has taken the argument seriously. . . .

A second reason is concerned with abortion as a medical procedure. When most criminal abortion laws were first enacted, the procedure was a hazardous one for the woman. This was particularly true prior to the development of antisepsis. Antiseptic techniques, of course, were based on discoveries by Lister, Pasteur, and others first announced in 1867, but were not generally accepted and employed until about the turn of the century. Abortion mortality was high. Even after 1900, and perhaps until as late as the development of antibiotics in the 1940's, standard modern techniques such as dilation and curettage were not nearly so safe as they are today. Thus it has been argued that a State's real concern in enacting a criminal abortion law was to protect the pregnant woman, that is, to restrain her from submitting to a procedure that placed her life in serious jeopardy.

Modern medical techniques have altered this situation. Appellants and various *amici* refer to medi-

cal data indicating that abortion in early pregnancy, that is, prior to the end of first trimester, although not without its risk, is now relatively safe. Mortality rates for women undergoing early abortions, where the procedure is legal, appear to be as low as or lower than the rates for normal childbirth. Consequently, any interest of the State in protecting the woman from an inherently hazardous procedure, except when it would be equally dangerous for her to forgo it, has largely disappeared. Of course, important state interests in the area of health and medical standards do remain. The State has a legitimate interest in seeing to it that abortion, like any other medical procedure, is performed under circumstances that insure maximum safety for the patient. This interest obviously extends at least to the performing physician and his staff, to the facilities involved, to the availability of after-care, and to adequate provision for any complication or emergency that might arise. The prevalence of high mortality rates at illegal "abortion mills" strengthens, rather than weakens, the State's interest in regulating the conditions under which abortions are performed. Moreover, the risk to the woman increases as her pregnancy continues. Thus the State retains a definite interest in protecting the woman's own health and safety when an abortion is performed at a late stage of pregnancy.

The third reason is the State's interest—some phrase it in terms of duty—in protecting prenatal life. Some of the argument for this justification rests on the theory that a new human life is present from the moment of conception. . . .

Parties challenging state abortion laws have sharply disputed in some courts the contention that a purpose of these laws, when enacted, was to protect prenatal life. Pointing to the absence of legislative history to support the contention, they claim that most state laws were designed solely to protect the woman. Because medical advances have lessened this concern, at least with respect to abortion in early pregnancy, they argue that with respect to such abortions the laws can no longer be justified by any state interest. There is some scholarly support for this view of original purpose. The few state courts called upon to interpret their laws in the late 19th and early 20th centuries did focus on the State's interest in protecting the woman's health rather than in preserving embryo and fetus. . . .

The Constitution does not explicitly mention any right of privacy. In a line of decisions, however, going back perhaps as far as *Union Pacific R. Co.* v. *Botsford,* 141 U.S. 250, 251 (1891), the Court has recognized that a right of personal privacy, or a guarantee of certain areas or zones of privacy, does exist under the Constitution. In varying contexts the Court or individual Justices have indeed found at least the roots of that right in the First Amendment, . . . in the Fourth and Fifth Amendments . . . in the penumbras of the Bill of Rights . . . in the Ninth Amendment . . . or in the concept of liberty guaranteed by the first section of the Fourteenth Amendment. . . . These decisions make it clear that only personal rights that can be deemed "fundamental" or "implicit in the concept of ordered liberty," . . . are included in this guarantee of personal privacy. They also make it clear that the right has some extension to activities relating to marriage, . . . procreation, . . . contraception, . . . family relationships, . . . and child rearing and education. . . .

This right of privacy, whether it be founded in the Fourteenth Amendment's concept of personal liberty and restrictions upon state action, as we feel it is, or, as the District Court determined, in the Ninth Amendment's reservation of rights to the people, is broad enough to encompass a woman's decision whether or not to terminate her pregnancy. . . .

. . . Appellants and some *amici* argue that the woman's right is absolute and that she is entitled to terminate her pregnancy at whatever time, in whatever way, and for whatever reason she alone chooses. With this we do not agree. Appellants' arguments that Texas either has no valid interest at all in regulating the abortion decision, or no interest strong enough to support any limitation upon the woman's sole determination, is unpersuasive. The Court's decisions recognizing a right of privacy also acknowledge that some state regulation in areas protected by that right is appropriate. As noted above, a state may properly assert important interests in safe-guarding health, in maintaining medical standards, and in protecting potential life. At some point in pregnancy, these respective interests become sufficiently compelling to sustain regulation of the factors that govern the abortion decision. The privacy right involved, therefore, cannot be said to be absolute. . . .

We therefore conclude that the right of personal privacy includes the abortion decision, but that this right is not unqualified and must be considered against important state interests in regulation.

We note that those federal and state courts that have recently considered abortion law challenges have reached the same conclusion. . . .

Although the results are divided, most of these courts have agreed that the right of privacy, however based, is broad enough to cover the abortion decision;

that the right, nonetheless, is not absolute and is subject to some limitations; and that at some point the state interests as to protection of health, medical standards, and prenatal life, become dominant. We agree with this approach.

The appellee and certain *amici* argue that the fetus is a "person" within the language and meaning of the Fourteenth Amendment. In support of this they outline at length and in detail the well-known facts of fetal development. If this suggestion of personhood is established, the appellant's case, of course, collapses, for the fetus' right to life is then guaranteed specifically by the Amendment. The appellant conceded as much on reargument. On the other hand, the appellee conceded on reargument that no case could be cited that holds that a fetus is a person within the meaning of the Fourteenth Amendment.

All this, together with our observation, *supra,* that throughout the major portion of the 19th century prevailing legal abortion practices were far freer than they are today, persuades us that the word "person," as used in the Fourteenth Amendment, does not include the unborn. . . . Indeed, our decision in *United States* v. *Vuitch,* 402 U.S. 62 (1971), inferentially is to the same effect, for we would not have indulged in statutory interpretation favorable to abortion in specified circumstances if the necessary consequence was the termination of life entitled to Fourteenth Amendment protection.

. . . As we have intimated above, it is reasonable and appropriate for a State to decide that at some point in time another interest, that of health of the mother or that of potential human life, becomes significantly involved. The woman's privacy is no longer sole and any right of privacy she possesses must be measured accordingly.

. . . We need not resolve the difficult question of when life begins. When those trained in the respective disciplines of medicine, philosophy, and theology are unable to arrive at any consensus, the judiciary, at this point in the development of man's knowledge, is not in a position to speculate as to the answer.

It should be sufficient to note briefly the wide divergence of thinking on this most sensitive and difficult question. There has always been strong support for the view that life does not begin until live birth. This was the belief of the Stoics. It appears to be the predominant, though not the unanimous, attitude of the Jewish faith. It may be taken to represent also the position of a large segment of the Protestant community, insofar as that can be ascertained; organized groups that have taken a formal position on the abortion issue have generally regarded abortion as a matter for the conscience of the individual and her family. As we have noted, the common law found greater significance in quickening. Physicians and their scientific colleagues have regarded that event with less interest and have tended to focus either upon conception or upon live birth or upon the interim point at which the fetus becomes "viable," that is, potentially able to live outside the mother's womb, albeit with artificial aid. Viability is usually placed at about seven months (28 weeks) but may occur earlier, even at 24 weeks. . . .

In areas other than criminal abortion the law has been reluctant to endorse any theory that life, as we recognize it, begins before live birth or to accord legal rights to the unborn except in narrowly defined situations and except when the rights are contingent upon live birth. . . . In short, the unborn have never been recognized in the law as persons in the whole sense.

In view of all this, we do not agree that, by adopting one theory of life, Texas may override the rights of the pregnant woman that are at stake. We repeat, however, that the State does have an important and legitimate interest in preserving and protecting the health of the pregnant woman, whether she be a resident of the State or a nonresident who seeks medical consultation and treatment there, and that it has still *another* important and legitimate interest in protecting the potentiality of human life. These interests are separate and distinct. Each grows in substantiality as the woman approaches term and, at a point during pregnancy, each becomes "compelling."

With respect to the State's important and legitimate interest in the health of the mother, the "compelling" point, in the light of present medical knowledge, is at approximately the end of the first trimester. This is so because of the now established medical fact . . . that until the end of the first trimester mortality in abortion is less than mortality in normal childbirth. It follows that, from and after this point, a State may regulate the abortion procedure to the extent that the regulation reasonably relates to the preservation and protection of maternal health. Examples of permissible state regulation in this area are requirements as to the qualifications of the person who is to perform the abortion; as to the licensure of that person; as to the facility in which the procedure is to be performed, that is, whether it must be a hospital or may be a clinic or some other place of less-than-hospital status; as to the licensing of the facility; and the like.

This means, on the other hand, that, for the period of pregnancy prior to this "compelling" point, the attending physician, in consultation with his patient, is free to determine, without regulation by the State, that in his medical judgment the patient's pregnancy should be terminated. If that decision is reached, the judgment may be effectuated by an abortion free of interference by the State.

With respect to the State's important and legitimate interest in potential life, the "compelling" point is at viability. . . . State regulation protective of fetal life after viability thus has both logical and biological justifications. If the State is interested in protecting fetal life after viability, it may go so far as to proscribe abortion during that period except when it is necessary to preserve the life or health of the mother. . . .

To summarize and repeat:

1. A state criminal abortion statute of the current Texas type, that excepts from criminality only a *life saving* procedure on behalf of the mother, without regard to pregnancy stage and without recognition of the other interests involved, is violative of the Due Process Clause of the Fourteenth Amendment.
   (a) For the stage prior to approximately the end of the first trimester, the abortion decision and its effectuation must be left to the medical judgment of the pregnant woman's attending physician.
   (b) For the stage subsequent to approximately the end of the first trimester, the State, in promoting its interest in the health of the mother, may, if it chooses, regulate the abortion procedure in ways that are reasonably related to maternal health.
   (c) For the stage subsequent to viability the State, in promoting its interest in the potentiality of human life, may, if it chooses, regulate, and even proscribe, abortion except where it is necessary, in appropriate medical judgment, for the preservation of the life or health of the mother.
2. The State may define the term "physician," as it has been employed in the preceding numbered paragraphs of this Part XI of this opinion, to mean only a physician currently licensed by the State, and may proscribe any abortion by a person who is not a physician as so defined.

. . . The decision leaves the State free to place increasing restrictions on abortion as the period of pregnancy lengthens, so long as those restrictions are tailored to the recognized state interests. The decision vindicates the right of the physician to administer medical treatment according to his professional judgment up to the points where important state interests provide compelling justifications for intervention. Up to those points the abortion decision in all its aspects is inherently, and primarily, a medical decision, and basic responsibility for it must rest with the physician. If an individual practitioner abuses the privilege of exercising proper medical judgment, the usual remedies, judicial and intraprofessional, are available. . . .

Dissent by Justice Byron R. White (Concurred in by Justice William H. Rehnquist)

At the heart of the controversy in these cases are those recurring pregnancies that pose no danger whatsoever to the life or health of the mother but are nevertheless unwanted for any one or more of a variety of reasons—convenience, family planning, economics, dislike of children, the embarrassment of illegitimacy, etc. The common claim before us is that for any one of such reasons, or for no reason at all, and without asserting or claiming any threat to life or health, any woman is entitled to an abortion at her request if she is able to find a medical advisor willing to undertake the procedure.

The Court for the most part sustains this position: During the period prior to the time the fetus becomes viable, the Constitution of the United States values the convenience, whim or caprice of the putative mother more than the life or potential life of the fetus; the Constitution, therefore, guarantees the right to an abortion as against any state law or policy seeking to protect the fetus from an abortion not prompted by more compelling reasons of the mother.

With all due respect, I dissent. I find nothing in the language or history of the Constitution to support the Court's judgment. . . . As an exercise of raw judicial power, the Court perhaps has authority to do what it does today; but in my view its judgment is an improvident and extravagant exercise of the power of judicial review which the Constitution extends to this Court.

The Court apparently values the convenience of the pregnant mother more than the continued existence and development of the life or potential life which she carries. . . .

It is my view, therefore, that the Texas statute is not constitutionally infirm because it denies abortions to those who seek to serve only their convenience rather than to protect their life or health. . . .

*PLANNED PARENTHOOD OF S.E. PENNSYLVANIA V. CASEY**

United States Supreme Court, 1992

Justice O'Connor, Justice Kennedy, and Justice Souter announced the judgment of the Court:

At issue in these cases are five provisions of the Pennsylvania Abortion Control Act of 1982 as amended in 1988 and 1989. The Act requires that a woman seeking an abortion give her informed consent prior to the abortion procedure, and specifies that she be provided with certain information at least 24 hours before the abortion is performed. For a minor to obtain an abortion, the Act requires the informed consent of one of her parents, but provides for a judi-

*112 S. Ct. 2791 (1992).

cial bypass option if the minor does not wish to or cannot obtain a parent's consent. Another provision of the Act requires that, unless certain exceptions apply, a married woman seeking an abortion must sign a statement indicating that she has notified her husband of her intended abortion. The Act exempts compliance with these three requirements in the event of a "medical emergency," which is defined in S 3203 of the Act. In addition to the above provisions regulating the performance of abortions, the Act imposes certain reporting requirements on facilities that provide abortion services. . . .

After considering the fundamental constitutional questions resolved by *Roe,* principles of institutional integrity, and the rule of stare decisis, we are led to conclude this: the essential holding of *Roe* v. *Wade* should be retained and once again reaffirmed.

It must be stated at the outset and with clarity that *Roe*'s essential holding, the holding we reaffirm, has three parts. First is a recognition of the right of the woman to choose to have an abortion before viability and to obtain it without undue interference from the State. Before viability, the State's interests are not strong enough to support a prohibition of abortion or the imposition of a substantial obstacle to the woman's effective right to elect the procedure. Second is a confirmation of the State's power to restrict abortions after fetal viability, if the law contains exceptions for pregnancies which endanger a woman's life or health. And third is the principle that the State has legitimate interests from the outset of the pregnancy in protecting the health of the woman and the life of the fetus that may become a child. These principles do not contradict one another; and we adhere to each. . . .

The Court's duty in the present case is clear. In 1973, it confronted the already divisive issue of governmental power to limit personal choice to undergo abortion, for which it provided a new resolution based on the due process guaranteed by the Fourteenth Amendment. Whether or not a new social consensus is developing on that issue, its divisiveness is no less today than in 1973, and pressure to overrule the decision, like pressure to retain it, has grown only more intense. A decision to overrule *Roe*'s essential holding under the existing circumstances would address error, if error there was, at the cost of both profound and unnecessary damage to the Court's legitimacy, and to the Nation's commitment to the rule of law. It is therefore imperative to adhere to the essence of *Roe*'s original decision, and we do so today. . . .

From what we have said so far it follows that it is a constitutional liberty of the woman to have some freedom to terminate her pregnancy. We conclude that the basic decision in *Roe* was based on a constitutional analysis which we cannot now repudiate. The woman's liberty is not so unlimited, however, that from the outset the State cannot show its concern for the life of the unborn, and at a later point in fetal development the State's interest in life has sufficient force so that the right of the woman to terminate the pregnancy can be restricted.

That brings us, of course, to the point where much criticism has been directed at *Roe,* a criticism that always inheres when the Court draws a specific rule from what in the Constitution is but a general standard. We conclude, however, that the urgent claims of the woman to retain the ultimate control over her destiny and her body, claims implicit in the meaning of liberty, require us to perform that function. Liberty must not be extinguished for want of a line that is clear. And it falls to us to give some real substance to the woman's liberty to determine whether to carry her pregnancy to full term.

We conclude the line should be drawn at viability, so that before that time the woman has a right to choose to terminate her pregnancy. We adhere to this principle for two reasons. First, as we have said, is the doctrine of stare decisis. Any judicial act of line-drawing may seem somewhat arbitrary, but *Roe* was a reasoned statement, elaborated with great care. We have twice reaffirmed it in the face of great opposition. Although we must overrule those parts of *Thornburgh* and *Akron I* which, in our view, are inconsistent with *Roe*'s statement that the State has a legitimate interest in promoting the life or potential life of the unborn, the central premise of those cases represents an unbroken commitment by this Court to the essential holding of *Roe.* It is that premise which we reaffirm today.

The second reason is that the concept of viability, as we noted in *Roe,* is the time at which there is a realistic possibility of maintaining and nourishing a life outside the womb, so that the independent existence of the second life can in reason and all fairness be the object of state protection that now overrides the rights of the woman. Consistent with other constitutional norms, legislatures may draw lines which appear arbitrary without the necessity of offering a justification. But courts may not. We must justify the lines we draw. And there is no line other than viability which is more workable. To be sure, as we have said, there may be some medical developments that affect the precise point of viability, but this is an imprecision within tolerable limits given that the medical community and all those who must apply its discoveries will continue to explore the matter. The viability line also has, as a practical matter, an element of fairness. In some broad sense it might be said that a woman who fails to act before viability has consented to the State's intervention on behalf of the developing child.

The woman's right to terminate her pregnancy before viability is the most central principle of *Roe* v. *Wade.* It is a rule of law and a component of liberty we cannot renounce. . . .

Yet it must be remembered that *Roe* v. *Wade* speaks with clarity in establishing not only the woman's liberty but also the State's "important and legitimate interest in potential life." That portion of the decision in *Roe* has been given too little acknowledgement and implementation by the Court in its subsequent cases. Those cases decided that any regulation touching upon the abortion decision must survive strict scrutiny, to be sustained only if drawn in narrow terms to further a compelling state interest. Not all of the cases decided under that formulation can be reconciled with the holding in *Roe* itself that the State has legitimate interests in the health of the woman and in protecting the potential life within her. In resolving this tension, we choose to rely upon *Roe,* as against the later cases.

Roe established a trimester framework to govern abortion regulations. Under this elaborate but rigid construct, almost no regulation at all is permitted during the first trimester of pregnancy; regulations designed to protect the woman's health, but not to further the State's interest in potential life, are permitted during the second trimester; and during the third trimester, when the fetus is viable, prohibitions are permitted provided the life or health of the mother is not at stake. Most of our cases since *Roe* have involved the application of rules derived from the trimester framework.

The trimester framework no doubt was erected to ensure that the woman's right to choose not become so subordinate to the State's interest in promoting fetal life that her choice exists in theory but not in fact. We do not agree, however, that the trimester approach is necessary to accomplish this objective. A framework of this rigidity was unnecessary and in its later interpretation sometimes contradicted the State's permissible exercise of its powers.

Though the woman has a right to choose to terminate or continue her pregnancy before viability, it does not at all follow that the State is prohibited from taking steps to ensure that this choice is thoughtful and informed. Even in the earliest stages of pregnancy, the State may enact rules and regulations designed to encourage her to know that there are philosophic and social arguments of great weight that can be brought to bear in favor of continuing the pregnancy to full term and that there are procedures and institutions to allow adoption of unwanted children as well as a certain degree of state assistance if the mother chooses to raise the child herself. "'[T]he Constitution does not forbid a State or city, pursuant to democratic processes, from expressing a preference for normal childbirth.'" *Webster* v. *Reproductive Health Services.* . . .

We reject the trimester framework, which we do not consider to be part of the essential holding of *Roe.* Measures aimed at ensuring that a woman's choice contemplates the consequences for the fetus do not necessarily interfere with the right recognized in *Roe,* although those measures have been found to be inconsistent with the rigid trimester framework announced in that case. A logical reading of the central holding in *Roe* itself, and a necessary reconciliation of the liberty of the woman and the interest of the State in promoting prenatal life, require, in our view, that we abandon the trimester framework as a rigid prohibition on all previability regulation aimed at the protection of fetal life. The trimester framework suffers from these basic flaws: in its formulation it misconceives the nature of the pregnant woman's interest; and in practice it undervalues the State's interest in potential life, as recognized in *Roe.*

As our jurisprudence relating to all liberties save perhaps abortion has recognized, not every law which makes a right more difficult to exercise is, ipso facto, an infringement of that right. An example clarifies the point. We have held that not every ballot access limitation amounts to an infringement of the right to vote. Rather, the States are granted substantial flexibility in establishing the framework within which voters choose the candidates for whom they wish to vote.

The abortion right is similar. Numerous forms of state regulation might have the incidental effect of increasing the cost or decreasing the availability of medical care, whether for abortion or any other medical procedure. The fact that a law which serves a valid purpose, one not designed to strike at the right itself, has the incidental effect of making it more difficult or more expensive to procure an abortion cannot be enough to invalidate it. Only where state regulation imposes an undue burden on a woman's ability to make this decision does the power of the State reach into the heart of the liberty protected by the Due Process Clause.

These considerations of the nature of the abortion right illustrate that it is an overstatement to describe it as a right to decide whether to have an abortion "without interference from the State," *Planned Parenthood of Central Mo.* v. *Danforth.* All abortion regulations interfere to some degree with a woman's ability to decide whether to terminate her pregnancy. It is, as a consequence, not surprising that despite the protestations contained in the original *Roe* opinion to the effect that the Court was not recognizing an absolute right, the Court's experience applying the trimester framework has led to the striking down of some abortion regulations which in no real sense deprived women of the ultimate decision. Those decisions went too far because the right recognized by *Roe* is a right "to be free from unwarranted governmental intrusion into matters so fundamentally affecting a person as the decision whether to bear or beget a child." *Eisenstadt* v. *Baird.* Not all governmental intrusion is of necessity unwarranted; and that brings us to the other basic flaw in the trimester framework: even in *Roe*'s terms, in practice it undervalues the State's interest in the potential life within the woman. *Roe* v. *Wade* was express in its recognition of the State's "important and legitimate interest[s] in preserving and protecting the health of the pregnant woman [and] in protecting the potentiality of human life." The trimester framework, however, does not fulfill *Roe*'s own promise that the State has an interest in protecting fetal life or potential life. *Roe* began the contradiction by using the trimester framework to forbid any regulation of abortion designed to advance that interest before viability. Before viability, *Roe* and subsequent cases treat all governmental attempts to influence a woman's decision on behalf of the potential life within her as unwarranted. This treatment is, in our judgment, incompatible with the recognition that there is a substantial state interest in potential life throughout pregnancy.

The very notion that the State has a substantial interest in potential life leads to the conclusion that not all regulations must be deemed unwarranted. Not all burdens on the right to decide whether to terminate a pregnancy will be undue. In our view, the undue burden standard is the appropriate means of reconciling the State's interest with the woman's constitutionally protected liberty.

A finding of an undue burden is a shorthand for the conclusion that a state regulation has the purpose or effect of placing a substantial obstacle in the path of a woman seeking an abortion of a nonviable fetus. A statute with this purpose is invalid because the means chosen by the State to further the interest in potential life must be calculated to inform the woman's free choice, not hinder it. And a statute which, while furthering the interest in potential life or some other valid state interest, has the effect of placing a substantial obstacle in the path of a woman's choice cannot be considered a permissible means of serving its legitimate ends. To the extent that the opinions of the Court or of individual Justices use the undue burden standard in a manner that is inconsistent with this analysis, we set out what in our view should be the controlling standard. In our considered judgment, an undue burden is an unconstitutional burden. . . .

Some guiding principles should emerge. What is at stake is the woman's right to make the ultimate decision, not a right to be insulated from all others in doing so. Regulations which do no more than create a structural mechanism by which the State, or the parent or guardian of a minor, may express profound respect for the life of the unborn are permitted, if they are not a substantial obstacle to the woman's exercise of the right to choose. Unless it has that effect on her right of choice, a state measure designed to persuade her to choose childbirth over abortion will be upheld if reasonably related to that goal. Regulations designed to foster the health of a woman seeking an abortion are valid if they do not constitute an undue burden.

Even when jurists reason from shared premises, some disagreement is inevitable. That is to be expected in the application of any legal standard which must accommodate life's complexity. We do not expect it to be otherwise with respect to the undue burden standard. We give this summary:

(a) To protect the central right recognized by *Roe* v. *Wade* while at the same time accommodating the State's profound interest in potential life, we will employ the undue burden analysis as explained in this opinion. An undue burden exists, and therefore a provision of law is invalid, if its purpose or effect is to place a substantial obstacle in the path of a woman seeking an abortion before the fetus attains viability.

(b) We reject the rigid trimester framework of *Roe* v. *Wade.* To promote the State's profound interest in potential life, throughout pregnancy the State may take measures to ensure that the woman's choice is informed, and measures designed to advance this interest will not be invalidated as long as their purpose is to persuade the woman to choose childbirth over abortion. These measures must not be an undue burden on the right.

(c) As with any medical procedure, the State may enact regulations to further the health or safety of a woman seeking an abortion. Unnecessary health regulations that have the purpose or effect of presenting a substantial obstacle to a woman seeking an abortion impose an undue burden on the right.

(d) Our adoption of the undue burden analysis does not disturb the central holding of *Roe* v. *Wade,* and we reaffirm that holding. Regardless of whether exceptions are made for particular circumstances, a State may not prohibit any woman from making the ultimate decision to terminate her pregnancy before viability.

(e) We also reaffirm *Roe*'s holding that "subsequent to viability, the State in promoting its interest in the potentiality of human life may, if it chooses, regulate, and even proscribe, abortion except where it is necessary, in appropriate medical judgment, for the preservation of the life or health of the mother." *Roe* v. *Wade,* 410 U.S., at 164-165, 93 S.Ct., at 732.

These principles control our assessment of the Pennsylvania statute. . . .

The Court of Appeals applied what it believed to be the undue burden standard and upheld each of the provisions except for the husband notification requirement. We agree generally with this conclusion. . . .

*BOWERS V. HARDWICK**

United States Supreme Court, 1986

Justice WHITE delivered the opinion of the Court.

In August 1982, respondent was charged with violating the Georgia statute criminalizing sodomy[1] by committing that act with another adult male in the bedroom of respondent's home. After a preliminary hearing, the District Attorney decided not to present the matter to the grand jury unless further evidence developed.

Respondent then brought suit in the Federal District Court, challenging the constitutionality of the statute insofar as it criminalized consensual sodomy.[2] He asserted that he was a practicing homosexual, that the Georgia sodomy statute, as administered by the defendants, placed him in imminent danger of arrest, and that the statute for several reasons violates the Federal Constitution. The District Court granted the defendants' motion to dismiss for failure to state a claim, relying on *Doe* v. *Commonwealth's Attorney*

for the City of Richmond, 403 F.Supp. 1199 (ED Va. 1975), which this Court summarily affirmed, 425 U.S. 901, 96 S.Ct. 1489, 47 L.Ed.2d 751 (1976).

A divided panel of the Court of Appeals for the Eleventh Circuit reversed. . . . The court first held that, because *Doe* was distinguishable and in any event had been undermined by later decisions, our summary affirmance in that case did not require affirmance of the District Court. Relying on our decisions in *Griswold* v. *Connecticut,* . . . *Eisenstadt* v. *Baird,* . . . *Stanley* v. *Georgia,* . . . and *Roe* v. *Wade,* . . . the court went on to hold that the Georgia statute violated respondent's fundamental rights because his homosexual activity is a private and intimate association that is beyond the reach of state regulation by reason of the Ninth Amendment and the Due Process Clause of the Fourteenth Amendment. The case was remanded for trial, at which, to prevail, the State would have to prove

---

*478 U.S. 186 (1986). Endnotes edited and renumbered.

that the statute is supported by a compelling interest and is the most narrowly drawn means of achieving that end.

Because other Courts of Appeals have arrived at judgments contrary to that of the Eleventh Circuit in this case, we granted the State's petition for certiorari questioning the holding that its sodomy statute violates the fundamental rights of homosexuals. We agree with the State that the Court of Appeals erred, and hence reverse its judgment.

This case does not require a judgment on whether laws against sodomy between consenting adults in general, or between homosexuals in particular, are wise or desirable. It raises no question about the right or propriety of state legislative decisions to repeal their laws that criminalize homosexual sodomy, or of state court decisions invalidating those laws on state constitutional grounds. The issue presented is whether the Federal Constitution confers a fundamental right upon homosexuals to engage in sodomy and hence invalidates the laws of the many States that still make such conduct illegal and have done so for a very long time. The case also calls for some judgment about the limits of the Court's role in carrying out its constitutional mandate.

We first register our disagreement with the Court of Appeals and with respondent that the Court's prior cases have construed the Constitution to confer a right of privacy that extends to homosexual sodomy and for all intents and purposes have decided this case. The reach of this line of cases was sketched in *Carey* v. *Population Services International,* . . . *Pierce* v. *Society of Sisters,* . . . and *Meyer* v. *Nebraska,* . . . were described as dealing with child rearing and education; *Prince* v. *Massachusetts,* . . . with family relationships; *Skinner* v. *Oklahoma ex xel. Williamson,* . . . with procreation; *Loving* v. *Virginia,* . . . with marriage; *Griswold* v. *Connecticut, supra,* and *Eisenstadt* v. *Baird, supra,* with contraception; and *Roe* v. *Wade,* . . . with abortion. The latter three cases were interpreted as construing the Due Process Clause of the Fourteenth Amendment to confer a fundamental individual right to decide whether or not to beget or bear a child. . . .

Accepting the decisions in these cases and the above description of them, we think it evident that none of the rights announced in those cases bears any resemblance to the claimed constitutional right of homosexuals to engage in acts of sodomy that is asserted in this case. No connection between family, marriage, or procreation on the one hand and homosexual activity on the other has been demonstrated, either by the Court of Appeals or by respondent. Moreover, any claim that these cases nevertheless stand for the proposition that any kind of private sexual conduct between consenting adults is constitutionally insulated from state proscription is unsupportable. Indeed, the Court's opinion in *Carey* twice asserted that the privacy right, which the *Griswold* line of cases found to be one of the protections provided by the Due Process Clause, did not reach so far. . . .

Precedent aside, however, respondent would have us announce, as the Court of Appeals did, a fundamental right to engage in homosexual sodomy. This we are quite unwilling to do. It is true that despite the language of the Due Process Clauses of the Fifth and Fourteenth Amendments, which appears to focus only on the processes by which life, liberty, or property is taken, the cases are legion in which those Clauses have been interpreted to have substantive content, subsuming rights that to a great extent are immune from federal or state regulation or proscription. Among such cases are those recognizing rights that have little or no textual support in the constitutional language. *Meyer, Prince,* and *Pierce* fall in this category, as do the privacy cases from *Griswold* to *Carey.*

Striving to assure itself and the public that announcing rights not readily identifiable in the Constitution's text involves much more than the imposition of the Justices' own choice of values on the States and the Federal government, the Court has sought to identify the nature of the rights qualifying for heightened judicial protection. In *Palko* v. *Connecticut,* . . . it was said that this category includes those fundamental liberties that are "implicit in the concept of ordered liberty," such that "neither liberty nor justice would exist if [they] were sacrificed." A different description of fundamental liberties appeared in *Moore* v. *East Cleveland,* . . . (opinion of POWELL, J.), where they are characterized as those liberties that are "deeply rooted in this Nation's history and tradition." . . .

It is obvious to us that neither of these formulations would extend a fundamental right to homosexuals to engage in acts of consensual sodomy. Proscriptions against that conduct have ancient roots. See generally, Survey on the Constitutional Right to Privacy in the Context of Homosexual Activity, 40 U.Miami L.Rev. 521, 525 (1986). Sodomy was a criminal offense at common law and was forbidden by the laws of the original thirteen States when they ratified the Bill of Rights. In 1868, when the Fourteenth Amendment was ratified, all but 5 of the 37 States in the Union had criminal sodomy laws. In fact, until 1961, all 50 States outlawed sodomy, and today, 24

States and the District of Columbia continue to provide criminal penalties for sodomy performed in private and between consenting adults. Survey, U.Miami L.Rev., *supra,* at 524, n. 9. Against this background, to claim that a right to engage in such conduct is "deeply rooted in this Nation's history and tradition" or "implicit in the concept of ordered liberty" is, at best, facetious.

Nor are we inclined to take a more expansive view of our authority to discover new fundamental rights imbedded in the Due Process Clause. The Court is most vulnerable and comes nearest to illegitimacy when it deals with judge-made constitutional law having little or no cognizable roots in the language or design of the Constitution. That this is so was painfully demonstrated by the face-off between the Executive and the Court in the 1930s, which resulted in the repudiation of much of the substantive gloss that the Court had placed on the Due Process Clause of the Fifth and Fourteenth Amendments. There should be, therefore, great resistance to expand the substantive reach of those Clauses, particularly if it requires redefining the category of rights deemed to be fundamental. Otherwise, the Judiciary necessarily takes to itself further authority to govern the country without express constitutional authority. The claimed right pressed on us today falls far short of overcoming this resistance.

Respondent, however, asserts that the result should be different where the homosexual conduct occurs in the privacy of the home. He relies on *Stanley* v. *Georgia,* . . . where the Court held that the First Amendment prevents conviction for possessing and reading obscene material in the privacy of his home: "If the First Amendment means anything, it means that a State has no business telling a man, sitting alone in his house, what books he may read or what films he may watch." . . .

Stanley did protect conduct that would not have been protected outside the home, and it partially prevented the enforcement of state obscenity laws; but the decision was firmly grounded in the First Amendment. The right pressed upon us here has no similar support in the text of the Constitution, and it does not qualify for recognition under the prevailing principles for construing the Fourteenth Amendment. Its limits are also difficult to discern. Plainly enough, otherwise illegal conduct is not always immunized whenever it occurs in the home. Victimless crimes, such as the possession and use of illegal drugs do not escape the law where they are committed at home. *Stanley* itself recognized that its holding offered no protection for

the possession in the home of drugs, firearms, or stolen goods. *Id.,* at 568, n. 11, 89 S.Ct., at 1249, n. 11. And if respondent's submission is limited to the voluntary sexual conduct between consenting adults, it would be difficult, except by fiat, to limit the claimed right to homosexual conduct while leaving exposed to prosecution adultery, incest, and other sexual crimes even though they are committed in the home. We are unwilling to start down that road.

Even if the conduct at issue here is not a fundamental right, respondent asserts that there must be a rational basis for the law and that there is none in this case other than the presumed belief of a majority of the electorate in Georgia that homosexual sodomy is immoral and unacceptable. This is said to be an inadequate rationale to support the law. The law, however, is constantly based on notions of morality, and if all laws representing essentially moral choices are to be invalidated under the Due Process Clause, the courts will be very busy indeed. Even respondent makes no such claim, but insists that majority sentiments about the morality of homosexuality should be declared inadequate. We do not agree, and are unpersuaded that the sodomy laws of some 25 States should be invalidated on this basis.

Accordingly, the judgment of the Court of Appeals is

Reversed.

Chief Justice BURGER, concurring.

I join the Court's opinion, but I write separately to underscore my view that in constitutional terms there is no such thing as a fundamental right to commit homosexual sodomy.

As the Court notes, *ante* at—, the proscriptions against sodomy have very "ancient roots." Decisions of individuals relating to homosexual conduct have been subject to state intervention throughout the history of Western Civilization. Condemnation of those practices is firmly rooted in Judaeo-Christian moral and ethical standards. Homosexual sodomy was a capital crime under Roman law. See Code Theod. 9.7.6; Code Just. 9.9.31. See also D. Bailey, Homosexuality in the Western Christian Tradition 70–81 (1975). During the English Reformation when powers of the ecclesiastical courts were transferred to the King's Courts, the first English statute criminalizing sodomy was passed. 25 Hen. VIII, c. 6. Blackstone described "the infamous crime against nature" as an offense of "deeper malignity" than rape, an heinous act "the very mention of which is a disgrace to human nature," and "a crime not fit to be named." Blackstone's Commentaries 215. The common law of England, including its prohibition of sodomy, became the received law of Georgia and the other Colonies. In 1816 the Georgia Legislature passed the statute at issue here, and that statute has been continuously in force in one form or another since that time. To hold that the act of homosexual sodomy is somehow protected as a fundamental right would be to cast aside millennia of moral teaching.

This is essentially not a question of personal "preferences" but rather of the legislative authority of the State. I find nothing in the Constitution depriving a State of the power to enact the statute challenged here.

Justice POWELL, concurring.

I join the opinion of the Court. I agree with the Court that there is no fundamental right—*i.e.,* no substantive right under the Due Process Clause—such as that claimed by respondent, and found to exist by the Court of Appeals. This is not to suggest, however, that respondent may not be protected by the Eighth Amendment of the Constitution. The Georgia statute at issue in this case, Ga.Code Ann. § 16-6-2, authorizes a court to imprison a person for up to 20 years for a single private, consensual act of sodomy. In my view, a prison sentence for such conduct—certainly a sentence of long duration—would create a serious Eighth Amendment issue. Under the Georgia statute a single act of sodomy, even in the private setting of a home, is a felony comparable in terms of the possible sentence imposed to serious felonies such as aggravated battery, § 16-5-24, first degree arson, § 16-7-60 and robbery, § 16-8-40.[3]

In this case, however, respondent has not been tried, much less convicted and sentenced. Moreover, respondent has not raised the Eighth Amendment issue below. For these reasons this constitutional argument is not before us.

Justice BLACKMUN, with whom Justice BRENNAN, Justice MARSHALL, and Justice STEVENS join, dissenting.

This case is no more about "a fundamental right to engage in homosexual sodomy," as the Court purports to declare, . . . than *Stanley* v. *Georgia,* . . . was about a fundamental right to watch obscene movies, or *Katz* v. *United States,* . . . was about a fundamental right to place interstate bets from a telephone booth. Rather, this case is about "the most comprehensive of

rights and the right most valued by civilized men," namely, "the right to be let alone." *Olmstead* v. *United States,* 277 U.S. 438, 478, 48 S.Ct. 564, 572, 72 L.Ed. 944 (1928) (Brandeis, J., dissenting).

The statute at issue, Ga.Code Ann. § 16-6-2, denies individuals the right to decide for themselves whether to engage in particular forms of private, consensual sexual activity. The Court concludes that § 16-6-2 is valid essentially because "the laws of . . . many States . . . still make such conduct illegal and have done so for a very long time." . . . But the fact that the moral judgments expressed by statutes like § 16-6-2 may be "natural and familiar . . . ought not to conclude our judgment upon the question whether statutes embodying them conflict with the Constitution of the United States." *Roe* v. *Wade,* . . . quoting *Lochner* v. *New York,* . . . (Holmes, J., dissenting). Like Justice Holmes, I believe that "[i]t is revolting to have no better reason for a rule of law than that so it was laid down in the time of Henry IV. It is still more revolting if the grounds upon which it was laid down have vanished long since, and the rule simply persists from blind imitation of the past." Holmes, The Path of the Law, 10 Harv.L.Rev. 457, 469 (1897). I believe we must analyze respondent's claim in the light of the values that underlie the constitutional right to privacy. If that right means anything, it means that, before Georgia can prosecute its citizens for making choices about the most intimate aspects of their lives, it must do more than assert that the choice they have made is an "'abominable crime not fit to be named among Christians,'" . . .

I

In its haste to reverse the Court of Appeals and hold that the Constitution does not confe[r] a fundamental right upon homosexuals to engage in sodomy," *ante,* at 2843, the Court relegates the actual statute being challenged to a footnote and ignores the procedural posture of the case before it. A fair reading of the statute and of the complaint clearly reveals that the majority has distorted the question this case presents.

First, the Court's almost obsessive focus on homosexual activity is particularly hard to justify in light of the broad language Georgia has used. Unlike the Court, the Georgia Legislature has not proceeded on the assumption that homosexuals are so different from other citizens that their lives may be controlled in a way that would not be tolerated if it limited the choices of those other citizens. . . . Rather, Georgia has provided that "[a] person commits the offense of sodomy when he performs or submits to any sexual act involving the sex organs of one person and the mouth or anus of another." Ga.Code Ann. § 16-6-2(a). The sex or status of the persons who engage in the act is irrelevant as a matter of state law. In fact, to the extent I can discern a legislative purpose for Georgia's 1968 enactment of § 16-6-2, that purpose seems to have been to broaden the coverage of the law to reach heterosexual as well as homosexual activity.[4] I therefore see no basis for the Court's decision to treat this case as an "as applied" challenge to § 16-6-2, . . . or for Georgia's attempt, both in its brief and at oral argument, to defend § 16-6-2 solely on the grounds that it prohibits homosexual activity. Michael Hardwick's standing may rest in significant part on Georgia's apparent willingness to enforce against homosexuals a law it seems not to have any desire to enforce against heterosexuals. . . . But his claim that § 16-6-2 involves an unconstitutional intrusion into his privacy and his right of intimate association does not depend in any way on his sexual orientation.

Second, I disagree with the Court's refusal to consider whether § 16-6-2 runs afoul of the Eighth or Ninth Amendments or the Equal Protection Clause of the Fourteenth Amendment. . . . Respondent's complaint expressly invoked the Ninth Amendment, see App. 6, and he relied heavily before this Court on *Griswold* v. *Connecticut,* . . . which identifies that Amendment as one of the specific constitutional provisions giving "life and substance" to our understanding of privacy. . . . More importantly, the procedural posture of the case requires that we affirm the Court of Appeals' judgment if there is *any* ground on which respondent may be entitled to relief. This case is before us on petitioner's motion to dismiss for failure to state a claim. . . . It is a well-settled principle of law that "a complaint should not be dismissed merely because a plaintiff's allegations do not support the particular legal theory he advances, for the court is under a duty to examine the complaint to determine if the allegations provide for relief on any possible theory." . . . Thus, even if respondent did not advance claims based on the Eighth or Ninth Amendments, or on the Equal Protection Clause, his complaint should not be dismissed if any of those provisions could entitle him to relief. I need not reach either the Eighth Amendment or the Equal Protection Clause issues because I believe that Hardwick has stated a cognizable

claim that § 16-6-2 interferes with constitutionally protected interests in privacy and freedom of intimate association. But neither the Eighth Amendment nor the Equal Protection Clause is so clearly irrelevant that a claim resting on either provision should be peremptorily dismissed.[5] The Court's cramped reading of the issue before it makes for a short opinion, but it does little to make for a persuasive one.

II

"Our cases long have recognized that the Constitution embodies a promise that a certain private sphere of individual liberty will be kept largely beyond the reach of government." *Thornburgh* v. *American Coll. of Obst. & Gyn.,* . . . In construing the right to privacy, the Court has proceeded along two somewhat distinct, albeit complementary, lines. First, it has recognized a privacy interest with reference to certain *decisions* that are properly for the individual to make. . . . Second, it has recognized a privacy interest with reference to certain *places* without regard for the particular activities in which the individuals who occupy them are engaged. . . . The case before us implicates both the decisional and the spatial aspects of the right to privacy.

A

The Court concludes today that none of our prior cases dealing with various decisions that individuals are entitled to make free of governmental interference "bears any resemblance to the claimed constitutional right of homosexuals to engage in acts of sodomy that is asserted in this case." . . . While it is true that these cases may be characterized by their connection to protection of the family, . . . the Court's conclusion that they extend no further than this boundary ignores the warning in *Moore* v. *East Cleveland,* . . . against "clos[ing] our eyes to the basic reasons why certain rights associated with the family have been accorded shelter under the Fourteenth Amendment's Due Process Clause." We protect those rights not because they contribute, in some direct and material way, to the general public welfare, but because they form so central a part of an individual's life. "[T]he concept of privacy embodies the 'moral fact that a person belongs to himself and not others nor to society as a whole.'" . . . And so we protect the decision whether to marry precisely because marriage "is an association that promotes a way of life, not causes; a harmony in living, not political faiths; a bilateral loyalty, not commercial or social projects." *Griswold* v. *Connecticut*. . . . We protect the decision whether to have a child because parenthood alters so dramatically an individual's self-definition, not because of demographic considerations or the Bible's command to be fruitful and multiply. Cf. *Thornburgh* v. *American Coll. of Obst. & Gyn., supra,*—U.S., at—,n. 6. 106 S.Ct., at 2188, n. 6 (STEVENS, J., concurring). And we protect the family because it contributes so powerfully to the happiness of individuals, not because of a preference for stereotypical households. . . . The Court recognized in *Roberts* . . . that the "ability independently to define one's identity that is central to any concept of liberty" cannot truly be exercised in a vacuum; we all depend on the "emotional enrichment of close ties with others." . . .

Only the most willful blindness could obscure the fact that sexual intimacy is "a sensitive, key relationship of human existence, central to family life, community welfare, and the development of human personality," . . . The fact that individuals define themselves in a significant way through their intimate sexual relationships with others suggests, in a Nation as diverse as ours, that there may be many "right" ways of conducting those relationships, and that much of the richness of a relationship will come from the freedom an individual has to *choose* the form and nature of these intensely personal bonds. See Karst, The Freedom of Intimate Association, 89 Yale L.J. 624, 637 (1980). . . .

In a variety of circumstances we have recognized that a necessary corollary of giving individuals freedom to choose how to conduct their lives is acceptance of the fact that different individuals will make different choices. For example, in holding that the clearly important state interest in public education should give way to a competing claim by the Amish to the effect that extended formal schooling threatened their way of life, the Court declared: "There can be no assumption that today's majority is 'right' and the Amish and others like them are 'wrong.' A way of life that is odd or even erratic but interferes with no rights or interests of others is not to be condemned because it is different." *Wisconsin* v. *Yoder*. . . . The Court claims that its decision today merely refuses to recognize a fundamental right to engage in homosexual sodomy; what the Court really has refused to recognize is the fundamental interest all individuals have in controlling the nature of their intimate associations with others.

B

The behavior for which Hardwick faces prosecution occurred in his own home, a place to which the Fourth Amendment attaches special significance. The Court's treatment of this aspect of the case is symptomatic of its overall refusal to consider the broad principles that have informed our treatment of privacy in specific cases. Just as the right to privacy is more than the mere aggregation of a number of entitlements to engage in specific behavior, so too, protecting the physical integrity of the home is more than merely a means of protecting specific activities that often take place there. Even when our understanding of the contours of the right to privacy depends on "reference to a 'place,'" . . . "the essence of a Fourth Amendment violation is 'not the breaking of [a person's] doors, and the rummaging of his drawers,' but rather is 'the invasion of his indefeasible right of personal security, personal liberty and private property.'" . . .

The Court's interpretation of the pivotal case of *Stanley* v. *Georgia*, . . . is entirely unconvincing. *Stanley* held that Georgia's undoubted power to punish the public distribution of constitutionally unprotected, obscene material did not permit the State to punish the private possession of such material. According to the majority here, *Stanley* relied entirely on the First Amendment, and thus, it is claimed, sheds no light on cases not involving printed materials. . . . But that is not what *Stanley* said. Rather, the *Stanley* Court anchored its holding in the Fourth Amendment's special protection for the individual in his home:

> "'*The makers of our Constitution undertook to secure conditions favorable to the pursuit of happiness. They recognized the significance of man's spiritual nature, of his feelings and of his intellect. They knew that only a part of the pain, pleasure and satisfactions of life are to be found in material things. They sought to protect Americans in their beliefs, their thoughts, their emotions and their sensations.*'
>
> "*These are the rights that appellant is asserting in the case before us. He is asserting the right to read or observe what he pleases—the right to satisfy his intellectual and emotional needs in the privacy of his own home.*" . . .

The central place that *Stanley* gives Justice Brandeis' dissent in *Olmstead*, a case raising *no* First Amendment claim, shows that *Stanley* rested as much on the Court's understanding of the Fourth Amendment as it did on the First. Indeed, in *Paris Adult The-*

atre I v. Slaton, . . . suggested that reliance on the Fourth Amendment not only supported the Court's outcome in *Stanley* but actually was *necessary* to it: "If obscene material unprotected by the First Amendment in itself carried with it a 'penumbra' of constitutionally protected privacy, this Court would not have found it necessary to decide *Stanley* on the narrow basis of the 'privacy of the home,' which was hardly more than a reaffirmation that 'a man's home is his castle.'" . . . "The right of the people to be secure in their . . . houses," expressly guaranteed by the Fourth Amendment, is perhaps the most "textual" of the various constitutional provisions that inform our understanding of the right to privacy, and thus I cannot agree with the Court's statement that "[t]he right pressed upon us here has no . . . support in the text of the Constitution," . . . Indeed, the right of an individual to conduct intimate relationships in the intimacy of his or her own home seems to me to be the heart of the Constitution's protection of privacy.

III

The Court's failure to comprehend the magnitude of the liberty interests at stake in this case leads it to slight the question whether petitioner, on behalf of the State, has justified Georgia's infringement on these interests. I believe that neither of the two general justifications for § 16-6-2 that petitioner has advanced warrants dismissing respondent's challenge for failure to state a claim.

First, petitioner asserts that the acts made criminal by the statute may have serious adverse consequences for "the general public health and welfare," such as spreading communicable diseases or fostering other criminal activity. . . . Inasmuch as this case was dismissed by the District Court on the pleadings, it is not surprising that the record before us is barren of any evidence to support petitioner's claim.[6] In light of the state of the record, I see no justification for the Court's attempt to equate the private, consensual sexual activity at issue here with the "possession in the home of drugs, firearms, or stolen goods," . . . to which *Stanley* refused to extend its protection. . . . None of the behavior so mentioned in *Stanley* can properly be viewed as "[v]ictimless," . . . drugs and weapons are inherently dangerous, . . . and for property to be "stolen," someone must have been wrongfully deprived of it. Nothing in the record before the Court provides any justification for finding the activity

forbidden by § 16-6-2 to be physically dangerous, either to the persons engaged in it or to others.

The core of petitioner's defense of § 16-6-2, however, is that respondent and others who engage in the conduct prohibited by § 16-6-2 interfere with Georgia's exercise of the "'right of the Nation and of the States to maintain a decent society,'" . . . Essentially, petitioner argues, and the Court agrees, that the fact that the acts described in § 16-6-2 "for hundreds of years, if not thousands, have been uniformly condemned as immoral" is a sufficient reason to permit a State to ban them today. . . .

I cannot agree that either the length of time a majority has held its convictions or the passions with which it defends them can withdraw legislation from this Court's scrutiny. . . . As Justice Jackson wrote so eloquently for the Court in *West Virginia Board of Education* v. *Barnette*, . . . "we apply the limitations of the Constitution with no fear that freedom to be intellectually and spiritually diverse or even contrary will disintegrate the social organization. . . . [F]reedom to differ is not limited to things that do not matter much. That would be a mere shadow of freedom. The test of its substance is the right to differ as to things that touch the heart of the existing order." See also Karst, 89 Yale L.J., at 627. It is precisely because the issue raised by this case touches the heart of what makes individuals what they are that we should be especially sensitive to the rights of those whose choices upset the majority.

The assertion that "traditional Judaeo-Christian values proscribe" the conduct involved, Brief for Petitioner 20, cannot provide an adequate justification for § 16-6-2. That certain, but by no means all, religious groups condemn the behavior at issue gives the State no license to impose their judgments on the entire citizenry. The legitimacy of secular legislation depends instead on whether the State can advance some justification for its law beyond its conformity to religious doctrine. . . . Thus, far from buttressing his case, petitioner's invocation of Leviticus, Romans, St. Thomas Aquinas, and sodomy's heretical status during the Middle Ages undermines his suggestion that § 16-6-2 represents a legitimate use of secular coercive power.[7] A State can no more punish private behavior because of religious intolerance than it can punish such behavior because of racial animus. "The Constitution cannot control such prejudices, but neither can it tolerate them. Private biases may be outside the reach of the law, but the law cannot, directly or indirectly, give them effect." . . . No matter how uncomfortable a certain group may make the majority of this

Court, we have held that "[m]ere public intolerance or animosity cannot constitutionally justify the deprivation of a person's physical liberty." . . .

Nor can § 16-6-2 be justified as a "morally neutral" exercise of Georgia's power to "protect the public environment," . . . Certainly, some private behavior can affect the fabric of society as a whole. Reasonable people may differ about whether particular sexual acts are moral or immoral, but "we have ample evidence for believing that people will not abandon morality, will not think any better of murder, cruelty and dishonesty, merely because some private sexual practice which they abominate is not punished by the law." H.L.A. Hart, Immorality and Treason, reprinted in The Law as Literature 220, 225 (L. Blom-Cooper ed. 1961). Petitioner and the Court fail to see the difference between laws that protect public sensibilities and those that enforce private morality. Statutes banning public sexual activity are entirely consistent with protecting the individual's liberty interest in decisions concerning sexual relations: the same recognition that those decisions are intensely private which justifies protecting them from governmental interference can justify protecting individuals from unwilling exposure to the sexual activities of others. But the mere fact that intimate behavior may be punished when it takes place in public cannot dictate how States can regulate intimate behavior that occurs in intimate places. See *Paris Adult Theatre I,* . . . ("marital intercourse on a street corner or a theater stage" can be forbidden despite the constitutional protection identified in *Griswold* v. *Connecticut.* . . .

This case involves no real interference with the rights of others, for the mere knowledge that other individuals do not adhere to one's value system cannot be a legally cognizable interest, . . . let alone an interest that can justify invading the houses, hearts, and minds of citizens who choose to live their lives differently.

IV

It took but three years for the Court to see the error in its analysis in *Minersville School District* v. *Gobitis* . . . and to recognize that the threat to national cohesion posed by a refusal to salute the flag was vastly outweighed by the threat to those same values posed by compelling such a salute. . . . I can only hope that here, too, the Court soon will reconsider its analysis and conclude that depriving individuals of the right to

choose for themselves how to conduct their intimate relationships poses a far greater threat to the values most deeply rooted in our Nation's history than tolerance of nonconformity could ever do. Because I think the Court today betrays those values, I dissent.

Justice STEVENS, with whom Justice BRENNAN and Justice MARSHALL join, dissenting.

Like the statute that is challenged in this case,[8] the rationale of the Court's opinion applies equally to the prohibited conduct regardless of whether the parties who engage in it are married or unmarried, or are of the same or different sexes. Sodomy was condemned as an odious and sinful type of behavior during the formative period of the common law. That condemnation was equally damning for heterosexual and homosexual sodomy. Moreover, it provided no special exemption for married couples.[9] The license to cohabit and to produce legitimate offspring simply did not include any permission to engage in sexual conduct that was considered a "crime against nature."

The history of the Georgia statute before us clearly reveals this traditional prohibition of heterosexual, as well as homosexual, sodomy.[10] Indeed, at one point in the 20th century, Georgia's law was construed to permit certain sexual conduct between homosexual women even though such conduct was prohibited between heterosexuals. The history of the statutes cited by the majority as proof for the proposition that sodomy is not constitutionally protected, . . . similarly reveals a prohibition on heterosexual, as well as homosexual, sodomy.

Because the Georgia statute expresses the traditional view that sodomy is an immoral kind of conduct regardless of the identity of the persons who engage in it, I believe that a proper analysis of its constitutionality requires consideration of two questions: First, may a State totally prohibit the described conduct by means of a neutral law applying without exception to all persons subject to its jurisdiction? If not, may the State save the statute by announcing that it will only enforce the law against homosexuals? The two questions merit separate discussion.

I

Our prior cases make two propositions abundantly clear. First, the fact that the governing majority in a State has traditionally viewed a particular practice as immoral is not a sufficient reason for upholding a law prohibiting the practice; neither history nor tradition could save a law prohibiting miscegenation from constitutional attack. Second, individual decisions by married persons, concerning the intimacies of their physical relationship, even when not intended to produce offspring, are a form of "liberty" protected by the Due Process Clause of the Fourteenth Amendment. *Griswold* v. *Connecticut. . . .* Moreover, this protection extends to intimate choices by unmarried as well as married persons. . . .

In consideration of claims of this kind, the Court has emphasized the individual interest in privacy, but its decisions have actually been animated by an even more fundamental concern. As I wrote some years ago:

> "*These cases do not deal with the individual's interest in protection from unwarranted public attention, comment, or exploitation. They deal, rather, with the individual's right to make certain unusually important decisions that will affect his own, or his family's, destiny. The Court has referred to such decisions as implicating 'basic values,' as being 'fundamental,' and as being dignified by history and tradition. The character of the Court's language in these cases brings to mind the origins of the American heritage of freedom—the abiding interest in individual liberty that makes certain state intrusions on the citizen's right to decide how he will live his own life intolerable. Guided by history, our tradition of respect for the dignity of individual choice in matters of conscience and the restraints implicit in the federal system, federal judges have accepted the responsibility for recognition and protection of these rights in appropriate cases."* . . .

Society has every right to encourage its individual members to follow particular traditions in expressing affection for one another and in gratifying their personal desires. It, of course, may prohibit an individual from imposing his will on another to satisfy his own selfish interests. It also may prevent an individual from interfering with, or violating, a legally sanctioned and protected relationship, such as marriage. And it may explain the relative advantages and disadvantages of different forms of intimate expression. But when individual married couples are isolated from observation by others, the way in which they voluntarily choose to conduct their intimate relations is a matter for them—not the State—to decide. The essential "liberty" that animated the development of the law in

cases like *Griswold, Eisenstadt,* and *Carey* surely embraces the right to engage in nonreproductive, sexual conduct that others may consider offensive or immoral.

Paradoxical as it may seem, our prior cases thus establish that a State may not prohibit sodomy within "the sacred precincts of marital bedrooms," *Griswold,* . . . or, indeed, between unmarried heterosexual adults. *Eisenstadt. . . .* In all events, it is perfectly clear that the State of Georgia may not totally prohibit the conduct proscribed by § 16-6-2 of the Georgia Criminal Code.

II

If the Georgia statute cannot be enforced as it is written—if the conduct it seeks to prohibit is a protected form of liberty for the vast majority of Georgia's citizens—the State must assume the burden of justifying a selective application of its law. Either the persons to whom Georgia seeks to apply its statute do not have the same interest in "liberty" that others have, or there must be a reason why the State may be permitted to apply a generally applicable law to certain persons that it does not apply to others.

The first possibility is plainly unacceptable. Although the meaning of the principle that "all men are created equal" is not always clear, it surely must mean that every free citizen has the same interest in "liberty" that the members of the majority share. From the standpoint of the individual, the homosexual and the heterosexual have the same interest in deciding how he will live his own life, and, more narrowly, how he will conduct himself in his personal and voluntary associations with his companions. State intrusion into the private conduct of either is equally burdensome.

The second possibility is similarly unacceptable. A policy of selective application must be supported by a neutral and legitimate interest—something more substantial than a habitual dislike for, or ignorance about, the disfavored group. Neither the State nor the Court has identified any such interest in this case. The Court has posited as a justification for the Georgia statute "the presumed belief of a majority of the electorate in Georgia that homosexual sodomy is immoral and unacceptable." . . . But the Georgia electorate has expressed no such belief—instead, its representatives enacted a law that presumably reflects the belief that *all sodomy* is immoral and unacceptable. Unless the Court is prepared to conclude that such a law is constitutional, it may not rely on the work product of the Georgia Legislature to support its holding. For the Georgia statute does not single out homosexuals as a separate class meriting special disfavored treatment.

Nor, indeed, does the Georgia prosecutor even believe that all homosexuals who violate this statute should be punished. This conclusion is evident from the fact that the respondent in this very case has formally acknowledged in his complaint and in court that he has engaged, and intends to continue to engage, in the prohibited conduct, yet the State has elected not to process criminal charges against him. As Justice POWELL points out, moreover, Georgia's prohibition on private, consensual sodomy has not been enforced for decades. The record of nonenforcement, in this case and in the last several decades, belies the Attorney General's representations about the importance of the State's selective application of its generally applicable law.

Both the Georgia statute and the Georgia prosecutor thus completely fail to provide the Court with any support for the conclusion that homosexual sodomy, *simpliciter,* is considered unacceptable conduct in that State, and that the burden of justifying a selective application of the generally applicable law has been met.

III

The Court orders the dismissal of respondent's complaint even though the State's statute prohibits all sodomy; even though that prohibition is concededly unconstitutional with respect to heterosexuals; and even though the State's *post hoc* explanations for selective application are belied by the State's own actions. At the very least, I think it clear at this early stage of the litigation that respondent has alleged a constitutional claim sufficient to withstand a motion to dismiss.

I respectfully dissent.

---

1. *Ga.Code Ann. § 16-6-2 (1984) provides, in pertinent part, as follows:*

    "(a) A person commits the offense of sodomy when he performs or submits to any sexual act involving the sex organs of one person and the mouth or anus of another. . . .

    "(b) A person convicted of the offense of sodomy shall be punished by imprisonment for not less than one nor more than 20 years. . . ."

2. *John and Mary Doe were also plaintiffs in the action. They alleged that they wished to engage in sexual activity proscribed by § 16-6-2 in the privacy of their home, App. 3, and that they had been "chilled and deterred" from engaging in such activity by both the existence of the statute and Hardwick's arrest. Id., at 5. The District Court held, however, that because they had neither sustained, nor were in immediate danger of sustaining, any direct injury from the enforcement of the statute, they did not have proper standing to maintain the action. Id., at 18. The Court of Appeals affirmed the District Court's judgment dismissing the Does' claim for lack of standing. 760 F.2d 1202, 1206–1207 (1985), and the Does do not challenge that holding in this Court.*

    The only claim properly before the Court, therefore, is Hardwick's challenge to the Georgia statute as applied to consensual homosexual sodomy. We express no opinion on the constitutionality of the Georgia statute as applied to other acts of sodomy.

3. *It was conceded at oral argument that, prior to the complaint against respondent Hardwick, there had been no reported decision involving prosecution for private homosexual sodomy under this statute for several decades. See Thompson v. Aldredge, 187 Ga. 467, 200 S.E. 799 (1939). Moreover, the State has declined to present the criminal charge against Hardwick to a grand jury, and this is a suit for declaratory judgment brought by respondents challenging the validity of the statute. The history of nonenforcement suggests the moribund character today of laws criminalizing this type of private, consensual conduct. Some 26 states have repealed similar statutes. But the constitutional validity of the Georgia*

statute was put in issue by respondents, and for the reasons stated by the Court, I cannot say that conduct condemned for hundreds of years has now become a fundamental right.

4. *Until 1968, Georgia defined sodomy as "the carnal knowledge and connection against the order of nature, by man with man, or in the same unnatural manner with woman." Ga. Crim.Code § 26-5901 (1933). In Thompson v. Aldredge, 187 Ga. 467, 200 S.E. 799 (1939), the Georgia Supreme Court held that § 26-5901 did not prohibit lesbian activity. And in Riley v. Garrett, 219 Ga. 345, 133 S.E.2d 367 (1963), the Georgia Supreme Court held that § 26-5901 did not prohibit heterosexual cunnilingus. Georgia passed the act-specific statute currently in force "perhaps in response to the restrictive court decisions such as Riley." Note, The Crimes Against Nature, 16 J.Pub.L. 159, 167, n. 47 (1967).*

5. *In Robinson v. California, 370 U.S. 660, 82 S.Ct. 1417, 8 L.Ed.2d 758 (1962), the Court held that the Eighth Amendment barred convicting a defendant due to his "status" as a narcotics addict, since that condition was "apparently an illness which may be contracted innocently or involuntarily." Id., at 667, 82 S.Ct., at 1420. In Powell v. Texas, 392 U.S. 514, 88 S.Ct. 2145, 20 L.Ed.2d 1254 (1968), where the Court refused to extend Robinson to punishment of public drunkenness by a chronic alcoholic, one of the factors relied on by Justice MARSHALL, in writing the plurality opinion, was that Texas had not "attempted to regulate appellant's behavior in the privacy of his own home." Id., at 532, 88 S.Ct., at 2154. Justice WHITE wrote separately:*

    "Analysis of this difficult case is not advanced by preoccupation with the label 'condition.' In Robinson the Court dealt with 'a statute which makes the "status" of narcotic addiction a criminal offense. . . .' 370 U.S., at 666 [82 S.Ct., at 1420]. By precluding criminal conviction for such a 'status' the Court was dealing with a condition brought about by acts remote in time from the application of the criminal sanctions contemplated, a condition which was relatively permanent in duration, and a condition of great magnitude and significance in terms of human behavior and values. . . . If it

were necessary to distinguish between 'acts' and 'conditions' for purposes of the Eighth Amendment, I would adhere to the concept of 'condition' implicit in the opinion in Robinson. . . . The proper subject of inquiry is whether volitional acts brought about the 'condition' and whether those acts are sufficiently proximate to the 'condition' for it to be permissible to impose penal sanctions on the 'condition.'" Id., 392 U.S., at 550–551, n. 2, 88 S.Ct., at 2163, n. 2.

Despite historical views of homosexuality, it is no longer viewed by mental health professionals as a "disease" or disorder. See Brief for American Psychological Association and American Public Health Association as Amici Curiae 8–11. But, obviously, neither is it simply a matter of deliberate personal election. Homosexual orientation may well form part of the very fiber of an individual's personality. Consequently, under Justice WHITE's analysis in Powell, the Eighth Amendment may pose a constitutional barrier to sending an individual to prison for acting on that attraction regardless of the circumstances. An individual's ability to make constitutionally protected "decisions concerning sexual relations," Carey v. Population Services International, 431 U.S. 678, 711, 97 S.Ct. 2010, 2029, 52 L.Ed.2d 675 (1977) (POWELL, J., concurring in part and concurring in the judgment), is rendered empty indeed if he or she is given no real choice but a life without any physical intimacy.

With respect to the Equal Protection Clause's applicability to § 16-6-2, I note that Georgia's exclusive stress before this Court on its interest in prosecuting homosexual activity despite the gender-neutral terms of the statute may raise serious questions of discriminatory enforcement, questions that cannot be disposed of before this Court on a motion to dismiss. See Yick Wo v. Hopkins, 118 U.S. 356, 373–374, 6 S.Ct. 1064, 1072–1073, 30 L.Ed. 220 (1886). The legislature having decided that the sex of the participants is irrelevant to the legality of the acts, I do not see why the State can defend § 16-6-2 on the ground that individuals singled out for prosecution are of the same sex as their partners. Thus, under the circumstances of this case, a claim under the Equal Protection Clause may well be available without having to reach the more controversial question whether homosexuals are a suspect class. See, e.g., Rowland v. Mad River Local School District,—U.S.—,—, 105 S.Ct. 1373,—, 84 L.Ed.2d 392 (1985) (BRENNAN, J., dissenting from denial of certiorari); Note, The Constitutional Status of Sexual Orientation: Homosexuality as a Suspect Classification, 98 Harv. L.Rev. 1285 (1985).

6. Even if a court faced with a challenge to § 16-6-2 were to apply simple rational-basis scrutiny to the statute, Georgia would be required to show an actual connection between the forbidden acts and the ill effects it seeks to prevent. The connection between the acts prohibited by § 16-6-2 and the harms identified by petitioner in his brief before this Court is a subject of hot dispute, hardly amenable to dismissal under Federal Rule of Civil Procedure 12(b)(6).

7. The theological nature of the origin of Anglo-American anti-sodomy statutes is patent. It was not until 1533 that sodomy was made a secular offense in England. 25 Hen. VIII, cap. 6. Until that time, the offense was, in Sir James Stephen's words, "merely ecclesiastical." 2 J. Stephen, A History of the Criminal Law of England 430 (1883). Pollock and Maitland similarly observed that "[t]he crime against nature . . . was so closely connected with heresy that the vulgar had but one name for both." 2 F. Pollock & F. Maitland, The History of English Law 554 (1895). The transfer of jurisdiction over prosecutions for sodomy to the secular courts seems primarily due to the alteration of ecclesiastical jurisdiction attendant on England's break with the Roman Catholic Church, rather than to any new understanding of the sovereign's interest in preventing or punishing the behavior involved. Cf. E. Coke, The Third Part of the Institutes of the Laws of England, ch. 10 (4th ed. 1797).

8. See Ga. Code Ann. § 16-6-2(a) (1984) ("A person commits the offense of sodomy when he performs or submits to any sexual act involving the sex organs of one person and the mouth or anus of another").

9. See J. May, The Law of Crimes § 203 (2d ed. 1893) ("Sodomy, otherwise called buggery, bestiality, and the crime against nature, is the unnatural copulation of two persons with each other, or of a human being with a beast. . . . It may be committed by a man with a man, by a man with a beast, or by a woman with a beast, or by a man with a woman—his wife, in which case, if she consents, she is an accomplice").

10. The predecessor of the current Georgia statute provided, "Sodomy is the carnal knowledge and connection against the order of nature, by man with man, or in the same unnatural manner with woman." Ga.Code, Tit. 1, Pt. 4, § 4251 (1861). This prohibition of heterosexual sodomy was not purely hortatory. See, eg., Comer v. State, 21 Ga.App. 306, 94 S.E. 314 (1917) (affirming prosecution for consensual heterosexual sodomy).

Freedom of Expression and Its Limits

LIMITS TO THE FREE EXPRESSION OF OPINION

Joel Feinberg

The purpose of this essay is to determine how the liberal principles that support free expression of opinion generally also define the limits to what the law can permit to be said. The liberal principle in question, put vaguely, is that state coercion is justified only to prevent personal or public harm. That more harm than good can be expected to come from suppression of dissenting opinions in politics and religion has been amply documented by experience and argument, but concentration on this important truth, despite its salutary practical effects, is likely to mislead us into thinking that the liberal "harm principle" is simple in its meaning and easy in its application. For that reason, this essay will only summarize (in Part I) the impressive case for total freedom of expression of opinions of certain kinds in normal contexts, and concentrate instead (in Part II) on the types of expressions excluded by the harm principle: defamation and "malicious truth," invasions of privacy, and expressions that cause others to do harm (those that cause panics, provoke retaliatory violence, or incite others to crime or insurrection). Part III will examine the traditional crime of "sedition," and conclude that it is not properly among the categories of expressions excluded by the harm principle. Among the other lessons that will emerge from these exercises, I hope, is that the harm principle is a largely empty formula in urgent need of supplementation by tests for determining the relative importance of conflicting interests and by measures of the degree to which interests are endangered by free expressions.

I The Case for Freedom

The classic case for free expression of opinion was made by John Stuart Mill.[1] Mill's purpose in his famous chapter "Of the Liberty of Thought and Discussion" was to consider, as a beginning, just one class of actions and how his "harm principle" applied to them. The actions in question were instances of expressing orally or in print opinions about matters of fact, and about historical, scientific, theological, philosophical, political, and moral questions. Mill's conclusion was that suppressing such expressions is always more harmful than the expressions themselves would be and therefore is never justified. But don't expressions of opinion *ever* harm others? Of course they do, and it would be silly to ascribe to Mill the absurd contrary view. Expressions of opinion harm others when they are: defamatory (libelous or slanderous), seditious, incitive to violence, malicious publications of damaging or embarrassing truths, or invasions of privacy. In fact, in classifying an expression under one of these headings, we are *ipso facto* declaring that it is harmful. Mill is not radical about this. Putting these obviously harmful expressions to one side (he is best understood as asking) is there any [further] ground for suppressing mere "opinions"? To *this* question Mill's answer is radical and absolutist: If an expression cannot be subsumed under one of these standard headings for harmfulness, then it can never be sufficiently injurious to be justifiably suppressed. Apart from direct harm to assignable persons, no other ground is ever a sufficient reason for overriding the presumption in favor of liberty. One may *never* properly suppress an expression on the grounds, for example, that it is immoral, shocking to sensibilities, annoying, heretical, unorthodox, or "dangerous," and especially not on the ground simply that it is false.

Expressions of opinion thus occupy a very privileged position, in Mill's view. That is because their suppression, he contends, is not only a private injury to the coerced party but also and inevitably a very serious harm to the public in general. The argument has two distinct branches. The first has us consider the possibility that the suppressed opinion is wholly or partially true. On this assumption, of course, repression will have the harmful social consequence of loss of truth.

The crucial contention in this wing of the argument, however, is much stronger than that. Mill contends that there is *always* a chance, for all we can know, that the suppressed opinion is at least partially true, so that the act of repression itself necessarily involves some risk. Moreover, the risk is always an unreasonable one, never worth taking, since the risk of its alternative—permitting free expression generally— to our interest in acquiring knowledge and avoiding error, is negligible. By letting every opinion, no matter how "certainly true," be challenged, we minimize the risk of permanent commitment to falsehood. In the process, of course, we allow some falsehoods to be expressed, but since the truth is not denied its champions either, there is very little risk that the tolerated falsehood will become permanently enthroned. The balance of favorable risks then is clearly on the side of absolute freedom of expression.

This argument is especially convincing in the world of science, where no hypothesis bears its evidence on its face, and old errors are continually exposed by new and easily duplicable evidence and by more careful and refined experimental techniques. Even totalitarian regimes have learned that it is in their own interest to permit physicists and plant geneticists to go their theoretical ways unencumbered by ideological restrictions. Sometimes, to be sure, the truth of a scientific theory is so apparent that it is well worth acting on even though it strains governmental priorities to do so and requires large investment of funds; but this very confidence, Mill argued, is justified only when every interested party has had an opportunity to refute the theory. In respect at least to scientific theories, the more open to attack an opinion is, the

more confident we can eventually be of its truth. That "no one has disproved it yet" is a convincing reason for accepting a theory only when everyone has been free to try.

To deny that it is possible for a given opinion to be true, Mill maintained, is to assume one's own infallibility. This is no doubt an overstatement, but what does seem clear is that to deny that a given proposition can possibly be true is to assume one's own infallibility with respect to *it,* though of course not one's infallibility generally. To say that one cannot possibly be wrong in holding a given belief is to say that one knows that one's knowledge of its truth is authentic. We claim to know infallibly when we claim to know that we know. It is also clear, I think, that we are sometimes justified in making such claims. I know that I know that $2 + 3 = 5$, that I am seated at my desk writing, and that New York is in the United States. In the face of challenges from the relentless epistemological skeptic, I may have to admit that I don't know *how* I know these things, but it doesn't follow from that that I don't know them. It seems then that there is no risk, after all, in suppressing some opinions, namely, the denials of such truisms.

Yet what could ever be the point of forbidding persons from denying that $2 + 3 = 5$ or that New York is in the United States? There is surely no danger that general confidence in these true propositions would be undermined. There is no risk of loss of truth, I suppose, in suppressing their denials, but also no risk in allowing them free circulation. Conceding that we can know truisms infallibly, therefore, can hardly commit us to approve of the suppression of their denials, at least so long as we adhere, with Mill, exclusively to the harm principle. More importantly, there are serious risks involved in granting any mere man or group of men the power to draw the line between those opinions that are known infallibly to be true and those not so known, in order to ban expression of the former. Surely, if there is one thing that is *not* infallibly known, it is how to draw *that* line.

In any case, when we leave tautologies and truisms behind and consider only those larger questions of substance, doctrines about which have in fact been banned by rulers in the past as certainly false (for example, the shape of the earth, the cause of disease, the wisdom of certain wars or economic policies, and the morality of certain kinds of conduct) our own fallibility is amply documented by history. The sad fact is that at every previous stage of history including the recent past there have been questions of the highest importance about which nearly *everyone,* including the wisest and most powerful, has been dead wrong. The more important the doctrines, then, the greater the risk we run in forbidding expressions of disagreement.

Mill's account, in this first wing of his argument, of the public interest in the discovery and effective dissemination of truth has many important practical implications. Mill himself thought that we should seek out our ideological enemies and offer them public forums in which to present and defend their views, or failing that, hire "devil's advocates" to defend unpopular positions in schools and in popular debates. Mill's reasons for these proposals also provide the grounding for the so-called "adversary theory of politics." The argument is (in the words of Zechariah Chafee): "Truth can be sifted out from falsehood only if the government is vigorously and constantly cross-examined. . . . Legal proceedings prove that an opponent makes the best cross-examiner."[2] This states the rationale of the two-party system exactly. The role of the out-party is like that of the prosecutor in a criminal trial, or plaintiff in a civil action. It is a vitally important role too. Numerous historical instances suggest that we are in grave danger when both parties agree. Witness, for example, the Vietnam debacle, which was the outcome of a twenty-year "bipartisan foreign policy." Foreign policy decisions are as difficult as they are important; hence the need for constant reexamination, probing for difficulties and soft spots, bringing to light new and relevant facts, and subjecting to doubt hitherto unquestioned first premises. Without these aids, we tend to drift quite complacently into dead ends and quagmires.[3]

The second branch of the argument has us assume that the unorthodox opinion we are tempted to suppress really is false anyway. Even in this case, Mill insists, we will all be the losers, in the end, for banning it. When people are not forced by the stimulus of dissent to rethink the grounds of their convictions, then their beliefs tend to wither and decay. The rationales of the tenets are forgotten, their vital direction and value lost, their very meaning altered, until at last they are held in the manner of dead dogmas rather than living truths.

No part of Mill's argument in *On Liberty* is more impressive than his case for totally free expression of opinion. It is especially ingenious in that it rests entirely on social advantages and foregoes all help that might come from appeals to "the inalienable right to say what one pleases whether it's good for society or not." But that very utilitarian ingenuity may be its Achilles heel; for if liberty of expression is justified only because it is socially useful, then some might think that it is justified only *when* it is socially useful. The possibility of special circumstances in which repression is still *more* useful is real enough to disturb allies of Mill who love liberty fully as much as he and would seek therefore a still more solid foundation for it. But even if the case for absolute liberty of opinion must rest ultimately on some theory of natural rights, Mill has given that case powerful utilitarian reinforcement.

II Limits to Freedom

Despite the impressive case for complete liberty of expression, there are obvious instances where permitting a person to speak his mind freely will cause more harm than good all around. These instances have been lumped together in various distinct legal categories whose names have come to stand for torts or crimes and to suggest, by a powerful linguistic convention, unpermitted wrongdoing. Thus, there can be no more right to defame or to incite to riot than there can be a right way, in Aristotle's example,[4] to commit adultery. Underlying these linguistic conventions, however, are a settled residue of interest weightings as well as actual and hypothetical applications of the harm principle, often filled in or mediated in various ways by principles of other kinds. The various categories of excluded expressions are worth examining not only for the light they throw on the harm principle, but also for the conceptual and normative problems each raises on its own for political theory.

1. *Defamation and "Malicious Truth."* Defamatory statements are those that damage a person's reputation by their expression to third parties in a manner that "tends to diminish the esteem in which the plaintiff is held, or to excite adverse feelings or opinions against him."[5] The primary mode of discouraging defamers in countries adhering to the common law has been the threat of civil liability to a court-enforced order to pay cash to the injured party in compensation for the harm done his reputation. In cases of especially malicious defamation, the defendant may be ordered to pay a stiff fine ("punitive damages") to the plaintiff as well. Only in the most egregious cases (and rarely even then) has criminal liability been imposed for defamation, but nevertheless the threat of civil suit as sufficient to entitle us to say that our law does not leave citizens (generally) free to defame one another. Here then is one clear limit to our freedom of expression.

Not all expressions that harm another's reputation, of course, are legally forbidden. Even when damaging defamation has been proved by the plaintiff, the defendant may yet escape liability by establishing one of two kinds of defense. He may argue that his utterance or publication was "privileged," or simply that it is *true*. The former defense is established by showing either that the defendant, in virtue of his public office or his special relation to the plaintiff, has been granted an absolute immunity from liability for defamation (for example, he spoke in a judicial or legislative proceeding, or he had the prior consent of the plaintiff), or that he had a prior immunity contingent on the reasonableness of his conduct. Examples of this category of privilege are the immunity of a person protecting himself or another by a warning that someone is of poor character, or of a drama, literary, or political critic making "fair comment" of an extremely unfavorable kind about a performance, a book, or a policy. These immunities are still other examples of public policies that protect an interest (in this case, the interest in reputation) just to the point where the protection interferes with interests deemed more important—either to the public in general or to other private individuals. These policies imply that a person's reputation is a precious thing that deserves legal protection just as his life, health, and property do, but on the other hand, a certain amount of rough handling of reputations is to be expected in courtrooms, in the heated spontaneous debates of legislative chambers, in reviews of works presented to the public for critical comment, and in the rough-and-tumble competition among eminent persons for power or public acclaim. To withhold immunities in these special contexts would be to allow nervous inhibitions to keep hard truths out of law courts to the detriment of justice, or out of legislatures to the detriment of the laws themselves; or to make critics overly cautious, to the detriment of those who rely on their judgments; or to make political commentators overly deferential to power and authority, to the detriment of reform.

There is, however, no public interest in keeping those who are not in these special contexts uninhibited when they speak or write about others. Indeed, we should all be nervous when we make unfavorable comments, perhaps not on the ground that feelings and reputations will simply be damaged (there may be both justice and social gain in such damage), but at least on the ground that the unfavorable comment may be *false*. In a way, the rationale for the defamation action at law is the opposite of Mill's case for the free expression of opinion. The great public interest in possessing the truth in science, philosophy, politics, and so on, is best served by keeping everyone uninhibited in the expression of his views; but there are areas where there is a greater interest in avoiding falsehood than in acquiring truth, and here we are best served by keeping people very nervous indeed when they are tempted to speak their minds.

Once the plaintiff has proved that the defendant has published a defamatory statement about him, the defendant may avoid liability in another way, namely, by showing that the statement in question is *true*. "Out of a tender regard for reputations," writes Professor Prosser, "the law presumes in the first instance that all defamation is false, and the defendant has the burden of pleading and proving its truth."[6] In the large majority of American jurisdictions, truth is a "complete defense" which will relieve the defendant of liability even when he published his defamation merely out of spite, in the absence of any reasonable social purpose. One wonders why this should be. Is the public interest in "the truth" so great that it should always override a private person's interest in his own reputation? An affirmative answer, I should think, would require considerable argument.

Most of the historical rationales for the truth defense worked out in the courts and in legal treatises will not stand scrutiny. They all founder, I think, on the following kind of case. A New York girl supports her drug addiction by working as a prostitute in a seedy environment of crime and corruption. After a brief jail sentence, she decides to reform, and travels to the Far West to begin her life anew. She marries a respectable young man, becomes a leader in civic and church affairs, and raises a large and happy family. Then twenty years after her arrival in town, her neurotically jealous neighbor learns of her past, and publishes a lurid but accurate account of it for the eyes of the whole community. As a consequence, her "friends" and associates snub her; she is asked to resign her post as church leader; gossip-mongers prattle ceaselessly about her; and obscene inscriptions appear on her property and in her mail. She dare not sue her neighbor for defamation since the defamatory report is wholly true. She has been wronged, but she has no legal remedy.

Applied to this case the leading rationales for the truth defense are altogether unconvincing. One argument claims that the true gravamen of the wrong in defamation is the deception practiced on the public in misrepresenting the truth, so that where there is no misrepresentation there is no injury—as if the injury to the reformed sinner is of no account. A variant of this argument holds the reformed sinner to be deserving of exposure on the ground that he (or she) in covering up his past deceives the public, thereby compounding the earlier delinquency. If this sort of "deception" is morally blameworthy, then so is every form of 'covering up the truth,' from cosmetics to window blinds! Others have argued that a delinquent plaintiff should not be allowed any standing in court because of his established bad character. A related contention is that "a person is in no position to complain of a reputation which is consistent with his actual character and behavior."[7] Both of these rationales apply well enough to the unrepentant sinner, but work nothing but injustice and suffering on the reformed person, on the plaintiff defamed in some way that does not reflect upon his character, or on the person whose "immoralities" have been wholly private and scrupulously kept from the public eye. It does not follow from the fact that a person's reputation is consistent with the truth that it is "deserved."

The most plausible kind of argument for the truth defense is that it serves some kind of overriding public interest. Some have argued that fear of eventual exposure can serve as effectively as the threat of punishment to *deter* wrongdoing. This argument justifies a kind of endless social penalty and is therefore more cruel than a system of criminal law, which usually permits a wrongdoer to wipe his slate clean. Others have claimed that exposure of character flaws and past sins protects the community by warning it of dangerous or untrustworthy persons. That argument is well put (but without endorsement) by Harper and James when they refer to ". . . the social desirability as a general matter, of leaving individuals free to warn the public of antisocial members of the community, provided only that the person furnishing the information take the risk of its being false."[8] (Blackstone went so far as to assert that the defendant who can show the truth of his defamatory remarks has rendered a public service in exposing the plaintiff and deserves the public's gratitude[9]). This line of argument is convincing enough when restricted to public-spirited defamers and socially dangerous plaintiffs; but it lacks all plausibility when applied to the malicious and useless exposure of past misdeeds, or to nonmoral failings and "moral" flaws of a wholly private and well-concealed kind.

How precious a thing, after all, is this thing denoted by the glittering abstract noun, the "Truth"? The truth in general is a great and noble cause, a kind of public treasury more important than any particular person's feelings; but the truth about a particular person may be of no great value at all except to that

person. When the personal interest in reputation outweighs the dilute public interest in truth (and there is no doubt that this is sometimes the case) then it must be protected even at some cost to our general knowledge of the truth. The truth, like any other commodity, is not so valuable that it is a bargain at *any* cost. A growing number of American states have now modified the truth defense so that it applies only when the defamatory statement has been published with good motives, or is necessary for some reasonable public purpose, or (in some cases) both. The change is welcome.

In summary, the harm principle would permit all harmless statements about others whether true or false (harmless statements by definition are not defamatory), but it would impose liability for all defamatory false statements and all seriously defamatory true statements except those that serve (or seem likely to serve) some beneficial social purpose.

2. *Invasions of Privacy.* Still other expressions are neither defamatory nor false, and yet they can unjustly wound the persons they describe all the same. These do not invade the interest in a good reputation so much as a special kind of interest in peace of mind, sometimes called a sense of dignity, sometimes the enjoyment of solitude, but most commonly termed the interest in personal privacy. As the legal "right to privacy" is now understood, it embraces a miscellany of things, protecting the right-holder not only from "physical intrusions upon his solitude" and "publicity given to his name or likeness or to private information about him" without his permission, but also from being placed "in a false light [but without defamation] in the public eye" and from the "commercial appropriation of elements of his personality."[10] (Some of these are really invasions of one's property rights through unpermitted commercial exploitation of one's name, image, personality, and so on. For that reason it has been urged that the invaded right in these cases be called "the right to publicity.") What concerns us here are statements conveying true and nondefamatory information about the plaintiff, of a very intimate and properly private kind, gathered and published without his consent, often to his shame and mortification. Business advantage and journalistic profit have become ever stronger motives for such statements, and the invention of tiny, very sensitive snooping devices has made the data easier than ever to come by.

Since the "invasion of privacy" tort has been recognized, plaintiffs have recovered damages from defendants who have shadowed them, looked into their windows, investigated their bank accounts, and tapped their telephone wires. In many of these cases, the court's judgment protected the plaintiff's interest in "being let alone," but in other cases the interest protected was not merely this, or not this at all, but rather the interest in *not being known about.* If there is a right not to be known about in some respects by anyone, then *a fortiori* there is a right not to be known about, in those respects by nearly everyone. Privacy law has also protected the interests of those who don't want details of their lives called to the public's attention and made the subject of public wonder, amusement, discussion, analysis, or debate. Hence some plaintiffs have recovered from defendants who have published embarrassing details of their illness or physical deformity; their personal letters or unpublished notes, or inventories of their possessions; their photographs in a "good looks" popularity contest, or in a "before and after" advertisement for baldness or obesity cures, or on the labels of tomato cans; and from defendants who have published descriptions of the plaintiffs' sexual relations, hygienic habits, and other very personal matters. No life, of course, can be kept wholly private, or immune from public inspection even in some of its most personal aspects. "No one enjoys being stared at," Harper and James remind us, yet if a person "goes out on the street he [can have] no legal objection to people looking at him."[11] On the other hand, life would be hardly tolerable if there were no secrets we could keep (away from "the street"), no preserve of dignity, no guaranteed solitude.

There would probably be very little controversy over the existence of a right to privacy were it not the case that the interest in being let alone is frequently in conflict with other interests that seem at least equally deserving of protection. Even where the right is recognized by law, it is qualified by the recognition of very large classes of privileged expressions. First of all, like most other torts and crimes, the charge of invasion of privacy is completely defeated by proof that the plaintiff gave his consent to the defendant's conduct. Secondly, and more interestingly, the right of privacy can conflict with the constitutionally guaranteed freedom of the press, which, according to Prosser, "justifies the publication of news and all other matters of legitimate public interest and concern."[12] For a court to adjudicate between a paper's right to publish and an individual's right to privacy then, it must employ some standard for determining what is of legitimate public concern or, what amounts to the same thing, which news about a person is "fit to print." Such legal standards are always in the making,

never finished, but the standard of "legitimate interest" has begun to take on a definite shape. American courts have decided, first of all, that "the person who intentionally puts himself in the public eye . . . has no right to complain of any publicity which reasonably bears on his activity."[13] The rationale for this judgment invokes the maxim that a person is not wronged by that to which he consents, or by that the risk of which he has freely assumed. The person who steps into the public spotlight ought to know what he is letting himself in for; hence the law presumes that he *does* know, and therefore that he is asking for it. Much the same kind of presumption lies behind the "fair comment" defense in defamation cases: The person who voluntarily publishes his own work is presumed to be inviting criticism and is therefore not entitled to complain when the criticism is adverse or harsh, providing only that it is relevant and not personally abusive. One can put oneself voluntarily into the public eye by running for or occupying public office; by becoming an actor, musician, entertainer, poet, or novelist; by inventing an interesting device or making a geographical or scientific discovery; or even by becoming wealthy. Once a person has become a public figure, he has sacrificed much of his right of privacy to the public's legitimate curiosity. Of course, one never forfeits *all* rights of privacy; even the public figure has a right to the privacy of his very most intimate affairs. (This may, however, be very small consolation to him.)

One cannot always escape the privilege of the press to invade one's privacy simply by avoiding public roles and offices, for the public spotlight can catch up with anyone. "Reluctant public characters" are nonetheless public and therefore, according to the courts, as legitimate objects of public curiosity as the voluntary public figures. Those unfortunates who attract attention unwillingly by becoming involved, even as victims, in accidents, or by being accused of crimes, or even as innocent bystanders to interesting events, have become "news," and therefore subject to the public's right to know. They maintain this unhappy status "until they have reverted to the lawful and unexciting life led by the great bulk of the community," but until then, "they are subject to the privileges which publishers have to satisfy the curiosity of the public as to their leaders, heroes, villains, and victims."[14] Again, the privilege to publish is not unlimited so that "the courts must somehow draw the distinction between conduct which outrages the common decencies and goes beyond what the public mores will tolerate, and that which the plaintiff must be expected in the circumstances to endure."[15]

When interests of quite different kinds head toward collisions, how can one determine which has the right of way? This problem, which lies behind the most puzzling questions about the grounds for liberty and coercion, tends to be concealed by broadly stated principles. The conflict between the personal interest in privacy and the public curiosity is one of the best illustrations of the problem, but it is hardly unique. In defamation cases, as we have seen, there is often a conflict between the public interest in truth and the plaintiff's interest in his own good name. In nuisance law, there is a conflict between the plaintiff's interest in the peaceful enjoyment of his land and the defendant's interest in keeping a hogpen, or a howling dog, or a small boiler factory. In suburban neighborhoods, the residents' interest in quiet often conflicts with motorcyclists' interest in cheap and speedy transportation. In buses and trains, one passenger's interest in privacy[16] can conflict with another's interest in listening to rock and roll music on a portable radio, or for that matter, with the interests of two nearby passengers in making unavoidably audible, but avoidably inane, conversation. The principle of "the more freedom the better" doesn't tell us whose freedom must give way in these competitive situations.

The invasion of privacy cases are among the very clearest examples of the inevitable clash of interests in populous modern communities. They are, moreover, examples that show that solving the problem is not just a matter of minimizing harm all around. Harm is the invasion of an interest, and invasions do differ in degree, but when interests of radically different kinds are invaded to the same degree, where is the greater harm? Perhaps we should say that some interests are more important than others in the sense that harm to them is likely to lead to greater damage to the whole economy of personal (or as the case may be, community) interests than harm to the lesser interest, just as harm to one's heart or brain will do more damage to one's bodily health than an "equal degree" of harm to less vital organs. Determining which interests are more "vital" in an analogous sense would be no easy task, but even if we could settle this matter, there would remain serious difficulties. In the first place, interests pile up and reinforce one another. My interest in peace and quiet may be more vital in my system than the motorcyclist's interests in speed, excitement, and economy are in his, but there is also the interest of the cyclist's employer in having workers efficiently transported to his factory, and the economic interest of the community in general (including me) in the flourishing of the factory owner's business; the inter-

est of the motorcycle manufacturers in their own profits; the interest of the police and others (perhaps including me) in providing a relatively harmless outlet for adolescent exuberance, and in not having a difficult rule to enforce. There may be nowhere near so great a buildup of reinforcing interests, personal and public, in the quietude of my neighborhood.

There is still another kind of consideration that complicates the delicate task of interest-balancing. Interests differ not only in the extent to which they are thwarted, in their importance or "vitality," and the degree to which they are backed up by other interests, but also in their inherent moral quality. Some interests, simply by reason of their very natures, we might think better worth protecting than others. The interest in knowing the intimate details of Brigitte Bardot's married sex life (the subject of a sensational lawsuit in France) is a morally repugnant peeping tom's interest. The sadist's interest in having others suffer pain is a morbid interest. The interest in divulging a celebrity's private conversations is a busybody's interest. It is probably not conducive to the public good to encourage development of the character flaws from which these interests spring, but even if there were social advantage in the individual vices, there would be a case against protecting their spawned interests, based upon their inherent unworthiness. The interests in understanding, diagnosing, and simply being apprised of newsworthy events might well outbalance a given individual's reluctance to be known about, but photographs and descriptions with no plausible appeal except to the morbid and sensational can have very little weight in the scales.

3. *Causing Panic.* Defamatory statements, "malicious truths," and statements that wrongfully invade privacy do harm to the persons they are about by conveying information or falsehood to third parties. Their publication tends to instill certain beliefs in others, and the very existence of those beliefs constitutes a harm to the person spoken or written about. Other classes of injurious expressions do harm in a rather different way, namely, by causing those who listen to them (or more rarely, those who read them) to act in violent or otherwise harmful ways. In these cases, the expressions need not be about any specifiable persons, or if they are about persons, those individuals are not necessarily the victims of the subsequent harm. When spoken words cause panic, breach the peace, or incite to crime or revolt, a variety of important interests, personal and social, will be seriously harmed. Such expressions, therefore, are typically proscribed by the criminal, and not merely the civil, law.

"The most stringent protection of free speech," wrote Holmes in his most celebrated opinion, "would not protect a man in falsely shouting fire in a theatre and causing a panic."[17] In some circumstances a person can cause even more harm by *truthfully* shouting "Fire!" in a crowded theater, for the flames and smoke might reinforce the tendency of his words to cause panic, and the fire itself might block exits, leading the hysterical crowds to push and trample. But we do not, and cannot fairly, hold the excited alarm sounder criminally responsible for his warning when it was in fact true and shouted with good intentions. We can hardly demand on pain of punishment that persons pick their words carefully in emergencies, when emotions naturally run high and there is no time for judicious deliberation. A person's warning shout in such circumstances is hardly to be treated as a full-fledged voluntary act at all. Perhaps it can be condemned as negligent, but given the mitigating circumstances, such negligence hardly amounts to the gross and wanton kind that can be a basis of criminal liability. The law, then, can only punish harmful words of this class when they are spoken or written with the intention of causing the harm that in fact ensues, or when they are spoken or written in conscious disregard of a high and unreasonable risk that the harm will ensue. The practical joker in a crowded auditorium who whispers to his comrade, "Watch me start a panic," and then shouts "Fire!" could be convicted for using words intentionally to cause a panic. The prankster who is willing to risk a general panic just for the fun of alarming one particular person in the audience could fairly be convicted for the grossly reckless use of dangerous words. Indeed, his recklessness is akin to that of the motorist who drives at an excessive speed just to frighten a timorous passenger.

Suppose, however, that the theater is virtually empty, and as the lights come on at the end of the film, our perverse or dim-witted jokester shouts "Fire! Fire!" just for the sake of confusing the three or four other patrons and alarming the ushers. The ushers quickly see through the ruse and suffer only a few moments of anxiety, and the patrons walk quickly to the exits and depart. No harm to speak of has been done; nor could any have reasonably been anticipated. This example shows how very important are the surrounding circumstances of an utterance to the question of its permissibility. Given the presumptive case for liberty in general, and especially the powerful social interest in leaving persons free to use *words* as they see fit, there can be a countervailing case for suppression on the grounds of the words' dangerous tendency only when the danger in fact is great and the tendency immediate. These matters are determined not only by the particular words used, but by the objective character of the surrounding circumstances— what lawyers call "the time, place, and manner" of utterance.

The question of legal permissibility should not be confused with that of moral blameworthiness or even with civil liability. The practical joker, even in relatively harmless circumstances, is no moral paragon. But then neither are the liar, the vulgarian, the rude man, and the scandalmonger, most of whose faults are not fit subjects for penal legislation. We cannot make every instance of mendacity, rudeness, and malicious gossip criminal, but we can protect people from the serious injury that comes from fraud, battery, or defamation. Similarly, practical jokers should be blamed but not punished, unless their tricks reach the threshold of serious danger to others. On the other hand, almost all lies, bad tales, jokes, and tricks create some risk, and there is no injustice in making the perpetrator compensate (as opposed to being punished) even his unlikely victim. Thus, if a patron in the nearly empty theater described above sprains an ankle in hurrying towards an exit, there is no injustice in requiring the jokester to pay the medical expenses.

It is established in our law that when words did not in fact cause harm the speaker may nevertheless be punished for having uttered them only if there was high danger when they were spoken that serious harm would result. This condition of course could be satisfied even though the harm in fact was averted: Not everything probable becomes actual. Similarly, for a person rightly to be punished even for harm in fact caused by his words, the harm in its resultant magnitude must have been an objectively probable consequence of the spoken words in the circumstances; otherwise the speaker will be punished for an unforeseeable fluke. In either case, then, the clear and present danger that serious harm will follow a speaker's words is necessary if he is rightly to be punished.

As we have seen, punishment for the harm caused by words is proper only if the speaker caused the harm either *intentionally* or *recklessly*. Both of these "mental conditions" of guilt require the satisfaction of the clear and present danger formula, or something like it. Consider recklessness first. For there to be recklessness there must really be a substantial risk consciously and unreasonably run. A speaker is not being reckless if he utters words that have only a remote and speculative tendency to cause panics or riots.

Intentional harm-causing by words raises more complications. Suppose an evil-minded person wishes to cause a panic and believes what is false and wholly unsupported by any real evidence, namely, that his words will have that effect. Imagine that he attends a meeting of the Policemen's Benevolent Association and, at what he takes to be the strategic moment, he stands up and shrieks, "There's a mouse under my chair!" Perhaps these words would cause a panic at a meeting of Girl Scouts but it merely produces a round of contemptuous laughter here. Wanting a panic and sincerely believing that one is causing a panic by one's words, then, are not sufficient. Suppose however we complicate the story so that by some wholly unforeseeable fluke the spoken words do precipitate a panic. The story is hard to invent at this point, but let us imagine that one patrolman laughs so hard that he tips over his chair causing another to drop his pipe, starting a fire, igniting live bullets, et cetera. Now, in addition to evil desire, and conscious belief in causal efficacy, we have a third important element: The words actually do initiate a causal process resulting in the desired panic. But these conditions still are not sufficient to permit us to say that the speaker *intentionally caused* a panic. Without the antecedent objective probability that a panic would follow these words in these circumstances, we have only a bizarre but tragic coincidence.

We would say much the same thing of a superstitious lady who "attempts" to start a riot by magic means. In an inconspicuous corner of a darkened theater, she sticks pins into a doll and mutters under her breath a magic incantation designed to produce a panic. Of course this doesn't work in the way intended, but a nearsighted and neurotic passerby observes her, takes the doll to be a real baby, and screams. The hoped-for panic then really follows. The evil lady cannot be found guilty of intentionally causing a panic, even though she intended to cause one and really did cause (or at least initiate a causal process that resulted in) one. She can be condemned for having very evil motives. But if people are sufficiently ignorant and impotent, the law, applying the harm principle, allows them to be as evil as they wish.

4. *Provoking Retaliatory Violence.* Suppose a person utters words which have as their unhappy effects violence directed *at him* by his angry audience, counterviolence by his friends and protectors, and escalation into a riotous breach of the peace. This is still another way of causing harm by words. Should the speaker be punished? In almost every conceivable case, the answer should be No. There is a sense, of course, in which the speaker did not start the physical violence. He used only words, and while words can sting and infuriate, they are not instruments of violence in the same sense that fists, knives, guns, and clubs are. If the law suppresses public speech, either by withholding permits in advance or punishing afterwards, simply on the ground that the expressed views are so unpopular that some auditors can be expected to start fighting, then the law punishes some for the criminal proclivities of others. "A man does not become a criminal because someone else assaults him . . . ," writes Zechariah Chafee. Moreover, he continues, on any such theory, "a small number of intolerant men . . . can prevent *any kind* of meeting. . . . A gathering which expressed the sentiment of a majority of law-abiding citizens would become illegal because a small gang of hoodlums threatened to invade the hall."[18] When violent response to speech threatens, the obvious remedy is not suppression, but rather increased police protection.

So much seems evident, but there may be some exceptions. Some words uttered in public places in the presence of many unwilling auditors may be so abusive or otherwise offensive as to be "reasonably considered a direct provocation to violence."[19] The captive auditor, after all, is not looking for trouble as he walks the public streets intent on his private errands. If he is forced to listen, as he walks past a street meeting, to speakers denouncing and ridiculing his religion, and forced to notice a banner with a large and abusive caricature of the Pope,[20] his blood might reasonably be expected to boil. Antireligious and anticlerical opinions, of course, no matter how unpopular, are entitled to the full protection of the law. Even abusive, virulent, and mocking expressions of such views are entitled to full protection if uttered to private gatherings, in private or privately reserved places. Such expressions become provocative only when made in public places to captive auditors.

What makes an expression "provocative?" Surely, if words are to be suppressed on the ground that they are provocative of violence, they must be more than merely "provoking," else all unpopular opinions will be suppressed, to the great public loss. As far as I know, the concept of provocation has received thorough legal elaboration only in the law of homicide, where provocation reduces a charge of murder to that of manslaughter, thus functioning as a kind of mitigating consideration rather than as a justification or complete excuse. In the common law, for there to be sufficient provocation to mitigate: (1) The behavior of the victim must have been so aggravating that it would have produced "such excitement and passion as would obscure the reason of an ordinary man and induce him ... to strike the blow."[21] (2) There must not have elapsed so much time between the provocation and the violence that a reasonable man's blood would have cooled. (3) But for the victim's provocation the violence would not have occurred. In short, provocation mitigates only when it in fact produces a reason-numbing rage in the attacker and is such that it could be expected to produce such a rage in any normal person in his circumstances. Nazi emblems might be expected to have this effect on a former inmate of a Nazi death camp, but the Democratic party line cannot be sufficiently provocative to excuse a violent Republican, and similarly the other way round. Indeed, in the law of homicide, *no mere words alone,* no matter how abusive or scurrilous, can be adequate provocation to justify or totally excuse killing as a response.

There would seem to be equally good reason not to consider mere words either as justifying or totally excusing nonlethal acts of violence. The "reasonable person" in a democracy must be presumed to have enough self-control to refrain from violent responses to odious words and doctrines. If he is followed, insulted, taunted, and challenged, he can get injunctive relief, or bring charges against his tormentor as a nuisance; if there is no time for this and he is backed to the wall he may be justified in using "reasonable force" in self-defense; or if he is followed to his own home, he can use the police to remove the nuisance. But if he is not personally harrassed in these ways, he can turn on his heels and leave the provocation behind, and this is what the law, perhaps, should require of him.

Only when public speech satisfies stringent tests qualifying it as "direct provocation to violence," (if that is possible at all) will the harm principle justify its suppression. But there are many possible modes of suppression, and some are far more restrictive of liberty than others. Orders to cease and desist on pain of arrest are most economical, for they permit the speaker to continue to air his views in a nonprovocative way or else retire with his audience to a less public place. Lawful removal of the provocation (as a public nuisance) may be more satisfactory than permitting violent response to it, and is infinitely preferable to punishing the speaker. Nowhere in the law where provocation is considered as a defense do the rules deem the proven provoker (the victim) a criminal himself! At best his conduct mitigates the crime of his attacker, who is the only criminal.

One final point. While it is conceivable that some public *speech* can satisfy the common law test for provocation by being so aggravating that even a reasonable person could be expected to lose control of his reason when exposed to it, this can never be true of books. One can always escape the provocation of the printed word simply by declining to read it, and where escape from provocation is that easy, no "reasonable person" will succumb to it.

5. *Incitement to Crime or Insurrection.* In the criminal law, anyone who "counsels, commands, or encourages another to commit a crime" is himself guilty of the resultant crime as an "accessory before the fact." Counseling, commanding, and encouraging, however, must consist in more than merely uttering certain words in the presence of others. Surely there must also be serious (as opposed to playful) intent and some possibility at least of the words having their desired effect. It is not possible that these conditions can be satisfied if I tell my secretary that she should overthrow the United States government, or if a speaker tells an audience of bank presidents that they should practice embezzlement whenever they can. These situations are analogous to the efforts to start a panic by magical means or to panic policemen with words about mice.

The problem of interpreting the meaning of a rule making the counseling of crime itself a crime is similar, I should think, to that raised by a statute forbidding the planting of a certain kind of plant. One does not violate such a statute if he scatters the appropriate kind of seeds on asphalt pavement or in barren desert, even with evil intent. (Again, if you are stupid enough, the law—insofar as it derives from the harm principle—can allow you to be as evil as you wish.) To violate the statute, either one would have to dig a little hole in the appropriate sort of soil, deposit the appropriate seeds, cultivate, fertilize, allow for sufficient water, protect against winds, worms, and dogs; *or* one would have to find suitable conditions ready-made, where the soil is already receptive and merely dropping the seeds will create a substantial likelihood that plants will grow and thrive. By analogy, even words of advice, if they are to count as incitements to crime, must fall on reasonably receptive ears. The harm principle provides a ready rationale for this requirement. If we permit coercive repression of nondangerous words we will confer such abundant powers on the repressive organs of the state that they are certain to be abused. Moreover, we will so inhibit persons in their employment of language as to discourage both spontaneity and serious moral discussion, thus doing a great deal of harm and virtually no good at all. (The only "gain," if it is that, to be expected from looser standards of interpretation would be that nondangerous persons with evil motives could be scooped up in the state's tighter nets and punished.)

Counseling others to crime is not the only use of speech that can be described as incitement. We must also come to terms with instigating, egging on, and inflaming others to violence. Even Mill conceded that the opinion that "corn dealers are starvers of the poor," which deserves protection when published in the press, may nevertheless "justly incur punishment when delivered orally to an excited mob assembled before the house of a corn dealer. . . ."[22] The metaphor of planting seeds in receptive soil is perhaps less apt for this situation than the commonly employed "spark and tinder" analogy. Words which merely express legitimate though unpopular opinion in one context become "incendiary" when addressed to an already inflammable mob. As Chafee put it: "Smoking is all right, but not in a powder magazine."[23] Of course the man who carries a cigar into a powder magazine may not know that the cigar he is carrying is lighted, or he may not know that he has entered a powder magazine. He may plead his lack of intention afterward (if he is still alive) as a defense. Similarly, the man who speaks his opinion to what he takes to be a calm audience, or an excited audience with *different* axes all ground fine, may plead his ignorance in good faith as a defense. But "the law" (as judges are fond of saying) "presumes that a man intends the natural and probable consequences of his actions," so that a defendant who denies that he intended to cause a riot may have the burden of proving his innocent intention to the jury.

In summary, there are two points to emphasize in connection with the punishment of inflammatory incitements. First, the audience must really be tinder, that is to say not merely sullen, but angry to the point of frenzy, and so predisposed to violence. A left-wing radical should be permitted to deliver a revolutionary tirade before the ladies of the D.A.R., even if his final words are "to the barricades!", for that would be to light a match not in a powder magazine but in a Turkish steam bath. Second, no one should be punished for inciting others to violence unless he used words intentionally, or at least recklessly, with respect to that consequence. Otherwise at best a speaker will be punished for his mere negligence, and at worst he will be punished though perfectly innocent.

There is one further problem raised by the concept of incitement as a crime. It might well be asked how one person—the inciter—can be held criminally responsible for the free and deliberate actions of another person—the one who is incited by his words. This problem is common to both kinds of incitement, counseling and inflaming or egging on, but it seems especially puzzling in the case of advising and persuading; for the deliberate, thoughtful, unforced, and undeceived acceptance of the advice of another person is without question itself a voluntary act. Yet there may well be cases which are such that had not the advice been given, the crime would never have been perpetrated, so that the advisor can truly be said to have "got" the advisee to do something he might otherwise never have done. In this case, the initiative was the advisor's, and his advice was the crucial causal factor that led to the criminal act, so that it would be no abuse of usage to call it "the cause." And yet, for all of that, no one *forced* the advisee to act; he could have rejected the advice, but he didn't.

If there is the appearance of paradox in this account, or in the very idea of one person's causing another to act voluntarily, it is no doubt the result of an unduly restrictive conception of what a cause is. There are, of course, a great many ways of causing another person to behave in a given way by the use of words. If we sneak up behind him and shout "boo!" we may startle him so that he jumps and shrieks. In this case our word functioned as a cause not in virtue of its meaning or the mediation of the other person's understanding, but simply as a noise, and the person's startled reaction to this physical stimulus was as involuntary as an eye-twitch or a knee-jerk. Some philosophers would restrict the notion of causing behavior to cases of this kind, but there is no good reason for such a restriction, and a strong case can be built against it based both on its capacity to breed paradox and on common sense and usage. I can "get" an acquaintance to say "Good morning" by putting myself directly in his line of vision, smiling, and saying "Good morning" to him. If I do these things and he predictably responds in the way I intended, I can surely say that my behavior was the cause, in those circumstances, of his behavior; for my conduct is not only a circumstance but for which his action would not have occurred, it is also a circumstance which, when added to those already present, made the difference between his speaking and remaining silent. Yet I did not force him to speak; I did not deceive him; I did not trick him. Rather I exploited those of his known policies and dispositions that made him antecedently "receptive" to my words. To deny that I caused him to act voluntarily, in short, is either to confuse causation with compulsion (a venerable philosophical mistake) or to regard one person's initiative as incompatible with another person's responsibility.[24]

In any case, where one person causes another to act voluntarily either by giving him advice or information or by otherwise capitalizing on his carefully studied dispositions and policies, there is no reason why *both* persons should not be held responsible for the act if it should be criminal. It is just as if the law made it criminal to contribute to a human explosion either by being human dynamite or by being a human spark: either by being predisposed by one's character to crime or by one's passions to violence, or else by providing the words or materials which could fully be anticipated to incite the violent or criminal conduct of others. It is surely no reasonable defense of the spark to say that but for the dynamite there would have been no explosion. Nor is it any more reasonable to defend the dynamite by arguing that but for the spark it should have remained forever quiescent.

There is probably even less reason for excluding from responsibility the speaker haranguing an inflammable mob on the grounds that the individuals in the throng are free adults capable of refraining from violence in the circumstances. A mob might well be understood as a kind of fictitious collective person whose passions are much more easily manipulated and whose actions more easily maneuvered than those of individual persons. If one looks at it this way, the caused behavior of an inflamed mob may be a good deal less than fully voluntary, even though the component individuals in it, being free adults, are all acting voluntarily on their own responsibility.

III Sedition

Causing panic, provoking violence, and inciting to crime or insurrection are all made punishable by what Chafee calls "the normal criminal law of words."[25] The relevant common law categories are riot, breach of the peace, solicitation, and incitement. All these crimes, as we have seen, require either intentionally harmful or reckless conduct, and all of them require, in addition—and for reasons partly derived from and explicable by the harm principle—that there be some objective likelihood that the relevant sort of harm will be produced by the words uttered in the circumstances. In addition to these traditional common law crimes, many governments have considered it necessary to create statutes making *sedition* a crime. It will be useful to consider the question of sedition against the background of the normal criminal law of words, for this will lead us quickly to two conclusions. The first is that sedition laws are wholly unnecessary to avert the harm they are ostensibly aimed at. The second is that if we must nevertheless put up with sedition laws, they must be applied by the courts in accordance with the same standards of objective likelihood and immediate danger that govern the application of the laws against provoking and inciting violence. Otherwise sedition statutes are likely to do far more social harm than good. Such laws when properly interpreted by enforcers and courts are at best legal redundancies. At worst they are corrosive of the values normally protected by freedom of expression.

The word "sedition," which in its oldest, prelegal sense meant simply divisiveness and strife, has never been the name of a crime in the English common law. Rather the adjective "seditious" forms part of the name of the common law crimes of "seditious words," "seditious libel," and "seditious conspiracy." Apparently the common ingredient in these offenses was so-called "seditious intent." The legal definition of "seditious intent" has changed over the centuries. In the beginning any spoken or written words which in fact had a tendency, however remote, to cause dissension or to weaken the grip of governmental authorities, and were spoken or published intentionally (with or without the further purpose of weakening the government or causing dissension) were held to manifest the requisite intent. In the fifteenth and sixteenth centuries, for example, publicly to call the king a fool, even in jest, was to risk capital punishment. There was to be less danger somewhat later for authors of *printed* words; for all books and printed papers had to be submitted in advance to the censorship (a practice denounced in Milton's eloquent *Areopagitica*), so that authors of politically dangerous words risked not punishment but only prior restraint. There is little evidence, however, that many of them felt more free as a consequence of this development.

The abandonment of the censorship in 1695 was widely hailed as a triumph for freedom of the press, but it was soon replaced by an equally repressive and far more cruel series of criminal trials for "seditious libel." Juries were permitted to decide only narrow factual questions, whereas the matter of "seditious intent" was left up to very conservative judges who knew well where their own personal interests lay. Moreover, truth was not permitted as a defense[26]— a legal restriction which in effect destroyed all right of adverse political criticism. Zechariah Chafee[27] has argued convincingly that the First Amendment to the United States Constitution was proposed and adopted by men who were consciously reacting against the common law of seditious libel, and in particular against the applications of that law in the English trials of the time. "Reform" (of sorts) came in England through Fox's Libel Act of 1792, which allowed juries to decide the question of seditious intent and permitted the truth defense if the opinions were published with good motives. (The ill-advised and short-lived American Sedition Act of 1798 was modeled after this act.) In the hysterical reaction to the French Revolution and the Napoleonic Wars, however, juries proved to be even more savage than judges, and hundreds were punished even for the mildest political unorthodoxy.

Throughout most of the nineteenth century, the prevailing definition of seditious intent in English law derived from a statute passed during the repressive heyday of the Fox Act sedition trials. Men were punished for publishing any words with:

> the intention of (1) exciting disaffection, hatred, or contempt against the sovereign, or the government and constitution of the kingdom, or either house of parliament, or the administration of justice, or (2) exciting his majesty's subjects to attempt, otherwise than by lawful means, the alteration of any matter in church or state by law established, or (3) to promote feelings of ill will and hostility between different classes.[28]

In short, the three possible modes of seditious libel were defamation of the institutions or officers of the government, incitement to unlawful acts, and a use of language that tends toward the breach of the peace "between classes." The normal criminal law of words sufficiently covers the last two modes; and the civil law of defamation would apply to the first. The criminal law, as we have seen, employs a clear and present danger test for incitement and breach of peace, and does so for good reasons derived from the harm principle and the analysis of "intentional causing." For other good reasons, also derived from the harm principle, the law of defamation privileges fair

comment on public officials, and gives no protection at all to institutions. So there would seem to be no further need, at least none demonstrated by the harm principle, for a criminal law of sedition.[29]

Still, many have thought that the harm principle requires sedition laws, and some still do. The issue boils down to the question of whether the normal law of words with its strict standard of immediate danger is too lax to prevent serious harms, and whether, therefore, it needs supplementing by sedition laws employing the looser standards of "bad tendency" and "presumptive intent." By the standard of bad tendency, words can be punished for their dangerous propensity "long before there is any probability that they will break out into unlawful acts";[30] and by the test of presumptive intent, it is necessary only that the defendant intended to publish his words, not that he intended further harm by them. It is clear that most authors of sedition statutes have meant them to be interpreted by the courts in accordance with the tests of bad tendency and presumptive intent (although the United States Supreme Court has in recent decades declared that such interpretations are contrary to the First Amendment of the Constitution). Part of the rationale for the older tests was that if words make a definite contribution to a situation which is on its way to being dangerous, it is folly not to punish them well before that situation reaches the threshold of actual harm. There may seem to be no harm in piling up twigs as such, but if this is done with the purpose (or even the likely outcome) of starting a fire eventually, why not stop it now before it is too late? Those who favor this argument have often employed the harm principle also to defend laws against institutional defamation. The reason why it should be unlawful to bring the Constitution or the courts (or even the *flag*) into disrepute by one's words, they argue, is not simply that such words are offensive, but rather that they tend to undermine respect and loyalty and thereby contribute to more serious harm in the long run.

The focus of the disagreement over sedition laws is the status of *advocacy*. The normal law of words quite clearly outlaws counseling, urging, or demanding (under certain conditions) that others resort to crime or engage in riots, assassinations, or insurrections. But what if a person uses language not directly to counsel or call for violence but rather (where this is different) to *advocate* it? In the wake of the Russian Revolution, many working class parties in America and Europe adopted some variant of an ideology which declared that the propertied classes derived their wealth from the systematic exploitation of the poor; capitalists controlled the major media of news and opinion as well as parliaments and legislators; the grievances of the workers therefore could not be remedied through normal political channels but required instead direct pressure through such means as general strikes, boycotts, and mass demonstrations; and that the working class would inevitably be triumphant in its struggle, expropriate the exploiters, and itself run industry. Spokesmen for this ideology were known for their flamboyant rhetoric, which invariably contained such terms as "arise," "struggle," "victory," and "revolution." Such persons were commonly charged with violations of the Federal Espionage Act during and after World War I, of state sedition laws during the 1920s, and, after World War II, of the Smith Act. Often the key charge in the indictment was "teaching or advocating" riot, assassination, or the violent overthrow of the government.

Trials of Marxists for advocacy of revolution tended to be extremely difficult and problematic partly because it was never clear whether revolution in any usual sense was something taught and approved by them, and partly because it was unclear whether the form of reference to revolution in the Marxist ideology amounted to "advocacy" of it. Marxists disagreed among themselves over the first point. Many thought that forms of group pressure well short of open violence would be sufficient to overturn the capitalists; others thought that "eventually" (when is that?), when conditions were at last ripe, a brief violent seizure of power might be necessary. Does this, in any case, amount to the advocacy of revolution? If it is criminal advocacy to teach that there are conceivable circumstances under which revolution would be justified, then almost everyone, including this author, "advocates" revolution. Suppose one holds further that the "conceivable justifying conditions" may one day become actual, or that it is even probable that they will be actual at some indeterminate future time. Is this to count as criminal advocacy?

Not according to Justice Holmes in his famous opinion in *U.S.* v. *Schenk.* Schenk and others had encouraged draft resistance in 1917 by mailing circulars denouncing conscription as unconstitutional and urging in very emotional prose that draft-eligible men "assert their rights." The lower court found this to be advocacy of unlawful conduct, a violation, in particular, of the Espionage Act of 1917. The Supreme Court upheld the conviction but nevertheless laid down in the words of O. W. Holmes the test which was to be

applied, in a more generous spirit, in later cases: "The question in every case is whether the words . . . are used in such circumstances and are of such a nature as to create a clear and present danger that they will bring about the substantive evils that Congress has a right to prevent." Since Congress has the right to raise armies, any efforts to interfere by words or action with the exercise of that right are punishable. But the clear and present danger standard brings advocacy under the same kind of test as that used for incitement in the normal law of words. One can "advocate" draft resistance over one's breakfast table to one's daughter (though perhaps not to one's son), but not to a sullen group waiting to be sworn in at the induction center.

There is, on the other hand, never any real danger in this country in permitting the open advocacy of *revolution,* except, perhaps, as Chafee puts it, "in extraordinary times of great tension." He continues:

> *The chances of success are so infinitesimal that the probability of any serious attempt following the utterances seems too slight to make them punishable. . . . This is especially true if the speaker urges revolution at some future day, so that no immediate check is needed to save the country.*[31]

Advocacy of assassination, on the other hand, is less easily tolerated. In the first place, the soil is always more receptive to that seed. It is not that potential assassins are more numerous than potential revolutionaries, although at most times that is true. Potential assassins include among their number persons who are contorted beyond reason by hate, mentally unstable persons, and unpredictable crackpots. Further, a successful assassination requires only one good shot. Since it is more likely to be tried and easier to achieve, its danger is always more "clear and present." There will be many circumstances, therefore, in which Holmes's test would permit advocacy of revolution but punish advocacy of assassination. Still in most contexts of utterance it would punish neither. It should no doubt be criminal for a prominent politician to advocate assassination of the president in a talk over national television, or in a letter to the *New York Times,*[32] but when a patron of a neighborhood tavern heatedly announces to his fellow drinkers that "the bum ought to be shot," the president's life will not be significantly endangered. There are times and places where it doesn't matter in the slightest how carelessly one chooses one's words, and others where one's choice of words can be a matter of life and death.

I shall, in conclusion, sketch a rationale for the clear and present danger test, as a kind of mediating standard for the application of the harm principle in the area of political expression. The natural challenge to the use of that test has been adumbrated above. It is true, one might concede, that the teaching of Communist ideology here and now will not create a clear and present danger of violent revolution. Every one knows that, including the Communists. Every trip, however, begins with some first steps, and that includes trips to forbidden destinations. The beginning steps are meant to increase numbers, add strength, and pick up momentum at later stages. To switch the metaphor to one used previously, the Communists are not just casting seeds on barren ground; their words are also meant to cultivate the ground and irrigate it. If the law prohibits planting a certain kind of shrub and we see people storing the forbidden seeds, garden tools, and fertilizer, and actually digging trenches for irrigation pipes, why wait until they are ready to plant the seed before stopping them? Even at these early stages of preparation, they are clearly attempting to achieve what is forbidden. So the argument goes.

The metaphor employed by the argument, however, is not very favorable to its cause. There is a world of difference between making plans and preparations for a future crime and actually launching an attempt, and this distinction has long been recognized by the ordinary criminal law. Mere preparations without actual steps in the direction of perpetration are not sufficient for the crime of attempt (though if preparation involves talking with collaborators, it may constitute the crime of conspiracy). Not even preliminary "steps" are sufficient; for "the act must reach far enough toward the accomplishment of the desired result to amount to the commencement of the consummation."[33] So the first faltering steps of a surpassingly difficult fifty-year trip toward an illegal goal can hardly qualify as an "attempt" in either the legal or the everyday sense.

If the journey is a collective enterprise, the participants could be charged with *conspiracy* without any violation of usage. The question is whether it would be sound public policy to suppress dissenting voices in this manner so long before they reach the threshold of public danger. The argument to the contrary has been given very clear statement in our time by Zechariah Chafee. Consider what interests are involved when the state employs some coercive technique to prevent a private individual or group from expressing an opinion on some issue of public policy,

or from teaching or advocating some political ideology. Chafee would have us put these various interests in the balance to determine their relative weights. In the one pan of the scale, there are the private interests of the suppressed individual or group in having their opinions heard and shared, and in winning support and eventual acceptance for them. These interests will be effectively squelched by state suppression. In the other pan is the public interest in peace and order, and the preservation of democratic institutions. These interests may be endangered to some degree by the advocacy of radical ideologies. Now if these are the only interests involved, there is no question that the public interest (which after all includes all or most private interests) sits heavier in the pan. There is, however, another public interest involved of very considerable weight. That is the public interest in the discovery and dissemination of all information that can have any bearing on public policy, and of all opinions about what public policy should be. The dangers that come from neglecting *that* interest are enormous at all times. (See Part I above.) And the more dangerous the times—the more serious the questions before the country's decision makers (and *especially* when these are questions of war and peace)—the more important it is to keep open all the possible avenues to truth and wisdom.

Only the interest in national safety can outweigh the public interest in open discussion, but *it sits in the scale only to the degree that it is actually imperiled*. From the point of view of the public interest alone, with no consideration whatever of individual rights, it would be folly to sacrifice the social benefits of free speech for the bare possibility that the public safety may be somewhat affected. The greater the certainty and imminence of danger, however, the more the interest in public safety moves on to the scale, until at the point of clear and present danger it is heavy enough to tip the scales its way.

The scales analogy, of course, is only an elaborate metaphor for the sorts of deliberations that must go on among enforcers and interpreters of the law when distinct public interests come into conflict. These clashes of interest are most likely to occur in times of excitement and stress when interest "balancing" calls for a clear eye, a sensitive scale, and a steady hand. At such times the clear and present danger rule is a difficult one to apply, but other guides to decision have invariably gone wrong, while the clear and present danger test has hardly ever been seriously tried. Perhaps that helps account, to some degree, for the sorry human record of cruelty, injustice, and war.

1. *In Chapter Two of* On Liberty, *not reprinted in this volume.*

2. *Zechariah Chafee, Jr.,* Free Speech in the United States *(1941), p. 33.*

3. *This point applies especially to discussions of moral, social, political, legal, and economic questions, as well as matters of governmental policy, domestic and foreign. "Cross-examination" in science and philosophy is perhaps less important.*

4. *Aristotle,* Nicomachean Ethics, *Bk. II, Chap. 6, 1107ª. "When a man commits adultery, there is no point in asking whether it was with the right woman or at the right time or in the right way, for to do anything like that is simply wrong."*

5. *William L. Prosser,* Handbook of the Law of Torts, *2nd ed. (St. Paul: West Publishing Co., 1955), p. 584.*

6. Ibid., *p. 631.*

7. *Fowler V. Harper and Fleming James, Jr.,* The Law of Torts *(Boston: Little, Brown and Co., 1956), Vol. I, p. 416. The authors do not endorse this view.*

8. Ibid.

9. *William Blackstone,* Commentaries on the Laws of England, *Vol. III, 1765 Reprint (Boston: Beacon Press, 1962), p. 125.*

10. Prosser, op. cit., *p. 644.*

11. Harper and James, op. cit., *p. 680.*

12. Prosser, op. cit., *p. 642.*

13. Loc. cit.

14. *American Law Institute,* Restatement of the Law of Torts *(St. Paul, 1934) § 867, comment c.*

15. Prosser, op. cit., *p. 644.*

16. *"There are two aspects of the interest in seclusion. First, the interest in preventing others from seeing and hearing what one does and says. Second, the interest in avoiding seeing and hearing what other people do and say. . . . It may be as distasteful to suffer the intrusions of a garrulous and unwelcome guest as to discover an eavesdropper or peeper."* Harper and James, op. cit., *p. 681. (Emphasis added.)*

17. *Schenck v. United States, 249 U.S. 47 (1919).*

18. Chafee, op. cit., *pp. 152, 161, 426. cf. Terminiello v. Chicago 337 U.S. 1, (1949).*

19. Chafee, op. cit., *p. 426.*

20. Ibid., *p. 161.*

21. *Toler v. State, 152 Tenn. 1, 13, 260 S.W. 134 (1923).*

22. Mill, op. cit., *pp. 67–8.*

23. Chafee, op. cit., *p. 397.*

24. *For a more detailed exposition of this view see my "Causing Voluntary Actions" in* Doing and Deserving *(Princeton, N.J.: Princeton University Press, 1970), p. 152.*

25. Chafee, op. cit., *p. 149.*

26. *In the words of the great common law judge, William Murray, First Earl of Mansfield, "The Greater the Truth, the Greater the Libel," hence Robert Burns's playful lines in his poem, "The Reproof":*
"Dost not know that old Mansfield
Who writes like the Bible,
Says the more 'tis a truth, sir,
The more 'tis a libel?"

27. Chafee, op. cit., *pp. 18–22.*

28. Ibid., *p. 506.*

29. *Such things, however, as patriotic sensibilities are capable of being highly offended by certain kinds of language. The rationale of sedition laws, therefore, may very well derive from the "offense-principle," which warrants prohibition of offensive behavior even when it is (otherwise) harmless.*

30. Chafee, op. cit., *p. 24.*

31. Ibid., *p. 175.*

32. *In which case the newspaper too would be criminally responsible for publishing the letter.*

33. *Lee v. Commonwealth, 144 Va. 594, 599, 131 S.E. 212, 214 (1926) as quoted in Rollin M. Perkins,* Criminal Law *(Brooklyn Foundation Press, 1957), p. 482.*

COHEN V. CALIFORNIA*

United States Supreme Court, 1971

Opinion of the Court

Mr. Justice Harlan delivered the opinion of the Court.

This case may seem at first blush too inconsequential to find its way into our books, but the issue it presents is of no small constitutional significance.

Appellant Paul Robert Cohen was convicted in the Los Angeles Municipal Court of violating that part of California Penal Code § 415 which prohibits "maliciously and willfully disturb[ing] the peace or quiet of any neighborhood or person . . . by . . . offensive conduct. . . ."[1] He was given 30 days' imprisonment. The facts upon which his conviction rests are detailed in the opinion of the Court of Appeal of California, Second Appellate District, as follows:

*408 U.S. 15 (1971). Some footnotes omitted. Citation omitted.

"On April 26, 1968, the defendant was observed in the Los Angeles County Courthouse in the corridor outside of division 20 of the municipal court wearing a jacket bearing the words 'Fuck the Draft' which were plainly visible. There were women and children present in the corridor. The defendant was arrested. The defendant testified that he wore the jacket knowing that the words were on the jacket as a means of informing the public of the depth of his feelings against the Vietnam War and the draft.

"The defendant did not engage in, nor threaten to engage in, nor did anyone as the result of his conduct in fact commit or threaten to commit any act of violence. The defendant did not make any loud or unusual noise, nor was there any evidence that he uttered any sound prior to his arrest."

In affirming the conviction the Court of Appeal held that "offensive conduct" means "behavior which has a tendency to provoke *others* to acts of violence or to in turn disturb the peace," and that the State had proved this element because, on the facts of this case, "[i]t was certainly reasonably foreseeable that such conduct might cause others to rise up to commit a violent act against the person of the defendant or attempt to forceably remove his jacket." The California Supreme Court declined review by a divided vote. We brought the case here, postponing the consideration of the question of our jurisdiction over this appeal to a hearing of the case on the merits. We now reverse.

I

In order to lay hands on the precise issue which this case involves, it is useful first to canvass various matters which this record does *not* present.

The conviction quite clearly rests upon the asserted offensiveness of the *words* Cohen used to convey his message to the public. The only "conduct" which the State sought to punish is the fact of communication. Thus, we deal here with a conviction resting solely upon "speech," not upon any separately identifiable conduct which allegedly was intended by Cohen to be perceived by others as expressive of particular views but which, on its face, does not necessarily convey any message and hence arguably could be regulated without effectively repressing Cohen's ability to express himself. Further, the State certainly lacks power to punish Cohen for the underlying content of the message the inscription conveyed. At least so long as there is no showing of an intent to incite disobedi-

ence to or disruption of the draft, Cohen could not, consistently with the First and Fourteenth Amendments, be punished for asserting the evident position on the inutility or immorality of the draft his jacket reflected.

Appellant's conviction, then, rests squarely upon his exercise of the "freedom of speech" protected from arbitrary governmental interference by the Constitution and can be justified, if at all, only as a valid regulation of the manner in which he exercised that freedom, not as a permissible prohibition on the substantive message it conveys. This does not end the inquiry, of course, for the First and Fourteenth Amendments have never been thought to give absolute protection to every individual to speak whenever or wherever he pleases, or to use any form of address in any circumstances that he chooses. In this vein, too, however, we think it important to note that several issues typically associated with such problems are not presented here.

In the first place, Cohen was tried under a statute applicable throughout the entire State. Any attempt to support this conviction on the ground that the statute seeks to preserve an appropriately decorous atmosphere in the courthouse where Cohen was arrested must fail in the absence of any language in the statute that would have put appellant on notice that certain kinds of otherwise permissible speech or conduct would nevertheless, under California law, not be tolerated in certain places. No fair reading of the phrase "offensive conduct" can be said sufficiently to inform the ordinary person that distinctions between certain locations are thereby created.[2]

In the second place, as it comes to us, this case cannot be said to fall within those relatively few categories of instances where prior decisions have established the power of government to deal more comprehensively with certain forms of individual expression simply upon a showing that such a form was employed. This is not, for example, an obscenity case. Whatever else may be necessary to give rise to the States' broader power to prohibit obscene expression, such expression must be, in some significant way, erotic. It cannot plausibly be maintained that this vulgar allusion to the Selective Service System would conjure up such psychic stimulation in anyone likely to be confronted with Cohen's crudely defaced jacket.

This Court has also held that the States are free to ban the simple use, without a demonstration of additional justifying circumstances, of so-called "fighting words," those personally abusive epithets which, when addressed to the ordinary citizen, are, as a matter of common knowledge, inherently likely to provoke violent reaction. While the four-letter word displayed by Cohen in relation to the draft is not uncommonly employed in a personally provocative fashion, in this instance it was clearly not "directed to the person of the hearer." No individual actually or likely to be present could reasonably have regarded the words on appellant's jacket as a direct personal insult. Nor do we have here an instance of the exercise of the State's police power to prevent a speaker from intentionally provoking a given group to hostile reaction. There is, as noted above, no showing that anyone who saw Cohen was in fact violently aroused or that appellant intended such a result.

Finally, in arguments before this Court much has been made of the claim that Cohen's distasteful mode of expression was thrust upon unwilling or unsuspecting viewers, and that the State might therefore legitimately act as it did in order to protect the sensitive from otherwise unavoidable exposure to appellant's crude form of protest. Of course, the mere presumed presence of unwitting listeners or viewers does not serve automatically to justify curtailing all speech capable of giving offense. While this Court has recognized that government may properly act in many situations to prohibit intrusion into the privacy of the home of unwelcome views and ideas which cannot be totally banned from the public dialogue, we have at the same time consistently stressed that "we are often 'captives' outside the sanctuary of the home and subject to objectionable speech." The ability of government, consonant with the Constitution, to shut off discourse solely to protect others from hearing it is, in other words, dependent upon a showing that substantial privacy interests are being invaded in an essentially intolerable manner. Any broader view of this authority would effectively empower a majority to silence dissidents simply as a matter of personal predilections.

In this regard, persons confronted with Cohen's jacket were in a quite different posture than, say, those subjected to the raucous emissions of sound trucks blaring outside their residences. Those in the Los Angeles courthouse could effectively avoid further bombardment of their sensibilities simply by averting their eyes. And, while it may be that one has a more substantial claim to a recognizable privacy interest when walking through a courthouse corridor than, for example, strolling through Central Park, surely it is nothing like the interest in being free from unwanted expression in the confines of one's own home. Given the subtlety and complexity of the factors involved, if

Cohen's "speech" was otherwise entitled to constitutional protection, we do not think the fact that some unwilling "listeners" in a public building may have been briefly exposed to it can serve to justify this breach of the peace conviction where, as here, there was no evidence that persons powerless to avoid appellant's conduct did in fact object to it, and where that portion of the statute upon which Cohen's conviction rests evinces no concern, either on its face or as construed by the California courts, with the special plight of the captive auditor, but, instead, indiscriminately sweeps within its prohibitions all "offensive conduct" that disturbs "any neighborhood or person."

II

Against this background, the issue flushed by this case stands out in bold relief. It is whether California can excise, as "offensive conduct," one particular scurrilous epithet from the public discourse, either upon the theory of the court below that its use is inherently likely to cause violent reaction or upon a more general assertion that the States, acting as guardians of public morality, may properly remove this offensive word from the public vocabulary.

The rationale of the California court is plainly untenable. At most it reflects an "undifferentiated fear or apprehension of disturbance [which] is not enough to overcome the right to freedom of expression." We have been shown no evidence that substantial numbers of citizens are standing ready to strike out physically at whomever may assault their sensibilities with execrations like that uttered by Cohen. There may be some persons about with such lawless and violent proclivities, but that is an insufficient base upon which to erect, consistently with constitutional values, a governmental power to force persons who wish to ventilate their dissident views into avoiding particular forms of expression. The argument amounts to little more than the self-defeating proposition that to avoid physical censorship of one who has not sought to provoke such a response by a hypothetical coterie of the violent and lawless, the States may more appropriately effectuate that censorship themselves.

Admittedly, it is not so obvious that the First and Fourteenth Amendments must be taken to disable the States from punishing public utterance of this unseemly expletive in order to maintain what they regard as a suitable level of discourse within the body politic. We think, however, that examination and reflection will reveal the shortcomings of a contrary viewpoint.

At the outset, we cannot overemphasize that, in our judgment, most situations where the State has a justifiable interest in regulating speech will fall within one or more of the various established exceptions, discussed above but not applicable here, to the usual rule that governmental bodies may not prescribe the form or content of individual expression. Equally important to our conclusion is the constitutional backdrop against which our decision must be made. The constitutional right of free expression is powerful medicine in a society as diverse and populous as ours. It is designed and intended to remove governmental restraints from the arena of public discussion, putting the decision as to what views shall be voiced largely into the hands of each of us, in the hope that use of such freedom will ultimately produce a more capable citizenry and more perfect polity and in the belief that no other approach would comport with the premise of individual dignity and choice upon which our political system rests.

To many, the immediate consequence of this freedom may often appear to be only verbal tumult, discord, and even offensive utterance. These are, however, within established limits, in truth necessary side effects of the broader enduring values which the process of open debate permits us to achieve. That the air may at times seem filled with verbal cacophony is, in this sense not a sign of weakness but of strength. We cannot lose sight of the fact that, in what otherwise might seem a trifling and annoying instance of individual distasteful abuse of a privilege, these fundamental societal values are truly implicated. That is why "[w]holly neutral futilities . . . come under the protection of free speech as fully as do Keats' poems or Donne's sermons," *Winters* v. *New York,* (1948) (Frankfurter, J., dissenting), and why "so long as the means are peaceful, the communication need not meet standards of acceptability," *Organization for a Better Austin* v. *Keefe,* (1971).

Against this perception of the constitutional policies involved, we discern certain more particularized considerations that peculiarly call for reversal of this conviction. First, the principle contended for by the State seems inherently boundless. How is one to distinguish this from any other offensive word? Surely the State has no right to cleanse public debate to the point where it is grammatically palatable to the most squeamish among us. Yet no readily ascertainable general principle exists for stopping short of that result were we to affirm the judgment below. For, while the particular four-letter word being litigated here is perhaps more distasteful than most others of its genre, it is nevertheless often true that one man's vulgarity is another's lyric. Indeed, we think it is largely because governmental officials cannot make principled distinctions in this area that the Constitution leaves matters of taste and style so largely to the individual.

Additionally, we cannot overlook the fact, because it is well illustrated by the episode involved here, that much linguistic expression serves a dual communicative function: it conveys not only ideas capable of relatively precise, detached explication, but otherwise inexpressible emotions as well. In fact, words are often chosen as much for their emotive as their cognitive force. We cannot sanction the view that the Constitution, while solicitous of the cognitive content of individual speech, has little or no regard for that emotive function which, practically speaking, may often be the more important element of the overall message sought to be communicated. Indeed, as Mr. Justice Frankfurter has said, "[o]ne of the prerogatives of American citizenship is the right to criticize public men and measures—and that means not only informed and responsible criticism but the freedom to speak foolishly and without moderation." *Baumgartner* v. *United States,* (1944).

Finally, and in the same vein, we cannot indulge the facile assumption that one can forbid particular words without also running a substantial risk of suppressing ideas in the process. Indeed, governments might soon seize upon the censorship of particular words as a convenient guise for banning the expression of unpopular views. We have been able, as noted above, to discern little social benefit that might result from running the risk of opening the door to such grave results.

It is, in sum, our judgment that, absent a more particularized and compelling reason for its actions, the State may not, consistently with the First and Fourteenth Amendments, make the simple public display here involved of this single four-letter expletive a criminal offense. Because that is the only arguably sustainable rationale for the conviction here at issue, the judgment below must be reversed.

Separate Opinion

Mr. Justice Blackmun, with whom The Chief Justice and Mr. Justice Black join.

I dissent, and I do so for two reasons:

1. Cohen's absurd and immature antic, in my view, was mainly conduct and little speech. The California Court of Appeal appears so to have described it, and I cannot characterize it otherwise. Further, the case appears to me to be well within the sphere of *Chaplinsky* v. *New Hampshire*, where Mr. Justice Murphy, a known champion of First Amendment freedoms, wrote for a unanimous bench. As a consequence, this Court's agonizing First Amendment values seems misplaced and unnecessary.

2. I am not at all certain that the California Court of Appeal's construction of § 415 is now the authoritative California construction. . . .

---

1. *The statute provides in full:*
"Every person who maliciously and willfully disturbs the peace or quiet of any neighborhood or person, by loud or unusual noise, or by tumultuous or offensive conduct, or threatening, traducing, quarreling, challenging to fight, or fighting, or who, on the public streets of any unincorporated town, or upon the public highways in such unincorporated town, run any horse race, either for a wager or for amusement, or fire any gun or pistol in such unincorporated town, or use any vulgar language within the presence or hearing of women or children, in a loud and boisterous manner, is guilty of a misdemeanor, and upon conviction by any Court of competent jurisdiction shall be punished by fine not exceeding two hundred dollars, or by imprisonment in the County Jail for not more than ninety days, or by both fine and imprisonment, or either, at the discretion of the Court."

2. *It is illuminating to note what transpired when Cohen entered a courtroom in the building. He removed his jacket and stood with it folded over his arm. Meanwhile, a policeman sent the presiding judge a note suggesting that Cohen be held in contempt of court. The judge declined to do so and Cohen was arrested by the officer only after he emerged from the courtroom.*

VILLAGE OF SKOKIE V. NATIONAL SOCIALIST PARTY OF AMERICA*

Supreme Court of Illinois, 1978

PER CURIAM:

Plaintiff, the village of Skokie, filed a complaint in the circuit court of Cook County seeking to enjoin defendants, the National Socialist Party of America (the American Nazi Party) and 10 individuals as "officers and members" of the party, from engaging in certain activities while conducting a demonstration within the village. The circuit court issued an order enjoining certain conduct during the planned demonstration. The appellate court modified the injunction order, and, as modified, defendants are enjoined from "[i]ntentionally displaying the swastika on or off their persons, in the course of a demonstration, march, or parade." . . . We allowed defendants' petition for leave to appeal. . . .

The pleadings and the facts adduced at the hearing are fully set forth in the appellate court opinion, and only those matters necessary to the discussion of the issues will be repeated here. The facts are not disputed.

It is alleged in plaintiff's complaint that the "uniform of the National Socialist Party of America consists of the storm trooper uniform of the German Nazi Party embellished with the Nazi swastika"; that the plaintiff village has a population of about 70,000 persons of which approximately 40,500 persons are of "Jewish

---

religion or Jewish ancestry" and of this latter number 5,000 to 7,000 are survivors of German concentration camps; that the defendant organization is "dedicated to the incitation of racial and religious hatred directed principally against individuals of Jewish faith or ancestry and non-Caucasians"; and that its members "have patterned their conduct, their uniform, their slogan and their tactics along the pattern of the German Nazi Party."

Defendants moved to dismiss the complaint. In an affidavit attached to defendants' motion to dismiss, defendant Frank Collin, who testified that he was "party leader," stated that on or about March 20, 1977, he sent officials of the plaintiff village a letter stating that the party members and supporters would hold a peaceable, public assembly in the village on May 1, 1977, to protest the Skokie Park District's requirement that the party procure $350,000 of insurance prior to the party's use of the Skokie public parks for public assemblies. The demonstration was to begin at 3 p.m., last 20 to 30 minutes, and consist of 30 to 50 demonstrators marching in single file, back and forth, in front of the village hall. The marchers were to wear uniforms which include a swastika emblem or armband. They were to carry a party banner containing a swastika emblem and signs containing such statements as "White Free Speech," "Free Speech for the White Man," and "Free Speech for White America." The demonstrators would not distribute handbills, make any derogatory statements directed to any ethnic or religious group, or obstruct traffic. They would cooperate with any reasonable police instructions or requests.

At the hearing on plaintiff's motion for an "emergency injunction" a resident of Skokie testified that he was a survivor of the Nazi holocaust. He further testified that the Jewish community in and around Skokie feels the purpose of the march in the "heart of the Jewish population" is to remind the two million survivors "that we are not through with you" and to show "that the Nazi threat is not over, it can happen again." Another resident of Skokie testified that as the result of defendants' announced intention to march in Skokie, 15 to 18 Jewish organizations, within the village and surrounding area, were called and a counter-demonstration of an estimated 12,000 to 15,000 people was scheduled for the same day. There was opinion evidence that defendants' planned demonstration in Skokie would result in violence.

The circuit court entered an order enjoining defendants from "marching, walking or parading in the uniform of the National Socialist Party of America;

marching, walking or parading or otherwise displaying the swastika on or off their person; distributing pamphlets or displaying any materials which incite or promote hatred against persons of Jewish faith or ancestry or hatred against persons of any faith or ancestry, race or religion" within the village of Skokie. The appellate court, as earlier noted, modified the order so that defendants were enjoined only from intentional display of the swastika during the Skokie demonstration.

The appellate court opinion adequately discussed and properly decided those issues arising from the portions of the injunction order which enjoined defendants from marching, walking, or parading, from distributing pamphlets or displaying materials, and from wearing the uniform of the National Socialist Party of America. The only issue remaining before this court is whether the circuit court order enjoining defendants from displaying the swastika violates the First Amendment rights of those defendants.

In defining the constitutional rights of the parties who come before this court, we are, of course, bound by the pronouncements of the United States Supreme Court in its interpretation of the United States Constitution. The decisions of that court, particularly *Cohen* v. *California* . . . in our opinion compel us to permit the demonstration as proposed, including display of the swastika.

"It is firmly settled that under our Constitution the public expression of ideas may not be prohibited merely because the ideas are themselves offensive to some of their hearers" . . . and it is entirely clear that the wearing of distinctive clothing can be symbolic expression of a thought or philosophy. The symbolic expression of thought falls within the free speech clause of the First Amendment . . . and the plaintiff village has the heavy burden of justifying the imposition of a prior restraint upon defendants' right to freedom of speech. . . . The village of Skokie seeks to meet this burden by application of the "fighting words" doctrine first enunciated in *Chaplinsky* v. *New Hampshire* (1942), . . . That doctrine was designed to permit punishment of extremely hostile personal communication likely to cause immediate physical response, "no words being 'forbidden except such as have a direct tendency to cause acts of violence by the persons to whom, individually, the remark is addressed.'" . . . In *Cohen* the Supreme Court restated the description of fighting words as "those personally abusive epithets which, when addressed to the ordinary citizen, are, as a matter of common knowledge, inherently likely to provoke violent reaction." . . . Plaintiff urges, and the appellate court has held, that the exhibition of the Nazi symbol, the swastika, addresses to ordinary citizens a message which is tantamount to fighting words. Plaintiff further asks this court to extend *Chaplinsky*, which upheld a statute punishing the use of such words, and hold that the fighting-words doctrine permits a prior restraint on defendants' symbolic speech. In our judgment we are precluded from doing so.

In *Cohen*, defendant's conviction stemmed from wearing a jacket bearing the words "Fuck the Draft" in a Los Angeles County courthouse corridor. The Supreme Court for reasons we believe applicable here refused to find that the jacket inscription constituted fighting words. That court stated:

> "The constitutional right of free expression is powerful medicine in a society as diverse and populous as ours. It is designed and intended to remove governmental restraints from the arena of public discussion, putting the decision as to what views shall be voiced largely into the hands of each of us, in the hope that use of such freedom will ultimately produce a more capable citizenry and more perfect polity and in the belief that no other approach would comport with the premise of individual dignity and choice upon which our political system rests. . . .
>
> To many, the immediate consequence of this freedom may often appear to be only verbal tumult, discord, and even offensive utterance. These are, however, within established limits, in truth necessary side effects of the broader enduring values which the process of open debate permits us to achieve. That the air may at times seem filled with verbal cacophony is, in this sense not a sign of weakness but of strength. We cannot lose sight of the fact that, in what otherwise might seem a trifling and annoying instance of individual distasteful abuse of a privilege, these fundamental societal values are truly implicated . . . 'so long as the means are peaceful, the communication need not meet standards of acceptability.' . . .
>
> Against this perception of the constitutional policies involved, we discern certain more particularized considerations that peculiarly call for reversal of this conviction. First, the principle contended for by the State seems inherently boundless. How is one to distinguish this from any other offensive word [emblem]? Surely the State has no right to cleanse public debate to the point where it is grammatically palatable to the most squeamish among us. Yet no readily ascertainable general principle exists for stopping short of that result were we to affirm the judgment below. For, while the particular four-letter word [emblem] being litigated here is perhaps more distasteful than most others of its genre, it is nevertheless often true that one man's vulgarity is another's lyric. Indeed, we think it is largely because governmental officials cannot make principled distinctions in this area that the Constitution leaves matters of taste and style so largely to the individual. . . .
>
> Finally, and in the same vein, we cannot indulge the facile assumption that one can forbid particular words without also running a substantial risk of suppressing ideas in the process. Indeed, governments might soon seize upon the censorship of particular words [emblems] as a convenient guise for banning the expression of unpopular views. We have been able, as noted above, to discern little social benefit that might result from running the risk of opening the door to such grave results." . . .

The display of the swastika, as offensive to the principles of a free nation as the memories it recalls may be, is symbolic political speech intended to convey to the public the beliefs of those who display it. It does not, in our opinion, fall within the definition of "fighting words," and that doctrine cannot be used here to overcome the heavy presumption against the constitutional validity of a prior restraint.

Nor can we find that the swastika, while not representing fighting words, is nevertheless so offensive and peace threatening to the public that its display can be enjoined. We do not doubt that the sight of this symbol is abhorrent to the Jewish citizens of Skokie, and that the survivors of the Nazi persecutions, tormented by their recollections, may have strong feelings regarding its display. Yet it is entirely clear that this factor does not justify enjoining defendants' speech. The *Cohen* court spoke to this subject:

> "Finally, in arguments before this Court much has been made of the claim that Cohen's distasteful mode of expression was thrust upon unwilling or unsuspecting viewers, and that the State might therefore legitimately act as it did in order to protect the sensitive from otherwise unavoidable exposure to appellant's crude form of protest. Of course, the mere presumed presence of unwitting listeners or

viewers does not serve automatically to justify curtailing all speech capable of giving offense. . . . While this Court has recognized that government may properly act in many situations to prohibit intrusion into the privacy of the home of unwelcome views and ideas which cannot be totally banned from the public dialogue, e.g., Rowan v. Post Office Dept., 397 U.S. 728, 90 S.Ct. 1484, 25 L.Ed.2d 736 (1970), we have at the same time consistently stressed that 'we are often "captives" outside the sanctuary of the home and subject to objectionable speech.' Id., at 738, 90 S.Ct. at 1491. The ability of government, consonant with the Constitution, to shut off discourse solely to protect others from hearing it is, in other words, dependent upon a showing that substantial privacy interests are being invaded in an essentially intolerable manner. Any broader view of this authority would effectively empower a majority to silence dissidents simply as a matter of personal predilections." . . .

Similarly, the Court of Appeals for the Seventh Circuit, in reversing the denial of defendant Collin's application for a permit to speak in Chicago's Marquette Park, noted that courts have consistently refused to ban speech because of the possibility of unlawful conduct by those opposed to the speaker's philosophy.

> *"Starting with* Terminiello *v.* City of Chicago, . . . *and continuing to* Gregory *v.* City of Chicago, . . . *it has become patent that a hostile audience is not a basis for restraining otherwise legal First Amendment activity. As with many of the cases cited herein, if the actual behavior is not sufficient to sustain a conviction under a statute, then certainly the anticipation of such events cannot sustain the burden necessary to justify a prior restraint."* . . .

Rockwell v. *Morris* . . . also involved an American Nazi leader, George Lincoln Rockwell, who challenged a bar to his use of a New York City park to hold a public demonstration where anti-Semitic speeches would be made. Although approximately 2½ million Jewish New Yorkers were hostile to Rockwell's message, the court ordered that a permit to speak be granted, stating:

> *"A community need not wait to be subverted by street riots and storm troopers; but, also, it cannot, by its policemen or commissioners,*

suppress a speaker, in prior restraint, on the basis of news reports, hysteria, or inference that what he did yesterday, he will do today. Thus, too, if the speaker incites others to immediate unlawful action he may be punished—in a proper case, stopped when disorder actually impends; but this is not to be confused with unlawful action from others who seek unlawfully to suppress or punish the speaker.

> *So, the unpopularity of views, their shocking quality, their obnoxiousness, and even their alarming impact is not enough. Otherwise, the preacher of any strange doctrine could be stopped; the anti-racist himself could be suppressed, if he undertakes to speak in 'restricted' areas; and one who asks that public schools be open indiscriminately to all ethnic groups could be lawfully suppressed, if only he choose to speak where persuasion is needed most."* . . .

In summary, as we read the controlling Supreme Court opinions, use of the swastika is a symbolic form of free speech entitled to First Amendment protections. Its display on uniforms or banners by those engaged in peaceful demonstrations cannot be totally precluded solely because that display may provoke a violent reaction by those who view it. Particularly is this true where, as here, there has been advance notice by the demonstrators of their plans so that they have become, as the complaint alleges, "common knowledge" and those to whom sight of the swastika banner or uniforms would be offense are forewarned and need not view them. A speaker who gives prior notice of his message has not compelled a confrontation with those who voluntarily listen.

As to those who happen to be in a position to be involuntarily confronted with the swastika, the following observations from *Erznoznik* v. *City of Jacksonville* . . . are appropriate:

> *"The plain, if at all times disquieting, truth is that in our pluralistic society, constantly proliferating new and ingenious forms of expression, 'we are inescapably captive audiences for many purposes.' . . . Much that we encounter offends our esthetic, if not our political and moral, sensibilities. Nevertheless, the Constitution does not permit government to decide which types of otherwise protected speech are sufficiently offensive to require protection for the unwilling listener or viewer. Rather, absent the narrow circumstances described above [home intrusion or captive audience], the bur-*

den normally falls upon the viewer to 'avoid further bombardment of [his] sensibilities simply by averting [his] eyes.'" . . .

Thus by placing the burden upon the viewer to avoid further bombardment, the Supreme Court has permitted speakers to justify the initial intrusion into the citizen's sensibilities.

We accordingly, albeit reluctantly, conclude that the display of the swastika cannot be enjoined under the fighting-words exception to free speech,

nor can anticipation of a hostile audience justify the prior restraint. Furthermore, *Cohen* and *Erznoznik* direct the citizens of Skokie that it is their burden to avoid the offensive symbol if they can do so without unreasonable inconvenience. Accordingly, we are constrained to reverse that part of the appellate court judgment enjoining the display of the swastika. That judgment is in all other respects affirmed.

Affirmed in part and reversed in part.

CLARK, Justice, dissenting.

*TEXAS V. JOHNSON**

United States Supreme Court, 1989

JUSTICE BRENNAN delivered the opinion of the Court.

After publicly burning an American flag as a means of political protest, Gregory Lee Johnson was convicted of desecrating a flag in violation of Texas law. This case presents the question whether his conviction is consistent with the First Amendment. We hold that it is not.

I

While the Republican National Convention was taking place in Dallas in 1984, respondent Johnson participated in a political demonstration dubbed the "Republican War Chest Tour." As explained in literature distributed by the demonstrators and in speeches made by them, the purpose of this event was to protest the policies of the Reagan administration and of certain Dallas-based corporations. The demonstrators marched through the Dallas streets, chanting political slogans and stopping at several corporate locations to stage "die-ins" intended to dramatize the consequences of nuclear war. On several occasions they

spray-painted the walls of buildings and overturned potted plants, but Johnson himself took no part in such activities. He did, however, accept an American flag handed to him by a fellow protestor who had taken it from a flag pole outside one of the targeted buildings.

The demonstration ended in front of Dallas City Hall, where Johnson unfurled the American flag, doused it with kerosene, and set it on fire. While the flag burned, the protestors chanted, "America, the red, white, and blue, we spit on you." After the demonstrators dispersed, a witness to the flag-burning collected the flag's remains and buried them in his backyard. No one was physically injured or threatened with injury, though several witnesses testified that they had been seriously offended by the flag-burning.

Of the approximately 100 demonstrators, Johnson alone was charged with a crime. The only criminal offense with which he was charged was the desecration of a venerated object in violation of Tex. Penal Code Ann. § 42.09 (a)(3) (1989).[1] After a trial, he was convicted, sentenced to one year in prison, and fined $2,000. The Court of Appeals for the Fifth District of Texas at Dallas affirmed Johnson's conviction, . . . but

---

*109 S.Ct. 2533 (1989). Only an excerpt has been included here from the dissenting opinion.

the Texas Court of Criminal Appeals reversed, . . . holding that the State could not, consistent with the First Amendment, punish Johnson for burning the flag in these circumstances.

The Court of Criminal Appeals began by recognizing that Johnson's conduct was symbolic speech protected by the First Amendment: "Given the context of an organized demonstration, speeches, slogans, and the distribution of literature, anyone who observed appellant's act would have understood the message that appellant intended to convey. The act for which appellant was convicted was clearly 'speech' contemplated by the First Amendment." *Id.,* at 95. To justify Johnson's conviction for engaging in symbolic speech, the State asserted two interests: preserving the flag as a symbol of national unity and preventing breaches of the peace. The Court of Criminal Appeals held that neither interest supported his conviction.

Acknowledging that this Court had not yet decided whether the Government may criminally sanction flag desecration in order to preserve the flag's symbolic value, the Texas court nevertheless concluded that our decision in *West Virginia Board of Education* v. *Barnette,* . . . (1943), suggested that furthering this interest by curtailing speech was impermissible. "Recognizing that the right to differ is the centerpiece of our First Amendment freedoms," the court explained, "a government cannot mandate by fiat a feeling of unity in its citizens. Therefore, that very same government cannot carve out a symbol of unity and prescribe a set of approved messages to be associated with that symbol when it cannot mandate the status or feeling the symbol purports to represent." . . . Noting that the State had not shown that the flag was in "grave and immediate danger," *Barnette, supra,* . . . of being stripped of its symbolic value, the Texas court also decided that the flag's special status was not endangered by Johnson's conduct. . . .

As to the State's goal of preventing breaches of the peace, the court concluded that the flag-desecration statute was not drawn narrowly enough to encompass only those flag-burnings that were likely to result in a serious disturbance of the peace. And in fact, the court emphasized, the flag-burning in this particular case did not threaten such a reaction. "'Serious offense' occurred," the court admitted, "but there was no breach of peace nor does the record reflect that the situation was potentially explosive. One cannot equate 'serious offense' with incitement to breach the peace." . . . The court also stressed that another Texas statute, Tex. Penal Code Ann. § 42.01 (1989), prohibited breaches of the peace. Citing *Boos*

v. *Barry,* . . . the court decided that § 42.01 demonstrated Texas' ability to prevent disturbances of the peace without punishing this flag desecration.

Because it reversed Johnson's conviction on the ground that § 42.09 was unconstitutional as applied to him, the state court did not address Johnson's argument that the statute was, on its face, unconstitutionally vague and overbroad. We granted certiorari, . . . and now affirm.

II

Johnson was convicted of flag desecration for burning the flag rather than for uttering insulting words.[2] This fact somewhat complicates our consideration of his conviction under the First Amendment. We must first determine whether Johnson's burning of the flag constituted expressive conduct, permitting him to invoke the First Amendment in challenging his conviction. . . . If his conduct was expressive, we next decide whether the State's regulation is related to the suppression of free expression. . . . If the State's regulation is not related to expression, then the less stringent standard we announced in *United States* v. *O'Brien* for regulations of noncommunicative conduct controls. . . . If it is, then we are outside of *O'Brien's* test, and we must ask whether this interest justifies Johnson's conviction under a more demanding standard.[3] . . . A third possibility is that the State's asserted interest is simply not implicated on these facts, and in that event the interest drops out of the picture.

The First Amendment literally forbids the abridgement only of "speech," but we have long recognized that its protection does not end at the spoken or written word. While we have rejected "the view that an apparently limitless variety of conduct can be labeled 'speech' whenever the person engaging in the conduct intends thereby to express an idea," . . . we have acknowledged that conduct may be "sufficiently imbued with elements of communication to fall within the scope of the First and Fourteenth Amendments."

In deciding whether particular conduct possesses sufficient communicative elements to bring the First Amendment into play, we have asked whether "[a]n intent to convey a particularized message was present, and [whether] the likelihood was great that the message would be understood by those who viewed it." . . . Hence, we have recognized the expressive nature of students' wearing of black armbands to protest American military involvement in

Vietnam, . . . of a sit-in by blacks in a "whites only" area to protest segregation, . . . of the wearing of American military uniforms in a dramatic presentation criticizing American involvement in Vietnam, . . . and of picketing about a wide variety of causes. . . .

Especially pertinent to this case are our decisions recognizing the communicative nature of conduct relating to flags. Attaching a peace sign to the flag, . . . saluting the flag, . . . and displaying a red flag, . . . we have held, all may find shelter under the First Amendment. See also *Smith* v. *Goguen* . . . (treating flag "contemptuously" by wearing pants with small flag sewn into their seat is expressive conduct). That we have had little difficulty identifying an expressive element in conduct relating to flags should not be surprising. The very purpose of a national flag is to serve as a symbol of our country; it is, one might say, "the one visible manifestation of two hundred years of nationhood."

Thus, we have observed:

> *"[T]he flag salute is a form of utterance. Symbolism is a primitive but effective way of communicating ideas. The use of an emblem or flag to symbolize some system, idea, institution, or personality, is a short cut from mind to mind. Causes and nations, political parties, lodges and ecclesiastical groups seek to knit the loyalty of their followings to a flag or banner, a color or design."*

. . . Pregnant with expressive content, the flag as readily signifies this Nation as does the combination of letters found in "America."

We have not automatically concluded, however, that any action taken with respect to our flag is expressive. Instead, in characterizing such action for First Amendment purposes, we have considered the context in which it occurred. In *Spence,* for example, we emphasized that Spence's taping of a peace sign to his flag was "roughly simultaneous with and concededly triggered by the Cambodian incursion and the Kent State tragedy." . . . The State of Washington had conceded, in fact, that Spence's conduct was a form of communication, and we stated that "the State's concession is inevitable on this record."

The State of Texas conceded for purposes of its oral argument in this case that Johnson's conduct was expressive conduct, . . . and this concession seems to us as prudent as was Washington's in *Spence.* Johnson burned an American flag as part—indeed, as the culmination—of a political demonstration that coincided with the convening of the Republican Party and its renomination of Ronald Reagan for President. The expressive, overtly political nature of this conduct was both intentional and overwhelmingly apparent. At his trial, Johnson explained his reasons for burning the flag as follows: "The American Flag was burned as Ronald Reagan was being renominated as President. And a more powerful statement of symbolic speech, whether you agree with it or not, couldn't have been made at that time. It's quite a just position [juxtaposition]. We had new patriotism and no patriotism." . . . In these circumstances, Johnson's burning of the flag was conduct "sufficiently imbued with elements of communication, . . . to implicate the First Amendment.

III

The Government generally has a freer hand in restricting expressive conduct than it has in restricting the written or spoken word. . . . It may not, however, proscribe particular conduct *because* it has expressive elements. "[W]hat might be termed the more generalized guarantee of freedom of expression makes the communicative nature of conduct an inadequate *basis* for singling out that conduct for proscription. A law *directed at* the communicative nature of conduct must, like a law directed at speech itself, be justified by the substantial showing of need that the First Amendment requires." . . . It is, in short, not simply the verbal or nonverbal nature of the expression, but the governmental interest at stake, that helps to determine whether a restriction on that expression is valid.

Thus, although we have recognized that where "'speech' and 'nonspeech' elements are combined in the same course of conduct, a sufficiently important governmental interest in regulating the nonspeech element can justify incidental limitations on First Amendment freedoms," . . . we have limited the applicability of *O'Brien*'s relatively lenient standard to those cases in which "the governmental interest is unrelated to the suppression of free expression." . . . In stating, moreover, that *O'Brien*'s test "in the last analysis is little, if any, different from the standard applied to time, place, or manner restrictions," . . . we have highlighted the requirement that the governmental interest in question be unconnected to expression in order to come under *O'Brien*'s less demanding rule.

In order to decide whether *O'Brien*'s test applies here, therefore, we must decide whether Texas has asserted an interest in support of Johnson's conviction that is unrelated to the suppression of expression. If we find that an interest asserted by the State is simply not implicated on the facts before us, we need not ask whether *O'Brien*'s test applies. . . . The State offers two separate interests to justify this conviction: preventing breaches of the peace, and preserving the flag as a symbol of nationhood and national unity. We hold that the first interest is not implicated on this record and that the second is related to the suppression of expression.

A

Texas claims that its interest in preventing breaches of the peace justifies Johnson's conviction for flag desecration.[4] However, no disturbance of the peace actually occurred or threatened to occur because of Johnson's burning of the flag. Although the State stresses the disruptive behavior of the protestors during their march toward City Hall, . . . it admits that "no actual breach of the peace occurred at the time of the flagburning or in response to the flagburning." . . . The State's emphasis on the protestors' disorderly actions prior to arriving at City Hall is not only somewhat surprising given that no charges were brought on the basis of this conduct, but it also fails to show that a disturbance of the peace was a likely reaction to Johnson's conduct. The only evidence offered by the State at trial to show the reaction to Johnson's actions was the testimony of several persons who had been seriously offended by the flag-burning.

The State's position, therefore, amounts to a claim that an audience that takes serious offense at particular expression is necessarily likely to disturb the peace and that the expression may be prohibited on this basis.[5] Our precedents do not countenance such a presumption. On the contrary, they recognize that a principal "function of free speech under our system of government is to invite dispute. It may indeed best serve its high purpose when it induces a condition of unrest, creates dissatisfaction with conditions as they are, or even stirs people to anger." . . . It would be odd indeed to conclude *both* that "if it is the speaker's opinion that gives offense, that consequence is a reason for according it constitutional protection," . . . *and* that the Government may ban the expression of certain disagreeable ideas on the unsupported presumption that their very disagreeableness will provoke violence.

Thus, we have not permitted the Government to assume that every expression of a provocative idea

will incite a riot, but have instead required careful consideration of the actual circumstances surrounding such expression, asking whether the expression "is directed to inciting or producing imminent lawless action and is likely to incite or produce such action." *Brandenburg* v. *Ohio,* . . . (reviewing circumstances surrounding rally and speeches by Ku Klux Klan). To accept Texas' arguments that it need only demonstrate "the potential for a breach of the peace, . . . and that every flag-burning necessarily possesses that potential," would be to eviscerate our holding in *Brandenburg.* This we decline to do.

Nor does Johnson's expressive conduct fall within that small class of "fighting words" that are "likely to provoke the average person to retaliation, and thereby cause a breach of the peace." . . . No reasonable onlooker would have regarded Johnson's generalized expression of dissatisfaction with the policies of the Federal Government as a direct personal insult or an invitation to exchange fisticuffs. . . .

We thus conclude that the State's interest in maintaining order is not implicated on these facts. The State need not worry that our holding will disable it from preserving the peace. We do not suggest that the First Amendment forbids a State to prevent "imminent lawless action." . . . And, in fact, Texas already has a statute specifically prohibiting breaches of the peace, Tex. Penal Code Ann. § 42.01 (1989), which tends to confirm that Texas need not punish this flag desecration in order to keep the peace. . . .

B

The State also asserts an interest in preserving the flag as a symbol of nationhood and national unity. In *Spence,* we acknowledged that the Government's interest in preserving the flag's special symbolic value "is directly related to expression in the context of activity" such as affixing a peace symbol to a flag. . . . We are equally persuaded that this interest is related to expression in the case of Johnson's burning of the flag. The State, apparently, is concerned that such conduct will lead people to believe either that the flag does not stand for nationhood and national unity, but instead reflects other, less positive concepts, or that the concepts reflected in the flag do not in fact exist, that is, we do not enjoy unity as a Nation. These concerns blossom only when a person's treatment of the flag communicates some message, and thus are related "to the suppression of free expression" within the meaning of *O'Brien.* We are thus outside of *O'Brien*'s test altogether.

IV

It remains to consider whether the State's interest in preserving the flag as a symbol of nationhood and national unity justifies Johnson's conviction.

As in *Spence*, "[w]e are confronted with a case of prosecution for the expression of an idea through activity," and "[a]ccordingly, we must examine with particular care the interests advanced by [petitioner] to support its prosecution." 418 U.S., at 411. Johnson was not, we add, prosecuted for the expression of just any idea; he was prosecuted for his expression of dissatisfaction with the policies of this country, expression situated at the core of our First Amendment values. . . .

Moreover, Johnson was prosecuted because he knew that his politically charged expression would cause "serious offense." If he had burned the flag as a means of disposing of it because it was dirty or torn, he would not have been convicted of flag desecration under this Texas law: federal law designates burning as the preferred means of disposing of a flag "when it is in such condition that it is no longer a fitting emblem for display," . . . and Texas has no quarrel with this means of disposal. . . . The Texas law is thus not aimed at protecting the physical integrity of the flag in all circumstances, but is designed instead to protect it only against impairments that would cause serious offense to others.[6] Texas concedes as much: "Section 42.09(b) reaches only those severe acts of physical abuse of the flag carried out in a way likely to be offensive. The statute mandates intentional or knowing abuse, that is, the kind of mistreatment that is not innocent, but rather is intentionally designed to seriously offend other individuals." . . .

Whether Johnson's treatment of the flag violated Texas law thus depended on the likely communicative impact of his expressive conduct.[7] Our decision in *Boos* v. *Barry* . . . tells us that this restriction on Johnson's expression is content-based. In *Boos*, we considered the constitutionality of a law prohibiting "the display of any sign within 50 feet of a foreign embassy if that sign tends to bring that foreign government into 'public odium' or 'public disrepute.'" . . . Rejecting the argument that the law was content-neutral because it was justified by "our international law obligation to shield diplomats from speech that offends their dignity," . . . we held that a "[t]he emotive impact of speech on its audience is not a 'secondary effect'" unrelated to the content of the expression itself. . . .

According to the principles announced in *Boos*, Johnson's political expression was restricted because of the content of the message he conveyed. We must therefore subject the State's asserted interest in preserving the special symbolic character of the flag to "the most exacting scrutiny."[8] . . .

Texas argues that its interest in preserving the flag as a symbol of nationhood and national unity survives this close analysis. Quoting extensively from the writings of this Court chronicling the flag's historic and symbolic role in our society, the State emphasizes the "'special place'" reserved for the flag in our Nation. . . . The State's argument is not that it has an interest simply in maintaining the flag as a symbol of *something*, no matter what it symbolizes; indeed, if that were the State's position, it would be difficult to see how that interest is endangered by highly symbolic conduct such as Johnson's. Rather, the State's claim is that it has an interest in preserving the flag as a symbol of *nationhood* and *national unity*, a symbol with a determinate range of meanings. . . . According to Texas, if one physically treats the flag in a way that would tend to cast doubt on either the idea that nationhood and national unity are the flag's referents or that national unity actually exists, the message conveyed thereby is a harmful one and therefore may be prohibited.[9]

If there is a bedrock principle underlying the First Amendment, it is that the Government may not prohibit the expression of an idea simply because society finds the idea itself offensive or disagreeable. . . .

We have not recognized an exception to this principle even where our flag has been involved. In *Street* v. *New York*, . . . we held that a State may not criminally punish a person for uttering words critical of the flag. Rejecting the argument that the conviction could be sustained on the ground that Street had "failed to show the respect for our national symbol which may properly be demanded of every citizen," we concluded that "the constitutionally guaranteed 'freedom to be intellectually . . . diverse or even contrary,' and the 'right to differ as to things that touch the heart of the existing order,' encompass the freedom to express publicly one's opinions about our flag, including those opinions which are defiant or contemptuous." . . . Nor may the Government, we have held, compel conduct that would evince respect for the flag. "To sustain the compulsory flag salute we are required to say that a Bill of Rights which guards the individual's right to speak his own mind, left it open to public authorities to compel him to utter what is not in his mind." . . .

In holding in *Barnette* that the Constitution did not leave this course open to the Government, Justice Jackson described one of our society's defining principles in words deserving of their frequent repetition: "If there is any fixed star in our constitutional constellation, it is that no official, high or petty, can prescribe what shall be orthodox in politics, nationalism, religion, or other matters of opinion or force citizens to confess by word or act their faith therein." . . . In *Spence,* we held that the same interest asserted by Texas here was insufficient to support a criminal conviction under a flag-misuse statute for the taping of a peace sign to an American flag. "Given the protected character of [Spence's] expression and in light of the fact that no interest the State may have in preserving the physical integrity of a privately owned flag was significantly impaired on these facts," we held, "the conviction must be invalidated." . . . See also *Goguen,* . . . (to convict a person who had sewn a flag onto the seat of his pants for "contemptuous" treatment of the flag would be "[t]o convict not to protect the physical integrity or to protect against acts interfering with the proper use of the flag, but to punish for communicating ideas unacceptable to the controlling majority in the legislature").

In short, nothing in our precedents suggests that a State may foster its own view of the flag by prohibiting expressive conduct relating to it.[10] To bring its argument outside our precedents, Texas attempts to convince us that even if its interest in preserving the flag's symbolic role does not allow it to prohibit words or some expressive conduct critical of the flag, it does permit it to forbid the outright destruction of the flag. The State's argument cannot depend here on the distinction between written or spoken words and nonverbal conduct. That distinction, we have shown, is of no moment where the nonverbal conduct is expressive, as it is here, and where the regulation of that conduct is related to expression, as it is here. . . . In addition, both *Barnette* and *Spence* involved expressive conduct, not only verbal communication, and both found that conduct protected.

Texas' focus on the precise nature of Johnson's expression, moreover, misses the point of our prior decisions: their enduring lesson, that the Government may not prohibit expression simply because it disagrees with its message, is not dependent on the particular mode in which one chooses to express an idea.[11] If we were to hold that a State may forbid flag-burning wherever it is likely to endanger the flag's

symbolic role, but allow it wherever burning a flag promotes that role—as where, for example, a person ceremoniously burns a dirty flag—we would be saying that when it comes to impairing the flag's physical integrity, the flag itself may be used as a symbol—as a substitute for the written or spoken word or a "short cut from mind to mind"—only in one direction. We would be permitting a State to "prescribe what shall be orthodox" by saying that one may burn the flag to convey one's attitude toward it and its referents only if one does not endanger the flag's representation of nationhood and national unity.

We never before have held that the Government may ensure that a symbol be used to express only one view of that symbol or its referents. Indeed, in *Schacht* v. *United States,* we invalidated a federal statute permitting an actor portraying a member of one of our armed forces to "'wear the uniform of that armed force if the portrayal does not tend to discredit that armed force.'" . . . This proviso, we held, "which leaves Americans free to praise the war in Vietnam but can send persons like Schacht to prison for opposing it, cannot survive in a country which has the First Amendment." . . .

We perceive no basis on which to hold that the principle underlying our decision in *Schacht* does not apply to this case. To conclude that the Government may permit designated symbols to be used to communicate only a limited set of messages would be to enter territory having no discernible or defensible boundaries. Could the Government, on this theory, prohibit the burning of state flags? Of copies of the Presidential seal? Of the Constitution? In evaluating these choices under the First Amendment, how would we decide which symbols were sufficiently special to warrant this unique status? To do so, we would be forced to consult our own political preferences, and impose them on the citizenry, in the very way that the First Amendment forbids us to do. . . .

There is, moreover, no indication—either in the text of the Constitution or in our cases interpreting it—that a separate juridical category exists for the American flag alone. Indeed, we would not be surprised to learn that the persons who framed our Constitution and wrote the Amendment that we now construe were not known for their reverence for the Union Jack. The First Amendment does not guarantee that other concepts virtually sacred to our Nation as a whole—such as the principle that discrimination on the basis of race is odious and destructive—will go unquestioned in the marketplace of ideas. . . . We decline, therefore, to create for the flag an exception to the joust of principles protected by the First Amendment.

It is not the State's ends, but its means, to which we object. It cannot be gainsaid that there is a special place reserved for the flag in this Nation, and thus we do not doubt that the Government has a legitimate interest in making efforts to "preserv[e] the national flag as an unalloyed symbol of our country." . . . We reject the suggestion, urged at oral argument by counsel for Johnson, that the Government lacks "any state interest whatsoever" in regulating the manner in which the flag may be displayed. . . . Congress has, for example, enacted precatory regulations describing the proper treatment of the flag, see 36 U.S.C. §§ 173–177, and we cast no doubt on the legitimacy of its interest in making such recommendations. To say that the Government has an interest in encouraging proper treatment of the flag, however, is not to say that it may criminally punish a person for burning a flag as a means of political protest. "National unity as an end which officials may foster by persuasion and example is not in question. The problem is whether under our Constitution compulsion as here employed is a permissible means for its achievement." . . .

We are fortified in today's conclusion by our conviction that forbidding criminal punishment for conduct such as Johnson's will not endanger the special role played by our flag or the feelings it inspires. To paraphrase Justice Holmes, we submit that nobody can suppose that this one gesture of an unknown man will change our Nation's attitude towards its flag. . . . Indeed, Texas' argument that the burning of an American flag "'is an act having a high likelihood to cause a breach of the peace,'" . . . and its statute's implicit assumption that physical mistreatment of the flag will lead to "serious offense," tend to confirm that the flag's special role is not in danger; if it were, no one would riot or take offense because a flag had been burned.

We are tempted to say, in fact, that the flag's deservedly cherished place in our community will be strengthened, not weakened, by our holding today. Our decision is a reaffirmation of the principles of freedom and inclusiveness that the flag best reflects, and of the conviction that our toleration of criticism such as Johnson's is a sign and source of our strength. Indeed, one of the proudest images of our flag, the one immortalized in our own national anthem, is of the bombardment it survived at Fort McHenry. It is the Nation's resilience, not its rigidity, that Texas sees reflected in the flag—and it is that resilience that we reassert today.

The way to preserve the flag's special role is not to punish those who feel differently about these matters. It is to persuade them that they are wrong. "To courageous, self-reliant men, with confidence in the power of free and fearless reasoning applied through the processes of popular government, no danger flowing from speech can be deemed clear and present, unless the incidence of the evil apprehended is so imminent that it may befall before there is opportunity for full discussion. If there be time to expose through discussion the falsehood and fallacies, to avert the evil by the processes of education, the remedy to be applied is more speech, not enforced silence." . . . And, precisely because it is our flag that is involved, one's response to the flag-burner may exploit the uniquely persuasive power of the flag itself. We can imagine no more appropriate response to burning a flag than waving one's own, no better way to counter a flag-burner's message than by saluting the flag that burns, no surer means of preserving the dignity even of the flag that burned than by—as one witness here did—according its remains a respectful burial. We do not consecrate the flag by punishing its desecration, for in doing so we dilute the freedom that this cherished emblem represents.

V

Johnson was convicted for engaging in expressive conduct. The State's interest in preventing breaches of the peace does not support his conviction because Johnson's conduct did not threaten to disturb the peace. Nor does the State's interest in preserving the flag as a symbol of nationhood and national unity justify his criminal conviction for engaging in political expression. The judgment of the Texas Court of Criminal Appeals is therefore

Affirmed.

CHIEF JUSTICE REHNQUIST, with whom JUSTICE WHITE and JUSTICE O'CONNOR join, dissenting.

In holding this Texas statute unconstitutional, the Court ignores Justice Holmes' familiar aphorism that "a page of history is worth a volume of logic." . . . For more than 200 years, the American flag has occupied a unique position as the symbol of our Nation, a uniqueness that justifies a governmental prohibition against flag burning in the way respondent Johnson did here. . . .

The Court concludes its opinion with a regrettably patronizing civics lecture, presumably addressed to the Members of both Houses of Congress, the members of the 48 state legislatures that enacted prohibitions against flag burning, and the troops fighting under that flag in Vietnam who objected to its being burned: "The way to preserve the flag's special role is not to punish those who feel differently about these matters. It is to persuade them that they are wrong." . . . The Court's role as the final expositor of the Constitution is well established, but its role as a platonic guardian admonishing those responsible to public opinion as if they were truant school children has no similar place in our system of government. The cry of "no taxation without representation" animated those who revolted against the English Crown to found our Nation—the idea that those who submitted to government should have some say as to what kind of laws would be passed. Surely one of the high purposes of a democratic society is to legislate against conduct that is regarded as evil and profoundly offensive to the majority of people—whether it be murder, embezzlement, pollution, or flag burning.

Our Constitution wisely places limits on powers of legislative majorities to act, but the declaration of such limits by this Court "is, at all times, a question of much delicacy, which ought seldom, if ever, to be decided in the affirmative, in a doubtful case." *Fletcher* v. *Peck,* 6 Cranch 87, 128 (1810) (Marshall, C. J.). Uncritical extension of constitutional protection to the burning of the flag risks the frustration of the very purpose for which organized governments are instituted. The Court decides that the American flag is just another symbol, about which not only must opinions pro and con be tolerated, but for which the most minimal public respect may not be enjoined. The government may conscript men into the Armed Forces where they must fight and perhaps die for the flag, but the government may not prohibit the public burning of the banner under which they fight. I would uphold the Texas statute as applied in this case.[12]

---

1. *Tex. Penal Code Ann. § 42.09 (1989) provides in full: "§ 42.09. Desecration of Venerated Object*

"(a) A person commits an offense if he intentionally or knowingly desecrates:

"(1) a public monument;

"(2) a place of worship or burial; or

"(3) a state or national flag.

"(b) For purposes of this section, 'desecrate' means deface, damage, or otherwise physically mistreat in a way that the actor knows will seriously offend one or more persons likely to observe or discover his action.

"(c) An offense under this section is a Class A misdemeanor."

2. *Because the prosecutor's closing argument observed that Johnson had led the protestors in chants denouncing the flag while it burned, Johnson suggests that he may have been convicted for uttering critical words rather than for burning the flag. Brief for Respondent 33–34. He relies on Street v. New York, 394 U.S. 576, 578 (1969), in which we reversed a conviction obtained under a New York statute that prohibited publicly defying or casting contempt on the flag "either by words or act" because we were persuaded that the defendant may have been convicted for his words alone. Unlike the law we faced in Street, however, the Texas flag-desecration statute does not on its face permit conviction for remarks critical of the flag, as Johnson himself admits. See Brief for Respondent 34. Nor was the jury in this case told that it could convict Johnson of flag desecration if it found only that he had uttered words critical of the flag and its referents.*

Johnson emphasizes, though, that the jury was instructed— according to Texas' law of parties—that " 'a person is criminally responsible for an offense committed by the conduct of another if acting with intent to promote or assist the commission of the offense, he solicits, encourages, directs, aids, or attempts to aid the other person to commit the offense.' " Brief for Respondent 2, n. 2, quoting 1 Record 49. The State offered this instruction because Johnson's defense was that he was not the person who had burned the flag. Johnson did not object to this instruction at trial, and although he challenged it on direct appeal, he did so only on the ground that there was insufficient evidence to support it. 706 S. W. 2d 120, 124 (Tex. App. 1986). It is only in this Court that Johnson has argued that the law-of-parties instruction might have led the jury to convict him for his words alone. Even if we were to find that this argument is properly raised here, however, we would conclude that it has no merit in these circumstances. The instruction would not have permitted a conviction merely for the pejorative nature of Johnson's words, and those words themselves did not encourage the burning of the flag as the instruction seems to require. Given the additional fact that "the bulk of the State's argument was premised on Johnson's culpability as a sole actor," ibid., we find it too unlikely that the jury convicted Johnson on the basis of this alternative theory to consider reversing his conviction on this ground.

3. *Although Johnson has raised a facial challenge to Texas' flag-desecration statute, we choose to resolve this case on the basis of his claim that the statute as applied to him violates the First Amendment. Section 42.09 regulates only physical conduct with respect to the flag, not the written or spoken word, and although one violates the statute only if one "knows" that one's physical treatment of the flag "will seriously offend one or more persons likely to observe or discover his action," Tex. Penal Code Ann. § 42.09(b) (1989), this fact does not necessarily mean that the statute applies only to expressive conduct protected by the First Amendment. Cf. Smith v. Goguen, 415 U.S. 566, 588 (1974) (WHITE, J., concurring in judgment) (statute prohibiting "contemptuous" treatment of flag encompasses only expressive conduct). A tired person might, for example, drag a flag through the mud, knowing that this conduct is likely to offend others, and yet have no thought of expressing any idea; neither the language nor the Texas courts' interpretations of the statute precludes the possibility that such a person would be prosecuted for flag desecration. Because the prosecution of a person who had not engaged in expressive conduct would pose a different case, and because we are capable of disposing of this*

case on narrower grounds, we address only Johnson's claim that § 42.09 as applied to political expression like his violates the First Amendment.

4. Relying on our decision in Boos v. Barry, 485 U.S. 312 (1988), Johnson argues that this state interest is related to the suppression of free expression within the meaning of United States v. O'Brien, 391 U.S. 367 (1968). He reasons that the violent reaction to flag-burnings feared by Texas would be the result of the message conveyed by them, and that this fact connects the State's interest to the suppression of expression. Brief for Respondent 12, n. 11. This view has found some favor in the lower courts. See Monroe v. State Court of Fulton County, 739 F. 2d 568, 574–575 (CA11 1984). Johnson's theory may overread Boos insofar as it suggests that a desire to prevent a violent audience reaction is "related to expression" in the same way that a desire to prevent an audience from being offended is "related to expression." Because we find that the State's interest in preventing breaches of the peace is not implicated on these facts, however, we need not venture further into this area.

5. There is, of course, a tension between this argument and the State's claim that one need not actually cause serious offense in order to violate § 42.09. See Brief for Petitioner 44.

6. Cf. Smith v. Goguen, 415 U.S., at 590–591 (BLACKMUN, J., dissenting) (emphasizing that lower court appeared to have construed state statute so as to protect physical integrity of the flag in all circumstances); id., at 597–598 (REHNQUIST, J., dissenting) (same).

7. Texas suggests that Johnson's conviction did not depend on the onlookers' reaction to the flag-burning because § 42.09 is violated only when a person physically mistreats the flag in a way that he "knows will seriously offend one or more persons likely to observe or discover his action." Tex. Penal Code Ann. § 42.09(b) (1969) (emphasis added). "The 'serious offense' language of the statute," Texas argues, "refers to an individual's intent and to the manner in which the conduct is effectuated, not to the reaction of the crowd." Brief for Petitioner 44. If the statute were aimed only at the actor's intent and not at the communicative impact of his actions, however, there would be little reason for the law to be triggered only when an audience is "likely" to be present. At Johnson's trial, indeed, the State itself seems not to have seen the distinction between knowledge and actual communicative impact that it now stresses; it proved the element of knowledge by offering the testimony of persons who had in fact been seriously offended by Johnson's conduct. Id., at 6–7. In any event, we find the distinction between Texas' statute and one dependent on actual audience reaction too precious to be of constitutional significance. Both kinds of statutes clearly are aimed at protecting onlookers from being offended by the ideas expressed by the prohibited activity.

8. Our inquiry is, of course, bounded by the particular facts of this case and by the statute under which Johnson was convicted. There was no evidence that Johnson himself stole the flag he burned, Tr. of Oral Arg. 17, nor did the prosecution or the arguments urged in support of it depend on the theory that the flag was stolen. Ibid. Thus, our analysis does not rely on the way in which the flag was acquired, and nothing in our opinion should be taken to suggest that one is free to steal a flag so long as one later uses it to communicate an idea. We also emphasize that Johnson was prosecuted only for flag desecration—not for trespass, disorderly conduct, or arson.

9. Texas claims that "Texas is not endorsing, protecting, avowing or prohibiting any particular philosophy." Brief for Petitioner 29. If Texas means to suggest that its asserted interest does not prefer Democrats over Socialists, or Republicans over Democrats, for example, then it is beside the point, for Johnson does not rely on such an argument. He argues instead that the State's desire to maintain the flag as a symbol of nationhood and national unity assumes that there is only one proper view of the flag. Thus, if Texas means to argue that its interest does not prefer any viewpoint over another, it is mistaken; surely one's attitude towards the flag and its referents is a viewpoint.

10. Our decision in Halter v. Nebraska, 205 U.S. 34 (1907), addressing the validity of a state law prohibiting certain commercial uses of the flag, is not to the contrary. That case was decided "nearly 20 years before the Court concluded that the First Amendment applies to the States by virtue of the Fourteenth Amendment." Spence v. Washington, 418 U.S. 405, 413, n. 7 (1974). More important, as we continually emphasized in Halter itself, that case involved purely commercial rather than political speech. 205 U.S., at 38, 41, 42, 45.

Nor does San Francisco Arts & Athletics v. Olympic Committee, 483 U.S. 522, 524 (1987), addressing the validity of Congress' decision to "authoriz[e] the United States Olympic Committee to prohibit certain commercial and promotional uses of the word 'Olympic,'" relied upon by the dissent, post, at 9, even begin to tell us whether the Government may criminally punish physical conduct towards the flag engaged in as a means of political protest.

11. The dissent appears to believe that Johnson's conduct may be prohibited and, indeed, criminally sanctioned, because "his act . . . conveyed nothing that could not have been conveyed and was not conveyed just as forcefully in a dozen different ways." Post, at 10. Not only does this assertion sit uneasily next to the dissent's quite correct reminder that the flag occupies a unique position in our society—which demonstrates that messages conveyed without use of the flag are not "just as forcefu[l]" as those conveyed with it—but it also ignores the fact that, in Spence, supra, we "rejected summarily" this very claim. See 418 U.S., at 411, n. 4.

12. In holding that the Texas statute as applied to Johnson violates the First Amendment, the Court does not consider Johnson's claims that the statute is unconstitutionally vague or overbroad. Brief for Respondent 24–30. I think those claims are without merit. In New York State Club Assn. v. City of New York, 487 U.S. —, — (1988), we stated that a facial challenge is only proper under the First Amendment when a statute can never be applied in a permissible manner or when, even if it may be validly applied to a particular defendant, it is so broad as to reach the protected speech of third parties. While Tex. Penal Code Ann. § 42.09 (1989) "may not satisfy those intent on finding fault at any cost, [it is] set out in terms that the ordinary person exercising ordinary common sense can sufficiently understand and comply with." CSC v. Letter Carriers, 413 U.S. 548, 579 (1973). By defining "desecrate" as "deface," "damage" or otherwise "physically mistreat" in a manner that the actor knows will "seriously offend" others, § 42.09 only prohibits flagrant acts of physical abuse and destruction of the flag of the sort at issue here—soaking a flag with lighter fluid and igniting it in public—and not any of the examples of improper flag etiquette cited in Respondent's brief.

CIVIL RIGHTS VERSUS CIVIL LIBERTIES:
The Case of Discriminatory Verbal Harassment*†

Thomas C. Grey

The expression of a change of aspect is the expression of a *new* perception and at the same time of the perception's being unchanged.

Wittgenstein, *Philosophical Investigations*[1]

American liberals believe that both civil liberties and civil rights are harmonious aspects of a basic commitment to human rights. But recently these two clusters of values have seemed increasingly to conflict—as, for example, with the feminist claim that the legal toleration of pornography, long a goal sought by civil libertarians, actually violates civil rights as a form of sex discrimination.

Here I propose an interpretation of the conflict of civil rights and civil liberties in its latest manifestation: the controversy over how to treat discriminatory verbal harassment on American campuses. I was involved with the controversy in a practical way at Stanford, where I helped draft a harassment regulation that was recently adopted by the university.

Like the pornography issue, the harassment problem illustrates the element of paradox in the conflict of civil-liberties and civil-rights perspectives or mentalities. This problem does not simply trigger familiar disagreements between liberals of a classical or libertarian orientation as against those of a welfare state or social democratic one—though it does sometimes do that. In my experience, the issue also has the power to appear to a single person in different shapes and suggest different solutions as it oscillates between being framed in civil-liberties and in civil-rights terms. At the same time, however, it remains recognizably

the same problem. It is thus a very practical and political example of the kind of tension noted by Wittgenstein in the aphorism that heads this essay—a puzzle of interpretive framing, of "seeing-as."

One of my aims in this essay is to bring the reader to share the sense of paradox that, for me, pervades the experience of trying to categorize and resolve the harassment issue. At the outset, let me sketch what I take to be the two main structural features of the clash between the civil-liberties and the civil-rights perspectives that this problem exemplifies.

First, the two approaches take contrasting views of intangible or psychic injury. The civil-liberties mentality, centrally concerned with protecting freedom of expression against censorship, tends to limit the kinds of harms that can justify abridgment of that freedom to traditionally recognized infringements of tangible interests in property and bodily security. In particular, claims that government can interfere with speech to protect sensibilities, emotional tranquility, or self-esteem—in general, *feelings*—are strongly disfavored. It is a "bedrock principle" of civil liberties that censorship is not justified to prevent even what is "deeply offensive to many."[2] The civil-libertarian counsel to fellow citizens is the traditional parental advice to the child wounded by insult or rejection: "Sticks and stones may break my bones, but words will never hurt me"—not hurt *enough,* that is, to justify the known costs of censorship.

By contrast, the civil-rights approach, with its roots in anti-discrimination law and social policy, is

---

*[Thomas C. Grey expresses] thanks for excellent research assistance . . . to William Boyle, Jay Fowler, and John Tweedy. And [he is] also grateful for the editorial suggestions of Barbara Babcock, Barbara Fried, Mark Kelman, Richard Posner, Robert Rabin, Carol Rose, James Weinstein, Steven Shiffrin, and Steven Winter; of those who attended [the] faculty workshop at Boalt Hall, University of California, Berkeley; and of Ellen Paul and the other editors of *Social Philosophy & Policy.* Finally, special thanks, for inspiration, to Charles Lawrence III.

†From Grey, Thomas, "Civil Rights and Civil Liberties: The Case of Discriminatory Verbal Harassment," in *Social Philosophy and Policy* (1991). Reprinted by permission of Blackwell Publishers.

centrally concerned with injuries of stigma and humiliation to those who are the victims of discrimination—
conduct generating "feelings of inferiority" that
damage "hearts and minds," in the language of the
most famous American civil rights case.[3] The point is
not so much to protect a sphere of autonomy or personal security from *intrusion* as to protect potentially
marginal members of the community from *exclusion*—
from relegation, that is, to the status of second-class
citizens.

The second contrast is a related one: it comes in
the treatment of the public-private distinction. The active state is traditionally conceived as the sole or dominant threat to civil liberties. Civil libertarians do not
spend much of their time or energy seeking ways to
positively empower dissenters, deviants, and nonconformists against the pressures brought on them by unorganized public opinion, or by private employers or
landlords. The catalogue of civil liberties is certainly
what Judge Richard Posner has called the Constitution: "a charter of negative rather than positive
liberties."[4]

"But [to continue with the same quotation from
Judge Posner] where the liberty asserted is the right to
equal treatment irrespective of race or sex, the analysis is more complex."[5] Under the civil-rights perspective, defense of basic human rights is by no means
simply a matter of limiting state power. Government
may deny equal protection by omission as well as by
action—for example, by refusing law enforcement
protection to minorities. The tendency of the civil-
rights mentality is to favor the prohibition of all invidious treatment that has the effect of "implying
inferiority in civil society" to individuals on the basis
of their membership in identifiable social groups.[6]
This "anti-discrimination principle" goes beyond
cleansing government action of bias; it also attacks
discrimination on the suspect bases of race, sex, and
so on, in the other major institutions of civil society.
Thus the identification of a new form of invidious discrimination today typically brings with it pressure for
legislation against private as well as official discrimination of that kind in housing, employment, and
education.[7]

When the conflict of civil-liberties and civil-rights
perspectives is described in terms of the structural features just sketched, it resonates with a number of the
binary oppositions of social philosophy: liberty against
equality; liberty against democracy; individualism
against collectivism; the methods of economics and
rational choice theory against those of sociology and
cultural anthropology. Though I hope what I have to

say here may intrigue those interested in the practical
implications of the standard theoretical dichotomies, I
do not analyze the harassment issue in these terms.

This is partly to avoid one of the temptations of
classic social philosophy, the urge to make it as nearly
as possible like geometry or physics. One seeks, using
this paradigm, to formulate contending theoretical
positions as models, stated as broadly and at the
same time as rigorously as possible. Adopting this
approach, one then sees an actual controversy that
brings these oppositions into play as simply a manifestation of underlying theoretical contradictions. The
practical issue serves the purpose of forcing choice
between the theories, just as crucial experiments are
supposed to force choice between rival scientific hypotheses. On the harassment issue, the structural conflict between civil-liberties and civil-rights approaches
then naturally appears as the vivid illustration of a
contradiction between, for example, opposed libertarian and egalitarian theories of liberalism. Intellectual rigor and respect for consistency would then
require forthright resolution of the contradiction, most
readily achieved by rejecting one of the conflicting
alternatives.

This seems to me the wrong way to deal with
the harassment problem; indeed, it generally seems
the wrong way to deal with most theoretical disagreements as they bear on social, political, and legal questions. Rarely can important theories in these areas be
plausibly formulated as models or axiom-systems precise enough to give rise to "contradictions." Much
more often the actual working theories are perspectives, approaches, or mentalities constituted of more
or less vague (but never completely open-ended)
clusters of goals, ideals, guidelines, and presumptions.
When theories this imprecise clash, no principle of
logic requires rejection of either one.

Methods of social philosophy that seek to formulate theories with maximum precision do so with
an eye to determinacy—they seek theories that can
actually *compel* results where they apply. Theories
that conflict over a practical issue then compel conflicting results; when a contradiction arises, one theory
must be chosen to the exclusion of the other. Yet in
problematic practical situations, each of the conflicting theories (perspectives, approaches, mentalities)
may have something valuable and even essential to
contribute to a resolution. In such situations, over-
sharpened theories tend to produce incomplete and
one-sided outcomes, whereas a pragmatist tolerance
of theoretical ambiguity and imprecision can conduce
to better results.

Such a situation is, it seems to me, presented by the issue of discriminatory harassment. This problem exemplifies something liberal pragmatists should accept as normal—a conflict between plural, sometimes incommensurable, structured clusters of values and principles, here the familiar ones surrounding the terms "civil liberties" and "civil rights." Where these conflicting approaches overlap, as they inevitably will, liberal democrats can identify a range of mediating solutions that respect the claims of both conflicting approaches. I offer the Stanford provision on discriminatory verbal harassment as an example of such a solution. But first I should more fully describe the practical issue and the opposed civil-rights and civil-liberties approaches to it.

I

There has recently been an upsurge in the number and intensity of reported incidents of racist, homophobic, and sexist abuse in American universities.[8] An extreme example was the incident reported at the University of Wisconsin in which white students followed a black woman student across campus shouting "We've never tried a nigger."[9] Perhaps less unequivocal in its implications was this exchange at Stanford: after a dormitory argument in which a black student had claimed that Ludwig van Beethoven was a mulatto and other students had objected to placing such stress on racial origins, two white students defaced a picture of the composer into a blackface caricature and posted it near the black student's room.[10]

The question is: what disciplinary action (if any) is appropriate in such cases? A pure civil-rights approach treats the conduct in question as discriminatory harassment. Then principles of equal treatment not only entitle but *require* universities to punish the behavior, at least if it becomes sufficiently widespread to create a pervasively hostile environment. The analogy is to employers' obligations to deal with racial or sexual harassment by fellow employees in the workplace. When black or female employees must endure a barrage of race- or sex-based insults from coworkers, an employer who ignores the situation may be guilty of unlawful (and if a public employer, unconstitutional) race or sex discrimination.[11] Again I quote Judge Posner, certainly no civil-rights extremist:

> By taking no steps to prevent sexual harassment, the city created a worse working environment for women than for men. . . .

> That is discrimination. . . . It is as if the city decided to provide restrooms for male but not female employees, and when pressed for a reason said it simply didn't care whether its female employees were comfortable or not.[12]

In the case in question, the sexual harassment included some physical contact and coercive sexual proposals by supervisors, as well as sexist obscenities and epithets from fellow workers. In discriminatory harassment cases, however, courts have not sharply differentiated between action and verbal abuse in evaluating claims by black or female employees. Typically, action and speech are blended together in a course of conduct that gives rise to liability for the employer when it creates an intolerably "hostile environment" for women or racial minority employees. In some cases, which the courts have not singled out for special treatment on this ground, harassment is found from speech alone—typically a stream of racist or sexist jokes, pictures, and epithets. To avoid liability, the employer must take reasonable steps to keep verbal as well as physical or otherwise coercive abuse below the level of a "sustained pattern of harassment."[13] The decisive question is not whether the harassment constitutes speech or action, but whether it is widespread and serious enough to go beyond what the courts judge must be tolerated as part of life's ordinary rough and tumble.

A civil rights approach to the verbal abuse problem on campus simply applies the doctrine of hostile environment discrimination to the university. Most educators, like most employers, are required by law (as they should feel required by fairness) to provide equal opportunity to women and students of color. Campus harassment can make the educational environment hostile, just as workplace harassment makes the employment environment so. Many campuses have already recognized this with respect to sexual harassment and have adopted disciplinary restrictions accordingly. There is no good reason why racial or anti-homosexual harassment should not be treated in the same way. As a legal matter, an unremedied "sustained pattern of harassment" might make the university itself guilty of unlawful discrimination.[14] Prudent and sensitive administrators will prohibit acts of harassment before the point at which the conduct cumulates into a sustained pattern and thus creates a legally actionable hostile environment.

An analysis like this can easily lead to a prohibition defined purely in terms of civil rights. Thus the University of Michigan, faced with an upsurge in racial harassment, enacted a prohibition against any "behavior, verbal or physical" that "stigmatizes or victimizes" an individual on the basis of race, sex, or other characteristics protected under the university's non-discrimination policy and that has the "reasonably foreseeable effect of interfering with an individual's academic efforts," or "[c]reates an intimidating, hostile or demeaning environment for educational pursuits." This is a prohibition drafted to track the form of injury dealt with by the civil-rights approach—conduct contributing to a hostile environment that denies equal educational opportunity.[15]

And yet, in the first major case involving the regulation of campus verbal harassment, a federal district court struck this provision down on First Amendment grounds.[16] Civil libertarians applauded the opinion; they qualified their applause at the result only because the case seemed so easy that it did not establish a particularly powerful precedent for other cases of regulation of campus harassment. And an easy case it was—as soon as it was considered from the angle of a civil-liberties, rather than a civil-rights, approach.

Viewed through a First Amendment lens, the Michigan regulation—now seen as a "hate speech" or "group defamation" rule rather than a harassment prohibition—was a dramatically overbroad incursion into core areas of protected speech. Consider just one example of the kind of speech prohibited by the regulation, taken from the guidelines the university distributed to student to explain the new policy:

> *A male student makes remarks in class like "Women just aren't as good in this field as men," thus creating a hostile learning atmosphere for female classmates.*[17]

From this one can readily extrapolate to other statements (made in class or in a dorm hallway debate) that would violate the standard: arguing on the basis of IQ data that blacks are less intelligent than whites; that homosexuality is "unnatural," or is a disease; that women are naturally less creative than men.[18] The expression of these opinions is certainly experienced as "stigmatizing" and "demeaning" by many, probably most, students belonging to the groups thus insulted; when cumulated to create a climate of opinion, comments like these might well foreseeably "interfere with the academic efforts" of the students whose basic humanity or equal mental capacity they deny.

Because the Michigan regulation has been so universally condemned, it is important to understand how campus authorities might have drafted and enforced it the way they did. They evidently viewed the problem of verbal harassment from one perspective only: the perspective of civil rights. Viewed solely through the lens provided by anti-discrimination law and policy, the kind of statements to which the regulation was applied might well appear as more polite but no less demeaning versions of the kind of racist, sexist, or homophobic insults routinely prohibited under anti-harassment codes in the employment area.

Indeed, the very "politeness" of these statements might rationally be thought to make them *more* disabling to the educational performance of those exposed to them than are the relatively rare incidents involving gutter epithets. At most universities, the victims of the crudest insults can partly discount them because they clearly transgress the dominant mores. By contrast, the more academically respectable forms of denigration of blacks, women, and gays can be supported by evidence and argument, the forms of discourse with maximum credibility in the university. And the damage such statements do is probably enhanced when the stereotypes they reinforce deny the ability of groups of students to study and learn whose members already feel marginal on many campuses. The discourse of "statistics show . . ." and "environmental factors cannot fully explain . . ." may much more effectively create a hostile educational environment than "[Epithet] go home!"

But as soon as a civil-liberties perspective is brought to bear, the kind of speech reached by the Michigan regulation is readily seen as close to the core of the First Amendment. The record in the federal court challenge to the regulation, with a large number of complaints processed, and many resolved informally to require apology (and, in some cases, what looks suspiciously like University of Beijing-style "re-education")[19] in response to speech expressing views on issues of public and campus concern, did indeed present an easy case. If questions that go to the core of human rights and social policy issues cannot be freely debated on campuses, what issues can?

The regulation established a general, content-based regime of censorship of politically and socially controversial speech, with speech concerning issues of race, gender, and sexual orientation subject to special restriction. Worse, within that content-defined field of regulation, the censorship regime imposed a viewpoint-specific orthodoxy: students were allowed to state radical or liberal, but not conservative or reactionary, views on controverted issues. They could say that the mental abilities of blacks were equal to or greater than those of whites, but not lesser; that homosexuality was a culturally formed category of sexual preference or a natural inclination, but not a disease or a sin; that women's genetic endowments made them equal or superior to men in socially valued activities, but not inferior.[20]

Viewed from the civil-liberties perspective, regulations such as these are highly suspect because they are aimed squarely at the content of speech rather than at its incidental injurious consequences. Under current First Amendment doctrine, no restriction focused on the communicative impact of speech is permissible unless it is necessary to prevent serious and imminent harm; the harm in question cannot be simply offense, however strong and justified, at what is said. Finally, any restriction within these narrow confines must be "viewpoint neutral."

The underlying idea is that there must be no ideological censorship—no official regime of screening utterances for the political, moral, or social acceptability of the message they deliver.[21] "The First Amendment recognizes no such thing as a 'false' idea."[22] The idea behind this slogan need not be a paralyzed relativism. It can be a historically-founded liberal suspicion that officials are peculiarly unlikely to accurately distinguish falsity from truth under a regime of censorship, as expressed in Justice Jackson's classic *Barnette* opinion:

> *If there is any star fixed in our constitutional constellation, it is that no official, high or petty, can prescribe what shall be orthodox in politics, nationalism, religion, or other matters of opinion . . .[23]*

Or it can be a republican faith in the citizenry's ability to respond to bad speech with better speech, as in Justice Brandeis's equally classic *Whitney* opinion:

> *Fear or serious injury alone cannot justify suppression of free speech. . . . Those who won our independence by revolution were not cowards. . . . If there be time to expose through discussion the falsehood and fallacies, to avert the evil by the processes of education, the remedy to be applied is more speech, not enforced silence.[24]*

The civil-liberties analytical framework tends to confine regulation of campus verbal harassment to prohibiting conduct verging on assault, including perhaps tortious "intentional infliction of emotional distress" and certain face-to-face insults that are especially likely to provoke immediate violence—so-called "fighting words." Further, the civil-liberties

framework requires that any speech regulations must be evenhanded; universities may not single out ideologically defined classes of provocations or verbal assaults for prohibition. This, let it be said, is the moderate civil-libertarian position. Civil-liberties purists find even the "emotional distress" and "fighting words" theories insufficiently content-neutral and so oppose *any* disciplinary measures against verbal harassment whatever—even in the extreme Wisconsin example I mentioned above.[25]

For some, of course, the civil-rights and civil-liberties approaches are not "perspectives" on this problem; rather, one or the other of these approaches simply states the reality of the situation. Thus on the civil-rights side, many students at Stanford were sincerely shocked when free speech concerns led university authorities not to prosecute the Beethoven poster episode at Stanford that I described above. A number of them described this as an instance of taking something that was clearly one thing—a racist atrocity, which if left unpunished established an officially condoned practice of discrimination—and "turning it into" a civil-liberties issue. Later in the year, when members of a left-activist student coalition seized (forcibly, but without causing personal injury or property damage) the office of the president of the university, they cited the Beethoven incident as one of their main grievances; when they were charged (and ultimately found guilty) under the university disciplinary code for the takeover, they said it was an irony that their "peaceful protest" had been punished while this clear incident of racist persecution had been treated as protected free speech.

On the other side, many civil libertarians simply do not see the problem as involving issues of civil rights or discrimination at all. It is *not* a clash of equal protection and free speech, they insist, but a pure civil-liberties issue, in which fragile free speech values are threatened by powerful political pressure groups on liberal campuses. For these civil libertarians, protecting discriminatory verbal harassment is no different from protecting flag-burning; it represents the principled defense of reason against the perennial collective emotional impulse to censor, rather than answer, the speech of unpopular and often unpleasant dissenters.[26]

My own view is that there are plenty of good reasons, and plenty of worthy passions, on both sides of the issue. And they seem to me really to be *sides*—mutually incommensurable perspectives—rather than the poles of a well-defined continuum along which negotiators may approach each other in search of a solution that measurably splits the difference between them.[27] The epigraph to this essay occurs in the course of Wittgenstein's famous discussion of the ambiguous "duck-rabbit" drawing, which can appear as either a duck or a rabbit, depending on how you look at it.[28] You can learn facility at shifting between seeing the figure as a duck and seeing it as a rabbit, but at any moment it appears only in one aspect or the other. The campus harassment issue has something of the same quality.

II

Let me now describe the proposal I originally drafted, which was recently adopted as a disciplinary rule covering discriminatory verbal harassment at Stanford.[29] The provision is an attempt to accommodate competing values, to mediate the incommensurable conflict of civil-liberties and civil-rights approaches on this issue. I am not confident that it is better than other mediating solutions, though I can give a reason for the choice of each of its elements. But I do believe that some such accommodating solution, as against a "principled" choice implementing one approach to the exclusion of the other, is needed.[30]

The first section of the provision restates Stanford's policy on free expression, including an insistence that students must learn to "tolerate even expression of opinions which they find abhorrent." Counterposed is a second section restating the university's existing policy against discrimination "in the administration of its educational policies" on the basis of "sex, race, color, handicap, religion, sexual orientation, or national and ethnic origin," and adding that harassment on the basis of these characteristics can, when cumulated, constitute hostile environment discrimination under the policy. The third section notes that the free expression and anti-discrimination policies conflict on the issue of verbal harassment; it provides that "protected free expression ends and prohibited discriminatory harassment begins" at the point where expression of opinion becomes "personal vilification" of a student on the basis of one of the characteristics stated in the anti-discrimination policy.

The operative part of the provision comes in the fourth and last section, which defines "personal vilification" as speech or other symbolic expression that (a) is intended to insult or stigmatize individuals on the basis of one of the designated characteristics;

(b) is "addressed directly" to those insulted or stigmatized; and (c) makes use of "insulting or 'fighting' words," defined (quoting from *Chaplinsky* v. *New Hampshire*[31]) as words (or non-verbal symbols) that "by their very utterance inflict injury or tend to incite to an immediate breach of the peace."

Finally, the proposal adds a narrowing proviso designed to adapt the *Chaplinsky* insulting-or-fighting words concept to civil-rights enforcement. In the context of discriminatory harassment, punishable words (or symbols) are defined as those "commonly understood to convey direct and visceral hatred or contempt for human beings on the basis of" the characteristics specified in the anti-discrimination policy—a phrase meant to capture the sense of the common expression "racial epithets" and to extend it to other prohibited forms of discrimination.

To summarize, the rule would punish speech directed to individuals: speech meant to insult them on the basis of a protected characteristic that also makes use of one of the gutter epithets of bigotry. It thus adopts one element of what I have called the "moderate civil libertarian" view of harassment regulation; it prohibits only expression that falls roughly within the categories of fighting words or intentional infliction of emotional distress doctrines. The provision therefore only prohibits a very narrow category of expression, immunizing even the vilest hate speech addressed generally to a campus audience as well as many serious face-to-face discriminatory verbal assaults. Many students of color and other civil-rights advocates at Stanford have opposed it, for these reasons, as too weak an anti-discrimination measure.

At the same time, narrow as it is, the proposal retains enough of the civil-rights approach to trouble most civil libertarians. It seems to violate the second central civil-liberties tenet: not only can speech be regulated only to the minimum extent necessary to prevent immediate and otherwise unremediable harm; further, any speech regulation must be *neutral*—generally neutral as to content, certainly neutral as to viewpoint. The provision's apparent violation of the neutrality constraint results directly from its being framed as civil-rights protection or anti-discrimination measure.

To bring out the neutrality problem, I need to describe more fully the legal underpinnings of the proposal. It does not precisely track either of the most common bases for narrow discriminatory harassment regulations: the "fighting words" or "intentional infliction of emotional distress" rationales, which have been adopted at other universities in the wake of the

Michigan case.[32] Rather, it draws on the relevant common elements in those two theories, adapting them to the context of a civil-rights–based campus harassment regulation.

In the *Chaplinsky* case, a unanimous Supreme Court excluded from First Amendment protection "insulting or 'fighting' words," those which "by their very utterance inflict injury" *or* that "tend to incite an immediate breach of the peace." Subsequent cases have focused on the "breach of the peace" half of the category, and the Court has made clear that its reach is narrow indeed; it has never affirmed a conviction under the doctrine since *Chaplinsky* itself in 1942.[33] During those years, the Court has also developed the "heckler's veto" doctrine as a counterweight to its "fighting words" proviso, putting the burden on law enforcement to protect speakers against threatened violence, rather than avoiding the violence by silencing the speaker.[34]

The heckler's veto analysis brings out the weakness in the "fighting words" doctrine as it was traditionally formulated. The concept seems to ask purely factual and predictive questions. Can imminent violence be expected from an audience? Are available law enforcement resources insufficient to protect the speaker? As many civil libertarians have argued, however, it seems inconsistent with free speech values to punish a speaker simply because the heckler's veto is made effective—because, that is, a sufficient number of thugs have plausibly threatened violence and available police protection is inadequate. A serious civil-libertarian presumption in favor of free speech seems to require some evaluation of what the speaker has said—are they really "*fighting* words"?—before silencing the speaker in the face of a hostile audience can be said to be a proper response.

The same requirement of normative evaluation of the speech must also apply, it seems, in the case of intentional infliction of emotional distress. And here, indeed, the evaluative element is explicitly built into the standard common law elements of the tort. The victim must foreseeably suffer severe emotional distress from what the defendant does or says, but this is not sufficient. In addition, the defendant's conduct must be, as Section 46 or the Torts Restatement puts it, in unmistakably evaluative terms, "beyond all possible bounds of decency" and "regarded as atrocious and utterly intolerable in a civilized community"—in short, "outrageous."[35]

I suggest that we interpret the *Chaplinsky* category of "insulting or 'fighting' words" as designating utterances that at least meet the standard set by Restatement Section 46. For free speech purposes, though, the Section 46 standard is *too* purely evaluative—too vague.[36] But if the vagueness problem can be met (by delineating a category of utterances that *are* "outrageous" and are given further and more objective definition), then it would be reasonable—under *Chaplinsky*—to treat those utterances as subject to prohibition because they are likely *either* to provoke violence or to cause severe emotional distress.

The Stanford provision thus interprets *Chaplinsky*'s dual formulation to suggest a category of speech, objectively "insulting" in character, that attacks the very identity of its victim in such a way as to stimulate the familiar "fight or flight reaction." Among certain classes of hearers, particularly young males socialized to be physically aggressive, the typical reaction to a vile personal insult may be "fight." For others — many men; perhaps most children, most older people, most women; invalids—the typical reaction to this kind of verbal assault is some combination of extreme fear, numbness, and impotent rage: reactions calculated to produce the sort of "severe emotional distress" to which the Restatement of Torts makes reference. We should read *Chaplinsky,* in my view, to have identified two distinct kinds of reactions (fight or flight) to the same category of intolerable speech when it speaks, respectively, of utterances that "tend to incite an immediate breach of the peace" and those that "by their very utterance inflict injury."

The Stanford provision identifies discriminatory "personal vilification" as a class of utterances of which any instance is particularly likely to produce one or the other of the kinds of injury covered by the "fighting words" and "emotional distress" analysis. These are, in Richard Delgado's phrase, "words that wound"—utterances directed to members of groups specially subject to discrimination, intended to insult or stigmatize them, and making use of the small class of commonly recognized words or symbols that have no other function but to convey hatred and contempt for these groups.[37]

Professor Delgado offers as the test for liability under his proposal the requirement that the words directed to the victim be such as "a reasonable person would recognize as a racial insult." In a campus context, where claims of insult and ideological debate are often intertwined, this phrasing raises special, and I think avoidable, civil-liberties problems. Some ideas might be taken as racial or ethnic insults by virtue of their content alone: for example, claims that the Holocaust never happened, or that blacks are genetically inferior to whites. To avoid banning ideas as such on the basis of propositional content, on campus or elsewhere, the Stanford regulation prohibits only verbal abuse including actual racial epithets, or their equivalents for other forms of discrimination.[38] These are the all-too-familiar words that carry with them so inseparable a message of hatred and contempt that apologies are in order for the affront involved in even quoting them: "nigger," "kike," "faggot," "cunt," and the like.[39]

Racial and other discriminatory hatred and contempt can be effectively expressed without using these words, of course, but (partly in the interests of avoiding vagueness and its chilling effect) such cases are not included under the regulation. A white student can tell a black student, face-to-face, "you people are inferior and should not be here," but not be guilty of harassment. In addition, even gutter epithets are immunized when uttered to the campus or public at large, in order to give the widest possible leeway for speech in the public forum; the Klan or the neo-Nazis may demonstrate and display their symbols and shout their words of hatred with impunity. This very much narrows the reach of the proposal and exposes it to the charge, mentioned before, that it is mere tokenism. But at the same time, it helps meet traditional and legitimate civil-liberties concerns about public political expression, and about vagueness and its accompanying chilling effect.[40]

The Stanford provision has also been drafted with an eye on another concern—one rooted in the civil-rights perspective, and often noted as well in civil-libertarian objections to "hate speech" or "group defamation" regulations.[41] The concern is illustrated by one of the cases that occurred under the Michigan regulation. A black woman law student, in the course of a heated argument, called a classmate "white trash." She was charged with a violation of the harassment rule; she ultimately agreed to write a formal letter of apology to the classmate in settlement of the charge.

Under the Stanford provision, calling a white student "white trash" would not constitute harassment. In its commonly understood meaning, the term is (like "redneck") derogatory to the poor whites of the rural South by virtue of their class, not their race.[42] If the student addressed came from that social background, and if class bias were a form of discrimination covered by the proposal (as it is not), there might be a disciplinary case. But as a white person, she is not a victim of discriminatory *racial* harassment; the term "white trash" is clearly not "commonly understood" to convey hatred or contempt for whites on the basis of their race as such—a requirement for

liability under the provision. This is not to deny that the black woman student intended to express race-based hatred or contempt, or that she may have effectively conveyed a racial insult, just as a white student does who tells a black student that "you people are inferior and shouldn't be here." In neither case, though, is the regulation violated, because in neither case is there use of one of the required "commonly understood" assaultive epithets or symbols of discriminatory contempt.

The point of the "white trash" case can be generalized, and in a way that is most troubling to civil-libertarian defenders of viewpoint neutrality. As best I can see, there are *no* epithets in this society at this time that are "commonly understood" to convey hatred and contempt for whites *as such*. The same can be said, I believe, of males as such, and heterosexuals as such.[43] If this is indeed a socio-linguistic fact, it is of course one not fixed in stone; on the other hand, it is no accident. The denigrating epithets covered by the Stanford provision are able to inflict the serious and distinctive injuries characteristic of legally prohibited invidious discrimination because they strike at groups subjected to longstanding and deep-rooted prejudices widely held and disseminated throughout our culture. American children grow up with the negative stereotypes of blacks, women, and homosexuals in their bones and in their souls. This is tragically true, too, of children who are black, female, or later identify themselves as homosexual.

The denigrating epithets draw their capacity to impose the characteristic civil-rights injury to "hearts and minds" from the fact that they turn the whole socially and historically inculcated weight of these prejudices upon their victim. Each hatemonger who invokes one of these terms summons a vicious chorus in his support. It is because, given our cultural history, no such *general* prejudices strike against the dominant groups that there exist no comparable terms of universally understood hatred and contempt applicable to whites, males, and heterosexuals as such.[44]

III

The Stanford provision, then, while neutral on its face, will foreseeably be asymmetric in its application. This aspect of the provision allows its interpretation to reflect a state of affairs central to civil-rights analysis— the continued existence of asymmetric social relations of group domination and subjugation in the United

States. Contrary to the democratic ideal, American society (like other societies) is still characterized by a hierarchy of relatively stable ascriptive status groups. To rephrase the point from the jargon of sociology to the rhetoric of movement politics, there still exist "oppressor" and "oppressed" (or, to lower the political pitch, "privileged" and "subordinated") groups, identified as such by characteristics such as race, gender, class, and sexual preference. Indeed, the civil-rights project can best be understood as at once premised on the existence of these groups' asymmetric power relations and aimed at the ultimate elimination of the asymmetries. (To describe it thus is not to decide in advance the debatable question of affirmative action—the question of whether symmetric or asymmetric policies are best suited to attain the goal.)

Given its narrow coverage, the Stanford provision obviously does not embody a particularly radical or utopian civil-rights approach. Its categories and its thrust largely reflect a civil-liberties perspective on the racial harassment problem. The exclusive remedy it contemplates for all but a tiny fraction of discriminatory speech is the one civil libertarians favor: more speech. But the features it adopts from a civil-rights approach still jar most civil libertarians; indeed, they jar me when I look at the problem through a civil-liberties lens. First, the provision lacks content-neutrality; it regulates only speech bearing on matters of race, gender, sexual orientation, and the like while neglecting other speech that might similarly provoke violence or cause similarly severe emotional distress. Second, and even more troubling, the rule bears asymmetrically on its restricted subject matter in a way that, to some, will seem inconsistent with viewpoint-neutrality.

That is, it may seem biased against the disfavored ideologies of racism, sexism, and homophobia, openly favoring "politically correct" egalitarians against their adversaries in the campus marketplace of opinion. It arguably takes from the bigots emotively powerful rhetorical weapons—the traditional hate epithets—without imposing comparable restrictions on the other side. It is as if terms like "commie" and "pinko" were barred from political debate, while "imperialist lackey" and "capitalist running dog" were allowed. This seems to violate official neutrality: the principle of "no orthodoxy in matters of opinion," "no such thing as a false idea."

This civil-libertarian objection helps bring out the deep structure of the conflict between the two approaches. From the civil rights perspective, there *are* false ideas and ideologies, among which white

supremacy and related forms of bigotry are the paradigm examples. The insult and stigma involved in the imposition of supremacist ideologies on those whom they oppress and exclude from full citizenship attacks what John Rawls has called the most fundamental of those "primary goods" that government is established to allow individuals to pursue—those that form the basis of self-respect.[45] The protection of the basis of the individual's capacity for self-respect against violation by socially authoritative humiliation is as much at the heart of equal protection as is official viewpoint-neutrality in regulating the marketplace of ideas that is at the heart of free expression.

The analysis of the civil-rights approach in terms of preventing exclusion by the social imposition of caste-based stigma supplies the standard rationale for the central doctrine of modern anti-discrimination law: the rejection of the "separate but equal" version of Jim Crow.[46] The doctrinal problem was this: A state supplies equal (but separate) facilities to whites and blacks—schools, public parks, beaches, buses, amenities in public buildings, etc. How does this equality-preserving separation of the races violate the Constitution's prohibition of racially *unequal* treatment? The *Brown* line of cases answers that the inequality inheres in the subordinating character of the *message* delivered by the separation—the material state action, separate but equal segregation, viewed in isolation from its communicative impact, fully preserves equality. *Plessy* had said that if black people felt insulted by the separation, that was only their interpretation; *Brown* finally (and realistically) accepted that the insulting interpretation was the only plausible one.[47]

But the *Plessy* formula is a quite appropriate response to a complaint of discriminatory segregation in some social contents. Separation sometimes stigmatizes no one. The maintenance of separate men's and women's restrooms in public buildings, for example, does not by itself constitute invidious sex discrimination. But in the context of this society and its history, the Jim Crow variety of racial segregation imposed inequality because it rested on the assumption, and hence delivered the message, that whites were a superior caste to be protected from the polluting contact of their black inferiors. The insulting message, the wound inflicted by the authoritative endorsement of the "false idea" of white supremacy and black unworthiness, was what made Jim Crow unconstitutional.[48]

Essentially the same wound is the injury inflicted on minority, female, and gay students or employees when endemic verbal abuse renders educational or work environment discriminatorily "hostile" within the terms of discrimination law. In this sense, the focus on symbolic injury to the "hearts and minds" of black children in the desegregation cases supplies the basic authority for campus verbal harassment regulation; *Brown,* as Charles Lawrence strikingly argues, "may be read as regulating the content of racist speech."[49]

The civil-libertarian, dedicated to a principle of liberal official neutrality in the marketplace of ideas, sees this as a perverse misstatement of *Brown.* It ignores two crucial distinctions, the argument runs: speech vs. action, and public vs. private.[50] First, the civil-libertarian insists that the *practice* of white (or male, or heterosexual) supremacy must be kept distinct from its *preaching;* while the former violates the anti-discrimination principle, the latter is protected by the principle of free expression. Questions of the boundary between speech and action may present difficulty, but the structure is clear.

The point is quite general: the Constitution certainly requires the *practice* of republican government, due process, and non-establishment of religion, as well as non-discrimination. But equally central is the principle of free expression, which includes the freedom to *preach* dictatorship, summary justice, theocracy—or even universal censorship. And so, the argument continues, the same principle guarantees freedom to advocate racist and other inegalitarian doctrines—as, indeed, many First Amendment decisions firmly establish.[51]

Second, the argument continues, the invocation of *Brown* to support the suppression of racist speech ignores the public-private distinction, which is essential to the maintenance not only of free speech but also of such other civil liberties as freedom of religion. If *Brown* does perhaps strike at certain "speech" (more precisely, at the communicative element in certain actions), it is only at *official* speech, which has never been thought protected by a principle of free expression. What the First Amendment protects is the right of *private* individuals to deliver those same messages.

While the equal protection clause might, for example, prohibit a legislature from placing a white supremacist slogan on a state's seal, flag, public buildings, and the like, the First Amendment just as firmly protects the freedom of private individuals to put that slogan into free competition against more egalitarian ones in the marketplace of ideas. Not only the flag, but also a copy of the *Brown* decision, or a picture of Martin Luther King, can be defaced in public with

impunity under the First Amendment—though of course, as the civil-libertarian usually adds, government officials should denounce such racist outrages, just as university authorities should denounce racist speech on campus while resolutely protecting it against coercive interference.

When we turn to look at the world through the civil-rights lens, though, we find much less clarity in the public-private distinction.[52] The civil-rights approach seeks to cleanse not only the state but civil society generally of racist and other bigoted practices. The formal constitutional expression of the public-private distinction, the state action doctrine, tends to break down in the area of discrimination law. Nothing approaching a clear line separates (prohibited) official encouragement or support of private discrimination on the one hand from (permissible) neutral toleration on the other. Judge Posner's words quoted earlier from the hostile environment discrimination case help make the point: states often deny the equal protection of the laws not by acting, but by omitting to act against private discriminatory action within such areas of responsibility as a government workplace. The point becomes more forceful as, with the growth of the modern welfare and regulatory state, government's sphere of activity broadens, and increased supervision of areas of private conduct brings with it more responsibility for that conduct.[53]

Further, when we look beyond formal constitutional doctrine, we find that our actual civil-rights practices place little weight on the public-private distinction. The social condemnation of a form of discrimination as invidious brings it within the anti-discrimination principle. This principle typically leads both to judicial prohibition of the official forms of prejudice and legislative prohibition where it appears "privately" in employment, housing, education, and public accommodations. By contrast, our civil-liberties practices exhibit no parallel tendency toward legislative protection of Nazis, Klansmen, and flag-burners against private discrimination. "Tolerance," a civil-rights word, and "toleration," a civil-liberties word, name quite different values.

And as I have already stressed, the civil-rights approach likewise does not sharply distinguish between speech and action. "Sticks and stones may break my bones, but words will never hurt me"—which expresses in homely form the First Amendment's Brandeisian ideal of self-reliant civic courage[54]—does not apply within a framework of analysis in which the central injury to be avoided is stigma and humiliation—injury to a socially constructed (and hence socially destructible) personality. Words and symbols are among the chief weapons for inflicting this form of injury. The point becomes clear when one reads the facts of some of the hostile environment discrimination cases; anyone will agree with Judge Posner that the victims in these cases have suffered discrimination in "terms and conditions of employment" as surely as if they had been made to do extra work for the same pay on account of their race or sex.[55]

These same hostile environment discrimination cases likewise provide some of the best examples of civil rights analysis that blur the "speech-action" as well as the "public-private" distinction. When a private employer is held liable under Title VII for not taking reasonable steps to prevent racist or sexist verbal assaults by employees on their fellow workers, the government is in effect imposing (as sovereign, not employer) a content- and viewpoint-specific regime of censorship on the speech of private employees. The American Civil Liberties Union has seen the point; it opposes liability for employers or schools who fail to prevent verbal sexual harassment that "has no other effect on its recipient than to create an unpleasant working [learning] environment."[56] But I have found that many good civil-libertarians see these hostile environment cases (at least in the employment context) through the civil-rights lens; they thus agree with current law in accepting that an employer should be obligated to police the workplace to some extent against even purely verbal abuse when it becomes so pervasive and differentially "unpleasant" on grounds of race or sex to affect employees' terms and conditions of employment.

IV

I have tried to suggest how the civil-liberties and civil-rights approaches overlap and clash on the issue of discriminatory harassment; apparently, no higher principle of comparable force and vitality can resolve their conflict.[57] Do these two approaches simply represent, respectively, right- and left-wing political tendencies within American liberalism? It is possible to tell the story that way: civil-liberties (and its marketplace of ideas) then represents a dying classical liberalism, while civil-rights (and its society of equal groups) represents a post-liberal social democracy struggling to be born. Or (to flip the political poles of the historical plot-line) civil liberties now represents the true liberal future at this moment of the end of history, while the asymmetric civil-rights project will be rejected along with other misguided attempts to inject communitarian ideals into the legal governance of free societies.

Both of these sketches operate on the "contradiction" hypothesis; they postulate, on the basis of the structural conflict between the civil-rights and civil-liberties approaches, that one should give way in the name of principled consistency. Following this analysis, one could press (from the right) toward a more formal and neutral "civil-liberties" style of anti-discrimination law or (from the left) toward a more substantive and result-oriented "civil-rights" version of free speech law.

The former move would incline toward an ideal of formal neutrality in civil-rights law, one that stressed not the abolition of caste or status-subordination by the elimination from law of "suspect classifications"—distinctions based upon individuals' immutable characteristics. The latter move would give a larger role in First Amendment law to correction of market imperfections in the marketplace of ideas, pursuing policies such as realistically equal access to media, opening debate to the participation of those previously silenced by social subordination, and so on. As this essay perhaps suggests, I am more inclined to go in the latter direction than in the former, but I am not inclined to go very far[58]—nothing like far enough to bring civil-liberties law into full consistency with the public-private and speech-action treatments characteristic of current civil-rights law.

What, then, is the alternative to seeing this incommensurable conflict as contradiction? My answer is already implicit in the body of the essay; it can be roughly captured by the slogan that the civil-rights approach embodies a *project,* which is to be carried on within a *framework* constituted by the civil-liberties approach. Civil rights has statable social goals, however utopian: the abolition of racism, sexism, and other forms of bigotry. It postulates disease-like social conditions and collective enemies; it then sets us the task of struggling against these and, ideally, eliminating them. The civil-rights mentality represents our collective self-commitment to a definite, though limited and negative, judgment about the nature of the good society, or at least the good society for us—it is one without castes (whether of race, or sex, or sexual orientation, or . . .). Civil-rights law is then conceived mainly as an *instrument* toward that end.

Note that this instrumental account of civil-rights doctrine characterizes even those who are unhappy with affirmative action and who tend to support a symmetric version of anti-discrimination law. First, in my experience, few adherents of this view support a wholehearted symmetry in practice. Second, the reason for this shows up in their arguments; they oppose affirmative action as counter-productive, as a poor strategy in the effort to attain what all concede to be the long-run goal: a caste-free society. To use race as a principle for distributing burdens and benefits, they argue, is to legitimize it as a ground for social action; this reinforces the tendency to revert to less benign uses in moments of social panic or pressure. These neutralists on civil rights are thus, at bottom, instrumentalists too; they share the same conception of the overriding goal, only disagreeing on the best means by which to pursue it.[59]

The civil-liberties approach, whether in its right- or left-wing versions, postulates no goal for society in the same sense. What would society look like if the "aims" of the First Amendment were achieved? It would be a society where people could in general say what they have to say, but this merely restates First Amendment doctrine in summary form without articulating a social goal at which it aims. Attempts to state positive goals for the First Amendment typically produce vague and eclectic wish-lists that are of little help in shaping free speech doctrine. A similar point could be made, I believe, of the free exercise clause and some aspects of the right of privacy. We cannot say anything very definite about how society would look if these civil-libertarian rights were fully realized.

We might fairly say that these provisions aim at an open society, but that is to say only that they aim at a society that might look like anything at all. Their very goallessness is in a sense the point of these provisions. They capture our skeptical sense that we do not, in general, know where we are going; we have no dominant *overall* collective project, and we want to keep it that way. The First Amendment, along with the other "civil liberties,"[60] is there to maintain possibilities, to keep the future open to the presently unpredictable workings of the human imagination. Its effective enforcement requires a strong dose of skepticism—not (a self-contradictory) "absolute relativism," but a skeptical *attitude* toward collectively-imposed substantive moral judgments. (This skepticism is not inconsistent with a fair degree of romanticism about the possible achievements of the unchecked human imagination.[61]) By contrast, the civil-rights approach,

on its more limited subject (the intolerability of a system of group subordination or caste), is not skeptical at all—no more skeptical than were the abolitionists. (Of course, a degree of skepticism about the possibility of authoritatively ranking human beings, hence of identifying "natural aristocrats," also lends support to this limited egalitarian absolutism.)

In this contrast between the dominant skepticism of the civil libertarian and the dominant confidence of the civil-rights advocate lies the best answer to the objection that a narrow prohibition of discriminatory harassment violates "viewpoint-neutrality" by discriminating in favor of the Left against the Right on issues relevant to civil-rights concerns. The answer is that if the prohibition has been framed narrowly enough, it does preserve practical neutrality—that is, it does *not* differentially deprive any significant element in American political life of its rhetorical capital. I would argue that this is the case with the Stanford provision. The Right has no special stake in the free face-to-face use of epithets that perform no other function except to portray whole classes of Americans as subhuman and unworthy of full citizenship.

V

In conclusion, I must return to answer an objection to the Stanford provision that I have heard from critics of both the civil-rights and civil-liberties persuasions. This has to do with the charge that the regulation is drafted so narrowly as to make it "merely symbolic," a point that evidently engages one of the key differences between the two approaches. I readily agree that the provision prohibits very little of the behavior that creates the significantly discriminatory hostile environment that faces students of color and others on many campuses. So why bother with it? The point is made with special force by civil libertarians, who think the proposal exacts a high cost in principle through its incursions into the indivisible fabric of the First Amendment. But egalitarians, on their side, can also object on principle to the provision as a form of tokenism.

I also concede that the main good the provision can do is through its educative or symbolic effect—though I would add that the harms its opponents see in it are likewise largely symbolic as well. The question then arises: why can we not get the same educative effect through official statements, declarations of concern, and the like, issued with appropriate vehemence by university authorities whenever serious incidents of racist verbal abuse occur? Let me suggest a partial answer by modifying a hypothetical situation I posed earlier.

Suppose a state legislature declared a "white supremacy day," perhaps invoking the descriptive and predictive terms of Justice Harlan's dissent in *Plessy* v. *Ferguson* as an ideal. ("The white race deems itself to be the dominant race in this country. And so it is. . . . So, I doubt not, it will continue for all time, if it remains true to its great heritage. . . ."[62]) That would be a terrible thing, but would it be unconstitutional? I think it would be—but I also admit there is at least some doubt as to the answer. On the other hand, there is no doubt at all that state imposition of racial segregation in public facilities, even if they maintain perfect material equality, are unconstitutional. Yet by hypothesis the injury, the stigma of official racial insult, is the same in both cases—or, if anything, more explicit and obvious in the case of "white supremacy day." Why is segregation more obviously unconstitutional?

One answer: because the government delivers the insult with more force (and hence compounds the injury) when the action expressing the insult *does* something, even if the thing done is (apart from the insult) not itself discriminatory. We think of government as primarily an instrument for the maintenance of law and order and the provision of material public goods.[63] Its ideological centrality in our lives derives mainly from its role as the primary repository of legitimated power in society. It provides such a "bully pulpit" largely *because* it already has so firm a grip on our attention through its coercive powers of taxation and law enforcement.

For this reason, government speaks most clearly when its message is delivered through the exercise of one of those powers, such as the provision of schools, parks, and the like. We think of joint resolutions designating state flowers and mayoral proclamations of schoolteacher week as quite apart from the serious business of government. The adoption of a racist resolution or motto, then, though unconstitutional, would not be as obviously so as would, say, resegregating the seats in the courthouse. When the government acts—when it does something—it puts its money where its mouth is.

Similarly, when a university administration backs its anti-racist pronouncements with action, it puts *its* money where its mouth is. The action, if it is to serve this purpose, must be independently justifiable—independently, that is, of the symbolic purpose. Author-

ities make the most effective statement when they are honestly concerned to do something *beyond* making a statement. And the action of punishing persons who violate the Stanford harassment regulation *is* justifiable independent of the statement it makes. It provides a remedy for an action that causes real pain and harm to real individuals while doing no good, and it may serve to deter such actions in the future.

Notice that the idea of the "main business of government" advanced here is derived from the classical liberal conception of the state, which in turn lies at the heart of the civil-liberties approach. In that conception, government exists to prevent private force and fraud and to supply tangible public goods by taxing and spending. And that is basically *all* it is there for; its other functions are either suspect or "merely symbolic." Yet throughout this essay I have contrasted that conception of government to one implicit in the civil-rights approach, which undermines traditional public-private distinctions as well as denying the automatic association of "merely" with "symbolic" or "intangible" when discussing of the kind of effects law and government should be centrally concerned with.

And yet, at the end, I revert to slogans involving a distinction between real state action and mere gesture! The point is that neither the civil-liberties nor the civil-rights approach will go away; sometimes, as here, one of them even feeds on the other. With that suggestion of the sometimes paradoxical interweaving of these perspectives, incommensurably co-existing at the heart of modern liberalism, let me call a halt to this very limited examination of their mutual relations.

Appendix: The Stanford Discriminatory Harassment Provision

Preamble

The Fundamental Standard requires that students act with "such respect for . . . the rights of others as is demanded of good citizens." Some incidents in recent years on campus have revealed doubt and disagreement about what this requirement means for students in the sensitive area where the right of free expression can conflict with the right to be free of invidious discrimination. The Student Conduct Legislative Council offers this interpretation to provide students and administrators with some guidance in this area.

Fundamental Standard Interpretation: Free Expression and Discriminatory Harassment

1. Stanford is committed to the principles of free inquiry and free expression. Students have the right to hold and vigorously defend and promote their opinions, thus entering them into the life of the University, there to flourish or wither according to their merits. Respect for this right requires that students tolerate even expression of opinions which they find abhorrent. Intimidation of students by other students in their exercise of this right, by violence or threat of violence, is therefore considered to be a violation of the Fundamental Standard.

2. Stanford is also committed to principles of equal opportunity and non-discrimination. Each student has the right of equal access to a Stanford education, without discrimination on the basis of sex, race, color, handicap, religion, sexual orientation, or national and ethnic origin. Harassment of students on the basis of any of these characteristics contributes to a hostile environment that makes access to education for those subjected to it less than equal. Such discriminatory harassment is therefore considered to be a violation of the Fundamental Standard.

3. This interpretation of the Fundamental Standard is intended to clarify the point at which protected free expression ends and prohibited discriminatory harassment begins. Prohibited harassment includes discriminatory intimidation by threats of violence, and also includes personal vilification of students on the basis of their sex, race, color, handicap, religion, sexual orientation, or national and ethnic origin.

4. Speech or other expression constitutes harassment by personal vilification if it:

a) is intended to insult or stigmatize an individual or a small number of individuals on the basis of their sex, race, color, handicap, religion, sexual orientation, or national and ethnic origin; and

b) is addressed directly to the individual or individuals whom it insults or stigmatizes; and

c) makes use of insulting or "fighting" words or non-verbal symbols.

In the context of discriminatory harassment, insulting or "fighting" words or non-verbal symbols are those "which by their very utterance inflict injury or tend to incite to an immediate breach of the peace," and which are commonly understood to convey direct and visceral hatred or contempt for human beings on the basis of their sex, race, color, handicap, religion, sexual orientation, or national and ethnic origin.

---

1. *Ludwig Wittgenstein,* Philosophical Investigations *196e (New York: Macmillan, 1958).*

2. United States *v.* Eichman, *110 S. Ct. 2404, 2410 (1990).*

3. Brown *v.* Board of Education, *347 U.S. 483, 494 (1954).*

4. Bohen *v.* City of East Chicago, *799 F.2d 1180, 1189–90 (7th Cir., 1986) (concurring opinion).*

5. *Ibid.*

6. Strauder *v.* West Virginia, *100 U.S. (10 Otto) 303, 308 (1880).*

7. *See Paul Brest, "Foreword: In Defense of the Antidiscrimination Principle,"* Harvard Law Review, *vol. 90 (1976), p. 1.*

8. *I will often make the oversimplifying assumption that all these forms of discrimination can and should be treated the same. Each form of insult has its own unique features and problems, however, and may ultimately generate its own distinct body of legal doctrine, as does each form of discrimination recognized as "invidious" under equal protection law and civil rights statutes. I will, moreover, put discrimination against gays and lesbians in with the rest, though it has not yet been recognized as invidious under federal constitutional law. A number of state and local civil rights laws, and the anti-discrimination policies of many public and private institutions (including Stanford) do prohibit sexual-preference discrimination, as in my view all should.*

9. Time, *May 23, 1989, p. 89.*

10. *I was faculty co-chair of the campus judicial council at Stanford when this incident occurred; no disciplinary charges were ultimately brought. Thereafter I worked on the drafting of a disciplinary standard to deal with racial harassment, which was adopted by the campus legislative body and became effective in June of 1990.*

The Beethoven incident is treated eloquently, strictly from a civil-rights perspective, in Patricia Williams, "The Obliging Shell: An Informal Essay on Formal Equal Opportunity," Michigan Law Review, *vol. 87 (1989), pp. 2128, 2133–37.*

11. *The applicable legal provisions are (for most private employers) Title VII of the Civil Rights Act of 1964, which prohibits employers from discriminating against employees on the basis of race or sex in the "terms or conditions of employment," and (for public employers) the Fourteenth Amendment's requirement that no state may "deny to any person the equal protection of the laws," which has been construed to prohibit race and sex discrimination in public employment.*

12. Bohen *v.* East Chicago, *p. 1191. Judge Posner alternatively analyzed the employer's inaction as analogous to a selective withdrawal of protection, as if a government denied police protection to blacks, or failed to punish rapes alone among violent crimes.*

13. *In sex discrimination cases under Title VII, the courts distinguish between "quid pro quo" harassment (efforts to extract sexual favors in return for job retention or promotion) and "hostile environment" harassment of the kind described in the text. Racial harassment takes only the latter form. The Supreme Court recognized hostile environment sexual harassment as a Title VII violation in* Meritor Savings Bank *v.* Vinson, *477 U.S. 57 (1986). On hostile environment discrimination, see* Rogers *v.* EEOC, *454 F.2d 234, 238 (5th Cir. 1971) ("sustained pattern of harassment");* Bundy *v.* Jackson, *641 F.2d 934 (D. C. Cir. 1981), and* Henson *v.* City of Dundee, *682 F.2d 897 (11th Cir. 1982) (sexual harassment cases involving mixed* quid pro quo *and pure verbal harassment*

incidents); Erebia v. Chrysler Plastics, *722 F.2d 1250 (6th Cir. 1985)*; EEOC v. Murphy Motor Freight Lines, *488 F. Supp. 381 (D. Minn. 1980)* (employer failure to take action against racist insults of black employee by fellow workers held unlawful discrimination).

14. As with public employers, the Fourteenth Amendment prohibits public universities from discriminating on the basis of race or sex in providing educational services. Private universities receiving federal grants are subject to similar prohibitions under Title IX of the Civil Rights Act of 1964. In some states, statutes also prohibit discriminatory practices by private universities. Finally, most private universities in the United States have committed themselves to non-discrimination policies, which may give rise to contractual liability when a student can show discrimination that would be unlawful for a public university.

15. Indeed it was evidently drafted on the model of the Equal Employment Opportunity Commission guidelines, which define sexual harassment to include "verbal or physical conduct of a sexual nature" that "has the purpose or effect of unreasonably interfering with an individual's work performance or creating an intimidating, hostile, or offensive working environment." *29 CFR § 1604.11(a)*.

16. Doe v. University of Michigan, *721 F. Supp. 852 (E. D. Mich. 1989).* See 856 for the text of the regulations.

17. Doe v. Michigan, p. 858. The Guide went on to warn students that "YOU are a harasser when . . . you comment in a derogatory way about a . . . group's . . . cultural origins, or religious beliefs"— a very sweeping restriction on the discussion of history and current events. Might not screening The Last Temptation of Christ or selling The Satanic Verses count as "derogatory comment" on a "group's religious beliefs"?

18. Under the University of Michigan regulation, a social work student was in fact prosecuted for expressing the view that homosexuality was a disease, for which he hoped to develop a counseling plan in a research class; Doe v. Michigan, p. 865. The other two statements propound views that I trust my readers will admit are widely held, or at least entertained, if relatively rarely expressed, on American campuses.

19. For example, a student who had recited a homophobic limerick in class plea-bargained the dropping of a charge against him under the Michigan regulations in return for a classroom apology, a letter of apology to the campus paper, and attendance at a "gay rap session;" Doe v. University of Michigan, p. 865. It has become a commonplace among civil-libertarian opponents of verbal harassment regulation to stress the utility of "education" (rather than disciplinary rules) as a remedy for campus discrimination, generally without much serious attention to the question of what such "education" may entail. In my own view, the worst of both worlds is achieved when multicultural sensitivity training (valuable as it can be when done well) is imposed as a penal sanction for harassment. I would sharply separate punishment of harassment (which should be confined to cases of intentional wrongdoing) from orientation efforts aimed at acquainting students and others with the diverse cultural backgrounds, expectations, and sensitivities they are likely to meet in the contemporary university.

20. The plaintiff in the Michigan case was a psychology graduate student working on the biological basis of differences in personality traits and mental abilities. He alleged, quite plausibly, that certain theories in his field could be perceived as sexist or racist, so that their discussion might be sanctionable under the policy. Doe v. Michigan, p. 858.

21. An excellent and often-cited doctrinal analysis, distinguishing the key terms of art's "communicative impact," "content," and "viewpoint," is Geoffrey Stone, "Content Regulation and the First Amendment," William and Mary Law Review, *vol. 25 (1983)*, p. 189.

22. Hustler Magazine v. Falwell, *108 S. Ct. 876, 879 (1988)*; compare Gertz v. Robert Welch, *418 U.S. 323, 339 (1974)*.

23. West Virginia State Board of Education v. Barnette, *319 U.S. 624, 643 (1943)*. Compare Texas v. Johnson, *109 S. Ct. 2533, 2544*: "If there is a bedrock principle underlying the First Amendment, it is that the government may not prohibit the expression of an idea because society finds the idea itself offensive or disagreeable."

24. Whitney v. California, *274 U. S. 357, 377 (1927)*.

25. The moderate view is especially well articulated, by a present General Counsel of the ACLU, in Nadine Strossen, "Regulating Campus Speech: A Modest Proposal," Duke Law Journal, p. 483. Strossen, like other moderates, is more skeptical of the "fighting words" than of the "emotional distress" rationale. The purist view is inferrable from Franklyn Haiman, Speech and Law in a Free Society (Chicago: University of Chicago, 1981). Haiman altogether rejects the "insulting or fighting words" doctrine, (pp. 132–35, 256–59); he would confine sanctions for verbal infliction of emotional distress to cases of injury through intentional factual misrepresentation (pp. 148–56).

26. It has been my personal experience in debating this issue with colleagues and students that few causes attract more powerful emotional adherence than does First Amendment absolutism. I make the point not to disparage this aspect of their commitment, but because civil libertarians frequently pose the verbal harassment issue (typically with analogy to the flag-burning issue) as a clash between "reason" on their side and "emotion" on the other. On the other side, not a few civil-rights egalitarians take up the same binary opposition between "reason" and "passion" and turn it around to accuse free speech defenders of the moral defect of cerebral and unfeeling elitism.

27. Incommensurable conflicts are, roughly, those we have to resolve in the absence of a satisfactory determining norm (substantive rule, agreed procedure, or common metric). They are not contradictions and need not be resolved "irrationally." A good discussion of value-incommensurability in the context of individual action can be found in Joseph Raz, The Morality of Freedom, *321–66 (Oxford: Clarendon Press, 1986)*.

28. Wittgenstein, Philosophical Investigations, p. 194.

29. The text of the Stanford regulation is given in the Appendix.

30. One example of an alternative mediating solution was the situation at Stanford before adoption of the harassment provision. The University's president and general counsel had said publicly that face-to-face use of racial epithets could be considered to violate the long-standing "Fundamental Standard" which required of students conduct manifesting such "respect for the rights of others as is expected of good citizens." Though that solution gave too little guidance to satisfy civil-liberties concerns in my view, it was in the same ballpark as the one later adopted. Other examples of mediating solutions include the regulation adopted at the University of California and the one proposed at the University of Texas. See note 32 below.

31. *315 U.S. 568, 572 (1942)*.

32. The University of California has adopted a prohibition on student harassment by "fighting words," defined as "those personally abusive epithets which, when directly addressed to any ordinary person are, in the context used and as a matter of common knowledge, inherently likely to provoke a violent reaction whether or not they actually do so." These "include, but are not limited to" terms abusive in terms of race, sex, or the other categories of discrimination law. Harassment occurs when fighting words are used to "create a hostile and intimidating environment" which the utterer should know will interfere with the victim's education.

A committee at the University of Texas has proposed a regulation of "racial harassment" tracking the Restatement of Torts definition of intentional infliction of emotional distress, with the addition of the element of intent to "harass, intimidate, or humiliate . . . on account of race, color or national origin." Establishing a violation requires an actual showing of "severe emotional distress" on the part of the victim.

33. See Cohen v. California, *403 U.S. 15 (1971)*; Gooding v. Wilson, *405 U.S. 518 (1972)*.

34. Compare Gregory v. Chicago, *394 U.S. 111 (1969)* with Feiner v. New York, *340 U.S. 315 (1951)*.

35. Restatement of Torts, *2d, sec. 46, comment (d)*.

36. "'Outrageousness' in the area of political and social discourse has an inherent subjectiveness about it which would allow a jury to impose liability on the basis of the jurors' tastes or views, or perhaps on the basis of their dislike of a particular expression." Hustler

Magazine *v.* Falwell, *108 S. Ct. 876, 882. The Court's decision, however, does not foreclose granting tort damages under the "outrageousness" test for infliction of emotional distress through speech alone in a private or face-to-face context, rather than in a published and nationally distributed lampoon of an important public figure, such as was involved in* Falwell.

37. *Richard Delgado, "Words that Wound: A Tort Action for Racial Insults, Epithets, and Name-calling,"* Harvard Civil Rights–Civil Liberties Law Review, *vol. 17 (1982), pp. 133–81. Professor Delgado has assembled on pp. 136–49 an impressive body of evidence and argument that supports the identification of racial verbal abuse as inflicting a distinctive and identifiable form of injury, and so qualifying as a distinctive wrong. His proposal is limited to racial insults.*

38. *Because I believe to this extent in the "no false ideas" strand of American First Amendment law, I reject group defamation and hate-speech prohibitions of the kind called for by the International Convention on the Elimination of All Forms of Racial Discrimination: "States Parties . . . shall declare as an offence publishable by law all dissemination of ideas based on racial superiority or hatred. . . ." Mari Matsuda ably argues the contrary view, urging modification of First Amendment law to permit the extension of a limited version of the international standard to this country in "Public Response to Racist Speech: Considering the Victim's Story,"* Michigan Law Review, *vol. 87 (1989), p. 2320. As Professor Matsuda's article documents, many Western countries have such laws. The Canadian hate-speech statute is currently under review by the Supreme Court of Canada for its consistency with the free expression guarantee of the recently adopted Canadian Charter of Rights and Freedoms.*

39. *It would be possible, in the interests of maximum clarity, to attempt a comprehensive list of the "discriminatory fighting words" and equivalent visual symbols (swastikas, burning crosses, etc.). I think this would be a mistake; new examples of such words and symbols are constantly being invented by the creativity of the collective bigoted mind. Even without a definitive list, however, the Stanford regulation gives clearer notice of what will count as an offense than any other similar proposal I know. I should add that as I understand the provision, derogatory epithets aimed at (white) national origin groups ("dago," "Polack," etc.) would come within its terms to the extent they were determined to be still "commonly understood" to "convey direct and visceral hatred or contempt" on the basis of national origin.*

40. *The narrow confinement of the harassment regulation to the use of the gutter epithets also emphasizes that it is meant as an anti-discrimination provision, not a "civility rule." As a teacher, I would not let students address each other in class using personally derogatory terms of any kind, and would exclude students who persisted in doing so. That is a civility rule, similar to those applied in most American parliamentary bodies. Such rules are, in my opinion, appropriate for campus-wide enforcement. The campus should be thought of as primarily a general public forum, and secondarily as a workplace (the work of education). I would add that values of residential privacy may justify more stringent regulation of offensive speech in student dormitories than in classrooms or in public campus areas, but this is a complex issue which I cannot treat adequately here.*

41. *This is the concern raised by Justice Black in his dissent from the Supreme Court's decision sustaining conviction of a white racist pamphleteer under a group libel statute: "If there be any minority groups who hail this holding as their victory, they might consider the possible relevance of this ancient remark: 'Another such victory and I am undone.' "* Beauharnais *v.* Illinois, *343 U.S. 250, 275 (1952).*

42. *Indeed in its usual sense, the term is implicitly racist toward people of color—with its implication of surprise that a* white *person would be "trash."*

43. *I realize that others might disagree with this, citing terms such as "honky," "gringo," "breeder," etc. But I myself do not know which of these terms are current and seriously-used epithets of hatred or contempt—evidence that they are not "commonly under-*

stood" as such. On the other side, no sentient black, Latino, or gay American has any doubt about the current standard insulting epithets for their groups.

44. *A similar analysis applies to the unjustified use of the term "white racist," which many of my white students have invoked as the equivalent, applied to them, of the standard racial epithets as applied to the students of color. Leaving to one side whether unjustified use of a term like this inflicts the same level of injury, it does not in any event come within the class of injuries that concern civil-rights law and policy. The term "white racist" does not denigrate whites as such, any more than "black separatist racist" denigrates blacks as such. In addition, strong civil-liberties considerations distinguish the cases. Terms of political abuse like "white racist" (or "Stalinist," "Nazi," "terrorist") are sometimes accurately and appropriately applied to individuals in robust debate; exactly when they properly apply, however, is politically controversial. In contrast, the Stanford provision rests on the premise that the racial (and other) discriminatory gutter epithets it deals with are never appropriately directed at individuals; enforcement of the provision, therefore, does not involve the politically charged task of discriminating between justified and unjustified uses.*

45. *John Rawls,* A Theory of Justice *(Cambridge: Harvard, 1971), pp. 178–79, 440–46, 543–47.*

46. Brown *v.* Board of Education, *347 U.S. 483 (1954); see also* Mayor of Baltimore *v.* Dawson, *350 U.S. 877 (1955) (beaches);* Gayle *v.* Browder, *352 U.S. 903 (1956) (buses);* Holmes *v.* City of Atlanta, *350 U.S. 879 (1955) (golf courses);* Johnson *v.* Virginia, *373 U.S. 61 (1963) (courthouses).*

47. Plessy *v.* Ferguson, *163 U.S. 537, 551 (1896), rejecting the claim that "the enforced separation of the two races stamps the colored race with a badge of inferiority" on the ground that "[i]f this be so, it is not by reason of anything found in the act, but solely because the colored race chooses to put that construction upon it." Compare* Brown *v.* Board of Education, *347 U.S. 483, 494 (1954).*

48. *Edmond Cahn early on offered this rationale as the proper interpretation of* Brown:

As is observed in the ancient Babylonian Talmud, to shame and degrade a fellow-creature is to commit a kind of psychic mayhem upon him. Like an assailant's knife, humiliation slashes his self-respect and human dignity. He grows pale, the blood rushes from his face just as thought it had been shed. That is why we are accustomed to say he feels "wounded." . . .

So one speaks in terms of the most familiar and universally accepted standards of right and wrong when one remarks (1) that racial segregation under government auspices inevitably inflicts humiliation, and (2) that official humiliation of innocent, law-abiding citizens is psychologically injurious and morally evil. . . .

"Jurisprudence," New York University Law Review, *vol. 30 (1955), pp. 148–59.*

49. *Charles Lawrence III, "If He Hollers Let Him Go: Regulating Racist Speech on Campus,"* Duke Law Journal, *vol. 1990, pp. 901, 909. My treatment of* Brown *has been much influenced by this excellent article.*

50. *Nadine Strossen contests the* Brown *analogy in these terms in her article cited above.*

51. Collin *v.* Smith, *578 F.2d 1197 (7th Cir. 1978), cert. denied 436 U.S. 953 (1978);* Brandenburg *v.* Ohio, *395 U.S. 444 (1969);* Terminiello *v.* Chicago, *337 U.S. 1 (1949). The Court has reiterated the point in significant dicta in the flag-burning cases. "The First Amendment does not guarantee that other concepts virtually sacred to our Nation as a whole—such as the principle that discrimination on the basis of race is odious and destructive—will go unchallenged in the marketplace of ideas."* Texas *v.* Johnson, *109 S. Ct. 2533, 2544 (1989). "We are aware that desecration of the flag is deeply offensive to many. But the same might be said, for example, of virulent ethnic and religious epithets [citing* Terminiello*]. . . ."* United States *v.* Eichman, *110 S. Ct. 2404, 2410 (1990).*

52. *The reliance of traditional civil-liberties law on a public-private distinction much stronger than we recognize elsewhere is the*

theme of Frank Michelman, "Conceptions of Democracy in American Constitutional Argument: The Case of Pornography Regulation," Tennessee Law Review, vol. 56 (1989), p. 291.

53. Thus in Shelley v. Kraemer, 334 U.S. 1 (1948), extensive legal supervision of the kinds of enforceable covenants running with the land rendered enforcement of a racially restrictive private covenant discriminatory state action; in Terry v. Adams, 345 U.S. 461 (1953), extensive state regulation of elections rendered the exclusionary practices of the formally private Texas Jaybird Democratic Club (in effect the white Democratic Party) discriminatory state action; in Burton v. Wilmington Parking Authority, 365 U.S. 715 (1961), public ownership and operation of a parking garage constitutionally entangled the state in the racial exclusion practiced by a privately-owned restaurant leasing space in the building.

54. See the language from Justice Brandeis's opinion in Whitney v. California, quoted in text accompanying note 24 above.

55. Thus in Bohen v. East Chicago, the plaintiff, a female fire department dispatcher, had to deal with a supervisor who was constantly "speaking to her entirely of sexual matters and describing his preferred sexual positions, Bohen's participation, and his expectations for her behavior." Further, she was "a continual target for obscene comments by firefighters and other male employees and was forced to listen to their filthy talk and descriptions of their sexual fantasies of which she was the object." A fire captain told her that "a forcible rape in some nearby flora would improve her disposition." 799 F.2d, pp. 1182–83.

In EEOC v. Murphy Motor Freight Lines, 488 F. Supp. 381 (D. Minn. 1980), Ray Wells, a black dockman, was subjected regularly to racial slurs on chalkboards attached to loading carts: "Ray Wells is a nigger," "The only good nigger is a dead nigger," "Niggers are a living example that Indians screwed buffalo." When Wells started eating in another room, his white co-workers wrote "niggers only" above the door. Management did nothing in response to complaints. See pp. 384–85.

56. Policy Guide of the ACLU (rev. ed. 1989), at 142, 400. The ACLU position requires distinguishing between (protected) verbal abuse that merely renders the environment "unpleasant" and that which crosses the line to inflicting actionable emotional distress— hardly a bright line. My thanks to Nadine Strossen for providing me the text of these ACLU provisions.

57. Which is not to say that verbal formulae may not be offered to supply formal or aesthetic resolution to liberal theory and hence

present it as a closed system. John Rawls attempts such a closure with his lexical ordering of liberty over equal opportunity in A Theory of Justice; the difficulty is to defend the substance of this firm hierarchy. Joseph Raz supplies an attractive overarching account of "autonomy" as the supreme liberal value, resolving liberty-equality conflicts, in The Morality of Freedom. I myself prefer the frank pluralism of Isaiah Berlin in "Two Concepts of Liberty," Four Essays on Liberty, pp. 167–72 (London: Oxford, 1969).

58. Thus I sympathize with Owen Fiss's suggestions for moving First Amendment doctrine in a more realistically democratic direction in his "Free Speech and Social Structure," Iowa Law Review, vol. 71 (1986), p. 1405. On the other hand, I stop short of endorsing civil-rights-based bans on potentially broad content-defined categories of speech: racist speech, as endorsed by Mari Matsuda, "Public Response"; or sexist pornography, as in the trafficking provisions of the Indianapolis anti-pornography ordinance invalidated in American Booksellers Assn'n v. Hudnut, 771 F.2d 323 (7th Cir. 1985).

59. Thus in the most "neutralist" of recent Supreme Court civil-rights decisions, City of Richmond v. J. A. Croson, 109 S. Ct. 706, 721 (1989), invalidating a municipal minority business set-aside program, the Court majority stated the grounds for treating even benign racial classifications as suspect in terms instrumental to an anti-caste goal: "Classifications based on race carry a danger of stigmatic harm. . . . They may in fact promote notions of racial inferiority and lead to a politics of racial hostility."

60. The First Amendment is also tied (as the free exercise and privacy rights are not) to the preservation of a functioning democratic system of government; however, there could conceivably be a working free speech guarantee, justified along the lines I suggest, even in a liberal but undemocratic state.

61. This romantic side of the civil-liberties mentality is very attractively presented in Steven Shiffrin, The First Amendment, Democracy, and Romance (Cambridge: Harvard University Press, 1990).

62. 163 U.S. 537, 559 (1896). Actual current controversies that raise this issue (though less starkly) include the continued official use by southern states of the Confederate flag.

63. This isn't true of government in all societies; see Clifford Geertz, Negara: The Theater State in Nineteenth Century Bali (Princeton: Princeton University Press, 1980).

Principles of Constitutional Interpretation

THE RIGHT OF PRIVACY:
The Construction of a Constitutional Time Bomb*

Robert H. Bork

The 1965 decision in *Griswold* v. *Connecticut*[1] was insignificant in itself but momentous for the future of constitutional law. Connecticut had an ancient statute making it criminal to use contraceptives. The state also had a general accessory statute allowing the punishment of any person who aided another in committing an offense. On its face, the statute criminalizing the use of contraceptives made no distinction between married couples and others. But the statute also had never been enforced against anyone who used contraceptives, married or not. There was, of course, no prospect that it ever would be enforced. If any Connecticut official had been mad enough to attempt enforcement, the law would at once have been removed from the books and the official from his office. Indeed, some Yale law professors had gotten the statute all the way to the Supreme Court a few years previously, and the Court had refused to decide it precisely because there was no showing that the law was ever enforced. The professors had some difficulty arranging a test case but finally managed to have two doctors who gave birth control information fined $100 apiece as accessories.

Such enforcement in the area as there was consisted of the occasional application of the accessory statute against birth control clinics, usually clinics that advertised. The situation was similar to the enforcement of many antigambling laws. They may cover all forms of gambling on their faces, but they are in fact enforced only against commercial gambling. An official who began arresting the priest at the church bingo party or friends having their monthly poker game at home would have made a most unwise career decision and would be quite unlikely to get a conviction. There are a number of statutes like these in various state codes, such as the statutes flatly prohibiting sodomy and other "unnatural practices," which apply on their faces to all couples, married or unmarried, heterosexual or homosexual. The statutes are never enforced, but legislators, who would be aghast at any enforcement effort, nevertheless often refuse to repeal them.

There is a problem with laws like these. They are kept in the codebooks as precatory statements, affirmations of moral principle. It is quite arguable that this is an improper use of law, most particularly of

---

criminal law, that statutes should not be on the books if no one intends to enforce them. It has been suggested that if anyone tried to enforce a law that had moldered in disuse for many years, the statute should be declared void by reason of desuetude or that the defendant should go free because the law had not provided fair warning.

But these were not the issues in *Griswold*. Indeed, getting off on such grounds was the last thing the defendants and their lawyers wanted. Since the lawyers had a difficult time getting the state even to fine two doctors as accessories, it seems obvious that the case was not arranged out of any fear of prosecution, and certainly not the prosecution of married couples. *Griswold* is more plausibly viewed as an attempt to enlist the Court on one side of one issue in a cultural struggle. Though the statute was originally enacted when the old Yankee culture dominated Connecticut politics, it was now quite popular with the Catholic hierarchy and with many lay Catholics whose religious values it paralleled. The case against the law was worked up by members of the Yale law school faculty and was supported by the Planned Parenthood Federation of America, Inc., the Catholic Council on Civil Liberties, and the American Civil Liberties Union. A ruling of unconstitutionality may have been sought as a statement that opposition to contraception is benighted and, therefore, a statement about whose cultural values are dominant. Be that as it may, the upshot was a new constitutional doctrine perfectly suited, and later used, to enlist the Court on the side of moral relativism in sexual matters.

Justice Douglas's majority opinion dealt with the case as if Connecticut had devoted itself to sexual fascism. "Would we allow the police to search the sacred precincts of marital bedrooms for telltale signs of the use of contraceptives? The very idea is repulsive to the notions of privacy surrounding the marriage relationship."[2] That was both true and entirely irrelevant to the case before the Court. Courts usually judge statutes by the way in which they are actually enforced, not by imagining horrible events that have never happened, never will happen, and could be stopped by courts if they ever seemed about to happen. Just as in *Skinner* he had treated a proposal to sterilize three-time felons as raising the specter of racial genocide, Douglas raised the stakes to the sky here by treating Connecticut as though it was threatening the institution of marriage. "We deal with a right of privacy older than the Bill of Rights—older than our political parties, older than our school system." The thought was incoherent. What the right of privacy's

age in comparison with that of our political parties and school system had to do with anything was unclear, and where the "right" came from if not from the Bill of Rights it is impossible to understand. No court had ever invalidated a statute on the basis of the right Douglas described. That makes it all the more perplexing that Douglas in fact purported to derive the right of privacy not from some pre-existing right or law of nature, but from the Bill of Rights. It is important to understand Justice Douglas's argument both because the method, though without merit, continually recurs in constitutional adjudication and because the "right of privacy" has become a loose canon in the law. Douglas began by pointing out that "specific guarantees in the Bill of Rights have penumbras, formed by emanations from those guarantees that help give them life and substance." There is nothing exceptional about that thought, other than the language of penumbras and emanations. Courts often give protection to a constitutional freedom by creating a buffer zone, by prohibiting a government from doing something not in itself forbidden but likely to lead to an invasion of a right specified in the Constitution. Douglas cited *NAACP* v. *Alabama*,[3] in which the Supreme Court held that the state could not force the disclosure of the organization's membership lists since that would have a deterrent effect upon the members' First Amendment rights of political and legal action. That may well have been part of the purpose of the statute. But for this anticipated effect upon guaranteed freedoms, there would be no constitutional objection to the required disclosure of membership. The right not to disclose had no life of its own independent of the rights specified in the first amendment.

Douglas named the buffer zone or "penumbra" of the First Amendment a protection of "privacy," although, in *NAACP* v. *Alabama*, of course, confidentiality of membership was required not for the sake of individual privacy but to protect the public activities of politics and litigation. Douglas then asserted that other amendments create "zones of privacy." These were the first, third (soldiers not to be quartered in private homes), fourth (ban on unreasonable searches and seizures), and fifth (freedom from self-incrimination). There was no particularly good reason to use the word "privacy" for the freedoms cited, except for the fact that the opinion was building toward those "sacred precincts of marital bedrooms." The phrase "areas of freedom" would have been more accurate since the provisions cited protect both private and public behavior.

None of the amendments cited, and none of their buffer or penumbral zones, covered the case before the Court. The Connecticut statute was not invalid under any provision of the Bill of Rights, no matter how extended. Since the statute in question did not threaten any guaranteed freedom, it did not fall within any "emanation." *Griswold* v. *Connecticut* was, therefore, not like *NAACP* v. *Alabama*. Justice Douglas bypassed that seemingly insuperable difficulty by simply asserting that the various separate "zones of privacy" created by each separate provision of the Bill of Rights somehow created a general but wholly undefined "right of privacy" that is independent of and lies outside any right or "zone of privacy" to be found in the Constitution. Douglas did not explain how it was that the Framers created five or six specific rights that could, with considerable stretching, be called "privacy," and, though the Framers chose not to create more, the Court could nevertheless invent a general right of privacy that the Framers had, inexplicably, left out. It really does not matter to the decision what the Bill of Rights covers or does not cover.

Douglas closed the *Griswold* opinion with a burst of passionate oratory. "Marriage is a coming together for better or for worse, hopefully enduring, and intimate to the degree of being sacred. It is an association that promotes a way of life, not causes; a harmony in living, not political faiths; a bilateral loyalty, not commercial or social projects. Yet it is an association for as noble a purpose as any involved in our prior decisions."[4] It is almost a matter for regret that Connecticut had not threatened the institution of marriage, or even attempted to prevent anyone from using contraceptives, since that left some admirable sentiments, expressed with rhetorical fervor, dangling irrelevantly in midair. But the protection of marriage was not the point of *Griswold*. The creation of a new device for judicial power to remake the Constitution was the point.

The *Griswold* opinion, of course, began by denying that any such power was being assumed. "[W]e are met with a wide range of questions that implicate the Due Process Clause of the 14th Amendment. Overtones of some arguments suggest that [*Lochner* v. *New York*] should be our guide. But we decline that invitation. . . . We do not sit as a super-legislature to determine the wisdom, need, and propriety of laws that touch economic problems, business affairs, or social conditions."[5] *Griswold*, as an assumption of judicial power unrelated to the Constitution is, however, indistinguishable from *Lochner*. And the nature of that

power, its lack of rationale or structure, ensured that it could not be confined.

The Court majority said there was now a right of privacy but did not even intimate an answer to the question, "Privacy to do what?" People often take addictive drugs in private, some men physically abuse their wives and children in private, executives conspire to fix prices in private, Mafiosi confer with their button men in private. If these sound bizarre, one professor at a prominent law school has suggested that the right of privacy may create a right to engage in prostitution. Moreover, as we shall see, the Court has extended the right of privacy to activities that can in no sense be said to be done in private. The truth is that "privacy" will turn out to protect those activities that enough Justices to form a majority think ought to be protected and not activities with which they have little sympathy.

If one called the zones of the separate rights of the Bill of Rights zones of "freedom," which would be more accurate, then, should one care to follow Douglas's logic, the zones would add up to a general right of freedom independent of any provision of the Constitution. A general right of freedom—a constitutional right to be free of regulation by law—is a manifest impossibility. Such a right would posit a state of nature, and its law would be that of the jungle. If the Court had created a general "right of freedom," we would know at once, therefore, that the new right would necessarily be applied selectively, and, if we were given no explanation of the scope of the new right, we would know that the "right" was nothing more than a warrant judges had created for themselves to do whatever they wished. That . . . is precisely what happened with the new, general, undefined, and unexplained "right of privacy."

Justice Black's dissent stated: "I like my privacy as well as the next one, but I am nevertheless compelled to admit that government has a right to invade it unless prohibited by some specific constitutional provision."[6] He found none. "The Court talks about a constitutional 'right of privacy' as though there is some constitutional provision or provisions forbidding any law ever to be passed which might abridge the 'privacy' of individuals. But there is not." He pointed out that there are "certain specific constitutional provisions which are designed in part to protect privacy at certain times and places with respect to certain activities." But there was no general right of the sort Douglas had created. Justice Stewart's dissent referred to the statute as "an uncommonly silly law" but noted that its asininity was not before the Court.[7] He could "find no such general right of privacy in the Bill of Rights, in any other part of the Constitution, or in any case ever before decided by this Court." He also observed that the "Court does not say how far the new

constitutional right of privacy announced today extends." That was twenty-four years ago, and the Court still has not told us.

----

1. *381 U.S. 479 (1965).*
2. Id. *at 485–86.*
3. *357 U.S. 449 (1958).*
4. *381 U.S. at 486.*

5. Id. *at 481–482.*
6. *381 U.S. at 507, 508, 510 (Black, J. dissenting).*
7. *381 U.S. at 527, 530m.7 (Stewart, J., dissenting).*

DISCOVERING FUNDAMENTAL VALUES*

John Hart Ely

[I]t remains to ask the hardest questions. Which values . . . qualify as sufficiently important or fundamental or whathaveyou to be vindicated by the Court against other values affirmed by legislative acts? And how is the Court to evolve and apply them?

— *Alexander Bickel*

No answer is what the wrong question begets. . . .

— *Alexander Bickel*

Since interpretivism[1]—at least a clause-bound version of interpretivism—is hoist by its own petard, we should look again, and more closely, at its traditional competitor. The prevailing academic line has held for some time that the Supreme Court should give content to the Constitution's open-ended provisions by identifying and enforcing upon the political branches those values that are, by one formula or another, truly important or fundamental. Indeed we are told this is inevitable: "there is simply no way for courts to review legislation in terms of the Constitution without re-

peatedly making difficult substantive choices among competing values, and indeed among inevitably controverted political, social, and moral conceptions." "[C]onstitutional law must now be understood as the means by which effect is given to those ideas that from time to time are held to be fundamental. . . ." The Court is "an institution charged with the evolution and application of society's fundamental principles," and its "constitutional function," accordingly, is "to define values and proclaim principles."

The Judge's Own Values

The ultimate test of the Justices' work, I suggest, must be goodness. . . .

— *J. Skelly Wright*

The view that the judge, in enforcing the Constitution, should use his or her *own values* to measure the judgment of the political branches is a methodology that is seldom endorsed in so many words. As we proceed

----

through the various methodologies that are, however, I think we shall sense in many cases that although the judge or commentator in question may be talking in terms of some "objective," nonpersonal method of identification, what he is really likely to be "discovering," whether or not he is fully aware of it, are his own values. It is thus important at the outset to understand just why a "judge's own values" approach is unacceptable: that understanding will illumine the unacceptability of the entire enterprise.

How might one arrive at such a view? Much of the explanation seems to involve what might be called the fallacy of transformed realism. About forty years ago people "discovered" that judges were human and therefore were likely in a variety of legal contexts consciously or unconsciously to slip their personal values into their legal reasonings. From that earth-shattering insight it has seemed to some an easy inference that that is what judges *ought* to be doing. Two observations are in order, both obvious. The first is that such a "realist" theory of adjudication is not a theory of adjudication at all, in that it does not tell us *which* values should be imposed. The second is that the theory's "inference" does not even remotely follow: that people have always been tempted to steal does not mean that stealing is what they should be doing. This is all plain as a pikestaff, which means something else has to be going on. People who tend to this extreme realist view must consciously or unconsciously be envisioning a Court staffed by justices who think as they do. That assumption takes care of both the problems I've mentioned. It tells you what values are to be imposed (the commentator's own) and also explains (at least to the satisfaction of the commentator) why such a Court would be desirable. But it's a heroic assumption, and the argument that seems to score most heavily against such a "realist" outlook is one that is genuinely realistic—that there is absolutely no assurance that the Supreme Court's life-tenured members (or the other federal judges) will be persons who share your values.

But let that pass and grant the realists their strange assumption. There remains the immense and obvious problem of reconciling the attitude under discussion with the basic democratic theory of our government. At this point a distinction is drawn. In America it would not be an acceptable position that appointed judges should run the country, and that is not the position of the commentators under discussion. Saying the judges should run the country is different, however, and many have argued that it is significantly different, from saying the judges should use their own values to give content to the Constitution's open texture. Consistency with democratic theory will supposedly be found in the idea that the judiciary isn't really in a position to make much of a difference to the way the country is run. This assumption has impressive historical roots, running back to Hamilton's *Federalist* 78:

> *Whoever attentively considers the different departments of power must perceive, that, in a government in which they are separated from each other, the judiciary, from the nature of its functions, will always be the least dangerous to the political rights of the Constitution; because it will be least in a capacity to annoy or injure them. . . . The judiciary . . . has no influence over either the sword or the purse; no direction either of the strength or of the wealth of the society; and can take no active resolution whatever. It may truly be said to have neither FORCE nor WILL, but merely judgment; and must ultimately depend upon the aid of the executive arm even for the efficacy of its judgments.*

This must have made a good bit of sense at the outset of our nation: in the absence of precedent, the lack of independent enforcement machinery and the various constitutional checks on the judiciary must have seemed sufficient to ensure that it would play a quite insignificant role. What are harder to justify are the "realist" literature's *contemporary* iterations of Hamilton's assurances, most unrealistically untouched by two hundred years of experience. The Court may be purseless and swordless, but its ability importantly to influence the way the nation functions has proved great, and seems to be growing all the time. It may be true that the Court cannot *permanently* thwart the will of a solid majority, but it can certainly delay its implementation for decades—workmen's compensation, child labor, and unionization are among the more obvious examples—and to the people affected, that's likely to be forever.

The formal checks on the Court have surely not proved to be of much consequence. Congress's control over the budget of the federal courts—note, though, that it cannot constitutionally reduce judicial salaries—has proved an instrument too blunt to be of any real control potential. The country needs functioning and competent federal courts, and everybody knows it does. Despite the two-thirds requirement, impeachment *might* have developed into an effective mode of controlling decision. However, in part precisely because of our allegiance to the idea of an independent judiciary, it didn't, and today it is understood to be a weapon reserved for the grossest of cases. (It is no easier to impeach a justice than a President, as Richard Nixon learned, from both sides.) Congress's theoretical power to withdraw the Court's jurisdiction over certain classes of cases is so fraught with constitutional doubt that although talked about from time to time, it has not been invoked for over one hundred years. Altering the size of, or "packing," the Court was quite popular in the nineteenth century, but only once, during the Grant Administration, is it even arguable that it had its desired effect. And that is the last time it's been done. Franklin Roosevelt tried it, and although he failed, the prevailing mythology for a time was that his effort had pressured the Court into mending its ways. More recently discovered Court records have indicated, however, that the Court's "switch" was independent of (in fact prior to) the announcement of his plan. The message is mixed, but what now seems important about the episode is that an immensely popular President riding an immensely popular cause had his lance badly blunted by his assault on judicial independence.

There is also the possibility of constitutional amendment, but even when this course works it takes time—during which the Court's roadblock stays in place—and in any event it seldom works. Our recent experience with the Equal Rights Amendment, endorsed by both major parties and hardly advancing a radical proposition, corroborates the difficulty of amending the Constitution. In all our history only four decisions of the Supreme Court have been reversed by constitutional amendment. It is also true that often, though by no means always, the cooperation of political officials is required to enforce Supreme Court decisions. But they generally go along, however grudgingly: it is, after all, their perceived legal duty to do so. (One inclined to regard failure to obey as a viable means of controlling the Court would do well to reflect on the fact that the President of the United States—one hardly renowned for his reverence to the rule of law—did surrender those fatal tapes.) What's left is the fact that the President appoints and the Senate confirms the new members of the Court, and certainly there is something there. But it generally takes several successive presidential terms, and the concurrence of several successive Senates, to replace a majority of the justices. It has also proved hard to predict how someone in another line of work will function as a justice and one sometimes wonders whether the ap-

pointee who turns out differently from the way the President who appointed him expected is not the rule rather then the exception. (Truman and Eisenhower are both reported to have regarded Supreme Court appointments—Clark and Warren, respectively—as the worst mistakes they had made as President.) Nor is it the least bit unusual for a justice to sit for decades during which the issues are likely to have shifted markedly from those the President had in mind when the appointment was made.

So it can't be the actual invocation of the formal checks the realists mean to rely on in assuring us that the Court is no threat to influence importantly the governance of the country. The point tends to be made more mysteriously, generally in the language of "destruction." Thus we are told that the Court's "essentially anti-democratic character keeps it constantly in jeopardy of destruction": it knows "that frequent judicial intervention in the political process would generate such widespread political reaction that the Court would be destroyed in its wake." Readers who are even passingly familiar with the literature on judicial review of the 1960s and 1970s will recognize the theme: it is incanted as an article of faith and forms the foundation for much conservative "realism." But what is it supposed to mean? What sort of "destruction" is it that lurks around the activist corner? We're never exactly told, but to be coherent the idea has to be that although the formal checks appear to the naive observer to have atrophied, the Court knows better, and understands that if it gets too rambunctious—if it too regularly exercises what the public will understand are properly political functions—those checks will be invoked.

This isn't the way it works, and the justices know it isn't. Throughout its history the Court has been told it had better stick to its knitting or risk destruction, yet somehow "[t]he possibility of judicial emasculation by way of popular reaction against constitutional review by the courts has not in fact materialized in more than a century and a half of American experience." The warnings probably reached their peak during the Warren years; they were not notably heeded; yet nothing resembling destruction materialized. In fact the Court's power continued to grow, and probably has never been greater than it has been over the past two decades. For public persons know that one of the surest ways to acquire power is to assert it. "[J]udicial activism feeds on itself," Professors Karst and Horowitz have written. "The public has come to expect the Court to intervene against gross abuses.

And so the Court must intervene." "*Must* intervene"? I'd argue not, at least not as the formula is stated here. But "can get away with intervening"? For sure.

It's because everybody down deep knows this that few come right out and argue for the judge's own values as a source of constitutional judgment. Instead the search purports to be objective and value-neutral; the reference is to something "out there" waiting to be discovered, whether it be natural law or some supposed value consensus of historical America, today's America, or the America that is yet to be.

Natural Law

"Well, what may seem like the truth to you," said the seventeen-year-old bus driver and part-time philosopher, "may not, of course, seem like the truth to the other fella, you know."

"THEN THE OTHER FELLOW IS WRONG, IDIOT!"

—*Philip Roth,* The Great American Novel

At the time the original Constitution was ratified, and during the period leading up to the Fourteenth Amendment as well, a number of people espoused the existence of a system of natural law principles. "This law of nature being coeval with mankind and dictated by God himself is of course superior in obligation to any other. It is binding over the whole globe, in all countries and at all times. No human laws are of any validity if contrary to this. . . ." Some sort of natural law theory (which need not necessarily be deistic) thus seems an obvious candidate in the search for a source of values to give content to the Constitution's open-ended provisions.

The historical record here is not so uncomplicated as it is sometimes made to appear. As noted above, some of our nation's founders did not find the concept intelligible in any context, and even those who did "were seldom, if ever, guilty of confusing law with natural right." It therefore seems no oversight that the Constitution at no point adverts to the concept. Of course the Declaration of Independence *had* spoken in such terms. Part of the explanation for the difference is undoubtedly that intellectual fashions had changed somewhat over that eventful decade and a half. But surely that can't be all there was to it— ideas do not come and go so fast—and a more important factor seems to have been the critical difference

in function between the two documents. The Declaration of Independence was, to put it bluntly, a brief (with certain features of an indictment). People writing briefs are likely, and often well advised, to throw in arguments of every hue. People writing briefs for revolution are obviously unlikely to have apparent positive law on their side, and are therefore well advised to rely on natural law.[2] This the argument for our Revolution did, combining natural law concepts with references to positive law, both English and colonial, to the genuine "will of the people," to the "rights of Englishmen"—in short, with references to anything that seemed to help. "It was the quarrel with Britain that forced Americans to reach upward and bring natural law down from the skies, to be converted into a political theory for use as a weapon in constitutional argument; in that capacity it was directed against British policies and was never intended as a method of analyzing the rights and wrongs of colonial life." The Constitution was not a brief, but a frame of government. A broadly accepted natural law philosophy surely could have found a place within it, presumably in the Bill of Rights. But such philosophies were not that broadly accepted. Since the earlier impetus that had moved the Declaration, the need to "make a case," was no longer present, these controversial doctrines were omitted, at least in anything resembling explicit form, from the later document.

Natural law was also part of the rhetoric of antislavery, but again it was just one arrow in the quiver. As suited their purposes, the abolitionists, like the revolutionaries before them, argued both positive law, now in the form of existing constitutional provisions, and natural law. And for them too, the latter reference was virtually unavoidable, since it took a purity of spirit that transcended judgment not to recognize that the original Constitution, candidly considered, not only did not outlaw slavery, but deliberately protected it. "When it was the fashion to speak and write of 'natural' law very few stopped to consider the exact significance of that commonplace of theological, economic, literary, and scientific, as well as political, thought. Particularly is this true of the use of theories of natural law in the heat of controversies. At such times it is the winning of a cause, not the discussion of problems of ontology, which occupies men's minds." *Justice Accused,* Robert Cover's fine recent book on antislavery and the judicial process, corroborates the conclusion that for early American lawyers, references to natural law and natural rights functioned as little more than signals for one's sense that the law was not as one felt it should be. This is not to say that "natural law" was entirely without perceived legal significance. It was thought to be invocable interstitially, when no aspect of positive law provided an applicable rule for the case at hand. But it was subordinate to applicable statutes and well-settled precedent as well as to constitutional provisions, and not generally perceived as a source of values on whose basis positive law could be constitutionally upset.

We shouldn't make too much of this historical record, though. If there is such a thing as natural law, and if it can be discovered, it would be folly, no matter what our ancestors did or didn't think, to ignore it as a source of constitutional values. It's not nice to fool Mother Nature, and even Congress and the President shouldn't be allowed to do so. The idea is a discredited one in our society, however, and for good reason. "[A]ll theories of natural law have a singular vagueness which is both an advantage and disadvantage in the application of the theories." The advantage, one gathers, is that you can invoke natural law to support anything you want. The disadvantage is that everybody understands that. Thus natural law has been summoned in support of all manner of causes in this country—some worthy, others nefarious—and often on both sides of the same issue. Perhaps the most explicit invocation of natural law in a Supreme Court opinion appears in Justice Bradley's 1872 opinion in *Bradwell v. Illinois*, denying Ms. Bradwell's application to become a lawyer:

> *[T]he civil law, as well as nature herself, has always recognized a wide difference in the respective spheres and destinies of man and woman. . . . The constitution of the family organization, which is founded in the divine ordinance, as well as in the nature of things, indicates the domestic sphere as that which properly belongs to the domain and functions of womanhood. . . . The paramount destiny and mission of woman are to fulfill the noble and benign offices of wife and mother. This is the law of the Creator.*

But in fact the list of causes natural law has supported is almost infinite.

> *[N]atural law has had as its content whatever the individual in question desired to advocate. This has varied from a defence of theocracy to a defence of the complete separation of church and state, from revolutionary rights in 1776 to liberty of contract in recent judicial opinions,*

> *from the advocacy of universal adult suffrage to a defence of rigid limitations upon the voting power, from philosophical anarchy in 1849 with Thoreau to strict paternalism five years later with Fitzhugh, from the advocacy of the inalienable right of secession to the assertion of the natural law of national supremacy, from the right of majority rule to the rights of vested interests.*

It was, indeed, invoked on both sides of the slavery question. Calhoun cited natural law to "prove" the inferiority of blacks, and the Kentucky Constitution of 1850 and the Kansas Constitution of 1857 declared the right to own slaves "before and higher than any constitutional sanction." Small wonder, then, that abolitionists like Wendell Phillips came to realize that "[b]ecause 'nature' no longer spoke with a single voice, only the judge's conscience ultimately determined the source of right."

It has thus become increasingly evident that the only propositions with a prayer of passing themselves off as "natural law" are those so uselessly vague that no one will notice—something along the "No one should needlessly inflict suffering" line. "[A]ll the many attempts to build a moral and political doctrine upon the conception of a universal human nature have failed. They are repeatedly trapped in a dilemma. Either the allegedly universal ends are too few and abstract to give content to the idea of the good, or they are too numerous and concrete to be truly universal. One has to choose between triviality and implausibility." The concept has consequently all but disappeared in American discourse. The influence of religion has declined, but that isn't the real point: even persons who count themselves religious are unlikely to hold that the Almighty speaks with a sufficiently unambiguous ethical voice to help with today's difficult issues of public policy. Perhaps physical laws will be found "out there," though even that faith is fraying, but in any event moral laws will not. In 1931 Benjamin Wright wrote, in *American Interpretations of Natural Law:* "Since the Civil War the concept has been of importance only in the field of constitutional law. Here certain of the traditional individual rights doctrines have been taken over and woven into the fabric of due process of law and liberty of contract. In systematic theory it has served almost solely as an object of criticism." One thing has changed since 1931: constitutional lawyers have gotten the message, and the concept is no longer respectable in that context either.

This is not to say that the arguments against "moral absolutism" have not been overstated. It is no fairer to cite the dissenting "morality" of Adolf Hitler to prove the nonexistence of moral truth than it would be to invoke the views of the Flat Earth Society to prove there is not a correct position on the shape of the world. There *are* ethical positions so hopelessly at odds with assumptions most of us hold that we would be justified in labeling them (if not with absolute precision) "irrational." But the set of such propositions will turn out to be the mirror image of the set of propositions sufficiently vague and uncontroversial to pass themselves as "natural law": an example here would be the proposition that the infliction of needless suffering is morally acceptable. The existence of such a set of plainly unentertainable ethical propositions will obviously be no more relevant to constitutional disputes than will their plainly undeniable counterparts. Constitutional litigation will involve an action that has been approved by the legislative branch of the government involved or someone ultimately accountable thereto, whose action in addition has seemed sufficiently acceptable to a government lawyers' office to result in governmental defense in court. Such actions will involve a *choice* of evils (or goods). They may involve the infliction of suffering for reasons whose sufficiency on balance is open to argument; they will not involve the infliction of suffering that can fairly be labeled needless.

Another point that is sometimes made in this context is that what appear on the surface to be ethical disputes will often turn out on analysis to be disagreements over what the facts are. This position can be overstated. Some disputes—cruelty to animals and abortion are two—are over the appropriate breadth of the moral universe and not over any factual claim. More often, an apparent ethical dispute will preeminently involve a balancing or comparison of two or more quite well understood costs—abortion again, once fetuses are admitted to the universe of moral concern, is an example—and this is a paradigmatically ethical dispute. It is undoubtedly true, however, that at least some apparent moral disagreements do hide different factual assumptions. What follows for the constitutional context, though? That courts should resolve the disputes, by finding the actual facts and applying to them what all, presumably, would then agree—let's pass *that* problem—was the appropriate moral principle? That can't be right. In the first place, it isn't clear why judges should be the ones to find the facts in such situations. Broad questions of public policy are likely to involve what are called, uncoinci-

dentally, "legislative facts," or broad factual generalizations, as opposed to specific "adjudicative facts." The conventional wisdom here, that courts are markedly worse than legislatures at determining legislative facts, surely can stand significant qualification—but at the same time there isn't any reason to suppose they are better at it. More fundamentally, these are likely to be situations in which the facts are inherently intractable, not susceptible to resolution in any way that would satisfy all observers. The ancient, and recently reheated, controversy over whether the death penalty actually deters homicides is a good example. It shows us what is genuinely likely to be at stake in public policy controversies, namely questions of *how public institutions should behave under conditions of empirical uncertainty*. That factual uncertainty is an element of a problem does not mean the problem is not a profoundly moral one, or that it is one courts have any superior claim to being able or entitled to solve.

When I was a lad studying philosophy in the late 1950s, epistemology and logic were all the rage, and moral and political philosophy were sneered at by knowledgeables: after all, one couldn't really *reason* about ethical issues, could one? That day, happily, has passed: people *do* reason about such issues and some of them number among our most renowned contemporary philosophers. But the kind of reasoning that is involved in the arguments of contemporary moral philosophers proceeds from ethical principles or conclusions it is felt the reader is likely already to accept to other conclusions or principles he or she might not previously have perceived as related in the way the writer suggests. Surely this is reasoning, for reasoning in other areas consists in nothing more. But note the critical appeal at the outset to acceptance of the initial proposition or conclusion: the inference proceeds, as it must, from one "ought" to another. We have learned once again that we *can* reason about moral issues, but reasoning about ethical issues is not the same as discovering absolute ethical truth. So we're where we were: our society does not, rightly does not, accept the notion of a discoverable and objectively valid set of moral principles, at least not a set that could plausibly serve to overturn the decisions of our elected representatives.

Neutral Principles

In 1959 Herbert Wechsler delivered a widely heralded lecture, which became a widely heralded article, entitled "Toward Neutral Principles of Constitutional Law." He argued that the Supreme Court, rather than functioning as a "naked power organ" simply announcing its conclusions ad hoc, should proceed on the basis of principles that transcend the case at bar and treat like cases alike. Having announced such a principle in one case, the Court should then proceed unflinchingly to apply it to all others it controls. Consciousness of this obligation to the future will obviously help shape the principle the Court will formulate, and thus the result it will reach, in the first case. (What he said, in short, is that the Court should act in a principled fashion.)

Even this suggestion has had its detractors. There are those who will wax quite eloquent on the byzantine beauty of what is sometimes called the common law method, one of reaching what instinctively seem the right results in a series of cases, and only later (if at all?) enunciating the principle that explains the pattern—a sort of connect-the-dots exercise. This quarrel is of no concern to us here, though obviously I wouldn't have written this book if I weren't with Wechsler on *that* point. What is relevant here is that as embellished by the subsequent literature, Wechsler's suggestion was given another dimension, one it is not entirely clear he intended. "Neutral principles" became not simply an appropriate *requirement* for judicial behavior but also, in the minds of much of the profession, a *source* of constitutional judgment—a sufficient as well as necessary condition of legitimate constitutional decision-making. The articulation of a neutral principle, the idea seems sometimes to run, is itself sufficient guarantee that the Court is behaving appropriately.

We needn't spend long on this suggestion. Its unambiguous endorsement has been rare, and its fallacy has been pointed out by others. An insistence on "neutral principles" does not by itself tell us anything useful about the appropriate content of those principles or how the Court should derive the values they embody. The requirement means initially—this much is easy in theory, though we all know people who don't abide by it—that a principle, once promulgated, is to be applied to all cases it controls and not just when one is in the mood. But that can't be enough: the principle that "Freedom of speech is guaranteed to Republicans" would not satisfy us as "neutral," no matter how unblinkingly it was applied. Thus some degree of generality must also be required to make a principle count as "neutral" in Wechsler's sense. Even in the unlikely event that we could agree on what degree of generality should be required, however, we

still would not have arrived at a formula that would guarantee the *appropriateness* of the principle. The principle that "Legislatures can do whatever they want"—even if (especially if) unblinkingly applied—would obviously be unacceptable, but hardly because of inadequate generality.

"Neutral principles" has often served as a code term for judicial conservatism, probably because Wechsler himself originally used the concept in criticizing *Brown* v. *Board of Education* as wrongly decided. But it needn't have been so: there are neutral principles of every hue. (How about "No racial segregation, ever"?) In fact the Warren Court probably came as close to the ideal as any of its predecessors: the problem for the commentators may actually have been too much generality, not too little. But however that may be, requirements of generality of principle and neutrality of application do not provide a source of substantive content.

Reason

> *If a society were to design an institution which had the job of finding the society's set of moral principles and determining how they bear in concrete situations, that institution would be sharply different from one charged with proposing policies. . . . It would provide an environment conducive to rumination, reflection, and analysis. "Reason, not Power" would be the motto over its door.*
>
> —Harry Wellington

The constitutional literature that has dominated the past thirty years has often insisted that judges, in seeking constitutional value judgments, should employ, in Alexander Bickel's words, "the method of reason familiar to the discourse of moral philosophy." "Judges have, or should have, the leisure, the training, and the insulation to follow the ways of the scholar in pursuing the ends of government." This view, like the others we are considering, seldom appears in unadulterated form. (Indeed, much of the point is that these various value sources, in their understandable confusion, fall all over one another.) It is, however, one of the more important presences.

Technically, of course, reason alone can't tell you anything: it can only connect premises to conclusions. To mean anything, the reference has to be somewhat richer, to implicate the invocation of premises along with the ways in which one reasons from them. The basic idea thus seems to be that moral philosophy is what constitutional law is properly about, that there exists a correct way of doing such philosophy, and that judges are better than others at identifying and engaging in it. Now I know lawyers are a cocky lot: the fact that our profession brings us into contact with many disciplines often generates the delusion that we have mastered them all. But surely the claim here cannot be that lawyers and judges are the best imaginable people to tell good moral philosophy from bad: members of the clergy, novelists, maybe historians, to say nothing of professional moral philosophers, all seem more sensible candidates for this job. I suppose that this isn't the relevant comparison, though, and that all that has to be demonstrated is that of the institutions existing in our government, courts are those best equipped to make moral judgments, in particular that they are better suited to the task than legislatures.

Since judges tend generally to be drawn from roughly the same ranks as legislators, the heart of the argument here is that moral judgments are sounder if made dispassionately, and that because of their comparative insulation judges are more likely so to make them. "[T]he environment in which legislators function makes difficult a bias-free perspective. It is often hard for law-makers to resist pressure from their constituents who react to particular events (a brutal murder, for instance) with a passion that conflicts with common morality." One might begin by questioning the alleged incompatibility between popular input on moral questions and "correct" moral judgment. In fact there are reasons for supposing that our moral sensors function *best* under the pressure of experience. Most of us did not fully wake up to the immorality of our most recent war until we were shown pictures of Vietnamese children being scalded by American napalm. Professor Bickel makes this point in what must have seemed to him an unrelated section of his book:

> There was an unforgettable scene . . . in one CBS newscast from New Orleans, of a white mother fairly foaming at the mouth with the effort to rivet her distracted little boy's attention and teach him how to hate. And repeatedly, the ugly, spitting curse, NIGGER! The effect, achieved on an unprecedented number of people with unprecedented speed, must have been something like what used to happen to individuals (the young Lincoln among them) at the sight of an actual slave auction, or like the

> slower influence on northern opinion of the fighting in "Bleeding Kansas" in 1854–55.

It is thus no surprise that the case that our "insulated" judiciary has done a better job of speaking for our better moral selves turns out to be historically shaky. "Can we really be sure that it was Marshall or Taney rather than Clay or Webster who did the better job of articulating values? Which of the Civil War Justices excelled Lincoln in voicing the hopes and goals of the republic? . . . Which Justice in the 1920's gave better tongue than Norris or LaFollette to the American dream?"

A more fundamental error underlies the view under consideration, however—an outsider's error, akin to the assumption nonlawyers frequently make that there is something called "the law" whose shape good lawyers will describe identically. (Whatever one's profession, I assume this phenomenon is recognizable.) The error here is one of assuming that something exists called "the method of moral philosophy" whose contours sensitive experts will agree on, that "there are only two kinds of reasoning—one is sound and the other is unsound." That is not the way things are. Some moral philosophers think utilitarianism is the answer; others feel just as strongly it is not. Some regard enforced economic redistribution as a moral imperative; others find it morally censurable. What may be the two most renowned recent works of moral and political philosophy, John Rawls's *A Theory of Justice* and Robert Nozick's *Anarchy, State and Utopia,* reach very different conclusions. There simply does not exist *a* method of moral philosophy.

Ronald Dworkin also succumbs to this error. Writing in 1972 he said:

> Constitutional law can make no genuine advance until it isolates the problem of rights against the state and makes that problem part of its own agenda. That argues for a fusion of constitutional law and moral theory, a connection that, incredibly, has yet to take place. It is perfectly understandable that lawyers dread contamination with moral philosophy, and particularly with those philosophers who talk about rights, because the spooky overtones of that concept threaten the graveyard of reason. But better philosophy is now available than the lawyers may remember. Professor Rawls of Harvard, for example, has published an abstract and complex book about justice which no constitutional lawyer will be able to ignore.

The invitation to judges seems clear: seek constitutional values in—that is, overrule political officials on the basis of—the writings of good contemporary moral philosophers, in particular the writings of Rawls. Rawls's book *is* fine. But how are judges to react to Dworkin's invitation when almost all the commentators on Rawls's work have expressed reservations about his conclusions? The Constitution may follow the flag, but is it really supposed to keep up with the *New York Review of Books?*

One might be tempted to suppose that there will be no systematic bias in the judges' rendition of "correct moral reasoning" aside from whatever derives from the philosophical axioms from which they begin. ("We like Rawls, you like Nozick. We win, 6–3. Statute invalidated.") That would certainly be bad enough, but the actual situation is likely to be somewhat worse. Experience suggests that in fact there will be a systematic bias in judicial choice of fundamental values, unsurprisingly in favor of the values of the upper-middle, professional class from which most lawyers and judges, and for that matter most moral philosophers, are drawn. People understandably think that what is important to them is what is important, and people like us are no exception.[3] Thus the list of values the Court and the commentators have tended to enshrine as fundamental is a list with which readers of this book will have little trouble identifying: expression, association, education, academic freedom, the privacy of the home, personal autonomy, even the right not to be locked in a stereotypically female sex role and supported by one's husband. But watch most fundamental-rights theorists start edging toward the door when someone mentions jobs, food, or housing: those are important, sure, but they aren't *fundamental*.

Thus the values judges are likely to single out as fundamental, to the extent that the selections do not simply reflect the political and ethical predispositions of the individuals concerned, are likely to have the smell of the lamp about them. They will be—and it would be unreasonable to expect otherwise if the task is so defined—the values of what Henry Hart without irony used to call "first-rate lawyers." The objection to "reason" as a source of fundamental values is therefore best stated in the alternative: either it is an empty source, in the same way "neutral principles" turned out to be an empty source, or, if not empty, it is so flagrantly elitist and undemocratic that it should be dismissed forthwith.[4] Our society did not make the constitutional decision to move to near-universal suffrage only to turn around and have superimposed on

popular decisions the values of first-rate lawyers. As Robert Dahl has observed, "After nearly twenty-five centuries, almost the only people who seem to be convinced of the advantages of being ruled by philosopher-kings are . . . a few philosophers."

Tradition

Running men out of town on a rail is at least as much an American tradition as declaring unalienable rights.

—Garry Wills

Tradition is an obvious place to seek fundamental values, but one whose problems are also obvious. The first is that people have come to understand that "tradition" can be invoked in support of almost any cause. There is obvious room to maneuver, along continua of both space and time, on the subject of which tradition to invoke. Whose traditions count? America's only? Why not the entire world's? (For some reason Justice Frankfurter liked to refer to the "traditions of the English-speaking people.") And what is the relevant time frame? All of history? Anteconstitutional only? Prior to the ratification of the provision whose construction is in issue? Why not, and indeed this seems the more usual reference, extending to the present day? (Once you're there, however, you're verging into a somewhat distinct approach.) And who is to say that the "tradition" must have been one endorsed by a majority? Is Henry David Thoreau an invocable part of American tradition? John Brown? John Calhoun? Jesus Christ? It's hard to see why not. Top all this off with the tremendous uncertainties in ascertaining anything very concrete about the intellectual or moral climates of ages passed, and you're in a position to prove almost anything to those who are predisposed to have it proved or, more candidly, to admit that tradition doesn't really generate an answer, at least not an answer sufficiently unequivocal to justify overturning the contrary judgment of a legislative body.[5]

The indications in *Regents of the University of California* v. *Bakke* that racial preferences for historically disadvantaged minorities are to be treated as (at least somewhat) constitutionally suspect were quite explicitly rooted in an appeal to tradition. "This perception of racial and ethnic distinctions is rooted in our Nation's constitutional and demographic history." And indeed Justice Powell was able to assemble a collection of historical statements to the effect that a person's legal status should not be affected by his race. Those statements, however, were made in the context of discussing whether whites should be permitted to advantage themselves at the expense of racial minorities: to quote them in the affirmative action context without taking account of that critical fact is to succumb to the understandable temptation to vary the relevant tradition's level of abstraction to make it come out right.

Even with respect to the use of racial discrimination to *dis*favor minorities, our country has two conflicting traditions: the egalitarian one to which most official documents have paid lip service over the past century, and the quite different and malevolent one that in fact has characterized much official and unofficial practice over the same period (and certainly before). Presumably no reader would wish to endorse the latter tradition, but I'd be interested to hear the argument that can make it go away. Assume that by some magic it will, however, and assume therefore a unitary American tradition against the use of racial classification to disadvantage minorities: even that contrivance will not, unless we cheat, generate a unitary tradition on the different question of whether racial minorities can be favored. In recent years there have been numerous official programs that give breaks of one sort or another to persons because of their minority race. It is true that in some earlier periods such programs did not exist, but that may have been because those concerned with improving the lot of minorities had their hands full attempting, generally unsuccessfully, to combat widespread official discrimination *against* minorities. In fact the only prior period during which affirmative action for racial minorities seems even to have been a realistic possibility was Reconstruction. Some did object, apparently in part on principle—the name of Andrew Johnson is one that comes to mind here—but it surely seems more relevant that the Reconstruction Congress, the same Congress that gave us the amendment under which Bakke brought his challenge, passed over Johnson's veto such explicit preferences for blacks as those contained in the Freedmen's Bureau Act of 1866. In the heat of debate one might attempt to identify Reconstruction as the relevant period from which to draw those traditions that should define our construction of the Fourteenth Amendment, and surely that seems no more disreputable than other appeals to tradition we have seen. The more honest conclusion, however, is that one must look elsewhere to decide what racial and other groups are to be permitted constitutionally to do to and for each other. There does not exist an unambiguous American tradition on the question of whether racial majorities can act to aid minorities, and one can make it seem there is only by quoting out of context.

It is never satisfactory to rest one's whole objection to a constitutional theory on grounds of indeterminacy, if only because the implications of *any* nontrivial theory will be open to debate. There are, however, serious theoretical problems with tradition as a source of constitutional values. Its overtly backward-looking character highlights its undemocratic nature: it is hard to square with the theory of our government the proposition that yesterday's majority, assuming it was a majority, should control today's. Of course part of the point of the Constitution is to check today's majority. This observation simply compounds the problems with making tradition a source of constitutional values, however, since the provisions for which we are seeking a source of values were phrased in open-ended terms to admit the possibility of growth. (If one wanted to freeze a tradition, the sensible course would be to write it down.) Moreover, "[i]f the Constitution protects only interests which comport with traditional values, the persons most likely to be penalized for their way of life will be those least likely to receive judicial protection," and that flips the point of the provisions exactly upside down. Reliance on tradition therefore seems consistent with neither the basic theory of popular control nor the spirit of the majority-checking provisions to which we are seeking to give content. For these reasons the reference is invariably a passing one, buttressing what turns out to be the most common reference-in-chief, the genuine consensus of contemporary American thought.

Consensus

Few of us would march our sons and daughters off to war to preserve the citizen's right to see "Specified Sexual Activities" exhibited in the theaters of our choice.
—United States Supreme Court (1976)

The idea that society's "widely shared values" should give content to the Constitution's open-ended provisions—that "constitutional law must now be understood as expressing contemporary norms" turns out to be at the core of most "fundamental values" positions. Just as those who talk about tradition usually wind up with something like "today's values viewed in the light of tradition," something like contemporary value consensus almost inevitably ends up giving content to the inherently contentless notions of "reason" and "principle." The reference has received its clearest recent articulation by Harry Wellington, who put it in terms of "conventional" or "common" morality: "The Court's task is to ascertain the weight of the principle in conventional morality and to convert the moral principle into a legal one by connecting it with the body of constitutional law."

In theory this approach solves two problems we have seen with earlier ones. In theory it is not incomplete. Consensus or conventional morality is postulated as something "out there" that can be discovered. And in theory it is not undemocratic. Quite to the contrary, it is billed by Wellington as a "reference to the people." F. A. Hayek elaborates: "Only a demagogue can represent as 'anti-democratic' the limitations which long-term decisions and the general principles held by the people impose upon the power of temporary majorities."

I guess this makes me a demagogue, but I think both claims—that judicial references to popular consensus are not incomplete and that they are not undemocratic—are wrong. As to the first, there is a growing literature that argues that in fact there is no consensus to be discovered (and to the extent that one may seem to exist, that is likely to reflect only the domination of some groups by others). It is sometimes said that the American consensus disintegrated in the 1960s. That would be rebuttal enough, but in fact it may be only the recognition that is recent:

> *The lack of common interest between master and slave is obvious. So is the relationship between the military during World War II and the Japanese-Americans who were herded into internment camps in an order whose constitutionality was upheld by the Supreme Court. Latter-day disputes concerning the legitimate role of race in governmental decision-making, whether for purposes of segregation or affirmative action, or the legitimacy of the state's allowing the cessation of the possibility of life, by abortion or euthanasia, also present differences of the greatest magnitude regarding conceptions of justice.*

Even if we assume, however—though it's virtually self-contradictory to do so—that there *is* a consensus lurking out there that contradicts the judgment of our elected representatives, there would still remain the point, sufficient in itself, that that consensus is not reliably discoverable, at least not by courts. As Louis Jaffe once inquired:

> *How does one isolate and discover a consensus on a question so abstruse as the existence of a fundamental right? The public may value a right and yet not believe it to be fundamental. The public may hold that the rights of parents are fundamental and yet have no view whether they include sending a child to a private school. There may be a profound ambiguity in the public conscience; it may profess to entertain a traditional ideal but be reluctant to act upon it. In such a situation might we not say that the judge will be free to follow either the traditional ideal or the existing practice, depending on the reaction of his own conscience? And in many cases will it not be true that there has been no general thinking on the issue?*

Thus when one gets down to cases, one finds much the same mix we found when the reference was to "natural law"—a mix of the uselessly general and the controversially specific. Roberto Unger's observation about references to tradition seems equally applicable here: "To make the doctrine plausible in the absence of divinely revealed moral truth, its proponents rely on references to moral opinions shared by men of many different ages and societies. The more concrete the allusions to this allegedly timeless moral agreement, the less convincing they become. Therefore, to make their case the proponents of objective value must restrict themselves to a few abstract ideals whose vagueness allows almost any interpretation." Express skepticism about the existence of moral consensus to someone who claims it means something, and you're likely to be given some jejune maxim like "No one should profit from his own wrong." Ask for an actual case where a constitutional court could legitimately overrule a legislative judgment on the basis of a moral consensus, and things get a little strange. In *Breithaupt* v. *Abram,* decided in 1957, the Supreme Court held that the drawing of twenty cubic centimeters of blood from the unconscious body of the obviously unconsenting petitioner, and the subsequent use of that blood to convict him of drunk driving, did not deny him due process. In doing so it rather explicitly employed a consensus methodology: "[D]ue process is not measured by the yardstick of personal reactions . . . but by that whole community sense of 'decency and fairness' that has been woven by common experience into the fabric of acceptable conduct. It is on this bedrock that this Court has established the concept of due process." Bedrock indeed: what the Court fails to note, for all its talk of community sense, is that three of the nine justices dissented. The doubtful attribution of consensus is not, I should hasten to add, a technique reserved for "conservative" causes. In their separate concurring opinions in *Furman* v. *Georgia* (1972), Justices Brennan and Marshall argued quite directly that the death penalty was unconstitutional because it was out of accord with contemporary community values. The risk in such a claim is obvious, and in this case it was tragically realized. Following *Furman* there was a virtual stampede of state reenactments of the death penalty, and the clarity of that community reaction surely had much to do with the Court's turnaround on the issue.

The commentators' readings of society's values are as questionable as those of the justices. Professor Bickel wrote: "I would assert that the rightness of the Court's decision in the *School Segregation Cases* can be demonstrated [in terms of an appeal to societal values]. I would deny, however, that any similar demonstration can be or was mounted . . . to show that a statute setting maximum hours or minimum wages violates fundamental presuppositions of our society." One can surely understand the goal that is evident here—to find a way of approving *Brown* while disapproving *Lochner*. And I think that combination can responsibly be defended, but not in these terms. I suppose it's possible, though in fact it seems unlikely, that by 1954 the values of most of the country—assuming, despite our federal system, that opinion nationwide is what should count here—had moved to the point of condemning "separate but equal" schooling. And obviously, given the existence of the legislation whose constitutionality was in issue, there were in some quarters serious reservations about laissez-faire capitalism around the time of *Lochner*. Bickel's *comparative* judgment, however, seems indefensible: racism of the sort that supported separate schools was into the 1950s (and remains today) a strong strain in American life, and laissez-faire capitalism was a philosophy that was very widely entertained around the turn of the century. Dean Wellington, developing the implications of his "conventional morality" approach, pronounces, if more hesitantly, the same dubious verdict as Bickel on *Lochner*'s roots in popular opinion. His ability to distinguish propositions that conventional morality supports from those it does not is displayed even more impressively, however, in the area of abortion:

> I take some comfort in the fact that the American Law Institute's Model Penal Code also would permit abortion for rape, to save the life of the mother, or if "the child would be born with grave physical or mental defect." The work of the Institute is a check of sorts. Its conclusions are some evidence of society's moral position on these questions. It is, indeed, better evidence than state legislation, for the Institute, while not free of politics, is not nearly as subject to the pressures of special interest groups as is a legislature.
>
> The Institute, however, would permit abortion in additional situations, most importantly where there was "a substantial risk that continuance of the pregnancy would gravely impair the physical or mental health of the mother." I would like to be able to find support for that position in conventional morality, for it surely coincides with my personal preference. But the Institute's position is here the best evidence there is and that does not seem enough. I do not understand how, by noticing commonly held attitudes, one can conclude that a healthy fetus is less important than a sick mother.

It's quite a slalom, but I doubt that there's room on it for anyone besides Wellington.

Examples could be multiplied, but it should by now be clear that by viewing society's values through one's own spectacles—resolving apparent inconsistencies in popular thinking in the "appropriate" direction by favoring the "emergent over the recessive," the "general over the particular," or whatever[6]—one can convince oneself that some invocable consensus supports almost any position a civilized person might want to see supported. As elsewhere, though, it is hard to claim that this alone adds up to a dispositive argument: there does not exist a nontrivial constitutional theory that will not involve judgment calls. In fact I think this one is worse than most in that regard, but in any event the comparative judgment is devastating: as between courts and legislatures, it is clear that the latter are better situated to reflect consensus. Sophisticated commentary never tires of reminding us that legislatures are only imperfectly democratic. Beyond the fact that the appropriate answer is to make them more democratic, however, the point is one that may on analysis backfire. The existing antimajoritarian influences in Congress and the state legislatures, capable though they may be of *blocking* legislation, are not well situated to get legislation passed in the face of majority opposition. That makes all the more untenable the suggestion under consideration, that courts should invalidate legislation in the name of a supposed contrary consensus. Beyond that, however, we may grant until we're blue in the face that legislatures aren't wholly democratic, but that isn't going to make courts more democratic than legislatures.

An appeal to consensus, or to consensus tempered by the judge's own values, may make some sense in a "common law" context, where the court is either filling in the gaps left by the legislature—"legislating interstitially," in Cardozo's phrase—or, perhaps, responding to a broad legislative delegation of decision-making authority. Since they are "standing in" for the legislature, courts presumably should try to behave as (good) legislatures behave, and that may involve combining their best estimate of popular opinion with their own best judgment. All too often commentators accustomed to working in fields other than constitutional law, fields where appeals to this sort of filtered consensus may make sense, seek to transfer their analytical techniques to the constitutional area without dropping a stitch. After all, the inference seems to run, law is law, isn't it, and if it made sense there it should make sense here. The problem is that the constitutional context is worlds away: the legislature has spoken, and the question is whether the court is to overrule it in a way that can be undone only by the cumbersome process of constitutional amendment. That is precisely what constitutional courts must do—quite often, I shall argue. But to do so on the theory that the legislature does not truly speak for the people's values, but the Court does, is ludicrous.

The notion that the genuine values of the people can most reliably be discerned by a nondemocratic elite is sometimes referred to in the literature as "the Führer principle," and indeed it was Adolf Hitler who said "My pride is that I know no statesman in the world who with greater right than I can say that he is the representative of his people." We know, however, that this is not an attitude limited to right-wing elites. "The Soviet definition" of democracy, as H. B. Mayo has written, also involves the "ancient error" of assuming that "the wishes of the people can be ascertained more accurately by some mysterious methods of intuition open to an elite rather than by allowing people

to discuss and vote and decide freely." Apparently moderates are not immune either.

The final problem, the most fundamental of all, comes into perspective when you step back a couple of paces and think about why we're engaging in this entire exercise. There are two possible reasons one might look to consensus to give content to the Constitution's open-ended provisions. One *might* say one was seeking to protect the rights of the majority by ensuring that legislation truly reflect popular values. If that were the purpose, however, the legislative process would plainly be better suited to it than the judicial. This leaves the other possible reason for the reference, to protect the rights of individuals and minority groups against the actions of the majority. That, of course, is what we've been about in this chapter. No one suggests that we look to "natural law" or "tradition" to ensure that the majority's will is in fact being worked; such references are instead calculated to protect minorities from the unchecked exercise of the majority's will. Now think again about consensus as a possible source, and the message will come clear: it makes no sense to employ the value judgments of the majority. The consensus approach therefore derives what apparent strength it has from a muddle: its methodology, which people slide into accepting because of its similarity to what courts may do properly in common law contexts, has nothing to do with the tasks they can legitimately set themselves in the area of constitutional adjudication.

Predicting Progress

In his 1969 Holmes Lectures, subsequently published as *The Supreme Court and the Idea of Progress,* the thinking of Alexander Bickel apparently took a new tack. The Warren Court, he claimed, had tried to prefigure the future, to shape its constitutional principles in accord with its best estimate of what tomorrow's observers would be prepared to credit as progress. In this, he argued, it had failed: already the Warren Court's "bets on the future" were coming up political losers. Bickel was somewhat elusive about whether he himself was prepared to accredit "tomorrow's values" as a source of constitutional judgment: his formal claim was that that had been the criterion of the Warren Court and that by its own criterion that Court had to be judged a failure. Though the point is arguable, I believe there was a good deal of prescription folded into Bickel's description. In any event others, before and after, have endorsed the method, even if Bickel did not mean to.

The problems with this approach are the familiar ones, in more aggravated form. First—assuming for the moment that we really are talking about a predictive task—there is no reason to suppose that judges are well qualified to foresee the future development of popular opinion. Professor Bickel, whose historical sensitivity surely exceeded that of most lawyers and judges, fell on his face—or so at least it seems as of 1980—explaining a decade ago how the Warren Court's great desegregation and reapportionment decisions had (already!) become irrelevant. That only proves he was human—we've all mistaken ripples for waves. But that's exactly the point: prediction is a risky enterprise for anyone, and there is no warrant for an appointed judge's supposing he is so much better at it than the legislature that he is going to declare their efforts unconstitutional on the basis of his predictions.

In addition, the reference is antidemocratic on its face. Controlling today's generation by the values of its grandchildren is no more acceptable than controlling it by the values of its grandparents: a "liberal accelerator" is neither less nor more consistent with democratic theory than a "conservative brake." Superimposed on this problem is one I noted in connection with a contemporary consensus approach: the imposition of allegedly majoritarian values is a mindless way of going about protecting minorities, and stipulating that the majority is to be a future majority does not suddenly make sense of it. But even assuming that by some miracle of logic we could convince ourselves that the sensible way to protect today's minorities from today's majority is to impose on today's majority the values of tomorrow's majority, it would remain a myth that "the values of tomorrow's majority" are data that prescient courts can discover in a value-neutral way. For today's judicial decision (no matter what its source of judgment) will inevitably have an important influence on the values of tomorrow's majority. The "prophecies" of people in power have an inevitably self-fulfilling character, even when what is being "prophesied" is popular opinion. This may or may not be a bad thing, but it does mean that the Court cannot be heard to plead value-neutrality on the theory that it is "taking its values from the future" rather than imposing its values *on* it: the fact that things turned out as the Supreme Court predicted may prove only that the Supreme Court is the Supreme Court. Thus by predicting the future the justices will unavoidably help shape it, and by shaping the future they will unavoidably, indeed this is the point of the methodology, shape the present. Assuming it works, that amounts to the imposition of the justices' own values. That's just what the fundamental value theorists promised they wouldn't do to us; the fact that it's done with mirrors shouldn't count as a defense. . . .

There are a couple of reasons why Alexander Bickel has been such a central character in this chapter. He was probably the most creative constitutional theorist of the past twenty years. And he ran the gamut of fundamental-value methodologies. His career[7] is thus a microcosm, and it testifies to the inevitable futility of trying to answer the wrong question: "Which values, among adequately neutral and general ones, qualify as sufficiently important or fundamental or whathaveyou to be vindicated by the Court against other values affirmed by legislative acts?" It wouldn't do, he acknowledged, for the justices simply to impose their own values: he recognized, as others have pretended not to, that given the enormous influence of the judiciary such a course would be fundamentally inconsistent with the first principles of our democracy. Nor did he suppose for a moment that there was some timeless set of objectively valid natural law principles out there to be discovered by judges or anyone else. And so he began his quest. He was one of the first to see that incanting "neutral principles" doesn't begin to tell you what those principles should be, and though he talked a lot about "reason" it was clear he understood that some other ingredient was needed. Tradition was too backward-looking, at least for a Robert Kennedy liberal, which is what Bickel was as late as 1968. Consensus—now that was promising, that could solve the countermajoritarian difficulty. But slowly he came to realize, though he never gave up on the idea altogether, that there probably wasn't any consensus respecting the sorts of issues that came before the Court, and that even if there had been, the Court was one of the last bodies we should trust to find it. Thus "the idea of progress." Bickel's posthumously published book, *The Morality of Consent,* suggests that he soon saw this too for what it was, a thinly veiled imposition of personal judicial values on the present and future. What, then, to fill the breach? Unfortunately, a pastiche of themes remembered, with particular stress this time on one that hadn't much attracted the young Alex Bickel: tradition. His good friend Robert Bork explained at Bickel's Memorial Service that this Burkean ending meant that Bickel had finally "resolved the tension" between his political liberalism and his judicial conservatism. "To read his *New Republic* piece on Edmund Burke is to see that his political philosophy had come into alignment with his legal philosophy." I remember choking as Bork said this, not because I disagreed that Bickel's politics had moved somewhat toward the end—I can't account for *The Morality of Consent* without that assumption either—but rather because of Bork's suggestion that there had been a contradiction to be resolved. For one perfectly well *can* be a genuine political liberal and at the same time believe, out of a respect for the democratic process, that the Court should keep its hands off the legislature's value judgments. I've calmed down, though, and now I can see how *someone who started with Bickel's premise,* that the proper role of the Court is the definition and imposition of values, might well after a lifetime of searching conclude that since nothing else works—since there isn't any impersonal value source out there waiting to be tapped—one might just as well "do the right thing" by imposing one's own values. It's a conclusion of desperation, but in this case an inevitable desperation. No answer is what the wrong question begets.

---

1. *The author earlier defined* interpretivism *as the view that "judges should confine themselves to enforcing norms that are stated or clearly implicit in the written Constitution."*—Editors' note.
2. *This is not a new insight. "If the written law tells against our case, clearly we must appeal to the universal law, and insist on its greater equity and justice." Aristotle, "Rhetoric" 1375a, in* The Basic Works of Aristotle *1374 (R. McKeon ed. 1941).*
3. *"And so we arrive at the result, that the pleasure of the intelligent part of the soul is the pleasantest of the three, and that he of us in whom this is the ruling principle has the pleasantest life.*
   "Unquestionably, he said, the wise man speaks with authority when he approves of his own life." Plato, The Republic, *Book IX, in* 2 The Dialogues of Plato *455 (4th ed. B. Jowett 1953).*
4. *The danger that upper-middle-class judges and commentators will find upper-middle-class values fundamental is obviously present irrespective of methodology. I think it's exacerbated when "reason" is the supposed value source, however, partly because the values we have mentioned are the values of the "reasoning class," and partly because "reason," being inherently an empty source, may lend itself unusually well to being filled in by the values of one's own kind.*
5. *A related technique is to discredit a practice by associating it with a disreputable tradition. See, e.g., Shaughnessy v. United States ex rel. Mezei, 345 U.S. 206, 217–18 (1953) (Black, J., dissenting). The techniques of association and dissociation can obviously be used in tandem. See, e.g., Poe v. Ullman, 367 U.S. 497, 542 (1961) (Harlan, J., dissenting) (emphasis added): "The balance of which I speak is the balance struck by this country, having regard to what history teaches are the traditions from which it developed as well as the traditions from which it broke." This tech-nique is virtually omnipotent, since there is no litmus that can separate prior practices that are properly regarded as part of our tradition from those the framers "must have been rebelling against" (though any commentator is likely almost automatically to assume that those of which he or she disapproves belong in the latter category).*
6. *Such techniques are evident in the work of consensus theorists generally, and are sometimes made explicit. Ronald Dworkin argues that community values must be refined by the judge in a way that removes prejudice, emotional reaction, rationalization, and "parroting," and in addition should be tested for sincerity and consistency. R. Dworkin, Taking Rights Seriously 126, 240–58 (1977). See also, e.g., Wellington, "Common Law Rules and Constitutional Double Standards: Some Notes on Adjudication," 83 Yale L. J. 221, 251 (1973) (courts "must be reasonably confident that they draw on conventional morality and screen out contemporary bias, passion, and prejudice, or indeed, that they distinguish cultivated taste from moral obligation"); Perry, "Substantive Due Process Revisited: Reflections on (and beyond) Recent Cases," 71 Nw. U. L. Rev. 417, 442 (1976) (distinction should be drawn between "the commands to which conventional moral culture subscribes and the commands to which it not only subscribes but believes should have the force of law"). Some such collection of "laundering" devices is plainly needed, lest one be forced to the conclusion that the law the legislature passed is likely to reflect the way contemporary community values bear on the issues in question. Cf. Note, "Legislative Purpose, Rationality, and Equal Protection," 82 Yale L. J. 123, 127–32, 135–37 (1972).*
7. *"Tragically foreshortened" is too trite for Alex, who was never trite, in intellectual or personal style.*

CONSTITUTIONAL INTERPRETATION AND ORIGINAL MEANING*

David Lyons

I. Constitutional Originalism

By "originalism" I mean the familiar approach to constitutional adjudication that accords binding authority to the text of the Constitution or the intentions of its adopters. At least since Marbury, *in which Chief Justice Marshall emphasized the significance of our Constitution's being a written document, originalism in one form or another has been a major theme in the American constitutional tradition.[1]*

Indeed, originalism can seem to be the only plausible approach to judicial review. One might reason as follows: "A court cannot decide whether an official decision conforms to the Constitution without applying its rules. The Constitution was written down to fix its content, and its rules remain unchanged until it is amended. Courts have not been authorized to change the rules. So courts deciding cases under the Constitution should follow the rules there laid down. By what right would courts decide constitutional cases on any other grounds?"

That challenge is conveyed by writings on judicial review that are regarded as originalist. But it is misleading. Most of the positions that are condemned by contemporary originalists accept the authority of the Constitution.[2] Although originalists present the issue as fidelity to the Constitution, it primarily concerns, I shall argue, how the Constitution is to be interpreted.

A distinctively originalist mode of interpretation assumes that the doctrinal content of the Constitution was completely determined when it was adopted and that constitutional doctrines can be identified by a value-free factual study of the text or of "original intent." It is part of my purpose to show that this type of theory is not only less plausible than its severest critics have suggested,[3] but that significant alternatives to it are available (sections II and III).

An approach to judicial review includes not only a theory of interpretation, which tells us how to understand the Constitution, but also a theory of adjudication, which tells us how to apply the Constitution so interpreted—how it should be used in constitutional cases. Originalist theory is not usually analyzed in this way, but we shall find that the distinction is needed when considering contemporary originalism.

One would expect a distinctively originalist approach to adjudication to hold that constitutional cases should be decided on the basis of doctrines in the "original" Constitution (that is, the Constitution interpreted in an originalist way), and on no other basis whatsoever. I shall show that contemporary theorists who present themselves as strict originalists accept rules for judicial review that cannot be found in or otherwise attributed to the "original" Constitution (sections IV–VI).

A third point I wish to make is that doctrines drawn from general philosophy—ideas about meaning and morals, for example—play a significant role in contemporary originalist theorizing. This point is important because these philosophical notions are dubious and controversial. It must be emphasized, however, that some of the same philosophical ideas have wide currency in legal theory generally.

Although originalism has relatively few defenders, its most prominent champions are highly placed within the federal government. These include Robert H. Bork,[4] Judge on the United States Court of Appeals

---

From Lyons, David. "Constitutional Interpretation and Original Meaning," in *Social Philosophy and Policy* (1987). Reprinted by permission of Blackwell Publishers.

for the District of Columbia Circuit, Edwin Meese III,[5] Attorney General of the United States, and William H. Rehnquist,[6] Associate Justice of the United States Supreme Court. It is important for us to recognize the quality of the constitutional theories that are embraced by these responsible officials.

This paper is, then, a critique of constitutional originalism. We need a better theory. Although I shall not offer one here, I shall suggest some requirements for an adequate theory of constitutional adjudication.

II. Original Intent

Paul Brest's definition of "originalism" mentions two variants—"textualism" and "intentionalism."[7] The difference between them is significant. This section deals with constitutional intentionalism, especially its need for justification and the difficulties of finding any.

An originalist mode of interpretation holds that the doctrinal content of the Constitution was fixed when (or by the time that) the Constitution was adopted,[8] and that constitutional doctrines can be identified by a value-free factual inquiry. An intentionalist version of originalism holds that we must understand the Constitution in terms of the "intentions" of its framers, adopters, or ratifiers,[9] such as the specific applications that they had in mind, those they would have been prepared to accept, or their larger purposes.[10]

Champions of "original intent" seem to regard that approach to constitutional interpretation as so obviously correct that it requires no justification; for none seems to be offered. So it will be useful to begin by noting some aspects of intentionalism that imply its need for justification.

Reference to "original intent" is inherently ambiguous. The following questions indicate some (but not all) of that ambiguity. Whose intentions count? The intentions of, for example, one who drafts a text or one who votes for it? Which intentions count? To establish as authoritative some particular text, or some text understood in a certain way, or to serve some identifiable larger purposes? Reference to original intent is problematic in other ways too. While two or more individuals can share an intention, it is by no means clear how (or whether it is always possible) to aggregate the relevant attitudes of the members of a group so as to determine their collective intentions.[11]

The answer that one gives to such questions should affect originalist interpretation, so the selection of any particular criterion of original intent as the basis for interpreting the Constitution requires specific justification. In the absence of a satisfactory rationale, we should regard any particular criterion of original intent as theoretically arbitrary. Sad to say, original intent theorists generally ignore these fundamental problems, despite their having systematically been surveyed in law reviews for at least two decades.[12]

But the differences among the various versions of originalist intentionalism do not chiefly concern us now. The point I would like to emphasize is that *any* intentionalist approach requires substantial justification. Intentionalism is a special theory of constitutional interpretation, not a platitude.

Early in our constitutional career, the Supreme Court refused to apply the Bill of Rights to the several states, holding that the first ten amendments restricted only the federal government, although their language does not explicitly limit most of those amendments in that way.[13] In so deciding, the Court made some reference to the intentions of "the framers." Although the Court's grounds for its decision went far beyond original intent, its reference to framers' intent might suggest that the Court followed that criterion of constitutional meaning instead of the apparent meaning of the authoritative text. If that were so, the Court would have followed a special theory of constitutional interpretation, and one that requires substantial justification.

In general, we recognize that we do not always mean what we say or write; *we* may mean something different from the meaning *of the language* that we use. This is reflected in our reading of legal instruments such as wills and contracts. It has also been observed, by advocates as well as critics of intentionalism, that the surest guide to authors' intent is the authoritative constitutional text itself. This is possible only because the text is understood to carry a meaning that stands on its own—that is independent of its authors' intentions.[14]

It follows that intentionalism is a special theory of constitutional interpretation, not a platitude. Either it derives from a failure to appreciate the distinction between the meaning of a text and what its authors meant to convey; or else it presupposes some reason for holding that the meaning of the constitutional text, unlike that of texts generally, is a matter of authors' intent. So intentionalism is either confused or else requires substantial justification.

What might justify intentionalist constitutional interpretation? Originalists might appeal to (1) the idea (not limited to law) that interpretation should generally be governed by authors' intentions; (2) a specifically legal canon of construction; or (3) some theory of political morality that implies that we are under an obligation to respect the intentions of the framers, adopters, or ratifiers.

(1) *Intentionalism as a general approach to interpretation.* The notion that textual interpretation seeks generally to determine authors' intentions is plausible when our primary concern is what some individual had in mind, as in the case of personal communications, studies of literary figures and, in law, wills and contracts. The question is whether our proper concern when interpreting an authoritative public text such as a constitution is to determine what its authors had in mind. The suggestion seems to me implausible.

I do not wish to deny that, just as a poem can be a political statement, law can be read as literature. But law's distinctive functions are significantly different from those of literature and personal communications. Law tells us what we must or must not do, threatening punishment for disobedience. It places the coercive power of the state behind some individuals' decisions. It quite literally regulates death and taxes, war and peace, debts and compensation, imprisonment, conscription and confiscation, and innumerable other matters of direct, vital interest to individuals, communities, and often all humanity. That is the explicit, normal business of the law, including the U.S. Constitution.

An important feature of law's normal business is that it requires justification. The same applies, of course, to judicial decisions, including those that turn upon legal interpretation. They require justification, too. The justification of judicial decisions, like the justification of the normal business of the law generally, cannot be understood in narrowly legalistic terms. Adequate justification concerns not merely whether something is required or allowed by law but, also, whether what the law does is what I have elsewhere called "defensible."[15] All of this suggests that the need for justification may properly regulate matters of legal and specifically constitutional interpretation and, thus, that these matters turn on political morality.

(2) *Intentionalism as a theory of legal interpretation.* Could intentionalism be based on a general canon of construction for legal instruments? The possibility is suggested by the fact that statutory construction is said to seek out "legislative intent." But there are several difficulties here. Insofar as constitutional intentionalism relies upon a canon of construction that derives from precedent or common law, there will be

some difficulty incorporating such a theory of interpretation into originalism, as I shall explain later.

Another problem is this. Conventions regulate the identification of "legislative intent," such as the authority given to official reports from legislative committees. Such conventions have only problematic application to the U.S. Constitution. The existence of such conventions suggests something else that seems important, namely, that the search for "legislative intent" is not a purely factual inquiry about a consensus that obtained at a particular historical moment. This is suggested also by the fact that statutory construction characteristically seeks to interpret legislation in as favorable a light as possible; for example, as a reasonable and legislatively legitimate means to a reasonable and legislatively legitimate means to be a reasonable and legislatively legitimate end. Such a normative bias can be explained by the fact that statutory construction seeks to provide, if possible, a grounding for judicial decisions that are justified. If what counts as "legislative intent" is in fact shaped by normative considerations, it could not serve as a model for "original intent," for those who endorse the latter as the criterion of constitutional meaning regard it as a plain matter of historical fact, accessible to a value-free inquiry.

Originalists assume that the Constitution is a morally adequate basis for judicial decisions (as well as for our political arrangements generally). The normative bias within interpretation to which I refer requires that we interpret the Constitution in such a way that it is, if possible, capable of performing that function.

If statutory construction is no help to constitutional intentionalism, what about the interpretation of other legal instruments, such as wills and contracts? The first point made about "legislative intent" applies here, too: insofar as constitutional intentionalism relies upon a canon of construction that derives from precedent or common law, there will be some difficulty incorporating such a theory of interpretation into originalism.

It might nonetheless be thought that an intentionalist interpretation of contracts[16] could serve as a model for constitutional intentionalism. That is because political rhetoric often refers to the Constitution as the upshot of a "social contract." Now, the idea of a "social contract" is invoked to argue for obedience to law, however objectionable on other grounds it might be, so long as it does not violate constitutional restrictions. This means that a "social contract" basis for intentionalism is dependent on a theory of political morality. To accept intentionalism on this basis, we must establish the legitimacy of a "social contract" argument and its valid application to this case.

(3) *Intentionalism as a theorem of political morality.* Our discussion suggests that we should seek a rationale for constitutional intentionalism in the political morality of constitutional creation and application, that is, in principles that explain why the Constitution is worthy of respect and morally binding. Two ideas are provided by political rhetoric. One, already noted, refers to a "social contract." Another, asserted within as well as outside the Constitution, holds that it comes from "the people."

The latter idea is promising because contemporary originalists, like most constitutional theorists, emphasize the predominantly "democratic" character of our constitutional arrangements. Representative government nicely complements popular sovereignty. Political rhetoric suggests that "the people" knowingly and freely agreed to respect government so long as it conforms to the Constitution, and that "the people" are accordingly bound by that agreement. But this does not yet yield the constitutional theory of original intent, which requires that the Constitution be understood in terms of the "intentions" of a special subclass of "the people," namely, the framers, adopters, or ratifiers, as opposed to (say) the understanding that one might have of the Constitution based on text meaning.

The present line of reasoning requires us to suppose, then, (a) that "the people" *contracted to accept the intentions of the authors,* by reference to which the Constitution must therefore be understood, and (b) that *this* makes the Constitution binding on us now. The theory seems fatally flawed.

(a) In the first place, only a small minority of the people of that time and place were permitted to participate in the original adoption process. We lack precise figures, but it should suffice for present purposes to observe that the process excluded not only many adult white males (and, of course, children) but also women, chattel slaves, and Native Americans. It could not have included more than a small fraction of the total population, and willing contractors would have amounted to a smaller fraction still.

In the second place, it is doubtful whether any such contractors would have been morally competent to create obligations to respect political arrangements that continued chattel slavery, second-class citizenship for women, and the subjugation of Native Americans. At the very least, those subject to such arrangements could not be bound by a constitution simply because it was agreeable to others.

(b) In the third place, it is unclear how contracts made by members of earlier generations can bind succeeding generations. This is not to suggest that law can bind only those who have given their consent. But the mere fact that some people some time in the past have accepted a political arrangement cannot by itself automatically bind others. More is required than that to show that later generations are bound.

But the rhetoric of popular sovereignty is nonetheless illuminating. It suggests a commitment to popular government, however narrowly that was at first conceived.[17] Furthermore, the Constitution is a piece of public, not private law. Our proper concern in interpreting it is not to implement the understanding of parties to a limited, private agreement or the personal wishes of a testator, but to establish the basis for political arrangements and justified judicial decisions that legitimately concern the community as a whole. Whatever else is needed for a theory of constitutional adjudication, the legitimate interest of the entire population strongly suggests that the primary criterion of constitutional meaning should be popular understanding, the basic index of which must be text meaning.

Consider the alternative. Interpretation in terms of the intentions of constitutional framers or ratifiers would seem to assume a conception of law like that of the classical legal positivists Bentham and Austin, according to which an exclusive subgroup of the population makes law for others to follow.[18] That is objectionable because of our interest in justification. Interpretation based on anything like that conception of the law will present formidable obstacles to justifying the Constitution, justifying compliance with morally deficient laws so long as they conform to the Constitution, and justifying judicial decisions that those laws require.

The upshot is that constitutional intentionalism is profoundly problematic. There is no obvious linguistic or moral basis for interpreting the Constitution by reference to the intentions of an exclusive political group, as opposed to the meaning of the text. When these considerations are combined with other substantial objections to intentionalism, the theory seems unpromising indeed.

III. Alternatives to Intentionalism

In this section, I argue that intentionalism does not win out by default, despite its deficiencies. According to Brest's typology, the originalist alternative to intentionalism is textualism, which comes in two varieties. "A strict textualist purports to construe words and phrases very narrowly and precisely."[19] Brest appears to argue that this is untenable both as textual interpretation and as originalism: "An originalist would hold that, because interpretation is designed to capture the original understanding, the text must be understood in the contexts of the society that adopted it."[20] This means that textualism must be "moderate" to be plausible. "A moderate textualist takes account of the open-textured quality of language and reads the language of provisions in their social and linguistic contexts."[21]

In other words, Brest judges the only legitimate originalist alternative to intentionalism[22] to be a reading of constitutional language as "open textured."[23] Unfortunately, Brest does not explain what he takes this to mean. But his reference to the spurious precision of "strict" textualism suggests that we might understand "moderate textualism" by reference to Hart's use of "open-textured" when he introduced that technical term into legal theory.[24]

Following the received wisdom of the time, Hart held that all terms in "natural" languages (which include the language of the law) are "open-textured." An "open-textured" word has a core of determinate meaning, encompassing fact situations to which it uncontroversially applies, and a "penumbra" encompassing fact situations to which the term neither clearly applies nor clearly does not apply. The idea of "open texture" assumes that the meaning of a word is indeterminate whenever there are reasons both for and against applying the word. This aspect of the theory of "open texture" provides a theoretical rationale for a view that is widely accepted by legal theorists, namely, that legal language has indeterminate meaning insofar as its proper application is unclear.

On this understanding, to characterize constitutional language as "open textured" is to imply that the doctrines given by that language are incompletely formed. Provisions that many theorists seem to believe fit this description to an extreme degree include the so-called "vague clauses" guaranteeing "free speech," "due process," "just compensation," "equal protection," and the like. On the "open texture" model, these provisions are seen as having tiny cores of clear (and therefore determinate) meaning and relatively wide unclear (and therefore indeterminate) penumbras.

This is a politically significant idea. For it implies that, insofar as the judicial process of "interpreting" the Constitution makes its proper application clearer,

the process really *changes* the Constitution by making its meaning more determinate. The clearer doctrines resulting from such "interpretations" could not then be attributed to the "original" Constitution. That is the view of constitutional language that Brest seems to regard as the ("moderate") originalist alternative to "strict" textualism.

Given this conception of the alternatives, we can better understand why originalists regard as most significant the dividing line between "strict" and "moderate" originalism. That is because moderate originalism appears to collapse into nonoriginalism.

Originalism regards the authority of the "original" Constitution as axiomatic, whereas nonoriginalism holds that adherence to the Constitution requires justification and that principles of political morality that are capable of providing such justification might also justify deviation from it.[25] To clarify this difference, we can distinguish two categories of doctrines that might be used in constitutional cases. Those that can and those that cannot truly be attributed to the Constitution may be called "constitutional" and "extra-constitutional," respectively. Nonoriginalism is prepared to consider using extra-constitutional doctrines in constitutional cases, whereas a distinctively originalist theory of adjudication would presumably reject any such use of them.

"Moderate" originalism regards unclear constitutional language as "open-textured," or inherently somewhat vague. It also accepts the judicial practice of deciding cases under unclear aspects of the Constitution. But it seems to regard the constitutional "interpretations" that are used as creating, and the resulting decisions as applying, doctrines that are extra-constitutional—judicial amendments to the "original" Constitution. On this view, "moderate" originalism's approach to deciding cases under unclear aspects of the Constitution *is equivalent to nonoriginalism*. Such decisions would be condemned by a "strict" originalist who holds that, as courts have no authority to amend the Constitution, they should refrain from doing so.[26]

It must be emphasized that the line of reasoning sketched in the last few paragraphs assumes that "moderate" textualism regards the Constitution as indeterminate insofar as its proper application is unclear. But we need not assume this; we need not accept the dubious assumption that the meaning of a text is indeterminate whenever it is unclear, or whenever interpretation of it would be controversial, so that the discovery of text meaning is impossible precisely when it is needed.

Instead of discussing these issues in the abstract, it will be useful to consider an approach which agrees that such language in the "original" Constitution does *not* provide *complete* doctrines of just compensation, free speech, and the like. This approach nevertheless provides grounds for attributing the doctrines resulting from sound interpretations to the Constitution. This will provide us with all that we require for present purposes, namely, an alternative to "strict" intentionalism that might justifiably assign meaning to the Constitution and enable courts to decide cases on constitutional grounds.

It has been suggested[27] that the so-called "vague clauses" incorporate "contested concepts." It is the nature of such a concept to admit of competing "conceptions" and thus routinely to *require* interpretation. Contested concepts do not have built-in criteria of application; they are more abstract than that. As a result, different people can use the same (contested) concept while accepting and employing different standards for its application. It would seem, for example, that general normative concepts, such as "right" and "wrong," "good" and "bad," "right" and "obligation," as well as more specific normative concepts, such as particular virtues and vices, are "contested" in this way. When people agree about the "facts" but disagree in their evaluations, their disagreement concerns the principles that determine the proper application of those concepts to particular cases.

The notion of a "contested concept" is explicitly used, for example, in Rawls's theory of social justice, the relevant part of which can be explained as follows. Imagine that you and I disagree about the substantive requirements of social justice. We then differ as to how the concept of justice applies; we differ, that is, about the principles of justice. This is possible if the concept of justice admits of different interpretations, or competing conceptions. That seems to be the case.

Rawls maintains that the mere concept of justice determines no detailed, substantive criteria of justice, only the skeletal requirement that there be no "arbitrary distinctions" between persons but, rather, "a proper balance between competing claims."[28] The task of a theory of justice is to show (not merely to claim) the superiority of one conception (one principle or set of principles) over competing conceptions as an interpretation of this requirement. The possibility of a uniquely correct interpretation of a provision incorporating the contested concept of justice, then, depends on the superior justifiability of a particular conception of justice.

Now consider a constitutional example. Past judicial interpretations aside,[29] a court applying the just compensation clause would not necessarily decide a case as the original authors would have done, nor would it automatically follow a more popular consensus of the time (even if either were possible). Instead, a court would understand the Constitution to mean precisely what it says and thus to require *just compensation*. A court would need to defend a particular conception of just compensation (that is, it would need to defend principles of justice appropriate to compensation) against the most plausible alternatives. It would then apply that conception to decide the case at bar.

Someone might be skeptical about the possibility of justifying such an interpretation. Someone might believe it is impossible to provide a rational defense of, say, principles of just compensation and might therefore claim that a court adopting this approach would inevitably impose its own arbitrary conception of just compensation instead of the conception embraced by the authors of the Constitution or by a broader "original" consensus. (It should be emphasized that, on this view, an "original" conception of just compensation is completely arbitrary and indefensible.) Someone might hold, in other words, that all such principles are inherently arbitrary, so that courts cannot possibly do what is required to implement this approach to the interpretation of "vague" constitutional language.[30] I shall not offer a general critique of such skepticism,[31] but I shall suggest below why it is reasonable to believe that there can be a best conception among competing conceptions of some contested concepts. I shall later show how philosophical skepticism about values is, in this context, incoherent.[32]

Contested concepts do not seem confined to morality and law. Their properties are at any rate similar to those of concepts referring to natural substances or phenomena, such as water and heat. On a plausible understanding of the development of science, for example, the caloric and kinetic theories of heat are (or at one time were) competing conceptions of the concept heat. This is suggested by the fact that "heat" refers to a physical phenomenon that is but partially and imperfectly identified by any prescientific verbal definition of the word, and that something very much like the idea of a contested concept is required to explain how there can be two theories of heat, that is, two different conceptions of the single concept heat.

If, as most people would agree, "heat" refers to a determinate physical phenomenon, there can be, in principle, a best theory of heat. This implies that there can be a best conception of a contested concept, at least in some cases. This suggests, in turn, that contested concepts in the Constitution might have best interpretations.

The kinetic theory of heat has displaced the caloric conception and is currently our best conception of heat. As this example implies, we may be justified in using *our* best conception even if it is not in fact *the* best. Similarly, just as our best conception of heat is liable to change, so we may expect change from time to time in our best conception of, say, just compensation. This involves no moral relativism.

Now if the idea that the Constitution includes contested concepts is correct, then to apply the Constitution in terms of their best interpretation is, in effect, to apply doctrines whose application is called for by the original Constitution. But, just as interpretation of the concept heat requires more than mere reflection, any interpretation of this type inevitably draws upon resources that are neither implicit in the text nor purely linguistic. It makes essential use of political argument, though at a relatively general or abstract level. So this alternative approach implies that a sound interpretation—one faithful to the meaning of the text—can include substantive doctrines that are not derivable from the text (even supplemented by its original social and linguistic context) but that are identifiable only by reasoning about political principles in the context of the federal system.

It is important to emphasize that this approach to constitutional interpretation, where applicable, requires that an interpreter go outside the "four corners" of the text, its strict linguistic implications, and the relatively specific intentions of its authors,[33] for interpretations and arguments supporting them. But, as this is done because it is understood to be required by the very nature of contested concepts found within the Constitution, both the strategy of argument and its results can claim fidelity to the Constitution. For this reason, the interpretive approach just sketched might reasonably be regarded as "originalist."

As usually understood, however, "originalism" assumes that constitutional doctrines must be identified by a value-free factual study of the text or of original intent and that doctrines that are not implicit in the "original" text or "understanding" cannot truly be attributed to the Constitution. It accordingly rejects without a hearing the possibility of attributing to the Constitution interpretations of those contested concepts that are in the Constitution. That possibility gives reason to withhold assent from the more familiar originalist theories.

IV. Originalist Adjudication

The Fourteenth Amendment says that no state "shall deny to any person within its jurisdiction the equal protection of the laws." The meaning of this provision is unclear. If (as some suggest) the provision does not have any determinate meaning, how should courts deal with cases under it? The Constitution does not tell us what we should then do.

As I have suggested, a comprehensive theory of judicial review can be understood as having two parts. A theory of interpretation purports to determine constitutional meaning. If well grounded, such a theory should be welcome when the text is unclear. Furthermore, anyone who holds the text to be misleading needs a good theory to justify such a claim.

But theories about judicial review go beyond straightforward interpretation; they include theories of adjudication, which purport to determine how the Constitution should be applied.[34] Such a theory is required if cases are decided when the meaning of the Constitution is undetermined, or to justify departure from the Constitution's implications.

To illustrate the latter possibility, consider Thayer's famous deferential doctrine.[35] Thayer argued that federal legislation should never be nullified by federal courts unless it cannot reasonably be doubted that the legislation violates the Constitution. He held that this judicial policy was needed to promote respect for federal law and to protect the courts from legislative interference.[36] Thayer did not assume that the Constitution has no determinate meaning when there is reasonable disagreement about its meaning. On the contrary, he insisted that the judiciary should not apply its best interpretation of the Constitution but should defer whenever it is possible to regard the legislature's actions as constitutional.

> [W]hen the ultimate question is . . . whether certain acts of another department, officer, or individual are legal or permissible, . . . the ultimate question is not what is the true meaning of the constitution, but whether legislation is sustainable or not.[37]

Thayer recommends, in effect, that the courts should sometimes refrain from enforcing the Constitution, even when they have a good, justifiable, and perhaps sound idea of what it means. That amounts to a special theory of adjudication (and, incidentally, one that seems decidedly extra-constitutional).

The distinctively originalist approach to adjudicating constitutional cases would seem to hold that they should be decided exclusively by doctrines that can be found in the "original" Constitution, that is, interpreted in an originalist way. There is a problem here. It is by no means clear that originalist theory can be found within the "original" Constitution. If originalism itself includes extra-constitutional doctrines, then insofar as a court applied and was guided by this theory of adjudication, it would decide cases in a non-originalist way!

It may accordingly seem reasonable to revise the originalist theory of adjudication so that originalism does not prohibit its own application. It would be modified to say that a doctrine may be applied within judicial review if, but only if, the doctrine either is attributable to the Constitution (in the sense required by an appropriate originalist theory of interpretation) or else is a doctrine of originalism itself.

That problem seemed easily solved. But it may suggest how difficult it is to embrace originalism unqualifiedly. Take another example. Raoul Berger's attack upon judicial decisions that fail to respect "framers' intent" leads him to suggest that courts should repudiate all decisions that cannot be grounded upon the Constitution so construed, regardless of "undesirable consequences."[38] But Berger hastily retreats from this proposal, saying:

> It would, however, be utterly unrealistic and probably impossible to undo the past in the face of the expectations that the segregation decisions, for example, have aroused in our black citizenry—expectations confirmed by every decent instinct. That is more than the courts should undertake and more, I believe, than the American people would desire.[39]

Berger's retreat appears unprincipled. At best, he invokes an undefined and undefended extra-constitutional principle of constitutional adjudication, which clashes with his originalist pretensions.

Henry Monaghan appears sensitive to Berger's problem. He too says that the school desegregation decisions should not be undone. Unlike Berger, however, Monaghan suggests a judicial principle that would permit leaving those decisions undisturbed, even though he questions their constitutional warrant. His solution is to advocate a doctrine of judicial precedent.[40]

The question now is whether a doctrine of judicial precedent can be attributed to the "original" Constitution. Monaghan appears not to think so. But he believes that such a doctrine can be justified because it serves "the long-run values of stability and predictability for ordering our most fundamental affairs."[41]

Monaghan does not seem to appreciate the awkwardness of his position. In offering a justification for a doctrine of precedent based on its desirable consequences, he commits himself to holding that judicial review may be regulated by *any* principles whose use would serve the same "long-run values." That would permit the use in judicial review of an indeterminate class of useful extra-constitutional principles.[42]

One might, alternatively, suggest that a doctrine of precedent was in fact provided by the "original" Constitution. For the Constitution was grafted upon a system whose common law heritage includes, of course, a doctrine requiring courts to respect judicial precedent.[43] The trouble with this way of reasoning, from an originalist perspective, is that it would render the Constitution much less limited doctrinally than originalists tend to view it. It would imply that the Constitution contains a multitude of common law principles.

Monaghan's predicament suggests the instability of originalism. If an originalist believes that there is justification for respecting a judicial principle that is no more controversial than precedent, he not only runs the risk of agreeing that constitutional cases may properly be decided by doctrines that cannot be attributed to the Constitution; he may become committed to accepting a relatively indeterminate theory of judicial review, incorporating all the principles of constitutional adjudication that can be justified by the criteria that are needed to justify a doctrine of precedent.

This point is generalizable. Contemporary originalists are often preoccupied with "restraining" the federal judiciary in constitutional cases and tend to embrace theories of adjudication that are designed in part to limit judicial nullification of decisions made by elected officials. The relevant judicial principles require justification. If such principles cannot be found in the "original" Constitution, they require justification by reference to some principles of political morality. The considerations that are adduced or required to justify such doctrines are capable of justifying an indefinite class of other doctrines that are relevant to constitutional adjudication. To endorse an extra-constitutional principle is to commit oneself to endorsing any other principle that is justifiable on the same grounds that justify the one endorsed. Such an approach to constitutional adjudication is hardly consistent with the spirit of originalism.

V. Democratic Sensibilities

Constitutional theorizing nowadays puts an emphasis upon "democracy" that we have so far neglected. It arises in contexts like the following. Intentionalists believe that our knowledge of constitutional meaning extends only so far as our knowledge of original intent. What remains unclear can be assigned no determinate meaning. If it is assumed that the "interpretation" and application of unclear aspects of the Constitution involves extra-constitutional doctrines, it would be natural for originalists to prefer that courts refrain from deciding such cases.

One who wishes to justify such a policy of "judicial restraint" might suggest that the defendant should win whenever law is unclear and therefore indeterminate, because then the burden of proof cannot effectively be shouldered by a plaintiff or appellant.[44] This reasoning seems warranted by the notion that courts should decide cases by reference to existing law. Not requiring extra-constitutional doctrines, it seems compatible with originalism.

But extensive use of the burden-of-proof rule would be problematic in our system. Suppose, for example, that district courts in different circuits, believing they had adequate constitutional grounds for doing so, decided similar cases, but did so differently. Suppose, further, that their decisions involved aspects of the Constitution that their respective circuit courts regarded as indeterminate because unclear. If the circuit courts invoked the burden-of-proof rule, the result would in effect establish conflicting constitutional doctrines in different circuits. The federal courts would seem to require some extra-constitutional doctrine to extricate us from that predicament.

The alternative basis for a policy of "judicial restraint" is an argument from "democracy," which concludes that nonelected judges should not nullify decisions made by "electorally accountable" officials. The reasoning may be understood as follows. Insofar

as political arrangements are subject to popular control through elections, they are regarded by many constitutional theorists as respecting democratic values. In addition, our system involves a division of political power under which popularly elected legislatures are authorized to make law and the judiciary is conventionally understood as authorized to interpret and apply, but not to make law.

One who assumes that unclear law is indeterminate will also believe that judges must "legislate" whenever they decide "hard cases." This practice is tolerable, or even desirable, when kept to a minimum, judges are elected and, most importantly, elected legislatures are able, if they wish, to modify the results by means of subsequent legislation. This would normally be the case except when courts must rule on limits to the legislature's authority.

From that perspective, judicial review by the federal courts of decisions made by elected officials is most problematic. In the first place, federal judges are not elected, but are appointed with indefinite tenure. Popular control is more limited over the federal judiciary than over elected officials (or, more generally, over those who are considered "electorally accountable"—those who, for example, are appointed but serve at the pleasure of elected officials). In the second place, such review concerns the constitutionality of nonjudicial decisions. Decisions made by electorally accountable officials are liable to be nullified by nonelected federal judges, and electorally accountable officials will be unable to override those judicial decisions. It is accordingly held by many constitutional theorists that such judicial review severely strains democratic principles.

These same democratic sensibilities are most seriously offended when judicial review is thought to be combined with "judicial legislation." Therefore, when constitutional cases turn upon the testing of nonjudicial decisions against unclear constitutional provisions, legal theorists tend to suppose that any substantive decision involves judicial revision of the Constitution itself. On the basis of such reasoning, contemporary originalists sometimes hold that decisions made by officials who are answerable to the electorate should not be nullified by nonelected judges unless it is clear that those decisions violate the Constitution.[45]

Some constitutional theorists are thought to lack such scruples. They are accused of claiming that courts may take it upon themselves to change the supreme law of the land. An example of such thinking is discussed by Justice Rehnquist, who quotes from a brief filed in federal court on behalf of state prisoners as follows:

> *We are asking a great deal of the Court because other branches of government have abdicated their responsibility. . . . Prisoners are like other "discrete and insular" minorities for whom the Court must spread its protective umbrella because no other branch of government will do so. . . . This Court, as the voice and conscience of contemporary society, as the measure of the modern conception of human dignity, must declare that the [named prison] and all it represents offends the Constitution of the United States and will not be tolerated.*[46]

Rehnquist understands this to imply that "nonelected members of the federal judiciary may address themselves to a social problem simply because other branches of government have failed or refused to do so."[47] Federal judges would then have "a roving commission to second-guess Congress, state legislatures, and state and federal administrative officers concerning what is best for the country."[48] Rehnquist accordingly describes such a view as "a formula for an end run around popular government, genuinely corrosive of the fundamental values of our democratic society."[49]

Rehnquist's rhetoric is fired by "democratic" flames, so let us look more closely at this argument from democracy. It challenges the legitimacy of judicial review. If we were to formulate the argument rigorously, its conclusion would amount to the following proposition:

> *Judicial review of a non-judicial decision violates democratic principles to the extent that the reviewing judiciary is less directly accountable to a popular electorate than is the non-judicial decision maker.*

To reach this conclusion, a premise like the following is needed:

> *Democratic principles imply that the more directly accountable an official decision maker is to a popular electorate, the greater the priority that should be given her official decisions.*

This claim is dubious. It assumes that democratic standards apply directly to the several branches of a political structure, although the several branches are supposed to complement each other so as to yield a structure that is democratic overall. On the contrary, just as various amendments to the Constitution can be understood as promoting the system's respect for democratic values, rather than compromising that commitment, judicial review may be instrumental in securing that respect.

The sort of premise that seems to be needed by the standard argument against judicial review invokes "democracy" in a problematic way. It seems to invoke a theory of the Constitution. But no attempt is made to explain what relation such a view must have to the Constitution if the former is to qualify as a theory of the latter, no less how a particular theory might be defended. This is especially important because it is uncertain whether any view can both qualify as a theory of the Constitution, to be used in constitutional interpretation, and be reconciled with "strict" originalism.

More generally, the premise of the standard argument from democracy fails to reflect any appreciation of the values that might explain the importance of accountability to a popular electorate. It is implausible to suppose that "electoral accountability" is a fundamental value. That it is not is suggested, for example, by the qualifications that one would reasonably place on electoral accountability before it could serve in such a role; for example, that elections be free and fair. This strongly suggests that electoral accountability derives its importance from some more fundamental value, such as the right to participate in shaping the rules that may be enforced against oneself or, perhaps, political equality. These values and their relation to electoral accountability require clarification. Until we understand the basic values at stake, we can hardly determine the relation between judicial review and a commitment to democracy. And yet the literature on judicial review is silent on such matters.

Now, a federal judge might find it awkward to endorse the argument from democracy. For it suggests that the constitutional system is "democratic" in such a way as to make judicial review illegitimate. One who endorses such an argument might find it difficult to function honestly in the federal judiciary, where judicial review is firmly established.

It turns out, however, that the argument from democracy is used not to block judicial review but, rather, to establish a presumption against it. It is thought to counsel "restraint." This is illustrated by Rehnquist's response to the argument from democracy. He does not reject judicial review. He endorses it on the ground that the constitutional arrangements including judicial review are given by "the people."[50] Unfortunately, Rehnquist's version of this claim is no more plausible than the one we considered in section II. A specious argument receives a glib reply.

It should be observed, finally, that Rehnquist charges those he criticizes as favoring "the substitution of some other set of values for those which may be derived from the language and intent of the framers."[51] As this formulation suggests, his argument really turns on how the Constitution is to be understood. The quoted brief claimed, after all, that courts have a special responsibility to protect "discrete and insular minorities." This is a proposition with which some constitutional scholars agree.[52] They hold this responsibility to be based on the Constitution, not created by judicial fiat. Rehnquist disagrees with this interpretation and treats its proponents as if they recommend infidelity to the Constitution.

VI. The Wages of Skepticism

An initially more promising argument regarding judicial review is presented by Professor (now Judge) Bork, who begins by rejecting the crude argument from democracy and by describing our constitutional system as "Madisonian":

> *A Madisonian system is not completely democratic, if by "democratic" we mean completely majoritarian. It assumes that in wide areas of life majorities are entitled to rule for no better reason than they are majorities. We need not pause here to examine the philosophical underpinnings of that assumption since it is a "given" in our society. . . .*[53]

Bork refrains from reflecting on the values that are at stake. This may be deliberate, for reasons that will emerge presently. But it is unfortunate because Bork, too, appears to offer us a theory of the Constitution.

Bork claims that "the Madisonian model" has two "premises." One is "majoritarian," the other "counter-majoritarian."

> *The model . . . assumes there are some areas of life a majority should not control. There are some things a majority should not do to us no matter how democratically it decides to do them.*[54]

To reconcile these "premises," we charge the Supreme Court to "define both majority and minority freedom through the interpretation of the Constitution."[55] Thus Bork accepts the legitimacy of judicial review. But, he says,

> *the Court's power is legitimate only if it has, and can demonstrate in reasoned opinions that it has, a valid theory, derived from the Constitution, of the respective spheres of majority and minority freedom. If it does not have such a theory but merely imposes its own value choices, or worse if it pretends to have a theory but actually follows its own predilections, the Court violates the postulates of the Madisonian model that alone justifies its power.*[56]

This passage suggests Bork's concern that the Court not impose its own "value choices."

He explains that concern in the course of an argument that appears more promising than Rehnquist's because it deals with the issues at a more fundamental level. Bork's argument may be summarized as follows:

1. Judicial decisions *should be* "principled."
2. Judicial decisions either *make* or *implement* "value choices."
3. Judicial decisions that *implement* "value choices" *can* be "principled."
4. There is *no* "principled" way to *make* a "value choice."
5. Judicial decisions *should implement,* rather than make, "value choices."
6. Law-creation, such as legislation or the framing of a constitution, involves *making* "value choices."
7. "Courts [reviewing legislation] must accept any value choice the legislature makes unless it clearly runs contrary to a choice made in the framing of the Constitution."[57]

This argument is originalist in spirit, if not entirely in content. An originalist theory of interpretation is suggested by the notion that certain "value choices" were made by the framers and are now available to be implemented by the courts. This corresponds to the idea that Constitutional doctrines are fixed when the document is framed. An originalist theory of adjudication is suggested too, as Bork comes near to claiming that only those doctrines embodying the "framers' value choices" should be applied by the Court.

Note that the last step in the argument appears to presuppose a nonoriginalist principle:

Whenever the Constitution is unclear, the Court should defer to the legislature.

What basis could there be for such a doctrine of "restraint"? Bork has no grounds for suggesting, for example, that the practice of judicial review should be confined because it suffers under a cloud of illegitimacy. For, as we have seen, he has rejected the dubious argument from democracy, endorsed the practice of judicial review, and assigned it an indispensable constitutional function.

Here is one possible explanation of that last step in Bork's reasoning. As we have observed, many legal theorists embrace assumptions about meaning which lead them to believe that law is indeterminate when it is unclear. As we shall presently see, Bork explicitly endorses an even more radical type of philosophical skepticism—about value judgments generally. It would therefore not be out of keeping for Bork to indulge in the semantical skepticism that leaps from "unclear" to "indeterminate." This would lead him to reason that, when (a) the Constitution does not *clearly* contain a doctrine that is violated by a piece of legislation, then (b) the Constitution contains *no* such doctrine, (c) the legislation does not violate the Constitution, and (d) the legislation should accordingly be accepted by the Court.[58]

But the most serious difficulty with Bork's reasoning derives from his value skepticism. To see this, we might begin by asking what is meant by a "value choice." This expression is so commonplace in constitutional theory that we may need to remind ourselves that it is an artifact of theory. Compare the expression with "value judgment." "Value choice" omits any reference to judgment, and so encourages the suggestion of arbitrariness and discourages any contrary suggestion of rational defensibility. The difference fits nicely into Bork's strategy of argument, which explicitly invokes a general philosophical doctrine of skepticism about the rational defensibility of value judgments.

As we have seen, Bork defines the central problem of "Madisonian democracy" as the need to strike a balance between "majority and minority freedom."[59] It is precisely in this context that he says, for example:

> *Every clash between a minority claiming freedom and a majority claiming power to regulate involves a choice between gratifications of the two groups. When the Constitution has not spoken, the Court will be able to find no scale, other than its own value preferences,*

> *upon which to weigh the respective claims to pleasure.*[60]

Bork has two examples. One is *Griswold,* which he views as a judicial choice between two "claims to pleasure" and their respective "gratifications." Another is "a hypothetical suit by an electric company and one of its customers to void a smoke pollution ordinance as unconstitutional. The cases are identical."[61]

To make Bork's position perfectly clear, we should consider a different example. Prior to the Fourteenth Amendment, Bork would presumably respond to a suit seeking invalidation of a law banning Jews and Catholics from certain occupations, as follows:

> *There is no way of deciding these matters other than by reference to some system of moral or ethical values that has no objective or intrinsic validity of its own and about which men can and do differ. Where the Constitution does not embody the moral or ethical choice, the judge has no basis other than his own values upon which to set aside the community judgment embodied in the statute.*[62]

My point is not that a refusal to invalidate the statute would have been unfaithful to the law, for the contrary interpretation is, unfortunately, plausible. My point is that Bork's express reason for a judicial policy of "restraint" is that all opposing positions, including the rejection of bigotry, are rationally indefensible, so that, lacking constitutional warrant, a judicial decision favoring one would be "unprincipled" *just because* any "preference" for one side or the other *could not be* "principled." Value "choices" are required to adjudicate between any two opposing views, because moral and political positions are in Bork's view equivalent to preferences. The judicial vindication of a morally motivated claim is likewise equivalent, in his eyes, to favoring one person's gratification over another's. But:

> *There is no principled way to decide that one man's gratifications are more deserving of respect than another's or that one form of gratification is more worthy than another.*[63]

Such "value choices" might be made by judges or derived from the Constitution. If made by judges, Bork maintains, the judicial decisions in which they are embodied are "unprincipled," because value judgments are in general "unprincipled."

> *Where constitutional materials do not clearly specify the value to be preferred, there is no*

principled way to prefer any claimed human value to any other.[64]

But if the "value choices" are derived from the Constitution, then the judicial decisions implementing them are "principled."

It is important to emphasize that in these passages Bork is *not* simply asserting the standard originalist claim that judges reviewing legislation should not impose their own values, but should apply doctrines derived from the Constitution. For that is what he is trying to prove. He is arguing, in effect, that *when the Constitution is unclear and interpretation of it may seem to require moral reasoning,* judges should defer to the legislature. His philosophical skepticism is deployed to show that judges should make no value judgments when deciding constitutional cases.

That is relevant to an earlier argument of this paper. The alternative to "strict" originalism that was sketched in section III requires that courts applying "vague clauses" of the Constitution interpret "contested concepts," which requires reasoning about moral or political principles. Bork's view that judges should not make "value choices" seems to mean that courts should not engage in any such reasoning. Bork reasons: judicial review should be neutral, principled, and nonarbitrary; it is impossible to make value judgments that are neutral, principled, or nonarbitrary; so judges should not incorporate value judgments into their constitutional decisions.

Bork's value skepticism is assumed and applied without justification.[65] Needless to say, value skepticism cannot be found within the Constitution. Indeed, the two are clearly incompatible. Thus Bork invokes an *anti*-constitutional doctrine to significant effect.

It is worth noting that Bork's skepticism renders his overall position incoherent. Consider his claim that judges *should* decide constitutional cases in a certain way—that (as he seems to argue) they are *under an obligation* to do so. Bork writes as if he is providing a rational defense for that sort of conclusion about the responsible, legitimate use of judicial power. He appears to believe that his reasoning excludes contrary conceptions of judicial obligation. In his terminology, however, to embrace such a doctrine is to make a "value choice," which according to his value skepticism is irremediably "unprincipled," or rationally indefensible.

The result is a dilemma for Bork. If it is possible to provide good reasons (as Bork purports to do) for his conception of the legitimate (justified, responsible) exercise of judicial power—reasons designed to show that his conception is superior to contrary conceptions—then "value choices" can be principled. On the one hand, the success of any argument for the attribution of an obligation to judges would refute his value skepticism and undermine his argument that value judgments have no legitimate place in constitutional adjudication. On the other hand, his wholesale value skepticism excludes the possibility that any conception of the legitimate exercise of judicial power might be rationally defensible; so his skepticism undermines his own argument for and resulting judgment about responsible adjudication.

Consider now Bork's notion that judges must rely upon the value judgments that are embedded in the Constitution if their decisions are to be "principled." Bork assumes that decisions involving the exercise of judicial review can be "principled" insofar as they are grounded upon constitutional doctrines. This apparently means that the decisions can be justified relative to, or conditional upon, those doctrines.

But conditional justification is only as good as its condition. Recall that one piece of Bork's argument goes as follows:

> *Law-creation, such as legislation or the framing of a constitution, involves making "value choices."*

Another piece says:

> *There is no principled way to make a "value choice."*

Put together, these pieces yield the conclusion that the "value choices" embodied in the Constitution and the corresponding doctrines are themselves "unprincipled" or, in other words, unjustifiable. But if the doctrines on which the justification of judicial decisions depends are themselves unjustifiable, then the same applies to those decisions.

This means that Bork is faced with another dilemma. On the one hand, if "value choices" are unjustifiable, then so are the "value choices" reflected in the Constitution, and the same applies to all that relies on them for justification. On the other hand, if some value judgments can be justified (such as the idea that the Constitution merits respect), then Bork's general value skepticism is unsound, and his main argument collapses.

Bork might seem to avoid this particular incoherence when he remarks that his value skepticism "is not applicable to legislation. Legislation requires value choice and cannot be principled in the sense under discussion."[66] Bork might seem to suggest that there is another sense of "principled" in which the "value choices" embodied in legislation (and thus the legislation itself) can be "principled." Bork might mean, for example, that, rationally defensible or not, legislation by popularly elected officials is *permissible* under both democratic principles and our constitutional system. He might also wish to infer from this that those subject to such laws are under an obligation to respect them.

But this interpretation would not enable Bork to avoid the dilemma. Either he accepts the idea that democratic standards *justify* political arrangements that satisfy them, or he rejects it, presumably because of his value skepticism. If he rejects the idea, then there is no apparent sense within Bork's skeptical system in which legislation or indeed our constitutional system can be justifiable; there is no apparent sense in which the Constitution can *truly* be said to merit respect, in which judges can *truly* be said to be under an obligation to respect it. If Bork believes that any of these value judgments can *truly* be justified, then he must forsake his objection based on value skepticism to the exercise of moral judgment within judicial review.

VII. Conclusion

Originalism seems to derive its initial plausibility from a simplified conception of how written constitutions work. Interpretation in terms of original intent promises a stable, uncontroversial version of the Constitution. But intentionalism faces overwhelming difficulties and appears to lack compensating justification, either in political or linguistic terms. Seeing no promising alternatives, opponents of strict originalism have accepted the need for extra-constitutional doctrines in constitutional adjudication. Originalists appear to reject such heterodoxy, but they unselfconsciously embrace a variety of extra-constitutional doctrines. Their theorizing about the Constitution tends toward the superficially descriptive and has yet to face the substantive value commitments implicit even in ritualistic appeals to democracy. Just as the Constitution cannot be value-free, so our understanding of it must be informed by reflection on the principles it serves.

---

1. *Brest,* The Misconceived Quest for the Original Understanding, *60 B.U. L. Rev. 204 (1980).*

2. *At the same time, it seems that most if not all theorists hold that constitutional cases may sometimes be decided by rules that cannot be attributed to the Constitution. We shall touch on "nonoriginalism" in section III.*

3. *See, e.g., John Ely,* Democracy and Distrust, *ch. 2 (1980); Brest,* The Misconceived Quest; *Dworkin,* The Forum of Principle, *56 N.Y.U. L. Rev. 469–500 (1981); and Schauer,* An Essay on Constitutional Language, *29 UCLA L. Rev. 797 (1982). MacCallum,* Legislative Intent, *75 Yale L.J. 754 (1966) applies here too.*

4. *Bork,* Neutral Principles and Some First Amendment Problems, *47 Indiana L.J. 1 (1971).*

5. *Meese,* Construing the Constitution, *19 U.C. Davis L. Rev. 22 (1985).*

6. *Rehnquist,* The Notion of a Living Constitution, *54 Texas L. Rev. 693 (1976).*

7. *Brest also draws a distinction between "strict" and "moderate" originalism, which I take up below.*

8. *On this view, the meaning of an amendment would presumably be fixed when (or by the time) it was ratified, and its incorporation into the Constitution would presumably modify (and in that sense fix anew) the doctrinal content of the Constitution as a whole.*

9. *I shall occasionally use "author" to refer to such an exclusive subclass of the population.*

10. *This covers both species of intentionalism in Brest's typology. "Strict intentionalism requires the interpreter to determine how the adopters would have applied a provision to a given situation, and to apply it accordingly." (Brest,* The Misconceived Quest, *p. 222) This permits "intentions" to include general principles, as most original intent theorists appear to accept. "A moderate intentionalist applies a provision consistent with the adopters' intent at a relatively high level of generality, consistent with what is sometimes*

called 'the purpose of the provision' " *(ibid., p. 223) The words I have emphasized suggest the view that "intentions" are relatively concrete or specific whereas "purposes" are relatively abstract or general, so that an appeal to original intent, strictly speaking, should be limited to the former. Brest does not defend this view, which does not square with his definition of "strict intentionalism" and is not required by the concept of intent. On the relevance of abstract intentions, see Dworkin,* The Forum of Principle.

11. *The most plausible criterion in such cases—which are, of course, most directly relevant here—would refer to the meaning of a text that has been adopted as authoritative. But that criterion would subordinate intentionalism to textualism and would make authors' intent a derivative rather than a basic determinant of meaning. I am here considering intentionalism as a basic general theory of constitutional interpretation. I am not considering, for example, the idea that considerations of original intent may for one reason or another properly play a secondary, subordinate, or supplementary role in constitutional interpretation.*

12. *See Ely,* Democracy and Distrust; *Brest,* The Misconceived Quest; *Dworkin,* The Forum of Principle; *Schauer,* An Essay on Constitutional Language; *and MacCallum,* Legislative Intent.

13. *Barron v.* The Mayor and City Council of Baltimore, *7 Pet. 243, 8 L. Ed. 672 (1833).*

14. *This point does not presuppose a general theory of text meaning. The argument of section III would seem to imply, however, that the meaning of a text is not determined solely by linguistic conventions.*

15. *See my* Derivability, Defensibility, and the Justification of Judicial Decisions, *68 The Monist 325 (1985).*

16. *Insofar as such interpretation is, in fact, intentionalist. It seems relevant that contractual interpretation is not purely a matter of actual intent, but is also regulated by legal norms.*

17. *The idea of popular sovereignty was reflected in constitutional rhetoric from early on. It became increasingly reflected in the constitutional system as time passed, as major changes occurred in the Republic, including of course major constitutional amendments.*

18. *This aspect of that theory is discussed by H. L. A. Hart, The Concept of Law 41–43 (1961).*

19. *Brest,* The Misconceived Quest, *p. 204.*

20. *ibid., p. 208.*

21. *ibid., p. 223.*

22. *Actually, Brest seems to believe that moderate* textualism *amounts to the only plausible originalist alternative to "strict" intentionalism, as he says that "moderate textualism and intentionalism closely resemble each other in methodology and results." ibid.*

23. *ibid., pp. 205, 223.*

24. *Hart,* The Concept of Law, *pp. 121–132.*

25. *Compare Brest,* The Misconceived Quest, *p. 225. For a work that might be considered "nonoriginalist," see M.J. Perry, The Constitution, the Courts, and Human Rights (1982).*

26. *We shall consider the originalist approach to this issue in section V.*

27. *R. Dworkin, Taking Rights Seriously 132–137 (1977). This suggestion is independent of other aspects of Dworkin's legal theory.*

28. *J. Rawls, A Theory Of Justice 5, 10 (1971).*

29. *If a court works under a doctrine of precedent, then the criterion of a justifiable interpretation cannot simply be fidelity to the "original" Constitution. In that case, past judicial interpretations can presumably affect the content of a justifiable interpretation, even when those past interpretations were mistaken. I ignore that complication here.*

30. *We should distinguish such philosophical skepticism about values from concern about the difficulty a court might have trying to identify the best conception of a contested political concept (even when the alternatives are severely limited in number) and from an appreciation of the fact that any attempt to identify the best conception is likely to be controversial. We may also assume that reasonable judges can differ in their interpretations. It should be emphasized, however, that approaches to judicial review that seek to avoid controversial interpretations of the Constitution cannot be assumed to be justifiable by reference to the "original" Constitution. That is precisely one of the points at issue here.*

31. *I address some aspects of this issue in Ethics and the Rule of Law, ch. 1 (1984).*

32. *Section VI.*

33. *Interpretation by reference to "original intent" also, of course, draws upon information outside the "four corners" of the text.*

34. *A theory of adjudication would seem to presuppose an independently determined interpretation of the Constitution, to fix whatever is (or is not) to be applied.*

35. *Thayer,* The Origin and Scope of the American Doctrine of Constitutional Law, *7 Harv. L. Rev. 129 (1893).*

36. *These are Thayer's chief arguments for judicial deference. Although he nods in the direction of democratic sentiments, he expresses little respect for the virtue, sense, or competence of legislators, but he fears their collective power.*

37. *Thayer,* The Origin, *p. 150 (emphasis in the original).*

38. *R. Berger, Government By Judiciary 412 (1977).*

39. *ibid., pp. 412–413.*

40. *Monaghan,* Our Perfect Constitution, *56 N.Y.U. L. Rev. 387–391 (1981); and* Taking Supreme Court Decisions Seriously, *39 Maryland L. Rev. 1–12 (1979).*

We are presumably concerned here with precedents on the same court level, as distinct from precedents that are binding due to the hierarchical structure of a layered court system.

41. *Monaghan,* Our Perfect Constitution, *p. 389; compare* Taking Supreme Court Decisions Seriously, *p. 7.*

Lawyers seem to favor consequentialist arguments for precedent over the notion that precedent is grounded upon the fairness of treating like cases alike. For a discussion of this alternative, see Lyons, Formal Justice and Judicial Precedent, *38 Vanderbilt L. Rev. 495 (1985).*

42. *Perhaps Monaghan would like to limit the use of consequentialist argument in some unexplained way. It will be difficult to show, however, that such limitations are not ad hoc. Indeed, Monaghan's consequentialist strategy of argument threatens to get completely out of hand. For his argument commits him to approving all principles whose use would serve any values that are as desirable as "stability and predictability." It may also be noted that insofar as originalist doctrine, such as strict intentionalism, appeals to past judicial practice, its originalist credentials must be as problematic as those of a doctrine of precedent.*

43. *Monaghan distinguishes the doctrine of precedent that is needed for constitutional cases from "common law analogies" because of differences in details, and he may infer from these differences that the constitutional doctrine could not be based on common law traditions;* Taking Supreme Court Decisions Seriously, *p. 12. But that reasoning is dubious.*

44. *See, e.g., Van Alstyne,* Interpreting This Constitution: The Unhelpful Contributions of Special Theories of Judicial Review, *35 U. Fla. L. Rev. 229 (1983).*

45. *This assumes, of course, that judicial review can be justified despite the argument from democracy. We shall return to that point presently.*

46. *Rehnquist,* The Notion of a Living Constitution, *54 Texas L. Rev. 695 (1976).*

47. *ibid.*

48. *ibid., p. 698.*

49. *ibid., p. 706.*

50. *ibid., p. 696.*

51. *ibid., p. 695.*

52. *See, e.g., Ely,* Democracy and Distrust.

53. *Bork,* Neutral Principles, *pp. 2–3.*

54. *ibid., p. 3.*

55. *ibid.*

56. *ibid.*

57. *ibid., pp. 10–11.*

58. *This assumes the use of a burden-of-proof rule discussed in section V.*

59. *Bork,* Neutral Principles, *p. 3.*

60. *ibid., p. 9.*

61. *ibid.*

62. *ibid., p. 10.*

63. *ibid., Bork's note explains: "The impossibility is related to that of making interpersonal comparisons of utilities." He apparently assumes that if there is any morally defensible criterion for making decisions (including those adjudicating interpersonal conflicts of interest), it is that they should maximize (in Bork's terms) "gratifications." The alleged impossibility to which he refers would make that criterion impossible to satisfy. Normative welfare economics avoids the problem by giving up the maximizing requirement and replacing it with a conception of economic efficiency, such as Pareto's, that requires no interpersonal comparisons of utility. Bork's note suggests that he is unaware of or refuses to consider either economic or deontological alternatives to classical utilitarianism.*

64. *ibid., p. 8.*

65. *But see note 63.*

66. *Bork,* Neutral Principles, *p. 8.*

PART THREE

Justice

The framework for discussing questions about justice comes to us rather directly from the ancient Greeks. Even when they disagreed strongly among themselves about the justice of particular political policies, the leading Greek philosophers were agreed that there is some basic connection between the ideas of justice and *equality*. But only the extreme radicals, those who called themselves "democrats," thought that in all the contexts of justice, benefits and burdens must be allocated with perfect equality. Aristotle maintained that distributive justice, for example, does not consist in absolute equality (that is, perfectly equal shares for all those among whom something is to be distributed) but rather in a proportionate equality, which is to say an equality of ratios. What justice requires, he insisted, is that equal cases be treated alike (equally), and that unequal cases be treated unalike (unequally) in direct proportion to the relevant differences (inequalities) between them, so that between any two persons the ratio between their shares (S_1 : S_2) should equal the ratio between their qualifying characteristics (C_1 : C_2).

Aristotle conceded that people disagree over which characteristics of persons should be taken into account in assessing their qualifications, but all parties to these disagreements (except those who insisted upon absolute equality) employed tacitly the notion of proportionate equality. However merit is conceived, for example, those for whom it would be the sole criterion in awarding shares would give one person twice as large a share of some benefit as they would to any other person deemed only half as meritorious. The common object of these distributors, even when they disagree over what merit is, is to divide shares into a ratio (2 : 1) equal to the ratio of the merits of the two persons (2 : 1). Such distributions are sometimes necessarily impressionistic (how can one person's merit be seen to be exactly one-half of another's?). But, when the criterion of merit is exactly definable, and the shares themselves can be measured in terms of money, the calculations can sometimes achieve a mathematical precision.

Since any two persons will be unequal in some respects and equal in others, Aristotle's theory of distributive justice is incomplete until he tells us which personal characteristics are *relevant* factors to be considered in the balancing of ratios. Various criteria of relevance have been proposed by writers of different schools. Some have held that A's share should be to B's share as A's ability is to B's ability, or as A's moral virtue is to B's, or as A's labor is to B's, and so on. All the above maxims could be said to specify different forms of merit, so that a meritarian theorist would be one who held that the only personal characteristics relevant to a just distribution of goods are such forms of personal merit. Aristotle was undoubtedly a meritarian in this broad sense. Meritarian social philosophers, then, can disagree among themselves over which forms of merit are relevant and over criteria for assessing a given form of merit. In addition, they might hold that some forms of merit are relevant to some types of distribution, and other merits to other types. A nonmeritarian theory would find exclusive relevance in personal characteristics (for example, needs) that are in no sense merits, and of course mixed theories are also possible. Even a "democratic" or "equalitarian" theory, one that is wholly nonmeritarian, might plausibly be said to employ tacitly Aristotle's *analysis* of distributive justice as proportionate equality while rejecting of course Aristotle's suggested criteria of relevance. Even a perfect equalitarian would presumably wish to endorse such maxims as: *A*'s share should be to *B*'s share as *A*'s needs are to *B*'s needs, or as *A*'s "infinite human worth" is to *B*'s "infinite human worth" (that is, the same). It seems likely, therefore, that all complete theories of social justice must contain maxims specifying relevant characteristics, and that all of them presuppose Aristotle's formal analysis of distributive justice as proportionate equality between shares and relevant characteristics.

The Machinery of Justice: Three Sample Procedural Problems

In the modern world the principles of justice often seem far removed from the procedures of a legal system in operation. Attempts to do justice generate further problems of justice, which philosophers of law can take up with equal relish.

The essay by John H. Langbein, "Torture and Plea Bargaining," describes the serious problems that surround the procedure for disposing of most criminal cases in America today. Criminal accusations are made the subject of negotiation rather than adjudication so that as little time, effort, and money as possible need be spent in dealing with criminal charges. Reducing the charge itself or reducing the sentence to be demanded on a particular charge is offered in exchange for a guilty plea so that the burdensome business of a trial can be avoided. The accused is very rarely a free bargaining agent, and the result is frequently a coerced conviction. In other cases where there is serious crime, insupportable leniency mocks the very reason for a system of criminal justice. The system encourages the plea bargainer to believe that after getting caught, it is a matter mainly of getting a good deal or not. This works against the cultivation of a general law-abiding attitude in that part of the community most prone to crime. The overdeveloped adversarial system makes plea bargaining in some form necessary, in Langbein's view, and its evils can only be escaped by fundamental reforms that take the sort of approach to criminal justice that is seen in European countries.

Kent Greenawalt discusses another problem for justice that arises through operation of somewhat rusty "machinery of justice": the dilemma of jury nullification. This is a problem only in countries that use the jury system as a way of finding the facts to which the relevant rules, as specified in the instructions of the judge, are to be applied. In the Anglo-American jury system, jurors are aware both that they have a duty to obey the judge's instructions and that they have a legal power to disobey those instructions when their consciences direct them to do so in the interest of justice to a defendant. Professor Greenawalt's proposed guide to the perplexed juror dovetails nicely with Joel Feinberg's essay on civil disobedience in Part One.

The final article in this subsection presents a procedural problem concerning the moral limits of certain methods of criminal law enforcement. For many years, and in many countries, police have set traps for criminals by providing them with apparent opportunities, not to mention temptations and inducements, to commit crimes. In the majority of these cases, where the victim was predisposed to commit the very crime he is "trapped" into committing, there is no problem for justice. But as Gerald Dworkin points out, it is sometimes morally disturbing to realize that, but for the police conduct, this particular prisoner would never have committed this crime, now or ever.

Justice and Compensation

Aristotle's concept of corrective justice (distinguished in the *Nichomachean Ethics* from distributive justice) is what we think of as the basis of compensation to an injured party when the one who injures is required to pay damages. Recently the foundations of the law of torts (and other areas of law) have been radically reinterpreted along lines of economic theory. The legal theorists who are doing the reinterpretation suggest that notions of justice can be better understood in terms of economic efficiency. In tort law perhaps more than in any other branch of law, the economic consequences of rules of liability seem to have great influence. Exactly what role, however, those consequences have played in the past or should play in the future is a matter of considerable dispute. In his article entitled "The Concept of Corrective Justice in Recent Theories of Tort law," Richard Posner, the leading figure among modern economic revisionist scholars, argues that the theory of wealth maximization (his cardinal principle of economic interpretation) leads to results in tort law that are virtually the same as the orthodox theory of corrective justice propounded by Aristotle. Posner even suggests that economic theory may well provide the reason lacking in Aristotle's work for a duty to redress injuries. In his initial reply to various critics, Posner provides the reader with illuminating discussion not only of Aristotle's theory, but also of points that must be resolved by any comprehensive theory of compensation. It is natural to feel that somehow this economic interpretation misses the most important considerations in doing justice between the parties. At any rate, even those who remain skeptical will be intrigued and challenged to explain the considerable coincidence of justice and economic efficiency reflected by judicial decisions in tort cases.

Jules Coleman, a leading philosopher who is also Professor of Law at the Yale law school and one of the leading critics of the "law and economics" school, defends his own theory of the law of torts against attempts to reduce the maxims of justice to the principle of economic efficiency. Coleman's account of the role of tort law in a modern community is based squarely on a principle of corrective justice that Coleman finds similar to, but not identical with, that of Aristotle. Among their many differences, then, Posner and Coleman share a qualified respect for Aristotle's analysis of corrective justice.

Justice and Contract

This subsection presents a basic part of one of the leading philosophical theories of the law of contracts, and two somewhat opposed articles about one of the most highly publicized controversies in our time to be raised by a contractual agreement. The theory is that of Charles Fried of the Harvard Law School, formerly solicitor general of the United States, as expressed in his readable volume, *Contract as Promise*. The controversial contract case is that which was decided by the New Jersey Supreme Court in 1986, *In the Matter of Baby M*. Professor Fried's general theory of contract may or may not help the student come to a reasoned conviction on the problem of surrogate motherhood contracts, but it is more than worth reading, in any case, for its independent insights, especially about the connection between legal policy and the moral reasons supporting promissory obligations.

Seldom has the justice of a private contract occasioned so much public debate as the agreement between Mr. and Mrs. Whitehead, on the one hand, and

Mr. and Mrs. Stern, on the other, in the celebrated case of Baby M, settled in 1986 by the New Jersey Supreme Court. A large complex of philosophical and moral issues were involved in this, as in most surrogate mother cases. The Baby M case, unfortunately, tended to blur these issues because it involved so many extraneous and unhappy elements—a badly drawn agreement, a predictable mind change, kidnapping, assault and battery, passion, anger, and noise. That is a shame, because even by 1986 there had been several hundred smooth and uneventful cases of women contracting, for an agreed-upon fee, to carry a baby that another woman was physically unable to bear to parturition. In the Baby M case Mr. Stern had fertilized Mrs. Whitehead's ovum by artificial insemination so that Baby M was descended genetically from the male adopter and the "gestational mother" (the woman who carried the child through gestation), but in other cases the ovum of the adopting woman herself is fertilized by her own husband's sperm and the resulting embryo is transferred to the surrogate's womb. In that kind of case the surrogate mother is not the biological mother.

Moral and policy issues involved in any case of surrogacy include the following: How can an act or transaction that is uncontroversially permissible when done without monetary charge be contrary to public policy, at the least, when done for money? How does money acquire this mysterious capacity to corrupt? (Prostitution is another example of this kind; so are sales by a next of kin of her deceased kinsman's healthy bodily organs, and sales, as opposed to charitable donations, of blood to hospitals.) Should lopsided contracts that protect the interests of one party far more than the other be enforceable, even at great cost to the naive and trusting weaker party? Or should the law be paternalistic and protect people from their own folly? Is there an important distinction between a court ordering damages for breach of contract and a court ordering specific performance? Can a woman ever give informed consent to an agreement that might lead her to relinquish a baby that she has (unforeseeably) decided to keep? Can we reconcile surrogacy contracts with the outright ban on new baby sales? The articles by Robin Fox and Bonnie Steinbock differ somewhat in emphasis and attitude: Fox is less impressed than Steinbock by the liberty to make contractual commitments. But both articles illustrate how philosophers who are both sensitive and sensible can hope to achieve agreement even on vexatious and emotional moral issues.

Justice, Affirmative Action, and Racial Quotas

Invidiously discriminatory treatment in the distribution of benefits (including opportunities) and burdens is the essential feature of what Aristotle called distributive injustice. In the United States grossly discriminatory rules and practices have only recently begun to crumble, and for the first time in centuries there is hope that the ideal of equal opportunity will one day be fulfilled. To expect the effects of racial and sexual discrimination to vanish overnight with the abrogation of ancient rules, however, would be exceedingly naive. Many reformers, in fact, have been urging that the elimination of discriminatory practices is not enough, and that a kind of reverse discrimination, especially in the allocation of educational and professional opportunities for such groups as blacks and women, is required by social justice. Programs of affirmative action (that is, of active recruitment of minorities even in some cases at the expense of apparently better qualified majority males) are full of moral dangers and raise many misgivings even among those of us who find racism utterly odious. Chief of these misgivings is the fear that injustice to one group is being sought by means that are unjust to another, and that that is not an effective way to promote the cause of justice generally. Others have feared the effects on the beneficiaries themselves, as they become targets of skeptical disrespect from those who infer that they have found success in the world only because of favoritism. That general suspicion especially hurts those many professionally successful blacks who more than hold their own in fair competition with whites.

Because of these and similar worries, defenders of affirmative action programs have felt obliged to argue that justice is on the side of affirmative action. Those arguments, even when winning plaudits from those already inclined to agree, have not won many converts from among the skeptics. By and large, the arguments for affirmative action have been of two kinds. Forward-looking arguments base their case on the long-term contributions of pump-priming efforts now to increased economic parity and political power for blacks in the future, greater respect for blacks as more and more of them achieve middle-class status without the aid of special advantages, and more social stability and freedom from disruptive violence. Among other such consequential benefits, one can mention the benefit to black children that comes from having black schoolteachers, doctors, and other professionals to deal with daily.

The second class of arguments for affirmative action are backward looking. They focus on the great wrongs committed against blacks in the past and the enormous debt whites have inherited. These debts, the arguments state, require whites to rectify those wrongs through a program of reparations in which affirmative action plays a central role. Some of the arguments in these two categories have genuine merit and have scored points. But none has been very convincing to the firemen, policemen, medical students, and professors who believe that they have lost their jobs, or their job security, just because their employers had to fill quotas assigned to minorities.

Both of the authors in this section are sympathetic to affirmative action, but dissatisfied with the way it has been defended in the past, partly because of its inadequate message to resentful displaced whites (Nagel's emphasis) and partly because unexamined possibilities for justification, quite apart from the future advantage and past-looking reparation categories, have been neglected (Hill's emphasis). Although Nagel's article was published twenty years ago (1973) it sounds like a fresh new voice, in harmony with that of Hill, in his very recent article (1991). Thomas Nagel is Professor of Philosophy and Law at New York University. Thomas Hill is Professor of Philosophy at the University of North Carolina, Chapel Hill.

Legal Injustices to Women: Feminist Analysis

The final subsection of Part Three has a title that may at first startle the reader: Legal Injustices to Women. The unifying theme is that our laws are mainly the work of men in courts and legislatures that rarely included women. There is no logical necessity, of course, that mostly male legislatures and judges must be unfair to women, but nonetheless there is a grave danger that men will not be able to share the point of view of women, that they will assume without thought that a woman's outlook on the world is essentially the same as their own in all particulars. In that event they will lack empathy with, and therefore understanding of, women in their roles as litigants in courts of law. As Kim Lane Scheppele puts it, "Women have experiences of the world that are not the same as men's," and failure to see the world through women's eyes leads first to misunderstanding and then, naturally enough, to injustice.

That is not to say that traditional legal rules are without exception entirely unfair to the women to whom they apply. Some of the cases considered in this section are genuinely controversial. But it is plain that many traditional legal rules—for example, those in the law of rape—have been severely unjust to women. Even these "plain" cases, however, are such that deciding how to improve things is complex and difficult, not at all obvious. The problems illustrated in the section are rape, sincere but unreasonable mistake as to consent, the battered-woman defense to homicide (and the so-called battered woman's syndrome, which can paralyze the resolve of women in serious danger from their husbands), and sexual harassment.

The final article, *"Michael M.* v. *Superior Court of Sonoma County,* can be interpreted as illustrating an injustice to males, or at least males like the defendant, Michael M. Perhaps it shows how gender injustice need not, in the very nature of things, victimize women only. The petitioner in this U.S. Supreme Court case claimed that the California statutory rape statute unlawfully discriminated on the basis of gender, since men alone were criminally liable under the statute. Among other matters, the primary issue was whether the ground for treating men and women under the age of eighteen differently was an arbitrary one or whether the different roles of men and women in sexual relations were highly relevant to a legitimate state purpose in treating them differently. Many of the reforms that have helped women's "liberation" in the last two decades have proceeded from arguments that certain differences between men and women are arbitrary ones, not relevant to any legitimate regulative concern. In this case Chief Justice Rehnquist found a way of arguing that a statute that can send a 17½-year-old male to prison for an "unlawful" sexual encounter with a 16½-year-old female, but can impose no criminal liability on the female, is not unconstitutional discrimination on the basis of gender.

The Machinery of Justice: Three Sample Procedural Problems

TORTURE AND PLEA BARGAINING*

John H. Langbein

The American system of plea bargaining is becoming a subject of immense academic and public attention. A dozen books have appeared in the last year or so describing plea bargaining as observed in one forum or another. The law reviews are full of writing about the details; a special issue of the *Law and Society Review* is now offering 20 more articles. The general theme of much of the current writing is that although, arguably, plea bargaining might be in need of various operational reforms, the basic institution is natural, inevitable, universal, and just.

In this essay I shall set forth some of the case against plea bargaining from a perspective that must appear bizarre, although I hope to show that it is illuminating. I am going to contrast the modern American system of plea bargaining with the medieval European law of torture. My thesis is that there are remarkable parallels in origin, in function, and even in specific points of doctrine, between the law of torture and the law of plea bargaining. I shall suggest that these parallels expose some important truths about how

criminal justice systems respond when their trial procedures fall into deep disorder.

The Law of Torture

For about half a millennium, from the middle of the thirteenth century to the middle of the eighteenth, a system of judicial torture lay at the heart of Continental criminal procedure. In our own day the very word "torture" is, gladly enough, a debased term. It has come to mean anything unpleasant, and we hear people speak of a tortured interpretation of a poem, or the torture of a dull dinner party. In discussions of contemporary criminal procedure we hear the word applied to describe illegal police practices or crowded prison conditions. But torture as the medieval European lawyers understood it had nothing to do with official misconduct or with criminal sanctions. Rather, the application of torture was a routine and judicially

*John H. Langbein, "Torture and Plea Bargaining," *The Public Interest*, No. 58, Winter 1980, pp. 43–61. Reprinted by permission of *The Public Interest*.

supervised feature of European criminal procedure. Under certain circumstances the law permitted the criminal courts to employ physical coercion against suspected criminals in order to induce them to confess. The law went to great lengths to limit this technique of extorting confessions to cases in which it was thought that the accused was highly likely to be guilty, and to surround the use of torture with other procedural safeguards that I shall discuss shortly.

This astonishing body of law grew up on the Continent as an adjunct to the law of proof—what we would call the system of trial—in cases of serious crime (for which the sanction was either death or severe physical maiming). The medieval law of proof was designed in the thirteenth century to replace an earlier system of proof, the ordeals, which the Roman Church effectively destroyed in the year 1215. The ordeals purported to achieve absolute certainty in criminal adjudication through the happy expedient of having the judgments rendered by God, who could not err. The replacement system of the thirteenth century aspired to achieve the same level of safeguard— absolute certainty—for human adjudication.

Although human judges were to replace God in the judgment seat, they would be governed by a law of proof so objective that it would make that dramatic substitution unobjectionable — a law of proof that would *eliminate human discretion* from the determination of guilt or innocence. Accordingly, the Italian Glossators who designed the system developed and entrenched the rule that conviction had to be based upon the testimony of two unimpeachable eyewitnesses to the gravamen of the crime—evidence that was, in the famous phrase, "clear as the noonday sun." Without these two eyewitnesses, a criminal court could not convict an accused who contested the charges against him. Only if the accused *voluntarily* confessed the offense could the court convict him without the eyewitness testimony.

Another way to appreciate the purpose of these rules is to understand their corollary: Conviction could not be based upon circumstantial evidence, because circumstantial evidence depends for its efficacy upon the subjective persuasion of the trier who decides whether to draw the inference of guilt from the evidence of circumstance. Thus, for example, it would not have mattered in this system that the suspect was seen running away from the murdered man's house and that the bloody dagger and the stolen loot were found in his possession. If no eyewitness saw him actually plunge the weapon into the victim, the court could not convict him.

In the history of Western culture no legal system has ever made a more valiant effort to perfect its safeguards and thereby to exclude completely the possibility of mistaken conviction. But the Europeans learned in due course the inevitable lesson. They had set the level of safeguard too high. They had constructed a system of proof that could as a practical matter be effective only in cases involving overt crime or repentant criminals. Because society cannot long tolerate a legal system that lacks the capacity to convict unrepentant persons who commit clandestine crimes, something had to be done to extend the system to those cases. The two-eyewitness rule was hard to compromise or evade, but the confession rule seemed to invite the subterfuge that in fact resulted. To go from accepting a voluntary confession to coercing a confession from someone against whom there was already strong suspicion was a step that began increasingly to be taken. The law of torture grew up to regulate this process of generating confessions.

The spirit of safeguard that had inspired the unworkable formal law of proof also permeated the subterfuge. The largest chapter of the European law of torture concerned the prerequisites for examination under torture. The European jurists devised what Anglo-American lawyers would today call a rule of probable cause, designed to assure that only persons highly likely to be guilty would be examined under torture. Thus, torture was permitted only when a so-called "half proof" had been established against the suspect. That meant either one eyewitness, or circumstantial evidence of sufficient gravity, according to a fairly elaborate tariff. In the example where a suspect was caught with the dagger and the loot, each of those indicia would be a quarter proof. Together they cumulated to a half proof, which was sufficient to permit the authorities to dispatch the suspect for a session in the local torture chamber.

In this way the prohibition against using circumstantial evidence was overcome. The law of torture found a place for circumstantial evidence, but a nominally subsidiary place. Circumstantial evidence was not consulted directly on the ultimate question, guilt or innocence, but on a question of interlocutory procedure—whether or not to examine the accused under torture. Even there the law attempted to limit judicial discretion by promulgating predetermined, ostensibly objective criteria for evaluating the indicia and assigning them numerical values (quarter proofs, half proofs, and the like). Vast legal treatises were compiled on this jurisprudence of torture to guide the examining magistrate in determining whether there was probable cause for torture.

In order to achieve a verbal or technical reconciliation with the requirement of the formal law of proof that the confession be voluntary, the medieval lawyers treated a confession extracted under torture as involuntary, hence ineffective, unless the accused repeated it free from torture at a hearing that was held a day or so later. Often enough the accused who had confessed under torture did recant when asked to confirm his confession. But seldom to avail: The examination under torture could thereupon be repeated. An accused who confessed under torture, recanted, and then found himself tortured anew, learned quickly enough that only a "voluntary" confession at the ratification hearing would save him from further agony in the torture chamber.

Fortunately, more substantial safeguards were devised to govern the actual application of torture. These were rules designed to enhance the reliability of the resulting confession. Torture was not supposed to be used to elicit an abject, unsubstantiated confession of guilt. Rather, torture was supposed to be employed in such a way that the accused would disclose the factual detail of the crime—information which, in the words of a celebrated German statute of the year 1532, "no innocent person can know." The examining magistrate was forbidden to engage in so-called suggestive questioning, in which the examiner supplied the accused with the detail he wanted to hear from him. Moreover, the information admitted under torture was supposed to be investigated and verified to the extent feasible. If the accused confessed to the slaying, he was supposed to be asked where he put the dagger. If he said he buried it under the old oak tree, the magistrate was supposed to send someone to dig it up.

Alas, these safeguards never proved adequate to overcome the basic flaw in the system. Because torture tests the capacity of the accused to endure pain, rather than his veracity, the innocent might (as one sixteenth-century commentator put it) yield to "the pain and torment and confess things that they never did." If the examining magistrate engaged in suggestive questioning, even accidentally, his lapse could not always be detected or prevented. If the accused knew something about the crime, but was still innocent of it, what he did know might be enough to give his confession verisimilitude. In some jurisdictions the requirement of verification was not enforced, or was enforced indifferently.

These shortcomings in the law of torture were identified even in the Middle Ages and were the subject of emphatic complaint in Renaissance and early modern times. The Europeans looked ever more admiringly at England, where the jury system—operating without the two-eyewitness rule—had never needed the law of torture. In the eighteenth century, as the law of torture was finally about to be abolished along with the system of proof that had required it, Beccaria and Voltaire became famous as critics of judicial torture; but they were latecomers to a critical legal literature nearly as old as the law of torture itself. Judicial torture survived the centuries not because its defects had been concealed, but in spite of their having been long revealed. The two-eyewitness rule had left European criminal procedure without a tolerable alternative. Having entrenched this unattainable level of safeguard in their formal trial procedure, the Europeans found themselves obliged to evade it through a subterfuge that they knew was defective. The coerced confession had to replace proof of guilt.

The Law of Plea Bargaining

I am now going to cross the centuries and cross the Atlantic in order to speak of the rise of plea bargaining in twentieth-century America. The account of the European law of torture that I just presented (which is based upon my monograph *Torture and the Law of Proof,* 1977), should stir among American readers an unpleasant sensation of the familiar, for the parallels between our modern plea bargaining system and the ancient system of judicial torture are many and chilling.

Let us begin by recollecting the rudiments of the American system of plea bargaining in cases of serious crime. Plea bargaining occurs when the prosecutor induces an accused criminal to confess guilt and to waive his right to trial in exchange for a more lenient criminal sanction than would be imposed if the accused were adjudicated guilty following trial. The prosecutor offers leniency either directly, in the form of a charge reduction, or indirectly, through the connivance of the judge, in the form of a recommendation for reduced sentence that the judge will follow. In exchange for procuring this leniency for the accused, the prosecutor is relieved of the need to prove the accused's guilt, and the court is spared having to adjudicate it. The court condemns the accused on the basis of his confession, without independent adjudication.

Plea bargaining is, therefore, a nontrial procedure for convicting and condemning the accused criminal. If you turn to the American Constitution in search of authority for plea bargaining, you will look in vain. Instead, you will find—in no less hallowed a place than the Bill of Rights—an opposite guarantee, a guarantee of trial. The Sixth Amendment provides: "In *all* criminal prosecutions, the accused shall enjoy the right to . . . trial . . . by an impartial jury . . ." (emphasis added).

In our day, jury trial continues to occupy its central place both in the formal law and in the mythology of the law. The Constitution has not changed, the courts pretend to enforce the defendant's right to jury trial, and television transmits a steady flow of dramas in which a courtroom contest for the verdict of the jury leads inexorably to the disclosure of the true culprit. In truth, criminal jury trial has largely disappeared in America. The criminal justice system now disposes of virtually all cases of serious crime through plea bargaining. In the major cities between 95 and 99 percent of felony convictions are by plea. This nontrial procedure has become the ordinary dispositive procedure of American law.

Why has our formal system of proof been set out of force and this nontrial system substituted for the trial procedure envisaged by the Framers? Scholars are only beginning to investigate the history of plea bargaining, but enough is known to permit us to speak with some confidence about the broad outline. In the two centuries from the mid-eighteenth to the mid-twentieth, a vast transformation overcame the Anglo-American institution of criminal jury trial, rendering it absolutely unworkable as an ordinary dispositive procedure and requiring the development of an alternative procedure, which we now recognize to be the plea bargaining system.

In eighteenth-century England jury trial was still a *summary proceeding*. In the Old Bailey in the 1730s we know that the court routinely processed between 12 and 20 jury trials for felony in a single day. A single jury would be impaneled and would hear evidence in numerous unrelated cases before retiring to formulate verdicts in all. Lawyers were not employed in the conduct of ordinary criminal trials, either for the prosecution or the defense. The trial judge called the witnesses (whom the local justice of the peace had bound over to appear), and the proceeding transpired as a relatively unstructured altercation between the witnesses and the accused. Plea bargaining was unknown—indeed, judges actively discouraged pleas of guilty even from defendants who tendered them voluntarily and without hope of sentencing concessions. In the 1790s, when the Americans were constitutionalizing English jury trial, it was still rapid and efficient. The trial of Hardy for high treason in 1794 was the first that ever lasted more than one day, and the court seriously considered whether it had any power to adjourn. By contrast, we may note that the trial of Patricia Hearst for bank robbery in 1976 lasted 40 days and that the average felony jury trial in Los Angeles in 1968 required 7.2 days of trial time. In the eighteenth century the most characteristic (and time-consuming) features of modern jury trial, namely adversary procedure and the exclusionary rules of the law of criminal evidence, were still primitive and uncharacteristic. The accused's right to representation by retained counsel was not generalized to all felonies until the end of the eighteenth century in America and the nineteenth century in England. Appellate review was very restricted into the twentieth century; counsel for indigent accused was not required until the middle of this century. The practices that so protract modern American jury trials—extended *voir dire* (pretrial probing of the views and backgrounds of individual jurors for juror challenges), exclusionary rules and other evidentiary barriers, motions designed to provoke and preserve issues for appeal, maneuvers and speeches of counsel, intricate and often incomprehensible instructions to the jury—all are late growths in the long history of common-law criminal procedure. No wonder, then, that plea bargaining appears to have been a late-nineteenth-century growth that was scarcely acknowledged to exist in the United States before the 1920s. (The English are only now facing up to the fact of their dependence on plea bargaining.)

Nobody should be surprised that jury trial has undergone great changes over the last two centuries. It desperately needed reform. The level of safeguard against mistaken conviction was in several respects below what civilized peoples now require. What we will not understand until there has been research directed to the question, is why the pressure for greater safeguards led in the Anglo-American procedure to the law of evidence and the lawyerization of the trial, reforms that ultimately destroyed the system in the sense that they made jury trial so complicated and time-consuming as to be unworkable as the routine dispositive procedure.

Similar pressures for safeguards were being felt on the Continent in the same period, but they led to reforms in nonadversarial procedure that preserved the institution of trial. In the middle of the nineteenth century, when Continental criminal procedure was being given its modern shape, the draftsmen of the

European codes routinely studied Anglo-American procedure as a reform model. They found much to admire and to borrow, but they resisted the temptation to adversary domination. Their experience with the way that their medieval rules of evidence had led to the law of torture also left them unwilling to imitate the nascent Anglo-American law of evidence. And they were unanimous in rejecting the institution of the guilty plea. As early as the 1850s German writers were saying that it was wrong for a court to sentence an accused on mere confession, without satisfying itself of his guilt.

Parallels to the Law of Torture

Let me now turn to my main theme—the parallels in function and doctrine between the medieval European system of judicial torture and our plea bargaining system. The starting point, which will be obvious from what I have thus far said, is that each of these substitute procedural systems arose in response to the breakdown of the formal system of trial that it subverted. Both the medieval European law of proof and the modern Anglo-American law of jury trial set out to safeguard the accused by circumscribing the discretion of the trier in criminal adjudication. The medieval Europeans were trying to eliminate the discretion of the professional judge by requiring him to adhere to objective criteria of proof. The Anglo-American trial system has been caught up over the last two centuries in an effort to protect the accused against the dangers of the jury system, in which laymen ignorant of the law return a one- or two-word verdict that they do not explain or justify. Each system found itself unable to recant directly on the unrealistic level of safeguard to which it had committed itself, and each then concentrated on inducing the accused to tender a confession that would waive his right to the safeguards.

The European law of torture preserved the medieval law of proof undisturbed for those easy cases in which there were two eyewitnesses or voluntary confession. But in the more difficult cases (where, I might add, safeguard was more important), the law of torture worked an absolutely fundamental change within the system of proof: It largely *eliminated the adjudicative function.* Once probable cause had been determined, the accused was made to concede his guilt rather than his accusers to prove it.

In twentieth-century America we have duplicated the central experience of medieval European criminal procedure. We have moved from an adjudicatory to a concessionary system. We coerce the accused against whom we find probable cause to confess his guilt. To be sure, our means are much more polite; we use no rack, no thumbscrew, no Spanish boot to mash his legs. But like the Europeans of distant centuries who did employ those machines, we make it terribly costly for an accused to claim his right to the constitutional safeguard of trial. We threaten him with a materially increased sanction if he avails himself of his right and is thereafter convicted. This sentencing differential is what makes plea bargaining coercive. There is, of course, a difference between having your limbs crushed if you refuse to confess, or suffering some extra years of imprisonment if you refuse to confess, but the difference is of degree, not kind. Plea bargaining, like torture, is coercive. Like the medieval Europeans, the Americans are now operating a procedural system that engages in condemnation without adjudication. The maxim of the medieval Glossators, no longer applicable to European law, now aptly describes American law: *Confessio est regina probationum,* confession is the queen of proof.

Supporters of plea bargaining typically maintain that a "mere" sentencing differential is not sufficiently coercive to pressure an innocent accused to convict himself. That point can be tested in the abstract simply by imagining a differential so great—for example, death versus a 50-cent fine—that any rational defendant would waive even the strongest defenses. The question of whether significant numbers of innocent people do plead guilty is not, of course, susceptible to empirical testing. It has been established that many of those who plead guilty claim that they are innocent. More importantly, prosecutors widely admit to bargaining hardest when the case is weakest, which is why the leading article on the subject, by Albert Alschuler ("The Prosecutor's Role in Plea Bargaining," University of Chicago Law Review, 1968), concluded that "the greatest pressures to plead guilty are brought to bear on defendants who may be innocent." Alschuler recounted one such case:

San Francisco defense attorney Benjamin M. Davis recently represented a man charged with kidnapping and forcible rape. The defendant was innocent, Davis says, and after investigating the case Davis was confident of an acquittal. The prosecutor, who seems to have shared the defense attorney's opinion on this point, offered to permit a guilty plea to simple battery. Conviction on this charge would not have led to a greater sentence than 30 days' imprisonment, and there was every likelihood that the defendant would be granted probation. When Davis informed his client of this offer, he emphasized that conviction at trial seemed highly improbable. The defendant's reply was simple: "I can't take the chance."

I do not think that great numbers of Americans plead guilty to offenses committed by strangers. (The European law of torture was also not supposed to apply in the easy cases where the accused could forthrightly explain away the evidence that might otherwise have given cause to examine him under torture.) I do believe that plea bargaining is used to coerce the waiver of tenable defenses, as in attorney Davis's example, and in cases where the offense has a complicated conceptual basis, as in tax and other white-collar crimes. Like the medieval law of torture, the sentencing differential in plea bargaining elicits confessions of guilt that would not be freely tendered, and some of the confessions are false. Plea bargaining is therefore coercive in the same sense as torture, although surely not in the same degree.

I do not mean to say that excesses of the plea bargaining system affect only the innocent who is coerced to plead guilty or the convict whose sentence is made more severe because he insisted on his right to trial. In other circumstances plea bargaining has been practiced in ways that result in unjustified leniency. Many observers have been struck by the extent of the concessions that prosecutors have been prepared to make in serious criminal cases in order to avoid having to go to trial. One Alaskan prosecutor told Alschuler in 1976 that "prosecutors can get rid of everything if they just go low enough. The police complained that we were giving cases away, and they were right."

I have said that European law attempted to devise safeguards for the use of torture that proved illusory; these measures bear an eerie resemblance to the supposed safeguards of the American law of plea bargaining. Foremost among the illusory safeguards of both systems is the doctrinal preoccupation with characterizing the induced waivers as voluntary. The Europeans made the torture victim repeat his confession "voluntarily," but under the threat of being tortured anew if he recanted. The American counterpart is Rule 11(d) of the Federal Rules of Criminal Procedure, which forbids the court from accepting a guilty plea without first "addressing the defendant personally in open court, determining that the plea is voluntary and

not the result of force or threats or of promises *apart from a plea agreement.*" Of course, the plea agreement is the *source* of the coercion and already embodies the involuntariness.

The architects of the European law of torture sought to enhance the reliability of a torture-induced confession with other safeguards designed to substantiate its factual basis. We have said that they required a probable-cause determination for investigation under torture and that they directed the court to take steps to verify the accuracy of the confession by investigating some of its detail. We have explained why these measures were inadequate to protect many innocent suspects from torture, confession, and condemnation. Probable cause is not the same as guilt, and verification, even if undertaken in good faith, could easily fail as a safeguard, either because the matters confessed were not susceptible of physical or testimonial corroboration, or because the accused might know enough about the crime to lend verisimilitude to his confession even though he was not in fact the culprit.

The American law of plea bargaining has pursued a similar chimera: the requirement of "adequate factual basis for the plea." Federal Rule 11(f) provides that "the court should not enter judgment upon [a guilty] plea without making such inquiry as shall satisfy it that there is a factual basis for the plea." As with the tortured confession, so with the negotiated plea: Any case that has resisted dismissal for want of probable cause at the preliminary hearing will rest upon enough inculpating evidence to cast suspicion upon the accused. The function of trial, which plea bargaining eliminates, is to require the court to adjudicate whether the facts proven support an inference of guilt beyond a reasonable doubt. Consider, however, the case of *North Carolina* v. *Alford,* decided in this decade, in which the U.S. Supreme Court found it permissible to condemn without trial a defendant who had told the sentencing court: "I pleaded guilty on second degree murder because they said there is too much evidence, but I ain't shot no man. . . . I just pleaded guilty because they said if I didn't they would gas me for it. . . . I'm not guilty but I plead guilty." I invite you to compare Alford's statement with the explanation of one Johannes Julius, seventeenth-century burgomaster of Bamberg, who wrote from his dungeon cell where he was awaiting execution, in order to tell his daughter why he had confessed to witchcraft "for which I must die. It is all falsehood and invention, so help me God. . . . They never cease to torture until one says something."

The tortured confession is, of course, markedly less reliable than the negotiated plea, because the degree of coercion is greater. An accused is more likely to bear false witness against himself in order to escape further hours on the rack than to avoid risking a longer prison term. But the resulting moral quandary is the same. Judge Levin of Michigan was speaking of the negotiated guilty plea, but he could as well have been describing the tortured confession when he said, "there is no way of knowing whether a particular guilty plea was given because the accused believed he was guilty, or because of the promised concession." Beccaria might as well have been speaking of the coercion of plea bargaining when he said of the violence of torture that it "confounds and obliterates those minute differences between things which enable us at times to know truth from falsehood." The doctrine of adequate factual basis for the plea is no better substitute for proof beyond reasonable doubt than was the analogous doctrine in the law of torture.

The factual unreliability of the negotiated plea has further consequences, quite apart from the increased danger of condemning an innocent man. In the plea bargaining that takes the form of charge bargaining (as opposed to sentence bargaining), the culprit is convicted not for what he did, but for something less opprobrious. When people who have murdered are said to be convicted of wounding, or when those caught stealing are nominally convicted of attempt or possession, cynicism about the processes of criminal justice is inevitably reinforced. This willful mislabelling plays havoc with our crime statistics, which explains in part why Americans—uniquely among Western peoples—attach so much importance to arrest records rather than to records of conviction. I think that the unreliability of the plea, the mislabelling of the offense, and the underlying want of adjudication all combine to weaken the moral force of the criminal law, and to increase the public's unease about the administration of criminal justice. The case of James Earl Ray is perhaps the best example of public dissatisfaction over the intrinsic failure of the plea bargaining system to establish the facts about crime and guilt in the forum of a public trial. Of course, not every trial resolves the question of guilt or innocence to public satisfaction. The Sacco-Vanzetti and Rosenberg cases continue to be relitigated in the forum of popular opinion. But plea bargaining leaves the public with what I believe to be a more pronounced sense of unease about the justness of results, because it avoids the open ventilation and critical evaluation of evidence that characterize public trial. (Just this con-

cern appears to have motivated the government in the plea-bargained bribery case of Vice President Agnew to take extraordinary steps to assure the disclosure of the substance of the prosecution case.) It is interesting to remember that in Europe in the age of Beccaria and Voltaire, the want of adjudication and the unreliability of the law of torture had bred a strangely similar cynicism towards the criminal justice system of that day.

The Moral Blunder

Because plea bargaining involves condemnation without adjudication, it undermines a moral postulate of the criminal justice system so basic and elementary that in past centuries Anglo-American writers seldom bothered to express it: Serious criminal sanctions should only be imposed when the trier has examined the relevant evidence and found the accused guilty beyond reasonable doubt.

Why have we been able to construct a nontrial procedure that is irreconcilable with this fundamental proposition? A major reason is that we have been beguiled by the similarities between civil and criminal litigation in our lawyer-dominated procedural system. "What's wrong with settling cases?" the argument runs. "Surely society is correct not to insist on full-scale adjudication of every private grievance. If the parties are satisfied with their deal, there is no social interest in adjudication. Likewise in criminal adjudication: If the prosecutor and the accused can reach agreement about the sanction, hasn't the matter been satisfactorily concluded?"

The answer is that because the social interest in criminal adjudication differs importantly from that in civil cases, the deeply embedded policy in favor of negotiated (nontrial) settlement of civil disputes is misapplied when transposed to the criminal setting. There is good reason for treating adjudication as the norm in the criminal law, but as a last and exceptional resort in private law. Kenneth Kipnis has provided a wry illustration of the distinction with an example drawn from neither. Kipnis asks us to imagine a system of "grade bargaining," in which the teacher would offer a student a favorable grade in exchange for a waiver of the student's right to have the teacher read his examination paper. The teacher would save time, thus conserve his resources, and the student would not accept the teacher's grade offer unless he calculated it to be in his interest by comparison with his expected results from conventional grading.

We see instantly what is wrong with grade bargaining. Because third parties rely upon grades in admissions and hiring decisions, the grade bargain would adversely affect the legitimate interests of these outsiders. And because the grade is meant to inform the student about the teacher's perception of the comparative quality of his performance, the grade bargain would disserve the larger interest of the student.

Quite analogous objections apply to plea bargaining. Criminal sanctions are imposed for public purposes: certainly in order to deter future crime, probably still with the object of reforming at least some offenders, and perhaps still in the interest of retribution. Sentences that satisfy the accused's wish to minimize the sanction and the prosecutor's need to reduce his trial caseload are arrived at with only passing attention to these social interests. In particular, the enormous sentence differential needed to sustain the plea bargaining system is repugnant to any tenable theory of sentencing. We can scarcely claim to be tailoring the sentence to the crime when one of the largest aggravating factors we consult is whether the accused had the temerity to ask for his right to trial. The truth is that when an accused is convicted following jury trial, we customarily punish him twice: once for the crime, and then more severely for what the Constitution calls "enjoy[ing] the right to . . . trial . . . by an impartial jury."

Twenty years ago in a celebrated article the late Henry Hart compared so-called "civil commitment" for mental or contagious disease with imprisonment for criminal conviction. Many a prison is more pleasant than a nearby asylum. Why, then, do we treat the decision to imprison as the more serious and surround it with safeguards that, at least in theory, are more substantial than those for the civil-commitment process? Notwithstanding the operational similarity between civil and criminal sanctions, said Hart, there is a profound difference in purpose. "The core of the difference is that the patient has not incurred the moral condemnation of his community, whereas the convict has." The very stigma of criminal conviction is the source of much of the deterrent and retributive power of the criminal sanction. I believe that this moral force of the criminal sanction is partially dependent on the sanction having been imposed after rational inquiry and decision on the facts. Adjudication alone legitimates the infliction of serious criminal sanctions, because it alone is adequate to separate the innocent from the guilty and to establish the basis for proportioning punishment to the degree of culpability. To assert (as a defender of plea bargaining must) the equivalency of waiver and of adjudication is to overlook the distinctive characteristic of the criminal law.

The Prosecutor

Our law of plea bargaining has not only recapitulated much of the doctrinal folly of the law of torture, complete with the pathetic safeguards of voluntariness and factual basis, but it has also repeated the main institutional blunder of the law of torture. Plea bargaining concentrates effective control of criminal procedure in the hands of a single officer. Our formal law of trial envisages a division of responsibility. We expect the prosecutor to make the charging decision, the judge and especially the jury to adjudicate, and the judge to set the sentence. Plea bargaining merges these accusatory, determinative, and sanctional phases of the procedure in the hands of the prosecutor. Students of the history of the law of torture are reminded that the great psychological fallacy of the European inquisitorial procedure of that time was that it concentrated in the investigating magistrate the powers of accusation, investigation, torture, and condemnation. The single inquisitor who wielded those powers needed to have what one recent historian has called "superhuman capabilities [in order to] . . . keep himself in his decisional function free from the predisposing influences of his own instigating and investigating activity."

The dominant version of American plea bargaining makes similar demands: It requires the prosecutor to usurp the determinative and sentencing functions, hence to make himself judge in his own cause. There are dangers in this concentration of prosecutorial power. One need not necessarily accept Jimmy Hoffa's view that Robert Kennedy was conducting a personal and political vendetta against him in order to appreciate the danger that he might have been. The power to prosecute as we know it carries within itself the power to persecute. The modern public prosecutor commands the vast resources of the state for gathering and generating accusing evidence. We allowed him this power in large part because the criminal trial interposed the safeguard of adjudication against the danger that he might bring those resources to bear against an innocent citizen—whether on account of honest error, arbitrariness, or worse. But the plea bargaining system has largely dissolved that safeguard.

While on the subject of institutional factors, I have one last comparison to advance. The point has been made, most recently by the Attorney General of Alaska, that preparing and taking cases to trial is much harder work than plea bargaining—for police, prosecutors, judges, and defense counsel. In short, convenience—or worse, sloth—is a factor that sustains plea bargaining. We suppose that this factor had a little to do with torture as well. As someone in India remarked to Sir James Fitzjames Stephen in 1872 about the proclivity of the native policemen for torturing suspects, "It is far pleasanter to sit comfortably in the shade rubbing red pepper into a poor devil's eyes than to go about in the sun hunting up evidence." If we were to generalize about this point, we might say that concessionary criminal-procedural systems like the plea bargaining system and the system of judicial torture may develop their own bureaucracies and constituencies. Here as elsewhere the old adage may apply that if necessity is the mother of invention, laziness is the father.

The Jurisprudence of Concession

Having developed these parallels between torture and plea bargaining, I want to draw some conclusions about what I regard as the lessons of the exercise. The most important is this: A legal system will do almost anything, tolerate almost anything, before it will admit the need for reform in its system of proof and trial. The law of torture endured for half a millennium although its dangers and defects had been understood virtually from the outset; and plea bargaining lives on although its evils are quite familiar to us all. What makes such shoddy subterfuges so tenacious is that they shield their legal systems from having to face up to the fact of breakdown in the formal law of proof and trial.

Why is it so hard for a legal system to reform a decadent system of proof? I think that there are two main reasons, one in a sense practical, the other ideological. From the standpoint of the practical, nothing seems quite so embedded in a legal system as the procedures for proof and trial, because most of what a legal system does is to decide matters of proof—what we call "fact finding." (Was the traffic light green or red? Was this accused the man who fired the shot or robbed the bank?) Blackstone emphasized this point in speaking of civil litigation, and it is even more true of criminal litigation. He said: "Experience will abundantly shew, that above a hundred of our lawsuits arise from disputed facts, for one where the law

is doubted of." Every institution of the legal system is geared to the system of proof; forthright reconstruction would disturb, at one level or another, virtually every vested interest.

The inertia, the resistance to change that is associated with such deep-seated interests, is inevitably reinforced by the powerful ideological component that underlies a system of proof and trial. Adjudication, especially criminal adjudication, involves a profound intrusion into the lives of affected citizens. Consequently, in any society the adjudicative power must be rested on a theoretical basis that makes it palatable to the populace. Because the theory of proof purports to govern and explain the application of the adjudicative power, it plays a central role in legitimating the entire legal system. The medieval European law of proof assured people that the legal system would achieve certainty. The Anglo-American jury system invoked the inscrutable wisdom of the folk to justify its results. Each of these theories was ultimately untenable—the European theory virtually from its inception, the Anglo-American theory after a centuries-long transformation of jury procedure. Yet the ideological importance of these theories prevented either legal system from recanting them. For example, I have elsewhere pointed out how in the nineteenth century the ideological attachment to the jury retarded experimentation with juryless trial—that is, what we now call bench trial—while the plea bargaining system of juryless nontrial procedure was taking shape out of public sight. Like the medieval European lawyers before us, we have been unable to admit that our theory of proof has resulted in a level of procedural complexity and safeguard that renders our trial procedure unworkable in all but exceptional cases. We have responded to the breakdown of our formal system of proof by taking steps to perpetuate the ideology of the failed system, steps that closely resemble those taken by the architects of the law of torture. *Like the medieval Europeans, we have preserved an unworkable trial procedure in form, we have devised a substitute nontrial procedure to subvert the formal procedure, and we have arranged to place defendants under fierce pressure to "choose" the substitute.*

That this script could have been played out in a pair of legal cultures so remote from each other in time and place invites some suggestions about the adaptive processes of criminal procedural systems. First, there are intrinsic limits to the level of complexity and safeguard that even a civilized people can tolerate. If those limits are exceeded and the repressive capacity of the criminal justice system is thereby endangered, the system will respond by developing subterfuges that overcome the formal law. But subterfuges are intrinsically overbroad, precisely because they are not framed in a careful, explicit, and principled manner directed to achieving a proper balance between repression and safeguard. The upshot is that the criminal justice system is saddled with a lower level of safeguard than it could and would have achieved if it had not pretended to retain the unworkable formal system.

The medieval Europeans insisted on two eyewitnesses and wound up with a law of torture that allowed condemnation with no witnesses at all. American plea bargaining, in like fashion, sacrifices just those values that the unworkable system of adversary jury trial is meant to serve: lay participation in criminal adjudication, the presumption of innocence, the prosecutorial burden of proof beyond reasonable doubt, the right to confront and cross-examine accusers, the privilege against self-incrimination. Especially in its handling of the privilege against self-incrimination does American criminal procedure reach the outer bounds of incoherence. We have exaggerated the privilege to senseless lengths in formal doctrine, while in the plea bargaining system—which is our routine procedure for processing cases of serious crime—we have eliminated practically every trace of the privilege.

Furthermore, the sacrifice of our fundamental values through plea bargaining is needless. In its sad plea bargaining opinions of the 1970s, the Supreme Court has effectively admitted that for reasons of expediency American criminal justice cannot honor its promise of routine adversary criminal trial, but the Court has simply assumed that the present nontrial plea bargaining procedure is the inevitable alternative. There is, however, a middle path between the impossible system of routine adversary jury trial and the disgraceful nontrial system of plea bargaining. That path is a streamlined nonadversarial trial procedure.

Routine Nonadversarial Trials

The contemporary nonadversarial criminal justice systems of countries like West Germany have long demonstrated that advanced industrial societies can institute efficient criminal procedures that neverthe-less provide for lay participation and for full adjudication in every case of serious crime. I have described the German system in detail in my *Comparative Criminal Procedure: Germany* (1977), and I have made no secret of my admiration for the brilliant balance that it strikes between safeguard and procedural effectiveness. Not the least of its achievements is that in cases of serious crime it functions with no plea bargaining whatsoever. Confessions are still tendered in many cases (41 percent in one sample), but they are not and cannot be bargained for; nor does a confession excuse the trial court from hearing sufficient evidence for conviction on what amounts to a beyond-reasonable-doubt standard of proof. In a trial procedure shorn of all the excesses of adversary procedure and the law of evidence, the time difference between trial without confession and trial with confession is not all that great. Because an accused will be put to trial whether he confesses or not, he cannot inflict significant costs upon the prosecution by contesting an overwhelming case. Confessions are tendered at trial not because they are rewarded, but because there is no advantage to be wrung from the procedural system by withholding them.

Plea bargaining is all but incomprehensible to the Europeans, whose ordinary dispositive procedure is workable without such evasions. In the German press, the judicial procedure surrounding the criminal conviction and resignation of Vice President Agnew was viewed with the sort of wonder normally inspired by reports of the customs of primitive tribes. The *Badische Zeitung* reported as the story unfolded in October 1973: "The resignation occurred as part of a 'cowtrade,' as it can only in the United States be imagined."

I hope that over the coming decades we who still live under criminal justice systems that engage in condemnation without adjudication will face up to the failure of adversary criminal procedure. I believe that we will find in modern Continental criminal procedure an irresistible model for reform. For the moment, however, I am left to conclude with a paradox. Today in lands where the law of torture once governed, peoples who live in contentment with their criminal justice systems look out across the sea in disbelief to the spectacle of plea bargaining in America, while American tourists come by the thousands each year to gawk in disbelief at the decaying torture chambers of medieval castles.

JURY NULLIFICATION*

Kent Greenawalt

The jury's power to nullify is the most obvious. In civil cases, a jury can decide against the party that has presented the most persuasive evidence; unless the evidence in favor of the losing party is extremely strong, the jury's decision will survive an appeal. Its power in criminal cases is more absolute; if it acquits, the constitutional rule against double jeopardy precludes further proceedings against the defendant. I will concentrate here on the role of the jury in criminal cases. Much of what is said also applies to civil cases, though, of course, the claim of the opposing party to have his lawful expectations satisfied is a powerful argument against subverting the rules of civil liability to his disadvantage.

Lay jurors in common-law countries can nullify the criminal law by acquitting a defendant they believe is guilty of the crime charged. They can also nullify the written law in a more moderate fashion, by returning a verdict for a lesser offense when they believe the defendant is guilty of the more serious offense with which he has been charged. One juror alone (or a minority of jurors in jurisdictions that allow conviction with less than unanimity) can, if sufficiently strong-willed and persistent, block application of the law to an offender by refusing to vote for conviction.

The Legal Authority of Juries

Whether or not jurors have legal authority to engage in such refusals to apply the law is a complex question. Their dispensing power has been a fundamental element of the administration of the criminal law since the medieval period, and indeed, because of the capital sentence for most homicides and thefts, was once a more integral aspect of the law's administration than it is now.[20] In the sixteenth and seventeenth centuries,

jurors were occasionally fined and imprisoned for refusals to convict,[21] now when they acquit, not only is their verdict unreviewable, they are immune from any punishment for failing to fulfill their temporary official duty. Nevertheless, jurors are instructed to apply the law as the judge gives it to them, and they take an oath that they will do so; and despite three narrowly interpreted state constitutional standards that grant jurors authority to determine the law,[22] the earlier dispute over whether jurors are the ultimate finders of law as well as fact has now been decisively resolved: jurors must take the law according to the judge's instructions. Defendant's counsel can neither argue that the jury should disregard those instructions nor present evidence in favor of the proposition that the defendant should be acquitted despite violating the law.

How is the legal duty of jurors to be understood? One view is that the power of acquittal establishes a right of acquittal. As Chancellor James Kent put it, "The law must . . . have intended, in granting this power to a jury, to grant them a lawful and rightful power, or it would have provided a remedy against the undue exercise of it."[23] Without more, however, this position is too simple. The law may confer unreviewable power for a variety of reasons. Judges of highest courts, for example, have essentially unreviewable authority to determine the law, because in a practical system of government such power must be placed somewhere. Yet certainly some interpretations of law could be so egregious, so far beyond permissible bounds, that we should say the judges who made them violated their legal duty and acted outside their authority. In cases in which substantial evidence is produced against the defendant, jurors have, as George Christie has pointed out, effective power to convict on less than the reasonable doubt standard.[24] That is to say, if the jurors consciously determine that the evidence does not meet that requisite, but the defendant is

---

probably guilty and is certainly a dangerous character who should be locked up, they can convict, and no other organ of government will be able to go behind their verdict and undo their finding of guilt. We should, nevertheless, hesitate to say that the jurors have legal authority to convict on less than beyond a reasonable doubt. Power does not necessarily demonstrate right.

The contrary position—that the jury's legal duty is always simply to apply the law as the judge instructs it—also presents some difficulties, because the undoubted power to acquit rests on something more than the impracticality of review. One of the historic arguments for jury trial is that a community check against enforcement of arbitrary laws and unduly harsh penalties is desirable; and jury refusals to convict publishers charged with seditious libel and petty thieves facing mandatory death penalties are celebrated as civilizing the administration of justice. Before the American Revolution, John Adams conceived the jury as introducing a democratic element into the executive function by which "the subject is guarded in the execution of the laws."[25] When the Supreme Court held that the Fourteenth Amendment required states to afford jury trials in criminal cases, the possibility of jury nullification was considered one of the characteristics making jury trial fundamental to our system of justice.[26] Since judges may direct judgment for either party in a civil case or acquittal in a criminal case, a judge's inability to direct a finding of guilt in a criminal trial rests not on impracticality, but on special solicitude for the criminal defendant—a sense that he should not be convicted without a supportive judgment by members of the community. Even such an apparently innocuous technique as requiring the jury to make particular findings of fact as well as returning a general verdict has been said to undercut its "historic function . . . of tempering rules of law by common sense."[27] Thus, the jury's power on occasion to nullify the law is viewed as a positive feature of its operation, one that is self-consciously protected by ancillary doctrines.

Finding each of the two simple competing views to be unsatisfactory, Mortimer and Sanford Kadish, in their insightful book *Discretion to Disobey,*[28] conclude that juries are under a legal obligation to follow instructions and have a legal right to disobey the instructions if the reasons for doing so are strong enough. Jurors are exemplars of officials who occupy "recourse roles" and who are permitted to depart from the prescribed means for exercising their roles when they believe the ends for which their roles are created will not be served if they fail to digress. The obligation to follow the prescribed means is like a promissory obligation in ordinary life—one that must be given considerable weight but can be overridden by very strong contrary reasons.

This account of the juror's responsibility under our system may make us somewhat uncomfortable, because we are used to thinking that the law forbids, requires, or permits actions. But the Kadish view reflects sophistication about subtle variations in the messages that may be conveyed to actors in a social enterprise.

One need only reflect on parental injunctions to small children to grasp the point. When my three boys have wanted to do things I regarded as part of the birthright of every youth but in later life saw as fraught with potential danger, such as walking on high walls, shooting metal clips with slingshots, throwing sticks and small rocks at the enemy of the moment, hitting brothers in assorted parts of the anatomy, and climbing out of windows, I have discovered that, whether I am presented with a fait accompli or involve myself before the event, my responses are modulated according to my feelings of danger and acceptability. For the actions I regard as the worst, I may say something like "This is absolutely forbidden. You should never do that. If you do it again, you will be seriously punished." On other occasions I say things like "That's a bad idea. You really shouldn't do that," or "That is really stupid. You know you can hurt someone (yourself) that way," or "I am very disappointed in you for doing X" (hitting a brother in a part of the body not absolutely forbidden), or "You really shouldn't do that, but if you must, be very careful." The last comment comes close to a grudging permission, but what I am struggling somehow to do in many instances is to avoid conveying a genuine permission, something that may connote approval or acceptance, and yet to steer clear of absolute prohibition. I should not want to make too much of this analogy, especially since what underlies my variations is a wish not to dilute the prohibitions of the worst acts or overburden the boys with absolute "no's" and a hope that their own sense of responsibility will develop—reasons quite different from those that underlie the uncertain signals the legal system conveys about jury responsibilities. But if a small amount of self-study reveals such variations in parental attempts to guide children, we should hardly be surprised that something as complicated as a legal system may not offer straightforward directions about the performance of some important responsibilities.

If the Kadishes are right that the legal authority of jurors cannot be described in simple terms, it does not follow that their own theoretical account is the most satisfactory. The thrust of their suggestions has a rather paradoxical air—that the obligation to apply the law faithfully continues in force even in those situations when nullification is warranted by the powerful reasons in its favor. As Kurt Baier has pointed out,[29] the conflict between possible nullification and applying the law is not just an ordinary conflict of obligations one cannot practically fulfill at the same time.[30] Nullification is logically incompatible with applying the law; if nullification is required by the ends of justice, one cannot conceivably fulfill that end of one's role and the obligation to apply the law. Without challenging the Kadish account of what jurors may do, Baier tries to dispel the element of paradox by suggesting that jurors should be thought to be under an obligation to follow instructions unless compliance would seriously frustrate some of the ends of their role.[31] In that event, they would cease to be under the obligation to apply the law faithfully.

I do not believe that Baier's revision is philosophically more compelling than the original account of the Kadishes. Having suggested that the obligations of promise and fair play may run into conflicts with more compelling duties of justice, I have assumed that obligations may be outweighed rather than cease, even when performance of the obligation is not logically compatible with satisfying the duty of justice. Imagine that A previously helped B to capture B's escaped slave; B has promised to do the same for A if the need arises. B, who has by now freed all his own slaves, sees A's escaped slave on his property. His obligations of promise and fair play toward A compete with his natural duties toward the slave. Performance of one duty is logically incompatible with performance of the other. I should say the promissory or fair play obligation is outweighed by the natural duty rather than nonexistent. Similarly, a jury's obligation to apply the law could be outweighed by its duty to do what is morally just in an individual case.

In any event, whatever the strength of Baier's position as an account of how outsiders should view the jury's responsibilities, it fails to capture the perplexities facing jurors themselves, who are not instructed about any authority to disregard instructions. Because no one tells them under what conditions they may nullify the law, they are likely to feel themselves being pulled in two different directions, with the uneasy feeling that whatever they do will be wrong from some point of view. The Kadish paradox is much more faithful to their disquieting dilemma than is Baier's simpler resolution.

Criteria for Nullification

Because judges do not instruct juries about their power to nullify the law, the dearth of writing on how conscientious jurors should exercise that power is not surprising; but I want to consider what standard might be applied by a thoughtful juror who is considering acquittal, even though he recognizes that application of the judge's instructions to the facts would yield a guilty verdict. Few now believe that lay jurors should supplant the judge's instructions with their own interpretations of the law, and such authority would be hard to defend. The authority that is implicitly conceded to jurors is rather that they may disregard the law when its application would be highly unjust. As the Kadishes put it, the jurors must place a "significant surcharge" on denial of their obligation to apply the law. A juror should not acquit unless he is firmly convinced that a gross injustice would be done by conviction. He must believe more than that the actor's motives were good or that the law is a bad one. He must think that the actor was performing an act that was clearly justified or was exercising an undeniable moral right. Ordinarily, he would have to think either that the law on which the prosecution is based is itself highly unjust or that the particular circumstances of the case are so far outside what the legislature had in mind that the law's application in this case would be unconscionable. In rare cases, for example, when jurors are strongly persuaded that protesters had an overwhelming powerful reason to break a law, acquittal may be warranted even though jurors do not consider the law itself unjust or the situation to be outside the legislature's intentions.

Perhaps the jury needs less strong reasons when the form of nullification is to reduce the crime involved (say from murder to manslaughter) without justification in the law and facts. Because the defendant will still be convicted and receive a sentence, the jury's defiance of the law in this situation is not quite so great.

One final distinction needs to be drawn. Some cases will present a genuine issue of guilt on the basis of the evidence, and an outsider may not be able to tell whether the jury honestly disbelieved the prosecutor's version of the facts or believed it but nevertheless determined not to convict. Indeed, the jurors voting for acquittal may represent both positions, and the jurors wishing to nullify may deceive the other jurors about the grounds for their votes. In such cases, nullification may be surreptitious; no one will be sure it has taken place.[32] Such violations of the ordinary premises of the system still require strong justification, but since the practical damage will be less if others are not aware of what has occurred, such manipulation may occasionally be warranted even if an open and clear nullification would not be.

The law itself supplies the guiding criteria for jury nullification only to a limited degree. In some cases, jurors may reach behind the letter of the broken law to its ascertainable spirit, perceiving that the individual violator was simply not a person that the legislature really wanted to penalize. In other instances, jurors may be aware that a particular prohibition is out of line with other, more important provisions of the law. For the most part, however, a juror must call on his own, individual sense of justice to decide if a legally warranted conviction would be so intolerable that he should not vote for it. Thus, if jury nullification is an instance in which agents "undertake actions outside the role's prescribed means to achieve the role's ends,"[33] the "ends" are general ones of justice and fairness. The jurors themselves will fill in the content of those ends, not from any special conception of the criminal law as it then exists, but from a less focused appreciation of when condemnation and punishment is acceptable.

Possible Reform

Practical interest in the status of jury nullification increased greatly with the trials of those who refused military service in Vietnam or protested the war there. Change in the present understanding of jury role could take place in either direction. Jury nullification could be more clearly labeled an illegitimate exercise of power, perhaps stripped of some of the support it now enjoys from tangential rules of law, no longer forming the basis of any constitutional doctrines about right to jury trial or providing a subject of admiration for thoughtful commentators. Conversely, jury nullification could be formally recognized, with juries instructed about their power and, perhaps, with lawyers presenting evidence and argument about the appropriateness of deciding against the law in particular cases.

There can be no doubt that jury nullification played a critical humanizing role during stages of English history when the substantive criminal law and its penalties were extremely harsh.[34] The lay jury has also served as an important safeguard against outright oppression. One can certainly conceive of systems of criminal justice that can do without lay jurors and their nullifying powers; but these systems would lack a significant check on official abuse. In any event, the tradition of such power is too deeply rooted in our law to be abandoned.

For the law implicitly to recognize and approve a power it does not admit to those who must exercise it is anomalous. Jurors lacking instructions about authority to nullify can hardly be expected to have reasonably compatible notions of when the duty to apply the law is outweighed by other considerations; on that score defendants are at the mercy of the private notions of members of their particular juries.

Formidable objections to a shift exist, however. If jury nullification could be effectively discouraged, jury power to prevent injustice would be diminished. If jury nullification were formally approved, the proper authority of the written law might be undermined. As all recognize, juries may nullify for bad reasons as well as good, and no one has yet thought of a formula that would produce nullification only in deserving cases. The sensible assumption is that if juries were instructed about their power to nullify, this would increase the instances of nullification; some of these would be just refusals to apply the law, others victories for prejudice or overly generous sympathy.

George Christie has made the further observation that such instructions would tend to have the undesirable effect of relieving the moral responsibility that jurors feel for nullification and increasing their sense of moral responsibility for convictions, because jurors could no longer view themselves as simple agents of the law sworn to do as it directs.[35] If defense attorneys could present evidence and argument in favor of nullification, the dangers of appeal to prejudice would be greatly enhanced, and trials of many political protesters would be turned into unconstrained debates over controversial political issues.

Some language should be discoverable that would alert all jurors to the existence of the nullification power but would indicate in the strongest terms that it should be reserved for only the most exceptional cases. Jurors might be told the following, for example: "Your basic responsibility is to apply the law as given in the judge's instructions. You do have the legal authority to acquit a defendant who is guilty under the law, but that should be done only in an extreme case of a terrible injustice." The gains in openness and consistency should outweigh any harm from a slight increase in instances of nullification. Because a crucial value of the law is its capacity to focus and narrow issues, however, to make cases turn on something other than the political and social sympathies of juries, no evidence or argument on the possibility of nullification should be permitted.

Judge Nullification

Judges in criminal cases also have some power to nullify the substantive law. In jury trials, they can direct jurors to acquit when evidence clearly supports a finding of guilt: when a trial is before the bench, a judge can acquit though persuaded of legal guilt. Such determinations are unreviewable, and the possibility of any disciplinary action for isolated instances of nullification is remote.

Judicial power to nullify the substantive law has never been suggested as a desirable feature of trial before judges, and the nonreviewability of their decisions to acquit may be thought to derive more from implications of the defendant's right against double jeopardy than from any sense that the judge is an appropriate agent to second guess the legislature about what behavior should be criminal. Judges are permanent officers of the law sworn to uphold the law, not representatives of community sentiment. In a system with jurors and judges, judges are much less appropriate candidates than jurors to assess the moral acceptability of applications of the law.[36] Perhaps in serious cases,[37] judges have no authority like that of the jury to engage in justified departures from the rules of the substantive law. If judges do have any authority to nullify the criminal law, it is much more limited than the parallel authority of juries.

Nevertheless, it is conceivable that some convictions would be so abhorrent that judicial defiance of the law would be defensible, and this conclusion may be true even if such action is considered to be outside the law in every sense. Given the judge's greater understanding of the law, its values may more fully inform his or her evaluation of possible justifications for nullification than will be true for jurors. Both because of the nature of the office and because they usually find a way of mitigating the rigors of the law through their sentencing power, judges will need much more powerful reasons than juries to engage in outright nullification.

Judges also have the power, in their roles as fact-finders, in their supervision of jurors, and even in their construal of the law, to achieve nullification of the civil law. Except when they resolve factual disputes, what trial court judges do is subject to appeal, but the reality often is that a case is not worth appealing and the powers of trial judges are frequently much greater than a formal analysis of their relation to appellate courts indicates. Nullification of the civil law means denial of legal rights to a litigant who is claiming them; but especially in areas of law in which the power of litigants is unequal, such as landlord-tenant, judges may sometimes be disposed to mitigate the rigor of applicable legal standards.

---

20. *See, generally,* T. A. Green, *Verdict According to Conscience* (1985).
21. *Id. at 209.*
22. *Ga. Const. Art. 1, 32–201; Ind. Constr. Art. 1, § 19; Mo. Const. Art XV, § 19.*
23. *See* M. Kadish and S. Kadish, *Discretion to Disobey 51 (1973).*
24. *Christie, Lawful Departures from Legal Rules: "Jury Nullification" and Legitimated Disobedience, 62 Calif. L. Rev. 1289 (1974).*
25. *See* J. Adams, *Works III, 481, quoted and discussed in* B. Bailyn, *The Ideological Origins of the American Revolution 74 (1967).*
26. *Duncan v.* Louisiana, *391 U.S. 145, 153 (1968).*
27. *United States v.* Spock, *416 F.2d 165, 181 (1st Cir. 1969).*
28. *See* note 23, *supra.*
29. *See* Baier, *Book Review, 124 U. Pa. L. Rev. 561, 576 (1975).* M. B. E. Smith has criticized the Kadishes' assumption that one can speak of legal obligations independently of moral obligations. Smith, *Concerning Lawful Illegality, 83 Yale L. J. 1534 (1974).*
30. *If A has promised to pay B his only $2000, he cannot both fulfill the promise and pay $2000 for C's badly needed operation, but no logical compatibility exists between the two actions.*
31. *Id. at 581.*
32. *The initial grand jury disposition of the Bernhard Goetz case illustrates the possible uncertainty. Outsiders cannot be sure whether grand jurors refused to indict for homicide because they genuinely believed Goetz had a good claim of self-defense or because they just did not want to see him convicted given the circumstances surrounding his shooting of four youths.*
33. *Kadish and Kadish, supra note 23 at 31.*
34. *See* Green, *note 20 supra.*
35. *Christie, note 24 supra at 1304.*
36. *An assessment based on established constitutional or legislative criteria is much more appropriate for a judge. Both the application of the necessity defense and the interpretation of constitutional standards can involve judges in such assessments.*
37. *With respect to some petty offenses, such as traffic violations, it may be thought that judges have an implicit authority to decline to hold technically guilty offenders criminally liable.*

THE SERPENT BEGUILED ME AND I DID EAT:
Entrapment and the Creation of Crime*

Gerald Dworkin

This paper examines the legitimacy of pro-active law enforcement techniques, i.e. the use of deception to produce the performance of a criminal act in circumstances where it can be observed by law enforcement officials. It argues that law enforcement officials should only be allowed to create the intent to commit a crime in individuals who they have probable cause to suppose are already engaged or intending to engage in criminal activity of a similar nature.

In the past few years a number of criminal prosecutions have brought to public attention the issue of entrapment: Abscam, the DeLorean cocaine trial, Operation Greylord, various sting fencing operations. The investigative techniques used in, say, Abscam while highly elaborate, expensive and ingenious are only one example of the range of investigative techniques with which I shall be concerned in this essay. What these techniques have in common is the use of deception to produce the performance of a criminal act under circumstances in which it can be observed by law enforcement officials. I shall use the term "pro-active enforcement" to cover such techniques and the question I shall be discussing is under what circumstances, if any, is the use of such measures legitimate.

1

Let me begin by saying something more about the nature of pro-active law enforcement and also by giving a fairly extensive sample of the use of such tech-niques. The sample will not only make clearer the nature of such operations but also provide a range of cases for testing judgments about the acceptability of such techniques.

Traditionally, law enforcement in our society has left most of the burden of reporting criminal offenses to private citizens. It is left to individuals, usually victims, to come forward with a complaint of criminal action and to provide much of the evidence in identifying and prosecuting the criminal. Government's role has been limited to various patrol activities and to reaction to complaint. Hence, the traditional notion of reactive law enforcement.

Recently the existence of "invisible offenses" has posed challenges to reactive law enforcement. Invisible offenses include not only the so-called victimless crimes, i.e. those crimes in which there are no complaints because all parties to the transaction are willing (drugs, vice, gambling) but also a variety of cases in which the victims are not aware of any criminal act. The patrons of a hotel are not aware of code violations whose existence is protected by the bribery of a building inspector. The purchasers of General Electric products were not aware of the fact that the price of the products they bought was affected by a price-fixing agreement. The customers of a bank are not aware of the loss of funds due to the embezzlement of a teller. There is another class of offenses which produces knowing victims but where, for a variety of reasons, the victims are not prepared to complain—blackmail, extortion, sexual harassment. We know from crime surveys that many victims of robbery and theft do not report these crimes either because of fear of harassment or because they believe it to be a waste of time.

*From Dworkin, Gerald. "The Serpent Beguiled Me and I Did Eat: Entrapment and the Creation of Crime," in *Law and Philosophy* vol. 4 (1985), pp. 17–39. Copyright ©

Faced with the failure of the traditional modes of notification and investigative aid, law enforcement officials have turned to modes of investigation in which the reporting, observation and testimony can be done by the officials themselves. Detection of crime and investigation of crime proceed simultaneously. This is the arena of pro-active law enforcement. Originally used mainly in drug and vice investigations such techniques are now being used increasingly for many other kinds of crime. I shall enumerate a list of such techniques.

Decoy Operations

The New York City Street Crime Unit is a unit of the New York City Police Department which specializes in the techniques of "decoying and blending." The decoy is a police officer who assumes the role of a potential victim. He (or she) may play the role of derelict, shopper, grandmother, drunk, "john," cab driver, potential rape victim. The decoy is placed in an area where experience indicates it is likely the decoy will become a victim. The back-up blends into the street area near the decoy. When the decoy indicates that a crime has been committed the back-up team moves in for the arrest. A similar idea using inanimate objects occurs when decoy letters are sent to trap postal thieves.

In most decoy cases the potential offender is not targeted. But the same techniques can be used against specific suspects. In one case a Manhattan dentist was targeted after three patients had complained that they had been molested while under anaesthesia. An undercover policewoman posed as a patient, accepted anaesthesia, and was kept under surveillance by a hidden camera. The dentist was arrested and the video evidence led to a conviction.

Sting Operations

Undercover agents take over a warehouse and announce that they are in the market to purchase stolen goods. They purchase goods brought to them and, after some period of time, arrest the sellers of the stolen property. Similar operations have involved running a pornographic bookstore in order to arrest film wholesalers.

Manna from Heaven Operations

Police leave a piece of luggage unattended at the Port Authority bus terminal and arrest those who attempt to walk off with it. As an integrity test for policemen money is left in an apartment, the door is left open, and an "open-door" call is put through to the police.

Honey-Pot Operations

Undercover agents provide opportunities for various criminal acts without actively soliciting them. They may, for example, open a garbage business in the hopes of becoming targets for extortion, or operate a bar in the hopes of being solicited for bribes by city inspectors.

Solicitation Operations

The most common mode of drug enforcement involves government agents offering to buy drugs from dealers. Similar methods are used to enforce laws against counterfeit currency and illegal firearms. In one of the more creative uses of such techniques the police fencing detail in Portland, Oregon purchased color television sets at wholesale prices (under an LEAA grant) and then made the rounds of bars offering to sell the sets very cheaply, claiming they were stolen. As part of the same operation randomly chosen appliance stores were approached with the same offer.

In the recent Operation Greylord in Cook County, Illinois, undercover agents staged a crime and arrest so that they could solicit offers to drop the charges for a payment.

In the course of soliciting a crime the government may play an active role in a criminal operation. In one extreme case involving liquor regulations an agent contacted two defendants with whom he had been previously involved in the production of bootleg alcohol and pressured them to re-establish operations. He offered to provide a still, a still-site, equipment and an operator. He then provided two thousand pounds of sugar at wholesale. The operation lasted for three years during which the government agent was the only customer.

Although the Ninth Circuit reversed this conviction it did not do so on grounds of entrapment. It did argue, however, that "the same underlying objections which render entrapment objectionable to American criminal justice are operative."[1] To see both why the court did not find entrapment, and what the underlying objectives referred to consist in, we must now examine the nature of the entrapment defense. Although my concern is with the normative issues raised by proactive law enforcement, the legal doctrine of entrapment has been the focus of much of the discussion of such issues, and many of the conceptual and normative distinctions are present in the legal discussion.

2

Entrapment is a defense to a criminal charge. The defendant asserts a claim that he ought not to be held legally liable for some criminal act. It is a defense which originally was a judicial creation although it has since been codified in a number of states including Illinois, New York and Alaska. It is also interesting to note that as a bar to criminal liability it is virtually exclusive to the criminal jurisprudence of the United States.

It is a very narrow defense in that it only applies when the entrapment is performed by a government agent. It is not available to those who are enticed into criminal acts by private citizens. The term government agents, however, includes all employees of government, and in certain circumstances private citizens working for a government agent will count as government agents.

Entrapment occurs when government agents procure the commission of a criminal act by someone who, except for the solicitation, persuasion, or enticement, would not have committed the crime. Both the conditions under which entrapment will be found and the theoretical foundations of the defense are matters of legal dispute. Originally, state and federal courts based the defense on estoppel and public policy. But in 1932 the Supreme Court replaced these with the legal fiction that Congress implicitly excludes entrapment whenever it enacts a criminal statute. The court held that if the police implant in the mind of an innocent person the disposition to commit an offense it is unfair to find such a person guilty. We see here the two elements which recur through the future development of the doctrine—the innocence or predisposition of the offender and the inducement to commit the offense.

Sorrells contains the two main views about the justification of the entrapment defense.[2] The majority focuses on entrapment as a defense in the standard sense of the term, i.e. as a factor affecting the culpability or innocence of the offender. If somebody is found innocent by virtue of entrapment then, on this view, it is similar to being found innocent by virtue of mistake of fact. The offender is not, or not as, culpable. As an excuse, entrapment is focused on the conduct of the defendant and his relative blameworthiness.

The concurring view, on the other hand, focuses not on the culpability of the offender but on the integrity of the judicial process and the legitimacy of the methods used by the police. The defendant is excused, not because he is less culpable, but because the government has acted in an illegitimate fashion. The point of the defense is not to exculpate offenders but to monitor police behavior.

Parallel to these different views of the nature and function of the defence has been the development of two different standards for the applicability of the defense. What has come to be called the "subjective" test concentrates on the offender's state of mind. With whom did the intent to commit the crime originate? Was the defendant predisposed to commit the crime? Would this particular defendant have committed this particular crime in the absence of the government's conduct? On the view that the defense affects culpability, only those not predisposed to commit the offense will be excused. That is why the defendant in Greene, who had a prior history of violation of liquor regulations, could not invoke entrapment.

The "objective" test, sometimes called the "hypothetical person" test focuses on the conduct of the police, not the defendant. It asks whether the methods used would have led a hypothetical law-abiding citizen to commit the crime in question. As the California Supreme Court put it:

> [We] are not concerned with who first conceived or who willingly, reluctantly, acquiesced in a criminal project. What we do care about is how much and what manner of persuasion, pressure and cajoling are brought to bear by law enforcement officials to induce persons to commit crime. . . . The proper test of entrapment in California is the following: was the conduct of the law-enforcement agent likely to induce a normally law-abiding person to commit the offense.[3]

Note that on this view it does not matter whether or not this defendant was predisposed. If a hypothetical non-predisposed person would have been likely to commit the crime because of the actions of the police this defendant is let off, not because he is innocent, but because the government conduct cannot be condoned.

The two views cannot be integrated into a single theory. For on the view which emphasizes the innocence of those induced to perform criminal acts it should be irrelevant whether or not the entrapping parties are government agents or private citizens. And on the view which emphasizes the conduct of government agents, it should be irrelevant whether or not the suspect was predisposed to commit the crime.

Because the dominant opinion in the Supreme Court has favored the subjective test of entrapment, and most defendants have a criminal record which makes it difficult to demonstrate lack of predisposition, the entrapment defense remains limited in scope, rarely used, and even less rarely successful.

The legal literature on entrapment consists almost exclusively in expositions of the Supreme Court's various views about the doctrine, and normative questions are usually confined to arguing the relative merits of subjective vs. objective tests.[4] The much larger and important issue of the legitimacy of government created crime is ignored. What values are threatened by the use of pro-active methods of law enforcement? Ought we to distinguish between public officials and private citizens as targets of such techniques? Ought criminals have a right to complain about efficient methods of investigating and detecting their crimes? If certain crimes, e.g. bribery, can only (or most efficiently) be detected by these methods then does a norm of equal enforcement of the law favor such techniques?

3

The central moral concern with pro-active law enforcement techniques is that they manufacture or create crime in order that offenders be prosecuted and punished. They do not discover criminal activity; they create it. I take it that there is some common understanding of these terms such that if this were an accurate and apt description of certain law enforcement methods there would be a decisive objection to their use.

Consider, for example, the scenario of *U.S.* v. *Ordner.*[5] Ordner, a commercial blaster and firearms manufacturer, with no previous history of lawbreaking, was approached by a government informer at a gun show. The informer, working with the government in the hope of reducing his sentence in a pending case, offered to introduce Ordner to a contractor who might have some blasting work for him. When Ordner went to meet the contractor, he was instead confronted with an elaborate scheme concocted by agents of the Bureau of Alcohol, Tax and Firearms to resemble a meeting of an underworld gang. Ordner eventually provided the blueprint and directed the assembly of five hundred "penguns." This is clearly an instance of the creation of criminal activity by law enforcement agents. What are the elements that distinguish the creation or manufacture of crime from its investigation and detection?

If one looks back at the range of operations listed earlier one sees that there are various means by which agents contrive to have criminal acts performed in their presence (other than maintaining surveillance of the suspect or a potential crime scene). They can suggest the crime be committed, offer various incentives, use coercion, provide some of the means needed to commit the crime, participate in the commission of the crime, arrange the presence of a potential victim, arrange the presence of a valuable object in an unsecure context, offer to buy or sell contraband, appeal to sentiments of friendship.

On at least one view all of these might count as the creation of criminal activity. Suppose we defined the creation of criminal activity as occurring whenever the police acted in such a way that they caused criminal activity to occur. According to one idea of cause which has played an important role in tort law, one event is said to cause another if it is a necessary condition for its occurrence. This is referred to as "but for" causation. But for the presence of the event in question the other event would not have occurred. Now it is a feature of all pro-active techniques that but for the actions of law enforcement officials the crime for which the defendants are charged would, almost certainly, not have been committed.

Thus, if a policeman rides on a bus with a wallet in his back pocket, and his pocket is picked, but for the actions of the policeman his wallet would not have been stolen. If an officer, suspecting short weighting, makes a purchase of meat at a supermarket, weighs it and finds it short weighted, then this particular fraudulent sale would not have been committed if the government had not acted. Yet, in these cases, it does not seem that the culpability of defendants is reduced, or that the methods go beyond some idea of what is fair.

One way to see this is to note that in an ordinary mugging the presence of the victim is a but for cause of the crime. If this little old lady had not been walking her dog in the park, her mugging would not have occurred. But, surely, she did not create or manufacture crime. The contribution of the state has to go beyond simply providing a potential victim, as in decoy operations.

If, however, the decoy is made to look particularly vulnerable and the "reward" particularly attractive, then questions of temptation and the overcoming of the will raise issues of causation and responsibility.

If the crime is made sufficiently "easier" or sufficiently attractive then, as social scientists who leave wallets lying about in phone booths find out, almost any of us is likely to commit a crime.

It is relevant here to note that the increased probability does not occur simply as a forseen consequence of governmental action. A case of this would be the decision to shift patrols to a high-crime area foreseeing that there would be an increase in crime in the section of town with reduced patrols. But in the cases we are considering the point of the action is to increase the likelihood that a crime will be committed in the presence of the police.

If somebody commits a crime, and would not have done so absent the efforts of the state to make the crime easier, has the state created crime? To help in thinking about this let us look at other parts of the law which have developed theory on similar matters. In tort law it is common to invoke the idea that if one neglects to take precautions against harm one is liable for the harm that comes about, even if the harm is brought about by others. Thus a house painter was held liable for the loss of goods stolen by a thief who entered when the painter failed to lock the front door. But the language of the courts in such cases is not that the negligent party causes the wrongdoer to do what he does, or that he causes the harm that results. Rather it is that one has a duty to guard against such harm. Providing others with the opportunity to do harm may ground liability but not because it causes the harm.

In the criminal law there is also a distinction drawn between providing an opportunity to commit a crime and inducing others to commit crime. With respect to criminal responsibility a person is only held to have caused another to act if he makes use of threats, lies or the exercise of authority to induce another to act.

With respect to civil liability for the acts of others the accepted view is that one individual must do something which is directly addressed to the other person such as uttering a threat, or making a false statement, or exploiting personal influence. It is only when the agent led to act is less than fully competent, as in the case of young children, that the mere providing of a temptation counts as causing another to act— as in the doctrine of "attractive nuisance."

Both on grounds of conformity with other legal doctrine and harmony with commonsense notions of causation it is reasonable not to count the mere provision of opportunity to commit a crime as the manufacture or creation of crime. It is only if the opportunity is made sufficiently attractive that creation of opportuni-

ties can be regarded as temptation. The danger of such techniques is that they may lead persons to commit crimes who have not engaged in similar activities before. The person who walks away with the "abandoned" suitcase in the Port Authority building may not have been disposed to steal anything at all. In such cases there is the danger that one may not merely shift the scene of criminal activity but create crime that otherwise would not have occurred.

The offer to buy drugs, sex or stolen goods from those already engaged in their sale, or letting it be known that one is available for a bribe, does more than merely make it easier to commit a crime. It invites the criminal to act. Again, this does not seem sufficient to categorize the activity as the creation of crime since although the particular sale might not have taken place had it not been for the offer to engage in the transaction, by hypothesis one is dealing with those already engaged in criminal activity. Leaving aside complications, such as the fact that sting fencing operations may encourage individuals to commit burglaries by providing a ready outlet at above-market prices, such offers are on the portion of the spectrum closer to shifting the scene of criminal activity.

An interesting comparison is between the offer to sell as opposed to buy contraband. This seems a more questionable practice but it is not apparent where the difference lies. It is a crime to buy as well as sell contraband. Both transactions rely on the willingness of an offender to engage in the transaction. While it is true that the danger to society is usually greater from the seller than the buyer this seems to be relevant to what crimes to aim at, not at which techniques are permissible. Moreover, it does not seem particularly outrageous to let it be known that one is willing to sell one's services as a contract murderer (for the purpose of apprehending a buyer of such services).

I believe this is explained by the contingent fact that the offer to sell is more likely to be made without knowledge that a particular individual is already embarked on a course of criminal conduct. This is why the Oregon case of going into bars and offering to sell supposedly stolen televisions seems to be the creation of crime, while the offer to sell one's services as a contract murderer does not. In the former the state is, in effect, making a random test of the corruptability of the general public.

The next step up from merely providing an opportunity, or merely offering to engage in a criminal transaction, is to provide the necessary means for the commission of a crime. Consider for example the facts in the Twigg case.[6] Robert Kubica after being arrested on charges of illegally manufacturing speed, pled guilty and agreed to assist the Drug Enforcement Administration in prosecuting other offenders. At the request of DEA officials he contacted an acquaintance, Henry Neville, and proposed they set up a laboratory for manufacturing speed. Kubica assumed responsibility for acquiring the necessary equipment, raw materials and a production site. The DEA supplied all of these plus an ingredient essential to the manufacture which, while legal, was difficult to obtain. Twigg joined the operation at the invitation of Neville. Kubica alone had the technical knowledge and skills necessary to manufacture the drug and had complete charge of the laboratory. The Court reversed on the grounds that when Kubica contacted him, Neville

> *was not engaged in any illicit drug activity. Using Kubica, and actively participating with him, the DEA agents deceptively implanted the criminal design in Neville's mind. . . . This egregious conduct on the part of government agents generated new crimes by the defendant merely for the sake of pressing criminal charges against him when, as far as the record reveals, he was lawfully and peacefully minding his own affairs. Fundamental fairness does not permit us to countenance such actions by law enforcement officials and prosecution for a crime so fomented will be barred.*[7]

I should suppose fundamental fairness would raise some problems about this case even if the intent to commit the crime arose in Neville. Imagine that he approached Kubica saying he would like to manufacture some speed but, unfortunately, lacked the raw materials, the technical skills, the capital, and the equipment. Kubica then supplies them all and Neville is then arrested. What is the harm that the state seeks to avoid by such prosecutions?

Nevertheless the court is focusing on the right factor in the creation of crime—the origin of criminal intent. The essential question for determining when crime has been created is what the role of government is in causing the offender to form the specific intent to commit the crime in question. The issue of predisposition, which runs through the entrapment commentary, is a red herring. We are not interested in the general willingness of an offender to commit crime but in whether he has formed the intent to engage in a specific crime if the opportunity presents itself. In so far as only an opportunity is offered, then if the of-

fender is using it to realize a pre-existing purpose the origin of intent is in him. If the government, in Learned Hand's phrase, "solicits, proposes, initiates, broaches or suggests" the offense then the origin of the intent lodges with the state.

Real situations are, of course, complicated by overdetermination. Suppose, for example, I form the intent to commit a crime if and only if I am solicited to do so by someone else. Or suppose I form the intent to steal something, but cannot overcome a residual fear of being apprehended, and it is only your encouragement that enables me to carry out the original intent.

The fact that there are difficult questions about determining the origin of intent only shows that the question of whether crime has been manufactured is often hard to settle. And that is something we already knew. If the ambiguities and difficulties in determining the origin of intent match those in deciding whether crime has been created that is all one can demand in terms of a satisfactory analysis.

Given our understanding of the idea of the creation of crime in terms of origin of intent we can now pass to the normative issues. Is it legitimate, and if so under what conditions, for the government to create criminal activity?

4

To answer this question one must have some general view about the underlying purpose and rules of fairness which are embedded in the particular system of criminal law-enforcement we have adopted. The legitimacy of particular law-enforcement techniques is necessarily relative to a particular conception or model of criminal justice. At most an argument for condemning particular modes of enforcement will be of the form "If you accept a particular ideal of the purposes and fairness of attaching criminal sanctions to rules of conduct, then these methods will be inconsistent or not cohere with such an ideal."

I shall sketch the outlines of what I believe to be an ideal of the principles of distribution applied to criminal sanctions embedded in our current practice and jurisprudence.

1. Criminal sanctions constitute an interference with the liberty of the members of a society.
2. They are justified, at least in part, by their contribution to the adherence of citizens to justifiable standards of conduct.
3. Individuals ought to have a broad area of auton-

omy, i.e. self-determination, in the choice of behavior and the formation of goals and purposes.

4. There is a conflict between maximizing autonomy and promoting fundamental human goods such as security of possessions, personal integrity and opportunity. One way of mitigating this conflict is to allow individuals to choose whether or not to become subject to criminal sanctions by presenting them with reasons against certain conduct (sanctions) and letting them make the decision to comply or not. Individuals who are legitimately punished have self-selected themselves for such treatment.

5. The criminal law is not to be thought of as a price system, i.e. as it being indifferent whether a citizen obeys the law or violates it but pays the price of the sanction. The criminal law is meant to be obeyed. Certain behaviors are forbidden and others are required, and while the citizen is given a choice (in the sense that the behaviors are not made impossible) his will is constrained to make the correct choice.

These propositions have implications for very different aspects of the criminal justice system. They affect the substantive content of legal standards, e.g. standards which are very difficult or impossible to obey would be ruled out. They affect procedural issues, e.g. laws should be prospective in application. They affect the excusing conditions we ought to allow. And they affect the types of law-enforcement techniques we should regard as legitimate.

In light of the above propositions the normative issue may be phrased in the following manner: what methods of apprehending and detecting offenders are consistent with the view of a system of criminal sanctions as a choosing system and as the enforcement of law, i.e. authoritative rules backed by sanctions. I am claiming that it is not consistent with such a system that law enforcement officials attempt to see if they can cause a person to commit a crime by suggesting or encouraging in any way that a crime be committed.

It is not that such suggestions are improper only if they are such as to overwhelm the will. The use of coercion, excessive temptation, and fraud are obviously inconsistent with the view that we are only entitled to punish those offenders who willingly choose to commit crimes. I am arguing for the much stronger view that it is not proper to solicit, encourage, or suggest crime even if this is done by no stronger means than verbal suggestion. It is not that the offender can complain after the fact that his will was overborne. It

is that we, any of us, can complain before the fact that it is not the purpose of officers of the law to encourage crime for the purpose of punishing it.

For the law is set up to forbid people to engage in certain kinds of behavior. In effect it is commanding "Do not do this." And it shows that it is commanding, as opposed to requesting or advising by saying that it will impose sanctions on those who refuse to conform. It will "humble the will" to use Fingarette's language.[8]

But for a law enforcement official to encourage, suggest, or invite crime is to, in effect, be saying "Do this." It is certainly unfair to the citizen to be invited to do that which the law forbids him to do. But it is more than unfair; it is conceptually incoherent. Of course this incoherence does not appear to the person being entrapped since he is not aware of the official capacity of his entrapper. And the incapacity is concealed from the official since he thinks of himself as trying to detect a criminal—the thought being that an honest citizen will simply refuse the invitation. From the standpoint of one trying to understand and evaluate the system, however, the conflict is clear.

It is important to note that we are not literally involved in a contradiction as we would be, for example, if the Statutes both commanded and forbade that a certain action be done. Nor is it a pragmatic contradiction, in the sense of being self-defeating. The person who says "P but I do not believe P" takes back with the latter part of his assertion what he implies with the former part. Nor is it self-defeating in the sense that it cannot be useful to engage in such behavior in order to increase overall compliance with the legal system. It is not as if one part of the criminal justice system (the police) are trying to undo what another part (the legislature) is trying to accomplish.

It is not always incoherent to invite someone to do the very act which one is trying to get them to avoid doing. Consider a parent trying to teach a child not to touch the stove. In the case of a particularly recalcitrant child the most effective technique might be to encourage the child to touch the stove in one's presence. The slight pain now will teach the child to avoid a greater pain later. But this is surely not the model being used by the police. They are interested either in deterring others or in punishing guilty people. The end being served is not that of the person being invited to commit the crime.

I suppose we can (barely) make sense of a system of rules forbidding certain behavior which is enforced by inviting people to commit the forbidden acts and then punishing them for doing so. But such a system violates elementary standards of coherence and fairness.

To encourage the commission of a crime in the absence of any reason to believe the individual is already engaged in a course of criminal conduct is to be a tester of virtue, not a detector of crime.

As a way of insuring against such testing of virtue I suggest that whenever the action of creating an intent to commit a criminal act would render a private citizen liable to criminal charges as accessory or co-conspirator, public officials should be allowed to perform such acts as would create such an intent only if they have probable cause to suppose that the individuals approached are already engaged or are intending to engage in activity of a similar nature. If they offer to buy contraband from specific individuals they should have probable cause to believe those individuals are already engaged in such transactions. If they offer to sell stolen goods to individuals, they ought to have probable cause to believe such individuals are already buying stolen goods. If they offer bribes to public officials, then they should have probable cause to suppose that the officials are already corrupt; not just corruptible.

To use an analogy we do not think it proper for police to engage in random searches of homes in order to detect possible criminal activity. Why then should we allow random solicitation or encouragement of criminal activity? I have heard it argued that on grounds of equitable law enforcement it is wrong to allow those who may have corrupt dispositions, but have been fortunate enough not to have been given the opportunity to exercise them, to escape punishment when their less fortunate counterparts are caught. After all if we had offered them a bribe they would have taken it. This counter-factual seems to me an interesting piece of data for God, but not for the FBI. Suggesting the commission of a crime, even to wicked people, is not a legitimate function of a system of law enforcement.[9, 10]

Although my discussion has been much broader than the topic of Abscam I would like to apply the discussion to Abscam, partly because it has caused so much controversy and partly because it is a difficult case to form a judgment about. Abscam is not one case but many since there were a number of different public officials involved. But basically the actual solicitation of crime involved either offering money to secure residency for the "shiek" or the offer to finance a titanium mine in return for using political office to secure government contracts. It is the latter case (Senator Williams) that I wish to focus upon.

The charges against Williams and his attorney related to a titanium mine and processing plant. Williams' investment group consisting of himself, his attorney Feinberg, Katz, Errichetti (the mayor of Camden) and Sandy Williams sought financing to acquire the titanium enterprise. Through Errichetti the group contacted Melvin Weinberg a convicted swindler who was working for the government, and an undercover agent, Anthony Amoroso. The latter pair posed as members of Abdul Enterprises, an investment firm pretending to represent wealthy Arabs. Criminal charges arose out of the promise requested by the undercover agent as a condition for the financing, that Williams would use his power and influence to obtain government contracts for purchasing the titanium to be produced.

My own reading of the trial transcripts and the due process hearings that followed the conviction of Williams convinces me that Senator Williams acted in a corrupt and morally indefensible manner. Quite independently of the outcome of the criminal charges the Senate Ethics Committee acted entirely correctly in recommending that Williams be expelled from the Senate—an outcome he avoided by resigning.

On the legal issue of entrapment the trial judge denied Williams's motions to dismiss the indictment on grounds of entrapment and the Supreme Court concurred. What this shows, in my view, is that the current legal doctrine of entrapment is too narrowly construed because I believe the best reading of the evidence shows that Williams's crime was created and manufactured by the state, that there was no probable cause for targeting Williams, and that, in accordance with my earlier argument, it was improper to procede with prosecution. I can, in this appendix, only briefly highlight what I believe to be the grounds supporting my reading of the evidence. I shall be ignoring various aspects of the investigation which raise due process questions of their own, such as the reliability of Weinberg, the chief government informant, the absence of control over Weinberg by government agents, the absence of written reports summarizing conversations that were not recorded. I will focus only on the entrapment issues.

Was there probable cause for targeting Williams? The U.S. Attorney who supervised the investigation stated that he "had no reason to question the integrity of Senator Harrison Williams." The Special

Agent in Charge, John Good, testified the government was "starting with a clean slate." Nowhere is there evidence of a predicate to investigate. It is the absence of such a predicate, not the question of predisposition, which I regard as crucial to the legitimacy of soliciting or encouraging crime.

As to the question of where the suggestion for criminal activity arose one has to read the evidence and note when and how often the suggestion for illegal conduct arose with the informant or government agents. The titanium venture itself was a legitimate business venture. The criminal elements included using political influence to get government contracts, concealing one's interest in the mine, and so forth. Consider these conversations. MW is Melvin Weinberg, the government informant. SW is Sandy Williams, friend and business associate of Senator Williams. TD is an FBI agent. AF is Williams attorney and business associate. GK is a business associate of Williams.

MW: Allright, now what about, uh, let me ask you a question. There's a lot of government contracts that, ya know, on the chemicals.

SW: Right.

MW: Now, can Williams get us the bids on them.

SW: Well, I don't know about that. The main thing is with this Cyanamid thing . . .

MW: Yeah.

SW: They've got customers they've had for twenty, thirty, forty years. . . . And if we wanna increase our business, we'll have to, we'll have to go into like Sherman-Williams and people like that and try to get their business away from somebody else.

TD: Is he going to be able to steer any kind of contracts from the Committees that he's going to get involved with? I mean . . .

AF: Well, this I didn't know until now I have to ask him that.

GK: He's not a guy, he's not a doer, you know, quietly behind the scene, you know, he, uh, may move a little bit . . . but let me tell you this here between you and me, he's in a very, very powerful position here, the committees that he heads, you understand?

MW: Yeah.

GK: But he doesn't use that power for any advantages.

MW: Oh, how can we make him use it?

In this exchange the associates of Williams did not raise the issue of government contracts, and in every case where the government did so, they acted in a neutral or discouraging fashion. With respect to concealing his interest in the mine notice how in this conversation between Feinberg, Weinberg and Da Vito, the suggestion of concealing the interest arises from the government.

MW: That's in the mine though. But on the other thing there he, in fact you may we may put the 20 percent in his name even. I don't think he can though.

TD: Well, if he puts . . .

AF: I don't know, we haven't decided yet. We're gonna both examine the law involving his side investments which he . . .

MW: I don't think he can.

AF: He can put it in his wife's name or someone else.

MW: They could chase that too fast.

TD: Yeah.

MW: Come on, you're an attorney, you know that.

AF: I know that.

TD: Any, anything that he puts . . .

AF: I'm not sure that he's forbidden.

MW: Sure he is if he's going to get us open doors. Come on, you know that's a conflict of interest. He'll be sitting with Nixon out in Clemente there.

Perhaps the most controversial aspect of the investigation involves the coaching session between Weinberg and Williams just prior to Williams's meeting with the "shiek." This is the backstage maneuvers before the on-camera performance. Here is Weinberg telling Williams what to say.

MW: Forget the mine. Don't even mention the mine. . . . [Tell him] how high you are in the Senate. . . . He's interested in you . . . Who you know in the Senate can do you favors. . . . Without you there is no deal. You are the deal. You put this together. You worked on this and you got the government contracts. Without me there is no government contracts. . . . Mention, you know, come on as strong as possible. . . . You gotta just play and blow your horn. The louder you blow and mention names, who you control. And that's it, it goes no further. It's all talk, all bullshit.

But with all this effort the meeting with the shiek proves inconclusive. In November 1979, the prosecutors held a meeting to review the evidence against Williams and came to the conclusion that further investigative efforts were required.

Relative to the matter concerning US Senator Harrison Williams of New Jersey, the following was decided:

1. It will be necessary to recontact US Senator Williams to attempt to obtain an overt action on his part regarding the sponsorship of some type of legislation, i.e. tax cover for titanium mine and/or import quotas for titanium mine.

2. It was also suggested that attempts should be made to elicit from US Senator Williams whether or not he wanted his shares hidden, through discussions concerning reporting of personal taxes and official acts that he promised to provide.

The prosecutors subsequently decided to add the "asylum scenario" that had been used so successfully against other Congressmen. A meeting between Williams and the shiek was held in which the shiek offered Williams money to obtain permanent residency in the United States. Williams refused the money, although he did go on to link his assistance on the immigration matter to the financing of the titanium venture. Incidentally, this meeting which was videotaped and observed by the investigators was interrupted at one point by a phone call by an FBI agent who instructed the shiek as to what he should say to Williams. The agent later testified as to the purpose of the interruption: "It was clear from the way the conversation was going on that it wasn't quite as specific as we would have liked it to have been."

I suggest that what we had in this case was not an investigation of whether Senator Williams was breaking the law but an effort to see if he could be induced to do so. That he was apparently quite willing to be so induced is not at issue. The issue is whether it is legitimate to substitute for the question. "Is this individual, who we have reason to suspect of corrupt activity, acting in a corrupt manner?" the question "Can we corrupt this individual who we have no reason to believe is corrupt?"

I do not deny that political corruption is a very difficult crime to detect by normal investigative techniques. I also do not believe that it is impermissible to use deception and trickery in the attempt to uncover such corruption. But I do not believe that it is legitimate to solicit and encourage such corruption unless we have evidence that the targeted individuals are already engaged in such corruption.

---

1. Greene v. United States, *454 F. 2nd 783 (9th Cir. 1971).*

2. Sorrells v. United States, *287 U.S. 435 (1932).*

3. People v. Barraza, *23 Cal. 3rd 675 (1979).*

4. *Some exceptions include Park,* The Entrapment Controversy, *60 Minn. L. Rev. 163 (1976).* Goldstein, For Harold Laswell: Some Reflections on Human Dignity, Entrapment, Informed Consent and the Plea Bargain, *84 Yale L.J. 683 (1975).* Causation and Intention in the Entrapment Defense, *28 UCLA Law J. 859 (1981).*

5. *554 F. 2d 24 (2d Circ.), 434 U.S. 824 (1977).*

6. U.S. v. Twigg, *558 F. 2d 373 (3d Cir. 1978).*

7. *Id. at 381.*

8. *H. Fingarette,* Punishment and Suffering, *Proceedings and Addresses of the American Philosophical Society, v. 50, 1977 p. 510.*

9. *I have ignored in my argument any discussion of the practical consequences of law enforcement officials engaging in the creation of crime. My argument has been addressed to matters of principle rather than practice. I believe, however, that considerations of likely consequences strengthens the argument. The work of* Gary Marx, *a sociologist from MIT, is the best source for the dangers of undercover police work in general. Here are some of the problems that he worries about.*

(a) The lack of effective supervision of informers and police.

(b) The possibility of damage to unwitting victims and third parties.

(c) The possibility of police participating in real crimes to gain the confidence of the targeted suspects.

(d) The use of selective targeting against political opponents.

(e) The corrupting effect on police of pretending to be corrupt.

(f) Excessive invasion of privacy.

(g) Stimulation of criminal activity, e.g. through offering to purchase stolen goods.

10. *A version of this paper was read at the Eastern Division Meetings of the American Philosophical Association. My commentators at the meeting were Gerald Postema and Patricia White. I am indebted to them, and in particular to Postema, for helpful suggestions and criticisms.*

Justice and Compensation

THE CONCEPT OF CORRECTIVE JUSTICE IN RECENT THEORIES OF TORT LAW*

Richard Posner

For the last 100 years, which is to say since the publication of Holmes's The Common Law,[1] *most tort scholars have thought that tort doctrines were, and should be, based on utilitarian (or, more recently, economic) concepts.[2] This was the view of Holmes, of Ames, and of Terry; of the draftsmen of the first and second* Restatement of Torts; *and of the legal realists who thought the focus of tort law should be on loss spreading rather than on assessment of fault.[3] It is also the view of economic analysts of tort law such as Guido Calabresi and myself. Writing in 1972 about tort scholarship, George Fletcher declared that "the fashionable questions of the time are instrumentalist: What social value does the rule of liability further in this case? Does it advance a desirable goal, such as compensation, deterrence, risk-distribution, or minimization of accident costs?"[4] It would be easy to show that the goals which he listed were regarded by their advocates as utilitarian, or sometimes economic, goals. Since he wrote, the economic approach to tort law has developed apace; at the same time, several scholars have joined Fletcher both in questioning the proposition that tort doctrines are or*

should be based on utilitarian or economic ideas, and in arguing that the tort law should be, and perhaps already is, based on the idea of corrective justice.

This article will examine the concept of corrective justice and its application to theories of tort law. Part I explains how the concept was defined by its inventor, Aristotle, whose treatment is still the "classic analysis."[5] Part II examines the use of the concept by recent torts scholars—besides Fletcher, by Richard Epstein, John Borgo, Jules Coleman, and Frederick Sharp. Borgo, Fletcher, and Sharp refer to Aristotle explicitly; Coleman and Epstein do not, but they echo the Aristotelian definition. All five scholars, I contend, misapply the Aristotelian concept to a greater or lesser extent. Part III of the article argues that the Aristotelian concept is compatible with, and indeed required by, the economic theory of tort and, incidentally, contract and criminal law. Parts II and III illustrate the analysis with the question of no-fault automobile accident compensation plans.

The advocates of the corrective justice approach contend variously that corrective

*From Posner, Richard. "The Concept of Corrective Justice in Recent Theories of Tort Law," 10 *Journal of Legal Studies* 187–206 ('81). Copyright © by the University of Chicago. Reprinted by permission of *The Journal of Legal Studies*.

justice is and that it should be the basis of tort law. While ordinarily the difference between positive and normative analysis is of great importance in discussions of law, it is in this instance irrelevant. My argument is not that the theory of corrective justice provides either an inaccurate description of or an unsound guide to principles of tort liability, but that those who believe it is necessarily a rival to the economic approach are mistaken; the Aristotelian concept, at least, is not.

Appearances to the contrary notwithstanding, this paper is not an essay in antiquarianism. The idea of corrective justice, stated by Aristotle and accepted by later writers in the Aristotelian sense, continues to exercise a powerful hold over the imagination of legal scholars. It is for some of these scholars a ground for rejecting a utilitarian or economic conception of law. It is in short a part of the contemporary debate over legal theory.

I. Aristotle's Concept of Corrective Justice

In Book V, Chapter 4, of the *Nicomachean Ethics*, Aristotle develops the concept of corrective justice.[6] He had discussed, in Chapter 3, distributive justice—that is, justice in the distribution by the state of money, honors, and other things of value—saying that such awards should be made according to merit (*kat' axian*). Chapter 4 discusses a contrasting concept of justice, the rectificatory or corrective (*diorthōtikos*—literally "making straight"), which he says applies to transactions (*sunallagmata*), both voluntary (*hekosia*) and involuntary (*akosia*); the distinction is roughly that between contracts and torts.[7] The crucial passage in Chapter 4 is the following:

> . . . *it makes no difference [from a corrective justice standpoint] whether a good man has defrauded a bad man or a bad man a good one, nor whether it is a good or a bad man that has committed adultery; the law looks only to the distinctive character of the injury, and treats the parties as equal, if one is in the wrong and the other is being wronged, and if one inflicted injury and the other has received it.*[8]

As far as remedy is concerned, Aristotle says that

> *the judge tries to equalize things by means of the penalty, taking away from the gain of the assailant. For the term 'gain' [kerdos] is applied generally to such cases—even if it be not a term appropriate to certain cases, e.g. to the person who inflicts a wound—and 'loss' [zēmia] to the sufferer; at all events, when the suffering has been estimated, the one is called loss and the other gain. . . . Therefore the just . . . consists in having an equal amount before and after the transaction.*[9]

There is more, but the chapter is short, and the part I have summarized and especially the passages I have quoted contain the gist of Aristotle's concept.

The *Nicomachean Ethics*, consisting as they do of classroom notes of Aristotle's lectures, are notoriously obscure and there is a fair amount of exegetic literature on Book V, Chapter 4.[10] But there is little controversy with regard to the basic features of his concept of corrective justice, summarized above. As paraphrased by Joachim,

> *If, for example, the thief was a gentleman and the injured party a beggar—a member of an inferior class in the State—this difference of rank is nothing to the law. . . . All that the law is concerned with is that, of two parties before it, one has got an unfair advantage and the other has suffered an unfair disadvantage. There is, therefore, a wrong which needs redress—an inequality which needs to be equalized.*[11]

Three points should be noted about Aristotle's concept of corrective justice:

1. The duty to rectify is based not on the fact of injury but on the conjunction of injury and wrongdoing. The injurer must do wrong (*adikei*) as well as do harm (*eblapsen*), and the victim must be wronged (*adiketei*) as well as harmed (*beblaptai*). Not all departures from distributive justice call for correction. Someone who voluntarily makes a bad bargain may end up worse off than the principles of distributive justice would, but for the bad bargain, dictate. But he has not been wronged, and he is not entitled to rectification. Moreover, what is wrongful or unjust—*adikos*—is not defined in Chapter 4; it is assumed. In Chapter 8 of Book V we learn that "Whether an act is or is not one of injustice (or of justice) is determined by its voluntariness or invol-

untariness."[12] But even within the class of voluntary acts, only those that are deliberate can be acts of injustice. Those done by misadventure (where "the injury takes place contrary to reasonable expectation") or by mistake (where, for example, "he threw not with intent to wound but only to prick") are not.[13]

2. The idea that distributive considerations do not count in a setting of corrective justice ("it makes no difference whether a good man has defrauded a bad man or a bad man a good one . . .") is a procedural principle. It is not equivalent to saying that distributive notions should not affect the definition of rights or even that they should not enter into the determination of what sorts of acts are unjust or wrongful. The point, rather, is that the judge is interested only in the character—whether it is wrongful—of the injury, rather than in the character of the parties apart from that of the injury: "the moral worth of persons . . . is ignored."[14]

3. Aristotle was writing against the background of the Athenian legal system of his day, where even suits to redress crimes were (with rare exceptions) instituted and prosecuted by private individuals, the victim or a member of his family, rather than by the state.[15] So he naturally assumed that redress for wrongful injuries was by means of private actions. But there is no indication in Chapter 4 that he thought there could be only one mode of rectification consistent with the concept of corrective justice—namely, a tort action, in which the judge orders the wrongdoer to pay a damages judgment to the victim. In fact, as we shall see in Part III, it is not even certain that Aristotle required that rectification involve full compensation of the victim.

To summarize, the main point in Chapter 4 is that if someone injures another wrongfully, he has behaved unjustly irrespective of his merit, relative to the victim's, evaluated apart from the wrongful injury itself. Chapter 4 is thus a corollary to Chapter 3, which discusses distributive justice. Chapter 4 makes clear that the rights of the superior individual do not include the right to injure an inferior person through wrongful conduct. This idea of "impartial legal correction"[16] is important, but it is more limited than the corrective justice concepts of recent tort scholars, to which I turn next. It is limited because it is part of what Aristotle called "particular" justice (in Chapter 2 of Book V), in contrast to universal justice which he equates to virtue in general.

II. Modern Tort Scholars on Corrective Justice

Professor Fletcher analyzes tort law under two competing "paradigms"—the "paradigm of reciprocity" and the "paradigm of reasonableness."[17] The former is derived from notions of corrective justice that Fletcher locates in Book V, Chapter 4 of the *Nicomachean Ethics*,[18] and the latter from utilitarian ideas. The paradigm of reasonableness corresponds in a rough way to the negligence standard, with its implicit (sometimes explicit[19]) balancing of the costs and benefits of risky activity. Under the paradigm of reciprocity, in contrast, "a victim has a right to recover for injuries caused by a risk greater in degree and different in order from those created by the victim and imposed on the defendant,"[20] irrespective of the social value of the defendant's or the plaintiff's activity giving rise to the injury. The choice between the two paradigms depends on "whether judges should look solely at the claims and interests of the parties before the court . . . without looking beyond the case at hand" (as corrective justice requires, according to Fletcher)—in which event they should choose the paradigm of reciprocity—or whether judges should "resolve seemingly private disputes in a way that serves the interests of the community as a whole,"[21] in which event they should choose the paradigm of reasonableness.

Fletcher's suggested rule of reciprocity has no basis in the concept of corrective justice expounded by Aristotle, the only authority on corrective justice to whom Fletcher refers. Nowhere does Aristotle suggest that the concept of wrongful or unjust conduct excludes consideration of the social value of conduct. To be sure, the Aristotelian judge is not to look "beyond the case at hand," but only in the sense that he is not to consider whether the defendant is a better man than the plaintiff, evaluated apart from the character of the injury; it does not follow that the social utility of the defendant's conduct that gave rise to the injury is irrelevant to whether the injury was wrongful.[22] There is no basis in the Aristotelian concept of corrective justice for Fletcher's conclusion that negligence is an inappropriate standard when the victim's conduct is less dangerous to the injurer than the injurer's is to the victim.

Professor Epstein began publishing articles on tort law the year after Fletcher wrote his article. Epstein initially did not base his concept of tort liability on corrective justice; the only reference to the term in the first article is in a footnote criticizing Fletcher—who Epstein, at this point at least, seems to have thought was playing a different sort of game.[23] Epstein's first article bases his idea that tort liability is, *prima facie,* strict liability on notions variously described as causation, common sense, ordinary language, liberty, and free will—not corrective justice. But the term is used repeatedly in the next article,[24] and by 1979, writing on nuisance, Epstein describes his "basic . . . framework" or "conceptual . . . ideal" as one based on the "principles of corrective justice: rendering to each person whatever redress is required because of the violation of his rights by another."[25] This is an acceptable paraphrase of the Aristotelian concept, but reading on one realizes that corrective justice means something different to Epstein from what it meant to Aristotle. Epstein speaks of "the distribution of vested rights demanded by a corrective justice theory" and says that "corrective justice principles still help us decide who is a wrongdoer and who is an innocent driver," and again that "corrective justice arguments identify the wrongdoer."[26] But the Aristotelian concept of corrective justice does not tell us who is a wrongdoer or who has vested rights; all it tells us is that a wrongful injury is not excused by the moral superiority of the injurer to the victim. More recently Epstein has described his conceptual ideal as "straight corrective justice-libertarian theory."[27] But unless the Aristotelian notion is to be abandoned completely, "corrective justice" and "libertarian" cannot be yoked in this way—the former referring as it does to the rectification of a wrong, the latter to a particular theory of wrongful conduct.

Epstein seems to associate two fundamental ideas with corrective justice. The first is that the victim of wrongdoing has a right to be compensated by the wrongdoer for injury resulting from the invasion.[28] The second is that the fact of injury "permits the plaintiff to show that the initial balance between the two parties is in need of redress because of the defendant's conduct."[29] The first idea, that of the wrongdoer's duty to compensate the victim of wrong, is certainly found in Book V, Chapter 4 of the *Nicomachean Ethics,* but I think as background rather than as a central principle of corrective justice. If one had said to Aristotle, "the best way to deal with wrongful conduct is to deter it through a heavy criminal penalty, rather than to allow private damage actions," there is no evidence that he would have regarded such a substitution as unjust. As to the second point, while the ideas of balance and redress are part of Aristotle's concept of corrective justice, Epstein's idea that the balance is disturbed by

injury alone is not. Aristotle requires, as the predicate for redress under a corrective justice theory, that the injurer be acting wrongfully *and* that the victim be harmed. These are two distinct requirements in Aristotle, not one as in Epstein.[30]

I do not criticize Epstein for not being an Aristotelian. But since the idea of corrective justice remains closely associated with the Aristotelian concept, it would promote clarity if modern writers wishing to use the term in a different sense would explain their meaning. No doubt they like the favorable connotations of the term "corrective justice"—why else use it? —but these favorable connotations properly belong to the Aristotelian usage, if only because the subsequent philosophical tradition accepted, and to this day accepts, that usage.[31]

I shall skip over Professor Coleman for a moment, though he is next chronologically, to discuss Professor Borgo, who builds his analysis of corrective justice on Epstein's. Borgo describes Epstein's concept of corrective justice as "the notion that when one man harms another the victim has a moral right to demand, and the injurer a moral duty to pay him, compensation for the harm,"[32] and Borgo accepts this as a correct statement of the Aristotelian concept, citing Book V, Chapter 4 of the *Nicomachean Ethics.*[33] But Aristotle does not suggest that a duty to compensate arises from the fact of harm; he states explicitly that the harm must be wrongful.

Borgo's mistake warps his entire analysis. Having defined the idea of corrective justice as requiring compensation paid for harm done, Borgo must do handsprings to come up with an idea of causation that will carry the moral freight that he associates with the idea of corrective justice. He states: "the linchpin of a system of corrective justice is a nonorthodox doctrine of causation. Such a doctrine makes it possible to focus analysis on the causal relation between the defendant's conduct and the plaintiff's harm. That relation in turn provides the basis for ascribing moral, and therefore legal, responsibility for harm."[34] If causation is defined as moral responsibility, so that the idea of harm is equated to the idea of wrongful harm, the Aristotelian concept is obtained. But this extraordinarily indirect route to the correct conclusion is necessary only because Borgo misreads Aristotle.

It is easy to see how Borgo was inveigled into taking this path by Professor Epstein, who uses the term corrective justice repeatedly, states that corrective justice principles require that a person be prima facie liable for any injury that he causes, and then, through the idea of "causal paradigms," imposes limitations on the meaning of "cause." In Epstein's view, the basic meaning of cause is captured in the paradigmatic example "*A* hit *B*." To be considered causal, a relationship must resemble closely this example. Using this method, Epstein can show, for example, that competition is not a tort, because the way in which harm occurs when one rival offers a lower price or superior product than another does not involve the use of force or anything enough like force to be assimilated to the *A*-hit-*B* example.[35]

Epstein's idea of causation is an unusual one, for there is no linguistic or conceptual difficulty in regarding a successful competitor as having "caused" the business losses of his less successful rival, and an unnecessary one, for it does not follow from the idea of corrective justice that competition is a tort merely because it causes injury; the idea of corrective justice does not imply that merely causing a harm creates a right to redress or rectification. But because Borgo thinks Epstein has defined the Aristotelian notion of corrective justice correctly, and hence that merely causing harm *does* entitle the victim to redress, Borgo must find some other, non-Epsteinian method of limiting the idea of cause, in order to avoid unacceptable results such as liability in the competition case. Borgo's method is to equate causation in tort law to moral or legal responsibility.[36] It is as curious a way of limiting the idea of causation as Epstein's. It is true that conclusions about causation are frequently influenced by normative considerations: that we may single out one necessary condition from all the others as "the cause" because it is the thing we want to change. But causation and responsibility are not synonyms. The competition example shows this. The successful competitor has indeed "caused" his rival's business losses, but no moral opprobrium, or legal liability, attaches to this injury, because social welfare is enhanced by competition. Only a misreading of Aristotle could make Borgo think it important to pour the idea of moral responsibility into the idea of causation in order to avoid unacceptable results.

Another way to read Epstein is that he believes the duty of corrective justice is triggered not by causing harm but by causing harm through the use of physical force or some closely related modality such as fraud.[37] In this reading Aristotle's distinction between the wrong and the injury is preserved, and the wrong is the use of force or fraud. But in not making this distinction explicit Epstein merges the issues of wrong and injury, with the result that the ethical basis of his system is unclear.[38] Early Epstein is a "responsibility" theorist,[39] as is Borgo; later Epstein, and

Fletcher, are "rights" theorists.[40] Although Epstein has used the term corrective justice to describe both stages of his thought, neither responsibility theories nor rights theories are theories of corrective justice. They are theories about the holdings or entitlements that people can legitimately claim. They belong to distributive rather than corrective justice.

Professor Jules Coleman has written a series of articles on tort law emphasizing what he calls compensatory or sometimes rectificatory justice, a term equivalent to Aristotle's corrective justice. Coleman states that "compensatory justice is concerned with eliminating undeserved or otherwise unjustifiable gains and losses. Compensation is therefore a matter of justice because it protects a distribution of wealth—resources or entitlements to them—from distortion through unwarranted gains and losses. It does so by requiring annulment of both."[41] Coleman recognizes that a duty of corrective justice is compatible with a substantive concept of unjust conduct based on economics or utilitarianism. The "distortion" of which he speaks comes about because the injurer has violated a standard of conduct and the standard could be "one of maximizing social utility."[42] This is an important point that is easily missed. If one equates retributive justice to punishment based on a nonutilitarian theory of desert, in the manner of Kant, and then equates retributive to corrective justice, then corrective justice will indeed seem necessarily inconsistent with utilitarianism. But even if the Kantian concept of retributive justice is accepted, the further step of equating retributive and corrective justice is unwarranted; Aristotle himself rejects retribution as a basis for punishment in Chapter 5 of Book V.

The twist that Coleman gives the concept of corrective justice is to emphasize the victim's deserts more than the injurer's guilt. If an injury is wrongful, the victim is entitled to be compensated, but not necessarily by the injurer; if the injurer did not gain from his wrongful act, corrective justice does not require that he be the source of the victim's compensation. But there is a problem: if the injurer is not the source of the compensation, then someone else, who is innocent, must be, and why is not that innocent party a victim of the wrongdoer's injurious conduct?

Defending no-fault automobile accident compensation plans against arguments based on corrective justice notions, Coleman argues that the victim of an accident in which the injurer was at fault is entitled to compensation and receives it under a no-fault system, but the injurer is not required as a matter of justice to be the source of the compensation because he does not gain by his wrongful act, as he would if we were speaking of a theft rather than an accident.[43] Both propositions—that the victim is compensated, and that the wrongdoer does not gain—can be questioned. Take the second first. The injurer avoids the costs of taking care. This cost saving is a gain to him; if his conduct (driving too fast, for example) is wrongful, it is a wrongful gain. Negligence under the Hand formula is a failure to take cost-justified precautions, and this failure involves a cost savings to the injurer which is a wrongful gain to him. Coleman has made not only a mistake in economics but a mistake about Aristotle, who used "gain" and "loss" to describe the relation between injurer and victim even when the term "gain" was (he thought) not quite appropriate, as in the case of a wounding.[44]

And is the victim really compensated? He receives the insurance proceeds, and let us assume they are sufficient to make him whole; but he paid for the insurance, so he just receives what is his. Potential victims as a class are clearly harmed by people who cause accidents; accident insurance premiums will be higher the higher the accident rate, and there will be no compensation by the wrongdoers for these higher premiums. Therefore, no-fault automobile accident compensation plans, which amount to eliminating liability and compelling potential victims to insure (at their own cost) against being hurt in automobile accidents, would appear to violate corrective justice because they do not redress injuries caused by wrongdoing.[45]

It does not follow that allowing people to buy *liability* insurance is inconsistent with the Aristotelian concept of corrective justice. It might appear that the effect of liability insurance is to shift the victim's costs resulting from the wrongdoer's action to the other members of the wrongdoer's risk pool, who become in effect uncompensated victims of his action. But they are compensated, albeit *ex ante,* by the opportunity which insurance affords them to shift some of their accident costs to other members of the risk pool. There is nothing in Aristotle to preclude this mode of compensation, indirect as it may seem; it is the principle of rectification, rather than the form it takes, that Aristotle insists on.

I come finally to Frederick Sharp, who has written an article applying "the ethical categories of Aristotle" to the question whether tort law should adopt "enterprise liability," defined as "liability without fault imposed on enterprises."[46] Corrective justice is one of these categories, but Sharp realizes that the Aristotelian concept of justice is not exhausted by

the discussion of corrective justice in Chapter 4 of Book V.

Sharp's discussion of *Rylands* v. *Fletcher*[47] illustrates his method and its shortcomings. He begins by suggesting that there is a problem in applying the Aristotelian categories to the case because, he says, the injury involved a loss to the victim but no gain to the injurer. This is the same economic error that Coleman made, but Sharp, here a sharper reader of Aristotle than Coleman, notes that Aristotle said that there is a duty of corrective justice even in cases where there is no apparent gain to the injurer. But Sharp faces another problem: "although the defendant [in *Rylands* v. *Fletcher*] inflicted injury on the plaintiff, he did not do so 'wrongfully' since [according to Book V, Chapter 8 of the *Nicomachean Ethics*] this requires knowledge."[48]

Sharp nevertheless concludes that corrective justice supports the result in *Rylands* v. *Fletcher*. His reasoning is complex, and as the only extended attempt among the writers we are considering to extract a substantive principle of justice from Aristotle's discussion of corrective justice deserves quotation in full:

> Between all citizens there is proportionality, which is altered when one suffers injury. It is unjust to suffer injury at the hands of another, and thus important that the injury be recompensed. But what to do if no one has gained by the injury? Mr. Justice Blackburn [in Rylands v. Fletcher] justified imposing liability on the defendant by the nature of his activity; "anything likely to do mischief if it escapes." Put in extended Aristotelian terms, anyone who carries on a hazardous activity which alters the social proportion of benefits by inflicting injury must bear the burden, because the nature of the activity has brought "gain" to the enterpriser. This is corrective justice in the sense that hazardous enterprises can cause injury disproportionate to the expectations of citizens living together by agreement in a commonwealth. A "gain" is imputed to the defendant in this case, since he departed from the restrictive standard of conduct owing to one's neighbours, and so potentially violated the social proportionality from the moment he embarked on the dangerous activity. It is thus that I argue Aristotle's support for the doctrine of enterprise liability for ultrahazardous activities, on the basis that industry must pay its own way.[49]

The key idea is that of proportion. There is indeed much discussion in Book V of the *Nicomachean Ethics*, as elsewhere in this great work, of proportion, balance, mean, and related terms. In particular, Aristotle makes a distinction between what he calls the "geometrical mean" and the "arithmetical mean,"[50] relating the first concept to distributive justice and the second to corrective justice. If there is some amount of money or of honors to be distributed by the state, it should be distributed in proportion to the relative merits of the citizens. Thus if A is twice as virtuous as B, and virtue is the standard of merit in the society, A should receive two-thirds of the distribution. This is the "geometrical mean." But if A steals a drachma from B, B is entitled to the return of the drachma—not just to one-third of a drachma. This is the "arithmetical mean."

In short, corrective justice requires annulling a departure from the preexisting distribution of money or honors in accordance with merit, but only when the departure is the result of *an act of injustice,* causing injury. Sharp omits this qualification. When he states, "It is unjust to suffer injury at the hands of another, and thus important that the injury be recompensed," he departs from the Aristotelian concept of corrective justice by failing to distinguish injury from wrong. The problem is not that the defendants in *Rylands* v. *Fletcher* did not gain from the injury—they did, at least in an economic analysis. The problem is that there is no basis in Aristotelian thought for regarding an injury that occurs without fault as unjust, and therefore as triggering a duty of corrective justice.[51] So we have a paradox: Epstein and Sharp (and also Fletcher) invoke corrective justice in support of enlarging the scope of strict liability as a principle of tort law, but if anything the Aristotelian concept suggests narrowing it, because the concept requires wrongful conduct as well as harmful result.

One could, I think, argue that strict liability would be consistent with the Aristotelian concept if it were shown to be simply a more efficient method of compensating the victims of wrongdoers; the fact that some injurers who were not wrongdoers would be mulcted in damages would not necessarily invalidate the argument. Yet Aristotle, with all the emphasis he places on the greatest good for man being happiness in activity, and not merely in disposition,[52] would probably have thought it odd to penalize the man of action by requiring him to compensate someone whom he injured while using due care. But this point, having to do with Aristotle's substantive conception of the good for man, cannot be adequately developed in the compass of this paper.

III. The Economic Basis of Corrective Justice

Once the concept of corrective justice is given its correct Aristotelian meaning, it becomes possible to show that it is not only compatible with, but required by, the economic theory of law. In that theory, law is a means of bringing about an efficient (in the sense of wealth-maximizing) allocation of resources by correcting externalities and other distortions in the market's allocation of resources.[53] The idea of rectification in the Aristotelian sense is implicit in this theory. If A fails to take precautions that would cost less than their expected benefits in accident avoidance, thus causing an accident in which B is injured, and nothing is done to rectify this wrong, the concept of justice as efficiency will be violated. The reason is discovered by considering the consequences of doing nothing. Since A does not bear the cost (or the full cost) of his careless behavior, he will have no incentive to take precautions in the future, and there will be more accidents than is optimal. Since B receives no compensation for his injury, he may be induced to adopt in the future precautions which by hypothesis (the hypothesis that the accident was caused by A's wrongful conduct, in an economic sense of "wrongful") are more costly than the precaution that A failed to take. B's precautions will reduce the number of accidents, thus partially offsetting the adverse consequences of A's continuing failure to take the precaution, but aggregate social welfare will be diminished by this allocation of care between the parties.

The substantive concept of "wrongful" conduct in this example is of course different from Aristotle's substantive concept of wrongful conduct as set forth in Chapter 8 of Book V. He did not consider negligence the kind of wrongful conduct that triggers a duty of rectification, because negligence is not a deliberate wrong; the negligent injurer does not desire to cause an injury. But the idea of corrective justice as redress for wrongful injury (Chapter 4) is logically separable from the idea of wrongful injury as *deliberately* wrongful (Chapter 8). By the same token, the act of injustice that triggers the duty of corrective justice could be defined more broadly than Aristotle, or a normative economist, would define it.

Although the economic theory of justice requires rectification in the above example and thus implies the Aristotelian concept of corrective justice, the precise mode of rectification remains, for the economist as for Aristotle, a secondary question having to do with the practical advantages and disadvantages of alternative modes. Aristotle assumed that the method of rectification would involve private actions, mainly for damages, because that was how things were done in his day. The situation today remains much the same and economists have presented arguments why the private damage action continues to be the cornerstone of the system of redress in most tort (and contract) settings.[54] But where private tort remedies are infeasible, as where injurers have no assets to levy on—not even what they wrongfully took from the victim— there is nothing in Aristotle to imply that an alternative mode of rectification, such as criminal punishment, would be unjust.

A more difficult case is where tort remedies, while feasible, are more costly than the alternatives. Suppose the advocates of no-fault automobile accident compensation plans are correct that a combination of criminal penalties for dangerous driving and compulsory accident insurance for potential victims would be a more efficient method of accident control, considering all relevant social costs—the costs of accidents, the costs of accident avoidance, and the costs of administering the accident-control system itself— than the present tort system. If the criminal penalties deterred all negligent driving, there would be no victims of wrongful conduct and so no problem with the abolition of liability. But not all negligent injuries would be deterred, so some victims of wrongful injury would go uncompensated. Would the no-fault system therefore violate corrective justice? Not necessarily. The concept of *ex ante* compensation, introduced earlier, is again relevant. If the no-fault system is really cheaper, potential victims (who are also drivers) may prefer to buy accident insurance and forgo their tort rights in exchange for not having to buy liability insurance.

But there is a simpler route to the conclusion that a no-fault plan would not necessarily violate the concept of corrective justice. If there are good reasons, grounded in considerations of social utility, for abolishing the wrong of negligently injuring another, then the failure to compensate for such an injury is not a failure to compensate for *wrongful* injury. To repeat an earlier point, corrective justice is a procedural principle; the meaning of wrongful conduct must be sought elsewhere.

Let us consider another example of arguable conflict between corrective justice and economics.

Suppose a favorite idea of economists was adopted, and a very high fine was set for some offense coupled with a very low probability of apprehension and conviction. Say the fine was $100—although the social cost of the offense was only $1—and the probability of apprehending and convicting an offender was set at one percent. Then in 99 out of 100 cases the offender would go scot-free. Would such a penalty scheme, though economically optimal, violate the principles of corrective justice? I think not. The expected cost of the offense is $1, which we said was its social cost. The offender has paid for the offense—in advance. To be sure, *ex post* there will be unequal treatment of offenders; *ex post,* some really will get off scot-free; but unless the *ex ante* perspective is inconsistent with the Aristotelian idea of corrective justice (and why should it be?), a failure of redress *ex post* is not necessarily a failure to do corrective justice.

Book V, Chapter 4 of the *Nicomachean Ethics* makes the point not only that a wrongful and injurious act requires rectification in some unspecified form—a point perilously close to being a tautology—but also, and more interestingly, that the duty of rectification is unaffected by the relative merit of injurer and victim considered apart from the injury; unaffected, that is, by distributive considerations. Distributive neutrality is also required by the economic analysis of law. Consider two otherwise identical accident cases, but in one the injurer and the victim have incomes of 100 (in present-value terms) and in the other the victim's income is only 60. The accident is the result of a wrong (in the economic sense of a failure to take a cost-justified precaution) by the injurer, and the victim is totally disabled from gainful work by the accident but not otherwise injured. Under the economic approach as under the Aristotelian, and assuming rectification takes the form of private damages actions, the first victim would be entitled to damages of 100 and the second to 60. If the second victim's damages were reduced by a further 60 percent—say on the ground that he is only 60 percent as meritorious as the injurer—there would be underdeterrence of accidents from an economic standpoint, because the injurer would not bear the full social costs of his accidents. Similarly, it would be wrong as a matter both of economics and corrective justice to award the same damages to both victims—notwithstanding the difference in their incomes—on the ground, for example, that they were in some sense equally good people. To adjust the compensation according to the relative merit of the injurer and the victim as persons would be contrary to Aristotle's concept of corrective justice, and it would also be inefficient because it would induce an inefficient level of precautions by one of the victims, or by both, or even by the injurer. For example, if victim A receives only 60 in damages, and victim B also 60, A will be undercompensated and will be led to take excessive precautions. If A and B each receive 100, there will be overdeterrence of injurers; in addition, B will have an incentive to act carelessly since he profits from being disabled. If each receives 80 (one-half their combined loss), then A will be undercompensated and B overcompensated, with inefficient results as just described. Thus, the distributive neutrality of the economic analysis of torts is not a merely adventitious characteristic of that analysis. Neutrality is required as a matter of justice, where justice is defined in terms of economic efficiency.

I am not arguing that Aristotle anticipated the economic analysis of law. He did not. Not only was his substantive concept of wrongful conduct too narrow from an economic standpoint, because limited to deliberate wrongs, but it is not clear whether his idea of corrective justice required that the victim of wrongful conduct be correctly (from an economic standpoint) compensated. The problem is most acute in the case where the wrongdoer's gain is less than the victim's loss. One commentator has suggested that if the wrongdoer gained 3 and the victim lost 7, Aristotle would have wanted the judge to award damages of 5.[55] Another commentator thinks Aristotle would have required full compensation.[56] The first suggestion would involve giving the victim an incentive to overinvest in safety.

The problem of asymmetrical gain and loss is common in contract as well as tort cases and helps explain why specific performance, as distinct from damages, is not necessarily required by the principles of corrective justice. At first glance it might seem that if someone has breached his contract, ordering him to perform it—specific performance—is the natural method of rectification. But suppose the reason he breached was that the cost of performance had become prohibitive; then specific performance would impose a cost on the wrongdoer that might be much greater than the loss to the victim of the breach, while a damages remedy might (depending on the rules of damages) compensate the victim fully.

Various rules of standing may seem to raise questions of conflict between corrective justice principles and economic principles. Take the rule that only a direct purchaser from a seller who is charging a price in violation of antitrust law can maintain a damages action against the seller. A purchaser from that purchaser—an indirect purchaser, in other words—is not allowed to sue even though the first purchaser may have passed on most of the overcharge to him.[57] The indirect purchaser is injured, and he is injured as the result of a wrongful act: must he not, therefore, be allowed to sue, if corrective justice is to be done? Professor Landes and I have argued that even in this case there is compensation *ex ante*.[58] If the direct purchaser has a right to collect the entire overcharge, the net cost to him of buying the good in question is lower, and he will pass on the saving to the indirect purchaser (or so much of the saving as he would pass on of the overcharge). Therefore, the indirect purchaser is compensated in advance for the expected cost of the antitrust overcharge passed on to him, by paying a lower price for the good. And the wrongdoer is punished, since he pays damages to the direct purchaser. The essentials of corrective justice are preserved.

But we also argued that the costs of allowing indirect purchasers to maintain damage actions provided an independent ground for denying such purchasers standing. Is cost a proper ground for refusing to do corrective justice? Consider this case. The theory of the second best teaches that sometimes the optimal way to improve the allocation of resources is to allow a compensating distortion. Suppose there is a cartel of widget producers, and they maintain a price far above cost, inducing some purchasers to switch to other products; this switching results in what the economist calls a "deadweight loss." One way of reducing the deadweight loss would be to raise the price of substitute products; then there would be less switching and less deadweight loss. Yet it would strain the ordinary meaning of the word "wrong" to say that the cartel's behavior was not wrongful, simply because society had decided to offset the wrong rather than correct it directly. Perhaps even in this case an argument based on *ex ante* compensation could be used, as in the earlier example of no-fault automobile accident compensation, to preserve corrective justice. But the more interesting question is whether corrective justice imposes duties regardless of cost. There is nothing in Aristotle to suggest that it does.

To all that I have said in this part of the paper two possible responses remain to be considered. The first is that I have limited discussion to *Aristotle's* concept of corrective justice and other concepts might lead to other results, perhaps inconsistent with the economic approach. This is of course possible, but while Aristotle's concept is not always followed, as I tried to show in Part II of this article, no alternative concept has, to my knowledge at least, been elaborated. Second, it may be argued that while both the Aristotelian concept and economic analysis result in the same or at least similar systems of redress, they do so for different reasons: the Aristotelian to carry out some ideal of justice, and the economic to maximize the wealth of society. But Aristotle did not explain *why* he thought there was a duty of corrective justice; he merely explained what that duty was.[59] Economic analysis supplies a reason why the duty to rectify wrongs, and the corollary principle of distributive neutrality in rectification, is (depending on the cost of rectification) a part of the concept of justice. Corrective justice is an instrument for maximizing wealth, and in the normative economic theory of the state—or at least in that version of the theory that I espouse—wealth maximization is the ultimate objective of the just state.

To summarize, my argument is not that Aristotle advocated an economic approach to law; it is that the concept of corrective justice in Book V, Chapter 4 of the *Nicomachean Ethics* is, and must be, a component of the economic theory of law. But whether this point is correct or not, those scholars who view the term "corrective justice" in a sense different from Aristotle's should explain and justify their unorthodox usage.

---

1. See Oliver Wendell Holmes, Jr., *The Common Law* (1881), especially at pp. 94–96.

2. On the utilitarian tradition in tort law see William M. Landes & Richard A. Posner, *The Economic Structure of Tort Law*, ch. 1 (1980) (unpublished manuscript at the Univ. of Chicago). I have argued that the law is economic rather than utilitarian, that what is and should be maximized by judges applying that law is wealth rather than utility; but wealth and utility are both aggregate measures of social welfare, and my normative economic approach can be described as one of constrained utilitarianism. See Richard A. Posner, *The Value of Wealth: A Comment on Dworkin and Kronman*, 9 J. Legal Stud. 243, 248 (1980); cf. Richard A. Posner, *Utilitarianism, Economics, and Legal Theory*, 8 J. Legal Stud. 103 (1979); Richard A. Posner, *The Economics of Justice*, chs. 3–4 (Harvard University Press, forthcoming 1981).

3. The usual justification of loss spreading, as by making business enterprises strictly liable for injuries caused by their defective products, is a utilitarian (or economic) one: that given diminishing marginal utility of income, and assuming that victims and nonvictims of accidents have on average the same utility functions, distributing a loss over a large number of consumers or shareholders of the enterprise that causes the injury will result in less disutility than if the same loss is concentrated on the victim of the injury. This is the economic rationale of insurance; and enterprise liability, in the usual form in which it is advocated as a desirable method of insuring against accidents caused by defective products, is defended primarily as a desirable method of insuring against accidents caused by defective products. Similar justifications are offered for no-fault automobile insurance.

4. George P. Fletcher, *Fairness and Utility in Tort Theory*, 85 Harv. L. Rev. 537, 538 (1972) (footnote omitted).

5. John Borgo, *Causal Paradigms in Tort Law* 8 J. Legal Stud. 419 n.3 (1979).

6. He introduces it briefly in Chapter 2.

7. Voluntary transactions he instances by "sale, purchase, loan for consumption, pledging, loan for use, depositing, letting"; involuntary by "theft, adultery, poisoning, procuring, enticement of slaves, assassination, false witness [,] assault, murder, robbery with violence, mutilation, abuse, insult." Aristotle, *The Nicomachean Ethics* 111–12 (David Ross trans., rev. ed. 1980).

8. *Id* at 114–15. The Greek (transliterated) is ouden gar diapherei, ei epieikēs phaulon apesterēsen ē phaulos epieikē, oud' ei emoicheusen epieikēs ē phaulos; alla pros tou blabous tēn diaphoran monon blepei ho nomos, kai chrētai hōs isois, ei ho men adikei ho d' adikeitai, kai ei eblapsen ho de beblaptai. *Aristotelis, Ethica Nicomachea* 96 (I. Bywater ed. 1894). Rendered more or less literally, this means: "for it makes no difference whether a fair [moderate, upper class, good, reasonable] man robs [bereaves, defrauds] a man of low [bad, inferior] station or a man of low station robs a fair man, or whether a fair man commits adultery [against a man of low station] or a man of low station [commits adultery against a fair man]; the law looks to the distinction alone of the injury, and treats as equals, if one acts unjustly and the other is wronged, and if one injures and the other is injured."

9. Aristotle, *supra* note 7, at 115, 117.

10. See 2 *The Ethics of Aristotle* 112–16 (Alexander Grant ed., 4th rev. ed. 1885); *The Ethics of Aristotle* 217–23 (John Burnet ed. 1904); *The Fifth Book of the Nicomachean Ethics of Aristotle* 82–86 (Henry Jackson ed. 1879); W. F. R. Hardie, *Aristotle's Ethical Theory* 192–95 (1968); H. H. Joachim, *Aristotle: The Nicomachean Ethics: A Commentary* 136–47 (D. A. Rees ed. 1951); D. G. Ritchie, *Aristotle's Subdivisions of "Particular Justice,"* 8 Classical Rev. 185 (1894); J. A. Stewart, 1 *Notes on the Nicomachean Ethics of Aristotle* 430–41 (1973). See also Max Hamburger, *Morals and Law: The Growth of Aristotle's Legal Theory* 46–47, 51 (1951); Konrad Marc-Wogau, *Aristotle's Theory of Corrective Justice and Reciprocity, in Philosophical Essays* 21–30 (1967).

11. Joachim, *supra* note 10, at 144.

12. Aristotle, *supra* note 7, at 125.

13. *Id.* at 126–27. Hamburger, *supra* note 10, at 70, equates the mistake category to negligence. See Edgar Bodenheimer, *Treatise on Justice* 210–13 (1967), for a discussion of the state-of-mind requirement in Aristotle's concept of acting unjustly.

14. 2 *The Ethics of Aristotle* 113 n.3 (Alexander Grant ed., 4th rev. ed. 1885).

15. See A. R. W. Harrison, *Aristotle's Nicomachean Ethics, Book V, and the Law of Athens*, 77 J. Hellenic Stud. 42, 45–46 (1957); Joachim, *supra* note 10, at 137; Richard A. Posner, *Retribution and Related Concepts of Punishment*, 9 J. Legal Stud. 71, 85 (1980), and references cited therein; 2 Paul Vinogradoff, *Outlines of Historical Jurisprudence* 45–51 (1922). See generally H. D. P. Lee, *The Legal Background of Two Passages in the* Nicomachean Ethics, 31 Classical Q. 129 (1937).

16. Delba Winthrop, *Aristotle and Theories of Justice*, 72 Am. Pol. Sci. Rev. 1201, 1205 (1978). See also Morris Ginsberg, *The Concept of Justice*, 38 Philosophy 99, 105 (1963); H. L. A. Hart, *The Concept of Law* 158–61 (1961).

17. Fletcher, *supra* note 4, at 540–42.

18. Or so I infer from a comparison of id. at 538 with id. at 547 n.40.

19. As in the Hand formula. See id. at 542 n.19; Richard A. Posner, *A Theory of Negligence*, 1 J. Legal Stud. 29, 32 (1972).

20. Fletcher, *supra* note 4, at 542.

21. *Id.* at 540.

22. As Rawls states:

"The more specific sense that Aristotle gives to justice, and from which the most familiar formulations derive, is that of refraining from pleonexia, that is, from gaining some advantage for oneself by seizing what belongs to another, his property, his reward, his office, and the like, or by denying a person that which is due to him, the fulfillment of a promise, the repayment of a debt, the showing of proper respect and so on. It is evident that this definition is framed to apply to actions, and persons are thought to be just insofar as they have, as one of the permanent elements of their character, a steady and effective desire to act justly. Aristotle's definition clearly presupposes, however, an account of what properly belongs to a person and of what is due to him. Now such entitlements are, I believe, very often derived from social institutions and the legitimate expectations to which they give rise. There is no reason to think that Aristotle would disagree with this, and certainly he has a conception of social justice to account for these claims."

John Rawls, A Theory of Justice 10–11 (1971) (footnote omitted). J. R. Lucas, On Justice 13–14 (1980), makes the general point well:

"Although the reasons on which a just decision is based have to be individualized reasons, they do not therefore have to exclude all general considerations. General considerations, e.g., of expediency or utility, can justify there being one general rule rather than another: what justice requires is that any such general considerations shall issue in rules that apply generally, and that their application in the individual case must be justified by reference to the facts of that case."

23. See Richard A. Epstein, A Theory of Strict Liability, 2 J. Legal Stud. 151, 165 n.42 (1973).

24. See Richard A. Epstein, Defenses and Subsequent Pleas in a System of Strict Liability, 3 J. Legal Stud. 165 (1974).

25. Richard A. Epstein, Nuisance Law: Corrective Justice and Its Utilitarian Constraints, 8 J. Legal Stud. 49, 50, 99 (1979).

26. Id. at 77, 101.

27. Richard A. Epstein, Causation and Corrective Justice: A Reply to Two Critics, 8 J. Legal Stud. 477, 496 (1979).

28. See Epstein, supra note 24, at 198–99 and n.87.

29. Id. at 167–68.

30. To be sure, Epstein's principle of strict liability is one only of prima facie liability, and he allows for various excuses. But if the defendant has no excuse (consent or self-defense or whatever), and he may not, then the fact of harm, by itself, is indeed a basis of redress. And this is not an Aristotelian idea.

31. See, e.g., William T. Blackstone, Reverse Discrimination and Compensatory Justice, 3 Soc. Theory & Practice 253, 254–55 (1975); Ginsberg, supra note 16, at 111–12; Hart, supra note 16, at 158–61, 251:2 Vinogradoff, supra note 15, at 45.

32. Borgo, supra note 5, at 419–20. See also id. at 454: "the defendant's prima facie moral responsibility is determined exclusively by the existence vel non of a causal relation between his conduct and the plaintiff's harm."

33. See id. at 419 n.3.

34. Id. at 454.

35. See Richard A. Epstein, Intentional Harms, 4 J. Legal Stud. 391, 431–32 (1975).

36. See Borgo, supra note 5, at 444.

37. See the repeated equation of causation and use of force in Epstein, supra note 27, at 480–81.

38. As Joseph Steiner has said of Epstein's tort theory, "The physical descriptions which constitute the paradigms of causation either have no normative content and cannot lead to normative conclusions or they employ words with implicit normative content thereby incorporating unstated, independent, normative premises which are the very principles we are seeking. In neither case do the paradigms, per se, give guidance on the assignment of rights." Joseph M. Steiner, Economics, Morality, and the Law of Torts, 26 U. Toronto L. J. 227, 246 (1976).

39. That is, Epstein, in his early work, and Borgo believe that questions of legal liability can be answered within a more general theory of personal responsibility, a theory based on causation. I am indebted for the term to Jules Coleman.

40. On Epstein, see Richard A. Posner, Epstein's Tort Theory: A

Critique, 8 J. Legal Stud. 457, 465–71 (1979); on Fletcher, see Jules Coleman, Justice and Reciprocity in Tort Theory, 14 W. Ontario L. Rev. 105, 117–18 (1975), explaining, and criticizing, Fletcher's derivation of the paradigm of reciprocity from a "security principle" analogous to one of John Rawls's principles of distributive justice.

41. Jules L. Coleman, Mental Abnormality, Personal Responsibility, and Tort Liability, in Mental Illness: Law and Public Policy 107, 123 (B. A. Brody & H. Tristam Engelhardt, Jr. eds. 1980) (reference omitted). For earlier discussion of his corrective justice approach to tort law see Jules L. Coleman, Justice and the Argument for No-Fault, 3 Soc. Theory & Practice 161, 173–78 (1975); Reply to Pilon, 59 The Personalist 307, 312–13 (1978); The Morality of Strict Tort Liability, 18 Wm. & Mary L. Rev. 259 (1976). Coleman acknowledges a debt to James W. Nickel, whose views may be found in Justice in Compensation, 18 Wm. & Mary L. Rev. 379 (1976).

42. Coleman, Mental Abnormality, Personal Responsibility, and Tort Liability, supra note 41, at 123.

43. "But in the case of accidental torts there is, in general, no gain on the wrongdoer's behalf that needs to be eliminated. That his conduct is wrongful supports the right of the victim to recompense, nothing more." Coleman, Justice and the Argument for No-Fault, supra note 41, at 177.

44. See text at note 9 supra. To be sure, as Coleman has pointed out to me, the gain in the negligence case is not triggered by the loss—it would be the same if the accident had not occurred—but I do not see what difference that makes so far as the wrongfulness of the injury is concerned. We would say that a robber who shot his victim injured him wrongfully, though it was no part of his plan to shoot him and he did so only because the victim resisted.

45. This assumes, of course, that negligence is wrongful. Aristotle would not have thought so, but, as Coleman and I both believe, Aristotle's idea of what constitutes wrongful conduct can be severed from his idea of corrective justice. More on this, and also on no-fault automobile accident compensation, in Part III.

46. Frederick L. Sharp, Aristotle, Justice and Enterprise Liability in the Law of Torts, 34 U. Toronto Faculty L. Rev. 84 and n.1 (1976).

47. (1868) L.R. 3 H.L. 330. This case imposed strict liability on the defendants for water damage to property caused by the collapse, not due to the defendants' negligence or other wrongdoing, of a reservoir on the defendants' property.

48. Sharp, supra note 46, at 89.

49. Id. at 90 (footnotes omitted).

50. The term "mean" is not used in the mathematical sense of average.

51. As Coleman notes:

"the principle of strict liability is inadequate as a basis of justice in compensation. On the strict liability model, a victim is entitled to recompense even if his injurer is not at fault (usually negligent) in causing him harm. Thus, the strict liability rule does not restrict recompense to those who have absorbed unjustifiable losses, and though compensating the general category of victims may be justified as a matter of general welfare or benevolence, compensation is not a matter of justice their right. The rule of fault liability, on the other hand, enables us to identify those victims for whom recompense is a matter of justice."

Coleman, Reply to Pilon, supra note 41, at 315 n.31 (emphasis in original).

52. See the Nicomachean Ethics at bk. I, ch. 8 & bk. X, ch. 6.

53. See, e.g., Richard A. Posner, Economic Analysis of Law, pt. II (2d ed. 1977).

54. See William M. Landes & Richard A. Posner, The Private Enforcement of Law, 4 J. Legal Stud. 1, 32, 35 (1975); Posner, supra note 19, at 48–52. A parallel argument to that in the text is possible for breach of contract. See Landes & Posner, supra, at 36. In fact, Aristotle's treatment of torts and contracts as involuntary and voluntary transactions parallels the modern economic view of these subjects. See, e.g., Posner, supra note 53, at 179–80. Aristotle would apparently have regarded a breach of contract, if deliberate, as an act of injustice. Cf. note 7 supra. In the common law, breach of contract is a strict-liability concept by and large (some excuses

are recognized, however—for example, where performance is impossible), but the difference between Aristotle's and the common law view has to do with the substantive concept of wrongdoing rather than with the duty to rectify a wrongful harm arising from a contractual relationship. The duty is common to both systems. Whether the wrong is a deliberate breach of contract, or any breach, does not affect the analysis of corrective justice.

55. See The Ethics of Aristotle 221n (John Burnet ed. 1904). In Burnet's actual example, the gain was 7 and the loss 3. In the example in the text I have reversed the numbers to make the example simpler to understand, but my basic analytical point is independent of this transposition. In Burnet's example, awarding the

victim 5 would give him an incentive to be injured, since the injury would yield him a profit of 2.

56. See Harrison, supra note 15, at 45.

57. See Illinois Brick Co. v. Illinois, 431 U.S. 720 (1977).

58. See William M. Landes & Richard A. Posner, Should Indirect Purchasers Have Standing to Sue under the Antitrust Laws? An Economic Analysis of the Rule of Illinois Brick, 46 U. Chi. L. Rev. 602, 605–08 (1979).

59. In fact, because adikos means unlawful as well as unjust, it is unclear to what extent Aristotle thought he was doing more than describing legal concepts that happened to be prevale in his society. See sources in note 15 supra.

CORRECTIVE JUSTICE AND WRONGFUL GAIN*

Jules Coleman

Richard Posner's essay "The Concept of Corrective Justice in Recent Theories of Tort Law"[1] falls into three distinct but related sections. In the first part of the paper Posner attempts to characterize the principle(s) of corrective justice. In the second part, he criticizes the efforts of a number of other tort theorists, including George Fletcher, Richard Epstein, and myself, who have attempted to ground the law of torts on a foundation of corrective justice. Having himself previously advanced an efficiency-based conception of the law of torts, Posner goes on to argue in the third part of the essay that the principle of corrective justice is itself required by the principle of efficiency. By laying an economic foundation for the principle of corrective justice, Posner argues not only for the compatibility of the most promising line of moral defense of tort law with the dominant economic one, but for the primacy of the latter as well.

Posner has graciously provided me with the opportunity to respond to his paper. In a series of essays, some of which have appeared in philosophy journals,[2] others of which have surfaced in law reviews,[3] and one of which has appeared as a chapter in a very overpriced book,[4] I have explored the moral foundations of tort law. It would not be unfair—indeed, it

may be too generous—to say that in these essays I have advanced a theory of torts based on the principle of corrective justice. In what follows I first summarize (in a very compressed fashion) my view of the role of corrective justice in tort theory, then briefly contrast it with those of Epstein and Fletcher, and finally consider Posner's objections to it.

I. Liability, Recovery, and a Conception of Corrective Justice

Central to my account of torts is the distinction between the grounds of liability and recovery—in other words, between the two questions (1) What are the grounds necessary and sufficient to justify a victim's claim to recompense? and (2) Under what conditions ought an injurer be obligated to provide compensation to his victims?[5] That the grounds of recovery and liability are at least analytically distinguishable is illustrated by the fact that a society could establish an insurance scheme to compensate all accident victims, while only those injurers who are at fault in causing an accident would be required to contribute to the insurance pool. Were we to separate liability and recovery in this way, being at fault in causing harm would be a necessary condition of liability, but not of the victim's case for recovery. Whether a system that separated liability from recovery in this particular way would be just or efficient remains to be worked out. For now the point is simply that the considerations that ground a claim to recompense need not coincide with those that ground the obligation to repair.

Once the distinction between the foundations of recovery and liability is drawn, the next question concerns the role of corrective justice in each. This in turn requires a conception of corrective justice. In my view, corrective or compensatory justice is concerned with the category of wrongful gains and losses. Rectification, in this view, is a matter of justice when it is necessary to protect a distribution of holdings (or entitlements) from distortions which arise from unjust enrichments and wrongful losses. The principle of corrective justice requires the annulments of both wrongful gains and losses.[6]

This conception of corrective justice puts a great burden on the concepts of wrongful gain and wrongful loss. Without offering a set of conditions necessary and sufficient for a loss or gain to count as wrongful I have tried in my previous work to characterize the basic idea by examples. Within the category of wrongful losses are those one suffers through the fault or wrongful conduct of another; within the class of unjust enrichments are those one secures through one's wrongdoing, as in many instances of fraud and theft. A compensable or undeserved loss need not, however, be the result of another's wrongdoing. Sometimes the justifiable (i.e., nonwrongful) taking of what another has a well-established right to justifies a claim to rectification.[7] An instance of a justifiable taking that creates a compensable loss is given by the following example of Joel Feinberg's:

> Suppose that you are on a back-packing trip in the mountain country when an unanticipated blizzard strikes the area with such ferocity that your life is imperiled. Fortunately, you stumble onto an unoccupied cabin, locked and boarded up for the winter, clearly somebody else's private property. You smash in a window, enter, and huddle in a corner for three days until the storm abates. During this period you help yourself to your unknown benefactor's food supply and burn his wooden furniture in the fireplace to keep warm. Surely you

> are justified in doing all these things, and yet you have infringed the clear rights of another person.[8]

Feinberg argues, and I concur, that in spite of the justifiability of what you have done, you owe the owner of the cabin compensation for his food and furniture.

Though these examples do not define in any strict sense the operative notion of wrongfulness, they help to characterize it sufficiently to make the notion a useful one.

Given this general conception of corrective justice, the above examples of wrongful gain and loss, as well as the central distinction between the grounds of recovery and liability, we can begin to spell out my account of the role of corrective justice in tort theory.

In torts a distinction is drawn between the rules of fault (or conditional) and strict (or unconditional) liability. In fault liability, a victim is not entitled to recover his loss unless it is the result of another's fault, and an injurer is liable only for those harms that are his fault. In strict liability, neither the victim's claim to recompense nor the injurer's responsibility to make repair requires that the injurer's conduct be at fault.

A. Corrective Justice and the Fault Principle

Consider first the role of corrective justice in grounding recovery and liability under the fault principle. Under the fault principle a victim is entitled to repair only if his loss results from another's fault. A loss that is the consequence of another's fault is, in the sense just characterized, a wrongful one. Since the principle of corrective justice requires annulling wrongful losses, it supports the victim's claim to recompense in fault liability.

The relationship between corrective justice and the principle that an individual ought to be liable for the untoward consequences of his fault is somewhat more complex. There are two kinds of cases in which the principle of corrective justice gives direct support to the principle of fault liability: (1) those cases in which an individual's fault results not only in another's loss, but in his gain as well; and (2) those cases in which an individual secures a wrongful gain through his fault, though his gain is not the result of another's loss. Unjust enrichment through fraud is an example of a wrongful gain secured at another's expense; non-harm-causing but nevertheless negligent motoring is often an example of conduct that creates wrongful gain in the absence of a corresponding wrongful loss.

Consider the case of negligent motoring more carefully. Negligent motoring may or may not result in an accident. Whether or not it does, individuals who drive negligently often secure a wrongful gain in doing so, namely, the "savings" from not taking adequate safety precautions—those required of the reasonable man of ordinary prudence. This form of wrongful gain is not, *ex hypothesi,* the result of anyone else's wrongful loss. On the other hand, if a negligent motorist causes another harm, he normally secures no *additional* wrongful gain in virtue of his doing so. In this respect faulty motoring differs from the usual case of fraud or theft. Because harmful, negligent motoring does not generally result in any wrongful gain (apart from that which is the result of negligence itself), the obligation to repair the victim's wrongful loss cannot be entirely grounded on a foundation of corrective justice. There is, in other words, no wrongful gain correlative of the wrongful loss the faulty injurer imposes upon his victim, and no reason, therefore, as a matter of corrective justice alone, for imposing the victim's loss upon his injurer. The wrongful gain negligent motorists secure is logically distinct from any loss they may cause others, and so the occasion of another's loss cannot be the moral basis for annulling these gains as a matter of justice.[9]

This is bound to appear controversial; some additional distinctions might make it appear less so. A full theory of justice in tort liability and recovery would distinguish among four issues: (1) the foundation of a claim that a person has suffered a compensable loss, or that he has secured an unjust gain; (2) the mode of rectification—that is, the manner in which unjust gains and losses are to be eliminated;[10] (3) the character of rectification—that is, whether a particular form of compensation (e.g., money) is always, sometimes, or rarely appropriate; and (4) the extent of rectification—that is, just how much of a person's loss (or gain) ought to be eliminated.[11]

The central claim of my thesis is the rather straightforward one (I believe) that determining whether a gain or loss is wrongful determines the answer only to the first of these issues. If there is a wrongful loss, it ought to be annulled; the same goes for wrongful or unwarranted gains. Nevertheless, the principle of corrective justice which enables us to identify compensable losses and unjust enrichments does not commit us to adopting any particular mode of rectification. The principle that determines which gains and losses are to be eliminated does not by itself

specify a means for doing so. Presumably there is more than one way of rectifying undeserved gains and losses. So when I claim that if an injurer who through his fault imposes a wrongful loss on another but who does not thereby gain has an obligation to repair, his obligation cannot derive directly from the principle of corrective justice, I mean only to be emphasizing the obvious fact that he has secured no gain which would be the concern of corrective justice to rectify. His victim's claim to recompense is on the other hand a matter of corrective justice. And if we feel that the injurer should rectify his victim's loss, it must be for reasons other than the fact that doing so is required by justice in order to annul his gain.

Once we have adopted a system of tort liability we have committed ourselves to a particular mode of rectifying wrongful gains and losses—a method that imposes victims' losses on their injurers whether or not the loss occasions a wrongful gain. That particular mode of rectification is in no sense required by the principle of corrective justice. There may be reasons other than those which derive from a theory of corrective justice for imposing an innocent victim's loss on his injurer. Consider three such arguments. First, one might argue from the principle of retributive justice for the imposition of liability of faulty injurers. Such an argument would hold that wrongdoing, whether or not it secures personal gain, is sinful and ought to be punished or sanctioned. Imposing liability in torts is a way of sanctioning mischief. Therefore liability is imposed on the faulty injurer not to rectify his gain—of which there may be none—but to penalize his moral wrong.[12] Or one could argue from the principle that claim rights impose correlative duties to the conclusion that the victim's right, which is grounded in corrective justice, imposes a correlative duty to repair on his injurer.[13] Or one might take yet another tack and seek to ground the injurer's obligation to repair in considerations of deterrence or accident cost avoidance. This argument might take the following form. To be at fault is to act in an inefficient manner; it is to fail to take appropriate accident-avoidance measures when the cost of doing so is less than the cost of the harm to the victim discounted by the probability of its occurrence. An injurer who is at fault in harming another is obligated to make restitution because his doing so provides him with an incentive to take such precautions as are reasonable and necessary in the future, and because doing so in general has the long-term effect of reducing the sum of accident and accident-avoidance costs.[14] Were one to take an "economic approach" to the liability of the faulty injurer and a "corrective-justice" approach to the right of his victim to secure recompense, the net result would be a merger of economic and moral theories of fault liability, albeit a more narrowly defined one than Posner contemplates.

B. Corrective Justice and Strict Liability

Consider now the relationship between the principle of corrective justice and liability and recovery under the rule of unconditional or strict liability. The conception of unwarranted or wrongful gain and loss central to the principle of corrective justice includes losses and gains that result from justified "takings." Unlike the wrongful losses in fault liability, the unwarranted losses in these cases are not the result of wrongdoing in the ordinary sense. The "taking" itself may be reasonable or justified, as it is in Feinberg's example, and as it is in cases like *Vincent* v. *Lake Erie Transp. Co.*[15] Consequently, there is no wrong in the doing; were there any wrong at all it would consist in taking what another has a legitimate right to (under specifiable circumstances) and not rendering adequate compensation for having done so.

Understood in this way, corrective justice may explain those strict liability cases that can adequately be modeled on the idea of a taking. Corrective justice might therefore explain *Vincent* v. *Lake Erie,* but probably not strict liability for either ultrahazardous activities or defective products. Just how much of strict liability the principle of corrective justice explains will depend on the proper analysis of what constitutes a taking—and that is no easy matter.

Again, one has to be careful to avoid misunderstanding the claim. It does not follow from what I have said that those areas of strict liability, like ultrahazardous or products liability, which do not involve takings in the ordinary sense cannot be justified or rationally explained. My point is simply that appealing to the principle of corrective justice—once it is properly understood—will not help to explain them. There may be other considerations, both of morality and economics, that neatly rationalize existing strict liability law. My purpose is simply to determine which, if any, of the existing law of torts might be defensible within a certain conception of corrective justice. If it turns out, as I think it does, that only certain well-defined areas of tort law can be comprehended by a single principle, so much the better for my view, for it demonstrates theoretically what we knew pretheoretically—namely, that the law of torts is extremely complex and that it resists simple analysis.[16]

II. Epstein and Fletcher on Corrective Justice

Considerations of corrective justice ground four claims related to liability and recovery in torts: (1) the claim to recompense of a victim of another's fault, (2) the liability of a faulty injurer who gains through his mischief, (3) the claim of a victim in strict liability for a takings-like loss, and (4) the injurer's liability for a taking. In contrast, both Epstein and Fletcher appear to believe that all, or nearly all, of torts can be explained by subsumption under a theory of corrective justice. The interesting question concerns how it is that the three of us, each of whom believes that corrective justice is central to an adequate analysis of torts, reach such different conclusions.

There really is not much of a mystery, however. The key difference is that both Epstein and Fletcher share a strategy which is first to identify an element common to both strict and fault liability, then to argue that this common element is central to liability and recovery, then finally to confer normativity upon this feature of both fault and strict liability by subsuming it under a particular conception of corrective justice. Fletcher and Epstein disagree about which element is the operative shared component in strict and fault liability. For Epstein it is the fact that in both fault and strict liability the injurer causes the victim's loss;[17] for Fletcher it is the fact that the injurer harmed the victim through his nonreciprocal risk taking.[18]

Epstein's arguments are motivated in part by a desire to deemphasize the role of fault in determining both liability and recovery. The desire to eliminate the centrality of fault to torts must be understood against the background of a failed moral theory of fault liability and an increasingly accepted economic account of it. Let me explain. At one time the prevailing moral theory of torts seized upon the introduction of the fault requirement in the mid nineteenth century as a shift away from the immoral criterion of strict liability to a moral foundation for liability. Instead of imposing liability without regard to the culpability or blameworthiness of the injurer—as was the case in strict liability—fault liability injected a concern for the moral character of the injurer's conduct into the formula that was to determine the appropriateness of imposing another's loss upon him.

The concern of torts for the moral character of the injurer's conduct has always been rather minimal, however. It is the lesson of *Vaughan* v. *Menlove*[19] that an individual may be at fault in torts even if he is not morally at fault for his conduct, his fault being determined by his failure to comply with a standard of reasonable care whether or not he is capable of compliance. Because moral culpability is not a condition of fault in torts, previous efforts to provide a moral account of fault liability have stalled. Moreover, by the early 1970s, the prevailing view had become that the only plausible, coherent account of fault in torts was an economic one: to be at fault is simply to fail to take the precautions necessary to avoid an inefficient (in cost/benefit terms) harm. In short, the standard of fault liability which moralists had hoped would anchor a moral theory of torts appeared not only to escape moral analysis, but to be firmly rooted in economic theory. Theorists intent on defending a moral account of torts were faced with a choice: either they could provide an alternative moral account of the fault principle, or they could reexamine, even eliminate, the role of fault in a moral theory of torts. (I have pursued the former route; Epstein and Fletcher have taken the latter.)

In reducing the role of fault liability Epstein focuses his attention on the fact that wherever liability is appropriate, someone has caused another harm. The moral freight which, in the traditional view, had been carried by the fault requirement is borne, in Epstein's view, by the causal condition. Unlike a theory of torts that relies on fault, the theory that relies on the causal condition can theoretically (at least) ground all of tort law under a comprehensive moral principle, since the causal condition, unlike the fault condition, is a necessary element in both fault and strict liability.

Though Epstein has always emphasized the causal condition as central to a moral account of tort liability, his view about the principle that confers moral significance on the causal condition has undergone subtle but significant changes.

In his early essay, "A Theory of Strict Liability,"[20] Epstein appears to have held the view that the best way to understand and (where possible) justify tort liability is by rooting it in a more comprehensive theory of personal responsibility. Tort liability is justly imposed provided the conditions of tort liability conform to the requirements of an agent's being responsible for his conduct. Epstein's view is that a satisfactory account of personal responsibility must be developed in terms of an analysis of causation and volition.

Running alongside the responsibility thesis in Epstein's early work is a very undeveloped argument which relies on corrective justice as the basis of tort liability. Prior to the incidence of harm, individuals are in a state of "equilibrium" or "balance." Liability in torts provides the mechanism for redressing imbalances caused by harmful conduct: liability and recovery in torts reestablish the previously existing equilibria. The causal condition remains central to a just theory of liability since the principle of corrective justice requires annulling gains and losses caused by harmful conduct.

Both the responsibility thesis and the simple corrective-justice accounts of tort liability are seriously flawed. I have argued that although considerations of personal responsibility are relevant to a full theory of torts, Epstein is mistaken in thinking that the analysis of responsibility (which would be a normative theory) could be adequately developed in terms of an analysis of causation (which would involve a natural or scientific theory).[21] One can be responsible not only for what one does, but for what one fails to do as well. If an individual wrongly fails to act he may be culpable for his failure to prevent harm. Though it would be philosophically confused to say that his failure to act caused the harm, there might be sufficient reasons for ascribing the resulting harm to him as his responsibility.

The problem with the theory of corrective justice that relies on the fact that *A* caused *B* harm as sufficient both for (*prima facie*) liability and recovery (respectively) is simply that not every way in which *A* harms *B* is wrongful. Not every loss *B* suffers at *A*'s hands is a wrongful one; not every gain *A* secures at *B*'s expense is an unjust one.

Epstein's most recent view emerges from these lines of criticism. In answering the charge that *A* may have a duty to prevent harm to *B* so that his failure to do so may be both wrongful and the resulting harm to *B* his responsibility, Epstein denies that *B* has any *right* to rescue against *A*. And in answering the objection to the corrective-justice theory that not every harm creates a wrongful loss, Epstein's response is that only those harms that involve invasions of property *rights* are compensable. In short, the emerging Epstein view is that corrective justice requires annulling only gains and losses owing to the invasion of an individual's rights.[22]

This account of corrective justice maintains a commitment to the causal requirement as central to a just theory of liability not because causing harm is sufficient to trigger the principle's application, but because the concept of a "right invasion" is to be spelled out in causal terms. Causation, then, is necessary to liability but no longer sufficient to justify even the *prima facie* case. For it is also necessary that the injurer's conduct invade one or more of the victim's rights.

I take up Epstein's latest view elsewhere,[23] so I will confine these remarks to a few observations. One way of understanding this view is as follows: Epstein has simply adopted my general conception of corrective justice—that wrongful gains and losses are to be annulled. He has then chosen to analyze the difficult and troublesome notion of wrongfulness in terms of the more basic idea of a property-right violation. Wrongful losses are those that result from the invasion of a property right. So what a judge in a tort case is deciding upon is whether B has a property right against A which A has failed adequately to respect. If the claim "A invaded B's right" is true, then it follows on this view that B has a further right against A to recompense for whatever loss A's invasion occasioned.

My view, which I will not defend here, is that the latest Epstein account is both too strong and too weak. It is too strong because it makes the fact that the victim's loss resulted from a right invasion a necessary condition of liability, whereas in fact not every compensable loss requires that the harm for which one seeks recovery results from the invasion of a right. It is too weak because it maintains that if a person's property rights are violated it follows that he is entitled to recompense, whereas it does not follow either as a matter of logic or moral argument that every right violation triggers a right to repair.

For Fletcher, the guiding principle in determining liability and recovery is the principle of nonreciprocity of risk. A person is entitled to recover whenever he is the victim of harm caused by another's nonreciprocal risk taking; an individual is liable in torts whenever he has no excuse for having caused another harm through his nonreciprocal risk taking. An individual imposes a nonreciprocal risk on others whenever it is different in degree or kind from those risks others impose on him. Examples of nonreciprocal risk taking include engaging in ultrahazardous activities and keeping wild animals on one's property (while one's neighbors confine their affections to traditional domestic pets). The principle of nonreciprocity of risk therefore explains strict liability for harms that result from such activities. Strict liability is appropriate in those cases in which one risk taker imposes risks different from those others in general impose upon him.

There are other activities, however, in which individuals generally impose a certain level of risk on one another. Motoring is one. Liability is not imposed whenever an individual motorist harms another. In Fletcher's view that is because activities like motoring involve a level of reciprocal risk taking. For such activities liability is not strict. In order for liability to be imposed a motorist must negligently harm another. In other words, liability is appropriate only for risks that exceed the general level of shared risk. These nonreciprocal risks are all that is meant, in Fletcher's view, by negligence.

In fault as well as in strict liability, the key to recovery is nonreciprocity of risk. The difference between fault and strict liability is to be understood in terms of the level of risk that constitutes the "background" against which the criterion of nonreciprocity is to be applied. The fault criterion is appropriate to activities of mutual involvement, like motoring, in which there exists a shared level of background or reciprocal risk taking. A faulty or negligent risk is one that exceeds the level of common or background risk. In activities that do not by nature involve participants imposing similar risks on one another, activities like blasting, strict liability is the appropriate criterion.[24]

Fletcher is considerably less clear about what it is that confers moral significance on nonreciprocity of risk. He cites Aristotle on corrective justice as the source of nonreciprocity of risk's claim to moral significance, but the actual argument he advances on its behalf relies on Rawls. The difference is important. Whereas Aristotle is concerned with corrective justice, Rawls is concerned with principles of distributive justice.

Citing Rawls, Fletcher argues for nonreciprocity of risk by constructing a principle of distributive justice that he takes to be an analogue of Rawls's first principle of justice. Fletcher contends that each individual is entitled to the maximum degree of security compatible with a like level of security for all. (The "analogy" is to Rawls's principle that each individual is entitled to the most extensive liberty compatible with a like liberty for all.) Fletcher goes on to define security as freedom from harm without compensation. So defined, everyone has a right not to be harmed without being compensated. If we take Fletcher at his word, it is the fact that one has suffered harm that entitles one to recompense, not the fact that one's harm results from another's nonreciprocal risk taking.

The principle that is supposed to impart moral significance on the criterion of nonreciprocity of risk actually has the effect of eliminating it. With nonreciprocity as a condition of liability out of the way, Fletcher's view collapses into Epstein's—in fact, into a less defensible version of Epstein's, since Epstein is committed to the weaker proposition that causing harm is sufficient to establish the *prima facie* case for liability only.

To maintain the centrality of nonreciprocity of risk in Fletcher's theory one must reformulate the principle that is to confer moral significance on it. This can be accomplished in a number of ways, each of which is problematic. First, one might redefine the notion of security more narrowly as freedom from exposure to nonreciprocal risk taking. An individual's right to security is then the freedom from having nonreciprocal risks imposed on him. If the right one has is to freedom from nonreciprocal risks, then the right to recover that is based upon it does not require that one actually suffer a harm. Exposure to nonreciprocal risk, whether or not it results in harm, triggers the right to recompense. The effect is to eliminate as central to liability what is currently necessary in both strict and fault liability: the requirement that one who seeks relief must establish a loss, not just the threat or risk of loss.

It will not do to redefine security even more narrowly as freedom from harm due to nonreciprocal risk, for that would trivialize the enterprise by restating the criterion of recovery as the principle that is supposed to justify it: people are entitled to recover for harms caused by nonreciprocal risk taking because there is a principle that people have such a right.

I want to develop a more sympathetic reading of Fletcher that involves ignoring his efforts to ground the principle of nonreciprocity of risk in a Rawlsian conception of distributive justice. I prefer to read Fletcher as follows: First, assume that he has adopted a conception of corrective justice like mine or Aristotle's. Then understand the criterion of nonreciprocity of risk as his way of characterizing wrongful gains and losses. In other words, ascribe to Fletcher the position that justice requires annulling wrongful gains and losses; then interpret his account of nonreciprocity of risk as a characterization of what it is that makes a gain or loss wrongful. Our views would then be much closer than they otherwise appear to be. The advantage of this would be that by identifying wrongful loss with losses that result from nonreciprocal risk taking, he can provide a criterion of wrongfulness that

is applicable to all of tort law—both strict and fault liability. My conception of wrongfulness is considerably more narrow and explains only a small area of strict liability law. The problem with his view might then be that the notion of nonreciprocity of risk is too broad a characterization of wrongfulness to function within the principle of corrective justice.

To sum up: Epstein, Fletcher, and myself reach different conclusions regarding the extent to which the principle of corrective justice could figure in an adequate theory of liability and recovery in torts for the following reasons. Epstein advances both a simple and a more complex theory of corrective justice. According to the simple theory, corrective justice requires annulling losses caused by harmful conduct. This conception of corrective justice is broad enough to make the fact that *A* caused *B* harm sufficient to trigger its application. Since causing harm is (presumably) a necessary element in both strict and fault liability, Epstein's conception of corrective justice turns out to be sufficient to ground all of liability and recovery in torts.

According to the more complex theory of corrective justice, the facts that *A* harmed *B* and that in doing so *A* invaded a right of *B*'s are both separately necessary and jointly sufficient to justify rectification. The best way to read this amendment to the simple view is as resulting from Epstein's sensitivity to the objection that not every harm one suffers at the hands of another creates a compensable loss. To meet that objection to the simple view Epstein restricts compensable losses to those occasioned by the invasion of a property right. Because Epstein must also believe that as a matter of fact all recoverable losses in torts involve property-right invasions, he can maintain the view that the principle of corrective justice grounds most, if not all, of tort law.

Fletcher does not explicitly put forward a conception of corrective justice, but it would be fair to ascribe to him a much narrower conception of it than the one Epstein first put forth, for example, one like mine or Aristotle's which requires that a loss or gain be wrongful in order to trigger its application. Fletcher and I differ because we have different conceptions of what makes a gain or loss a wrongful one. Because Fletcher believes that nonreciprocity of risk is central to both strict and fault liability, and because nonreciprocity of risk is one way of fleshing out the notion of wrongfulness in the principle of corrective justice, Fletcher, like Epstein (but for different reasons), is led to the conclusion that corrective justice explains most of torts.

When the emerging Epstein view and the principle of reciprocity are understood in the way in which I have been suggesting, it would be fair to ascribe to both Epstein and Fletcher the same conception of the principle of corrective justice I have advanced. The differences between us could be pinpointed as involving the ways which each of us analyzes the notion of wrongfulness. Whereas Fletcher and I may be said to adopt the same principle of corrective justice, the principle of nonreciprocity of risk constitutes a much broader conception of what makes a gain or loss compensable or wrongful than does the account I have been developing. Epstein's theory of wrongful losses as involving invasions of property rights is both broader and narrower than my own. It is narrower in the sense that my view allows compensation for losses even where the invasion of a property right is not established; it is broader in the sense that he believes that as a matter of fact every compensable loss in torts involves the invasion of a property right.

Let me close this section by saying something about the difference between my view and Aristotle's. In my view, the principle of corrective justice explains a good deal more of tort law than it would for Aristotle. While Aristotle's conception of corrective justice is very similar to mine, he appears to have held that a wrongful gain or loss requires that a wrong has been done. In that case, the principle of corrective justice could not explain any of strict liability. In contrast, my view is that a loss or gain may sometimes be wrongful, as in a justified taking, even if the conduct that creates it is not wrongful. Moreover, Aristotle appears to have further limited the notion of a wrong to deliberate or intentional wrongdoing. In that case the principle of corrective justice would be unable to account for much of fault liability in which liability is imposed for what one unintentionally but negligently does.

III. Posner's Objections

I come finally to Posner's objections. Though Posner appears to find much to recommend the position he ascribes to me, he finds fault with three related components of my argument. Two of his objections concern the limitations I place on the argument for liability from the principle of corrective justice; the third concerns the question of whether requiring potential victims to purchase first-party insurance coverage actually enables them to secure full compensation in the event of injury.

One of the central points of my thesis is that, whereas the victim of another's fault has a claim as a matter of corrective justice to recompense, the obligation to make him whole may or may not be as a matter of corrective justice the injurer's responsibility. Objecting to this claim Posner asks rhetorically, "If the injurer is not the source of the compensation, someone else, who is innocent, must be, and why is not that innocent party a victim of the wrongdoer's injurious conduct?"[25] Again, after ascribing to me the view that "the victim of an accident in which the injurer was at fault is entitled to compensation . . . the injurer is not required as a matter of justice to be the source of compensation because he does not gain by his wrongful act, as he would if we were speaking of a theft rather than an accident," Posner argues that because faulty injurers avoid the costs of taking adequate safety precautions, they in fact gain by their injurious conduct.[26] Because they gain by their wrongdoing, liability is appropriately imposed upon them.

In sum, Posner's objections are: (1) if a faulty injurer is not the source of compensation, some "innocent" third party must be, and this constitutes an injustice; and (2) each faulty injurer gains from his wrongdoing in a sense sufficient to warrant imposing the victim's loss upon him as a matter of corrective justice.

Taken together these points constitute a serious challenge to central features of my argument. Consider the second objection first. Surely Posner is right in thinking that by and large faulty injurers gain by their failing to satisfy the standard of reasonable care. In fact, their gain, the savings from failing to exercise the care required of others, is a wrongful one, since it is the consequence of their fault. Nevertheless, as I have already pointed out to Posner, and earlier in this paper, this gain in savings is secured by negligent individuals whether or not their negligence results in another's loss. The gain in savings is not triggered by the harm a particular individual's negligence causes another. In contrast to a theft, it is not a gain that results from another's loss. Posner acknowledges the distinction, but goes on to say that he fails to understand the importance of distinguishing between wrongful gains that result from another's loss and those which do not in determining whether an individual's conduct is wrongful.[27]

Posner's response misses the point, however. The distinction is not relevant to determining if an individual's gain from his actions is wrongful; I did not suggest that it was. The distinction may play an important role, however, in determining whether the victims's loss should be imposed upon his particular injurer. In making *that* determination it is relevant to inquire whether the injurer's gain is correlative of the victim's loss, for if the injurer's gain exists independently of the victim's loss, then it is not the victim's loss that provides the moral basis for annulling the injurer's gain.

Furthermore, there are ways other than imposing the victim's loss on him of annulling the gain faulty injurers secure by avoiding the costs of adequate precautions: for example, by imposing fines for negligence. Indeed, because the gains owing to taking inadequate precautions accrue to all negligent individuals, it is in fact more appropriate to annul the gain in savings by fines imposed on each. In this way we can treat this category of wrongful gains similarly by not imposing any additional burden on those particular faulty injurers who, though they do not gain further by their mischief, are unfortunate enough to cause another harm. In short, Posner is right to insist upon the fact that wrongful gain is sufficient to impose as a matter of corrective justice a victim's loss on his negligent injurer.

Posner's other objection is that if the faulty injurer is not required to compensate his victim, an innocent individual—either the victim or some third party—will be forced to do so, and that imposing the loss on an innocent individual constitutes an injustice. (Indeed, Posner goes so far as to refer to these innocent individuals as "victims" of the faulty party's conduct.) This objection goes astray from the start. It simply does not follow in a system in which faulty injurers were not made liable to victims of their mischief that innocent individuals would be coerced into doing so in their stead. Surely, it is at least logically possible that everyone would agree *ex ante* to distribute accident costs without regard to fault—for example, in accordance with a deep-pocket or risk-spreading principle. In such a system individuals other than those at fault in causing particular accidents would help to pay for the costs of accidents, though no injustice of the sort Posner imagines would exist. Alternatively, the costs of accidents as they accumulate over time could be allocated among faulty individuals—whether or not the fault of each results in harm—without any individual being liable to any particular victim of his fault. Instead, each negligent motorist, for example, would pay according to the degree of his fault rather than according to the extent of the damage his fault causes. (After all, minor faults often occasion major damage, and serious wrongdoing may result in little, if any, damage at all.) In both

counterexamples to Posner's objection, the negligent motorist is not obligated to his victim, yet the result is not that some innocent third party is unjustly held liable instead.

Both of these counterexamples imagine modes of rectifying wrongful losses other than the tort system. Perhaps Posner's objection is more telling if we limit ourselves to the tort system. Then his objection appears to be the following: In torts, the victim of another's wrongdoing has a right to recompense. This right constitutes a valid claim against someone. If the obligation to repair is not imposed upon the faulty injurer, the victim's loss will fall on some innocent party or other. According to Posner, my view is that if the faulty injurer does not gain from his conduct, he has no obligation as a matter of corrective justice to render compensation. Absent such an obligation, the victim's loss must indeed fall on someone else (i.e., an innocent person). Therefore (given the tort system as the appropriate mode of rectification), my position generates injustice.

Though more promising, this line of argument fails as well. The argument begins by assuming a particular mode of rectification, namely, that the desired way of annulling undeserved gains and losses is by conferring on victims a right to redress and by imposing on their injurers the corresponding obligation to repair. There is nothing in my view that is incompatible with establishing a tort system to annul wrongful losses. Given the tort system, it would be my view that the obligation to repair the victim's loss falls upon his faulty injurer. It is also my view, however, that it cannot logically be any part of the reason for imposing the duty to repair on the faulty victim in such cases that in doing so we rectify or annul his wrongful gain. He simply enjoys no gain that needs to be rectified. The duty to repair his victim's loss, in other words, may be rightly his responsibility in a tort system, though it is not a duty of corrective justice.

These objections to my view rest on an ambiguity concerning whether the tort system as a particular mode of rectification is to be assumed, or whether instead it needs some sort of justification. I take the latter approach; and because I do, I emphasize the fact that in the absence of wrongful gain the tort system will not be required by corrective justice. Some other principles must therefore ground our choice of this particular mode of rectification. Posner's last objection takes the tort system as given, then chides me for not being able to explain the faulty injurer's liability as rooted in corrective justice and accuses me of imposing the obligation to repair on an innocent third party.

But if we take the tort system as given, my view does in fact impose the obligation to repair upon the faulty injurer; and though it imposes the obligation to repair upon the faulty injurer, it does not explain that obligation as required by the principle of corrective justice itself. Instead, whatever principle it is that leads us to adopt the tort system as the desired means of rectification (and I am not sure we should be driven in that direction) will be the principle that explains why we impose the victim's loss on his injurer. But to deny that the relevant principle is one of corrective justice is not tantamount to asserting that I cannot provide an explanation of the injurer's liability.

Given the tort system, one might object that I am making far too much of these subtle distinctions among the various ways of grounding the injurer's liability. After all, or so the argument might go, I am not denying that (under these circumstances) the faulty injurer has an obligation to make his victim whole. Provided the injurer is obligated to repair, why should it matter whether the duty derives from corrective justice, deterrence, or from a principle like Posner's? It does matter, however, for two very different reasons.

First, the concern of my work has been in part to explore the limits of the corrective-justice theory of torts. The limits on the role of corrective justice in imposing liability are therefore important. Second, it is important, I think, to distinguish between the question of whether a particular individual has a duty and the question of whether justice requires that the encumbered individual, rather than someone else, discharge the duty. If the faulty injurer's duty to repair is a matter of corrective justice, that means, in my view, that he has secured a wrongful gain. If someone else discharges the duty on his behalf, that is, compensates his victim, an injustice remains since the injurer's gain is left unrectified. In contrast, if the faulty injurer's duty does not derive from the principle of corrective justice, that means that his victim's loss does not translate into his wrongful gain. If someone other than the faulty injurer fully compensates the victim, no corrective injustice is done, since there exists no wrongful gain that is left unrectified.

The distinction I insist on among the various sources of one's obligation to repay is relevant in determining whether principles of justice permit or prohibit various means for compensating victims. Certain debts of repayment, like the criminal's debt to society, cannot, consistent with principles of justice, be discharged by others, for example, through an insurance scheme for criminal liability. The debt of repayment one has in virtue of the wrongful gain one secures at another's expense is another debt that must as a matter of justice be discharged by the encumbered party. Failure to do so leaves a wrongful gain unrectified. On the other hand, if I am right, the debt of repayment a faulty injurer who does not gain by his mischief owes his victim is one that can, consistent with the principle of corrective justice, be discharged by another. This feature of the debt of repayment in torts is, I have argued, central to any defense of no-fault insurance schemes.[28]

---

1. Richard Posner, The Concept of Corrective Justice, 10 J. Legal Stud. 187 (1981).

2. Jules Coleman, On the Moral Argument for the Fault System, 71 J. Phil. 473 (1974), and Justice and the Argument for No-Fault, 3 Soc. Theory Practice 161 (1974).

3. Jules Coleman, The Morality of Strict Tort Liability, 18 Wm. & Mary L. Rev. 259 (1976).

4. Jules Coleman, Mental Abnormality, Personal Responsibility and Tort Liability, in Mental Illness: Law and Public Policy 107 (Baruch A. Brody & H. Tristram Engelhardt, Jr., eds. 1980).

5. The question of whether my analysis is intended to be normative or positive often comes up in connection with my insistence upon this distinction—a distinction which appears to play little role in existing tort practice. An honest answer is that my analysis is intended to be both normative and positive. It is normative in the sense that were I a legislator charged with the task of doing justice in the allocation of accident costs, I would be concerned first with identifying the relevant principles of justice, then with inquiring whether the current tort system or some alternative to it would best be able to meet the demands of justice. It is positive in that I believe many features of the existing law of torts can be understood as enforcing some plausible conception of corrective justice. I do not argue that the principle of corrective justice explains everything that goes on in torts, and to this extent my position is more modest than those of other proponents of corrective-justice accounts of tort law. Proponents of the economic analysis of torts, in particular, my friends Richard Posner and William Landes, have asked me why it is that I adhere to an account of torts that by my own admission explains only certain elements of the law, especially when there exists an alternative analysis—the economic one—that explains nearly all of tort law. This is a fair question that merits at least some response in the context of a reply to an essay by a major proponent of the economic analysis. First, I take as a starting point the common-sense view that in resolving disputes judges try to do justice—not economics—though they may fail to do either or both very well. Given the ordinary person's view that in resolving controversial disputes judges attempt to do justice, I have tried to get a handle on exactly what sort of justice they do by developing an analysis of corrective justice that seems to make sense of a fair amount of what they do. Second, in response to the claim that economics makes sense out of more of what judges in torts do, my response is that it does not make better sense of it. The economic theory of adjudication is incompatible with any defensible analysis of judicial competence or authority. For it ascribes to judges the role of fixing rights and duties in particular disputes in order to serve the social goal of efficiency, when a proper theory of adjudi-

cation would (in my view anyway) restrict judicial authority to resolving disputes in terms of the respective claim litigants have against one another. Finally, the efficiency analysis of torts cannot explain why it is that judges impose the costs of harms on either of the litigants to the dispute. The efficient outcome might be secured by imposing the costs on some third party who, though not party to the dispute, may be the cheapest cost avoider. Economics, in other words, cannot explain the most basic feature of tort law, namely, the implicit decision to allocate losses as between respective litigants.

6. In my previous work I did not use the terms "wrongful gain" or "wrongful loss." Instead, I talked about unwarranted, undeserved, or unjustified losses and gains. I am using "wrongful" here as a catch phrase to cover all such compensable losses and rectifiable gains.

7. I owe the reader an account of how it is that justifiable or right conduct can sometimes create wrongful or compensable losses. That is, if what A does to B is justifiable or legitimate, why would we say that the losses B might suffer as a consequence are "wrongful" ones, or why would we feel that A has a duty to make good B's losses? I have suggested that the basic concept may be that of a "taking" which only shifts the burden to an analysis of which loss impositions are takings in the sense that requires compensation. I do not have a fully worked out analysis of a "taking," but I did not want the reader to think that I had not realized the importance of developing one.

8. Joel Feinberg, *Voluntary Euthanasia and the Right to Life,* 7 Phil. Pub. Aff. 93 (1978).

9. For a different view, see Posner, supra note 1, at 198 and n. 44.

10. There are means other than a tort system for rectifying wrongful gains and losses, for example, general insurance pools of the sort I have discussed elsewhere (*On the Moral Argument for the Fault System,* supra note 2). With respect to the matter of modes of rectification, I want to draw attention to a serious error in Posner's article. After noting the distinction between grounds and modes of rectification, Posner claims that there is nothing in Aristotle's view that would prohibit him from endorsing a system of penal sanctions as the best means of rectifying both wrongful losses and gains. Surely this is confused, since punishing an offender, by itself, does not annul his gain, and even if punishment deters future wrongs, reducing the incidence of wrongful gains is logically distinct from rectifying the gains and losses wrongs occasion.

11. Questions concerning the appropriate extent of rectification arise in determining damages and in explaining the principle of comparative negligence.

12. I have discussed and rejected the defense of fault liability in *On the Moral Argument for the Fault System,* supra note 2.

13. One obvious problem with this line of defense is that it assumes a particular mode of rectifying the innocent victim's wrongful loss, namely, by conferring upon him a claim right to recompense. Such a claim right logically imposes a duty on someone—usually the injurer. Assuming a system of correlative rights and duties, that is, a tort system, begs the justificatory question, namely, Why choose this rather than some other mode of rectification?

14. This line of argument is intended to be a "catchall" for the wide variety of economic analyses of fault liability. Whatever their differences, these accounts all believe that fault is a criterion of economic efficiency and that liability is imposed on the basis of fault to reduce inefficient costs.

15. *10 Minn. 456, 124 NW 221 (1910).*

16. When I presented a version of this paper at the University of Chicago Law School, Richard Posner expressed a powerful objection to my account which I want to share and discuss here. The objection relies on contrasting two cases. In the first case, Jones wrongfully injures Smith for no reason other than to have Smith suffer loss. Jones secures no gain in virtue of his misconduct; indeed, he may have arranged things to preclude the very possibility

of his securing any gain other than the satisfaction he would derive from Smith's suffering. In the second case, in order to save valuable property (and perhaps life), Jones is compelled by good sense to harm Smith in some nontrivial but not terribly disastrous way. Suppose now that the second case falls within the takings analogy that I have suggested can be employed to explain aspects of strict tort liability. If that is the case, Jones is obligated to compensate Smith in the second case though he acted reasonably—even admirably. This obligation to render compensation is, in my view, apparently a matter of corrective justice. In the first case, however, Jones has no such obligation—since he did not gain in virtue of his mischief—though his conduct is hardly admirable, or even defensible. It (apparently) turns out that, in my view, right conduct may not free one from liability, but wrongful conduct can. Surely this is counterintuitive. The objection misses its mark, however. First, it is not my view that there are no grounds upon which to impose an obligation to repair in the first case. The fact that Jones intentionally injured Smith for no good reason may itself be reason enough for imposing Smith's loss upon him. But this response is inadequate, for Posner will argue that the real problem is not that we cannot develop some other reason for holding Jones liable in the first case; the problem is that my theory of corrective justice is unable to generate such an obligation. What's worse, corrective justice not only fails to impose an obligation where doing so is appropriate; it imposes one where doing so is inappropriate—in the second case. If this is the objection, then the problem with it is that it misunderstands my view. For my view need not impose an obligation in either case; that will depend on the mode of rectification. In the first case, there simply is no wrongful gain which it is the concern of corrective justice to rectify. There is, however, a wrongful loss. In this sort of case the appropriate mode of rectification may well be to impose the victim's loss on his injurer—though it is my view that the principle of corrective justice does not require that we do so. In the second case, there is once again wrongful loss. But is there wrongful gain as well? I am not sure. In Feinberg's example there is a gain that the mountain climber secures in virtue of his destroying the cabin owner's furniture and emptying his shelves: he stays alive. Does justice require that we annul that advantage—that we kill him? I do not think so. In Vincent v. Lake Erie, the ship and its goods are saved because the captain secured the boat to the dock, thereby causing the dock to suffer damage during the subsequent storm. Does justice require the ship owner to eliminate his gain in virtue of such conduct? I doubt it. So I am not clear that there is a wrongful gain in all such cases, though there is a gain that would not have occurred but for the loss others have suffered. (In some cases of nonwrongful conduct there can be wrongful gain or advantage which should as a matter of justice be annulled. Suppose unwittingly I wrongly step in front of you while we are queueing up for the theater. As it turns out, by stepping in front I get in and you do not. Justice does require that both my gain and your loss be rectified in some manner—probably by my getting out of and your getting into the theater.) When we have wrongful loss, but no wrongful gain, as we very well might in the second case, my view does not necessarily impose the victim's loss on the injurer. Indeed, even if we had both wrongful gain and loss in a case involving nonwrongful conduct, it still would not follow that on my view the "injurer" would be obligated to his victim. Once again, that would depend on the chosen mode of rectification. It would be the case, in my view, that there is a gain and a loss to be rectified, but that would be the only way in which the first and second cases would differ. Whether there would be an obligation to repair imposed on the injurer in either, both, or neither of the cases is, I emphasize, another matter.

17. Richard Epstein's views seem to have changed somewhat. See the discussion in text at notes 20–24.

18. George Fletcher, *Fairness and Utility in Tort Theory,* 85 Harv. L. Rev. 537 (1972).

19. *3 Bing. (N.C.) 468 132 Eng. Rep. 490 (1837).*

20. Richard Epstein, *A Theory of Strict Liability,* 2 J. Legal Stud. 151 (1973).

21. *See my Mental Abnormality, Personal Responsibility and Tort Liability, supra note 4.*

22. *Nuisance Law: Corrective Justice and Its Utilitarian Constraints, 8 J. Legal Stud. 49 (1979).*

23. *See Jules Coleman, Moral Theories of Torts: Their Scope and Limits, Law & Philosophy, forthcoming.*

24. *I raise doubts about the plausibility of nonreciprocity of risk as a standard of liability in Justice and Reciprocity in Tort Theory, 14 U. Western Ont. L. Rev. 105 (1975).*

25. *Posner, supra note 1, at 197.*

26. *Id. at 198.*

27. *Id. at n. 44.*

28. *See my Justice and the Argument for No-Fault, supra note 2.*

Justice and Contract

CONTRACT AS PROMISE*

Charles Fried

It is a first principle of liberal political morality that we be secure in what is ours—so that our persons and property not be open to exploitation by others, and that from a sure foundation we may express our will and expend our powers in the world. By these powers we may create good things or low, useful articles or luxuries, things extraordinary or banal, and we will be judged accordingly—as saintly or mean, skillful or ordinary, industrious and fortunate or debased, friendly and kind or cold and inhuman. But whatever we accomplish and however that accomplishment is judged, morality requires that we respect the person and property of others, leaving them free to make their lives as we are left free to make ours. This is the liberal ideal. This is the ideal that distinguishes between the good, which is the domain of aspiration, and the right, which sets the terms and limits according to which we strive. This ideal makes what we achieve our own and our failures our responsibility too—however much or little we may choose to share our good fortune and however we may hope for help when we fail.[1]

Everything must be available to us, for who can deny the human will the title to expand even into the remotest corner of the universe? And when we forbear to bend some external object to our use because of its natural preciousness we use it still, for it is to our judgment of its value that we respond, our own conception of the good that we pursue. Only other persons are not available to us in this way—they alone share our self-consciousness, our power of self-determination; thus to use them as if they were merely part of external nature is to poison the source of the moral power we enjoy. But others *are* part of the external world, and by denying ourselves access to their persons and powers, we drastically shrink the scope of our efficacy. So it was a crucial moral discovery that free men may yet freely serve each others' purposes: the discovery that beyond the fear of reprisal or the hope of reciprocal favor, morality itself might be enlisted to assure not only that you respect me and mine but that you actively serve my purposes.[2] When my confidence in your assistance derives from my conviction that you will do what is right (not just what is prudent), then I trust you, and trust becomes a powerful tool for our working our mutual wills in the world. So remarkable a tool is trust that in the end we pursue it for its own sake; we prefer doing things cooperatively when we might have relied on fear or interest or worked alone.[3]

The device that gives trust its sharpest, most palpable form is promise. By promising we put in another man's hands a new power to accomplish his will, though only a moral power: What he sought to do alone he may now expect to do with our promised help, and to give him this new facility was our very

*Reprinted by permission of the publishers from *Contract as Promise, A Theory of Contractual Obligation* by Charles Fried, Cambridge, Mass.: Harvard University Press, Copyright © 1981 by the President and Fellows of Harvard College.

purpose in promising. By promising we transform a choice that was morally neutral into one that is morally compelled. Morality, which must be permanent and beyond our particular will if the grounds for our willing are to be secure, is itself invoked, molded to allow us better to work that particular will. Morality then serves modest, humdrum ends: We make appointments, buy and sell, harnessing this loftiest of all forces.

What is a promise, that by my words I should make wrong what before was morally indifferent? A promise is a communication—usually verbal; it says something. But how can my saying something put a moral charge on a choice that before was morally neutral? Well, by my misleading you, or by lying.[4] Is lying not the very paradigm of doing wrong by speaking? But this won't do, for a promise puts the moral charge on a *potential* act—the wrong is done later, when the promise is not kept—while a lie is a wrong committed at the time of its utterance. Both wrongs abuse trust, but in different ways. When I speak I commit myself to the truth of my utterance, but when I promise I commit myself to *act,* later. Though these two wrongs are thus quite distinct there has been a persistent tendency to run them together by treating a promise as a lie after all, but a particular kind of lie: a lie about one's intentions. Consider this case:

I. I sell you a house, retaining an adjacent vacant lot. At the time of our negotiations, I state that I intend to build a home for myself on that lot. What if several years later I sell the lot to a person who builds a gas station on it? What if I sell it only one month later? What if I am already negotiating for its sale as a gas station at the time I sell the house to you?[5]

If I was already negotiating to sell the lot for a gas station at the time of my statement to you, I have wronged you. I have lied to you about the state of my intentions, and this is as much a lie as a lie about the state of the plumbing.[6] If, however, I sell the lot many years later, I do you no wrong. There are no grounds for saying I lied about my intentions; I have just changed my mind. Now if I had *promised* to use the lot only as a residence, the situation would be different. Promising is more than just truthfully reporting my present intentions, for I may be free to change my mind, as I am not free to break my promise.

Let us take it as given here that lying is wrong and so that it is wrong to obtain benefits or cause harm by lying (including lying about one's intentions). It does not at all follow that to obtain a benefit or cause harm by breaking a promise is also wrong. That my act procures me a benefit or causes harm all by itself proves nothing. If I open a restaurant near your hotel and prosper as I draw your guests away from the standard hotel fare you offer, this benefit I draw from you places me under no obligation to you. I should make restitution only if I benefit *unjustly,* which I do if I deceive you—as when I lie to you about my intentions in example I.[7] But where is the injustice if I honestly intend to keep my promise at the time of making it, and later change my mind? If we feel I owe you recompense in that case too, it cannot be because of the benefit I have obtained through my promise: We have seen that benefit even at another's expense is not alone sufficient to require compensation. If I owe you a duty to return that benefit it must be because of the promise. It is the promise that makes my enrichment at your expense unjust, and not the enrichment that makes the promise binding. And thus neither the statement of intention nor the benefit explains why, if at all, a promise does any moral work.

A more common attempt to reduce the force of a promise to some other moral category invokes the harm you suffer in relying on my promise. My statement is like a pit I have dug in the road, into which you fall. I have harmed you and should make you whole. Thus the tort principle might be urged to bridge the gap in the argument between a statement of intention and a promise: I have a duty just because I could have foreseen (indeed it was my intention) that you would rely on my promise and that you would suffer harm when I broke it. And this wrong then not only sets the stage for compensation of the harm caused by the misplaced reliance, but also supplies the moral predicate for restitution of any benefits I may have extracted from you on the strength of my promise.[8] But we still beg the question. If the promise is no more than a truthful statement of my intention, why am *I* responsible for harm that befalls you as a result of my change of heart? To be sure, it is not like a change in the weather—I might have kept to my original intention—but how does this distinguish the broken promise from any other statement of intention (or habit or prediction of future conduct) of mine of which you know and on which you choose to rely? Should your expectations of me limit my freedom of choice? If you rent the apartment next to mine because I play chamber music there, do I owe you more than an expression of regret when my friends and I decide to meet instead at the cellist's home? And in general, why should my liberty be constrained by the harm you would suffer from the disappointment of the expectations you choose to entertain about my choices?

Does it make a difference that when I promise you do not just happen to rely on me, that I communicate my intention to you and therefore can be taken to know that changing my mind may put you at risk? But then I might be aware that you would count on my keeping to my intentions even if I myself had not communicated those intentions to you. (*You* might have told me you were relying on me, or you might have overheard me telling some third person of my intentions.) It might be said that I become the agent of your reliance by telling you, and that this makes my responsibility clearer: After all, I can scarcely control all the ways in which you might learn of my intentions, but I *can* control whether or not I tell you of them. But we are still begging the question. If promising is no more than my telling you of my intentions, why do we both not know that I may yet change my mind? Perhaps, then, promising is like telling you of my intention and telling you that I don't intend to change my mind. But why can't I change my mind about the latter intention?

Perhaps the statement of intention in promising is binding because we not only foresee reliance, we invite it: We intend the promisee to rely on the promise. Yet even this will not do. If I invite reliance on my stated intention, then that is all I invite. Certainly I may hope and intend, in example I, that you buy my house on the basis of what I have told you, but why does that hope bind me to do more than state my intention honestly? And that intention and invitation are quite compatible with my later changing my mind. In every case, of course, I should weigh the harm I will do if I do change my mind. If I am a doctor and I know you will rely on me to be part of an outing on which someone may fall ill, I should certainly weigh the harm that may come about if that reliance is disappointed. Indeed I should weigh that harm even if you do not rely on me, but are foolish enough not to have made a provision for a doctor. Yet in none of these instances am I bound as I would be had I promised.[9]

A promise invokes trust in my future actions, not merely in my present sincerity. We need to isolate an additional element, over and above benefit, reliance, and the communication of intention. That additional element must *commit* me, and commit me to more than the truth of some statement. That additional element has so far eluded our analysis.

It has eluded us, I believe, because there is a real puzzle about how we can commit ourselves to a course of conduct that absent our commitment is mor-

ally neutral. The invocation of benefit and reliance are attempts to explain the force of a promise in terms of two of its most usual effects, but the attempts fail because these effects depend on the prior assumption of the force of the commitment. The way out of the puzzle is to recognize the bootstrap quality of the argument: To have force in *a particular case* promises must be assumed to have force generally. Once that general assumption is made, the effects we intentionally produce by a particular promise may be morally attributed to us. This recognition is not as paradoxical as its abstract statement here may make it seem. It lies, after all, behind every conventional structure: games,[10] institutions and practices, and most important, language.

Let us put to one side the question of how a convention comes into being, or of when and why we are morally bound to comply with its terms, while we look briefly at what a convention is and how it does its work. Take the classical example of a game. What the players do is defined by a system of rules—sometimes quite vague and informal, sometimes elaborate and codified. These rules apply only to the players— that is, to persons who invoke them. These rules are a human invention, and their consequences (castling, striking out, winning, losing) can be understood only in terms of the rules. The players may have a variety of motives for playing (profit, fun, maybe even duty to fellow players who need participants). A variety of judgments are applicable to the players—they may be deemed skillful, imaginative, bold, honest, or dishonest—but these judgments and motives too can be understood only in the context of the game. For instance, you can cheat only by breaking rules to which you pretend to conform.

This almost canonical invocation of the game example has often been misunderstood as somehow applying only to unserious matters, to play, so that it is said to trivialize the solemn objects (like law or promises) that it is used to explain. But this is a mistake, confusing the interests involved, the reasons for creating and invoking a particular convention, with the logical structure of conventions in general. Games are (often) played for fun, but other conventions—for instance religious rituals or legal procedures—may have most earnest ends, while still other conventions are quite general. To the last category belongs language. The conventional nature of language is too obvious to belabor. It is worth pointing out, however, that the various things we do with language—informing, reporting, promising, insulting, cheating, lying— all depend on the conventional structure's being firmly in place. You could not lie if there were not both understanding of the language you lied in and a general convention of using that language truthfully. This point holds irrespective of whether the institution of language has advanced the situation of mankind and of whether lying is sometimes, always, or never wrong.

Promising too is a very general convention—though less general than language, of course, since promising is itself a use of language.[11] The convention of promising (like that of language) has a very general purpose under which we may bring an infinite set of particular purposes. In order that I be as free as possible, that my will have the greatest possible range consistent with the similar will of others, it is necessary that there be a way in which I may commit myself. It is necessary that I be able to make nonoptional a course of conduct that would otherwise be optional for me. By doing this I can facilitate the projects of others, because I can make it possible for those others to count on my future conduct, and thus those others can pursue more intricate, more far-reaching projects. If it is my purpose, my will that others be able to count on me in the pursuit of their endeavor, it is essential that I be able to deliver myself into their hands more firmly than where they simply predict my future course. Thus the possibility of commitment permits an act of generosity on my part, permits me to pursue a project whose content is that *you* be permitted to pursue *your* project. But of course this purely altruistic motive is not the only motive worth facilitating. More central to our concern is the situation where we facilitate each other's projects, where the gain is reciprocal. Schematically the situation looks like this:

You want to accomplish purpose *A* and I want to accomplish purpose *B*. Neither of us can succeed without the cooperation of the other. Thus I want to be able to commit myself to help you achieve *A* so that you will commit yourself to help me achieve *B*.

Now if *A* and *B* are objects or actions that can be transferred simultaneously there is no need for commitment. As I hand over *A* you hand over *B*, and we are both satisfied. But very few things are like that. We need a device to permit a trade over time: to allow me to do *A* for you when you need it, in the confident belief that you will do *B* for me when I need it. Your commitment puts your future performance into my hands in the present just as my commitment puts my future performance into your hands. A future exchange is transformed into a present exchange. And

in order to accomplish this all we need is a conventional device which we both invoke, which you know I am invoking when I invoke it, which I know that you know I am invoking, and so on.

The only mystery about this is the mystery that surrounds increasing autonomy by providing means for restricting it. But really this is a pseudomystery. The restrictions involved in promising are restrictions undertaken just in order to increase one's options in the long run, and thus are perfectly consistent with the principle of autonomy—consistent with a respect for one's own autonomy and the autonomy of others. To be sure, in getting something for myself now by promising to do something for you in the future, I am mortgaging the interest of my future self in favor of my present self. How can I be sure my future self will approve?* This is a deep and difficult problem about which I say more later in this chapter. Suffice it to say here that unless one assumes the continuity of the self and the possibility of maintaining complex projects over time, not only the morality of promising but also any coherent picture of the person becomes impossible.

The Moral Obligation of Promise

Once I have invoked the institution of promising, why exactly is it wrong for me then to break my promise?

My argument so far does not answer that question. The institution of promising is a way for me to bind myself to another so that the other may expect a future performance, and binding myself in this way is something that I may want to be able to do. But this by itself does not show that I am morally obligated to perform my promise at a later time if to do so proves inconvenient or costly. That there should be a system of currency also increases my options and is useful to me, but this does not show why I should not use counterfeit money if I can get away with it. In just the same way the usefulness of promising in general does not show why I should not take advantage of it in a particular case and yet fail to keep my promise. That the convention would cease to function in the long run, would cease to provide benefits if everyone felt free

---

*Note that this problem does not arise where I make a present sacrifice for a future benefit, since by hypothesis I am presently willing to make that sacrifice and in the future I only stand to gain.

to violate it, is hardly an answer to the question of why I should keep a particular promise on a particular occasion.

David Lewis has shown[12] that a convention that it would be in each person's interest to observe if everyone else observed it will be established and maintained without any special mechanisms of commitment or enforcement. Starting with simple conventions (for example that if a telephone conversation is disconnected, the person who initiated the call is the one who calls back) Lewis extends his argument to the case of language. Now promising is different, since (unlike language, where it is overwhelmingly in the interest of all that everyone comply with linguistic conventions, even when language is used to deceive) it will often be in the interest of the promisor *not* to conform to the convention when it comes time to render his performance. Therefore individual self-interest is not enough to sustain the convention, and some additional ground is needed to keep it from unraveling. There are two principal candidates: external sanctions and moral obligation.

David Hume sought to combine these two by proposing that the external sanction of public opprobrium, of loss of reputation for honesty, which society attaches to promise-breaking, is internalized, becomes instinctual, and accounts for the sense of the moral obligation of promise.[13] Though Hume offers a possible anthropological or psychological account of how people feel about promises, his is not a satisfactory *moral* argument. Assume that I can get away with breaking my promise (the promisee is dead), and I am now asking why I should keep it anyway in the face of some personal inconvenience. Hume's account of obligation is more like an argument *against* my keeping the promise, for it tells me how any feelings of obligation that I may harbor have come to lodge in my psyche and thus is the first step toward ridding me of such inconvenient prejudices.

Considerations of self-interest cannot supply the moral basis of my obligation to keep a promise. By an analogous argument neither can considerations of utility. For however sincerely and impartially I may apply the utilitarian injunction to consider at each step how I might increase the sum of happiness or utility in the world, it will allow me to break my promise whenever the balance of advantage (including, of course, my own advantage) tips in that direction. The possible damage to the institution of promising is only one factor in the calculation. Other factors are the alternative good I might do by breaking my promise, whether and by how many people the breach might

be discovered, what the actual effect on confidence of such a breach would be. There is no *a priori* reason for believing that an individual's calculations will come out in favor of keeping the promise always, sometimes, or most of the time.

Rule-utilitarianism seeks to offer a way out of this conundrum. The individual's moral obligation is determined not by what the best action at a particular moment would be, but by the rule it would be best for him to follow. It has, I believe, been demonstrated that this position is incoherent: Either rule-utilitarianism requires that rules be followed in a particular case even where the result would not be best all things considered, and so the utilitarian aspect of rule-utilitarianism is abandoned; or the obligation to follow the rule is so qualified as to collapse into act-utilitarianism after all.[14] There is, however, a version of rule-utilitarianism that makes a great deal of sense. In this version the utilitarian does not instruct us what our individual moral obligations are but rather instructs legislators what the best rules are.[15] If legislation is our focus, then the contradictions of rule-utilitarianism do not arise, since we are instructing those whose decisions can *only* take the form of issuing rules. From that perspective there is obvious utility to rules establishing and enforcing promissory obligations. Since I am concerned now with the question of individual obligation, that is, moral obligation, this legislative perspective on the argument is not available to me.

The obligation to keep a promise is grounded not in arguments of utility but in respect for individual autonomy and in trust. Autonomy and trust are grounds for the institution of promising as well, but the argument for *individual* obligation is not the same. Individual obligation is only a step away, but that step must be taken.[16] An individual is morally bound to keep his promises because he has intentionally invoked a convention whose function it is to give grounds—moral grounds—for another to expect the promised performance.[17] To renege is to abuse a confidence he was free to invite or not, and which he intentionally did invite. To abuse that confidence now is like (but only *like*) lying: the abuse of a shared social institution that is intended to invoke the bonds of trust. A liar and a promise-breaker each *use* another person. In both speech and promising there is an invitation to the other to trust, to make himself vulnerable; the liar and the promise-breaker then abuse that trust. The obligation to keep a promise is thus similar to but more constraining than the obligation to tell the truth. To avoid lying you need only believe in the truth of what you say when you say it, but a promise binds into the future, well past the moment when the promise is made. There will, of course, be great social utility to a general regime of trust and confidence in promise and truthfulness. But this just shows that a regime of mutual respect allows men and women to accomplish what in a jungle of unrestrained self-interest could not be accomplished. If this advantage is to be firmly established, there must exist a ground for mutual confidence deeper than and independent of the social utility it permits.

The utilitarian counting the advantages affirms the general importance of enforcing *contracts*. The moralist of duty, however, sees *promising* as a device that free, moral individuals have fashioned on the premise of mutual trust, and which gathers its moral force from that premise. The moralist of duty thus posits a general obligation to keep promises, of which the obligation of contract will be only a special case—that special case in which certain promises have attained legal as well as moral force. But since a contract is first of all a promise, the contract must be kept because a promise must be kept.

To summarize: There exists a convention that defines the practice of promising and its entailments. This convention provides a way that a person may create expectations in others. By virtue of the basic Kantian principles of trust and respect, it is wrong to invoke that convention in order to make a promise, and then to break it.

What a Promise Is Worth

If I make a promise to you, I should do as I promise; and if I fail to keep my promise, it is fair that I should be made to hand over the equivalent of the promised performance. In contract doctrine this proposition appears as the expectation measure of damages for breach. The expectation standard gives the victim of a breach no more or less than he would have had had there been no breach—in other words, he gets the benefit of his bargain.[18] Two alternative measures of damage, reliance and restitution, express the different notions that if a person has relied on a promise and been hurt, that hurt must be made good; and that if a contract-breaker has obtained goods or services, he must be made to pay a fair (just?) price for them.[19] Consider three cases:

II-A. I enter your antique shop on a quiet afternoon and agree in writing to buy an expensive chest I

see there, the price being about three times what you paid for it a short time ago. When I get home I repent of my decision, and within half an hour of my visit—before any other customer has come to your store—I telephone to say I no longer want the chest.

II-B. Same as above, except in the meantime you have waxed and polished the chest and had your delivery van bring it to my door.

II-C. Same as above, except I have the use of the chest for six months, while your shop is closed for renovations.

To require me to pay for the chest in case II-A (or, if you resell it, to pay any profit you lost, including lost business volume) is to give you your expectation, the benefit of your bargain. In II-B if all I must compensate is your effort I am reimbursing your reliance, and in II-C to force me to pay a fair price for the use I have had of the chest is to focus on making me pay for, restore, an actual benefit I have received.

The assault on the classical conception of contract, the concept I call contract as promise, has centered on the connection—taken as canonical for some hundred years—between contract law and expectation damages. To focus the attack on this connection is indeed strategic. As the critics recognize and as I have just stated, to the extent that contract is grounded in promise, it seems natural to measure relief by the expectation, that is, by the promise itself. If that link can be threatened, then contract itself may be grounded elsewhere than in promise, elsewhere than in the will of the parties. In his recent comprehensive treatise, *The Rise and Fall of Freedom of Contract*, Patrick Atiyah makes the connection between the recourse to expectation damages and the emerging enforceability of executory contracts—that is, contracts enforced, though no detriment has been suffered in reliance and no benefit has been conferred. (Case II-A is an example of an executory contract.) Before the nineteenth century, he argues, a contractual relation referred generally to one of a number of particular, community-sanctioned relations between persons who in the course of their dealings (as carriers, innkeepers, surgeons, merchants) relied on each other to their detriment or conferred benefits on each other. It was these detriments and benefits that had to be reimbursed, and an explicit promise—if there happened to be one—was important primarily to establish the reliance or to show that the benefit had been conferred in expectation of payment, not officiously or as a gift. All this, Atiyah writes, turned inside out when the promise itself came to be seen as the basis of obligation, so that neither benefit nor reliance any longer seemed necessary and the proper measure of the obligation was the promise itself, that is, the expectation. The promise principle was embraced as an expression of the principle of liberty—the will binding itself, to use Kantian language, rather than being bound by the norms of the collectivity—and the award of expectation damages followed as a natural concomitant of the promise principle.

The insistence on reliance or benefit is related to disputes about the nature of promising. As I have argued, reliance on a promise cannot alone explain its force: There is reliance because a promise is binding, and not the other way around. But if a person is bound by his promise and not by the harm the promisee may have suffered in reliance on it, then what he is bound to is just its performance. Put simply, I am bound to do what I promised you I would do—or I am bound to put you in as good a position as if I had done so. To bind me to do no more than to reimburse your reliance is to excuse me to that extent from the obligation I undertook. If your reliance is less than your expectation (in case II-A there is no reliance), then to that extent a reliance standard excuses me from the very obligation I undertook and so weakens the force of an obligation I chose to assume. Since by hypothesis I chose to assume the obligation in its stronger form (that is, to render the performance promised), the reliance rule indeed precludes me from incurring the very obligation I chose to undertake at the time of promising. The most compelling of the arguments for resisting this conclusion and for urging that we settle for reliance is the sense that it is sometimes harsh and ungenerous to insist on the full measure of expectancy. (This is part of Atiyah's thrust when he designates the expectation standard as an aspect of the rigid Victorian promissory morality.) The harshness comes about because in the event the promisor finds the obligation he assumed too burdensome.

This distress may be analyzed into three forms: (1) The promisor regrets having to pay for what he has bought (which may only have been the satisfaction of promising a gift or the thrill of buying a lottery ticket or stock option), though he would readily do the same thing again. I take it that this kind of regret merits no sympathy at all. Indeed if we gave in to it we would frustrate the promisor's ability to engage in his own continuing projects and so the promisor's plea is, strictly speaking, self-contradictory. (2) The

promisor regrets his promise because he was mistaken about the nature of the burdens he was assuming—the purchaser in case II-A thought he would find the money for the antique but in fact his savings are depleted, or perhaps the chest is not as old nor as valuable as he had imagined, or his house has burned down and he no longer needs it. All of these regrets are based on mistaken assumptions about the facts as they are or as they turn out to be. As we shall see . . . , the doctrines of mistake, frustration, and impossibility provide grounds for mitigating the effect of the promise principle without at all undermining it.

Finally there is the most troublesome ground of regret: (3) The promisor made no mistake about the facts or probabilities at all, but now that it has come time to perform he no longer values the promise as highly as when he made it. He regrets the promise because he regrets the value judgment that led him to make it. He concludes that the purchase of an expensive antique is an extravagance. Compassion may lead a promisee to release an obligation in such a case, but he releases as an act of generosity, not as a duty, and certainly not because the promisor's repentance destroys the force of the original obligation. The intuitive reason for holding fast is that such repentance should be the promisor's own responsibility, not one he can shift onto others. It seems too easy a way of getting out of one's obligations. Yet our intuition does not depend on suspicions of insincerity alone. Rather we feel that holding people to their obligations is a way of taking them seriously and thus of giving the concept of sincerity itself serious content. Taking this intuition to a more abstract level, I would say that respect for others as free and rational requires taking seriously their capacity to determine their own values. I invoke again the distinction between the right and the good. The right defines the concept of the self as choosing its own conception of the good. Others must respect our capacity as free and rational persons to choose our own good, and that respect means allowing persons to take responsibility for the good they choose. And, of course, that choosing self is not an instantaneous self but one extended in time, so that to respect those determinations of the self is to respect their persistence over time. If we decline to take seriously the assumption of an obligation because we do not take seriously the promisor's prior conception of the good that led him to assume it, to that extent we do not take him seriously as a person. We infantilize him, as we do quite properly when we release the very young from the consequences of their choices.[20]

Since contracts invoke and are invoked by promises, it is not surprising that the law came to impose on the promises it recognized the same incidents as morality demands. The connection between contract and the expectation principle is so palpable that there is reason to doubt that its legal recognition is a relatively recent invention. It is true that over the last two centuries citizens in the liberal democracies have become increasingly free to dispose of their talents, labor, and property as seems best to them. The freedom to bind oneself contractually to a future disposition is an important and striking example of this freedom (the freedom to make testamentary dispositions or to make whatever present use of one's effort or goods one desires are other examples), because in a promise one is taking responsibility not only for one's present self but for one's future self. But this does not argue that the promise principle itself is a novelty—surely Cicero's, Pufendorf's and Grotius's discussions of it[21] show that it is not—but only that its use has expanded greatly over the years.

Remedies in and Around the Promise

Those who have an interest in assimilating contract to the more communitarian standards of tort law have been able to obscure the link between contract and promise because in certain cases the natural thing to do *is* to give damages for the harm that has been suffered, rather than to give the money value of the promised expectation. But it does not follow from these cases that expectation is not a normal and natural measure for contract damages. First, these are situations in which the harm suffered is the measure of damages because it is hard to find the monetary value of the expectation. A leading case, *Security Stove & Mfg. Co.* v. *American Railway Express Co.,*[22] illustrates the type. The plaintiff stove manufacturer had arranged to have a new kind of stove shipped by the defendant express company to a trade convention, at which the plaintiff hoped to interest prospective buyers in his improved product. The president and his workmen went to the convention, but the defendant failed to deliver a crucial part of the exhibit in time, and they had nothing to show. Plaintiff brought suit to recover the cost of renting the booth, the freight charges, and the time and expenses lost as a result of the fruitless trip to the convention. The recovery of

these items of damages, which (with the possible exception of the prepaid booth rental) seem typical examples of reliance losses, is generally agreed to have been appropriate. There was no way of knowing what results the plaintiff would have obtained had he succeeded in exhibiting his product at the convention. There was no way of knowing what his expectancy was, and so the court gave him his loss through reliance. But this illustrates only that where expectancy cannot be calculated, reliance may be a reasonable surrogate. It is reasonable to suppose that the plaintiff's expectation in *Security Stove* was at least as great as the monies he put out to exhibit his goods—after all, he was a businessman and is assumed to have been exhibiting his goods to make an eventual profit. If it could somehow be shown that the exhibit would have been a failure and the plaintiff would have suffered a net loss, the case for recovery would be undermined, and most authorities would then deny recovery.*[23]

Second are the cases in which the amount needed to undo the harm caused by reliance is itself the fairest measure of expectation.

III-A. Buyer approaches manufacturer with the specifications of a small, inexpensive part—say a bolt—for a machine buyer is building. Manufacturer selects the part and sells it to buyer. The bolt is badly made, shears, and damages the machine.

The value of the thing promised, a well-made bolt, is negligible, but to give buyer his money back and no more would be a grave injustice. Here it does seem more natural to say that the manufacturer induced buyer's reasonable reliance and should compensate the resulting harm. But it is equally the case that it is a fair implication of the simple-seeming original transaction that manufacturer not only delivered and promised to transfer good title to the bolt, but promised at

---

*A case like this may be seen as involving no more than the allocation of the burden of proof as to the expectation. The plaintiff shows his reliance costs and says that *prima facie* his expectation was at least that great. The burden then shifts to the defendant to show that indeed this was a losing proposition and the expectation was less than the reliance. It seems only fair that since the defendant's breach prevented the exhibition from taking place and thus prevented the drama on which the expectation depended from being played out, the defendant should at least bear the risk of showing that the venture would have been a failure.

the same time that the bolt would do the job it was meant to do.*[24]

It is for the (perhaps wholly innocent) breach of this implied promise that we hold manufacturers liable. The soundness of this analysis is brought home if we vary the facts slightly:

III-B. Same as above, except buyer purchases the bolt over the counter in a local hardware store, saying nothing about its use.

To make the owner of the hardware store or the manufacturer of the bolt responsible for large damages in this case seems unfair. One can say that this is because they could not *foresee* harm of this magnitude arising out of their conduct. (A tort locution: The man who negligently jostles a package containing a bomb could not *foresee* and is not responsible for harm of the ensuing magnitude when the package explodes.) But one can as well cast the matter again in contractual terms, saying that they did not undertake this measure of responsibility. After all, if in the first version of this example the buyer and manufacturer had agreed that manufacturer would be responsible only up to a certain amount, say ten times the cost of the bolt, such a limitation would generally be respected. So in certain cases tort and contract ideas converge on the same result.[25] In III-A we may say that buyer justifiably relied on manufacturer. He relied in part because of the (implied) promise or warranty, and of course it *is* a primary function of promises to induce reliance.

Consider finally this variation:

III-C. Manufacturer makes not bolts but tinned goods. Buyer buys a can of peas at a grocer's and serves them to a guest who chips a tooth on a stone negligently included in the can.

Manufacturer promised the guest nothing. (In legal terminology there is between them no privity of con-

tract.) Yet manufacturer should be responsible for the guest's injuries, just as the driver of a car should be responsible for the injuries of a pedestrian whom he negligently hits, though there too privity of contract is lacking.[26] One may say that the guest reasonably relied on the purity of the peas he ate, just as a pedestrian must rely on the due care of motorists. But I never argued that promise is the *only* basis of reliance or that contract is the only basis of responsibility for harms to others.

Third, there are cases in which wrongs are committed and loss is suffered in and around the attempt to make an agreement. In these cases too reliance is the best measure of compensation. A striking example is *Hoffman* v. *Red Owl Stores:*[27] A prospective Red Owl supermarket franchisee sold his previously owned business and made other expenditures on the assumption that his negotiations to obtain a Red Owl franchise would shortly be concluded. The award of reliance damages was not a case of enforcement of a promise at all, since the parties had not reached the stage where clearly determined promises had been made. Reliance damages were awarded because Red Owl had not dealt fairly with Hoffman. It had allowed him to incur expenses based on hopes that Red Owl knew or should have known were imprudent and that Red Owl was not prepared to permit him to realize. Red Owl was held liable not in order to force it to perform a promise, which it had never made, but rather to compensate Hoffman for losses he had suffered through Red Owl's inconsiderate and temporizing assurances.[28] There is nothing at all in my conception of contract as promise that precludes persons who behave badly and cause unnecessary harm from being forced to make fair compensation. Promissory obligation is not the only basis for liability; principles of tort are sufficient to provide that people who give vague assurances that cause foreseeable harm to others should make compensation. Cases like *Hoffman* are seen to undermine the conception of contract as promise: If contract is really discrete and if it is really based in promise, then whenever there has been a promise in the picture (even only a potential promise) contractual principles must govern the whole relation. To state the argument is to reveal it as a non sequitur. It is a logical fallacy of which the classical exponents of contract as promise were themselves supremely guilty in their reluctance to grant relief for fraud or for mistakes that prevented a real agreement from coming into being. Modern critics of contractual freedom have taken the classics at their word. Justice often requires relief and adjustment in cases of accidents in

---

*In law the latter promise is called a warranty—a promise not merely that the promisor will do something in the future, but a taking of responsibility over and above the responsibility of well-meaning honesty that something is the case. For instance, a dealer may warrant that a violin is a Stradivarius. This means more than that he in good faith believes it to be one: he is promising that if it is not, he will be responsible. Uniform Commercial Code (hereafter cited as UCC) § 2-714. Cf. *Smith* v. *Zimbalist,* 2 Cal. App.2d 324, 38 P.2d 170 (1934), hearing denied 17 Jan. 1935.

and around the contracting process, and the critics have seen in this a refutation of the classics' major premise. . . . Here it is sufficient to introduce the notion that contract as promise has a distinct but neither exclusive nor necessarily dominant place among legal and moral principles. A major concern of this book is the articulation of the boundaries and connection between the promissory and other principles of justice.*

The tendency to merge promise into its adjacent concepts applies also to the relation between it and the principle of restitution, which holds that a person who has received a benefit at another's expense should compensate his benefactor, unless a gift was intended. This principle does indeed appeal to a primitive intuition of fairness. Even where a gift was intended, the appropriateness at least of gratitude if not of a vague duty to reciprocate is recognized in many cultures. Aristotle refers the principle to the imperative that some balance be retained among members of a society, but this seems to restate the proposition rather than to explain it.[29] Since restitution, like reliance, is a principle of fairness that operates independently of the will of the parties, the attempt to refer promissory obligation to this principle is another attempt to explain away the self-imposed character of promissory obligation. I have already argued that this cannot be done without begging the question. Certainly the restitution principle cannot explain the force of a promise for which no benefit has yet been or ever will be given in return. (The legal recognition of such gift promises is tangled in the confusions of the doctrine of consideration. . . .) The reduction of promise to restitution (or to restitution plus reliance) must fail. There are nevertheless breaches of promise for which restitution is the correct principle of relief.[30]

IV. In a case like *Security Stove,* where the freight charges have been prepaid but the goods

never picked up or delivered as agreed, let us suppose the express company could show that the contemplated exhibit would have been a disaster and that the stove company was much better off never having shown at the fair. Perhaps in such a case there should be no award of reliance damages, but should the express company be allowed to keep the prepayment? Should it be able to argue that the stove company is lucky there was a breach?

In terms of both expectation and harm the stove company should get nothing. Its expectation is shown to be negative, and it suffered no harm. And yet it is entirely clear that Railway Express should make restitution. They did nothing for the money and should not keep it. But is this enforcing the promise? Not at all.

V. I owe my plumber ten dollars, so I place a ten-dollar bill in an envelope, which I mistakenly address and send to you.

On what theory can I get my ten dollars back from you? You made no promise to me. You have *done* me no wrong, and so that is not the ground of my demand that you return the money—though you wrong me now if you do not accede to my demand. The principle is a general one: It is wrong to retain an advantage obtained without justification at another's expense. And what justification can you offer for keeping the ten dollars?*[31] What justification can Railway Express offer for keeping the freight charges in case IV? That it has done the stove company a favor by spoiling the exhibit? But this is no favor the stove company asked for and not one that Railway Express had a right to thrust on it. And surely Railway Express cannot say it received the money properly under a contract, since it has utterly repudiated that contract. The contract drops out leaving Railway Express without a justification. In this state of affairs the stove company wins.

Promise and restitution are distinct principles. Neither derives from the other, and so the attempt to dig beneath promise in order to ground contract in restitution (or reliance, for that matter) is misconceived. Contract is based on promise, but when something goes wrong in the contract process—when

*There is a category of cases that has become famous in the law under the rubric of promissory estoppel or detrimental reliance. In these cases there has indeed generally been a promise, but the basis for *legal* redress is said to be the plaintiff's detrimental reliance on the promise. Courts now tend to limit the amount of the redress in such cases to the detriment suffered through reliance. But these cases also do not show that reliance and harm are the general basis for contractual recovery. Rather these cases should be seen for what they are: a belated attempt to plug a gap in the general regime of enforcement of promises, a gap left by the artificial and unfortunate doctrine of consideration. See . . . Fuller and Eisenberg, supra note 25, at 159–161.

*That you thought it was a present, spent it, and would now have to dip into the grocery budget to pay me back? Well, that might be a justification if it were true.

people fail to reach agreement, or break their promises—there will usually be gains and losses to sort out. The *Red Owl* case is one illustration. Here is another:

I. Britton signs on to work for Turner for a period of one year at an agreed wage of $120 to be paid at the end of his service. After nine months of faithful service he quits without justification, and Turner without difficulty finds a replacement for him.

On one hand Britton has not kept his promise; on the other Turner has had a substantial benefit at his expense.[32] The promise and restitution principles appear to point in opposite directions in this situation. . . . For the present it is sufficient to note that it is the very distinctness of the principles that causes such questions to arise. Certainly nothing about the promise principle, the conception of contract as promise, entails that all disputes between people who have tried but failed to make a contract or who have broken a contract must be decided solely according to that principle.

---

1. *On the right and the good the critical discussion is John Rawls,* A Theory of Justice *§§ 68, 83–85 (Cambridge, 1971), which harks back to Immanuel Kant,* Groundwork of the Metaphysics of Morals *(Paton trans., Harper Torchbooks ed. New York, 1964) where the contrast is made between the right and happiness. See also W. D. Ross,* The Right and the Good *(Oxford, 1930); Ronald Dworkin, "Liberalism," in* Public and Private Morality *(S. Hampshire ed. Cambridge, England, 1978). On the relation between liberalism and responsibility, see Friedrich Hayek,* The Constitution of Liberty *ch. 5 (Chicago, 1960); Charles Fried,* Right and Wrong *124–126 (Cambridge, 1978); Rawls, supra at 519. For a different view see C. B. Macpherson,* The Political Theory of Possessive Individualism—Hobbes to Locke *(Oxford, 1962).*

2. *Immanuel Kant,* The Metaphysical Elements of Justice *54–55 (Ladd trans. Indianapolis, 1965).*

3. *See Charles Fried,* An Anatomy of Values *81–86 (Cambridge, 1970); Henry Sidgwick,* Elements of Politics, *quoted in Friedrich Kessler and Grant Gilmore,* Contracts *4 (2d ed. Boston, 1970).*

4. *Sissela Bok,* Lying: Moral Choice in Public Life *(New York, 1978); Fried, supra note 1, ch. 3.*

5. *This example is based on* Adams v. Gillig, *199 N.Y. 314, 92 N.E. 670 (1930).*

6. *See generally Page Keeton, "Fraud: Statements of Intention," 15 Texas L. Rev. 185 (1937).*

7. *See generally Robert Goff and Gareth Jones,* The Law of Restitution *ch. 1 (2d. ed. London, 1978).*

8. *For a strong statement of the tort and benefit principles as foundations of contract law, see Patrick Atiyah,* The Rise and Fall of Freedom of Contract *1–7 (Oxford, 1979). A remarkable article stating the several moral principles implicit in contract law is George Gardner, "An Inquiry into the Principles of the Law of Contracts," 46 Harv. L. Rev. 1 (1932).*

9. *For a review of Anglo-American writing on promise from Hobbes to modern times, see Atiyah, supra note 8, at 41–60, 649–659. There has been a lively debate on the bases for the moral obligation of promises in recent philosophical literature. Some philosophers have taken a line similar to that of Atiyah and Gilmore, deriving the obligation of promise from the element of reliance. The strongest statement is Neil MacCormick, "Voluntary Obligations and Normative Powers," Proceedings of the Aristotelian Society, supp. vol. 46, at 59 (1972). See also Pall Ardal, "And That's a Promise," 18 Phil. Q. 225 (1968); F. S. McNeilly, "Promises Demoralized," 81 Phil. Rev. 63 (1972). G. J. Warnock,* The Object of Morality *ch. 7 (London, 1971), offers an effective refutation along the lines in the text, but his affirmative case proposes that the obligation of a promise rests on the duty of veracity, the duty to make the facts correspond to the promise. For an excellent discussion of this last suggestion and a proposal that accords with my own, see Don Locke, "The Object of Morality and the Obligation to Keep a Promise," 2 Canadian J. of Philosophy 135 (1972). Locke's emphasis on*

trust seems a clearer and sounder version of H. A. Prichard's proposal that the obligation of a Promise rests on a more general "agreement to keep agreements." *Moral Obligation ch. 7 (Oxford, 1957).*

10. *A number of the philosophers who disagree with the Atiyah-MacCormick argument emphasize the conventional aspect of the invocation of the promissory form, as well as the self-imposed nature of the obligation. E.g. Joseph Raz, "Voluntary Obligations," Proceedings of the Aristotelian Society, supp. vol. 46, at 79 (1972); Raz, "Promises and Obligations," in* Law, Morality and Society *(Hacker, Raz eds. Oxford, 1977); John Searle,* Speech Acts *33–42, 175–188 (Cambridge, 1969); Searle, "What Is a Speech Act?" in* The Philosophy of Language *(John Searle ed. Oxford, 1971). The locus classicus of this view of promising is John Rawls, "Two Concepts of Rules," 64 Phil. Rev. 3 (1955). The general idea goes back, of course, to Ludwig Wittgenstein,* Philosophical Investigations *§ 23. For Hume's account of the conventional nature of promissory obligation, see* A Treatise of Human Nature *516–525 (Selby-Bigge ed. Oxford, 1888).*

11. *Stanley Cavell's contention in* The Claim of Reason *293–303 (Oxford, 1979) that promising is not a practice or an institution, because unlike the case of a game one cannot imagine setting it up or reforming it and because promising is not an office, seems to me beside the point. Kant's discussion, supra note 2, shows that morality can mandate that there be a convention with certain general features, as does Hume's discussion supra note 10, though Hume's morality is a more utilitarian one.*

12. *David Lewis,* Convention *(Cambridge, 1969).*

13. *Supra note 10.*

14. *Here I side with David Lyons,* The Forms and Limits of Utilitarianism *(Oxford, 1965) in a continuing debate. For the most recent statement of the contrary position, see Richard Brandt,* A Theory of the Good and Right *(Oxford, 1979). For an excellent introduction, see J. J. C. Smart and Bernard Williams,* Utilitarianism: For and Against *(Cambridge, England, 1973). I argue that it is a mistake to treat Rawls's discussion of promising in "Two Concepts of Rules," supra note 10, as an instance of rule-utilitarianism in my review of Atiyah, 93 Harv. L. Rev. 1863n18 (1980). See also Charles Landesman, "Promises and Practices," 75 Mind (n.s.) 239 (1966).*

15. *This was in fact Bentham's general perspective. See also Brandt, supra note 14.*

16. *Compare Rawls, supra note 1, ch. 6, where it is argued that (a) the deduction of the principles of justice for institutions, and (b) a showing that a particular institution is just are not sufficient to generate an obligation to comply with that institution. Further principles of natural duty and obligation must be established.*

17. *See Locke, supra note 9; Prichard, supra note 9; Raz, supra note 10.*

18. *American Law Institute,* Restatement (1st) of the Law of Contracts *[hereafter cited as* Restatement *(1st) or (2d)], § 329, Com-*

ment a: "In awarding compensatory damages, the effort is made to put the injured party in as good a position as that in which he would have been put by full performance of the contract . . ."; E. Allan Farnsworth, "Legal Remedies for Breach of Contract," 70 Colum. L. Rev. 1145 (1970); Gardner, supra note 8; Charles Goetz and Robert Scott, "Enforcing Promises: An Examination of the Basis of Contract," 80 Yale L. J. 1261 (1980).

19. See Fuller and Perdue, "The Reliance Interest in Contract Damages," 46 Yale L. J. 52, 373 (1936, 1937); Gardner, supra note 8.

20. For discussions of these issues see Fried, supra note 3, at 169–177; Rawls, supra note 1, § 85; and the essays in The Identities of Persons (Amelie Rorty ed. Berkeley, 1976) and Personal Identity (John Perry ed. Berkeley, 1975).

21. See Atiyah, supra note 8, at 140–141 for a discussion of these early sources. See my review of Atiyah, 93 Harv. L. Rev. 1858, 1864–1865 (1980) for a further discussion of these and other early sources.

22. 227 Mo. App. 175, 51 S.W.2d 572 (1932).

23. Restatement (1st) § 333(d).

24. Gardner, supra note 8, at 15, 22–23.

25. This is the problem that is standardly dealt with in contract texts under the rubric of consequential damages, or the principle in Hadley v. Baxendale 9 Exch. 341 (1854). See Gardner, supra note 8, at 28–30. Holmes, in Globe Refining Co. v. Landa Cotton Oil Co., 190 U.S. 540 (1903) explained the limitation of liability for consequential damages in terms of the agreement itself: The defendant is liable only for those risks he explicitly or tacitly agreed to

assume. This conception has been generally rejected in favor of a vaguer standard by which defendant is liable for any risks of which he had "reason to know" at the time of the agreement. UCC § 2–715 comment 2. Holmes's test seems more consonant with the thesis of this work. See Pothier, The Law of Obligations, quoted in Lon Fuller and Melvin Eisenberg, Basic Contract Law 27 (3rd ed. St. Paul, 1972). The difference between the two positions is not great: first, because it is always within the power of the parties to limit or expand liability for consequential damages by the agreement itself, UCC § 2–719(3); second, because the "reason to know" standard means that the defendant at least has a fair opportunity to make such an explicit provision.

26. UCC § 2–318; William Prosser, Torts ch. 17 (4th ed. St. Paul, 1971).

27. 133 N.W.2d 267, 26 Wis.2d 683 (1965).

28. See Stanley Henderson, "Promissory Estoppel and Traditional Contract Doctrine," 78 Yale L. J. 343, 357–360 (1969); see generally Friedrich Kessler and Edith Fine, "Culpa in Contrahendo, Bargaining in Good Faith, and Freedom of Contract: A Comparative Study," 77 Harv. L. Rev. 401 (1964).

29. Nicomachean Ethics, bk. V, iv–v.

30. See John Dawson, "Restitution or Damages?" 20 Ohio St. L. J. 175 (1959); Gardner, supra note 8, at 18–27. For a fuller discussion of restitution and contracts see chapter 8 infra.

31. Goff and Jones, supra note 7, at 69; the problem raised in the footnote is treated at 88–89.

32. Britton v. Turner, 6 N.H. 281 (1834).

BABIES FOR SALE:
Reflections on the Baby M Case*

Robin Fox

Can you write a commercial contract for a baby? Can a man buy his own child? Who owns the frozen embryos of a dead woman; can they be willed to third parties? It has been five years since the controversial and emotional "Baby M" case was legally settled, but we have barely begun to understand its implications.

The public read the headlines and moved on. But given advances in the so-called "New Birth Technologies" we are faced with a bewildering future for the very definition of the family, if not of the individual. In a world awash with rhetoric about family values, there are lessons to be learned from a close examination of the case and the public reaction to it.

We are a civilization obsessed with the model of the individual contractor as the ultimate social unit. In some ways, as Sir Henry Maine forcefully reminded us, the shift from social relations based on Status— what sociologists would now call "ascribed status"—

---

*From Fox, Robin. "Babies for Sale," in *The Public Interest*, no. 111 ('93), pp. 14–40. Reprinted here by permission of National Affairs, Inc.

to those based on Contract is the major shift in Western society over the historic period. The model for relations of Status was of course kinship—the family. A king was the father of his nation; God was the father of his people; the Church was the mother of us all. In the world of Contract, however, all parties are equal and autonomous contractors bound by their agreements. Society itself is such a contractual arrangement. The islands of Status, like slavery, have gradually been swept away, especially in the United States. Here, as Lawrence Friedman so graphically describes it, King Contract triumphed in the nineteenth and twentieth centuries as the model for *all* agreements between those acting rationally in their own interests.

One area held out for Status: the family. Or did it? This is the issue the Baby M case raised. And while there was indeed a settlement of sorts, it was an uneasy one, and one that was not convincing to a large segment of the American public. For Mary Beth Whitehead had not just demanded to keep "her" baby; she had challenged the power of almighty Contract. She issued this challenge in the name of motherhood. But as we shall see, motherhood, for all its hype, is a slender reed in the contractual wind.

A Contract Forbidding Bonds

In March 1986 a baby girl was born to Mary Beth Whitehead, a housewife in Brick Township, New Jersey. It was her third child—she already had a girl (Tuesday) and a boy (Ryan); she called it Sara Elizabeth. Mr. Whitehead, however—at that point employed as a garbage collector—was not Sara's father. The baby had been conceived and born as a result of a contractual agreement between the Whiteheads and William and Elizabeth Stern, a biochemist and physician respectively, of Tenafly, New Jersey, whereby Mrs. Whitehead was artificially inseminated with Mr. Stern's sperm. The contract was drawn up on February 6, 1985 by a lawyer, Noel Keane, of The Infertility Center of New York, a private organization concerned with bringing together infertile couples and potential surrogate mothers. The Center's fee for this service was $7,500.

The motives of the parties seemed fairly clear at the time. Mrs. Stern was unable to bear children for medical reasons. Mr. Stern had lost all his family in the Nazi genocide and desperately wanted to have a child of his own blood as a kind of psycho-physical replacement for the lost kin. Mrs. Whitehead saw an adver-

tisement for the clinic, and considering her family's marginal economic condition and the relative ease and pleasure with which she had already twice given birth, felt capable of performing as a surrogate mother. She was to receive $10,000 for her services and all expenses would be paid by the Sterns. The parties met, Bill and Betsy liked Mary Beth, and she felt well-disposed to them. Richard Whitehead at first was dubious but eventually agreed. The contract—or "Surrogate Parenting Agreement"—was accepted and signed.

Let us pause here to consider this all-important contract. Right up front it states, in Clause 2, that "the sole purpose of this Agreement is to enable William Stern and his infertile wife to have a child which is biologically related to William Stern." In the next clause it puts the whole issue on the line:

> *MARY BETH WHITEHEAD, Surrogate, represents that she is capable of conceiving children. MARY BETH WHITEHEAD understands and agrees that in the best interests of the child, she will not form or attempt to form a parent-child relationship with any child or children she may conceive, carry to term and give birth to, pursuant to the provisions of this Agreement, and shall freely surrender custody to WILLIAM STERN, Natural Father, immediately upon birth of the child and terminate all parental rights to said child pursuant to this agreement.*

So before any of the details—even before any mention of the artificial insemination—the contract insists that the natural mother of the child who must "conceive, carry to term and give birth to" it, should not "form a parent-child relationship" with it. Clearly this must refer to the post-birth situation since, we must immediately ask, how can the mother *not* form a relationship with the child to whom she has been so intimately attached for nine months? And if, as there is much evidence to show, the most fundamental point of this parent-fetus bonding process occurs at birth itself, then short of bypassing the actual birth process how can the mother voluntarily refuse to form such a bond?

The contract, however, not only assumes she can but makes this the most fundamental of its conditions. It is as if the designer (Keane) knew in advance that the most difficult part of such an agreement was not the numerous medical details, but the prohibition of a natural process: that it was this that was most likely to derail the proceedings and therefore had to be gotten out of the way first.

The next provision obtains Richard Whitehead's agreement to the same conditions and to the artificial insemination, and "rebut[s] the presumption of paternity of any offspring conceived and born pursuant to aforementioned agreement." This is because the law, in the absence of proof to the contrary, does assume any children born to a wife to be the natural children of her husband. (This goes back to Roman law. *Pater est quem nuptiae demonstrant:* the legal father of a child is he who can show marriage to the mother.) The third provision of this clause enjoins Mrs. Whitehead to cooperate in medical examinations, carry the baby to term, and surrender all parental rights.

The next clause concerns the payment of the fees and expenses, and includes agreement to paternity testing. If Stern is found not to be the father, then the deal is off, and the Whiteheads must reimburse the Sterns for all expenses incurred.

Clause 5 asks the Whiteheads to "understand and assume all risks, including the risk of death, which are incidental to conception, pregnancy and childbirth, including, but not limited to, postpartum complications." Clause 6 demands "psychiatric evaluations" of the Whiteheads, and permits a release of these to ICNY or the Sterns. The evaluation was indeed made and the psychiatrist, Joan Einwohner, concluded thus:

> It is the examiner's impression that Ms. Whitehead is sincere in her plan to become a surrogate mother and that she has thought extensively about the plan. However, I do have some concern about her tendency to deny feelings and think it would be important to explore with her in somewhat more depth whether she will be able to relinquish the child in the end.

There was more to this effect. The explorations in more depth never took place, and this evaluation was never communicated to the Sterns by ICNY.

The issue of miscarriage was then addressed. If the miscarriage occurred before the fifth month—no compensation for the mother; if after the fifth month, she would receive $1,000 for her services. Physical examinations and the possibility of no pregnancy were then dealt with. Then, in Clause 13, came the matter of abortion:

> MARY BETH WHITEHEAD, Surrogate, agrees that she will not abort the child once conceived except, if in the professional medical opinion of the inseminating physician, such action is necessary for the physical health of MARY BETH WHITEHEAD or the child has been determined by said physician to be physiologically abnormal. MARY BETH WHITEHEAD further agrees, upon the request of said physician to undergo amniocentesis or similar tests to detect genetic and congenital defects. In the event that said test reveals that the fetus is genetically or congenitally abnormal, MARY BETH WHITEHEAD, Surrogate, agrees to abort the fetus upon demand of WILLIAM STERN, Natural Father, in which case the fee paid to the Surrogate will be in accordance with paragraph 10. If MARY BETH WHITEHEAD refuses to abort the fetus upon demand of WILLIAM STERN, his obligations as stated in this agreement shall cease forthwith, except as to obligations of paternity imposed by statute.

Thus the contract was not for a child as such but for *a genetically and physiologically perfect child.* Anything less could lead to a demand for abortion, and if this was refused, then the "surrogate" was stuck with the defective infant, no fee, and no expenses. The "natural father" would be in the clear. The next clause does admit that some such defects cannot be detected in advance, and if these occur then Stern "assumes the legal responsibility" for any such child. This is remarkably vague compared with the harsh specificity of the conditions imposed on the mother. Does "legal responsibility" extend to permanent custody or refer only to acknowledgement of paternity and child support?

In Clause 15, the "surrogate" agrees not to "smoke cigarettes, drink alcoholic beverages, use illegal drugs or take non-prescription medications," etc. And in the final clause Richard Whitehead agrees to execute a "refusal of consent" form. In this, Richard expressly refuses his consent to the artificial insemination while agreeing to all the other clauses. This is necessary so that Richard cannot be "declared or considered to be the legal father of the child conceived thereby."

I have spelled out the conditions of the contract for several reasons. Without knowing precisely what was in the contract it would be hard to have any sensible discussion (although much passionate debate was undertaken by parties who had never read the contract and had no idea what the specific provisions were). Also, as we have seen, the contract was loaded in favor of the "natural father" from the start, as one might expect since he was paying the fees. With a stroke of the pen, and the payment of a hefty sum of money, he appeared to gain enormous control over "the surrogate": He could require insemination, amniocentesis, the regulation of maternal habits, prevention of the formation of parent-child bonds, risk of death, and even abortion (if the child were imperfect). Very few of those who insisted that "a contract was a contract" and that Mrs. Whitehead was bound to submit to its clauses, knew the clauses even existed in this form.

This was a contract, for a monetary consideration, concerning the conception, gestation, birth, and custody of a human being, in which a natural mother was asked to agree not to develop any maternal feelings, and to turn over her child unconditionally to the sperm donor who had paid for this privilege. But there it was. She had "freely entered into" the contract. She was of sound mind. She was not coerced by anything but financial need.

Bonds Negate the Contract

But when Sara was born on March 27, 1986, the arrangement fell apart. Mrs. Whitehead did not want to give up the baby. She was flooded with feelings of guilt over surrendering Sara as well as guilt over disappointing the Sterns. But it came to her with overpowering strength that she was selling her baby "like a slave." She couldn't do it. The bond was simply too strong. She was allowed to take the baby home, but the Sterns insisted on their rights and eventually, with grief and desperation, Mrs. Whitehead gave up the child. The Sterns immediately named it Melissa and started the adoption process. Mrs. Whitehead refused to go through with the adoption and would not accept the $10,000. She was in such a distraught state that on March 30 the Sterns agreed to let her have the child "for a few days." When she again refused to relinquish the baby, the Sterns, armed with a lawyer (Gary Skolof), adoption papers, and the agreement, successfully applied for a court order to claim Sara/Melissa.

Their claim was heard by Superior Court Judge Harvey Sorkow on May 5th. Mrs. Whitehead had been breast-feeding the baby for forty days at this point. She was not represented at the hearings and the judge never interviewed her. He depended solely on the testimony of the Sterns' lawyer. The judge apparently had no qualms about the legitimacy of the contract

and issued an *ex parte* order giving the Sterns sole custody. The grounds were that Mary Beth Whitehead had shown "mental instability" in her refusal to honor the contract, and that she might flee with the baby.

A bizarre scenario followed, almost Kafkaesque in its details, many of which cannot be given here since it is not the drama that concerns us but the legal issues. In summary, on May 5th, immediately after obtaining the order, the Sterns alerted the local police in Brick Township and descended on the Whitehead home with their court order. They produced the order, which demanded the surrender of one "Melissa Elizabeth Stern." They were monentarily stalled when the Whiteheads claimed no such baby existed and showed a legal birth certificate for "Sara Elizabeth Whitehead." While the police puzzled over this discrepancy, the infant was passed through a back window to Mr. Whitehead, who indeed fled with her to Mary Beth's parents' home in Florida. Once the disappearing trick was discovered, Mrs. Whitehead was handcuffed and arrested by the police, who later released her since they could not find any actual basis for arrest. Once released she too fled to Florida to join her husband and the baby and she resumed breast-feeding.

They stayed successfully in hiding, making fifteen moves over the course of almost three months, during which time Mrs. Whitehead repeatedly called William Stern to try to persuade him to stop the hunt and let her keep the baby, promising joint custody if he agreed. He refused to agree, taped the conversations (including Mary Beth's threats of suicide) on the advice of his lawyer, and hired private detectives to find the Whiteheads. Judge Sorkow had frozen the Whiteheads' bank account, the bank was about to foreclose on their mortgage, and they were out of funds. A judge in Florida issued an order, based on Sorkow's *ex parte* order, for repossession of the child. Later, when faced with all the facts, he rescinded the order, but by then it was too late.

The Sterns waited until Mrs. Whitehead was in a hospital being treated for an infection, then sent in armed private detectives and local police to the Florida home. Mary Beth's mother was manhandled and thrown to the ground. The baby was pulled from her crib, taken back to the police station, and handed over to the Sterns, who took her back to New Jersey. She had been breast-feeding for 123 days at this point, and the judge ordered her weaned by the police. The Whiteheads returned to New Jersey, but were not allowed to see her for more than five weeks, when the judge allowed twice-weekly visits of one hour in a supervised facility with guards present. Mrs. White-head was specifically prohibited from breastfeeding her baby; her children were not allowed to see their sister. The Whiteheads by this time had a lawyer—on a *pro bono* basis, since they had no money—and they sued for custody. Suits, countersuits, motions, and petitions followed, until at last the trial date, before the same judge whose order had set in motion this bizarre train of events, was set for January 5, 1987, in the New Jersey Superior Court, Family Division, in Hackensack.

When Is a Deal Not a Deal?

The story so far is bizarre enough, but the layman may be excused for wondering why the courts could not quickly and easily settle the issue. Yet the baby was conceived and born under circumstances for which no exact legal precedent existed. Nor was there any state or federal legislation which entirely covered the case. It was not unequivocally a simple custody matter, nor was it just an issue of legal adoption, nor was it a blatant case of "baby selling." States have laws covering these cases, but the surrogate mother case was, to say the least, murky. No statute or precedent seemed to cover it clearly. Hence the intense general, legal, and media interest in the "Baby M" trial as it had now become.

Whose baby was she? Did she belong to the mother who bore her, and hence the mother's legal husband, or did she belong to the genetic father who had a contract for her? Seventy percent of the public, according to polls by the *Bergen Record* and *Newsweek,* believed that "she signed a contract, she should hand over the baby." The minority (less than 20 percent) felt "a baby can't be taken from its natural mother, contract or no contract." The law had no immediate answer.

The response of the overwhelming public majority is interesting. The sanctity of contracts was elevated over the sanctity of motherhood. And indeed the law does by and large encourage contracts and holds the keeping of them to be a good thing. But the public was misled in thinking that if a contract or agreement is signed, then that is that: The conditions must be met. In fact, while any contract may be drawn up, the courts may or may not decide to honor it in the event of a breach of the contract by one party. They may very well decide that the contract was not legal in the first place, since there are some things about which we may not write contracts. But even if they decide it was legal, the issue then becomes: What kind of restitution will they order to the injured party? In the case in question, Mary Beth Whitehead (and her husband) might well have been in breach of the contract, but the question remained: Would the courts order "specific performance" of the contract—that is, the handing over of the child to the injured parties (the Sterns)—or would they decide that a monetary penalty (damages) and costs to the injured party would suffice?

Contrary to public opinion, courts have traditionally been reluctant to order specific performance. And this reluctance has been particularly strong in what are called "personal service" contracts—typically contracts of employment. They have been reluctant because to enforce such a contract is tantamount to enforcing servitude. If someone breaks a contract of employment, by leaving a job before the specified time for example, then a court will certainly award damages to the employer, but it will rarely insist that the term of service be completed, since this would interfere with what is seen as a basic constitutional right to freedom of movement. Employees are not serfs. Similarly with the contract of marriage: If one partner breaches this contract, then damages may be awarded to the other, but the court will never insist that the partner in breach of the contract be forced to continue in the marriage. People who hold the "a deal is a deal" principle rarely seem to invoke this when it comes to their own divorces.

New Jersey, following this general rule, is reluctant to enforce specific performance of personal service contracts. In fact the standard as applied in New Jersey is particularly exacting compared to other states. New Jersey further insists that specific performance should not be granted when it is either contrary to the public interest or would require the court to act inequitably. The New Jersey Supreme Court had ruled that specific performance should be denied if it violates basic principles of human dignity or would be "harsh and oppressive" to one of the parties. Thus with contracts to bear children and renounce parental rights, courts should be unwilling to enforce compliance when one or both parties are resistant.

But for the moment we are simply trying to establish that there is no simple "a deal is a deal" doctrine as far as the law is concerned, and that in this the law is a lot wiser than the public. But then, that is one reason we have the law in the first place: to protect us against our own worst instincts (or perhaps, more exactly, our own worst social and historical constructs).

As far as specific performance is concerned, the law seems clear: If there exists a market where one can obtain an adequate substitute, then the contract should not be enforced. And "subjective harm" is not the issue. That you desperately wanted the specific item in question (sentimental value, perhaps) is not at issue. You can get an adequate substitute. This establishes that performance of a contract is by no means automatic, and one might well argue that a sperm-donor father has a "market" out there in which he can obtain an adequate substitute. The substitute will still be his child. As A. Corbin, an expert on contract law, has stated, the onus is on the party seeking specific performance to prove that "a substantial equivalent for all practical purposes" is not readily obtainable from others in exchange for a monetary payment.

It is again remarkable how many people, presented with this argument, respond that it is "repugnant" to discuss a child in this manner—as the subject of a monetary agreement. These are often the same people who saw nothing wrong with the contract in the first place and insisted passionately that it should be upheld!

Equally, we have to consider the issue of "informed consent." A valid contract is unenforceable if one of the parties was, for example, under duress, or if relevant information was withheld from any of the parties, or for any reason that renders one of the parties not in a position to give "informed consent" to the document. Thus if you have a gun to my head when I sign, or if I am legally insane, then even though my signature is on the contract the court will declare it void. In this case, even if we regard the contract as valid in establishing parental rights for Mr. Stern, can we hold it as valid in *extinguishing* the parental rights of Mary Beth Whitehead? Can a woman in fact ever give "informed consent" to a promise to relinquish the child of her body? When it comes to giving up a child for adoption, for example, every state except Wyoming holds that *consent to adoption prior to birth is invalid unless ratified after birth.*

The question, then, is open: Should a surrogate mother have fewer rights in this matter than the mother of a baby put up for adoption? There is here, it might be argued, a genetic father with rights in the child. This is not disputed. In the adoption case there is a genetic father also, but he is rarely ever consulted. The issue is, as we have said, whether an agreement is sufficient to extinguish the mother's parental rights.

Nor must we lose sight of the overriding consideration of the "best interests of the child"—fondly known in legal circles as "BIC." BIC arises only if the issue of custody is reached, that is, if the courts decide that parental rights reside in both father and mother. This would require a fitness hearing in which the court would try to determine which of the parents was most fit to have custody, and would probably allow visitation rights by the other parent, much as in a divorce case.

More to the point, perhaps, in countering the "a deal is a deal" mentality is the issue of what contracts can legally be written. All states and the federal government have statutes which specifically rule out certain things as subjects of contracts. Thus prostitution, slavery, and baby selling are prohibited in all states. Any contract, for example, to provide sexual services or to sell a baby could indeed be written and signed, but if a party defaulted and was sued, the suit would get nowhere and the plaintiffs might even be open to criminal prosecution.

Can a Father Buy His Baby?

In the various surrogate mother cases around the country that had cropped up, the specific issue of a mother refusing to give up her child had not arisen, so the Baby M case was to set an important precedent. But in anticipation of such cases, and in response to other issues in surrogate mothering being brought to court, many states had given relevant judgments and advanced legal opinions through their attorneys general. One of the most popular opinions was that surrogate mothering violates state "baby selling" statutes. Is this a fair analogy? Is surrogate mothering a form of baby selling?

Legal opinion largely said "yes." At the time, Kentucky provided the best testing ground since the courts at different levels had taken different views and so aired most of the possibilities. The attorney general of Kentucky believed that surrogate mothering constitutes illegal baby selling. A Kentucky court, however, held that surrogate arrangements are very different from adoption arrangements. Kentucky did indeed have strong laws against selling children, but the court asked how a natural father could be characterized as either adopting or buying his own baby. He pays not for the child per se, but for the *services* of the surrogate in carrying and bearing the child. Since he cannot be buying his own child, the arrangement does not violate baby selling laws. The Kentucky Court of Appeals finally agreed with the attorney general: This *is* an adoption procedure (by the father's wife at least); money changes hands; it does contravene Kentucky laws.

Looking to the Constitution

Thus any such contract must first get over the hurdle of whether or not it is "void as contrary to public policy." Even if it makes it past that test, the issue of "specific performance" is still open. But there is yet another hurdle. Such a contract may still be void if it infringes one or other of the parties' constitutional rights. What relevant constitutional issues might the surrogate mother cases raise? This has been much discussed but boils down essentially to three issues: the constitutional prohibition of slavery (the Thirteenth Amendment and Anti-Peonage Act); the "right to privacy" derived from the Fifth Amendment and applied, for example, to a woman's right to abortion in the famous *Roe* v. *Wade* case; and the equally derivative "right to procreate" with its corollary the "right to marry." The "right to procreate" is ambiguous insofar as it does not specify whether it extends automatically to custody rights over the results of its exercise. This case was to test just how far a right to procreate went. Then there is the mother's "right to the companionship of her children." And we could go on.

The fact is that often these basic constitutional rights (or basic rights derived from the Constitution) seem to be obscure or in conflict. They only become definitive through court rulings in specific cases. And these rulings can appear to conflict in turn. Much ingenious ink is spilled by eager students in law journal "notes" in attempts to reconcile the varying interpretations of the Constitution. For our purposes it is enough to note that the contract and its enforcement have to face the constitutional hurdles mentioned. Some commentaries, for example, have insisted that since the child is being given up to its father, it is not being enslaved, and therefore the Thirteenth Amendment is not infringed. But this overlooks the issue of whether the contract effectively enslaves the mother. The whole issue is muddied by the fact that family relationships have always been treated by all courts as special cases: Thus children are, according to some ultra-liberal critics, effectively enslaved to their parents with the acquiescence of the courts, and marriage contracts are treated differently from ordinary commercial contracts.

As I have mentioned, one of the most interesting aspects of the surrogate parenting issue is precisely this blurring of what have traditionally been separate areas: family relationships and contractual commercial relationships. The writers of "surrogate parenting" contracts seem to want to have it both ways: They want the contracts upheld as commercial documents, and at the same time they want constitutional protections for the privileged "parental" (i.e., non-commercial) status of the "father."

The combination of unprecedented consequences of non-coital reproductive techniques and the clash of principles in contract versus motherhood, as well as the specifics of the human drama in New Jersey, was what I believe made the Baby M case so intensely interesting to the world. We were not just deciding the fate of one baby, but perhaps getting close to redefining the nature of the family, and even the individual, in a world of Lockean contractual relations gone haywire.

The Court Convenes

I shall not dwell in detail on the trial, since it rapidly became a media circus with the world press corps and all the major television networks in noisy attendance. For three weeks it was the nation's favorite soap opera. The details then are known to the world. And in any case, it is not so much the trial per se as the judge's decision that concerns us here. But we must look briefly at his conduct of the case, because his view reflected closely the majority opinion in the media and the polls. This opinion was of course largely middle-class opinion, and the middle-class commentators, with some notable exceptions, were uncompromisingly on the side of their peers the Sterns, and almost contemptuous of the claims of the feckless, working-class Catholic Whiteheads (who were, of course, never described as such).

For a start, the judge managed to rule out a great deal of testimony that might have been relevant, and to include a great deal that was not. He refused to hear experts who lacked direct knowledge of the parties in the case. Thus the authors of influential books on parent-infant bonding were barred from speaking, while a number of low-level and in some cases grossly incompetent "experts" were allowed to testify because they had interviewed the Whiteheads and/or the Sterns. Evidence about the long-term harm to a mother of losing a child was not allowed, because the purported harm to *this* mother had yet to occur and was therefore "hypothetical."

Mary Beth Whitehead faced other obstacles. A guardian *ad litem*—Lorraine Abrahams—had been appointed to represent Baby M. This meant that a further set of "experts" could be called to testify, without breaking ranks, against Mrs. Whitehead. Their testimony was supposed to be independent—and the guardian swore to this in court—but in fact they met for a total of more than twenty-four hours with the guardian, before and during the trial, and were obviously working in tandem. Together with the experts called by the Sterns they hammered away at Mary Beth's character.

Somewhere in all this the contract issue got lost. The judge initially had ordered two trials: one on the contract, one on custody. The Appeals Court ordered only one trial, so the judge decided, with almost theological finesse, that it should be one trial but in two parts. The first part was heard in a matter of hours, with each counsel arguing the case for and against the legitimacy of the contract. The judge barred any expert testimony on the contractual issue, and insisted that he was not going to get "mired in inquiries dealing with ethics, morality and theology." This meant that the first part of the trial was going to be very brief indeed. As the judge and Skolof wanted, the trial moved quickly into the custody phase, which in turn became a battle over Mrs. Whitehead's character.

Skolof was a custody lawyer, and before the trial he had announced that his tactic was to turn this into a custody battle, which he "knew how to win." First, he delayed the trial as long as possible with numerous requests for more time. The longer Baby M was with the Sterns, the less likely was any court to order her return "in the best interests of the child." This tactic worked perfectly, and it took an order of the Supreme Court of New Jersey to get the trial started on January 5th.

Skolof's next tactic was to present a picture of the Sterns as an upright, middle-class, well-educated professional couple who could give an excellent home to to the baby (including trips to Bloomingdale's), as against the working-class, impoverished, unreliable Whiteheads who could not. In particular, the calm, serious, and capable Mrs. Stern (pediatrician), was to be contrasted with the whimsical, manipulative, dishonest, overprotective, and undereducated Mrs. Whitehead (ex-Go-Go dancer). Harold Cassidy, the Whitehead's *pro bono* lawyer, refused to meet Skolof on his own terms. He would not indulge in "expert" mud-slinging against the Sterns; instead, he tried to build up a good picture of Mrs. Whitehead as a wife, mother, and neighbor, with his experts doing their best to counter the accusations of the Sterns' (and the guardian's) highly paid witnesses. The result of this mismatch was a foregone conclusion, and it is to that result we must now turn.

Parens Patriae Super

Judge Harvey Sorkow rendered his judgment on March 31, 1987, after a three month trial of unprecedented media attention and world-wide publicity. He set the tone from the start:

> *The primary issue to be determined by this litigation is what are the best interests of a child until now called "Baby M." All other concerns raised by counsel constitute commentary.*

This attitude was to determine the whole judgment. Most of the legal issues discussed at length earlier were dismissed by Judge Sorkow as "non-issues." As Skolof had wanted, the trial became a custody battle and the judgment a custody judgment. There can be no equitable justice for the adult parties in the case, said the judge, and in any case it wasn't his place to find it. "The court will seek to achieve justice for the child." It will do this on the basis of the doctrine of *parens patriae,* roughly, "the country as parent."

One must remember that Sorkow was essentially a family court judge, not a contract lawyer or a constitutional expert. He saw his business therefore as the subordination of any other consideration to the "best interests of the child," this being the traditional matter of family court disputes. His dismissal of contract and constitutional issues as "mere commentary" reflected this stance.

> *[A]ll should listen again to the plea of the infant as voiced so poignantly by several of the professional witnesses, statements with which this court agrees to such an extent that it will use its total authority if required to accomplish these ends.*

Thus dominated by the notion of *parens patriae,* and clearly of the opinion that the Whiteheads were unsuitable parents while the Sterns were exemplary, he proceeded to validate the contract, terminate Mrs. Whitehead's parental rights, order the adoption by Mrs. Stern of Baby M, and grant sole custody to the Sterns with no rights of visitation for the Whiteheads. Everything was premised on the "best interests of the

child." For example, on the issue of "specific performance" the judge ruled:

> *This court holds that whether there will be*
> *specific performance . . . depends on whether*
> *doing so is in the child's best interest. . . . We*
> *find by clear and convincing evidence, indeed*
> *by a measure of evidence reaching beyond*
> *reasonable doubt, that Melissa's best interest*
> *will be served by being placed in her father's*
> *sole custody.*

So much for specific performance. On the contract itself, the judge leaned heavily on the fact that
there was no New Jersey statute covering surrogacy as
such. Laws against baby selling did not apply, he said,
because the baby was not sold to her natural father,
who only paid for the surrogate's services. The surrogate was indeed a rented uterus. Adoption statutes did
not apply, he said, because Mr. Stern did not need
to adopt his own child, and, he noted, adoption by
Mrs. Stern was not mentioned in the contract. Failing
any statutes to govern the case, he argued, the contract should be treated as an ordinary commercial
contract, regardless of the peculiar nature of its conditions. Thus, when it came to the issue of Mrs. Whitehead's parental rights, the judge refused to accept that
statutory tests, as in adoption cases, applied. There is
a presumption, in law, that the biological mother is
the fit parent unless a hearing specifically finds her to
be unfit, that is, engaged in active, harmful behavior
with regard to the child. Mrs. Whitehead was not entitled to such a presumption, said the judge, because
in the contract she agreed not to be a "mother." So
presumptions about motherhood could not apply to
her. She had signed away her rights to maternity.

Constitutional matters got equally short shrift,
although the judge was more cautious here. While the
best interests of the child should dominate all other
concerns *once the child was conceived,* he argued, it
was indeed an invasion of privacy and unconstitutional to enforce any of the clauses up to the time of
conception. And even after conception, it was clearly
unconstitutional to enforce the abortion clause. But all
the other clauses, including the all-important termination of parental rights clause, must be "specifically
performed."

> *The sole legal concepts that control are* parens
> patriae *and the best interests of the child. To*
> *wait for birth, to plan, pray and dream of the*
> *joy it will bring and then be told that the child*

> *will not come home, that a new set of rules ap-*
> *plies and to ask a court to approve such a re-*
> *sult deeply offends the conscience of this court.*

Nothing is said about the destructive effects on
the mother who may wish to keep the child of her
body. In fact this is dismissed as another non-issue.
She can just go back to where she was, he says. She
didn't really want any other children of her own anyway, and her husband had had a vasectomy to this
end. Therefore, it was in no way harsh or inequitable
to enforce specific performance here. The "right to
procreate" issue again is interpreted entirely in favor
of the father. In fact, the judge held, any state interference with this right of the father to specific performance would itself be unconstitutional.

The essential provisions of Sorkow's decision
were as follows:

(1) The surrogate parenting agreement of February 6,
1985, will be specifically enforced.
(2) The prior order of the court giving temporary custody to Mr. Stern is herewith made permanent.
Prior orders of visitation are vacated.
(3) The parental rights of the defendant Mary Beth
Whitehead are terminated.
(4) Mr. Stern is formally adjudged the father of Melissa Stern.
(5) The New Jersey Department of Health [is] directed
to amend all records of birth to reflect the paternity and name of the child to be Melissa Stern.
(6) The defendants (Whiteheads) . . . must refrain
from interfering with the parental and custodial
rights of the plaintiff.

Enlightenment in Trenton

Most people, in my experience, stopped following the
trial at this point. If they knew anything of the appeal
to the New Jersey Supreme Court it was what the media chose to stress: that the Supreme Court confirmed
the grant of custody of Baby M to the Sterns. But the
court's verdict deserves closer consideration, because
on every other point it was a stunning reversal of the
lower court's decision. On February 3, 1988, in a
unanimous opinion written by Chief Justice C. J. Wil-
enz, the court:

(1) Found the contract to be invalid and contrary to
New Jersey law and public policy;

(2) Found the *ex parte* order giving temporary custody to the Sterns to have been invalid;

(3) Voided the adoption of Baby M by Mrs. Stern;

(4) Restored Mrs. Whitehead's parental rights;

(5) Affirmed the order giving custody of Baby M to Mr. Stern; and

(6) Remanded to the lower court—but with a different judge—the question of the nature and extent of Mrs. Whitehead's future visitation rights.

Note my original argument was that even if the contract were found valid, it should not be enforced. Yet since the court, however, invalidated the contract largely on the basis of its incompatibility with New Jersey law, the question of its enforceability did not arise.

The court was firm in its rejection of surrogacy contracts:

> *We invalidate the surrogacy contract because it conflicts with the law and public policy of this State . . . we find the payment of money to a "surrogate" mother illegal, perhaps criminal, and potentially degrading to women. . . . [W]e void both the termination of the surrogate mother's parental rights and the adoption of the child by the wife/stepparent. We thus restore the "surrogate" as the mother of the child.*

The illegality of the contract stems from its use of money to procure an adoption through private placement.

> *Its use of money for this purpose—and we have no doubt whatsoever that the money is being paid to obtain an adoption and not, as the Sterns argue, for the personal services of Mary Beth Whitehead—is illegal and perhaps criminal.*

In addition, the court decided, the contract was in fact "coercive." Prior even to conception, the mother agreed irrevocably to surrender the child to the adoptive couple. She also illegally agreed to surrender her parental rights. The court turned the "best interests of the child" argument—used by the lower court entirely to boost the Stern's case—completely around. The contract itself, the court said, totally ignored the "best interests of the child."

> *In this case a termination of parental rights was obtained not by proving the statutory prerequisites but by claiming the benefit of contractual provisions. . . . The contract's basic premise, that the natural parents can decide in advance of birth which one is to have custody of the child, bears no relationship to the settled law that the child's best interests shall determine custody. . . .*

In other words, the contract preempted the right to decide custody "in the best interest of the child" that can only lie in the power of the courts. It was not the child's interests that the contract sought to protect, but the father's. The rights of the child were never considered. Indeed: "The surrogacy contract guarantees permanent separation of the child from one of its natural parents," thus running contrary to public policy in the state. "The surrogacy contract violates the policy of this State that the rights of natural parents are equal concerning their child, the father's right no greater than the mother's. . . . The whole purpose of the surrogacy contract was to give the father the exclusive right to the child by destroying the rights of the mother. . . ."

But above all, the court reserved its severest condemnation for the issue mentioned above: the failure of the contract to give any regard for the best interests of the child, which, ironically, as we have seen, was the doctrine central to Judge Sorkow's decision. "There is not the slightest suggestion that any enquiry will be made at any time to determine the fitness of the Sterns as custodial parents, of Mrs. Stern as an adoptive parent, their superiority to Mrs. Whitehead, or the effects on the child of not living with its natural mother."

They conclude severely: "This is the sale of a child, or, at the very least, the sale of a mother's right to her child, the only mitigating factor being that one of the purchasers is the father." So the father here is buying his own child, the court says; he is paying money to obtain exclusive rights to it. He can't do that under the law. The contract is invalid from beginning to end.

On the issue of "informed consent," they found that no potential surrogate could be said to be fully informed in advance of pregnancy and birth:

> *Under the contract, the natural mother is irrevocably committed before she knows the strength of her bond with her child. She never makes a totally voluntary, informed decision, for quite clearly any decision prior to the baby's birth is, in the most important sense, uninformed, and any decision after that . . . is less than voluntary.*

The justices also recognized the potential harm to the mother otherwise ignored by Judge Sorkow:

> The long-term effects of surrogacy contracts are not known, but feared—the impact on the child who learns she was bought . . . ; the impact on the natural mother as the full weight of her isolation is felt along with the full reality of the sale of her body and her child. . . .

As regards the father's "right to procreate" they insisted that it was "no more than that." It was fulfilled by the artificial insemination and did not extend to the right to custody. This latter right had to be independently established (as in this case they felt it had been).

On the crucial point of the *ex parte* order, which had started the whole thing rolling, they argued as follows:

> When father and mother are separated and disagree, at birth, on custody, only in an extreme, truly rare, case should the child be taken from its mother pendente lite, i.e., only in the most unusual case should the child be taken from the mother before the dispute is finally determined by the court on its merits. The probable bond between mother and child, and the child's need, not just the mother's, to strengthen that bond, along with the likelihood, in most cases, of a significantly lesser, if any, bond with the father—all counsel against temporary custody in the father.

It should also be noted that the court went out of its way to repudiate at length the "too harsh" judgment of Mrs. Whitehead's character and even, surprisingly, faced up to the otherwise taboo issue of social class—something that the lower court, the public, and most of the commentators had tried to ignore, treating obvious class differences between the Sterns and Whiteheads as though they were personal merits and defects of the individuals involved.

> We have a further concern regarding the trial court's emphasis on the Sterns' interest in Melissa's education as compared to the Whiteheads'. That this difference is a legitimate factor to be considered we have no doubt. But it should not be overlooked that a best-interests test is designed to create not a new member of the intelligentsia but rather a well-integrated person who might reasonably be expected to be happy with life. "Best interests" does not con-
> tain within it any idealized lifestyle; the question boils down to a judgement, consisting of many factors, about the likely future happiness of a human being. Stability, love, family happiness, and, ultimately, support of independence—all rank much higher in predicting future happiness than the likelihood of a college education. . . .

One might have been forgiven at this point for expecting a resounding decision in Mrs. Whitehead's favor on the custody question. But in the end the court ducked from this issue. While Mary Beth might provide love, she might also not provide stability or the possibility of autonomy. The Sterns' experts were against her; her own witnesses were divided; and above all, "most convincingly, the three experts chosen by the court-appointed guardian *ad litem* of Baby M, each clearly free of all bias and interest, unanimously and persuasively recommended custody in the Sterns." This is the only place where this otherwise extraordinarily well-argued judgment falls into absurdity. But it was clear that the members of the court, for all their good sense and sound argument, could not, like most of the rest of middle-class America, find it in their hearts to deprive little Melissa (as she now was) of her trips to Bloomingdale's. Having dumped the major expert—Judge Sorkow—without ceremony, they fell back on the other experts to save them from the consequences of their own logic and enable them to deliver Baby M up to the Sterns in her own "best interest."

At the same time, the court restored fully Mrs. Whitehead's parental rights and hence her rights to visitation. She is the "legal mother," they said, and added somewhat ironically that she should not be "punished one iota because of the [illegal and possibly criminal] surrogacy contract." This was of course only with respect to visitation; she had already been punished since the illegal and criminal contract was what caused the issuance of the original *ex parte* order, which is what led to Baby M being kept in the primary custody of the Sterns for a year and a half, which in turn became a major argument for leaving her there so as not to disturb her settled situation.

Offspring Without Sex

Our brief on the details of Baby M really ends here. But we have to recognize that "surrogate parenting" is only one of several New Reproductive Technologies

(NRTs), all of which raise some similar issues. So-called *in vitro* fertilization, where sperm and egg are brought together in a petri dish, and the resulting fertilized egg implanted in the womb of, say, an infertile woman, has raised hopes for "curing" infertility ever since the technique was developed in Oldham, England, in 1978. But the egg of an infertile woman, together with her husband's sperm, can also be implanted by simple artificial insemination techniques into a surrogate mother.

This raises an interesting conundrum, since the surrogate in this case does not contribute any genetic material to the child she bears. Yet she is still the "genetrix" in our sense, and the *in utero* bonding and bonding at birth will still have taken place. How would her claim stand up in court? There could be no issue of breach of the adoption laws here since the wife of the sperm donor—the equivalent of Elizabeth Stern—would be also the genetic mother of the child. How should the claim of the totally genetic parents here stack up against resistance by the genetically unrelated surrogate? Does the contribution of a bit of the male donor's limitless supply of sperm, and the flushing out of a few ova from the female donor's fallopian tubes match up to nine months gestation and the risks of childbearing and childbirth? Is the surrogate in this case going to feel the child is any the less "hers" because she did not contribute the egg?

Even more bizarre scenarios can be considered. Take the case of an infertile husband with a wife who is fertile but cannot, for some reason, give birth. Her flushed-out ovum could be combined with sperm from a donor and implanted in a surrogate. Here we would have four people involved: a genetic mother married to a prospectively social father plus a genetic father (probably unknown) and an actual genetrix or birth mother. One can run around the possibilities, with the most bizarre being sperm and eggs from unknown donors being externally fused and then implanted in a surrogate who surrenders the eventual child for adoption to two other (possibly infertile) social parents: five people, none of whom had sex with any of the others. In the case of frozen sperm, a child could be that of a dead man; and with frozen embryos a child could be born to long dead parents. With frozen sperm and ova from dead parents being combined, children could technically be orphans at the moment of conception. It will only take a breakthrough in incubator technology to bypass the surrogate mother altogether, and produce offspring not only without sex but without mothers either; then we are truly in Huxley land. For the moment, however, the "rented womb" is still needed and hence will run into all the problems discussed in this chapter should the genetrix lay claim to the child.

Several countries have now introduced legislation to control or outlaw such procedures, so injurious do they seem to accepted notions of love, marriage and the family, and to the "normality" of parent-child relationships. The British Parliament has endorsed embryo research but criminalized surrogacy. The issues evoke deep feelings everywhere, and there is no consensus. On the one side the scientists and doctors, and an increasing number of infertile couples, claim "progress," while the opposition claims everything from "inhumanity" to the gross "unnaturalness" of the whole business. (The Catholic Church is a leading voice in this opposition.) Feminists seem to be divided on this issue. Some see surrogacy as freeing women from the necessity of childbirth to pursue careers and self-fulfillment, others see surrogacy as the apotheosis of sisterhood and cooperation among women, and yet others see it as an attack on the woman in her role as mother and a handing over of even more patriarchal control to males—especially the medical profession, which particularly excites their indignation (and not without reason).

It is scarcely surprising that there should be such passionate debate. This great leap forward in technology leaves us unprepared for what appears to be a total redefinition of the family, of marriage and "lawful procreation," and even of the individual. How much of himself—and in this case certainly herself—does the individual own, for example? If I may sell an ovum to some third party, have I any rights and duties towards the end product? If I donate sperm (actually I would be more likely to sell it) do I have paternal (or even contractual) obligations to its eventual bawling and gurgling consequences? The majority of us simply find these possibilities too remote from our traditional (and often religiously backed) notions of family and parenthood and love for offspring.

But how can we attack or defend such practices as "unnatural" if we have no established standards of what is "natural" in the first place? And how can we have these standards if relativism informs all our enquiries and tells us that whatever definitions we come up with will be merely social or cultural constructs? I would agree, for example, with those who say that the nuclear family is not a sacrosanct "natural" entity but simply one kind of institutional possibility. I have been saying so for thirty years or more. But as a student of mammalian behavior I would have to disagree that "motherhood" is a similar construct, depending on context for its meaning. A hard look at the mammals (including ourselves) tells us that no matter what the genetic link may be, the genetrix does indeed bond with the child in the womb and at parturition, and hence has a "natural" claim to it. If this is true, it at least gives us somewhere to start.

Thus a woman who has gone through gestation and parturition will be "primed" to bond with her child. If the bond takes, then she is not likely to repudiate it simply because she knows the genes in the child are not her own. The child is already eliciting "mothering" responses, as indeed a non-related adopted infant will do for the parents who take it into their care. Claims of genetic relatedness, then, should not take precedence over those involving powerful proximate—especially bonding—mechanisms.

Other cultures take in stride the idea that a child may not have a father or that children can be born to a dead man. These are not the important things. All these cultures still try to satisfy the basic individual needs for sex, shelter, provisioning, property, dominance, companionship, love, bonding, respect, kinship, children, etc. The various institutional forms by which they do this can vary widely—they are indeed "cultural constructs"—but they are forms which still must answer basic individual needs or risk severe cultural dislocation. This is where relativism fails. Cultural constructs must be rooted in biological reality or they will surely collapse. The NRTs will survive only insofar as they acknowledge these basic realities. We have looked at only one example—if we try to force bonded mothers to give up their children in the name of contract (a cultural construct) we will fail, or at least deserve to fail. But the same principle can be extended to any of the other NRTs. Do they help or hinder the pursuit of those proximate motivations that are programmed into us by evolution to ensure the production of future generations? Here comparative enthnography may help us in showing the limits of human tolerance for variation—which are in fact quite wide. We have to learn how to rewrite the old rules to meet the new circumstances, and to control the new circumstances in the face of timeless realities.

Efforts so far to deal with the issue of NRTs have been largely legislative and restrictive. Surrogacy, for example, simply gets outlawed. Legislators—and social scientists—are happiest as philosopher-kings. But as the Baby M case has shown, we often do not know in advance what the problems will be. Thus a case by case approach may well generate more workable solutions to actual problems than will grand schemes of legislation aiming to solve hypothetical problems all at once. If I may venture an opinion on the surrogacy issue: I do not think surrogacy should be banned, since it has been proven to work in many cases with quite satisfactory results. I do obviously think, however, that a surrogate mother (even if genetically unrelated to her child) should not be required to give up the baby if she does not wish to. That seems to me to be the moral of this case. We can deal with the case of the unfrozen embryo, the product of a long-dead billionaire (and his mistress) whose fortune has already been divided among the other heirs excluding the unstable great-niece in whom the revived embryo has been implanted by an unscrupulous lawyer, when it arises. Michael Crichton is probably already at work on the novel.

An American Dilemma

Thus we come round full circle to the issue that the Baby M case thrust into our unwilling consciousness: How far are we willing to take our insistence on the dominance of the model of contract in social relationships? In a secular society, which is nevertheless riddled with sentimental religiosity, are there still some areas that we consider sacred and off-limits to the rules of contract? The advocates of traditional family values seem to think so, and are horrified when children are allowed to sue parents for breaches of implied "family contracts." We are in a socially schizophrenic state. We cling on the one hand to the secular contract model as the only model compatible with our individualist assumptions about how society should work. On the other hand, we seem to want certain areas declared out-of-bounds to the basic rule of contract.

But we simply can't decide where the boundaries are. Even the boundaries of the contracting individual are now becoming fuzzy, and organic products of one's own body (or parts fused with those from other bodies) become commodities subject to contractual agreements. This dilemma cuts across the usual liberal and conservative distinctions. Conservatives are as likely to be confused about the relative weights of contract and status as liberals are. Those who vociferously defend "family values" are equally likely to be those who stoutly defend the sanctity of contracts and the autonomy of the individual. And as we have seen, the issue divides feminists at least three ways.

For the moment, given the New Jersey precedent, it is illegal to write a commercial contract for a baby. But for frozen fertilized ova? The kinds of decisions we are faced with are decisions not just about specific cases, but about the kind of society we want to be. The winning of a revolutionary war provoked us to rethink this problem in the late eighteenth century. The issue of slavery prompted us to rethink it yet again in the late nineteenth century. Perhaps the stubbornness of a New Jersey mother, in her love for her newborn child, will be the catalyst for a new such rethinking in the late twentieth century. We now have the advantage of a profounder understanding of the evolutionary basis of human nature and the limitations of social constructs. But we are very unhappy with the idea of such limitations, particularly when they affect our most cherished ideas. The chances of our getting it right are not good.

SURROGATE MOTHERHOOD AS PRENATAL ADOPTION*

Bonnie Steinbock

The recent case of "Baby M" has brought surrogate motherhood to the forefront of American attention. Ultimately, whether we permit or prohibit surrogacy depends on what we take to be good reasons for preventing people from acting as they wish. A growing number of people want to be, or hire, surrogates; are there legitimate reasons to prevent them? Apart from its intrinsic interest, the issue of surrogate motherhood provides us with an opportunity to examine different justifications for limiting individual freedom.

In the first section of this article, I examine the Baby M case and the lessons it offers. In the second section, I examine claims that surrogacy is ethically unacceptable because it is exploitive, inconsistent with human dignity, or harmful to the children born of such arrangements. I conclude that these reasons justify restrictions on surrogate contracts, rather than an outright ban.

Baby M

Mary Beth Whitehead, a married mother of two, agreed to be inseminated with the sperm of William Stern and to give up the child to him for a fee of $10,000. The baby (whom Ms. Whitehead named Sara, and the Sterns named Melissa) was born on March 27, 1986. Three days later, Ms. Whitehead took her home from the hospital and turned her over to the Sterns.

Then Ms. Whitehead changed her mind. She went to the Sterns' home, distraught, and pleaded to have the baby temporarily. Afraid that she would kill herself, the Sterns agreed. The next week, Ms. Whitehead informed the Sterns that she had decided to keep the child, and threatened to leave the country if court action was taken.

At that point, the situation deteriorated into a cross between the Keystone Kops and Nazi stormtroopers. Accompanied by five policemen, the Sterns

---

*From Steinbock, Bonnie. "Surrogate Motherhood as Prenatal Adoption," in *Law, Medicine, and Health Care,* v. 16, no. 1, ('88), pp. 44–50. Reprinted here by permission of American Society of Law, Medicine and Ethics.

went to the Whitehead residence armed with a court order giving them temporary custody of the child. Ms. Whitehead managed to slip the baby out of a window to her husband, and the following morning the Whiteheads fled with the child to Florida, where Ms. Whitehead's parents lived. During the next three months, the Whiteheads lived in roughly twenty different hotels, motels, and homes to avoid apprehension. From time to time, Ms. Whitehead telephoned Mr. Stern to discuss the matter: he taped these conversations on advice of counsel. Ms. Whitehead threatened to kill herself, to kill the child, and to falsely accuse Mr. Stern of sexually molesting her older daughter.

At the end of July 1986, while Ms. Whitehead was hospitalized with a kidney infection, Florida police raided her mother's home, knocking her down, and seized the child. Baby M was placed in the custody of Mr. Stern, and the Whiteheads returned to New Jersey, where they attempted to regain custody. After a long and emotional court battle, Judge Harvey R. Sorkow ruled on March 31, 1987, that the surrogacy contract was valid, and that specific performance was justified in the best interests of the child. Immediately after reading his decision, he called the Sterns into his chambers so that Mr. Stern's wife, Dr. Elizabeth Stern, could legally adopt the child.

This outcome was unexpected and unprecedented. Most commentators had thought that a court would be unlikely to order a reluctant surrogate to give up an infant merely on the basis of a contract.[1] Indeed, if Ms. Whitehead had never surrendered the child to the Sterns, but had simply taken her home and kept her there, the outcome undoubtedly would have been different. It is also likely that Ms. Whitehead's failure to obey the initial custody order angered Judge Sorkow, and affected his decision.

The decision was appealed to the New Jersey Supreme Court, which issued its decision on February 3, 1988. Writing for a unanimous court, Chief Justice Wilentz reversed the lower court's ruling that the surrogacy contract was valid. The court held that a surrogacy contract that provides money for the surrogate mother, and that includes her irrevocable agreement to surrender her child at birth, is invalid and unenforceable. Since the contract was invalid, Ms. Whitehead did not relinquish, nor were there any other grounds for terminating, her parental rights. Therefore, the adoption of Baby M by Dr. Stern was improperly granted, and Ms. Whitehead remains the child's legal mother.

The court further held that the issue of custody is determined solely by the child's best interests, and

it agreed with the lower court that it was in Melissa's best interests to remain with the Sterns. However, Ms. Whitehead, as Baby M's legal as well as natural mother, is entitled to have her own interest in visitation considered. The determination of what kind of visitation rights should be granted to her, and under what conditions, was remanded to the trial court.

The distressing details of this case have led many people to reject surrogacy altogether. Do we really want police officers wrenching infants from their mothers' arms, and prolonged custody battles when surrogates find they are unable to surrender their children, as agreed? Advocates of surrogacy say that to reject the practice wholesale, because of one unfortunate instance, is an example of a "hard case" making bad policy. Opponents reply that it is entirely reasonable to focus on the worst potential outcomes when deciding public policy. Everyone can agree on at least one thing: this particular case seems to have been mismanaged from start to finish, and could serve as a manual of how not to arrange a surrogate birth.

First, it is now clear that Mary Beth Whitehead was not a suitable candidate for surrogate motherhood. Her ambivalence about giving up the child was recognized early on, although this information was not passed on to the Sterns.[2] Second, she had contact with the baby after birth, which is usually avoided in "successful" cases. Typically, the adoptive mother is actively involved in the pregnancy, often serving as the pregnant woman's coach in labor. At birth, the baby is given to the adoptive, not the biological mother. The joy of the adoptive parents in holding their child serves both to promote their bonding and to lessen the pain of separation of the biological mother.

At Ms. Whitehead's request, no one at the hospital was aware of the surrogacy arrangement. She and her husband appeared as the proud parents of "Sara Elizabeth Whitehead," the name on her birth certificate. Ms. Whitehead held her baby, nursed her, and took her home from the hospital—just as she would have done in a normal pregnancy and birth. Not surprisingly, she thought of Sara as her child, and she fought with every weapon at her disposal, honorable and dishonorable, to prevent her being taken away. She can hardly be blamed for doing so.[3]

Why did Dr. Stern, who supposedly had a very good relation with Ms. Whitehead before the birth, not act as her labor coach? One possibility is that Ms. Whitehead, ambivalent about giving up her baby, did not want Dr. Stern involved. At her request, the Sterns' visits to the hospital to see the newborn baby were unobtrusive. It is also possible that Dr. Stern was ambivalent about having a child. The original idea of hiring a surrogate was not hers, but her husband's. It was Mr. Stern who felt a "compelling" need to have a child related to him by blood, having lost all his relatives to the Nazis.

Furthermore, Dr. Stern was not infertile, as was stated in the surrogacy agreement. Rather, in 1979 she was diagnosed by two eye specialists as suffering from optic neuritis, which meant that she "probably" had multiple sclerosis. (This was confirmed by all four experts who testified.) Normal conception was ruled out by the Sterns in late 1982, when a medical colleague told Dr. Stern that his wife, a victim of multiple sclerosis, had suffered a temporary paralysis during pregnancy. "We decided the risk wasn't worth it," Mr. Stern said.[4]

Ms. Whitehead's lawyer, Harold J. Cassidy, dismissed the suggestion that Dr. Stern's "mildest case" of multiple sclerosis determined the Sterns' decision to seek a surrogate. He noted that she was not even treated for multiple sclerosis until after the Baby M dispute had started. "It's almost as though it's an afterthought," he said.[5]

Judge Sorkow deemed the decision to avoid conception "medically reasonable and understandable." The Supreme Court did not go so far, noting that Dr. Stern's "anxiety appears to have exceeded the actual risk, which current medical authorities assess as minimal."[6] Nonetheless, the court acknowledged that her anxiety, including fears that pregnancy might precipitate blindness and paraplegia, was "quite real." Certainly, even a woman who wants a child very much may reasonably wish to avoid becoming blind and paralyzed as a result of pregnancy. Yet is it believable that a woman who really wanted a child would decide against pregnancy *solely* on the basis of *someone else's* medical experience? Would she not consult at least one specialist on her *own* medical condition before deciding it wasn't worth the risk? The conclusion that she was at best ambivalent about bearing a child seems irresistible.

This possibility conjures up many people's worst fears about surrogacy: that prosperous women, who do not want to interrupt their careers, will use poor and educationally disadvantaged women to bear their children. I will return shortly to the question of whether this is exploitive. The issue here is psychological: what kind of mother is Dr. Stern likely to be? If she is unwilling to undergo pregnancy, with its discomforts, inconveniences, and risks, will she be willing to make the considerable sacrifices that good

parenting requires? Ms. Whitehead's ability to be a good mother was repeatedly questioned during the trial. She was portrayed as immature, untruthful, hysterical, overly identified with her children, and prone to smothering their independence. Even if all this is true—and I think that Ms. Whitehead's inadequacies were exaggerated—Dr. Stern may not be such a prize either. The choice for Baby M may have been between a highly strung, emotional, overinvolved mother, and a remote, detached, even cold one.[7]

The assessment of Ms. Whitehead's ability to be a good mother was biased by the middle-class prejudices of the judge and of the mental health officials who testified. Ms. Whitehead left school at fifteen, and is not conversant with the latest theories on child rearing: she made the egregious error of giving Sara teddy bears to play with, instead of the more "age-appropriate," expert-approved pans and spoons. She proved to be a total failure at patty-cake. If this is evidence of parental inadequacy, we're all in danger of losing our children.

The Supreme Court felt that Ms. Whitehead was "rather harshly judged" and acknowledged the possibility that the trial court was wrong in its initial award of custody. Nevertheless, it affirmed Judge Sorkow's decision to allow the Sterns to retain custody, as being in Melissa's best interests. George Annas disagrees with the "best interests" approach. He points out that Judge Sorkow awarded temporary custody of Baby M to the Sterns in May 1986, without giving the Whiteheads notice or an opportunity to obtain legal representation. That was a serious wrong and injustice to the Whiteheads. To allow the Sterns to keep the child compounds the original unfairness: "justice requires that reasonable consideration be given to returning Baby M to the permanent custody of the Whiteheads."[8]

But a child is not a possession, to be returned to the rightful owner. It is not fairness to all parties that should determine a child's fate, but what is best for her. As Chief Justice Wilentz rightly stated, "The child's interests come first: we will not punish it for judicial errors, assuming any were made."[9]

Subsequent events have substantiated the claim that giving custody to the Sterns was in Melissa's best interests. After losing custody, Ms. Whitehead, whose husband had undergone a vasectomy, became pregnant by another man. She divorced her husband and married Dean R. Gould last November. These developments indicate that the Whiteheads were not able to offer a stable home, although the argument can be made that their marriage might have survived if not for the strains introduced by the court battle and the loss of Baby M. But even if Judge Sorkow had no reason to prefer the Sterns to the Whiteheads back in May 1986, he was still right to give the Sterns custody in March 1987. To take her away then, at nearly eighteen months of age, from the only parents she had ever known would have been disruptive, cruel, and unfair to her.

Annas' preference for a just solution is premised partly on his belief that there *is* no "best interest" solution to this "tragic custody case." I take it that he means that however custody is resolved, Baby M is the loser. Either way, she will be deprived of one parent. However, a best-interests solution is not a perfect solution. It is simply the solution that is on balance best for the child, given the realities of the situation. Applying this standard, Judge Sorkow was right to give the Sterns custody, and the Supreme Court was right to uphold the decision.

The best-interests argument is based on the assumption that Mr. Stern has at least a *prima facie* claim to Baby M. We certainly would not consider allowing a stranger who kidnapped a baby and managed to elude the police for a year to retain custody on the grounds that he was providing a good home to a child who had known no other parent. However, the Baby M case is not analogous. First, Mr. Stern is Baby M's biological father and, as such, has at least some claim to raise her, which no non-parental kidnapper has. Second, Mary Beth Whitehead *agreed* to give him their baby. Unlike the miller's daughter in *Rumpelstiltskin,* the fairy tale to which the Baby M case is sometimes compared, she was not forced into the agreement. Because both Mary Beth Whitehead and Mr. Stern have *prima facie* claims to Baby M, the decision as to who should raise her should be based on her present best interests. Therefore we must, regretfully, tolerate the injustice to Ms. Whitehead, and try to avoid such problems in the future.

It is unfortunate that the court did not decide the issue of visitation on the same basis as custody. By declaring Ms. Whitehead-Gould the legal mother, and maintaining that she is entitled to visitation, the court has prolonged the fight over Baby M. It is hard to see how this can be in her best interests. This is no ordinary divorce case, where the child has a relation with both parents that it is desirable to maintain. As Mr. Stern said at the start of the court hearing to determine visitation, "Melissa has a right to grow and be happy and not be torn between two parents."[10]

The court's decision was well-meaning but internally inconsistent. Out of concern for the best interests of the child, it granted the Sterns custody. At the same time, by holding Ms. Whitehead-Gould to be the legal mother, with visitation rights, it precluded precisely what is most in Melissa's interest, a resolution of the situation. Further, the decision leaves open the distressing possibility that a Baby M situation could happen again. Legislative efforts should be directed toward ensuring that this worst-case scenario never occurs.

Should Surrogacy Be Prohibited?

On June 27, 1988, Michigan became the first state to outlaw commercial contracts for women to bear children for others.[11] Yet making a practice illegal does not necessarily make it go away: witness black-market adoption. The legitimate concerns that support a ban on surrogacy might be better served by careful regulation. However, some practices, such as slavery, are ethically unacceptable, regardless of how carefully regulated they are. Let us consider the arguments that surrogacy is intrinsically unacceptable.

Paternalistic Arguments

These arguments against surrogacy take the form of protecting a potential surrogate from a choice she may later regret. As an argument for banning surrogacy, as opposed to providing safeguards to ensure that contracts are freely and knowledgeably undertaken, this is a form of paternalism.

At one time, the characterization of a prohibition as paternalistic was a sufficient reason to reject it. The pendulum has swung back, and many people are willing to accept at least some paternalistic restrictions on freedom. Gerald Dworkin points out that even Mill made one exception to his otherwise absolute rejection of paternalism: he thought that no one should be allowed to sell himself into slavery, because to do so would be to destroy his future autonomy.

This provides a narrow principle to justify some paternalistic interventions. To preserve freedom in the long run, we give up the freedom to make certain choices, those that have results that are "far-reaching, potentially dangerous and irreversible."[12] An example would be a ban on the sale of crack. Virtually everyone who uses crack becomes addicted and, once addicted, a slave to its use. We reasonably and willingly give up our freedom to buy the drug, to protect our ability to make free decisions in the future.

Can a Dworkian argument be made to rule out surrogacy agreements? Admittedly, the decision to give up a child is permanent, and may have disastrous effects on the surrogate mother. However, many decisions may have long-term, disastrous effects (e.g., postponing childbirth for a career, having an abortion, giving a child up for adoption). Clearly we do not want the state to make decisions for us in all these matters. Dworkin's argument is rightly restricted to paternalistic interferences that protect the individual's autonomy or ability to make decisions in the future. Surrogacy does not involve giving up one's autonomy, which distinguishes it from both the crack and selling-oneself-into-slavery examples. Respect for individual freedom requires us to permit people to make choices they may later regret.

Moral Objections

Four main moral objections to surrogacy were outlined in the Warnock Report.[13]

1) It is inconsistent with human dignity that a woman should use her uterus for financial profit.
2) To deliberately become pregnant with the intention of giving up the child distorts the relationship between mother and child.
3) Surrogacy is degrading because it amounts to child-selling.
4) Since there are some risks attached to pregnancy, no woman ought to be asked to undertake pregnancy for another in order to earn money.[14]

We must all agree that a practice that exploits people or violates human dignity is immoral. However, it is not clear that surrogacy is guilty on either count.

Exploitation The mere fact that pregnancy is *risky* does not make surrogate agreements exploitive, and therefore morally wrong. People often do risky things for money; why should the line be drawn at undergoing pregnancy? The usual response is to compare surrogacy and kidney-selling. The selling of organs is prohibited because of the potential for coercion and exploitation. But why should kidney-selling be viewed as intrinsically coercive? A possible explanation is that no one would do it, unless driven by poverty. The choice is both forced and dangerous, and hence coercive.[15]

The situation is quite different in the case of the race-car driver or stuntman. We do not think that they are *forced* to perform risky activities for money: they

freely choose to do so. Unlike selling one's kidneys, these are activities that we can understand (intellectually, anyway) someone choosing to do. Movie stuntmen, for example, often enjoy their work, and derive satisfaction from doing it well. Of course they "do it for the money," in the sense that they would not do it without compensation; few people are willing to work "for free." The element of coercion is missing, however, because they enjoy the job, despite the risks, and could do something else if they chose.

The same is apparently true of most surrogates. "They choose the surrogate role primarily because the fee provides a better economic opportunity than alternative occupations, but also because they enjoy being pregnant and the respect and attention that it draws."[16] Some may derive a feeling of self-worth from an act they regard as highly altruistic: providing a couple with a child they could not otherwise have. If these motives are present, it is far from clear that the surrogate is being exploited. Indeed, it seems objectionally paternalistic to insist that she is.

Human dignity It may be argued that even if womb-leasing is not necessarily exploitive, it should still be rejected as inconsistent with human dignity. But why? As John Harris points out, hair, blood, and other tissue is often donated or sold; what is so special about the uterus?[17]

Human dignity is more plausibly invoked in the strongest argument against surrogacy, namely, that it is the sale of a child. Children are not property, nor can they be bought or sold.[18] It could be argued that surrogacy is wrong because it is analogous to slavery, and so is inconsistent with human dignity.

However, there are important differences between slavery and a surrogate agreement.[19] The child born of a surrogate is not treated cruelly or deprived of freedom or resold; none of the things that make slavery so awful are part of surrogacy. Still, it may be thought that simply putting a market value on a child is wrong. Human life has intrinsic value; it is literally priceless. Arrangements that ignore this violate our deepest notions of the value of human life. It is profoundly disturbing to hear in a television documentary on surrogacy the boyfriend of a surrogate say, quite candidly, "We're in it for the money."

Judge Sorkow accepted the premise that producing a child for money denigrates human dignity, but he denied that this happens in a surrogate agreement. Ms. Whitehead was not paid for the surrender of the child to the father: she was paid for her willingness to be impregnated and carry Mr. Stern's child to term. The child, once born, is his biological child. "He cannot purchase what is already his."[20]

This is misleading, and not merely because Baby M is as much Ms. Whitehead's child as Mr. Stern's. It is misleading because it glosses over the fact that the surrender of the child was part—indeed, the whole point—of the agreement. If the surrogate were paid merely for being willing to be impregnated and carrying the child to term, then she would fulfill the contract upon giving birth. She could take the money *and* the child. Mr. Stern did not agree to pay Ms. Whitehead merely to *have* his child, but to provide him with a child. The New Jersey Supreme Court held that this violated New Jersey's laws prohibiting the payment or acceptance of money in connection with adoption.

One way to remove the taint of baby-selling would be to limit payment to medical expenses associated with the birth or incurred by the surrogate during pregnancy (as is allowed in many jurisdictions, including New Jersey, in ordinary adoptions).[21] Surrogacy could be seen, not as baby-selling, but as a form of adoption. Nowhere did the Supreme Court find any legal prohibition against surrogacy when there is no payment, and when the surrogate has the right to change her mind and keep the child. However, this solution effectively prohibits surrogacy, since few women would become surrogates solely for self-fulfillment or reasons of altruism.

The question, then, is whether we can reconcile paying the surrogate, beyond her medical expenses, with the idea of surrogacy as prenatal adoption. We can do this by separating the terms of the agreement, which include surrendering the infant at birth to the biological father, from the justification for payment. The payment should be seen as compensation for the risks, sacrifice, and discomfort the surrogate undergoes during pregnancy. This means that if, through no fault on the part of the surrogate, the baby is stillborn, she should still be paid in full, since she has kept her part of the bargain. (By contrast, in the Stern-Whitehead agreement, Ms. Whitehead was to receive only $1,000 for a stillbirth).[22] If, on the other hand, the surrogate changes her mind and decides to keep the child, she would break the agreement, and would not be entitled to any fee or to compensation for expenses incurred during pregnancy.

The Right of Privacy

Most commentators who invoke the right of privacy do so in support of surrogacy.[23] However, George An-

nas makes the novel argument that the right to rear a child you have borne is also a privacy right, which cannot be prospectively waived. He says:

> *[Judge Sorkow] grudgingly concedes that [Ms. Whitehead] could not prospectively give up her right to have an abortion during pregnancy. . . . This would be an intolerable restriction on her liberty and under* Roe v. Wade, *the state has no constitutional authority to enforce a contract that prohibits her from terminating her pregnancy. But why isn't the same logic applicable to the right to rear a child you have given birth to? Her constitutional rights to rear the child she has given birth to are even stronger since they involve even more intimately, and over a lifetime, her privacy rights to reproduce and rear a child in a family setting.*[24]

Absent a compelling state interest (such as protecting a child from unfit parents), it certainly would be an intolerable invasion of privacy for the state to take children from their parents. But Baby M has two parents, both of whom now want her. It is not clear why only people who can give birth (i.e., women) should enjoy the right to rear their children.

Moreover, we do allow women to give their children up for adoption after birth. The state enforces those agreements even if the natural mother, after the prescribed waiting period, changes her mind. Why should the right to rear a child be unwaivable before, but not after, birth? Why should the state have the constitutional authority to uphold postnatal, but not prenatal, adoption agreements? It is not clear why birth should affect the waivability of this right or have the constitutional significance that Annas attributes to it.

Nevertheless, there are sound moral and policy, if not constitutional, reasons to provide a postnatal waiting period in surrogate agreements. As the Baby M case makes painfully clear, the surrogate may underestimate the bond created by gestation and the emotional trauma caused by relinquishing the baby. Compassion requires that we acknowledge these findings, and not deprive a woman of the baby she has carried because, before conception, she underestimated the strength of her feelings for it. Providing a waiting period, as in ordinary postnatal adoptions, will help protect women from making irrevocable mistakes, without banning the practice.

Some may object that this gives too little protection to the prospective adoptive parents. They cannot be sure that the baby is theirs until the waiting period is over. While this is hard on them, a similar burden is placed on other adoptive parents. If the absence of a guarantee serves to discourage people from entering surrogacy agreements, that is not necessarily a bad thing, given all the risks inherent in such contracts. In addition, this requirement would make stricter screening and counseling of surrogates essential, a desirable side-effect.

Harm to Others

Paternalistic and moral objections to surrogacy do not seem to justify an outright ban. What about the effect on the offspring of such contracts? We do not yet have solid data on the effects of being a "surrogate child." Any claim that surrogacy creates psychological problems in the children is purely speculative. But what if we did discover that such children have deep feelings of worthlessness from learning that their natural mothers deliberately created them with the intention of giving them away? Might we ban surrogacy as posing an unacceptable risk of psychological harm to the resulting children?

Feelings of worthlessness are harmful. They can prevent people from living happy, fulfilling lives. However, a surrogate child, even one whose life is miserable because of these feelings, cannot claim to have been harmed by the surrogate agreement. Without the agreement, the child would never have existed. Unless she is willing to say that her life is not worth living because of these feelings, that she would be better off never having been born, she cannot claim to have been harmed by being born of a surrogate mother.[25]

Elsewhere I have argued that children can be *wronged* by being brought into existence, even if they are not, strictly speaking, *harmed.*[26] They are wronged if they are deprived of the minimally decent existence to which all citizens are entitled. We owe it to our children to see that they are not born with such serious impairments that their most basic interests will be doomed in advance. If being born to a surrogate is a handicap of this magnitude, comparable to being born blind or deaf or severely mentally retarded, then surrogacy can be seen as wronging the offspring. This would be a strong reason against permitting such contracts. However, it does not seem likely. Probably the problems arising from surrogacy will be like those faced by adopted children and children whose parents divorce. Such problems are not trivial, but neither

are they so serious that the child's very existence can be seen as wrongful.

If surrogate children are neither harmed nor wronged by surrogacy, it may seem that the argument for banning surrogacy on grounds of its harmfulness to the offspring evaporates. After all, if the children themselves have no cause for complaint, how can anyone else claim to reject it on their behalf? Yet it seems extremely counter-intuitive to suggest that the risk of emotional damage to the children born of such arrangements is not even relevant to our deliberations. It seems quite reasonable and proper—even morally obligatory—for policy-makers to think about the possible detrimental effects of new reproductive technologies, and to reject those likely to create physically or emotionally damaged people. The explanation for this must involve the idea that it is wrong to bring people into the world in a harmful condition, even if they are not, strictly speaking, harmed by having been brought into existence.[27] Should evidence emerge that surrogacy produces children with serious psychological problems, that would be a strong reason for banning the practice.

There is some evidence on the effect of surrogacy on the other children of the surrogate mother. One woman reported that her daughter, now seventeen, who was eleven at the time of the surrogate birth, "is still having problems with what I did, and as a result she is still angry with me." She explains: "Nobody told me that a child could bond with a baby while you're still pregnant. I didn't realize then that all the times she listened to his heartbeat and felt his legs kick that she was becoming attached to him."[28]

A less sentimental explanation is possible. It seems likely that her daughter, seeing one child given away, was fearful that the same might be done to her. We can expect anxiety and resentment on the part of children whose mothers give away a brother or sister. The psychological harm to these children is clearly relevant to a determination of whether surrogacy is contrary to public policy. At the same time, it should be remembered that many things, including divorce, remarriage, and even moving to a new neighborhood, create anxiety and resentment in children. We should not use the effect on children as an excuse for banning a practice we find bizarre or offensive.

Conclusion

There are many reasons to be extremely cautious of surrogacy. I cannot imagine becoming a surrogate, nor would I advise anyone else to enter into a contract so fraught with peril. But the fact that a practice is risky, foolish, or even morally distasteful is not sufficient reason to outlaw it. It would be better for the state to regulate the practice, and minimize the potential for harm, without infringing on the liberty of citizens.

---

1. *See, for example, "Surrogate Motherhood Agreements: Contemporary Legal Aspects of a Biblical Notion,"* University of Richmond Law Review, *16 (1982): 470; "Surrogate Mothers: The Legal Issues,"* American Journal of Law & Medicine, *7 (1981): 338, and* Angela Holder, Legal Issues in Pediatrics and Adolescent Medicine *(New Haven: Yale University Press, 1985), 8: "Where a surrogate mother decides that she does not want to give the baby up for adoption, as has already happened, it is clear that no court will enforce a contract entered into before the child was born in which she agreed to surrender her baby for adoption." Emphasis added.*

2. *Had the Sterns been informed of the psychologist's concerns as to Ms. Whitehead's suitability to be a surrogate, they might have ended the arrangement, costing the Infertility Center its fee. As Chief Justice Wilentz said, "It is apparent that the profit motive got the better of the Infertility Center." In the matter of Baby M, Supreme Court of New Jersey, A-39, at 45.*

3. *"[W]e think it is expecting something well beyond normal human capabilities to suggest that this mother should have parted with her newly born infant without a struggle. . . . We . . . cannot conceive of any other case where a perfectly fit mother was expected to surrender her newly born infant, perhaps forever, and was then told she was a bad mother because she did not." Id.: 79.*

4. *"Father Recalls Surrogate Was 'Perfect,'"* New York Times, *Jan. 6, 1987, B2.*

5. *Id.*

6. *In the matter of Baby M, supra note 2, at 8.*

7. *This possibility was suggested to me by Susan Vermazen.*

8. *George Annas, "Baby M: Babies (and Justice) for Sale,"* Hastings Center Report, *17, no. 3 (1987): 15.*

9. *In the matter of Baby M, supra note 2, at 75.*

10. *"Anger and Anguish at Baby M Visitation Hearing,"* New York Times, *March 29, 1988, 17.*

11. New York Times, *June 28, 1988, A20.*

12. *Gerald Dworkin, "Paternalism," in R. A. Wasserstrom, ed.,* Morality and the Law *(Belmont, Cal.: Wadsworth, 1971); reprinted in J. Feinberg and H. Gross, eds.,* Philosophy of Law, *3d ed. (Belmont, Cal.: Wadsworth, 1986), 265.*

13. *M. Warnock, chair,* Report of the Committee of Inquiry into Human Fertilisation and Embryology *(London: Her Majesty's Stationery Office, 1984).*

14. *As summarized in J. Harris,* The Value of Life *(London: Routledge & Kegan Paul, 1985), 142.*

15. *For an argument that kidney-selling need not be coercive, see B. A. Brody and H. T. Engelhardt, Jr.,* Bioethics: Readings and Cases *(Englewood Cliffs, N.J.: Prentice-Hall, 1987), 331.*

16. *John Robertson, "Surrogate Mothers: Not So Novel after All,"* Hastings Center Report, *13, no. 5 (1983): 29; citing P. Parker, "Surrogate Mother's Motivations: Initial Findings,"* American Journal of Psychiatry, *140 (1983): 1.*

17. *Harris, supra note 14, at 144.*

18. *Several authors note that it is both illegal and contrary to public policy to buy or sell children, and therefore contracts that contemplate this are unenforceable. See B. Cohen, "Surrogate Mothers: Whose Baby Is It?,"* American Journal of Law & Medicine, *10 (1984): 253; "Surrogate Mother Agreements: Contemporary Legal Aspects of a Biblical Notion,"* University of Richmond Law Review, *16 (1982): 469.*

19. *Robertson makes a similar point, supra note 16, at 33.*

20. *In re Baby "M," 217 N.J. Super. 372, 525 A.2d 1157 (1987).*

21. *Cohen, supra note 18. See also Angela Holder, "Surrogate Motherhood: Babies for Fun and Profit,"* Law, Medicine & Health Care, *12 (1984): 115.*

22. *Annas, supra note 8, at 14.*

23. *See, for example, Robertson, supra note 16, at 32; and S. R. Gersz, "The Contract in Surrogate Motherhood: A Review of the Issues,"* Law, Medicine & Health Care, *12 (1984): 107.*

24. *Annas, supra note 8.*

25. *For discussion of these issues, see D. Parfit, "On Doing the Best for Our Children," in M. D. Bayles, ed.,* Ethics and Population *(Cambridge, Mass.: Schenkman, 1976); M. D. Bayles, "Harm to the Unconceived,"* Philosophy & Public Affairs, *5 (1976): 292; J. Glover,* Causing Death and Saving Lives *(Harmondsworth, Eng.: Penguin, 1977), 67; John Robertson, "In Vitro Conception and Harm to the Unborn,"* Hastings Center Report, *8 (1978): 13; J. Feinberg,* Harm to Others *(Oxford: Oxford University Press, 1984), 95.*

26. *Bonnie Steinbock, "The Logical Case for 'Wrongful Life',"* Hastings Center Report, *16, no. 2 (1986): 15.*

27. *For the distinction between being harmed and being in a harmful state, see Feinberg, supra note 25, at 99.*

28. *"Baby M Case Stirs Feelings of Surrogate Mothers,"* New York Times, *March 2, 1987, B1.4*

Justice, Affirmative Action, and Racial Quotas

EQUAL TREATMENT AND COMPENSATORY DISCRIMINATION*

Thomas Nagel

It is currently easier, or widely thought to be easier, to get certain jobs or to gain admission to certain educational institutions if one is black or a woman than if one is a white man. Whether or not this is true, many people think it should be true, and many others think it should not. The question is: If a black person or a woman is admitted to a law school or medical school, or appointed to a certain academic or administrative post, in preference to a white man who is in other respects better qualified,[1] and if this is done in pursuit of a preferential policy or to fill a quota, is it unjust? Can the white man complain that he has been unjustly treated? It is important to investigate the justice of such practices, because if they are unjust, it is much more difficult to defend them on grounds of social utility. I shall argue that although preferential policies are not required by justice, they are not seriously unjust either—because the system from which they depart is already unjust for reasons having nothing to do with racial or sexual discrimination.

I

In the United States, the following steps seem to have led us to a situation in which these questions arise. First, and not very long ago, it came to be widely accepted that deliberate barriers against the admission of blacks and women to desirable positions should be abolished. Their abolition is by no means complete, and certain educational institutions, for example, may be able to maintain limiting quotas on the admission of women for some time. But deliberate discrimination is widely condemned.

Secondly, it was recognized that even without explicit barriers there could be discrimination, either consciously or unconsciously motivated, and this gave support to self-conscious efforts at impartiality, careful consideration of candidates belonging to the class discriminated against, and attention to the proportions of blacks and women in desirable positions, as evidence that otherwise undetectable bias might be influencing the selections. (Another, related consideration is that criteria which were good predictors of performance for one group might turn out to be poor predictors of performance for another group, so that the continued employment of those criteria might introduce a concealed inequity.)

The third step came with the realization that a social system may continue to deny different races or sexes equal opportunity or equal access to desirable positions even after the discriminatory barriers to those positions have been lifted. Socially-caused inequality in the capacity to make use of available opportunities or to compete for available positions may persist, because the society systematically provides to one group more than to another certain educational, social, or economic advantages. Such advantages improve one's competitive position in seeking access to jobs or places in professional schools. Where there has recently been widespread deliberate discrimination in many areas, it will not be surprising if the formerly excluded group experiences relative difficulty in gaining access to newly opened positions, and it is plausible to explain the difficulty at least partly in terms of disadvantages produced by past discrimination. This leads to the adoption of compensatory measures, in the form of special training programs, or financial support, or day-care centers, or apprenticeships, or tutoring. Such measures are designed to qualify those whose reduced qualifications are due to racial or sexual discrimination, either because they have been the direct victims of such discrimination, or because they are deprived as a result of membership in a group or community many of whose other members have been discriminated against. The second of these types of influence covers a great deal, and the importance of the social contribution is not always easy to establish. Nevertheless its effects typically include the loss of such goods as self-esteem, self-confidence, motivation, and ambition—all of which contribute to competitive success and none of which is easily restored by special training programs. Even if social injustice has produced such effects, it may be difficult for society to eradicate them.

This type of justification for compensatory programs raises another question. If it depends on the claim that the disadvantages being compensated for are the product of social injustice, then it becomes important how great the contribution of social injus-

tice actually is, and to what extent the situation is due to social causes not involving injustice, or to causes that are not social, but biological. If one believes that society's responsibility for compensatory measures extends only to those disadvantages due to social injustice, one will assign political importance to the degree, if any, to which racial differences in average I.Q. are genetically influenced, or the innate contribution, if any, to the statistical differences, if any, in emotional or intellectual characteristics between men and women. Also, if one believes that among socially-produced inequalities, there is a crucial distinction for the requirement of compensation between those which are produced unjustly and those which are merely the incidental results of just social arrangements, then it will be very important to decide exactly where that line falls: whether, for example, certain intentions must be referred to in arguing that a disadvantage has been unjustly imposed. But let me put those issues aside for the moment.

The fourth stage comes when it is acknowledged that some unjustly caused disadvantages, which create difficulties of access to positions formally open to all, cannot be overcome by special programs of preparatory or remedial training. One is then faced with the alternative of either allowing the effects of social injustice to confer a disadvantage in the access to desirable positions that are filled simply on the basis of qualifications relevant to performance in those positions, or else instituting a system of compensatory discrimination in the selection process to increase access for those whose qualifications are lower at least partly as a result of unjust discrimination in other situations and at other times (and possibly against other persons). This is a difficult choice, and it would certainly be preferable to find a more direct method of rectification, than to balance inequality in one part of the social system by introducing a reverse inequality at a different point. If the society as a whole contains serious injustices with complex effects, there is probably, in any case, no way for a single institution within that society to adjust its criteria for competitive admission or employment so that the effects of injustice are nullified as far as that institution is concerned. There is consequently considerable appeal to the position that places should be filled solely by reference to the criteria relevant to performance, and if this tends to amplify or extend the effects of inequitable treatment elsewhere, the remedy must be found in a more direct attack on those differences in qualifications, rather than in the introduction of irrelevant criteria of appointment or admission which will also sacrifice efficiency, productivity, or effectiveness of the institution in its specific tasks.

At this fourth stage we therefore find a broad division of opinion. There are those who believe that nothing further can legitimately be done in the short run, once the *remediable* unjust inequalities of opportunity between individuals have been dealt with: the irremediable ones are unjust, but any further steps to counterbalance them by reverse discrimination would also be unjust, because they must employ irrelevant criteria. On the other hand, there are those who find it unacceptable in such circumstances to stay with the restricted criteria usually related to successful performance, and who believe that differential admission or hiring standards for worse-off groups are justified because they roughly, though only approximately, compensate for the inequalities of opportunity produced by past injustice.

But at this point there is some temptation to resolve the dilemma and strengthen the argument for preferential standards by proceeding to a fifth stage. One may reflect that if the criteria relevant to the prediction of performance are not inviolable it may not matter whether one violates them to compensate for disadvantages caused by injustice or disadvantages caused in other ways. The fundamental issue is what grounds to use in assigning or admitting people to desirable positions. To settle that issue, one does not have to settle the question of the degree to which racial or sexual discrepancies are socially produced, because the differentials in reward ordinarily correlated with differences in qualifications are not the result of natural justice, but simply the effect of a competitive system trying to fill positions and perform tasks efficiently. Certain abilities may be relevant to filling a job from the point of view of efficiency, but they are not relevant from the point of view of justice, because they provide no indication that one deserves the rewards that go with holding that job. The qualities, experience, and attainments that make success in a certain position likely do not in themselves merit the rewards that happen to attach to occupancy of that position in a competitive economy.

Consequently it might be concluded that if women or black people are less qualified, for *whatever* reason, in the respects that lead to success in the professions that our society rewards most highly, then it would be just to compensate for this disadvantage, within the limits permitted by efficiency, by having suitably different standards for these groups, and thus bringing their access to desirable positions more into line with that of others. Compensatory discrimination would not, on this view, have to be tailored to deal only with the effects of past injustice.

But it is clear that this is not a stable position. For if one abandons the condition that to qualify for compensation an inequity must be socially caused, then there is no reason to restrict the compensatory measures to well-defined racial or sexual groups. Compensatory selection procedures would have to be applied on an individual basis, within as well as between such groups—each person, regardless of race, sex, or qualifications, being granted equal access to the desirable positions, within limits set by efficiency. This might require randomization of law and medical school admissions, for example, from among all the candidates who were above some minimum standard enabling them to do the work. If we were to act on the principle that different abilities do not merit different rewards, it would result in much more equality than is demanded by proponents of compensatory discrimination.

There is no likelihood that such a radical course will be adopted in the United States, but the fact that it seems to follow naturally from a certain view about how to deal with racial or sexual injustice reveals something important. When we try to deal with the inequality in advantages that results from a disparity in qualifications (however produced) between races or sexes, we are up against a pervasive and fundamental feature of the system, which at every turn exacts costs and presents obstacles in response to attempts to reduce the inequalities. We must face the possibility that the primary injustice with which we have to contend lies in this feature itself, and that some of the worst aspects of what we now perceive as racial or sexual injustice are merely conspicuous manifestations of the great social injustice of differential reward.

II

If differences in the capacity to succeed in the tasks that any society rewards well are visibly correlated, for whatever reason, with other characteristics such as race or religion or social origin, then a system of liberal equality of opportunity will give the appearance of supporting racial or religious or class injustice. Where there is no such correlation, there can be the appearance of justice through equal opportunity. But in reality, there is similar injustice in both cases, and it lies in the schedule of rewards.

The liberal idea of equal treatment demands that people receive equal opportunities if they are equally qualified by talent or education to utilize those opportunities. In requiring the relativization of equal treatment to characteristics in which people are very unequal, it guarantees that the social order will reflect and probably magnify the initial distinctions produced by nature and the past. Liberalism has therefore come under increasing attack in recent years, on the ground that the familiar principle of equal treatment, with its meritocratic conception of relevant differences, seems too weak to combat the inequalities dispensed by nature and the ordinary workings of the social system.

This criticism of the view that people deserve the rewards that accrue to them as a result of their natural talents is not based on the idea that no one can be said to deserve anything.[2] For if no one deserves anything, then no inequalities are contrary to desert, and desert provides no argument for equality. Rather, I am suggesting that for many benefits and disadvantages, certain characteristics of the recipient *are* relevant to what he deserves. If people are equal in the relevant respects, that by itself constitutes a reason to distribute the benefit to them equally.[3]

The relevant features will vary with the benefit or disadvantage, and so will the weight of the resulting considerations of desert. Desert may sometimes, in fact, be a rather unimportant consideration in determining what ought to be done. But I do wish to claim, with reference to a central case, that differential abilities are not usually among the characteristics that determine whether people *deserve* economic and social benefits (though of course they determine whether people *get* such benefits). In fact, I believe that nearly all characteristics are irrelevant to what people deserve in this dimension, and that most people therefore deserve to be treated equally.[4] Perhaps voluntary differences in effort or moral differences in conduct have some bearing on economic and social desert. I do not have a precise view about what features are relevant. I contend only that they are features in which most people do not differ enough to justify very wide differences in reward.[5] (While I realize that these claims are controversial, I shall not try to defend them here, nor to defend the legitimacy of the notion of desert itself. If these things make no sense, neither does the rest of my argument.)

A decision that people are equally or unequally deserving in some respect is not the end of the story. First of all, desert can sometimes be overridden, for example by liberty or even by efficiency. In some cases the presumption of equality is rather weak, and not much is required to depart from it. This will be so if the interest in question is minor or temporally circumscribed, and does not represent an important value in the subject's life.

Secondly, it may be that although an inequality is contrary to desert, no one can benefit from its removal: all that can be done is to worsen the position of those who benefit undeservedly from its presence. Even if one believes that desert is a very important factor in determining just distributions, one need not object to inequalities that are to no one's disadvantage. In other words, it is possible to accept something like Rawls's Difference Principle from the standpoint of an egalitarian view of desert.[6] (I say it is possible. It may not be required. Some may reject the Difference Principle because they regard equality of treatment as a more stringent requirement.)

Thirdly (and most significantly for the present discussion), a determination of relative desert in the distribution of a particular advantage does not even settle the question of *desert* in every case, for there may be other advantages and disadvantages whose distribution is tied to that of the first, and the characteristics relevant to the determination of desert are not necessarily the same from one advantage to another. This bears on the case under consideration in the following way. I have said that people with different talents do not thereby deserve different economic and social rewards. They may, however, deserve different opportunities to exercise and develop those talents.[7] Whenever the distribution of two different types of benefit is connected in this way, through social or economic mechanisms or through natural human reactions, it may be impossible to avoid a distribution contrary to the conditions of desert in respect of at least one of the benefits. Therefore it is likely that a dilemma will arise in which it appears that injustice cannot be entirely avoided. It may then be necessary to decide that justice in the distribution of one advantage has priority over justice in the distribution of another that automatically goes with it.

In the case under discussion, there appears to be a conflict between justice in the distribution of educational and professional opportunities and justice in the distribution of economic and social rewards. I do not deny that there is a presumption, based on something more than efficiency, in favor of giving equal opportunities to those equally likely to succeed. But if the presumption in favor of economic equality is considerably stronger, the justification for departing from it must be stronger too. If this is so, then when "educational" justice and economic justice come into conflict, it will sometimes be necessary to sacrifice the former to the latter.

III

In thinking about racial and sexual discrimination, the view that economic justice has priority may tempt one to proceed to what I have called the fifth stage. One may be inclined to adopt admission quotas, for example, proportional to the representation of a given group in the population, because one senses the injustice of differential rewards per se. Whatever explains the small number of women or blacks in the professions, it has the result that they have less of the financial and social benefits that accrue to members of the professions, and what accounts for those differences cannot justify them. So justice requires that more women and blacks be admitted to the professions.

The trouble with this solution is that it does not locate the injustice accurately, but merely tries to correct the racially or sexually skewed economic distribution which is one of its more conspicuous symptoms. We are enabled to perceive the situation as unjust because we see it, e.g., through its racial manifestations, and race is a subject by now associated in our minds with injustice. However, little is gained by merely transferring the same system of differential rewards, suitably adjusted to achieve comparable proportions, to the class of blacks or the class of women. If it is unjust to reward people differentially for what certain characteristics enable them to do, it is equally unjust whether the distinction is made between a white man and a black man or between two black men, or two white women, or two black women. There is no way of attacking the unjust reward schedules (if indeed they are unjust) of a meritocratic system by attacking their racial or sexual manifestations directly.

In most societies reward is a function of demand, and many of the human characteristics most in demand result largely from *gifts* or *talents*. The greatest injustice in this society, I believe, is neither racial nor sexual but intellectual. I do not mean that it is unjust that some people are more intelligent than others. Nor do I mean that society rewards people differentially simply on the basis of their intelligence: usually it does not. Nevertheless it provides on the average much larger rewards for tasks that require superior intelligence than for those that do not. This is simply the way things work out in a technologically advanced society with a market economy. It does not reflect a social judgment that smart people *deserve* the opportunity to make more money than dumb people. They may deserve richer educational opportunity, but they do not therefore deserve the material wealth that goes with it. Similar things could be said about society's differential reward of achievements facilitated by other talents or gifts, like beauty, athletic ability, musicality, etc. But intelligence and its development by education provide a particularly significant and pervasive example.

However, a general reform of the current schedule of rewards, even if they are unjust, is beyond the power of individual educational or business institutions, working through their admissions or appointments policies. A competitive economy is bound to reward those with certain training and abilities, and a refusal to do so will put any business enterprise in a poor competitive position. Similarly, those who succeed in medical school or law school will tend to earn more than those who do not—whatever criteria of admission the schools adopt. It is not the procedures of appointment or admission, based on criteria that predict success, that are unjust, but rather what happens as a result of success.

No doubt a completely just solution is not ready to hand. If, as I have claimed, different factors are relevant to what is deserved in the distribution of different benefits and disadvantages, and if the distribution of several distinct advantages is sometimes connected even though the relevant factors are not, then inevitably there will be injustice in some respect, and it may be practically impossible to substitute a principle of distribution which avoids it completely.

Justice may require that we try to reduce the automatic connections between material advantages, cultural opportunity, and institutional authority. But such changes can be brought about, if at all, only by large alterations in the social system, the system of taxation, and the salary structure. They will not be achieved by modifying the admissions or hiring policies of colleges and universities, or even banks, law firms, and businesses.

Compensatory measures in admissions or appointment can be defended on grounds of justice only to the extent that they compensate for specific disadvantages which have themselves been unjustly caused, by factors distinct from the general meritocratic character of the system of distribution of advantageous positions. Such contributions are difficult to verify or estimate; they probably vary among individuals in the oppressed group. Moreover, it is not obvious that where a justification for preferential treatment exists, it is strong enough to create an obligation, since it is doubtful that one element of a pluralistic society is obliged to adopt discriminatory measures to counteract injustice due to another element, or even to the society as a whole,

IV

These considerations suggest that an argument on grounds of justice for the imposition of racial or sexual quotas would be difficult to construct without the aid of premises about the source of unequal qualifications between members of different groups. The more speculative the premises, the weaker the argument. But the question with which I began was not whether compensatory discrimination is *required* by justice, but whether it is *compatible* with justice. To that question I think we can give a different answer. If the reflections about differential reward to which we have been led are correct, then compensatory discrimination need not be seriously unjust, and it may be warranted not by justice but by considerations of social utility. I say not *seriously* unjust, to acknowledge that a departure from the standards relevant to distribution of intellectual opportunities *per se* is itself a kind of injustice. But its seriousness is lessened because the factors relevant to the distribution of intellectual opportunity are irrelevant to the distribution of those material benefits that go with it. This weakens the claim of someone who argues that by virtue of those qualities that make him likely to succeed in a certain position, he deserves to be selected for that position in preference to someone whose qualifications make it likely that he will succeed less well. He cannot claim that justice requires the allocation of positions on the basis of ability, because the result of such allocation, in the present system, is serious injustice of a different kind.

My contention, then, is that where the allocation of one benefit on relevant grounds carries with it the allocation of other, more significant benefits to which those grounds are irrelevant, the departure from those grounds need not be a serious offense against justice. This may be so for two reasons. First, the presumption of equal treatment of relevantly equal persons in respect of the first benefit may not be very strong to begin with. Second, the fairness of abiding by the presumption may be overshadowed by the unfairness of the other distribution correlated with

it. Consequently, it may be acceptable to depart from the "relevant" grounds for undramatic reasons of social utility, that would not justify more flagrant and undiluted examples of unfairness. Naturally a deviation from the usual method will appear unjust to those who are accustomed to regarding ability to succeed as the correct criterion, but this appearance may be an illusion. That depends on how much injustice is involved in the usual method, and whether the reasons for departing from it are good enough, even though they do not correct the injustice.

The problem, of course, is to say what a good reason is. I do not want to produce an argument that will justify not only compensatory discrimination on social grounds, but also ordinary racial or sexual discrimination designed to preserve internal harmony in a business, for instance. Even someone who thought that the system of differential economic rewards for different abilities was unjust would presumably regard it as an *additional* unjustice if standard racial, religious, or sexual discrimination were a factor in the assignment of individuals to highly rewarded positions.

I can offer only a partial account of what makes systematic racial or sexual discrimination so exceptionally unjust. It has no social advantages, and it attaches a sense of reduced worth to a feature with which people are born.[8] A psychological consequence of the systematic attachment of social disadvantages to a certain inborn feature is that both the possessors of the feature and others begin to regard it as an essential and important characteristic, and one which reduces the esteem in which its possessor can be held.[9] Concomitantly, those who do not possess the characteristic gain a certain amount of free esteem by comparison, and the arrangement thus constitutes a gross sacrifice of the most basic personal interests of some for the interests of others, with those sacrificed being on the bottom. (It is because similar things can be said about the social and economic disadvantages that attach to low intelligence that I am inclined to regard that, too, as a major injustice.)

Reverse discrimination need not have these consequences, and it can have social advantages. Suppose, for example, that there is need for a great increase in the number of black doctors, because the health needs of the black community are unlikely to be met otherwise. And suppose that at the present average level of premedical qualifications among black applicants, it would require a huge expansion of total medical school enrollment to supply the desirable absolute number of black doctors without adopting differential admission standards. Such an expansion may be unacceptable either because of its cost or because it would produce a total supply of doctors, black and white, much greater than the society requires. This is a strong argument for accepting reverse discrimination, not on grounds of justice but on grounds of social utility. (In addition, there is the salutary effect on the aspirations and expectations of other blacks, from the visibility of exemplars in formerly inaccessible positions.)

The argument in the other direction, from the point of view of the qualified white applicants who are turned away, is not nearly as strong as the argument against standard racial discrimination. The self-esteem of whites as a group is not endangered by such a practice, since the situation arises only because of their general social dominance, and the aim of the practice is only to benefit blacks, and not to exclude whites. Moreover, although the interests of some are being sacrificed to further the interests of others, it is the better placed who are being sacrificed and the worst placed who are being helped.[10] It is an important feature of the case that the discriminatory measure is designed to favor a group whose social position is exceptionally depressed, with destructive consequences both for the self-esteem of members of the group and for the health and cohesion of the society.[11]

If, therefore, a discriminatory admissions or appointments policy is adopted to mitigate a grave social evil, and it favors a group in a particularly unfortunate social position, and if for these reasons it diverges from a meritocratic system for the assignment of positions which is not itself required by justice, then the discriminatory practice is probably not unjust.[12]

It is not without its costs, however. Not only does it inevitably produce resentment in the better qualified who are passed over because of the policy, but it also allows those in the discriminated-against group who would in fact have failed to gain a desired position in any case on the basis of their qualifications to feel that they may have lost out to someone less qualified because of the discriminatory policy. Similarly, such a practice cannot do much for the self-

esteem of those who know they have benefited from it, and it may threaten the self-esteem of those in the favored group who would in fact have gained their positions even in the absence of the discriminatory policy, but who cannot be sure that they are not among its beneficiaries. This is what leads institutions to lie about their policies in this regard, or to hide them behind clouds of obscurantist rhetoric about the discriminatory character of standard admissions criteria. Such concealment is possible and even justified up to a point, but the costs cannot be entirely evaded, and discriminatory practices of this sort will be tolerable only so long as they are clearly contributing to the eradication of great social evils.

V

When racial and sexual injustice have been reduced, we shall still be left with the great injustice of the smart and the dumb, who are so differently rewarded for comparable effort. This would be an injustice even if the system of differential economic and social rewards had no systematic sexual or racial reflection. On the other hand, if the social esteem and economic advantages attaching to different occupations and educational achievements were much more uniform, there would be little cause for concern about racial, ethnic, or sexual patterns in education or work. But of course we do not at present have a method of divorcing professional status from social esteem and economic reward, at least not without a gigantic increase in total social control, on the Chinese model. Perhaps someone will discover a way in which the socially produced inequalities (especially the economic ones) between the intelligent and the unintelligent, the talented and the untalented, or even the beautiful and the ugly, can be reduced without limiting the availability of opportunities, products and services, and without resort to increased coercion or decreased liberty in the choice of work or style of life. In the absence of such a utopian solution, however, the familiar task of balancing liberty against equality will remain with us.[13]

---

1. By saying that the white man is "in other respects better qualified" I mean that if, e.g., a black candidate with similar qualifications had been available for the position, he would have been selected in preference to the black candidate who was in fact selected; or, if the choice had been between two white male candidates of corresponding qualifications, this one would have been selected. Ditto for two white or two black women. (I realize that it may not always be easy to determine similarity of qualifications, and that in some cases similarity of credentials may give evidence of a difference in qualifications—because, e.g., one person had to overcome more severe obstacles to acquire those credentials.)

2. *Rawls appears to regard this as the basis of his own view. He believes it makes sense to speak of positive desert only in the context of distributions by a just system, and not as a pre-institutional conception that can be used to measure the justice of the system. John Rawls, A Theory of Justice (Cambridge, Mass., 1971), pp. 310–313.*

3. *Essentially this view is put forward by Bernard Williams in "The Idea of Equality," in Philosophy, Politics, and Society (Second Series), ed. P. Laslett and W. G. Runciman (Oxford, 1964), pp. 110–131.*

4. *This is distinct from a case in which nothing is relevant because there is no desert in the matter. In that case the fact that people differed in no relevant characteristics would not create a presumption that they be treated equally. It would leave the determination of their treatment entirely to other considerations.*

5. *It is not my view that we cannot be said to deserve the results of anything which we do not deserve. It is true that a person does not deserve his intelligence, and I have maintained that he does not deserve the rewards that superior intelligence can provide. But neither does he deserve his bad moral character or his above-average willingness to work, yet I believe that he probably does deserve the punishments or rewards that flow from those qualities. For an illuminating discussion of these matters, see Robert Nozick, Anarchy, State, and Utopia (New York, Basic Books: forthcoming), chap. 7.*

6. *Rawls, op. cit., pp. 75–80.*

7. *Either because differences of ability are relevant to degree of desert in these respects or because people are equally deserving of opportunities proportional to their talents. More likely the latter.*

8. *For a detailed and penetrating treatment of this and a number*

of other matters discussed here, see Owen M. Fiss, "A Theory of Fair Employment Laws," University of Chicago Law Review 38 (Winter 1971): 235–314.

9. *This effect would not be produced by an idiosyncratic discriminatory practice limited to a few eccentrics. If some people decided they would have nothing to do with anyone left-handed, everyone else, including the left-handed, would regard it as a silly objection to an inessential feature. But if everyone shunned the left-handed, left-handedness would become a strong component of their self-image, and those discriminated against would feel they were being despised for their essence. What people regard as their essence is not independent of what they get admired and despised for.*

10. *This is a preferable direction of sacrifice if one accepts Rawls's egalitarian assumptions about distributive justice. Rawls, op. cit., pp. 100–103.*

11. *It is therefore not, as some have feared, the first step toward an imposition of minimal or maximal quotas for all racial, religious, and ethnic subgroups of the society.*

12. *Adam Morton has suggested an interesting alternative, which I shall not try to develop: namely, that the practice is justified not by social utility, but because it will contribute to a more just situation in the future. The practice considered in itself may be unjust, but it is warranted by its greater contribution to justice over the long term, through eradication of a self-perpetuating pattern.*

13. *I have presented an earlier version of this paper to the New York Group of the Society for Philosophy and Public Affairs, the Princeton Undergraduate Philosophy Club, and the Society for Ethical and Legal Philosophy, and I thank those audiences for their suggestions.*

THE MESSAGE OF AFFIRMATIVE ACTION

Thomas E. Hill, Jr.

Affirmative action programs remain controversial, I suspect, partly because the familiar arguments for and against them start from significantly different moral perspectives. Thus I want to step back for a while from the details of debate about particular programs and give attention to the moral viewpoints presupposed in different *types* of argument. My aim, more specifically, is to compare the "messages" expressed when affirmative action is defended from different moral perspectives. Exclusively forward-looking (for example, utilitarian) arguments, I suggest, tend to express the wrong message, but this is also true of

exclusively backward-looking (for example, reparation-based) arguments. However, a moral outlook that focuses on cross-temporal narrative values (such as mutually respectful social relations) suggests a more appropriate account of what affirmative action should try to express. Assessment of the message, admittedly, is only one aspect of a complex issue, but it is a relatively neglected one. My discussion takes for granted some common-sense ideas about the communicative function of action, and so I begin with these.

Actions, as the saying goes, often *speak* louder than words. There are times, too, when only actions

*From Hill, Jr., Thomas E. "The Message of Affirmative Action," in *Social Philosophy and Policy*, vol. 8, issue 2,

(1991) pp. 108–129. Reprinted by permission of Blackwell Publishers.

can effectively communicate the message we want to convey and times when giving a message is a central part of the purpose of action. What our actions say to others depends largely, though not entirely, upon our avowed reasons for acting; and this is a matter for reflective decision, not something we discover later by looking back at what we did and its effects. The decision is important because "the same act" can have very different consequences, depending upon how we choose to justify it. In a sense, acts done for different reasons are not "the same act" even if they are otherwise similar, and so not merely the consequences but also the moral nature of our acts depends in part on our decisions about the reasons for doing them.

Unfortunately, the message actually conveyed by our actions does not depend only on our intentions and reasons, for our acts may have a meaning for others quite at odds with what we hoped to express. Others may misunderstand our intentions, doubt our sincerity, or discern a subtext that undermines the primary message. Even if sincere, well-intended, and successfully conveyed, the message of an act or policy does not by itself justify the means by which it is conveyed; it is almost always a relevant factor, however, in the moral assessment of an act or policy.

These remarks may strike you as too obvious to be worth mentioning; for, even if we do not usually express the ideas so abstractly, we are all familiar with them in our daily interactions with our friends, families, and colleagues. Who, for example, does not know the importance of the message expressed in offering money to another person, as well as the dangers of misunderstanding? What is superficially the same "act" can be an offer to buy, an admission of guilt, an expression of gratitude, a contribution to a common cause, a condescending display of superiority, or an outrageous insult. Since all this is so familiar, the extent to which these elementary points are ignored in discussions of the pros and cons of social policies such as affirmative action is surprising. The usual presumption is that social policies can be settled entirely by debating the rights involved or by estimating the consequences, narrowly conceived of as separate from the messages that we want to give and those that are likely to be received.

I shall focus attention for a while upon this relatively neglected issue of the message of affirmative action. In particular, I want to consider what message we *should try* to give with affirmative action programs and what messages we should try to avoid. What is the best way to convey the intended message, and

indeed whether it is likely to be heard, are empirical questions that I cannot settle; but the question I propose to consider is nonetheless important, and it is a *prior* question. What do we want to say with our affirmative action programs, and why? Since the message that is received and its consequences are likely to depend to some extent on what we decide, in all sincerity, to be the rationale for such programs, it would be premature and foolish to try to infer or predict these outcomes without adequate reflection on what the message and rationale should be. Also, for those who accept the historical/narrative perspective described in Section IV, there is additional reason to focus first on the desired message; for that perspective treats the message of affirmative action not merely as a minor side effect to be weighed in, for or against, but rather as an important part of the legitimate purpose of affirmative action.

Much useful discussion has been devoted to the constitutionality of affirmative action programs, to the relative moral rights involved, and to the advantages and disadvantages of specific types of programs.[1] By deemphasizing these matters here, I do not mean to suggest that they are unimportant. Even more, my remarks are not meant to convey the message, "It doesn't matter what we do or achieve, all that matters is what we *say*." To the contrary, I believe that mere gestures are insufficient and that universities cannot even communicate what they should by affirmative action policies unless these are sincerely designed to result in increased opportunities for those disadvantaged and insulted by racism and sexism.

I divide my discussion as follows. *First,* I describe briefly two affirmative action programs with which I am acquainted, so that we can have in mind some concrete examples before we turn to controversial principles. *Second,* I summarize why I think that affirmative action programs need not be illegitimate forms of "reverse discrimination" that violate the rights of non-minority males. This is a large issue, well discussed by others, but it must be considered at least briefly in order to open the way for more positive considerations. *Third,* I discuss two familiar strategies for justifying affirmative action and give some reasons for thinking that these should not be considered the whole story. One strategy, the "forward-looking," appeals exclusively to the good results expected from such programs; the other, the "backward-looking," focuses on past injustice and demands reparation. One of my main points is that this very division leads us to overlook some other important considerations. *Fourth,* in a brief philosophical interlude, I sketch a mode of evaluation that seems to provide a helpful alternative or supplement to the traditional sorts of evaluation that have dominated discussions of affirmative action. This suggestion draws from recent work in ethical theory that stresses the importance of historical context, narrative unity, and interpersonal relations. *Fifth,* combining these ideas with my proposal to consider the message of affirmative action, I present some analogies that point to an alternative perspective on the aims of affirmative action programs. Seen from this perspective, programs that stress outreach, encouragement, and development opportunities appear in a more favorable light than those that simply alter standards to meet quotas.

I. Samples of Affirmative Action Programs

Affirmative action programs take various forms and are used in many different contexts. Here, however, I shall concentrate on hiring and admission policies in universities and colleges. Even in this area there are many complexities that must be taken into account in the assessment of particular programs. It may matter, for example, whether the program is voluntary or government-mandated, quota-based or flexible, fixed-term or indefinite, in a formerly segregated institution or not, and so on. Obviously it is impossible to examine all these variations here. It is also unnecessary, for my project is not to defend or criticize specific programs but to raise general questions about how we should approach the issue. Nonetheless, though a full range of cases is not needed for this purpose, it may prove useful to sketch some sample programs that at least illustrate what the more abstract debate is about.

A common feature of affirmative action programs is that they make use of the categories of race and gender (more specifically, blacks and women) in their admissions and hiring policies, and they do so in a way that gives positive weight to being in one or the other of these latter categories. Policies use these classifications in different ways, as is evident in the cases described below.

When I taught at Pomona College in 1966–68, for example, the faculty/student Admissions Committee was blessed, or cursed, with applications numbering several times the number of places for new students. After a careful study of the correlation between grade-point averages of graduating seniors and data available in their initial application dossiers, a professor had devised a formula for predicting "success" at the college, where success was measured by the student's academic average at graduation from college. The predictive factors included high school grades, national test scores, and a ranking of the high school according to the grades its previous graduates received at the college. All applicants were then ranked according to this formula, which was supposed purely to reflect academic promise. The top ten percent were automatically admitted; a cut-off point was established below which candidates were deemed incapable of handling the college curriculum. Then committee members made a "subjective" evaluation of the remaining (middle) candidates in which the members were supposed to give weight to special talents, high-minded ambition, community service, intriguing personality, and (more generally) the likelihood of contributing to the sort of college community that the evaluators thought desirable. Another cut was made, reflecting both the "pure academic" criteria and the subjective evaluations. Next (as I recall) the football coach, the drama instructor, the orchestra leader, and others were invited to pick a specified number from those above the minimum cut-off if they needed a quarterback, a lead actor, a tuba player, or whatever. Then those identified as minorities but above the minimum cut-off line were admitted, if they had not been already, by a procedure that started with the most qualified academically, moving down the list until the minority applicants to be admitted made up at least a certain percentage of the final number of students to be admitted (10 percent, as I recall). The rest were admitted by their place on the academic list.

Pomona College is a private institution, but some state colleges and universities have adopted policies that are similar in important respects. At the University of California at Los Angeles in the 1970s, I became familiar with a significantly different kind of affirmative action regarding graduate student admissions and faculty hiring and promotion. The emphasis here was on positive efforts to seek out and encourage qualified minority applicants—for example, through recruitment letters, calls, and campus visits. Special funds were allocated to create new faculty positions for qualified minority candidates, and special fellowships were made available to release minority faculty from some teaching duties prior to tenure. Teaching and research interests in race and gender problems were officially recognized as relevant to hiring and promotion decisions in certain departments, provided the usual academic standards were maintained. Guidelines and watchdog committees were established to require departments to prove that, each time they hired a non-minority male, they did so only after a thorough search for and examination of minority and female candidates. Since decisions to hire and promote were still determined by the judgments of diverse individuals, I suspect that some deans, department heads, and voting faculty members carried affirmative action beyond the guidelines, some countered this effect by negative bias, and some simply refused to deviate from what they perceived as "color-blind" and "sex-blind" criteria.

II. Affirmative Action or Reverse Discrimination?

Is affirmative action *necessarily* a morally illegitimate form of "reverse discrimination" that violates the rights of white male applicants?

The question here is not whether some particular affirmative action program is illegitimate, for example, because it uses quotas or causes the deliberate hiring of less qualified teachers; the question, rather, is whether making gender and race a relevant category in university policy is *in itself* unjust. If so, we need not go further with our discussion of the message of affirmative action and its advantages and disadvantages: for however important the need is to communicate and promote social benefits, we should not do so by unjust means.

Some think that the injustice of all affirmative action programs is obvious or easily demonstrated. Two facile but confused arguments seem to have an especially popular appeal. The first goes this way: "Affirmative action, by definition, gives preferential treatment to minorities and women. This is discrimination in their favor and against non-minority males. All discrimination by public institutions is unjust, no matter whether it is the old kind or the newer 'reverse discrimination.' So all affirmative action programs in public institutions are unjust."

This deceptively simple argument, of course, trades on an ambiguity. In one sense, to "discriminate" means to "make a distinction," to pay attention to a difference. In this evaluatively neutral sense, of course, affirmative action programs do discriminate. But public institutions must, and justifiably do, "discriminate" in this sense—for example, between citizens and non-citizens, freshmen and seniors, the tal-

ented and the retarded, and those who pay their bills and those who do not. Whether it is unjust to note and make use of a certain distinction in a given context depends upon many factors: the nature of the institution, the relevant rights of the parties involved, the purposes and effects of making that distinction, and so on.

All this would be obvious except for the fact that the word "discrimination" is also used in a pejorative sense, meaning (roughly) "making use of a distinction in an unjust or illegitimate way." To discriminate in this sense is obviously wrong; but now it remains an open question whether the use of race and gender distinctions in affirmative action programs is really "discrimination" in this sense. The simplistic argument uses the evaluatively neutral sense of "discrimination" to show that affirmative action discriminates; it then shifts to the pejorative sense when it asserts that discrimination is always wrong. Although one may, in the end, *conclude* that all public use of racial and gender distinctions is unjust, to do so requires more of an *argument* than the simple one (just given) that merely exploits an ambiguity of the word "discrimination."

A slightly more sophisticated argument runs as follows: "Affirmative action programs give special benefits to certain individuals 'simply because they are women or blacks.' But one's color and gender are morally irrelevant features of a person. It is unjust for public institutions to give special benefits to individuals solely because they happen to have certain morally irrelevant characteristics. Hence affirmative action programs are always unjust."

A special twist is often added to this argument, as follows: "What was wrong with Jim Crow laws, denial of the vote to women and blacks, and segregation in schools and public facilities was just the fact that such practices treated people differently simply because they happened to have certain morally irrelevant characteristics. Affirmative action programs, however well-intentioned, are doing exactly the same thing. So they are wrong for the same reason."

Now people who argue in this way may well be trying to express something important, which should not be dismissed; but, as it stands, the argument is confused, unfair, and historically inaccurate. The confusion and unfairness lie in the misleading use of the expression "*simply* because they are women or blacks." It is true that typical affirmative action programs, such as those I described earlier, use the categories of "black" (or "minority") and "female" as an instrumental part of a complex policy. This does not mean, however, that the fundamental reason, purpose, or justification of the policy is nothing more than "this individual is black (or female)." To say that someone favors a person "*simply because* that person is black (or female)" implies that there is no further reason, purpose, or justification, as if one merely had an utterly arbitrary preference for dark skin as opposed to light or female anatomy over male anatomy. But no serious advocate of affirmative action thinks the program is justified by such personal preferences. On the contrary, advocates argue that, given our historical situation, quite general principles of justice or utility justify the temporary classificatory use of race and gender. That being black or white, male or female, does not in itself make anyone morally better or more deserving is acknowledged on all sides.

Thus even if one should conclude that the attempts to justify affirmative action fail, the fair and clear way to express this would be to say that the grounds that have been offered for using race and gender categories as affirmative action programs do are unconvincing. Unlike the rhetorical claim that they favor individuals "merely because they are black (or female)," this does not insinuate unfairly that the programs were instituted for no reason other than personal taste. And, of course, those of us who believe that there are good reasons for affirmative action policies, with their sorting by gender and race, have even more reason to reject the misleading and insulting description that we advocate special treatment for individuals *merely because* they are blacks or women.

The argument we have been considering is objectionable in another way as well. As Richard Wasserstrom points out, the moral wrongs against blacks and women in the past were not wrong just because people were classified and treated differently according to the morally irrelevant features of gender and color.[2] There was this sort of arbitrary treatment, of course, but the main problem was not that women and blacks were treated differently *somehow* but that they were *treated as no human being should be treated*. Segregation, for example, was in practice not merely a pointless sorting of individuals, like separating people according to the number of letters in their names. It was a way of expressing and perpetuating white contempt for blacks and preserving social structures that kept blacks from taking full advantage of their basic human rights. The mistreatment of women was not merely that they were arbitrarily selected for the more burdensome but still legitimate social roles. It was, in large part, that the practices expressed an attitude towards women that subtly undermined their chances

of making use of even the limited opportunities they had. The proper conclusion, then, is not that any current program that makes use of race and gender categories is simply committing the same old wrongs in reverse. The worst wrongs of the past went far beyond merely the arbitrary use of these categories; moreover, it has yet to be established that the new use of these categories in affirmative action is in fact arbitrary (like the old use). An arbitrary category is one used without good justification; the charge that affirmative action programs use race and gender categories unjustifiably is just what is at issue, not something we can assume at the start.

Another argument to show that affirmative action is unjust is that it violates the rights of white males who apply for admission or jobs in the university. This is a complex issue, discussed at length in journals and before the Supreme Court; rather than review that debate, I will just mention a few of the considerations that lead me to think that, though certain *types* of affirmative action may violate the rights of white males, appropriately designed affirmative action programs do not.

First, no individual, white male or otherwise, has an absolute right to a place in a public university—that is, a right independent of complex considerations of the functions of the university, the reasonable expectations of actual and potential taxpayers and other supporters, the number of places available, the relative merits of other candidates, and so on. What rights does an applicant have? Few would dispute that each individual has a right to "formal justice."[3] That is, one should not be arbitrarily denied a place to which one is entitled under the existing and publicly-declared rules and regulations. Any university must have rules concerning residency, prior education, submission of application forms, taking of entrance tests, and the like, as well as more substantive standards and policies for selecting among those who satisfy these minimal requirements. Formal justice requires that individual administrators do not deviate from the preestablished rules and standards currently in effect, whether from personal preference or high-minded social ideals. But this is not to say that old policies cannot reasonably be changed. One does not, for example, necessarily have a right to be treated by the rules and standards in force when one was born or when one first thought about going to college.

Formal justice is quite limited, however, for it is compatible with substantively unjust rules and standards. In addition to formal justice, each individual citizen has a right that the rules and standards of the university to which he or she applies be made (and, when necessary, changed) only for good reasons, consistent with the purposes of the university and the ideals of justice and basic human equality. This is a more stringent standard; it does establish a *presumption* against using race and gender categories in policies which affect the distribution of opportunities, such as jobs and student status. This is because race and gender, like height and musculature, are not *in themselves* morally relevant characteristics. Considered in isolation from their connections with other matters, they do not make anyone more, or less, deserving of anything. As the Supreme Court says, they are classifications that are "suspect."[4] But this does not mean that it is always unjust to use them, but only that their use stands in need of justification. What counts as a justification depends crucially upon our assessment of the legitimate purposes of the institution that uses the categories.

No one denies that the education of citizens and the pursuit of knowledge are central among the purposes of public universities. But, when resources are limited, decisions must be made as to what knowledge is to be pursued and who is to be offered education in each institution. Here we must consider the roles that universities play as parts of a complex network of public institutions (of many kinds) in a country committed to democratic ideals and faced with deep social problems. It has never been the practice of universities to disregard their social roles in the name of "purely academic" concerns; given current social problems, few would morally defend such disregard now. The more serious issue is not whether this role should be considered but rather whether the role is better served by affirmative action or by admission and hiring policies that admit only classification by test scores, grades, and past achievements. To decide this, we must look more closely at the purposes that affirmative action is supposed to serve.

III. Strategies of Justification: Consequences and Reparations

Some arguments for affirmative action look exclusively to its future benefits. The idea is that what has happened in the past is not in itself relevant to what we should do; at most, it provides clues as to what acts and policies are likely to bring about the best future. The philosophical tradition associated with this approach is utilitarianism, which declares that the morally right act is whatever produces the best consequences. Traditionally, utilitarianism evaluated consequences in terms of happiness and unhappiness, but the anticipated consequences of affirmative action are often described more specifically. For example, some argue that affirmative action will ease racial tensions, prevent riots, improve services in minority neighborhoods, reduce unemployment, remove inequities in income distribution, eliminate racial and sexual prejudice, and enhance the self-esteem of blacks and women. Some have called attention to the fact that women and minorities provide alternative perspectives on history, literature, philosophy, and politics, and that this has beneficial effects for both education and research.

These are important considerations, not irrelevant to the larger responsibilities of universities. For several reasons, however, I think it is a mistake for advocates of affirmative action to rest their case exclusively on such forward-looking arguments. First, critics raise reasonable doubts about whether affirmative action is necessary to achieve these admirable results. The economist Thomas Sowell argues that a free-market economy can achieve the same results more efficiently; his view is therefore that even if affirmative action has beneficial results (which he denies), it is not necessary for the purpose.[5] Though Sowell's position can be contested, the controversy itself tends to weaken confidence in the entirely forward-looking defense of affirmative action.

An even more obvious reason why affirmative action advocates should explore other avenues for its defense is that the exclusively forward-looking approach must give equal consideration to possible negative consequences of affirmative action. It may be, for example, that affirmative action will temporarily increase racial tensions, especially if its message is misunderstood. Even legitimate use of race and sex categories may encourage others to abuse the categories for unjust purposes. If applied without sensitive regard to the educational and research purposes of the university, affirmative action might severely undermine its efforts to fulfill these primary responsibilities. *If* affirmative action programs were to lower academic standards for blacks and women, they would run the risk of damaging the respect that highly qualified blacks and women have earned by leading others to suspect that these highly qualified people lack the merits of white males in the same positions. This could also be damaging to the self-respect of those who accept affirmative action positions. Even programs that disavow "lower standards" unfortunately arouse the suspicion that they don't really do so, and this by itself can cause problems. Although I believe that well-designed affirmative action programs can minimize these negative effects, the fact that they are a risk is a reason for not resting the case for affirmative action on a delicate balance of costs and benefits.

Reflection on the *message* of affirmative action also leads me to move beyond entirely forward-looking arguments. For if the sole purpose is to bring about a brighter future, then we give the wrong message to both the white males who are rejected and to the women and blacks who are benefited. To the latter what we say, in effect, is this: "Never mind how you have been treated. Forget about the fact that your race or sex has in the past been actively excluded and discouraged, and that you yourself may have had handicaps due to prejudice. Our sole concern is to bring about certain good results in the future, and giving you a break happens to be a useful means for doing this. Don't think this is a recognition of your rights as an individual or your disadvantages as a member of a group. Nor does it mean that we have confidence in your abilities. We would do the same for those who are privileged and academically inferior if it would have the same socially beneficial results."

To the white male who would have had a university position but for affirmative action, the exclusively forward-looking approach says: "We deny you the place you otherwise would have had simply as a means to produce certain socially desirable outcomes. We have not judged that others are more deserving, or have a right, to the place we are giving them instead of you. Past racism and sexism are irrelevant. The point is just that the sacrifice of your concerns is a useful means to the larger end of the future welfare of others."

This, I think, is the wrong message to give. It is also unnecessary. The proper alternative, however, is not to ignore the possible future benefits of affirmative action but rather to take them into account as a part of a larger picture.

A radically different strategy for justifying affirmative action is to rely on backward-looking arguments. Such arguments call our attention to certain events in the past and assert that *because* these past events occurred, we have certain duties now. The modern philosopher who most influentially endorsed such arguments was W.D. Ross.[6] He argued that there are duties of fidelity, justice, gratitude, and reparation that have a moral force independent of any tendency these may have to promote good consequences. The fact that you have made a promise, for example, gives you a strong moral reason to do what you promised, whether or not doing so will on balance have more beneficial consequences. The Rossian principle that is often invoked in affirmative action debates is a principle of reparation. This says that those who wrongfully injure others have a (*prima facie*) duty to apologize and make restitution. Those who have wronged others owe reparation.

James Forman dramatically expressed this idea in New York in 1969 when he presented "The Black Manifesto," which demanded five hundred million dollars in reparation to American blacks from white churches and synagogues.[7] Such organizations, the Manifesto contends, contributed to our history of slavery and racial injustice; as a result, they incurred a debt to the black community that still suffers from its effects. Objections were immediately raised: for example, both slaves and slave-owners are no longer alive; not every American white is guilty of racial oppression; and not every black in America was a victim of slavery and its aftermath.

Bernard Boxill, author of *Blacks and Social Justice,* developed a more sophisticated version of the backward-looking argument with a view to meeting these objections.[8] Let us admit, he says, that both the perpetrators and the primary victims of slavery are gone, and let us not insist that contemporary whites are guilty of perpetrating further injustices. Some do, and some do not, and public administrators cannot be expected to sort out the guilty from the non-guilty. However, reparation, or at least some "compensation,"[9] is still owed, because contemporary whites have reaped the profits of past injustice to blacks. He asks us to consider the analogy with a stolen bicycle. Suppose my parent stole your parent's bicycle some time ago, both have since died, and I "inherited" the bike from my parent, the thief. Though I may be innocent of any wrongdoing (so far), I am in possession of stolen goods rightfully belonging to you, the person who would have inherited the bike if it had not been stolen. For me to keep the bike and declare that I owe you nothing would be wrong, even if I was not the cause of your being deprived. By analogy, present-day whites owe reparations to contemporary blacks, not because they are themselves guilty of causing the disadvantages of blacks, but because they are in possession of advantages that fell to them as a result of the gross injustices of their ancestors. Special advantages continue to fall even to innocent whites because of the ongoing prejudice of their white neighbors.

Although it raises many questions, this line of argument acknowledges some important points missing in most exclusively forward-looking arguments: for example, it stresses the (intrinsic) relevance of past injustice and it calls attention to the rights and current disadvantages of blacks (in contrast with future benefits for others). When developed as an argument for affirmative action, it does not accuse all white males of prejudice and wrongdoing; at the same time, however, it sees the fundamental value as justice. As a result, it avoids giving the message to either rejected white males or reluctant affirmative action applicants that they are "mere means" to a social goal that is largely independent of their rights and interests as individuals.

There are, however, serious problems in trying to justify affirmative action by this backward-looking argument, especially if it is treated as the exclusive or central argument. Degrees of being advantaged and disadvantaged are notoriously hard to measure. New immigrants have not shared our history of past injustices, and so the argument may not apply to them in any straightforward way. The argument appeals to controversial ideas about property rights, inheritance, and group responsibilities. Some argue that affirmative action tends to benefit the least disadvantaged blacks and women; though this does not mean that they are owed nothing, their claims would seem to have lower priority than the needs of the most disadvantaged. Some highly qualified blacks and women object that affirmative action is damaging to their reputations and self-esteem, whereas the reparation argument seems to assume that it is a welcome benefit to all blacks and women.

If we focus on the message that the backward-looking argument sends, there are also some potential problems. Though rightly acknowledging past injustice, the argument (by itself) seems to convey the message that racial and sexual oppression consisted primarily in the loss of tangible goods, or the deprivation of specific rights and opportunities, that can be "paid back" in kind. The background idea, which goes back at least to Aristotle, is that persons wrongfully deprived of their "due" can justly demand an "equivalent" to what they have lost.[10] But, while specific deprivations were an important part of our racist and sexist past, they are far from the whole story. Among the worst wrongs then, as now, were humiliations and contemptuous treatment of a type that cannot, strictly, be "paid back." The problem was, and is, not just that specific rights and advantages were denied, but that prejudicial attitudes damaged self-esteem, undermined motivations, limited realistic options, and made even "officially open" opportunities seem undesirable. Racism and sexism were (and are) *insults,* not merely tangible *injuries.*[11] These are not the sort of thing that can be adequately measured and repaid with equivalents. The trouble with treating insulting racist and sexist practices on a pure reparation model is not merely the practical difficulty of identifying the offenders, determining the degree of guilt, assessing the amount of payment due, etc. It is also that penalty payments and compensation for lost benefits are not the only, or primary, moral responses that are called for. When affirmative action is defended exclusively by analogy with reparation, it tends to express the misleading message that the evils of racism and sexism are all tangible losses that can be "paid off"; by being silent on the insulting nature of racism and sexism, it tends to add insult to insult.

The message suggested by the reparation argument, by itself, also seems objectionable because it conveys the idea that higher education, teaching, and doing research are mainly benefits awarded in response to self-centered demands. The underlying picture too easily suggested is that applicants are a group of self-interested, bickering people, each grasping for limited "goodies" and insisting on a right to them. When a university grants an opportunity through affirmative action, its message would seem to be this. "We concede that you have a valid claim to this benefit and we yield to your demand, though this is not to suggest that we have confidence in your abilities or any desire to have you here." This invitation seems too concessive, the atmosphere too adversarial, and the emphasis too much on the benefits rather than the responsibilities of being a part of the university.

IV. Philosophical Interlude: An Alternative Perspective

Here I want to digress from the explicit consideration of affirmative action in order to consider more abstract philosophical questions about the ways we evaluate acts and policies. At the risk of oversimplifying, I want to contrast some assumptions that have, until recently, been dominant in ethical theory with alternatives suggested by contemporary philosophers who emphasize historical context, narrative unity, and community values.[12] Although these alternatives, in my opinion, have not yet been adequately developed, there seem to be at least four distinguishable themes worth considering.

First, when we reflect on what we deeply value, we find that we care not merely about the present moment and each future moment in isolation but also about how our past, present, and future cohere or fit together into a life and a piece of history. Some of our values, we might say, are cross-time wholes, with past, present, and future parts united in certain ways. Thus, for example, the commitments I have made, the projects I have begun, what I have shared with those I love, the injuries I have caused, and the hopes I have encouraged importantly affect both whether I am satisfied with my present and how I want the future to go.

Second, in reflecting on stretches of our lives and histories, we frequently use evaluative concepts drawn more from narrative literature than from accounting. Thus, for example, we think of our lives as having significant beginnings, crises, turning points, dramatic tension, character development, climaxes, resolutions, comic interludes, tragic disruptions, and eventually fitting (or unfitting) endings. The value of any moment often depends on what came before and what we anticipate to follow. And since our lives are intertwined with others in a common history, we also care about how our moments cohere with others' life stories. The past is seen as more than a time of accumulated debts and assets, and the future is valued as more than an opportunity for reinvesting and cashing in assets.

Third, evaluation must take into account one's particular historical context, including one's cultural, national, and ethnic traditions, and the actual individuals in one's life. Sometimes this point is exaggerated, I think, to suggest a dubious cultural relativism or "particularism" in ethics: for example, the thesis that what is valuable for a person is defined by the person's culture or that evaluations imply no general reasons beyond particular judgments, such as "That's *our* way" and "John is *my* son."[13] But, construed modestly as a practical or epistemological point, it seems obvious enough, on reflection, that we should take into account the historical context of our acts and that we are often in a better position to judge what is appropriate in particular cases than we are to articulate universally valid premises supporting the judgment. We can sometimes be reasonably confident about what is right in a particular context without being sure about whether or not there are relevant differences blocking the same judgment in seemingly similar but

less familiar contexts. We know, as a truism, that the same judgment applies if there are no relevant differences, but in practice the particular judgment may be more evident than the exact scope of the moral generalizations that hold across many cases. Thus, though giving reasons for our judgments in particular contexts commits us to acknowledging their potential relevance in other contexts, moral judgment cannot be aptly represented simply as deducing specific conclusions from clear and evident general principles.

Fourth, when we evaluate particular acts and policies as parts of lives and histories, what is often most important is the value of the whole, which cannot always be determined by "summing up" the values of the parts. Lives, histories, and interpersonal relations over time are what G.E. Moore called "organic unities"—that is, wholes the value of which is not necessarily the sum of the values of the parts.[14] The point here is not merely the obvious practical limitation that we cannot measure and quantify values in this area. More fundamentally, the idea is that it would be a mistake even to try to evaluate certain unities by assessing different parts in isolation from one another, then adding up all their values. Suppose, for example, a woman with terminal cancer considered two quite different ways of spending her last days. One way, perhaps taking a world cruise, might seem best when evaluated in terms of the quality of each future moment, in isolation from her past and her present ties; but another way, perhaps seeking closure in projects and with estranged family members, might seem more valuable when seen as a part of her whole life.

Taken together, these ideas cast doubt on both the exclusively forward-looking method of assessment and the standard backward-looking alternative. Consequentialism, or the exclusively forward-looking method, attempts to determine what ought to be done at present by fixing attention entirely on future results. To be sure, any sensible consequentialist will consult the past for lessons and clues helpful in predicting future outcomes: for example, recalling that you offended someone yesterday may enable you to predict that the person will be cool to you tomorrow unless you apologize. But beyond this, consequentialists have no concern with the past, for their "bottom line" is always "what happens from now on," evaluated independently of the earlier chapters of our lives and histories. For the consequentialist, assessing a life or history from a narrative perspective becomes impossible or at least bizarre, as what must be evaluated at each shifting moment is "the story from now on" independently of what has already been written.[15]

The standard Rossian alternative to this exclusively forward-looking perspective is to introduce certain (*prima facie*) *duties* to respond to certain past events in specified ways—for example, pay debts, keep promises, pay reparation for injuries. These duties are supposed to be self-evident and universal (though they are *prima facie*), and they do not hold because they tend to promote anything good or valuable. Apart from aspects of the acts mentioned in the principles (for example, fulfilling a promise, returning favors, not injuring, etc.), details of historical and personal context are considered irrelevant.

By contrast, the narrative perspective sketched above considers the past as an integral part of the valued unities that we aim to bring about, not merely as a source of duties. If one has negligently wronged another, Ross regards this past event as generating a duty to pay reparations even if doing so will result in nothing good. But from the narrative perspective, the past becomes relevant in a further way. One may say, for example, that the *whole* consisting of your life and your relationship with that person from the time of the injury into the future will be a better thing if you acknowledge the wrong and make efforts to restore what you have damaged. For Ross, the duty is generated by the past and unrelated to bringing about anything good; from the narrative perspective, however, the requirement is just what is required to bring about a valuable connected whole with past, present, and future parts—the best way to complete a chapter, so to speak, in two intersecting life-stories.

So far, neither the Rossian nor the narrative account has told us much about the ultimate reasons for their evaluations, but they reveal ways to consider the matter. The Rossian asks us to judge particular cases in the light of "self-evident" general principles asserting that certain past events tend to generate present (or future) duties. The alternative perspective calls for examining lives and relationships, over time, in context, as organic unities evaluated (partly) in narrative terms.

To illustrate, consider two persons, John and Mary. John values having Mary's trust and respect, and conversely Mary values having John's; moreover, John values the fact that Mary values being trusted and respected by him, and conversely Mary values the same about John.[16]

Now suppose that other people have been abusive and insulting to Mary, and that John is worried that Mary may take things he had said and done as similarly insulting, even though he does not think that he consciously meant them this way. Though he is worried, Mary does not seem to suspect him; he fears that he may only make matters worse if he raises the issue, creating suspicions she did not have or focusing on doubts that he cannot allay. Perhaps, he thinks, their future relationship would be better served if he just remained silent, hoping that the trouble, if any, will fade in time. If so, consequentialist thinking would recommend silence. Acknowledging this, he might nonetheless feel that duties of friendship and fidelity demand that he raise the issue, regardless of whether or not the result will be worse. Then he would be thinking as a Rossian.

But, instead, he might look at the problem from an alternative perspective, asking himself what response best affirms and contributes to the sort of ongoing relationship he has and wants to continue with Mary. Given their history together, it is important to him to do his part towards restoring the relationship if it indeed has been marred by perceived insults or suspicions. To be sure, he wants *future* relations of mutual trust and respect, but not at any price and not by just any means. Their history together is not irrelevant, for what he values is not merely a future of a certain kind, but that their relationship over time be of the sort he values. He values an ongoing history of mutual trust and respect that *calls for* an explicit response in this current situation, not merely as a means to a brighter future but as a present affirmation of what they value together. Even if unsure which course will be best for the future, he may be reasonably confident that the act that best expresses his respect and trust (and his valuing hers, etc.) is to confront the problem, express his regrets, reaffirm his respect, ask for her trust, be patient with her doubts, and welcome an open dialogue. If the insults were deep and it is not entirely clear whether or not he really associated himself with them, then mere words may not be enough to convey the message or even to assure himself of his own sincerity. Positive efforts, even at considerable cost, may be needed to express appropriately and convincingly what needs to be said. How the next chapter unfolds is not entirely up to him, and he would not be respectful if he presumed otherwise by trying to manipulate the best future unilaterally.

The example concerns only two persons and their personal values, but it illustrates a perspective that one can also take regarding moral problems involving many persons.

V. Mutual Respect, Fair Opportunity, and Affirmative Action

Turning back to our main subject, I suggest that some of the values that give affirmative action its point are best seen as cross-time values that fall outside the exclusively forward-looking and backward-looking perspectives. They include having a history of racial and gender relations governed, so far as possible, by the ideals of mutual respect, trust, and fair opportunity for all.

Our national history provides a context of increasing recognition and broader interpretation of the democratic ideal of the equal dignity of all human beings—an ideal that has been flagrantly abused from the outset, partially affirmed in the bloody Civil War, and increasingly extended in the civil rights movement, but is still far from being fully respected. More specifically, blacks and women were systematically treated in an unfair and demeaning way by public institutions, including universities, until quite recently, and few could confidently claim to have rooted out racism and sexism even now.[17] The historical context is not what grounds or legitimates democratic values, but it is the background of the current problem, the sometimes admirable and often ugly way the chapters up until now have been written.

Consider first the social ideal of mutual respect and trust among citizens. The problem of implementing this in the current context is different from the problem in the two-person example discussed above, for the history of our racial and gender relations is obviously not an idyllic story of mutual respect and trust momentarily interrupted by a crisis. Even so, the question to ask is not merely, "What will promote respectful and trusting racial and gender relations in future generations?", but rather, "Given our checkered past, how can we appropriately express the social value of mutual respect and trust that we want, so far as possible, to characterize our history?" We cannot change our racist and sexist past, but we also cannot express full respect for those present individuals who live in its aftermath if we ignore it. What is called for is not merely repayment of tangible debts incurred by past injuries, but also a message to counter the deep insult inherent in racism and sexism.

Recognizing that problems of this kind are not amenable to easy solutions deduced from self-evident moral generalizations, we may find it helpful instead to reflect on an analogy. Suppose you return to the hometown you left in childhood, remembering with pride its Fourth of July speeches about the values of community, equality, and fairness for all. You discover, however, that the community was never as perfect as you thought. In fact, for years—until quite recently—certain families, who had been disdainfully labeled "the Barefeet," had not only been shunned by most folk but had also been quietly terrorized by a few well-placed citizens. The Barefeet had been arrested on false charges, beaten, raped, and blackmailed into silent submission. The majority, perhaps, would never have done these things, but their contempt for the Barefeet was such that most would have regarded these crimes less important than if they had been done to insiders. Fortunately, the worst offenders have died, and so have the victims of the most outrageous crimes. Majority attitudes have changed somewhat, though often only from open contempt to passive disregard. Some new citizens have come to town, and a few of the Barefeet (now more politely called "Cross-towners") have managed to become successful. Nonetheless, the older Cross-towners are still fearful and resigned, and the younger generation is openly resentful and distrustful when officials proclaim a new commitment to democratic ideals. It is no surprise, then, that few Cross-towners take full advantage of available opportunities and that the two groups tend to isolate themselves from each other.

Now suppose you, as one of the majority, could persuade the rest to give a message to the Cross-towners, a message appropriate to the majority's professed value of being a community committed to mutual respect and trust. What would you propose? And, assuming that doing so would violate no one's rights, what means would you think best to convey that message sincerely and effectively? Some would no doubt suggest simply forgetting about the past and hoping that time will heal the wounds. But, whether effective in the future or not, this plan fails to express full respect for the Cross-towners now. Others might suggest a more legalistic approach, trying to determine exactly who has been the disadvantaged, the degree of loss, which citizens are most responsible, etc., in order to pay off the debt. But this, taken by itself, faces the sorts of disadvantages we have already considered. If, instead, the value of mutual respect and trust is the governing ideal, the appropriate message would be to acknowledge and deplore the past openly, to affirm a commitment to promote mutual respect and trust in the future, to welcome full interchange and participation with the Cross-towners, and to urge them to undertake the risks of overcoming their understandable suspicions by joining in a common effort to work towards fulfilling the ideal. This would address not merely the injury but also the insult implicit in the town's history.

The more difficult question, however, is how we might express such a message effectively and with evident sincerity in an atmosphere already poisoned by the past. Mere words will be taken as mere words; they may in fact turn out to be just that. What is needed is more positive action—concrete steps to prove commitment, to resist backsliding, and to overcome reluctance on both sides. The sort of affirmative action taken in the U.C.L.A. program described in Section I seems especially appropriate for this purpose. Here the emphasis was on outreach, increasing awareness of opportunities, accountability and proof of fairness in procedures, and allocating resources (fellowships, release time, etc.) in a way that showed trust that, if given an adequate chance, those formerly excluded would enrich the university by fully appropriate standards. These seem the most natural way to give force to the message, though arguably other methods may serve the purpose as well.

There is another historical value that is also relevant and seems to favor even more radical steps in affirmative action. The issue is too complex to address adequately here, but it should at least be mentioned. What I have in mind might be called "fair opportunity." That is, implicit in our democratic ideals is the idea that our public institutions should be so arranged that they afford to each person, over time, more or less equal opportunities to develop and make use of his or her natural talents and to participate and contribute to those institutions. The idea is hard to make precise, but it clearly does not mean that all should have equal chances to have a desirable position, regardless of effort and natural aptitude. The physically handicapped and the mentally retarded suffer from natural misfortunes; though society should not ignore them, they cannot expect standards to be rigged to ensure the former equal odds at making the basketball team or the latter equal odds of being appointed to the faculty. Similarly, those who choose not to make the effort to develop their capacities have no right to expect public institutions to include them in a pool from which candidates are selected by lot. But when persons have been disadvantaged by social injustice, having had their initial chances diminished by the network of public institutions themselves, then positive steps are needed to equalize their opportunities over time.

This ideal calls for something more than efforts to ensure that future generations do not suffer from the same disadvantages, for those efforts fail to respond to the unfairness to the present individuals. But, for obvious practical reasons, legal efforts to remedy precisely identifiable disadvantages incurred by individuals are bound to be quite inadequate to address the many subtle losses of opportunity caused by past institutional racism and sexism. Since no perfect solution is possible, we need to choose between this inadequate response and policies that address the problem in a less fine-grained way. Affirmative action programs that employ a working presumption that women and minorities generally have had their opportunities restricted to some degree by institutional racism and sexism will admittedly risk compensating a few who have actually had, on balance, as much opportunity as white males. But the practical alternatives, it seems, are to accept this risk or to refuse to respond at all to the innumerable ways that institutional racism and sexism have undermined opportunities too subtly for the courts to remedy.

Given these options, what would be the message of choosing to limit redress to precisely identifiable losses? This would say, in effect, to women and minorities, "We cannot find a way to ensure *precisely* that each talented and hard-working person has an equal opportunity over time; and, given our options, we count it more important to see that *none* of you women and minorities are overcompensated than to try to see that the *majority* of you have more nearly equal opportunities over your life-time. Your grievances are too subtle and difficult to measure, and your group may be harboring some who were not disadvantaged. We would rather let the majority of white males enjoy the advantages of their unfair head start than risk compensating one of you who does not deserve it."

Now *if* it had been established on antecedent grounds that the affirmative action measures in question would violate the *rights* of white male applicants, then one could argue that these coarse-grained efforts to honor the ideal of fair opportunity are illegitimate. But that premise, I think, has not been established. Affirmative action programs would violate the rights of white males only if, all things considered, their guidelines temporarily favoring women and minorities were arbitrary, not serving the legitimate social role of universities or fulfilling the ideals of fairness and respect for all. The considerations offered here, however, point to the conclusion that some affirmative action programs, even those involving a degree of preferential treatment, are legitimated by ideals of mutual respect, trust, and fair opportunity.

Conclusion

All this, I know, is too brief, loose, and incomplete; I hope it is worth considering nonetheless. The main suggestion is that, ideally, a central purpose of affirmative action would be to communicate a much-needed message, sincerely and effectively. The message is called for not just as a means to future good relations or a dutiful payment of a debt incurred by our past. It is called for by the ideal of being related to other human beings over time, so that our histories and biographies reflect the responses of those who deeply care about fair opportunity, mutual trust, and respect for all.

If so, what should public universities try to say to those offered opportunities through affirmative action? Perhaps something like this: "Whether we individually are among the guilty or not, we acknowledge that you have been wronged—if not by specific injuries which could be named and repaid, at least by the humiliating and debilitating attitudes prevalent in our country and our institutions. We deplore and denounce these attitudes and the wrongs that spring from them. We acknowledge that, so far, most of you have had your opportunities in life diminished by the effects of these attitudes, and we want no one's prospects to be diminished by injustice. We recognize your understandable grounds for suspicion and mistrust when we express these high-minded sentiments, and we want not only to ask respectfully for your trust but also to give concrete evidence of our sincerity. We welcome you respectfully into the university community and ask you to take a full share of the responsibilities as well as the benefits. By creating special opportunities, we recognize the disadvantages you have probably suffered; we show our respect for your talents and our commitment to the ideals of the university, however, by not faking grades and honors for you. Given current attitudes about affirmative action, accepting this position will probably have drawbacks as well as advantages.[18] It is an opportunity and a responsibility offered neither as charity nor as entitlement, but rather as part of a special effort to welcome

and encourage minorities and women to participate more fully in the university at all levels. We believe that this program affirms some of the best ideals implicit in our history without violating the rights of any applicants. We hope that you will choose to accept the position in this spirit as well as for your own benefit."

The appropriate message is no doubt harder to communicate to those who stand to lose some traditional advantages under a legitimate affirmative action program. But if we set aside practical difficulties and suppose that the proper message could be sincerely given and accepted as such, what would it say? Ideally, it would convey an understanding of the moral reasoning for the program; perhaps, in conclusion, it would say something like the following.

"These are the concerns that we felt made necessary the policy under which the university is temporarily giving special attention to women and minorities. We respect your rights to formal justice and to a policy guided by the university's education and research mission as well as its social responsibilities. Our policy in no way implies the view that your opportunities are less important than others', but we estimate (roughly, as we must) that as a white male you have probably had advantages and encouragement that for a long time have been systematically, unfairly, insultingly unavailable to most women and minorities. We deplore invidious race and gender distinctions; we hope that no misunderstanding of our program will prolong them. Unfortunately, nearly all blacks and women have been disadvantaged to some degree by bias against their groups, and it is impractical for universities to undertake the detailed investigations that would be needed to assess how much particular individuals have suffered or gained from racism and sexism. We appeal to you to share the historical values of fair opportunity and mutual respect that underlie this policy; we hope that, even though its effects may be personally disappointing, you can see the policy as an appropriate response to the current situation."

Unfortunately, as interests conflict and tempers rise, it is difficult to convey this idea without giving an unintended message as well. White males unhappy about the immediate effects of affirmative action may read the policy as saying that "justice" is the official word for giving preferential treatment to whatever group one happens to favor. Some may see a subtext insinuating that blacks and women are naturally inferior and "cannot make it on their own." Such cynical readings reveal either misunderstanding or the willful refusal to take the moral reasoning underlying affirmative action seriously. They pose serious obstacles to the success of affirmative action—practical problems that may be more intractable than respectful moral disagreement and counter-argument. But some types of affirmative action invite misunderstanding and suspicion more than others. For this reason, anyone who accepts the general case for affirmative action suggested here would do well to reexamine in detail the means by which they hope to communicate its message.[19]

---

1. *See, for example, the following: John Arthur, ed.*, Morality and Moral Controversies, *2nd ed. (Englewood Cliffs: Prentice-Hall, Inc., 1986). ch. 11, pp. 305–47; William T. Blackstone and Robert D. Heslep, eds.*, Social Justice and Preferential Treatment *(Athens: The University of Georgia Press, 1977); Bernard Boxill*, Blacks and Social Justice *(Totowa: Rowman and Allanheld, 1984); Marshall Cohen, Thomas Nagel, and Thomas Scanlon, eds.*, Equality and Preferential Treatment *(Princeton: Princeton University Press, 1977); Robert K. Fullinwider*, The Reverse Discrimination Controversy *(Totowa: Rowman and Littlefield, 1980); Alan H. Goldman*, Justice and Reverse Discrimination *(Princeton: Princeton University Press, 1979); Kent Greenawalt*, Discrimination and Reverse Discrimination *(New York: Alfred A. Knopf, 1983). Barry R. Gross, ed.*, Reverse Discrimination *(Buffalo: Prometheus Press, 1977); Thomas A. Mappes and Jane S. Zembaty, eds.*, Social Ethics *(2nd ed.; New York: McGraw-Hill Book Company, 1982), ch. 5, pp. 159–98.*

2. *See Richard Wasserstrom, "Racism and Sexism," "Preferential Treatment" in his* Philosophy and Social Issues *(Notre Dame: University of Notre Dame Press, 1980).*

3. *William K. Frankena, "The Concept of Social Justice," in* Social Justice, *ed. Richard B. Brandt (Englewood Cliffs: Prentice-Hall, Inc., 1962), pp. 8–9; Henry Sidgwick*, Methods of Ethics, *7th ed. (London: Macmillan, 1907), pp. 379, 386ff.; John Rawls*, A Theory of Justice *(Cambridge: Harvard University Press, 1971), pp. 56–60, 180, 235–239, 504ff.*

4. Regents of the University of California *v.* Allan Bakke, *98 S.Ct. 2733, 46 L.W. 4896 (1978). Reprinted in Wasserstrom, ed.*, Today's Moral Issues, *2nd ed. (New York: Macmillan Publishing Co., 1975), pp. 149–207, esp. pp. 156–57.*

5. *Thomas Sowell*, Race and Economics *(New York: David McKay Co., 1975), ch. 6;* Markets and Minorities *(New York: Basic Books, Inc., 1981), pp. 114–15.*

6. *W.D. Ross*, The Right and the Good *(Oxford: Clarendon Press, 1930).*

7. *James Forman was at the time director of international affairs for SNCC (Student Nonviolent Coordinating Committee). The "Black Manifesto" stems from an economic development conference sponsored by the Interreligious Foundation for Community Organizations, April 26, 1969, and presented by Forman at the New York Interdominational Riverside Church on May 4, 1969. Later the demand was raised to three billion dollars. See Robert S. Lecky and H. Elliot Wright*, Black Manifesto *(New York: Sheed and Ward Publishers, 1969), pp. vii, 114–26.*

8. *Bernard Boxill, "The Morality of Reparation,"* Social Theory and Practice, *vol. 2, no. 1 (1972), pp. 113–22, and* Blacks and Social Justice, *ch. 7.*

9. *In the article cited above, Boxill calls what is owed "reparation," but in the book (above) he calls it "compensation." The latter term, preferred by many, is used more broadly to cover not only restitution for wrongdoing but also "making up" for deficiencies and losses that are not anyone's fault (for example, naturally caused physical handicaps, or damages unavoidably resulting from legitimate and necessary activities). We could describe the backward-looking arguments presented here as demands for "compensation" rather than "reparation," so long as we keep in mind that the compensation is supposed to be due as the morally appropriate response to past wrongdoing.*

10. *Aristotle*, Nicomachean Ethics, *tr. A. K. Thomson (Baltimore: Penguin Books, Inc., 1955), bk. V, esp. pp. 143–55.*

11. *See Boxill*, Blacks and Social Justice, *pp. 132ff., and Ronald Dworkin, "Reverse Discrimination," in* Taking Rights Seriously *(Cambridge: Harvard University Press, 1978), pp. 231ff.*

12. *See, for example, Alasdair MacIntyre*, After Virtue *(Notre Dame: Notre Dame University Press, 1981). Similar themes are found in Carol Gilligan's* In A Different Voice *(Cambridge: Harvard University Press, 1982) and in Lawrence Blum*, Friendship, Altruism, and Morality *(Boston: Routledge and Kegan Paul, 1980).*

13. *Regarding cultural and moral relativism see, for example, David B. Wong*, Moral Relativity *(Berkeley and Los Angeles: University of California Press, 1984), with an excellent bibliography, and Richard B. Brandt*, Ethical Theory *(Englewood Cliffs: Prentice-Hall, Inc., 1959), ch. 11, pp. 271–94. Versions of particularism are presented in Andrew Oldenquist, "Loyalties,"* The Journal of Philosophy, *vol. 79 (1982), pp. 173–93; Lawrence Blum,* Friendship, Altruism, and Morality; *and Bernard Williams, "Persons, Character and Morality" in* Moral Luck *(New York: Cambridge University Press, 1981), pp. 1–19.*

14. *G. E. Moore*, Principia Ethica *(Cambridge: Cambridge University Press, 1912), pp. 27ff.*

15. *That is, the evaluation is independent of the past in the sense that the past makes no intrinsic difference to the final judgment and the future is not evaluated as a part of a temporal whole including the past. As noted, however, consequentialists will still look to the past for lessons and clues about how to bring about the best future.*

16. *For an interesting illustration of reciprocal desires (e.g., A wanting B, B wanting A, A wanting B to want A, B wanting A to want B, A wanting B to want A to want B, etc.), see Thomas Nagel, "Sexual Perversion,"* The Journal of Philosophy, *vol. 66 (1969).*

17. *Racism and sexism present significantly different problems, but I shall not try to analyze the differences here. For the most part (and especially in the analogy to follow) my primary focus is on racism, but the relevance of the general type of moral thinking considered here to the problems of sexism should nonetheless be evident.*

18. *How severe these drawbacks are will, of course, depend upon the particular means of affirmative action that are selected and how appropriate these are for the situation. For example, if, to meet mandated quotas, highly-ranked colleges and universities offer special admission to students not expected to succeed, then they may well be misleading those students into a wasteful and humiliating experience when those students could have thrived at lower-ranked educational institutions. This practice was explicitly rejected in the policies at Pomona College and at U.C.L.A. described in Section I, but William Allen (a contributor to this volume) suggested to me in discussion that, in his opinion, the practice is quite common. The practice, I think, is unconscionable, and my argument in no way supports it.*

Geoffrey Miller . . . described in discussion another possible affirmative action program that would be quite inappropriate to the circumstances but is again not supported by the line of argument I have suggested. He asks us to imagine a "permanent underclass" of immigrants who are "genetically or culturally deficient" and as a result fail to succeed. Since we do not share a common social and cultural history of injustice resulting in their condition, the historical dimension of my case for affirmative action is missing. And since they are a "permanent" underclass, and thus the "genetic or cultural deficiencies" that result in their failure cannot be altered, one cannot argue that universities can help them or even can sincerely give them an encouraging "message" through affirmative action. This does not mean, however, that there are not other reasons for society to extend appropriate help. Also, any suggestion that certain urban populations that are now called a "permanent underclass" are accurately and fairly described by the "fictional" example is politically charged and needs careful examination.

19. Although my aim in this paper has been to survey general types of arguments for thinking that some sort of affirmative action is needed, rather than to argue for any particular program, one cannot reasonably implement the general idea without considering many contextual factors that I have set aside here. Thus, though the moral perspective suggested here seems to favor the second method described in Section I (recruitment, special funds, accountability) over the first method (proportionality, given a fixed lower standard), the need for more detailed discussion is obvious.

Legal Injustices to Women

THE REASONABLE WOMAN*

Kim Lane Scheppele

In the intense tribalism of our times, empathy seems in short supply, but also in little demand. Newly or partially empowered groups use their small and fragile power to say, "You can't understand me unless you're *like* me," where "like" means of a similar gender or race or other social grouping now acutely aware of its own historical disempowerment. "You can't understand me" sounds like an accusation, and also a warning not to try.

But it is simply not true that people can't understand those whose experiences and values are very different from their own. It isn't easy; it requires work; it takes a certain humility to learn how much of one's own way of seeing the world is dependent on features of oneself that one cannot easily imagine away. But it is possible, with concentrated effort, much willingness to listen to others, and genuine good faith. So perhaps "you can't understand me" shouldn't be understood as a statement about what's possible. Instead it might be heard as a demand that statements about me must be heard in my voice, or at least in the voice of someone who shares my experience and my point of view. "You can't understand me" is a way of saying that you can't flatten my perspective into your perspective on the world. It is a call to stop the effort to find the "view from nowhere" or the apparently point-of-viewless point of view. It is an attack on the conception of objectivity that sees one unitary and coherent point of view as privileged over all the others.

A serious problem for the legitimacy of public institutions occurs when truths become multiple, when stories proliferate in incommensurable versions, when different people with different ways of seeing become empowered to be heard in public debate. The problem is particularly evident in the law. How do courts continue to figure out "what happened" for the purposes of finding a resolution in disputes when the ideal in a multicultural society is no longer a single unassailable truth, but plural and various truths?

We can see the problem of multiple truths most clearly by focusing on consent. Consent is crucial to the legal status of many actions. Consent transforms actions from criminal to legal. For example, a surgical operation is converted from a severe battery to a legitimate procedure by the consent of the patient. Taking someone's car is converted from theft to borrowing by the consent of the owner. Determining whether relevant people have consented is, then, a crucial part of judging actions to be legal. And where disputants diverge over how consent is to be imagined, disputants will also diverge over basic issues of legitimacy.

People with different backgrounds and experiences have different experiences of consent. Consent is often associated with choice, but a great deal of the legitimating force of choice depends on how the choices are seen. Most people would agree that the gunman who approaches and says "Your money or your life" is giving you a choice, but it's hard to say

---

*From Kim Lane Scheppele, "The Reasonable Woman," in *The Responsive Community, Rights, and Responsibilities*, vol. I, issue 4, 1991. Reprinted here in abridged form by permission of *The Responsive Community*.

that you consented if you hand over your wallet. That's because it is widely recognized that almost everyone would see the "life" option as an unattractive choice. Handing over money feels, understandably, compelled, not chosen. But assume that the choice is between living with someone who beats you or moving out. Moving out sounds like the clear choice—unless you have no money, little chance of supporting yourself, and no independent support system to help you through the transition—and you believe that if you leave, the person you're living with will track you down and beat you worse than before. Men who are self-supporting and physically strong will tend to see that choice differently from women who are not. And if judges are men who assume their partial views represent the only truth, they may see women as having consented to stay, because, after all, the women chose to do so when they could have done otherwise. A judge who decides this way has no empathic imagination. He fails to see the choice as someone else might. He assumes that there is some single right answer in the choice, a right answer whose very claim to universality disguises the partiality of his own perspective. And with this totalizing point of view, his version of consent wins out over the real experience of feeling that one has no choice.

Rape is an area of law in which consent is crucial. If an accused rapist can demonstrate that the victim consented, sex is no longer rape. Many accused rapists use the consent defense at trial, forcing the focus of the trial onto the actions of the victim, who is almost always (and in some states has to be by statute) a woman. Though consent is defense to other crimes as well—theft, for example, or battery—consent poses a particular problem in rape cases, because consent to sex is often thought to be more problematic than consent to being beaten or having one's possessions taken. Sex, after all, is almost always emotionally complicated, and there may well be reasons for appearing to consent at the time and appearing not to have consented later. At least, that's what those who judge often think. This, of course, already tells us something crucial about consent—whether it will be believed in a particular context depends on its plausibility, judged against a set of implicit background standards. But those background standards may not always be shared by all those concerned, particularly the victims. Women have experiences of the world that are not the same as men's, especially when it comes to sex. And given the different perceptions of what is going on, women's views about consent in sex differ systematically from men's.

Let's look at one example. In *Rusk* v. *State*, a Maryland case, Eddie Rusk was convicted by a jury of raping a woman, referred to in the opinions only as Pat, whom he had met at a singles bar. When she said she was leaving, shortly after meeting him, Rusk asked Pat to drive him home. She agreed, drove him to his apartment in a part of the city that she didn't know, and refused his several invitations to come in. He took the car keys from the ignition and invited her in again. At the trial, Pat said that she was stranded in a strange and dangerous part of Baltimore. She said she believed it was unsafe to try to escape on foot and that she hoped to be able to convince Rusk to give back her car keys and to let her go. She followed him into his room and made no attempt to leave, even when he went down the hall to go to the bathroom. She asked for her car keys back and, when he refused, begged to be able to leave with her car. Rusk repeatedly said she couldn't, but he had no weapon and did not use overwhelming physical force. Rusk pulled her onto the bed and undressed her. Pat started to cry and Rusk put his hands on her throat and "started lightly to choke" her. She then asked, "If I do what you want, will you let me go without killing me?" and he answered yes. She performed oral sex, and then they had sexual intercourse, after which he gave her back the car keys and said she could leave. Charged with rape, Rusk claimed she had consented to sex with him. The appeals courts were called upon to determine whether her actions counted as consent.

This is where the 20 judges who heard the case on appeal (13 in the Court of Special Appeals, the intermediate appeals court in Maryland, and 7 in the Court of Appeals, the state supreme court) split all over the map. In the Court of Special Appeals, in 1979, the vote went 8–5 in favor of reversing the conviction, and in the Court of Appeals, in 1981, the vote was 4–3 in favor of reinstatement. The judges who wanted to overturn the conviction said that Rusk had not used enough force to overcome Pat's resistance if she had really meant not to consent; those who wanted to uphold the conviction said that Pat was afraid enough to make consent implausible.

The judges who found that Pat consented saw her options very differently from the way she reported them. Judge Thompson, for the Court of Special Appeals, noted that she could have sought help or tried to leave without her car. He minimized her reports that she was in a completely strange part of town and was frightened. Justice Cole, dissenting in the Maryland Court of Appeals, stressed that Pat was on an ordinary city street, that she was with a man who did not "grapple with her," and that she *followed* this man (Justice Cole's emphasis) into his apartment knowing what would happen if she did. "She certainly had to realize that they were not going upstairs to play Scrabble," Justice Cole observed.

The judges who found that Pat had *not* consented saw her options at the time more the way Pat said she did. Judge Wilner, dissenting in the Court of Special Appeals, quoted Pat's own words frequently throughout his description of the facts, and emphasized that Rusk's theft of her car keys was equivalent to a threat of force. And Justice Murphy, writing for the Court of Appeals, concluded Pat was "badly frightened . . . unable to think clearly . . . and believ[ed] that she had no other choice in the circumstances."

What these four opinions disagree about is precisely how to see her options and how she might have "reasonably" considered them. But, where the person whose consent is being constructed sees the world very differently from the judges, should judges be using universal (i.e., apparently point-of-viewless) standards that represent how a "reasonable man" would have acted at the time? Or should they consider how Pat herself, or a reasonable person with Pat's background, should have acted?

Good-faith efforts to understand the multiplicity of perspectives and the serious incommensurability of many points of view should make some difference here. Consent matters precisely because the consenter's point of view is crucial to the legitimacy of the actions she takes. To substitute what some hypothetical consenter unlike the particular person whose consent is being sought *would have* done in that circumstance undermines the very idea that makes consent a moral force—respect for the person's self-believed descriptions are checked not against the world that the individual sees but against a world that she does not see because she has a different socially grounded perspective.

In a number of areas of the law, courts already find ways to incorporate the distinctive social knowledge of socially diverse actors. In tort cases, for example, courts adopt some formulation, either explicitly or implicitly, that inquires into what the reasonable man would have done under the circumstances. As tort doctrine has evolved, the unitary reasonable man has multiplied into the reasonably prudent doctor, the reasonable pilot, and the ordinarily careful horse trainer, among other characters recognizable in law. This multiplication of types of persons shows that existing legal doctrine and con-

siderations of fairness do not require that everyone's perceptions be measured against the same social standard of reasonableness. But the law only incompletely recognizes that special knowledge is acquired not only in occupations but also in other sociological categories that give rise to different ways of seeing the world. The few cases that do mention a reasonable woman in tort law do so only for grammatical consistency, because one of the parties happens to be a woman, not because anything different results from noticing the gender of the parties. The reasonable woman is just like the reasonable man, only with a different pronoun.

But the reasonable woman could be a more sociologically powerful construction if we believed that everyone has "expertise" obtained from living a particular life in a particular social environment. Some of that expertise comes from living as a woman or a person of color. The choices each of us makes, and the degree of consent we express in those choices, depend on how our expertise tells us to evaluate the availability and attractiveness of alternatives. Being female or a person of color in this society is relevant to one's social point of view, and the law would better serve everyone if it recognized that the melting pot no longer melts all points of view into one, if indeed it ever did.

Considering a reasonable woman standard with gender-specific content is, in some ways, nothing new, though it is still controversial. In some areas of legal doctrine, women's unique perspectives have already been taken into account in this way, though only quite recently. In sexual harassment cases, a number of courts have said that the point of view of the reasonable woman should be adopted in determining whether men's behavior in the workplace is disruptive enough to qualify as sexual harassment. In *Ellison* v. *Brady* (1991), for example, the Ninth Circuit Court of Appeals found that any reasonable woman would have found the persistent and threatening "love letters" from her co-worker objectionable, reasoning:

> *We adopt the perspective of a reasonable woman primarily because we believe that a sex-blind reasonable person standard tends to be male-biased and tends to systematically ignore the experiences of women. The reasonable woman standard does not establish a higher level of protection for women than men. . . . Instead, a gender-conscious examination of sexual harassment enables women to*

*participate in the workplace on an equal foot-
ing with men.*

The reasonable woman was also decisive in *Robinson* v. *Jacksonville Shipyards* (Federal District Court,
Middle District in Florida, 1991), and in *Yates* v. *Avco
Corp* (6th Circuit, 1987). And it's not only in sexual
harassment cases that the reasonable woman makes
an appearance. She appears in murder or assault cases
where a woman has killed or injured her attacker. In
State v. *Wanrow* (1977), the Supreme Court of Washington reversed Yvonne Wanrow's conviction for assault and murder of a man who had allegedly molested her children. The court reversed because the
jury had been instructed to consider the woman defendant's actions according to the standard of the reasonable man:

> *[The jury instruction] not only establishes an
> objective standard, but through the persistent
> use of the masculine gender leaves the jury
> with the impression the objective standard to
> be applied is that applicable to an altercation
> between two men. The impression created—
> that a 5'4" woman with a cast on her leg and
> using a crutch must, under the law, somehow
> repel an assault by a 6'2" intoxicated man
> without employing weapons in her defense,
> unless the jury finds her determination of the
> degree of danger to be objectively reasonable—
> constitutes a separate and distinct misstate-
> ment of the law and, in the context of this case,
> violates the respondent's right to equal protec-
> tion of the law. The respondent was entitled to
> have the jury consider her actions in the light
> of her own perceptions of the situation, includ-
> ing those perceptions which were the product
> of our nation's "long and unfortunate history
> of sex discrimination."*

The "reasonable woman," then, has been accepted by
some judges (though rejected by others) when the
standard would involve importing a substantive judgment into the law that is different from the judgment
of the reasonable man. But the places where the reasonable woman has already won some qualified acceptance in legal doctrine present fewer serious
challenges to business-as-usual in the law than the
rape cases do. In sexual harassment complaints, the
relevant law is Title VII of the Civil Rights Act of 1964,
whose primary purpose is to remedy past discrimination by stopping present and future discrimination.

Seeing the harm from the point of view of the class
explicitly protected by the statute is not a radical
move, particularly given that the litigated complaints
are civil cases. In the criminal cases with women defendants, the *mens rea* ("guilty mind") requirement
for almost all crimes already focuses inquiry on the
point of view of *this particular defendant*. If this particular defendant happened to be a woman, it would
stand to reason that her perspective should be given
due consideration without radically challenging existing law. Neither the civil cases involving sexual harassment nor the criminal cases involving women
defendants contest the point of view already built into
the doctrine for other reasons. But the rape cases are
different.

Using the reasonable woman standard in rape
cases like *Rusk* means asking the court to see the criminal nature of the defendant's conduct as dependent
upon the *victim's* point of view. This is a radical departure for the criminal law, which customarily considers the victim to be just another witness at the trial
and which privileges the perspective of the defendant
through the *mens rea* requirement. But most crimes
have as part of their definitions the lack of consent of
the victim. For example, as we have seen, theft becomes borrowing if the owner consents, and battery
becomes legitimate surgery with the consent of the
patient. Usually consent isn't at issue in criminal trials
for battery or theft. But in rape cases, consent is used
frequently as a defense, and consent in rape has been
taken as consent from men's point of view. Eleven of
the 20 judges who heard the *Rusk* case adopted this
perspective and the conviction was upheld only because the highest court had a slim majority in Pat's
favor. Given the overwhelming focus in criminal cases
on the defendant's perceptions of events (even if the
defendant is a woman, as we have seen), introducing
the perspective of the reasonable woman as a victim
represents a major change.

The reasonable woman victim is not in the
usual cast of characters of rape cases. Instead, the consent of the rape victim is usually assumed to be a flat
fact that can be determined by an outsider's assessment of the evidence: Did she kick and scream? Did
she try every avenue of escape? Was her fear the sort
of fear I (the judge) would have had under the circumstances? Under these questions, the power of legiti-
mation that consent is supposed to bring evaporates.
The consent that is found does not respect the potential consenter's perspective. And if consent is to have
the moral force assigned to it in liberal moral theory,
the consent must not be imposed by someone who

does not attempt to understand the potential consenter's point of view.

Does this mean that a search for consent should always be a quest for what *this* particular person thought at *that* particular time, no matter what the reasonableness of the perception? It would be easy, using the sort of perspective I've been encouraging here, to have as many standards as there are potential consenters and to make the legitimacy of actions requiring consent rest on detailed inquiries in individual instances. And that would be the best possible result for women who are victims of sexual assault. But there are some claims that defendants can make here that need to be considered as well. Criminal law is a vehicle for the expression of the moral standards of the community. The penalties are harsh and the stigma great for criminal conviction. As a result, criminal prosecutions are more serious for the defendants than ordinary civil trials. To base criminal convictions on potentially idiosyncratic perceptions of victims is unfair to those accused. If a woman says yes while meaning no, for example, we cannot expect the accused rapist to figure out what she means. This is why the reasonable woman standard has something to offer here. Adopting the reasonable woman as a social construct in the law allows women's views to have a strong impact on the outcome of rape trials while simultaneously putting men on notice that they must consider how women's perceptions of sexualized situations may be very different from their own. The reasonable woman standard does not require men to guess what is in each woman's mind, but it does require men to respect that women have the right to claim difference. It requires men to see the world through women's eyes.

For women, politically disadvantaged in the construction of sexuality, gender crucially shapes the world. As we saw in the *Rusk* case, Pat, like most women, learned to fear city streets, to count on the men she knew to protect her from lurking dangers.

Women don't sexualize situations as quickly as men do, and so they may be slower to recognize danger in the first place. Pat's choice to go into Rusk's room because she was frightened to walk alone at night was an understandable choice, in the same way that the choice to stay in a dreadful living situation is understandable when the alternative is a reasonably seen threat of homelessness. Pat said "no" to sex. Rusk tried to override that "no" by limiting her means of escape. Pat decided it was less dangerous to go with Rusk and not fight him off physically than to risk the streets alone at night. The fact that she chose this option doesn't mean that she consented to sex with him. Her "no" meant no. The reasonable man, who does not fear city streets the way a reasonable woman does and who can fight physically with the expectation of success, may have tried to leave or fight. He would have had other options to reinforce what he meant by "no."

Women, people of color, and other politically disadvantaged groups are ill-served by a standardized concept of a reasonable man or an average person or a point-of-viewless point of view. So, the multiplication of standards against which perception might be judged is crucial to deciding whether women or people of color might have in fact consented to the conditions that the law holds them responsible for. And for starters, women in rape cases will see the world differently than men who face similar choices.

The intense tribalism of our time is a sign that conditions are improving for those whose voices have been silenced in the past. Women and people of color are calling for the recognition of multiple truths and many versions to replace the false unity of totalizing standards. We all owe each other a good-faith attempt to understand how people differently situated in the social order may reasonably see the same set of choices differently. In a pluralistic community, empathy is one of our most crucial resources. Extending the standard of the reasonable woman would be one good way to bring empathy to the law.

STATE V. RUSK*

Court of Appeals of Maryland, 1981

Murphy, C.J. Edward Rusk was found guilty by a jury . . . of second degree rape in violation of Maryland Code Art. 27, § 463(a)(1), which provides in pertinent part:

> *A person is guilty of rape in the second degree if the person engages in vaginal intercourse with another person:*
> *(1) By force or threat of force against the will and without the consent of the other person. . . .*

On appeal, the Court of Special Appeals, sitting en banc, reversed the conviction; it concluded by an 8–5 majority that in view of the prevailing law as set forth in *Hazel* v. *State,* 221 Md. 464, 157 A.2d 922 (1960), insufficient evidence of Rusk's guilt had been adduced at the trial to permit the case to go to the jury. We granted certiorari to consider whether the Court of Special Appeals properly applied the principles of *Hazel.* . . .

At the trial, the 21-year-old prosecuting witness, Pat, testified that on the evening of September 21, 1977, she attended a high school alumnae meeting where she met a girl friend, Terry. After the meeting, Terry and Pat agreed to drive in their respective cars to Fells Point to have a few drinks. . . . They went to a bar where . . . Rusk approached and said "hello" to Terry. Terry, who was then conversing with another individual, momentarily interrupted her conversation and said "Hi, Eddie." Rusk then began talking with Pat and during their conversation both of them acknowledged being separated from their respective spouses and having a child. Pat told Rusk that she had to go home . . . [and] Rusk requested a ride to his apartment. Although Pat did not know Rusk, she thought that Terry knew him. She thereafter agreed to give him a ride. Pat cautioned Rusk on the way to the car that "I'm just giving a ride home, you know, as a friend, not anything to be, you know, thought of other than a ride." . . .

After a twenty-minute drive, they arrived at Rusk's apartment. . . . Pat testified that she was totally unfamiliar with the neighborhood. She parked the car at the curb . . . but left the engine running. Rusk asked Pat to come in, but she refused. . . . Pat said that Rusk was fully aware that she did not want to accompany him to his room. Notwithstanding her repeated refusals, Pat testified that Rusk reached over and turned off the ignition to her car and took her car keys. He got out of the car, walked over to her side, opened the door and said, "Now, will you come up?" Pat explained her subsequent actions:

> *At that point, because I was scared, because he had my car keys. I didn't know what to do. I was someplace I didn't even know where I was. It was in the city. I didn't know whether to run. I really didn't think at that point, what to do.*
> *Now, I know that I should have blown the horn. I should have run. There were a million things I could have done. I was scared, at that point, and I didn't do any of them.*

Pat testified that at this moment she feared that Rusk would rape her. She said: "[I]t was the way he looked at me, and said 'Come on up, come on up'; and when he took the keys, I knew that was wrong."

It was then about 1 A.M. Pat accompanied Rusk across the street into a totally dark house. . . . Rusk unlocked the door to his one-room apartment, and turned on the light. According to Pat, he told her to sit down. She sat in a chair beside the bed. Rusk sat on the bed. After Rusk talked for a few minutes, he left the room for about one to five minutes. Pat remained seated in the chair. She made no noise and did not attempt to leave. She said that she did not notice a telephone in the room. When Rusk returned,

*289 Md. 230, 424 A.2d 720 (1981). Endnotes omitted.

he turned off the light and sat down on the bed. Pat asked if she could leave; she told him that she wanted to go home and "didn't want to come up." She said, "Now, [that] I came up, can I go?" Rusk, who was still in possession of her car keys, said he wanted her to stay.

Rusk then asked Pat to get on the bed with him. He pulled her by the arms to the bed and began to undress her. . . . Pat removed the rest of her clothing, and then removed Rusk's pants because "he asked me to do it." After they were both undressed Rusk started kissing Pat as she was lying on her back. Pat explained what happened next:

> *I was still begging him to please let, you know, let me leave. I said, "you can get a lot of other girls down there, for what you want," and he just kept saying, "no"; and then I was really scared, because I can't describe, you know, what was said. It was more the look in his eyes; and I said, at that point—I didn't know what to say; and I said, "If I do what you want, will you let me go without killing me?" Because I didn't know, at that point, what he was going to do; and I started to cry; and when I did, he put his hands on my throat, and started lightly to choke me; and I said, "If I do what you want, will you let me go?" And he said, yes, and at that time, I proceeded to do what he wanted me to.*

Pat testified that Rusk made her perform oral sex and then vaginal intercourse.

Immediately after the intercourse, Pat asked if she could leave. She testified that Rusk said, "Yes," after which she got up and got dressed and Rusk returned her car keys. She said that Rusk then

> *walked me to my car, and asked if he could see me again; and I said, "Yes"; and he asked me for my telephone number; and I said, "No, I'll see you down Fells Point sometime," just so I could leave.*

Pat testified that she "had no intention of meeting him again." She asked him for directions out of the neighborhood and left.

. . . As she sat in her car reflecting on the incident, Pat said she began to

> *wonder what would happen if I hadn't of done what he wanted me to do. So I thought the right thing to do was to go report it, and I went from there to Hillendale to find a police car.*

She reported the incident to the police at about 3:15 A.M. . . .

Rusk and two of his friends, Michael Trimp and David Carroll, testified on his behalf. According to Trimp, they went in Carroll's car to Buggs' bar to dance, drink and "tr[y] to pick up some ladies." Rusk stayed at the bar, while the others went to get something to eat.

Trimp and Carroll next saw Rusk walking down the street arm-in-arm with a lady whom Trimp was unable to identify. . . .

Carroll's testimony corroborated Trimp's. He saw Rusk walking down the street arm-in-arm with a woman. He said "[s]he was kind of like, you know, snuggling up to him like. . . . She was hanging all over him then." Carroll was fairly certain that Pat was the woman who was with Rusk. . . .

According to Rusk, when they arrived in front of his apartment Pat parked the car and turned the engine off. They sat for several minutes "petting each other." . . . Rusk testified that Pat came willingly to his room and that at no time did he make threatening facial expressions. . . . Rusk explained that after the intercourse, Pat "got uptight."

> *Well, she started to cry. She said that—she said, "You guys are all alike," she says, "just out for," you know, "one thing." . . . And she said, that she just wanted to leave; and I said, "Well, okay"; and she walked out to the car. I walked out to the car. She got in the car and left.*

Rusk denied placing his hands on Pat's throat or attempting to strangle her. He also denied using force or threats of force to get Pat to have intercourse with him.

In reversing Rusk's second degree rape conviction, the Court of Special Appeals quoting from *Hazel*, noted that:

> *Force is an essential element of the crime [of rape] and to justify a conviction, the evidence must warrant a conclusion either that the victim resisted and her resistance was overcome by force or that she was prevented from resisting by threats to her safety.*

Writing for the majority, Judge Thompson said:

> *In all of the victim's testimony we have been unable to see any resistance on her part to the sex acts and certainly can we see no fear as would overcome her attempt to resist or escape*

as required by Hazel. *Possession of the keys by the accused may have deterred her vehicular escape but hardly a departure seeking help in the rooming house or in the street. We must say that "the way he looked" fails utterly to support the fear required by* Hazel.

. . . Of course, due process requirements mandate that a criminal conviction not be obtained if the evidence does not reasonably support a finding of guilt beyond a reasonable doubt. However, as the Supreme Court made clear in *Jackson* v. *Virginia,* 443 U.S. 307 (1979), the reviewing court does not ask itself whether *it* believes that the evidence established guilt beyond a reasonable doubt; rather, the applicable standard is "whether, after viewing the evidence in the light most favorable to the prosecution, *any* rational trier of fact could have found the essential elements of the crime beyond a reasonable doubt." (emphasis in original). . . .

The Court [in *Hazel*] noted that lack of consent is generally established through proof of resistance or by proof that the victim failed to resist because of fear. The degree of fear necessary to obviate the need to prove resistance, and thereby establish lack of consent, was defined in the following manner: "The kind of fear which would render resistance by a woman unnecessary to support a conviction of rape includes, but is not necessarily limited to, a fear of death or serious bodily harm, or a fear so extreme as to preclude resistance, or a fear which would well nigh render her mind incapable of continuing to resist, or a fear that so overpowers her that she does not dare resist."

. . . While *Hazel* made it clear that the victim's fear had to be genuine, it did not pass upon whether a real but unreasonable fear of imminent death or serious bodily harm would suffice. The vast majority of jurisdictions have required that the victim's fear be reasonably grounded in order to obviate the need for either proof of actual force on the part of the assailant or physical resistance on the part of the victim. We think that, generally, this is the correct standard. . . .

We think the reversal of Rusk's conviction by the Court of Special Appeals was in error for the fundamental reason so well expressed in the dissenting opinion by Judge Wilner when he observed that the majority had "trampled upon the first principle of appellate restraint [because it had] substituted [its] own view of the evidence (and the inferences that may fairly be drawn from it) for that of the judge and jury

[and had thereby] improperly invaded the province allotted to those tribunals." In view of the evidence adduced at the trial, the reasonableness of Pat's apprehension of fear was plainly a question of fact for the jury to determine. . . . Quite obviously, the jury disbelieved Rusk and believed Pat's testimony. From her testimony, the jury could have reasonably concluded that the taking of her car keys was intended by Rusk to immobilize her alone, late at night, in a neighborhood with which she was not familiar; that after Pat had repeatedly refused to enter his apartment, Rusk commanded in firm tones that she do so; that Pat was badly frightened and feared that Rusk intended to rape her; . . . that Pat was afraid that Rusk would kill her unless she submitted; that she began to cry and Rusk then put his hands on her throat and began "lightly to choke" her; that Pat asked him if he would let her go without killing her if she complied with his demands; that Rusk gave an affirmative response, after which she finally submitted.

Just where persuasion ends and force begins in cases like the present is essentially a factual issue. . . . Considering all of the evidence in the case, with particular focus upon the actual force applied by Rusk to Pat's neck, we conclude that the jury could rationally find that the essential elements of second degree rape had been established and that Rusk was guilty of that offense beyond a reasonable doubt. . . .

COLE, J., dissenting. [W]hen one of the essential elements of a crime is not sustained by the evidence, the conviction of the defendant cannot stand as a matter of law.

The majority, in applying this standard, concludes that "[i]n view of the evidence adduced at the trial, the reasonableness of Pat's apprehension of fear was plainly a question of fact for the jury to determine." In so concluding, the majority has skipped over the crucial issue. It seems to me that whether the prosecutrix's fear is reasonable becomes a question only after the court determines that the defendant's conduct under the circumstances was reasonably calculated to give rise to a fear on her part to the extent that she was unable to resist. . . .

While courts no longer require a female to resist to the utmost or to resist where resistance would be foolhardy, they do require her acquiescence in the act of intercourse to stem from fear generated by something of substance. She may not simply say, "I was really scared," and thereby transform consent or mere unwillingness into submission by force. These words do not transform a seducer into a rapist. She must follow the natural instinct of every proud female to resist, by more than mere words, the violation of her person by a stranger or an unwelcomed friend. She must make it plain that she regards such sexual acts as abhorrent and repugnant to her natural sense of pride. She must resist unless the defendant has objectively manifested his intent to use physical force to accomplish his purpose. The law regards rape as a crime of violence. The majority today attenuates this proposition. It declares the innocence of an at best distraught young woman. It does not demonstrate the defendant's guilt of the crime of rape.

. . . The majority suggests that "from her testimony the jury could have reasonably concluded that the taking of her keys was intended by Rusk to immobilize her alone, late at night, in a neighborhood with which she was unfamiliar. . . ." But on what facts does the majority so conclude? There is no evidence descriptive of the tone of his voice; her testimony indicates only the bare statement quoted above. . . .

She also testified that she was afraid of "the way he looked," and afraid of his statement, "come on up, come on up." But what can the majority conclude from this statement coupled with a "look" that remained undescribed? There is no evidence whatsoever to suggest that this was anything other than a pattern of conduct consistent with the ordinary seduction of a female acquaintance who at first suggests her disinclination. . . .

The majority relies on the trial court's statement that the defendant responded affirmatively to her question "If I do what you want, will you let me go without killing me?" The majority further suggests that the jury could infer the defendant's affirmative response. The facts belie such inference since by the prosecutrix's own testimony the defendant made *no* response. *He said nothing!*

She then testified that she started to cry and he "started lightly to choke" her, whatever that means. Obviously, the choking was not of any persuasive significance. During this "choking" she was able to talk. She said "If I do what you want will you let me go?" It was at this point that the defendant said yes.

I find it incredible for the majority to conclude that on these facts, without more, a woman was *forced* to commit oral sex upon the defendant and then to engage in vaginal intercourse.

[T]here are no acts or conduct on the part of the defendant to suggest that these fears were created by the defendant or that he made any objective, identifiable threats to her which would give rise to this woman's failure to flee, summon help, scream, or make physical resistance. . . .

In my judgment the State failed to prove the essential element of force beyond a reasonable doubt and, therefore, the judgment of conviction should be reversed. . . .

REGINA V. MORGAN*

House of Lords, 1976

The defendant Morgan and three other defendants were convicted of the forcible rape of Morgan's wife. Morgan's liability rested on his having aided and abetted the three others. The Court of Appeals affirmed all the convictions but certified the following question to the House of Lords:

Whether in rape the defendant can properly be convicted notwithstanding that he in fact believed that the woman consented, if such a belief was not based on reasonable grounds.

[The applicable statute stated simply: "*Rape—* (1) It is a felony for a man to rape a woman."]

---

*[1976] A.C. 182. Endnotes deleted.

LORD HAILSHAM of St. Marylebone. . . . The question arises in the following way. The appellant Morgan and his three co-appellants, who were all members of the RAF, spent the evening of 15th August 1973 in one another's company. The appellant Morgan was significantly older than the other three, and considerably senior to them in rank. He was . . . married to the alleged victim, but not, it seems, at the time habitually sleeping in the same bed. [B]y the time the appellants arrived at Morgan's house, Mrs. Morgan was already in bed and asleep, until she was awoken by their presence.

According to the version of the facts which she gave in evidence, and which was evidently accepted by the jury, she was aroused from her sleep, . . . held by each of her limbs, . . . while each of the three young appellants in turn had intercourse with her in the presence of the others. . . .

According to Mrs. Morgan she consented to none of this and made her opposition to what was being done very plain indeed. . . .

All four appellants explained in the witness box that they had spent the evening together in Wolverhampton, and by the time of the alleged offences had had a good deal to drink. Their original intention had been to find some women in the town but, when this failed, Morgan made the surprising suggestion to the others that they should all return to his home and have sexual intercourse with his wife. According to the three younger appellants (but not according to Morgan who described this part of their story as "lying") Morgan told them that they must not be surprised if his wife struggled a bit, since she was "kinky" and this was the only way in which she could get "turned on." However this may be, it is clear that Morgan did invite his three companions home in order that they might have sexual intercourse with his wife and, no doubt, he may well have led them in one way or another to believe that she would consent to their doing so. This, however, would only be matter predisposing them to believe that Mrs. Morgan consented, and would not in any way establish that, at the time, they believed she did consent whilst they were having intercourse.

I need not enter into the details of what the appellants said happened after they had arrived at the house. As I have said they admitted that some degree of struggle took place in the wife's bedroom. But all asserted that after she got into the double bedroom she not merely consented to but actively co-operated with and enjoyed what was being done. . . .

The choice before the jury was thus between two stories each wholly incompatible with the other, and in my opinion it would have been quite sufficient for the judge, after suitable warnings about the burden of proof, corroboration, separate verdicts and the admissibility of the statements only against the makers, to tell the jury that they must really choose between the two versions. . . .

The certified question arises because counsel for the appellants raised the question whether, even if the victim [objected], the appellants may . . . have honestly believed that she did [not]. [I]n the summing-up [to the jury] . . . [t]he learned judge said:

> [T]he prosecution have to prove that each defendant intended to have sexual intercourse with this woman without her consent. Not merely that he intended to have intercourse with her but that he intended to have intercourse without her consent. Therefore if the defendant believed or may have believed that Mrs. Morgan consented to him having sexual intercourse with her, then there would be no such intent in his mind and he would be not guilty of the offence of rape, but such a belief must be honestly held by the defendant in the first place. He must really believe that. And, secondly, his belief must be a reasonable belief; such a belief as a reasonable man would entertain if he applied his mind and thought about the matter. It is not enough for a defendant to rely upon a belief, even though he honestly held it, if it was completely fanciful; contrary to every indication which could be given which would carry some weight with a reasonable man.

It is on the second proposition about the mental element that the appellants concentrate their criticism. An honest belief in consent, they contend, is enough. It matters not whether it be also reasonable. No doubt a defendant will wish to raise argument or lead evidence to show that this belief was reasonable, since this will support its honesty. No doubt the prosecution will seek to cross-examine or raise arguments or adduce evidence to undermine the contention that the belief is reasonable, because, in the nature of the case, the fact that a belief cannot reasonably be held is a strong ground for saying that it was not in fact held honestly at all. Nonetheless, the appellants contend, the crux of the matter, the factum probandum, or rather the fact to be refuted by the prosecution, is honesty and not honesty plus reasonableness. . . .

The beginning of wisdom in all the "mens rea" cases to which our attention was called is, as was pointed out by Stephen, J., in *R. v. Tolson,* [23 Q.B.D. 168 (1889)], that "mens rea" means a number of quite different things in relation to different crimes. . . .

Once one has accepted, what seems to me abundantly clear, that the prohibited act in rape is non-consensual sexual intercourse, and that the guilty state of mind is an intention to commit it, it seems to me to follow as a matter of inexorable logic that there is no room either for a "defence" of honest belief or mistake, or of a defence of honest and reasonable belief and mistake. Either the prosecution proves that the accused had the requisite intent, or it does not. In the former case it succeeds, and in the latter it fails. Since honest belief clearly negatives intent, the reasonableness or otherwise of that belief can only be evidence for or against the view that the belief and therefore the intent was actually held. . . .

For the above reasons I would answer the question certified in the negative, but would apply the proviso to s. 2(1) of the Criminal Appeal Act 1968 on the ground that no miscarriage of justice has or conceivably could have occurred. In my view, therefore these appeals should be dismissed.

LORD FRASER of Tulleybelton. . . . The argument for the Crown in support of an affirmative answer to the question in this case was not supported by any English decision on rape. It was supported by reference to English decisions in relation to other offences which are more or less analogous to rape. . . . The English case upon which most reliance was placed was *Reg. v. Tolson,* 23 Q.B.D. 168, which was concerned with bigamy, and which decided that a bona fide belief *on reasonable grounds* in the death of the husband at the time of the second marriage afforded a good defence to the indictment for bigamy. The main argument in the case was concerned with the question whether a mistaken belief could be a defence to a charge of bigamy at all, and comparatively little attention was given to the subsidiary point of whether the belief had to be based upon reasonable grounds. The case seems to me therefore of only limited assistance for the present purpose. . . . The difficulty of arguing by analogy from one offence to another is strikingly illustrated by reference to the case of *Reg. v. Prince* (1875) 13 Cox C.C. 138. That case dealt with abduction of a girl under the age of 16, an offence created by section 55 of the Act of 1861. Bramwell, B., with whom five other judges concurred, held that a mistaken and reasonable belief by the defendant that the abducted girl was aged 16 or more was no excuse, because abduction of a young girl was immoral as well as illegal, although a mistaken and reasonable belief by the defendant that he had the consent of the girl's father would have been an excuse. If such differences can exist about mistaken beliefs of different facts in one offence, it is surely dangerous to argue from one offence to another. No doubt a rapist, who mistakenly believes that the woman is consenting to intercourse, must be behaving immorally, by committing fornication or adultery. But those forms of immoral conduct are not intended to be struck at by the law against rape; indeed, they are not now considered appropriate to be visited with penalties of the criminal law at all. There seems therefore to be no reason why they should affect the consequences of the mistaken belief. . . .

For these reasons, I am of the opinion that there is no authority which compels me to answer the question in what I would regard as an illogical way. I would therefore answer the question in the negative—i.e. in favour of the accused. But for the reasons stated by . . . Lord Hailsham . . . I would apply the proviso to the Criminal Appeal Act of 1968 . . . and I would refuse the appeal. APPEALS DISMISSED.

STATE V. KELLY*

Supreme Court of New Jersey, 1984

WILENTZ, C.J. . . . On May 24, 1980, defendant, Gladys Kelly, stabbed her husband, Ernest, with a pair of scissors. He died shortly thereafter at a nearby hospital. . . .

Ms. Kelly was indicted for murder. At trial, she did not deny stabbing her husband, but asserted that her action was in self-defense. To establish the requisite state of mind for her self-defense claim, Ms. Kelly called Dr. Lois Veronen as an expert witness to testify about the battered-woman's syndrome. After hearing a lengthy voir dire examination of Dr. Veronen, the trial court ruled that expert testimony concerning the syndrome was inadmissible on the self-defense issue. . . .

Mrs. Kelly was convicted of reckless manslaughter. [We] reverse.

The Kellys had a stormy marriage. Some of the details of their relationship, especially the stabbing, are disputed. The following is Ms. Kelly's version of what happened—a version that the jury could have accepted and, if they had, a version that would make the proffered expert testimony not only relevant, but critical.

The day after the marriage, Mr. Kelly got drunk and knocked Ms. Kelly down. Although a period of calm followed the initial attack, the next seven years were accompanied by periodic and frequent beatings, sometimes as often as once a week. During the attacks, which generally occurred when Mr. Kelly was drunk, he threatened to kill Ms. Kelly and to cut off parts of her body if she tried to leave him. Mr. Kelly often moved out of the house after an attack, later returning with a promise that he would change his ways. Until the day of the homicide, only one of the attacks had taken place in public.

The day before the stabbing, Gladys and Ernest went shopping. They did not have enough money to buy food for the entire week, so Ernest said he would give his wife more money the next day.

The following morning he left for work. Ms. Kelly next saw her husband late that afternoon at a friend's house. She had gone there with her daughter, Annette, to ask Ernest for money to buy food. He told her to wait until they got home, and shortly thereafter the Kellys left. After walking past several houses, Mr. Kelly, who was drunk, angrily asked "What the hell did you come around here for?" He then grabbed the collar of her dress, and the two fell to the ground. He choked her by pushing his fingers against her throat, punched or hit her face, and bit her leg.

A crowd gathered on the street. Two men from the crowd separated them, just as Gladys felt that she was "passing out" from being choked. Fearing that Annette had been pushed around in the crowd, Gladys then left to look for her. . . .

After finding her daughter, Ms. Kelly then observed Mr. Kelly running toward her with his hands raised. Within seconds he was right next to her. Unsure of whether he had armed himself while she was looking for their daughter, and thinking that he had come back to kill her, she grabbed a pair of scissors from her pocketbook. She tried to scare him away, but instead stabbed him.[1]

The central question in this case is whether the trial court erred in its exclusion of expert testimony on the battered-woman's syndrome. That testimony was intended to explain defendant's state of mind and bolster her claim of self-defense. We shall first examine the nature of the battered-woman's syndrome and then consider the expert testimony proffered in this case and its relevancy. . . .

As the problem of battered women has begun to receive more attention, sociologists and psychologists have begun to focus on the effects a sustained pattern of physical and psychological abuse can have on a woman. The effects of such abuse are what some scientific observers have termed "the battered-woman's syndrome," a series of common characteris-

---

*478 A.2d 364 (1984). Endnotes deleted. Text originally appearing as a footnote now appears as an endnote.

tics that appear in women who are abused physically and psychologically over an extended period of time by the dominant male figure in their lives. Dr. Lenore Walker, a prominent writer on the battered-woman's syndrome, defines the battered woman as one

> *who is repeatedly subjected to any forceful physical or psychological behavior by a man in order to coerce her to do something he wants her to do without concern for her rights. Battered women include wives or women in any form of intimate relationships with men. Furthermore, in order to be classified as a battered woman, the couple must go through the battering cycle at least twice. Any woman may find herself in an abusive relationship with a man once. If it occurs a second time, and she remains in the situation, she is defined as a battered woman. [L. Walker, The Battered Woman (1979) at xv].*

According to Dr. Walker, relationships characterized by physical abuse tend to develop battering cycles. Violent behavior directed at the woman occurs in three distinct and repetitive stages that vary both in duration and intensity depending on the individuals involved.

Phase one of the battering cycle is referred to as the "tension-building stage," during which the battering male engages in minor battering incidents and verbal abuse while the woman, beset by fear and tension, attempts to be as placating and passive as possible in order to stave off more serious violence.

Phase two of the battering cycle is the "acute battering incident." At some point during phase one, the tension between the battered woman and the batterer becomes intolerable and more serious violence inevitable. The triggering event that initiates phase two is most often an internal or external event in the life of the battering male, but provocation for more severe violence is sometimes provided by the woman who can no longer tolerate or control her phase-one anger and anxiety.

Phase three of the battering cycle is characterized by extreme contrition and loving behavior on the part of the battering male. During this period the man will often mix his pleas for forgiveness and protestations of devotion with promises to seek professional help, to stop drinking, and to refrain from further violence. For some couples, this period of relative calm may last as long as several months, but in a battering relationship the affection and contrition of the man will eventually fade and phase one of the cycle will start anew.

The cyclical nature of battering behavior helps explain why more women simply do not leave their abusers. The loving behavior demonstrated by the batterer during phase three reinforces whatever hopes these women might have for their mate's reform and keeps them bound to the relationship. R. Langley & R. Levy, Wife Beating: The Silent Crisis 112–14 (1977).

Some women may even perceive the battering cycle as normal, especially if they grew up in a violent household. . . . Other women, however, become so demoralized and degraded by the fact that they cannot predict or control the violence that they sink into a state of psychological paralysis and become unable to take any action at all to improve or alter the situation. There is a tendency in battered women to believe in the omnipotence or strength of their battering husbands and thus to feel that any attempt to resist them is hopeless.

In addition to these psychological impacts, external social and economic factors often make it difficult for some women to extricate themselves from battering relationships. A woman without independent financial resources who wishes to leave her husband often finds it difficult to do so because of a lack of material and social resources. . . . Thus, in a violent confrontation where the first reaction might be to flee, women realize soon that there may be no place to go. Moreover, the stigma that attaches to a woman who leaves the family unit without her children undoubtedly acts as a further deterrent to moving out.

In addition, battered women, when they want to leave the relationship, are typically unwilling to reach out and confide in their friends, family, or the police, either out of shame and humiliation, fear of reprisal by their husband, or the feeling they will not be believed.

Dr. Walker and other commentators have identified several common personality traits of the battered woman: low self-esteem, traditional beliefs about the home, the family, and the female sex role, tremendous feelings of guilt that their marriages are failing, and the tendency to accept responsibility for the batterer's actions.

Finally, battered women are often hesitant to leave a battering relationship because, in addition to their hope of reform on the part of their spouse, they harbor a deep concern about the possible response leaving might provoke in their mates. They literally become trapped by their own fear. Case histories are replete with instances in which a battered wife left her husband only to have him pursue her and subject her to an even more brutal attack.

The combination of all these symptoms—resulting from sustained psychological and physical trauma compounded by aggravating social and economic factors—constitutes the battered-woman's syndrome. Only by understanding these unique pressures that force battered women to remain with their mates, despite their long-standing and reasonable fear of severe bodily harm and the isolation that being a battered woman creates, can a battered woman's state of mind be accurately and fairly understood.

The voir dire testimony of Dr. Veronen, sought to be introduced by defendant Gladys Kelly, conformed essentially to this outline of the battered-woman's syndrome. . . .

In addition, Dr. Veronen was prepared to testify as to how, as a battered woman, Gladys Kelly perceived her situation at the time of the stabbing, and why, in her opinion, defendant did not leave her husband despite the constant beatings she endured.

Whether expert testimony on the battered-woman's syndrome should be admitted in this case depends on whether it is relevant to defendant's claim of self-defense, and, in any event, on whether the proffer meets the standards for admission of expert testimony in this state. We examine first the law of self-defense and consider whether the expert testimony is relevant.

. . . The use of force against another in self-defense is justifiable "when the actor reasonably believes that such force is immediately necessary for the purpose of protecting himself against the use of unlawful force by such other person on the present occasion." N.J.S.A. 2C:3–4(a). Further limitations exist when deadly force is used in self-defense. The use of such deadly force is not justifiable

> *unless the actor reasonably believes that such force is necessary to protect himself against death or serious bodily harm. . . . [N.J.S.A. 2C: 3–4(b)(2)].*

Gladys Kelly claims that she stabbed her husband in self-defense, believing he was about to kill her. The gist of the State's case was that Gladys Kelly was the aggressor, that she consciously intended to kill her husband, and that she certainly was not acting in self-defense.

The credibility of Gladys Kelly is a critical issue in this case. If the jury does not believe Gladys Kelly's account, it cannot find she acted in self-defense. The expert testimony offered was directly relevant to one of the critical elements of that account, namely, what Gladys Kelly believed at the time of the stabbing, and was thus material to establish the honesty of her stated belief that she was in imminent danger of death. . . .

As can be seen from our discussion of the expert testimony, Dr. Veronen would have bolstered Gladys Kelly's credibility. Specifically, by showing that her experience, although concededly difficult to comprehend, was common to that of other women who had been in similarly abusive relationships, Dr. Veronen would have helped the jury understand that Gladys Kelly could have honestly feared that she would suffer serious bodily harm from her husband's attacks, yet still remain with him. This, in turn, would support Ms. Kelly's testimony about her state of mind (that is, that she honestly feared serious bodily harm) at the time of the stabbing. . . .

We also find the expert testimony relevant to the reasonableness of defendant's belief that she was in imminent danger of death or serious injury. We do not mean that the expert's testimony could be used to show that it was understandable that a battered woman might believe that her life was in danger when indeed it was not and when a reasonable person would not have so believed. . . . Expert testimony in that direction would be relevant solely to the honesty of defendant's belief, not its objective reasonableness. Rather, our conclusion is that the expert's testimony, if accepted by the jury, would have aided it in determining whether, under the circumstances, a reasonable person would have believed there was imminent danger to her life.

At the heart of the claim of self-defense was defendant's story that she had been repeatedly subjected to "beatings" over the course of her marriage. . . . When that regular pattern of serious physical abuse is combined with defendant's claim that the decedent sometimes threatened to kill her, defendant's statement that on this occasion she thought she might be killed when she saw Mr. Kelly running toward her could be found to reflect a reasonable fear; that is, it could so be found if the jury believed Gladys Kelly's story of the prior beatings, if it believed her story of the prior threats, and, of course, if it believed her story of the events of that particular day.

The crucial issue of fact on which this expert's testimony would bear is why, given such allegedly severe and constant beatings, combined with threats to kill, defendant had not long ago left decedent. Whether raised by the prosecutor as a factual issue or not, our own common knowledge tells us that most of us, including the ordinary juror, would ask himself or herself just such a question. [O]ne of the common myths, apparently believed by most people, is that battered wives are free to leave. To some, this misconception is followed by the observation that the battered wife is masochistic, proven by her refusal to leave despite the severe beatings; to others, however, the fact that the battered wife stays on unquestionably suggests that the "beatings" could not have been too bad for if they had been, she certainly would have left. The expert could clear up these myths, by explaining that one of the common characteristics of a battered wife is her *inability* to leave despite such constant beatings; her "learned helplessness"; her lack of anywhere to go; her feeling that if she tried to leave, she would be subjected to even more merciless treatment; her belief in the omnipotence of her battering husband; and sometimes her hope that her husband will change his ways. . . .

The difficulty with the expert's testimony is that it *sounds* as if an expert is giving knowledge to a jury about something the jury knows as well as anyone else, namely, the reasonableness of a person's fear of imminent serious danger. That is not at all, however, what this testimony is *directly* aimed at. It is aimed at an area where the purported common knowledge of the jury may be very much mistaken, an area where jurors' logic, drawn from their own experience, may lead to a wholly incorrect conclusion. . . . After hearing the expert, instead of saying Gladys Kelly could not have been beaten up so badly for if she had, she certainly would have left, the jury could conclude that her failure to leave was very much part and parcel of her life as a battered wife. The jury could conclude that instead of casting doubt on the accuracy of her testimony about the severity and frequency of prior beatings, her failure to leave actually reinforced her credibility.

Since a retrial is necessary, we think it advisable to indicate the limit of the expert's testimony on this issue of reasonableness. It would not be proper for the expert to express the opinion that defendant's belief on that day was reasonable, not because this is the ultimate issue, but because the area of *expert* knowledge relates, in this regard, to the reasons for defendant's failure to leave her husband. Either the jury accepts or rejects that explanation and, based on that, credits defendant's stories about the beatings she suffered. No expert is needed, however, once the jury has made up its mind on those issues, to tell the jury the logical conclusion, namely, that a person who has in fact been severely and continuously beaten might very well reasonably fear that the imminent beating she was about to suffer could be either life-threatening or pose a risk of serious injury. What the expert could state was that defendant had the battered-woman's syndrome, and could explain that syndrome in detail, relating its characteristics to defendant, but only to enable the jury better to determine the honesty and reasonableness of defendant's belief. Depending on its content, the expert's testimony might also enable the jury to find that the battered wife, because of the prior beatings, numerous beatings, as often as once a week, for seven years, from the day they were married to the day he died, is particularly able to predict accurately the likely extent of violence in any attack on her. That conclusion could significantly affect the jury's evaluation of the reasonableness of defendant's fear for her life.

Having determined that testimony about the battered-woman's syndrome is relevant, we now consider whether Dr. Veronen's testimony satisfies the limitations placed on expert testimony by Evidence Rule 56(2) and by applicable case law. . . . In effect, this Rule imposes three basic requirements for the admission of expert testimony: (1) the intended testimony must concern a subject matter that is beyond the ken of the average juror; (2) the field testified to must be at a state of the art such that an expert's testimony could be sufficiently reliable; and (3) the witness must have sufficient expertise to offer the intended testimony. . . .

As previously discussed, a battering relationship embodies psychological and societal features that are not well understood by lay observers. . . . It is clear that this subject is beyond the ken of the average juror. . . .

The second requirement that must be met before expert testimony is permitted is a showing that the proposed expert's testimony would be reliable. . . .

Dr. Veronen, the proffered expert, testified that the battered-woman's syndrome is acknowledged and accepted by practitioners and professors in the fields of psychology and psychiatry. Dr. Veronen also brought to the court's attention the findings of several researchers who have published reports confirming the presence of the battered-woman's syndrome. . . . Briefs submitted to this Court indicate that there are at least five books and almost seventy scientific articles and papers about the battered-woman's syndrome.

Thus, the record before us reveals that the battered woman's syndrome has a sufficient scientific basis to produce uniform and reasonably reliable results. . . . However, while the record before us could require such a ruling, we refrain from conclusively ruling that Dr. Veronen's proffered testimony about the battered-woman's syndrome would satisfy New Jersey's standard of acceptability for scientific evidence. This is because the State was not given a full opportunity in the trial court to question Dr. Veronen's

methodology in studying battered women or her implicit assertion that the battered-woman's syndrome has been accepted by the relevant scientific community. . . .

[Reversed and remanded.]

---

1. *This version of the homicide—with a drunk Mr. Kelly as the aggressor both in pushing Ms. Kelly to the ground and again in rushing at her with his hands in a threatening position after the two had been separated—is sharply disputed by the State. The prosecution presented testimony intended to show that the initial scuffle* *was started by Gladys; that upon disentanglement, while she was restrained by bystanders, she stated that she intended to kill Ernest; that she then chased after him, and upon catching up with him stabbed him with a pair of scissors taken from her pocketbook.*

IS SEXUAL HARASSMENT COERCIVE?*

Larry May and John C. Hughes

A number of recent lawsuits filed under Title VII of the 1964 Civil Rights Act have brought the problem of sexual harassment into the footlights of contemporary political and moral discussion.[1] Is sexual harassment a purely private matter between two individuals, or is it a social problem? If sexual harassment is to be treated as something more than a purely personal dispute, how do we distinguish the social problem from benevolent forms of social interaction between members of a work hierarchy? We will further argue here that sexual harassment of women workers is a public issue because it is inherently coercive, regardless of whether it takes the form of a threat for noncompliance, or of a reward for compliance. We will further argue that the harm of harassment is felt beyond the individuals immediately involved because it contributes to a pervasive pattern of discrimination and exploitation based on sex.

The term *sexual harassment* refers to the intimidation of persons in subordinate positions by those holding power and authority over them in order to exact sexual favors that would ordinarily not have been granted. Sexual harassment of male subordinates by female superiors is conceivable, and probably occurs, albeit infrequently. Positions of authority are more likely to be occupied by males, while women are predominantly relegated to positions of subservience and dependency. Furthermore, strong cultural patterns induce female sexual passivity and acquiescence to male initiative.[2] These factors combine to produce a dominant pattern of male harassment of females. However, it might be reflecting that the poisoning of the work environment that may result from sexual intimidation may affect members of both sexes, so that sexual harassment should be viewed as more than merely a woman's issue.

---

*From Larry May and John C. Hughes, "Is Sexual Harassment Coercive?" Reprinted from *Moral Rights in the Workplace* by Gertrude Ezorsky by permission of the State University of New York Press. Copyright © 1987 by the State University of New York.

Truly systematic empirical studies of the incidence of sexual harassment are yet to be done. Most of the studies by social scientists to date suffer from severe methodological flaws. Nevertheless, they reveal a pattern of sexual harassment of working women that is too strong to ignore. . . .

I

Like most interpersonal transactions, sexual advances may take many forms. There is of course the sincere proposal, motivated by genuine feeling for another, made in a context of mutual respect for the other's autonomy and dignity. Such offers are possible between members of a work hierarchy, but are of no concern here. Rather, we are interested in advances that take the following forms: (1) Sexual threat: "If you don't provide a sexual benefit, I will punish you by withholding a promotion or a raise that would otherwise be due, or ultimately fire you." (2) Sexual offer: "If you provide a sexual benefit, I will reward you with a promotion or a raise that would otherwise not be due." There are also sexual harassment situations that are merely annoying, but without demonstrable sanction or reward. It is worth noting at the outset that all three forms of sexual harassment have been proscribed under recently promulgated Equal Employment Opportunity Commission guidelines implementing Title VII.[3]

Sexual harassment in the form of threats is coercive behavior that forces the employee to accept a course of conduct she wouldn't otherwise accept. What is wrong with this? Why can't she simply resist the threats and remain as before? Viewed in this abstract, one can seemingly resist threats, for unlike physical restraint, threatening does not completely deny individual choice over her alternatives. A person who is physically restrained is literally no longer in control of her own life. The victim is no longer reaching decisions of her own and autonomously carrying them out. Threats do not have this dramatic effect on a person's autonomy. Rather, the effect of the threat is that the recipient of a threat is much less inclined to act as she would have absent the threat—generally out of fear. Fear is the calculation of expected harm and the decision to avoid it. Reasonably prudent individuals will not, without a sufficiently expected possibility of gain, risk harm. The first thing wrong with sexual threats then is that, for the reasonable person,

it now takes a very good reason to resist the threat, whereas no such strength of reasoning was required before to resist a sexual advance.

Sexual threats are coercive because they worsen the objective situation the employee finds herself in. To examine this claim, consider her situation before and after the threat has been made (preproposition stage and postproposition stage).[4] In the preproposition stage, a secretary, for example, is judged by standards of efficiency to determine whether she should be allowed to retain her job. She would naturally view her employer as having power over her, but only in the rather limited domain concerning the job-related functions she performs. Her personal life would be her own. She could choose her own social relationships, without fear that these decisions might adversely affect her job. In the postproposition stage, she can no longer remain employed under the same conditions while not choosing to have relations with her employer. Further, the efficient performance of job-related functions is no longer sufficient for the retention of her job. She can no longer look to her supervisor as one who exercises power merely over the performance of her office duties. He now wields power over a part of her personal life. . . . [She] cannot simply go on as before, for [her] new situation is correctly perceived as worse than the old situation.

It is the worsening of the woman's situation after the threat has been made that contributes to the likelihood of her acquiescence to the threat. The perception of job insecurity created by the threat can only be alleviated by her acceptance of the sexual proposition. But what of the woman who prefers to have a sexual relationship with her employer than not to do so? Has this woman also been made objectively worse off then she was before the threat occurred? We contend that she has, for before the threat was made she could pursue her preference without feeling forced to do so. If the liaison developed and then turned sour, she could quit the relationship and not so clearly risk a worsening of her employment situation. Now, however, her continued job success might be held ransom to the continued sexual demands of her employer. This also may adversely affect other women in the business organization. What the employer has done is to establish a precedent for employment decisions based upon the stereotype that values women for their sexuality rather than for their job skills. This has a discriminatory impact on women individually and as a group. Focusing on this effect will shed some light on the harm of both sexual threats and sexual offers.

II

Consider the following case.[5] Barnes was hired as an administrative assistant by the director of a federal agency. In a preemployment interview, the director, a male, promised to promote Barnes, a female, within ninety days. Shortly after beginning her job, (1) the director repeatedly asked her for a date after work hours, even though she consistently refused; (2) made repeated remarks to her that were sexual in nature; and (3) repeatedly told her that if she did not cooperate with him by engaging in sexual relations, her employment status would be affected. After consistently rebuffing him, she finally told him she wished for their relationship to remain a strictly professional one. Therefore the director, sometimes in concert with others, began a campaign to belittle and demean her within the office. Subsequently she was stripped of most of her job duties, culminating in the eventual abolition of her job. Barnes filed suit, claiming that these actions would not have occurred but for the fact that she was a woman.

Under Title VII, it is now widely accepted that the kind of sexual threat illustrated by this case is an instance of sex discrimination in employment.[6] Such threats treat women differently than men in employment contexts even though gender is not a relevantly applicable category for making employment-related decisions. The underlying principle here is that like persons should be treated alike. Unless there are relevant differences among persons, it is harmful to disadvantage one particular class of persons. In the normal course of events, male employees are not threatened sexually by employers or supervisors. The threats disadvantage a woman in that an additional requirement is placed in her path for successful job retention, one not placed in the path of male employees. When persons who are otherwise similarly situated are distinguished on the basis of their sex, and rewards or burdens are apportioned according to these gender-based classifications, illegal sex discrimination has occurred. Applying this theory of discrimination to Barnes's complaint, the federal appellate court ruled:

> So it was, by her version, that retention of her job was conditioned upon submission to sexual relations—an exaction which the supervisor would not have made of any male. It is much too late in the day to contend that Title VII does not outlaw terms of employment for women which differ appreciably from those set for men and which are not genuinely and reasonably related to the performance on the job. . . . Put another way, she became the target of her superior's sexual desires because she was a woman and was asked to bow to demands as the price for holding her job.[7]

There is a second way in which this behavior might be viewed as discriminatory. Sexual threats also contribute to a pervasive pattern of disadvantaged treatment of women as a group. Under this approach, the harm is not viewed as resulting from the arbitrary and unfair use of gender as a criterion for employment decisions. Rather, emphasis is on the effect the classification has of continuing the subordination of women as a group. The harm results regardless of whether the specific incident could be given an employment rationale or not. Sexual harassment perpetuates sex discrimination, and illustrates the harm that occurs for members of a group that have historically been disadvantaged. This theory was applied to sexual harassment in another federal lawsuit, *Tomkins* v. *Public Service Gas and Electric Co*.[8] The plaintiff's lawyers argued that employer tolerance of sexual harassment and its pattern of reprisals had a disparate impact upon women as an already disadvantaged group and was inherently degrading to all women.

Sexual threats are harmful to the individual woman because she is coerced and treated unfairly by her employer, disadvantaging her for no good reason. Beyond this, such practices further contribute to a pervasive pattern of disadvantaged status for her and all women in society. The sexual stereotyping makes it less likely, and sometimes impossible, that women will be treated on the basis of job efficiency, intelligence, or administrative skill. These women must now compete on a very different level, and in the case where sexual threats are common or at least accepted, this level is clearly inferior to that occupied by men. The few male employees who are harassed in the workplace suffer the first harm but not the second. We shall next show that there are also two harms of sexual offers in employment, only one of which can also be said to befall men.

III

The harm of sexual offers is much more difficult to identify and analyze. Indeed, some may even see sexual offers as contributing to a differentiation based on sex that advantages rather than disadvantages women, individually and as a group. After all, males cannot normally gain promotions by engaging in sexual relations with their employers. We shall argue, on the contrary, that a sexual offer disadvantages the woman employee by changing the work environment so that she is viewed by others, and may come to view herself, less in terms of her work productivity and more in terms of her sexual allure. This change, like the threat, makes it unlikely that she can return to the preproposition stage even though she might prefer to do so. Furthermore, to offset her diminished status and to protect against later retaliation, a prudent woman would feel that she must accept the offer. Here, sexual offers resemble the coercive threat. The specific harm to women becomes clearer when one looks at the group impact of sexual offers in employment. Women are already more economically vulnerable and socially passive than men. When sexual offers are tendered, exploitation of a woman employee is accomplished by taking advantage of a preexisting vulnerability males generally do not share.

Seduction accomplished through sexual offers and coercive threats blend together most clearly in the mixed case of the sexual offer of a promotion with the lurking threat of retaliation if the offer is turned down. Both combine together to compel the woman to engage in sexual relations with her employer. Gifts are so rare in economic matters that it is best to be suspicious of all offers and to look for their hidden costs. . . .

Why are the clearly mixed cases, where there is both an offer and a (sometimes only implied) threat, coercive rather than noncoercive? To return to our initial discussion, why is it that one is made worse off by the existence of these proposals? In one sense they enable women to do things they couldn't otherwise do, namely, get a promotion that they did not deserve, thus seeming to be noncoercive. On the other hand, if the woman prefers not having sexual relations with her employer (while retaining her job) to having sexual relations with him (with ensuing promotion), then it is predominantly a threat and more clearly coercive. The best reason for not preferring the postproposition stage is that she is then made worse off if she rejects the proposition, and if she accepts, she nonetheless risks further harm or retaliation. This latter condition is also true for more straightforward offers, as we shall now show.

A number of contemporary philosophers have argued that offers place people in truly advantageous positions, for they can always be turned down with the ensuing return to the preoffer stage.[9] In the case of sexual offers, however, the mere proposal of a promotion in exchange for sexual relations changes the work environment. Once sexual relations are seriously proposed as a sufficient condition for employment success, the woman realizes that this male employer sees her (and will probably continue to see her) as a sex object as well as an employee. A prudent woman will henceforth worry that she is not being regarded as an employee who simply happens to be a woman, but rather as a woman made more vulnerable by the fact that she happens to be an employee. If she accepts the offer, she lends credence to the stereotype, and because of this, it is more likely that she may experience future offers or even threats. She would thus worry about her ability to achieve on the basis of her work-related merits. If she rejects the offer, she would still worry about her employer's attitude toward her status as a worker. Furthermore, because of the volatility of sexual feelings, these offers cannot be turned down without the risk of offending or alienating one's employer, something any employee would wish to avoid. She may reasonably conclude from these two considerations that neither postoffer alternative is desirable. This is one of the hidden costs of sexual offers in the workplace.

It may be claimed that such environmental changes are no different for men who can also be the objects of sexual offers in the workplace. One needs to show that the changed environment is worse for those who are women. Sexual employment offers take advantage of unequal power relations that exist between employer and employee so as to force a particular outcome further benefitting those who are already in advantageous positions. But beyond this, sexual offers are doubly exploitative for female employees, because women already enter the employment arena from a position of vulnerability. As we have indicated, this is true because of the history of their economic powerlessness and because of their culturally ingrained passivity and acquiescence in the face of male initiatives. Women enter the employment arena much more ripe for coercion than their male colleagues. Thus, women are more likely to be harmed by these offers.

. . . Men are not similarly harmed by sexual offers because they do not have the same history of sexual exploitation. Men are likely to regard such seductive offers either humorously or as insults to be aggressively combatted, while women have been socialized to be passive rather than combative in such situations. The woman to whom the offer is made becomes less sure of her real abilities by virtue of the proposal itself. This self-denigrating response to an unwelcomed proposal is a vestige of women's history of subordination. Even without the veiled threat, sexual offers can cause women to act in ways they would not choose to act otherwise. To this extent, these sexual offers are coercive.

Most offers are not coercive because one would prefer to have the offer made. This is because one of the postoffer alternatives (rejecting the offer) is equivalent to the preoffer alternative (having no offer at all). Sexual offers made by male employers to female employees are different, however, because they more closely resemble threats than ordinary offers.[10] As we have shown, the preoffer alternative, being employed, unpromoted, yet able to obtain promotion according to one's merits—is different from, and preferable to,

either of the postoffer alternatives—accepting the promotion, and having sexual relations with her employer, with all of its negative consequences, or rejecting the offer of promotion, but with the risk that the promotion may now prove unobtainable on the basis of merit. By blocking a return to the more preferable preoffer alternative, the male employer has acted similarly to the employer who uses sexual threats. The woman is forced to choose between two undesirable alternatives because she cannot have what she would have chosen before the proposal was made. Stressing these hidden costs, which are much greater for women than for men, exposes the coercive element inherent in sexual offers as well as in sexual threats. We are thus led to conclude that both of these employment practices are harmful to women and recently were properly proscribed by the U.S. Equal Employment Opportunity Commission.

---

1. *For a careful analysis of these cases we recommend Catharine MacKinnon's book,* Sexual Harassment of Working Women *(New Haven, Conn.: Yale University Press, 1979).*

2. *For the historical evidence, see William Chaffe,* Women and Equality *(New York: Oxford University Press, 1977). For the sociological evidence, see J. R. Feagin and C. B. Feagin,* Discrimination American Style *(Englewood Cliffs, N.J.: Prentice-Hall, 1978).*

3. *45 Fed. Reg. 74, 677 (1980); 29 C.F.R. 1604.11(a).*

4. *We proceed from the general analysis developed by Robert Nozick, "Coercion,"* Philosophy, Science and Method, *Morgenbesser, Suppes, and White, eds. (New York: St. Martin's Press, 1969). A very large literature has grown out of this analysis. We recommend the essays by Bernard Gert, Michael Bayles, and especially Virginia Held, collected in* NOMOS XIV: Coercion *(New York: Lieber Atherton, 1973).*

5. *Summary of the facts for* Barnes v. Costel, *561 F.2d 984 (D.C. Cir. 1977).*

6. *For more elaboration, see Section II of our essay, "Sexual Harassment,"* Social Theory and Practice *(1980), pp. 256–68.*

7. *561 F.2d 989, 990, 992 n. 68 (D.C. Cir. 1977).*

8. *568 F.2d 1044 (3rd Cir. 1977).*

9. *See Michael Bayles, "Coercive Offers and Public Benefits,"* The Personalist *55 (1974); Donald Vandeveer, "Coercion, Seduction and Rights,"* The Personalist *58 (1977); and Nozick, "Coercion," among others.*

10. *Some other employment offers have been seen as coercive also. See David Zimmerman, "Coercive Wage Offers,"* Philosophy and Public Affairs *10 (1981).*

BARED BUTTOCKS AND FEDERAL CASES*

Ellen Frankel Paul

Women in American society are victims of sexual harassment in alarming proportions. Sexual harassment is an inevitable corollary to class exploitation; as capitalists exploit workers, so do males in positions of authority exploit their female subordinates. Male professors, supervisors, and apartment managers in ever

---

*From *Society* v. 28, issue no. 4, pp. 4–7. Copyright 1991 by Transaction. Reprinted by permission.

increasing numbers take advantage of the financial dependence and vulnerability of women to extract sexual concessions.

These are the assertions that commonly begin discussions of sexual harassment. For reasons that will be adumbrated below, dissent from the prevailing view is long overdue. Three recent episodes will serve to frame this disagreement.

Valerie Craig, an employee of Y & Y Snacks, Inc., joined several co-workers and her supervisor for drinks after work one day in July of 1978. Her supervisor drove her home and proposed that they become more intimately acquainted. She refused his invitation for sexual relations, whereupon he said that he would "get even" with her. Ten days after the incident she was fired from her job. She soon filed a complaint of sexual harassment with the Equal Employment Opportunity Commission (EEOC), and the case wound its way through the courts. Craig prevailed, the company was held liable for damages, and she received back pay, reinstatement, and an order prohibiting Y & Y from taking reprisals against her in the future.

Carol Zabowicz, one of only two female forklift operators in a West Bend Co. warehouse, charged that her co-workers over a four year period from 1978–1982 sexually harassed her by such acts as: asking her whether she was wearing a bra; two of the men exposing their buttocks between ten and twenty times; a male co-worker grabbing his crotch and making obscene suggestions of growling; subjecting her to offensive and abusive language; and exhibiting obscene drawings with her initials on them. Zabowicz began to show symptoms of physical and psychological stress, necessitating several medical leaves, and she filed a sexual harassment complaint with the EEOC. The district court judge remarked that "The sustained, malicious, and brutal harassment meted out . . . was more than merely unreasonable; it was malevolent and outrageous." The company knew of the harassment and took corrective action only after the employee filed a complaint with the EEOC. The company was, therefore, held liable, and Zabowicz was awarded back pay for the period of her medical absence, and a judgment that her rights were violated under the Civil Rights Act of 1964.

On September 17, 1990, Lisa Olson, a sports reporter for the *Boston Herald,* charged five football players of the just-defeated New England Patriots with sexual harassment for making sexually suggestive and offensive remarks to her when she entered their locker room to conduct a post-game interview. The

incident amounted to nothing short of "mind rape," according to Olson. After vociferous lamentations in the media, the National Football League fined the team and its players $25,000 each. The National Organization of Women called for a boycott of Remington electric shavers because the owner of the company, Victor Kiam, also owns the Patriots and who allegedly displayed insufficient sensitivity at the time when the episode occurred.

All these incidents are indisputably disturbing. In an ideal world—one needless to say far different from the one that we inhabit or are ever likely to inhabit—women would not be subjected to such treatment in the course of their work. Women, and men as well, would be accorded respect by co-workers and supervisors, their feelings would be taken into account, and their dignity would be left intact. For women to expect reverential treatment in the workplace is utopian, yet they should not have to tolerate outrageous, offensive sexual overtures and threats as they go about earning a living.

One question that needs to be pondered is: What kinds of undesired sexual behavior women should be protected against by law? That is, what kind of actions are deemed so outrageous and violate a woman's rights to such [an] extent that the law should intervene, and what actions should be considered inconveniences of life, to be morally condemned but not adjudicated? A subsidiary question concerns the type of legal remedy appropriate for the wrongs that do require redress. Before directly addressing these questions, it might be useful to diffuse some of the hyperbole adhering to the sexual harassment issue.

Surveys are one source of this hyperbole. If their results are accepted at face value, they lead to the conclusion that women are disproportionately victims of legions of sexual harassers. A poll by the Albuquerque *Tribune* found that nearly 80 percent of the respondents reported that they or someone they knew had been victims of sexual harassment. The Merit Systems Protection Board determined that 42 percent of the women (and 14 percent of men) working for the federal government had experienced some form of unwanted sexual attention between 1985 and 1987, with unwanted "sexual teasing" identified as the most prevalent form. A Defense Department survey found that 64 percent of women in the military (and 17 percent of the men) suffered "uninvited and unwanted sexual attention" within the previous year. The United Methodist Church established that 7 percent of its clergywomen experienced incidents of sexual harassment, with 41 percent of these naming a pastor or colleague as the perpetrator, and 31 percent mentioning church social functions as the setting.

A few caveats concerning polls in general, and these sorts of polls in particular, are worth considering. Pollsters looking for a particular social ill tend to find it, usually in gargantuan proportions. (What fate would lie in store for a pollster who concluded that child abuse, or wife beating, or mistreatment of the elderly had dwindled to the point of negligibility!) Sexual harassment is a notoriously ill-defined and almost infinitely expandable concept, including everything from rape to unwelcome neck massaging, discomfiture upon witnessing sexual overtures directed at others, yelling at and blowing smoke in the ears of female subordinates, and displays of pornographic pictures in the workplace. Defining sexual harassment, as the United Methodists did, as "any sexually related behavior that is unwelcome, offensive or which fails to respect the rights of others," the concept is broad enough to include everything from "unsolicited suggestive looks or leers [or] pressures for dates" to "actual sexual assaults or rapes." Categorizing everything from rape to "looks" as sexual harassment makes us all victims, a state of affairs satisfying to radical feminists, but not very useful for distinguishing serious injuries from the merely trivial.

Yet, even if the surveys exaggerate the extent of sexual harassment, however defined, what they do reflect is a great deal of tension between the sexes. As women in ever increasing numbers entered the workplace in the last two decades, as the women's movement challenged alleged male hegemony and exploitation with ever greater intemperance, and as women entered previously all-male preserves from the board rooms to the coal pits, it is lamentable, but should not be surprising, that this tension sometimes takes sexual form. Not that sexual harassment on the job, in the university, and in other settings is a trivial or insignificant matter, but a sense of proportion needs to be restored and, even more importantly, distinctions need to be made. In other words, sexual harassment must be de-ideologized. Statements that paint nearly all women as victims and all men and their patriarchal, capitalist system as perpetrators, are ideological fantasy. Ideology blurs the distinction between being injured—being a genuine victim—and merely being offended. An example is this statement by Catharine A. MacKinnon, a law professor and feminist activist:

Sexual harassment perpetuates the interlocked structure by which women have been kept sexually in thrall to men and at the bottom of the labor market. Two forces of American society converge: men's control over women's sexuality and capital control over employees' work lives. Women historically have been required to exchange sexual services for material survival, in one form or another. Prostitution and marriage as well as sexual harassment in different ways institutionalize this arrangement.

Such hyperbole needs to be diffused and distinctions need to be drawn. Rape, a nonconsensual invasion of a person's body, is a crime clear and simple. It is a violation of the right to the physical integrity of the body (the right to life, as John Locke or Thomas Jefferson would have put it). Criminal law should and does prohibit rape. Whether it is useful to call rape "sexual harassment" is doubtful, for it makes the latter concept overly broad while trivializing the former.

Intimidation in the workplace of the kind that befell Valerie Craig—that is, extortion of sexual favors by a supervisor from a subordinate by threatening to penalize, fire, or fail to reward—is what the courts term *quid pro quo* sexual harassment. Since the mid-1970s, the federal courts have treated this type of sexual harassment as a form of sex discrimination in employment proscribed under Title VII of the Civil Rights Act of 1964. A plaintiff who prevails against an employer may receive such equitable remedies as reinstatement and back pay, and the court can order the company to prepare and disseminate a policy against sexual harassment. Current law places principal liability on the company, not the harassing supervisor, even when higher management is unaware of the harassment and, thus, cannot take any steps to prevent it.

Quid pro quo sexual harassment is morally objectionable and analogous to extortion: the harasser extorts property (i.e., use of the woman's body) through the leverage of fear for her job. The victim of such behavior should have legal recourse, but serious reservations can be held about rectifying these injustices through the blunt instrument of Title VII. In [outrageous] cases the victim is left less than whole (for back pay will not compensate for her ancillary losses), and no prospect for punitive damages are offered to deter would-be harassers. Even more distressing about Title VII is the fact that the primary target of litigation is not the actual harasser, but rather the employer. This places a double burden on a company. The employer is swindled by the supervisor because he spent his time pursuing sexual gratification and thereby impairing the efficiency of the workplace by mismanaging his subordinates, and the employer must endure lengthy and expensive litigation, pay damages, and suffer loss to its reputation. It would be fairer to both the company and the victim to treat sexual harassment as a tort—that is, as a private wrong or injury for which the court can assess damages. Employers should be held vicariously liable only when they know of an employee's behavior and do not try to redress it.

As for the workplace harassment endured by Carol Zabowicz—the bared buttocks, obscene portraits, etc.—that too should be legally redressable. Presently, such incidents also fall under the umbrella of Title VII, and are termed hostile environment sexual harassment, a category accepted later than *quid pro quo* and with some judicial reluctance. The main problem with this category is that it has proven too elastic: cases have reached the courts based on everything from off-color jokes to unwanted, persistent sexual advances by co-workers. A new tort of sexual harassment would handle these cases better. Only instances above a certain threshold of egregiousness or outrageousness would be actionable. In other words, the behavior that the plaintiff found offensive would also have to be offensive to the proverbial "reasonable man" of the tort law. That is, the behavior would have to be objectively injurious rather than merely subjectively offensive. The defendant would be the actual harasser not the company, unless it knew about the problem and failed to act. Victims of scatological jokes, leers, unwanted offers of dates, and other sexual annoyances would no longer have their day in court.

A distinction must be restored between morally offensive behavior and behavior that causes serious harm. Only the latter should fall under the jurisdiction of criminal or tort law. Do we really want legislators and judges delving into our most intimate private lives, deciding when a look is a leer, and when a leer is a Civil Rights Act offense? Do we really want courts deciding, as one recently did, whether a school principal's disparaging remarks about a female school district administrator was sexual harassment and, hence, a breach of Title VII, or merely the act of a spurned and vengeful lover? Do we want judges settling disputes such as the one that arose at a car dealership after a female employee turned down a male co-worker's offer of a date and his colleagues retaliated by calling her offensive names and embarrassing her in front of customers? Or another case in which a female shipyard worker complained of an "offensive working environment" because of the prevalence of pornographic material on the docks? Do we want the state to prevent or compensate us for any behavior that someone might find offensive? Should people have a legally enforceable right not to be offended by others? At some point, the price for such protection is the loss of both liberty and privacy rights.

Workplaces are breeding grounds of envy, personal grudges, infatuation, and jilted loves, and beneath a fairly high threshold of outrageousness, these travails should be either suffered in silence, complained of to higher management, or left behind as one seeks other employment. No one, female or male, can expect to enjoy a working environment that is perfectly stress-free, or to be treated always and by everyone with kindness and respect. To the extent that sympathetic judges have encouraged women to seek monetary compensation for slights and annoyances, they have not done them a great service. Women need to develop a thick skin in order to survive and prosper in the work force. It is patronizing to think that they need to be recompensed by male judges for seeing a few pornographic pictures on a wall. By their efforts to extend sexual harassment charges to even the most trivial behavior, the radical feminists send a message that women are not resilient enough to ignore the run-of-the-mill, churlish provocation from male co-workers. It is difficult to imagine a suit by a longshoreman complaining of mental stress due to the display of nude male centerfolds by female co-workers. Women cannot expect to have it both ways: equality where convenient, but special dispensations when the going gets rough. Equality has its price and that price may include unwelcome sexual advances, irritating and even intimidating sexual jests, and lewd and obnoxious colleagues.

[Outrageous] acts—sexual harassment per se—must be legally redressable. Lesser but not trivial offenses, whether at the workplace or in other more social settings, should be considered moral lapses for which the offending party receives opprobrium, disciplinary warnings, or penalties, depending on the setting and the severity. Trivial offenses, dirty jokes, sexual overtures, and sexual innuendoes do make many women feel intensely discomfited, but, unless they become outrageous through persistence or content, these too should be taken as part of life's annoyances. The perpetrators should be either endured, ignored, rebuked, or avoided, as circumstances and personal inclination dictate. Whether Lisa Olson's experience in the locker room of the New England

Patriots falls into the second or third category is debatable. The media circus triggered by the incident was certainly out of proportion to the event.

As the presence of women on road gangs, construction crews, and oil rigs becomes a fact of life, the animosities and tensions of this transition period are likely to abate gradually. Meanwhile, women should "lighten up," and even dispense a few risqué barbs of their own, a sure way of taking the fun out of it for offensive male bores.

MICHAEL M. V. SUPERIOR COURT OF SONOMA COUNTY*

United States Supreme Court, 1981

Justice REHNQUIST announced the judgment of the Court and delivered an opinion, in which THE CHIEF JUSTICE, Justice STEWART, and Justice POWELL joined.

The question presented in this case is whether California's "statutory rape" law, violates the Equal Protection Clause of the Fourteenth Amendment. Section 261.5 defines unlawful sexual intercourse as "an act of sexual intercourse accomplished with a female not the wife of the perpetrator, where the female is under the age of 18 years." The statute thus makes men alone criminally liable for the act of sexual intercourse.

In July 1978, a complaint was filed in the Municipal Court of Sonoma County, Cal., alleging that petitioner, then a 17½-year-old male, had had unlawful sexual intercourse with a female under the age of 18, in violation of § 261.5. The evidence, adduced at a preliminary hearing showed that at approximately midnight on June 3, 1978, petitioner and two friends approached Sharon, a 16½-year-old female, and her sister as they waited at a bus stop. Petitioner and Sharon, who had already been drinking, moved away from the others and began to kiss. After being struck in the face for rebuffing petitioner's initial advances, Sharon submitted to sexual intercourse with petitioner. Prior to trial, petitioner sought to set aside the information on both state and federal constitutional grounds, asserting that § 261.5 unlawfully discriminated on the basis of gender. The trial court and the California Court of Appeal denied petitioner's request for relief and petitioner sought review in the Supreme Court of California.

The Supreme Court held that "section 261.5 discriminates on the basis of sex because only females may be victims, and only males may violate the section." The court then subjected the classification to "strict scrutiny," stating that it must be justified by a compelling state interest. It found that the classification was "supported not by mere social convention but by the immutable physiological fact that it is the female exclusively who can become pregnant." Canvassing "the tragic human costs of illegitimate teenage pregnancies," including the large number of teenage abortions, the increased medical risk associated with teenage pregnancies, and the social consequences of teenage childbearing, the court concluded that the State has a compelling interest in preventing such pregnancies. Because males alone can "physiologically cause the result which the law properly seeks to avoid," the court further held that the gender classification was readily justified as a means of identifying offender and victim. For the reasons stated below, we affirm the judgment of the California Supreme Court.

As is evident from our opinions, the Court has had some difficulty in agreeing upon the proper approach and analysis in cases involving challenges to gender-based classifications. The issues posed by such challenges range from issues of standing to the appropriate standard of judicial review for the sub-

---

*450 U.S. 464, 67 L.Ed.2d 437. Citations and endnotes deleted from text.

stantive classification. Unlike the California Supreme Court, we have not held that gender-based classifications are "inherently suspect" and thus we do not apply so-called "strict scrutiny" to those classifications. Our cases have held, however, that the traditional minimum rationality test takes on a somewhat "sharper focus" when gender-based classifications are challenged. In *Reed* v. *Reed,* for example, the Court stated that a gender-based classification will be upheld if it bears a "fair and substantial relationship" to legitimate state ends, while in *Craig* v. *Boren,* the Court restated the test to require the classification to bear a "substantial relationship" to "important governmental objectives."

Underlying these decisions is the principle that a legislature may not "make overbroad generalizations based on sex which are entirely unrelated to any differences between men and women or which demean the ability or social status of the affected class." But because the Equal Protection Clause does not "demand that a statute necessarily apply equally to all persons" or require "'things which are different in fact . . . to be treated in law as though they were the same,'" this Court has consistently upheld statutes where the gender classification is not invidious, but rather realistically reflects the fact that the sexes are not similarly situated in certain circumstances. As the Court has stated, a legislature may "provide for the special problems of women."

Applying those principles to this case, the fact that the California Legislature criminalized the act of illicit sexual intercourse with a minor female is a sure indication of its intent or purpose to discourage that conduct. Precisely why the legislature desired that result is of course somewhat less clear. This Court has long recognized that "[i]nquiries into congressional motives or purposes are a hazardous matter," and the search for the "actual" or "primary" purpose of a statute is likely to be elusive. Here, for example, the individual legislators may have voted for the statute for a variety of reasons. Some legislators may have been concerned about preventing teenage pregnancies, others about protecting young females from physical injury or from the loss of "chastity," and still others about promoting various religious and moral attitudes towards premarital sex.

The justification for the statute offered by the State, and accepted by the Supreme Court of California, is that the legislature sought to prevent illegitimate teenage pregnancies. That finding, of course, is entitled to great deference. And although our cases establish that the State's asserted reason for the enactment

of a statute may be rejected, if it "could not have been a goal of the legislation." This is not such a case.

We are satisfied not only that the prevention of illegitimate pregnancy is at least one of the "purposes" of the statute, but also that the State has a strong interest in preventing such pregnancy. At the risk of stating the obvious, teenage pregnancies, which have increased dramatically over the last two decades, have significant social, medical, and economic consequences for both the mother and her child, and the State. Of particular concern to the State is that approximately half of all teenage pregnancies end in abortion. And of those children who are born, their illegitimacy makes them likely candidates to become wards of the State.

We need not be medical doctors to discern that young men and young women are not similarly situated with respect to the problems and the risks of sexual intercourse. Only women may become pregnant, and they suffer disproportionately the profound physical, emotional and psychological consequences of sexual activity. The statute at issue here protects women from sexual intercourse at an age when those consequences are particularly severe.

The question thus boils down to whether a State may attack the problem of sexual intercourse and teenage pregnancy directly by prohibiting a male from having sexual intercourse with a minor female. We hold that such a statute is sufficiently related to the State's objectives to pass constitutional muster.

Because virtually all of the significant harmful and inescapably identifiable consequences of teenage pregnancy fall on the young female, a legislature acts well within its authority when it elects to punish only the participant who, by nature, suffers few of the consequences of his conduct. It is hardly unreasonable for a legislature acting to protect minor females to exclude them from punishment. Moreover, the risk of pregnancy itself constitutes a substantial deterrence to young females. No similar natural sanctions deter males. A criminal sanction imposed solely on males thus serves to roughly "equalize" the deterrents on the sexes.

We are unable to accept petitioner's contention that the statute is impermissibly underinclusive and must, in order to pass judicial scrutiny, be *broadened* so as to hold the female as criminally liable as the male. It is argued that this statute is not *necessary* to deter teenage pregnancy because a gender-neutral statute, where both male and female would be subject to prosecution, would serve that goal equally well. The relevant inquiry, however, is not whether the statute is drawn as precisely as it might have been, but whether the line chosen by the California Legislature is within constitutional limitations.

In any event, we cannot say that a gender-neutral statute would be as effective as the statute California has chosen to enact. The State persuasively contends that a gender-neutral statute would frustrate its interest in effective enforcement. Its view is that a female is surely less likely to report violations of the statute if she herself would be subject to criminal prosecution. In an area already fraught with prosecutorial difficulties, we decline to hold that the Equal Protection Clause requires a legislature to enact a statute so broad that it may well be incapable of enforcement.

We similarly reject petitioner's argument that § 261.5 is impermissibly overbroad because it makes unlawful sexual intercourse with prepubescent females, who are, by definition, incapable of becoming pregnant. Quite apart from the fact that the statute could well be justified on the grounds that very young females are particularly susceptible to physical injury from sexual intercourse, it is ludicrous to suggest that the Constitution requires the California Legislature to limit the scope of its rape statute to older teenagers and exclude young girls.

There remains only petitioner's contention that the statute is unconstitutional as it is applied to him because he, like Sharon, was under 18 at the time of sexual intercourse. Petitioner argues that the statute is flawed because it presumes that as between two persons under 18, the male is the culpable aggressor. We find petitioner's contentions unpersuasive. Contrary to his assertions, the statute does not rest on the assumption that males are generally the aggressors. It is instead an attempt by a legislature to prevent illegitimate teenage pregnancy by providing an additional deterrent for men. The age of the man is irrelevant since young men are as capable as older men of inflicting the harm sought to be prevented.

In upholding the California statute we also recognize that this is not a case where a statute is being challenged on the grounds that it "invidiously discriminates" against females. To the contrary, the statute places a burden on males which is not shared by females. But we find nothing to suggest that men, because of past discrimination or peculiar disadvantages, are in need of the special solicitude of the courts. Nor is this a case where the gender classification is made "solely for . . . administrative convenience," or rests on "the baggage of sexual stereotypes." As we have held, the statute instead reasonably reflects the fact that the consequences of sexual intercourse and pregnancy fall more heavily on the female than on the male.

Accordingly, the judgment of the California Supreme Court is

Affirmed.

Justice STEWART, concurring.

Section 261.5, on its face, classifies on the basis of sex. A male who engages in sexual intercourse with an underage female who is not his wife violates the statute; a female who engages in sexual intercourse with an underage male who is not her husband does not. The petitioner contends that this state law, which punishes only males for the conduct in question, violates his Fourteenth Amendment right to the equal protection of the law. The Court today correctly rejects that contention.

A

At the outset, it should be noted that the statutory discrimination, when viewed as part of the wider scheme of California law, is not as clearcut as might at first appear. Females are not freed from criminal liability in California for engaging in sexual activity that may be harmful. It is unlawful, for example, for any person, of either sex, to molest, annoy, or contribute to the delinquency of anyone under 18 years of age. All persons are prohibited from committing "any lewd or lascivious act," including consensual intercourse, with a child under 14. And members of both sexes may be convicted for engaging in deviant sexual acts with anyone under 18. Finally, females may be brought within the proscription of § 261.5 itself, since a female may be charged with aiding and abetting its violation.

Section 261.5 is thus but one part of a broad statutory scheme that protects all minors from the problems and risks attendant upon adolescent sexual activity. To be sure, § 261.5 creates an additional measure of punishment for males who engage in sexual intercourse with females between the ages of 14 and 17. The question then is whether the Constitution prohibits a state legislature from imposing this *additional* sanction on a gender-specific basis.

B

The Constitution is violated when government, state or federal, invidiously classifies similarly situated people on the basis of the immutable characteristics with which they were born. Thus, detrimental racial classifications by government always violate the Constitution, for the simple reason that, so far as the Constitution is concerned, people of different races are always similarly situated. By contrast, while detrimental gender classifications by government often violate the Constitution, they do not always do so, for the reason that there are differences between males and females that the Constitution necessarily recognizes. In this case we deal with the most basic of these differences: females can become pregnant as the result of sexual intercourse; males cannot.

As was recognized in *Parham* v. *Hughes,* "a State is not free to make overbroad generalizations based on sex which are entirely unrelated to any differences between men and women or which demean the ability or social status of the affected class." Gender-based classifications may not be based upon administrative convenience, or upon archaic assumptions about the proper roles of the sexes. But we have recognized that in certain narrow circumstances men and women are *not* similarly situated; in these circumstances a gender classification based on clear differences between the sexes is not invidious, and a legislative classification realistically based upon those differences is not unconstitutional. "[G]ender-based classifications are not invariably invalid. When men and women are not in fact similarly situated in the area covered by the legislation in question, the Equal Protection Clause is not violated."

Applying these principles to the classification enacted by the California Legislature, it is readily apparent that § 261.5 does not violate the Equal Protection Clause. Young women and men are not similarly situated with respect to the problems and risk associated with intercourse and pregnancy, and the statute is realistically related to the legitimate state purpose of reducing those problems and risks.

C

As the California Supreme Court's catalog shows, the pregnant unmarried female confronts problems more numerous and more severe than any faced by her male partner. She alone endures the medical risks of pregnancy or abortion. She suffers disproportionately the social, educational, and emotional consequences of pregnancy. Recognizing this disproportion, California has attempted to protect teenage females by prohibiting males from participating in the act necessary for conception.

The fact that males and females are not similarly situated with respect to the risks of sexual intercourse applies with the same force to males under 18 as it does to older males. The risk of pregnancy is a significant deterrent for unwed young females that is not shared by unmarried males, regardless of their age. Experienced observation confirms the commonsense notion that adolescent males disregard the possibility of pregnancy far more than do adolescent females. And to the extent that § 261.5 may punish males for intercourse with prepubescent females, that punishment is justifiable because of the substantial physical risks for prepubescent females that are not shared by their male counterparts.

D

The petitioner argues that the California Legislature could have drafted the statute differently, so that its purpose would be accomplished more precisely. "But the issue, of course, is not whether the statute could have been drafted more wisely, but whether the lines chosen by the . . . [l]egislature are within constitutional limitations." That other States may have decided to attack the same problems more broadly, with gender-neutral statutes, does not mean that every State is constitutionally compelled to do so.

E

In short, the Equal Protection Clause does not mean that the physiological differences between men and women must be disregarded. While those differences must never be permitted to become a pretext for invidious discrimination, no such discrimination is presented by this case. The Constitution surely does not require a State to pretend that demonstrable differences between men and women do not really exist.

Justice BLACKMUN, concurring in the judgment.

It is gratifying that the plurality recognizes that "[a]t the risk of stating the obvious, teenage pregnancies . . . have increased dramatically over the last two decades" and "have significant social, medical, and economic consequences for both the mother and her child, and the State." There have been times when I have wondered whether the Court was capable of this perception, particularly when it has struggled with the different but not unrelated problems that attend abortion issues.

Some might conclude that the two uses of the criminal sanction—here flatly to forbid intercourse in order to forestall teenage pregnancies, and in *Matheson* to prohibit a physician's abortion procedure except upon notice to the parents of the pregnant minor—are vastly different proscriptions. But the basic social and privacy problems are much the same. Both Utah's statute in *Matheson* and California's statute in this case are legislatively created tools intended to achieve similar ends and addressed to the same societal concerns: the control and direction of young people's sexual activities. The plurality opinion impliedly concedes as much when it notes that "approximately half of all teenage pregnancies end in abortion," and that "those children who are born" are "likely candidates to become wards of the State."

I, however, cannot vote to strike down the California statutory rape law, for I think it is a sufficiently reasoned and constitutional effort to control the problem at its inception. For me, there is an important difference between this state action and a State's adamant and rigid refusal to face, or even to recognize, the "significant . . . consequences"—to the woman— of a forced or unwanted conception. I have found it difficult to rule constitutional, for example, state efforts to block, at that later point, a woman's attempt to deal with the enormity of the problem confronting her, just as I have rejected state efforts to prevent women from rationally taking steps to prevent that problem from arising. In contrast, I am persuaded that, although a minor has substantial privacy rights in intimate affairs connected with procreation, California's efforts to prevent teenage pregnancy are to be viewed differently from Utah's efforts to inhibit a woman from dealing with pregnancy once it has become an inevitability.

Craig v. *Boren* was an opinion which, in large part, I joined. The plurality opinion in the present case points out the Court's respective phrasings of the applicable test in *Reed* v. *Reed*. I vote to affirm the judgment of the Supreme Court of California and to uphold the State's gender-based classification on that test and as exemplified by those two cases and by *Schlesinger* v. *Ballard*.

I note, also, that § 261.5 of the California Penal Code is just one of several California statutes intended to protect the juvenile. Justice STEWART, in his concurring opinion, appropriately observes that § 261.5 is "but one part of a broad statutory scheme that protects all minors from the problems and risks attendant upon adolescent sexual activity."

I think, too, that it is only fair, with respect to this particular petitioner, to point out that his partner, Sharon, appears not to have been an unwilling participant in at least the initial stages of the intimacies that took place the night of June 3, 1978. Petitioner's and Sharon's nonacquaintance with each other before the incident; their drinking; their withdrawal from the others of the group; their foreplay, in which she willingly participated and seems to have encouraged; and the closeness of their ages (a difference of only one year and 18 days) are factors that should make this case an unattractive one to prosecute at all, and especially to prosecute as a felony, rather than as a misdemeanor chargeable under § 261.5. But the State has chosen to prosecute in that manner, and the facts, I reluctantly conclude, may fit the crime.

Justice BRENNAN, with whom Justices WHITE and MARSHALL join, dissenting.

I

It is disturbing to find the Court so splintered on a case that presents such a straightforward issue: Whether the admittedly gender-based classification in Cal. Penal Code Ann. § 261.5 bears a sufficient relationship to the State's asserted goal of preventing teenage pregnancies to survive the "mid-level" constitutional scrutiny mandated by *Craig* v. *Boren*. Applying the analytical framework provided by our precedents, I am convinced that there is only one proper resolution of this issue: the classification must be declared unconstitutional. I fear that the plurality opinion and Justices STEWART and BLACKMUN reach the opposite result by placing too much emphasis on the desirability of achieving the State's asserted statutory goal—prevention of teenage pregnancy—and not enough emphasis on the fundamental question of whether the sex-based discrimination in the California statute is *substantially* related to the achievement of that goal.

II

After some uncertainty as to the proper framework for analyzing equal protection challenges to statutes containing gender-based classifications, this Court settled upon the proposition that a statute containing a gender-based classification cannot withstand constitutional challenge unless the classification is substantially related to the achievement of an important governmental objective.

The State of California vigorously asserts that the "important governmental objective" to be served by § 261.5 is the prevention of teenage pregnancy. It claims that its statute furthers this goal by deterring sexual activity by males—the class of persons it considers more responsible for causing those pregnancies. But even assuming that prevention of teenage pregnancy is an important governmental objective and that it is in fact an objective of § 261.5, California still has the burden of proving that there are fewer teenage pregnancies under its gender-based statutory rape law than there would be if the law were gender neutral. To meet this burden, the State must show that because its statutory rape law punishes only males, and not females, it more effectively deters minor females from having sexual intercourse.

The plurality assumes that a gender-neutral statute would be less effective than § 261.5 in deterring sexual activity because a gender-neutral statute would create significant enforcement problems. The plurality thus accepts the State's assertion that

> "a female is surely less likely to report violations of the statute if she herself would be subject to criminal prosecution. In an area already fraught with prosecutorial difficulties, we decline to hold that the Equal Protection Clause requires a legislature to enact a statute so broad that it may well be incapable of enforcement."

However, a State's bare assertion that its gender-based statutory classification substantially furthers an important governmental interest is not enough to meet its burden of proof under *Craig* v. *Boren*. Rather, the State must produce evidence that will persuade the court that its assertion is true.

The State has not produced such evidence in this case. Moreover, there are at least two serious flaws in the State's assertion that law enforcement problems created by a gender-neutral statutory rape law would make such a statute less effective than a gender-based statute in deterring sexual activity.

First, the experience of other jurisdictions, and California itself, belies the plurality's conclusion that a gender-neutral statutory rape law "may well be incapable of enforcement." There are now at least 37 States that have enacted gender-neutral statutory rape laws. Although most of these laws protect young per-

sons (of either sex) from the sexual exploitation of older individuals, the laws of Arizona, Florida, and Illinois permit prosecution of both minor females and minor males for engaging in mutual sexual conduct. California has introduced no evidence that those States have been handicapped by the enforcement problems the plurality finds so persuasive. Surely, if those States could provide such evidence, we might expect that California would have introduced it.

In addition, the California Legislature in recent years has revised other sections of the Penal Code to make them gender-neutral. For example, Cal. Penal Code Ann. §§ 286(b)(1) and 288a(b)(1), prohibiting sodomy and oral copulation with a "person who is under 18 years of age," could cause two minor homosexuals to be subjected to criminal sanctions for engaging in mutually consensual conduct. Again, the State has introduced no evidence to explain why a gender-neutral statutory rape law would be any more difficult to enforce than those statutes.

The second flaw in the State's assertion is that even assuming that a gender-neutral statute would be more difficult to enforce, the State has still not shown that those enforcement problems would make such a statute less effective than a gender-based statute in deterring minor females from engaging in sexual intercourse. Common sense, however, suggests that a gender-neutral statutory rape law is potentially a *greater* deterrent of sexual activity than a gender-based law, for the simple reason that a gender-neutral law subjects both men and women to criminal sanctions and thus arguably has a deterrent effect on twice as many potential violators. Even if fewer persons were prosecuted under the gender-neutral law, as the State suggests, it would still be true that twice as many persons would be *subject* to arrest. The State's failure to prove that a gender-neutral law would be a less effective deterrent than a gender-based law, like the State's failure to prove that a gender-neutral law would be difficult to enforce, should have led this Court to invalidate § 261.5.

III

Until very recently, no California court or commentator had suggested that the purpose of California's statutory rape law was to protect young women from the risk of pregnancy. Indeed, the historical development of § 261.5 demonstrates that the law was initially enacted on the premise that young women, in contrast to young men, were to be deemed legally incapable of consenting to an act of sexual intercourse. Because their chastity was considered particularly precious, those young women were felt to be uniquely in need of the State's protection. In contrast, young men were assumed to be capable of making such decisions for themselves; the law therefore did not offer them any special protection.

It is perhaps because the gender classification in California's statutory rape law was initially designed to further these outmoded sexual stereotypes, rather than to reduce the incidence of teenage pregnancies, that the State has been unable to demonstrate a substantial relationship between the classification and its newly asserted goal. But whatever the reason, the State has not shown that Cal. Penal Code § 261.5 is any more effective than a gender-neutral law would be in deterring minor females from engaging in sexual intercourse. It has therefore not met its burden of proving that the statutory classification is substantially related to the achievement of its asserted goal.

I would hold that § 261.5 violates the Equal Protection Clause of the Fourteenth Amendment, and I would reverse the judgment of the California Supreme Court.

Justice STEVENS, dissenting.

Local custom and belief—rather than statutory laws of venerable but doubtful ancestry—will determine the volume of sexual activity among unmarried teenagers. The empirical evidence cited by the plurality demonstrates the futility of the notion that a statutory prohibition will significantly affect the volume of that activity or provide a meaningful solution to the problems created by it. Nevertheless, as a matter of constitutional power, unlike my Brother BRENNAN I would have no doubt about the validity of a state law prohibiting all unmarried teenagers from engaging in sexual intercourse. The societal interests in reducing the incidence of venereal disease and teenage pregnancy are sufficient, in my judgment, to justify a prohibition of conduct that increases the risk of those harms.

My conclusion that a nondiscriminatory prohibition would be constitutional does not help me answer the question whether a prohibition applicable to only half of the joint participants in the risk-creating conduct is also valid. It cannot be true that the validity of a total ban is an adequate justification for a selective prohibition; otherwise, the constitutional objection to discriminatory rules would be meaningless. The question in this case is whether the difference between males and females justifies this statutory discrimination based entirely on sex.

The fact that the Court did not immediately acknowledge that the capacity to become pregnant is what primarily differentiates the female from the male does not impeach the validity of the plurality's newly found wisdom. I think the plurality is quite correct in making the assumption that the joint act that this law seeks to prohibit creates a greater risk of harm for the female than for the male. But the plurality surely cannot believe that the risk of pregnancy confronted by the female—any more than the risk of venereal disease confronted by males as well as females—has provided an effective deterrent to voluntary female participation in the risk-creating conduct. Yet the plurality's decision seems to rest on the assumption that the California Legislature acted on the basis of that rather fanciful notion.

In my judgment, the fact that a class of persons is especially vulnerable to a risk that a statute is designed to avoid is a reason for making the statute applicable to that class. The argument that a special need for protection provides a rational explanation for an exemption is one I simply do not comprehend.

In this case, the fact that a female confronts a greater risk of harm than a male is a reason for applying the prohibition to her—not a reason for granting her a license to use her own judgment on whether or not to assume the risk. Surely, if we examine the problem from the point of view of society's interest in preventing the risk-creating conduct from occurring at all, it is irrational to exempt 50% of the potential violators. See dissent of Justice BRENNAN. And, if we view the government's interest as that of a *parens patriae* seeking to protect its subjects from harming themselves, the discrimination is actually perverse. Would a rational parent making rules for the conduct of twin children of opposite sex simultaneously forbid the son and authorize the daughter to engage in conduct that is especially harmful to the daughter? That is the effect of this statutory classification.

If pregnancy or some other special harm is suffered by one of the two participants in the prohibited act, that special harm no doubt would constitute a legitimate mitigating factor in deciding what, if any, punishment might be appropriate in a given case. But from the standpoint of fashioning a general preventive rule—or, indeed, in determining appropriate punishment when neither party in fact has suffered any special harm—I regard a total exemption for the members of the more endangered class as utterly irrational.

In my opinion, the only acceptable justification for a general rule requiring disparate treatment of the two participants in a joint act must be a legislative judgment that one is more guilty than the other. The risk-creating conduct that this statute is designed to prevent requires the participation of two persons—one male and one female. In many situations it is probably true that one is the aggressor and the other is either an unwilling, or at least a less willing, participant in the joint act. If a statute authorized punishment of only one participant and required the prosecutor to prove that that participant had been the aggressor, I assume that the discrimination would be valid. Although the question is less clear, I also assume, for the purpose of deciding this case, that it would be permissible to punish only the male participant, if one element of the offense were proof that he had been the aggressor, or at least in some respects the more responsible participant in the joint act. The statute at issue in this case, however, requires no such proof. The question raised by this statute is whether the State, consistently with the Federal Constitution, may always punish the male and never the female when they are equally responsible or when the female is the more responsible of the two.

It would seem to me that an impartial lawmaker could give only one answer to that question. The fact that the California Legislature has decided to apply its prohibition only to the male may reflect a legislative judgment that in the typical case the male is actually the more guilty party. Any such judgment must, in turn, assume that the decision to engage in the risk-creating conduct is always—or at least typically—a male decision. If that assumption is valid, the statutory classification should also be valid. But what is the support for the assumption? It is not contained in the record of this case or in any legislative history or scholarly study that has been called to our attention. I think it is supported to some extent by traditional attitudes toward male-female relationships. But the possibility that such a habitual attitude may reflect nothing more than an irrational prejudice makes it an insufficient justification for discriminatory treatment that is otherwise blatantly unfair. For, as I read this statute, it requires that one, and only one, of two equally guilty wrongdoers be stigmatized by a criminal conviction.

I cannot accept the State's argument that the constitutionality of the discriminatory rule can be saved by an assumption that prosecutors will commonly invoke this statute only in cases that actually involve a forcible rape, but one that cannot be established by proof beyond a reasonable doubt. That assumption implies that a State has a legitimate interest in convicting a defendant on evidence that is constitutionally insufficient. Of course, the State may create a lesser-included offense that would authorize punishment of the more guilty party, but surely the interest in obtaining convictions on inadequate proof cannot justify a statute that punishes one who is equally or less guilty than his partner.

Nor do I find at all persuasive the suggestion that this discrimination is adequately justified by the desire to encourage females to inform against their male partners. Even if the concept of a wholesale informant's exemption were an acceptable enforcement device, what is the justification for defining the exempt class entirely by reference to sex rather than by reference to a more neutral criterion such as relative innocence? Indeed, if the exempt class is to be composed entirely of members of one sex, what is there to support the view that the statutory purpose will be better served by granting the informing license to females rather than to males? If a discarded male partner informs on a promiscuous female, a timely threat of prosecution might well prevent the precise harm the statute is intended to minimize.

Finally, even if my logic is faulty and there actually is some speculative basis for treating equally guilty males and females differently, I still believe that any such speculative justification would be outweighed by the paramount interest in even-handed enforcement of the law. A rule that authorizes punishment of only one of two equally guilty wrongdoers violates the essence of the constitutional requirement that the sovereign must govern impartially.

I respectfully dissent.

PART FOUR

Responsibility

One convenient way of dividing up the subject matter of law is to begin by distinguishing between private and public law. The function of private law is to provide an authoritative way to resolve disputes between private parties. When one party, the plaintiff, makes a claim against another, the defendant, that the defendant has violated a contractual agreement, or taken possession of land that belongs to the plaintiff, or caused the plaintiff personal injuries by negligent or reckless conduct or, even worse, by deliberately intending such harm, then the apparatus of private law is brought into play to settle the issue. The branches of the private law include the law of torts and the law of contracts. The law of torts decides whether the plaintiff has suffered harms that should be compensated for by payments from the defendant and, if so, how large the compensatory payments should be. The law of contracts can require compensatory monetary payments for breach of contract or in some cases compel specific performance of the action promised but not yet done by the defendant. The aim of public law, on the other hand, is not compensation but rather criminal punishment. In criminal law the party that claims to have been wronged by the defendant is not called the plaintiff, but rather the state or the crown or the people. Those wrongful acts that not only injure private parties but also set back widely shared public interests are called crimes.

Whether we are talking about crimes and the issue of punishment or torts and the issue of compensation, we come immediately to an appreciation of the court's role in protecting the rights of the defendant, who is being accused of some kind of wrongful conduct and threatened either with punishment or with legal pressure to make often costly compensation. If

the defendant is to have civil liability imposed on him or her or convicted of a crime, the defendant must be shown to be responsible for what she did or for the harm suffered by the plaintiff. That means that the defendant's conduct must be shown to have satisfied the definition of the tort or crime she is accused of, that the defendant can be shown to have acted or omitted to act in the appropriately voluntary way, that her conduct was appropriately faulty, and that the faulty action was the cause of a harm or of an unreasonable risk of a harm. Moreover, the defendant must be allowed to cite one or more recognized defenses to the charges. To begin with, she can deny the facts alleged in the accusation or argue that the prosecution (in criminal law) or the plaintiff (in tort law) has not successfully borne the assigned burden of proof (a "failed proof defense"). The defendant can do this by presenting evidence that tends to undermine the case against her. There is thus something essentially negative about this kind of defense since it aims to negate (or to "negative" as lawyers often put it) the case of the plaintiff (in torts) or the prosecution (in a criminal trial). In contrast some important defenses are labeled affirmative defenses. The defendant argues in these instances that, even if the other side has successfully shown that the defendant's conduct satisfied the defining elements of the crime or tort charged, there are independent reasons for acquittal (in the case of a crime) or release from civil liability (for harm). At this point, typically, the burden switches to the defendant to plead and prove the affirmative defense (usually with a lighter burden of proof). Defenses of this kind in the criminal law are divided into two subcategories, justifications and excuses. (This terminology is used less frequently in the law of torts than in contract law, and the terms are especially difficult to apply to defenses to negligence, though the terminology fits comfortably enough with various defenses to intentional torts, such as self-defense and consent.)

To justify one's conduct is to show that it was in the circumstances legally right or correct, or at least all right, or permissible—that is, not wrong. Thus a justification, in George Fletcher's words, "renders a nominal violation of the criminal law lawful, and therefore exempt from criminal sanctions."[1] The most common criminal justifications are self-defense, defense of others, defense of property, justified use of force in law enforcement, and necessity (forced choice of the lesser evil). An excuse, on the other hand, does not deny that the defendant has done something prohibited by law and that he did it without justification. The excuse claims only that the defendant could not help doing what he did or didn't know what he was doing—in short, that the defendant was not responsible and therefore is not to blame. Indeed, the criminal action cannot be imputed to the defendant at all, as his doing, without qualification. The most common excuses are infancy (imagine a two-year-old charged with homicide), duress, provocation (a mitigation only), insanity, and intoxication.

Responsibility, Negligence, and Causation

That the defendant's action, or perhaps the defendant's faulty action, was the cause of a harm to the plaintiff, is a necessary condition for tort liability.[2] It is also a necessary condition for some, but not all, kinds of criminal liability. One cannot commit murder, for example, unless one's action caused the death of a victim, but one can commit attempted murder, without actually causing a death or any other injury to one's would-be victim. The causal condition is more constant in torts because deciding on compensation is the whole object of a tort proceeding. Unless a harm has been caused, there is nothing to be compensated.

Even when it is clear that the defendant was at fault in acting as she did (for example, that the defendant acted negligently, without due care) and equally clear that the plaintiff was harmed, it may be extremely difficult to know whether that faulty act or omission was the cause of the harm. Sometimes it is

not difficult to know that the act was a necessary condition of the harm or a *conditio sine qua non,* or equivalently a "but for cause." (But for the act, the harm would not have happened.) But that is not enough to warrant pinning the label *cause* on it. But for the actor's father meeting the actor's mother, the harm would not have occurred, because the actor would never have come into existence. And but for the act in this case, the victim would not have gone to the drugstore to buy his newly prescribed medication, and would not have met the woman there whom he was eventually to marry. Thus the offspring of that marriage, another human being now in existence, would never have been born, with further consequences on into the infinite future. In order to avoid commitment to the proposition that the liability of a negligent defendant can extend to all those losses that would not have occurred but for the defendant's negligence, legal theorists have urged that legal cause—or proximate cause, as they call it—be understood as a severe restriction of "but for cause," confining it to necessary conditions that are significant and important, or proximate, or near and immediate, or directly traceable, or foreseeable. It is usually acknowledged that whether an act is a "but for cause" of some consequence is a question of fact. Still another common term for causally necessary condition then, is cause-in-fact, and that phrase is often used to contrast "but for cause" with legal cause, the latter being only partly factual and partly decisional—partly a matter of legal policy rather than entirely a matter of fact.

A popular belief in the first half of the twentieth century was that legal, or proximate, cause is simply a blend of cause-in-fact and policy. A court's decision to permit or exclude a given necessary condition as a proximate cause of a plaintiff's harm, it was often said, is a policy decision disguised as a factual discovery. Hart and Honoré, in the work from which their selection is drawn, try to find an alternative to that view. They argue that the common-sense concept of a cause, complex though it may be, provides a framework for determinations of proximate cause that are policy neutral.

In 1928, according to a leading writer on the law of torts, ". . . a bombshell burst upon this field when the New York Court of Appeals, forsaking 'proximate cause,' stated the issue of foreseeability in terms of duty" [the duty of care *to* someone or other that helps define negligence].[3] The reference is to the case of *Palsgraf* v. *Long Island Railroad Company,* which has since become "the most discussed and debated of all torts cases."[4] This case is the second selection in Part

Four. Since 1928 the *Palsgraf* decision has gradually established itself as the prevailing precedent for tort cases with so-called "unforeseeable plaintiffs," but the deep issues in the case are still controversial among theorists, probably because of a vexatious conundrum about justice at the heart of the dispute between the majority and minority opinions in that case. On the one hand, we are inclined to say that a negligent defendant, being the party at fault, ought to compensate wholly innocent people, like Mrs. Palsgraf. To be sure, in cases like *Palsgraf,* the negligent party could not have reasonably anticipated any possibility of injury to so remote and unlikely a plaintiff. It is unfair to make them liable to a party who was situated well outside the limits of the genuine risks their negligence had created. On the other hand, we must remember that Mrs. Palsgraf was wholly faultless in this episode and, if there are no alternatives between forcing a negligent railroad company to pay for her injuries or leaving them for her to deal with, justice would seem to favor her claim against the company. Still it must be remembered that the accumulated harm from a minor sort of negligence, if we include harm to those who were well outside the risk created and also those who are not members of the class to whom the risk was created, can be out of all proportion to the defendant's fault. The best rule for cases like this, it might be said, is the one that protects defendants from liability for results beyond their fault and finds a nonarbitrary "place to stop short of infinite liability."[5] Justice Cardozo's majority opinion provides such a place. After all, the railroad did not fulfill its duty of care to the last-minute passenger trying to board, but there was no duty to Mrs. Palsgraf that it left unfulfilled.

The problem of determining the scope of liability for negligence is dramatized by the *Palsgraf* case, but there are many other kinds of troublesome cases that illustrate it too, so a kind of general theory is in order. The third selection, Robert Keeton's description and analysis of "the basic rule of legal cause in negligence cases," will help students keep in focus problems that they may never before have encountered. Keeton chooses to approach the problem via a theory of legal causation, but causation as he understands it deviates considerably from the commonsense principles applied by Hart and Honoré. His notion of causation is interesting and challenging in part because it permits us to speak of negligence, or of "negligent aspects" of conduct as causes—a conception that many philosophers of causation will have trouble attempting to accommodate.

Responsibility for Results

Judith Thomson calls our attention to what she calls "the decline of cause" in the law—that is, the weakening, especially in tort law, of the requirement that the defendant's faulty act or omission was the cause of the harm or loss suffered by the plaintiff. In recent times, in some types of cases, it has become sufficient that the faulty act or omission created an unreasonable risk of the kind of harm that actually resulted. It may be that the plaintiff is unable to prove, after the passage of many years, that, say a drug company's proven negligence to persons of a certain class which includes her, was the actual cause of the actual harms she suffered. But more and more persons have begun to ask why that should be necessary at all.

Thomson connects this new skepticism about the causal condition for liability to some recent developments in moral theory. Some moral philosophers (Thomson calls them "moral sophisticates") now maintain that a negligent actor does no more than create the risk of a harm, and is not responsible for the full harm that results. For beyond the risk, the actual results are in large part a matter of luck, for which the actor deserves neither credit nor blame. Suppose we compare two cases in which the blame for wrongful risk creation is equal, harm resulting nevertheless in the one but not in the other case. In these cases only luck, not moral merit or demerit, distinguishes the two actors. Thomson notes how contrary this is to the moral responses of the man and woman in the street, who make sharply different moral appraisals of the actors, depending on the actual results of their risk creation. In this essay Thomson tries to support their commonsense moral judgments with philosophical argument.

The problem of explaining the moral significance, if any, of actual results also arises in the criminal law. The most familiar example is that of two persons, each intending to kill an enemy. With identical motives and intentions, and in perfectly parallel circumstances, each fires, but only the first succeeds in killing the victim. Unknown to the second assassin, the would-be victim is wearing a bulletproof vest. Thomson offers an argument, not just for continuing our practice of punishing murder more than attempted murder, but also for regarding the successful murderer as more blameworthy. This conclusion is the target of the article by Richard Parker. Parker, concentrating on the criminal law, concludes that the significance of actual harmful results, in both law and morals, is greatly overrated—the man and woman in the street notwithstanding.

Responsibility for Non-Intervention

Both the criminal law and the law of torts in the English-speaking countries hold people responsible for certain wrongful interventions in the lives of others. But the Anglo-American law has never helped persons civilly or criminally responsible for their noninterventions in the activities of people to whom they stand in no special legal relation. In this respect the English-speaking countries (including 47 of the 50 American states) differ markedly from most of the rest of the world. Most nations have criminal sanctions requiring citizens to attempt "easy rescues" even of total strangers. It is a different matter when the person in a position to rescue an endangered party is related to that person (say, as parent to child) or has special duties to attempt rescue (as, for example, those of a paid lifeguard toward the specific persons who bathe on the guard's assigned stretch of beach), or has contracted with the endangered person to offer constant protection. A morally sensitive person might wonder why there should be duties to rescue *only* in these special cases and not in the case of unrelated parties. Thomas Babington Macaulay, in the very brief selection included here, addresses his remarks primarily to that query. Most British and American legal writers in the last century and a half have agreed that Macaulay satisfactorily defended the Anglo-American practice. On the same subject, John Kleinig sketches some of the developments in legal thought since Macaulay's time.

Some Criminal Defenses

The remainder of the selections in Part Four discuss moral or philosophical problems raised by various defenses to criminal liability. The defenses discussed here are not exhaustive, but they are fairly representative. There are two negativing defenses claiming that the prosecution has failed to shoulder the burden of proving beyond a reasonable doubt that all of the definitional elements of the crime have been satisfied. The remainder of the defenses here illustrated, interpreted and in some cases evaluated, are affirmative defenses; two of these are justifications, and two are excuses.

People v. *Young* is a criminal case involving a very serious mistake of fact. Mr. Young's mistaken belief was that the two ununiformed men he saw beating a third were ordinary thugs, in fact, they were plainclothes policemen trying to make an arrest. His defense involved presenting evidence meant to create a reasonable doubt that all of the elements of the crime he had been charged with were satisfied. In particular, he claimed that he lacked *mens rea,* an appropriately guilty mind. He *did* attack policemen and interfere with their legitimate work, but he did not do that act purposely, or knowingly, though it might be argued that he did that act recklessly or possibly even negligently. Another question that arises is whether the court should instruct the jury to use an objective or a subjective standard in appraising Young's false belief. Are they to compare it with the beliefs, whether true or false, of a "reasonable man" in his circumstances? Does the law require his beliefs to be true or only reasonable? Similarly, does the law require his false beliefs to be reasonable or only sincere, honest, and genuine? There are important policy issues behind these questions, as well as the difficult question of fairness to a courageous if quixotic person of good intentions. (Compare this case with *Regina* v. *Morgan,* in Part Three.)

If *Palsgraf* is the most discussed noncriminal real case in our legal history, Lon Fuller's "The Case of the Speluncean Explorers" is certainly the most discussed fictitious criminal case, even though it was composed as recently as 1948. The fictitious defendants in that case might have tried a number of defenses, but the most promising one was necessity (or forced choice of the lesser evil). That is, they could have argued, as some members of the specially appointed judicial panel that heard their case did argue, that they were forced by circumstances beyond their control to choose whether to die of starvation or to select by voluntary lottery a victim to be killed and cannibalized. Following one alternative, four would live and one would die; following the other, all five would die. Their choice of the lesser evil, they could claim, was a justified choice. At least, they might say, that it is not consistent to admit that self-defense can justify homicide while equally threatening impersonal necessity cannot. One of Professor Fuller's former students, Anthony D'Amato, wrote a fictitious sequel to this case in 1980. From this sequel, "Further Proceedings," we have taken the opinion of one expert, Professor Wun, to supplement those of Fuller's five judges.

People v. *Goetz* is one of the leading cases in

our recent past in which self-defense is the defendant's declared justification. Goetz had shot five relatively unarmed black youths in a New York subway train. He claimed the youths were threatening him. The complicated facts in the case make it very difficult to decide. They also reveal some of the difficulties in formulating adequate rules for the legal justification called self-defense. (See also *State* v. *Kelly,* in Part Three.)

The crime at issue in the fictitious tale "The Case of Lady Eldon's French Lace" is attempted smuggling. The attempt was not successful because, unknown to Lady Eldon, the British government had removed French lace from the duty list the day before she tried to smuggle it. It is impossible, so it is said, to commit a crime by doing something that is completely legal. If one is charged with attempt in those circumstances, then one can argue in one's defense that the *actus reus* (guilty act) specified in the definition of the crime has not been satisfied (a failed proof defense). The *mens rea* condition, however, is sometimes satisfied in spades! There are dozens of exquisitely comical examples in the casebooks of defendants struggling mightily to do something they think is illegal while all of the time the act they labor to complete is perfectly legal. Why shouldn't a guilty mind (when it is *that* guilty) be sufficient for criminal liability (as it clearly is for moral guilt)? And is it really impossible to attempt to do something that is impossible?

The remaining selections in Part Four concern the bewildering criminal excuse of insanity. The famous M'Naghten Rules and its leading American rival, the American Law Institute's *Model Penal Code,* are here reprinted, along with Hyman Gross's article on mental abnormality as an excuse. The main issue in *State* v. *Guido* is "What constitutes a disease?" This question must be answered before a key element in the M'Naghten Rules, that which requires a "disease of the mind," can be considered. Behind these questions, according to Chief Justice Weintraub, lies the assumption that, even if we leave insanity out of the picture, "some wrongdoers are sick and some are bad." How to distinguish between these two classes, if Weintraub's assumption is correct, has proven to be the most difficult—perhaps because the most fundamental—of the puzzles about responsibility.

The concluding selection, "Two Views of the Psychopathic Personality," contains excerpts from the first important study of the psychopathic personality, that of the physician Hervey Cleckley; from two social scientists, William and Joan McCord, who have a theory of how children come to grow into psychopaths; and some comments by Joel Feinberg. If ever any people have straddled the ill-drawn line between sane wrongdoers who are sick, and sane wrongdoers who are bad, the psychopaths do. One of the many reasons for studying them, therefore, is to better understand the distinction, if there really is one, between mental illness and pure badness.

---

1. *George Fletcher, "Justification," in* Encyclopedia of Crime and Justice, *p. 941.*
2. *This bold statement in the text is no longer universally true. See Judith Thomson, "The Decline of Cause."*
3. *Prosser and Keeton on* The Law of Torts, *5th edition (St. Paul: West Publishing Co., 1984), p. 284.*
4. Loc. cit.
5. Ibid., *p. 287.*

Responsibility for Results

CAUSATION AND RESPONSIBILITY*

H. L. A. Hart and A. M. Honoré

I. Responsibility in Law and Morals

We have so far traced the outline of a variety of causal concepts the diversity of which is to be seen in such familiar examples of the use of causal language as the following: "The explosion of gas caused the building to collapse," "He made him hand over his money by threatening to shoot," "The consequence of leaving the car unlocked was that it was stolen," "The strike was the cause of the drop in profits."

The main structure of these different forms of causal connection is plain enough, and there are many situations constantly recurring in ordinary life to which they have a clear application; yet it is also true that like many other fundamental notions these have aspects which are vague or indeterminate; they involve the weighing of matters of degree, or the plausibility of hypothetical speculations, for which no exact criteria can be laid down. Hence their application, outside the safe area of simple examples, calls for judgment and is something over which judgments often differ. Even the type of case which is most familiar, and most nearly approximates to Mill's model for "cause and effect," where causal connection between a physical event and some earlier initiating event or human action is traced through a series of physical events, involves an implicit judgment on such imprecise issues as the *normal* condition of the thing concerned and the *abnormality* of what is identified as

the cause. Very often, in particular where an omission to take common precautions is asserted to be the cause of some disaster, a speculation as to what *would have* happened had the precaution been taken is involved. Though arguments one way or another over such hypothetical issues may certainly be rational and have more or less "weight," there is a sense in which they cannot be conclusive. When such areas of dispute are reached, the decision whether to describe the facts of a case in the terms of some given form of causal connection will be influenced very much by factors connected with the context and purpose of making the causal statement.

Hitherto we have discussed only one principal purpose for which causal language is used: i.e., when an explanation is sought or provided of some puzzling or unusual occurrence. But as well as this explanatory context, in which we are concerned with what *has* happened, there are many others. Our deliberations about our own conduct often take the form of an inquiry as to the future consequences of alternative actions; here causal connections are *ex hypothesi* bounded by the horizon of the foreseeable. But even if we confine ourselves to causal statements about the past there are still different contexts and purposes to be discriminated. Thus it would be wrong to think of the historian as using causal notions only when he is explaining. The movement of his thought is not always from the later problematic event to something

*© H.L.A. Hart and Tony Honoré 1959, 1985. Reprinted from *Causation in the Law* by H.L.A. Hart and A.M. Honoré (2nd ed. 1985) by permission of Oxford University Press.

earlier which explains it and in using causal language he is not always engaged in diagnosis. His thought very often takes the contrary direction; for in addition to providing explanations (answers to the question "why?") he is also concerned to trace the outcome, the results, or the consequences of the human actions and omissions which are his usual starting-points, though he may also work out the "effects" of natural events. So he will discuss the consequences of a king's policy or the effects of the Black Death. This is so because the narrative of history is scarcely ever a narrative of brute sequence, but is an account of the roles played by certain factors and especially by human agents. History is written to satisfy not only the need for explanation, but also the desire to identify and assess contributions made by historical figures to changes of importance; to triumphs and disasters, and to human happiness or suffering. This assessment involves tracing "consequences," "effects," or "results," and these are more frequently referred to than "causes" which has a primarily diagnostic or explanatory ring. In one sense of "responsibility" the historian determines the responsibility of human beings for certain types of change; and sometimes he does this with an eye to praising or blaming or passing other forms of moral judgment. But this need not be so; the historian, though concerned to trace the consequences of human action, need not be a moralist.

In the moral judgments of ordinary life, we have occasion to blame people because they have caused harm to others, and also, if less frequently, to insist that morally they are bound to compensate those to whom they have caused harm. These are the moral analogues of more precise legal conceptions; for, in all legal systems, liability to be punished or to make compensation frequently depends on whether actions (or omissions) have caused harm. Moral blame is not of course confined to such cases of causing harm. We blame a man who cheats or lies or breaks promises, even if no one has suffered in the particular case: this has its legal counterpart in the punishment of abortive attempts to commit crimes, and of offences constituted by the unlawful possession of certain kinds of weapons, drugs, or materials, for example, for counterfeiting currency. When the occurrence of harm is an essential part of the ground for blame the connection of the person blamed with the harm may take any of the forms of causal connection we have examined. His action may have initiated a series of physical events dependent on each other and culminating in injury to persons or property, as in wounding and kill-

ing. These simple forms are the paradigms for the lawyer's talk of harm "directly" caused. But we blame people also for harm which arises from or is the consequence of their neglect of common precautions; we do this even if harm would not have come about without the intervention of another human being deliberately exploiting the opportunities provided by neglect. The main legal analogue here is liability for "negligence." The wish of many lawyers to talk in this branch of the law of harm being "within the risk of" rather than "caused by" the negligent conduct manifests appreciation of the fact that a different form of relationship is involved in saying that harm is the consequence, on the one hand, of an explosion and, on the other, of a failure to lock the door by which a thief has entered. Again, we blame people for the harm which we say is the consequence of their influence over others, either exerted by non-rational means or in one of the ways we have designated "interpersonal transactions." To such grounds for responsibility there correspond many important legal conceptions: the instigation of crimes ("commanding" or "procuring") constitutes an important ground of criminal responsibility and the concepts of enticement and of inducement (by threats or misrepresentation) are an element in many civil wrongs as well as in criminal offences.

The law, however, especially in matters of compensation, goes far beyond these causal grounds for responsibility in such doctrines as the vicarious responsibility of a master for his servant's civil wrongs and that of the responsibility of an occupier of property for injuries suffered by passers-by from defects of which the occupier had no knowledge and which he had no opportunity to repair. There is a recognition, perhaps diminishing, of this non-causal ground of responsibility outside the law; responsibility is sometimes admitted by one person or group of persons, even if no precaution has been neglected by them, for harm done by persons related to them in a special way, either by family ties or as members of the same social or political association. Responsibility may be simply "placed" by moral opinion on one person for what others do. The simplest case of such vicarious moral responsibility is that of a parent for damage done by a child; its more complex (and more debatable) form is the moral responsibility of one generation of a nation to make compensation for their predecessors' wrong, such as the Germans admitted in payment of compensation to Israel.

At this point it is necessary to issue a caveat about the meaning of the expression "responsible" if only to avoid prejudicing a question about the character of *legal* determinations of causal connection. . . . Usually in discussion of the law and occasionally in morals, to say that someone is responsible for some harm means that in accordance with legal rules or moral principles it is at least permissible, if not mandatory, to blame or punish or exact compensation from him. In this use[1] the expression "responsible for" does not refer to a factual connection between the person held responsible and the harm but simply to his liability under the rules to be blamed, punished, or made to pay. The expressions "answerable for" or "liable for" are practically synonymous with "responsible for" in *this* use, in which there is no implication that the person held responsible actually *did* or *caused* the harm. In this sense a master is (in English law) responsible for the damage done by his servants acting within the scope of their authority and a parent (in French and German law) for that done by his children; it is in this sense that a guarantor or surety is responsible for the debts or the good behaviour of other persons and an insurer for losses sustained by the insured. Very often, however, especially in discussion of morals, to say that someone is responsible for some harm is to assert (*inter alia*) that he *did* the harm or *caused* it, though such a statement is perhaps rarely confined to this for it usually also carries with it the implication that it is at least permissible to blame or punish him. This double use of the expression no doubt arises from the important fact that doing or causing harm constitutes not only the most usual but the primary type of ground for holding persons responsible in the first sense. We still speak of inanimate or natural causes such as storms, floods, germs, or the failure of electricity supply as "responsible for" disasters; this mode of expression, now taken only to mean that they caused the disasters, no doubt originated in the belief that all that happens is the work of spirits when it is not that of men. Its survival in the modern world is perhaps some testimony to the primacy of causal connection as an element in responsibility and to the intimate connection between the two notions.

We shall consider later an apparent paradox which interprets in a different way the relationship between cause and responsibility. Much modern thought on causation in the law rests on the contention that the statement that someone has caused harm either means no more than that the harm would not have happened without ("but for") his action or where (as in normal legal usage and in all ordinary speech), it apparently means more than this, it is a disguised way of asserting the "normative" judgment that he is responsible in the first sense, i.e. that it is proper or just to blame or punish him or make him pay. On this view to say that a person caused harm is not really, though ostensibly it is, to give a *ground* or *reason* for holding him responsible in the first sense; for we are only in a position to say that he has caused harm when we have decided that he is responsible. Pending consideration of the theories of legal causation which exploit this point of view we shall use the expression "responsible for" only in the first of the two ways explained, i.e. without any implication as to the type of factual connection between the person held responsible and the harm; and we shall provisionally, though without prejudicing the issue, treat statements that a person caused harm as one sort of non-tautologous ground or reason for saying that he is responsible in this sense.

If we may provisionally take what in ordinary life we say and do at its face value, it seems that there coexist in ordinary thought, apart from the law though mirrored in it, several different types of connection between a person's action and eventual harm which render him responsible for it; and in both law and morals the various forms of causal connection between act or omission and harm are the most obvious and least disputable reasons for holding anyone responsible. Yet, in order to understand the extent to which the causal notions of ordinary thought are used in the law, we must bear in mind the many factors which must differentiate moral from legal responsibility in spite of their partial correspondence. The law is not only not bound to follow the moral patterns of attribution of responsibility but, even when it does, it must take into account, in a way which the private moral judgment need not and does not, the general social consequences which are attached to its judgments of responsibility; for they are of a gravity quite different from those attached to moral censure. The use of the legal sanctions of imprisonment, or enforced monetary compensation against individuals, has such formidable repercussions on the general life of society that the fact that individuals have a type of connection with harm which is adequate for moral censure or claims for compensation is only *one* of the factors which the law must consider, in defining the kinds of connection between actions and harm for which it will hold individuals legally responsible. Always to follow the private moral judgment here would be far too expensive for the law: not only in the crude sense that it would entail a vast machinery of courts and officials, but in the more important sense that it would inhibit or discourage too many other valuable activities of society. To limit the *types* of harm which the law will recognize is not enough; even if the types of harm are limited it would still be too much for any society to punish or exact compensation from individuals whenever their connection with harm of such types would justify moral censure. Conversely, social needs may require that compensation should be paid and even (though less obviously) that punishment be inflicted where no such connection between the person held responsible and the harm exists.

So causing harm of a legally recognized sort or being connected with such harm in any of the ways that justify moral blame, though vitally important and perhaps basic in a legal system, is not and should not be either always necessary or always sufficient for legal responsibility. All legal systems in response either to tradition or to social needs both extend responsibility and cut it off in ways which diverge from the simpler principles of moral blame. In England a man is not guilty of murder if the victim of his attack does not die within a year and day. In New York a person who negligently starts a fire is liable to pay only for the first of several houses which it destroys.[2] These limitations imposed by legal policy are *prima facie* distinguishable from limitations due to the frequent requirement of legal rules that responsibility be limited to harm caused by wrongdoing. Yet a whole school of thought maintains that this distinction does not exist or is not worth drawing.

Apart from this, morality can properly leave certain things vague into which a legal system must attempt to import some degree of precision. Outside the law nothing requires us, when we find the case too complex or too strange, to say whether any and, if so, which of the morally significant types of connection between a person's action and harm exists; we can simply say the case is too difficult for us to pass judgment, at least where moral condemnation of others is concerned. No doubt we evade less easily our questions about our own connection with harm, and the great novelists have often described, sometimes in language very like the lawyers, how the conscience may be still tortured by uncertainties as to the *character* of a part in the production of harm, even when all the facts are known.[3] The fact that there is no precise system of punishments or rewards for common sense to administer, and so there are no "forms of action" or "pleadings" to define precise heads of responsibility for harm, means that the principles which guide common-sense attributions of responsibility give precise answers only in relatively simple types of case.

II. Tracing Consequences

"To consequences no limit can be set": "Every event which would not have happened if an earlier event had not happened is the consequence of that earlier event." These two propositions are not equivalent in meaning and are not equally or in the same way at variance with ordinary thought. They have, however, both been urged sometimes in the same breath by the legal theorist[4] and the philosopher: they are indeed sometimes said by lawyers to be "the philosophical doctrine" of causation. It is perhaps not difficult even for the layman to accept the first proposition as a truth about certain physical events; an explosion may cause a flash of light which will be propagated as far as the outer nebulae; its effects or consequences continue indefinitely. It is, however, a different matter to accept the view that whenever a man is murdered with a gun his death was the consequence of (still less an "effect" of or "caused by") the manufacture of the bullet. The first tells a perhaps unfamiliar tale about unfamiliar events; the second introduces an unfamiliar, though, of course, a possible way of speaking about familiar events. It is not that this unrestricted use of "consequence" is unintelligible or never found; it is indeed used to refer to bizarre or fortuitous connections or coincidences: but the point is that the various causal notions employed for the purposes of explanation, attribution of responsibility, or the assessment of contributions to the course of history carry with them implicit limits which are similar in these different employments.

It is, then, the second proposition, defining consequence in terms of "necessary condition," with which theorists are really concerned. This proposition is the corollary of the view that, if we look into the past of any given event, there is an infinite number of events, each of which is a necessary condition of the given event and so, as much as any other, is its cause. This is the "cone"[5] of causation, so called because, since any event has a number of simultaneous conditions, the series fans out as we go back in time. The justification, indeed only partial, for calling this "the philosophical doctrine" of causation is that it resembles Mill's doctrine that "we have no right to give the name of cause to one of the conditions exclusive of the others of them." It differs from Mill's view in taking the essence of causation to be "necessary condition" and not "the sum total"[6] of the sufficient conditions of an event.

Legal theorists have developed this account of cause and consequence to show what is "factual," "objective," or "scientific" in these notions: this they call "cause in fact" and it is usually stressed as a preliminary to the doctrine that any more restricted application of these terms in the law represents nothing in the facts or in the meaning of causation, but expresses fluctuating legal policy or sentiments of what is just or convenient. Moral philosophers have insisted in somewhat similar terms that the consequences of human action are "infinite": this they have urged as an objection against the Utilitarian doctrine that the rightness of a morally right action depends on whether its consequences are better than those of any alternative action in the circumstances. "We should have to trace as far as possible the consequences not only for the persons affected directly but also for those indirectly affected and to these no limit can be set."[7] Hence, so the argument runs, we cannot either inductively establish the Utilitarian doctrine that right acts are "optimific" or use it in particular cases to discover what is right. Yet, however vulnerable at other points Utilitarianism may be as an account of moral judgment, this objection seems to rest on a mistake as to the sense of "consequence." The Utilitarian assertion that the rightness of an action depends on its consequences is not the same as the assertion that it depends on all those later occurrences which would not have happened had the action not been done, to which indeed "no limit can be set." It is important to see that the issue here is not the linguistic one whether the word "consequence" would be understood if used in this way. The point is that, though we could, we do not think in this way in tracing connections between human actions and events. Instead, whenever we are concerned with such connections, whether for the purpose of explaining a puzzling occurrence, assessing responsibility, or giving an intelligible historical narrative, we employ a set of concepts restricting in various ways what counts as a consequence. These restrictions colour *all* our thinking in causal terms; when we find them in the law we are not finding something invented by or peculiar to the law, though of course it is for the law to say when and how far it will use them and, where they are vague, to supplement them.

No short account can be given of the limits thus placed on "consequences" because these limits vary, intelligibly, with the variety of causal connection asserted. Thus we may be tempted by the generalization

that consequences must always be something intended or foreseen or at least foreseeable with ordinary care: but counterexamples spring up from many types of context where causal statements are made. If smoking is shown to cause lung cancer this discovery will permit us to describe past as well as future cases of cancer as the effect or consequence of smoking even though no one foresaw or had reasonable grounds to suspect this in the past. What is common and commonly appreciated and hence foreseeable certainly controls the scope of consequences in certain varieties of causal statement but not in all. Again the voluntary intervention of a second person very often constitutes the limit. If a guest sits down at a table laid with knife and fork and plunges the knife into his hostess's breast, her death is not in any context other than a contrived one[8] thought of as caused by, or the effect or result of the waiter's action in laying the table; nor would it be linked with this action as its consequence for any of the purposes, explanatory or attributive, for which we employ causal notions. Yet as we have seen there are many other types of case where a voluntary action or the harm it does are naturally treated to the consequence of to some prior neglect of precaution. Finally, we may think that a simple answer is already supplied by Hume and Mill's doctrine that causal connection rests on general laws asserting regular connection; yet, even in the type of case to which this important doctrine applies, reference to it alone will not solve our problem. For we often trace a causal connection between an antecedent and a consequent which themselves very rarely go together: we do this when the case can be broken down into intermediate stages, which themselves exemplify different generalizations, as when we find that the fall of a tile was the cause of someone's death, rare though this be. Here our problem reappears in the form of the question: When can generalizations be combined in this way?

We shall examine first the central type of case where the problem is of this last-mentioned form. Here the gist of the causal connection lies in the general connection with each other of the successive stages; and is not dependent on the special notions of one person providing another with reasons or exceptional opportunities for actions. This form of causal connection may exist between actions and events, and between purely physical events, and it is in such cases that the words "cause" and "causing" used of the antecedent action or event have their most obvious application. It is convenient to refer to cases of the first type where the consequence is harm as cases of "causing harm," and to refer to cases where harm is the consequence of one person providing another with reasons or opportunities for doing harm as cases of "inducing" or "occasioning" harmful acts.[9] In cases of the first type a voluntary act, or a conjunction of events amounting to a coincidence, operates as a limit in the sense that events subsequent to these are not attributed to the antecedent action or event as its consequence even though they would not have happened without it. Often such a limiting action or coincidence is thought of and described as "intervening": and lawyers speak of them as "superseding" or "extraneous" causes "breaking the chain of causation." To see what these metaphors rest on (and in part obscure) and how such factors operate as a limit we shall consider the detail of three simple cases.

(i) A forest fire breaks out, and later investigation shows that shortly before the outbreak A had flung away a lighted cigarette into the bracken at the edge of the forest, the bracken caught fire, a light breeze got up, and fanned the flames in the direction of the forest. If, on discovering these facts, we hesitate before saying that A's action caused the forest fire this would be to consider the alternative hypothesis that in spite of appearances the fire only succeeded A's action in point of time, that the bracken flickered out harmlessly and the forest fire was caused by something else. To dispose of this it may be necessary to examine in further detail the process of events between the ignition of the bracken and the outbreak of fire in the forest and to show that these exemplified certain types of continuous change. If this is shown, there is no longer any room for doubt: A's action *was* the cause of the fire, whether he intended it or not. This seems and is the simplest of cases. Yet it is important to notice that even in applying our general knowledge to a case as simple as this, indeed in regarding it as simple, we make an implicit use of a distinction between types of factor which constitute a limit in tracing consequences and those which we regard as mere circumstances "through" which we trace them. For the breeze which sprang up after A dropped the cigarette, and without which the fire would not have spread to the forest, was not only subsequent to his action but entirely independent of it: it was, however, a common recurrent feature of the environment, and, as such, it is thought of not as an "intervening" force but as merely part of the circumstances in which the cause "operates." The decision so to regard it is implicitly taken when we combine our knowledge of the successive stages of the process and assert the connection.

It is easy here to be misled by the natural metaphor of a causal "chain," which may lead us to think that the causal process consists of a series of single events each of which is dependent upon (would not have occurred without) its predecessor in the "chain" and so is dependent upon the initiating action or event. In truth in any causal process we have at each phase not single events but complex sets of conditions, and among these conditions are some which are not only subsequent to, but independent of the initiating action or event. Some of these independent conditions, such as the evening breeze in the example chosen, we classify as mere conditions in or on which the cause operates; others we speak of as "interventions" or "causes." To decide how such independent elements shall be classified is also to decide how we shall combine our knowledge of the different general connections which the successive stages exemplify, and it is important to see that nothing *in* this knowledge itself can resolve this point. We may have to go to science for the relevant general knowledge before we can assert with proper confidence that A's action did cause the fire, but science, though it tells us that an air current was required, is silent on the difference between a current in the form of an evening breeze and one produced by someone who deliberately fanned the flames as they were flickering out in the bracken. Yet an air current in this deliberately induced form is not a "condition" or "mere circumstance" through which we can trace the consequence; its presence would force us to revise the assertion that A caused the fire. Conversely if science helped us to identify as a necessary factor in producing the fire some condition or element of which we had previously been totally ignorant, e.g. the persistence of oxygen, this would leave our original judgment undisturbed if this factor were a common or pervasive feature of the environment or of the thing in question. There is thus indeed an important sense in which it is true that the distinction between cause and conditions is not a "scientific" one. It is not determined by laws or generalizations concerning connections between events.

When we have assembled all our knowledge of the factors involved in the fire, the residual question which we then confront (the attributive question) may be typified as follows: Here is A's action, here is the fire: can the fire be attributed to A's action as its consequence given that there is also this third factor (the breeze or B's intervention) without which the fire would not have happened? It is plain that, both in raising questions of this kind and in answering them, ordinary thought is powerfully influenced by the analogy between the straightforward cases of causal attribution (where the elements required for the production of harm in addition to the initiating action are all "normal" conditions) and even simpler cases of responsibility which we do not ordinarily describe in causal language at all but by the simple transitive verbs of action. These are the cases of the direct manipulation of objects involving changes in them or their position: cases where we say "He pushed it," "He broke it," "He bent it." The cases which we do confidently describe in causal language ("The fire was caused by his carelessness," "He caused a fire") are cases where no other human action or abnormal occurrence is required for the production of the effect, but only normal conditions. Such cases appear as mere long-range or less direct versions or extensions of the most obvious and fundamental case of all for the attribution of responsibility: the case where we can simply say "He did it." Conversely in attaching importance to thus causing harm as a distinct ground of responsibility and in taking certain kinds of factor (whether human interventions or abnormal occurrences), without which the initiating action would not have led to harm, to preclude the description of the case in simple causal terms, common sense is affected by the fact that here, because of the manner in which the harm eventuates, the outcome cannot be represented as a mere extension of the initiating action; the analogy with the fundamental case for responsibility ("He did it") has broken down.

When we understand the power exerted over our ordinary thought by the conception that causing harm is a mere extension of the primary case of doing harm, the interrelated metaphors which seem natural to lawyers and laymen, in describing various aspects of causal connection, fall into place and we can discuss their factual basis. The persistent notion that some kinds of event required in addition to the initiating action for the production of harm "break the chain of causation" is intelligible, if we remember that though such events actually *complete* the *explanation* of the harm (and so *make* rather than *break* the causal explanation) they do, unlike mere normal conditions, break the *analogy* with cases of simple actions. The same analogy accounts for the description of these factors as "new actions" (*novus actus*) or "new causes," "superseding," "extraneous," "intervening forces": and for the description of the initiating action when "the chain of causation" is broken as "no longer operative," "having worn out," *functus officio*.[10] So too when the "chain" is held not to be "broken" the initiating action

is said to be still "potent,"[11] "continuing," "contributing," "operative," and the mere conditions held insufficient to break the chain are "part of the background,"[12] "circumstances in which the cause operates,"[13] "the stage set," "part of the history."

(ii) *A* throws a lighted cigarette into the bracken which catches fire. Just as the flames are about to flicker out, *B*, who is not acting in concert with *A*, deliberately pours petrol on them. The fire spreads and burns down the forest. *A*'s action, whether or not he intended the forest fire, was not the cause of the fire: *B*'s was.

The voluntary intervention of a second human agent, as in this case, is a paradigm among those factors which preclude the assimilation in causal judgments of the first agent's connection with the eventual harm to the case of simple direct manipulation. Such an intervention displaces the prior action's title to be called the cause and, in the persistent metaphors found in the law, it "reduces" the earlier action and its immediate effects to the level of "mere circumstances" or "part of the history." *B* in this case was not an "instrument" through which *A* worked or a victim of the circumstances *A* has created. He has, on the contrary, freely exploited the circumstances and brought about the fire without the co-operation of any further agent or any chance coincidence. Compared with this the claim of *A*'s action to be ranked the cause of the fire fails. That this and not the moral appraisal of the two actions is the point of comparison seems clear. If *A* and *B* both intended to set the forest on fire, and this destruction is accepted as something wrong or wicked, their moral wickedness, judged by the criterion of intention, is the same. Yet the causal judgment differentiates between them. If their moral guilt is judged by the outcome, this judgment though it would differentiate between them cannot be the source of the causal judgment; for it presupposes it. The difference just is that *B* has caused the harm and *A* has not. Again, if we appraise these actions as good or bad from different points of view, this leaves the causal judgments unchanged. *A* may be a soldier of one side anxious to burn down the enemy's hideout: *B* may be an enemy soldier who has decided that his side is too iniquitous to defend. Whatever is the moral judgment passed on these actions by different speakers it would remain true that *A* had not caused the fire and *B* had.

There are, as we have said, situations in which a voluntary action would not be thought of as an intervention precluding causal connection in this way. These are the cases discussed further below where an opportunity commonly exploited for harmful actions is negligently provided, or one person intentionally provides another with the means, the opportunity, or a certain type of reason for wrongdoing. Except in such cases a voluntary intervention is a limit past which consequences are not traced. By contrast, actions which in any of a variety of different ways are less than fully voluntary are assimilated to the means by which or the circumstances in which the earlier action brings about the consequences. Such actions are not the outcome of an informed choice made without pressure from others, and the different ways in which human action may fall short in this respect range from defective muscular control, through lack of consciousness or knowledge, to the vaguer notions of duress and of predicaments, created by the first agent for the second, in which there is no "fair" choice.

In considering examples of such actions and their bearing on causal judgments there are three dangers to avoid. It would be folly to think that in tracing connections through such actions instead of regarding them, like voluntary interventions, as a limit, ordinary thought has clearly separated out their non-voluntary aspect from others by which they are often accompanied. Thus even in the crude case where A lets off a gun (intentionally or not) and startles B, so that he makes an involuntary movement of his arm which breaks a glass, the commonness of such a reaction as much as its compulsive character may influence the judgment that A's action was the cause of the damage.

Secondly we must not impute to ordinary thought all the fine discriminations that could be made and in fact are to be found in a legal system, or an equal willingness to supply answers to complex questions in causal terms. Where there is no precise system of punishment, compensation or reward to administer, ordinary men will not often have faced such questions as whether the injuries suffered by a motorist who collides with another in swerving to avoid a child are consequences attributable to the neglect of the child's parents in allowing it to wander on to the road. Such questions courts have to answer and in such cases common judgments provide only a general, though still an important indication of what are the relevant factors.

Thirdly, though very frequently non-voluntary actions are assimilated to mere conditions or means by which the first agent brings about the consequences, the assimilation is never quite complete. This is manifested by the general avoidance of many causal locutions which are appropriate when the consequences are traced (as in the first case) through purely physical events. Thus even in the case in which the second agent's role is hardly an "action" at all, e.g. where A hits B, who staggers against a glass window and breaks it, we should say that A's blow made B stagger and break the glass, rather than that A's blow caused the glass to break, though in any explanatory or attributive context the case would be *summarized* by saying that A's action was the cause of the *damage*.

In the last two cases where B's movements are involuntary in the sense that they are not part of any action which he chose or intended to do, their connection with A's action would be described by saying that A's blow *made B* stagger or *caused* him to stagger or that the noise of A's shot *made* him jump. This would be true, whether A intended or expected B to react in this way or not, and the naturalness of treating A's action as the cause of the ultimate damage is due to the causal character of this part of the process involving B's action. The same is, however, true where B's actions are not involuntary movements but A is considered to have made or caused B to do them by less crude means. This is the case if, for example, A uses threats or exploits his authority over B to make B do something, e.g. knock down a door. At least where A's threats are serious harm, or B's act was unquestionably within A's authority to order, he too has made or forced or (in formal quasi-legal parlance) "caused" B to act.

Outside the area of such cases, where B's will would be said either not to be involved at all, or to be overborne by A, are cases where A's act creates a predicament for B *narrowing* the area of choice so that he has either to inflict some harm on himself or others, or sacrifice some important interest or duty. Such cases resemble coercion in that A narrows the area of B's choice but differ from it in that this predicament need not be intentionally created. A sets a house on fire (intentionally or unintentionally): B to save himself has to jump from a height involving certain injury, or to save a child rushes in and is seriously burned. Here, of course, B's movements are not involuntary; the "necessity" of his action is here of a different order. His action is the outcome of a choice between two evils forced on him by A's action. In such cases, when B's injuries are thought of as the consequences of the fire, the implicit judgment is made that his action was the lesser of two evils and in this sense a "reasonable" one which he was obliged to make to avoid the greater evil. This is often paradoxically, though understandably, described by saying that here the agent "had no choice" but to do what he did. Such judgments involve a comparison of the importance of the respective interests sacrificed and preserved, and the final assertion that A's action was the cause of the injuries rests on evaluations about which men may differ.

Finally, the ground for treating some harm which would not have occurred without B's action as the consequence of A's action may be that B acted in ignorance of or under a mistake as to some feature of the situation created by A. Poisoning offers perhaps the simplest example of the bearing on causal judgments of actions which are less than voluntary in this Aristotelian sense. If A intending B's death deliberately poisons B's food and B, knowing this, deliberately takes the poison and dies, A has not, unless he coerced B into eating the poisoned food, caused B's death: if, however, B does not know the food to be poisoned, eats it, and dies, A has caused his death, even if he put the poison in unwittingly. Of course only the roughest judgments are passed in causal terms in such cases outside law courts, where fine degrees of "appreciation" or "reckless shutting of the eyes" may have to be discriminated from "full knowledge." Yet, rough as these are, they indicate clearly enough the controlling principles.

Though in the foregoing cases A's initiating action might often be described as "the cause" of the ultimate harm, this linguistic fact is of subordinate importance to the fact that, for whatever purpose, explanatory, descriptive, or evaluative, consequences of an action are traced, discriminations are made (except in the cases discussed later) between free voluntary interventions and less than voluntary reactions to the first action or the circumstances created by it.

(iii) The analogy with single simple actions which guides the tracing of consequences may be broken by certain kinds of conjunctions of physical events. A hits B who falls to the ground stunned and bruised by the blow; at that moment a tree crashes to the ground and kills B. A has certainly caused B's bruises but not his death: for though the fall of the tree was, like the evening breeze in our earlier example, independent of and subsequent to the initiating action, it would be differentiated from the breeze in any description in causal terms of the connection of B's death with A's action. It is to be noticed that this is not a matter which turns on the intention with which A struck B. Even if A hit B inadvertently or accidentally his blow would still be the cause of B's bruises: he would have caused them, though unintentionally. Conversely even if A had intended his blow to kill, this would have been an attempt to kill but still not the cause of B's death, unless A knew that the tree was

about to fall just at that moment. On this legal and ordinary judgments would be found to agree; and most legal systems would distinguish for the purposes of punishment[14] an attempt with a fatal upshot, issuing by such chance or anomalous events, from "causing death"—the terms in which the offenses of murder and manslaughter are usually defined.

Similarly the causal description of the case does not turn on the moral appraisal of A's action or the wish to punish it. A may be a robber and a murderer and B a saint guarding the place A hoped to plunder. Or B may be a murderer and A a hero who has forced his way into B's retreat. In both cases the causal judgment is the same. A had caused the minor injuries but not B's death, though he tried to kill him. A may indeed be praised or blamed but not for causing B's death. However intimate the connection between responsibility and causation, it does not determine causal judgments in this simple way. Nor does the causal judgment turn on a refusal to attribute grave consequences to actions which normally have less serious results. Had A's blow killed B outright and the tree, falling on his body, merely smashed his watch we should still treat the coincidental character of the fall of the tree as determining the form of causal statement. We should then recognize A's blow as the cause of B's death but not the breaking of the watch.

The connection between A's action and B's death in the first case would naturally be described in the language of *coincidence*. "It was a coincidence: it just happened that, at the very moment when A knocked B down, a tree crashed at the very place where he fell and killed him." The common legal metaphor would describe the fall of the tree as an "extraneous" cause. This, however, is dangerously misleading, as an analysis of the notion of coincidence will show. It suggests merely an event which is subsequent to and independent of some other contingency, and of course the fall of the tree has both these features in relation to A's blow. Yet in these respects the fall of the tree does not differ from the evening breeze in the earlier case where we found no difficulty in tracing causal connection. The full elucidation of the notion of a coincidence is a complex matter for, though it is very important as a limit in tracing consequences, causal questions are not the only ones to which the notion is relevant. The following are its most general characteristics. We speak of a coincidence whenever the conjunction of two or more events in certain spatial or temporal relations (1) is very unlikely by ordinary standards and (2) is for some reason significant or important, provided (3) that they occur without human contrivance and (4) are independent of each other. It is therefore a coincidence if two persons known to each other in London meet without design in Paris on their way to separate independently chosen destinations; or if two persons living in different places independently decide to write a book on the same subject. The first is a coincidence of time and place ("It just happened that we were at the same place at the same time"), and the second a coincidence of time only ("It just happened that they both decided to write on the subject at the same time").

Use of this general notion is made in the special case when the conjunction of two or more events occurs in temporal and/or spatial relationships which are significant, because, as our general knowledge of causal processes shows, this conjunction is required for the production of some given further event. In the language of Mill's idealized model, they form a necessary part of a complex set of jointly sufficient conditions. In the present case the fall of the tree just as B was struck down within its range satisfies the four criteria for a coincidence which we have enumerated. First, though neither event was of a very rare or exceptional kind, their conjunction would be rated very unlikely judged by the standards of ordinary experience. Secondly, this conjunction was causally significant for it was a necessary part of the process terminating in B's death. Thirdly, this conjunction was not consciously designed by A; had he known of the impending fall of the tree and hit B with the intention that he should fall within its range B's death would not have been the result of any coincidence. A would certainly have caused it. The common-sense principle that a contrived conjunction cannot be a coincidence is the element of truth in the legal maxim (too broadly stated even for legal purposes) that an intended consequence cannot be too "remote." Fourthly, each member of the conjunction in this case was independent of the other; whereas if B had fallen against the tree with an impact sufficient to bring it down on him, this sequence of physical events, though freakish in its way, would not be a coincidence and in most contexts of ordinary life, as in the law, the course of events would be summarized by saying that in this case, unlike that of the coincidence, A's act was the cause of B's death, since each stage is the effect of the preceding stage. Thus, the blow forced the victim against the tree, the effect of this was to make the tree fall and the fall of the tree killed the victim.

One further criterion in addition to these four must be satisfied if a conjunction of events is to rank as a coincidence and as a limit when the consequences of the action are traced. This further criterion again shows the strength of the influence which the analogy with the case of the simple manipulation of things exerts over thought in causal terms. An abnormal *condition* existing at the time of a human intervention is distinguished both by ordinary thought and, with a striking consistency, by most legal systems from an abnormal event or conjunction of events subsequent to that intervention; the former, unlike the latter, are not ranked as coincidences or "extraneous" causes when the consequences of the intervention come to be traced. Thus A innocently gives B a tap over the head of a normally quite harmless character, but because B is then suffering from some rare disease the tap has, as we say, "fatal results." In this case A has caused B's death though unintentionally. The scope of the principle which thus distinguishes contemporaneous abnormal conditions from subsequent events is unclear; but at least where a human being initiates some physical change in a thing, animal, or person, abnormal physical states of the object affected, existing at the time, are ranked as part of the circumstances in which the cause "operates." In the familiar controlling imagery these are part of "the stage already set" before the "intervention."

Judgments about coincidences, though we often agree in making them, depend in two related ways on issues incapable of precise formulation. One of these is patent, the other latent but equally important. Just how unlikely must a conjunction be to rank as a coincidence, and in the light of what knowledge is likelihood to be assessed? The only answer is: "very unlikely in the light of the knowledge available to ordinary men." It is, of course, the indeterminacies of such standards, implicit in causal judgments, that make them inveterately disputable, and call for the exercise of discretion or choice by courts. The second and latent indeterminacy of these judgments depends on the fact that the things or events to which they relate do not have pinned to them some uniquely correct description always to be used in assessing likelihood. It is an important pervasive feature of all our empirical judgments that there is a constant possibility of more or less specific description of any event or thing with which they are concerned. The tree might be described not simply as a "tree" but as a "rotten tree" or as a "fir tree" or a "tree sixty feet tall." So too its fall might be described not as a "fall" but as a fall of a specified distance at a specified velocity. The likelihood of conjunctions framed in these different terms would be differently assessed. The criteria of appropriate description like the standard of likelihood are supplied by consideration of common knowledge. Even if the scientist knew the tree to be rotten and could have predicted its fall with accuracy, this would not change the judgment that its fall at the time when *B* was struck down within its range was a coincidence; nor would it make the description "rotten tree" appropriate for the assessment of the chances involved in this judgment. There are other controls over the choice of description derived from the degree of specificity of our interests in the final outcome of the causal process. We are concerned with the fall of an object sufficient to cause "death" by impact and the precise force or direction which may account for the detail of the wounds is irrelevant here.

Opportunities and Reasons

Opportunities The discrimination of voluntary interventions as a limit is no longer made when the case, owing to the commonness or appreciable risk of such harmful intervention, can be brought within the scope of the notion of providing an opportunity, known to be commonly exploited for doing harm. Here the limiting principles are different. When *A* leaves the house unlocked the range of consequences to be attributed to this neglect, as in any other case where precautions are omitted, depends primarily on the way in which such opportunities are commonly exploited. An alternative formulation of this idea is that a subsequent intervention would fall within the scope of consequences if the likelihood of its occurring is one of the reasons for holding *A*'s omission to be negligent.

It is on these lines that we would distinguish between the entry of a thief and of a murderer; the opportunity provided is believed to be sufficiently commonly exploited by thieves to make it usual and often morally or legally obligatory not to provide it. Here, in attributing consequences to prior actions, causal judgments are directly controlled by the notion of the risk created by them. Neglect of such precautions is both unusual and reprehensible. For these reasons it would be hard to separate the two ways in which such neglect deviates from the "norm." Despite this, no simple identification can be made of the notion of responsibility with the causal connection which is a ground for it. This is so because the provision of an opportunity commonly taken by others is ranked as the cause of the outcome independently of

the wish to praise or blame. The causal judgment may be made simply to assess a contribution to some outcome. Thus, whether we think well or ill of the use made of railways, we would still claim that the greater mobility of the population in the nineteenth century was a consequence of their introduction.

It is obvious that the question whether any given intervention is a sufficiently common exploitation of the opportunity provided to come within the risk is again a matter on which judgments may differ, though they often agree. The courts, and perhaps ordinary thought also, often describe those that are sufficiently common as "natural" consequences of the neglect. They have in these terms discriminated the entry of a thief from the entry of a man who burnt the house down, and refused to treat the destruction of the house as a "natural" consequence of the neglect.[15]

We discuss later . . . the argument that this easily intelligible concept of "harm within the risk," overriding as it does the distinctions between voluntary interventions and others, should be used as the general test for determining what subsequent harm should be attributed for legal purposes to prior action. The merits of this proposal to refashion the law along these simple lines are perhaps considerable, yet consequences of actions are in fact often traced both in the law and apart from it in other ways which depend on the discrimination of voluntary interventions from others. We distinguish, after all, as differing though related grounds of responsibility, causing harm by one's own action and providing opportunities for others to do harm, where the guiding analogy with the simple manipulation of things, which underlies causal thought, is less close. When, as in the examples discussed above, we trace consequences through the nonvoluntary interventions of others our concern is to show that certain stages of the process have a certain type of connection with the preceding stages, and not, as when the notion of risk is applied, to show that the ultimate outcome is connected in some general way with the initiating action. Thus, when *A*'s shot makes *B* start and break a glass it is the causal relationship described by the expression "made *B* start" that we have in mind and not the likelihood that on hearing a shot someone may break a glass. Causal connection may be traced in such cases though the initiating action and the final outcome are not contingencies that commonly go together.

Apart from these conceptual reasons for distinguishing these related grounds for responsibility, it is clear that both in the law . . . and apart from it we constantly treat harm as caused by a person's action though it does not fall "within the risk." If, when *B* broke the glass in the example given above, a splinter flew into *C*'s eye, blinding him, *A*'s action is indeed the cause of *C*'s injury though we may not always blame him for so unusual a consequence.

Reasons   In certain varieties of interpersonal transactions, unlike the case of coercion, the second action is quite voluntary. *A* may not threaten *B* but may bribe or advise or persuade him to do something. Here, *A* does not "cause" or "make" *B* do anything: the strongest words we should use are perhaps that he "induced" or "procured" *B*'s act. Yet the law and moral principles alike may treat one person as responsible for the harm which another free agent has done "in

consequence" of the advice or the inducements which the first has offered. In such cases the limits concern the range of those actions done by *B* which are to rank as the consequence of *A*'s words or deeds. In general this question depends on *A*'s intentions or on the "plan of action" he puts before *B*. If *A* advises or bribes *B* to break in and steal from an empty house and *B* does so, he acts in consequence of *A*'s advice or bribe. If he deliberately burns down the house this would not be treated as the consequence of *A*'s bribe or advice, legally or otherwise, though it may in some sense be true that the burning would not have taken place without the advice or bribe. Nice questions may arise, which the courts have to settle, where *B* diverges from the detail of the plan of action put before him by *A*.

---

1. *Cf.* OED sub tit. *Responsible: Answerable, accountable* (to another for *something); liable to be called to account: "being responsible to the King for what might happen to us," 1662; Hart, "Varieties of Responsibility" (1967) 83* LQR *346, reprinted with additions as "Responsibility and Retribution" in* Hart, Punishment and Responsibility *(Oxford, 1968), chap. IX.*

2. *The rule is defended on the ground that, most houseowners being insured, it promotes efficient loss distribution: Harper and James,* Torts, *s. 20.6 n. 1.*

3. *See the following passage from* The Golden Bowl *by Henry James. (Mrs. Assingham, whose uncertain self-accusation is described here, had, on the eve of the Prince's marriage, encouraged him to resume an old friendship with Charlotte Stant. The relationship which developed came to threaten the marriage with disaster.) "She had stood for the previous hour in a merciless glare, beaten upon, stared out of countenance, it fairly seemed to her, by intimations of her mistake. For what she was most immediately feeling was that she had in the past been active for these people to ends that were now bearing fruit and that might yet bear a greater crop. She but brooded at first in her corner of the carriage: it was like burying her exposed face, a face too helplessly exposed in the cool lap of the common indifference . . . a world mercifully unconscious and unreproachful. . . . The sense of seeing was strong in her, but she clutched at the comfort of not being sure of what she saw. Not to know what it would represent on a longer view was a help in turn to not making out that her hands were embrued; since*

if she had stood in the position of a producing cause she should surely be less vague about what she had produced. This, further, in its way, was a step toward reflecting that when one's connection with any matter was too indirect to be traced, it might be described also as too slight to be deplored" (The Golden Bowl, *Book 3, chap. 3). We are much indebted to Dame Mary Warnock for this quotation.*

4. *Lawson,* Negligence in the Civil Law, *p. 53.*

5. *Glanville Williams,* Joint Torts and Contributory Negligence, *p. 239.*

6. *Mill, Book III, chap. v, s. 2.*

7. *Ross,* The Right and the Good, *p. 36.*

8. *E.g. if the guest was suspected of being a compulsive stabber and the waiter had therefore been told to lay only a plastic knife in his place.*

9. *In Chaps. VI, VII, XII, XIII of* Causation and the Law *we distinguish these different relationships in the law.*

10. Davies *v.* Swan Motor Co. *[1947] 2 KB 291, 318.*

11. Minister of Pensions *v.* Chennell *[1947] KB 250, 256. Lord Wright (1950), 13* MLR *3.*

12. Norris *v.* William Moss & Son Ltd. *[1954] 1 WLR 46, 351.*

13. Minister of Pensions *v.* Chennel *[1947] KB 250, 256.*

14. *For the bearing of the principles of punishment on such problems see Chap. XIV of our book,* Causation in the Law.

15. Bellows *v.* Worcester Storage Co. *(1937) 297 Mass. 188, 7 NE 2d 588.*

PALSGRAF V. THE LONG ISLAND RAILROAD CO.*

New York Court of Appeals, 1928

CARDOZO, Ch. J. Plaintiff was standing on a platform of defendant's railroad after buying a ticket to go to Rockaway Beach. A train stopped at the station, bound for another place. Two men ran forward to catch it. One of the men reached the platform of the car without mishap, though the train was already moving. The other man, carrying a package, jumped aboard the car, but seemed unsteady as if about to fall. A guard on the car, who had held the door open, reached forward to help him in, and another guard on the platform pushed him from behind. In this act, the package was dislodged, and fell upon the rails. It was a package of small size, about fifteen inches long, and was covered by a newspaper. In fact it contained fireworks, but there was nothing in its appearance to give notice of its contents. The fireworks when they fell exploded. The shock of the explosion threw down some scales at the other end of the platform, many feet away. The scales struck the plaintiff, causing injuries for which she sues.

The conduct of the defendant's guard, if a wrong in its relation to the holder of the package, was not a wrong in its relation to the plaintiff, standing far away. Relatively to her it was not negligence at all. Nothing in the situation gave notice that the falling package had in it the potency of peril to persons thus removed. Negligence is not actionable unless it involves in the invasion of a legally protected interest, the violation of a right. "Proof of negligence in the air, so to speak, will not do." "Negligence is the absence of care, according to the circumstances." The plaintiff as she stood upon the platform of the station might claim to be protected against intentional invasion of her bodily security. Such invasion is not charged. She might claim to be protected against unintentional invasion by conduct involving in the thought of reasonable men an unreasonable hazard that such invasion would ensue. These, from the point of view of the law, were the bounds of her immunity, with perhaps some

rare exceptions, survivals for the most part of ancient forms of liability, where conduct is held to be at the peril of the actor (*Sullivan* v. *Dunham,* 161 N.Y. 290). If no hazard was apparent to the eye of ordinary vigilance, an act innocent and harmless, at least to outward seeming, with reference to her, did not take to itself the quality of a tort because it happened to be a wrong, though apparently not one involving the risk of bodily insecurity, with reference to someone else. "In every instance, before negligence can be predicated of a given act, back of the act must be sought and found a duty to the individual complaining, the observance of which would have averted or avoided the injury." "The ideas of negligence and duty are strictly correlative." (BOWEN, L. J., in *Thomas* v. *Quartermaine,* 18 Q.B.D. 685, 694.) The plaintiff sues in her own right for a wrong personal to her, and not as the vicarious beneficiary of a breach of duty to another.

A different conclusion will involve us, and swiftly too, in a maze of contradictions. A guard stumbles over a package which has been left upon a platform. It seems to be a bundle of newspapers. It turns out to be a can of dynamite. To the eye of ordinary vigilance, the bundle is abandoned waste, which may be kicked or trod on with impunity. Is a passenger at the other end of the platform protected by the law against the unsuspected hazard concealed beneath the waste? If not, is the result to be any different, so far as the distant passenger is concerned, when the guard stumbles over a valise which a truckman or a porter has left upon the walk? The passenger far away, if the victim of a wrong at all, has a cause of action, not derivative, but original and primary. His claim to be protected against invasion of his bodily security is neither greater nor less because the act resulting in the invasion is a wrong to another far removed. In this case, the rights that are said to have been violated, the interests said to have been invaded, are not even of

*248 N.Y. 339 (1928). Citations omitted.

the same order. The man was not injured in his person nor even put in danger. The purpose of the act, as well as its effect, was to make his person safe. If there was a wrong to him at all, which may very well be doubted, it was a wrong to a property interest only, the safety of his package. Out of this wrong to property, which threatened injury to nothing else, there has passed, we are told, to the plaintiff by derivation or succession a right of action for the invasion of an interest of another order, the right to bodily security. The diversity of interests emphasizes the futility of the effort to build the plaintiff's right upon the basis of a wrong to someone else. The gain is one of emphasis, for a like result would follow if the interests were the same. Even then, the orbit of the danger as disclosed to the eye of reasonable vigilance would be the orbit of the duty. One who jostles one's neighbor in a crowd does not invade the rights of others standing at the outer fringe when the unintended contact casts a bomb upon the ground. The wrongdoer, as to them is the man who carries the bomb, not the one who explodes it without suspicion of the danger. Life will have to be made over, and human nature transformed, before prevision so extravagant can be accepted as the norm of conduct, the customary standard to which behavior must conform.

The argument for the plaintiff is built upon the shifting meanings of such words as "wrong" and "wrongful," and shares their instability. What the plaintiff must show is "a wrong" to herself, *i.e.,* a violation of her own right, and not merely a wrong to someone else, nor conduct "wrongful" because unsocial, but not "a wrong" to anyone. We are told that one who drives at reckless speed through a crowded city street is guilty of a negligent act and, therefore, of a wrongful one irrespective of the consequences. Negligent the act is, and wrongful in the sense that it is unsocial, but wrongful and unsocial in relation to other travelers, only because the eye of vigilance perceives the risk of damage. If the same act were to be committed on a speedway or a race course, it would lose its wrongful quality. The risk reasonably to be perceived defines the duty to be obeyed, and risk imports relation; it is risk to another or to others within the range of apprehension (Seavey, Negligence, Subjective or Objective, 41 H. L. Rv. 6; *Boronkay* v. *Robinson & Carpenter,* 247 N.Y. 365). This does not mean, of course, that one who launches a destructive force is always relieved of liability if the force, though known to be destructive, pursues an unexpected path. It was not necessary that the defendant should have had notice of the particular method in which an accident would occur, if the possibility of an accident was clear to the ordinarily prudent eye. Some acts, such as shooting, are so imminently dangerous to any one who may come within reach of the missile, however unexpectedly, as to impose a duty of prevision not far from that of an insurer. Even today, and much oftener in earlier stages of the law, one acts sometimes at one's peril. Under this head, it may be, fall certain cases of what is known as transferred intent, an act willfully dangerous to A resulting by misadventure in injury to B. These cases aside, wrong is defined in terms of the natural or probable, at least when unintentional. The range of reasonable apprehension is at times a question for the court, and at times, if varying inferences are possible, a question for the jury. Here, by concession, there was nothing in the situation to suggest to the most cautious mind that the parcel wrapped in newspaper would spread wreckage through the station. If the guard had thrown it down knowingly and willfully, he would not have threatened the plaintiff's safety, so far as appearances could warn him. His conduct would not have involved, even then, an unreasonable probability of invasion of her bodily security. Liability can be no greater where the act is inadvertent.

Negligence, like risk, is thus a term of relation. Negligence in the abstract, apart from things related, is surely not a tort, if indeed it is understandable at all. Negligence is not a tort unless it results in the commission of a wrong, and the commission of a wrong imports the violation of a right, in this case, we are told, the right to be protected against interference with one's bodily security. But bodily security is protected, not against all forms of interference or aggression, but only against some. One who seeks redress at law does not make out a cause of action by showing without more that there has been damage to his person. If the harm was not willful, he must show that the act as to him had possibilities of danger so many and apparent as to entitle him to be protected against the doing of it though the harm was unintended. Affront to personality is still the keynote of the wrong. Confirmation of this view will be found in the history and development of the action on the case. Negligence as a basis of civil liability was unknown to medieval law. For damage to the person, the sole remedy was trespass, and trespass did not lie in the absence of aggression, and that direct and personal. Liability for other damage, as where a servant without orders from the master does or omits something to the damage of another, is a plant of later growth. When it emerged out of the legal soil, it was thought of as a variant of trespass, an offshoot of the parent stock. This appears in the form of action, which was known as trespass on the case. The victim does not sue derivatively, or by right of subrogation, to vindicate an interest invaded in the person of another. Thus to view his cause of action is to ignore the fundamental difference between tort and crime. He sues for breach of a duty owing to himself.

The law of causation, remote or proximate, is thus foreign to the case before us. The question of liability is always anterior to the question of the measure of the consequences that go with liability. If there is no tort to be redressed, there is no occasion to consider what damage might be recovered if there were a finding of a tort. We may assume, without deciding, that negligence, not at large or in the abstract, but in relation to the plaintiff, would entail liability for any and all consequences, however novel or extraordinary. There is room for argument that a distinction is to be drawn according to the diversity of interests invaded by the act, as where conduct negligent in that it threatens an insignificant invasion of an interest in property results in an unforeseeable invasion of an interest of another order, as *e.g.,* one of bodily security. Perhaps other distinctions may be necessary. We do not go into the question now. The consequences to be followed must first be rooted in a wrong.

The judgment of the Appellate Division and that of the Trial Term should be reversed, and the complaint dismissed, with costs in all courts.

ANDREWS, J. (dissenting). Assisting a passenger to board a train, the defendant's servant negligently knocked a package from his arms. It fell between the platform and the cars. Of its contents the servant knew and could know nothing. A violent explosion followed. The concussion broke some scales standing a considerable distance away. In falling they injured the plaintiff, an intending passenger.

Upon these facts may she recover the damages she has suffered in an action brought against the master? The result we shall reach depends upon our theory as to the nature of negligence. Is it a relative concept—the breach of some duty owing to a particular person or to particular persons? Or where there is an act which unreasonably threatens the safety of others, is the doer liable for all its proximate consequences, even where they result in injury to one who would generally be thought to be outside the radius of danger? This is not a mere dispute as to words. We might not believe that to the average mind the dropping of the bundle would seem to involve the probability of harm to the plaintiff standing many feet away whatever might be the case as to the owner or to

one so near as to be likely to be struck by its fall. If, however, we adopt the second hypothesis we have to inquire only as the relation between cause and effect. We deal in terms of proximate cause, not of negligence.

Negligence may be defined roughly as an act or omission which unreasonably does or may affect the rights of others, or which unreasonably fails to protect oneself from the dangers resulting from such acts. Here I confine myself to the first branch of the definition. Nor do I comment on the word "unreasonable." For present purposes it sufficiently describes that average of conduct that society requires of its members.

There must be both the act or the omission, and the right. It is the act itself, not the intent of the actor, that is important. In criminal law both the intent and the result are to be considered. Intent again is material in tort actions, where punitive damages are sought, dependent on actual malice—not on merely reckless conduct. But here neither insanity nor infancy lessens responsibility.

As has been said, except in cases of contributory negligence, there must be rights which are or may be affected. Often though injury has occurred, no rights of him who suffers have been touched. A licensee or trespasser upon my land has no claim to affirmative care on my part that the land be made safe. Where a railroad is required to fence its tracks against cattle, no man's rights are injured should he wander upon the road because such fence is absent. An unborn child may not demand immunity from personal harm.

But we are told that "there is no negligence unless there is in the particular case a legal duty to take care, and this duty must be one which is owed to the plaintiff himself and not merely to others." This, I think too narrow a conception. Where there is the unreasonable act, and some right that may be affected there is negligence whether damage does or does not result. That is immaterial. Should we drive down Broadway at a reckless speed, we are negligent whether we strike an approaching car or miss it by an inch. The act itself is wrongful. It is a wrong not only to those who happen to be within the radius of danger but to all who might have been there—a wrong to the public at large. Such is the language of the street. Such the language of the courts when speaking of contributory negligence. Such again and again their language in speaking of the duty of some defendant and discussing proximate cause in cases where such a discussion is wholly irrelevant on any other theory. As was said by Mr. Justice HOLMES many years ago, "the mea-

sure of the defendant's duty in determining whether a
wrong has been committed is one thing, the measure
of liability when a wrong has been committed is another." Due care is a duty imposed on each one of us
to protect society from unnecessary danger not to protect *A, B* or *C* alone.

It may well be that there is no such thing as
negligence in the abstract. "Proof of negligence in the
air, so to speak, will not do." In an empty world negligence would not exist. It does involve a relationship
between man and his fellows. But not merely a relationship between man and those whom he might
reasonably expect his act would injure. Rather, a relationship between him and those whom he does in fact
injure. If his act has a tendency to harm some one, it
harms him a mile away as surely as it does those on
the scene. We now permit children to recover for the
negligent killing of the father. It was never prevented
on the theory that no duty was owing to them. A husband may be compensated for the loss of his wife's
services. To say that the wrongdoer was negligent as
to the husband as well as to the wife is merely an
attempt to fit facts to theory. An insurance company
paying a fire loss recovers its payment of the negligent
incendiary. We speak of subrogation—of suing in the
right of the insured. Behind the cloud of words is the
fact they hide, that the act, wrongful as to the insured,
has also injured the company. Even if it be true that
the fault of father, wife or insured will prevent recovery, it is because we consider the original negligence
not the proximate cause of the injury.

In the well-known *Polemis Case* (1921, 3 K.B.
560), SCRUTTON, L.J., said that the dropping of a plank
was negligent for it might injure "workman or cargo
or ship." Because of either possibility the owner of the
vessel was to be made good for his loss. The act being wrongful the doer was liable for its proximate results. Criticized and explained as this statement may
have been, I think it states the law as it should be and
as it is.

The proposition is this. Every one owes to the
world at large the duty of refraining from those acts
that may unreasonably threaten the safety of others.
Such an act occurs. Not only is he wronged to whom
harm might reasonably be expected to result, but he
also who is in fact injured, even if he be outside what
would generally be thought the danger zone. There
needs be duty due the one complaining but this is not
a duty to a particular individual because as to him
harm might be expected. Harm to someone being the
natural result of the act, not only that one alone, but

all those in fact injured may complain. We have never,
I think, held otherwise. Indeed in the *Di Caprio* case
we said that a breach of a general ordinance defining
the degree of care to be exercised in one's calling is
evidence of negligence as to every one. We did not
limit this statement to those who might be expected to
be exposed to danger. Unreasonable risk being taken,
its consequences are not confined to those who might
probably be hurt.

If this be so, we do not have a plaintiff suing by
"derivation or succession." Her action is original and
primary. Her claim is for a breach of duty to herself—
not that she is subrogated to any right of action of the
owner of the parcel or of a passenger standing at the
scene of the explosion.

The right to recover damages rests on additional
considerations. The plaintiff's rights must be injured,
and this injury must be caused by the negligence. We
build a dam, but are negligent as to its foundations.
Breaking, it injures property down stream. We are not
liable if all this happened because of some reason
other than the insecure foundation. But when injuries
do result from our unlawful act we are liable for the
consequences. It does not matter that they are unusual, unexpected, unforeseen and unforeseeable. But
there is one limitation. The damages must be so connected with the negligence that the latter may be said
to be the proximate cause of the former.

These two words have never been given an inclusive definition. What is a cause in a legal sense, still
more what is a proximate cause, depend in each case
upon many considerations, as does the existence of
negligence itself. Any philosophical doctrine of causation does not help us. A boy throws a stone into a
pond. The ripples spread. The water level rises. The
history of that pond is altered to all eternity. It will be
altered by other causes also. Yet it will be forever the
resultant of all causes combined. Each one will have
an influence. How great only omniscience can say.
You may speak of a chain, or if you please, a net. An
analogy is of little aid. Each cause brings about future
events. Without each the future would not be the
same. Each is proximate in the sense it is essential.
But that is not what we mean by the word. Nor on
the other hand do we mean sole cause. There is no
such thing.

Should analogy be thought helpful, however, I
prefer that of a stream. The spring, starting on its journey, is joined by tributary after tributary. The river,
reaching the ocean, comes from a hundred sources.
No man may say whence any drop of water is derived.

Yet for a time distinction may be possible. Into the clear creek, brown swamp water flows from the left. Later, from the right comes water stained by its clay bed. The three may remain for a space, sharply divided. But at last, inevitably no trace of separation remains. They are so commingled that all distinction is lost.

As we have said, we cannot trace the effect of an act to the end, if end there is. Again, however, we may trace it part of the way. A murder at Sarajevo may be the necessary antecedent to an assassination in London twenty years hence. An overturned lantern may burn all Chicago. We may follow the fire from the shed to the last building. We rightly say the fire started by the lantern caused its destruction.

A cause, but not the proximate cause. What we do mean by the word "proximate" is, that because of convenience, of public policy, of a rough sense of justice, the law arbitrarily declines to trace a series of events beyond a certain point. This is not logic, it is practical politics. Take our rule as to fires. Sparks from my burning haystack set on fire my house and my neighbor's. I may recover from a negligent railroad. He may not. Yet the wrongful act as directly harmed the one as the other. We may regret that the line was drawn just where it was, but drawn somewhere it had to be. We said the act of the railroad was not the proximate cause of our neighbor's fire. Cause it surely was. The words we used were simply indicative of our notions of public policy. Other courts think differently. But somewhere they reach the point where they cannot say the stream comes from any one source.

Take the illustration given in an unpublished manuscript by a distinguished and helpful writer on the law of torts. A chauffeur negligently collides with another car which is filled with dynamite, although he could not know it. An explosion follows. *A,* walking on the sidewalk nearby, is killed. *B,* sitting in a window of a building opposite, is cut by flying glass. *C,* likewise sitting in a window a block away, is similarly injured. And a further illustration. A nursemaid, ten blocks away, startled by the noise, involuntarily drops a baby from her arms to the walk. We are told that *C* may not recover while *A* may. As to *B* it is a question for court or jury. We will all agree that the baby might not. Because, we are again told, the chauffeur had no reason to believe his conduct involved any risk of injuring either *C* or the baby. As to them he was not negligent.

But the chauffeur, being negligent in risking the collision, his belief that the scope of the harm he might do would be limited is immaterial. His act unreasonably jeopardized the safety of anyone who might be affected by it. *C's* injury and that of the baby were directly traceable to the collision. Without that, the injury would not have happened. *C* had the right to sit in his office, secure from such dangers. The baby was entitled to use the sidewalk with reasonable safety.

The true theory is, it seems to me, that the injury to *C,* if in truth he is to be denied recovery, and the injury to the baby is that their several injuries were not the proximate result of the negligence. And here not what the chauffeur had reason to believe would be the result of his conduct, but what the prudent would foresee, may have a bearing. May have some bearing, for the problem of proximate cause is not to be solved by any one consideration.

It is all a question of expediency. There are no fixed rules to govern our judgment. There are simply matters of which we may take account. We have in somewhat different connection spoken of "the stream of events." We have asked whether that stream was deflected—whether it was forced into new and unexpected channels. This is rather rhetoric than law. There is in truth little to guide us other than common sense.

There are some hints that may help us. The proximate cause, involved as it may be with many other causes, must be, at the least, something without which the event would not happen. The court must ask itself whether there was a natural and continuous sequence between cause and effect. Was the one a substantial factor in producing the other? Was there a direct connection between them, without too many intervening causes? Is the effect of cause on result not too attenuated? Is the cause likely, in the usual judgment of mankind, to produce the result? Or by the exercise of prudent foresight could the result be foreseen? Is the result too remote from the cause, and here we consider remoteness in time and space, where we passed upon the construction of a contract—but something was also said on this subject. Clearly we must so consider, for the greater the distance either in time or space, the more surely do other causes intervene to affect the result. When a lantern is overturned the firing of a shed is a fairly direct consequence. Many things contribute to the spread of the conflagration—the force of the wind, the direction and width of street, the character of intervening structures, other factors. We draw an uncertain and wavering line, but draw it we must as best we can.

Once again, it is all a question of fair judgment, always keeping in mind the fact that we endeavor to make a rule in each case that will be practical and in keeping with the general understanding of mankind.

Here another question must be answered. In the case supposed it is said, and said correctly, that the chauffeur is liable for the direct effect of the explosion although he had no reason to suppose it would follow a collision. "The fact that the injury occurred in a different manner than that which might have been expected does not prevent the chauffeur's negligence from being in law the cause of the injury." But the natural results of a negligent act—the results which a prudent man would or should foresee—do have a bearing upon the decision as to proximate cause. We have said so repeatedly. What should be foreseen? No human foresight would suggest that a collision itself might injure one a block away. On the contrary, given an explosion, such a possibility might be reasonably expected. I think the direct connection, the foresight of which the courts speak, assumes prevision of the explosion, for the immediate results of which, at least, the chauffeur is responsible.

It may be said this is unjust. Why? In fairness he should make good every injury flowing from his negligence. Not because of tenderness toward him we say he need not answer for all that follows his wrong. We look back to the catastrophe, the fire kindled by the spark, or the explosion. We trace the consequences—not indefinitely, but to a certain point. And to aid us in fixing that point we ask what might ordinarily be expected to follow the fire or the explosion.

This last suggestion is the factor which must determine the case before us. The act upon which defendant's liability rests is knocking an apparently harmless package onto the platform. The act was negligent. For its proximate consequences the defendant is liable. If its contents were broken, to the owner; if it fell upon and crushed a passenger's foot, then to him. If it exploded and injured one in the immediate vicinity, to him also as to A in the illustration. Mrs. Palsgraf was standing some distance away. How far cannot be told from the record—apparently twenty-five or thirty feet. Perhaps less. Except for the explosion, she would not have been injured. We are told by the appellant in his brief "it cannot be denied that the explosion was the direct cause of the plaintiff's injuries." So it was a substantial factor in producing the result—there was here a natural and continuous sequence—direct connection. The only intervening cause was that instead of blowing her to the ground the concussion smashed the weighing machine which in turn fell upon her. There was no remoteness in time, little in space. And surely, given such an explosion as here it needed no great foresight to predict that the natural result would be to injure one on the platform at no greater distance from its scene than was the plaintiff. Just how no one might be able to predict. Whether by flying fragments, by broken glass, by wreckage of machines or structures no one could say. But injury in some form was most probable.

Under these circumstances I cannot say as a matter of law that the plaintiff's injuries were not the proximate result of the negligence. That is all we have before us. The court refused to so charge. No request was made to submit the matter to the jury as a question of fact, even would that have been proper upon the record before us.

The judgment appealed from should be affirmed, with costs.

POUND, LEHMAN and KELLOGG, JJ., concur with CARDOZO, CH. J.; ANDREWS, J., dissents in opinion in which CRANE and O'BRIEN, JJ., concur.

Judgment reversed, etc.

THE BASIC RULE OF LEGAL CAUSE IN NEGLIGENCE CASES*

Robert E. Keeton

Diverse Formulations of the Risk Rule

Statement and Illustration of Three Formulations

The defendant, proprietor of a restaurant, placed a large, unlabeled can of rat poison beside cans of flour on a shelf near a stove in a restaurant kitchen. The victim, while in the kitchen making a delivery to the restaurant, was killed by an explosion of the poison. Assume that the defendant's handling of the rat poison was negligent because of the risk that someone would be poisoned but that defendant had no reason to know of the risk that the poison would explode if left in a hot place. Is the defendant liable for the death of the victim?[1]

This question illustrates the central problem of scope of liability for negligence. The problem is commonly subdivided into issues associated with, first, the foreseeability of any kind of harm to the victim who, in fact, was harmed and, second, the foreseeability of the particular harm or kind of harm that occurred.

The predominant theme in judicial utterances on the scope of liability in negligence cases is expressed in a proposition that, for convenience, will be referred to as *the Risk Rule*. This rule, quite commonly expressed in substance both in charges to the jury and in appellate opinions, is as follows:

A negligent actor is legally responsible for that harm, and only that harm, of which negligence *is a cause in fact.*

Some explanatory comments are in order. First, this rule is addressed not only to matters uniformly classified as problems of legal cause but also to other matters sometimes classified as problems of duty. Comments directed specifically to this choice of terminology are reserved for the second and third chapters.[2]

Other explanatory comments that seem necessary at the outset are concerned with the meaning of the words "actor" and "negligence." "Actor" is used here to signify the person whose "conduct" is being judged, whether plaintiff or defendant, and whether charged with acting negligently or with negligently failing to act. "Conduct" is used in a sense that includes both "acting" and "failing to act." "Negligence," in the context of this rule, must be understood in a more precise sense than merely "the negligent actor's conduct." This statement of the Risk Rule makes no sense unless interpreted as meaning that the actor's *conduct* during the period of his negligence may be a cause of harm of which his *negligence* is not a cause. For example, in the case of the explosive rat poison, it is not enough to ask whether the defendant's conduct in placing the poison where he did was a cause of the death of the victim. We should, as well, ask whether the defendant's negligence was a cause of the death. As a means of arriving at a satisfactory answer to that question, it will be useful to consider another.

What was that aspect of the conduct of the defendant that caused it to be characterized as negligence? Placing rat poison on a shelf may or may not be negligence. The negligence here consisted of placing the poison where it was likely to be mistaken for something intended for human consumption. This description says nothing about the proximity of the shelf to heat. That circumstance is omitted because of the assumption that the defendant had no reason to know of the explosive character of the poison; in such a situation it would not have been negligent to put the

---

poison in a place that happened to be near heat, provided it was not a place where the poison was likely to be mistaken as something intended for human consumption. Thus, the defendant's *negligence* (his placing the poison where it was likely to be mistaken for something intended for human consumption) was not a *sine qua non* of the harm. For present purposes I draw no distinction between the several expressions "but-for cause," "necessary antecedent," and "*sine qua non*."[3] That is, I am speaking simply of the concept that it cannot be said that the harm of death from explosion would not have occurred but for defendant's placing the poison where it was likely to be mistaken for something intended for human consumption. Defendant's negligence was not in this sense a but-for cause, or a necessary antecedent, or a *sine qua non* of the death. But his conduct (placing the poison near heat) was, at least in a qualified sense, a *sine qua non*.

The qualification is concerned with the hypothetical character of the assertion. That is, the assertion that the harm would not have occurred but for the defendant's conduct is a hypothetical assertion the accuracy of which is not subject to demonstration. For example, how are we to know that, had the poison been placed elsewhere than near a hot stove, it would not have been exploded by some other source of heat that might have happened to be applied to the poison while the victim was present? Also, imbedded in the hypothetical assertion of what would not have happened are ambiguities in the meaning of "conduct" and "harm." Does "conduct" refer to placing the poison in the exact spot where it was placed? If so, might it not be said that the conduct was not a *sine qua non* since death at the same time and place might have occurred if the poison had been placed near a hot radiator rather than the stove? Does "the harm" refer merely to death of the victim, or to the time, place, and manner of death in all their detail, or to something between these extremes? In some instances, the ambiguity and hypothetical character of the assertion will present serious difficulty.[4] But, in the case of the explosive rat poison, we can readily understand and accept, in at least a rough sense, the assertion that the defendant's conduct was a *sine qua non* of the harm because there appears to have been no substantial possibility either that the harm in all its details would have occurred or that something generally resembling it would have occurred in the absence of defendant's conduct of placing the rat poison near heat. Also, no doubt, we can agree that if defendant's negligence is defined in the limited sense of that quality of his

conduct consisting of his placing the poison where it was likely to be mistaken for something intended for human consumption, his negligence was not a *sine qua non*.

There is yet another difficulty, however, in the assertion that one aspect of his conduct was a cause of harm and another aspect of the same conduct, the same single action of putting down a can of poison, was not a cause of the harm. It is more normal, perhaps, to think of the conduct as indivisible and to reject the suggestion that the negligent aspect can be separated from other aspects for an inquiry into causal relation. Perhaps it will be helpful in this respect to think of negligence as the creation of unreasonable risks[5] and, rather than thinking of harm itself as the focus of the concept of risk, to think of a risk as a set of forces and conditions and circumstances that might foreseeably bring about harm.[6] No special point is made here regarding the choice among the terms "force," "condition," and "circumstance" to convey the intended idea, though the word "circumstance" seems the most congenial to the separation of aspects of a single state of affairs. Negligence, then, consists of creating a set of unduly risky forces or conditions or circumstances, and the negligence is a *sine qua non* of subsequent harm only if some force or condition or circumstance within this set is a *sine qua non*. In the case of the rat poison, the negligence consisted of creating a force or condition or circumstance of having a poisonous substance where it might be mistaken as something intended for human consumption. That circumstance was not a cause of the harm, though the coexisting circumstance of having an explosive substance near heat was a cause.

This focus upon the negligent aspect of conduct as the meaning of the unqualified word "negligence" in the statement of the Risk Rule presented above suggests a second, perhaps less ambiguous, formulation of exactly the same meaning:

> *A negligent actor is legally responsible for that harm, and only that harm, of which the* negligent aspect of his conduct *is a cause in fact.*

In many cases it is less easy than in the case of the explosive rat poison to extract the negligent aspect from the total conduct. To meet this difficulty, still another formulation of the Risk Rule is helpful. A moment ago, we were thinking of risk with a focus upon the forces or conditions or circumstances that might produce harm. Shift the focus now to the harm that might be produced. With this focus, in order to find that the negligence (that is, the negligent aspect of the conduct) bears a causal relation to the harm, we must find that the harm that came about was one of the things that was risked. Another way of expressing the same idea is to say that the harm must be a result within the scope of at least one of the risks on the basis of which the actor is found to be negligent. Thus the Risk Rule of legal cause as stated in the first and second formulations above may be restated in a third formulation without change of meaning:

> A negligent actor is legally responsible for the harm, and only the harm, that not only (1) is caused in fact by his conduct but also (2) is a result within the scope of the risks by reason of which the actor is found to be negligent.

In the case of the explosive rat poison, injury by explosion was not a result within the scope of the risks by reason of which the defendant was found to be negligent, though injury by poisoning would have been.

The third formulation of the rule is often expressed in the statement that the actor is responsible only for "results within the risk." Among those who remain constantly alert to its meaning, there is no objection to use of such a shorthand expression. But this cryptic phrase is apt to be misleading to the unsophisticated because it does not designate the point of view from which the composite of risks is defined. The concept of "risk" and the cognate concept of "probability" are founded on prediction from some selected point of view. But they do not necessarily imply any particular point of view, such as that of a reasonable man in the position of the actor. Thus, results that in the wisdom of hindsight are said to have been "probable" may yet have been beyond the scope of those risks by reason of which the actor's conduct is found to have been negligence. Also, such concepts as "risk," "probability," and "foreseeability" imply a point of view involving a degree of ignorance about the factors at work in a situation. To one who knows all, a future event is not "probable" or merely "foreseeable" but either certain to occur or certain not to occur. When we say a result was "probable" as a matter of hindsight, we are using a point of view that is neither that of a reasonable person in the actor's position nor that of an omniscient observer after the fact. It is a point of view based on foresight in the face of incomplete knowledge, but with greater knowledge or greater mental capacity than that of the actor or that of the standard man in the actor's circumstances. As used in the Risk Rule, on the other hand, "risk" implies a standard based on foresight from the point of view of the standard man in the actor's circumstances at the time of the conduct that is being judged.

As we examine the policy foundation of the Risk Rule, reasons will appear for using, in relation to problems of legal cause, this standard of foresight that is also used in determining whether the actor was negligent. But, first, we digress for further explanation of the use of three formulations of the Risk Rule.

Why Three Formulations?

The first formulation of the Risk Rule tracks language found in many jury charges today, as well as in appellate opinions, though supplemented usually by elaborations upon the theme and occasionally by qualifications. The third formulation tracks the rationale of exponents of what has come to be known as the risk theory of legal cause, and of Professor Seavey in particular.[7] Professors Harper and James also recommended an inquiry in terms generally consistent with the rationale expressed in the third formulation,[8] though they appear less happy than Professor Seavey with adherence to the limitation on scope of liability implicit in accepting this as the basic rule of legal cause. They also observed that in essence this is the same inquiry as the question whether there is causal relation "between *that aspect of the defendant's conduct which is wrongful* and the injury."[9] Thus, the second formulation offered here is supported by their analysis. This formulation is offered as a transitional bond between the first and the third, in the belief that the intended substance of these different expressions is the same. Candor requires disclosure that Professor Seavey dislikes both the first and the second formulations because of a concern, as I understand him, that they are more likely to mislead than to clarify. His disfavor is firm, though expressed in the warmhearted spirit that has characterized his rigorous intellectual assaults upon the ideas of generations of students, colleagues, and judges. At the risk of suffering an intermeddler's unhappy fate, I persist in offering the second formulation and in marshaling the three together in the hope of improving relations between adherents of two ways of thought that I believe to be compatibly directed toward the same goal.

The Risk Rule As a Rule of Causation

Perhaps a secondary benefit of this focus on three formulations of one rule is to expose rather persuasive evidence that the Risk Rule is indeed a rule of causation in a cause-in-fact sense. There are various deviations from the Risk Rule—some toward greater liability, some toward less—that are founded in notions beyond causation. But the predominant theme represented by the Risk Rule is a theme of causation. It concerns cause-in-fact relation between the negligent aspect of the conduct and the harm.

This conclusion is supported by only a few of the multitude of authors on legal cause—among them Professor Carpenter,[10] and, more recently, Professors Harper and James.[11] Even these three appear not willing to carry the separation of aspects of the conduct as far as is suggested here. The following passage from Harper and James is relevant:

> But there are cases where causal relation exists between defendant's fault and the injury, yet where liability will not be imposed. Thus in Gorris v. Scott, L.R. 9 Ex. 125 (1874), defendants' wrongful failure to have pens for cattle on shipboard was the cause in fact of their being washed overboard in a heavy sea. There was no liability, however, since the statutory requirement was designed to protect the cattle only from perils from contagious disease, a hazard which was not encountered and from which their loss did not result. See Carpenter, Workable Rules for Determining Proximate Cause, 20 Calif. L. Rev. 396, 408 (1932).[12]

The claim of negligence in Gorris v. Scott was violation of orders issued pursuant to the Contagious Diseases (Animals) Act of 1869, the violation being failure to provide battens or footholds for the animals and failure to provide pens not larger than 9 by 15 feet each. Under the analysis suggested in this chapter, the negligent aspect of the conduct was not the circumstance that absence of such pens and footholds placed the cattle in position to be washed overboard. No doubt, reluctance to declare that there is no causal connection between the negligent aspect of the conduct and the result in these circumstances arises from the difficulty of imagining facts in which compliance with the required safeguards against disease would not also protect the cattle against being washed overboard. The case is thus unlike that of the speeding automobile that strikes a child who could not have been avoided by a driver proceeding at a reasonable speed; in that situation, speed causes the automobile to be at the scene at the critical time, but we can imagine the defendant's starting sooner and arriving in time to strike the child though he drives at a reasonable speed throughout the journey. Perhaps the converse

point of view is also relevant, however. That is, perhaps we should consider not only whether situations can be imagined in which the required safeguard would have been ineffectual to prevent the particular kind of harm of which plaintiff is complaining but also whether situations can be imagined in which despite absence of the required safeguards the plaintiff would have been fully protected against this kind of harm. This is not to say that a required safeguard is intended to be an exclusive safeguard against the dangers to which it is directed. But this point of view does suggest that, when we treat one circumstance (that absence of pens placed the cattle in position to be washed overboard) as an aspect of the conduct separate from another circumstance (that absence of pens placed the cattle in position to be subject to an increased risk of contagious disease), we are no more attempting to separate inseparable aspects of a single faulty course of conduct than in the converse situation illustrated by the case of excessive speed. Pursuing this line of thought, we may observe that it would have been possible in Gorris v. Scott to have larger pens and no footholds and yet have the cattle protected against the risk of being washed overboard. In any event, the negligence was concerned with the circumstance that absence of the required safeguards increased the risks of disease, including the risk that affected cattle would communicate the disease widely among animals not separated into small groups by use of small enclosures. It was not concerned with the circumstance that the cattle were in position to be washed overboard. Thus, there was no causal relation between the negligent aspect of the conduct and the harm.

Possibly some passages in the recent broad study of causation by a distinguished pair of English scholars, Hart and Honoré, can also be fairly interpreted as supporting the assertion that the Risk Rule is concerned with causal relation between the negligent aspect of conduct and the harm of which plaintiff complains.[13] Yet, elsewhere they may be thought to be saying that foreseeability is a policy factor, that causal principles are policy neutral, and that use of foreseeability as a test for scope of liability is a departure from use of causal criteria.[14] They argue that the foreseeability test breaks down, especially in cases of what they call "ulterior" harm (e.g., harm following a foreseeable impact on an unforeseeably thin skull), and that causal criteria must be used instead.[15] Perhaps these several passages can be reconciled on the basis that Hart and Honoré mean not to declare that the foreseeability test is unconcerned with causal relation between the negligent aspect of the conduct and the harm but only that in some situations, especially those of "ulterior" harm, the scope of liability is fixed by a test of causal relation between conduct and harm rather than between negligent aspect of conduct and harm. If this reading of their book is proper, then the views of Hart and Honoré tend to support the assertion that the three separate formulations of the Risk Rule are in essence expressions of one idea and that this idea is concerned with cause-in-fact relation between the negligent aspect of the conduct and the harm.

To the contrary, other writers, probably a majority, have insisted that doctrines of legal cause generally, and the result-within-the-risk formulation in particular, are based on policy considerations having nothing to do with cause in fact.[16] The insight produced by a focus upon the relation between the negligent aspect of conduct and the ensuing harm is nevertheless persuasive. The persistence of courts in dealing with this problem under the rubric of causation is perhaps more than evidence of a judicial instinct for right results; perhaps it is also evidence that on occasion judicial perception surpasses that of the majority of reflective critics. This accolade to the courts is not intended to imply a preference for the first or the second formulation of the Risk Rule over the third. It does, however, express a conviction that the first and second formulations offer added illumination on the problem though the third is generally the more manageable in difficult applications. Inevitably, different formulations are likely to produce different nuances and connotations. Since all three formulations are expressions of a single theme, it will often be an aid to deliberate and rational choice to examine the implications of the Risk Rule from the several points of view of all three formulations.

The Policy Foundation of the Risk Rule

Scope of Liability Commensurate with the Basis of Liability

The policy foundation of the Risk Rule can be summarized in this way: The factors determining that the actor is liable for unintended harm caused by his conduct should also determine the scope of his liability. There is surely an interest of public policy in formulating rules that do not impose crushing liability.[17] Since the unintended consequences of one's conduct go on indefinitely, some limit of responsibility is a practical necessity. The theory of the Risk Rule is that the scope of liability should be commensurate with the basis of liability. "Prima facie at least, the reasons for creating liability should limit it."[18]

Opponents of the Risk Rule have argued that in applying the risk concept first to the issue of liability and again to the issue of scope of liability a court gives the defendant an unwarranted advantage by applying twice a restrictive test of foreseeability of harm.[19] The argument is not persuasive. In the first place, the test is expansive rather than restrictive if we start with the assumption that the burden is on the plaintiff to prove some good reason for entering a loss-shifting judgment. That is, when the test for negligence is found to have been fulfilled, liability is expanded in the sense of establishment of an obligation not previously acknowledged. Only if we make a comparison with an assumed state of broader liability, or if we start with the assumption that there is a burden on the defendant to prove nonliability, can we think of an application of the test of foreseeability of harm as restrictive rather than expansive. This is true whether it be applied to the liability issue alone, to the scope of liability issue as well, or to the combination as a unit. In the second place, separating the issues of liability and scope of liability is simply a means of organizing thought. There is no more reason for characterizing the process as a double application of a standard, either restrictive or expansive, when the issues are separated than when they are merged into one issue of liability for how much—none, all, or something between. This double-advantage argument is a conclusion derived from the premise that the scope of liability *should be* governed by a separate test. The opposing premise on which the Risk Rule is founded—the premise that the scope of liability should be limited by the factors accounting for liability—has been described as the view that there is only one question in negligence cases, not two.[20]

Relation to the Principle That Liability Is Based on Fault

The policy argument underlying use of the Risk Rule in negligence cases is a corollary of the foundation of tort law on fault. Generally one is not liable for an unintended harm caused by his nonnegligent conduct. If negligence in one respect were to make the actor liable for all unintended harms to follow, the legal consequences would be disproportionate to the fault. For example, suppose the defendant's negligence consisted of his transporting dynamite in an unmarked truck, otherwise carefully operated, and the only harm caused was injury to one who, without negligence, fainted, fell into the path of the truck, and was run down. Defendant was negligent with respect to risks of explosion but not with respect to risks of an injury of the kind that occurred. The policy judgment underlying the Risk Rule is that with respect to the kind of injury that occurred, the defendant was not at fault.

It may be argued that, as between a negligent defendant and a nonnegligent plaintiff, a loss of which defendant's conduct was a cause in fact ought to be imposed upon the defendant irrespective of whether it was a kind of loss within the risks by reason of which his conduct is characterized as negligence. But if it is relevant to take into account defendant's fault with respect to a risk different from any that would include the harm plaintiff has suffered, then would it not also be relevant to take into account his other faults as well? And would it not seem equally relevant to consider plaintiff's shortcomings? Shall we fix legal responsibility by deciding who is the better and who the worse person? An affirmative answer might involve us, and quickly too, in the morality of run-of-the-ranch TV drama, where the good guys always win.

If we reject this standard of judgment, then so long as liability is to be based on fault, should we not limit the scope of legal responsibility to those consequences with respect to which the actor was negligent—to those consequences of which the negligent aspect of his conduct was a cause? An affirmative answer implies, in relation to the hypothetical case of the transportation of explosives, that legal responsibility should be limited to damages caused by explosion or by conduct responsive to the explosion risk, rather than being extended to injuries that would have occurred even if the driver had used warning signs or had transported no explosives, while acting in other respects exactly as he did.

The policy foundation for the Risk Rule, though applicable more broadly to all problems of results outside the risk, is seen in its most persuasive context in relation to *persons outside the risk*. In this context Judge Learned Hand expressed the philosophy

of the rule in an opinion that is especially illuminating on matters of legal cause. After noting that there are in tort law some instances of strict liability, he said:

> *But so long as it is an element of imposed liability that the wrongdoer shall in some degree disregard the sufferer's interests, it can only be an anomaly, and indeed vindictive, to make him responsible to those whose interests he has not disregarded.*[21]

Perhaps this is as forcefully as one can fairly state the policy justification for the Risk Rule. Indeed, it is easy to exaggerate the weight of this argument as brought to bear upon one of those close cases about which dispute is likely. In the first place, this policy argument is essentially one of blameworthiness, resting distinctly on moral judgment. The twilight zones of disputed legal judgment are also zones of disputed moral judgment, not alone in the minds of judges, but as well in the views of the community at large.[22] Uncertainty is increased by the multiplicity of influences that bear on judgments of blameworthiness. Moreover, even aside from this element of uncertainty about which way underlying moral justifications point for a particular case in the twilight zone, the very fact that the policy is one based on a moral judgment exerts a restraint upon its influence, because we are less content today with moral justifications for our legal rules than with political, economic, and social justifications. It is characteristic of our time to be discomfited about the imposition of our moral judgments on others, especially judgments concerning individual rather than group morality.

One may disagree with the policy argument underlying the Risk Rule, or he may believe that it has been too widely influential, or he may believe that we should now move beyond the Risk Rule in sympathetic conformity with a trend away from liability based on fault and toward strict liability. But to believe that the Risk Rule is without rational policy foundation is to misunderstand, and to deny the existence of that foundation because of aversion to its moralizing quality is to misrepresent. Its force may be doubtful in a range of close cases; and, like most policy arguments, it falls short of providing a firm guide to decision in close cases. But demonstration of these uncertainties on the fringe leaves the hard core of the policy argument intact. This hard core continues to serve as the basic theme of decisions on legal cause.

1. *Cf.* Larrimore v. American Nat'l Ins. Co., *184 Okla. 614, 89 P.2d 340 (1939).* This hypothetical variation upon the facts of that case is chosen for the purpose of eliminating possible grounds of decision other than those to which attention is directed here.

2. *The author's reference is to his discussion of the* Palsgraf *case—Eds.*

3. *Challenges to some of the common assumptions about these expressions appear in Hart & Honoré,* Causation in the Law *19 n.1, 84 n.2, 103–22 (1959); and in Becht & Miller, The Test of Factual Causation in Negligence and Strict Liability Cases 13–21 (1961). See also Williams,* Causation in the Law, *1961 Camb. L. J. 62, 63–79, for comments evoked by the Hart & Honoré book.*

4. *See, e.g., Hart & Honoré,* Causation in the Law *95–96 (1959); 2 Harper & James, Torts 1138 (1956). Compare Becht & Miller, The Test of Factual Causation in Negligence and Strict Liability Cases 21–25 (1961), discussing the hypothetical character of any assertion that an omission was a cause of a subsequent occurrence. Their discussion is addressed to what might be thought of as the converse of the problem referred to here. Here the issue is, Would the same thing have happened if the actor had not engaged in the conduct (whether described as an act, an omission, or a combination) alleged to be negligent? The issue they discuss is, Would the same thing have happened if the actor had done a particular thing he omitted doing? Both inquiries are hypothetical.*

5. *In the context of this discussion of legal cause, the plural, "risks," is chosen in preference to the more commonly used singular form as a means of avoiding the confusion that the risk within which the result falls must be such that, standing alone, it would make the conduct unreasonable. A composite of substantial, foreseeable risks is weighed against utility in judging whether the conduct is unreasonable.*

6. *Cf. P. Keeton,* Negligence, Duty, and Causation in Texas, *16 Texas L. Rev. 1, 11–12 (1937). Though the idea expressed in the text above was suggested to me by the cited passage, the subsequent development in that article of the meaning of "force" (id. at 12–14) indicates that its author might not regard the present idea as one of the legitimate progeny of his teaching.*

7. *E.g., see Seavey,* Cogitations on Torts *31–36 (1954); Seavey* Principles of Torts, *56 Harv. L. Rev. 72, 90–93 (1942); Seavey, Mr. Justice Cardozo and the Law of Torts, 39 Colum. L. Rev. 20, 29–39; 52 Harv. L. Rev. 372, 381–91; 48 Yale L.J. 390, 399–409 (1939). For expressions of generally compatible points of view from the other side of the Atlantic, see Goodhart,* Liability and Compensation, *76 L.O. Rev. 567 (1960) and Williams,* The Risk Principle, *77 L.Q. Rev. 179 (1961).*

8. *2 Harper & James, Torts 1138 (1956).*

9. *Ibid. (emphasis in original).*

10. *Carpenter,* Workable Rules for Determining Proximate Cause, *20 Calif. L. Rev. 229, 231, 408–19 (1932).*

11. *2 Harper & James, Torts 1138 (1956). Perhaps some degree of support for this thesis can be found in the analysis of Becht and Miller, which, for the purpose of inquiries into "factual causation," distinguishes between conduct and the "negligent segment" of it. See Becht & Miller, The Test of Causation in Negligence and Strict Liability Cases 25–28 (1961). But both the explanation of their distinction and the applications of it in their book indicate that it is a physical, rather than a qualitative, distinction. That is, a segment of conduct is an act or an omission among the many acts and omissions that make up the conduct, rather than an unreasonably risky quality of either the total conduct or some part of it. Thus, their distinction is not directed to the question whether the Risk Rule concerns cause-in-fact relation between the harm and the negligent aspect of conduct, as that concept is developed here. Moreover, in some situations where their thesis produces a finding of causal relation between the negligent segment of the conduct and the harm (and either supports liability or else explains nonliability on the "policy" ground that the harm is not within the type against*

which the rule of conduct is directed), the present thesis produces a finding of no causal relation between the negligent aspect of the conduct and the harm. E.g., *they find that the negligent segment of a plaintiff's conduct in sitting on an unsafe wall was a cause of the injury he suffered when the wall was knocked down by a careless motorist whose conduct would have caused the same injuries if the wall had been safe. See* id. at 182–84, *where they criticize the view of Hart and Honoré that the plaintiff's negligence in this situation was causally irrelevant. Under the thesis presented here, as under the thesis of Hart and Honoré apparently, the plaintiff's negligence consisted of placing himself where he was likely to be injured by the collapse of the wall, either without an external impact or under an external impact insufficient to cause the collapse of a safe wall. This aspect of his conduct was not a* sine qua non *of the injury he suffered.*

12. *2 Harper & James, Torts 1138 n. 15 (1956).*

13. *Hart & Honoré,* Causation in the Law *110–12, 192–93 (1959).*

14. *See, e.g.,* id. at 231–38, 259, and 266.

15. *See* id. at 259.

16. *E.g., Green,* The Causal Relation Issue in Negligence Law, *60 Mich. L. Rev. 543, 576 (1962) ("the only cause issue is the connection between the defendant's conduct and the victim's injury"; the issue of causal relation should be unloaded of other considerations [emphasis in the original]); Prosser,* Torts *252, 258, 266 (2d ed. 1955), (proximate cause "is nearly always a matter of various considerations of policy which have nothing to do with the fact of causation"; the problem of scope of liability for unforeseeable consequences "is in no way one of causation, and it does not arise until causation has been established"; the problem of intervening causes is one of policy, not causation); Restatement,* Torts *§ 433, Reason for Changes (1948 Supp.), (Legal cause consists of two elements: 'the substantial factor' element deals with causation in fact"; the second element is concerned with whether there is a rule of law restricting "liability for harm occurring in the particular manner" at issue, and "deals with a legal policy relieving the actor of liability for harm he has, as a matter of fact, caused"; "[i]t is completely faulty analysis" to confuse "the question of policy with the question of fact"). Insistence that the result-within-the-risk problem is not one of causation is found even among advocates of the principle expressed in the several formulations of the Risk Rule. For example, Professor Goodhart declares: "But consequences cannot 'flow' from negligence. Consequences 'flow' from an act or an omission." Goodhart,* Liability for the Consequences of a "Negligent Act," *in* Cambridge Legal Essays *101, 105–6 (1926), reprinted in Goodhart,* Essays in Jurisprudence and the Common Law *110, 114 (1931). See also Foster, Grant & Green,* The Risk Theory and Proximate Cause—A Comparative Study, *32 Neb. L. Rev. 72, 79–80 (1952) (advocating the risk theory and the "relational" quality of negligence, but declaring that "proximate cause often has little if anything to do with causation in fact, except that no issue of proximate cause arises unless actual causation is present," and observing of a typical case that if defendant is held not liable "it is not because its fault was not a cause of the disaster").*

17. *Cf. 2 Harper & James, Torts 1132–33 (1956).*

18. *Seavey,* Mr. Justice Cardozo and the Law of Torts, *39 Colum. L. Rev. 20, 34; 52 Harv. L. Rev. 372, 386; 48 Yale L. J. 390, 404 (1939).*

19. *E.g., Smith,* Legal Cause in Actions of Tort, *25 Harv. L. Rev. 103, 223, 245 (1912). Cf. Green,* Foreseeability in Negligence Law, *61 Colum. L. Rev. 1401, 1408 (1961), noting that there are numerous devices for controlling decisions of both liability and damages, and asserting that "the foreseeability formula" need not "reach beyond the negligence issue" into the area of other limitations on scope of liability.*

20. *See Pound,* Causation, *67 Yale L. J. 1, 10 (1957), referring to Pollock's view. Pollock stated the question as one "whether the accepted test of liability for negligence in the first instance is or not*

also the proper measure of liability for the consequences of proved or admitted default." Pollock, Liability for Consequences, 38 L. Q. Rev. 165 (1922).

21. Sinram v. Pennsylvania R.R., *61 F.2d 767, 770 (2d Cir. 1932).*
22. *Cf. Morris,* Proximate Cause in Minnesota, *34 Minn L. Rev. 185, 207 (1950).*

THE DECLINE OF CAUSE*

Judith Jarvis Thomson

I

Once upon a time there was a simple way of characterizing tort law. It could in those days be said that the defendant will be declared liable for the plaintiff's loss if and only if the plaintiff proves the following three things: (1) that he suffered a loss, (2) that an act or failure to act on the part of the defendant was proximate cause of the plaintiff's suffering that loss, and (3) that the defendant was at fault in so acting or failing to act. Proximate cause was a messy business, of course, but one thing that was clear was that a person's act or omission was not proximate cause of another person's loss unless it caused the loss.

So much for once upon a time. Fault went first: it began to be possible in certain kinds of cases for a plaintiff to win his suit if he proved (1) that he suffered a loss, and (2) that an act or failure to act on the part of the defendant proximately caused his loss, even though he did not prove (3) that the defendant was at fault in so acting or failing to act. Now cause is going. In a number of cases in recent years the plaintiff has won his suit on proof (1) that he suffered a loss, and (2) that there was a faulty act or omission on the part of the defendant, but without proving (3) that the defendant's faulty act or omission caused the loss. No doubt the plaintiff has to prove *some* connection between his loss and the defendant's faulty act. If I prove I lost my legs this morning, and that you hit your little brother with a brick yesterday, *that* certainly will not suffice for me to win a suit against you for damages for the loss of my legs. The plaintiff has to connect the

faulty act with the loss. But in the kind of case I have in mind, the connection he makes need not be causation.

Which kind of case? A good example is *Sindell* v. *Abbott Laboratories,*[1] which was decided by the California Supreme Court in 1980. The plaintiff alleged she could prove that she developed cancer as a result of the DES taken by her mother while pregnant; she alleged she could prove also that the defendants— eleven drug companies — knew or should have known that DES would cause cancer in the daughters of mothers who took it. In other words, she alleged she could prove (1) that she was harmed, and (2) that the defendant drug companies were at fault. But she was unable to prove, after the passage of so many years, which drug company had marketed the very DES her mother took, so she was unable to prove about any of the drug companies (3) that *its* acts had caused the harm she suffered. All the same, she won the right to get a jury on the fact she alleged she could prove, and the right to win if she could prove them.

An earlier California case—*Summers* v. *Tice,*[2] decided in 1948—presented the problem that confronted the plaintiff in *Sindell* much more starkly and cleanly. The plaintiff Summers had gone hunting with the two defendants, Tice and Simonson. A quail was flushed, and, as Summers alleged, the defendants fired negligently in Summers' direction; as he also alleged, one of the two wounded him. But he was unable to prove which, since the defendants had fired similar pellets from similar guns. Loss yes, fault yes,

From Judith Jarvis Thomson, "The Decline of Cause," in 76 *Georgetown Law Journal* 137. Reprinted with the permission of the publisher, © 1987 The Georgetown Law Journal Association and Georgetown University.

but causality could not be proved. However he too won his suit.

My own impression is that cases like *Summers* and *Sindell*—in which loss and fault are clear, but causality cannot be proved—were very rarely won until recently. Why are they being won now? It is an excellent question, with, I am sure, a great many answers. Chief among them is probably a mix of four things: first, the very fact that causality *is* hard to prove in them; together with, second, the felt need to regulate the increasing number of activities which impose risk as a byproduct of technological advance; third, an increasing public acceptance of egalitarianism; and fourth, the absence as yet of a mechanism other than the tort suit to regulate those activities and secure a measure of compensation for those who may be being victimized by them.[3]

II

A related phenomenon—at least I think it really must be related—is the increasing dismissiveness about causality that can be seen in legal theorizing. Here are Landes and Posner in an article published in 1983: "causation in the law is an inarticulate groping for economically sound solutions. . . ."[4] In an article published in 1975, Calabresi defends the idea that certain concepts related to causality have a role to play in law, but his defense of that idea would have puzzled many lawyers fifty years ago. He says:

> [I]n law *the term "cause" is used in different guises but always to identify those pressure points that are most amenable to the social goals we wish to accomplish. . . . [U]se of such [causal] concepts has great advantages over explicit identification and separation of the goals. Terms with an historical, common law gloss [like "cause"] permit us to consider goals (like spreading) that we do not want to spell out or too obviously assign to judicial institutions.*[5]

This dismissiveness about causality is not visible only in those whose legal theorizing is influenced by economics.[6]

III

I am not competent to speak to the question why the law and legal theory have been developing in these ways, or even to the question exactly what forms these developments have taken. What I want to do instead is to mull over one of the sources of the welcome with which these developments have been received by many of the moral philosophers who have taken note of them.

What I have in mind is that there has been a phenomenon equally entitled to be called "The Decline of Cause" in moral theorizing.

The moral sophisticate nowadays is nowhere near as enamored of causality as the ignorant rest of us. Here is an example. Yesterday, Alfred backed his car out of his driveway without looking. Bad of him!—one ought not do that. Today, Bert backed his car out of his driveway without looking, but lo and behold there was a child at the end of the driveway, and Bert ran over the child and crushed its legs. Horrendous—much worse. Or so many people think.

The moral sophisticate regards that as a vulgar error. "Look," he says, "both Alfred and Bert behaved negligently, indeed equally negligently. Bert crushed a child's legs and Alfred did not, but that was just bad luck for Bert, and good luck for Alfred. After all, it wasn't Bert's fault that there was a child at the foot of his driveway; all Bert was at fault for is exactly what Alfred was at fault for, namely backing his car out of his driveway without looking. So Bert acted no worse than Alfred did, and—other things being equal—Bert is no worse a person than Alfred is."

The moral sophisticate may concede that the law does well to mark a difference between Alfred and Bert in the following two ways: (1) imposing a more severe punishment on Bert than on Alfred, and (2) making Bert, and not Alfred, compensate the child's parents. But if so, he says it is for reasons extraneous to the *moral* valuation proper to them and their acts.

It is clear that the moral sophisticate is going to hold this same view in other pairs of cases too. Murder and attempted murder, of course. Yesterday Charles fired a gun at a man, to kill him; Charles'[s] intended victim was wearing a bullet proof vest, so Charles did not kill him. Today David fired a gun at a man, to kill him; David's intended victim was not wearing a bullet proof anything, so David did kill him. David murdered a man, and Charles only attempted murder, but the moral sophisticate says that David acted no worse than Charles did—for after all, it was just bad luck for Charles that his intended victim was wearing that vest, and thus nothing that Charles can take any credit for.

It seems to me three principles lie behind this moral attitude. The first concerns itself with *acts*. What we do in the world depends on the world as well as on us. If you fire a gun at a man to kill him, then the question whether you do not merely fire a gun at him, but also kill him turns on whether the world cooperates—thus on whether the bullet actually reaches him, as it might not if some third party intervenes, and on whether it enters him when it reaches him, as it might not if he is wearing bullet proof clothes. The first principle I have in mind says that the moral value of what you do in the world turns on and only on that part of it which is *entirely* under your control. When you fire a gun at a man, what is under your control is at most such things as the kind of gun you fire, the time and place at which you fire it, the direction in which you fire it, and the intention with which you fire it—merely to scare your victim, or merely to wound him, or positively to kill him. The rest that happens is up to the world, and is not something that has any bearing on the moral value of your act.

I said "at most." Let us look again at the kind of gun you fire. Is it new? Is it clean? Is it sufficiently powerful to do the work you want it to do? Strictly speaking, that the gun you fire does or does not have these features is not entirely under your control. What is under your control is only that you have made an effort to be sure that you are firing a suitable gun and now think you are: After all, somebody might have secretly replaced your carefully chosen gun with a different one—whether a person did or did not do this is not under your control. Similarly for the time and place at which you fire the gun, and the direction in which you fire it: Somebody might have secretly altered your clocks and roadmaps, and substituted distorting glasses for the glasses you normally wear—whether a person did or did not do this is also not under your control.

Strictly speaking, all that is entirely under your control are your intentions in acting—what you are at any given time setting yourself to be doing. That is not to say that setting yourself to do this or that is all you actually *do;* it is to say that the normal value of what you do *by* setting yourself to act in this or that way turns entirely on the moral value of those settings of yourself to act.

The second of the three principles concerns itself with *failures to act,* or omissions, for short. Consider two switchmen on different railways, Edward and Frank. Both were under a duty to throw a switch at ten this morning, and both failed to do so because they did not want to be bothered. Edward's omission caused a terrible train crash; Frank's omission caused nothing untoward at all, since the train Frank's switch-

throwing was to turn had luckily stalled before the fork in the track. If you think murder no worse than attempted murder, you will surely think Edward's omission no worse than Frank's. It was, after all, no credit to Frank, it was merely good luck for him, that his train had stalled. The second principle says that the moral value of an omission—as of an act—turns on and only on what is entirely under the agent's control. If you could have set yourself to do a thing, and ought to have done so, then your failure to do so is equally bad no matter what your omission does or does not cause.

The cases of Alfred and Bert with which I began are cases to which both principles apply. Alfred and Bert both acted, for they backed their cars down their driveways; and both failed to act, for they failed to look while doing so. Given the two principles, the fact that Bert's acting while failing to act caused a child's legs to be crushed has no bearing at all on the moral value of what he did.

The third of the three principles has to do with the moral value of *persons.* We do think of some people as morally better than others; on what does this judgment turn? Presumably in part on the moral value of what a person does or fails to do. Given the first two principles, however, that is a function only of the moral value of a person's settings of himself to do this or that, and his failures to set himself to do this or that.

But only in part, for there is something else that a friend of these ideas should think bears on a person's moral value. What I have in mind is that if you think that good and bad luck has no bearing on the moral value of an act or omission *or* person, then you should grant that the truth or falsehood of certain counterfactuals is relevant. For example, I do not drive, and a fortiori have never backed a car out of a driveway with *or* without looking. If I had driven, would I on occasion have backed my car out of my driveway without looking? Isn't that relevant to the question how good or bad a person I am?

I am sure that all of us have faced temptations to act badly, and that many of those temptations we have resisted, though some we have not. Most people, however, are lucky enough never to be tempted to do something truly dreadful. For example, I am sure that none of us has ever been in a position of power over prisoners in a concentration camp. I am sure that none of us has been lost at sea in a lifeboat with no provisions other than a plump cabin boy. We have been lucky. How would we behave if we were in such situations? Surely that we would or would not behave in this or that way has a bearing on our moral value as people. One reason why Stanley Milgram's experiments[7] were found so shocking was that they uncovered the fact that a lot of perfectly ordinary people were quite ready to set themselves to cause others a great deal of pain simply on being told by an authority figure in a white coat to do so. Milgram's readers did not think for a moment that the actual absence of pain excused the subjects of the experiments; and they took it that what Milgram had shown was a deep moral failing which may be present in perfectly ordinary people, though without ever in fact showing itself.

How good a person are you? The third principle tells us that to the extent to which you do not know what you would set yourself to do in situations you have been so far lucky as not to have faced, you just do not know how good a person you are.

I described the person who holds these views as the "moral sophisticate," because I think we do think these views more sophisticated than those which tell us to look merely at what happens, more sophisticated even than those which tell us to look *both* at what happens *and* at what is internal to a person—what he sets himself to do, and what he would set himself to do if he were in situations he has never faced. But I might just as well have described the person who holds these views as a Kantian, because it is directly from Kant that they come down to us today. Kant said: "The good will is not good because of what it effects or accomplishes or because of its adequacy to achieve some proposed end; it is good only because of its willing, i.e., it is good of itself. . . . Usefulness or fruitlessness can neither diminish or augment [its] worth."[8] And so similarly for the bad will: it is not bad because of what it causes, but only of itself. We might redescribe the decline of cause in moral philosophy as the triumph of Kant.

That Kant has triumphed seems clear enough. For example, I rather fancy that all of you have at least some inclination to agree with the three principles I drew attention to. I certainly do.

It is of interest to notice that these Kantian ideas are visible even in contemporary defenders of the most un-Kantian moral theory of all. I have Utilitarianism in mind, of course. Classical Utilitarians—such as John Stuart Mill and G.E. Moore—took the view that you have acted wrongly if and only if your act causes there to be less good in the world than you could have caused by choosing some other alternative act which was open to you at the time. Whether you knew it or not. Mill did explicitly grant that a man's intentions in acting do have a bearing on the moral

evaluation proper to *him;* but Mill insisted that the morality of a man's *act* turns on, and only on, a comparison between what it does in fact cause, and what his other available alternatives would have caused. But hardly anyone is a Classical Utilitarian nowadays. Those in favor of its spirit say that the morality of a man's act turns, not on what it in fact causes, but on what he expects it to cause. In short, the morality of action turns, not on actual, but on expected utilities.

Now I think that these Kantian ideas are one source of the welcome with which many moral philosophers have received those developments in law and legal theory that I mentioned at the outset. For example, they think that all of the defendants were at fault in *Sindell* and *Summers*—equally at fault, regardless of whoever in fact caused the harm. So they think that no one can object, on *moral* grounds, to the plaintiffs' winning, and to the defendants' therefore having to share in the plaintiffs' costs.[9]

IV

What should *we* think of all this? It is swimming upstream to try to fight it, but my own feeling is that it smells too much of the study and too little of the open air. Adam Smith said, very plausibly, I think,

> But how well soever we may seem to be persuaded of the truth of [these ideas], when we consider [them] after this manner, in abstract, yet when we come to particular cases, the actual consequences which happen to proceed from any action, have a very great effect upon our sentiments concerning its merit or demerit, and almost always either enhance or diminish our sense of both.[10]

Alfred backed his car out of his driveway without looking, and luckily for him, nothing untoward happened in consequence. Bad of him, we think. But not horrendous. People do that kind of thing often enough. They ought not, but they do, and it seems no great sin. Bert also backed his car out of his driveway without looking, but *he* ran a child down and crushed its legs. As Adam Smith said, we just *do* think that what Bert did was worse than what Alfred did. How can any philosophy be right which tells us we are mistaken in thinking this?

On the other hand, I think that Adam Smith's remark would not have been at all plausible if he had not said "almost always." He said: "the actual consequences which happen to proceed from any action, have a very great effect upon our sentiments concerning its merit or demerit, and *almost always* either enhance or diminish our sense of both."[11] There seem to me to be two kinds of case in which they do not.

To get at the first kind, let me draw your attention to the fact that in every example I have given, right from the outset, the agent whose act did cause a harm was at fault. In the two court cases I began with, all of the defendants were at fault, the drug companies in *Sindell,* the negligent hunters in *Summers.* Alfred and Bert were both careless. Charles and David, each of whom shot at a man to kill him, were both at least attempting murder. And so on. But what of an agent who causes someone to suffer a harm, but not by negligence or intention or by any wrong at all? A child runs out into the street and is run down by a truck driver who is entirely without fault—he has taken all due care to ensure that his truck, and in particular, his brakes, were in good order, and he was driving with all due care. The child simply ran too suddenly, too close, into the path of his truck. Does the very fact that he caused harm to the child diminish our sense of the merit of his actions? I think not. This example comes from Thomas Nagel, and he says about it: "The driver, if he is entirely without fault, will feel terrible about his role in the event, but will not have to reproach himself."[12] Nor will we reproach him. There is nothing to reproach him for. So here is a case of the first kind I had in mind: it is a case in which an agent was not at fault at all in acting, and that a bad consequence happens to flow from his action does not affect our sense of its merit or demerit. In particular, the bad consequence does not make us think worse of his driving than we would have thought had that bad consequence not flowed from it.

Symmetrically, we might imagine someone who does something of no particular merit, and something good just happens to flow from his doing it. For example, suppose a man is standing at a street corner, waiting for a bus. As he waits, he is idly tapping his foot. Through some freak of nature, his tapping his foot causes three lives to be saved. This good consequence does not affect our sense of the merit or demerit of his tapping his foot. In particular, it does not make us think better of his tapping his foot than we would have thought had that good consequence not flowed from it.

Let us go back to that truck driver, whom I will call Unlucky No Fault Driver. His not having been at fault must be the crucial fact about him which makes him an exception to Adam Smith's remarks. For let us now contrast him with two other truck drivers. Both of them were at fault. They were supposed to check their brakes before leaving the garage, but did not want to be bothered. So both went out with bad brakes. In the case of the first, nothing untoward happened, and I will call him Lucky Fault Driver. I will call the second Unlucky Fault Driver. A child ran in front of Unlucky Fault Driver's truck and he ran it down. I want to have it be clear about Unlucky Fault Driver that he ran the child down not because the child ran too suddenly, too close into the path of his truck, but because his brakes were not in good working order. Had his brakes been in good working order, he would have been able to stop his truck in time; but they were not, so he was not. Lucky Fault Driver acted badly, of course; but I think we do feel that Unlucky Fault Driver acted worse. The fact that a bad consequence flowed from his action does seem to affect our sense of its demerit.

Why? I think the answer is quite simply that Unlucky Fault Driver is to blame for the death he caused. Unlucky No Fault Driver also caused a death; but he is not to blame for it, since he was in no way at fault for causing it. It seems right to say that that is why the bad consequence which flowed from Unlucky No Fault Driver's action does not make us think it worse than we would have thought it had that bad consequence not flowed from it. More generally, it seems right to say that a bad consequence of an action makes that action worse *only* where the agent is to blame for that bad consequence which his action causes.

I am sure that the Kantian moral sophisticate would say at this point, "But surely it was mere bad luck for Unlucky Fault Driver that he caused a child's death. And surely one can't plausibly think a man to blame for something that he caused merely out of bad luck." There is a mistake here, and I think it the main source of the trouble. For it was not *mere* bad luck for Unlucky Fault Driver that he caused a child's death. We need a clearer grip on how bad luck figures in these cases. Unlucky No Fault Driver was in two ways unlucky. It was a piece of bad luck for him that a child ran into his path; and second, it was a piece of bad luck for him that a child ran into his path; but it was not a piece of bad luck for him that he was unable to stop his truck in time. Unlucky Fault Driver was unlucky in only the first of those two ways. It was a piece of bad luck for him that he was unable to stop his truck in time. His being unable to stop his truck in time was due to his bad brakes, and thus to his own negligence. Lucky Fault Driver did not have that first piece of bad luck, so it remains a counterfactual truth about him that *if* he had had it, then he too would have been unable to stop his truck in time. His being unable to stop would not have been a mere piece of bad luck for him, but would, instead, have been due to his negligence.

And it is the very same thing—namely Unlucky Fault Driver's negligence—that makes it not *mere* bad luck for him that he caused the child's death, that also makes him to blame for the child's death. Unlucky No Fault Driver, by contrast, was not at fault; and that is why it was mere bad luck for him that he caused a child's death, and therefore also why he is not to blame for the death of the child he killed.

The Kantian moral sophisticate could of course insist that a man cannot be thought to blame for something if bad luck entered *in any way at all* into the history of his bringing it about. But that seems to me even on its face implausible. Consider, for example, a man who is brought to trial for murder. "Look," his lawyer says to the court, "I grant that the victim's death is not *mere* bad luck for my client, since my client fired a gun at him with the intention of killing him. But the victim's death is in part due to my client's bad luck. For unbeknownst to my client, the victim almost always wore a bullet proof vest, and it was just bad luck for my client that the victim's bullet proof vest happened to be at the cleaners' on the day my client shot at him. So my client cannot be thought to blame for his victim's death." Whatever else will work in a court, *that* won't.

Let us go back now and look again at the first of the three principles that I said lie behind the moral attitude of the Kantian moral sophisticate. The first principle is: the moral value of what you do in the world turns on and only on that part of it which is entirely under your control. That seems to me to be false, and for the reason I have pointed to. Admittedly the two faulty drivers, Lucky Fault Driver and Unlucky Fault Driver, both acted equally negligently, and the difference between them has its source in the fact that one had good luck, the other bad luck. All the same, the difference which has that source is a moral difference, and of a very grave order. For the one is *by* his negligence to blame for a death, and the other is not.

A similar point surely holds of failures to act. Edward and Frank both failed to throw the switch; Edward's (but not Frank's) negligence caused a crash, for which he is therefore to blame. That, I think, is why we think that what he did was worse than what Frank did.

It seems to me, however, that we should be more sympathetic to the third of the three principles I

mentioned, which yields that Unlucky Fault Driver is no worse a person than Lucky Fault Driver is, and that Edward is no worse a person than Frank. Counterfactual truths about what people would have done and been to blame for if they had been in circumstances which they were lucky enough to have avoided really are important to us in assessing how good a person is—as important, I think, as truths about what they in fact did and in fact are to blame for.

This difference between our judgments of acts on the one hand and the people who perform them on the other hand may perhaps be due to the fact that different kinds of consequences flow from our arriving at these two different kinds of judgments. When we learn that someone is a bad person—untrustworthy, unreliable, prone to acting without thought for others—what flows from this judgment? Well, our attitude toward him changes, and in consequence we will behave differently toward him in many more or less delicate ways in the future. This reaction is appropriate whether the judgment is provoked by what he actually did *or* by what we have come to learn he would do if he were in circumstances he has not in fact been in. By contrast, some of the consequences of learning that a person has actually acted badly are backward looking. If we learn he is to blame for a dreadful outcome, we do not merely alter our behavior toward him in future, we may also lock him up for what he did, or exact compensation for it from him, or both.[13]

V

Candor, however, compels me to mention a difficulty for what I have been saying. Let us go back to Adam Smith. He said: "the actual consequences which happen to proceed from any action, have a great effect upon our sentiments concerning its merit or demerit, and *almost always* either enhance or diminish our sense of both."[14] I mentioned one class of exceptions. Unlucky No Fault Driver, for example, was merely unlucky. He caused a child's death, but because this was through no fault of his own, we do not think the worse of his actions. Where there is fault, however, I said that consequences do make a difference. We do think worse of Unlucky Fault Driver's actions than of Lucky Fault Driver's actions, and that is because the one is, and the other is not, to blame for a bad outcome.

But there is yet another class of exceptions to Adam Smith's remarks, which makes trouble for any simple treatment of these issues. The simplest example comes from a case I mentioned at the outset, namely *Summers* v. *Tice*.[15] (That is a wonderful case. If it had not occurred, we would have had to invent it.) The two defendants, Tice and Simonson, both fired negligently in Summers' direction, and one of them shot Summers, but we cannot tell which. Who should pay Summers' bills? Most people feel it right that Tice and Simonson should split the costs. The actual outcome in court was joint and several liability, but arguably that comes to roughly the same thing given the possibility of a suit for contribution, and in any case there are reasons to think that outcome fairer to Summers than a division of the costs. So far so good, nothing puzzling yet.

Now for the source of the puzzlement. Suppose that during the course of the trial evidence came forward which made it as certain as empirical matters ever are that the pellet that caused Summers' injury came from Tice's gun, so that it is Tice who is to blame for Summers' injury. We do, I think, take it to be clear that Simonson should now be dismissed from the suit: no doubt he acted badly, but he is not to blame for the injury, and hence he is not appropriately held liable for its costs.[16] But our *moral* assessment of Tice and Simonson does not shift. We do not think the worse of Tice, or even of Tice's acts, because he, as it turns out, is to blame for the harm; and we do not think the better of Simonson, or of Simonson's acts, because *he,* as it turns out, is not to blame for the harm. Our moral attitude does not shift in any way by virtue of the discovery that it is Tice who actually caused the harm. So we really seem to have a second kind of exception to Adam Smith's remarks.

It could of course be said that it is just irrational on our part to fail to distinguish between Tice and Simonson in the way in which we do distinguish between Lucky and Unlucky Fault Drivers. But it does not *feel* irrational. And the moral views of the man and woman in the street are deserving of great respect: they ought not be dismissed as irrational unless it really does turn out that there is no rationale for them.

What bubbles up in us men-and-women-in-the-street is, I think, this: "Simonson nearly caused the very same harm that Tice caused." It is not true of Lucky Fault Driver that he nearly caused the very same harm that Unlucky Fault Driver caused. Or at least you were not thinking of him as having done so. One driver goes out in one part of town, the other in another; they both have bad brakes; a child runs in front of one, no child runs in front of the other. So far so

good. One is to blame for a death and the other is not, and we feel very differently about what they did.

But now let the two drivers set out from the same part of town, down the same street. A child runs in front of both. Both come to a long screeching halt. The child is hit by one truck and not by the other. If the child had been running *ever* so slightly slower, it would have been hit by the other truck. Now the drivers seem to us like Tice and Simonson: we think no worse of what the one did than of what the other did.

This suggests that something else is at work in these cases, possibly two things, in fact.

In the first place, Tice and Simonson did not merely act equally negligently; they each imposed roughly the same risk of harm on a person. Similarly for the two truck drivers who set out from the same part of town, and in front of both of whom one child runs. Not so for two truck drivers who set out from different parts of town. If they both set out with bad brakes, they acted equally negligently; but if a child runs in front of one, and no child so much as gets near the other, they do not in fact impose even roughly the same risk of harm on anyone.

This does make a difference to us. Suppose you back your car out of your driveway without looking, but no child was anywhere near you. Perhaps you will feel bad later on thinking the matter over: after all, it is negligent to back out without looking. But you will not *dwell* on what you did; it would be irrational to lie awake at night shuddering at the thought of what you *might* have caused. But suppose you back your car out of your driveway without looking, and there was a child in the vicinity; indeed, you nearly hit it, and would have hit it but for the child's having noticed a penny up ahead and run faster to get to it. Here the shudder is not out of place. We all know what that terrible, nagging thought is like: it is not merely of what you might have caused, but of what you nearly did cause. You do not feel as bad as you would if you had actually hit the child; but you do feel considerably worse than you would if there had been no child in the vicinity at all.

Adam Smith said that the bad consequences of an act affect our sense of its merit or demerit, and I agreed that this is so if the act was faulty: for the bad things an act causes are things that its agent is to blame for, if his act was faulty. What seems to come out here is that it is not merely the actual bad consequences of an act that affect our sense of its demerit: the higher the risk of bad consequences that the act actually imposes on others, the greater the demerit of the act.

It is puzzling that this should be so, however. Your negligence in backing out of your driveway without looking is no greater or worse if there is a child in the vicinity than if there is not; and since you did not actually hit the child, [you] cannot explain [your] feeling that what you did was worse by appeal to the fact that you are to blame for a harm to the child. *Nobody* was harmed. So there is a gap here, and I hope you will find it as interesting a question as I do just how it is to be filled.

I said it is possible that there are two further things at work in these cases. The second of them is this: Tice and Simonson did not merely act equally negligently, and they did not merely each impose roughly the same risk of harm on *a* person; they each imposed roughly the same risk of harm on one and the same person, namely Summers. Similarly for the two truck drivers who set out from the same part of town, and in front of both of whom one child runs. Does *that* matter to us? I do not find it clear that it does. Dickenson fired his shotgun negligently last Wednesday, and nearly hit someone. He feels awful about what he did, and we think it right that he feel awful about it. Do we think worse of what Simonson did, given he nearly hit someone on Thursday, *and* given also that the person Simonson nearly hit was in fact hit by Tice? Perhaps so. But it is even harder, I think, to see why that should be so—if it is.

VI

Let me now try to pull this material together just briefly. I began by drawing attention to two phenomena in law—more precisely, one in law itself, the other in legal theory—which seem to warrant saying that as far as tort law is concerned at any rate, there has been a decline of cause. Many people think that if cause declines in law, law to that extent departs from morality. It therefore seemed to me worth drawing attention to the fact that there has been a decline of cause in moral theory too. That decline in part explains why moral theorists who interest themselves in law have welcomed those developments in law and legal theory. But it is of interest for its own sake. As Adam Smith said, when you think about these matters in the abstract, the philosophers seem to be right; but when you come out of the study, they seem to be wrong. Moral theorists must of course ask themselves why that is, and whether there is a rationale for it; that is the job of the moral theorist. But I hope that lawyers will find these questions of interest too. The law certainly is not, and need not be, an exact reflection of the morality of those governed by it; but responsible government tries to be sure it has a sound rationale whenever it departs from that morality, and therefore does well to try to become clear about what that morality is.

1. *26 Cal. 3d 88, 163 Cal. Rptr. 132, 607 P.2d 924*, cert. denied, *449 U.S. 912 (1980).*

2. *33 Cal. 2d 80, 199 P.2d 1 (1948).*

3. *For an interesting discussion of these and related matters, which brings out their bearing on a particular case, see P. Shuck, Agent Orange on Trial, Mass Toxic Disasters in the Courts (1986).*

4. *Landes & Posner*, Causation in Tort Law: An Economic Approach, *12 J.L. Stud. 109, 131 (1983).*

5. *Calabresi*, Concerning Cause and the Law of Torts: An Essay for Harry Kalven, Jr., *43 U. Chi. L. Rev. 69, 106–07 (1975) (emphasis in original).*

6. See, e.g., *Kelman*, The Necessary Myth of Objective Causation Judgments in Liberal Political Theory, *63 Chi-Kent L. Rev 579 (1987).*

7. See *S. Milgram, Obedience to Authority (1974) (summarizing results of Milgram's experiments).*

8. *I. Kant, Foundations of the Metaphysics of Morals 12–13 (Bobbs-Merill ed. 1969).*

9. See, e.g., *Fischer & Ennis*, Causation and Liability, *15 Phil. & Pub. Affairs 33 (1986); Kagan*, Causation, Liability, and Internalism, *15 Phil. & Pub. Affairs 41 (1986).*

10. *A. Smith, The Theory of Moral Sentiments 134 (Arlington House ed. 1969).*

11. *The emphasis is mine.*

12. *T. Nagel, Mortal Questions 28–29 (1979).*

13. *As I wrote in part III, the moral sophisticate may say that while the law does well to mark a difference between Alfred and Bert (punishing Bert more severely than Alfred, exacting compensation for the injury from Bert), this is for reasons extraneous to the moral valuation proper to them and their acts. I think it is one thing to say the moral valuation proper to them does not warrant differential legal consequences: Bert is surely no worse a person than Alfred is. But it is another thing to say the moral valuation proper to their acts does not warrant differential legal consequences: Bert, after all, is to blame for a harm and Alfred is not, so there really is a moral difference between what Bert did and what Alfred did.*

14. *A. Smith, supra note 10, at 134. The emphasis is mine.*

15. *33 Cal. 2d 80, 199 P.2d 1 (1948).*

16. *Why this should be so is discussed in Thomson*, Remarks on Causation and Liability, *13 Phil. & Pub. Affairs 101 (1984). Criticism of that discussion may be found in Fischer & Ennis, supra note 9, and in Kagan, supra note 9.*

BLAME, PUNISHMENT, AND THE ROLE OF RESULT*

Richard Parker

Rasputin, the story goes, was poisoned with cyanide, shot with pistols, bludgeoned, stabbed, emasculated, then tied with cords, wrapped in cloth and dumped through a hole in the ice in the Neva River. When the body was found, it was discovered that he had worked part way out of his bonds before he succumbed; the cause of death was drowning. Let us suppose for a moment that the object of these horrors had proved, incredibly, to be an even more recalcitrant victim than he was and that he had actually survived his ordeal. Clearly, this supposition has no effect at all with respect to the intentions of Prince Yusupov and his cohorts, the perpetrators of the crime, nor does it affect their conduct in any substantial way—they did everything they could to ensure Rasputin's death, employing means well beyond those ordinarily required. Had he survived, due to his own incredible efforts and constitution, would that diminish the seriousness of the crime committed against him? However we decide to answer this question, it is clear that Rasputin's survival would substantially change the culpability and statutory punishability of Yusupov and company in practically every jurisdiction within the scope of Anglo-American law. It is true, of course, that the parties guilty of such a crime could be punished very severely under existing statutes, but, compared to the penalty for murder, the sanctions attached to aggravated assault, attempted murder, battery, and mayhem—the offenses for which Yusupov is most likely indictable on our supposition—are clearly less forbidding.

I bring up this rather exotic example from the history of homicide to introduce what seems to me to be a serious difficulty in our system of criminal justice. The difficulty, in its most general form, can be put in terms of a question: on what rational grounds can we proportion punishment to the results of an actor's conduct when those results are largely or entirely beyond the actor's control? The distinction between attempts and completed crimes is only the most visible of many which call up this question. Felony-murder, misdemeanor-manslaughter, and reckless or negligent conduct of many kinds involve the same or an analogous problem. In what follows I'll concentrate on a few rather more mundane examples than the Rasputin incident, with particular attention to certain moral aspects of the issues.

I

It is often said that one who engages in criminal wrongdoing thereby incurs a debt to society; the wrongdoer's punishment is conceived as the coin in which the debt is payable. That he owes the debt to *society* rather than to some private individual or collective (who may have suffered a loss at his hands) is often said to be the key to the distinction between criminal law and tort law, or, perhaps better, between criminal harm and tortious harm. Lawrence Becker has discussed this matter[1] with helpful results especially with respect to the analysis of criminal or "social" harm and the role this notion should rightly play in the law of attempts. The position he takes is that it is the *attempt* to accomplish harm, whether the attempt succeed or fail, which is properly the concern of the society and hence the business of criminal law. Attempts, Becker argues, produce as much justifiable social volatility—his phrase for upset, anxiety, fear, and generally unfavorable reaction—as do successful crimes.[2] Hence the criminal law should make no distinction as regards punishability between a full-fledged attempt and a success, other things being equal.

*Richard Parker, "Blame, Punishment, and the Role of Result," a revision of a paper in *American Philosophical Quarterly*, vol. 21, no. 3 (1984), pp. 1–11. Reprinted by permission of the author and *American Philosophical Quarterly*.

In a few moments, I shall argue for Becker's conclusion on other, but related, grounds. First, though, I should point out how strongly this conclusion runs counter to both current practice and popular opinion.

In the history of criminal law, the punishment of unsuccessful attempts and other conduct which fails to produce harm is a relatively recent development.[3] Indeed, among the "basic premises which underlie the whole of Anglo-American criminal law" is the statement that, "since the criminal law aims to prevent harm to the public, there can be no crime without harm."[4] Clearly, we do not follow this dictum to the letter, as the law defines many criminal offenses which merely *tend* to have harmful consequences (such as forgery) or which merely produce dangerous situations (such as reckless driving). Still, the emphasis put on actual harm caused is a principal ingredient of the method we use to grade the seriousness of crimes and to determine the severity of punishments.[5] It can also make the difference between criminal and noncriminal conduct.[6]

As is usually the case with the substantive criminal law, there seems to be a connection between the law's emphasis on harm and certain moral intuitions which many people apparently share. It may strike us as gratuitous, for example, to punish a person for an action which in fact caused nobody any harm. What are we punishing him for? one might ask. On the other hand, there is a clear answer to this question if a harmful result is actually produced: he is punished for causing that result. Furthermore, since the criminal law is connected to moral blameworthiness (at least in a way that tort law is not),[7] it is not surprising that most people seem to find it easier to blame one who causes harm more than one who does not. I believe that blameworthiness and punishability should where possible run parallel in the law, but I think it is false that results are generally relevant either to one's blameworthiness or to his punishability.

Consider the following story: you and I attend a party and get roaring drunk. In our host's den we discover a pair of loaded rifles and decide to find out which of us is the better shot by firing out a window at a lamp across the street. Each of us takes several shots, with no ill effect on the lamp. One of your shots, however, ricochets off the lamppost or by some similar means finds its way into a citizen who, unknown to us, happened to be nearby. The citizen dies as a result of his wound. Now, given the similarity of our conduct, it seems perfectly appropriate to claim equal blameworthiness on our parts. This can be made quite clear, I think, by varying the case a bit. Suppose first that it is not immediately known which of our bullets, yours or mine, that caused the fatal result. It seems strange that we should have to wait to apportion blame until this determination is made, for most people would surely agree that what is necessary to make this apportionment is present in this case before we know whose bullet caused the death. If we *never* discover whose bullet did the fatal damage, is there some hesitancy, some cloudiness of our intuition with respect to how much comparative blame the two of us deserve? I think not. I think most people would be satisfied with equal blame between us, and, importantly, nobody would worry much about a mistake having been made—the mistake of one of us being blamed for something he didn't do or the other for not being blamed for something he did do. If unequal blame is due us, the pain of inconsistency can be avoided only by showing a relevant difference between us. And, if it can be shown that the only difference is that made by the fact that one fired the fatal bullet and one did not, and if it can further be determined that this difference is due to chance (which would be the case if, e.g., only a ballistics test could show whose bullet it was), then there clearly is no *morally* relevant difference between us at all. Hence we are equally blameworthy despite the unequal results of our conduct.

A possible argument on the other side goes this way: one of us is *more blameable* because he is blameable *for more*.[8] I believe that either this argument is question begging, in which case it is valid but has a premise that is false, or else it is a non sequitur. The second alternative is simpler to explain. "Blameable for" is connected in obvious ways to "caused." If you, in our story of a while ago, are said to be blameable for more merely in the sense that you caused more harm, then I have no objection beyond the remark that this way of putting it is misleading. But in this case it simply doesn't follow that you are more blameable in the sense of *morally* blameable. The alternative view of the argument has an individual being blameworthy, in the straightforward moral sense, for the *result* of the action as well as the action itself. The blameworthiness for these *two* items is apparently supposed to "add up" to more blame. Now, there is an obvious distinction between an actor's conduct on one hand and, on the other, that chain of events that begins where his conduct stops and which continues on indefinitely. The view I am urging here is that, properly speaking, only an actor's conduct can be blameworthy. I do not believe that it makes good sense to blame a person for the consequences that in fact flow from his conduct even if they are within the risk of that conduct.[9] I hasten to add that I do not mean that he cannot be held responsible for harm caused that is within the risk of his conduct. I maintain only that such harm is tortious rather than criminal and should be actionable only as such. A burden may rightfully be placed on a person for the harm he causes, but this is conceptually distinct from punishment and does not entail blameworthiness. The individual is blameworthy and punishable, on my view, only for the conduct itself, where conduct is construed as a combination of overt action, state of mind (including intention, knowledge, etc.) and circumstances. Common sense will have to serve here as a guide, and there is good reason to believe that it can.

Consider another example. Imagine that A takes a rifle to a place overlooking a stadium where he knows an event is underway and recklessly fires the weapon in the direction of the grandstands. Let us suppose the fortunate consequence of the bullet's striking the bleachers harmlessly after narrowly missing members of the crowd. Compare this with the situation of B, who takes his rifle to the same spot on a day when he knows there is no event scheduled and in fact believes the grandstands to be entirely empty. He too fires toward the seats but with unfortunate results: a lone custodian is present policing the stands and he is struck and killed by B's bullet. It takes either a considerable stretch of the imagination or adherence to a bad theory, or both, to want to hold B more blameworthy than A. Truly, the harm caused by B's conduct far outweighs that cause by A's, the latter being negligible. But it is A, on the view I am defending, who is the more blameworthy and whose desert is the greater punishment.

The last example makes it clear what I want to use as a substitute for harm as the device for determining blameworthiness and punishment: the *risk* of harm that the conduct creates.

In the example as described there is another relevant factor: A's *knowingly* creating the risk—he knew there was a crowd in the stands—and B's ignorance of the custodian's presence. In the usual terminology, these circumstances are captured by saying that A's conduct was reckless while B's was negligent. And it is true that we generally find more fault in the former than in the latter. There are at least two things to be said about that. First, I would hold the same view of A's and B's blameworthiness and punishability if B's behavior were reckless instead of merely negligent; if, that is, he had known about the presence of

the custodian. In such case, both A and B knowingly create risks, but A creates the greater risk and hence is more punishable. Second, it seems very plausible to believe that one reason why we judge reckless behavior more culpable than negligent behavior is that the former is riskier. A person who will perform an action *knowing* it is likely to cause harm is more apt to actually cause harm than one who would act only if he were ignorant of the likely harm, and this is the case even if the latter *should* have been aware of the harmful prospects (i.e., he is negligent by the standard of the reasonable man).

In cases of recklessness and negligence, it is fair and accurate to speak of the person who causes harm and, on current practice, is punished for it beyond what he would have been had no harm resulted, as being punished for his bad luck. (And it is his bad luck that he is being punished!) Seen this way, I think it is plain that the "extra" punishment is impossible to justify morally. In fact, if there is *something* wrong with punishing for harm caused in cases like these, then there is *everything* wrong with it. Let me borrow a statement of the relevant principle from Hyman Gross—the principle that liability ought to match culpability, a "general principle of proportion between crime and punishment,"

> is a principle of just desert that serves as the foundation of every criminal sentence that is justifiable. . . . Indeed, the requirement that punishment not be disproportionately great, which is a corollary of just desert, is dictated by the same principle that does not allow punishment of the innocent, for any punishment in excess of what is deserved for the criminal conduct is punishment without guilt.[10]

I need to add only that nobody is ever guilty of having bad luck, at least not in any relevant sense of "guilty."

In the recent examples, the person causing the harm in each case might indeed be said to be guilty by misfortune. The other side of this coin are those who are innocent by good fortune. Attempters, among others, fall into this category, and the position I advocate in such cases is in principle the same as that regarding negligently and recklessly caused harm. Whether we are talking about intentional or unintentional creation of risk, that is to say, has nothing to do with the point at issue: a person who performs a last step attempt—that is, one who does everything within his power that he believes necessary to complete a crime—and whose failure is due to a chance event not within his control, is no less blameworthy and ought to be no less punishable than one who is successful in bringing his intended result about. The reason is exactly analogous to those in the earlier cases: there are no grounds for punishing the attempter and the successful offender differently aside from the already criticized grounds of punishing for whatever good or bad luck attends one's activities. Punishment on these grounds is no less immoral than unequal punishment for unequal results in cases of negligence. For, if a given punishment is the just desert for a completed crime, then no less a punishment is the just desert of at least some attempts to commit that crime.[11] On the other hand, if we punish the attempter less than the successful offender, we punish the latter "in excess of what is deserved for the criminal conduct." Indeed, the punishment we visit on the successful criminal beyond that which we visit on the attempter is nothing less than "punishment without guilt."

II

The conclusion just reached may seem strange at first. If it does it is probably because of an underlying conceptual shift entailed by the present view. The shift is as follows. I've said that it is the risk-creating aspect of conduct that makes it punishable and not the results of that conduct. Implicit in that claim is a change in the very notion of a crime. For anything that counts as a *result* of conduct rather than a *part of* that conduct ought not strictly speaking be a part of a crime; only conduct can be criminal. This produces some admittedly strange results. For example, on the view I present, there can be no such crime as murder, at least as it is currently conceived, because on the current view the production of a corpse is, in a crucial sense, an irrelevant feature. (The sense in which it *is* relevant will be noted in a moment.) What is crucially relevant is the *likelihood* of a death resulting from the conduct in question. Consider the case of A, who produces a water pistol and begins squirting water at B, confident in his belief that he can kill B by eroding him to death.[12] We are not quick to find A guilty of a serious crime because, despite his intention and his action, he has done little that is likely to produce serious harm to B. Possibly more serious is the case of C, who puts a harmless drug in D's drink, thinking it is strychnine. The kind of conduct of which C is guilty may be dangerous indeed; exactly how dangerous it is depends largely upon what measures he took to ensure that the drug was strychnine. If it was incompetence that pro-

duced the mistake—he was suffering from the delusion that strychnine was contained in the sugar bowl on D's dinner table, for example—then the seriousness, and the likelihood of his harming D, is minimal. If it was chance—e.g., he happened to pick up an unlabeled bottle of saccharin that was next to his unlabeled strychnine bottle—then the seriousness and the dangerousness of the conduct escalate dramatically.

Gross provides a notion of harmful conduct that helps clarify matters. Harmful conduct is conduct that may or may not cause actual harm, but, if it does not, this fortunate consequence is due merely to chance.[13] This notion allows a concise statement of the primary claim I seek to defend: conduct is blameworthy and may create liability for punishment because and to the extent that it is harmful. There is also the corollary that an act may be deemed a crime to the extent that it is harmful.[14]

This principle (or these principles) may, with luck, capture the intuitions of those who were persuaded by the earlier claim that we ought not to punish those whose actions produce harm as the result of chance any more than those whose similar actions produce no harm. But it is important to notice that an action performed with evil intent is as well included under this principle as one performed negligently; we are talking about the entire array of criminal activity because we are talking about the very notion of a crime.

I indicated that the harm actually produced by conduct is not always irrelevant to an evaluation of the culpability attributable to that conduct, even on the theory proposed here. The relevance of a harmful result is in the form of evidence that the conduct in question was indeed harmful. In the case of the drunken shooting match that you and I held a few pages back, there is a claim that I can make that you cannot, i.e., that I *knew* that my bullets would not strike anybody. Under the circumstances described I would hardly be able to give any grounds for it, but it might, with corroborating evidence, provide a defense under circumstances where my conduct was not *ex hypothesi* as risky as that which actually produced the fatal harm. In general, the production of a harmful result is *prima facie* evidence that the conduct that produced it was likely to produce it. Such a result, or lack of one, would ordinarily help to locate properly a burden of proof on the defense or the prosecution, respectively. This, it seems to me, is the proper function of result. If it actually played this role, the conceptual scheme in many criminal cases would be substantially different from what it is currently. For example, the crime of involuntary manslaughter—a felony in most states—would be stricken from the books. A person who, on current practice, is indictable for such a crime would stand trial, on my view, for an offense of negligence or recklessness, and the death he caused would be offered as evidence of the negligence or recklessness of his conduct.

III

Let's next take a brief look at what seems to be behind most of the opposition to the view I have presented. There are two items that bear scrutiny in the accepted opinion. First, there is the view that, when an individual does something that might cause harm, he is taking a gamble of a sort, and when one gambles there are times when he wins and times when he loses. If one wins, so much the better; there is no harm done and nothing to pay for. If he loses, then he should be prepared to pay for it. After all, one hears, life itself is a gamble. This view has very little to recommend it. While it is true that we all take risks whether we get out of bed in the morning or not, surely we do not want to increase the amount of risk to which we are subject by building them into our system of criminal justice. We ought not to gear punishment to actual harm caused for exactly the same reason that we ought not to determine whether a person should be punished by flipping a coin or casting dice. Fortune may make us healthy, wealthy, or wise, but it ought not determine whether we go to prison.

A second point has to do with an explanation of why, in the common view, we fixate so readily on result when we consider the enormity or triviality of a crime. The result, when it is produced, provides a focus for our attention—it provides something tangible for us to get upset about. We do take the business of punishment seriously, and, given the kind of creatures we are, we are hesitant about punishing a person when we do not *feel* an actual loss of some sort. Take the person who drunkenly drives his automobile at a high rate of speed, jumps a curb, and careens down a sidewalk. We may think of the harm he *might* have caused, but that brings only a kind of "abstract" loss to mind. If he actually strikes and kills a child, however, there is a particular harm caused, and this gives our attention—our fears, our sense of outrage—a focal point: it was *this* child's life that was lost. And this is something that operates more powerfully in us,

something that sets off our "retributive urge."[15] The point is confirmed, I think, by what we ordinarily do in the case of a near miss. Should the drunkenly driven automobile narrowly miss a child walking down the sidewalk, we are apt to be more outraged by the driver's conduct than if no child had been present. In such a case we have something more than an abstraction (an imagined child that might have been on the sidewalk when in fact none was nearby) on which to focus—the details of what might have happened are more clear. "You might have killed *that* child," we want to say, whereas we have nobody to refer to if there is no near miss. But, if we carefully consider what is operating here, I think we will conclude that what the presence of the child who is narrowly missed really furnishes us is *evidence* that the driver was in no position to avoid hitting whomever might have been in the way. The evidence is simply greater when a death or injury actually occurs. If ample evidence can be given that the driver would have killed a person on the sidewalk, had there been one there, then we have as much *right* to be upset—and to punish— as if there actually had been a victim, even if in fact we are less inclined to be upset—and to punish—in such a case. But the proper conclusion is stronger than this; we are bound by the principle of justice that like cases be treated alike to punish the same whether there is a child struck, a child narrowly missed, or nobody on the sidewalk at all, provided the evidence is sufficient to show that the driver would have done what he did regardless of anyone's presence in his path. So the difference in emotional response is understandable but not really relevant to the culpability of the offender.

The fact that we respond emotionally to results of offenses has sometimes been offered as a reason for grading and creating offenses on the basis of their results. J.F. Stephen criticized (and managed to get amended) the Indian Penal Code for the omission of the crime of negligent manslaughter. The omission failed to recognize "the effect which an offense produces on the feelings and imagination of mankind."[16] Stephen admitted that result might be due purely to fortune and that it had nothing to do with the punishment one might deserve. But still, in a case where two negligent actors produce different results, "it gratifies a natural public feeling to choose out for punishment that one who actually has caused great harm, and the effect in the way of preventing a repetition of the offense is much the same as if both were punished."[17] Stephen's first point hardly requires rebuttal; it might gratify a public feeling to stage gladiatorial contests on television but it is not therefore the business of the government to produce them. True, public sentiment must be taken into some account in the structure of the system, but it is as much the business of that system to lead and to mold public opinion as it is to gratify public feelings.

Deterrence does not help the other side either. Let's distinguish between special deterrence (deterring *this* offender from repeating his offense) and general deterrence (deterring other members of the society). With respect to the first, unequal punishment appears to accomplish nothing; a lighter penalty for an attempt or nonharmful result could hardly discourage an offender from repeating his conduct, and, other things being equal, it is not at all clear that he is less apt to commit the offense again than one who actually causes harm—my suspicion is that quite the contrary is true. Other factors than result are almost certainly more relevant to determining the likelihood of repetition: the offender's personality, background, etc. In the case of general deterrence a number of problems arise, many of them speculative or empirical in nature and too complex to be dealt with here.[18] From a moral point of view, however, we might note that a general deterrence justification of unequal treatment has the criminal justice system *using* an individual to accomplish a general social end not directly connected with his own culpability.[19] The situation is no different from unusually harsh "exemplary" sentences and no less unjust.

To close, let me sum up. I take the principle that like cases should be treated alike to be a main part of the notion of justice that operates in our treatment of criminal offenders as well as in society at large. It is a person's conduct, I contend, for which we may properly blame him and hold him liable for punishment. Harm that results from a person's conduct is not strictly speaking a part of that conduct and does not provide grounds for distinguishing between culpabil-

ity and nonculpability, nor does it form a basis for grading offensive conduct with respect to liability for punishment. This becomes especially clear when we notice how much the results of conduct are susceptible to the intervention of chance—factors not a part of the actor's conduct and not within his direct control. The extent to which a given offense, consequences aside, is culpable and merits punishment depends, among other factors, upon the likelihood that harm will result from it. Whatever harm is actually produced should serve only as the basis for a rebuttable claim about the likelihood of such harm.

When result is allowed to form the basis for unequal punishment in otherwise similar cases, I have argued, the effect is to punish one whose action produces harm beyond what is that person's just desert. And this provides a moral ground for ruling out result as a factor in determining the severity of punishment.

Implicit in this view is a conceptual change in the notion of a crime. In principle, this notion should not include reference to harm actually caused but be restricted solely to conduct. The problem of determining more or less exactly what the scope and limits of conduct are looms large, but it is present already in many regions of the criminal law and common sense, properly directed, will serve sufficiently as a reliable guide.

The principle of liability for risk-creating or harmful conduct (in the sense of "harmful" described above) should serve as a guiding principle in the definitions of crimes and in the determination of appropriate sentences. At a bare minimum, it requires the elimination of certain current statutory provisions that mandate unequal punishment for offenses that are otherwise distinguished only by fortune. Otherwise we must simply face the rude fact that one of the most crucial elements of our system—indeed, our *notion*—of criminal justice is blind luck.

A slightly different version of this paper appeared in the American Philosophical Quarterly, *volume 21, number 3, July 1984. The first draft was written with support from a grant from the National Endowment for the Humanities.*

  1. *In "Criminal Attempt and the Theory of the Law of Crimes,"* Philosophy and Public Affairs, *vol. 3 (1974), pp. 262–94.*

  2. *Ibid., pp. 271–75.*

  3. *See W. LaFave and A. Scott,* Criminal Law *(St. Paul, 1972), p. 423.*

  4. *Ibid., p. 7.*

  5. *Attempt is punishable in California by a maximum of one-half the maximum term for the completed crime. The Model Penal Code* of the American Law Institute makes a misdemeanor of reckless conduct which creates a risk of injury if no harm or even bodily injury occurs; but if death occurs, the offense is manslaughter, a second degree felony. §§ 211.1 (1)(a), 211.2, 210.3 (Official Draft, 1962).

  6. *"Negligent conduct, not criminal in the absence of harm, becomes a misdemeanor if bodily injury occurs under some limited circumstances, and a felony of the third degree if death results."* J. Schulhofer, discussing the Model Penal Code in "Harm and Punishment," *University of Pennsylvania Law Review, vol. 122 (1974), p. 1499.*

  7. *LaFave and Scott, op. cit., pp. 9ff. Hart argues that the criminal*

law must not be permitted to create crimes out of conduct that lacks the blameworthiness deserving of moral condemnation. See H. M. Hart, Jr., "The Aims of the Criminal Law," in Law and Contemporary Problems, vol. 23 (1958), pp. 401, 404–6.

8. This argument was once suggested to me, not very enthusiastically, by the late F. A. Siegler.

9. A harm is "within the risk" of an action if, under the circumstances, it is a reasonably expectable or foreseeable (some say "natural") consequence of that action.

10. A Theory of Criminal Justice (Oxford, 1978), p. 436.

11. For some attempts it would not be the just desert, or we could not know that it was, because of an evidentiary point that is discussed later.

12. The example is cribbed from Richard Wasserstrom, whom I thank for discussions on this topic.

13. Gross, op. cit., pp. 428ff.

14. It may not be a crime simply because it may not be against the law.

15. The phrase is due to John Junker, who is also responsible for stimulating my initial interest in this topic.

16. History of the Criminal Law, vol. III (London, 1883), pp. 311ff.

17. Ibid.

18. A treatment of several aspects of the problem is available in Schulhofer, op. cit., pp. 1572–77.

19. See Gross, op. cit., pp. 390ff.

Responsibility for Nonintervention

NOTES ON THE INDIAN PENAL CODE*

Thomas Babington Macaulay

Early in the progress of the Code it became necessary for us to consider the following question: When acts are made punishable on the ground that those acts produce, or are intended to produce, or are known to be likely to produce, certain evil effects, to what extent ought omissions which produce, which are intended to produce, or which are known to be likely to produce, the same evil effects to be made punishable?

Two things we take to be evident; first, that some of these omissions ought to be punished in exactly the same manner in which acts are punished; secondly, that not all these omissions ought to be punished. It will hardly be disputed that a jailer who voluntarily causes the death of a prisoner by omitting to supply that prisoner with food, or a nurse who voluntarily causes the death of an infant entrusted to her care by omitting to take it out of a tub of water into which it has fallen, ought to be treated as guilty of murder. On the other hand, it will hardly be maintained that a man should be punished as a murderer because he omitted to relieve a beggar, even though there might be the clearest proof that the death of the beggar was the effect of this omission, and that the man who omitted to give the alms knew that the death of the beggar was likely to be the effect of the omission. It will hardly be maintained that a surgeon ought to be treated as a murderer for refusing to go from Calcutta to Meerut to perform an operation, although it should be absolutely certain that this surgeon was the only person in India who could perform it, and that if it were not performed, the person who required it would die. It is difficult to say whether a penal code which should put no omissions on the same footing with acts, or a penal code which should put all omissions on the same footing with acts, would produce consequences more absurd and revolting. There is no country in which either of these principles is adopted. Indeed, it is hard to conceive how, if either were adopted, society could be held together.

It is plain, therefore, that a middle course must be taken; but it is not easy to determine what that middle course ought to be. The absurdity of the two extremes is obvious. But there are innumerable intermediate points; and wherever the line of demarcation may be drawn it will, we fear, include some cases which we might wish to exempt, and will exempt some which we might wish to include. . . .

What we propose is this, that where acts are made punishable on the ground that they have caused, or have been intended to cause, or have been known to be likely to cause, a certain evil effect, omissions which have caused, which have been intended to cause, or which have been known to be likely to cause the same effect, shall be punishable in the same manner, provided that such omissions were, on other grounds, illegal. An omission is illegal . . . if it be an offense, if it be a breach of some direction of law, or if it be such a wrong as would be a good ground for a civil action.

*From *Works of Lord Macaulay*, Trevelyan, ed., vol. 7 (1866), pp. 493–97.

We cannot defend this rule better than by giving a few illustrations of the way in which it will operate. *A* omits to give *Z* food, and by that omission voluntarily causes *Z*'s death. Is this murder? Under our rule it is murder if *A* was *Z*'s gaoler, directed by the law to furnish *Z* with food. It is murder if *Z* was the infant child of *A,* and had, therefore, a legal right to sustenance, which right a Civil Court would enforce against *A*. It is murder if *Z* was a bedridden invalid, and *A* a nurse hired to feed *Z*. It is murder if *A* was detaining *Z* in unlawful confinement, and had thus contracted . . . a legal obligation to furnish *Z*, during the continuance of the confinement, with necessaries. It is not murder if *Z* is a beggar, who has no other claim on *A* than that of humanity.

A omits to tell *Z* that a river is swollen so high that *Z* cannot safely attempt to ford it, and by this omission voluntarily causes *Z*'s death. This is murder, if *A* is a peon stationed by authority to warn travellers from attempting to ford the river. It is a murder if *A* is a guide who had contracted to conduct *Z*. It is not murder if *A* is a person on whom *Z* has no other claim than that of humanity.

A savage dog fastens on *Z*. *A* omits to call off the dog, knowing that if the dog not be called off, it is likely that *Z* will be killed. *Z* is killed. This is murder in *A,* if the dog belonged to *A,* inasmuch as his omission to take proper order with the dog is illegal. But if *A* be a mere passerby, it is not murder.

We are sensible that in some of the cases which we have put, our rule may appear too lenient; but we do not think that it can be made more severe without disturbing the whole order of society. It is true that the man who, having abundance of wealth, suffers a fellow creature to die of hunger at his feet, is a bad man, a worse man, probably, than many of those for whom we have provided very severe punishment. But we are unable to see where, if we make such a man legally punishable, we can draw the line. If the rich man who refuses to save a beggar's life at the cost of a little copper is a murderer, is the poor man just one degree above beggary also to be a murderer if he omits to invite the beggar to partake his hard-earned rice? Again, if the rich man is a murderer for refusing to save the beggar's life at the cost of a little copper, is he also to be a murderer if he refuses to save the beggar's life at the cost of a thousand rupees? Suppose *A* to be fully convinced that nothing can save *Z*'s life unless *Z* leave Bengal and reside a year at the Cape; is *A,* however wealthy he may be, to be punished as a murderer because he will not, at his own expense, send *Z* to the Cape? Surely not. Yet it will be difficult to say on what principle we can punish *A* for not spending an anna to save *Z*'s life, and leave him unpunished for not spending a thousand rupees to save *Z*'s life. The distinction between a legal and an illegal omission is perfectly plain and intelligible; but the distinction between a large and a small sum of money is very far from being so, not to say that a sum which is small to one man is large to another.

The same argument holds good in the case of the ford. It is true that none but a very depraved man would suffer another to be drowned when he might prevent it by a word. But if we punish such a man, where are we to stop? How much exertion are we to require? Is a person to be a murderer if he does not go fifty yards through the sun of Bengal at noon in May in order to caution a traveller against a swollen river? Is he to be a murderer if he does not go a hundred yards?—if he does not go a mile?—if he does not go ten? What is the precise amount of trouble and inconvenience which he is to endure? The distinction between the guide who is bound to conduct the traveller as safely as he can, and a mere stranger is a clear distinction. But the distinction between a stranger who will not give a halloo to save a man's life, and a stranger who will not run a mile to save a man's life, is very far from being equally clear.

It is, indeed, most highly desirable that men should not merely abstain from doing harm to their neighbours, but should render active services to their neighbours. In general, however, the penal law must content itself with keeping men from doing positive harm, and must leave to public opinion, and to the teachers of morality and religion, the office of furnishing men with motives for doing positive good. It is evident that to attempt to punish men by law for not rendering to others all the service which it is their duty to render to others would be preposterous. We must grant impunity to the vast majority of those omissions which a benevolent morality would pronounce reprehensible, and must content ourselves with punishing such omissions only when they are distinguished from the rest by some circumstance which marks them out as peculiarly fit objects of penal legislation. Now, no circumstance appears to us so well fitted to be the mark as the circumstance which we have selected. It will generally be found in the most atrocious cases of omission; it will scarcely ever be found in a venial case of omission; and it is more clear and certain than any other mark that has occurred to us. That there are objections to the line which we propose to draw, we have admitted. But there are objections to every line which can be drawn, and some lines must be drawn. . . .

GOOD SAMARITANISM*

John Kleinig

The parable of the Good Samaritan was originally told in part-answer to the question, What shall I do to inherit eternal life?[1] But the Samaritan's example has now been absorbed into the general moral traditions of our culture. Over the past 130 years it has increasingly been made a legal requirement. In the Russian Criminal Code of 1845 and, since then, in almost every continental European country, the failure to be a Good Samaritan has been declared a criminal offense.[2] The glaring exceptions to this trend have been those countries within the Anglo-American legal tradition. This has been no mere oversight, but a matter of policy. In the words of C. J. Carpenter:

> With purely moral obligations, the law does not deal. For example, the priest and the Levite who passed by on the other side were not, it is supposed, liable at law for the continued suffering of the man who fell among thieves, which they might and morally ought to have prevented or relieved. Suppose A, standing close by a railroad, sees a two-year old babe on the track and a car approaching. He can easily rescue the child with entire safety to himself. And the instincts of humanity require him to do so. If he does not, he may perhaps justly be styled a ruthless savage and a moral monster, but he is not liable in damages for the child's injury or indictable under the statute for its death.[3]

Though the position is slowly changing in torts, the criminal law situation remains substantially the same. "The law does not compel active benevolence between man and man. It is left to one's conscience whether he shall be the Good Samaritan or not."[4]

The refusal of Anglo-American law to proscribe Bad Samaritanism needs to be distinguished (for the time being) from its growing willingness to allow actions against "Bad Levitism." Certain institutionalized relationships are recognized in torts as giving rise to special duties to care for others.[5] Doctors, nurses, policemen, firemen, and lifeguards are committed by their *vocational* skills to render aid. Even so, such obligations are less than clear-cut. A doctor who commences but then abandons the treatment of a patient is held liable in tort, but one who ignores a call for help is not always held liable. Duties to render aid also devolve upon those bearing certain *contractual* relationships to each other. Employers and employees, carriers and passengers, innkeepers and guests, fall into this category. Where the harm occurs in the context of such a relationship, the employer or carrier or innkeeper is bound to render assistance. The same is becoming true where there are institutionally recognized *personal* relationships, such as those between husband and wife, parent and child. Here the failure to aid has been made criminally indictable as well. In *R. v. Russell*, the defendant was found guilty of the manslaughter of his wife, who had drowned (herself ?), when he could have easily rendered aid.[6] Finally, a duty to render aid is now upheld in cases where a person has *accidentally caused* another's peril. If my car stalls just below the brow of a hill, I am required to take steps (by moving the car, or signaling to other travelers) to ensure that it does not constitute a hazard. In addition, a person may be held criminally liable for failure to stop and assist at the scene of an accident in which he has been involved, whether or not he was negligent. Bad Levites, unlike Bad Samaritans, are not complete strangers to a victim. By virtue of professional, contractual, or other circumstances, they stand in some kind of antecedently determinable relationship with those whose welfare is imperiled, even though they may never have met. But the Samaritan's appearance on the scene or knowledge of the peril may be entirely fortuitous. That is more or less how

*Excerpts from John Kleinig, "Good Samaritanism," in *Philosophy and Public Affairs*, vol. 5. Copyright © 1975 by Princeton University Press. Reprinted by permission of Princeton University Press.

Anglo-American law stands and in this respect it reflects the tradition of Roman law.

Two obvious questions are raised by the foregoing: (a) whether the Anglo-American rejection of Good Samaritan legislation is justified; and (b) whether this rejection is consistent with the proscription of Bad Levitism. . . .

Bad Samaritanism is a failure in humanitarian concern. But this is not sufficient to justify its criminalization. Lack of consideration, apathy, failure to lend assistance, unwillingness to extend friendship and selfishness are also failures of this kind, yet only when they constitute substantial harms to others does the law take cognizance of them. That might appear to hold equally for Bad Samaritanism in those systems which proscribe it. It is not legally required that help be given in every case of unfortunate circumstance or harm, but only where there is "great danger" or "grave peril of life, person or health."

History of the Discussion

In attempting to understand the current Anglo-American position with regard to Good Samaritan legislation, it is instructive to look at some of the debate which has led to it, since it has not come about without opposition.

Even in the eighteenth century, before Russia became the first continental European country to incorporate Good Samaritanism into its criminal code, there was some effort made to persuade the legislatures of England and the United States of the propriety of requiring Good Samaritanism. Bentham, for example, in his *Introduction to the Principles of Morals and Legislation,* asked the question: "In cases where the person is in danger, why should it not be made the duty of every man to save another from mischief, when it can be done without prejudicing himself, as well as abstain from bringing it on him?"[7] Undoubtedly, he felt that no satisfactory answer could be given:

> A woman's head-dress catches fire, water is at hand: a man, instead of assisting to quench the fire, looks on, and laughs at it. A drunken man, falling with his face downwards into a puddle, is in danger of suffocation: lifting his head a little to one side would save him: another man sees this and lets him lie. A quantity of gunpowder lies scattered about a room: a man is going into it with a lighted candle:

> another, knowing this, lets him go in without warning. Who is there that in any of these cases would think punishment misapplied?

Later developments were to wipe the rhetorical confidence from Bentham's question. He does not make it clear why the law should interfere in such cases, though his earlier discussion of the ability of negative acts to be "productive of material consequences" probably provides the clue. Whatever it was, he felt strongly enough about it to include Good Samaritanism in his *Specimen of a Penal Code:*

> Every man is bound to assist those who have need of assistance, if he can do it without exposing himself to sensible inconvenience. This obligation is stronger, in proportion as the danger is the greater for the one, and the trouble of preserving him the less for the other.[8]

Mill, who on matters of social policy remained close to Bentham, was more explicit about the rationale for Good Samaritan legislation. Soon after enunciating his harm principle in *On Liberty,* Mill points out that there are also "many positive acts for the benefit of others" which a person may "rightly be compelled to perform." Among these he includes

> certain acts of individual beneficence, such as saving a fellow creature's life, or interposing to protect the defenceless against ill-usage, things which whenever it is obviously a man's duty to do, he may rightfully be made responsible to society for not doing. A person may cause evil to others not only by his actions but by his inaction, and in either case he is justly accountable to them for the injury.[9]

On Mill's view, it is our duty to render aid because, by not doing so, we *harm another.*

> The same view is taken by Bentham's American disciple, Edward Livingston. In his (draft) Code of Crimes and Punishments, certain cases of Bad Samaritanism in which death occurred were proscribed as "homicides by omission."[10] If I see a blind man walking towards a precipice and do not warn him; if I see someone about to drink from a glass which I know to contain poison and make no attempt to prevent him; if I leave an infant or other helpless person in a forest on a winter's night; if I know that an infant is on a busy highway, and do not do anything about it; and if in any of these cases death results, though I could have inter-

vened "without personal danger or pecuniary loss," I am guilty of homicide by omission.

The most influential reaction came from Lord Macaulay et al. In their *Notes on the Indian Penal Code,* a Code heavily indebted to Livingston, Macaulay criticized the proposal of an offense of homicide by omission. His criticism is of the practicability of such legislation, though towards the end of his discussion he seems, somewhat inconsistently, to hint at a theoretical objection. . . .

The bulk of Macaulay's argument seems to be directed to the impracticability of Good Samaritan legislation. But in his final remarks new considerations are smuggled in:

> It is, indeed, most highly desirable that men should not merely abstain from doing harm to their neighbours, but should render active services to their neighbours. In general, however, the penal law must content itself with keeping men from doing positive harm, and must leave to public opinion, and to the teachers of morality and religion, the office of furnishing men with motives for doing positive good. It is evident that to attempt to punish men by law for not rendering to others all the services which it is their duty to render others would be preposterous. We must grant impunity to the vast majority of those omissions which a benevolent morality would pronounce reprehensible, and must content ourselves with punishing such omissions only when they are distinguished from the rest by some circumstance which marks them out as peculiarly fit objects of penal legislation.

There is a suggestion here, contrary to earlier statements, that Bad Samaritanism does not constitute the causing of harm, but only the withholding of a positive good. And therefore, since the function of law is to prevent harm and not to enforce benevolence, it would be improper for the law to require Good Samaritanism.[11] The point was put with force and sophistication by Stephen, whose support firmly established it in English legal opinion:

> The idea of killing by an omission implies, in the first place, the presence of an opportunity of doing the act the omission of which causes death. It would be extravagant to say that a man who having food in London omits to give it to a person starving to death in China has killed the man in China by omitting to feed him; but it would be natural to say that a nurse who being supplied with food for a sick person under her care omits to give it, and thereby causes the sick person's death, has killed that person. Whether a person, who being able to save the life of another without inconvenience or risk refuses to do so, even in order that he may die, can be said to have killed him is a question of words, and also a question of degree. A man who caused another to be drowned by refusing to hold out his hand to save him probably would in common language be said to have killed him, and many similar cases might be put, but the limit of responsibility is soon reached. It would hardly be said that a rich man who allowed a poor man to die rather than give, say £5, which the rich man would not miss, in order to save his life, had killed him, and though it might be cowardly not to run some degree of risk for the purpose of saving the life of another, the omission to do it could hardly be described as homicide. A number of people who stand around a shallow pond in which a child is drowning, and let it drown without taking the trouble to ascertain the depth of the pond, are no doubt, shameful cowards, but they can hardly be said to have killed the child.[12]

Several arguments are embedded in this debate, but undoubtedly the most important concerns the causal relevance of not rendering aid. . . .

However, I think another, rather different fear underlies Macaulay's opposition to Good Samaritan legislation. Made explicit by later writers, it is basically the fear that Good Samaritan legislation will substantially diminish freedom. In a culture steeped in individualism, nothing produces more hysteria than measures which encroach on individual liberty. "You owe me nothing; I owe you nothing. You stay out of my way, and I'll stay out of yours." That is an extreme expression, but it constitutes an important thread within the Anglo-American sociomoral fabric. . . .

The freedom to pursue one's interests is not, as Mill and Bentham clearly saw, unlimited. Where the pursuit of one's interests is a causal factor in another's harm, or threatens additional harm, as in Bad Samaritanism, we have the important beginnings of a case for justifiable state interference. . . .

1. *Luke 10:25–37.*

2. *For surveys, see Note, "The Failure to Rescue: A Comparative Survey,"* Columbia Law Review *52 (1952): pp. 631–647; A.W. Rudzinski, "The Duty to Rescue: A Comparative Analysis," in* The Good Samaritan and the Law, *ed. J. M. Ratcliffe (New York, 1966), pp. 91–134; F.J.M. Feldbrugge, "Good and Bad Samaritans: A Comparative Survey of Criminal Law Provisions Concerning Failure to Rescue,"* American Journal of Comparative Law *14 (1966): pp. 630–657.*

3. Buch *v.* Amory Manufacturing Co., *69 N.H. 257; 44 Atl. 809 (1897). For a partial catalogue of the grisly possibilities of such a policy, see W. L. Prosser,* Handbook of the Law of Torts, *4th ed. (St. Paul, Minn. 1971), chap. 9, #56, and references.*

4. *J. B. Ames, "Law and Morals," reprinted in* The Good Samaritan and the Law, *p. 19.*

5. *What follows is to be taken as a very general statement of the present situation. There is a good deal of variation between states and countries within the Anglo-American tradition. In England and Australia one may now be held guilty of misprision of felony—"the concealment of any information about a felony from the law-enforcement authorities by one who has a reasonable opportunity to make such disclosure." See the discussion and notes in L. Waller, "Rescue and the Common Law: England and Australia," in* The Good Samaritan and the Law, *pp. 148–152. In Hahn v.* Conley *(1971) 45 ALJR 631, C. J. Barwick held that even in the case of a parent any duty to the child springs out of the particular situation,* parenthood as such not being the source of the duty. This represents an important development, and reflects the judgment of Lord Atkin in the celebrated case of Donohue v. Stevenson (1932) A.C. 562: "The rule that you are to love your neighbor becomes in law, you must not injure your neighbor; and the lawyer's question, Who is my neighbor? receives a restricted reply. . . . The answer seems to be persons who are so closely and directly affected by my act that I ought reasonably to have them in contemplation as being so affected when I am directing my mind to acts or omissions which are called in question." Though a significant advance in torts, this represents only a small step towards the criminalization of Bad Samaritanism.*

6. R. *v.* Russell, *[1933] V.L.R. 59.*

7. *Bentham,* An Introduction to the Principles of Morals and Legislation, *ed. J.H. Burns and H.L.A. Hart (London, 1970), p. 293.*

8. *Bentham,* Specimen of a Penal Code, *in* Works, *ed. J. Bowring (Edinburgh, 1843), vol. I, p. 164.*

9. *J. S. Mill,* On Liberty, *in* Utilitarianism, . . . , *ed. M. Warnock (London, 1962), pp. 136–137.*

10. *E. Livingston,* Code of Crime and Punishments, *in* Complete Works *(New York: National Prison Association of U.S.A., 1873), vol. 2, pp. 126–127.*

11. *In torts this has frequently been couched in terms of the notorious distinction between misfeasance and nonfeasance.*

12. *J. F. Stephen,* History of the Criminal Law in England *(London, 1883), vol. 3, pp. 9–10.*

Some Criminal Defenses

*PEOPLE V. YOUNG**

New York Court of Appeals, 1962

Per Curiam. Whether one, who in good faith aggressively intervenes in a struggle between another person and a police officer in civilian dress attempting to effect the lawful arrest of the third person, may be properly convicted of assault in the third degree is a question of law of first impression here.

The opinions in the court below in the absence of precedents in this State carefully expound the opposing views found in other jurisdictions. The majority in the Appellate Division have adopted the minority rule in the other States that one who intervenes in a struggle between strangers under the mistaken but reasonable belief that he is protecting another who he assumes is being unlawfully beaten is thereby exonerated from criminal liability. The weight of authority holds with the dissenters below that one who goes to the aid of a third person does so at his peril.

While the doctrine espoused by the majority of the court below may have support in some States, we feel that such a policy would not be conducive to an orderly society. We agree with the settled policy of law in most jurisdictions that the right of a person to defend another ordinarily should not be greater than such person's right to defend himself. Subdivision 3 of section 246 of the Penal Law does not apply as no offense was being committed on the person of the one resisting the lawful arrest. Whatever may be the public policy where the felony charged requires proof of a specific intent and the issue is justifiable homicide, it is not relevant in a prosecution for assault in the third degree where it is only necessary to show that the defendant knowingly struck a blow.

In this case there can be no doubt that the defendant intended to assault the police officer in civilian dress. The resulting assault was forceful. Hence motive or mistake of fact is of no significance as the defendant was not charged with a crime requiring such intent or knowledge. To be guilty of third degree assault "It is sufficient that the defendant voluntarily intended to commit the unlawful act of touching" (1 Wharton's Criminal Law and Procedure [1957], § 338, p. 685). Since in these circumstances the aggression was inexcusable the defendant was properly convicted.

Accordingly, the order of the Appellate Division should be reversed and the information reinstated.

Froessel, J. (dissenting). The law is clear that one may kill in defense of another when there is reasonable, though mistaken, ground for believing that the person slain is about to commit a felony or to do some great personal injury to the apparent victim (Penal Law, § 1055); yet the majority now hold, for the first time, that in the event of a simple assault under similar circumstances, the mistaken belief, no matter how reasonable, is no defense.

Briefly, the relevant facts are these: On a Friday afternoon at about 3:40, Detectives Driscoll and Murphy, not in uniform, observed an argument taking place between a motorist and one McGriff in the street in front of premises 64 West 54th Street, in midtown

*11 N.Y.S. 2d 274 (1962). Citations omitted.

Manhattan. Driscoll attempted to chase McGriff out of the roadway in order to allow traffic to pass, but McGriff refused to move back; his actions caused a crowd to collect. After identifying himself to McGriff, Driscoll placed him under arrest. As McGriff resisted, defendant "came out of the crowd" from Driscoll's rear and struck Murphy about the head with his fist. In the ensuing struggle Driscoll's right kneecap was injured when defendant fell on top of him. At the station house, defendant said he had not known or thought Driscoll and Murphy were police officers.

Defendant testified that while he was proceeding on 54th Street he observed two white men, who appeared to be 45 or 50 years old, pulling on a "colored boy" (McGriff), who appeared to be a lad about 18, whom he did not know. The men had nearly pulled McGriff's pants off, and he was crying. Defendant admitted he knew nothing of what had transpired between the officers and McGriff, and made no inquiry of anyone; he just came there and pulled the officer away from McGriff.

Defendant was convicted of assault third degree. In reversing upon the law and dismissing the information, the Appellate Division held that one is not "criminally liable for assault in the third degree if he goes to the aid of another whom he mistakenly, but *reasonably,* believes is being unlawfully beaten, and thereby injures one of the apparent assaulters" (emphasis supplied). While in my opinion the majority below correctly stated the law, I would reverse here and remit so that the Appellate Division may pass on the question of whether or not defendant's conduct was reasonable in light of the circumstances presented at the trial (Code Crim. Pro., §§ 543-a, 543-b).

As the majority below pointed out, assault is a crime derived from the common law (*People* v. *Katz,* 290 N.Y. 361, 365). Basic to the imposition of criminal liability both at common law and under our statutory law is the existence in the one who committed the prohibited act of what has been variously termed a guilty mind, a *mens rea* or a criminal intent.

Criminal intent requires an awareness of wrongdoing. When conduct is based upon mistake of fact reasonably entertained, there can be no such awareness and, therefore, no criminal culpability. In *People ex rel. Hegeman* v. *Corrigan* (195 N.Y. 1, 12) we stated: "it is very apparent that the innocence or criminality of the intent in a particular act generally depends on the knowledge or belief of the actor at the time. An honest and *reasonable* belief in the existence of circumstances which, if true, would make the

act for which the defendant is prosecuted innocent, would be a good defense." (Emphasis supplied.)

It is undisputed that defendant did not know that Driscoll and Murphy were detectives in plain clothes engaged in lawfully apprehending an alleged disorderly person. If, therefore, defendant *reasonably* believed he was lawfully assisting another, he would not have been guilty of a crime. Subdivision 3 of section 246 of the Penal Law provides that it is not unlawful to use force "When committed either by the party about to be injured or *by another person in his aid or defense, in preventing or attempting to prevent an offense against his person,* if the force or violence used is not more than sufficient to prevent such offense" (emphasis supplied). The law is thus clear that if defendant entertained an "honest and reasonable belief " (*People ex rel. Hegeman* v. *Corrigan,* 195 N.Y. 1, 12 *supra*) that the facts were as he perceived them to be, he would be exonerated from criminal liability.

By ignoring one of the most basic principles of criminal law—that crimes *mala in se* require proof of at least general criminal intent—the majority now hold that the defense of mistake of fact is "of no significance." We are not here dealing with one of "a narrow class of exceptions" (*People* v. *Katz,* 290 N.Y. 361, 365, *supra*) where the Legislature has created crimes which do not depend on *criminal* intent but which are complete on the mere intentional doing of an act *malum prohibitum.* (9 N Y 2d 51, 58; *People* v. *Werner,* 174 N.Y. 132, *supra*).

There is no need, in my opinion, to consider the law of other States, for New York policy clearly supports the view that one may act on appearances reasonably ascertained, as does New Jersey. Our Penal Law (§ 1055), to which I have already alluded, is a statement of that policy. The same policy was expressed by this court in *People* v. *Maine* (166 N.Y. 50). There, the defendant observed his brother fighting in the street with two other men; he stepped in and stabbed to death one of the latter. The defense was justifiable homicide under the predecessor of section 1055. The court held it reversible error to admit into evidence the declarations of the defendant's brother, made before defendant happened upon the scene, which tended to show that the brother was the aggressor. We said (p. 52): "Of course the acts and conduct of the defendant must be judged solely with reference to the situation as it was when he first and afterwards saw it." Mistake of relevant fact, reasonably entertained, is thus a defense to homicide under section 1055 (*People* v. *Governale,* 193 N.Y. 581, 588), and one who kills in defense of another and proffers this defense of justification is to be judged according to the circumstances as they appeared to him.

The mistaken belief, however, must be one which is reasonably entertained, and the question of reasonableness is for the trier of the facts. "The question is not merely what did the accused believe, but also, what did he have the right to believe?" (*People* v. *Rodawald,* 177 N.Y. 408, 427.) Without passing on the facts of the instant case, the Appellate Division had no right to assume that defendant's conduct was reasonable, and to dismiss the information as a matter of law. Nor do we have the right to reinstate the verdict without giving the Appellate Division the opportunity to pass upon the facts (Code Crim. Pro., § 543-b).

Although the majority of our court are now purporting to fashion a policy "conducive to an orderly society," by their decision they have defeated their avowed purpose. What public interest is promoted by a principle which would deter one from coming to the aid of a fellow citizen who he has reasonable ground

to apprehend is in imminent danger of personal injury at the hands of assailants? Is it reasonable to denominate, as justifiable homicide, a slaying committed under a mistaken but reasonably held belief, and deny this same defense of justification to one using less force? Logic, as well as historical background and related precedent, dictates that the rule and policy expressed by our Legislature in the case of homicide, which is an assault resulting in death, should likewise be applicable to a much less serious assault not resulting in death.

I would reverse the order appealed from and remit the case to the Appellate Division pursuant to section 543-b of the Code of Criminal Procedure "for determination upon the questions of fact raised in that court."

Chief Judge Desmond and Judges Dye, Fuld, Burke and Foster concur in *Per Curiam* opinion; Judge Froessel dissents in an opinion in which Judge Van Voorhis concurs.

Order reversed, etc.

THE CASE OF THE SPELUNCEAN EXPLORERS*

Lon L. Fuller

The defendants, having been indicted for the crime of murder, were convicted and sentenced to be hanged by the Court of General Instances of the County of Stowfield. They bring a petition of error before this Court. The facts sufficiently appear in the opinion of the Chief Justice.

TRUEPENNY, C.J. The four defendants are members of the Speluncean Society, an organization of amateurs interested in the exploration of caves. Early in May of 4299 they, in the company of Roger Whetmore, then also a member of the Society, penetrated into the interior of a limestone cavern of the type found in the

Central Plateau of this Commonwealth. While they were in a position remote from the entrance to the cave, a landslide occurred. Heavy boulders fell in such a manner as to block completely the only known opening to the cave. When the men discovered their predicament they settled themselves near the obstructed entrance to wait until a rescue party should remove the detritus that prevented them from leaving their underground prison. On the failure of Whetmore and the defendants to return to their homes, the Secretary of the Society was notified by their families. It appears that the explorers had left indications at the

*Lon L. Fuller, "The Case of the Speluncean Explorers," *Harvard Law Review,* vol. 62 (1949), pp. 616–645. Reprinted by permission of the *Harvard Law Review* and Mr. John N. Roche.

headquarters of the Society concerning the location of the cave they proposed to visit. A rescue party was promptly dispatched to the spot.

The task of rescue proved one of overwhelming difficulty. It was necessary to supplement the forces of the original party by repeated increments of men and machines, which had to be conveyed at great expense to the remote and isolated region in which the cave was located. A huge temporary camp of workmen, engineers, geologists, and other experts was established. The work of removing the obstruction was several times frustrated by fresh landslides. In one of these, ten of the workmen engaged in clearing the entrance were killed. The treasury of the Speluncean Society was soon exhausted in the rescue effort, and the sum of eight hundred thousand frelars, raised partly by popular subscription and partly by legislative grant, was expended before the imprisoned men were rescued. Success was finally achieved on the thirty-second day after the men entered the cave.

Since it was known that the explorers had carried with them only scant provisions, and since it was also known that there was no animal or vegetable matter within the cave on which they might subsist, anxiety was early felt that they might meet death by starvation before access to them could be obtained. On the twentieth day of their imprisonment it was learned for the first time that they had taken with them into the cave a portable wireless machine capable of both sending and receiving messages. A similar machine was promptly installed in the rescue camp and oral communication established with the unfortunate men within the mountain. They asked to be informed how long a time would be required to release them. The engineers in charge of the project answered that at least ten days would be required even if no new landslides occurred. The explorers then asked if any physicians were present, and were placed in communication with a committee of medical experts. The imprisoned men described their condition and the rations they had taken with them, and asked for a medical opinion whether they would be likely to live without food for ten days longer. The chairman of the committee of physicians told them that there was little possibility of this. The wireless machine within the cave then remained silent for eight hours. When communication was reestablished the men asked to speak again with the physicians. The chairman of the physicians' committee was placed before the apparatus, and Whetmore, speaking on behalf of himself and the defendants, asked whether they would be able to survive for ten days longer if they consumed the flesh of one of their number. The physicians' chairman reluctantly answered this question in the affirmative. Whetmore asked whether it would be advisable for them to cast lots to determine which of them should be eaten. None of the physicians present was willing to answer the question. Whetmore then asked if there were among the party a judge or other official of the government who would answer this question. None of these attached to the rescue camp was willing to assume the role of advisor in this matter. He then asked if any minister or priest would answer their question, and none was found who would do so. Thereafter no further messages were received from within the cave, and it was assumed (erroneously, it later appeared) that the electric batteries of the explorers' wireless machine had become exhausted. When the imprisoned men were finally released it was learned that on the twenty-third day after their entrance into the cave Whetmore had been killed and eaten by his companions.

From the testimony of the defendants, which was accepted by the jury, it appears that it was Whetmore who first proposed that they might find the nutriment without which survival was impossible in the flesh of one of their own number. It was also Whetmore who first proposed the use of some method of casting lots, calling the attention of the defendants to a pair of dice he happened to have with him. The defendants were at first reluctant to adopt so desperate a procedure, but after the conversations by wireless related above, they finally agreed on the plan proposed by Whetmore. After much discussion of the mathematical problems involved, agreement was finally reached on a method of determining the issue by the use of the dice.

Before the dice were cast, however, Whetmore declared that he withdrew from the arrangement, as he had decided on reflection to wait for another week before embracing an expedient so frightful and odious. The others charged him with a breach of faith and proceeded to cast the dice. When it came Whetmore's turn, the dice were cast for him by one of the defendants, and he was asked to declare any objections he might have to the fairness of the throw. He stated that he had no such objections. The throw went against him, and he was then put to death and eaten by his companions.

After the rescue of the defendants, and after they had completed a stay in a hospital where they underwent a course of treatment for malnutrition and shock, they were indicted for the murder of Roger Whetmore. At the trial, after the testimony had been concluded, the foreman of the jury (a lawyer by profession) inquired of the court whether the jury might not find a special verdict, leaving it to the court to say whether on the facts as found the defendants were guilty. After some discussion, both the Prosecutor and counsel for the defendants indicated their acceptance of this procedure, and it was adopted by the court. In a lengthy special verdict the jury found the facts as I have related them above, and found further that if on these facts the defendants were guilty of the crime charged against them, then they found the defendants guilty. On the basis of this verdict, the trial judge ruled that the defendants were guilty of murdering Roger Whetmore. The judge then sentenced them to be hanged, the law of our Commonwealth permitting him no discretion with respect to the penalty to be imposed. After the release of the jury, its members joined in a communication to the Chief Executive asking that the sentence be commuted to an imprisonment of six months. The trial judge addressed a similar communication to the Chief Executive. As yet no action with respect to these pleas has been taken, as the Chief Executive is apparently awaiting our disposition of this petition of error.

It seems to me that in dealing with this extraordinary case the jury and the trial judge followed a course that was not only fair and wise, but the only course that was open to them under the law. The language of our statute is well known: "Whoever shall willfully take the life of another shall be punished by death." N.C.S.A. (N.S.) § 12-A. This statute permits of no exception applicable to this case, however our sympathies may incline us to make allowance for the tragic situation in which these men found themselves.

In a case like this the principle of executive clemency seems admirably suited to mitigate the rigors of the law, and I propose to my colleagues that we follow the example of the jury and the trial judge by joining in the communications they have addressed to the Chief Executive. There is every reason to believe that these requests for clemency will be heeded, coming as they do from those who have studied the case and had an opportunity to become thoroughly acquainted with all its circumstances. It is highly improbable that the Chief Executive would deny these requests unless he were himself to hold hearings at least as extensive as those involved in the trial below, which lasted for three months. The holding of such hearings (which would virtually amount to a retrial of the case) would scarcely be compatible with the function of the Executive as it is usually conceived. I think we may therefore assume that some form of clemency will be extended to these defendants. If this is done, then justice will be accomplished without impairing either the letter or spirit of our statutes and without offering any encouragement for the disregard of law.

FOSTER, J. I am shocked that the Chief Justice, in an effort to escape the embarrassments of this tragic case, should have adopted, and should have proposed to his colleagues, an expedient at once so sordid and so obvious. I believe something more is on trial in this case than the fate of these unfortunate explorers; that is the law of our Commonwealth. If this Court declares that under our law these men have committed a crime, then our law is itself convicted in the tribunal of common sense, no matter what happens to the individuals involved in this petition of error. For us to assert that the law we uphold and expound compels us to a conclusion we are ashamed of, and from which we can only escape by appealing to a dispensation resting within the personal whim of the Executive, seems to me to amount to an admission that the law of this Commonwealth no longer pretends to incorporate justice.

For myself, I do not believe that our law compels the monstrous conclusion that these men are murderers. I believe, on the contrary, that it declares them to be innocent of any crime. I rest this conclusion on two independent grounds, either of which is of itself sufficient to justify the acquittal of these defendants.

The first of these grounds rests on a premise that may arouse opposition until it has been examined candidly. I take the view that the enacted or positive law of this Commonwealth, including all of its statutes and precedents, is inapplicable to this case, and that the case is governed instead by what ancient writers in Europe and America called "the law of nature."

This conclusion rests on the proposition that our positive law is predicated on the possibility of men's coexistence in society. When a situation arises in which the coexistence of men becomes impossible, then a condition that underlies all of our precedents and statutes has ceased to exist. When that condition disappears, then it is my opinion that the force of our positive law disappears with it. We are not accustomed to applying the maxim *cessante ratione legis, cessat et ipsa lex* to the whole of our enacted law, but I believe that this is a case where the maxim should be so applied.

The proposition that all positive law is based on the possibility of men's coexistence has a strange sound, not because the truth it contains is strange, but simply because it is a truth so obvious and pervasive that we seldom have occasion to give words to it. Like the air we breathe, it so pervades our environment that we forget that it exists until we are suddenly deprived of it. Whatever particular objects may be sought by the various branches of our law, it is apparent on reflection that all of them are directed toward facilitating and improving men's coexistence and regulating with fairness and equity the relations of their life in common. When the assumption that men may live together loses its truth, as it obviously did in this extraordinary situation where life only became possible by the taking of life, then the basic premises underlying our whole legal order have lost their meaning and force.

Had the tragic events of this case taken place a mile beyond the territorial limits of our Commonwealth, no one would pretend that our law was applicable to them. We recognize that jurisdiction rests on a territorial basis. The grounds of this principle are by no means obvious and are seldom examined. I take it that this principle is supported by an assumption that it is feasible to impose a single legal order upon a group of men only if they live together within the confines of a given area of the earth's surface. The premise that men shall coexist in a group underlies, then, the territorial principle, as it does all of law. Now I contend that a case may be removed morally from the force of a legal order, as well as geographically. If we look to the purposes of law and government, and to the premises underlying our positive law, these men when they made their fateful decision were as remote from our legal order as if they had been a thousand miles beyond our boundaries. Even in a physical sense, their underground prison was separated from our courts and writ-servers by a solid curtain of rock that could be removed only after the most extraordinary expenditures of time and effort.

I conclude, therefore, that at the time Roger Whetmore's life was ended by these defendants, they were, to use the quaint language of the nineteenth-century writers, not in a "state of civil society" but in a "state of nature." This has the consequence that the law applicable to them is not the enacted and established law of this Commonwealth, but the law derived from those principles that were appropriate to their condition. I have no hesitancy in saying that under those principles they were guiltless of any crime.

What these men did was done in pursuance of an agreement accepted by all of them and first proposed by Whetmore himself. Since it was apparent that their extraordinary predicament made inapplica-

ble the usual principles that regulate men's relations with one another, it was necessary for them to draw, as it were, a new charter of government appropriate to the situation in which they found themselves.

It has from antiquity been recognized that the most basic principle of law or government is to be found in the notion of contract or agreement. Ancient thinkers, especially during the period from 1600 to 1900, used to base government itself on a supposed original social compact. Skeptics pointed out that this theory contradicted the known facts of history, and that there was no scientific evidence to support the notion that any government was ever founded in the manner supposed by the theory. Moralists replied that, if the compact was a fiction from a historical point of view, the notion of compact or agreement furnished the only ethical justification on which the powers of government, which include that of taking life, could be rested. The powers of government can only be justified morally on the ground that these are powers that reasonable men would agree upon and accept if they were faced with the necessity of constructing anew some order to make their life in common possible.

Fortunately, our Commonwealth is not bothered by the perplexities that beset the ancients. We know as a matter of historical truth that our government was founded upon a contract or free accord of men. The archaeological proof is conclusive that in the first period following the Great Spiral the survivors of that holocaust voluntarily came together and drew up a charter of government. Sophistical writers have raised questions as to the power of those remote contractors to bind future generations, but the fact remains that our government traces itself back in an unbroken line to that original charter.

If, therefore, our hangmen have the power to end men's lives, if our sheriffs have the power to put delinquent tenants in the street, if our police have the power to incarcerate the inebriated reveler, these powers find their moral justification in that original compact of our forefathers. If we can find no higher source for our legal order, what higher source should we expect these starving unfortunates to find for the order they adopted for themselves?

I believe that the line of argument I have just expounded permits of no rational answer. I realize that it will probably be received with a certain discomfort by many who read this opinion, who will be inclined to suspect that some hidden sophistry must underlie a demonstration that leads to so many unfamiliar conclusions. The source of this discomfort is, however, easy to identify. The usual conditions of human existence incline us to think of human life as an absolute value, not to be sacrificed under any circumstances. There is much that is fictitious about this conception even when it is applied to the ordinary relations of society. We have an illustration of this truth in the very case before us. Ten workmen were killed in the process of removing the rocks from the opening to the cave. Did not the engineers and government officials who directed the rescue effort know that the operations they were undertaking were dangerous and involved a serious risk to the lives of the workmen executing them? If it was proper that these ten lives should be sacrificed to save the lives of five imprisoned explorers, why then are we told it was wrong for these explorers to carry out an arrangement which would save four lives at the cost of one?

Every highway, every tunnel, every building we project involves a risk to human life. Taking these projects in the aggregate, we can calculate with some precision how many deaths the construction of them will require; statisticians can tell you the average cost in human lives of a thousand miles of a four-lane concrete highway. Yet we deliberately and knowingly incur and pay this cost on the assumption that the values obtained for those who survive outweigh the loss. If these things can be said of a society functioning above ground in a normal and ordinary manner, what shall we say of the supposed absolute value of a human life in the desperate situation in which these defendants and their companion Whetmore found themselves?

This concludes the exposition of the first ground of my decision. My second ground proceeds by rejecting hypothetically all the premises on which I have so far proceeded. I concede for purposes of argument that I am wrong in saying that the situation of these men removed them from the effect of our positive law, and I assume that the Consolidated Statutes have the power to penetrate five hundred feet of rock and to impose themselves upon these starving men huddled in their underground prison.

Now it is, of course, perfectly clear that these men did an act that violates the literal wording of the statute which declares that he who "shall willfully take the life of another" is a murderer. But one of the most ancient bits of legal wisdom is the saying that a man may break the letter of the law without breaking the law itself. Every proposition of positive law, whether contained in a statute or a judicial precedent, is to be interpreted reasonably, in the light of its evident pur-

pose. This is a truth so elementary that it is hardly necessary to expatiate on it. Illustrations of its application are numberless and are to be found in every branch of the law. In *Commonwealth* v. *Staymore* the defendant was convicted under a statute making it a crime to leave one's car parked in certain areas for a period longer than two hours. The defendant had attempted to remove his car, but was prevented from doing so because the streets were obstructed by a political demonstration in which he took no part and which he had no reason to anticipate. His conviction was set aside by this Court, although his case fell squarely within the wording of the statute. Again, in *Fehler* v. *Neegas* there was before this Court for construction a statute in which the word "not" had plainly been transposed from its intended position in the final and most crucial section of the act. This transposition was contained in all the successive drafts of the act, where it was apparently overlooked by the draftsmen and sponsors of the legislation. No one was able to prove how the error came about, yet it was apparent that, taking account of the contents of the statute as a whole, an error had been made, since a literal reading of the final clause rendered it inconsistent with everything that had gone before and with the object of the enactment as stated in its preamble. This Court refused to accept a literal interpretation of the statute, and in effect rectified its language by reading the word "not" into the place where it was evidently intended to go.

The statute before us for interpretation has never been applied literally. Centuries ago it was established that a killing in self-defense is excused. There is nothing in the wording of the statute that suggests this exception. Various attempts have been made to reconcile the legal treatment of self-defense with the words of the statute, but in my opinion these are all merely ingenious sophistries. The truth is that the exception in favor of self-defense cannot be reconciled with the *words* of the statute, but only with its *purpose*.

The true reconciliation of the excuse of self-defense with the statute making it a crime to kill another is to be found in the following line of reasoning. One of the principal objects underlying any criminal legislation is that of deterring men from crime. Now it is apparent that if it were declared to be the law that a killing in self-defense is murder such a rule could not operate in a deterrent manner. A man whose life is threatened will repel his aggressor, whatever the law may say. Looking therefore to the broad purposes of criminal legislation, we may safely declare that this statute was not intended to apply to cases of self-defense.

When the rationale of the excuse of self-defense is thus explained, it becomes apparent that precisely the same reasoning is applicable to the case at bar. If in the future any group of men ever find themselves in the tragic predicament of these defendants, we may be sure that their decision whether to live or die will not be controlled by the contents of our criminal code. Accordingly, if we read this statute intelligently it is apparent that it does not apply to this case. The withdrawal of this situation from the effect of the statute is justified by precisely the same considerations that were applied by our predecessors in office centuries ago to the case of self-defense.

There are those who raise the cry of judicial usurpation whenever a court, after analyzing the purpose of a statute, gives to its words a meaning that is not at once apparent to the casual reader who has not studied the statute closely or examined the objectives it seeks to attain. Let me say emphatically that I accept without reservation the proposition that this Court is bound by the statutes of our Commonwealth and that it exercises its powers in subservience to the duly expressed will of the Chamber of Representatives. The line of reasoning I have applied above raises no question of fidelity to enacted law, though it may possibly raise a question of the distinction between intelligent and unintelligent fidelity. No superior wants a servant who lacks the capacity to read between the lines. The stupidest housemaid knows that when she is told "to peel the soup and skim the potatoes" her mistress does not mean what she says. She also knows that when her master tells her to "drop everything and come running" he has overlooked the possibility that she is at the moment in the act of rescuing the baby from the rain barrel. Surely we have a right to expect the same modicum of intelligence from the judiciary. The correction of obvious legislative errors or oversights is not to supplant the legislative will, but to make that will effective.

I therefore conclude that on any aspect under which this case may be viewed these defendants are innocent of the crime of murdering Roger Whetmore, and that the conviction should be set aside.

TATTING, J. In the discharge of my duties as a justice of this Court, I am usually able to dissociate the emotional and intellectual sides of my reactions, and to decide the case before me entirely on the basis of the latter. In passing on this tragic case I find that my usual resources fail me. On the emotional side I find myself torn between sympathy for these men and a feeling of abhorrence and disgust at the monstrous act they committed. I had hoped that I would be able to put these contradictory emotions to one side as irrelevant, and to decide the case on the basis of a convincing and logical demonstration of the result demanded by our law. Unfortunately, this deliverance has not been vouchsafed for me.

As I analyze the opinion just rendered by my brother Foster, I find that it is shot through with contradictions and fallacies. Let us begin with his first proposition: these men were not subject to our law because they were not in a "state of civil society" but in a "state of nature." I am not clear why this is so, whether it is because of the thickness of the rock that imprisoned them, or because they were hungry, or because they had set up a "new charter of government" by which the usual rules of law were to be supplanted by a throw of the dice. Other difficulties intrude themselves. If these men passed from the jurisdiction of our law to that of "the law of nature," at what moment did this occur? Was it when the entrance to the cave was blocked, or when the threat of starvation reached a certain undefined degree of intensity, or when the agreement for the throwing of the dice was made? These uncertainties in the doctrine proposed by my brother are capable of producing real difficulties. Suppose, for example, one of these men had had his twenty-first birthday while he was imprisoned within the mountain. On what date would we have to consider that he had attained his majority—when he reached the age of twenty-one, at which time he was, by hypothesis, removed from the effects of our law, or only when he was released from the cave and became again subject to what my brother calls our "positive law"? These difficulties may seem fanciful, yet they only serve to reveal the fanciful nature of the doctrine that is capable of giving rise to them.

But it is not necessary to explore these niceties further to demonstrate the absurdity of my brother's position. Mr. Justice Foster and I are the appointed judges of a court of the Commonwealth of Newgarth, sworn and empowered to administer the laws of that Commonwealth. By what authority do we resolve ourselves into a Court of Nature? If these men were indeed under the law of nature, whence comes our authority to expound and apply that law. Certainly *we* are not in a state of nature.

Let us look at the contents of this code of nature that my brother proposes we adopt as our own and apply to this case. What a topsy-turvy and odious code it is! It is a code in which the law of contracts is more fundamental than the law of murder. It is a code under which a man may make a valid agreement empowering his fellows to eat his own body. Under the provisions of this code, furthermore, such an agreement once made is irrevocable, and if one of the parties attempts to withdraw, the others may take the law into their own hands and enforce the contract by violence—for though my brother passes over in convenient silence the effect of Whetmore's withdrawal, this is the necessary implication of his argument.

The principles my brother expounds contain other implications that cannot be tolerated. He argues that when the defendants set upon Whetmore and killed him (we know not how, perhaps by pounding him with stones) they were only exercising the rights conferred upon them by their bargain. Suppose, however, that Whetmore had had concealed upon his person a revolver, and that when he saw the defendants about to slaughter him he had shot them to death in order to save his own life. My brother's reasoning applied to these facts would make Whetmore out to be a murderer, since the excuse of self-defense would have to be denied to him. If his assailants were acting rightfully in seeking to bring about his death, then of course he could no more plead the excuse that he was defending his own life than could a condemned prisoner who struck down the executioner lawfully attempting to place the noose about his neck.

All of these considerations make it impossible for me to accept the first part of my brother's argument. I can neither accept his notion that these men were under a code of nature which this Court was bound to apply to them, nor can I accept the odious and perverted rules that he would read into that code. I come now to the second part of my brother's opinion, in which he seeks to show that the defendants did not violate the provisions of N.C.S.A. (N.S.) § 12-A. Here the way, instead of being clear, becomes for me misty and ambiguous, though my brother seems unaware of the difficulties that inhere in his demonstrations.

The gist of my brother's argument may be stated in the following terms: No statute, whatever its language, should be applied in a way that contradicts its purpose. One of the purposes of any criminal statute is to deter. The application of the statute making it a crime to kill another to the peculiar facts of this case would contradict this purpose, for it is impossible to believe that the contents of the criminal code could operate in a deterrent manner on men faced with the alternative of life or death. The reasoning by which this exception is read into the statute is, my brother

observes, the same as that which is applied in order to provide the excuse of self-defense.

On the face of things this demonstration seems very convincing indeed. My brother's interpretation of the rationale of the excuse of self-defense is in fact supported by a decision of this court, *Commonwealth* v. *Parry,* a precedent I happened to encounter in my research on this case. Though *Commonwealth* v. *Parry* seems generally to have been overlooked in the texts and subsequent decisions, it supports unambiguously the interpretation my brother has put upon the excuse of self-defense.

Now let me outline briefly, however, the perplexities that assail me when I examine my brother's demonstration more closely. It is true that a statute should be applied in the light of its purpose and that *one* of the purposes of criminal legislation is recognized to be deterrence. The difficulty is that other purposes are also ascribed to the law of crimes. It has been said that one of its objects is to provide an orderly outlet for the instinctive human demand for retribution. *Commonwealth* v. *Scape.* It has also been said that its object is the rehabilitation of the wrongdoer. *Commonwealth* v. *Makeover.* Other theories have been propounded. Assuming that we must interpret a statute in the light of its purpose, what are we to do when it has many purposes or when its purposes are disputed?

A similar difficulty is presented by the fact that although there is authority for my brother's interpretation of the excuse of self-defense, there is other authority which assigns to that excuse a different rationale. Indeed, until I happened on *Commonwealth* v. *Parry* I had never heard of the explanation given by my brother. The taught doctrine of our law schools, memorized by generations of law students, runs in the following terms: The statute concerning murder requires a "willful" act. The man who acts to repel an aggressive threat to his own life does not act "willfully," but in response to an impulse deeply ingrained in human nature. I suspect that there is hardly a lawyer in this Commonwealth who is not familiar with this line of reasoning, especially since the point is a great favorite of the bar examiners.

Now the familiar explanation for the excuse of self-defense just expounded obviously cannot be applied by analogy to the facts of this case. These men acted not only "willfully" but with great deliberation and after hours of discussing what they should do. Again we encounter a forked path, with one line of reasoning leading us in one direction and another in a direction that is exactly the opposite. This perplexity is in this case compounded, as it were, for we have to set off one explanation, incorporated in a virtually unknown precedent of this Court, against another explanation, which forms a part of the taught legal tradition of our law schools, but which, so far as I know, has never been adopted in any judicial decision.

I recognize the relevance of the precedents cited by my brother concerning the displaced "not" and the defendant who parked overtime. But what are we do with one of the landmarks of our jurisprudence, which again my brother passes over in silence? This is *Commonwealth* v. *Valjean*. Though the case is somewhat obscurely reported, it appears that the defendant was indicted for the larceny of a loaf of bread, and offered as a defense that he was in a condition approaching starvation. The court refused to accept this defense. If hunger cannot justify the theft of wholesome and natural food, how can it justify the killing and eating of a man? Again, if we look at the thing in terms of deterrence, is it likely that a man will starve to death to avoid a jail sentence for the theft of a loaf of bread? My brother's demonstrations would compel us to overrule *Commonwealth* v. *Valjean*, and many other precedents that have been built on that case.

Again, I have difficulty in saying that no deterrent effect whatever could be attributed to a decision that these men were guilty of murder. The stigma of the word "murderer" is such that it is quite likely, I believe, that if these men had known that their act was deemed by the law to be murder they would have waited for a few days at least before carrying out their plan. During that time some unexpected relief might have come. I realize that this observation only reduces the distinction to a matter of degree, and does not destroy it altogether. It is certainly true that the element of deterrence would be less in this case than is normally involved in the application of the criminal law.

There is still a further difficulty in my brother Foster's proposal to read an exception into the statute to favor this case, though again a difficulty not even intimated in his opinion. What shall be the scope of this exception? Here the men cast lots and the victim was himself originally a party to the agreement. What would we have to decide if Whetmore had refused from the beginning to participate in the plan? Would a majority be permitted to overrule him? Or, suppose that no plan were adopted at all and the others simply conspired to bring about Whetmore's death, justifying their act by saying that he was in the weakest condition. Or again, that a plan of selection was followed but one based on a different justification than the one

adopted here, as if the others were atheists and insisted that Whetmore should die because he was the only one who believed in an afterlife. These illustrations could be multiplied, but enough have been suggested to reveal what a quagmire of hidden difficulties my brother's reasoning contains.

Of course I realize on reflection that I may be concerning myself with a problem that will never arise, since it is unlikely that any group of men will ever again be brought to commit the dread act that was involved here. Yet, on still further reflection, even if we are certain that no similar case will arise again, do not the illustrations I have given show the lack of any coherent and rational principle in the rule my brother proposes? Should not the soundness of a principle be tested by the conclusions it entails, without reference to the accidents of later litigational history? Still, if this is so, why is it that we of this Court so often discuss the question whether we are likely to have later occasion to apply a principle urged for the solution of the case before us? Is this a situation where a line of reasoning not originally proper has become sanctioned by precedent, so that we are permitted to apply it and may even be under an obligation to do so?

The more I examine this case and think about it, the more deeply I become involved. My mind becomes entangled in the meshes of the very nets I throw out for my own rescue. I find that almost every consideration that bears on the decision of the case is counterbalanced by an opposing consideration leading in the opposite direction. My brother Foster has not furnished to me, nor can I discover for myself, any formula capable of resolving the equivocations that beset me on all sides.

I have given this case the best thought of which I am capable. I have scarcely slept since it was argued before us. When I feel myself inclined to accept the view of my brother Foster, I am repelled by a feeling that his arguments are intellectually unsound and approach mere rationalization. On the other hand, when I incline toward upholding the conviction, I am struck by the absurdity of directing that these men be put to death when their lives have been saved at the cost of the lives of ten heroic workmen. It is to me a matter of regret that the Prosecutor saw fit to ask for an indictment for murder. If we had a provision in our statutes making it a crime to eat human flesh, that would have been a more appropriate charge. If no other charge suited to the facts of this case could be brought against the defendants, it would have been wiser, I think, not to have indicted them at all. Unfortunately, however, the men have been indicted and tried, and we have therefore been drawn into this unfortunate affair.

Since I have been wholly unable to resolve the doubts that beset me about the law of this case, I am with regret announcing a step that is, I believe, unprecedented in the history of this tribunal. I declare my withdrawal from the decision of this case.

KEEN, J. I should like to begin by setting to one side two questions which are not before this Court.

The first of these is whether executive clemency should be extended to these defendants if the conviction is affirmed. Under our system of government, that is a question for the Chief Executive, not for us. I therefore disapprove of that passage in the opinion of the Chief Justice in which he in effect gives instructions to the Chief Executive as to what he should do in this case and suggests that some impropriety will attach if these instructions are not heeded. This is a confusion of governmental functions—a confusion of which the judiciary should be the last to be guilty. I wish to state that if I were the Chief Executive I would go farther in the direction of clemency than the pleas addressed to him propose. I would pardon these men altogether, since I believe that they have already suffered enough to pay for any offense they may have committed. I want it to be understood that this remark is made in my capacity as a private citizen who by the accident of his office happens to have acquired an intimate acquaintance with the facts of this case. In the discharge of my duties as judge, it is neither my function to address directions to the Chief Executive, nor to take into account what he may or may not do, in reaching my own decision, which must be controlled entirely by the law of this Commonwealth.

The second question that I wish to put to one side is that of deciding whether what these men did was "right" or "wrong," "wicked" or "good." That is also a question that is irrelevant to the discharge of my office as a judge sworn to apply, not my conceptions of morality, but the law of the land. In putting this question to one side I think I can also safely dismiss without comment the first and more poetic portion of my brother Foster's opinion. The element of fantasy contained in the arguments developed there has been sufficiently revealed in my brother Tatting's somewhat solemn attempt to take those arguments seriously.

The sole question before us for decision is whether these defendants did, within the meaning of N.C.S.A. (N.S.) § 12-A, willfully take the life of Roger Whetmore. The exact language of the statute is as follows: "Whoever shall willfully take the life of another shall be punished by death." Now I should suppose that any candid observer, content to extract from these words their natural meaning, would concede at once that these defendants did "willfully take the life" of Roger Whetmore.

Whence arise all the difficulties of the case, then, and the necessity for so many pages of discussion about what ought to be so obvious? The difficulties, in whatever tortured form they may present themselves, all trace back to a single source, and that is a failure to distinguish the legal from the moral aspects of this case. To put it bluntly, my brothers do not like the fact that the written law requires the conviction of these defendants. Neither do I, but unlike my brothers I respect the obligations of an office that requires me to put my personal predilections out of my mind when I come to interpret and apply the law of this Commonwealth.

Now, of course, my brother Foster does not admit that he is actuated by a personal dislike of the written law. Instead he develops a familiar line of argument according to which the court may disregard the express language of a statute when something not contained in the statute itself, called its "purpose," can be employed to justify the result the court considers proper. Because this is an old issue between myself and my colleague, I should like, before discussing his particular application of the argument to the facts of this case, to say something about the historical background of this issue and its implications for law and government generally.

There was a time in this Commonwealth when judges did in fact legislate very freely, and all of us know that during that period some of our statutes were rather thoroughly made over by the judiciary. That was a time when the accepted principles of political science did not designate with any certainty the rank and function of the various arms of the state. We all know the tragic issue of that uncertainty in the brief civil war that arose out of the conflict between the judiciary, on the one hand, and the executive and the legislature, on the other. There is no need to recount here the factors that contributed to that unseemly struggle for power, though they included the unrepresentative character of the Chamber, resulting from a division of the country into election districts that no longer accorded with the actual distribution of the population, and the forceful personality and wide popular following of the then Chief Justice. It is enough to observe that those days are behind us, and that in place of the uncertainty that then reigned we now have a clear-cut principle, which is the supremacy of the legislative branch of our government. From that principle flows the obligation of the judiciary to enforce faithfully the written law, and to interpret that law in accordance with its plain meaning without reference to our personal desires or our individual conceptions of justice. I am not concerned with the question whether the principle that forbids the judicial revision of statutes is right or wrong, desirable or undesirable; I observe merely that this principle has become a tacit premise underlying the whole of the legal and governmental order I am sworn to administer.

Yet though the principle of the supremacy of the legislature has been accepted in theory for centuries, such is the tenacity of professional tradition and the force of fixed habits of thought that many of the judiciary have still not accommodated themselves to the restricted role which the new order imposes on them. My brother Foster is one of that group; his way of dealing with statutes is exactly that of a judge living in the 3900's.

We are all familiar with the process by which the judicial reform of disfavored legislative enactments is accomplished. Anyone who has followed the written opinions of Mr. Justice Foster will have had an opportunity to see it at work in every branch of the law. I am personally so familiar with the process that in the event of my brother's incapacity I am sure I could write a satisfactory opinion for him without any prompting whatever, beyond being informed whether he liked the effect of the terms of the statute as applied to the case before him.

The process of judicial reform requires three steps. The first of these is to divine some single "purpose" which the statute serves. This is done although not one statute in a hundred has any such single purpose, and although the objectives of nearly every statute are differently interpreted by the different classes of its sponsors. The second step is to discover that a mythical being called "the legislator," in the pursuit of this imagined "purpose," overlooked something or left some gap or imperfection in his work. Then comes the final and most refreshing part of the task, which is, of course, to fill in the blank thus created. . . .

My brother Foster's penchant for finding holes in statutes reminds one of the story told by an ancient author about the man who ate a pair of shoes. Asked how he liked them, he replied that the part he liked best was the holes. That is the way my brother feels about statutes; the more holes they have in them the better he likes them. In short, he doesn't like statutes.

One could not wish for a better case to illustrate the specious nature of this gap-filling process than the one before us. My brother thinks he knows exactly what was sought when men made murder a crime, and that was something he calls "deterrence." My brother Tatting has already shown how much is passed over in that interpretation. But I think the trouble goes deeper. I doubt very much whether our statute making murder a crime really has a "purpose" in any ordinary sense of the term. Primarily, such a statute reflects a deeply-felt human conviction that murder is wrong and that something should be done to the man who commits it. If we were forced to be more articulate about the matter, we would probably take refuge in the more sophisticated theories of the criminologists, which, of course, were certainly not in the minds of those who drafted our statute. We might also observe that men will do their own work more effectively and live happier lives if they are protected against the threat of violent assault. Bearing in mind that the victims of murders are often unpleasant people, we might add some suggestion that the matter of disposing of undesirables is not a function suited to private enterprise, but should be a state monopoly. All of which reminds me of the attorney who once argued before us that a statute licensing physicians was a good thing because it would lead to lower life insurance rates by lifting the level of general health. There is such a thing as overexplaining the obvious.

If we do not know the purpose of § 12-A, how can we possibly say there is a "gap" in it? How can we know what its draftsmen thought about the question of killing men in order to eat them? My brother Tatting has revealed an understandable, though perhaps slightly exaggerated revulsion to cannibalism. How do we know that his remote ancestors did not feel the same revulsion to an even higher degree? Anthropologists say that the dread felt for a forbidden act may be increased by the fact that the conditions of a tribe's life create special temptations toward it, as incest is most severely condemned among those whose village relations make it most likely to occur. Certainly the period following the Great Spiral was one that had implicit in it temptations to anthropophagy. Perhaps it was for that very reason that our ancestors expressed their prohibition in so broad and unqualified a form. All of this is conjecture, of course, but it remains abundantly clear that neither I nor my brother Foster knows what the "purpose" of § 12-A is.

Considerations similar to those I have just outlined are also applicable to the exception in favor of self-defense, which plays so large a role in the reasoning of my brothers Foster and Tatting. It is of course true that in *Commonwealth* v. *Parry* an obiter dictum justified this exception on the assumption that the purpose of criminal legislation is to deter. It may well also be true that generations of law students have been taught that the true explanation of the exception lies in the fact that a man who acts in self-defense does not act "willfully," and that the same students have passed their bar examinations by repeating what their professors told them. These last observations I could dismiss, of course, as irrelevant for the simple reason that professors and bar examiners have not as yet any commission to make our laws for us. But again the real trouble lies deeper. As in dealing with the statute, so in dealing with the exception, the question is not the conjectural *purpose* of the rule, but its *scope*. Now the scope of the exception in favor of self-defense as it has been applied by this Court is plain: it applies to cases of resisting an aggressive threat to the party's own life. It is therefore too clear for argument that this case does not fall within the scope of the exception, since it is plain that Whetmore made no threat against the lives of these defendants.

The essential shabbiness of my brother Foster's attempt to cloak his remaking of the written law with an air of legitimacy comes tragically to the surface in my brother Tatting's opinion. In that opinion Justice Tatting struggles manfully to combine his colleague's loose moralisms with his own sense of fidelity to the written law. The issue of this struggle could only be that which occurred, a complete default in the discharge of the judicial function. You simply cannot apply a statute as it is written and remake it to meet your own wishes at the same time.

Now I know that the line of reasoning I have developed in this opinion will not be acceptable to those who look only to the immediate effects of a decision and ignore the long-run implications of an assumption by the judiciary of a power of dispensation. A hard decision is never a popular decision. Judges have been celebrated in literature for their sly prowess in devising some quibble by which a litigant could be deprived of his rights where the public thought it was wrong for him to assert those rights. But I believe that judicial dispensation does more harm in the long run than hard decisions. Hard cases may even have a certain moral value by bringing home to the people their own responsibilities toward the law that is ultimately their creation, and by reminding them that there is no principle of personal grace that can relieve the mistakes of their representatives.

Indeed, I will go farther and say that not only are the principles I have been expounding those *which are soundest for our present conditions,* but that we would have inherited a better legal system from our forefathers if those principles had been observed from the beginning. For example, with respect to the excuse of self-defense, if our courts had stood steadfast on the language of the statute the result would undoubtedly have been a legislative revision of it. Such a revision would have drawn on the assistance of natural philosophers and psychologists, and the resulting regulation of the matter would have had an understandable and rational basis, instead of the hodgepodge of verbalisms and metaphysical distinctions that have emerged from the judicial and professorial treatment.

These concluding remarks are, of course, beyond any duties that I have to discharge with relation to this case, but I include them here because I feel deeply that my colleagues are insufficiently aware of the dangers implicit in the conceptions of the judicial office advocated by my brother Foster.

I conclude that the conviction should be affirmed.

HANDY, J. I have listened with amazement to the tortured ratiocinations to which this simple case has given rise. I never cease to wonder at my colleagues' ability to throw an obscuring curtain of legalisms about every issue presented to them for decision. We have heard this afternoon learned disquisitions on the distinction between positive law and the law of nature, the language of the statute and the purpose of the statute, judicial functions and executive functions, judicial legislation and legislative legislation. My only disappointment was that someone did not raise the question of the legal nature of the bargain struck in the cave—whether it was unilateral or bilateral, and whether Whetmore could not be considered as having revoked an offer prior to action taken thereunder.

What have all these things to do with the case? The problem before us is what we, as officers of the government, ought to do with these defendants. That is a question of practical wisdom, to be exercised in a context, not of abstract theory, but of human realities. When the case is approached in this light, it becomes, I think, one of the easiest to decide that has ever been argued before this Court.

Before stating my own conclusions about the merits of the case, I should like to discuss briefly some of the more fundamental issues involved—issues on which my colleagues and I have been divided ever since I have been on the bench.

I have never been able to make my brothers see that government is a human affair, and that men are ruled, not by words on paper or by abstract theories, but by other men. They are ruled well when their rules understand the feelings and conceptions of the masses. They are ruled badly when that understanding is lacking.

Of all branches of the government, the judiciary is the most likely to lose its contact with the common man. The reasons for this are, of course, fairly obvious. Where the masses react to a situation in terms of a few salient features, we pick into little pieces every situation presented to us. Lawyers are hired by both sides to analyze and dissect. Judges and attorneys vie with one another to see who can discover the greatest number of difficulties and distinctions in a single set of facts. Each side tries to find cases, real or imagined, that will embarrass the demonstrations of the other side. To escape this embarrassment, still further distinctions are invented and imported into the situation. When a set of facts has been subjected to this kind of treatment for a sufficient time, all the life and juice have gone out of it and we have left a handful of dust.

Now I realize that wherever you have rules and abstract principles lawyers are going to be able to make distinctions. To some extent the sort of thing I have been describing is a necessary evil attaching to any formal regulation of human affairs. But I think that the area which really stands in need of such regulation is greatly overestimated. There are, of course, a few fundamental rules of the game that must be accepted if the game is to go on at all. I would include among these the rules relating to the conduct of elections, the appointment of public officials, and the term during which an office is held. Here some restraint on discretion and dispensation, some adherence to form, some scruple for what does and what does not fall within the rule, is, I concede, essential. Perhaps the area of basic principle should be expanded to include certain other rules, such as those designed to preserve the free civilmoign system.

But outside of these fields I believe that all government officials, including judges, will do their jobs best if they treat forms and abstract concepts as instruments. We should take as our model, I think, the good administrator, who accommodates procedures and principles to the case at hand, selecting from among the available forms those most suited to reach the proper result.

The most obvious advantage of this method of government is that it permits us to go about our daily tasks with efficiency and common sense. My adherence to this philosophy has, however, deeper roots. I believe that it is only with the insight this philosophy gives that we can preserve the flexibility essential if we are to keep our actions in reasonable accord with the sentiments of those subject to our rule. More governments have been wrecked, and more human misery caused, by the lack of this accord between ruler and ruled than by any other factor that can be discerned in history. Once we drive a sufficient wedge between the mass of people and those who direct their legal, political, and economic life, our society is ruined. Then neither Foster's law of nature nor Keen's fidelity to written law will avail us anything.

Now when these conceptions are applied to the case before us, its decision becomes, as I have said, perfectly easy. In order to demonstrate this I shall have to introduce certain realities that my brothers in their coy decorum have seen fit to pass over in silence, although they are just as acutely aware of them as I am.

The first of these is that this case has aroused an enormous public interest, both here and abroad. Almost every newspaper and magazine has carried articles about it; columnists have shared with their readers confidential information as to the next governmental move; hundreds of letters-to-the-editor have been printed. One of the great newspaper chains made a poll of public opinion on the question, "What do you think the Supreme Court should do with the Speluncean explorers?" About ninety percent expressed a belief that the defendants should be pardoned or let off with a kind of token punishment. It is perfectly clear, then, how the public feels about the case. We could have known this without the poll, of course, on the basis of common sense, or even by observing that on this Court there are apparently four-and-a-half men, or ninety percent, who share the common opinion.

This makes it obvious, not only what we should do, but what we must do if we are to preserve between ourselves and public opinion a reasonable and decent accord. Declaring these men innocent need not involve us in any undignified quibble or trick. No principle of statutory construction is required that is not consistent with the past practices of this Court. Certainly no layman would think that in letting these men off we had stretched the statute any more than our ancestors did when they created the excuse of self-defense. If a more detailed demonstration of the method of reconciling our decision with the statute is required, I should be content to rest on the arguments developed in the second and less visionary part of my brother Foster's opinion.

Now I know that my brothers will be horrified by my suggestion that this Court should take account of public opinion. They will tell you that public opinion is emotional and capricious, that it is based on half-truths and listens to witnesses who are not subject to cross-examination. They will tell you that the law surrounds the trial of a case like this with elaborate safeguards, designed to insure that the truth will be known and that every rational consideration bearing on the issues of the case has been taken into account. They will warn you that all of these safeguards go for naught if a mass opinion formed outside this framework is allowed to have any influence on our decision.

But let us look candidly at some of the realities of the administration of our criminal law. When a man is accused of crime, there are, speaking generally, four ways in which he may escape punishment. One of these is a determination by a judge that under the applicable law he has committed no crime. This is, of course, a determination that takes place in a rather formal and abstract atmosphere. But look at the other three ways in which he may escape punishment. These are: (1) a decision by the Prosecutor not to ask for an indictment; (2) an acquittal by the jury; (3) a pardon or commutation of sentence by the executive. Can anyone pretend that these decisions are held within a rigid and formal framework of rules that prevents factual error, excludes emotional and personal factors, and guarantees that all the forms of the law will be observed?

In the case of the jury we do, to be sure, attempt to cabin their deliberations within the area of the legally relevant, but there is no need to deceive ourselves into believing that this attempt is really successful. In the normal course of events the case now before us would have gone on all of its issues directly to the jury. Had this occurred we can be confident that there would have been an acquittal or at least a division that would have prevented a conviction. If the jury had been instructed that the men's hunger and their agreement were no defense to the charge of murder, their verdict would in all likelihood have ignored this instruction and would have involved a good deal more twisting of the letter of the law than any that is likely to tempt us. Of course the only reason that didn't occur in this case was the fortuitous circumstance that the foreman of the jury happened to be a lawyer. His learning enabled him to devise a form of words that would allow the jury to dodge its usual responsibilities.

My brother Tatting expresses annoyance that the Prosecutor did not, in effect, decide the case for him by not asking for an indictment. Strict as he is himself in complying with the demands of legal theory, he is quite content to have the fate of these men decided out of court by the Prosecutor on the basis of common sense. The Chief Justice, on the other hand, wants the application of common sense postponed to the very end, though like Tatting, he wants no personal part in it.

This brings me to the concluding portion of my remarks, which has to do with executive clemency. Before discussing that topic directly, I want to make a related observation about the poll of public opinion. As I have said, ninety percent of the people wanted the Supreme Court to let the men off entirely or with a more or less nominal punishment. The ten percent constituted a very oddly assorted group, with the most curious and divergent opinions. One of our university experts has made a study of this group and has found that its members fall into certain patterns. A substantial portion of them are subscribers to "crank" newspapers of limited circulation that gave their readers a distorted version of the facts of the case. Some thought that "Speluncean" means "cannibal" and that anthropophagy is a tenet of the Society. But the point I want to make, however, is this: although almost every conceivable variety and shade of opinion was represented in this group, there was, so far as I know, not one of them, nor a single member of the majority of ninety percent, who said, "I think it would be a fine thing to have the courts sentence these men to be hanged, and then to have another branch of the government come along and pardon them." Yet this is a solution that has more or less dominated our discussions and which our Chief Justice proposes as a way by which we can avoid doing an injustice and at the same time preserve respect for law. He can be assured that if he is preserving anybody's morale, it is his own, and not the public's, which knows nothing of his distinctions. I mention this matter because I wish to emphasize once more the danger that we may get lost in the patterns of our own thought and forget that these patterns often cast not the slightest shadow on the outside world.

I come now to the most crucial fact in this case, a fact known to all of us on this Court, though one that my brothers have seen fit to keep under the cover of their judicial robes. This is the frightening likelihood that if the issue is left to him, the Chief Executive will refuse to pardon these men or commute their sentence. As we all know, our Chief Executive is a man now well advanced in years, of very stiff notions. Public clamor usually operates on him with the reverse of the effect intended. As I have told my brothers, it happens that my wife's niece is an intimate friend of his secretary. I have learned in this indirect, but, I think, wholly reliable way, that he is firmly determined not to commute the sentence if these men are found to have violated the law.

No one regrets more than I the necessity for relying in so important a matter on information that could be characterized as gossip. If I had my way this would not happen, for I would adopt the sensible course of sitting down with the Executive, going over the case with him, finding out what his views are, and perhaps working out with him a common program for handling the situation. But of course my brothers would never hear of such a thing.

Their scruple about acquiring accurate information directly does not prevent them from being very perturbed about what they have learned indirectly. Their acquaintance with the facts I have just related explains why the Chief Justice, ordinarily a model of decorum, saw fit in his opinion to flap his judicial robes in the face of the Executive and threaten him with excommunication if he failed to commute the sentence. It explains, I suspect, my brother Foster's feat of levitation by which a whole library of law books was lifted from the shoulders of these defendants. It explains also why even my legalistic brother Keen emulated Pooh-Bah in the ancient comedy by stepping to the other side of the stage to address a few remarks to the Executive "in my capacity as a private citizen." (I may remark, incidentally, that the advice of Private Citizen Keen will appear in the reports of this court printed at taxpayer's expense.)

I must confess that as I grow older I become more and more perplexed at men's refusal to apply their common sense to problems of law and government, and this truly tragic case has deepened my sense of discouragement and dismay. I only wish that I could convince my brothers of the wisdom of the principles I have applied to the judicial office since I first assumed it. As a matter of fact, by a kind of sad rounding of the circle, I encountered issues like those involved here in the very first case I tried as Judge of the Court of General Instances in Fanleigh County.

A religious sect had unfrocked a minister who, they said, had gone over to the views and practices of a rival sect. The minister circulated a handbill making charges against the authorities who had expelled him.

Certain lay members of the church announced a public meeting at which they proposed to explain the position of the church. The minister attended this meeting. Some said he slipped in unobserved in a disguise; his own testimony was that he had walked in openly as a member of the public. At any rate, when the speeches began he interrupted with certain questions about the affairs of the church and made some statements in defense of his own views. He was set upon by members of the audience and given a pretty thorough pommeling, receiving among other injuries a broken jaw. He brought a suit for damages against the association that sponsored the meeting and against ten named individuals who he alleged were his assailants.

When we came to the trial, the case at first seemed very complicated to me. The attorneys raised a host of legal issues. There were nice questions on the admissibility of evidence, and, in connection with the suit against the association, some difficult problems turning on the question whether the minister was a trespasser or a licensee. As a novice on the bench I was eager to apply my law school learning and I began studying these questions closely, reading all the authorities and preparing well-documented rulings. As I studied the case I became more and more involved in its legal intricacies and I began to get into a state approaching that of my brother Tatting in this case. Suddenly, however, it dawned on me that all these perplexing issues really had nothing to do with the case, and I began examining it in the light of common sense. The case at once gained a new perspective, and I saw that the only thing for me to do was to direct a verdict for the defendants for lack of evidence.

I was led to this conclusion by the following considerations. The melee in which the plaintiff was injured had been a very confused affair, with some people trying to get to the center of the disturbance, while others were trying to get away from it; some striking at the plaintiff, while others were apparently trying to protect him. It would have taken weeks to find out the truth of the matter. I decided that nobody's broken jaw was worth that much to the Commonwealth. (The minister's injuries, incidentally, had meanwhile healed without disfigurement and without any impairment of normal faculties.) Furthermore, I felt very strongly that the plaintiff had to a large extent brought the thing on himself. He knew how inflamed passions were about the affair, and could easily have found another forum for the expression of his views. My decision was widely approved by the press and public opinion, neither of which could tolerate the views and practices that the expelled minister was attempting to defend.

Now, thirty years later, thanks to an ambitious Prosecutor and a legalistic jury foreman, I am faced with a case that raises issues which are at bottom much like those involved in that case. The world does not seem to change much, except that this time it is not a question of a judgment for five or six hundred frelars, but of the life or death of four men who have already suffered more torment and humiliation than most of us would endure in a thousand years. I conclude that the defendants are innocent of the crime charged, and that the conviction and sentence should be set aside.

TATTING, J. I have been asked by the Chief Justice whether, after listening to the two opinions just rendered, I desire to re-examine the position previously taken by me. I wish to state that after hearing these opinions I am greatly strengthened in my conviction that I ought not to participate in the decision of this case.

The Supreme Court being evenly divided, the conviction and sentence of the Court of General Instances is *affirmed*. It is ordered that the execution of the sentence shall occur at 6 A.M., Friday, April 2, 4300, at which time the Public Executioner is directed to proceed with all convenient dispatch to hang each of the defendants by the neck until he is dead.

Postscript

Now that the court has spoken, the reader puzzled by the choice of date may wish to be reminded that the centuries which separate us from the year 4300 are roughly equal to those that have passed since the Age of Pericles. There is probably no need to observe that the *Speluncean Case* itself is intended neither as a work of satire nor as a prediction in any ordinary sense of the term. As for the judges who make up Chief Justice Truepenny's court, they are, of course, as mythical as the facts and precedents with which they deal. The reader who refuses to accept this view, and who seeks to trace out contemporary resemblances where none is intended or contemplated, should be warned that he is engaged in a frolic of his own, which may possibly lead him to miss whatever modest truths are contained in the opinions delivered by the Supreme Court of Newgarth. The case was constructed for the sole purpose of bringing into a common focus certain divergent philosophies of law and government. These philosophies presented men with live questions of choice in the days of Plato and Aristotle. Perhaps they will continue to do so when our era has had its say about them. If there is any element of prediction in the case, it does not go beyond a suggestion that the questions involved are among the permanent problems of the human race.

THE SPELUNCEAN EXPLORERS: Further Proceedings*

Anthony D'Amato

Lon L. Fuller's *The Case of the Speluncean Explorers*[1] is a classic in jurisprudence. Set in the Supreme Court of Newgarth in the year 4300 the case presents five judicial opinions which clash with each other and pro-

*From Anthony D'Amato, "The Speluncean Explorers—Further Proceedings," 32 *Stanford Law Review* 467 (1980). Reprinted by permission of the author.

duce for the reader an exhilarating excursion into fundamental theories of law and the state and the role of courts vis-à-vis legislatures and executives. Though the issues articulated by Professor Fuller in 1949 are timeless, the past thirty years in jurisprudential scholarship have produced at least one major new vantage point—the "rights thesis" as advanced by Professor Dworkin and others.[2] Simply stated, the rights thesis holds that there is a "right" answer, and only one right answer, in every case. The litigants have a "right" to that and finally—to add one more shade of meaning to the comprehensive term "right"—the answer thus arrived at is dictated by general requirements of justice. Since justice is a branch of morality, the "right" answer is not only correct but also right in a moral sense.

My purpose here is to examine how the rights thesis would apply to the Speluncean Case, and to do so in the spirit of my former teacher's presentation. Therefore, let us imagine that, right after the decision in the Speluncean Case was handed down, the Chief Executive of Newgarth constituted a Special Commission of three law professors at the University of Newgarth School of Law to present a recommendation on the question whether executive clemency should be extended to the convicted defendants.[3]

Opinion of Professor Wun

When I received news of the decision in this case, I was relieved that the Court had reached the only proper result. But later, as I read the opinions of the Justices, I realized how fragile the Court's decision really was. To recap the vote, Justices Handy and Foster voted for acquittal, Tatting withdrew from the case, and although Keen and Truepenny voted to affirm the finding of guilty they engaged in powerful pleas to the Chief Executive to extend clemency to the convicted defendants. Not one of them came even close to believing, as I do, that the defendants were clearly guilty of murder. Perhaps the most egregiously bankrupt opinion illustrating the Court's true feeling is that of Justice Keen, who found it necessary to resort to the old and discredited theory of positivism to prop up his conclusion. He insisted upon a separation between law and morality, holding that "the law" required a finding of guilty even though his own morality would lead to a different result. Without repeating familiar arguments against this positivistic stance, it may suf-

fice to ask what morality compels Justice Keen to insist upon a separation between law and morality.

Since I believe that matters of right cannot be separated from matters of law, I might most efficiently begin by showing that what these defendants did is murder as a matter of morality, and only after that turn to the legal conclusion that murder was committed. As moral arguments are often best proved by analogies, let us consider four persons on the brink of death due to, respectively, a defective heart, diseased lungs, a destroyed liver, and a nonfunctioning kidney. Since their lives are at stake their "need" to have these organs replaced by healthy ones could not possibly be greater. We will assume that there are no replacement organs available. The four persons thereupon decide that they will kidnap a stranger who is in good health, take him to a medical office where they have several highly paid doctors waiting, kill the stranger, and have the doctors transplant his four healthy organs into the four conspirators. Four lives will thus be saved at the cost of only one, and the result can be said to have been objectively compelled by "necessity" and not by any personal malice toward the stranger or any wish to harm him.

I will assume that anyone would immediately conclude that these four persons would be morally guilty of murdering the stranger (and, consequently, that they should be prosecuted under the law for murder). But then, of course, we must ask whether there is any significant difference between the hypothetical and the speluncean explorers. Certainly not because the victim was a stranger whereas Whetmore was known to the explorers. For the case would not be morally improved if the four persons needing organ transplants had instead selected a victim who had been friendly with them. But, one might object, Whetmore was involved in the same enterprise as the other explorers; that surely makes a difference. Yet consider the following alteration: The four persons, partners in a research team, had their vital organs damaged because their machine had broken and emitted omicron rays. A fifth coworker was also present, but miraculously she was not hurt. Are the four damaged individuals thereby entitled to kill her and transplant her organs simply because she was involved in the same enterprise and at the same time as they?

What of another possible distinction: that Whetmore was going to die shortly of malnutrition anyway, whereas the stranger in the hypothetical case was in good health? Does that fact give the explorers a moral right to kill Whetmore? What if the persons needing transplants read in the papers that doctors had informed a certain individual that he had only six more months left to live? Would they be justified in kidnapping and killing that individual because his interest in living only six months is negligible in comparison with the four of them surviving for many years if they can have his organs? But even the six months can be questioned. The doctors might have been in error as to his good health; or the doctors may have been correct but a month later a cure could be discovered. Possibilities always exist, and they existed even for Whetmore. For the explorers trapped in the cave could not be *certain* that they would not be rescued the next day or even the next hour. Suppose the engineers had been wrong or that another entrance to the cave had been found and the defendants had been rescued two hours after they had killed and eaten Whetmore; would the Justices of our Supreme Court have been as sympathetic about the murder?

Let us look more deeply at estimating the possibility of survival for the four defendants trapped in the cave and the four persons needing organ transplants in the hypothetical case. Surely we cannot coerce *them* to be optimistic about the chance of rescue or of some dramatic medical breakthrough. They have the right to assess the odds for themselves. My contention is simply that they cannot force their version of the odds for survival upon Whetmore or upon the individual who was told he had six months to live.

But such a conclusion does not mean that we should give them a privilege of acting "out of necessity" to harm or kill someone else. At the very most they might decide upon a procedure to save most of their own lives at the expense of one or more of their own number. For example, since each of the four persons needing transplants needed a different organ, any three of them could survive with the healthy organs of the fourth. Suppose the four of them are in the medical office and they put on the table four identical-looking pills, three of which are placebos and the fourth an instantaneous deadly poison. If each selects a pill one would die and his or her organs could immediately be transplanted to the others. Such a procedure, incidentally, would not involve any of them actually killing any of the others; at worst they would each be guilty of attempted suicide and the victim would be guilty of actual suicide. But from a moral point of view, I tend to believe at the present time—unless someone persuades me that I have not refined my personal code of morality sufficiently and that further thought would lead to a different conclusion—

that the four persons had a moral right to decide that three survivors would be better than no survivors and that such a procedure would thus be justifiable. Note that the decision to go ahead with the pill-taking was the result of the informed consent of all four persons, each of whom arrived independently at the conclusion that the odds of survival if no action was taken were negligible. The willingness to go ahead with this desperate procedure would prove the genuineness of each individual's decision as to the odds of survival.

Let us apply analogous reasoning to the explorers. Roger Whetmore, for his own reasons, which may have included optimism in a greater degree than any of the other explorers about the chances of an early rescue, did not want to participate in the cannibalism scheme. To be sure there are complicating elements: Whetmore first proposed such a scheme, he carried the dice used to cast lots, and he initially agreed to participate. Yet surely none of these points either in themselves or when taken together estops Whetmore to withdraw, or set up some sort of reliance by the others such that Whetmore could not fairly withdraw from the scheme. Their charging him with a "breach of faith" is outrageous. Such a charge might properly be levelled at one who attempted to withdraw from the scheme *after* being designated the victim, but it cannot be applied to a person who withdrew prior to the throw. Although the Justices of our Supreme Court have glossed over the significance of Whetmore's withdrawal, to me the point is of critical importance. By withdrawing, Whetmore both avoided the risk of being killed by the others and denied himself the chance to survive if the others went ahead with their plan. He chose to risk nothing and had nothing to gain. Certainly such an action cannot be labelled as unfair to others.

The others, however, *did have something to gain* by including Whetmore. To be sure, by including Whetmore, the others were taking a risk that Whetmore might end a winner. Curiously, however, when we examine the odds involved, the fact that Whetmore could be a winner is not as significant as the fact that he could be the loser. Consider the four men only. If one of them is to die so that the others will be saved, then each man's chance of dying is one in four, or 25%. If we include Whetmore, each man's chance of dying now becomes one in five, or 20%. In short, each of the four defendants in this case calculated—and they certainly did so calculate, for we know from the testimony that there was much discussion of the mathematical problems involved—that his own chance of survival *increased* by five percentage points from 75% to 80% if Whetmore was included. The forcible inclusion of Whetmore was distinctly in their self-interest. The motive for murder is clear.

Additionally we should not lose sight of the fact that the others had to *kill* Whetmore. A suicide procedure analogous to the pill-taking hypothetical might have been preferable in itself, but *such a procedure was not available to them.* We know Whetmore refused to throw the dice. Clearly he would have refused to take a pill. By his refusal to participate, Whetmore placed the burden of action upon the others. They had to kill him. In fact, they murdered him.

Although I believe that the preceding arguments establish the defendants' moral guilt, I recognize the possible objection that my position against the "necessity" excuse in criminal law proves too much. Surely there are situations where necessity is a legitimate excuse. What if Whetmore discovered on the twentieth day that his pickaxe, which he purchased with his own money, had a hollow handle filled with condensed food pills to be used in case of emergency. Assume that there are enough pills so that Whetmore and his companions could survive for another two weeks. Assume further that Whetmore had come to loathe his companions and offers only to sell them food pills at astronomical prices. When his companions *accept* his price, Whetmore decides that they could not be trusted to pay once they are freed from the cave, and so he asks for immediate payment in cash. At this point, would his companions have the moral right to take some of the pills away from Whetmore by force? I would say yes. But the distinguishing feature of this hypothetical is that a *property right* is being sacrificed to save one or more lives, whereas in the real case we are considering that a *life* can be sacrificed to save other lives. In short, property-for-life involves rights on a different level, whereas life-for-life involves rights on the same level. And when we operate on the same level, necessity is not a justification. Even in a property-for-property case, for example, a man facing bankruptcy cannot justifiably steal money from someone else so that he can save his own property.

At first blush my analysis may appear to be challenged by *Commonwealth* v. *Valjean,* a case cited by Justice Tatting, which refused to accept the excuse that the defendant stole a loaf of bread because he was starving. I suppose the court paused seriously over the trade between property and life in that case, but must have decided as it did because a decision in the defendant's favor would have had enormously

disruptive consequences for society. For if the law were to allow the theft of property by a starving man, many people might soon put themselves into a condition approaching starvation (for example, by first squandering their money in a gambling parlor) and then use that condition as an excuse for stealing food or money without restraint. Thus the harshness of the result to the defendant in *Valjean* is dictated by the need to deter others from exploiting such an "excuse." In contrast, the facts of the speluncean explorers clearly preclude the possibility of general exploitation for the purpose of obtaining nutriment.

Suppose we alter my hypothetical so that Whetmore finds enough pills only to keep one person alive for two weeks. Then if the others force him to share the pills, each will be kept alive for two or three days, but not until the rescue team breaks in ten days later. In that case, Whetmore would be justified in keeping all the pills for himself. But then this is not a case of property winning over lives, it is still a life-for-life case. For if the others forcibly took away from Whetmore the pills he needed to survive, they would be killing him, even though they may have then redistributed to Whetmore a two- or three-day supply equal to each of theirs. Thus even the *Valjean* case, upon further reflection, may be seen as a life-for-life case and thus explainable as directly analogous to the real case of the speluncean explorers. For if hungry people could steal loaves of bread, farmers would not grow as much wheat and bakers would not make loaves of bread for sale to others. The shortage of food would mean that all would starve, including the farmer, since starving men would take away all of his wheat. Allowing theft not only destroys the incentive to produce in order to sell to others, but also destroys the ability to grow wheat for one's own consumption, since as soon as it is grown it will be stolen by hordes of starving people. In brief, it may be very hard to find a true "necessity" case. And if my first pickaxe hypothetical example is such a case, it is different from that of the speluncean explorers.

Let us turn now to the legal analysis, which is coincident with the moral argument previously given. Clearly the statute under which the defendants were convicted covers the present case. Section 12-A of the Consolidated Statutes of Newgarth, N.C.S.A. (N.S.) § 12-A, provides: "Whoever shall willfully take the life of another shall be punished by death." I do not have to explore the question whether this statute admits of exceptions, and I need not repeat the arguments of the Justices of our Supreme Court on the question whether self-defense is one such exception. Suffice it to say that if the statute does allow for exceptions, "necessity" is not one of them since it is a life-for-life and not a property-for-life case.

Nor am I troubled by Justice Foster's argument that the explorers, trapped in the cave, were removed from the jurisdiction of Newgarth and hence the law cannot be applied to them. For one thing, the explorers are nationals and citizens of Newgarth, and on that basis our criminal laws may be extended to them even if they were outside the territorial limits of Newgarth. (Of course they were not; they were in a cave within the Commonwealth.) Second, they killed a national of Newgarth and thereby harmed the Commonwealth itself; accordingly Newgarth has a right of vindication through its criminal law process. Third, the defendants expected to be rescued by citizens of Newgarth, and hence their "captors"—the first persons who would have jurisdiction over them—would be persons subject to our laws. Fourth, the taking of the life of another is the gravest possible violation of a human right enjoyed by everyone wherever located. Even if Judge Foster were correct that legislative power did not reach these explorers in their cave, our laws would provide a statutory and administrative basis for enforcing the universal prohibition against murder wherever perpetrated.

Finally, legal analysis requires us to consider the purpose of the statute. The purpose of the present or any other criminal statute is not primarily to punish someone for a past act, but to deter the act from ever taking place. Such statutes institutionalize rights—the rights accorded to every person to *not* be the victim of criminal acts. The purpose of the statute in the present case, therefore, is to give to potential murder victims the protective power of the state. We might imagine Roger Whetmore saying something like the following to the four explorers as they advanced upon him: "What you are about to do is to commit murder. If you do so, and you survive and are rescued from this cave, the Commonwealth of Newgarth will try, convict, and execute you for murder. So do not attempt to kill me. I have not participated in your casting of lots, and you have no rights against me. Either try to hold out a while longer, as I have decided to do, or else do whatever you feel you must among the four of you alone. But do not include me; the law protects me against death at your hands."

Some such statement, I submit, is the only protection that the Whetmores of this Commonwealth may have when they are outnumbered and cannot protect themselves. As I have said earlier, the situation need not be so rare as explorers trapped in a cave; it includes my organ-transplant hypothetical, and any situation where a potential victim must rely on the law for protection. Our Supreme Court has upheld the law. Certainly as Chief Executive you should not undercut the sanction provided by the statute by commuting the sentence. What the defendants did in this case they did willfully. They acted out of self-interest, to increase the odds of their individual survival by forcibly including Whetmore. Now each defendant should pay fully for the murder he committed to advance his self-interest at the expense of the life of another.

---

1. Fuller, The Case of the Speluncean Explorers, *62 Harv. L. Rev. 616 (1949).*
2. See *R. Dworkin, Taking Rights Seriously (1977); R. Sartorius, Individual Conduct and Social Norms 163–210 (1975);* Jurisprudence Symposium, *11 Ga. L. Rev. 969–1424 (1977).* See also *D'Amato, Judicial Legislation, 1 Cardozo L. Rev. 63 (1979).*
3. *Five members of the Speluncean Society—the four defendants and Roger Whetmore—left indications at the headquarters of the Society concerning the location of a cave they proposed to explore. Upon their failure to return, the Secretary of the Society organized a rescue party. The rescue party found that a landslide had blocked the only known entrance to the cave, sealing the explorers inside. The task of rescue proved to be greatly expensive, new landslides occurred, several rescuers perished, and success was only achieved on the thirty-second day.*

On the twentieth day of their imprisonment the explorers established radio contact with the rescue camp. The engineers outside informed them that it would take at least ten days to release them even if no new landslides occurred. The explorers then asked for a medical opinion whether they would be likely to survive without food; the reply was that there was little possibility of survival. Whetmore, speaking on behalf of himself and the others, asked whether they would be able to survive for ten days longer if they consumed
the flesh of one of their number. The physicians reluctantly answered in the affirmative. Whetmore then asked whether it would be advisable for them to cast lots to determine which of them should be eaten, but no one in the rescue camp was willing to answer. When the imprisoned men were released it was learned that on the twenty-third day Whetmore had been killed and eaten by his four companions.

Testimony established that Whetmore first proposed that cannibalism might make it possible for four members to survive. He also was the one who first proposed the use of some method of casting lots. The defendants were reluctant to adopt so desperate a procedure, but after deliberation, including much discussion of the mathematical problems involved, agreement was finally reached on a method of determining the issue by the use of dice.

Before the dice were cast, however, Whetmore withdrew from the arrangement, as he had decided on reflection to wait for another week before embracing an expedient so frightful and odious. The others charged him with a breach of faith and proceeded to cast the dice. When it came Whetmore's turn, the defendants cast the dice for him, and he was asked to declare any objections he might have to the fairness of the throw. He stated that he had no such objections. The throw went against him, and he was put to death and eaten by his companions. See *Fuller, supra* note 1, at 616–18.

PEOPLE V. GOETZ*

New York Court of Appeals, 1986

WACHTLER, C.J. A Grand Jury has indicted defendant on attempted murder, assault, and other charges for having shot and wounded four youths on a New York City subway train after one or two of the youths approached him and asked for $5. The lower courts, concluding that the prosecutor's charge to the Grand Jury on the defense of justification was erroneous, have dismissed the attempted murder, assault and weapons possession charges. We now reverse and reinstate all counts of the indictment.

The precise circumstances of the incident giving rise to the charges against defendant are disputed, and ultimately it will be for a trial jury to determine what occurred. We feel it necessary, however, to provide some factual background to properly frame the legal issues before us. Accordingly, we have summarized the facts as they appear from the evidence before the Grand Jury. We stress, however, that we do not purport to reach any conclusions or holding as to exactly what transpired or whether defendant is blameworthy. The credibility of witnesses and the reasonableness of defendant's conduct are to be resolved by the trial jury.

On Saturday afternoon, December 22, 1984, Troy Canty, Darryl Cabey, James Ramseur, and Barry Allen boarded an IRT express subway train in The Bronx and headed south toward lower Manhattan. The four youths rode together in the rear portion of the seventh car of the train. Two of the four, Ramseur and Cabey, had screwdrivers inside their coats, which they said were to be used to break into the coin boxes of video machines.

Defendant Bernhard Goetz boarded this subway train at 14th Street in Manhattan and sat down on a bench towards the rear section of the same car occupied by the four youths. Goetz was carrying an unlicensed .38 caliber pistol loaded with five rounds of ammunition in a waistband holster. The train left the 14th Street station and headed towards Chambers Street.

It appears from the evidence before the Grand Jury that Canty approached Goetz, possibly with Allen beside him, and stated "give me five dollars." Neither Canty nor any of the other youths displayed a weapon. Goetz responded by standing up, pulling out his handgun and firing four shots in rapid succession. The first shot hit Canty in the chest; the second struck Allen in the back; the third went through Ramseur's arm and into his left side; the fourth was fired at Cabey, who apparently was then standing in the corner of the car, but missed, deflecting instead off of a wall of the conductor's cab. After Goetz briefly surveyed the scene around him, he fired another shot at Cabey, who then was sitting on the end bench of the car. The bullet entered the rear of Cabey's side and severed his spinal cord.

All but two of the other passengers fled the car when, or immediately after, the shots were fired. The conductor, who had been in the next car, heard the shots and instructed the motorman to radio for emergency assistance. The conductor then went into the car where the shooting occurred and saw Goetz sitting on a bench, the injured youths lying on the floor or slumped against a seat, and two women who had apparently taken cover, also lying on the floor. Goetz told the conductor that the four youths had tried to rob him.

While the conductor was aiding the youths, Goetz headed towards the front of the car. The train had stopped just before the Chambers Street station and Goetz went between two of the cars, jumped onto the tracks and fled. Police and ambulance crews arrived at the scene shortly thereafter. Ramseur and Canty, initially listed in critical condition, have fully recovered. Cabey remains paralyzed, and has suffered some degree of brain damage.

*68 N.Y.2d 96, 497 N.E.2d 41 (1986).

On December 31, 1984, Goetz surrendered to police in Concord, New Hampshire. . . . [A]fter receiving *Miranda* warnings, he made two lengthy statements, both of which were tape recorded with his permission. In the statements . . . Goetz admitted that he had been illegally carrying a handgun in New York City for three years. He stated that he had first purchased a gun in 1981 after he had been injured in a mugging. Goetz also revealed that twice between 1981 and 1984 he had successfully warded off assailants simply by displaying the pistol.

According to Goetz's statement, the first contact he had with the four youths came when Canty, sitting or lying on the bench across from him, asked "how are you," to which he replied "fine." Shortly thereafter, Canty, followed by one of the other youths, walked over to the defendant and stood to his left, while the other two youths remained to his right, in the corner of the subway car. Canty then said "give me five dollars." Goetz stated that he knew from the smile on Canty's face that they wanted to "play with me." Although he was certain that none of the youths had a gun, he had a fear, based on prior experiences, of being "maimed."

Goetz then established "a pattern of fire," deciding specifically to fire from left to right. His stated intention at that point was to "murder [the four youths], to hurt them, to make them suffer as much as possible." When Canty again requested money, Goetz stood up, drew his weapon, and began firing, aiming for the center of the body of each of the four. Goetz recalled that the first two he shot "tried to run through the crowd [but] they had nowhere to run." Goetz then turned to his right to "go after the other two." One of these two "tried to run through the wall of the train, but . . . he had nowhere to go." The other youth (Cabey) "tried pretending that he wasn't with [the others]" by standing still, holding on to one of the subway hand straps, and not looking at Goetz. Goetz nonetheless fired his fourth shot at him. He then ran back to the first two youths to make sure they had been "taken care of." Seeing that they had both been shot, he spun back to check on the latter two. Goetz noticed that the youth who had been standing still was now sitting on a bench and seemed unhurt. As Goetz told the police, "I said '[y]ou seem to be all right, here's another,'" and he then fired the shot which severed Cabey's spinal cord. Goetz added that "if I was a little more under self-control . . . I would have put the barrel against his forehead and fired." He also admitted that "if I had had more [bullets], I would have shot them again, and again, and again." . . .

Penal Law article 35 recognizes the defense of justification, which "permits the use of force under certain circumstances." One such set of circumstances pertains to the use of force in defense of a person, encompassing both self-defense and defense of a third person. Penal Law § 35.15 (1) sets forth the general principles governing all such uses of force: "[a] person may . . . use physical force upon another person when and to the extent he *reasonably believes* such to be necessary to defend himself or a third person from what he *reasonably believes* to be the use or imminent use of unlawful physical force by such other person" (emphasis added).

Section 35.15 (2) sets forth further limitations on these general principles with respect to the use of "deadly physical force": "A person may not use deadly physical force upon another person under circumstances specified in subdivision one unless (a) He *reasonably believes* that such other person is using or about to use deadly physical force . . . or (b) He *reasonably believes* that such other person is committing or attempting to commit a kidnapping, forcible rape, forcible sodomy or robbery" (emphasis added). . . .

Because the evidence before the second Grand Jury included statements by Goetz that he acted to protect himself from being maimed or to avert a robbery, the prosecutor correctly chose to charge the justification defense in section 35.15 to the Grand Jury. The prosecutor properly instructed the grand jurors to consider whether the use of deadly physical force was justified to prevent either serious physical injury or a robbery, and, in doing so, to separately analyze the defense with respect to each of the charges. He elaborated upon the prerequisites for the use of deadly physical force essentially by reading or paraphrasing the language in Penal Law § 35.15. The defense does not contend that he committed any error in this portion of the charge.

When the prosecutor had completed his charge, one of the grand jurors asked for clarification of the term "reasonably believes." The prosecutor responded by instructing the grand jurors that they were to consider the circumstances of the incident and determine "whether the defendant's conduct was that of a reasonable man in the defendant's situation." It is this response by the prosecutor—and specifically his use of "a reasonable man"—which is the basis for the dismissal of the charges by the lower courts. As expressed repeatedly in the Appellate Division's plurality opinion, because section 35.15 uses the term "*he* reasonably believes," the appropriate test, according to that court, is whether a defendant's beliefs and re-

actions were "reasonable to *him*." Under that reading of the statute, a jury which believed a defendant's testimony that he felt that his own actions were warranted and were reasonable would have to acquit him, regardless of what anyone else in defendant's situation might have concluded. Such an interpretation defies the ordinary meaning and significance of the term "reasonably" in a statute, and misconstrues the clear intent of the Legislature, in enacting section 35.15, to retain an objective element as part of any provision authorizing the use of deadly physical force.

Penal statutes in New York have long codified the right recognized at common law to use deadly physical force, under appropriate circumstances, in self-defense. These provisions have never required that an actor's belief as to the intention of another person to inflict serious injury be correct in order for the use of deadly force to be justified, but they have uniformly required that the belief comport with an objective notion of reasonableness. . . .

In 1961 the Legislature established a Commission to undertake a complete revision of the Penal Law and the Criminal Code. The impetus for the decision to update the Penal Law came in part from the drafting of the Model Penal Code by the American Law Institute, as well as from the fact that the existing law was poorly organized and in many aspects antiquated. . . . While using the Model Penal Code provisions on justification as general guidelines . . . the drafters of the new Penal Law did not simply adopt them verbatim.

The provisions of the Model Penal Code with respect to the use of deadly force in self-defense reflect the position of its drafters that any culpability which arises from a mistaken belief in the need to use such force should be no greater than the culpability such a mistake would give rise to if it were made with respect to an element of a crime. Accordingly, under Model Penal Code § 3.04 (2) (b), a defendant charged with murder (or attempted murder) need only show that he "*believed[d]* that [the use of deadly force] was necessary to protect himself against death, serious bodily injury, kidnapping or [forcible] sexual intercourse" to prevail on a self-defense claim (emphasis added). If the defendant's belief was wrong, and was recklessly, or negligently formed, however, he may be convicted of the type of homicide charge requiring only a reckless or negligent, as the case may be, criminal intent (see, Model Penal Code § 3.09 . . .).

New York did not follow the Model Penal Code's equation of a mistake as to the need to use deadly force with a mistake negating an element of a crime, choosing instead to use a single statutory section which would provide either a complete defense or no defense at all to a defendant charged with any crime involving the use of deadly force. The drafters of the new Penal Law adopted in large part the structure and content of Model Penal Code § 3.04, but, crucially, inserted the word "reasonably" before "believes."

The plurality below agreed with defendant's argument that the change in the statutory language from "reasonable ground," used prior to 1965, to "he reasonably believes" in Penal Law § 35.15 evinced a legislative intent to conform to the subjective standard contained in Model Penal Code § 3.04. This argument, however, ignores the plain significance of the insertion of "reasonably." Had the drafters of section 35.15 wanted to adopt a subjective standard, they could have simply used the language of section 3.04. "Believes" by itself requires an honest or genuine belief by a defendant as to the need to use deadly force. Interpreting the statute to require only that the defendant's belief was "reasonable to *him*," as done by the plurality below, would hardly be different from requiring only a genuine belief; in either case, the defendant's own perceptions could completely exonerate him from any criminal liability.

We cannot lightly impute to the Legislature an intent to fundamentally alter the principles of justification to allow the perpetrator of a serious crime to go free simply because that person believed his actions were reasonable and necessary to prevent some perceived harm. To completely exonerate such an individual, no matter how aberrational or bizarre his thought patterns, would allow citizens to set their own standards for the permissible use of force. . . .

We can only conclude that the Legislature retained a reasonableness requirement to avoid giving a license for such actions. . . .

Goetz also argues that the introduction of an objective element will preclude a jury from considering factors such as the prior experiences of a given actor and thus, require it to make a determination of "reasonableness" without regard to the actual circumstances of a particular incident. This argument, however, falsely presupposes that an objective standard means that the background and other relevant characteristics of a particular actor must be ignored. To the contrary, we have frequently noted that a determination of reasonableness must be based on the "circumstances" facing a defendant or his "situation." Such terms encompass more than the physical movements of the potential assailant. [T]hese terms include any relevant knowledge the defendant had about that per-

son. They also necessarily bring in the physical attributes of all persons involved, including the defendant. Furthermore, the defendant's circumstances encompass any prior experiences he had which could provide a reasonable basis for a belief that another person's intentions were to injure or rob him or that the use of deadly force was necessary under the circumstances. . . .

The prosecutor's instruction to the second Grand Jury that it had to determine whether, under the circumstances, Goetz's conduct was that of a reasonable man in his situation was thus essentially an accurate charge. . . .

Accordingly, the order of the Appellate Division should be reversed, and the dismissed counts of the indictment reinstated.

THE CASE OF LADY ELDON'S FRENCH LACE:
A Hypothetical Decision on a Hypothetical State of Facts*

Sanford H. Kadish and Stephen J. Schulhofer

A perennial in the crop of attempt hypotheticals was suggested by Dr. Wharton.[1] "Lady Eldon, when traveling with her husband on the Continent, bought what she supposed to be a quantity of French lace, which she hid, concealing it from Lord Eldon in one of the pockets of the coach. The package was brought to light by a customs officer at Dover. The lace turned out to be an English manufactured article, of little value, and of course, not subject to duty. Lady Eldon had bought it at a price vastly above its value, believing it to be genuine, intending to smuggle it into England." Dr. Wharton, supra, and Professor Sayre[2] conclude that she could be found guilty of an attempt since she intended to smuggle dutiable lace into England. Professor Keedy disagrees, finding the fallacy of the argument in the failure to recognize "that the particular lace which Lady Eldon intended to bring into England was not subject to duty and therefore, although there was the wish to smuggle, there was not the intent to do so."[3]

Keedy was employing the distinction he has advanced between intent, on the one hand, and motive, desire, and expectation, on the other,[4] a distinction

that served as the linchpin of the decision in *People* v. *Jaffe* . . . and *United States* v. *Berrigan*. . . . As he sees it, what people intend to do on a particular occasion is to be determined by what they do in fact, rather than by what they thought they were doing. The lace was in fact not dutiable; thus, there was no intent on the part of Lady Eldon to smuggle dutiable French lace into the country, and there could be no conviction of the crime of attempt to do so, since what she intended to do on this view was not a crime—a straightforward case of legal impossibility. Professor Perkins has not, so far as we can tell, addressed himself to this particular case. But from what he has written it is clear that he would concur with Keedy. Presumably his analysis would rest on his distinction between primary and secondary intent.[5] Only the former may be considered in determining the existence of the necessary intent to establish an attempt. It, like Keedy's term *intent,* is determined by what the actor objectively and in fact did. What the actor believed he was doing, on the level of the facts as the actor took them to be, constitutes secondary intent. Apparently the latter is basically the same in description and

---

*From Sanford H. Kadish and Stephen J. Schulhofer, "The Case of Lady Eldon's French Lace," in *Criminal Law and Its Processes,* by Sanford Kadish and Stephen Schulhofer,

(Boston: Little, Brown and Co., 1989), pp. 669–675. Reprinted by permisison of Little, Brown and Company.

function as what Keedy refers to as the motive, desire, or expectation.

We concur with Wharton and Sayre.

We submit, with respect, that Keedy and Perkins, and the courts that follow their reasoning, have been guilty of some plain silliness in supporting their position. Their conclusion that Lady Eldon must be acquitted rests on the premise that what a person intends to do is what he actually does, even if that was the furthest thing from the person's mind:

"You're eating my salad."

"Sorry, I didn't mean to; I thought it was mine."

"You might have *thought* it was yours. But in fact it was mine. Therefore you intended to eat mine. You should be ashamed!"

Surely this is an extraordinary way of regarding what a person intended, quite at odds with common sense and common language. Where a circumstance is not known to the actor, there is no way consistent with straight thought that his act can be regarded as intentional as to that circumstance.

But, of course, it is hardly unknown for courts to adopt strained and artificial reasoning in support of a sound result otherwise thought beyond their reach. Is that the case here? Is it sound to conclude that the type of conduct engaged in by Lady Eldon should not be made criminal? Let us consider if it is.

Suppose Lady Eldon believed she had purchased an inexpensive English lace but in fact had purchased an expensive French lace. Certainly she could not be found guilty of smuggling if she got past the customs inspector or of an attempt if she failed. The reason is that the intent to smuggle French lace, necessary to establish either offense, does not exist. (We are assuming this is not a crime of absolute liability.) And it does not exist because her intent is judged by what she believed she was doing and not by what she in fact did. Now why should it make any more difference in Wharton's hypothetical that her act was objectively lawful than it does in our variation that her act was objectively unlawful? Why in both cases should not the intent be judged by the same standard, what she believed she was doing, rather than what she did in fact?

It may be answered that while an innocent mind can exculpate, a criminal mind simpliciter cannot implicate. The reasoning might be as follows: There is no legitimate purpose to be served by punishing those who mean to act blamelessly; and while a purpose could be served by punishing a person who decides to commit a crime (to the extent that all must first decide to commit an intentional crime before ac-

tually committing it, some will thereby be prevented from committing it, at this or another occasion) other considerations make it inexpedient and undesirable to do so. What are those considerations? They are those, presumably, which underlie the principle which forbids punishing a man for his thoughts alone; i.e., that thinking evil is not a reliable indication that a man will do evil and the criminal law may properly concern itself only with acts. . . .

But can this be said of Lady Eldon? Has she merely *thought* to smuggle French lace? Or rather has she *done* everything in her power and all she thought necessary to smuggle French lace? Has she shown herself to be less eligible for the imposition of criminal sanctions because, through no fault of her own, she failed? Surely not.

From the basic postulate that the law concerns itself with acts and not thoughts, it may be argued that the law is concerned not with what a person *may* do but with what he in fact *does*. This, however, is quite erroneous. There are many crimes that may be established without proof that acts have occurred that have invaded the interest sought to be protected. The law of attempts and conspiracy are prime examples. It is what is apprehended that the actor would subsequently do and not what he has done that constitutes the basis of criminality. As Holmes has pointed out, even larceny may be viewed in this way, since there is no requirement that the possessor be permanently deprived of his property, only that the actor intend to deprive him of it.[7] Looked at objectively, apart from intent, the acts done may be wholly innocuous—like striking a match or having a quiet conversation. The innocuous acts are made criminal because, combined with the requisite intent of the actor, they demonstrate him to be sufficiently likely to commit the injury that the law seeks to prevent, to justify the application of criminal sanctions.

Perhaps it may be argued that there is a different policy consideration supporting exculpation in cases like Lady Eldon's—namely, that in real cases, as opposed to hypotheticals, intention must be proved rather than supposed, and it is too dangerous to the innocent to permit juries to speculate on a defendant's intent in the absence of actions that strongly evidence that intent. One may fully agree with this, however, without concluding that Lady Eldon should be acquitted. Of course it would be evidentiary of Lady Eldon's intent to smuggle if she had been found with dutiable French lace at the border. (But only evidentiary—after all, she might have thought it was English lace, or it might have been put with her things by her maid without her knowledge.) But why should it be held, as it was in *United States* v. *Oviedo* . . . that, since the lace was nondutiable in fact, a finding of intent will necessarily be suspect, regardless of the strength of the evidence? Is it not perfectly possible that a reasonable jury could find this intent beyond a reasonable doubt even if the lace was nondutiable? Suppose, for example, that the lace were carefully secreted in a specially tailored, concealed pocket of the coach; that the coachman testified to incriminating statements Lady Eldon made to Lord Eldon; that a letter from her to her sister, which described her newly bought "French lace" in exquisite and appreciative detail, had been introduced; that her receipt showed she paid a price appropriate for French lace rather than for the vastly less expensive English lace. There would seem little danger to the innocent in allowing a jury to find an attempt to smuggle French lace on these facts. Indeed, in cases like *Jaffe* and *Berrigan*, "attempt" is charged only because of the involvement of an undercover agent, whose participation prevents completion of the intended crime. Whatever else one may say about such investigatory tactics, they do not necessarily render suspect the evidence of the defendant's intent; indeed, in practice, they usually render that evidence far *less* speculative than it otherwise would be. The proper remedy for speculative and unreliable jury findings of intent is a court alert to preclude such findings in particular cases where the evidence is insufficient.

In the end, then, the arguments in favor of Lady Eldon (and those which have been used to reverse conviction in cases like *Jaffe, Oviedo,* and *Berrigan*) are founded on unpersuasive policy considerations rationalized by a peculiar and Pickwickian interpretation of what it means to intend to do an act, one that is utterly at odds both with the common usage of our language and its usage elsewhere in the criminal law.[8] *We conclude that the innocuous character of the action actually done (innocuous in the sense that it could not constitute a crime under the actual circumstances) will not save her from an attempt conviction if she believed that the circumstances were otherwise, and, had her belief been correct, what she set out to do would constitute a crime.* This is the principle that has found favor in virtually every serious statutory effort to deal with the problem, and in numerous decisions reached without benefit of a specific statute to tell the court that a person intends to do what he thinks he intends to do.

We must say a few words more about the final qualification to the principle just asserted; namely, that "had her belief (in the circumstances) been correct, what she set out to do would constitute a crime." The point can best be made by altering the hypothetical. Suppose the lace that Lady Eldon had purchased was in fact the expensive French lace she meant to buy. The customs officer at Dover brings it to light. He then says to Lady Eldon: "Lucky for you you returned to England today rather than yesterday. I just received word this morning that the government has removed French lace from the duty list." Could Lady Eldon be held for attempt to smuggle in these circumstances?[9] Certainly what she did and what she intended to do were not different simply because she acted one day later, when French lace was removed from the duty list. But there is this important difference: that at the time she acted, *what* she intended to do (always judged, of course, from her own perspective) was not a violation of the criminal law, even though she thought it was. Of course, in doing what she did she showed that she was a person who would break a law. But what law? The law against smuggling French lace? There no longer was such a law. The criminal laws generally? Fortunately our law has not gone so far in accepting that *any* possibility for social protection is sufficient to justify criminal punishment. A mere disposition to engage in conduct thought to be criminal is much too speculative a basis for inferring that the actor will engage in some other kind of conduct that *is* illegal. At least for purposes of criminal liability (as opposed to sentencing) we are not prepared to generalize proclivities beyond the proclivity to commit the specific crime charged.[10] And, as Professor Williams has pointed out, "if the legislature has not seen fit to prohibit the consummated act, a mere approach to consummation should a fortiori be guiltless. Any other view would offend against the principle of legality; in effect the law of attempt would be used to manufacture a new crime, when the legislature has left the situation outside the ambit of the law." Glanville Williams, Criminal Law: The General Part 633–634 (2d ed. 1961). Had the criminal law been changed as supposed in our variation of the Lady Eldon hypothetical, therefore, it would be just as wrong to convict her as to convict an abortionist of attempted abortion where the abortion was committed, unknown to the defendant, after the abortion law was repealed or held invalid. These are the true cases of legal impossibility.

But, it should be noted, these situations are totally different from cases like *Jaffe* and *Berrigan*, even though the courts in each case made it seem otherwise, by asserting that what the defendants intended to do could not have constituted a crime. What the abortionist intended to do (and did) could not constitute a crime because there was no such crime. What Jaffe and Berrigan intended to do (and thought they did) was indeed a crime. It is only through a perverse use of intent that we can say that Jaffe intended to receive honestly obtained property or that Berrigan intended to send out a letter the warden knew about, and that therefore they intended to do what was no crime at all.

Lady Eldon, in the actual hypothetical, in contrast to the hypothetical hypothetical, presents no more a case of genuine legal impossibility than do *Jaffe* and *Berrigan*. She will be convicted of attempt to smuggle French lace.

COMMENT, 5 Hypothetical L. Rev. 1, 3–4 (1962–1989): The hypothetical *Lady Eldon* decision is a good effort, but it doesn't quite work.

First: Consider the case of a voodoo practitioner who practices his art upon a doll firmly intending to kill his victim and believing he will succeed. Or consider a safecracker who tries to open a safe with magic incantations. Under the formulation of *Lady Eldon,* each of these defendants, more pathetic than dangerous, would be guilty of attempt. Conviction of the defendants in these cases would be no less absurd than their own actions.

The Model Penal Code, in recognition of this problem, gives a court the power to dismiss a prosecution or decrease the penalty if "the particular conduct charged to constitute a criminal attempt . . . is so inherently unlikely to result or culminate in the commission of a crime that neither such conduct nor the actor presents a public danger." Section 5.05(2). But this is to commend the matter to the discretion of the judge; it is not a statement of a rule of law. A better approach is that taken by the revised Minnesota Criminal Code which states an exception to its rule that impossibility is no defense where the "impossibility would have been clearly evident to a person of normal understanding." Minn. Stat. Ann. § 609.17.2. A similar solution has been developed by Professor Robbins, who proposes that a person be guilty of attempt only when "he purposely does or omits to do anything that, *under the circumstances as a reasonable person would believe them to be,*" is a substantial step in a course of conduct planned to culminate in commission of the crime.[11]

Second: The effort to deal with the so-called "true legal impossibility" problem comes off more smoothly than convincingly. Consider the following case. Two friends, Mr. Fact and Mr. Law, go hunting in the morning of October 15 in the fields of the state of Dakota, whose law makes it a misdemeanor to hunt any time other than from October 1 to November 30. Both kill deer on the first day out, October 15. Mr. Fact, however, was under the erroneous belief that the date was September 15, and Mr. Law was under the erroneous belief that the hunting season was confined to the month of November, as it was the previous year. Under the *Lady Eldon* formulation, Mr. Fact could be convicted of an attempt to hunt out of season, but Mr. Law could not be. We fail to see how any rational system of criminal law could justify convicting one and acquitting the other on so fragile and unpersuasive a distinction that one was suffering under a mistake of fact, and the other under a mistake of law. Certainly if the ultimate test is the dangerousness of the actor (i.e., readiness to violate the law), as *Lady Eldon* would have it, no distinction is warranted—Mr. Law has indicated himself to be no less "dangerous" than Mr. Fact.

Third: In formulating a rule that would eliminate the defense of factual impossibility in all cases, the opinion overlooks the strong case for retaining the defense in one class of cases. These are the cases in which the acts done by the defendant are as consistent with an innocent as with a culpable state of mind. Take for example the old saw about the professor who takes his own umbrella thinking it belongs to his colleague. The act is utterly neutral. A man taking his own umbrella conveys no evidence of guilt. Now of course the matter changes if it can be *proven* that he believed it was his colleague's umbrella. But proof of state of mind where there are only ambiguous acts to support the inference is inherently unreliable.

Consider how the Model Penal Code deals with this very concern when it addresses itself to a different problem, i.e., drawing the line between preparation and attempt. This is typically the situation in which the actor has not yet completed all he set out to do. In Section 5.01, the Model Penal Code not only reflects existing law in requiring some substantial step toward commission of the crime. It also requires that the step at the same time be "strongly corroborative of the actor's criminal purpose." Why is this required? It may be supposed that the primary function of this requirement is to avoid the risk of false convictions; the animating idea is that where the evidence of intent falls below a certain level we are not willing to allow the jury to speculate.

Now both the *Lady Eldon* opinion and the Model Penal Code are shortsighted for not seeing that the same concern may exist in the class of impossibility cases under discussion. In this respect the court in *Oviedo* . . . and cases that have followed its lead,[12] are on very solid ground. If apprehension of false convictions calls for the requirement that the acts strongly corroborate the intent in those cases where the acts fall short of what was intended by the actor, then the same concern calls for the same requirement where the actor has done all he meant to do. If it is answered that in the latter cases the completed pattern of conduct carries the criminal intent on its face, the response must be that while this is generally so, it need

not be so. The professor taking his own umbrella surely is such a case.

To put the suggestion in statutory form, we suggest the following amendment to the Model Penal Code's Section 5.01:

"A person is guilty of an attempt to commit a crime if, acting with the kind of culpability otherwise required for commission of the crime, he: (a) purposely engages in conduct that *strongly corroborates the required culpability and* would constitute the crime if the attendant circumstances were as he believes them to be. . . ."

---

1. *Criminal Law* 304 n. 9 (12th ed. 1932).
2. *Criminal Attempts, 41 Harv. L. Rev. 821, 852 (1928).*
3. *Criminal Attempts at Common Law, 102 U. Pa. L. Rev. 464, 477 n. 85 (1954).*
4. *Id. at 466–468.*
5. *Rollin M. Perkins, Criminal Attempt and Related Problems, 2 U.C.L.A.L. Rev. 319, 330–332 (1955).*
6. *The Common Law 72 (1881).*
7. *Consider the Missouri court's justification for reversing the conviction of a hunter for attempting to take a deer out of season where the evidence showed that he shot a stuffed deer, placed in the woods by a game warden, believing it to be alive: "If the state's evidence showed an attempt to take the dummy, it fell far short of proving an attempt to take a deer." State v. Guffey, 262 S.W.2d 152 (Mo. App. 1953).*
8. *For an actual prosecution presenting just this problem, see Regina v. Taaffe, page 270 supra. Consider also a news story that appeared during the 1974 sugar shortage in England: "Travellers trying to beat Britain's sugar shortage are smuggling more and more of it into this country. They do not know that importing sugar is legal. A woman filled a shoebox with sugar and wrapped it like a gift, with fancy ribbons and bright paper. Another woman had sugar in a can marked 'face powder.' Customs officials chuckled at the reaction of sugar smugglers when they found out there was nothing wrong in what they were doing." N.Y. Herald Tribune, Oct.*

22, 1974, reprinted in Glanville Williams, Textbook of Criminal Law 398 (1978).
9. *See the discussion in Chapter 1, pages 26–36 supra, concerning the use of evidence of other crimes committed by the defendant.*
10. *Ira P. Robbins, Attempting the Impossible: The Emerging Consensus, 23 Harv. J. Legisl. 377, 441 (1986) (emphasis added). See also N.J. Stat. Ann. §; 2C:5-1a(1). . . .*
11. *E.g.,* United States v. Bagnariol, *665 F.2d 877 (9th Cir. 1981).*
12. *On the issues raised by this statutory proposal, see Robbins, footnote 1 supra at 400–12:. . . Thomas Weigend, Why Lady Eldon Should Be Acquitted: The Social Harm in Attempting the Impossible, 27 De Paul L. Rev. 231 (1979). A related proposal has been developed by Professor Fletcher, who suggests that attempts be punishable only when two conditions are satisfied: "the actor must attempt an act punishable under the law, and, further, this attempt must be dangerous on its face." George P. Fletcher, Constructing a Theory of Impossible Attempts, 5 Crim. J. Ethics 53, 67 (1986) (emphasis added). Professor Fletcher locates his proposal in "a theory that stresses the individual's right to an autonomous sphere free of state intrusion. Being suspected of dangerous propensities does not in itself justify the state's incursions into our private sphere. The minimal demand is that the actor's dangerousness express itself in an objectively dangerous act that treads upon the rights of others." Id.*

THE M'NAGHTEN RULES*

House of Lords, 1843

(Q.I.) "What is the law respecting alleged crimes committed by persons afflicted with insane delusion in respect of one or more particular subjects or persons: as for instance, where, at the time of the commission of

---

*10 Cl. 2nd F. 200 at p. 209.

the alleged crime, the accused knew he was acting contrary to law, but did the act complained of with a view, under the influence of insane delusion, of redressing or revenging some supposed grievance or injury, or of producing some supposed public benefit?"

(A.I.) "Assuming that your lordships' inquiries are confined to those persons who labor under such partial delusions only, and are not in other respects insane, we are of opinion that notwithstanding the accused did the act complained of with a view, under the influence of insane delusion, of redressing or avenging some supposed grievance or injury, or of producing some public benefit, he is nevertheless punishable, according to the nature of the crime committed, if he knew at the time of committing such crime that he was acting contrary to law, by which expression we understand your lordships to mean the law of the land."

(Q.II.) "What are the proper questions to be submitted to the jury where a person alleged to be afflicted with insane delusion respecting one or more particular subjects or persons is charged with the commission of a crime (murder, for example), and insanity is set up as a defence?"

(Q.III.) "In what terms ought the question to be left to the jury as to the prisoner's state of mind at the time when the act was committed?"

(A.II and A.III.) "As these two questions appear to us to be more conveniently answered together, we submit our opinion to be that the jury ought to be told in all cases that every man is presumed to be sane, and to possess a sufficient degree of reason to be responsible for his crimes, until the contrary be proved to their satisfaction; and that to establish a defence on the ground of insanity it must be clearly proved that, at the time of committing the act, the accused was labouring under such a defect of reason, from disease of the mind, as not to know the nature and quality of the act he was doing, or, if he did know it, that he did not know he was doing what was wrong. The mode of putting the latter part of the question to the jury on these occasions has generally been whether the ac-

cused at the time of doing the act knew the difference between right and wrong: which mode, though rarely, if ever, leading to any mistake with the jury, is not, as we conceive, so accurate when put generally and in the abstract as when put with reference to the party's knowledge of right and wrong, in respect to the very act with which he is charged. If the question were to be put as to the knowledge of the accused solely and exclusively with reference to the law of the land, it might tend to confound the jury, by inducing them to believe that an actual knowledge of the law of the land was essential in order to lead to conviction: whereas, the law is administered upon the principle that everyone must be taken conclusively to know it, without proof that he does know it. If the accused was conscious that the act was one that he ought not to do, and if that act was at the same time contrary to the law of the land, he is punishable; and the usual course, therefore, has been to leave the question to the jury, whether the accused had a sufficient degree of reason to know that he was doing an act that was wrong; and this course we think is correct, accompanied with such observations and explanations as the circumstances of each particular case may require."

(Q.IV.) "If a person under an insane delusion as to existing facts commits an offence in consequence thereof, is he thereby excused?"

(A.IV.) "The answer must, of course, depend on the nature of the delusion; but making the same assumption as we did before, namely, that he labors under such partial delusion only, and is not in other respects insane, we think he must be considered in the same situation as to responsibility as if the facts with respect to which the delusion exists were real. For example, if under the influence of his delusion he supposes another man to be in the act of attempting to take away his life, and he kills that man, as he supposes in self-defence, he would be exempt from punishment. If his delusion was that the deceased had inflicted a serious injury to his character and fortune, and he killed him in revenge for such supposed injury, he would be liable to punishment."

THE INSANITY DEFENSE*

The American Law Institute

Article 4, Responsibility

Section 4.01. Mental Disease or Defect Excluding Responsibility

(1) A person is not responsible for criminal conduct if at the time of such conduct as a result of mental disease or defect he lacks substantial capacity either to appreciate the criminality of his conduct or to conform his conduct to the requirements of law.

(2) The terms "mental disease or defect" do not include an abnormality manifested only by repeated criminal or otherwise antisocial conduct.

Alternative formulations of paragraph (1)

(a) A person is not responsible for criminal conduct if at the time of such conduct as a result of mental disease or defect his capacity either to appreciate the criminality of his conduct or to conform his conduct to the requirements of law is so substantially impaired that he cannot justly be held responsible.

(b) A person is not responsible for criminal conduct if at the time of such conduct as a result of mental disease or defect he lacks substantial capacity to appreciate the criminality of his conduct or is in such state that the prospect of conviction and punishment cannot constitute a significant restraining influence upon him.

* * *

Comments § 4.01. Article 4. Responsibility

Section 4.01. Mental Disease or Defect Excluding Responsibility

The Problem of Defining the Criteria of Irresponsibility

1. No problem in the drafting of a penal code presents larger intrinsic difficulty than that of determining when individuals whose conduct would otherwise be criminal ought to be exculpated on the ground that they were suffering from mental disease or defect when they acted as they did. What is involved specifically is the drawing of a line between the use of public agencies and public force to condemn the offender by conviction, with resultant sanctions in which there is inescapably a punitive ingredient (however constructive we may attempt to make the process of correction) and modes of disposition in which that ingredient is absent, even though restraint may be involved. To put the matter differently, the problem is to discriminate between the cases where a punitive-correctional disposition is appropriate and those in which a medical-custodial disposition is the only kind the law should allow.

2. The traditional M'Naghten rule resolves the problem solely in regard to the capacity of the individual to know what he was doing and to know that it was wrong. Absent these minimal elements of rationality, condemnation and punishment are obviously both unjust and futile. They are unjust because the individual could not, by hypothesis, have employed reason to restrain the act; he did not and he could not know the facts essential to bring reason into play. On the same ground, they are futile. A madman who believes that he is squeezing lemons when he chokes his wife or thinks that homicide is the command of God is plainly beyond reach of the restraining influence of law; he needs restraint but condemnation is entirely meaningless and ineffective. Thus the attacks on the M'Naghten rule as an inept definition of insanity or as an arbitrary definition in terms of special symptoms are entirely misconceived. The *rationale* of the position is that these are cases in which reason cannot operate and in which it is totally impossible for individuals to be deterred. Moreover, the category defined by the rule is so extreme that to the ordinary man the

exculpation of the persons it encompasses bespeaks no weakness in the law. He does not identify such persons and himself; they are a world apart.

Jurisdictions in which the M'Naghten test has been expanded to include the case where mental disease produces an "irresistible impulse" proceed on the same *rationale*. They recognize, however, that cognitive factors are not the only ones that preclude inhibition; that even though cognition still obtains, mental disorder may produce a total incapacity for self-control. The same result is sometimes reached under M'Naghten proper, in the view, strongly put forth by Stephen, that "knowledge" requires more than the capacity to verbalize right answers to a question, it implies capacity to function in the light of knowledge. Stephen, *History of English Criminal Law,* Vol. 2, p. 171. . . . In modern psychiatric terms, the "fundamental difference between verbal or purely intellectual knowledge and the mysterious other kind of knowledge is familiar to every clinical psychiatrist; it is the difference between knowledge divorced from affect and knowledge so fused with affect that it becomes a human reality." Zilboorg, "Misconceptions of Legal Insanity," 9 *Am. J. Orthopsychiatry,* pp. 540, 552. . . .

3. The draft accepts the view that any effort to exclude the nondeterrables from strictly penal sanctions must take account of the impairment of volitional capacity no less than of impairment of cognition; and that this result should be achieved directly in the formulation of the test, rather than left to mitigation in the application of M'Naghten. It also accepts the criticism of the "irresistible impulse" formulation as inept in so far as it may be impliedly restricted to sudden, spontaneous acts as distinguished from insane propulsions that are accompanied by brooding or reflection. . . .

Both the main formulation recommended and alternative (a) deem the proper question on this branch of the inquiry to be whether the defendant is without capacity to conform his conduct to the requirements of law. . . .

Alternative (b) states the issue differently. Instead of asking whether the defendant had capacity to conform his conduct to the requirements of law, it asks whether, in consequence of mental disease or defect, the threat of punishment could not exercise a significant restraining influence upon him. To some extent, of course, these are the same inquiries. To the extent that they diverge, the latter asks a narrower and harder question, involving the assessment of capacity to respond to a single influence, the threat of punish-

ment. Both Dr. Guttmacher and Dr. Overholser considered the assessment of responsiveness to this one influence too difficult for psychiatric judgment. Hence, though the issue framed by the alternative may well be thought to state the question that is most precisely relevant for legal purposes, the Reporter and the Council deemed the inquiry impolitic upon this ground. In so far as nondeterrability is the determination that is sought, it must be reached by probing general capacity to conform to the requirements of law. The validity of this conclusion is submitted, however, to the judgment of the Institute.

4. One further problem must be faced. In addressing itself to impairment of the cognitive capacity, M'Naghten demands that impairment be complete: the actor must *not* know. So, too, the irresistible impulse criterion presupposes a complete impairment of capacity for self-control. The extremity of these conceptions is, we think, the point that poses largest difficulty to psychiatrists when called upon to aid in their administration. The schizophrenic, for example, is disoriented from reality; the disorientation is extreme; but it is rarely total. Most psychotics will respond to a command of someone in authority within the mental hospital; they thus have some capacity to conform to a norm. But this is very different from the question whether they have the capacity to conform to requirements that are not thus immediately symbolized by an attendant or policeman at the elbow. Nothing makes the inquiry into responsibility more unreal for the psychiatrist than limitation of the issue to some ultimate extreme of total incapacity, when clinical experience reveals only a graded scale with marks along the way. . . .

We think this difficulty can and must be met. The law must recognize that when there is no black and white it must content itself with different shades of gray. The draft, accordingly, does not demand *complete* impairment of capacity. It asks instead for *substantial* impairment. This is all, we think, that candid witnesses, called on to infer the nature of the situation at a time that they did not observe, can ever confidently say, even when they know that a disorder was extreme.

If substantial impairment of capacity is to suffice, there remains the question whether this alone should be the test or whether the criterion should state the principle that measures how substantial it must be. To identify the degree of impairment with precision is, of course, impossible both verbally and logically. The recommended formulation is content to rest upon the term "substantial" to support the weight of judgment; if capacity is greatly impaired, that presumably should be sufficient. Alternative (a) proposes to submit the issue squarely to the jury's sense of justice, asking expressly whether the capacity of the defendant "was so substantially impaired that he cannot justly be held responsible." Some members of the Council deemed it unwise to present questions of justice to the jury, preferring a submission that in form, at least, confines the inquiry to fact. The proponents of the alternative contend that since the jury normally will feel that it is only just to exculpate if the disorder was extreme, that otherwise conviction is demanded, it is safer to invoke the jury's sense of justice than to rest entirely on the single word "substantial," imputing no specific measure of degree. The issue is an important one and it is submitted for consideration by the Institute.

5. The draft rejects the formulation warmly supported by psychiatrists and recently adopted by the Court of Appeals for the District of Columbia in *Durham* v. *United States,* 214, F. 2d 862 (1954), namely, "that an accused is not criminally responsible if his unlawful act was the product of mental disease or defect." . . .

The difficulty with this formulation inheres in the ambiguity of "product." If interpreted to lead to irresponsibility unless the defendant would have engaged in the criminal conduct even if he had not suffered from the disease or defect, it is too broad: an answer that he would have done so can be given very rarely; this is intrinsic to the concept of the singleness of personality and unity of mental processes that psychiatry regards as fundamental. If interpreted to call for a standard of causality less relaxed than but-for cause, there are but two alternatives to be considered: (1) a mode of causality involving total incapacity or (2) a mode of causality which involves substantial incapacity. See Wechsler, "The Criteria of Criminal Responsibility," 22 *U. of Chi. L. Rev.* (1955), p. 367. But if

either of these causal concepts is intended, the formulation ought to set it forth.

The draft also rejects the proposal of the majority of the recent Royal Commission on Capital Punishment, namely, "to leave to the jury to determine whether at the time of the act the accused was suffering from disease of the mind (or mental deficiency) to such a degree that he ought not to be held responsible." *Report* (1953), par. 333, p. 116. While we agree, as we have indicated, that mental disease or defect involves gradations of degree that should be recognized, we think the legal standard ought to focus on the *consequences* of disease or defect that have a bearing on the justice of conviction and of punishment. The Royal Commission proposal fails in this respect.

6. Paragraph (2) of section 4.01 is designed to exclude from the concept of "mental disease or defect" the case of so-called "psychopathic personality." The reason for the exclusion is that, as the Royal Commission put it, psychopathy "is a statistical abnormality; that is to say, the psychopath differs from a normal person only quantitatively or in degree, not qualitatively; and the diagnosis of psychopathic personality does not carry with it any explanation of the causes of the abnormality." While it may not be feasible to formulate a definition of "disease," there is much to be said for excluding a condition that is manifested only by the behavior phenomena that must, by hypothesis, be the result of disease for irresponsibility to be established. Although British psychiatrists have agreed, on the whole, that psychopathy should not be called "disease," there is considerable difference of opinion on the point in the United States. Yet it does not seem useful to contemplate the litigation of what is essentially a matter of terminology; nor is it right to have the legal result rest upon the resolution of a dispute of this kind.

MENTAL ABNORMALITY AS A CRIMINAL EXCUSE*

Hyman Gross

I

A person's mental condition at the time he engages in criminal conduct may relieve him from criminal liability. When this is the case, we say that he is not criminally liable because he was not a responsible person at the time of the offense. To say that one was not responsible in this sense is to assert the most personal of all excuses. What interests us is not something about the performance but something about the actor. The actor is said not to have had available those personal resources that are necessary to qualify him as accountable for his conduct. Since he is not accountable he cannot be faulted for his conduct and so enjoys exemption from judgments of culpability.

Mental abnormality of a sort relevant to excusing exists, then, when mental resources necessary for accountability are lacking. There are four varieties of relevant abnormality: One is mental illness that, formerly in medical literature and still in legal literature, would be characterized as a *disease* of the mind, by virtue of a sufficiently definite pathology and sufficiently pronounced morbidity. Intoxication, whatever its source, is another variety. Mental defectiveness is a third sort of relevant abnormality, encompassing cases of serious deficiency mainly in intelligence but including deficiency of any mental capacity necessary to control behavior. Finally, there is a variety of abnormality that may be conveniently referred to as automatism, which includes behavioral phenomena diverse in origin but which all are instances of a gross separation of consciousness and action such as exists during hypnosis, somnambulism, and epileptic seizures.

Relevant impairments of mental capacity may have an origin which is extrapsychic or intrapsychic. Drugs, alcohol, hypnotic suggestion, a blow on the head, emotional shock, an extra chromosome, or a brain tumor are all ways in which incapacitation may

be produced by external interventions upon normal mental functioning. It is clear that a person may himself be responsible for some of these interventions by doing something to himself or allowing others to. When this is the case, he is deemed responsible for the resulting condition he is in, though not otherwise. Still, one's being responsible for his condition does not always entail being criminally liable for what he does while in that condition. If he suffers mental incapacitation sufficient for him not to be responsible, he is then treated as one who is not, regardless of his having been a responsible person with reference to putting himself in that condition. A person may ultimately cause himself to suffer sieges of delirium tremens by the gradual effects of his own alcoholic indulgence. Yet he is entitled to be treated as not responsible regarding acts done during those sieges no less than a person whose delusions have an origin utterly beyond his control. But if a person while responsible does things to put himself in a state of incapacitation in which harmful conduct is expectable— he intoxicates himself to a dangerous degree—he may be liable for that when the harm occurs or, even without it occurring, when he engages in conduct that threatens the harm. The reason is that incapacitating himself while still a responsible person is itself a dangerous act, and so may be regarded as culpable. Other examples would be persons who willingly submit to drugs or hypnosis under circumstances portending harm, or who place themselves in dangerous situations knowing they are epileptics or sleepwalkers prone to violence. Culpability in such cases properly extends only to conduct that produces the loss of capacity and not the further conduct that is engaged in while the person is not responsible. One person may kill another quite deliberately under delusions produced by drugs taken quite deliberately, yet culpability is not for deliberate killing because the accused is

---

*This essay appears in a slightly altered version at pages 293–316 of *A Theory of Criminal Justice,* by Hyman Gross (Oxford University Press, 1979).

not responsible at all for his homicidal conduct but only for the act of taking the drugs. Not without some awkwardness in principle, the lesser culpability is usually reflected in the criminal law by liability for homicide of a lesser degree.

When mental impairment is intrapsychic in origin, the excuse based on it is received more charily. The same debilitation which would easily pass muster for an excuse if externally induced is regarded with skepticism when its origin is not palpably outside the mind of the actor. Initial suspicion is indeed warranted because of increased opportunity for deception. But even after genuineness of the psychopathology is established, there is often lingering skepticism regarding its significance for judgments of responsibility. This skepticism is justified to the extent that it reflects sound opinion that the actor was quite capable of doing otherwise in spite of his illness. But it is not justified when it reflects the belief that a person is in some measure responsible for his mental illness since its origins are within him and, unlike the case of mental abnormalities having identifiable physical causes, it pertains to him in an especially intimate way because of its purely psychic character. Holding a person responsible for his mental illness is in general even more unjust than holding him responsible for his physical illness. Such medical knowledge as we have bearing on the etiology of serious mental illness makes it quite clear that in most cases the sick person could not reasonably be expected to do such things as would probably have prevented the onset of his illness, while in the case of physical illness effective precautions often might quite easily have been taken.

II

It is not any mental abnormality that excuses. Even when the abnormality is of a kind that is relevant to responsibility, certain conditions of incapacitation must be met if there is to be an excuse. In the criminal law these conditions have been formulated as rules which govern the insanity defense. These rules look mainly to mental illness and defectiveness, but the conditions for excusing under them have a rationale which extends to mental abnormality of whatever variety. Four basic versions of this defense have developed in the criminal law and, as shall be shown, the conditions required by each are less dissimilar from those required by the others than would appear from the terms used in formulating each. The first ver-

sion, which dominates among Anglo-American jurisdictions, turns out to be too meager. The second of these versions (which in some form is now the law in a third of the American jurisdictions and under the Model Penal Code) represents the most satisfactory statement. The third and fourth versions, though lending themselves to suitably restrictive interpretation, as they stand offer too great opportunity for unwarranted excuses and in fact are the versions most often preferred by those advocating unsound excuses. First, each version will be briefly scanned and then good reasons will be distinguished from bad among excuses of this sort. The concern here is only with why a person is not responsible, and so the very difficult medical questions having to do with exactly what states of abnormality leave a person in a condition in which he is not responsible will remain unexplored. Only the more basic question of what it means not to be responsible is taken up here. But without answers to that, one does not know what exculpatory significance, if any, to attach ultimately to the medical facts.

The first version of the insanity defense is represented by the M'Naghten rules. Stated in their original terms, these rules provide that a person has a defense of insanity if he did not know the nature and quality of the act he was doing, or did not know that it was wrong, because laboring under a defect of reason from disease of the mind. There was in the original M'Naghten rules a further proviso that, even if not so afflicted, a person would have a defense if at the time of his act he was suffering from an insane delusion about something such that if—but only if—it were in fact the case, it would furnish a defense. This part of the M'Naghten rules has been generally disregarded because of the limitation it places on delusions which may excuse, though as we shall see the right reason for ignoring the rule on these grounds has not been generally apprehended. There has been a continuing need for a rule extending the defense generally to all those who have insane delusions about the circumstances under which they act, and this requirement has encouraged strained applications of the remainder of the M'Naghten doctrine to cover such cases.

Despite variations in language and differences in fine points of interpretation, the gist of the M'Naghten formula has remained unchanged in the many jurisdictions that have adopted it since its introduction in England well over a century ago. Serious incapacitation may make it impossible for the actor to be sufficiently aware of what he is doing so that he could choose to do otherwise. It may deprive him of appreciation of the harmfulness of his conduct, or of appreciation of the harm itself, so that a normal disposition to restrain harmful conduct is not aroused. It may deprive him of the ability to comprehend the circumstances in which he acts and so make it impossible for him to choose not to do what under the circumstances is not justifiable. It may make him incapable of knowing that the law prohibits what he does, when only the fact of legal prohibition is a reason for not doing it. In any of these cases, because of a failure of personal resources he cannot help what he does.

The second version of the insanity defense consists of some form of M'Naghten to which is added an excuse based on grossly deficient inhibitory capacity. This additional part is usually referred to as the irresistible impulse rule, though any suggestion that the act need be impulsive to qualify would be seriously misleading. Under this provision, if the accused was incapable of restraining himself from doing what he knew he was doing and knew he ought not to be doing, he may invoke as an excuse his inability to exercise self-control.

The gravamen of this excuse is again the actor's helplessness in being unable to avoid doing or causing harm. The excuse is even stronger than the claim of compulsion that is asserted when one has been forced to do something harmful. Instead of succumbing to pressures which one is nevertheless able to resist, the person without significant capacity for inhibition is simply unable to resist. The excuse is sometimes misconceived, however, so that it is the untoward urge rather than the inhibitory failure which receives primary attention. This distorts the rationale of the excuse. We do not excuse because the actor wanted very desperately to do what he did. By itself powerful determination to do harm is not grounds for exemption from judgments of culpability. On the contrary, it is grounds for a judgment of greater culpability.

The third version of the insanity defense makes mental disease or defect, *when it produces criminal conduct,* the basis of an excuse for that conduct. This version has been adopted in four American jurisdictions (though recently discarded in the one that gave it the name by which it is best known), enjoys considerable psychiatric advocacy, and is generally referred to as the Durham rule. It relies heavily in practice on the same rationale of excuse as the previous version, but offers opportunities for the troublesome departures that will be discussed shortly.

A final version is constituted by those criminal insanity provisions in which mental derangement or deficiency at the time of the act is itself an excuse. The actor need only be seriously defective or not in possession of his faculties in order for his conduct in such a state to be excusable. Unlike the previous version, the relation between the abnormality and the criminal conduct is not of concern here so long as the two are contemporaneous. This version has in somewhat primitive forms preceded M'Naghten in the common law and now appears in the criminal law of some civil law jurisdictions. It enjoys strong support among those of the medical profession who are interested in these forensic matters and is probably even more congenial to psychiatric views of the insanity defense than is the Durham version. As with Durham there is heavy reliance in practice on the same rationale of excuse that support M'Naghten and irresistible impulse; but again, as with Durham, opportunities for excusing on other grounds are made possible, and these call for careful investigation.

III

The preceding discussion has shown what grounds the law has recognized for an excuse of mental abnormality when the excuse is presented in its most dramatic form as the insanity defense. Many of those who favor the third or fourth version of the insanity defense think it a good defense simply that a person was mentally ill at the time of his criminal act, or that his criminal conduct was a result of the mental illness he suffered at the time. There are three important arguments here, one grounded in moral considerations regarding avoidance of cruelty, and the other two in exculpatory considerations thought to apply to sick persons.

The first contention is that it is wrong to punish a person *when he is sick*. It is generally regarded as inhumane to neglect the suffering of those who are in a debilitated condition and even more inhumane to inflict further suffering on them. It would therefore be barbarous if the criminal law not only withheld comfort and cure from the sick who are subject to its processes but imposed upon such persons a penal regime. Directed to present concerns, this principle of humane treatment clearly requires that a person mentally abnormal at the time of his crime not be subjected to punitive treatment while he continues to be in such a state, but that instead he receive medical treatment.

The principle of humane treatment is unquestionably sound and must be given full effect at all times. It does not, however, confer a cloak of immunity on persons who are sick when committing a crime. Conduct may be culpable even though the actor had chicken pox, pneumonia or multiple sclerosis. It may be culpable when the disorder is mental rather than physical. When a sick person's conduct is culpable, he is to be treated for his illness so long as it lasts by those in whose hands he is placed by virtue of liability for such culpable conduct. But liability for culpable conduct is not avoided by the mere fact of sickness. It is also true that even determination of liability to punishment must be postponed if the continuing illness of the accused makes impossible the proceedings necessary for a just determination of liability, and that those having custody of him must during this time abide by the imperatives of humane treatment. But again there is nothing in this to entitle the accused to exemption from liability.

A second argument derives from general requirements for culpability. It is wrong to punish someone *for being sick*. The reason is that in being sick a person has not done anything blameworthy. Since merely falling ill does not constitute culpable conduct, it may not be punished. (A person might indeed be rightly blamed for making himself sick, or allowing himself to become or to be made sick, and we might well decide that such conduct then deserves punishment when it was understood that the well-being of others depended upon the fitness of the one who became sick. In such a case there is culpability because the accused could have acted to prevent his illness.)

But insofar as a person is being punished for his conduct and not for his disorder, the requirement of culpability is not transgressed. Nevertheless, it is sometimes claimed that when a mentally disordered person is punished for his conduct, he is being punished for his disorder since the conduct is a symptom of it. Such claims are especially prominent in arguments advocating extension of a mental abnormality defense to those persons, often characterized as psychopaths or sociopaths, whose dedication to wrongdoing is especially strong and free of internal conflicts. This claim rests on a misunderstanding of what it means to be punished for something. A person may be punished for a criminal act and that act may in various other perspectives be viewed quite accurately as a symptom of his illness, or indeed of society's illness, as an act of dedicated self-sacrifice, or as an act to advance a socially worthwhile cause. Still in all these cases we are punishing him only for his culpable conduct. We may punish in spite of causes, motives,

or intentions, so long as they do not furnish an excuse or other reason for not punishing.

The third argument is that it is wrong to punish someone for what he does *as a result of being mentally sick*. Unlike the previous argument, the position here is not that it is wrong to punish someone for the illness evidenced by criminal conduct, but rather that it is wrong to punish someone for his conduct when it is *produced* by the disorder. The criminal conduct is not viewed as part of a pattern of behavior such that if one so behaves one must by that very fact be judged to be abnormal. Rather the conduct is viewed as determined by the abnormality in the sense that but for the abnormality there would have been no warrant for expecting such conduct.

Treating the fact that conduct resulted from mental abnormality as a reason to excuse the conduct leaves us with no principle on which to rest the excuse. Exculpation by way of justification would indeed be warranted by a principle that what is morbidly determined is not wrong, but there are no good reasons for recognizing as a justifying principle the proposition that condemnation ought to be restricted to healthy determinations to act harmfully. It is true that a person's mental abnormality, if it is to excuse his criminal conduct, must in some significant way be related to that conduct as its cause. This may be put in an even stronger form by saying that we ought to excuse when, but only when, conduct is the "product" of abnormality in the sense that the abnormality is a sufficient condition for the conduct. In that case, but only in that case, the accused was unable to do otherwise because of the abnormality and so is entitled to be excused. It is not true that we ought to excuse simply because the wrong thing that was done would likely not have been done but for the abnormality. Otherwise we should have to excuse anyone who acted from some untoward tendency attributable to a mental abnormality whenever it is unlikely that he would have done the act if he were normal, even in cases where he was quite as capable of acting otherwise as is a normal person subject to the same tendency. This would mean that a bank employee ought to be excused when he embezzles money only because of powerful unconscious wishes to be caught which he could effectively have chosen not to succumb to, although another employee who embezzles only because tempted by healthy fantasies of a life of leisure ought not to be excused.

There is a fourth argument for not punishing wrongdoers who suffered from mental abnormality that in effect requires for an excuse too much rather than too little. It has eminent philosophical credentials and is to be found in the best legal circles as well. The argument derives from general considerations bearing on justification of punishment.

It is pointed out that prescribing punishment for what the insane do is futile since the threat of punishment can have no deterrent effect on such persons. Anyone, therefore, who considers the practice of punishment to be justified by its deterrent effect must hold punishment of the insane to be unjustified and, in fact, a purposeless infliction of suffering. It has been argued in reply that punishment of the insane may still have a deterrent effect on sane persons since it deprives them of hope of escaping punishment by successfully advancing fraudulent claims of having been insane at the time of their offense. That answer is good only to the extent that crimes are committed after decisions to commit them which include deliberation on possible legal tactics to avoid conviction. But since most crimes are committed without decisions of this sort, the deterrent effect of a threat of punishment that makes no allowance for insanity is in any event largely otiose.

There are, however, other answers to the "no deterrence" objection to punishing the insane that do not require belief in such fictitious deliberations by would-be criminals.

If it is being suggested that nondeterrability has been the rationale for the insanity defense in the law as it has developed, we may ask why the law does not refuse by the same rationale to punish those who were genuinely and blamelessly ignorant of the law they broke. Such persons were in a position indistinguishable from the insane with respect to the futility of prospective punishment, and so to punish them is equally a purposeless infliction of suffering. Yet, as we know, in the law as it stands such innocent ignorance does not excuse, and this inconsistency must raise doubts about this rationale for the insanity defense.

But there is a more cogent objection than one based on inconsistency. It is not the case that all, or perhaps even most, insane persons are incapable of being deterred by threat of punishment. Under the prevailing Anglo-American insanity defense, the M'Naghten rules, there is an excuse if the accused by virtue of a defect of reason from disease of the mind did not know he was doing what was wrong. The Model Penal Code similarly establishes as a defense a person's lack of substantial capacity to appreciate the criminality of his conduct (which means more than mere knowledge that it is criminally prohibited) as a result of mental disease or defect. There are many persons who fit these specifications in being unable to appreciate that what they do is wrong and in fact think it for some reason justified, yet are aware and in awe of the threat of punishment quite as much as normal persons. In some of the most notable cases of the insanity defense, the defendant committed murder under the delusion that he was carrying out a divine command, or was giving his due to a man believed to be very wicked, or was killing someone who was bent on harming him. Less dramatic but far more frequent are the family and sex intrigue homicides where the killing was done in a suitably extreme abnormal mental state—usually spoken of as temporary insanity—in which the accused was likewise at the time convinced that he was justified. There is no reason to believe that in general their abnormality rendered the accused in these insanity cases incapable of being deterred by the threat of punishment, though of course like many normal defendants they were not in fact deterred by it. There is, further, every reason to believe that certain abnormal persons who would be entitled to exoneration on grounds of insanity were in fact deterred, just as normal persons would be because the law has made the conduct they contemplated punishable. If these things were not so, the insanity defense could consist simply in establishing the one point that by reason of mental abnormality the accused could not at the time of his crime be deterred by the threat of punishment. In fact what distinguishes the sane from the insane under criminal law standards is the inability of the insane to appreciate the *culpability,* not the punishability, of their conduct. Because of their abnormality the insane cannot at the time apprehend what justifies condemnation of their conduct. Even though amenable to threats of punishment, they lack a resource of appreciation that is necessary if one is to have a reason apart from avoidance of punishment for not doing what the law prohibits. Punishing such persons is indeed a useless infliction of suffering, for it can not serve to uphold the standards that the criminal law exists to preserve.

There is one other argument against mental abnormality defenses that should be noted here. Again it is an argument that by implication requires too much rather than too little for excuse. Many persons who are mentally ill and have committed crimes are dangerous, yet the very abnormality that is evidence of his being dangerous serves to shield the accused from liability. Those who see confinement of dangerous persons as a principal purpose of the criminal law are particularly distressed by this, for in effect just those who are thought to be most properly the concern of the criminal law are allowed to escape its restraints.

The answer to this argument is that not all restraint by the state need be based on criminal liability. If a person is dangerous because of mental abnormality, he may be prevented from doing harm by noncriminal commitment regardless of whether his conduct provided a basis for criminal liability. It is true that persons usually are not found to be a menace for purposes of commitment unless they have done something which would at least provide the substance of a criminal charge. But it is still dangerousness of the person and not criminality of his conduct that warrants deprivation of liberty. Since determinations of dangerousness and determinations of criminal liability are independent matters, a defense of insanity to a criminal charge does not weigh against the accused's subsequent liability to commitment because he is dangerous. Conversely, elimination or postponement of the question of insanity when determining liability would result in branding as criminals persons, whether dangerous or not, who are not to blame for what they did.

IV

The rationale of excusing for mental abnormality may be summarized in this way. Certain forms of mental incapacity deprive a person of ability to act other than the way he does because resources for an effective choice are lacking. When a person lacks capacity to tell what he is doing, whether it is offensive, or what is likely to happen; or lacks capacity to appreciate its harmful significance, or to restrain himself, he is in such a condition. It is apparent that a person incapacitated in any of these ways lacks a resource necessary for control and so necessary for culpable conduct. It is for this reason that an excuse of mental abnormality preempts the field of excuse and makes excuses going directly to culpability inappropriate. There is no point in being concerned about whether something was intentional, when whether it is intentional or not the actor was not a responsible agent. And conversely, when there is a complement of those personal resources that are necessary for responsible conduct, there is a duty to draw upon such resources to avoid harmful conduct. It follows that when a normal person claims he did not at the time appreciate the significance of sticking a knife into another person—his mind was elsewhere—he offers a different kind of

excuse than the mentally abnormal man who makes the same claim. The normal man can only expect by showing less culpability to blunt an accusation of conduct of a higher degree of culpability—he didn't harm the victim knowingly, but only negligently through absentmindedness in failing to pay attention to the dangers of what he was occupied in doing. But the man who establishes that his failure of appreciation was due to a lack of necessary mental resources exempts himself from any judgment of culpability.

The distinction and connections between lack of responsibility and mere lack of culpability are important with regard to several difficulties surrounding the insanity defense.

We have already mentioned the usually discarded third part of the original M'Naghten rule. It provided that even if the accused person who suffered a defect of reason from disease of the mind could know the nature and quality of his act, and even if he could know that what he was doing was wrong, he still might have a defense if at the time of his act he suffered from a delusion such that had it been a correct belief it would have afforded a defense. This part of the rule has been dropped, but not in order to exclude insanity defenses based on delusion; in fact, delusion cases have always been recognized as paradigms of criminal insanity and are allowed in all M'Naghten rule jurisdictions by strained interpretations of the other parts. It is the limitation upon the kinds of delusion which are acceptable that has been found objectionable. The usual argument is that the limitation leads to absurd results. For example, in accordance with conventional legal rules that preclude criminal jurisdiction for crimes of foreign nationals committed in foreign countries, a homicide defendant in England who in a delusion at the time of his crime believed himself to be Bluebeard reenacting one of his murders in France would have a good defense. But a homicide defendant also in England who in his similar delusion believed himself to be Jack the Ripper would not. Even when the rule has been confined to delusions which bear on exculpatory claims (typically provocation and self-defense), as undoubtedly it was intended to be by its original proponents, criticism has not abated though the reason for rejecting the rule is less clear.

It seems, in fact, that the original rule was a sound one based on the premises concerning the facts of mental abnormality which the M'Naghten judges accepted, but that these premises are incorrect. The mistake from which the rule proceeded has been characterized as the doctrine of partial insanity. It holds that a person whose insanity consists merely in delusions is still capable of choosing to act in conformity with the law that governed the situation as he perceived it. He therefore is to be held accountable for not acting in conformity with law as it would apply to the situation he perceived, though by virtue of his inability to perceive the situation correctly he could not be held accountable for breaking the law with respect to the situation as it actually was. However, according to better medical knowledge, the fact of the matter is that such persons in the grip of their delusions are normally so severely incapacitated that they cannot even choose to act otherwise. We therefore cannot hold them responsible when they act as their delusion dictates and so must consider them ineligible for blame. Questions about matters of culpability (usually matters of justification) which the original rule raises are for this reason superfluous.

A second problem concerns what is meant by "wrong" under the terms of the M'Naghten rule. If the accused, because of a defect of reason from disease of the mind, did not know that what he was doing was wrong he has a defense on grounds of insanity. The question which has persistently troubled courts both in England and the United States is whether the failure of knowledge required is of legal or of moral wrong. Does a psychotic person who knows murder is a crime but believes he may nevertheless commit it because divinely commanded have a defense? What about a mental defective who knows he is not supposed to hurt other people but cannot even comprehend what a criminal law is? The Model Penal Code speaks of the accused's lack of capacity to appreciate the criminality of his conduct, but the difficulty remains, for appreciating the criminality of conduct is not the equivalent of knowing that it has been made a crime. Indeed the final draft of the Code provision offers "wrongfulness" as an optional substitute for "criminality."

The difficulty is removed by recognizing that what is crucial is capacity to know, rather than knowledge; and that it is a capacity to know something that is necessary for culpability. In a just legal system conduct ought not to be treated as legally culpable unless reasonable opportunity exists to become aware of its legal interdiction. Such opportunity for awareness has significance only if there also is ability to take advantage of it. That in turn depends on ability to appreciate the untowardness of conduct, ability to be aware of the range of normal concerns of the law, as well as the ability to become acquainted with the law itself. If there is disabling incapacity with respect to any of these necessary conditions the person incapacitated is not responsible, for to that degree he lacks ability to take advantage of the opportunity to become aware of criminal liabilities and so his conduct cannot be deemed culpable. It turns out, then, that it is misleading to ask whether legal or moral wrong is meant. The question to be answered is whether the accused was deprived of any abilities that are necessary to take advantage of the opportunity of becoming aware of criminal liability.

Another difficulty concerns the irresistible impulse defense. There has been great hesitation in legal circles in admitting as an excuse an inability to exercise self-restraint. It challenges common sense appreciation of behavior to assert that a person possessed of all the abilities necessary to control what he is doing, nevertheless does not have the self-control to choose effectively not to do it. The excuse is therefore often construed as a direct denial of culpability analogous to external compulsion—he didn't mean to do that, he was forced to—rather than as a denial of responsibility by virtue of incapacity. The excuse so construed is then rejected as being too easy a way out for persons who either have not chosen to resist with sufficient determination powerful untoward urges or have failed to take precaution against succumbing to the urge and are therefore no less culpable than persons who lose their temper and, while in the grip of their rage, commit crimes.

But this excuse of no responsibility becomes plausible as understanding of human pathology advances, and it becomes increasingly clear that there are serious mental abnormalities which consist in inability either by repression or precaution to inhibit acting on certain urges. The claim of irresistible impulse is then no longer construed as one simply of not having effectively chosen to do otherwise, but rather more, as not having the personal resources that are necessary to choose effectively.

V

A stark separation according to mental abnormality of those who are responsible from those who are not seems at times unsatisfactory. We are bound to recognize that sometimes there is not sheer incapacity with regard to elements of control, yet there is deviation from normal capacities great enough to make desirable a limitation on accountability. Accordingly, there has developed in the law a doctrine of diminished (or partial) responsibility which, though still only little and narrowly accepted, offers a path for receiving into the law continuing insights respecting varieties of limited impairment bearing on control of conduct. The most notable legal recognition so far has been in the English Homicide Act of 1957, which reduces what otherwise would be murder to culpable homicide when the accused suffered from such abnormality of mind as "substantially impaired his mental responsibility" for his acts. The rationale for diminished responsibility is simple. If a person who is incapacitated is ineligible for blame, a person who is seriously impaired though not incapacitated is eligible to be blamed only within limits. While not utterly bereft of resources required for accountability, his resources of control are diminished to a point where full faulting according to the tenor of the conduct is inappropriate. But for reasons previously given, it would be a serious mistake to construe the defense of diminished responsibility as a declaration that the somewhat sick, simply because they are sick, ought not to be held to a liability as great as that of the healthy person. Indeed, perfectly healthy persons who have perfectly natural reactions that put them in an abnormal emotional state may rightly claim diminished responsibility. Typically, this is the case when a person acts under the influence of extreme anger or fear because provoked or threatened.

Mental abnormality may affect culpability in a more direct way, however, and some confusion about this has arisen in discussions of diminished responsibility. By virtue of his abnormality, a person may be unable to act in a way that is criminally culpable, or at least not as culpable as the conduct charged. Or, though capable of such conduct, he may simply not have been acting in the way charged but rather was acting in some other way dictated by his abnormal processes. In either case he may lodge an exculpatory claim that his conduct is different than alleged with respect to elements bearing on culpability, and he would rely on the evidence of his mental abnormality to establish this. Such an exculpatory claim in essence is no different from the sort that is appropriate when a normal person has not acted culpably, but the kind of argument which supports the claim is different. Instead of evidence indicating simply that the accused was engaged in a somewhat different enterprise than alleged, the evidence indicates that by virtue of his abnormal mental condition at the time, the accused could not or simply did not engage in the enterprise alleged. Two exculpatory claims are made in this way. Both of them have as their point what in the language of traditional criminal law theory would be called a lack of *mens rea*.

Suppose a prisoner attacks a guard with a knife and inflicts serious wounds. The prisoner is charged with first degree assault, an element of which is intent to cause serious physical injury. It is claimed on his behalf that he was at the time suffering severe paranoid anxieties which led him to misinterpret a routine warning as a sign that he was about to be attacked by the guard, and that he slashed at the guard only to fend off what he believed to be imminent blows. Evidence of his abnormal state would tend to show that he did not have the specific intent to cause serious physical injury. This would mean that while admittedly he exercised control in conducting an assault, he did not exercise control with regard to those features of it that produced the serious injury. The act done, therefore, was something less culpable than the act charged. The same would hold true for a person accused of burglary, which requires an intent to commit a felony, and who at the time of breaking and entering a home was in such a mental condition as to be incapable of having any definite further purpose.

The other challenge to culpability by way of abnormality does not concern the purpose which informs the act, but rather the earlier stages of planning the accomplishment of objectives and attending to the course of conduct while it is in progress. Such operational design and supervision as is referred to by "malice aforethought," "premeditation," "deliberation," "willfully," and "knowingly" may be beyond the accused's capacities or may simply be nonexistent by virtue of his abnormality. Powerful effects of intoxication or of lingering mental illness may render a person unable or unconcerned to form the plan or to remain in control of its execution, and so one is required to conclude that his homicidal attack was not designed with reference to the death of his victim. The Model Penal Code extends this variety of abnormality defense to all cases where evidence of mental disease or defect is relevant to the question of whether the accused had a required state of mind at the time of the crime, so that even recklessness or negligence may be disproved by evidence of appropriate abnormality.

In both of these "criminal intent" challenges based on mental abnormality, it is not responsibility that properly is said to be diminished. Culpability is what is really claimed to be diminished, and diminished to a point where the conduct is less culpable than is required for the offense charged.

VI

The excuse of insanity has presented far greater difficulties than any other for the criminal process. The main reason is that the point of the proceedings is lost sight of and confusion arises in deciding who may appropriately answer the very different kinds of questions involved, and also in deciding what the consequences of accepting or rejecting the excuse ought to be.

Much of the controversy in which medical and legal views of the insanity defense appear to be at odds results from a failure to appreciate that the law must ultimately be concerned not with who is sick but with whose conduct is excusable. Deciding that issue requires several subsidiary decisions that fall peculiarly within either medical or legal competence. There must, in the first place, be standards which set forth generally the nature of the incapacities that render a person not responsible. It is these standards that constitute the rules of the insanity defense, and deciding upon them is the responsibility of those with legislative and judicial authority who must make the law. It bears emphasis that what is called for here is not some general description of relevant clinical abnormalities in language lawyers are used to. What is required is a statement of the kinds of mental failures (due to mental illness or defectiveness) that entitle us to conclude for purposes of criminal liability that the accused could not help doing what he did. Once there are such standards of mental abnormality, proceedings to judge the abnormalities of a particular defendant with reference to such standards are possible. Then it is the opinion of medical experts which must first be looked to in order to determine the nature of the defendant's debilitation and the extent to which it affects capacities necessary for responsible conduct. Such expert opinion may be critically examined by lawyers, as indeed any expert opinion may be in a legal proceeding to determine a disputed issue. But that is not a means of substituting an inexpert for an expert opinion, but only a way of ensuring that its acceptance is ultimately based on reason rather than authority. There is finally a decision of vast discretion that is normally made by the jury. It is a conclusion about whether, according to the expert account of the mental condition that is finally accepted, there is debilitation sufficient to excuse according to the legal standards. Asking psychiatrists for expert opinions about whether such standards of incapacity are met is asking them to perform a role which is not within their special professional competence. But the job to be done in making the ultimate determination does require specialized skill in sifting among psychiatric opinions to arrive at a sound appreciation of the defendant's mental condition with reference to those features that are significant for judgments of responsibility. The paramount procedural problem of the insanity defense is to combine this specialist's appreciation with the layman's considered views about when choices to act are no longer meaningful or even possible. There is for this reason a great deal to recommend in principle suggestions, such as H.L.A. Hart's, that we adopt an "apparently coarser grained technique of exempting persons from liability to punishment if they fall into certain recognized categories of mental disorder," on the model of exemption from liability for persons under a specified age. But the establishment of a comprehensive scheme of clear categories seems at the present state of medical art a remote prospect.

Another sort of misapprehension deflects concern from responsibility to other matters, at the cost of both justice and humaneness in the administration of the criminal law. It is assumed that determining the accused to be responsible and so liable to have his conduct judged culpable is a warrant for treating him punitively rather than therapeutically. But in fact, it is said, many persons who meet legal standards for responsible conduct are nevertheless quite sick and sending them to a prison rather than a hospital is uncivilized. It is urged that the mentally ill ought therefore not to be treated as criminally responsible.

The mistake here is in giving priority to existing institutional arrangements and then attempting to have rules of liability which are humane in their effect under those arrangements. A rational and morally concerned society designs its institutions to treat in a humane way those who are liable according to just principles of liability. When a person who is liable according to proper standards of responsibility and culpability is also sick, principles of humane treatment, which are in no way inferior moral considerations, require that he be treated as sick. To the extent that inappropriate treatment may at present be expected under existing institutional arrangements and regimes, that is cause for reform of institutional arrangements and regimes, not of the rules of criminal liability.

STATE V. GUIDO*

New Jersey Supreme Court, 1963

WEINTRAUB, C.J. Adele Guido was convicted of murder in the second degree and sentenced to imprisonment for a minimum of 24 years and a maximum of 27 years. She appeals directly to this Court. . . .

The victim was defendant's husband. When they first met, she was a young girl and he a professional fighter of some success. . . .

All the details of the marital discord need not be stated. [Defendant] wanted a divorce, while decedent insisted upon holding on to her notwithstanding he would not or could not end his extra marital romance and assume the role of a responsible husband and parent. . . . In the early morning of April 17, 1961, after deceased fell asleep on a couch in the living room while watching television, defendant, according to her testimony, took the gun and went into her room, intending to end her life. Deciding that suicide would be no solution, she returned to the living room to put the weapon back in the suitcase, but when her eyes fell upon Guido, she raised the weapon and fired until it was empty.

With respect to physical abuse, the jury could find that although there were only a few incidents of actual injury, there was the constant threat of it from a man who had to have his way and who would not let go of a woman who had had her fill. It appears that on several occasions shortly before the homicide defendant called the local police to express her fear of harm. . . .

Defendant claimed "temporary" insanity. She was examined by two court-appointed psychiatrists. [Their] report contained sundry medical findings and ultimately the opinion that defendant was "legally" sane at the time of the shooting. Mr. Saltzman [defense counsel] met with the psychiatrists, and after some three hours of debate the psychiatrists changed their opinion as to "legal" insanity although their underlying medical findings remained the same. They then retyped the last page of their report.

On cross-examination of the first defense psychiatrist, it was developed that the original report had been revised. We do not know how the prosecutor learned of the change. The record shows that on its own initiative the court immediately directed that "Counsel shall produce the original report to the prosecutor." . . . What followed was some high drama that the occasion did not warrant.

Mr. Saltzman . . . returned from his office with the original report. The court undertook to interrogate him [out of the presence of the jury] with respect to the receipt of the changed last page. . . . With much formality the trial court . . . elicited step by step the receipt and transmittal of the papers. . . . The trial then resumed before the jury. . . .

Defense counsel and defense psychiatrists were thus subjected to a humiliating experience. Later the prosecutor berated them in his summation. He said "the defense in this case—I am sorry to say this—has been concocted"; . . . that Mr. Saltzman was "in cahoots with Doctors Galen and Chodosh and perpetrated a fraud on this Court"; and "how, how can you believe a woman who lends herself to the deception that was practiced on the Court, on this Court by the doctors and her attorney? Certainly she knew about it."

The trial judge did not stop this unjustifiable attack. On the contrary he intervened in a way that tended to sustain it. . . .

When the basis of the change in the experts' opinion was explored, it quickly appeared that the change was thoroughly consistent with honesty however mistaken it might be. In the minds of the witnesses the change involved no alteration whatever in their medical findings. Rather it stemmed from an altered understanding of the law's concept of insanity. Specifically, the doctors originally understood that the "disease of the mind" required by the *M'Naghten* concept of legal insanity to which we adhere, means a

*40 N.J. 191, 191 A.2d 45 (1963).

psychosis and not some lesser illness or functional aberration. As the result of their pretrial debate with Mr. Saltzman, the doctors concluded they had had too narrow a view of M'Naghten and that the "anxiety neurosis" they had found did qualify as a "disease" within the legal rule, and hence when the anxiety reached a "panic" state, "meaning simply a severe disorganizing degree of anxiety," defendant did not know right from wrong and she did not know what she was doing was wrong because of that "disease." . . .

The change in the opinions of the defense psychiatrists simply focuses attention upon an area of undeniable obscurity. As we have said, the *M'Naghten* rule requires a "disease of the mind." The competing concepts of legal insanity also require a disease (or defect) of the mind. . . . But the hard question under any concept of legal insanity is, What constitutes a "disease"? . . . The postulate is that some wrongdoers are sick while others are bad, and that it is against good morals to stigmatize the sick. Who then are the sick whose illness shows they are free of moral blame? We cannot turn to the psychiatrist for a list of illnesses which have that quality because, for all his insight into the dynamics of behavior, he has not solved the riddle of blame. The question remains an ethical one, the answer to which lies beyond scientific truth.

The *M'Naghten* rule does not identify the disease which will excuse, but rather stresses a specific effect of disease, i.e., that at the time of the committing of the act the accused was laboring under a defect of reason such as not to know the nature and quality of the act he was doing, or, if he did know it, that he did not know what he was doing was wrong. But although emphasis is thus upon a state of mind, it is nonetheless required that that state be due to "disease" and not something else. So our cases contrast that concept of insanity with "emotional insanity" or "moral insanity" which, upon the dichotomy mentioned above, is attributed to moral depravity or weakness and hence will not excuse the offender even if his rage was so blinding that he did not really appreciate what he was doing or that it was wrong. . . . Yet the traditional charge of the *M'Naghten* rule to the jury does not attempt to say what is meant by "disease," and [there is a] rather universal reluctance to assay a definition. . . .

Our cases seem not to have explored the question. . . . And so here, . . . we should not finally decide whether the testimony of the psychiatrists revealed a disease. . . . We have described the problem, not to resolve it, but simply to reveal the room for disputation, to the end of demonstrating the unfairness of charging defendant, her attorney, and her witnesses with a fraud when the change in the experts' opinion, however frivolous it may be in law, involved no departure from prior medical findings but rather a change in the witnesses' understanding of what the law means by "disease." . . .

The judgment is reversed. . . .

TWO VIEWS OF THE PSYCHOPATHIC PERSONALITY

Joel Feinberg

Given the strict tests for insanity, many intellectually or emotionally impaired persons are held fully responsible for their crimes; their impairments are not judged to be so great as to prevent these persons from conforming to the law. Still, their impaired capacities may make it more difficult for them than for "normal" people to avoid criminal conduct. In some cases it may be unreasonable to expect obedience from them. One name for persons of this type is psychopath *(frequently interchanged with* sociopath*). This article will review two important works in the field of clinical psychopathy and serve as a forum for me to introduce my own commentary. Under the headings that begin with the word "Commen-*

tary," the text is all mine. The text under the heading "The Mask of Sanity" *is largely derived from the work of Hervey Cleckley; the text under* "The Psychopath" *is, for the most part, a quotation from William and Joan McCord.*

Commentary: The Ones in Between

Many legally sane persons who do know what they are doing and can tell the difference between right and wrong, who can appreciate the wrongfulness of their conduct when it is wrong, and who can conform their conduct to the requirements of the law, are nonetheless psychologically troubled and likely in time to commit crimes. One way to conceive of this large and diverse class of persons is to think of them as capable of being perfectly law abiding if they choose, yet as laboring under such emotional burdens or with such character-dispositions that, to stay on the right side of the law, they must exert a far greater amount of self-discipline and restraint than ordinary criminals must exert to do the same. If there is a kind of spectrum of lawbreakers stretching from legally insane persons at one extreme, to "the ordinary purposeful criminal, or cold opportunist who, in pursuit of selfish ends, merely disregards ethical considerations and the rights of others,"[1] at the other extreme, then the legally sane but psychologically disordered and dangerous persons of whom we speak are scattered throughout the middle area of the dispersion.

Some of these people may seem simply "bad." They cluster near the "ordinary criminal" end, although those who are thought of as sheerly wicked may actually be very difficult to distinguish from the psychotic or legally insane people clustered at the other end. The scales of wickedness and mental illness seem actually to circle back and culminate at the same place, and although the moral and the medical diagnoses are supposed to be diametrically opposed—the more wicked, the more responsible and blameworthy; and the more sick, the less responsible and the less blameworthy—we find that the *extremely* wicked persons tend to resemble the most bizarre and crazy ones. The more bizarre, unrewarding, and incomprehensible the crime, the more sick it seems to ordinary people on its face. Thus, Jeffrey Daumer—who invited unsuspecting persons into his apartment, seduced them or abused them sexually, murdered them, dismembered them, and cannibalized them—

seems as sick as a criminal can be. Indeed, we can cognize his conduct only by thinking of it as essentially inhuman, either superhuman—diabolical, demonic, or fiendish—or else subhuman—that is, beastly or monstrous. Devils and wild animals are not sick human beings; they are inhuman beings. In short, both the "sick" and the "bad" in their most extreme forms are likely to appear inhuman, and almost indistinguishably so.

Other occupants of the middle ground are less dramatic, but no less dysfunctional and unhappy. There is no inevitability that any of these people will become criminals, but the statistical probabilities that they will are much higher than those of randomly selected groups. Among others there are extremely neurotic, but not psychotic or disoriented persons; those with post-traumatic stress disorder, which is common among veterans of military combat; diabetic or hypoglycemic individuals who are subject to spasmodic violence when their blood sugar is low; women with premenstrual syndrome, an affliction of an estimated 20 percent of the female population (a fact posited by medical researchers trying to account for the amazing fact, revealed in numerous studies, that upward of 50 percent of all serious crimes by women are committed eight days before menses[2]). Other categories interspersed between the bad and the sick include various forms of automatism; other conditions caused by hormone imbalances; various neurotic compulsions or obsessions, such as compulsive gambling disorder; and other conditions that substantially impair behavior controls.

People who fear for the future of personal responsibility in this country are understandably uncomfortable about this proliferation of syndromes and personality disorders. (One wag even invented obnoxious personality syndrome, a fictitious disorder to excuse obnoxious people from moral judgment.) It sometimes seems that there has been a veritable population explosion of criminal excuses, so that any exposure to circumstances that might incline a defendant toward crime (a mean mother, a drunken father, the divorce of parents, juvenile poverty, fancied rejection by the other sex, childhood nightmares, and more) by the same token would provide him or her with an excuse. There is a danger, and a great one, of accepting as a mitigating excuse almost anything that makes the crime a little more intelligible, so that in the end we have no idea where to draw a line between excusable and inexcusable behavior. Every time a lawyer thinks of a uniform pattern of criminal responses—and there must be dozens of prominent correlations between various histories, or personal experiences, and certain types of emotional response—he or she can refer to the pattern or type as a syndrome ("things that occur together and usually form an identifiable pattern"). Or, if the lawyer dare not cite the syndrome as a disease, he or she can call it a personality disorder, which is apparently the vogue diagnosis for a mitigating condition that is neither medical symptom nor moral flaw.

Nevertheless, if we are to be realistic, we must acknowledge that a great many criminals are neither at the "ordinary selfish" end of the spectrum, where moral language is most relevant, nor at the insane end, where psychological language has an exclusive application. Capacities to appreciate wrongfulness and to conform one's conduct to the requirements of law are matters of degree. If we restrict our attention to the rational calculating bad guy and the sick or demented insane person, we will be leaving behind a major part of the problem in any criminal justice system: the ones in between. For that reason some legal theorists have advocated that mental health evidence be admissible at a criminal trial "quite apart from its bearing on the insanity issue" and that American courts follow the British example and adopt the doctrine of diminished responsibility. According to this doctrine, some mentally disturbed defendants are entitled to a reduction of their sentences, "even though the prosecution has proved all the legal elements technically required for conviction."[3] A general scheme of diminished responsibility might have sentencing judges assign a kind of "gross figure sentence" recommended, say, by a sentencing commission for the type of crime under consideration before discounting it for diminished responsibility. So, if the gross figure is ten years, a judge might then multiply that number by a fraction of the number one according to how diminished the responsibility has been shown to be. (Compare the article by Robert Nozick in Part Five of this book.) So, if the defendant is declared insane, he or she would not be imprisoned because the formula applied would yield a zero-year term ($10 \times 0 = 0$). For the same crime, an ordinary rational criminal might be sentenced to ten years ($10 \times 1 = 10$), whereas one of the neglected disturbed types in between might be sentenced to five years ($10 \times 0.5 = 5$).

The most challenging of all the "in between" disorders is that called the psychopathic personality. The first and still the most thorough description of this type of criminal was given in 1941 by Hervey Cleckley, a medical doctor from Georgia, in his remarkable book, *The Mask of Sanity*.

The Mask of Sanity*

The psychopathic personality, as that term is now most commonly understood, is a man or a woman with a clearly recognized pattern of traits that lead to a lifetime of almost continuous anti-social behavior. To those who examine and treat psychopaths it seems quite impossible that people with their character-dispositions could be anything other than chronic troublemakers and petty criminals, at best. A minority composed of the more extreme psychopaths commit serious crimes too, although these are never properly called crimes of passion, since the psychopath never experiences genuine passion of any kind, and, unlike the psychoneurotic, suffers no anxiety ever. His or her characteristic behavior seems "free" enough, noncompulsive, nonobsessive, often stubbornly willful. Many but not all psychopaths are highly intelligent. Typically, they have learned how to be charming, witty, and shrewdly manipulative. These "social skills" enable them to win releases quickly from mental hospitals when they are transferred there by desperate prison authorities who are utterly frustrated by the psychopath's disruption of prison discipline and routine. Hospital authorities, especially after repeated experiences with the same person, are even more eager to have him or her discharged as soon as possible, lest the doctors are driven to changing places with the mental patients. As a consequence, in hundreds of cases, the psychopath over his or her life's history will have a record of more than a hundred convictions, incarcerations, and transfers to and quick releases from mental health facilities.[4] The cycle goes on and on. It seems that the psychopath is not fit to be free and not fit to be tied.[5]

It is true by definition that psychopaths have no superego (conscience); that they have no experience of affect beyond momentary irritations and attractions but never any deep major emotions such as love and hate, fear and depression, rage and joy; that they are totally irresponsible and untrustworthy; that even their own future is "unreal" to them (they show as little concern for their own condition one day into the future as for that of others—that is to say, nil); that

*From *The Mask of Sanity*, Third Edition (1955), by Harvey Cleckley. Reprinted here by permisison of Mrs. Emily S. Cleckley who, along with Dr. Corbett H. Thigpen, assisted Dr. Cleckley in his preparation of the current edition: Harvey Cleckley, *The Mask of Sanity*, Fifth Edition (Augusta, Georgia: Emily S. Cleckley, Publisher, 1988).

they are totally incapable of experiencing empathy, the putting of oneself imaginatively into the other person's shoes and thus coming to know how the other person feels (a prerequisite to *caring* how the other feels); that they are crafty, shy, and slick, the world's most accomplished liars.

Dr. Cleckley describes from his medical records case after case where the same syndrome is evident. The reader, bombarded by all these data, can quickly understand why psychopaths are automatically certified as sane and also how "their behavior demonstrates an irrationality and incompetence that are gross and obvious."[6] Max has a desire to show off, and "egotism and factiousness" that lead him into quarrels and fisticuffs with strangers almost daily. However, he "always took care not to challenge an antagonist who might get the upper hand."[7] In that way his behavior resembles that of the schoolyard bully. But some mornings he wakes up in a deserted alley or park, dirty, bloody, aching and sore, after a late night bar room quarrel with a better fighter. And of course on other mornings he wakes up in jail. "In his encounters with the law, he has usually appeared in the role of petty bully, sharper, thief, and braggart."[8]

> *Some months later I . . . testified at court when efforts were being made to have Max committed by law as "insane." . . . In trying to explain briefly and comprehensibly that I believed this man, while not suffering from a psychosis that could be named, or any of the technical symptoms of one, was entirely unsuited to be at large, the sense of futility was oppressive. Max, neat and well groomed, insouciant, witty, alert, and splendidly rational, rose, beaming, to hear again the verdict of freedom.[9]*

Tom liked alcohol and drugs as only a person for whom there is no tomorrow can, and he frequently overindulged. He could not keep a job for more than two days. Usually his frustrated employer would be extremely angry when sacking him, only to become angrier still when he learned that Tom had had his hand in the till. Then Tom would forge his uncle's check and proceed, in his elderly uncle's words, "to launch himself on another pot-valiant and fatuous rigadoon."[10] Tom is not neurotic in the traditional psychiatric sense, for like all psychopaths, he is "very sharply characterized by the lack of anxiety (remorse, uneasy anticipation, apprehensive scrupulousness, the sense of being under stress or strain). . . ." Tom and his fellow psychopaths are also to be contrasted and not confused with "the ordinarily dissipated or

profligate person," in that "the profligate is after what everyone can see is a kind of pleasure, or seeking simple relief from [psychic] pain . . . while the psychopath seldom drives at anything that looks very much like pleasure or necessary analgesia."[11] Neither can the psychopathic personalities described by Dr. Cleckley "consistently pursue what . . . is called evil [like the 'bad' criminals at one end of our initial criminal spectrum]; their exploits are fitful, buffoonist, and unsustained by any obvious purpose. Hatred of others [a motivating force in many 'bad' people], is not a guiding line in their life scheme."[12]

The lack of anxiety that was typical of Tom was a feature in the case of Roberta, another psychopath Cleckley describes.[13] (Although Cleckley's book contains more examples of male psychopaths than of female psychopaths, it presents numerous examples of psychopathic women.) Roberta was an un–self-conscious girl with a sort of "easy security" about her, apparently candid without effort. She cleverly exploited her appearance of unfeigned artlessness, winning credence for the most outrageous lies. Cleckley relates her history of petty shoplifting, charging expensive clothes to the account of her unsuspecting father, and her "spectacular and persistent" truancy from school. He also makes it clear that she experienced "no great thrill or consummation in a theft, nor found in it relief from uncomfortable stress," a feeling she never knew. Next came unauthorized "borrowings" from classmates and teachers, expulsion from high school, and long disappearances from home. She took a job and then "used her skill at figures and a good deal of ingenuity to make off with considerable sums." Then she would tell one of her natural, relaxed lies and thus win the forgiveness of her victims. These various episodes were "always without adequate motive or extraneous causes."

The properties that are uniformly present in psychopaths as Dr. Cleckley defines them include most importantly: "inadequately motivated antisocial behavior"; "pathologic egocentricity and incapacity for love"; "general poverty in major affective reactions"; "sex life impersonal, trivial, and poorly integrated"; "failure to follow any life plan."[14]

The most basic of all the deficiencies in the psychopath, however, are two that mark him or her apart from both the ordinary "bad" criminal and most of the mentally ill ones, short of insanity. (Dr. Cleckley judges that the psychopath is just as incompetent at running his own life as either of these other groups is.) These two deficiencies are the incapacities to experience empathy and affect, to really *care* about anything—whether self and personal future or the good of anyone else. Dr. Cleckley writes:[15]

> It is most difficult to believe that he is reacting to powerful drives which force or compel him into obviously disastrous actions. On the contrary, everything about him suggests a drifting approach, a casual and weak impulse, a half-hearted whim rather than an explosive release of passion in the forbidden deed. Instead of a pathologic intensity of drive there seems instead to be a pathologic devaluation of life, a complex deficiency, confusion, or malfunction in what chooses, aims, and directs impulse.
>
> Nothing that he expresses or that can be observed about him suggests a great stress or inner conflict in which strong opposing forces clash and from which emerges deep instinctual gratification as he makes off with a stolen automobile, thoroughly cleans out an opponent by fraud in crap shooting, saddles his father with a heavy debt, or drains his bottle and brawlingly defies the police. Nor is there anything yet detected about him that suggests true relief of inner tension as he reacts to society's restraints and retaliations. If these are his fundamental mechanisms they are so deeply concealed that they show no surface or subsurface repercussion of emotion that suggests in the least their nature or their existence.

Finally, a line from Dr. Cleckley that sums it all up: "let us then assume as a hypothesis that the psychopath's disorder or his difference from the whole, or normal, or integrated personality consists of an unawareness, and a persistent lack of ability to become aware, of what the most important experiences in life mean to others."[16]

How do the psychopaths get that way? Is there some lesson parents can learn from psychopaths' lives? There is no perfect consensus among social scientists about the etiology of psychopathy, but the theory of Doctors William and Joan McCord has won substantial support. Their shorter definition of psychopathy is similar to that of Cleckley: "The psychopath is an asocial, aggressive, highly impulsive person, who feels little or no guilt[17] and is unable to form lasting bonds of affection with other human beings."[18] The McCords are willing to complicate their account of the cause of psychopathy by recognizing other types of causal factors, but by and large it is what they call the environmental theory that carries the day.

The McCords' theory, which supplements Cleckley's, is presented in the next section. The McCords' words are given, for the most part, verbatim.

The Psychopath*

The environmentalist research has contributed many important insights. Through their analyses of rejection and affectional isolation, as well as their studies of psychopaths, the environmentalists have indicated that:

> The vast majority of psychopaths have been rejected in childhood. Aggression is the dominant reaction to rejection. Rejected or institutionalized children often, but not invariably, exhibit the psychopathic syndrome. They lack normal guilt feelings; they are impulsive, aggressive, . . . and they seem incapable of relating to other people. . . .

Because all psychopaths have been at least mildly rejected, rejection seems to be prerequisite in the development of the syndrome. But not all rejected children become psychopaths. Thus rejection, while necessary, is not a sufficient cause. Either a particular type of rejection or some additional factor must tip the balance toward psychopathy. Studies of rejected and institutionalized children have shown a correlation between severity of rejection and psychopathy. Severe rejection, though not complete isolation, seems to account for many cases of psychopathy. . . .

Thus, there seem to be three causal patterns:

1. Severe rejection, by itself, can cause psychopathy.
2. Mild rejection, in combination with damage to the brain area (possibly the hypothalamus), which normally inhibits behavior, causes psychopathy.
3. Mild rejection, in the absence of neural disorder, can result in psychopathy if certain other influences in the environment fail to provide alternatives.

Specifically, in this third case, [the McCords] hypothesize that an environment characterized by mild rejection and, in addition, by a psychopathic parental

---

*From William McCord and Joan McCord, *The Psychopath: An Essay on the Criminal Mind.* (Princeton, NJ: Van Nostrand Co., Inc., 1964). Reprinted by permission of Van Nostrand Reinhold and Joan McCord.

model, by erratically punitive discipline, and by an absence of adult supervision results in a psychopathic pattern. This theory, [they] believe, reasonably synthesizes the superficially conflicting discoveries about the psychopath. Rejection, sometimes severe and sometimes complemented by neural or environmental defects, plays the paramount role. The psychopathic syndrome evolves from this rejection.

The psychopath's *inability to maintain close relations* seems due to his inexperience with affectional bonds. As a child, the psychopath was consistently rebuffed. He did not experience the satisfactions which accompany emotional attachment. Since he never developed ties of affection, he never acquired the ability to empathize. Because he early learned that the world offered him no love, the psychopath reacts to other human beings with suspicious indifference. He doubts the sincerity of those who may seek to establish close relations. Though the psychopath might wish to develop an emotional attachment, he lacks the necessary techniques. His erratic, uninhibited, and aggressive behavior drives people from him.

Failure to develop a conscience flows logically from the psychopath's lovelessness. Almost all social scientists believe that the internalization of moral controls takes place primarily through the child's acceptance of his parents. The child and the parents strike an unconscious bargain: in return for the child's conformity to social restrictions, the parents give the child love. If the child fails to conform, disapproval follows. In time, the child looks ahead to the consequences of his acts. If he is about to misbehave, a gnawing fear warns that his parents might stop loving him. Thus the inner anxiety eventually results in internalization of the parent's morality. The child has developed a rudimentary conscience.

There is, of course, a more positive aspect in this development of inner controls: not only does the child fear withdrawal of love, he also identifies with his parents. He loves them, and he wishes to emulate them. As Gordon Allport has pointed out, children who fear the loss of love develop the concept of "must," but the "ought" of behavior comes only through identification with parents and other moral symbols.

In a rejectant environment, love, the central element, is missing. Because the rejected child does not love his parents and they do not love him, no identification takes place. Nor does the rejected child fear the loss of love—a love which he never had—when he

violates moral restrictions. Without love, the socializing agent, the psychopath remains *asocial*. And if love is too weak to countermand brain lesions which make socialization difficult, the child becomes a psychopath.

Since there is no real conscience in the psychopath, he allows uninhibited expression to whatever aggressive urges he has. *Aggression* seems intensified in the psychopath, although recent research with psychopathic children indicates that their aggressive drives may be no more pressing than the normal person's. Since he does not have strong emotional ties, the psychopath does not understand the effects of his aggression on other people.

Impulsivity is also intimately connected with early rejection. As a child, parental love did not compensate the psychopath for moderating his behavior and, in at least some cases, neurological dysfunctioning weakened his inhibitory faculties. Thus, as an adult, his impulsivity is unchecked.

Although inconsistent and purposeless behavior is a product of impulsivity, it may also be due to a deficiency in the psychopath's ego. Harrison Gough (among many others) believes that the normal person's self-concept arises through emotional interaction with other people. The child records the evaluations of those around him and gradually absorbs these into his feeling toward himself. If these early evaluations are missing or are inconsistent, the child is unable to develop a coherent attitude about himself. Absence of long-range goals and erratic impulsivity may be due to the psychopath's underdeveloped attitude toward his self.

The psychopath's *pleasure seeking,* like his other traits, seems primarily due to his early experiences. His emotional frustration, in all probability, increased the intensity of his desires. Because he so seldom experienced it, the psychopath craves pleasure with heightened intensity. Uninhibited by either conscience or attachment to others, the psychopath seeks immediate satisfaction for his whims.

Aggression, pleasure seeking, and impulsivity cause the psychopath to violate society's rules. These traits, in turn, come from deeper deficiencies: warped ability to form relations and consequent lack of conscience.

Thus, the psychopathic syndrome can be traced to early deficiency in affectional relations. Extreme emotional deprivation or moderate rejection coupled with other environmental conditions or with neural damage to inhibitive centers, best account for the development of psychopathy. Although this position obviously requires the confirmation of empirical research, the theory reconciles the two major discoveries: that all psychopaths are, in some degree, rejected, and that many psychopaths have a neural disorder.

Commentary: Moral and Philosophical Perplexity About Psychopathy

If Cleckley is right, most of the crimes committed by psychopaths are relatively minor. Occasionally, however, a psychopath—on impulse or whim—might join a group of thieves, or beat and severely injure a weakling who dared impugn his manhood as part of some banal persiflage, or shoot and kill almost routinely, without giving it much thought or ever regretting it. A psychopathic woman frequently abandons a child born to her out of wedlock, and she does so almost casually. When the crime is serious, and the perpetrator's motivation so trivial, then he can seem either more blameworthy than ordinary criminals or less blameworthy, depending on how we look at him. On the one hand, he is the very model of a cold-blooded conscienceless killer (or mugger, burglar, defrauder, etc.). On the rare occasions when he kills he acts not from anger, hate, or zeal (all states of mind foreign to him). He knows no guilt feelings, although he may feel something akin to shame if he should happen to kill awkwardly, unintelligently, or unnecessarily. Only in this sense is there anything like honor among psychopaths. He is totally incapable of feeling remorse, which is a blend of regret, self-loathing, guilt, and concern for one's victim, all saturated with intense affect. In short, those respects in which the psychopath differs from other wrongdoers generally make him a morally worse person.

On the other hand, the psychopath's crimes seem rarely to produce any benefit for himself; they proceed from no long-range scheme, no premeditated strategy for gaining profit or advantage for himself. He is not the rational calculating egoist traditionally assumed by the criminal law. He seems as much beyond the reach of the law, however, as any criminal in the other categories. And most importantly, like someone who suffers from a severe mental illness, he seems immensely handicapped. He seems doomed to the pointless, self-defeating life he leads.

Indeed, in the most common understanding of the concept of an illness, psychopaths *are* ill. In that conception an illness in the generic sense is the impaired functioning of some necessary element of an organic system. An organic system in turn, whether it be a machine like an automobile or a living thing like an animal or vegetable (and of course only the animal organisms are ever *literally* sick), is a complex of component parts related in such a way that the macroscopic functioning of the whole complex assemblage depends on the microscopic functioning of its parts, and to an important extent, vice versa. Thus the health of a human being's body depends on each component part—each gland, organ, and nerve doing its job—but on the other side, each component part, if *it* is to be healthy and function properly, requires the general good health of the body as a whole.

Diagnoses of health and sickness, it is interesting to note, though they may seem to be entirely factual matters, have in reality certain irreducibly normative aspects.[19] This is shown by the inescapability in all functional analyses of such terms as "doing its job," "function properly," "adequate, effective, or proper working order,"[20] and so on.

If mental illness shares the generic character of sickness, it must then consist in the disabling impairment of some vital mental function, such as reasoning, remembering, feeling, or imagining. The most conspicuous mental illnesses are those that involve impairment of the cognitive faculties and consequent chronic irrationality of one kind or another. Most forms of "proper functioning" are quite impossible for a person whose memory has totally failed, or who is incapable of drawing inferences or of distinguishing fact from fantasy. There is general agreement among us that the sorts of incapacities directly consequent upon these functional failures constitute "being out of proper working order" and, therefore, being sick.

Much more difficult questions are posed by the mental dysfunctions that are noncognitive. Persons are now commonly called mentally ill when their affective or emotional or volitional faculties are awry, even when there is no attendant cognitive dysfunction. If one's superego is a mental faculty and it fails to instruct or restrain, is its possessor mentally ill? Surely, there is one obvious sense in which no person can function "properly" if he has no conscience. And one might argue that any person who commits batteries, thefts, and murders is not in "good working order" and that certain moral norms, therefore, must be included among the criteria for proper functioning. If failure to act in accordance with the norms of a rational morality is the necessary consequence of some misfunction of mental faculty—such as failure of memory, deformity of conscience, caprice of will, hollowness of affect, perhaps even persistent deviant desires—then such immoral acts are, by definition, "sick." And, indeed, how can any organic system be out of proper working order unless there is some component that is misfiring? If an automobile won't run or runs only with great difficulty, it cannot possibly be that all its parts and component systems are in good working order. By this mode of argument, inclusion of noncognitive faculties among the components, whose failure can cause overall malfunction, leads us to the brink of the theory that all patently immoral behavior is sick and, therefore, excused.[21]

An athlete whose liver is not in good working order will not be able to perform well in the 10,000-meter run. A scholar whose brain is not functioning properly will not function properly in her capacity as a scholar. A laborer with a broken arm will be unable to perform his proper job (function) so long as his "component part" cannot do its job of lifting and pushing. If we can say these things, why can we not, by parity of reasoning, say that the psychopath cannot be expected to behave properly so long as his vitally necessary component part—his superego, or conscience—is not functioning properly? But once we say that, aren't we committed to the belief that the entire distinction between sickness and sin must break down? Perhaps that is too strong. But if we subtract from the ranks of those who are fully responsible for what they do, not only the insane psychotics but the hordes of psychopaths, we seem to be left primarily with those rational calculating wrongdoers whose superegos are still more or less intact and functioning properly, and who, nevertheless choose voluntarily to act contrary to the dictates of their conscience. Perhaps *these* are the criminals who are the most wicked, since they appreciate the wrongfulness of what they plan to do, and then, in defiance of internalized moral authority, they do it anyway. But then again, this group contains mostly individuals who know what guilt feelings are and are capable of suffering remorse for what they have done. Perhaps, then, an intact conscience—instead of aggravating the wrongfulness of its possessor's crime—is actually a mitigation, making it possible for him or her to deserve forgiveness and redemption. There seem to be arguments both ways. Perhaps that shows that there is something wrong with our conceptions of moral blameworthiness, illness, and the way they fit together.

The intelligent psychopath, having followed this long and inconclusive discussion of his character, might show his truly psychopathic indifference to the outcome by quoting the Duke of Coffin Castle in James Thurber's *The Thirteen Clocks:* "We all have our flaws, and mine is being wicked." The psychopath does seem to have a point there. His severely flawed character is just *there,* a part of his original nature, an essential component of his identity. He is wicked in the way the rest of us are all flawed, and there is nothing for him to do but accept that fact about himself, for nothing can be done about it, any more than something can be done for the person born without some essential bodily organ.

Perhaps that is so, though it is self-serving and unseemly for *him* to say so. But we can play the quoting game too, and cite to our psychopathic devil Robert Louis Stevenson's dialogue between the Devil and the innkeeper:[22]

> *"Now I am going to thrash you," said the innkeeper.*
>
> *"You have no right to be angry with me," said the Devil; "I am only the Devil and it is in my nature to do wrong."*
>
> *"Is that so," said the innkeeper.*
>
> *"Fact I assure you," said the Devil.*
>
> *"You really cannot help doing ill?" asked the innkeeper.*
>
> *"Not in the smallest," said the Devil. "It would be useless cruelty to thrash a thing like me."*
>
> *"It would indeed," said the innkeeper. And he made a noose and hanged the Devil.*
>
> *"There!" said the innkeeper.*

---

1. *Hervey Cleckley,* The Mask of Sanity, *3rd Edition (St. Louis: The C.V. Mosby Company, 1955), p. 44.*

2. *See "Premenstrual Syndrome: A New Criminal Defense?" by Lawrence Taylor and Katharina Dalton, California Western Law Review 19 (1983), 269–287.*

3. *Sanford Kadish and Stephen J. Schulhofer,* Criminal Law and its Processes, *5th Edition (Boston: Little Brown, 1989), p. 1053.*

4. *Op. cit.*

5. *G.N. Thompson is quoted by Cleckley as follows: ". . . The administrative officers of penal institutions attempt to have such*

individuals transferred to mental hospitals because they believe them to be mentally ill. Knowing how little they can do for them and what difficult problems they are, the superintendents of mental hospitals attempt to get rid of them as soon as possible and transfer them back to the prison as 'not psychotic.' Pushed from prison to hospital and back again, wanted in neither, the psychopathic delinquent is essentially the orphan of both penology and psychiatry." Quoted from The Psychopathic Delinquent and Criminal *by G.N. Thompson, in* The Mask of Sanity, supra, *p. 509.*

6. *Cleckley,* op. cit., *p. 19.*
7. Ibid, p. 53.
8. Ibid., *p. 67.*
9. Ibid., *p. 68.*
10. Ibid., *p. 100.*
11. Ibid., *p. 362.*

12. Ibid., *p. 370.*
13. Ibid., *pp. 69–79.*
14. Ibid., *p. 380.*
15. Ibid., *pp. 171–72.*
16. Ibid., *p. 424.*
17. *William and Joan McCord,* The Psychopath, *p. 14.*
18. Ibid., *p. 3.*
19. *See Joel Feinberg,* Doing and Deserving *(Princeton, N.J.: Princeton University Press, 1970), pp. 253–55.*
20. *Carl Hempel, "The Logic of Functional Analysis," in* Symposium on Sociological Theory, *ed. Lewelyn Gross (New York: Harper & Row, 1959), p. 99.*
21. *This paragraph is borrowed from Joel Feinberg,* op. cit., *pp. 255–56.*
22. *Robert Louis Stevenson, "The Devil and the Innkeeper."*

PART FIVE

Punishment

What distinguishes criminal law from the various branches of private law is that criminal law's assigned function is to determine whether or not an accused person is properly to be *punished* for prior conduct. Tort law, in contrast—except in hybrid judgments of punitive damages—is unconcerned with punishment. Its assigned function is to determine which of two contending parties is to pay the bill for damages produced when the one party's flawed conduct seemed to be the cause of the other party's loss or injury. The philosophy of criminal law, then, must commence with an analysis of the concept of punishment, just as tort theory must begin by coming to terms with the idea of compensation. Punishment is what defines and distinguishes criminal law; it is what that branch of the law is for, "the name of its game," its "bottom line."

For that reason the concept of legal punishment, in its own right, is of central theoretical importance to a philosopher of law. In addition, solutions to the puzzles it poses for the philosopher are also presupposed by problems, both theoretical and practical, throughout the substantive criminal law. Questions about the necessary conditions of criminal liability, for example, are often answered in different ways by philosophers with differing conceptions of the nature and moral grounding of punishment. That these two types of disagreement should appear together is no mere coincidence. Differing views about the conditions of criminal responsibility can derive specifically from prior disagreements over the nature of punishment. Even in the practical contexts in which law cases are adjudicated, decisions often hinge upon which definition of *punishment* a judge's argument endorses.

What Is Legal Punishment?

In the 1950s there seemed for a time to be promise of a resolution of the traditional impasse in the philosophy of punishment. The promising new developments were primarily due to more careful definitions of the term *legal punishment*. Largely through the examples of Anthony Flew, Stanley Benn, Herbert Hart, and John Rawls, philosophers began to distinguish between defining and justifying punishment, between particular instances of punishment and punishment as a general practice within an institutional structure, and between moral and legal guilt—among other things. The hope was that the new distinctions and more accurate definitions would permit reformulations of ancient unitary questions now seen to be separable. No one view carried the day, but people were especially excited by the idea that the general practice of punishment is something retributive in its defining operations and utilitarian in its justifying aims. The influential definition from Flew had five conditions. To paraphrase, one party's treatment of another can properly be called legal punishment only if (1) it is hard treatment (2) inflicted for a violation of legal rules (3) on the actual or supposed violator (4) imposed and administered by human beings other than the supposed violator himself (5) who have the authority to do so under the rules of the governing legal system. If the sense of punishment captured by the Flew's definition is the "general practice" sense, then the practice it analyzes seems clearly justifiable by its likely deterrence of would-be violators. But, unlike other utilitarian theories, it does not define a practice whose internal or constitutive rules could ever permit the punishment of the innocent. That kind of barbarism, in fact, is explicitly ruled out by condition (3) of the definition.

Joel Feinberg, in his 1964 article, "The Expressive Function of Punishment," had no quarrel with the basic Flew strategy. Feinberg argued, however, that Flew's definition was inadequate—though not in a way directly relating to Flew's main purpose. Feinberg argued that the five-pronged Flew definition was too broad. Although all the legal practices we would normally call punishment are indeed punishment according to Flew's definition, some of the practices we would not call punishment ("in the strict and narrow sense of special interest to the moralist") also fall within the scope of the definition. Feinberg had in mind as properly excludable the sanctions he called "mere penalties," such as parking tickets, taxes, and football penalties. To exclude them from the class of dealings properly called punishments, he proposed that a sixth condition be added to Flew's definition: namely, that proper punishments, unlike mere penalties, express (often through their conventional symbolism) resentment, disapproval, condemnation or reprobation. Now the definition seemed neither too broad nor too narrow.

That it is an essential feature of legal punishment to convey attitudes (say, of resentment) and judgments (of condemnation) and to send complex "messages" to the one who is punished and his victims is a view that has now become commonplace. Each "expressionist" theorist, however, seems to find in legal punishment his or her own message and expressive mechanism. Igor Primoratz, in his useful article, traced this development from Emil Durkheim, a century ago, to recent writers such as Jean Hampton and R.A. Duff. Primoratz listed the advantages and the hazards of the various "expressionist" approaches to punishment.

What, If Anything, Justifies Legal Punishment?

We have already mentioned the impasse over the justification of legal punishment, but we have failed to mention the three-sided nature of the disagreement. As "The Classic Debate," by Feinberg, describes, more and more writers have come to regard both the pure retributivist theory and the pure utilitarian theory as too extreme to be credible. They have opted instead

for a mixed theory.* According to that theory, since moral guilt is said to be a necessary condition for an act of legal punishment to be justified, then social utility cannot, by itself, be sufficient; and since social utility is deemed necessary, it follows that moral guilt, all by itself, cannot be sufficient. Since the pure retributivist holds that moral guilt *is* sufficient to justify punishment, even in the absence of expected good consequences for *anybody,* then that theory is false. And since the pure utilitarian holds that social utility *is* sufficient, even without moral guilt, to justify legal punishment, then this theory is false too. Thus, both pure theories would have to give up their claims that their favorite justifying factors (moral guilt in the one case, social utility in the other) are sufficient for successful justification. The mixed theory would then hold that (1) moral guilt is necessary, but not alone sufficient; (2) social utility is necessary, but not alone sufficient; (3) moral guilt and social utility are severally necessary and jointly sufficient.

The adherent of the mixed theory is then relieved of the burden of defending two of the most difficult claims customarily made by philosophers of punishment. The first is the claim of Immanuel Kant (1724–1804) that, even if a desert island community were to disband and scatter throughout the world, they have a right, indeed a *duty,* to execute all the convicted murderers in their custody, their moral guilt being sufficient warrant. The second possibly embarrassing claim is that which must be defended by the pure utilitarian, at least according to the opponents of that theory. The utilitarian must either justify the occasional punishment of the innocent, it is commonly alleged, or rebut the accusation that pure utilitarian theory logically implies that the innocent may, in certain rare circumstances, properly be punished. The circumstances described in the "embarrassing example" put forth by the opponents of pure utilitarianism sometimes go beyond being rare. They sometimes are so incredibly unlikely that they appear "fantastic," in the manner of sloppily contrived science fiction. So long as these fictitious descriptions are not logically contradictory or violative of laws of nature and hence impossible on their face, philosophers have shown little hesitation in using counterexamples against one another. The Chinese-Australian philosopher C. L. Ten, in his selection here, considers precisely this question:

*In regard to Feinberg's terminology in "The Classic Debate": Some minor revision is necessary in this discussion of Feinberg's terminology if the mixed theory is to be coherent.

Do fantastic counterexamples, despite their being fantastic, undermine or discredit somehow the philosophical theses they are aimed at? Ten concludes his sensitive discussion by offering a set of fantastic counterexamples of his own against utilitarianism.

The mixed theory of punishment has more difficulty dealing with the third question distinguished by Feinberg in his "Classic Debate" article: "How should we determine how much punishment is the correct amount?" or put differently, "How should we interpret the requirement that 'the punishment must fit the crime?'" Insofar as the mixed theory is committed *both* to retributive and to utilitarian considerations, it must find a way to blend those normally irreconcilable factors in deciding how much punishment to dish out. And that is not easy to do.

Until recently the only important representatives of pure moralistic retributivism were the nineteenth-century German philosophers Immanuel Kant and Friedrich Hegel, and their followers. But their writings are typically so obscure that they perplex rather than stimulate students. But in Michael Moore's recent article on the subject, included here, we have a work marked not only by profundity and subtlety, but also clarity. This work, we think, even if it is not totally convincing, deserves to become a classic. (It is quite long, however, and should be read in at least two installments.) Moore's essay is all the more valuable in being uncompromising. He knows very well what rehabilitation theory is, and he rejects it. He knows what vengeance is, and he rejects it. He knows what mixed theories are, and he rejects them. He is the pure retributivist of Feinberg's "Classic Debate" article, a person who will not back away from the sufficiency thesis.

Moore's article is especially important for the way it responds to arguments against retributivism. He deals with one of these arguments, in particular, in detail—the argument whose first prominent spokesman was the German writer Friedrich Nietzche (1844–1900). Retributive punishments have been associated with some of the most unsavory of human emotions. Not only do these emotions produce the attitudes and judgments that are then embodied in retributivist punishments, but they are themselves strengthened by the retributive practices and made even more disreputable. Nietzche is a marvelously insightful literary psychologist who can be quite convincing even as he explains and exposes the typical mechanism by which people acquire the emotional dispositions that he lumps under the French term *ressentiment:* "resentment, fear, anger, cowardice, hostility, aggression, cruelty, sadism, envy, jealousy, guilt, self-loathing, hypocrisy, and [especially] self-deception."

Moore could have taken the quick way with the Nietzchean argument and simply convict its proponents of committing "the genetic fallacy"—inferring the falsity of a proposition from some truths about how people come to acquire a belief in that proposition. No matter how unsavory the emotions that lead one to believe some proposition, that proposition might yet be true. It is a fallacy to affirm its falsehood on the sole basis of the way people come to acquire a belief in it, just as it is a fallacy to infer its falsity from the unsavoriness of the emotions it may come in time to encourage. Moore, however, doesn't leave it at that. He treats the Nietzchean argument with great respect and devotes many pages of his own to an account of the moral and immoral emotions, the epistemic and psychological import of emotions in general, and particularly in relation to our moral judgments. One of his most effective devices is to turn the argument back on his opponents by showing how anti-retributive judgments can be motivated by some of the most unsavory human emotions. Very likely no conclusive proofs are given on either side of the debate about the morality of punishment, if only because of confusion about where the initial burden of proof belongs in this kind of debate. But at least two great benefits result from Moore's treatment of the issues. First, he identifies pivotal issues and clarifies arguments on both sides. Second, he treats us to one of the most thorough and sensitive discussions of the relations between moral judgment and emotion since Aristotle proclaimed that the realm of moral philosophy concerns not only our dispositions to *act* in certain ways in certain kinds of circumstances, but also our dispositions to have the *feelings* that are appropriate to the various situations in which we may find ourselves.

One of the most influential of the efforts in the 1950s to reconcile the retributive and utilitarian justificatory principles was that of John Rawls in his article "Punishment," only a small part of which is reprinted here. It may surprise readers who are familiar with Rawls's later work to learn that he had earlier defended utilitarianism—what came to be called rule utilitarianism—in this article. The word *defend,* however, is easy to misunderstand. Rawls does not argue here that the general moral theory called utilitarianism is true, but only that it can be reformulated in such a way that it is strengthened against one traditional type of objection to it. In particular, the selection from Rawls's article "defends" the general utilitarian theory from the argument that, in its application to legal punishment, it "justifies too much" and that in some "rare" circumstances it could be used to justify the punishment of the innocent. Rawls then suggests that this seems to be the case only because utilitarianism has been presented as an answer to the wrong question. It is a quite plausible answer to the question "What are the only acceptable reasons for having a legal system with criminal sanctions (that is, with the general practice of punishing criminals)?" But it is a preposterous answer to a similar question asked about individual cases—for example, "How can we justify sending John Gotti to prison?" The answer to the first question is that the justification of the general practice of punishing is that it makes credible the threat made by the law in support of the behavior it requires of us, and thereby diminishes the amount of crime and the pain suffered by the victims of crime. *That* is why we have prisons. But that isn't why we sent John Gotti to prison. We did that because Gotti broke the rules that punishment enforces. Once we agree to play the "baseball" game, we must abide by the three-strike-and-out rule. We cannot change the rule right in the middle of the game, no matter how good the reasons for doing so may seem on utilitarian, or any other, grounds. Similarly, once we agree to play the punishment game, we are not free to change the rules, right in the middle of the game, to send an innocent person to prison for Gotti's crimes, no matter how strong a utilitarian case there may seem to be in favor of doing so.

Like other rule-utilitarians, Rawls takes the charge that utilitarianism would justify punishing the innocent to be a judgment about the relative merits of two rival legal practices that are themselves defined by rules, not about the direct application of one of those rules to some individual case, like Gotti's. Clearly the rules of criminal procedure now in place do not authorize the framing of an innocent person for Gotti's crimes. That is an easy judgment. But it is also an easy judgment that a general practice, like our general practice of punishment, would be a better practice, on utilitarian grounds, than a similar practice—call it "telishment"—that differed from it only in authorizing certain officials in appropriate circumstances (themselves spelled out in the rule) to frame a person known to them to be innocent. In short, we cannot knowingly punish John Dotti for John Gotti's crimes because the rules of the game, as we now play it, will not permit it. And a good thing it is, generally speaking, that we choose to play *that* game rather than (say) the telishment game, for even though we

might in some special situation have to sacrifice a gain in human happiness, clearly in the long run we would be better off, more secure, more confident, more free, for playing the punishment game.

Victims' Rights: Restitution or Vengeance?

Another highly influential recent article, Randy E. Barnett's "Restitution: A New Paradigm of Criminal Justice," is like Rawls's in spirit, insofar as both try to reconcile conflicting approaches. But in advocating a new paradigm for punishment, Barnett is more radical, even revolutionary. He does not, of course, advocate violent revolution, but only the kind of conceptual transformation that Thomas Kuhn, the great historian of science, called a change in the "paradigm"—central idea—of a particular discipline or practice. In this respect Barnett appears to be considerably less enthusiastic than Rawls about the punishment game as it has evolved over the past few centuries. He advocates nothing less than the substitution of a new central idea in our design of the institutions of punishment. If even a tautology can sometimes be useful, and "All punishment must be punitive"[1] is such a tautology (compare "Business is business," "Enough is enough"), then Barnett's proposed revisions of punishment would change it into something that is not punishment at all.

Traditionally, as we have seen, the basis of the distinction between torts and contracts, on the one side, and criminal law, on the other, has been that torts and contracts have been thought to be a "private" matter, in which the interests of a small group of individuals are clearly at stake; the state offers its services only as an arbiter of conflicts and an enforcer of resolutions and agreements. Criminal law, on the other hand, was thought to be concerned with interests in which a whole community has a direct stake. Private individuals are direct victims of crimes, to be sure. But so is the state and, at least fractionally, so is everybody, if only because of the universal interest in seeing justice and/or vengeance done. Thus the state will often try an accused criminal against the wishes of a victim who does not personally wish to bring charges. And so the paradigm became set. Restitution is private and has no place in the criminal law; punishment is public and has no place in tort law (except for punitive damages). Against that background, Barnett advocates his revolutionary change. He would make restitution the primary concern of private and public law, insofar as any basis for that distinction is left at all, and do away altogether with the practices that define what for centuries has been called punishment.

The new paradigm would be as simple as it is radical. It would have the whole system of criminal justice shift its focus from criminal to victim: "Where we once saw an offense against society, we now see an offense against an individual victim. In a way it is a commonsense view of crime. *The armed robber did not rob society; he robbed the victim*. His debt therefore is not to society, it is to the victim." The rest of Barnett's article is simply a working out of the details. After a trial according to due process at which he is found guilty, the offender would be "sentenced" to make restitution to the victim. If he can afford to pay the whole debt immediately, he may thus discharge his whole liability at one stroke. If he is unable to pay it all at once, there are a variety of alternative tracks open to the authorities: garnishment of future wages, "a new type of confinement," mandatory labor for some privately owned company. Further practical details involve insurance companies and other third parties. Barnett's listing of advantages of the new scheme is especially persuasive. They include benefits for victims, first and foremost, but also more efficient law enforcement, more effective rehabilitation, even great savings to the taxpayers. But the establishment and maintenance of a proper ratio of suffering to moral blameworthiness would have no place in the system (contrary to what practice-retributivism would hold to be the chief justificatory aim of state punishment). The restitutional theorist would stoutly deny that retribution as a goal is any business of the state at all.

Restitutional justice is by no means the only process by which the state can promote the interests of crime victims. Another line of argument, consistent with, but distinguishable from, restitutionalism, employs what Feinberg in "The Classic Debate" called the "vindictive theory of punishment." That theory has never been popular with philosophers because it gives a major role in the justification of legal punishment to vengeance, a response that most philosophers regard as primitive, superstitious, and arational. Retributivists especially have taken great pains to distance themselves from any theory that even tolerates vengeance, much less to one that enshrines it near the top of the hierarchy of justificatory aims for punishment. Retributivists have been constantly challenged

to answer the utilitarian accusation that retribution is merely vengeance in disguise, a charge that does not always go away when the retributivist rejoins by indicting his or her critic for committing the "genetic fallacy." In recent years, perhaps under the growing influence of the victims' rights movement, there has been something of a change in this scenario. Formerly, retributivists unanimously abhorred vengeance; now some of them, instead of denying the connection between retribution and vengeance, suggest that vengeance need not be as disreputable as philosophers have long believed. In particular, *victims* of crimes are in a position to demand vengeance, since nonvictims—though they can demand that there be a return of the criminal's wrongdoing back on him "out of principle," or to "restore a moral equilibrium," or for some similarly impersonal moral reason—cannot themselves be the ones to enjoy retaliating or getting even. Also, if vengeance is thought to be a way of coping with such barely tolerable intense emotions as wrath and hatred, it belongs uniquely to a victim, if anyone.

The selections from Robert Nozick (Harvard), the late J.L. Mackie, Jeffrie G. Murphy (Arizona State), and law professor David R. Dow (The University of Houston) all deal with some aspect of the rights we can ascribe to the victims of crimes as such. Nozick gives one of the clearest and most comprehensive accounts yet of the very real distinction between retribution and revenge, before sketching his own original retributive theory. Mackie, who as an ethical subjectivist denies that there are objective moral truths, discusses the evolutionary advantages of retributive sentiments. Murphy deals more directly with the current demands of the politically active victims' rights movement and the point of the metaphor of "getting even." Dow also deals with those matters but much less sympathetically. As a lawyer he is interested in several United States Supreme Court opinions that have been interpreted as victories for the victims' rights movement, but strike Dow as a maze of confusions and a pandering to political forces. Not everyone will agree with Dow, especially not admirers of Justices Rehnquist and Scalia. But the issue is well joined, and the author cannot be faulted for characterizing that issue as both crucial and philosophical. It seems almost as if every major issue in this text regarding criminal law is involved in the debate in *Payne* v. *Tennessee*. This case involves the admissibility of victim impact statements and Justice Scalia's insistence that "the harm caused by criminal acts must be considered in assessing responsibility," even when the occurrence or nonoccurrence of the harm is such that some would call a "matter of luck." (See in Part Four, for example, the contributions of Richard Parker and Judith Thomson.)

The Death Penalty

The final section in this part concerns one specific criminal punishment—the death penalty. It deserves its own section because the disagreements it inspires between abolitionists and defenders of death as a punishment are perhaps the most intractable in our public life, not to mention the halls of academe. Almost all the abstract philosophical principles of the criminal law, those debated in the chapters on justice and responsibility as well as this chapter on punishment, are here applied to one specific problem, and difficult as the abstract issues are, the concrete issue in which they collide is more difficult still. (This is evident in the two cases that begin this subsection, *Furman* v. *Georgia* and *Woodson* v. *North Carolina.*) That, no doubt, is partly because "death is different." The sentence of death is irrevocable and its errors are uncorrectable. Also contributing to the difficulty is an argument that cuts both ways. On the one hand, killing a person seems to be a uniquely inappropriate way of imparting the moral teaching that killing people is morally wrong (a consideration that tells against the death penalty). Yet our failure to reserve the most extreme of all the morally acceptable punishments in our system for the most serious crime is a poor way of registering the extreme seriousness with which we regard this most horrifying of crimes. We give appropriate symbolism to that seriousness when we solemnly exact the greatest penalty for its commission. Anything less would misrepresent our feelings by trivializing them (relatively speaking).

Still another reason why the capital punishment debate seems so difficult to resolve is that on both sides can be found such gifted philosophers as Ernest van den Haag (in favor of capital punishment) and Stephen Nathanson (opposed). We cannot run away from a problem, however, even when it is, like this one, philosophical at its roots, just because disagreements among the learned seem to be intractable. In any event, the Supreme Court keeps returning to the problem, so it is hardly ever likely to drop from public view.

Many opponents of capital punishment during the 1960s, following the lead of Professor Charles Black of the Yale Law School,[2] argued that the selection by our system of only a small handful of convicted murderers (and at that time occasional rapists and traitors) strongly suggested that such selection was in large part a process characterized by "arbitrariness and caprice." Justice would require that morally relevant differences among the particular criminal acts being punished should be treated in proportionately different ways and that the death penalty be reserved for the most egregious ("morally aggravated") crimes. But in fact the differential treatment accorded the prisoners seemed to have no relation whatever to any "morally relevant differences" among their actions. They appeared as a group almost as if they had been selected randomly, by a process no more related to justice than a lottery is.

The North Carolina legislature evaded judicial efforts to reform its sentencing procedures by passing a bill making mandatory the sentence of death for *all* first-degree murders. No one could accuse *them* of arbitrariness, the legislators thought, since they treated all their murderers exactly alike: they executed all of them. But in the case of *Woodson* v. *North Carolina,* the Supreme Court gave its reasons for holding mandatory death penalties unconstitutional, apart from a reason that suggests itself immediately: to treat all murderers exactly alike is to imply that there are no morally relevant differences among them, a proposition that will amaze all students of moral philosophy.

Furman v. *Georgia,* decided by the Court in 1972, gave some moderate encouragement to the abolitionists, but not great excitement, for there were nine separate opinions delivered! Two justices of the five endorsing the majority opinion argued that *all* capital punishment is "cruel and unusual" and therefore forbidden by the Eighth Amendment. The remaining three members of the majority argued, with minor variations among them, that it is only the way capital punishment is currently administered that makes it unconstitutional, in effect citing arbitrariness rather than cruelty as the ground of unconstitutionality. The court's rejection of capital punishment was really only temporary and provisional. The death penalty is unconstitutional basically because "out of a large number of persons 'eligible' in law for the punishment of death a few were selected as if at random, by no stated (or perhaps statable) criteria, while all the rest suffered the lesser penalty of imprisonment."[3] The remaining four justices, those in the minority, argued that there were no sufficient reasons, at least not now, for finding the death penalty unconstitutional. That gave abolitionists very little to cheer about.

Almost immediately various state legislatures tried to get around *Furman* v. *Georgia* by revising the sentencing provisions in their penal codes. Two tactics were used. Some, like North Carolina, tried to make death sentences nonarbitrary by making them mandatory for some crimes. That evasive path was soon closed. The other method was to change their sentencing provisions so that they accorded more closely with the reasoning in *Furman*. Separate trials allowing juries to decide sentences after the regular trial at which the defendant was convicted was another new idea. In some states bills were passed containing lists of aggravating and mitigating circumstances and requirements that some score tallied up

from those lists must lead juries either to the death penalty or imprisonment, whichever is most appropriate given the score. Such criteria of nonarbitrariness were refined in many judicial test cases and legislative debates throughout the country. These eventually received the stamp of approval from the Supreme Court. Soon the number of court-approved sentencing procedures was large. Eventually the worst criminals (according to the plan) or the unluckiest ones (not according to the plan) began once more to be hanged, gassed, and electrocuted. And we are back to where we were before 1962. There is probably less arbitrariness in the system now, but very little less cruelty. Whether the death penalty is never, sometimes, or always cruel, in itself or in its context, and whether it is cruel enough in any case to be unconstitutional is a problem for the Supreme Court. But that does not mean that philosophers may not second-guess.

---

1. *Compare California's Determinate Sentencing Law (1976), whose preamble begins with this statement: "The legislature finds and declares that the purpose of imprisonment for crime is punishment." [This rules out rehabilitation, deterrence, incapacitation, moral education, and restitution.] But Barnett's purpose is not to state. the conditions under which traditional punishment is justi-*

fied. Rather he advocates an end to punishment as traditionally conceived.
2. *Charles L. Black,* Capital Punishment: The Inevitability of Caprice and Mistake *(New York: W.W. Norton & Co., 1974).*
3. *Ibid., p. 12.*

What Is Legal Punishment?

THE EXPRESSIVE FUNCTION OF PUNISHMENT*

Joel Feinberg

It might well appear to a moral philosopher absorbed in the classical literature of his discipline, or to a moralist sensitive to injustice and suffering, that recent philosophical discussions of the problem of punishment have somehow missed the point of his interest. Recent influential articles[1] have quite sensibly distinguished between questions of definition and justification, between justifying general rules and particular decisions, between moral and legal guilt. So much is all to the good. When these articles go on to *define* "punishment," however, it seems to many that they leave out of their ken altogether the very element that makes punishment theoretically puzzling and morally disquieting. Punishment is defined, in effect, as the infliction of hard treatment by an authority on a person for his prior failing in some respect (usually an infraction of a rule or command).[2] There may be a very general sense of the word "punishment" which is well expressed by this definition; but even if that is so, we can distinguish a narrower, more emphatic sense that slips through its meshes. Imprisonment at hard labor for committing a felony is a clear case of punishment in the emphatic sense; but I think we would be less willing to apply that term to parking tickets, offside penalties, sackings, flunkings, and disqualifications. Examples of the latter sort I propose to call *penalties* (merely), so that I may inquire further what distinguishes punishment, in the strict and narrow sense that interests the moralist, from other kinds of penalties.[3]

One method of answering this question is to focus one's attention on the class of nonpunitive penalties in an effort to discover some clearly identifiable characteristic common to them all, and absent from all punishments, on which the distinction between the two might be grounded. The hypotheses yielded by this approach, however, are not likely to survive close scrutiny. One might conclude, for example, that mere penalties are less severe than punishments, but although this is generally true, it is not necessarily and universally so. Again we might be tempted to interpret penalties as mere "price-tags" attached to certain types of behavior that are generally undesirable, so that only those with especially strong motivation will be willing to pay the price.[4] So, for example, deliberate efforts on the part of some western states to keep roads from urban centers to wilderness areas few in number and poor in quality are essentially no different from various parking fines and football penalties. In each case a certain kind of conduct is discouraged without being absolutely prohibited: Anyone who desires strongly enough to get to the wilderness (or park overtime, or interfere with a pass) may do so provided he is willing to pay the penalty (price). On this view penalties are, in effect, licensing fees, different from other purchased permits in that the price is often paid

---

*Joel Feinberg, *Doing and Deserving* (Princeton, N.J.: Princeton University Press, 1970), pp. 95–118.

afterward rather than in advance. Since a similar interpretation of punishments seems implausible, it might be alleged that this is the basis of the distinction between penalties and punishments. However, while a great number of penalties can, no doubt, plausibly be treated as retroactive license fees, this is hardly true of all of them. It is certainly not true, for example, of most demotions, firings, and flunkings, that they are "prices" paid for some already consumed benefit; and even parking fines are sanctions for rules "meant to be taken seriously as . . . standard[s] of behavior,"[5] and thus are more than mere public parking fees.

Rather than look for a characteristic common and peculiar to the penalties on which to ground the distinction between penalties and punishments, we would be better advised, I think, to cast our attention to the examples of punishments. Both penalties and punishments are authoritative deprivations for failures; but apart from these common features, penalties have a miscellaneous character, whereas punishments have an important additional characteristic in common. That characteristic, or specific difference, I shall argue, is a certain expressive function: Punishment is a conventional device for the expression of attitudes of resentment and indignation, and of judgments of disapproval and reprobation, either on the part of the punishing authority himself or of those "in whose name" the punishment is inflicted. Punishment, in short, has a *symbolic significance* largely missing from other kinds of penalties.

The reprobative symbolism of punishment and its character as "hard treatment," while never separate in reality, must be carefully distinguished for purposes of analysis. Reprobation is itself painful, whether or not it is accompanied by further "hard treatment"; and hard treatment, such as fine of imprisonment, because of its conventional symbolism, can itself be reprobatory; but still we can conceive of ritualistic condemnation unaccompanied by any *further* hard treatment, and of inflictions and deprivations which, because of different symbolic conventions, have no reprobative force. It will be my thesis in this essay that (1) both the hard treatment aspect of punishment and its reprobative function must be part of the *definition* of legal punishment; and (2) each of these aspects raises its own kind of question about the *justification* of legal punishment as a general practice. I shall argue that some of the jobs punishment does, and some of the conceptual problems it raises, cannot be intelligibly described unless (1) is true; and that the incoherence of a familiar form of the retributive theory results from failure to appreciate the force of (2).

I. Punishment As Condemnation

That the expression of the community's condemnation is an essential ingredient in legal punishment is widely acknowledged by legal writers. Henry M. Hart, for example, gives eloquent emphasis to the point:

> What distinguishes a criminal from a civil sanction and all that distinguishes it, it is ventured, is the judgment of community condemnation which accompanies . . . its imposition. As Professor Gardner wrote not long ago, in a distinct but cognate connection:
> "The essence of punishment for moral delinquency lies in the criminal conviction itself. One may lose more money on the stock market than in a courtroom; a prisoner of war camp may well provide a harsher environment than a state prison; death on the field of battle has the same physical characteristics as death by sentence of law. It is the expression of the community's hatred, fear, or contempt for the convict which alone characterizes physical hardship as punishment."
> If this is what a "criminal" penalty is, then we can say readily enough what a "crime" is. . . . It is conduct which, if duly shown to have taken place, will incur a formal and solemn pronouncement of the moral condemnation of the community. . . . Indeed the condemnation plus the added [unpleasant physical] consequences may well be considered, compendiously, as constituting the punishment.[6]

Professor Hart's compendious definition needs qualification in one respect. The moral condemnation and the "unpleasant consequences" that he rightly identifies as essential elements of punishment are not as distinct and separate as he suggests. It is not always the case that the convicted prisoner is first solemnly condemned and then subjected to unpleasant physical treatment. It would be more accurate in many cases to say that the unpleasant treatment itself expresses the condemnation, and that this expressive aspect of his incarceration is precisely the element by reason of which it is properly characterized as punishment and not mere penalty. The administrator who regretfully suspends the license of a conscientious but accident-prone driver can inflict a deprivation without any scolding, express or implied; but the reckless motorist who is sent to prison for six months is thereby inevitably subject to shame and ignominy—the very walls of his cell condemn him and his record becomes a stigma.

To say that the very physical treatment itself expresses condemnation is to say simply that certain forms of hard treatment have become the conventional symbols of public reprobation. This is neither more nor less paradoxical than to say that certain words have become conventional vehicles in our language for the expression of certain attitudes, or that champagne is the alcoholic beverage traditionally used in celebration of great events, or that black is the color of mourning. Moreover, particular kinds of punishment are often used to express quite specific attitudes (loosely speaking, this is part of their "meaning"); note the differences, for example, between beheading a nobleman and hanging a yeoman, burning a heretic and hanging a traitor, hanging an enemy soldier and executing him by firing squad.

It is much easier to show that punishment has a symbolic significance than to say exactly what it is that punishment expresses. At its best, in civilized and democratic countries, punishment surely expresses the community's strong *disapproval* of what the criminal did. Indeed it can be said that punishment expresses the *judgment* (as distinct from any emotion) of the community that what the criminal did was wrong. I think it is fair to say of our community, however, that punishment generally expresses more than judgments of disapproval; it is also a symbolic way of getting back at the criminal, of expressing a kind of vindictive resentment. To any reader who has in fact spent time in a prison, I venture to say, even Professor Gardner's strong terms—"hatred, fear, or contempt for the convict"—will not seem too strong an account of what imprisonment is universally taken to express. Not only does the criminal feel the naked hostility of his guards and the outside world—that would be fierce enough—but that hostility is self-righteous as well. His punishment bears the aspect of legitimized vengefulness; hence there is much truth in J. F. Stephen's celebrated remark that "The criminal law stands to the passion of revenge in much the same relation as marriage to the sexual appetite."[7]

If we reserve the less dramatic term "resentment" for the various vengeful attitudes, and the term "reprobation" for the stern judgment of disapproval, then perhaps we can characterize *condemnation* (or denunciation) as a kind of fusing of resentment and reprobation. That these two elements are generally to be found in legal punishment was well understood by the authors of the Report of the Royal Commission on Capital Punishment:

> *Discussion of the principle of* retribution *is apt to be confused because the word is not always used in the same sense. Sometimes it is intended to mean vengeance, sometimes reprobation. In the first sense the idea is that of satisfaction by the State of a wronged individual's desire to be avenged; in the second it is that of the State's* marking its disapproval *of the breaking of its laws by a punishment proportionate to the gravity of the offense [my italics].*[8]

II. Some Derivative Symbolic Functions of Punishment

The relation of the expressive function of punishment to its various central purposes is not always easy to trace. Symbolic public condemnation added to deprivation may help or hinder deterrence, reform, and rehabilitation—the evidence is not clear. On the other hand, there are other functions of punishment, often lost sight of in the preoccupation with deterrence and reform, that presuppose the expressive function and would be impossible without it.

1. *Authoritative disavowal.* Consider the standard international practice of demanding that a nation whose agent has unlawfully violated the complaining nation's rights should punish the offending agent. For example, suppose that an airplane of nation *A* fires on an airplane of nation *B* while the latter is flying over international waters. Very likely high authorities in nation *B* will send a note of protest to their counterparts in nation *A* demanding, among other things, that the transgressive pilot be punished. Punishing the pilot is an emphatic, dramatic, and well understood way of *condemning* and thereby *disavowing* his act. It tells the world that the pilot had no right to do what he did, that he was on his own in doing it, that his government does not condone that sort of thing. It testifies thereby to government *A*'s recognition of the violated rights of government *B* in the affected area, and therefore to the wrongfulness of the pilot's act. Failure to punish the pilot tells the world that government *A* does not consider him to have been personally at fault. That in turn is to claim responsibility for the act, which in effect labels that act as an "instrument of deliberate national policy," and therefore an act of

war. In that case either formal hostilities or humiliating loss of face by one side or the other almost certainly follows. None of this makes any sense without the well understood reprobative symbolism of punishment. In quite parallel ways punishment enables employers to disavow the acts of their employees (though not civil liability for those acts), and fathers the destructive acts of their sons.

2. *Symbolic nonacquiescence: "Speaking in the name of the people."* The symbolic function of punishment also explains why even those sophisticated persons who abjure resentment of criminals and look with small favor generally on the penal law are likely to demand that certain kinds of conduct be punished when or if the law lets them go by. In the state of Texas, so-called "paramour killings" are regarded by the law as not merely mitigated, but completely justifiable.[9] Many humanitarians, I believe, will feel quite spontaneously that a great injustice is done when such killings are left unpunished. The sense of violated justice, moreover, might be distinct and unaccompanied by any frustrated *schaden-freude* toward the killer, lust for blood or vengeance, or metaphysical concern lest the universe stay "out of joint." The demand for punishment in cases of this sort may instead represent the feeling that paramour killings deserve to be *condemned,* that the law in condoning, even approving of them, speaks for all citizens in expressing a wholly inappropriate attitude toward them. For, in effect, the law expresses the judgment of the "people of Texas," in whose name it speaks, that the vindictive satisfaction in the mind of the cuckolded husband is a thing of greater value than the very life of his wife's lover. The demand that paramour killings be punished may simply be the demand that this lopsided value judgment be withdrawn and that the state *go on record* against paramour killings, and the law *testify to the recognition* that such killings are wrongful. Punishment no doubt would also help deter killers. This too is a desideratum and a closely related one, but it is not to be identified with reprobation; for deterrence might be achieved by a dozen other techniques, from simple penalties and forfeitures to exhortation and propaganda; but effective public denunciation and, through it, symbolic nonacquiescence in the crime, seem virtually to require punishment.

This symbolic function of punishment was given great emphasis by Kant, who, characteristically, proceeded to exaggerate its importance. Even if a desert island community were to disband, Kant argued, its members should first execute the last murderer left in its jails, "for otherwise they might all be regarded as participators in the [unpunished] murder. . . ."[10] This Kantian idea that in failing to punish wicked acts society endorses them and thus becomes *particeps criminis* does seem to reflect, however dimly, something embedded in common sense. A similar notion underlies whatever is intelligible in the widespread notion that all citizens share the responsibility for political atrocities. Insofar as there is a coherent argument behind the extravagant distributions of guilt made by existentialists and other literary figures, it can be reconstructed in some such way as this: To whatever extent a political act is done "in one's name," to that extent one is responsible for it. A citizen can avoid responsibility in advance by explicitly disowning the government as his spokesman, or after the fact through open protest, resistance, and so on. Otherwise, by "acquiescing" in what is done in one's name, one incurs the responsibility for it. The root notion here is a kind of "power of attorney" a government has for its citizens.

3. *Vindication of the law.* Sometimes the state goes on record through its statutes, in a way that might well please a conscientious citizen in whose name it speaks, but then through official evasion and unreliable enforcement, gives rise to doubts that the law really means what it says. It is murder in Mississippi, as elsewhere, for a white man intentionally to kill a Negro; but if grand juries refuse to issue indictments or if trial juries refuse to convict, and this is well understood by most citizens, then it is in a purely formal and empty sense indeed that killings of Negroes by whites are illegal in Mississippi. Yet the law stays on the books, to give ever-less-convincing lip service to a noble moral judgment. A statute honored mainly in the breach begins to lose its character as law, unless, as we say, it is *vindicated* (emphatically reaffirmed); and clearly the way to do this (indeed the only way) is to punish those who violate it.

Similarly, *punitive damages,* so-called, are sometimes awarded the plaintiff in a civil action, as a supplement to compensation for his injuries. What more dramatic way of vindicating his violated right can be imagined than to have a court thus forcibly condemn its violation through the symbolic machinery of punishment?

4. *Absolution of others.* When something scandalous has occurred and it is clear that the wrongdoer must be one of a small number of suspects, then the state, by punishing one of these parties, thereby relieves the others of suspicion, and informally absolves

them of blame. Moreover, quite often the absolution of an accuser hangs as much in the balance at a criminal trial as the inculpation of the accused. A good example of this can be found in James Gould Cozzen's novel, *By Love Possessed*. A young girl, after an evening of illicit sexual activity with her boyfriend, is found out by her bullying mother, who then insists that she clear her name by bringing criminal charges against the boy. He used physical force, the girl charges; she freely consented, he replies. If the jury finds him guilty of rape, it will by the same token absolve her from (moral) guilt; and her reputation as well as his rides on the outcome. Could not the state do this job without punishment? Perhaps, but when it speaks by punishing, its message is loud, and sure of getting across.

III. The Constitutional Problem of Defining Legal Punishment

A philosophical theory of punishment that, through inadequate definition, leaves out the condemnatory function, not only will disappoint the moralist and the traditional moral philosopher; it will seem offensively irrelevant as well to the constitutional lawyer, whose vital concern with punishment is both conceptual, and therefore genuinely philosophical, and practically urgent. The distinction between punishment and mere penalties is a familiar one in the criminal law, where theorists have long engaged in what Jerome Hall calls "dubious dogmatics distinguishing 'civil penalties' from punitive sanctions, and 'public wrongs' from crimes."[11] Our courts now regard it as true (by definition) that all criminal statutes are punitive (merely labeling an act a crime does not make it one unless sanctions are specified); but to the converse question whether all statutes specifying sanctions are *criminal* statutes, the courts are reluctant to give an affirmative reply. There are now a great number of statutes that permit "unpleasant consequences" to be inflicted on persons and yet are surely not criminal statutes—tax bills, for example, are aimed at regulating, not forbidding, certain types of activity. How to classify borderline cases as either "regulative" or "punitive" is not merely an idle conceptual riddle; it very quickly draws the courts into questions of great constitutional import. There are elaborate constitutional safeguards for persons faced with the prospect of punishment; but these do not, or need not, apply when the threatened hard treatment merely "regulates an activity."

The 1960 Supreme Court case of *Flemming* v. *Nestor*[12] is a dramatic (and shocking) example of how a man's fate can depend on whether a government-inflicted deprivation is interpreted as a "regulative" or "punitive" sanction. Nestor had immigrated to the United States from Bulgaria in 1913, and in 1955 became eligible for old-age benefits under the Social Security Act. In 1956, however, he was deported in accordance with the Immigration and Nationality Act, for having been a member of the Communist Party from 1933 to 1939. This was a hard fate for a man who had been in America for forty-three years and who was no longer a Communist; but at least he would have his social security benefits to support him in his exiled old age. Or so he thought. Section 202 of the amended Social Security Act, however,

> provides for the termination of old-age, survivor, and disability insurance benefits payable to . . . an alien individual who, after September 1, 1954 (the date of enactment of the section) is deported under the Immigration and Nationality Act on any one of certain specified grounds, including past membership in the Communist Party.[13]

Accordingly, Nestor was informed that his benefits would cease.

Nestor then brought suit in a District Court for a reversal of the administrative decision. The court found in his favor and held § 202 of the Social Security Act unconstitutional, on the grounds that

> termination of [Nestor's] benefits amounts to punishing him without a judicial trial, that [it] constitutes the imposition of punishment by legislative act rendering § 202 a bill of attainder; and that the punishment exacted is imposed for past conduct not unlawful when engaged in, thereby violating the constitutional prohibition on ex post facto *laws*.[14]

The Secretary of Health, Education, and Welfare, Mr. Flemming, then appealed this decision to the Supreme Court.

It was essential to the argument of the District Court that the termination of old-age benefits under § 202 was in fact punishment, for if it were properly classified as nonpunitive deprivation, then none of the cited constitutional guarantees was relevant. The constitution, for example, does not forbid all retroactive laws, but only those providing punishment. (Retroactive tax laws may also be hard and unfair, but they are not unconstitutional.) The question before the Supreme Court then was whether the hardship imposed by § 202 was punishment. Did this not bring the Court face to face with the properly philosophical question "What is punishment?" and is it not clear that under the usual definition that fails to distinguish punishment from mere penalties, this particular judicial problem could not even arise?

The fate of the appellee Nestor can be recounted briefly. The five man majority of the court held that he had not been punished—this despite Mr. Justice Brennan's eloquent characterization of him in a dissenting opinion as "an aging man deprived of the means with which to live after being separated from his family and exiled to live among strangers in a land he quit forty-seven years ago."[15] Mr. Justice Harlan, writing for the majority, argued that the termination of benefits, like the deportation itself, was the exercise of the plenary power of Congress incident to the regulation of an activity.

> Similarly, the setting by a State of qualifications for the practice of medicine, and their modification from time to time, is an incident of the State's power to protect the health and safety of its citizens, and its decision to bar from practice persons who commit or have committed a felony is taken as evidencing an intent to exercise that regulatory power, and not a purpose to add to the punishment of ex-felons.[16]

Mr. Justice Brennan, on the other hand, argued that it is impossible to think of any purpose the provision in question could possibly serve except to "strike" at "aliens deported for conduct displeasing to the lawmakers."[17]

Surely Justice Brennan seems right in finding in the sanction the expression of Congressional reprobation, and therefore "punitive intent"; but the sanction itself (in Justice Harlan's words, "the mere denial of a noncontractual governmental benefit"[18]) was not a conventional vehicle for the expression of censure, being wholly outside the apparatus of the criminal law. It therefore lacked the reprobative symbolism essential to punishment generally, and was thus, in its hybrid character, able to generate confusion and judicial disagreement. It was as if Congress had "condemned" a certain class of persons privately in stage whispers, rather than by pinning the infamous label of criminal on them and letting that symbol do the condemning in an open and public way. Congress without question "intended" to punish a certain class of

aliens and did indeed select sanctions of appropriate severity for that use; but the deprivation they selected was not of an appropriate kind to perform the function of public condemnation. A father who "punishes" his son for a displeasing act the father had not thought to forbid in advance, by sneaking up on him from behind and then throwing him bodily across the room against the wall, would be in much the same position as the legislators of the amended Social Security Act, especially if he then denied to the son that his physical assault on him had had any "punitive intent," asserting that it was a mere exercise of his parental prerogative to rearrange the household furnishings and other objects in his own living room. This would be to tarnish the paternal authority and infect all later genuine punishments with hollow hypocrisy. This also happens when legislators go outside the criminal law to do the criminal law's job.

In 1961 the New York State Legislature passed the so-called "Subversive Drivers Act" requiring "suspension and revocation of the driver's license of anyone who has been convicted, under the Smith Act, of advocating the overthrow of the Federal government." *The Reporter* magazine[19] quoted the sponsor of the bill as admitting that it was aimed primarily at one person, Communist Benjamin Davis, who had only recently won a court fight to regain his driver's license after his five year term in prison. *The Reporter* estimated that at most a "few dozen" people would be kept from driving by the new legislation. Was this punishment? Not at all, said the bill's sponsor, Assemblyman Paul Taylor. The legislature was simply exercising its right to regulate automobile traffic in the interest of public safety:

> Driving licenses, Assemblyman Taylor explained . . . are not a "right" but a "valuable privilege." The Smith Act Communists, after all, were convicted of advocating the overthrow of the government by force, violence, or assassination. ("They always leave out the assassination," he remarked. "I like to put it in.") Anyone who was convicted under such an act had to be "a person pretty well dedicated to a certain point of view," the assemblyman continued, and anyone with that particular point of view "can't be concerned about the rights of others." Being concerned about the rights of others, he concluded, "is a prerequisite of being a good driver."[20]

This shows how transparent can be the effort to mask punitive intent. The Smith Act ex-convicts were treated with such severity and in such circumstances that no nonpunitive legislative purpose could *plausibly* be maintained; yet that *kind* of treatment (quite apart from its severity) lacks the reprobative symbolism essential to clear public denunciation. After all, aged, crippled, and blind persons are also deprived of their licenses, so it is not *necessarily* the case that reprobation attaches to that kind of sanction. And so victims of a cruel law understandably claim that they have been punished, and retroactively at that. Yet strictly speaking they have not been *punished;* they have been treated much worse.

IV. The Problem of Strict Criminal Liability

The distinction between punishments and mere penalties, and the essentially reprobative function of the former, can also help clarify the controversy among writers on the criminal law about the propriety of so-called "strict liability offenses"—offenses for the conviction of which there need be no showing of "fault" or "culpability" on the part of the accused. If it can be shown that he committed an act proscribed by statute then he is guilty irrespective of whether he had justification or excuse for what he did. Perhaps the most familiar examples come from the traffic laws: Leaving a car parked beyond the permitted time in a restricted zone is automatically to violate the law, and penalties will be imposed however good the excuse. Many strict liability statutes do not even require an overt act; these proscribe not certain conduct but certain *results*. Some make mere unconscious possession of contraband, firearms, or narcotics a crime, others the sale of misbranded articles or impure foods. The liability for so-called "public welfare offenses" may seem especially severe:

> . . . with rare exceptions, it became definitely established that mens rea is not essential in the public welfare offenses, indeed that even a very high degree of care is irrelevant. Thus a seller of cattle feed was convicted of violating a statute forbidding misrepresentation of the percentage of oil in the product, despite the fact that he had employed a reputable chemist to make the analysis and had even understated the chemist's findings.[21]

The rationale of strict liability in public welfare statutes is that violation of the public interest is more likely to be prevented by unconditional liability than by liability that can be defeated by some kind of excuse; that even though liability without "fault" is severe, it is one of the known risks incurred by businessmen; and that besides, the sanctions are *only fines,* hence not really "punitive" in character. On the other hand, strict liability to *imprisonment* (or "punishment proper") "has been held by many to be incompatible with the basic requirements of our Anglo-American, and indeed, any civilized jurisprudence."[22] Why should this be? In both kinds of case, defendants may have sanctions inflicted upon them even though they are acknowledged to be without fault; and the difference cannot be simply that imprisonment is always and necessarily a greater hurt than fine, for this is not always so. Rather, the reason why strict liability to imprisonment (punishment) is so much more repugnant to our sense of justice than is strict liability to fine (penalty) is simply that imprisonment in modern times has taken on the symbolism of public reprobation. In the words of Justice Brandeis, "It is . . . imprisonment in a penitentiary, which now renders a crime infamous."[23] We are familiar with the practice of penalizing persons for "offenses" they could not help. It happens every day in football games, business firms, traffic courts, and the like. But there is something very odd and offensive in *punishing* people for admittedly faultless conduct; for not only is it arbitrary and cruel to *condemn* someone for something he did (admittedly) without fault, it is also self-defeating and irrational.

Though their abundant proliferation[24] is a relatively recent phenomenon, statutory offenses with nonpunitive sanctions have long been familiar to legal commentators, and long a source of uneasiness to them. This is "indicated by the persistent search for an appropriate label, such as "public torts," "public welfare offenses," "prohibitory laws," "prohibited acts," "regulatory offenses," "police regulations," "administrative misdemeanors," "quasi-crimes," or "civil offences.""[25] These represent alternatives to the unacceptable categorization of traffic infractions, inadvertent violations of commercial regulations, and the like, as *crimes,* their perpetrators as *criminals,* and their penalties as *punishments*. The drafters of the new Model Penal Code have defined a class of infractions of penal law forming no part of the substantive criminal law. These they call "violations," and their sanctions "civil penalties."

Section 1.04. Classes of Crimes: Violations

(1) An offense defined by this code or by any other statute of this State, for which a sentence of [death or of] imprisonment is authorized, constitutes a crime. Crimes are classified as felonies, misdemeanors, or petty misdemeanors.

[(2), (3), (4) define felonies, misdemeanors, and petty misdemeanors.]

(5) An offense defined by this Code or by any other statute of this State constitutes a violation if it is so designated in this Code or in the law defining the offense or if no other sentence than a fine, or fine and forfeiture or other civil penalty is authorized upon conviction or if it is defined by a statute other than this Code which now provides that the offense shall not constitute a crime. A violation does not constitute a crime and conviction of a violation shall not give rise to any disability or legal disadvantage based on conviction of a criminal offense.[26]

Since violations, unlike crimes, carry no social stigma, it is often argued that there is no serious injustice if, in the interest of quick and effective law enforcement, violators are held unconditionally liable. This line of argument is persuasive when we consider only parking and minor traffic violations, illegal sales of various kinds, and violations of health and safety codes, where the penalties serve as warnings and the fines are light. But the argument loses all cogency when the "civil penalties" are severe—heavy fines, forfeitures of property, removal from office, suspension of a license, withholding of an important "benefit," and the like. The condemnation of the faultless may be the most flagrant injustice, but the good natured, noncondemnatory infliction of severe hardship on the innocent is little better. It is useful to distinguish violations and civil penalties from crimes and punishments; but it does not follow that the safeguards of culpability requirements and due process which justice demands for the latter are always irrelevant encumbrances to the former. Two things are morally wrong: (1) to condemn a faultless man while inflicting pain or deprivation on him however slight (unjust punishment); and (2) to inflict unnecessary and severe suffering on a faultless man even in the absence of condemnation (unjust civil penalty). To exact a two dollar fine from a hapless violator for overtime parking, however, even though he could not possibly have helped it, is to do neither of these things.

V. Justifying Legal Punishment; Letting the Punishment Fit the Crime

Public condemnation, whether avowed through the stigmatizing symbolism of punishment or unavowed but clearly discernible (mere "punitive intent"), can greatly magnify the suffering caused by its attendant mode of hard treatment. Samuel Butler keenly appreciated the difference between reprobative hard treatment (punishment) and the same treatment sans reprobation:

> . . . we should hate a single flogging given in the way of mere punishment more than the amputation of a limb, if it were kindly and courteously performed from a wish to help us out of our difficulty, and with the full consciousness on the part of the doctor that it was only by an accident of constitution that he was not in the like plight himself. So the Erewhonians take a flogging once a week, and a diet of bread and water for two or three months together, whenever their straightener recommends it.[27]

Even floggings and imposed fastings do not constitute punishments, then, where social conventions are such that they do not express public censure (what Butler called "scouting"); and as therapeutic treatments simply, rather than punishments, they are easier to take.

Yet floggings and fastings do hurt, and far more than is justified by their Erewhonian (therapeutic) objectives. The same is true of our own State Mental Hospitals where criminal psychopaths are often sent for "rehabilitation": Solitary confinement may not hurt *quite* so much when called "the quiet room," or the forced support of heavy fire extinguishers when called "hydrotherapy";[28] but their infliction on patients can be so cruel (whether or not their quasimedical names mask punitive intent) as to demand justification.

Hard treatment and symbolic condemnation, then, are not only both necessary to an adequate definition of "punishment"; each also poses a special problem for the justification of punishment. The reprobative symbolism of punishment is subject to attack not only as an independent source of suffering but as the vehicle of undeserved responsive attitudes and unfair judgments of blame. One kind of skeptic, granting that penalties are needed if legal rules are to be enforced, and also that society would be impossible without general and predictable obedience to such rules, might nevertheless question the need to add condemnation to the penalizing of violators. Hard treatment of violators, he might grant, is an unhappy necessity, but reprobation of the offender is offensively self-righteous and cruel; adding gratuitous insult to necessary injury can serve no useful purpose. A partial answer to this kind of skeptic has already been given. The condemnatory aspect of punishment does serve a socially useful purpose: It is precisely the element in punishment that makes possible the performance of such symbolic functions as disavowal, nonacquiescence, vindication, and absolution.

Another kind of skeptic might readily grant that the reprobative symbolism of punishment is necessary to and justified by these various derivative functions. Indeed, he may even add deterrence to the list, for condemnation is likely to make it clear where it would not otherwise be so that a penalty is not a mere price-tag. Granting that point, however, this kind of skeptic would have us consider whether the ends that justify public condemnation of criminal conduct might not be achieved equally well by means of less painful symbolic machinery. There was a time, after all, when the gallows and the rack were the leading clear symbols of shame and ignominy. Now we condemn felons to penal servitude as the way of rendering their crimes infamous. Could not the job be done still more economically? Isn't there a way to stigmatize without inflicting any further (pointless) pain to the body, to family, to creative capacity?

One can imagine an elaborate public ritual, exploiting the trustiest devices of religion and mystery, music and drama, to express in the most solemn way the community's condemnation of a criminal for his dastardly deed. Such a ritual might condemn so very emphatically that there could be no doubt of its genuineness, thus rendering symbolically superfluous any further hard physical treatment. Such a device would preserve the condemnatory function of punishment while dispensing with its usual physical forms— incarceration and corporal mistreatment. Perhaps this is only idle fantasy; perhaps there is more to it. The question is surely open. The only point I wish to make here is one about the nature of the question. The problem of justifying punishment, when it takes this form, may really be that of justifying our particular symbols of infamy.

Whatever the form of skeptical challenge to the institution of punishment, however, there is one traditional answer to it that seems to me to be incoherent.

I refer to that form of the Retributive Theory which mentions neither condemnation nor vengeance, but insists instead that the ultimate justifying purpose of punishment is to match off moral gravity and pain, to give each offender exactly that amount of pain the evil of his offense calls for, on the alleged principle of justice that the wicked should suffer pain in exact proportion to their turpitude.

I will only mention in passing the familiar and potent objections to this view.[29] The innocent presumably deserve *not* to suffer just as the guilty are supposed to deserve to suffer; yet it is impossible to hurt an evil man without imposing suffering on those who love or depend on him. Deciding the right amount of suffering to inflict in a given case would require an assessment of the character of the offender as manifested through his whole life, and also his total lifelong balance of pleasure and pain, an obvious impossibility. Moreover, justice would probably demand the abandonment of general rules in the interests of individuation of punishment since there will inevitably be inequalities of moral guilt in the commission of the same crime, and inequalities of suffering from the same punishment. If not dispensed with, however, general rules must list all crimes in the order of their moral gravity, all punishments in the order of their severity, and the matchings between the two scales. But the moral gravity scale would have to list motives and purposes, not simply types of overt acts, for a given crime can be committed from any kind of "mental state," and its "moral gravity" in a given case surely must depend in part on its accompanying motive. Condign punishment then would have to match suffering to motive (desire, belief, etc.), not to dangerousness or to amount of harm done. Hence some petty larcenies would be punished more severely than some murders. It is not likely we should wish to give power to judges and juries to make such difficult moral judgments. Worse than this, the judgments required are not merely "difficult," they are in principle impossible. It may seem "self-evident" to some moralists that the passionate impulsive killer, for example, deserves less suffering for his wickedness than the scheming deliberate killer; but if the question of comparative *dangerousness* is left out of mind, reasonable men not only can but will disagree in their appraisals of comparative blameworthiness, and there appears no rational way of resolving the issue.[30] Certainly, there is no rational way of demonstrating that one deserves exactly twice or three-eighths or twelve-ninths as much suffering as the other; yet on some forms, at least, of this theory, the amount of suffering inflicted for any two crimes should stand in exact proportion to the "amounts" of wickedness in the criminals.

For all that, however, the pain-fitting-wickedness version of the retributive theory does erect its edifice of moral superstition on a foundation in moral common sense, for justice *does* require that in some (other) sense "the punishment fit the crime." What justice requires is that the *condemnatory aspect* of the punishment suit the crime, that the crime be of a kind that is truly worthy of reprobation. Further, the degree of disapproval expressed by the punishment should "fit" the crime only in the unproblematic sense that the more serious crimes should receive stronger disapproval than the less serious ones, the seriousness of the crime being determined by the amount of harm it

generally causes and the degree to which people are disposed to commit it. That is quite another thing than requiring that the hard treatment component, considered apart from its symbolic function, should "fit" the moral quality of a specific criminal act, assessed quite independently of its relation to social harm. Given our conventions, of course, condemnation is expressed by hard treatment, and the degree of harshness of the latter expresses the degree of reprobation of the former; still this should not blind us to the fact that it is social disapproval and its appropriate expression that should fit the crime, and not hard treatment (pain) as such. Pain should match guilt only insofar as its infliction is the symbolic vehicle of public condemnation.

---

1. *See especially the following: A. Flew, "The Justification of Punishment," Philosophy, 29 (1954), 291–307; S. I. Benn, "An Approach to the Problems of Punishment," Philosophy, 33 (1958), 325–341; and H. L. A. Hart, "Prolegomenon to the Principles of Punishment," Proceedings of the Aristotelian Society, 60 (1959–60), 1–26.*

2. *Hart and Benn both borrow Flew's definition. In Hart's paraphrase, punishment "(i) . . . must involve pain or other consequences normally considered unpleasant. (ii) It must be for an offense against legal rules. (iii) It must be of an actual or supposed offender for his offense. (iv) It must be intentionally administered by human beings other than the offender. (v) It must be imposed and administered by an authority constituted by a legal system against which the offense is committed." (op. cit., p. 4.)*

3. *The distinction between punishments and penalties was first called to my attention by Dr. Anita Fritz of the University of Connecticut. Similar distinctions in different terminologies have been made by many. Pollock and Maitland speak of "true afflictive punishments" as opposed to outlawry, private vengeance, fine, and emendation. (History of English Law, 2d ed., II, pp. 451 ff.) The phrase "afflictive punishment" was invented by Bentham (Rationale of Punishment, London, 1830): "These [corporal] punishments are almost always attended with a portion of ignominy, and this does not always increase with the organic pain, but principally depends upon the condition [social class] of the offender." (p. 83.) James Stephen says of legal punishment that it "should always connote . . . moral infamy." (History of the Criminal Law, II, p. 171.) Lasswell and Donnelly distinguish "condemnation sanctions" and "other deprivations." ("The Continuing Debate over Responsibility: An Introduction to Isolating the Condemnation Sanction," Yale Law Journal, 68, 1959.) The traditional common law distinction is between "infamous" and "noninfamous" crimes and punishments. Conviction of an "infamous crime" rendered a person liable to such postpunitive civil disabilities as incompetence to be a witness.*

4. *That even punishments proper are to be interpreted as taxes on certain kinds of conduct is a view often associated with O. W. Holmes, Jr. For an excellent discussion of Holmes's fluctuations on this question see Mark De Wolfe Howe, Justice Holmes, The Proving Years (Cambridge, Mass., 1963), pp. 74–80. See also Lon Fuller, The Morality of Law (New Haven, 1964), Chap. II, part 7, and H. L. A. Hart, The Concept of Law (Oxford, 1961), p. 39, for illuminating comparisons and contrasts of punishment and taxation.*

5. *H. L. A. Hart, loc. cit.*

6. *Henry M. Hart, "The Aims of the Criminal Law," Law and Contemporary Problems, 23 (1958), II, A, 4.*

7. General View of the Criminal Law of England, *First ed. (London, 1863), p. 99.*

8. *(London, 1953), pp. 17–18.*

9. *The Texas Penal Code (Art. 1220) states: "Homicide is justifiable when committed by the husband upon one taken in the act of adultery with the wife, provided the killing takes place before the parties to the act have separated. Such circumstances cannot justify a homicide when it appears that there has been on the part of the husband, any connivance in or assent to the adulterous connection." New Mexico and Utah have similar statutes. For some striking descriptions of perfectly legal paramour killings in Texas, see John Bainbridge,* The Super-Americans *(Garden City, 1961), pp. 238 ff.*

10. The Philosophy of Law, *trans. W. Hastie (Edinburgh, 1887), p. 198.*

11. General Principles of Criminal Law, *2d ed. (Indianapolis, 1960), p. 328, hereafter cited as GPCL.*

12. Flemming v. Nestor *80 S. Ct. 1367 (1960).*

13. Ibid., *p. 1370.*

14. Ibid., *p. 1374 (interspersed citations omitted).*

15. Ibid., *p. 1385.*

16. Ibid., *pp. 1375–6.*

17. Ibid., *p. 1387.*

18. Ibid., *p. 1376.*

19. The Reporter *(May 11, 1961), p. 14.*

20. Loc. cit.

21. *Jerome Hall, GPCL, p. 329.*

22. *Richard A. Wasserstrom, "Strict Liability in the Criminal Law,"* Stanford Law Review, *12 (1960), p. 730.*

23. United States v. Moreland, *258 U.S. 433, 447–48. Quoted in Hall, GPCL, p. 327.*

24. *"A depth study of Wisconsin statutes in 1956 revealed that of 1113 statutes creating criminal offenses [punishable by fine, imprisonment, or both] which were in force in 1953, no less than 660 used language in the definitions of the offenses which omitted all reference to a mental element, and which therefore, under the canons of construction which have come to govern these matters, left it open to the courts to impose strict liability if they saw fit." Colin Howard, "Not Proven," Adelaide Law Review, 1 (1962), 274. The study cited is: Remington, Robinson and Zick, "Liability Without Fault Criminal Statutes," Wisconsin Law Review (1956), 625, 636.*

25. *Rollin M. Perkins, Criminal Law (Brooklyn, 1957), pp. 701–2.*

26. *American Law Institute, Model Penal Code, Proposed Official Draft (Philadelphia, 1962).*

27. *Erewhon (London, 1901), Chapter 10.*

28. *These two examples are cited by Francis A. Allen in "Criminal Justice, Legal Values and the Rehabilitative Ideal,"* Journal of Criminal Law, Criminology and Police Science, *50 (1959), 229.*
29. *For more convincing statements of these arguments, see* iter alia: *W. D. Ross,* The Right and the Good *(Oxford, 1930), pp. 56–65; J. D. Mabbott, "Punishment,"* Mind, *49 (1939); A. C. Ewing,*

The Morality of Punishment *(London, 1929), Chap. 1; and F. Dostoevsky,* The House of the Dead.
30. *Cf. Jerome Michael and Herbert Wechsler,* Criminal Law and Its Administration *(Chicago, 1940), "Note on Deliberation and Character," pp. 170–2.*

PUNISHMENT AS LANGUAGE*

Igor Primoratz

I

A number of philosophers and legal scholars have pointed out a fact about punishment that had not been sufficiently appreciated by many traditional accounts, utilitarian, retributive, or "mixed": that evil inflicted on the person punished is not an evil *simpliciter,* but rather the expression of an important social message—that punishment is a kind of language. The message which it is seen to communicate can broadly be described as condemnation by society of the crime committed. In what is still the only attempt at a general *and* critical discussion—Anthony Skillen's "How to Say Things with Walls"[1]—this way of understanding punishment is termed "expressionism." In this paper I propose to sort out the main varieties of expressionism in the philosophy of punishment, and to discuss some of their pros and cons.

One variety of expressionism is represented by Joel Feinberg's influential paper on "The Expressive Function of Punishment." Feinberg's point of departure is an important deficiency he finds in the "Flew–Benn–Hart" definition of punishment, which has been generally accepted in philosophical debates since the fifties. To define punishment as hard treatment intentionally inflicted on a person who has offended against a legal rule, by an authority constituted by the relevant legal system, is to miss an essential element of punishment as distinguished from a mere penalty

such as a parking ticket. That element is its *symbolic significance.* Punishment proper is "a conventional device for the expression of attitudes of resentment and indignation, and of judgments of disapproval and reprobation, on the part either of the punishing authority himself or of those 'in whose name' the punishment is inflicted."[2] The "hard treatment" involved in punishment and its expressive aspect in reality go together—the unpleasant treatment itself expresses the condemnation, "the very walls of his cell condemn him"[3]—but for purposes of analysis the two should be distinguished. Feinberg's thesis is that a definition of punishment must include both. Otherwise it may be suitable for dealing with such purposes of punishment as deterrence, reform, or rehabilitation, but not with some of its other functions, which are possible only by virtue of the expressive nature of punishment. Feinberg distinguishes four such functions: authoritative disavowal of the crime committed, symbolic nonacquiescence in it, vindication of the law which has been broken, and placing blame squarely on the culprit and thereby absolving anyone else who might have been suspected.

Feinberg's analysis of the expressive aspect of punishment and the tasks it performs *qua* expressive is largely convincing and very helpful. Its main limitation is just that—that it is solely an analysis. Feinberg's concern is with the definition of punishment, not with its moral legitimacy; his expressionist account is

*From Igor Primoratz, "Punishment as Language," in Philosophy, vol. 64 (1989), pp. 187–205. Copyright © 1989 by

The Royal Institute of Philosophy. Reprinted with the permission of Cambridge University Press.

offered as a contribution towards a more comprehensive understanding of the practice of punishment, and not as a justification (complete or partial) of that practice. Despite certain nods in the utilitarian direction, Feinberg's expressionism is ultimately neutral between competing ethical theories of punishment.

II

In the philosophy of punishment, an account such as Feinberg's is but a prolegomenon to the main part of the inquiry. Once the expressive character of punishment is acknowledged and its various potentialities specified, the question to ask is, What is the point— the justification—of expressing society's condemnation of crime by inflicting the evil of punishment? In the rest of this paper I shall be discussing the main varieties of expressionism as possible answers to this question, i.e. the main varieties of *normative* expressionism.

One of them is the theory of punishment of James Fitzjames Stephen. Stephen points out that moral indignation, vindictive feelings and hatred of the criminal are the usual response to crime in all societies we know of, and goes on to claim that they are also natural and healthy. They cannot be preached away by moralists who want us to learn to turn the other cheek instead, for they are too deeply rooted in human nature. They are also fully legitimate; the whole criminal law is based on the principle that it is morally right to hate criminals. The central function of punishment is to express these feelings in a regular, public, legal way.

More specifically, punishment embodies and emphatically expresses our moral indignation aroused by the crime, and the hatred and vindictiveness we feel towards its perpetrator. As these sentiments are expressed in punishment, they are thereby given satisfaction as well. Furthermore, punishment ratifies these feelings; in Stephen's memorable words, "the criminal law stands to the passion of revenge in much the same relation as marriage to the sexual appetite."[4] (In this analogy, and in Stephen's insistence that indignation and vindictive sentiments of the public be given expression in a regular, public and legal manner, there is an implication that otherwise they are liable to be expressed in socially unregulated and disruptive ways.) Finally, punishment endows the indignation and vindictiveness it expresses with definite

and lasting significance and impact: ". . . the sentence of the law is to the moral sentiment of the public in relation to any offence what a seal is to hot wax. It converts into a permanent final judgment what might otherwise be a transient sentiment."[5]

Punishment also aims at preventing crime. This is effected by its deterrent impact and by way of disabling the criminal from breaking the law again. But the expressive and deterrent functions of punishment are in no way inconsistent: the former reinforces the latter, disgrace deters. A thief is deterred by the prospect of six months in jail; would he be equally deterred by the prospect of catching an illness which causes the same amount of confinement, inconvenience and financial loss?

Another major statement of expressionism is found in the writings of Emile Durkheim. The background of Durkheim's account of punishment, as of his discussion of other social practices, is his theory of collective conscience as the basis of social cohesion. This conscience is a set of collective beliefs and sentiments that, for a given social system, are found in all healthy individual consciences with a certain degree of definiteness and force. Crime is an act that shocks a deeply ingrained and clearly defined collective sentiment. Such a sentiment derives all its authority and force from the fact that it is shared by all; it is strong because it is uncontested. A crime challenges and thereby damages this unanimity. If it is to be defended, if it is to survive, this unanimity must be reasserted. Individual consciences offended by the crime must "unite themselves to give mutual evidence of their communion . . . reinforce themselves by mutual assurances that they are always agreed" and that the act challenging this agreement is anomalous.[6] This can be done only by common action: by passionate reaction of the outraged common sentiments, of the shocked collective conscience, to the offending act. This reaction is punishment.

Punishment involves the infliction of suffering, but this is not its essential characteristic. Essentially, punishment is "the palpable symbol" of an inner state, "a notation, a language, through which is expressed the feeling inspired by the disapproved behaviour."[7] This feeling is "unanimous aversion"; its expression through punishment signifies that the offended sentiments are and remain collective. Thus the main function of punishment is not so much to reform or deter, but rather to maintain social cohesion by safeguarding a vigorous collective conscience. Challenged by crime, the latter "would necessarily lose its energy, if an emotional reaction of the community did not come to compensate its loss, and it would result in a break-down of social solidarity."[8]

But the most fully developed and philosophically the most interesting formulation of expressionism is Alfred Cyril Ewing's "educative theory" of punishment. Its central claim is that punishment is "a kind of language intended to express moral disapproval."[9] It is a language painful to listen to for the immediate addressee; but the pain has a moral significance and a moral function. It is both a symbol of the wickedness of his action and an expression of society's moral condemnation of it. And its aim is to help the criminal realize the wrongness of his action and mend his ways. For the criminal to be reformed, and not merely deterred,

> he must realize the badness of what he has been doing, and since his previous actions make it very doubtful whether he will do so of his own accord, this badness must be "brought home to him" and the consciousness of it stamped on his mind by suffering. The infliction of pain is society's way of impressing on him that he has done wrong.[10]

This is the distinctively moral influence of punishment. It also sends the same moral message and exerts a moralizing influence in another direction; that of the public at large. To be sure, people do not need the state to tell them that it is morally wrong to steal or kill by punishing those who do so. But we know that some are liable to commit such acts in the future, and that shows that not everybody realizes strongly and vividly enough just how very wrong such acts are. Those who do not are in need of the kind of moral education that is provided when thieves and murderers are punished. The theory of punishment need not take into account really upright people anyway, but rather their "weaker brethren" who are "hovering on the borderline of crime."[11]

These, then, are the main points in three expressionist accounts of punishment. The differences between them concern both the contents of the expression and the process of expressing these contents. According to Stephen and Durkheim, what are expressed through punishment are *feelings, sentiments* of the public; the expression *vents* these feelings. For Ewing, it is a moral *judgment* that is being *communicated* through punishment. Further differences have to do with the purpose and justification of using the language of punishment. Stephen offers a secularized version of the religious vision of the just rejoicing in heaven at the torments of sinners in hell: the aim of punishment is *gratification* of the vindictive feelings of the public. These feelings are natural, healthy and strong, and their satisfaction is good in itself. According to Durkheim, the purpose of giving vent to collective sentiments through punishment is to *reinforce* these sentiments, and thereby maintain *social solidarity* and *cohesion*. Ewing is more intellectualistic: punishment as expressive of society's moral condemnation *teaches* a moral lesson in order to *reform* the criminal and *educate* the public, thus contributing to the reduction of crime. The ethical diagnosis of the state of the public is also different in the three accounts. Neither Stephen nor Durkheim thinks that the public is in need of moral enlightenment. The former has no doubt that the public *knows* well enough what is right and what is wrong; its need to express and gratify its hatred of the criminal is supervenient on this knowledge. The latter would refuse to talk in terms of moral knowledge, for he holds that an act is wrong *in virtue of being disapproved* by society; what society needs is to vent its disapproval on appropriate occasions, and thereby reinforce it. Ewing, on the other hand, sees a significant part of the public *lacking in moral understanding* and in need of education; this is provided when punishment expresses the moral condemnation of crime by that part of society which has the right moral beliefs ingrained deeply enough.

III

But the differences of detail are not important for the point I want to make. The important things are two basic features common to these statements of expressionism. Punishment is seen as valuable not in itself, but as a means. And the end which it serves is social not only in the sense that it is an end *of* society, but also in that it is achieved by directly *affecting* society (or part of it) in a certain way. Stephen and Durkheim have hardly anything to say about the individual punished; whatever is done to him is significant and justified primarily in terms of what this does for others. The latter expressly says that punishment is designed above all to act on decent, law-abiding citizens: as it is meant to heal the wounds inflicted on collective sentiments, it can be effective only where these sentiments exist. Ewing takes into account the reformative effects of punishment on the individual punished, but makes it clear that its main object and primary justification is its educative influence on the public. The ultimate concern in punishing is to reduce crime;

therefore education comes first and reform second, both for the obvious reason that the actual criminal is but one while there are many potential criminals in the public, and because punishment is much more efficient in promoting the former objective than in achieving the latter.

There is another major theory of punishment that has both these features: the deterrent theory. Because it sees the *sole* justification of punishment in its contribution to crime control through its deterrent effects, the theory is exposed to the criticism that it severs the connection between punishment and considerations of justice and desert, and is liable to legitimize various unjust punishments whenever these turn out to be efficient *and* economical means of deterrence. The list of types of injustice which may prove socially expedient and therefore also morally right from the point of view of the deterrent theory is long; here I want to mention only two: punishment of the innocent and the merely apparent punishment of the guilty. While the argument on punishment of the innocent has been in the focus of confrontations between utilitarians and retributivists for quite some time now, the one on punishing the guilty in appearance only should perhaps be explicated. Within the context of the deterrent theory one must distinguish, with Bentham, between real and apparent punishment—punishment actually inflicted on someone, and the idea of that punishment formed in the minds of others—and acknowledge that it is apparent punishment that secures the desired deterrent effects on the public, which is the principal target. In this respect, real punishment is merely an expense, necessary for the sake of appearance. Therefore the proportion between the two should be as much as possible in favour of appearance as against reality. And the ultimate achievement of efficiency *and* economy in punishing would be to reap the fruits of apparent punishment without paying for them at all in the currency of human suffering of which real punishment consists: "If hanging a man *in effigy* would produce the same salutary impression of terror upon the minds of the people, it would be folly or cruelty ever to hang a man *in person*."[12]

Both Stephen and Durkheim criticize the deterrent theory for its unacceptable implications regarding the severity of punishment, and offer their own accounts as an alternative. Both seem to take it for granted that punishment as expressive will always be addressed to the guilty and only the guilty. Ewing is more cautious in this matter. He subjects the deterrent view to detailed critical analysis, marshalling against

it the punishment-of-the-innocent argument, among others. He then presents his own educative theory as an alternative—as a theory that effects a reconciliation of utilitarianism and retributivism by taking into account both the social utility of punishment and considerations of justice and desert. If punishment is to be socially useful—if it is to reform the criminal and educate the public by communicating society's condemnation of the crime—the communication must be true and delivered to the right address, i.e. meted out for a wrong act and to its perpetrator. If it is inflicted on an innocent person, it can have no desirable effects, neither on him nor on the public; it can only confuse, embitter and corrupt both the person punished and everyone else. If it is to be socially useful in the relevant sense, punishment must be deserved and just.

Nevertheless, the kind of expressionism advanced by these authors is exposed to the arguments on punishing the innocent and punishing the guilty in appearance only no less than the deterrent theory. For the vindictive feelings of the public to be vented and gratified, or for the collective sentiments to be given expression and thus reinforced, the person punished need not *be* guilty; it is enough that he be *believed* to be guilty by the public. For the moral lesson taught by punishment to be successful, the person punished need not *be* guilty; it is enough that the public should *think* that he is. (This is true only with respect to the educative effects of punishment; but on Ewing's theory achieving these effects is the primary aim of punishment and its main justification.)

Again, it is apparent punishment that gratifies the vindictive feelings of the public, or gives vent to, and thereby reinforces, collective sentiments. It is apparent punishment that helps educate the public about the true moral standing of crime. Real punishment is needed only for the sake of producing appearance. So whenever we can secure the desired effects of apparent punishment without paying the price in terms of real punishment, and no considerations of special prevention apply—no effects in this direction by way of deterrence, disablement, or reform can, or need, be achieved—we should stage a show of punishment without actually inflicting it. In such cases it would be both stupid and cruel not to hang an effigy and let the murderer off.

These unattractive implications are the result of two basic traits of expressionism of the kind advanced by Stephen, Durkheim and Ewing: the view of punishment as valuable as a means only, and as social in the sense that its immediate effects on society are what count most. So the way to defend expressionism would be to try to modify it with regard to one or both of these traits.

It might seem that a very recent statement of expressionism, Jean Hampton's "moral education theory of punishment," is not open to these objections. According to this theory, punishment should be seen as a sort of electrified fence marking a moral boundary. The pain this fence inflicts on those who try to cross it communicates a moral message to beings who are capable of reflecting on the reasons for the fence's standing where it does: the message that there is a barrier fencing off certain ways of acting *because* they are morally wrong. Thus punishment teaches both the criminal and the public that the crime is prohibited because it is morally wrong, and must not be perpetrated for this reason. By teaching this lesson, punishment helps prevent crimes.

Hampton takes up the question whether this theory might not imply that under certain circumstances an innocent person should be punished in order to teach the public the required lesson, and gives two arguments for denying this. First, educating the public and educating the criminal are "inextricably linked": "if the state aims to convey a moral lesson to the community about how other human beings should be treated, it will completely fail to do so if it inflicts pain on someone innocent of any wrongdoing—indeed, it would send a message exactly contrary to the one it had intended."[13] Hampton's theory is rather like Ewing's in its main points, and here she makes the same mistaken move as Ewing made, assuming that the public knows that the person punished is innocent. This is a surprising assumption, considering that in that case punishment could hardly serve even as a means of deterrence. Of course, no matter against which particular theory it is marshalled, the argument on punishing the innocent assumes just the opposite—that the public can be deceived into believing the accused to be guilty.

Second, Hampton claims that we can preserve the connection of punishment with guilt by making moral education of the criminal lexically prior to that of the public; for we know that the criminal is in need of it, while we are "less sure" about the public. This does not seem convincing either. In view of what we know about human beings and crime in general, and about crime in our own society in particular (from criminal statistics, for instance), it is a safe bet that most of the more usual crimes will be committed in no small numbers in the future. The difference on which Hampton builds her case is not so much in the degree of reliability of our knowledge that there is a need for

a moral lesson to be taught by punishment, but only in that in one case we know the name of the individual who could profit by such a lesson, while in the other case we only know that there are quite a few persons whom we cannot identify at present who are also in need of the same piece of education. Furthermore, if the principal concern in punishing is the prevention of crimes—as Hampton herself repeatedly says it is—then it is clear that we cannot in consistency assign lexical priority to exerting moral influence on the criminal. On the contrary, educating the public must be more important.

One might try to rebut at least the argument on staging shows of punishment without actually inflicting it, by granting that there may be cases in which reasons of special deterrence or disablement do not apply, but refusing to admit that there can ever be a case in which there is no hope of moral reform of the criminal. This is the view of another recent expressionist, Antony Duff. To refuse to punish a criminal on the ground that he is a hopeless case, says Duff,

> *is to give up any respect or hope for him as a moral agent; and this we may not do. The point here is not that we can never have empirically adequate grounds for believing that punishment will not in fact bring a criminal to repentance: it is rather that we can never have* morally *adequate grounds—nothing could count as morally adequate grounds—for treating a person as being beyond redemption. We owe it to every moral agent to treat him as one who can be brought to reform and redeem himself—to keep trying, however vainly, to reach the good that is in him, and to appeal to his capacity for moral understanding and concern.*[14]

This way of securing actual punishment of the guilty strikes me as farfetched. In view of the degree which wilful, unrepentant wickedness has reached in some criminals, claims such as these seem almost otherworldly. To take just two very recent examples, is it plausible to say of Klaus Barbie or Andrija Artuković, that we must not think of them as morally hopeless, but ought to respect them as moral agents? Do we really owe it to them to keep trying to reach the good that is in them? It seems obvious to me that to Barbie, Artuković, and the likes of them, we owe nothing of the sort.

Therefore the two objections to extrinsic expressionism stand. If this theory is the truth about punishment—if the primary purpose of punishment is to affect the public in a certain way, and if it is morally justified in so far as it achieves this purpose—then we must say that sometimes it will be morally right to punish the innocent, while at other times the morally right thing to do will be to refrain from actually inflicting punishment on the guilty, and to stage shows of their being punished instead.

IV

The view of punishment as expressive of society's emphatic moral condemnation of crime can be construed in a very different way. It can be claimed that punishment, so conceived, need not serve a purpose external to it and be justified in terms of its instrumental value, because it is *intrinsically* appropriate, justified and called for.[15]

One might be tempted to see this claim, with H. L. A. Hart, as "representing as a value to be pursued at the cost of human suffering the *bare* expression of moral condemnation," and to ask whether "the *mere* expression of moral condemnation [is] a thing of value in itself to be pursued at this cost."[16] The reply to this is that to disconnect punishment as expressive of society's condemnation of crime from all those forward-looking, consequentialist considerations referred to in various versions of extrinsic expressionism is not tantamount to reducing it to a *bare* or *mere* expression. For in expressing emphatic condemnation of the crime committed, punishment *vindicates* the law which has been broken, *reaffirms* the right which has been violated, and *demonstrates* that the misdeed was indeed a crime.

Rules that state standards of behaviour and command categorically imply that actions violating them are wrong, and that such actions are to be condemned, denounced, repudiated. Expressions of this condemnation and repudiation are the index of the validity of the rules and of the acceptance of the conviction that their breaches are wrong in society. If actions of a certain kind can be done without bringing about such a response from society, this indicates that no rule prohibiting such actions is accepted as a valid and binding standard of behaviour.

Moral standards, expressed by moral rules, evolve in society in a diffuse, non-institutional way, rely on the moral authority of society and conscience of its members, and are used as criteria of moral judgment by any and all of its members without any special authorization or qualification. Thus the question

whether a certain kind of action is considered to be morally wrong in a society, whether a society adheres to standard prohibiting that kind of action, will be settled by finding out whether ordinary members of that society condemn actions of that sort. Their condemnation vindicates the standard, and demonstrates that its violations are indeed held to be morally wrong.

Criminal laws are similar to moral rules in that they also state standards of behaviour. But these are standards of society organized into a state with its legal order; they presuppose the authority of the state and its legal order. They are authoritatively formulated and applied solely through formalized procedures in appropriate institutions. Legislative institutions of the state pass criminal laws which determine some of our most important legal rights, and turn their infringements into crimes. It is then up to criminal courts and institutions that carry out sentences passed in these courts to condemn actions that violate such laws and infringe the rights determined by them. This condemnation is expressed by punishment. By giving expression to it, punishment vindicates the law broken, reaffirms the right violated, and demonstrates that its violation was indeed a crime. Thus, if there are to be rights sanctioned by the criminal law, if some actions are to be crimes, if there is to be criminal law at all, there must be punishment as well. Where there is no punishment, there are no crimes, no criminal law, no rights determined and sanctioned by such law.

To be sure, if a thief who has stolen from me is never caught, tried in court and punished, this will not *in itself* show that what he did was not a crime, and that I actually had no right sanctioned by criminal law to the piece of property stolen. But if the state and the legal order did not even try to apprehend and punish him and other thieves, if thieves *as a rule* were not prosecuted and punished, the conclusion would have to be drawn that theft is not really a crime, and that property rights do not really obtain, at least in the sense of rights determined and guaranteed by the criminal law.

This kind of expressionism might easily be misunderstood. In order to avoid that, let me emphasize that the connection between the expression of condemnation of the crime through punishment, and the notions of crime, a right determined by the criminal law, and the criminal law itself, is not predicated on the function of this condemnation as a means of prevention of crimes. The prevention of crime is something distinct from punishment, something that may stand in a certain causal, i.e. contingent, relation to it, something that may be achieved in the future *by means* of it. The understanding and justification of punishment presented above is entirely backward-looking. If by punishing we prevent the commission of crimes in the future, so much the better; but neither such effects, nor the intention to bring them about, are *inherent* to the enterprise. The vindication of law, re-affirmation of right and demonstration that the action was a crime, on the other hand, *are* inherent to punishment: they are not things distinguished from punishment and achieved by means of it, but rather tasks accomplished *in* punishing. We shall have demonstrated that an action was a crime, and reaffirmed the right infringed and the law broken by it, even if the condemnation expressed through punishment proves inefficient in preventing future crimes of the same kind.

This means that, *if* the state has a right to pass criminal laws, to determine certain rights by such laws, and to proclaim that certain actions are crimes, it has also a right to punish. It has a duty to punish as well; for its failure to do so would be incompatible with the law it promulgates and the rights it proclaims, and would belie its professed conviction that their violation is a crime.

V

There are several objections which might be brought up against this version of expressionism.

(1) It might be said that the above argument at most exhibits a connection between standards of behaviour stated by criminal laws and *condemnation* by society of breaches of these standards. But this does not amount to a justification of *punishment,* for we still do not see why society's condemnation has to be punitive. As H. L. A. Hart put it, the "normal way" of expressing moral condemnation is by words, "and it is not clear, if denunciation is really what is required, why a solemn public statement of disapproval would not be the most 'appropriate' or 'emphatic' means of expressing this. Why should a denunciation take the form of punishment?"[17]

Before I take up this criticism squarely, two minor points should be made. What Hart says is not completely accurate even with regard to moral condemnation pure and simple. True, we convey moral condemnation verbally most of the time—but not always; there are non-verbal ways of expressing it, and they are no less normal for it. We also express condemnation by adopting a cool, formal demeanor; by reducing the scope and intensity of our relations with the person concerned; by failing to render help or support in situations in which, were it not for the moral offence committed, these would be forthcoming without ado; in the most extreme cases, by breaking off all contact and communication. A community may resort to boycott or ostracism as the ultimate expressions of moral repugnance. All these are actions, not words; and they are used to express moral condemnation when mere words do not seem up to the task.

Moreover, the connection between society's condemnation of crime and punishment as its expression may be somewhat less arbitrary than is often suggested. When characterizing punishment as expressive, some authors tend to use the word "symbol." Feinberg, in particular, repeatedly emphasizes the conventional nature of the relation between the condemnation and hard treatment of which punishment consists. According to him, certain forms of hard treatment are "conventional symbols" of public reprobation in the same way that the drinking of champagne is a conventional symbol of celebration, and black clothes are symbolic of mourning. It seems to me that Skillen is right in saying that punishment is a natural expression of condemnation, repudiation, and similar feelings and attitudes, rather than a conventional device for expressing them:

> *Whereas black is arguably neutral in itself and only contextually and conventionally constituted as mourning wear . . . it is pretty clear that losing money, years of liberty, or parts of one's body is hardly neutral in that way. [. . .] Feinberg vastly underrates the natural appropriateness, the non-arbitrariness, of certain forms of hard treatment to be the expression or communication of moralistic and punitive attitudes. Such practices* embody *punitive hostility, they do not merely "symbolize" it.*[18]

But even if it is granted that the connection between society's condemnation of crime and punishment is stronger than that of mere convention, that it is somehow natural and appropriate to express condemnation of crime by punishment, the question remains: Why not express it verbally nevertheless? Even if this is a less "natural" and "appropriate" way, it is *a* possibility. Is it not the possibility to be preferred, in view of the evil inflicted by expressing it in the most "natural" and "appropriate" manner?

The answer to this is that merely verbal condemnation is not likely to reach its immediate addressee and to be fully understood by him. Regrettably, although perhaps not surprisingly, many criminals are oblivious to mere words. They do not care for the standards of society; otherwise they would not be committing crimes. They are lacking in respect for others; otherwise they would not be violating their rights. They are deficient in human sympathy; otherwise they would not be harming others. But they are endowed with as lively an appreciation of their own interest as is everyone else. So if society's condemnation of their misdeeds is really to reach them, if they are really to understand how wrong their actions are, it will have to be translated into the one language they are sure to understand: the language of self-interest. This translation is accomplished by punishment.

Moreover, punishment is not like a private letter; it is rather like a poster put up on a billboard on a busy street. The immediate addressee of the message punishment conveys, the criminal punished, is not the only one for whom the message is meant; it is also meant for the victim of the crime and for the public at large. Now *they* would surely see purely verbal condemnation of crime, however public and solemn, as half-hearted and unconvincing. The state would be seen as promulgating laws which determine some of our most important rights—to life, bodily integrity, property—and pronouncing their violations to be crimes, and then responding to their violations only by issuing verbal statements of disapproval. It would be seen as desisting from activating its apparatus of force and coercion, which is surely one of its essential, defining features.[19] And there would be a striking dissimilarity and disproportion between crimes, which normally affect their victims very palpably, and the merely verbal response to them on the part of the state and the legal order, which might not reach the person to whom it is addressed at all, let alone impress or affect him. In view of all this, it seems to me that both those whose rights were being violated and those violating them, and everyone else for that matter, could not fail to draw the conclusion that those rights were not valid after all, were not really recognized, at least as rights defined and guaranteed by the criminal law, in any serious manner. The notion "taking X seriously" in this kind of context seems to preclude radical dissimilarity and disproportion between X and whatever is done by way of responding to it. An action cannot be shown to be a crime, the right infringed and the law broken by it cannot be reasserted and vindicated, if the response supposed to do this is by its nature so dissimilar to the action, and so disproportionate to it in weight, as a mere verbal condemnation, however public and solemn, would be. The necessary seriousness and weight can be secured only by punishment.

(2) Another objection that might be advanced against intrinsic expressionism is that it fails to accommodate considerations of justice and desert, and accordingly could legitimize, no less than the extrinsic variety of the theory, punishment of the innocent or merely apparent punishment of the guilty.

Extrinsic expressionism is liable to justify such courses of action because it sees moral condemnation expressed by punishment solely as a means to an end. If condemnation is merely a means, we shall condemn an action, refrain from condemning it, or even praise it, depending on how that end is best served under the circumstances. Intrinsic expressionism, on the other hand, does not construe the expression of moral condemnation that is punishment as a means to an end external to it, but as intrinsically right and proper. The right violated by the crime is reaffirmed, the law broken by it is vindicated, and the deed itself is shown to be a crime, *in* punishment as expressive of condemnation, and not *by means* of it. So the conditions punishment has to satisfy are not dictated by an extrinsic end it is made to serve and the ever-changing circumstances in which it does so; they are determined solely by the nature of moral condemnation. It has to be appropriate *as* moral condemnation. It has to be truthful, just and deserved, and to be seen as such, by everyone involved: by those conveying it, and by all those to whom it is being conveyed.

In this respect, punishment of the innocent as a communicative enterprise would be radically morally flawed at two crucial points. The expression of moral condemnation would be morally polluted at its very source: the judge, who is supposed to embody the moral authority of the law when acting in its name, would be knowingly and deliberately faking the moral condemnation of its violation—the condemnation which is the index of the law's acceptance in society, the condition of its presence in the life of society as a valid and binding standard of conduct. And it would be morally stained in a deep, irreparable manner in the eyes of the innocent person punished. It would be seen by him, if by no one else, for the lie that it is; it would be experienced by him, as Bradley put it in a different context, as "a gross immorality, a crying injustice, an abominable crime, and not what it pretends to be."[20]

It seems to me that if we knew of a case of deliberate punishment of the innocent in which the public was deceived into believing that the person punished was the culprit, we would not say that the law broken had been vindicated, the right infringed reasserted, and the misdeed shown to be a crime. We would rather say that the public *mistakenly believed* that all this took place, while what really happened was something quite different: that the condemnation expressed by the punishment was a lie and an injustice; that punishment as expressive of society's moral condemnation of crime was not properly applied, but rather abused; that the law broken was not vindicated, that the right violated was not reasserted, but rather insulted and made a mockery of yet one more time; that the action which had occasioned the whole proceedings was not properly shown to be a crime, but a new crime was committed instead.

What I have just said refers to the way punishment of the innocent would have to be judged from the standpoint of intrinsic expressionism; the argument on staging shows of punishing the guilty instead of actually punishing them could be refuted along the same lines.

(3) It was clear from the beginning that the distinction between the two types of expressionism is similar to that between the two traditional approaches to punishment, the utilitarian and the retributive: that extrinsic expressionism is a variety of utilitarianism, while intrinsic expressionism has a certain affinity with retributivism, at least in that both justify punishment in terms of backward-looking considerations. My discussion of the punishment-of-the-innocent argument advanced as an objection to intrinsic expressionism shows that this affinity is much stronger: that in claiming that punishment is *intrinsically* right and called for *qua* expressive of moral condemnation of crime, the adherent of intrinsic expressionism commits himself to just those considerations of justice and desert on which the retributivist insists. So it would seem that the two varieties of expressionism are just as mutually opposed as the traditional utilitarian and retributive accounts of punishment.

However, it has been claimed that this is not so, since intrinsic expressionism actually presupposes the validity of extrinsic expressionism and would be meaningless if it turned out that the claims of the latter concerning the instrumental value of punishment as expressive of society's condemnation of crime were false. This is the argument put forward by John Charvet, who construes punishment as a sort of criticism—the sort appropriate to the breaking of legal rules:

The purpose of having a rule is to secure the general realization of the conduct it prescribes. Therefore the existence of rules presupposes the possibility of affecting people's future actions. It is in this context that criticism operates, for it would indeed be meaningless and futile to criticize people for their actions, if such criticism never did or ever could have an effect on their future conduct. But since criticism is only relevant where rules exist, and since rules exist only where it is possible to affect people's actions by means of the rules, criticism is assured of having such general effects. Thus criticism does always in part look forward to the future actions of the rule-breaker and the other members of the community, as the Utilitarians have always insisted that punishment must.[21]

This, however, is too quick. It is true that criticism of any kind makes sense only against a background of rules. It is also true that rules are forward-looking. Finally, it is true that rules make sense only where there is a possibility that they will influence people's actions. But from all this it does not follow that criticism in general, or the particular kind of criticism that is punishment, must be forward-looking and efficient in affecting people's actions, or capable of doing so. Criticism that did not satisfy these conditions would be futile, and analytically so. But it would not necessarily be meaningless—no more so than an act of gratitude, performed although there are no good utilitarian reasons for performing it, would thereby be made meaningless. Let me bring up once again the cases of Klaus Barbie and Andrija Artuković. The facts in these two cases are such that no considerations of particular prevention apply: the men are beyond moral reform, while at the same time too old, feeble and isolated to need to be deterred from committing the same crimes again. As for the effects on society at large, be it in terms of deterrence, as Charvet would have it, moral education of the public, as in Ewing and Hampton, reinforcement of collective sentiments, as in Durkheim, or gratification of hatred and indignation, as in Stephen—any and all of these might be achieved by hanging the effigies instead of the men themselves. So what is the point of actually punishing in these cases, instead of securing the desired effects by apparent punishment, and sending the two to some far-away places to live out the remaining years of their natural lives in peace and comfort, after having grown beards and been provided with new names and passports? If the point of punishment is identified with its end, i.e.

with a state of affairs distinct from it, which is to be attained in the future *by means of it,* actually punishing Barbie or Artuković *is* pointless. But the point of doing something is not necessarily the end to be achieved by doing it, and it seems to me that there is no great difficulty in seeing the point here. *In* condemning their misdeeds in the serious way appropriate to their moral status, i.e. *in* punishing them, we shall vindicate the laws they broke, reaffirm the rights of their victims which they violated, and demonstrate to any and all, as well as bring home in no uncertain terms to the two men themselves, that their deeds were indeed crimes.

(4) The preceding criticisms are of the immanent type. But intrinsic expressionism might also be questioned by questioning the background of the theory: the social morality which is in part codified in the criminal law, and whose condemnation of crime punishment is taken to express. One might have doubts as to its validity, its homogeneity, and the consistency and authenticity of the judgment it passes on crime through punishment.

The expressionist might be taken to believe uncritically that the positive morality of society—any society—is self-authenticating, that its principles are moral axioms, and that punishment is conclusively justified once it is shown to express the emphatic moral condemnation of actions offending against these principles. But what if that morality itself is morally flawed? If the social morality of a multi-racial society sees "separate development" of races as a moral requirement, and the majority of people feel badly enough about the immorality of mixed marriages to prohibit them by law, are we to accept punishments based on that law as morally legitimate in virtue of expressing such attitudes? As Anthony Skillen has remarked, "'expression' itself is no adequate ethic, any more than is sincerity. Some of the worst deeds have been, no doubt, sincere expressions."[22]

It might be thought that the expressionist is assuming that social morality is a much more homogeneous set of beliefs and attitudes than the reality of most contemporary societies would warrant. Contemporary society is as typically pluralistic and conflict-ridden in the field of morals as in other areas. On many moral issues we are likely to find not one generally accepted stand, but two or more different and even mutually opposed views, espoused by significant sections of society. Which of them is to be expressed in law and in punishments for offending against it?[23]

There may also be problems of authenticity of the condemnation conveyed through punishment. It may well be that it is only capital punishment that expresses emphatically enough the moral condemnation of murder. Now murder is presumably so very wrong because human life is such a paramount value. But what are we to say of a society which provides for the death penalty as the appropriate punishment for murder, and at the same time, for instance, does not bother very much about those social and economic conditions which are known to breed crime, including the crime of murder? Or does not testify very convincingly to its high regard for the value of human life in fields such as medical care, or traffic regulations and the maintenance of roads? Or is given to using unadvisedly its armed forces in promoting its foreign policy and foreign trade objectives? In such cases, as Skillen says, "questions of sham and hypocrisy can arise," and one might suspect that punishment is not much more than a "fetishistic surrogate" for a value which is not given expression in other areas of life.[24]

Some statements of expressionism are certainly exposed to criticism along these lines. Authors such as Stephen and Durkheim seem to espouse an uncritical view of social morality, both in the sense of not being alive to the possibility that the moral outlook of a society may itself be morally questionable, and with respect to the degree of internal consistency they assume for it. But these are faults of specific formulations of expressionism, not its inherent flaws. The criticism is not damaging to expressionism as such, but rather points out the conditions of its proper applications. Therefore it should be welcome to a critical adherent of the theory. Such an adherent should say that this view will provide the justification of punishment in a society whose morals—or that part of its morals which is coextensive with its criminal law—are basically sound. If we cannot accept the moral outlook of a society, we shall withhold moral support when it expresses moral condemnation through punishment.

Similarly, intrinsic expressionism offers an account of punishment which assumes that there is a measure of moral consensus in society. It will justify those punishments that are based on this consensus (provided that its contents are sound), and refuse justification to those that go beyond it. Society may legitimately express moral condemnation by punishment only when its conscience speaks strongly and unequivocally, with one voice.

Finally, the theory will legitimize punishment on further condition that it is not "sham" in the sense of expressing allegiance to certain values in a specific, narrow context, while these same values are disregarded or flouted in other fields of social life. In these

matters, as elsewhere, sincerity is not enough; but it is surely necessary.[25]

---

1. *A. J. Skillen, "How to Say Things with Walls,"* Philosophy *55 (1980),* 509–523.

2. *J. Feinberg, "The Expressive Function of Punishment,"* Doing and Deserving *(Princeton University Press, 1970), 98.*

3. *Ibid., 100.*

4. *J. F. Stephen,* A General View of the Criminal Laws of England *(London: Macmillan, 1863), 99.*

5. *J. F. Stephen,* A History of the Criminal Law of England *(London: Macmillan, 1883), Vol. 2, 81.*

6. *E. Durkheim,* The Division of Labor in Society, *trans. by G. Simpson (New York: The Free Press, 1964), 103.*

7. *E. Durkheim,* Moral Education, *E. K. Wilson (ed.), trans. by E. K. Wilson and H. Schnurer (Glencoe: The Free Press, 1961), 176.*

8. *E. Durkheim,* The Division of Labor in Society, *108.*

9. *A. C. Ewing, "Punishment as Viewed by the Philosopher,"* The Canadian Bar. Review *21 (1943), 116.*

10. *A. C. Ewing,* The Morality of Punishment *(London: Kegan Paul, Trench, Trubner & Co., 1929), 84.*

11. *A. C. Ewing, "Punishment as Moral Agency,"* Mind *36 (1927), 297.*

12. *J. Bentham,* Principles of Penal Law, Works, *J. Bowring (ed.) (New York: Russell & Russell, 1962), Vol. I, 398.*

13. *J. Hampton, "The Moral Education Theory of Punishment,"* Philosophy and Public Affairs *13 (1984), 230.*

14. *R. A. Duff,* Trials and Punishments *(Cambridge University Press, 1986), 266. (Duff's version of expressionism is not of the extrinsic type.)*

15. *In this section and at the beginning of the next I draw on section VI of my "The Middle Way in the Philosophy of Punishment," R. Gavison (ed.),* Issues in Contemporary Legal Philosophy: The Influence of H. L. A. Hart *(Oxford University Press, 1987).*

16. *H. L. A. Hart,* Law, Liberty and Morality *(Oxford University Press, 1963), 65 (emphasis added).*

17. *Ibid., 66.*

18. *A. J. Skillen, op. cit., 517.*

19. *Cf. e.g. M. Weber, "Politics as a Vocation," H. H. Gerth and C. Wright Mills (eds.),* From Max Weber: Essays in Sociology *(London: Routledge & Kegan Paul, 1967), 77–78.*

20. *F. H. Bradley,* Ethical Studies, *2nd edn (London: Oxford University Press, 1962), 26.*

21. *J. Charvet, "Criticism and Punishment,"* Mind *75 (1966), 578.*

22. *A. J. Skillen, op. cit., 521.*

23. *Cf. H. L. A. Hart,* The Morality of the Criminal Law *(Jerusalem: The Magnes Press, 1964), 39–41.*

24. *A. J. Skillen, op. cit., 521–522.*

25. *An earlier, much shorter version of this paper was read at the 12th International Wittgenstein Symposium in Kirchberg am Wechsel, Austria, in August 1987.*

What, If Anything, Justifies Legal Punishment?

THE CLASSIC DEBATE*

Joel Feinberg

The traditional debate among philosophers over the justification of legal punishment has been between partisans of the "retributive" and "utilitarian" theories. Neither the term "retributive" nor the term "utilitarian" has been used with perfect uniformity and precision, but, by and large, those who have been called utilitarians have insisted that punishment of the guilty is at best a necessary evil justified only as a means to the prevention of evils even greater than itself. "Retributivism," on the other hand, has labeled a large miscellany of theories united only in their opposition to the utilitarian theory. It may best serve clarity, therefore, to define the utilitarian theory with relative precision (as above) and then define retributivism as its logical contradictory, so that the two theories are not only mutually exclusive but also jointly exhaustive. Discussion of the various varieties of retributivism can then proceed.

Perhaps the leading form of the retributive theory includes major elements identifiable in the following formulations:

> It is an end in itself that the guilty should suffer pain. . . . The primary justification of punishment is always to be found in the fact that an offense has been committed which deserves the punishment, not in any future advantage to be gained by its infliction.[1]
>
> Punishment is justified only on the ground that wrongdoing merits punishment. It is morally fitting that a person who does wrong should suffer in proportion to his wrongdoing. That a criminal should be punished follows from his guilt, and the severity of the appropriate punishment depends on the depravity of the act. The state of affairs where a wrongdoer suffers punishment is morally better than one where he does not, and is so irrespective of consequences.[2]

Justification, according to these accounts, must look backward in time to guilt rather than forward to "advantages"; the formulations are rich in moral terminology ("merits," "morally fitting," "wrongdoing," "morally better"); there is great emphasis on *desert*. For those reasons, we might well refer to this as a "moralistic" version of the retributive theory. As such it can be contrasted with a "legalistic" version, according to which punishment is for lawbreaking, not (necessarily) for wrongdoing. Legalistic retributivism holds that the justification of punishment is always to be found in the fact that a rule has been broken for

---

*Published in previous editions as part of the introduction to this section.

the violation of which a certain penalty is specified, whether or not the offender incurs any moral guilt. The offender, properly apprised in advance of the penalty, voluntarily assumes the risk of punishment, and when he or she receives comeuppance, he or she can have no complaint. As one recent legalistic retributivist put it,

> *Punishment is a corollary not of law but of lawbreaking. Legislators do not choose to punish. They hope no punishment will be needed. Their laws would succeed even if no punishment occurred. The criminal makes the essential choice: he "brings it on himself."*[3]

Both moralistic and legalistic retributivism have "pure" and "impure" variants. In their pure formulations, they are totally free of utilitarian admixture. Moral or legal guilt (as the case may be) is not only a necessary condition for justified punishment, it is quite sufficient "irrespective of consequences." In the impure formulation, both guilt (moral or legal) and conducibility to good consequences are necessary for justified punishment, but neither is sufficient without the other. This mixed theory could with some propriety be called "impure utilitarianism" as well as "impure retributivism." Since we have stipulated, however, that a retributive theory is one which is not wholly utilitarian, we are committed to the latter usage.

A complete theory of punishment will not only specify the conditions under which punishment should and should not be administered, it will also provide a general criterion for determining the amount or degree of punishment. It is not only unjust to be punished undeservedly and to be let off although meriting punishment, it is also unfair to be punished severely for a minor offense or lightly for a heinous one. What is the right amount of punishment? There is one kind of answer especially distinctive of retributivism in all of its forms: an answer in terms of fittingness or proportion. The punishment must *fit* the crime; its degree must be *proportionate* to the seriousness or moral gravity of the offense. Retributivists are often understandably vague about the practical interpretations of the key notions of fittingness, proportion, and moral gravity. Sometimes aesthetic analogies are employed (such as matching and clashing colors, or harmonious and dissonant chords). Some retributivists, including Immanuel Kant, attempt to apply the ancient principle of *lex talionis* (the law of retaliation): The punishment should match the crime not only in the degree of harm inflicted on its victim, but also in the mode and manner of the infliction: fines for larceny, physical beatings for battery, capital punishment for murder. Other retributivists, however, explicitly reject the doctrine of retaliation in kind; hence, that doctrine is better treated as a logically independent thesis commonly associated with retributivism rather than as an essential component of the theory.

Defined as the exhaustive class of alternatives to the utilitarian theory, retributivism of course is subject to no simple summary. It will be useful to subsequent discussions, however, to summarize that popular variant of the theory which can be called *pure moralistic retributivism* as consistent (at least) of the following propositions:

1. Moral guilt is a necessary condition for justified punishment.
2. Moral guilt is a sufficient condition ("irrespective of consequences") for justified punishment.
3. The proper amount of punishment to be inflicted upon the morally guilty offender is that amount which fits, matches, or is proportionate to the moral gravity of the offense.

That it is never justified to punish a morally blameless person for his or her "offense" (thesis 1) may not be quite self-evident, but it does find strong support in moral common sense. Thesis 2, however, is likely to prove an embarrassment for the pure retributivist, for it would have him or her approve the infliction of suffering on a person (albeit a *guilty* person) even when no good to the offender, the victim, or society at large is likely to result. "How can two wrongs make a right, or two evils a good?" he or she will be asked by the utilitarian, and in this case it is the utilitarian who will claim to speak for "moral common sense." In reply, the pure retributivist is likely to concede that inflicting suffering on an offender is not "good in itself," but will also point out that single acts cannot be judged simply "in themselves" with no concern for the context in which they fit and the events preceding them which are their occasion. Personal sadness is not a "good in itself" either, and yet when it is a response to the perceived sufferings of another it has a unique appropriateness. Glee, considered "in itself," looks much more like an intrinsically good mental state, but glee does not morally fit the perception of another's pain any more than an orange shirt aesthetically fits shocking pink trousers. Similarly, it may be true (the analogy is admittedly imperfect) that "while the moral evil in the offender and the pain of the punishment are each considered separately evils, it is intrinsically good that a certain relation exist or be established between them."[4] In this way the pure retributivist, relying on moral intuitions, can deny that a deliberate imposition of suffering on a human being is either good in itself or good as a means, and yet find it justified, nevertheless, as an essential component of an intrinsically good relation. Perhaps that is to put the point too strongly. All the retributivist needs to establish is that the complex situation preceding the infliction of punishment can be made better than it otherwise would be by the addition to it of the offender's suffering.

The utilitarian is not only unconvinced by arguments of this kind, he or she is also likely to find a "suspicious connection" between philosophical retributivism and the primitive lust for vengeance. The moralistic retributivist protests that he or she eschews anger or any other passion and seeks not revenge, but justice and the satisfaction of desert. Punishment, after all, is not the only kind of treatment we bestow upon persons simply because we think they deserve it. Teachers give students the grades they have earned with no thought of "future advantage," and with eyes firmly fixed on past performance. There is no necessary jubilation at good performance or vindictive pleasure in assigning low grades. And much the same is true of the assignments of rewards, prizes, grants, compensation, civil liability, and so on. Justice requires assignment on the basis of desert alone. To be sure, there is

> a great danger of revengeful and sadistic tendencies finding vent under the unconscious disguise of a righteous indignation calling for just punishment, since the evil desire for revenge, if not identical with the latter, bears a resemblance to it sufficiently close to deceive those who want an excuse.[5]

Indeed, it is commonly thought that our modern notions of retributive justice have grown out of earlier practices, like the vendetta and the law of deodand, that were through and through expressions of the urge to vengeance.[6] Still, the retributivist replies, it is unfair to *identify* a belief with one of its corruptions, or a modern practice with its historical antecedents. The latter mistake is an instance of the "genetic fallacy" which is committed whenever one confuses an account of how something came to be the way it is with an analysis of what it has become.

The third thesis of the pure moralistic retributivist has also been subject to heavy attack. Can it really be the business of the state to ensure that happiness and unhappiness are distributed among citizens in proportion to their moral deserts? Think of the practical difficulties involved in the attempt simply to apportion pain to moral guilt in a given case, with no help from utilitarian considerations. First of all, it is usually impossible to punish an offender without inflicting suffering on those who love or depend upon him and may themselves be entirely innocent, morally speaking. In that way, punishing the guilty is self-defeating from the moralistic retributive point of view. It will do more to increase than to diminish the disproportion between unhappiness and desert throughout society. Secondly, the aim of apportioning pain to guilt would in some cases require punishing "trivial" moral offenses, like rudeness, as heavily as more socially harmful crimes, since there can be as much genuine wickedness in the former as the latter. Thirdly, there is the problem of accumulation. Deciding the right amount of suffering to inflict in a given case would entail an assessment of the character of the offender as manifested throughout his or her whole life (and not simply at one weak moment) and also an assessment of his or her total lifelong balance of pleasure and pain. Moreover, there are inevitably inequalities of moral guilt in the commission of the same crime by different offenders, as well as inequalities of suffering from the same punishment. Application of the pure retributive theory then would require the abandonment of fixed penalties for various crimes and the substitution of individuated penalties selected in each case by an authority to fit the offender's uniquely personal guilt and vulnerability.

The utilitarian theory of punishment holds that punishment is never good in itself, but is (like bad-tasting medicine) justified when, and only when, it is a means to such future goods as *correction* (reform) of the offender, *protection* of society against other offenses from the same offender, and *deterrence* of other would-be offenders. (The list is not exhaustive.) Giving the offender the pain he deserves because of his wickedness is either not a coherent notion, on this theory, or else not a morally respectable independent reason for punishing. In fact, the utilitarian theory arose in the eighteenth century as part of a conscious reaction to cruel and uneconomical social institutions (including prisons) that were normally defended, if at all, in righteously moralistic terms.

For purposes of clarity, the utilitarian theory of punishment should be distinguished from utilitarianism as a general moral theory. The standard of right conduct generally, according to the latter, is conducibility to good consequences. Any act at all, whether that of a private citizen, a legislator, or a judge, is morally right if and only if it is likely, on the best evidence, to do more good or less harm all around than any alternative conduct open to the actor. (The standard for judging the goodness of consequences, in turn, for Jeremy Bentham and the early utilitarians was the amount of human happiness they contained, but many later utilitarians had more complicated conceptions of intrinsic value.) All proponents of general utilitarianism, of course, are also supporters of the utilitarian theory of punishment, but there is no logical necessity that in respect to punishment a utilitarian be a general utilitarian across the board.

The utilitarian theory of punishment can be summarized in three propositions parallel to those used above to summarize pure moralistic retributivism. According to this theory:

1. Social utility (correction, prevention, deterrence, et cetera) is a necessary condition for justified punishment.
2. Social utility is a sufficient condition for justified punishment.
3. The proper amount of punishment to be inflicted upon the offender is that amount which will do the most good or the least harm to all those who will be affected by it.

The first thesis enjoys the strongest support from common sense, though not so strong as to preclude controversy. For the retributivist, as has been seen, punishing the guilty is an end in itself quite apart from any gain in social utility. The utilitarian is apt to reply that if reform of the criminal could be secured with no loss of deterrence by simply giving him or her a pill that would have the same effect, then nothing would be lost by not punishing him or her, and the substitute treatment would be "sheer gain."

Thesis 2, however, is the utilitarian's greatest embarrassment. The retributivist opponent argues forcefully against it that in certain easily imaginable circumstances it would justify punishment of the (legally) innocent, a consequence which all would regard as a moral abomination. Some utilitarians deny that punishment of the innocent could *ever* be the alternative that has the best consequences in social utility, but this reply seems arbitrary and dogmatic. Other utilitarians claim that "punishment of the innocent" is a self-contradiction. The concept of punishment, they argue,[7] itself implies hard treatment imposed upon the guilty as a conscious and deliberate response to their guilt. That guilt is part of the very definition of punishment, these writers claim, is shown by the absurdity

of saying "I am punishing you for something you have not done," which sounds very much like "I am curing you even though you are not sick." Since all punishment is understood to be for guilt, they conclude, they can hardly be interpreted as advocating punishing without guilt. H. L. A. Hart[8] calls this move a "definitional stop," and charges that it is an "abuse of definition," and indeed it is, if put forward by a proponent of the general utilitarian theory. If the right act in all contexts is the one which is likely to have the best consequences, then conceivably the act of framing an innocent man could sometimes be right; and the question of whether such mistreatment of the innocent party could properly be called "punishment" is a mere question of words having no bearing on the utilitarian's embarrassment. If, on the other hand, the definitional stop is employed by a defender of the utilitarian theory of the justification of punishment who is not a utilitarian across the board, then it seems to be a legitimate argumentative move. Such a utilitarian is defending official infliction of hard treatment (deprivation of liberty, suffering, et cetera) on *those who are legally guilty,* a practice to which he or she refers by using the word "punishment," as justified when and only when there is probably social utility in it.

No kind of utilitarian, however, will have plausible recourse to the definitional stop in defending thesis 3 from the retributivist charge that it would, in certain easily imaginable circumstances, justify excessive and/or insufficient penalties. The appeal again is to moral common sense: It would be manifestly unfair to inflict a mere two dollar fine on a convicted murderer or life imprisonment, under a balance of terror policy, for parking offenses. In either case, the punishment imposed would violate the retributivist's thesis 3, that the punishment be proportional to the moral gravity of the offense. And yet, if these were the penalties likely to have the best effects generally, the utilitarian in the theory of punishment would be committed to their support. He or she could not argue that excessive or deficient penalties are not "really" punishments. Instead he would have to argue, as does Jeremy Bentham, that the proper employment of the utilitarian method simply could not lead to penalties so far out of line with our moral intuitions as the retributivist charges.

So far vengeance has not been mentioned except in the context of charge and countercharge between theorists who have no use for it. There are writers, however, who have kind words for vengeance and give it a central role in their theories of the justification of punishment. We can call these approaches the Vindictive Theory of Punishment (to distinguish them from legalistic and moralistic forms of retributivism) and then subsume its leading varieties under either the utilitarian or the retributive rubrics. Vindictive theories are of three different kinds: (1) The *escape-valve version,* commonly associated with the names of James Fitzjames Stephen and Oliver Wendell Holmes, Jr., and currently in favor with some psychoanalytic writers, holds that legal punishment is an orderly outlet for aggressive feelings, which would otherwise demand satisfaction in socially disruptive ways. The prevention of private vendettas through a state monopoly on vengeance is one of the chief ways in which legal punishment has social utility. The escape-valve theory is thus easily assimilated by the utilitarian theory of punishment. (2) The *hedonistic version* of the vindictive theory finds the justification of punishment in the pleasure it gives people (particularly the victim of the crime and his or her loved ones) to see the criminal suffer for the crime. For most utilitarians, and certainly for Bentham, any kind of pleasure—even spiteful, sadistic, or vindictive pleasure, just insofar as it *is* pleasure—counts as a good in the computation of social utility, just as pain—any kind of pain—counts as an evil. (This is sufficient to discredit hedonistic utilitarianism thoroughly, according to its retributivist critics.) The hedonistic version of the vindictive theory, then, is also subsumable under the utilitarian rubric. Finally, (3) the *romantic version* of the vindictive theory, very popular among the uneducated, holds that the justification of punishment is to be found in the emotions of hate and anger it expresses, these emotions being those allegedly felt by all normal or right-thinking people. I call this theory "romantic," despite certain misleading associations of that word, because, like any philosophical theory so labeled, it holds that certain emotions and the actions they inspire are self-certifying, needing no further justification. It is therefore not a kind of utilitarian theory and must be classified as a variety of retributivism, although in its emphasis on feeling it is in marked contrast to more typical retributive theories that eschew emotion and emphasize proportion and desert.

Some anthropologists have traced vindictive feelings and judgments to an origin in the "tribal morality" which universally prevails in primitive cultures, and which presumably governed the tribal life of our own prehistoric ancestors. If an anthropologist turned his attention to our modern criminal codes, he would discover evidence that tribalism has never entirely vacated its position in the criminal law. There are some provisions for which the vindictive theory (in any of its forms) would provide a ready rationale, but for which the utilitarian and moralistic retributivist theories are hard put to discover a plausible defense. Completed crimes, for example, are punished more severely than attempted crimes that fail for accidental reasons. This should not be surprising since the more harm caused the victim, his or her loved ones, and those of the public who can identify imaginatively with them, the more anger there will be at the criminal. If the purpose of punishment is to satisfy that anger, then we should expect that those who succeed in harming will be punished more than the bunglers who fail, even if the motives and intentions of the bunglers were every bit as wicked.

---

1. *A. C. Ewing,* The Morality of Punishment *(London: Kegan Paul, 1929), p. 13.*
2. *John Rawls, "Concepts of Rules,"* The Philosophical Review, *LXIV (1955), pp. 4, 5.*
3. *J. D. Mabbott, "Punishment,"* Mind, *LXVIII (1939), p. 161.*
4. *A. C. Ewing,* Ethics *(New York: Macmillan, 1953), pp. 169–70.*
5. *Ewing,* Morality of Punishment, *p. 27.*
6. *See O. W. Holmes, Jr.,* The Common Law *(Boston: Little, Brown, 1881) and Henry Maine,* Ancient Law. *1861 Reprint. (Boston: Beacon Press, 1963).*
7. *See, for example, Anthony Quinton, "On Punishment,"* Analysis, *XIV (1954), pp. 1933–42.*
8. *H. L. A. Hart,* Punishment and Responsibility *(New York and Oxford: Oxford University Press, 1968), pp. 5, 6.*

FANTASTIC COUNTEREXAMPLES AND THE UTILITARIAN THEORY*

C. L. Ten

2.1. The Effects of Punishment

The utilitarian theory justifies punishment solely in terms of the good consequences produced. There are disagreements among utilitarians about the nature of the good consequences which punishment is supposed to produce. Some utilitarians may even believe that the harm done by punishment outweighs the good, and hence punishment is not justified. But many utilitarians see the main beneficial effects of punishment in terms of the reduction of crime, and believe that punishing offenders will have at least some, if not all, of the following good effects. First, punishment acts as a deterrent to crime. The deterrent effects can be both individual and general. Punishment deters the offender who is punished from committing similar offences in future, and it also deters potential offenders. The offender who is punished is supposed to be deterred by his experience of punishment and the threat of being punished again if he re-offends and is convicted. This is the individual deterrent effect. The general deterrent effect of punishment on potential offenders works through the threat of their being subjected to the same kind of punishment that was meted out to the convicted offender.

Secondly, punishment is supposed to have reformative or rehabilitative effects.[1] This is confined to the offender who is punished. He is reformed in the sense that the effect of punishment is to change his values so that he will not commit similar offences in future because he believes such offences to be wrong. But if he abstains from criminal acts simply because he is afraid of being caught and punished again, then he is deterred rather than reformed and rehabilitated by punishment. So the effects of individual deterrence and rehabilitation are the same. What distinguishes them is the difference in motivation.

The third good consequence of punishment is its incapacitative effect. When an offender is serving his sentence in prison, he is taken out of general social circulation and is therefore prevented from committing a variety of offences, even though he may neither be deterred nor reformed by punishment. Of course punishment would not have an overall incapacitative effect if the offender would not have re-offended even if he were free, or if his incarceration led someone else, who would not otherwise have done so, to engage in criminal activity, perhaps as his replacement in a gang. While in prison, the offender might still commit certain offences: he might assault a fellow prisoner or a prison guard. But his opportunities are generally reduced. In some cases, however, his contacts with other prisoners would create opportunities for further involvement in crime when he is released. The incapacitative effect, though perhaps most likely in the case of imprisonment, may also be present in other forms of punishment. For example, parole may have some incapacitative effect in that although the offender is free, the fact that he is under supervision may restrict his opportunities for criminal activities.

The empirical evidence of the effects of punishment is very complex, but a brief survey will be of some use.

It looks as if the present state of our knowledge provides no basis for claiming that punishment by imprisonment reforms or rehabilitates the criminal, or that it is an individual deterrent. The position is well summed up by the Report of the Panel of the National Research Council in the United States on Research on Deterrent and Incapacitative Effects, hereafter referred to as the Panel:

*From C. L. Ten, *Crime, Guilt, and Punishment* (1987), pp. 7–37. Reprinted by permission of Oxford University Press.

The available research on the impact of various treatment strategies both in and out of prison seems to indicate that, after controlling for initial selection differences, there are generally no statistically significant differences between the subsequent recidivism of offenders, regardless of the form of "treatment." This suggests that neither rehabilitative nor criminogenic effects operate very strongly. Therefore, at an aggregate level, these confounding effects are probably safely ignored.[2]

By "criminogenic effects" the Panel refers to the undesirable effects of imprisonment in either increasing the criminal's propensity to commit crimes or to extend the duration of his criminal career. Such effects are the opposite of the rehabilitative effects. So the present evidence seems to suggest that in general the effect of imprisonment, or of the various programmes for rehabilitation which accompany imprisonment, is neither to make the criminal a better nor a worse person with respect to the standards of behaviour set by the criminal law.

The evidence also suggests that in general punishment has no individual deterrent effect. Daniel Nagin points out that at the observational level it is difficult to distinguish between individual (or what he calls special) deterrence and rehabilitation. He concludes that, "The figures suggest that recidivism rates cannot be affected by varying the severity of the punishment, at least within acceptable limits."[3] But Nagin cautiously adds that the evidence is only preliminary.

In a few specific cases there is indeed some evidence of the individual deterrent effect of punishment. Thus Johannes Andenaes draws attention to a study of amateur shoplifters which shows that detection and arrest, even without prosecution, produces serious shock. There is little or no recidivism among those who are apprehended and interrogated by the store police and then set free without being formally charged.[4] A study of drunk driving in Sweden also shows that those drivers who had been arrested estimated the risk of being arrested as many times higher than other drivers.[5]

There is disagreement about the general deterrent effects of punishment. Johannes Andenaes believes that, "In general terms it can only be stated that general deterrence works well in some fields and works poorly or not at all in other fields."[6] But in 1974 Gordon Tullock published an article, "Does Punishment Deter Crime?," in which he surveyed the work done by economists and sociologists.[7] Tullock points

out that economists began their work under the impression that punishment would deter crime because demand curves slope downwards showing that if the cost of a good is increased then less of it will be consumed. So if the cost of committing crime is increased by more severe punishment, then there will be fewer crimes. Sociologists, on the other hand, started out with the intention of confirming what was then the accepted view in their discipline that punishment would not deter crime. But Tullock argues that, although their starting points and assumptions were radically different, both economists and sociologists, after analysing the evidence, came to the same conclusion that punishment did indeed deter crime. After surveying their studies Tullock himself is convinced that "the empirical evidence is clear," and he states his conclusion unequivocally: "Even granting the fact that most potential criminals have only a rough idea as to the frequency and severity of punishment, multiple regression studies show that increasing the frequency or severity of the punishment does reduce the likelihood that a given crime will be committed."[8]

However, Tullock's confidence about the clarity of the empirical evidence is not shared by the Panel. The Panel argues that although the evidence consistently establishes a negative association between crime rates and sanctions (as measured by the risks of apprehension, conviction, or imprisonment), that is higher crime rates are associated with lower sanctions and vice versa, this does not necessarily show the general deterrent effect of sanctions. The negative association may be partly or wholly explained in terms of lower sanctions being the effect rather than the cause of higher crime rates. Higher crime rates may so overburden the resources of the criminal justice system that they reduce its ability to deal with new offenders. Overburdened judges and prosecuters may use their discretion to dismiss or reduce charges, or to offer attractive plea bargains.[9] Overcrowding of prisons may lead to a reduction in the time served in prison as more prisoners are released early on parole. The sanctions imposed on certain crimes may be reduced. So unless one can separate out the effect of higher crime rates on sanctions from the deterrent effect of sanctions on crime, one cannot interpret the evidence as establishing the presence of the general deterrent effect of punishment. The Panel's cautious assessment of the evidence is summed up in its remark that "we cannot yet assert that the evidence warrants an affirmative conclusion regarding deterrence," but the Panel adds that "the evidence certainly favours a proposition supporting deterrence more than it favours one asserting that deterrence is absent."[10] On the other hand, the Panel believes that the evidence does not even show a significant negative association between crime rates and the severity of punishment as measured by the time served in prison, but suggests that this may partly be accounted for in terms of various distortions.[11]

Moving from the analysis of statistics to the experimental evidence, the Panel identifies three studies which are not methodologically flawed. Of these, two show that the level of crime decreased significantly with increases in the level of sanctions, while one showed that the removal of criminal sanctions for abortions in Hawaii did not affect the incidence of abortions.[12] So it looks as if the present experimental evidence does not permit the drawing of general conclusions. But much of the experimental evidence is consistent with the operation of deterrence, as has been noted by Nigel Walker.[13]

Finally, we turn to the incapacitative effect of punishment. In her review of the literature for the Panel, Jacqueline Cohen suggests that disagreements about the magnitude of that effect can be attributed almost entirely to the different estimates of the average crime rate of prisoners.[14] The estimate of the increase in crime if current prison use were reduced or eliminated has been as low as five per cent.[15] Estimating the incapacitative effect of present prison policies is one thing. There is also the different question as to what we can expect the incapacitative effect to be if present policies are changed. Here one estimate is of a five fold decrease in crime, but Cohen points out that this can only be achieved by increasing the prison population by between 355 per cent and 567 per cent.[16] The incapacitative effect will not be the same for all crimes. Cohen points out that using the assumptions made by the available models, the increase in prison population required to reduce violent crimes is much less than the increases needed for similar reductions in other crimes. Violent crimes can be reduced by 10 per cent with less than 30 per cent increase in prison population.[17] This kind of consideration has led to an increasing interest in the use of selective incapacitation in which the focus of imprisonment is on certain types of offenders who are identified as having a high rate of committing crimes.[18]

We see that the evidence is perhaps more hospitable to the claim that punishment has some general deterrent effect and some incapacitative effect than it is to the claim that it has individual deterrent effect or that it rehabilitates offenders. This will no doubt be puzzling to some, but it provides a basis for caution in responding to a high rate of recidivism. Where there is such a high rate, it shows that punishment does not deter those who are punished. But it does not show that potential offenders are not in fact deterred by punishment, or that punishment does not incapacitate.

2.2. Punishing the Innocent

Let us now assume that the beneficial consequences of punishment outweigh the suffering that it inflicts on offenders. Critics of the utilitarian theory argue that if punishment is to be justified solely in terms of its good consequences, then punishment cannot be confined to offenders. There might be situations in which punishing an innocent person would produce better consequences than alternative courses of action. The utilitarian is therefore committed to punishing the innocent person. This objection has played an important role in the rejection of the utilitarian theory.

Let us consider an example made famous in the literature by H.J. McCloskey.[19] Suppose that in a particular town with a mixed population a man from one racial group rapes a woman from the other group. Because of existing racial tensions the crime is likely to produce racial violence with many people being injured, unless the guilty man is apprehended quickly. Suppose further that the sheriff of the town can prevent the violence by framing an innocent man who was near the scene of the crime, and who will be accepted by the community as the guilty person. Surely, it is argued, the best consequences will be produced by the sheriff's fabrication of evidence against him which will result in his conviction and severe punishment. But the critics maintain that the sheriff's act and the subsequent punishment of the innocent man are both wrong.

There are many ways in which utilitarians, or those sympathetic to them, can respond to this objection, and I shall consider some of their main arguments. First, it is argued that "punishing the innocent" is a logical contradiction because punishment implies guilt. Secondly, the premises of the objection are challenged. It is suggested that punishing the innocent man will not in fact produce the best consequences if we take into account all the consequences of such punishment including the long-term and less obvious consequences. Thirdly, it is claimed that the only situations in which punishing the innocent is optimific are hypothetical and "fantastic" situations rather than situations which arise, or are likely to occur, in the real world. It is then argued that for a variety of reasons, utilitarians should not be worried by what they are committed to in such fantastic situations. In discussing this third response, I shall also consider the views of those utilitarians who maintain that the punishment of the innocent would indeed be justified in situations where it produces the best consequences. If "commonsense morality" or our intuitions disagree, so much the worse for them.

2.3. Punishment and Guilt

In his well-known paper, "On Punishment," Anthony Quinton argues that the notion of "punishment" implies guilt in the sense that "punishment" is defined in part as the infliction of suffering on the guilty.[20] So when suffering is inflicted on innocent people, this cannot be properly described as punishment but as something else—judicial terrorism or social surgery. If we inflict suffering on an innocent man and try to pass it off as punishment, we are guilty of lying since we make a lying imputation that he is guilty and responsible for an offence. Part of Quinton's argument seems to rest on the importance of distinguishing between, for example, typhoid carriers and criminals even though both may sometimes be treated in rather similar ways. Thus a typhoid carrier, or a person with an infectious disease, will be quarantined. He will lose his freedom in much the same way that a criminal is deprived of his freedom when he is jailed. And yet we do not call quarantine a form of punishment precisely because the disease carrier is not guilty of an offence.

It is certainly true that in the typical cases of punishment it is inflicted on a person guilty of an offence. But the crucial issue is whether we can extend the notion of punishment to the infliction of suffering on the innocent without at the same time losing the distinction between punishment and various activities like the quarantine of disease carriers and certain kinds of medical or dental treatment which are painful.

In all these cases there is the infliction of some unpleasantness or suffering, but it is only in the case of punishment that the unpleasantness is essential to what is to be done. As Wasserstrom puts it "the point of the imposition of a deprivation when it is unmistak-

ably a punishment is that it is being imposed because it is a deprivation, because the person upon whom it is being imposed should thereby be made to suffer and in that respect be worse off than before."[21] On the other hand, the unpleasantness experienced by those who are quarantined, or by those undergoing medical treatment, is only incidental, and not essential to what needs to be done. Advances in medical technology may lead to the replacement of painful forms of treatment by pleasant, but still effective, treatment. Medical treatment does not have to be painful at all: a sweet pill is as much a medicine as a bitter pill. Similarly, quarantine implies a degree of isolation to prevent the spread of the infection, and that in itself will be unpleasant. But it can, if resources permit, be greatly outweighed by the pleasures of the surroundings in which one is put. But punishment implies at least an overall degree of unpleasantness. So we can distinguish between punishment and quarantine without falling back on the notion that the person who is punished must be guilty, or must at least be supposed to be guilty, of an offence.

However, the truth of the matter seems to be a bit more complex than we have so far acknowledged, and Quinton's argument, though mistaken, is interesting because it gestures towards that truth. Consider the difference between a monetary fine, which is a form of punishment, and a tax which is not. Arguably both are essentially unpleasant although both may be accepted or approved of as fully justified. What then is the difference between them? In *The Concept of Law* H. L. A. Hart points out that punishment involves "an offence or breach of duty in the form of violation of a rule set up to guide the conduct of ordinary citizens."[22] When someone is punished, he has violated a standard of conduct to which he is supposed to conform. But when he pays a tax, he has not breached any such standard of conduct. The main purpose of taxes is to raise revenue and not to set up a standard of correct conduct. Indeed the revenue-raising function of a tax would be defeated if people generally reacted to income tax by not working, or to Value Added Tax by not eating in restaurants. On the other hand, the purpose of punishment is not defeated if, as a result of it, people cease to breach the relevant standard of conduct. On the contrary, the threat of punishment is most effective when it is unnecessary to carry it out. This important difference between punishment and a tax can be blurred, as Hart acknowledges, when, for example, those running a business simply assimilate the relatively small fines for breaches of rules into the costs of the goods they produce, and pass them on to their consumers. It is also blurred in the other direction when a government imposes a tax on luxury goods partly in order to discourage their use.

A related difference between punishment and other forms of deprivation or unpleasant treatment is that punishment expresses condemnation or disapproval of the conduct punished.[23] The person punished is blamed for what he did, and this explains the peculiar unfairness of punishing the innocent who are of course blameless.

But now, if we accept the idea that punishment involves the breach of a standard of conduct, how is this different from Quinton's point that punishment is always for an offence? The element of truth in Quinton's position is that there must be some wrongdoing or some offence for there to be punishment. But this is not to say that the person punished must be the offender. An innocent person can be punished for an offence committed by someone else. This can happen not only when the legal authority makes a mistake and punishes the wrong person, but also when it deliberately frames an innocent person.

But suppose now that my arguments fail, and Quinton's analysis of the concept of punishment is correct. It certainly does not follow that it is wrong to imprison innocent people or even to execute them. What follows is merely that we cannot *describe* these acts as *punishing* the innocent. But the real issue is a moral issue as to whether we are justified in inflicting suffering on innocent persons. Admittedly this is not exactly the same issue as whether we should *punish* the innocent which raises the additional problem of whether we may unjustly blame the blameless, but none the less it is a serious moral issue. Quinton argues that "the suffering associated with punishment *may* not be inflicted on them, firstly, as brutal and secondly, if it is represented as punishment, as involving a lie."[24] The second objection does not hold if we do not represent the infliction of suffering on the innocent as a form of punishment. And the first objection is not one of which utilitarians can avail themselves if the brutal treatment of the innocent will in fact produce the best consequences. So the argument against the utilitarian can now be reformulated as follows: why should we confine ourselves to punishment in those cases where the infliction of suffering on the innocent will produce the best consequences?

The objection to the utilitarian position is clearly moral, and hence it cannot be evaded by appealing even to a correct definition of the notion of punish-

ment. A proper regard for the way in which terms are used will enable us to describe correctly the moral problem which confronts us, but it cannot solve that problem for us.

2.4. The Disutility of Punishing the Innocent

The second utilitarian response to the charge that utilitarians are committed to punishing the innocent draws our attention to the less obvious bad consequences of punishing innocent persons, and argues that on balance the punishment of the innocent will always produce worse consequences than the failure to do so. For example, it is claimed that the fact that an innocent man has been punished will soon leak out, and when that happens, there will be a loss of confidence in the sheriff and widespread fear among the population that any one of them might be the next innocent victim of the sheriff's attempt to prevent similar violence in future. Furthermore, the sheriff himself will have his sensibilities blunted once the barrier against framing and punishing the innocent has been removed. He is more likely to adopt a similar policy the next time he faces a problem of maintaining order, and on that occasion, there may be no strong utilitarian case for punishing an innocent person. It is also not certain that there will in fact be racial violence if an innocent person is not punished. On the other hand, the suffering of the innocent person who is punished is very real. The suffering of the innocent man is likely to be greater than that of the guilty. The punishment will come as a big shock to the innocent man, and he will be angered and distressed in a way that the guilty person will not be.[25]

But at each point of this utilitarian response, the critic can counter by tightening up the description of the example under consideration. Thus the sheriff suffers from a sudden fatal illness soon after the punishment of the innocent man, and he makes no deathbed confessions. No one else knows about the fabrication of evidence and the secret is buried with the sheriff. The innocent man who is punished has no relatives or close friends, and he himself is well endowed with an unusual temperament which faces unexpected disaster with calm resignation. We must not forget the unconvicted real offender who is still free and conceivably could give the whole show away. So he dies unexpectedly when he is run over by a bus on his way to the sheriff's funeral. Now we are back where we started with an example in which the punishment of an innocent person produces the best consequences and so should be accepted by the utilitarian.

2.5. Fantastic Examples and Moral Principles

But at this stage of the debate, the utilitarian will introduce a new, and by far the most complex and exciting, argument. He or she will argue that the nearer the critic gets to producing a water-tight example in which it is certain that punishing an innocent person will be optimific, the more fantastic the example becomes. The utilitarian moral theory cannot be defeated by the production of fantastic examples which are irrelevant to everyday moral argument in the real world.

It is strange that the rejection of fantastic examples has come to play such an important part in the writings of some utilitarian writers. In a radio talk "Does Oxford Moral Philosophy Corrupt Youth?" Anscombe attacked the use of such examples by utilitarian-minded philosophers. She parodied their method of argument with an example in which you have to decide what you ought to do when you have to move forward but "stepping with your right foot means killing twenty-five fine young men while stepping with your left foot would kill fifty drooling old ones."[26] Rising to the occasion, Anscombe gives the answer: "Obviously the right thing to do would be to jump and polish off the lot."[27] Today the attacks on the use of fantastic examples in moral argument are much more likely to come from utilitarians, irritated by attempts to undermine their moral principles which proceed by way of showing that in some conceivable, but very unlikely, situations, they are committed to all sorts of monstrous and outrageous acts— the punishment and killing of innocent people, torture, racial and religious persecutions, etc.

I want to argue that there is an important role for fantastic examples in moral argument. I shall, for the time being at least, assume that it is only in fantastic situations that the punishment of the innocent will produce the best consequences.

Suppose that you make a moral judgement: "It's wrong to stick knives into people."[28] A philosopher replies: "But suppose that human beings are so constructed that whenever you stick knives into their bodies you trigger off a mechanism which stimulates the pleasure-centres of their brains such that they experience very pleasurable sensations. Now surely it would then not be wrong to stick knives into them. Indeed mightn't it sometimes be obligatory to do so?" Is the philosopher just a smart Alec? Not necessarily. He or she may be trying to draw a distinction between, on the one hand, a subordinate or secondary moral principle, and on the other hand, a fundamental or ultimate moral principle. Sticking knives into people is only a subordinate moral principle: it is wrong only because it harms them. In the fantastic world imagined by the philosopher it would therefore not be wrong to stick knives into people. On the other hand the principle that we should not harm people may be a fundamental moral principle, and if it is, then, unlike a subordinate moral principle, it still holds good even in the fantastic world. In that world, it would not be wrong to stick knives into people, but it would still be wrong to harm them. Suppose that in the fantastic world, shaking hands would cause enormous pain. We would then have a new subordinate principle, applicable to that world, but not to our real world, that one ought not to shake hands unless both parties were masochists.

A subordinate moral principle is one which has to be justified in terms of another moral principle, whereas a fundamental moral principle is not justified by appealing to another moral principle. For the utilitarian, there is only one fundamental moral principle and that is the principle that one should always produce the best consequences. Thus from the utilitarian point of view the wrongness of punishing innocent people is only subordinate. It derives its justification from the fundamental utilitarian principle. It is wrong to punish the innocent only in so far as such punishment produces worse consequences than an alternative course of action. But for some non-utilitarians punishing the innocent is itself a fundamental moral principle. Our discussion of the philosopher's example suggests that fundamental moral principles apply even to fantastic situations. If this is correct, then we have a good reason for using fantastic examples to test the fundamental utilitarian principle. Utilitarians cannot therefore claim that their principle is only applicable to the real world and thereby refuse to consider the implications of the principle in fantastic situations. They can only fall back on this argument if the principle is subordinate, but it is not.

Furthermore, since subordinate principles do not apply to all situations whereas fundamental principles do, we can use fantastic situations to help us decide whether a particular principle is subordinate or fundamental. The principle that we are presently interested in is about the wrongness of punishing the innocent. We want to decide whether this principle is derivable from the utilitarian principle. If it is, then it is a subordinate principle. But if it is wrong to punish the innocent even when such punishment will produce the best consequences, then the utilitarian principle cannot be the only fundamental moral principle. We will not have shown that the wrongness of punishing the innocent is itself fundamental, for it may be based on a non-utilitarian fundamental moral principle. But even showing that much is enough to refute the utilitarian theory of punishment as providing the only basis for the justification of punishment.

In an interesting defence of consequentialism against moral absolutism, Kai Nielsen argues: "What is brutal or vile, for example, throwing a knife at a human being just for the fun of it, would not be so, if human beings were invulnerable to harm from such a direction because they had a metallic exoskeleton. Similarly, what is, as things are, morally intolerable, for example, the judicial killing of the innocent, need not be morally intolerable in all conceivable circumstances."[29] The two cases are however different in that the wrongness of throwing a knife at a human being just for the fun of it is clearly subordinate to some fundamental principle like that of not harming innocent human beings. On the other hand, for some non-utilitarians, the injunction against the judicial killing of the innocent is not a subordinate principle but an instance of a fundamental non-utilitarian moral principle against the killing of the innocent. Even if Nielsen is right that such a non-utilitarian principle may be violated in some conceivable circumstances, this does not show that the principle derives its force from consequentialist considerations. A non-utilitarian fundamental moral principle need not be absolutist in the sense that it must never be violated no matter what the consequences. It may sometimes be overridden by utilitarian considerations. But even when it is overridden, it "applies" or "holds good" in the sense that it embodies a morally relevant consideration which has to be taken into account in deciding what to do. (It has "the dimension of weight" that Ronald Dworkin attributes to legal principles as opposed to legal rules, so that even when a legal principle does not determine or necessitate a particular decision, it still states a reason that argues in one direction rather than another.)[30]

Thus some moderate non-utilitarians will side with utilitarian against the absolutist when for example the failure to punish or to harm an innocent person produces very much worse consequences to others than the harm caused to the innocent. In such a case although moderate non-utilitarians give a negative moral weight to punishing or harming the innocent, which is independent of utilitarian considerations, the weight may not be good enough to outweigh the positive weight which both they and the utilitarian give to avoidance of a great deal of suffering to others. But sometimes the consequences of punishing or harming the innocent can be *clearly better* than the consequences of not punishing or harming even though they are not *much better,* and in such situations whereas the utilitarian would still punish or harm the innocent, the moderate non-utilitarian would not. This difference has not been sufficiently appreciated because of the ambiguity in the claim that the consequences of one act are clearly better than those of all alternative acts. Sometimes what we mean is that the consequences are much better. But sometimes the difference is clearly better when it is only slightly better, but it is clear that it is slightly better. The clarity here refers not to the size of the difference but to the vividness of our perception of the difference. Thus under appropriate conditions, a person who is 5'8" tall can be clearly taller than a person who is 5'7" because, although the difference in height is small, it is clear that there is a small difference. The relevance of this to our discussion is that in situations where the consequences of punishing or harming the innocent, relative to all other alternative courses of action, are clearly, even though only slightly, better in this sense, the utilitarian would regard such punishment or harm as justifiably inflicted. But now moderate non-utilitarians would disagree because the independent negative weight they give to punishing or harming the innocent is enough to override the slightly better consequences.

If, as we are now assuming to be true, there are no actual situations in which the punishment of the innocent will produce the best consequences, then we have a good reason for appealing to fantastic situations. In the real world both the utilitarian and the non-utilitarian will, for different reasons, believe it wrong to punish the innocent. We need therefore a fantastic situation in which the utilitarian and non-utilitarian responses will diverge to discover which is more plausible. In this context the role played by fantastic examples is rather like that of controlled experiments in science. Suppose that when two factors, A and B, are present together we get an effect E. But suppose further that in the natural world A and B are inseparable. Scientists may wish to find out whether it is *A* or *B* singly, or the combination of them, which causes the effect *E*. To do this they will artificially create in the laboratory situations in which *A* and *B* are isolated from each other and then see whether *E* will still be produced. To object to the scientists' work on the ground that in the natural world *A* and *B* are inseparable is to show a considerable misunderstanding of what is going on. Of course the analogy is appropriate only up to a point. The fantastic example is supposed to separate what in the real world is inseparable, namely, the very bad consequences of punishing the innocent and the injustice of such punishment. But the fantastic example cannot provide a conclusive argument against the utilitarian principle because it is always open to the utilitarian to reject the view that punishing the innocent is still wrong when it produces the best consequences, in the way that it is not open for someone to claim that *A* alone causes *E* when it is shown that *B* singly can also cause *E*. But confronting utilitarians with a situation that they will not face in the real world helps them, and others who may be attracted by their view, to appreciate more clearly its implications. It is one thing to know in the abstract that we are committed to all sorts of actions which promote the best consequences. But it is quite another thing to know in vivid detail some of the numerous implications that our principle has in various circumstances. Well chosen fantastic examples will help us to understand the nature of our fundamental moral principles and their underlying assumptions.

But I have said enough to explain why I think that there is a place for fantastic examples in moral argument. I cannot therefore accept the vigorous attack on fantastic examples put forward by Sprigge, who argues: "A utilitarian will see no point in trying to imagine oneself looking with approval on the imaginary situation, since this is likely to weaken the feelings while not serving as a preparation for any actual situation."[31] His point is that if in the real world the punishment of the innocent will never produce the best consequences, then the utilitarian will develop strong feelings of aversion towards such punishment. They cause unnecessary harm. But if we now confront the utilitarian with a fantastic situation in which the punishment of the innocent is justified on utilitarian grounds, then the utilitarian will acknowledge this fact. But he will be uneasy because he has an aversion towards punishing the innocent which was built up through his experience in the real world. He does not wish to dwell on fantastic examples because they will weaken his strong feelings against punishing the in-

nocent. He has every reason to sustain these feelings since he is not ever going to be confronted with a situation in the real world in which he would endorse the punishment of the innocent.

But Sprigge's argument seems to miss the point about the use of fantastic example. He *assumes* that the utilitarian principle is the correct fundamental principle and uses it to decide what disposition he should cultivate. If one takes for granted that utilitarianism is correct, then one would have utilitarian reasons for doing or abstaining from many actions. For example one might decide not even to argue with non-utilitarians for fear that this might weaken one's utilitarian dispositions. But the issue with which we are concerned is whether utilitarianism is a correct moral doctrine. Fantastic examples will help us decide by illuminating the assumptions and implications of utilitarianism and of alternative principles. Even though a fantastic situation will never occur in the real world, it can, by presenting us with relatively simple and sharp alternatives, help us to understand the nature and strength of our commitment to various values. Even a person already inclined towards utilitarianism cannot afford to allow dispositions based on the acceptance of subordinate moral principles to develop into prejudices with a life of their own, and cut off from the fundamental utilitarian principle which is for him their ultimate justification. As situations in the world change, new subordinate moral principles are necessary to replace old ones or to supplement them. But fundamental principles do not change and hence it is important that we decide the status of various principles.

But Sprigge has another argument against the use of fantastic examples. He points out that we may not be able to focus properly on a fantastic example. Certain features of the real world are absent in the fantastic example, but because we are used to these features, we may unwittingly smuggle them into the fantastic example. Thus in the real world punishing an innocent person will produce very bad consequences. However, in a fantastic example, such bad consequences are explicitly ruled out and it is, on the other hand, stipulated that there will be some very good consequences. But Sprigge points out, "If one finds oneself still half-inclined to call such punishment wrong, it may well be because one does not really succeed in envisaging the situation just as described, but surrounds it with those circumstances of real life which would in fact create a greater probability of unhappiness in its consequences than happiness."[32]

There is certainly some truth in Sprigge's comments and we can bring this out more clearly by considering the details of a type of fantastic example which is sometimes used against the hedonistic utilitarian. The hedonistic utilitarian believes that pleasure is the only thing intrinsically good, or good in itself, and pain is the only thing intrinsically bad, and that we should always act to maximize the total amount of pleasure. Imagine a world in which there are nurses and doctors who are dedicated to their patients, but who secretly get a peculiar form of sadistic pleasure out of the patients' suffering. This sadism is peculiar because it does not affect the conduct of the nurses and doctors towards their patients. They never allow their patients to suffer one moment longer than is necessary. Nor do they display their enjoyment of their patients' suffering in any way that will distress others. So perhaps we are to imagine them having their tea-breaks in some remote corner of the hospital and rejoicing at their patients' suffering, but then returning with renewed vigour to attend to the patients. If the hedonistic utilitarian had a choice between creating two worlds, one in which there are these doctors and nurses, and another in which there are these doctors and nurses, and another in which everything else is exactly the same except that the doctors and nurses are not sadistic, then he or she would create the first world. But the critic points out that this is surely wrong in spite of the fact that there will be more pleasure in the first world. If we agree with the critic, can we be sure that our preference for the second world is not based on our failure to envisage the first world exactly as it has been presented to us? Perhaps we tend to smuggle into the first world the wide-ranging effects that sadism normally has. We might therefore find it difficult to come to terms with the innocent sadism of the doctors and nurses. Perhaps we do not fully appreciate that their innocent sadism is good only for a few harmless laughs, and there is no danger of the doctors and nurses prolonging the suffering of their patients when no one else is around. And if we clearly confront the fantastic example as it is described then perhaps we may well agree with the hedonistic utilitarian that we ought to create the first world in preference to the second. Sprigge's argument does appear to be quite powerful when applied to this kind of fantastic example. But it is not an argument which shows that fantastic examples as such have no place in moral reasoning. What the argument does is to warn us of the dangers of not considering fantastic examples as they are described, and of using fantastic examples which involve too radical a change in human nature

or in the world in which we live. Thus although it is logically possible for there to be "innocent sadists," it is difficult to imagine why they will not prolong the suffering of their patients if they gain so much pleasure from the suffering. But this difficulty may in the end be purely subjective, and the example may still be usefully employed in arguing with some people. In any case, examples can be fantastic in the sense of being very unlikely to occur in the real world even though they do not involve radical distortions of human nature or the world in which we live. An unusual combination of individually familiar circumstances may be most unlikely, but there is normally no difficulty in imagining its occurrence. Cases in real life may involve too complex assessments of the consequences of our actions, and those with different views will be bogged down in purely factual disagreements. So there is sometimes an advantage in using a fantastic example in which we can stipulate the consequences of certain actions so that discussion can then focus on the fundamental moral issues at stake.

Another attack on the use of fantastic examples is made by R. M. Hare in his stimulating defence of utilitarianism particularly in his book *Moral Thinking: Its Levels, Method and Point*.[33] Hare makes an important and illuminating distinction between two levels of moral thinking—the intuitive level and the critical level. We need relatively simple moral principles to help us decide what to do in everyday life when we are faced with new situations which resemble past situations in some important respects. Without such principles we will have to face each new situation from scratch and decide what to do without the benefit of useful dispositions developed through the adoption and application of such principles. These principles will also protect us from the temptation to special pleading which leads us to think in a manner which suits our own interests at the expense of the interests of others. Thus if we do not adopt the principle that lying is wrong, we are likely to persuade ourselves that in a particular situation the benefit of a lie to us is enormous and the harm to others only slight when in fact, if we view the situation impartially, we will discover that the lie causes much greater harm than good. So far we are operating at the intuitive level where our thinking is constrained by limitations of time and knowledge. But moral thinking cannot end at this level for there may be conflicts in the moral principles which we adopt at the intuitive level and these have to be resolved at another level, the critical level, where we are not subject to the limitations present at the intuitive level. Critical thinking is also necessary to determine whether a principle at the intuitive level is applicable to a new situation which differs from the cases covered by the principle in some important respects, and more generally to decide on the right course of action in unusual situations. Hare thinks that at the critical level the principle to be adopted is one which calls for the maximization of the satisfaction of preferences or desires, and this is a version of utilitarianism that is sometimes called preference utilitarianism. I shall not be concerned here with his argument for utilitarianism. But in the light of his distinction between the two levels of moral thinking, Hare would relegate the principle that it is wrong to punish the innocent to the intuitive level.[34]

Principles at the intuitive level are selected by critical thinking. We select those principles whose acceptance will produce actions which will best approximate to those actions which an archangel with superhuman qualities and no human weaknesses will recommend when he engages in critical thinking. For Hare, this means that the principles to be accepted at the intuitive level are those which will best promote the utilitarian end of maximizing the satisfaction of desires in the actual world.

Hare points out that the opponents of utilitarianism use fantastic examples in order to show that in such cases the utilitarian answers as to how we should act conflict with our common intuitions grounded on the acceptance of principles at the intuitive level.[35] But such conflicts do not undermine utilitarianism because our common intuitions about, for example, the wrongness of punishing the innocent, are designed for the actual world, and might not be appropriate to fantastic situations which do not occur in the actual world. So if, in fantastic situations, utilitarianism recommends the punishment of the innocent, then this does not show that utilitarianism is in any way defective. Hare challenges the critic of utilitarianism to specify the level at which his fantastic examples are to be considered. If they are brought in at the intuitive level then they are irrelevant since they do not refer to situations which will occur in the actual world. Hare maintains that fantastic examples are admissible at the critical level, but argues that at this level no appeal can be made to moral intuitions which cannot cope with such unusual cases.[36]

Hare's insistence that the discussion should be conducted *either* at the intuitive level *or* at the critical level is a little unfair. This is because a principle about the wrongness of punishing innocent people is simple enough to be used at the intuitive level, but at the same time it might also embody moral considerations which have an irreducible role to play at the critical level. At the critical level, it might well be, as we shall see later, that the intuitive principle, couched in exceptionless terms, would need to be qualified. But this does not mean that the moral consideration embodied in the principle is only derivative from other considerations and does not itself make an independent moral claim on us. As a utilitarian, Hare has a critical principle which specifies only one type of moral consideration as relevant, the maximization of the satisfaction of desires. This is the utilitarian end, and the intuitive principles are selected on the basis of their relative superiority in promoting this end in the actual world. These intuitive principles can be specified independently of the utilitarian end. The formulations of the principles do not *require* any reference to the maximization of desires. The relation between them and utilitarianism is simply that of means to end. The intuitive principles therefore cannot be chosen on the basis of the critical principle alone, but must be sensitive to the social situations in the actual world in which intuitive principles are to be applied. It is likely that in different societies different intuitive principles will be selected. But those non-utilitarians who believe that certain actions are intrinsically right or wrong, and that punishing the innocent is one such type of intrinsically wrong act, will view the relation between critical and intuitive principles differently. At least some of their intuitive principles will be relatively constant across cultural and social differences, and they will represent a more generalized version of their critical principles. They are not means to the realization of the non-utilitarian critical principles but rather imperfect exemplifications of those principles. They are imperfect because at the critical level the intuitive principles would have to be qualified since there are situations in which two such principles may conflict. Thus at the critical level we might discover that we are prepared to override the unqualified wrongness of punishing the innocent if large enough harms are avoided by such punishment. But this does not mean that the wrongness of punishing the innocent is simply dependent on the badness of the consequences it produces. Both the utilitarian and the non-utilitarian might agree at the intuitive level without also agreeing at the critical level. Hare allows the appeal to fantastic examples at the critical level, and such appeals may be necessary to clarify the nature of the principles that we are prepared to accept at that level. Thus a fundamental issue to be settled at that level is whether critical moral thinking is controlled by one principle, as Hare and other utilitarians suggest, or whether it has to find room for an irreducible plurality of moral principles as many non-utilitarians believe.[37]

But now once the discussion shifts to the critical level, are we not caught in the grips of Hare's argument that even though fantastic examples are permissible, the appeal to moral intuitions is not? So the fact that utilitarianism conflicts with our moral intuitions cannot be used as an argument against utilitarianism. Hare sometimes refers disparagingly to these anti-utilitarian moral intuitions as "the received opinion" and argues that they have no probative force.[38] Thus he points out that as recently as the early twentieth century the received opinion was against "mixed bathing" even though "mixed bathing" had a utilitarian justification.[39] The example is well chosen for at a time when nude bathing is the issue, and when some energy-conscious bodies are urging us to have "mixed showers," it is unlikely that anyone today would share the previously received opinion that there was something wrong with men and women, amply clothed, enjoying the same beaches together. The example shows that received opinion can embody prejudices, and therefore moral intuitions of this kind should not be used at the critical level. Indeed, Hare argues that moral intuitions should be modified by critical thinking which will inculcate the *right* intuitions whether or not these coincide with the received opinions.[40]

Hare's argument is successful against those who use moral intuitions as bed-rock considerations round which critical thinking must be constructed. But that is not the way that fantastic examples have featured in our discussion so far. I have pointed out that we appeal to fantastic examples to better appreciate the implications of our fundamental moral commitments. If we cannot accept some of these implications then we have to give up or modify our fundamental moral values. Thus utilitarians would have to accept all the implications of utilitarianism in actual and hypothetical situations, and if they want us to accept utilitarianism, then they must also persuade us that none of these implications is unacceptable to us. Fantastic examples have an honourable role to play even within the framework of Hare's moral theory. For in his theory to accept a moral judgement is to accept a universal prescription, and to accept a prescription is to act on it. The utilitarian principle that one ought always to produce the best consequences is itself a generalized moral judgement which identifies only one feature of actions as being relevant, namely the consequences produced. This being the case, anyone who accepts that principle must be prepared to act in all situations, actual or fantastic, in which the action will produce the best consequences. Fantastic examples help to test the genuineness and the strength of a person's commitment to utilitarianism. It is inadequate for a utilitarian to respond, in advance of a consideration of specific examples, that he or she is prepared to accept all the implications of utilitarianism. The utilitarian can of course be sure that whenever utilitarianism is inconsistent with a particular moral judgement others are inclined to accept, then that particular moral judgement will involve the acceptance of a course of action which will not produce the best consequences. But it is one thing to know this in general terms; it is quite another thing to repudiate all such particular judgements in the vast variety of situations in which they involve the non-production of the best consequences. Utilitarians may well find that in a particular case their insufficiently tested faith in their ability to resist recalcitrant counter-examples is in fact misplaced. Their moral beliefs may be more complex than they suppose, and utilitarianism may not be able to impose an order on their thinking.[41] What is true of the professed utilitarian will also be true of any person engaged in moral thinking. Fantastic examples probe the depths of our thinking. In using such examples, we are not appealing to the received opinion, but to the reflective judgement of each party to a moral argument as to how he or she would respond to particular situations. No matter how moral agents arrive at their critical moral principles, they still have to be sure that they know and can accept the implications of these principles.

2.6. Moral Dilemmas and Complexities

I have so far only been concerned to explain and justify the use of fantastic examples in moral argument. But we cannot assume that once fantastic examples are introduced, utilitarianism rather than non-utilitarian moral beliefs will be in difficulties. The conclusion that it is sometimes right to punish the innocent is one to which utilitarians are committed, but this may well be the correct conclusion. I have already mentioned this possibility earlier in our discussion. There are different ways of reaching the same moral conclusion in a particular case, and I shall now argue that even if the utilitarian's answer in a particular case, fantastic or otherwise, is correct, his or her reasoning to that answer may not be as illuminating as a non-utilitarian approach.

Let us consider a different example in which some non-utilitarians will also agree with the utilitarian that the normally strong moral injunction against torturing human beings may have to be violated. Anthony Quinton gives the example of "a man planting a bomb in a large hospital, which no one but he knows how to defuse and no one dare touch for fear of setting it off."[42] Quinton thinks that torturing the man could be justifiable given that it is an emergency situation with no time to resort to other methods, and there is no doubt about the bomb-planter's responsibility for, or capacity to produce, the violent act. The bomb-planter's responsibility for the act, and the fact that a much greater degree of suffering will be experienced by the innocent patients and staff of the hospital if the bomb were not defused in time, are certainly morally relevant features of the situation. But it is unclear whether these features can best be accounted for within the utilitarian framework of thinking. The example suggests that utilitarianism can mount a powerful attack on at least some forms of moral absolutism which share the view that there are certain kinds of acts, of which torture is one, which are always wrong, irrespective of the consequences.

But suppose now that the bomb-planter shows a considerable capacity for withstanding or evading torture (perhaps he conveniently faints whenever he is about to be tortured). There is very little time left, but it is discovered that the bomb-planter has a wife to whom he is very attached. If a moderate amount of physical pain were inflicted on her, the bomb-planter will defuse the bomb. Would it be wrong to harm his wife? This is in some ways like a case in which the punishment of an innocent person will prevent very bad consequences from occurring. If the pain to be inflicted on the innocent wife is very much less than the suffering of the people in the hospital, then both utilitarians and some non-utilitarians will agree that the act is justifiable. But does it follow that, other things being equal, we would be prepared to inflict the same amount of physical suffering on the wife as we would on the bomb-planter himself? Suppose we had a choice between torturing the bomb-planter and inflicting slightly less suffering on his innocent wife to achieve the same result. The fact that he is responsible for planting the bomb whereas she is innocent should be sufficient for us to choose him rather than her. This shows that we attach some weight, independent of utilitarian considerations, to not using innocent people unjustly for the benefit of others. On the other hand, there is no similar injustice in making the bomb-planter suffer if it is through his own act that we are

confronted with the situation in which his suffering is the lesser of two evils. We would of course regret that we had to choose between two evils, and some might also regard torture as an evil requiring a special justification. Utilitarianism cannot adequately capture the injustice of using innocent people as means towards desirable ends because it treats the difference between torturing the bomb-planter and torturing his innocent wife as merely a difference in the consequences of the respective acts.

Let us pursue further the claim that utilitarianism does not do justice to the complexity of moral thinking. Suppose now that our notorious bomb-planter has placed a peculiar bomb in a large children's hospital such that if the bomb exploded it will release a gas which will cause all those in the hospital to experience an unpleasant itch for just a couple of minutes. But the side effects are that all future direct descendants of the inhabitants of the hospital will also, once in a lifetime, each experience a two-minute unpleasant itch. There is no possibility of a cure, but there are no bad consequences. In a few generations, the total undesirable consequences of the bomb's explosion is that thousands of people will have each experienced such two-minute itches. Let us assume that the only way to prevent the explosion of the bomb is to torture the innocent child of the bomb-planter. In such a situation it would be wrong to torture the innocent child no matter how many other people would each suffer two-minute itches if we did not torture. But this is precisely the conclusion that the utilitarian cannot accept because although each person suffers only a little, if there are many such sufferers, the bad consequences when added together, will sooner or later exceed the great suffering of the tortured child. As the well-known rhymes go:

> Little drops of water,
>   Little grains of sand,
> Make the mighty ocean
>   And the pleasant land.

So too, little two-minute itches can add up to one mighty pain.

If pleasures and pains can be aggregated, as utilitarians believe, then the lesser pains of many people can exceed the much greater pain of one person. No matter how great the suffering of being tortured, it is still a finite amount that can be exceeded. No matter how slight the unpleasantness of an itch may be, if there are enough people experiencing it, then the aggregate will exceed the agony of one person being tortured. The only way in which utilitarians can get round this is by introducing certain discontinuities of scale in which, for example, no aggregate of the much lesser pains of many persons can outweigh the great suffering caused by the torture of one person. But this would be an *ad hoc* device which can find no motivation within utilitarianism itself, and will destroy some of its distinctive features. It is irrelevant from the utilitarian point of view that in the case of the tortured child all the great suffering is experienced by one person, whereas in the case of the little itches the unpleasantness is spread out very thinly over many people, and no single person experiences the total suffering.[43] Utilitarians are only interested in the distribution of good and bad consequences when this affects the total. An equal distribution of benefits and burdens is not in itself better than a very unequal one if the two distributions yield the same total happiness or welfare. In the actual world, differences in distribution will of course often affect the total welfare, but the fantastic example helps to bring out the point that in certain situations utilitarians are committed to sacrificing the major interest of one person in order to promote the minor interests of many persons. In practice this commitment would lead to the justification of the exemplary punishment of an offender for a relatively trivial offence if this would deter many others from committing similar offences. This is an issue to which we will return.

Let me summarize my objections to the utilitarian theory because these objections have to be taken into account in constructing a more acceptable theory of punishment. The first objection is that the utilitarian theory does not give any independent weight to the injustice of punishing the innocent. If the theory regards such punishment as wrong, then it is wrong simply in virtue of the fact that it produces bad consequences. Secondly, there are situations in which the utilitarian theory permits and even requires us to inflict great suffering on one person in order to prevent many other persons from each experiencing a very much smaller amount of suffering.

2.7. A Return to the Real World

I have so far assumed, for the sake of argument, that it is only in fantastic situations that utilitarians are committed to punishing the innocent. But it is now time to say something about this assumption. Most utilitarians seem to make the assumption. Thus Hare writes: "The retributivists are right at the intuitive level, and the utilitarians at the critical level."[44] But contrast this with David Richards's claim in *The Moral Criticism of Law* that the utilitarian theory of punishment "clearly seems to allow and even require the punishment of the innocent, since it is very plausible that a higher degree of criminal deterrence would be achieved by punishing the children or relatives or friends or lovers of criminals in addition to or even in place of the criminal. Primitive systems of law often do exactly this, . . ."[45] In the face of these conflicting claims, two remarks are appropriate. First, no one can claim with confidence that, on the balance of probabilities, there are no actual cases in which punishing the innocent will produce the best consequences. But secondly, the strength of our conviction, which is shared by many utilitarians, that punishing the innocent in the real world is unjustified, cannot be accounted for simply on the basis of utilitarian considerations. If we were guided by purely utilitarian considerations, we would not be entitled to be as confident as we in fact are that such punishment in the real world is wrong, and we should indeed be prepared to experiment with limited proposals for the punishment of the innocent.

Indeed we can go further and argue that in the present state of our knowledge, surveyed earlier, the evidence of the desirable effects of punishment is not always as firmly based as is often assumed, and this presents some difficulties for a purely utilitarian justification of punishment. From the utilitarian point of view punishing offenders produces bad consequences which are certain and not speculative, namely the suffering inflicted directly by punishment on offenders and indirectly on their friends and relatives. Against this, there is no equally firm evidence, in all cases where punishment is thought to be justified, of its countervailing good effects. There is some evidence of incapacitative effects although the extent of these effects varies with different types of offences, and the evidence is also consistent with there being some general deterrent effect. Again, there is good reason to think that the total abandonment of the practice of punishment would have unfortunate results. But there are specific crimes in which the utilitarian case for punishment, while not ruled out, is not particularly strong. It is then unclear what we should do in the present state of our knowledge if we were guided by purely utilitarian considerations. In fact our thinking on these matters is also guided by non-utilitarian considerations. Other things being equal, we think it better that the guilty should suffer through punishment than that there should be similar suffering by the innocent victims of crime. Again, given that the practice of punishment has some utilitarian justification, there will also be offenders who may justifiably be punished by appealing to non-utilitarian considerations. For example, if the punishment for some offences can be justified on utilitarian grounds in terms of the general deterrent effect and the incapacitative effect of such punishment, then it is unfair to allow those who have committed more serious offences to go unpunished even if in these latter cases the existing evidence is inadequate to show that punishment has similar good effects.

I do not believe that the practice of punishment would be justified if there were a decisive utilitarian case against it, or if it did not at least have some utilitarian support. But this is not to say that all desirable aspects of that practice can be justified in purely utilitarian terms.

---

1. *Jack P. Gibbs distinguishes between "rehabilitation" and "reformation." An offender is "rehabilitated" if he ceases to violate the law as a result of non-punitive means, whereas he is "reformed" if he ceases to violate the law as a result of punishment, but for reasons independent of the fear of punishment. See* Crime, Punishment, and Deterrence *(New York, 1975), p. 72. I use the two terms interchangeably and broadly to refer to cases in which the offender, after serving a sentence, no longer commits crimes because he believes that criminal behaviour is wrong and not because he fears punishment. His changed values can be brought about by punishment itself or by non-punitive means. Jean Hampton develops a sophisticated version of the moral education view of punishment according to which punishment communicates a moral message aimed at educating both the wrongdoer and the rest of society about the immorality of the offence. She is eager to distinguish her view from rehabilitative theories of punishment both in terms of the different ends to be achieved and the methods used to attain those ends. According to her, the aim of rehabilitation is to make the offender accept society's mores and operate successfully in society, and the pursuit of these goals is not constrained by respect for the autonomy of the wrongdoer. See "The Moral Education Theory of Punishment,"* Philosophy & Public Affairs, *13 (1984).*

2. *Alfred Blumstein, Jacqueline Cohen, and Daniel Nagin (eds.),* Deterrence and Incapacitation: Estimating the Effects of Criminal Sanctions on Crime Rates, *National Academy of Sciences, Panel on Research on Deterrent and Incapacitative Effects (Washington, 1978), p. 66. Hereafter this book will be referred to as The Panel.*

3. *Daniel Nagin, "General Deterrence: A Review of the Empirical Evidence," in* The Panel, *p. 96.*

4. *Johannes Andenaes, "Does Punishment Deter Crime?" in Gertrude Ezorsky (ed.),* Philosophical Perspectives on Punishment *(Albany, 1972), p. 354.*

5. *Ibid., p. 354.*

6. *Ibid., p. 346.*

7. *Gordon Tullcock, "Does Punishment Deter Crime?" The Public Interest (1974), pp. 103–11.*

8. *Ibid., p. 109.*

9. *The Panel, p. 39.*

10. *Ibid., p. 7.*

11. *Ibid., pp. 37–8.*

12. *Ibid., p. 55.*

13. *Nigel Walker,* Punishment, Danger and Stigma *(Oxford, 1980), pp. 77–80.*

14. *Jacqueline Cohen, "The Incapacitative Effect of Imprisonment: A Critical Review of the Literature," in* The Panel, *p. 209.*

15. *Ibid., p. 188.*

16. *Ibid., p. 218.*

17. *Ibid., p. 227.*

18. *See Mark H. Moore, Susan R. Estrich, Daniel McGillis, and William Spelman,* Dangerous Offenders: The Elusive Target of Justice *(Cambridge, 1984). I discuss the problem of dangerous offenders in Ch. 6.*

19. *See H. J. McCloskey, "A Non-utilitarian Approach to Punishment," in Michael D. Bayles (ed.),* Contemporary Utilitarianism *(New York, 1968). Some of the details of my example in the text differ from McCloskey's examples.*

20. *Anthony M. Quinton, "On Punishment," in H. B. Acton (ed.),* The Philosophy of Punishment *(London, 1969), pp. 58–9.*

21. *Richard A. Wasserstrom, "Capital Punishment as Punishment: Some Theoretical Issues and Objections,"* Midwest Studies in Philosophy, *7 (1982), p. 476. See also H. J. McCloskey, "The Complexity of the Concepts of Punishment,"* Philosophy, *37 (1962), p. 323.*

22. *H. L. A. Hart,* The Concept of Law *(Oxford, 1961), p. 39.*

23. *For an excellent discussion of this feature of punishment, see Joel Feinberg, "The Expressive Function of Punishment," in Hyman Gross and Andrew von Hirsch (eds.),* Sentencing *(New York & Oxford, 1981).*

24. *"On Punishment," p. 59.*

25. *Some of these utilitarian objections to punishing the innocent are voiced by T. L. S. Sprigge, "A Utilitarian Reply to Dr. McCloskey," in Michael D. Bayles (ed.),* Contemporary Utilitarianism *(New York, 1968), pp. 278–82.*

26. *G. E. M. Anscombe, "Does Oxford Moral Philosophy Corrupt Youth?"* The Listener *(14 February 1957), p. 267.*

27. *Ibid., p. 267.*

28. *See the interesting discussion in Kai Nielsen, "Against Moral Conservatism," in Karsten J. Struhl and Paula Rothenberg Struhl (eds.),* Ethics in Perspective *(New York, 1975), especially pp. 119–20. This article is reprinted from* Ethics, *82 (1971–2), pp. 219–31.*

29. *Ibid., p. 120.*

30. *Ronald Dworkin,* Taking Rights Seriously *(London, 1978), pp. 26–7.*

31. *T. L. S. Sprigge, "A Utilitarian Reply to Dr. McCloskey," p. 275.*

32. *Ibid., p. 276.*

33. *R. M. Hare,* Moral Thinking: Its Levels, Method and Point *(Oxford, 1981), esp. Chs. 1–3 and 8–9.*

34. *Ibid., pp. 162–3. Hare's argument for utilitarianism is critically discussed by Bernard Williams,* Ethics and the Limits of Philosophy *(London, 1985), pp. 82–92.*

35. *Ibid., pp. 48–9.*

36. *Ibid., pp. 131–2.*

37. *See Stuart Hampshire,* Two Theories of Morality *(Oxford, 1977).*

38. Moral Thinking: Its Levels, Method and Point, *op. cit., p. 12. See also "The Argument from Received Opinion," in R. M. Hare,* Essays on Philosophical Method *(London, 1971), p. 122.*

39. *"The Argument from Received Opinion," p. 127.*

40. Moral Thinking: Its Levels, Method and Point, *p. 142. A different view of the relation between intuitions and general moral principles or ethical theories is given by Bernard Williams,* Ethics and the Limits of Philosophy, *Ch. 6.*

41. *See Stuart Hampshire,* Two Theories of Morality, *pp. 26–7.*

42. *Anthony M. Quinton, "Views,"* The Listener *(2 December 1971), p. 758.*

43. *Some critics have accused utilitarianism of ignoring "the*

separateness of persons." For an illuminating discussion, see H. L. A. Hart, "Between Utility and Rights," in H. L. A. Hart, Essays in Jurisprudence and Philosophy (Oxford, 1983).

44. *Moral Thinking: Its Levels, Method and Point, p. 163.*
45. *David A. J. Richards,* The Moral Criticism of Law *(Encino & Belmont, 1977), pp. 232–3.*

THE MORAL WORTH OF RETRIBUTION*

Michael S. Moore

Retributivism and the Possible Modes of its Justification

Since I will in this chapter seek to justify the retributive theory of punishment, I will first say what such a theory is. *Retributivism* is the view that punishment is justified by the moral culpability of those who receive it. A retributivist punishes because, and only because, the offender deserves it. Retributivism thus stands in stark contrast to utilitarian views that justify punishment of past offenses by the greater good of preventing future offenses. It also contrasts sharply with rehabilitative views, according to which punishment is justified by the reforming good it does the criminal.

Less clearly, retributivism also differs from a variety of views that are often paraded as retributivist, but that in fact are not. Such views are typically put forward by people who cannot understand how anyone could think that moral desert by itself could justify punishment. Such persons scramble about for other goods that punishment achieves and label these, quite misleadingly, "retributivism." The leading confusions seem to me to be seven in number.

1. First, retributivism is sometimes identified with a particular measure of punishment such as *lex talionis,* an eye for an eye (e.g., Wilson and Herrnstein, 1985, p. 496), or with a kind of punishment such as the death penalty. Yet retributivism answers a question prior to the questions to which these could be answers. True enough, retributivists at some point have to answer the "how much" and "what type" questions for specific offenses, and they are committed to the principle that punishment should be graded in proportion to desert; but they are not committed to any particular penalty scheme nor to any particular penalty as being deserved. Separate argument is needed to answer these "how much" and "what type" questions, *after* one has described why one is punishing at all. It is quite possible to be a retributivist and to be against both the death penalty and *lex talionis,* the idea that crimes should be punished by like acts being done to the criminal.

2. Contrary to Anthony Quinton (1954) and others (see Hart, 1968), retributivism is *not* "the view that only the guilty are to be punished." A retributivist will subscribe to such a view, but that is not what is distinctive about retributivism. The distinctive aspect of retributivism is that the moral desert of an offender is a *sufficient* reason to punish him or her; the principle Quinton advocates make such moral desert only a *necessary* condition of punishment. Other reasons— typically, crime prevention reasons—must be added to moral desert, in this view, for punishment to be justified. Retributivism has no room for such additional reasons. That future crime might also be prevented by punishment is a happy surplus for a retributivist, but no part of the justification for punishing.

3. Retributivism is not the view that punishment of offenders satisfies the desires for vengeance of their

victims. The harm that is punishment can be justified by the good it does psychologically to the victims of crime, whose suffering is thought to have a special claim on the structuring of the criminal justice system (see Honderich, 1969, p. 30). To me, this is not retributivism. A retributivist can justify punishment as deserved even if the criminal's victims are indifferent (or even opposed) to punishing the one who hurt them. Indeed, a retributivist should urge punishment on all offenders who deserve it, even if *no* victims wanted it.

4. Relatedly, retributivism is not the view that the preferences of all citizens (not just crime victims) should be satisfied. A preference utilitarian might well believe, as did Sir James Fitzjames Stephen (1967 at p. 152), that punishment should be exacted "for the sake of gratifying the feeling of hatred—call it revenge, resentment, or what you will—which the contemplation of such [criminal] conduct excites in healthily constituted minds . . . ," or that "the feeling of hatred and the desire of vengeance . . . are important elements of human nature which ought . . . to be satisfied in a regular public and legal manner." Yet a retributivist need not believe such things, but only that morally culpable persons should be punished, irrespective of what other citizens feel, desire, or prefer.

5. Relatedly, retributivism is not the view that punishment is justified because without it vengeful citizens would take the law into their own hands. Usually it is those who are hostile to retributivism, such as Justice Marshall (1976), who link it to this indefensible idea. Punishment for a retributivist is not justified by the need to prevent private violence, which is an essentially utilitarian justification. Even in the most well-mannered state, those criminals who deserve punishment should get it, according to retributivism.

6. Nor is retributivism to be confused with denunciatory theories of punishment (Feinberg, 1971). In this latter view punishment is justified because punishment is the vehicle through which society can express its condemnation of the criminal's behavior. This is a utilitarian theory, not a retributive one, for punishment is in this view to be justified by the good consequences it achieves—either the psychological satisfactions denunciation achieves, or the prevention of private violence, or the prevention of future crimes through the education benefits of such denunciation. A retributivist justifies punishment by none of these supposed good consequences of punishing.

7. Finally, retributivism should not be confused with a theory of formal justice (the treating of like cases alike). Retributivism is not, as McCloskey (1965) has urged, "a particular application of a general principle of justice, namely, that equals should be treated equally and unequals unequally." True, a retributivist who also subscribes to the principle of formal justice is committed to punishing equally those persons who are equally deserving. However, the principle of formal justice says nothing about punishing anybody for anything; such a principle only dictates that, *if* we punish anyone, we must do so equally. Why we should punish anyone is the question retributivism purports to answer, a question not answered by the distinct principle of formal justice.

Retributivism is a very straightforward theory of punishment: We are justified in punishing because and only because offenders deserve it. Moral culpability ("desert")[1] is in such a view both a sufficient as well as a necessary condition of liability to punitive sanctions. Such justification gives society more than merely a right to punish culpable offenders. It does this, making it not unfair to punish them, but retributivism justifies more than this. For a retributivist, the moral culpability of an offender also gives society the *duty* to punish. Retributivism, in other words, is truly a theory of justice such that, if it is true, we have an obligation to set up institutions so that retribution is achieved.

Retributivism, so construed, joins corrective justice theories of torts, natural right theories of property, and promissory theories of contract as deontological alternatives to utilitarian justifications; in each case, the institutions of punishment, tort compensation, property, and contract are justified by the rightness or fairness of the institution in question, not by the good consequences such institution may generate. Further, for each of these theories, moral desert plays the crucial justificatory role: Tort sanctions are justified whenever the plaintiff does not deserve to suffer the harm uncompensated and the defendant by his or her conduct has created an unjust situation that permits corrective action; property rights are justified whenever one party, by his or her labor, first possession, or intrinsic ownership of his or her own body, has come by such actions or status morally to deserve such entitlements; and contractual liability is justified by the fairness of imposing it on one who deserves it (because of his or her voluntary undertaking, but subsequent and unexcused breach).

Once the deontological nature of retributivism is fully appreciated, it is often concluded that such a view cannot be justified. You either believe punishment to be inherently right, or you do not, and that is all there is to be said about it. As Hugo Bedau (1978) once put it:

Either he [the retributivist] appeals to something else—some good end—that is accomplished by the practice of punishment, in which case he is open to the criticism that he has a nonretributivist, consequentialist justification for the practice of punishment. Or his justification does not appeal to something else, in which case it is open to the criticism that it is circular and futile.

Such a restricted view of the justifications open to a retributivist leads theorists in one of two directions: Either they hang on to retributivism, urging that it is to be justified "logically" (i.e., non-morally), as inherent in the ideas of punishment (Quinton, 1954) or of law (Fingarette, 1977); or they give up retributivism as an inherently unjustifiable view (Benn and Peters, 1959). In either case, retributivism is unfairly treated, since the first alternative trivializes it and the second eliminates it.

Bedau's dilemma is surely overstated. Retributivism is no worse off in the modes of its possible justification than any other deontological theory. In the first place, one might become (like Bedau himself, apparently) a kind of "reluctant retributivist." A reluctant retributivist is someone who is somewhat repelled by retributivism but who nonetheless believes: (1) that there should be punishment; (2) that the only theories of punishment possible are utilitarian, rehabilitative, retributive, or some mixture of these; and (3) that there are decisive objections to utilitarian and rehabilitative theories of punishment, as well as to any mixed theory that uses either of these views in any combination. Such a person, as I have argued elsewhere (Moore, 1982b; also Moore, 1984, chap. 6), becomes, however reluctantly, a retributivist by default.

In the second place, positive arguments can be given for retributivism that do not appeal to some good consequences of punishing. It simply is not true that "appeals to authority apart, we can justify rules and institutions only by showing that they yield advantages" or that "to justify is to provide reasons in terms of something else accepted as valuable" (Benn and Peters, 1959, pp. 175–6). Coherence theories of justification in ethics allow two nonconsequentialist possibilities here:

1. We might justify a principle such as retributivism by showing how it follows from some yet more general principle of justice that we think to be true.
2. Alternatively, we can justify a moral principle by showing that it best accounts for those of our more

particular judgments that we also believe to be true.

In a perfectly coherent moral system, the retributive principle would be justified in both these ways, by being part of the best theory of our moral sentiments, considered as a whole.

The first of these deontological argument strategies is made familiar to us by arguments such as that of Herbert Morris (1976), who urges that retributivism follows from some general ideas about reciprocal advantage in social relations. Without assessing the merits of these proposals one way or another, I wish to pursue the other strategy. I examine the more particular judgments that seem to be best accounted for in terms of a principle of punishment for just deserts.

These more particular judgments are quite familiar. I suspect that almost everyone at least has a tendency—one that he may correct as soon as he detects it himself, but at least a tendency—to judge culpable wrongdoers as deserving of punishment. Consider some examples Mike Royko has used to get the blood to the eyes of readers of his newspaper column:

The small crowd that gathered outside the prison to protest the execution of Steven Judy softly sang "We Shall Overcome.". . .

But it didn't seem quite the same hearing it sung out of concern for someone who, on finding a woman with a flat tire, raped and murdered her and drowned her three small children, then said that he hadn't been "losing any sleep" over his crimes. . . .

I remember the grocer's wife. She was a plump, happy woman who enjoyed the long workday she shared with her husband in their ma-and-pa store. One evening, two young men came in and showed guns, and the grocer gave them everything in the cash register.

For no reason, almost as an afterthought, one of the men shot the grocer in the face. The woman stood only a few feet from her husband when he was turned into a dead, bloody mess.

She was about 50 when it happened. In a few years her mind was almost gone, and she looked 80. They might as well have killed her too.

Then there was the woman I got to know after her daughter was killed by a wolfpack gang during a motoring trip. The mother called me occasionally, but nothing that I said could ease her torment. It ended when she took her own life.

A couple of years ago I spent a long evening with the husband, sister and parents of a fine young woman who had been forced into the trunk of a car in a hospital parking lot. The degenerate who kidnapped her kept her in the trunk, like an ant in a jar, until he got tired of the game. Then he killed her.

[Reprinted by permission: Tribune Media Services]

Most people react to such atrocities with an intuitive judgment that punishment (at least of some kind and to some degree) is warranted. Many will quickly add, however, that what accounts for their intuitive judgment is the need for deterrence, or the need to incapacitate such a dangerous person, or the need to reform the person. My own view is that these addenda are just "bad reasons for what we believe on instinct anyway," to paraphrase Bradley's general view of justification in ethics.

To see whether this is so, construct a thought experiment of the kind Kant (1965, p. 102) originated. Imagine that these same crimes are being done, but that there is no utilitarian or rehabilitative reason to punish. The murderer has truly found Christ, for example, so that he or she does not need to be reformed; he or she is not dangerous for the same reason; and the crime can go undetected so that general deterrence does not demand punishment (alternatively, we can pretend to punish and pay the person the money the punishment would have cost us to keep his or her mouth shut, which will also serve the ends of general deterrence). In such a situation, should the criminal still be punished? My hypothesis is that most of us still feel some inclination, no matter how tentative, to punish. That is the particular judgment I wish to examine. (For those persons—saints or moral lepers, we shall see which—who do not have even a tentative inclination to punish, I argue that the reason for affirming such inclinations are also reasons to feel such inclinations.)

The Case Against Retributive Judgments

The puzzle I put about particular retributive judgments is this: Why are these particular judgments so

suspect—"primitive," "barbarous," "a throwback"—when other judgments in terms of moral desert are accorded places of honor in widely accepted moral arguments? Very generally, there seem to me to be five explanations (and supposed justifications) for this discriminatory treatment of retributive judgments about deserved punishment.

1. First and foremost there is the popularly accepted belief that punishment for its own sake does no good. "By punishing the offender you cannot undo the crime," might be the slogan for this point of view. I mention this view only to put it aside, for it is but a reiteration of the consequentialist idea that only further good consequences achieved by punishment could possibly justify the practice. Unnoticed by those who hold this position is that they abandon such consequentialism when it comes to other areas of morals. It is a sufficient justification not to scapegoat innocent individuals, that they do not deserve to be punished; the injustice of punishing those who do not deserve it seems to stand perfectly well by itself as a justification of our practices, without need for further good consequences we might achieve. Why do not we similarly say that the injustice of the guilty going unpunished can equally stand by itself as a justification for punishment, without need of a showing of further good consequences? It simply is not the case that justification always requires the showing of further good consequences.

Those who oppose retributivism often protest at this point that punishment is a clear harm to the one punished, and the intentional causing of this harm requires some good thereby achieved to justify it; whereas *not* punishing the innocent is not a harm and thus does not stand in need of justification by good consequences. Yet this response simply begs the question against retributivism. Retributivism purports to be a theory of justice, and as such claims that punishing the guilty achieves something good—namely, justice—and that therefore reference to any other good consequences is simply beside the point. One cannot defeat the central retributivist claim—that justice is achieved by punishing the guilty—simply by assuming that it is false.

The question-begging character of this response can be seen by imagining a like response in areas of tort, property, or contract law. Forcing another to pay tort or contract damages, or to forgo use and possession of some thing, is a clear harm that corrective justice theories of tort, promissory theories of contract, or natural right theories of property are willing to impose on defendants. Suppose no one gains anything of economic significance by certain classes of such impositions—as, for example, in cases where the plaintiff has died without heirs after his cause of action accrued. "It does no good to force the defendant to pay," interposed as an objection to corrective justice theories of tort, promissory theories of contract, or natural right theories of property simply denies what these theories assert: that something good *is* achieved by imposing liability in such cases— namely, that justice is done.

This "harm requires justification" objection thus leaves untouched the question of whether the rendering of justice cannot in all such cases be the good that justifies the harm all such theories impose on defendants. I accordingly put aside this initial objection to retributivism, relying as it does either on an unjustifiable discrimination between retributivism and other deontological theories, or upon a blunderbuss assault on deontological theories as such.

2. A second and very popular suspicion about retributive judgments is that they presuppose an indefensible objectivism about morals. Sometimes this objection is put metaphysically: There is no such thing as desert or culpability (J. Mackie, 1982). More often the point is put as a more cautious epistemological modesty: "Even if there is such a thing as desert, we can never know who is deserving." For religious people, this last variation usually contrasts us to God, who alone can know what people truly deserve. As Beccaria (1964, pp. 17–18) put it centuries ago:

> [W]hat insect will dare take the place of divine justice . . . ? The gravity of sin depends upon the inscrutable wickedness of the heart. No finite being can know it without revelation. How then can it furnish a standard for the punishment of crimes?

We might call this the "don't play God" objection.

One way to deal with this objection is to show that moral judgments generally (and judgments about culpability particularly) are both objectively true and knowable by persons. Showing both is a complicated business, and since I have attempted such a showing elsewhere (Moore, 1982a), let me try a different tack. A striking feature of the "don't play God" objection is how inconsistently it is applied. Let us revert to our use of desert as a limiting condition on punishment: We certainly seem confident both that it is true and that we can know that it is true, that we should not punish the morally innocent because they do not deserve it. Neither metaphysical skepticism nor episte-

mological modesty gets in our way when we use lack of moral desert as a reason not to punish. Why should it be different when we use presence of desert as a reason to punish? If we can know when someone does *not* deserve punishment, mustn't we know when someone *does* deserve punishment? Consider the illogic in the following passages from Karl Menninger (1968):

> The very word justice *irritates scientists. No surgeon expects to be asked if an operation for cancer is just or not. No doctor will be reproached on the grounds that the dose of penicillin he has prescribed is less or more than* justice *would stipulate. (p. 17)*
>
> It does not advance a solution to use the word justice. It is a subjective emotional word. . . . The concept is so vague, so distorted in its applications, so hypocritical, and usually so irrelevant that it offers no help in the solution of the crime problem which it exists to combat but results in its exact opposite—injustice, injustice to everybody. (pp. 10–11)

Apparently Dr. Karl knows injustice when he sees it, even if justice is a useless concept.

Analogously, consider our reliance on moral desert when we allocate initial property entitlements. We think that the person who works hard to produce a novel deserves the right to determine when and under what conditions the novel will be copied for others to read. The novelist's labor gives him or her the moral right. How can we know this—how can it be true—if desert can be judged only by those with God-like omniscience, or worse, does not even exist? Such skepticism about just deserts would throw out a great deal that we will not throw out. To me, this shows that no one really believes that moral desert does not exist or that we could not know it if it did. Something else makes us suspect our retributive judgments than supposed moral skepticism or epistemological modesty.

3. One particular form of moral skepticism merits separate attention in this context: This is the skepticism that asserts that no one is really responsible for anything because everything we do is caused by factors over which we have no control, and therefore none of us is really guilty or deserving of punishment. "Tout comprendre c'est tout pardonner," as the folk wisdom has it.

The main problem with this bit of folk wisdom is that it is false. To understand all (the causes of behavior) is not to forgive all. To match proverb for proverb: "Everybody has a story," as many convicts well know, realizing that such stories hardly excuse (Morse, 1984, p. 1499).

To do more than match proverbs against this objection to retributivism requires an extended excursion into compatibilist moral psychology. Having done that recently (Moore, 1985a), I will not recapitulate the argument defending the view that most people are responsible for what they do irrespective of the truth of determinism. In any case, if retributivism is to be rejected on hard determinist grounds, all justice theories in property, contract, and torts would have to be rejected as well, since no one could act in a way (viz., freely) so as to deserve anything.

4. A fourth popular suspicion about using moral desert as a justification to punish takes the opposite tack from the last objection. Here the thought is not that *none* of us are guilty, but rather that *all* of us are guilty—so that if we each got what we truly deserved, we would all be punished. How, then, can such a ubiquitous human condition be used to single out some but not all for punishment? Christ, of course, is the most famous purveyor of this argument when he dissuades the Pharisees from stoning an adulteress with an explicit appeal to their own guilt: "He that is without sin among you, let him first cast a stone at her" (John 8:3–11).

If we take this literally (I will give it a more charitable interpretation later), this is pretty clumsy moral philosophy. It is true that all of us are guilty of some immoralities, probably on a daily basis. Yet for most people reading this essay, the immoralities in question are things like manipulating others unfairly; not caring deeply enough about another's suffering; not being charitable for the limitations of others; convenient lies; and so forth (Shklar, 1984). Few of us have raped and murdered a woman, drowned her three small children, and felt no remorse about it afterward, to revert to one of Royko's examples. It is simply false—and obviously so—to equate guilt at the subtle immoralities of personal relationships with the gross violations of persons that violent crime represents. We do not all deserve the punishment of a murderer for the simple and sufficient reason that we are not all murderers, or anything like murderers in culpability.

One can of course quote more scripture here—"He that lusts after a woman has already committed adultery with her"—but that also is to miss some obvious and basic moral distinctions. Freud is surely to be preferred to scripture here, when he urged that we must give credit where credit is due: If our conscience is such that we do not allow ourselves to act on our admittedly wicked fantasies, that makes us a better person than one who not only dreams of such atrocities, but brings them about (see Moore, 1980, p. 1629, n. 198; compare Fingarette, 1955; Morris, 1976, p. 124).

The short of it is that desert is not such an ubiquitous feature of human personality that it cannot be a marker of punishment. To think otherwise is to gloss over obvious moral distinctions, a glossing that to me is so obviously wrong that it can only be a cover for a judgment made on other grounds.

5. It is often said that retributive judgments are "irrational." They are irrational, it is said, because they are based on "emotion rather than reason." Such irrational emotion cannot be the basis for justifying a legal institution such as punishment. Legal institutions can be justified only by reason, not by yielding to irrational emotions, whether ours or others'. Henry Weihofen (1956, pp. 130–1) once stated this objection forthrightly:

> It is not only criminals who are motivated by irrational and emotional impulsions. The same is true also of lawyers and judges, butchers and bakers. And it is especially true on such a subject as punishment of criminals. This is a matter on which we are all inclined to have deep feelings. When a reprehensible crime is committed, strong emotional reactions take place in all of us. Some people will be impelled to go out at once and work off their tensions in a lynching orgy. Even the calmest, most law-abiding of us is likely to be deeply stirred. . . . It is one of the marks of a civilized culture that it has devised legal procedures that minimize the impact of emotional reactions and strive for calm and rational disposition. But lawyers, judges and jurors are still human, and objective, rational inquiry is made difficult by the very irrationality of the human mind itself. . . . Consciously we want to be rational. We prefer to think of ourselves as governed by reason rather than as creatures swept by irrational emotions. . . .
>
> [Excerpt from The Urge to Punish by Henry Weihofen. Copyright © 1956 by Henry Weihofen. Reprinted by permission of Farrar, Straus and Giroux, Inc.]

This objection, as stated, proves far too much for its own good. Think for a moment about the intimate connection between our emotions and morality, a matter we explore later in this chapter. Although Kantian beings who could know morality without relying upon their emotions are perhaps conceivable—just barely—that surely is not us. We need our emotions to know about the injustice of racial discrimination, the unfairness of depriving another of a favorite possession, the immorality of punishing the innocent. Our emotions are our main heuristic guide to finding out what is morally right.

We do both of them and morality a strong disservice when we accept the old shibboleth that emotions are opposed to rationality. There is, as I have argued elsewhere (Moore, 1982a, 1984; see also de Sousa, 1980; Scruton, 1980), a rationality of emotions that can make them trustworthy guides to moral insight. Emotions are rational when they are intelligibly proportionate in their intensity to their objects, when they are not inherently conflicted, when they are coherently orderable, and instantiate over time an intelligible character. We also judge when emotions are appropriate to their objects; that is, when they are *correct*.

The upshot is that unless one severs any connection of our legal institutions to morals, one cannot condemn an institution because it is based on "emotion." Some emotions generate moral insights our legal system could hardly do without, such as the insight that it is outrageously unfair to punish an innocent person. Imagine condemning the legal ban on punishing the innocent because it is based on emotion and not on reason.

To be sure, there is also a sense of rationality opposed to emotionality (Moore, 1984, pp. 107–8). This is the sense in which we view rationality as reason and will and see these faculties as "unhinged" by powerful emotional storms. It is this sense of emotionality we use when we partially excuse a killer because the act was the product of extreme passion, not cool rationality. It is also this sense of rationality versus emotionality that is sometimes played upon by those making this objection to retributivism. The picture is one in which the retributivist emotions unhinge our reason by their power.

Karen Horney's assumption that vindictiveness is always neurotic (and thus always undesirable) is based upon this kind of characterization:

> *Often there is no more holding back a person driven toward revenge than an alcoholic determined to go on a binge. Any reasoning meets with cold disdain. Logic no longer prevails. Whether or not the situation is appropriate does not matter. It overrides prudence. Consequences for himself and others are*

> *brushed aside. He is as inaccessible as anybody who is in the grip of a blind passion. (Horney, 1948, p. 5).*

There is more than a little truth to this conception of the emotional base of retributivism. Literature is rich in faithful depictions of otherwise rational and moral people being unhinged by an urge to punish another for a wrong. Susan Jacoby (1984) recounts the tale of Michael Kohlhaas, written into a novel in 1806 by Heinrich von Kleist. Kohlhaas is depicted as a benevolent man, a horse dealer, friendly, kind, loyal to those around him, but one whose life is altered by the dominating passion of revenge. Kohlhaas's animals are maltreated by his neighbor—a man of higher social position—and Kohlhaas, in his unbending quest to make the offending squire pay, "eventually destroys his business and his marriage (his wife is killed by the enemies he has made); burns down the squire's house; murders innocent inhabitants of the castle; and incites a revolt that lays waste to much of the surrounding countryside" (pp. 51–2).

This is pathological and is fairly described as reason being overcome by a domineering, obsessive emotion. Yet it is surely not the case that the retributive urge always operates like this. Pathological cases can be found for any emotions, including benevolent ones. We should not judge the moral worth of an emotion by cases where it dominates reason, unless we are willing to say that such an emotion typically leads to such pathology; and the retributive intuition described here does not. One can have the intuition that the guilty deserve punishment, and one can have emotional outrage when they do not get it, without having one's reason dominated by an emotional storm. We may feel morally outraged at some guilty criminal going unpunished, but that need be no more unhinging of our reason than our outrage at the innocent being punished. In both cases, intense emotions may generate firm moral convictions; in each case, the emotions can get out of hand and dominate reason—but that is not reason to discount the moral judgments such emotions support when they do *not* get out of hand.

Despite the foregoing, I think that the most serious objection to retributivism as a theory of punishment lies in the emotional base of retributive judgments. As thus far construed, the objection is, as we have seen, ill-fated. If stated as an objection to there being an emotional base at all to judgments about deserved punishment, the objection is far too broad to be acceptable. All moral judgments would lose to such a charge if it were well founded. If stated as an objection to the unhinging quality of retributive emotions, the objection is psychologically implausible. Any emotion in pathological cases can unhinge reason, and there is nothing about retributive emotions that make it at all plausible that they always unhinge our reason when we experience them. The objection thus needs a third construction, which is this: The emotions that give rise to retributive judgments are always pathological—not in their intensity or their ability to unhinge our reason, but in their very nature. Some emotions, such as racial prejudice, have no moral worth even if typically experienced in a not very intense way. The true objection here is that the retributive urge is one such emotion.

In discussing this version of the objection to the emotional base of retributivism, I shall by and large rely on Nietzsche, who to my mind remains one of the most penetrating psychologists of the unsavory side of our emotional life. He is also one of the few thinkers to have delved deeply into the psychology of revenge. There is surprisingly little written on revenge in modern psychiatry, in large part because psychiatrists regard revenge "like sex before Freud . . . , condemned as immature and undesirable and thus unworthy of serious scientific investigation" (Harvey Lomas, quoted in Jacoby, 1984, p. 169).

"Mistrust," Nietzsche's Zarathustra advises us, "all in whom the impulse to punish is powerful" (*Zarathustra*, p. 212). Nietzsche clearly believes that the retributive emotions can get in the way of that celebration of life that makes us better—I would say virtuous—human beings. As he said in *The Gay Science*: "I do not want to wage war against what is ugly. I do not want to accuse; I do not even want to accuse those who accuse. *Looking away* shall be my only negation" (p. 223). And as he repeated later: "Let us not become darker ourselves on their [criminals'] account, like all those who punish others and feel dissatisfied. Let us sooner step aside. Let us look away" (p. 254).

What is the awful vision from which we should avert our gaze? If Nietzsche is right, truly a witch's brew: resentment, fear, anger, cowardice, hostility, aggression, cruelty, sadism, envy, jealousy, guilt, self-loathing, hypocrisy and self-deception—those "reactive affects" that Nietzsche sometimes lumped under the French term *ressentiment* (*Genealogy*, p. 74). All this, Nietzsche believed, lies behind our judgments of retributive justice.

Consider first resentment. One of Nietzsche's deepest insights into moral genealogy (Danto, 1965) is how much the retributive urge is based on resentment. As Max Scheler (1961, p. 46), once explained Nietzsche's insight here: "Revenge . . . , based as it is upon an experience of impotence, is always primarily a matter of those who are 'weak' in some respect." If we feel physically, psychologically, or politically weak, we will feel threatened by those we perceive to be stronger, such as those willing and able to use physical violence. Moreover, if we are actually or vicariously injured by such stronger persons, our weakness may prevent us from venting in the most direct way the anger such violation generates. Rather than either venting such anger directly through our own action (of retaliation), or at least feeling able to do so but choosing to refrain, our real or perceived helplessness transforms the anger into the brooding resentment of those who lack power. Such resentment, Nietzsche rightly thinks, can poison the soul, with its unstable equilibrium of repressed anger and repressing fear. A resentful person is burdened with an emotional conflict that is both ugly and harmful. It is better for us, because of this, to "look away" rather than to brood about revenge.

Our weakness and its accompanying emotions of fear and resentment can also make our retributive inclination seem cowardly, herdlike, and weak. As Nietzsche observed at one point: "'Punishment' . . . is simply a copy . . . of the normal attitude toward a hated, disarmed, prostrated enemy, who has lost not only every right and protection, but all hope of quarter as well . . ." (*Genealogy*, pp. 72–3). Yet unlike the victor in a fight who has won and who can afford to be merciful to a vanquished foe, those who wish to punish may feel that this is their first opportunity to get back, an opportunity they cannot afford to pass up. When Christ talks about throwing stones, it is not because we are all equally guilty that we should not throw the stones; rather, there is something cowardly in a group of persons throwing stones at one who is now helpless. Such cowardice can be exhibited by the need of such persons for group reinforcement (which is why avengers may refuse to throw the *first* stone—it would set one apart from the group). It is no accident that the retributive urge calls up images of mobs, groups who together finally find the strength to strike back at an only now helpless foe. Our fear and our resentment of criminals can make us look small and cowardly in our retaliation in a way that immediate retaliation by one without fear or resentment does not.

Our fear of criminals need not always be due to our sense of their power to hurt; sometimes we may feel such fears just because they are different. For some people, there is a link between fear of strangers and fear of criminals, a link partly reflected by the extraordinary group reinforcement they receive when their retributive urges are shared. Such a link is also reflected in the we–they attitude many adopt about criminals, an attitude suggesting that criminals are fundamentally different and outside the group about whom we need be concerned. This is the criminal as outlaw, an attitude that, although neither causing nor caused by prejudice and bigotries of various kinds, nonetheless invites such other fears of differences to get expressed in retributive judgments.

Even when we do not feel weak and threatened by criminals, we may find other emotions underlying our retributive judgments that are not very pretty. Surely one of the uglier spectacles of our times are the parties by fraternity boys outside the gates of prisons when an execution is taking place. What makes such spectacles so ugly is the cruelty and sadistic pleasure at the suffering of others that they express. Such people feel entitled to let go of the normal constraints on expressing such unsavory emotions because the legitimacy of retribution licenses it. It is all right to enjoy the suffering of criminals, because it is deserved suffering. Deserved punishment, as Nietzsche perceived, can be "a warrant for and title to cruelty" (*Genealogy*, p. 65). It can give us "the pleasure of being allowed to vent [our] power freely upon one who is powerless, the voluptuous pleasure of doing evil for the pleasure of doing it, the enjoyment of violation" (p. 65). Our retributive judgments, in such a case, look like a rationalization of, and excuse for, venting emotions we would be better off without.

There are admittedly other avenues in this society for people to vent sadistic enjoyment of another's suffering. One that comes to mind are such films as *The Texas Chainsaw Massacre*. Reported audience reaction to a scene depicting a helpless female about to be dismembered by a chainsaw included cries of "Cut the bitch." The unrestrained sadism in such reactions is a deep sickness of the soul. To the extent that our inclinations to punish are based on a like emotion, it too, as Menninger says (1968, p. 201), lines us "up with the Marquis de Sade, who believed in pleasure, especially the pleasure derived from making someone else feel displeasure."

There is also envy and jealousy sometimes to be found lying at the emotional base of our retributive inclinations (*Zarathustra*, p. 213). We seem to have some admiration for criminals, an admiration reflected in the attention we give them in the media and the

arts. We may admire their strength and courage; criminals, as Herbert Morris (1976, p. 132) aptly describes it, may manifest "what we too often do not, power and daring, a willingness to risk oneself for the satisfaction of strong desires." Thackeray had the same insight, writing *Vanity Fair* in large part to show us how much more we admire strength (Becky) than we do more conventional moral virtues (Amelia). Moreover, within the breasts of most of us beat some criminal desires. Not only may we admire the strength of will criminals may exhibit, but we may also be excited by the desires they allow themselves to satisfy. We thus may suffer a double dose of envy, both of the desires acted on and the strength that is exhibited in acting on them. Such envy and jealousy fuels the retributive urge, because punishment will tear down the object of such feelings.

Guilt has an interesting relationship to envy here. If criminals sometimes do what we might like to do but restrain ourselves from doing by our guilt, crime may excite a particularly virulent kind of envy. We may be envious not only of the power and the satisfaction of desires represented by criminal behavior, but even more of the freedom from guilt we may attribute to the criminal. Our own guilt in such a case may be challenged by apparent examples of such guiltless freedom to act on forbidden desires; if so, our defense is to transform the envy into the desire to destroy that which so challenges our own precarious balance between good and evil.

Guilt can give rise to our retributive judgments about others without the "good offices" of the emotions of envy and jealousy. Such retributivist judgments may simply project our own guilt onto the criminal and by doing so, lessen our guilt feelings because we are better than he. Henry Weihofen (1956, p. 138) aptly describes this Freudian insight about retribution:

> No one is more ferocious in demanding that the murderer or the rapist "pay" for his crime than the man who has felt strong impulses in the same direction. No one is more bitter in condemning the "loose" woman that the "good" women who have on occasion guiltily enjoyed some purple dreams themselves. It is never he who is without sin who casts the first stone.
>
> Along with the stone, we cast our own sins onto the criminal. In this way we relieve our own sense of guilt without actually having to suffer the punishment—a convenient and even

pleasant device for it not only relieves us of sin, but makes us feel actually virtuous.

The retributive urge often seems to be accompanied by the additional nonvirtues of self-deception and hypocrisy. Few people like to think of themselves as weak and resentful, fearful, cowardly, cruel and sadistic, envious, jealous, and guilt-ridden. Accordingly, if they possess such emotions and traits when they make retributive judgments, they have every reason to deceive themselves about it. Such self-deception Nietzsche thought to be "the masterpiece of these black magicians, who make whiteness, milk, and innocence of every blackness . . ." (*Genealogy*, p. 47; see also Horney, 1948, p. 4). "These cellar rodents full of vengefulness and hatred" have reconceived their black emotions into an abstract virtue:

> *"We good men—we are the just"—what they desire they call, not retaliation, but "the triumph of justice"; what they hate is not their enemy, no! They hate "injustice," they hate "godlessness"; what they believe in and hope for is not the hope of revenge . . . but the victory of God, of the* just *God, over the godless. . . .* (Genealogy, *p. 48)*

Self-deception and hypocrisy themselves are vices, and to the extent that our retributive judgments encourage them—because we cannot affirm the emotional base of such judgments—we would be better without them.

To this basically Nietzschean indictment of the emotions on which retributive judgments seem to be based, we may add the insight of some feminists that the urge to retaliate is an instance of a male and macho stereotype that is itself no virtue. As Susan Jacoby (1984, chap. 6) points out, there are actually two not entirely consistent stereotypes that operate here. One is that revenge is a male prerogative because it is the manly thing to do. The other is that women are the greatest avengers because (harking back to Nietzsche) their physical and political weakness demands subtler, more repressed, and thus more intense modes of retaliation. Such views are compliments neither to men nor to women. Such stereotypes, like racial prejudice and other differences mentioned earlier, do not cause our retributive judgments so much as they find in such judgments a vehicle for their expression.

Finally, consider the kind of "scoring mentality" that accompanies retributive judgments. As Scheler (1961, p. 46) noted: "It is of the essence of revenge that it always contains the *consciousness* of 'tit for tat,'

so that it is never a mere emotional reaction." Nietzsche too scorned the "shopkeeper's scales and the desire to balance guilt and punishment" (*Dawn,* p. 86) as a part of the retributive urge. Retributivism requires a kind of keeping track of another's moral ledger that seems distasteful. Retributive judgments seem legalistic, a standing on one's rights or a satisfaction with "doing one's duty" that psychologically crowds out more virtuous modes of relating to others. "Bother justice," E.M. Forster has his protagonist exclaim in *Howard's End.* Margaret later goes on to say that she will have "none of this absurd screaming about justice. . . . Nor am I concerned with duty. I'm concerned with the character of various people whom we know, and how, things being as they are, things may be made a little better" (p. 228). Aristotle (Book VII) understood the same point in his familiar thought that "between friends there is no need of justice." Relate to others in a way that does not concern itself with giving them their just deserts, positive or negative. Those who keep track of favors owed, debts due, or punishments deserved cut themselves off from modes of relating to others that can be both more virtuous (because supererogatory) and also more rewarding than demanding rights or acting on duties.

There is no question, I think, that insofar as the retributive urge is based on such emotions as these, or causes us to instantiate traits such as self-deception, the urge is bad for us. It makes us less well formed, less virtuous human beings to experience such emotions—or, more accurately, to be the sort of person who has such emotions. This insight about what are and what are not virtuous emotions to have persuades many people that they ought not to make retributive judgments. For it is natural to feel that such judgments are contaminated by their black emotional sources. Defense lawyers have long recognized our tendency to withdraw or soften our retributive demands once we see the emotional base for them. Consider Clarence Darrow's appeals to Judge Caverly's virtue in Darrow's famous closing argument in the Loeb and Leopold sentencing hearing:

> *I have heard in the last six weeks nothing but the cry for blood. I have heard from the office of the State's Attorney only ugly hate. I have heard precedents quoted which would be a disgrace to a savage race.*
>
> . . .
>
> *[Y]our Honor stands between the future and past. I know the future is with me. . . . I am*

*pleading for life, understanding, charity, kind-
ness, and the infinite mercy that considers all.
I am pleading that we overcome cruelty with
kindness and hatred with love. . . . I am pleading for a time when hatred and cruelty will not
control the hearts of men. When we can learn
by reason and judgment and understanding
and faith that . . . mercy is the highest attribute
of man. . . . If I can succeed . . . I have done
something to help human understanding, to
temper justice with mercy, to overcome hate
with love. I was reading last night of the aspiration of the old Persian poet, Omar Khayyam.
It appealed to me as the highest that I can vision. I wish it was in my heart, and I wish it
was in the hearts of all. "So I be written in the
Book of Love, I do not care that Book above,
erase my name or write it as you will, so I be
written in the Book of Love." (Hicks, 1925,
pp. 995, 1084)*

Persuasive words. For who does not want to be written in the Book of Love? Who wants to be written in
the books of hate, cruelty, cowardice, envy, resentment, and the like? Judge Caverly certainly did not,
and decided against a death sentence for Loeb or
Leopold.

Yet the more one looks at this argument, the
more questionable it becomes. What does the virtue
of the holder of a judgment have to do with the
truth (or lack of it) of that judgment? Why should we
think that Judge Caverly's damaging his virtue by deciding against Loeb and Leopold—increasing his virtue if he decides the other way—has anything to do
with the truth of the judgment "Loeb and Leopold
deserve to die"? How can a judge expect to reach
sound moral conclusions about Loeb and Leopold by
focusing on which decision will most enhance *his*
(the judge's) virtue? This seems to be a form of ad
hominem argument, and a rather selfish version to
boot, given its narcissistic preoccupation with one's
own virtue.

The most persuasive case against retributivism
is thus in danger of complete collapse. The charge is
this: Even if it makes us morally worse to make retributive judgments—because of the emotions that give
rise to such judgments—that lack of virtue on our part
is simply irrelevant to the assessment of whether retributive judgments are true. To assess this issue requires that we look in greater detail at the connections
between our emotions and our moral judgments,
which I propose to do next.

Morality and the Emotions

The charge laid at the end of the last section is a form
of the "genetic fallacy" objection. Such an objection
urges that it is fallacious to infer the falsity of a proposition from some truths (no matter how unsavory)
about the genesis of people's belief in that proposition. A common example is to infer the falsity of our
moral beliefs from the fact that they are caused by an
education that could easily have been otherwise (see
Moore, 1982a, pp. 1097–101). The ad hominem argument presented in the last section is like this, because it infers the falsity of retributivism from the
unnice emotional origins of people's belief in retributivism.

To respond adequately to this genetic fallacy
objection, the antiretributivist must establish that the
emotional base of a moral judgment is relevant to that
judgment's truth. If we leave ethics for a moment, one
can see that sometimes it is no fallacy to infer the falsity of a judgment from the truth of some explanation
of why people come to such judgment. Suppose the
proposition in question was: "Sticks become bent
when immersed in water, straight again when removed." Suppose the common explanation for why
people believe this proposition to be true is in terms
of their perceptual experience with sticks partly immersed in water—namely, they look bent to them. If
we have grounds to believe that these perceptual experiences as a class are unreliable—an "illusion"—
then it is no fallacy to infer the falsity of the proposition from an explanation of people's beliefs showing
such beliefs to be the product of an illusion. Knowing
what we do about the unreliability of perceptual experience when light is refracted in mediums of different density, we are entitled to disbelieve those who
rely on such experiences in coming to their beliefs
about sticks in liquid.

The antiretributivist would make a similar construction of the Nietzschean case against retributivism,
likening Nietzsche's explanation of people's beliefs in
retributivism (as due to the emotions of *ressentiment*)
to an explanation of a perceptual belief in terms of a
known illusion or hallucination. Whether there can be
such a thing as a moral hallucination or illusion, and
if so, whether the emotions of *ressentiment* should
be seen as such hallucinating experiences, depends
upon an affirmative answer to two questions:

1. Are any emotions epistemically relevant to the
   truth of moral judgments?

2. If so, is it the virtuous nature of an emotion that tells us whether it has epistemic import?

I shall consider these questions in order.

With respect to the first question, we should distinguish four different views on how the emotions are relevant either to the discovery or to the justification of moral judgments.

1. One is suggested by Kant's famous remarks in the *Groundwork* (1964, pp. 65–7) to the effect that moral worth is found in actions motivated only by reverence for the moral law, not in actions motivated by the inclinations, no matter how benevolent or virtuous. Such a view would make the emotions that generate a moral belief irrelevant to the truth of that belief. Good emotions could as easily generate false beliefs as true ones, and bad emotions could as easily generate true beliefs as false ones. The truth of a moral proposition would be governed solely by reasoning from the categorical imperative or other supreme principle of morality itself discoverable by reason alone, not from any emotional experience.

In this view there is no analogy between the relation of the emotions and moral truth, on the one hand, and the relation of perceptual experiences and scientific truth, on the other. Accordingly, a Kantian about this should find the genetic fallacy objection conclusive when applied to Nietzsche; the lack of virtue of the emotions that generate retributivism has nothing to do with the truth of retributivism because the emotions generally have no epistemic import for the truth of moral judgments. In this view the emotions are relevant neither to justifying a moral judgment as true nor to discovering it to be true.

2. An opposite conclusion about the force of the genetic fallacy objection in this context should be drawn by those who think that the emotions have everything to do with moral truth. This second view about the connection of the emotions to moral truth is the view of the conventionalist (or relativist) about morals. Lord Devlin's writings (1971) on the morality of homosexual behavior provide a convenient example. According to Devlin, homosexual behavior is immoral (and may be legally prohibited) whenever enough people feel deeply enough that it is bad. "It is not nearly enough," Devlin reminds us, "to say that a majority dislike a practice, there must be a real feeling of reprobation. . . . No society can do without intolerance, indignation, and disgust; they are the forces behind the moral law. . ." (p. 40).

In this view, the emotions of a people constitute moral truth. If most people feel deeply enough that a practice is immoral, then it is immoral, in this conventionalist view. This means that if the emotional base for some moral belief is undermined, then necessarily the belief cannot be true. If Nietzsche, for example, can show that the emotions that generate retributivist beliefs are contaminated, then necessarily retributivism is not morally right.

How could Devlin admit the possibility of this kind of undermining of the emotional base of retributivism, given the total absence of reason checking emotion in his conventionalist view of morals? For someone like Devlin, after all, morals just *are* feelings shared by a majority. Yet such majority feelings can be changed if that majority can be emotionally repelled by a subset of its own emotions. And if enough people are repelled enough by the Nietzschean case against *ressentiment,* then the retributive urge must be excluded from those conventions of shared feelings that constitute morality.

This conventionalist view about morality results in there being no genetic fallacy objection to be interposed against Nietzsche. To attack the emotional base of retributivism would be to attack retributivism itself.

Yet such a strong epistemic connection of the emotions to moral truth cannot be sustained. That a large percentage of Americans, perhaps a majority, have feelings of disgust, fear, and hatred of gays does not end a moral inquiry into the truth or falsity of the proposition that gays may be discriminated against, in housing, employment, or elsewhere. A person seeking to arrive at the truth about just treatment for minorities cannot accept his or her own emotional reactions as settling the issue (nor, more obviously, can the person accept the emotional reactions of others). Each must judge for himself or herself whether those emotions are harbingers of moral insight or whether they are the "hallucinations" of the emotional life that must be discarded in our search for the truth. The same, of course, is true for our sense perceptions vis-à-vis scientific truths. Sticks may look bent when partly immersed in water, but that does not mean that they really are bent. Our sense perception is not veridical, and there is no reason to suppose that our emotions are any better guarantors of knowledge.

3. This analogy of the emotions to sensory perception suggests a third way of thinking of the epistemic connection of the emotions to morality, a conception that is also, unfortunately, misleading. This is the route of intuitionism. An intuitionist, as I am here using the word, believes that the emotions stand to moral judgment in a relation exactly analogous to the relation between perceptual experience and scientific

judgment. For an intuitionist, the analogy is only an analogy, however, for such a person sees morals and science as distinct realms of knowledge, each with their own distinct experiential base. Such an intuitionist will usually be a metaphysical dualist, believing that such distinct modes of knowing must imply that there are distinct modes of being. (An example of this is how introspectionism goes hand in hand with dualism in the philosophy of mind.)

In any case, the intuitionist will regard emotions as crucial to morals, for they are the data from which moral theory is constructed. Without the emotions generating intuitions, there could be no moral insight, for this kind of intuitionist. An intuitionist is not committed to the emotions being veridical; indeed, to maintain the parallel to sensory perception, the intuitionist should say that the felt justice of punishing for its own sake is *good evidence* that it is just to punish for its own sake, but allow that the inference could be mistaken.

4. I must confess there is much in the intuitionist's account that I find tempting. Still, the dead ends of dualistic metaphysics and the lumpy epistemology of discrete cognitive realms is sufficient reason to avoid intuitionism and nonnaturalism in ethics, as it is to avoid introspectionism and dualism in psychology (Moore, 1985, 1987). We can avoid this metaphysical and epistemological lumpiness by thinking of the emotions as heuristic guides to moral insight, but not as the experience out of which moral theory is constructed. In this view, moral knowledge does not rest on its own unique experiential base, the emotions. Such a view could even concede the empiricist idea that all knowledge (moral knowledge included) rests on sensory experience and the inferences drawable from it.

Consider a judgment that another is morally culpable for some harm. An intuitionist would view culpability as a special kind of property not observable by the senses (a "nonnatural" property), and known only by that special faculty of intuition provided by our emotional life. I think, on the contrary, that culpability is not a property in some special realm. True, we cannot see it but must infer its existence from other properties, such as voluntariness of action, accountability, intention, causation, lack of excuse or justification. But then we cannot see those properties either. We infer the existence of an intention in another from behavioral clues; we do not see causal relations, but infer their existence as well. Culpability is no less a natural property of persons than is intentionality, voluntariness, and so on; none are visible properties, all

must be inferred from other evidence. Yet these facts do not demand a special mode of existence, and a special mode of knowing, for any of such properties (see my response to Mackie's well-known "queerness" objection in Moore, 1982a).

If we think of (moral) properties such as culpability in this way, then the emotions are not strictly necessary for there to be moral knowledge. We can imagine a being who could make correct inferences about culpability, as about other things such as intentionality, even if he or she were devoid of any relevant emotional life. True, the being would not *feel* about, for example, justice as we feel about it; yet he or she could know injustice, in the sense of being able to pick it out, as well as we.

The emotions are thus heuristic guides for us, an extra source of insight into moral truths beyond the knowledge we can gain from sensory and inferential capacities alone. One might think of them as I would think of conscious experience vis-à-vis knowledge of mind: My conscious experience of deciding to get a haircut is one way I can come to know that I intend to get a haircut; yet I or others can come to know that I intend to get a haircut in a variety of other ways, including perhaps someday by physiological measurements. My introspective, "privileged access" is only a heuristic guide to learning about my sensations, intentions, and so on that others do not possess. It is not essential to an intention that I be conscious of it, any more than it is essential to the injustice of an institution that I or others feel negatively toward it. The usual judgments I make about my intentions may be judgments reached by reflection on my conscious deliberative processes, just as my usual judgments about justice may be reached via some strong feelings; but the usual route to knowledge—of minds or morals— is not to be confused with what mental states or moral qualities *are*.

The upshot of this is that our emotions are important but not essential in our reaching moral truths. Contra Kant, there is an epistemic connection between our emotions and morality, but it is neither of the strong connections that conventionalism or intuitionism would posit. In the present context, the payoff of seeing this latter point lies in seeing when we may find some emotions wanting as epistemic indicators of moral truth. It is possible, in this last view, for there to be emotions that are "moral hallucinations," and it is therefore open to a Nietzschean to claim that our retributive inclinations are of this kind.

We come, then, to the second question—is the virtue of possessing an emotion relevant to that emotion's epistemic import? We should begin by being clear about the two different ways in which the emotions may be connected to morality before we inquire into the relation between them. We have hitherto been discussing what I would call the epistemic connection of the emotions to morality, distinguishing strong views of this connection (like Devlin's) from weaker views, such as my own or Kant's. Yet there is another possible way in which morality is related to our emotional life. This is where the emotions are themselves the objects of moral judgment. I call this the substantive connection of morality to the emotions.

The substantive connection can be grasped by reflecting on the judgments we make when we are not concerned with ascribing legal liability. The part of morality that is incorporated into our criminal law is by and large the morality of will and reason, by virtue of which we make the crudest of responsibility ascriptions. Voluntariness of action, accountability, intentionality, causation, justification, and excuse are the primary categories in terms of which we judge someone as morally culpable and thus legally punishable (Moore, 1984, chap. 2). Compare the less legalistic moral judgments we make in daily life: We often think of ourselves or others as more or less virtuous, depending on what emotions we feel on what occasions (Lyons, 1980; Dent, 1984). We make judgments, in other words, not just about the wrong actions a bad person wills, but also about the evil emotions a bad person feels. As Bernard Williams (1973, p. 207) has noted, there is a morality

> . . . about what a man ought or ought not to feel in certain circumstances, or, more broadly, about the ways in which various emotions may be considered as distinctive, mean or hateful, while others appear as creative, generous, admirable, or—merely—such as one would hope for from a decent human being. Considerations like these certainly play a large part in moral thought, except perhaps in that of the most restricted and legalistic kind. . . .

Consider a person who feels little or no compassion for others less fortunate. This person's behavior need not be that of a scrooge—he may do all the morally acceptable things, such as donate to charities, help blind persons across the street, not inflict needless suffering, and so on. Yet he does such things out of a priggish concern for propriety, including the propriety he attains by having a good opinion of himself. He does not feel any compassion for the objects of his charity; indeed, he regards them as inferior beings who exist for him mainly to be the objects of his virtue. Such a person is morally inferior to—less virtuous than—another whose actions may be no better but whose emotional life includes compassion (Blum, 1980).

Contrast this collection of the emotions and morality with the epistemic connection. Staying with the example of compassion: We may take our feelings of compassion for some disadvantaged persons to be the harbingers of a moral insight about what that group deserves. Suppose you travel to India and find the poverty of many Indians to be distressing. You might take that feeling of compassion to be the originator of a moral insight about the nature of distributive justice—namely, that the geographic limits you had previously observed in applying some ideal of distributive justice seem arbitrary, a matter of political expediency at best. In such a case, the emotional experience of compassion may generate a firm moral conviction that distributive justice knows no political boundaries or geographical limits, but extends to all persons.

The epistemic connection of the emotions to morality is quite different from the substantive connection. With the latter, we judge the emotions as virtuous or not; the emotions in such a case are the object of moral evaluation. With the former, we are not seeking to judge the moral worth of an emotion as a virtue; rather, we seek to learn from such emotions the correct moral judgments to make about some other institution, practice, act, or agent.

Having distinguished the two connections of morality to the emotions, it remains to inquire whether there is not some relation between them. One wishing to use Nietzsche's kind of insights to attack retributivism, and yet escape the genetic fallacy objection, must assert that there is some such relation. The idea is that we use our own virtue in possessing an emotion as the touchstone of whether that emotion is "hallucinatory" or not: If the possession of an emotion makes us more virtuous, then that emotion is a good heuristic for coming to moral judgments that are true; if the possession of an emotion makes us less virtuous, then that emotion is a good heuristic for coming to moral judgments that are false. This possibility, of course, would complete the antiretributivist's answer to the genetic fallacy charge. For then the vice of possessing the emotions of *ressentiment* gives us good reason to suppose that the moral judgments to which those emotions give rise—namely, retributive judgments—are false.

This is possible, but what reason do we have to think that such a connection—between the judge's virtue, and the truth of the judgment he or she is making—holds? Counterexamples certainly spring to mind; consider two of them.

1. As Herbert Morris has examined . . . there is such a thing as nonmoral guilt. Think, for example, of the guilt one might feel at having made a tragic choice: There were only two options, neither happy ones, and one chose to do the lesser evil. Using Philippa Foot's much-discussed example: A railroad switchman can only turn a moving trolley car onto one line or another, but he cannot stop it; he chooses to turn the car onto the line where only one trapped workman will be killed; on the other line, five workmen were trapped and would have been killed had the trolley car gone their way. The switchman is not morally culpable in directing the trolley on the line where only one workman would be killed. The alternative being even worse, the switchman was justified in doing what he did. Still the switchman should feel regret, remorse, and even guilt at killing the one workman. The switchman who experiences such emotions is a more virtuous person than one who has a "don't cry over what can't be helped" attitude toward the whole affair.

If both moral judgments are right—the switchman is not culpable (guilty), but his feeling guilty is virtuous—then we cannot say that the emotions that make us virtuous are necessarily the emotions that are good heuristic guides to moral truth. For if the latter were true, this switchman's (virtuous) feeling guilty should mean that the associated judgment, "I am guilty," is true; but it is not.

2. Just as some emotions are virtuous even though their associated judgments are not true, so some emotions that are not virtuous to possess may nonetheless spawn judgments that are true. Think of the institution of private property and its Lockean justifications in terms of the exercised liberty of one who mixes her labor with a thing. I think that the Lockean judgment, "she deserves the property right because she created the thing in the first place," to be true when applied to a novelist seeking copyright protections for a novel. Yet I also think that the emotions that are my heuristic guide to that judgment are suspect, at the least, in their enhancement of my virtue.

For are not the emotions that call to mind Lockean intuitions about deserved property entitlements essentially selfish emotions that make us worse for possessing them? (See E.M. Forster, 1936, pp. 22–6;

Becker, 1977, p. 96). We are entitled, from what we have done, to exclude others from the enjoyment of the products of our labor. My intuition is that this is true, but I am not proud of the selfish emotions that generate this intuition. They seem to consist too much of pride and self-congratulation to be virtues. To me at least, the nonvirtuous nature of the emotional base of Lockean property theories does not make me doubt their truth; it would be unfair to deprive another of the products of his or her labor, however much it would be better if we (and the other) did not beat our chests so much about our own accomplishments.

These examples are perhaps controversial, but I doubt that the point they illustrate is. The virtue (or lack of it) in the possession of our emotion is not an infallible guide to the epistemic import such as emotion may possess.

Is the first even a *fallible* guide to the second? A defender of retributivism might well think not. Such a person might compare the situation in science: What is the relevance, he or she might ask, of the virtue of a perceptual experience (say one induced by drugs) to the epistemic import of such an experience? What possible reason is there to think that the moral worth of a visual experience will correlate with its epistemic import? Tripping on LSD and looking at pornography may be equally lacking in virtue, but only one of them is likely to produce untrue beliefs about, for example, anatomical features of human beings.

Yet what if we substituted an example where the virtue in question is not so obviously removed from the truth of any scientific judgments? Suppose we focused on what might be called the "virtues of a scientist," traits such as analytical capacity, creativity, curiosity, being careful, and ambition. It is not nearly so implausible to think that beliefs produced through the exercise of these traits are more likely true, and that those produced by the analytically dull, the plodding, the mechanical, the careless or the lazy are more likely false.

Similarly, in ethics we should recognize that the virtue of (or vice) of an emotion may often, but not always, be taken as an indication of the truth (or falsity) of the judgment to which it leads. Indeed, would it not be remarkable to think that one could arrive at the judgments about science or morals only through emotions or traits that made one morally odious? Although not contradictory, it would surely be an oddly cohering morality that valued, say, equal treatment and also extolled the virtue of those prejudiced attitudes that typically produce discriminating judgments.

We value moral and scientific truth too highly to think that there could be any virtues so counterproductive to the attainment of truth.

In any case, what other criterion could there be for the epistemic reliability of the emotions? If such reliability had nothing to do with the virtue of such emotions, what would be our test? Rawls (1971, p. 48) suggests that we look to those "conditions favorable for deliberation and judgment in general" when we seek to isolate those "considered judgments" that in reflective equilibrium justify his two principles of justice. Which conditions are these?

> [We] can discard those judgments made with hesitation, or in which we have little confidence. Similarly, those given when we are upset or frightened, or when we stand to gain one way or the other can be left aside. All these judgments are likely to be erroneous or to be influenced by an excessive attention to our own interests. (p. 47; see also Copp, 1984)

Yet this test is too dispassionate, too judicial. Rawls's test for *judgments* that have epistemic import cannot be turned into a test for *emotions* because Rawls, like Kant, pretty much ignores the emotional base of moral judgment.

If we look in this way for a purely cognitive test for when emotions are epistemically reliable, my suspicion is that we will always end up slighting the role of the emotions in generating moral insight. We will do this because a purely cognitive test will inevitably seek to derive a criterion of epistemic warrant that is independent of any theory generated from the emotions themselves. It is like attempting to set up a criterion of epistemic warrant for perceptual experiences without using any theory derived from such experiences. Yet surely in science we do not expect to have to come up with some prescientific test for the epistemic import of sensory experience *before* we meld those experiences into a scientific theory. Rather, we rely on the body of scientific theory itself to justify exclusions of experience from the data. It is because we know what we do about optics that leads us to discount the illusion that a stick partly immersed in water looks bent; it is because we know what we do about drugs, mental disease, sensory deprivation, and the like, that we discount hallucinatory perceptual experiences. In science we quite literally explain such experiences away by using the very theories of which such experiences are part of the data. We are entitled to make the parallel move in ethics, so that our sub-

stantive moral theories—not some pale, preliminary, judicial, nonmoral litmus test—give us the criteria for weeding out emotions with misleading epistemic import. Those substantive theories of what justice is, for example, make it very unlikely that prejudice could be a virtue, or that compassion could not.

The upshot of all of this is that the genetic fallacy objection with which we began this section is inconclusive when interposed by the retributivist against the Nietzschean analysis of the retributive urge. If Nietzsche is right in asserting that our retributive beliefs are always motivated by the emotions of *ressentiment,* and right that the possession of those emotions makes us less virtuous, then we have grounds to reject retributivism as a philosophy of punishment. True, such a Nietzschean argument could not be a knockdown winner—from what has been said, it is possible that the nonvirtuous emotions of *ressentiment* nonetheless generate true moral judgments about what wrongdoers deserve. Yet this would have to be established by justifying the retributive principle in some way other than by showing it to be the best expression of our more particular judgments about criminals. Without such independent justification of retributivism, Nietzsche gives us reason to believe the retributive principle to be false when he shows us how lacking in virtue are the emotions that generate retributive judgments. For without such an independent justification, here as elsewhere we are entitled to rely on the connection that generally (but not inevitably) holds between the virtue in possessing an emotion and the truth of the judgment that that emotion generates.

The Correctness of Retributive Judgments

As previewed in the first part of this chapter, there are two justificatory routes a coherentist might use in justifying retributivism. First, because of the Nietzschean attack on the retributive urge, a retributivist might abandon the justificatory route that begins with our particular judgments about punishment in individual cases, and instead focus on how retributivism is justified because of its coherence with other, more general moral beliefs we are prepared to accept. He or she might show how there is an odd lacunae in our moral judgments about desert if the retributive principle is not accepted. That is, when passing out rewards, the desert of those whose labor produced them is (for Lockeans) both a necessary and a sufficient condition for allocating a property entitlement in them. The presence of such desert justifies giving the reward to them; the absence of such desert justifies withholding it from them. Similarly, when passing out legal duties to pay for harms caused, the culpability of he or she who caused the harm and the lack of culpability of he or she who suffers the harm, is (in standard corrective justice theories) both necessary and sufficient to justify tort liability. It is only with punishment that we have an asymmetry; namely (as even most nonretributivists will assert), that desert is a necessary condition of punishment, but not sufficient by itself to justify punishment.

Such an asymmetry does not by itself render a deontologist's social theory incoherent if he or she rejects retributivism (although it might if one isolated a general principle of just deserts common to corrective justice, property allocations, and retributive justice). My only point here is that if there were such incoherence without retributivism, the latter would be justified even if the retributive urge is unworthy of us. Nothing in the Nietzschean case against retributivism could prevent this. Still, since my approach is to justify retributivism by using our more particular judgments about punishment, I need to take seriously the Nietzschean case against those judgments.

The problem with the Nietzschean case against retributivism does not lie, as we have seen, in its presupposition that generally there is a strong connection between virtuous emotions and true moral judgments, vices and false moral judgments. The real problem for the Nietzschean critic is to show that retributive judgments are *inevitably* motivated by the black emotions of *ressentiment*. For if the critic cannot show this, then much of the contamination of those particular judgments is lifted. It is lifted because the retributive judgment would then not arise out of the kind of moral hallucination nonvirtuous emotions typically represent; rather, the retributive judgment would be only the vehicle for the expression of the emotions of *ressentiment*—dangerous for that reason, but not lacking in epistemic import for that reason.

Consider an analogy in meta ethics. The position I have defended elsewhere (Moore, 1982a), moral realism, is an admittedly dangerous view about which to proselytize. It is dangerous because many people use moral realism as a vehicle to express intolerance and contempt for autonomy. Many people may even accept moral realism because it seems to them to have

this potential for intolerant imperialism against the differing moral beliefs of others. Yet these psychological facts, to my mind, constitute no argument against the truth of moral realism. They do not because I am able to separate moral realism from intolerance: logically I see that a moral realist can defend tolerance, pluralism, and autonomy as much (more?) as anyone, and psychologically I do not see any inevitability in my moral realist views being motivated by intolerance. Making these separations, the fact that many people use moral realism to express their intolerance—or even are motivated to moral realist beliefs by their intolerance—loses any epistemic sting. It makes me cautious about holding forth about moral realism with intolerant audiences, but it does not give me reason to be cautious about the truth of moral realism.

As much seems to me to be true about retributivism. I shall make the argument in three steps: First, that the inevitability of linking *ressentiment* emotions to retributive judgments is weakened when one notes, as Nietzsche himself did, that *anti*retributive judgments are also often motivated by some of those same nonvirtuous emotions; second, that in our own individual cases we can imagine being motivated to make retributive judgments by the virtuous emotions of guilt and fellow feeling; and third, that because punishment is a social institution, unlike private vengeance, it can help us to control the emotions retributive punishment expresses by controlling the aspects of punishment that all too easily allow it to express *ressentiment*.

1. A paraphrase of Zarathustra, of which Nietzsche no doubt would have approved, would be that we should beware all those in whom the urge to punish is either actually, or claimed to be, nonexistent. As Nietzsche does tell us:

> *if you are cursed, I do not like it that you want to bless. Rather, join a little in the cursing. And if you have been done a great wrong, then quickly add five little ones: a gruesome sight is a person single-mindedly obsessed by a wrong. . . . A wrong shared is half right. . . . A little revenge is more human than no revenge.* (Zarathrustra, p. 180)

Everyone gets angry when their bodily integrity or other important interests are violated by another. If they care about other human beings, they are vicariously injured when someone close to them—or distant, depending on the reach of their empathy—is wronged. It is human to feel such anger at wrongful violation, and Nietzsche's thought is that not to express the anger in some retaliation is a recipe for *ressentiment* itself.

One might of course think that retaliation is a second best solution; better not to feel the anger at all so that the choice of expressing it in action, or of repressing it into the subtle revenge of pity, is not necessary (see Horney, 1948, p. 3). Leaving aside whether such willing away of anger is possible, is it desirable? While it has a saintly ring to it to turn the other cheek so long as it is one's own cheek that has just been slapped, is it virtuous to feel nothing stronger than sympathy for the suffering of others at the hands of wrongdoers? Where is that compassionate concern for others that is outraged because another person could have so unnecessarily caused such suffering?

Karen Horney concluded that "[t]he vindictive person thus is egocentric . . . because he has more or less severed his emotional relations to other human beings" (1948, p. 12). Yet isn't this even more often true of one who feels anger only when he himself suffers at the hands of a wrongdoer, not when others suffer? An egocentric lack of compassion for others may explain the antiretributivist, forgiving attitude as easily as it may explain the desire for vengeance.

Sometimes the compassion for victims is not absent, but gets transferred to the person who is now about to suffer; namely, the wrongdoer. Such a transfer of compassion is not justified by the relative merits of the two classes of persons, unless we are to think that there is some reason to prefer wrongdoers to victims as the appropriate objects of compassion. "Out of sight, out of mind" is the reason that suggests itself, but this psychological tendency can hardly justify forgetting those who have suffered at the hands of others. My own view is that such a transfer of concern from victim to criminal occurs in large part because of our unwillingness to face our own revulsion at what was done (Gaylin, 1983, p. 123). It allows us to look away from the horror that another person was willing to cause.

We almost cannot bear the sight. We invent for the wrongdoers a set of excusing conditions that we would not tolerate for a moment in ourselves. When they transgress, virtuous people know how ill it lies to "excuse" themselves by pointing to their own childhood or past, their lack of parental love, their need for esteem, and other causes (Moore, 1985a). Virtuous people do not use the childish "something made me do it" because they know that that denies their essential freedom in bringing about some harm. They know that they did it, chose to do it, caused though that choice surely was by factors themselves unchosen.

Yet we cannot stand to apply to criminals the same standard of responsibility that we apply to ourselves because we cannot stand to acknowledge that there is such a thing as evil in the world—and, worst of all, that it is not "inhuman" but a part of creatures not so different from ourselves. Lack of anger at criminals, if it does not represent simple indifference to the sufferings of others, may represent our self-deception about the potential for evil in humanity.

Such lack of anger may also represent the same fear of criminals that can motivate retributive judgments. Nietzsche:

> *There is a point in the history of society when it becomes so pathologically soft and tender that among other things it sides even with those who harm it, criminals, and does this quite seriously and honestly. Punishing somehow seems unfair to it, and it is certain that imagining "punishment" and "being supposed to punish" hurts it, arouses fear in it. "It is not enough to render him* undangerous? Why still *punish? Punishing itself is terrible." With this question, herd morality, the morality of timidity, draws its ultimate consequence. . . . The imperative of herd timidity: "We want that some day there should be nothing anymore to be afraid of!"* (Beyond Good and Evil, *p. 114)*

By repressing anger at wrongful violation, we may be attempting to deny that we live in a society in which there really are fearful and awful people.

Yet again, our transfer of fellow-feeling from victim to criminal, and its accompanying elimination of anger, may represent something other than indifference or inability to face evil or our own fears. It may represent a narcissism that is itself no virtue. A criminal, after all, represents an opportunity to exercise (and display, a separate point) one's virtue. The virtue in question is compassion for someone now threatened with harm. Yet such egoistic compassion becomes something other than compassion. It becomes just what Nietzsche said it becomes, the elevation of self by pity. Remarkably, one can lose compassionate concern for another by the self-conscious egoistic caricature of compassion we distinguish as pity. In pity we do not care about the other any more for his own sake, but only insofar as he allows *us* to become, in our own and others' eyes, better. We should beware, to adopt yet another paraphrase of Nietzsche, this one by Philippa Foot (1973, p. 168), all those who find others best when they find them most in need. We should beware of them because such people lack precisely the ability to feel that compassion whose outward form they ape.

2. Resentment, indifference to others, self-deception, fear, cowardice, and pity are not virtues. They do not perhaps add up to the witches' brew of a full batch of the *ressentiment* emotions, but to the extent they motivate antiretributive judgments, they make such judgments suspect. If one accepts, as Nietzsche did, that both retributive and antiretributive judgments are often motivated by, or at least expressions of, nonvirtuous emotions, where does that leave us? It should leave us asking whether we cannot make our judgments about punishment in such a way that they are not motivated by either set of unworthy emotions.

When we make a retributive judgment—such as that Stephen Judy deserved the death penalty for his rape-murder of a young mother and his murder of her three children—we need not be motivated by the *ressentiment* emotions. Nor is the alternative some abstract, Kantian concern for justice, derived by reason alone and unsullied by any strong emotional origin. Our concern for retributive justice might be motivated by very deep emotions that are nonetheless of a wholly virtuous nature. These are the feelings of guilt we would have if we did the kinds of acts that fill the criminal appellate reports of any state.

The psychiatrist Willard Gaylin interviewed a number of people closely connected to the brutal hammering death of Bonnie Garland by her jilted boyfriend, Richard Herrin. He asked a number of those in a Christian order that had been particularly forgiving of Richard whether they could imagine themselves performing such an act under any set of circumstances. Their answer was uniformly "Yes." All of us can at least find it conceivable that there might be circumstances under which we could perform an act like Herrin's—not exactly the same, perhaps, but something pretty horrible. All of us do share this much of our common nature with the worst of criminals. (For those with a greater we–they attitude toward criminals, the thought experiment that follows must be run with a somewhat less horrible act than Richard's.)

Then ask yourself: What would you feel like if it was you who had intentionally smashed open the skull of a 23-year-old woman with a claw hammer while she was asleep, a woman whose fatal defect was a desire to free herself from your too clinging embrace? My own response, I hope, would be that I would feel guilty unto death. I couldn't imagine any suffering that could be imposed upon me that would be unfair because it exceeded what I deserved.

Is that virtuous? Such deep feelings of guilt seem to me to be the only tolerable response of a moral being. "Virtue" is perhaps an odd word in the context of extreme culpability, but such guilt seems, at the least, very appropriate. One ought to feel so guilty one wants to die. Such sickness unto death is to my mind more virtuous than the nonguilty state to which Richard Herrin brought himself, with some help from Christian counseling about the need for self-forgiveness. After three years of prison on an eight- to twenty-five-year sentence for "heat of passion" manslaughter, Richard thought he had suffered quite enough for the killing of Bonnie:

HERRIN: I feel the sentence was excessive.

GAYLIN: Let's talk about that a little.

HERRIN: Well, I feel that way now and after the first years. The judge had gone overboard. . . .

Considering all the factors that I feel the judge should have considered: prior history of arrest, my personality background, my capacity for a productive life in society—you know, those kinds of things—I don't think he took those into consideration. He looked at the crime itself and responded to a lot of public pressure or maybe his own personal feelings, I don't know. I'm not going to accuse him of anything, but I was given the maximum sentence. This being my first arrest and considering the circumstances, I don't think I should have been given eight to twenty-five years.

GAYLIN: What do you think would have been a fair sentence?

HERRIN: Well, after a year or two in prison, I felt that was enough. . . .

GAYLIN: How would you answer the kind of person who says, for Bonnie, it's her whole life; for you it's eight years. What's eight years compared to the more years she might have had?

HERRIN: I can't deny that it's grossly unfair to Bonnie but there's nothing I can do about it. . . .

She's gone—I can't bring her back. I would rather that she had survived as a complete person, but she didn't. I'm not, again . . . I'm not saying that I shouldn't have been punished, but the punishment I feel is excessive. I feel I have five more years to go, and I feel that's just too much. There's no . . . I don't see any purpose in it. It's sad what happened, but it's even sadder to waste another life. I feel I'm being wasted in here.

GAYLIN: But what about the people who say, Look, if you got two years, then someone who robs should get only two days. You know, the idea of commensurate punishment. If it is a very serious crime it has to be a very serious punishment. Are you saying two years of prison is a very serious punishment considering what you did?

HERRIN: For me, yes.

[From W. Gaylin, *The Killing of Bonnie Garland,* pp. 325–7. Copyright © 1982 by Pip Enterprises, Inc. Reprinted by permission of Simon & Schuster, Inc.]

Compared to such shallow, easily obtained self-absolution for a horrible violation of another, a deep sense of guilt looks very virtuous indeed.

To be sure, there is an entire tradition that regards guilt as a useless passion (see Kaufmann, 1973). For one thing, it is always backward-looking rather than allowing one to get on with life. For another, it betrays an indecision that Nietzsche among others found unattractive: "The bite of conscience is indecent," Nietzsche thought (*Twilight,* p. 467), because it betrays the earlier decision about which one feels guilty. Yet Nietzsche and his followers are simply wrong here. Guilt feelings are often a virtue precisely because they do look to the past. As Herbert Morris (1976, p. 108) has argued, morality itself—including the morality of good character—has to take the past seriously. The alternative, of not crying over spilt milk (or blood), is truly indecent. A moral being *feels* guilty when he or she *is* guilty of past wrongs.

The virtue of feeling guilty is not raised so that punishment can be justified by its capacity to induce guilt. That is a possible retributive theory of punishment—a kind of moral rehabilitative theory—but it is not mine (see Morris, 1981). Rather, the virtue of our own imagined guilt is relevant because of the general connection between the virtue of an emotion and its epistemic import. We should trust what our imagined guilt feelings tell us; for acts like those of Richard Herrin, that if we did them we would be so guilty that some extraordinarily severe punishment would be deserved. We should trust the judgments such imagined guilt feelings spawn because nonneurotic guilt, unlike *ressentiment,* comes with good epistemic credentials.

Next, we need to be clear just what judgments it is that our guilt feelings validate in this way. First and foremost, to *feel* guilty causes the judgment that we *are* guilty, in the sense that we are morally culpable. Second, such guilt feelings typically engender the judgment that we deserve punishment. I mean this not only in the weak sense of desert—that it would not be unfair to be punished—but also and more important in the strong sense that we *ought* to be punished.

One might think that this second judgment of desert (in either its weak or its strong sense) is uncalled for by our feelings of guilt, that the judgment to which our guilt feelings lead is the judgment that we ought to repair as best we can the damage we have done. Such a view would justify corrective justice theories of punishment, but not retributive theories. Yet I think that this puts too nice a face on our guilt feelings. They do not generate only a judgment that we ought to make amends in this compensatory way. Rather—and this is what troubles many critics of guilt as an emotion—to feel guilty is to judge that we must suffer. We can see this plainly if we imagine ourselves having made provisions for Bonnie's family, comforting them in any way possible, and then feeling that our debt for killing her has been paid. It is so clear that such corrective actions do *not* satisfy guilt that to feel that they do is not to have felt guilty to begin with.

Our feelings of guilt thus generate a judgment that we deserve the suffering that is punishment. If the feelings of guilt are virtuous to possess, we have reason to believe that this last judgment is correct, generated as it is by emotions whose epistemic import is not in question.

Last, we should ask whether there is any reason not to make the same judgment about Richard Herrin's actual deserts as we are willing to make about our own hypothetical deserts. If we experience any reluctance to transfer the guilt and desert *we* would possess, had we done what Richard Herrin did, to Herrin himself, we should examine that reluctance carefully. Doesn't it come from feeling more of a person than Richard? We are probably not persons who grew up in the barrio of East Los Angeles, or who found Yale an alien and disorienting culture. In any case, we certainly have never been subject to the exact same stresses and motivations as Richard Herrin. Therefore, it may be tempting to withhold from Richard the benefit each of us gives himself or herself: the benefit of being the subjective seat of a will that, although caused, is nonetheless capable of both choice and responsibility (Moore, 1985a).

Such discrimination is a temptation to be resisted, because it is no virtue. It is elitist and condescending toward others not to grant them the same responsibility and desert you grant to yourself. Admittedly, there are excuses the benefit of which others as well as yourself may avail themselves. Yet that is not the distinction invoked here. Herrin had no excuse the rest of us could not come up with in terms of various causes for our choices. To refuse to grant him the same responsibility and desert as you would grant yourself is thus an instance of what Sartre called bad faith, the treating of a free, subjective will as an object (see also Strawson, 1968). It is a refusal to admit that the rest of humanity shares with us that which makes us most distinctively human, our capacity to will and reason—and thus to be and do evil. Far from evincing fellow feeling and the allowing of others to participate in our moral life, it excludes them as less than persons.

Rather than succumbing to this elitism masquerading as egalitarianism, we should ask ourselves what Herrin deserves by asking what *we* would deserve had we done such an act. In answering this question we should listen to our guilt feelings, feelings whose epistemic import is not in question in the same way as are those of *ressentiment*. Such guilt feelings should tell us that to do an act like Herrin's is to forfeit forever any lighthearted idea of going on as before. One should feel so awful that the idea of again leading a life unchanged from before, with the same goals and hopes and happiness, should appear revoltingly incomprehensible.[2]

3. It is admittedly not an easy task to separate the emotions one feels, and then in addition, discriminate which of them is the cause of one's retributive judgments. We can no more choose which emotion it will be that causes our judgments or actions than we can choose the reason for which we act. We can choose whether to act or not and whether to judge one way or another, but we cannot make it be true that some particular reason or emotion caused our action or our judgment. We must look inward as best we can to detect, but not to will, which emotions bring about our judgments; and here there is plenty of room for error and self-deception.

When we move from our judgments about the justice of retribution in the abstract, however, to the justice of a social institution that exists to exact retribution, perhaps we can gain some greater clarity. For if we recognize the dangers retributive punishment presents for the expression of resentment, sadism, and so on, we have every reason to design our punishment institutions to minimize the opportunity for such feelings to be expressed. There is no contradiction in attempting to make a retributive punishment system humane; doing so allows penitentiaries to be faithful to their names—places for penance, not excuses for sadism, prejudice, hatred, and the like.

Even the old biblical injunction—"Vengeance is mine, saith the Lord"—has something of this insight behind it. Retributive punishment is dangerous for individual persons to carry out, dangerous to their virtue and, because of that, unclear in its justification. But implicit in the biblical injunction is a promise that retribution will be exacted. For those like myself who are not theists, that cleansing function must be performed by the state, not God. If the state can perform such a function, it removes from retributive punishment, not the guilt, as Nietzsche (*Genealogy,* p. 95) and Sartre (1955) have it, but the ressentiment.

---

1. *"Moral culpability" as I am here using the phrase does not presuppose that the act done is morally bad, only that it is legally prohibited. An actor is culpable in this conception when, in doing an action violating some criminal prohibition, he or she satisfies those conditions of fair fault ascription. On this, see Moore (1985b), pp. 14–15. Usually, of course, most serious crimes are also serious moral breaches.*
2. *One may have noticed that the thought experiment just concluded has six steps to it. It is perhaps helpful to separate them explicitly: (1) The psychological presupposition that it is possible to engage in the thought experiment at all—that we can imagine we could do an act like Richard Herrin's. (2) The psychological question of what we would feel if we did such an action—guilty and deserving of punishment. (3) The moral question of the virtue of that feeling—that guilt is a virtuous emotion to feel when we have done such a wrongful act. (4) The psychological question of what judgments are typically caused by the emotions of guilt—the judg-* ments that we are guilty (culpable) and that we deserve to be punished. (5) The moral question of the correctness of the first person judgment that we deserve to be punished—as an inference drawn from the virtue of the emotion of guilt that spawns such a judgment. (6) The moral question of the correctness of the third person judgment that Richard Herrin deserves to be punished—as an inference drawn from the fact that we would deserve to be punished if we had done the act that Herrin did. One might believe that the thought experiment requires a seventh step—namely, that the state ought to punish those who deserve it. And in terms of a complete justification of a retributive theory of punishment, this last step is a necessary one. My aim throughout this paper has been more limited: to validate particular judgments, such as that Stephen Judy deserved the death penalty. The thought experiment is designed to get us only this far, leaving for further argument (hinted at in the text that closes this section) that the state has the right and the duty to set up institutions which give persons their just deserts.

References

Beccaria, *On Crimes and Punishments* (J. Grigson, trans.), in A. Manzoni (ed.), *The Column of Infamy* (Oxford: Oxford University Press, 1964).

L. Becker, *Property Rights* (London: Routledge and Kegan Paul, 1977).

H. Bedau, "Retribution and the Theory of Punishment," *Journal of Philosophy,* Vol. 75 (1978): 601–20.

S. I. Benn and R. S. Peters, *Social Principles and the Democratic State* (London: Allen and Unwin, 1959).

L. Blum, "Compassion," in A. Rorty (ed.), *Explaining Emotions* (Berkeley and Los Angeles: University of California Press, 1980).

C. Calhoun, "Cognitive Emotions?" in C. Calhoun and R. Soloman (eds.), *What Is an Emotion?* (Oxford: Oxford University Press, 1984).

D. Copp, "Considered Judgments and Moral Justification: Conservatism in Moral Theory," in D. Copp and D. Zimmerman (eds.), *Morality, Reason and Truth* (Totowa, NJ: Rowman and Allenheld, 1984).

A. Danto, *Nietzsche as Philosopher* (New York: Macmillan, 1965).

M. Dent, *The Moral Psychology of the Virtues* (Cambridge: Cambridge University Press, 1984).

P. Devlin, "Morals and the Criminal Law," in R. Wasserstrom (ed.), *Morality and the Law* (Belmont, CA: Wadsworth, 1971).

J. Feinberg, "The Expressive Function of Punishment," in his *Doing and Deserving* (Princeton, NJ: Princeton University Press, 1971).

H. Fingarette, "Punishment and Suffering," *Proc. Amer. Phil. Assoc.,* Vol. 50 (1977): 499–525.

"Psychoanalytic Perspectives on Moral Guilt and Responsibility: A Re-evaluation," *Philos. and Phenomenological Research,* Vol. 16 (1955): 18–36.

P. Foot, "Nietzsche: The Revaluation of Values," in R. Solomon (ed.), *Nietzsche: A Collection of Critical Essays* (Garden City, NY: Doubleday Anchor Books, 1973).

E. M. Forster, *Howard's End* (New York: Knopf, 1921).

"My Woods," in his *Abinger Harvest* (New York: Harcourt, Brace and World, 1936).

W. Gaylin, The Killing of Bonnie Garland (New York: Penguin Books, 1983).

H. L. A. Hart, *Punishment and Responsibility* (Oxford: Oxford University Press, 1968).

C. E. Hicks (ed.), *Famous American Jury Speeches* (St. Paul, MN: West Publishing, 1925).

T. Honderich, *Punishment: The Supposed Justifications* (London: Hutchinson, 1969).

K. Horney, "The Value of Vindictiveness," *Amer. Journal of Psychoanalysis,* Vol. 8 (1948): 3–12.

S. Jacoby, *Wild Justice: The Evolution of Revenge* (New York: Harper and Row, 1984).

I. Kant, *Groundwork of the Metaphysics of Morals* (Paton trans.) (New York: Harper, 1964).

The Metaphysical Elements of Justice (J. Ladd trans.) (Indianapolis: Bobbs-Merrill, 1965).

W. Kaufmann, *Without Guilt and Justice* (New York: Dell, 1973).

W. Lyons, *Emotion* (Cambridge: Cambridge University Press, 1980).

H. J. McCloskey, "A Non-Utilitarian Approach to Punishment," *Inquiry,* Vol. 8 (1965): 249–63.

J. Mackie, "Morality and the Retributive Emotions," *Criminal Justice Ethics,* Vol. 1 (1982): 3–10.

T. Marshall, concurring in *Gregg* v. *Georgia,* 428 U.S. 153 (1976).

K. Menninger, *The Crime of Punishment* (New York: Viking Press, 1968).

M. Moore, "Responsibility and the Unconscious," *Southern California Law Review,* Vol. 53 (1980): 1563–675.

"Moral Reality," *Wisconsin Law Review,* Vol. [1982]: 1061–1156 (1982a).

"Closet Retributivism," *USC Cites,* Vol. [Spring–Summer 1982]: 9–16 (1982b).

Law and Psychiatry: Rethinking the Relationship (Cambridge: Cambridge University Press, 1984).

"Causation and the Excuses," *California Law Review,* Vol. 73 (1985a): 201–59.

"The Moral and Metaphysical Sources of the Criminal Law," in J. R. Pennock and J. Chapman (eds.), *Nomos XXVII: Criminal Justice* (New York: New York University Press, 1985b).

"Mind, Brain, and Unconscious," in C. Wright and P. Clark (eds.), *Mind, Psychoanalysis, and Science* (Oxford: Blackwell, 1987).

H. Morris, *On Guilt and Innocence* (Berkeley and Los Angeles: University of California Press, 1976).

"Nonmoral Guilt," this volume," Chapter 9.

"A Paternalistic Theory of Punishment," *Amer. Phil. Quarterly,* Vol. 18 (1981): 263–71.

S. Morse, "Justice, Mercy, and Craziness," *Stanford Law Review,* Vol. 36 (1984): 1485–1515.

F. Nietzsche, *Beyond Good and Evil* (Kaufmann, trans.) (New York: Vintage, 1966).

Thus Spoke Zarathustra, in W. Kaufmann (ed.), *The Portable Nietzsche* (New York: Viking, 1954).

The Dawn, in W. Kaufmann (ed.), *The Portable Nietzsche* (New York: Viking, 1954).

The Gay Science (Kaufmann, trans.) (New York: Vintage, 1974).

On the Genealogy of Morals (Kaufmann, trans.) (New York: Vintage, 1969).

Twilight of the Idols, in W. Kaufmann (ed.), *The Portable Nietzsche* (New York: Viking, 1954).

A. Quinton, "On Punishment," *Analysis,* Vol. 14 (1954): 1933–42.

J. Rawls, *A Theory of Justice* (Cambridge, MA: Harvard University Press, 1971).

Mike Royko, "Nothing Gained by Killing a Killer? Oh Yes, There Is," *Los Angeles Times,* March 13, 1981, Sec. II, p. 7.

J.-P. Sartre, *The Flies,* in *No Exit and Three Other Plays* (New York: Vintage, 1955).

M. Scheler, *Ressentiment* (Holdheim trans.) (New York: Free Press, 1961).

R. Scruton, "Emotion, Practical Knowledge, and Common Culture," in A. Rorty (ed.), *Explaining Emotions* (Berkeley and Los Angeles: University of California Press, 1980).

J. Shklar, *Ordinary Vices* (Cambridge, MA: Harvard University Press, 1984).

R. de Sousa, "The Rationality of the Emotions," in A. Rorty (ed.), *Explaining Emotions* (Berkeley and Los Angeles: University of California Press, 1980).

Sir James Stephen, *Liberty, Equality, Fraternity* (Cambridge: Cambridge University Press, 1967).

P. F. Strawson, "Freedom and Resentment," in his *Studies in the Philosophy of Thought and Action* (Oxford: Oxford University Press, 1968).

H. Weihofen, *The Urge to Punish* (New York: Farrar, Straus and Cudahy, 1956).

B. Williams, "Morality and the Emotions," in his *Problems of Self* (Cambridge: Cambridge University Press, 1973).

J. Wilson and R. Herrnstein, *Crime and Human Nature* (New York: Simon and Schuster, 1985).

PUNISHMENT*

John Rawls

Two Concepts of Rules

In this paper I want to show the importance of the distinction between justifying a practice[1] and justifying a particular action falling under it, and I want to explain the logical basis of this distinction and how it is possible to miss its significance. While the distinction has frequently been made,[2] and is now becoming commonplace, there remains the task of explaining the tendency either to overlook it altogether, or to fail to appreciate its importance.

To show the importance of the distinction I am going to defend utilitarianism against those objections which have traditionally been made against it in connection with punishment and the obligation to keep promises. I hope to show that if one uses the distinction in question then one can state utilitarianism in a way which makes it a much better explication of our considered moral judgments than these traditional objections would seem to admit.[3] Thus the importance of the distinction is shown by the way it strengthens the utilitarian view regardless of whether that view is completely defensible or not.

To explain how the significance of the distinction may be overlooked, I am going to discuss two conceptions of rules. One of these conceptions conceals the importance of distinguishing between the justification of a rule or practice and the justification of a particular action falling under it. The other conception makes it clear why this distinction must be made and what is its logical basis.

The subject of punishment, in the sense of attaching legal penalties to the violation of legal rules, has always been a troubling moral question.[4] The trouble about it has not been that people disagree as to whether or not punishment is justifiable. Most peo-

*From "Two Concepts of Rules" by John Rawls, *The Philosophical Review*, Vol. 64 (1955), pp. 3–13. Reprinted by permission of the author and the publisher.

ple have held that, freed from certain abuses, it is an acceptable institution. Only a few have rejected punishment entirely, which is rather surprising when one considers all that can be said against it. The difficulty is with the justification of punishment: various arguments for it have been given by moral philosophers, but so far none of them has won any sort of general acceptance; no justification is without those who detest it. I hope to show that the use of the aforementioned distinction enables one to state the utilitarian view in a way which allows for the sound points of its critics.

For our purposes we may say that there are two justifications of punishment. What we may call the retributive view is that punishment is justified on the grounds that wrongdoing merits punishment. It is morally fitting that a person who does wrong should suffer in proportion to his wrongdoing. That a criminal should be punished follows from his guilt, and the severity of the appropriate punishment depends on the depravity of his act. The state of affairs where a wrongdoer suffers punishment is morally better than the state of affairs where he does not; and it is better irrespective of any of the consequences of punishing him.

What we may call the utilitarian view holds that on the principle that bygones are bygones and that only future consequences are material to present decisions, punishment is justifiable only by reference to the probable consequences of maintaining it as one of the devices of the social order. Wrongs committed in the past are, as such, not relevant considerations for deciding what to do. If punishment can be shown to promote effectively the interest of society it is justifiable, otherwise it is not.

I have stated these two competing views very roughly to make one feel the conflict between them: one feels the force of *both* arguments and one wonders how they can be reconciled. From my introductory remarks it is obvious that the resolution which I am going to propose is that in this case one must distinguish between justifying a practice as a system of rules to be applied and enforced, and justifying a particular action which falls under these rules; utilitarian arguments are appropriate with regard to questions about practices, while retributive arguments fit the application of particular rules to particular cases.

We might try to get clear about this distinction by imagining how a father might answer the question of his son. Suppose the son asks, "Why was *J* put in jail yesterday?" The father answers, "Because he robbed the bank at *B*. He was duly tried and found guilty. That's why he was put in jail yesterday." But suppose the son had asked a different question, namely, "Why do people put other people in jail?" Then the father might answer, "To protect good people from bad people" or "To stop people from doing things that would make it uneasy for all of us; for otherwise we wouldn't be able to go to bed at night and sleep in peace." There are two very different questions here. One question emphasizes the proper name: It asks why *J* was punished rather than someone else, or it asks what he was punished for. The other question asks why we have the institution of punishment: Why do people punish one another rather than, say, always forgiving one another?

Thus the father says in effect that a particular man is punished, rather than some other man, because he is guilty, and he is guilty because he broke the law (past tense). In his case the law looks back, the judge looks back, the jury looks back, and a penalty is visited upon him for something he did. That a man is to be punished, and what his punishment is to be, is settled by its being shown that he broke the law and that the law assigns that penalty for the violation of it.

On the other hand we have the institution of punishment itself, and recommend and accept various changes in it, because it is thought by the (ideal) legislator and by those to whom the law applies that, as a part of a system of law impartially applied from case to case arising under it, it will have the consequence, in the long run, of furthering the interests of society.

One can say, then, that the judge and the legislator stand in different positions and look in different directions: one to the past, the other to the future. The justification of what the judge does, *qua* judge, sounds like the retributive view; the justification of what the (ideal) legislator does, *qua* legislator, sounds like the utilitarian view. Thus both views have a point (this is as it should be since intelligent and sensitive persons have been on both sides of the argument); and one's initial confusion disappears once one sees that these views apply to persons holding different offices with different duties, and situated differently with respect to the system of rules that make up the criminal law.[5]

One might say, however, that the utilitarian view is more fundamental since it applies to a more fundamental office, for the judge carries out the legislator's will so far as he can determine it. Once the legislator decides to have laws and to assign penalties for their violation (as things are there must be both the law and the penalty) an institution is set up which involves a retributive conception of particular cases. It is part of the concept of the criminal law as a system of rules that the application and enforcement of these rules in particular cases should be justifiable by arguments of a retributive character. The decision whether or not to use law rather than some other mechanism of social control, and the decision as to what laws to have and what penalties to assign, may be settled by utilitarian arguments; but if one decides to have laws then one has decided on something whose working in particular cases is retributive in form.[6]

The answer, then, to the confusion engendered by the two views of punishment is quite simple: One distinguishes two offices, that of the judge and that of the legislator, and one distinguishes their different stations with respect to the system of rules which make up the law; and then one notes that the different sorts of considerations which would usually be offered as reasons for what is done under the cover of these offices can be paired off with the competing justifications of punishment. One reconciles the two views by the time-honored device of making them apply to different situations.

But can it really be this simple? Well, this answer allows for the apparent intent of each side. Does a person who advocates the retributive view necessarily advocate, as an *institution,* legal machinery whose essential purpose is to set up and preserve a correspondence between moral turpitude and suffering? Surely not.[7] What retributionists have rightly insisted upon is that no man can be punished unless he is guilty, that is, unless he has broken the law. Their fundamental criticism of the utilitarian account is that, as they interpret it, it sanctions an innocent person's being punished (if one may call it that) for the benefit of society.

On the other hand, utilitarians agree that punishment is to be inflicted only for the violation of law. They regard this much as understood from the concept of punishment itself.[8] The point of the utilitarian account concerns the institution as a system of rules: utilitarianism seeks to limit its use by declaring it justifiable only if it can be shown to foster effectively the good of society. Historically it is a protest against the indiscriminate and ineffective use of the criminal law.[9] It seeks to dissuade us from assigning to penal institutions the improper, if not sacrilegious, task of matching suffering with moral turpitude. Like others, utilitarians want penal institutions designed so that, as far as humanly possible, only those who break the law run afoul of it. They hold that no official should have discretionary power to inflict penalties whenever he thinks it for the benefit of society; for on utilitarian

grounds an institution granting such power could not be justified.[10]

The suggested way of reconciling the retributive and the utilitarian justifications of punishment seems to account for what both sides have wanted to say. There are, however, two further questions which arise, and I shall devote the remainder of this section to them.

First, will not a difference of opinion as to the proper criterion of just law make the proposed reconciliation unacceptable to retributionists? Will they not question whether, if the utilitarian principle is used as the criterion, it follows that those who have broken the law are guilty in a way which satisfies their demand that those punished deserve to be punished? To answer this difficulty, suppose that the rules of the criminal law are justified on utilitarian grounds (it is only for laws that meet his criterion that the utilitarian can be held responsible). Then it follows that the actions which the criminal law specifies as offenses are such that, if they were tolerated, terror and alarm would spread in society. Consequently, retributionists can only deny that those who are punished deserve to be punished if they deny that such actions are wrong. This they will not want to do.

The second question is whether utilitarianism doesn't justify too much. One pictures it as an engine of justification which, if consistently adopted, could be used to justify cruel and arbitrary institutions. Retributionists may be supposed to concede that utilitarians *intend* to reform the law and to make it more humane; that utilitarians do not *wish* to justify any such thing as punishment of the innocent; and that utilitarians may appeal to the fact that punishment presupposes guilt in the sense that by punishment one understands an institution attaching penalties to the infraction of legal rules, and therefore that it is logically absurd to suppose that utilitarians in justifying *punishment* might also have justified punishment (if we may call it that) of the innocent. The real question, however, is whether the utilitarian, in justifying punishment, hasn't used arguments which commit him to accepting the infliction of suffering on innocent persons if it is for the good of society (whether or not one calls this punishment). More generally, isn't the utilitarian committed in principle to accepting many practices which he, as a morally sensitive person, wouldn't want to accept? Retributionists are inclined to hold that there is no way to stop the utilitarian principle from justifying too much except by adding to it a principle which distributes certain rights to individuals. Then the amended criterion is not the greatest benefit of society *simpliciter* [simply], but the greatest benefit of society subject to the constraint that no one's rights may be violated. Now while I think that the classical utilitarians proposed a criterion of this more complicated sort, I do not want to argue that point here.[11] What I want to show is that there is *another* way of preventing the utilitarian principle from justifying too much, or at least of making it much less likely to do so: namely, by stating utilitarianism in a way which accounts for the distinction between the justification of an institution and the justification of a particular action falling under it.

I begin by defining the institution of punishment as follows: a person is said to suffer punishment whenever he is legally deprived of some of the normal rights of a citizen on the ground that he has violated a rule of law, the violation having been established by trial according to the due process of law, provided that the deprivation is carried out by the recognized legal authorities of the state, that the rule of law clearly specifies both the offense and the attached penalty, that the courts construe statutes strictly, and that the statute was on the books prior to the time of the offense.[12] This definition specifies what I shall understand by punishment. The question is whether utilitarian arguments may be found to justify institutions widely different from this and such as one would find cruel and arbitrary.

This question is best answered, I think, by taking up a particular accusation. Consider the following from Carritt:

> . . . the utilitarian must hold that we are justified in inflicting pain always and only to prevent worse pain or bring about greater happiness. This, then, is all we need to consider in so-called punishment, which must be purely preventive. But if some kind of very cruel crime becomes common, and none of the criminals can be caught, it might be highly expedient, as an example, to hang an innocent man, if a charge against him could be so framed that he were universally thought guilty; indeed this would only fail to be an ideal instance of utilitarian "punishment" because the victim himself would not have been so likely as a real felon to commit such a crime in the future; in all other respects it would be perfectly deterrent and therefore felicific.[13]

Carritt is trying to show that there are occasions when a utilitarian argument would justify taking an action which would be generally condemned; and thus that utilitarianism justifies too much. But the failure of Carritt's argument lies in the fact that he makes no distinction between the justification of the general system of rules which constitutes penal institutions and the justification of particular applications of these rules to particular cases by the various officials whose job it is to administer them. This becomes perfectly clear when one asks who the "we" are of whom Carritt speaks. Who is this who has a sort of absolute authority on particular occasions to decide that an innocent man shall be "punished" if everyone can be convinced that he is guilty? Is this person the legislator, or the judge, or the body of private citizens, or what? It is utterly crucial to know who is to decide such matters, and by what authority, for all of this must be written into the rules of the institution. Until one knows these things one doesn't know what the institution is whose justification is being challenged; and as the utilitarian principle applies to the institution one doesn't know whether it is justifiable on utilitarian grounds or not.

Once this is understood it is clear what the countermove to Carritt's argument is. One must describe more carefully what the *institution* is which his example suggests, and then ask oneself whether or not it is likely that having this institution would be for the benefit of society in the long run. One must not content oneself with the vague thought that, when it's a question of *this* case, it would be a good thing if *somebody* did something even if an innocent person were to suffer.

Try to imagine, then, an institution (which we may call "telishment") which is such that the officials set up by it have authority to arrange a trial for the condemnation of an innocent man whenever they are of the opinion that doing so would be in the best interests of society. The discretion of officials is limited, however, by the rule that they may not condemn an innocent man to undergo such an ordeal unless there is, at the time, a wave of offenses similar to that with which they charge him and telish him for. We may imagine that the officials having the discretionary authority are the judges of the higher courts in consultation with the chief of police, the minister of justice, and a committee of the legislature.

Once one realizes that one is involved in setting up an *institution,* one sees that the hazards are very great. For example, what check is there on the officials? How is one to tell whether or not their actions are authorized? How is one to limit the risks involved in allowing such systematic deception? How is one to avoid giving anything short of complete discretion to the authorities to telish anyone they like? In addition to these considerations, it is obvious that people will come to have a very different attitude towards their penal system when telishment is adjoined to it. They will be uncertain as to whether a convicted man has been punished or telished. They will wonder whether or not they should feel sorry for him. They will wonder whether the same fate won't at any time fall on them. If one pictures how such an institution would actually work, and the enormous risks involved in it, it seems clear that it would serve no useful purpose. A utilitarian justification for this institution is most unlikely.

It happens in general that as one drops off the defining features of punishment one ends up with an institution whose utilitarian justification is highly doubtful. One reason for this is that punishment works like a kind of price system: By altering the prices one has to pay for the performance of actions, it supplies a motive for avoiding some actions and doing others. The defining features are essential if punishment is to work in this way; so that an institution which lacks these features, for example, an institution which is set up to "punish" the innocent, is likely to have about as much point as a price system (if one may call it that) where the prices of things change at random from day to day and one learns the price of something after one has agreed to buy it.[14]

If one is careful to apply the utilitarian principle to the institution which is to authorize particular actions, then there is *less* danger of its justifying too much. Carritt's example gains plausibility by its indefiniteness and by its concentration on the particular case. His argument will only hold if it can be shown that there are utilitarian arguments which justify an institution whose publicly ascertainable offices and powers are such as to permit officials to exercise that kind of discretion in particular cases. But the requirement of having to build the arbitrary features of the particular decision into the institutional practice makes the justification much less likely to go through.

---

1. I use the word "practice" throughout as a sort of technical term meaning any form of activity specified by a system of rules which defines offices, roles, moves, penalties, defenses, and so on, and which gives the activity its structure. As examples one may think of games and rituals, trials and parliaments.

2. The distinction is central to Hume's discussion of justice in A Treatise of Human Nature, bk. III, pt. ii, esp. secs. 2–4. It is clearly stated by John Austin in the second lecture of Lectures on Jurisprudence (4th ed.; London, 1873), I, 116ff. (1st ed., 1832). Also it may be argued that J. S. Mill took it for granted in Utilitarianism; on this point cf. J. O. Urmson, "The Interpretation of the Moral Philosophy of J. S. Mill," Philosophical Quarterly, vol. III (1953). In addition to the arguments given by Urmson there are several clear statements of the distinction in A System of Logic (8th ed.; London, 1872), bk. VI, ch. xii pars. 2, 3, 7. The distinction is fundamental to J. D. Mabbott's important paper, "Punishment," Mind, n.s., vol. XLVIII (April, 1939). More recently the distinction has been stated with particular emphasis by S. E. Toulmin in The Place of Reason in Ethics (Cambridge, 1950), see esp. ch. xi, where it plays a major part in his account of moral reasoning. Toulmin doesn't explain the basis of the distinction, nor how one might overlook its importance, as I try to in this paper, and in my review of this book (Philosophical Review, vol. LX [October, 1951]), as some of my criticisms show, I failed to understand the force of it. See also H. D. Aiken, "The Levels of Moral Discourse," Ethics, vol. LXII (1952), A. M. Quinton, "Punishment," Analysis, vol. XIV (June, 1954), and P. H. Nowell-Smith, Ethics (London, 1954), pp. 236–239, 271–273.

3. On the concept of explication see the author's paper Philosophical Review, vol. LX (April, 1951).

4. While this paper was being revised, Quinton's appeared; footnote 2 supra. There are several respects in which my remarks are similar to his. Yet as I consider some further questions and rely on somewhat different arguments, I have retained the discussion of punishment and promises together as two test cases for utilitarianism.

5. Note the fact that different sorts of arguments are suited to different offices. One way of taking the differences between ethical theories is to regard them as accounts of the reasons expected in different offices.

6. In this connection see Mabbott, op. cit., pp. 163–164.

7. On this point see Sir David Ross, The Right and the Good (Oxford, 1930), pp. 57–60.

8. See Hobbe's definition of punishment in Leviathan, ch. xxviii; and Bentham's definition in The Principle of Morals and Legislation, ch. xii, par. 36, ch. xv, par. 28, and in The Rationale of Punishment, (London, 1830), bk. I, ch. i. They could agree with Bradley that: "Punishment is punishment only when it is deserved. We pay the penalty, because we owe it, and for no other reason; and if punishment is inflicted for any other reason whatever than because it is merited by wrong, it is a gross immorality, a crying injustice, an abominable crime, and not what it pretends to be." Ethical Studies (2nd ed.; Oxford, 1927), pp. 26–27. Certainly by definition it isn't what it pretends to be. The innocent can only be punished by mistake; deliberate "punishment" of the innocent necessarily involves fraud.

9. Cf. Leon Radzinowicz, A History of English Criminal Law: The Movement for Reform 1750–1833 (London, 1948), esp. ch. xi on Bentham.

10. Bentham discusses how corresponding to a punitory provision of a criminal law there is another provision which stands to it as an antagonist and which needs a name as much as the punitory. He calls it, as one might expect, the anaetiosostic, and of it he says: "The punishment of guilt is the object of the former one: the preservation of innocence that of the latter." . . .

11. By the classical utilitarians I understand Hobbes, Hume, Bentham, J. S. Mill, and Sidgwick.

12. All these features of punishment are mentioned by Hobbes; cf. Leviathan, ch. xxviii.

13. Ethical and Political Thinking (Oxford, 1947), p. 65.

14. The analogy with the price system suggests an answer to the question how utilitarian considerations insure that punishment is proportional to the offense. It is interesting to note that Sir David Ross, after making the distinction bewteen justifying a penal law and justifying a particular application of it, and after stating that utilitarian considerations have a large place in determining the former, still holds back from accepting the utilitarian justification of punishment on the grounds that justice requires that punishment be proportional to the offense, and that utilitarianism is unable to

account for this. Cf. The Right and the Good, pp. 61–62. I do not claim that utilitarianism can account for this requirement as Sir David might wish, but it happens, nevertheless, that if utilitarian considerations are followed penalties will be proportional to offenses in this sense: the order of offenses according to seriousness can be paired off with the order of penalties according to severity. Also the absolute level of penalties will be as low as possible. This fol-lows from the assumption that people are rational (i.e., that they are able to take into account the "prices" the state puts on actions), the utilitarian rule that a penal system should provide a motive for preferring the less serious offense, and the principle that punishment as such is an evil. All this was carefully worked out by Bentham in The Principles of Morals and Legislation, chs. xiii–xv.

Victims' Rights:
Restitution or Vengeance?

RESTITUTION:
A New Paradigm of Criminal Justice*

Randy E. Barnett

This paper will analyze the breakdown of our system of criminal justice in terms of what Thomas Kuhn would describe as a crisis of an old paradigm—punishment. I propose that this crisis could be solved by the adoption of a new paradigm of criminal justice—restitution. The approach will be mainly theoretical, though at various points in the discussion the practical implications of the rival paradigms will also be considered. A fundamental contention will be that many, if not most, of our system's ills stem from errors in the underlying paradigm. Any attempt to correct these symptomatic debilities without a reexamination of the theoretical underpinnings is doomed to frustration and failure. Kuhn's theories deal with the problems of science. What made his proposal so startling was its attempt to analogize scientific development to social and political development. Here, I will simply reverse the process by applying Kuhn's framework of scientific change to social, or in this case, legal development.[1]

In the criminal justice system we are witnessing the death throes of an old and cumbersome paradigm, one that has dominated Western thought for more than 900 years. While this paper presents what is hoped to be a viable, though radical alternative, much would be accomplished by simply prompting the reader to reexamine the assumptions underlying the present system. Only if we are willing to look at our old problems in a new light do we stand a chance of solving them. This is our only hope, and our greatest challenge.

The Crisis in the Paradigm of Punishment

"Political revolutions are inaugurated by a growing sense, often restricted to a segment of the political

*Reprinted with permission from *Ethics,* vol. 87, no. 4, 1977. Copyright © 1977 by the University of Chicago. (Footnotes have been updated.) Randy E. Barnett is Professor of Law at the Boston University School of Law. For other writings by the author, on restitution, see *Assessing the Criminal: Restitution, Retribution and the Legal Process,* ed. Randy E. Barnett and John Hagel (Cambridge, MA: Ballinger Publishing Co. 1977); Randy E.

Barnett, "The Justice of Restitution," *American Journal of Jurisprudence* 25 (1980): 117–32; Randy E. Barnett, "Pursuing Justice in a Free Society: Part One—*Power* v. *Liberty,* 4 (Summer/Fall 1985): 50–72; Randy E. Barnett, "Pursuing Justice in a Free Society: Part Two—Crime Prevention and the Legal Order," 5 (Winter/Spring 1986): 28–53.

community, that existing institutions have ceased adequately to meet the problems posed by an environment they have in part created. . . . In both political and scientific development the sense of malfunction that can lead to crisis is prerequisite to revolution."[2] Kuhn's description of the preconditions for scientific and political revolutions could accurately describe the current state of the criminal law. However, simply to recognize the existence of a crisis is not enough. We must look for its causes. The Kuhnian methodology suggests that we critically examine the paradigm of punishment itself.

The problems which the paradigm of punishment is supposed to solve are many and varied. A whole literature on the philosophy of punishment has arisen in an effort to justify or reject the institution of punishment. For our purposes the following definition from the *Encyclopedia of Philosophy* should suffice: "Characteristically punishment is unpleasant. It is inflicted on an offender because of an offense he has committed; it is deliberately imposed, not just the natural consequence of a person's action (like a hangover), and the unpleasantness is *essential* to it, not an accompaniment to some other treatment (like the pain of the dentist's drill)."[3]

Two types of arguments are commonly made in defense of punishment. The first is that punishment is an appropriate means to some justifiable end such as, for example, deterrence of crime. The second type of argument is that punishment is justified as an end in itself. On this view, whatever ill effects it might engender, punishment for its own sake is good.

The first type of argument might be called the *political* justification of punishment, for the end which justifies its use is one which a political order is presumably dedicated to serve: the maintenance of peaceful interactions between individuals and groups in a society. There are at least three ways that deliberate infliction of harm on an offender is said to be politically justified.

1. One motive for punishment, especially capital punishment and imprisonment, is the "intention to deprive offenders of the power of doing future mischief."[4] Although it is true that an offender cannot continue to harm society while incarcerated, a strategy of punishment based on disablement has several drawbacks.

    Imprisonment is enormously expensive. This means that a double burden is placed on the innocent who must suffer the crime and, in addition, pay through taxation for the support of the

offender and his family if they are forced onto welfare. Also, any benefit of imprisonment is temporary; eventually, most offenders will be released. If their outlook has not improved—and especially if it has worsened—the benefits of incarceration are obviously limited. Finally, when disablement is permanent, as with capital punishment or psychosurgery, it is this very permanence, in light of the possibility of error, which is frightening. For these reasons, "where disablement enters as an element into penal theories, it occupies, as a rule, a subordinate place and is looked upon as an object subsidiary to some other end which is regarded as paramount."[5]

2. Rehabilitation of a criminal means a change in his mental *habitus* so that he will not offend again. It is unclear whether the so-called treatment model which views criminals as a doctor would view a patient is truly a "retributive" concept. Certainly it does not conform to the above definition characterizing punishment as deliberately and essentially unpleasant. It is an open question whether any end justifies the intentional, forceful manipulation of an individual's thought processes by anyone, much less the state. To say that an otherwise just system has incidentally rehabilitative effects which may be desirable is one thing, but it is quite another to argue that these effects themselves justify the system. The horrors to which such reasoning can lead are obvious from abundant examples in history and contemporary society.[6]

    Rehabilitation as a reaction against the punishment paradigm will be considered below, but one aspect is particularly relevant to punishment as defined here. On this view, the visiting of unpleasantness itself will cause the offender to see the error of his ways; by having "justice" done him, the criminal will come to appreciate his error and will change his moral outlook. This end, best labeled "reformation," is speculative at best and counterfactual at worst. On the contrary, "it has been observed that, as a rule . . . ruthless punishments, far from mollifying men's ways, corrupt them and stir them to violence."[7]

3. The final justification to be treated here—deterrence—actually has two aspects. The first is the deterrent effect that past demonstrations of punishment have on the future conduct of others; the second is the effect that threats of future punishment have on the conduct of others. The distinction assumes importance when some advocates argue that future threats lose their deterrent effect when

there is a lack of past demonstrations. Past punishment, then, serves as an educational tool. It is a substitute for or reinforcement of threats of future punishment.

As with the goals mentioned above, the empirical question of whether punishment has this effect is a disputed one.[8] I shall not attempt to resolve this question here, but will assume *arguendo* that punishment even as presently administered has some deterrent effect. It is the moral question which is disturbing. Can an argument from deterrence alone "justify" in any sense the infliction of pain on a criminal? It is particularly disquieting that the actual levying of punishment is done not for the criminal himself, but for the educational impact it will have on the community. The criminal act becomes the occasion of, but not the reason for, the punishment. In this way, the actual crime becomes little more than an excuse for punishing.

Surely this distorts the proper functioning of the judicial process. For if deterrence is the end it is unimportant whether the individual actually committed the crime. Since the public's perception of guilt is the prerequisite of the deterrent effect, all that is required for deterrence is that the individual is "proved" to have committed the crime. The actual occurrence would have no relevance except insofar as a truly guilty person is easier to prove guilty. The judicial process becomes, not a truth-seeking device, but solely a means to legitimate the use of force. To treat criminals as means to the ends of others in this way raises serious moral problems. This is not to argue that men may never use others as means but rather to question the use of force against the individual because of the effect such use will have on others. It was this that concerned del Vecchio when he stated that "the human person always bears in himself something sacred, and it is therefore not permissible to treat him merely as a means towards an end outside of himself."[9]

Finally, deterrence as the ultimate justification of punishment cannot rationally limit its use. It "provides *no* guidance until we're told *how much* commission of it is to be deterred."[10] Since there are always some who commit crimes, one can always argue for more punishment. Robert Nozick points out that there must be criteria by which one decides how much deterrence may be inflicted.[11] One is forced therefore to employ "higher" principles to evaluate the legitimacy of punishment.

It is not my thesis that deterrence, reformation, and disablement are undesirable goals. On the contrary, any criminal justice system should be critically examined to see if it is having these and other beneficial effects. The view advanced here is simply that these utilitarian benefits must be incidental to a just system; they cannot, alone or in combination, justify a criminal justice system. Something more is needed. There is another more antiquated strain of punishment theory which seeks to address this problem. The *moral* justifications of punishment view punishment as an end in itself. This approach has taken many forms.[12] On this view, whatever ill or beneficial results it might have, punishment of lawbreakers is good for its own sake. This proposition can be analyzed on several levels.

The most basic question is the truth of the claim itself. Some have argued that "the alleged absolute justice of repaying evil with evil (maintained by Kant and many other writers) is really an empty sophism. If we go back to the Christian moralists, we find that an evil is to be put right only by doing good."[13] This question is beyond the scope of this treatment. The subject has been extensively dealt with by those more knowledgeable than I.[14] The more relevant question is what such a view of punishment as a good can be said to imply for a system of criminal justice. Even assuming that it would be good if, in the nature of things, the wicked got their "come-uppance," what behavior does this moral fact justify? Does it justify the victim authoring the punishment of his offender? Does it justify the same action by the victim's family, his friends, his neighbors, the state? If so what punishment should be imposed and who should decide?

It might be argued that the natural punishment for the violation of natural rights is the deserved hatred and scorn of the community, the resultant ostracism, and the existential hell of *being* an evil person. The question then is not whether we have the right to inflict some "harm" or unpleasantness on a morally contemptible person—surely, we do; the question is not whether such a punishment is "good"—arguably, it is. The issue is whether the "virtue of some punishment" justifies the *forceful* imposition of unpleasantness on a *rights violator* as distinguished from the morally imperfect. Any *moral* theory of punishment must recognize and deal with this distinction. Finally, it must be established that the state is the legitimate author of punishment, a proposition which further assumes the moral and legal legitimacy of the state. To raise these issues is not to resolve them, but it would seem that the burden of proof is on those seeking to justify the use of force against the individual.

Suffice it to say that I am skeptical of finding any theory which justifies the deliberate, forceful imposition of punishment within or without a system of criminal justice.

The final consideration in dealing with punishment as an end in itself is the possibility that the current crisis in the criminal justice system is in fact a crisis of the paradigm of punishment. While this, if true, does not resolve the philosophical issues, it does cast doubt on the punishment paradigm's vitality as the motive force behind a system of criminal justice. Many advocates of punishment argue that its apparent practical failings exist because we are not punishing enough. All that is needed, they say, is a crackdown on criminals and those victims and witnesses who shun participation in the criminal justice system; the only problem with the paradigm of punishment is that we are not following it.[15] This response fails to consider *why* the system doggedly refuses to punish to the degree required to yield beneficial results and instead punishes in such a way as to yield harmful results. The answer may be that the paradigm of punishment is in eclipse, that the public lacks the requisite will to apply it in anything but the prevailing way.

Punishment, particularly state punishment is the descendant of the tradition which imparts relious and moral authority to the sovereign and, through him, the community. Such an authority is increasingly less credible in a secular world such as ours. Today there is an increasing desire to allow each individual to govern his own life as he sees fit provided he does not violate the rights of others. This desire is exemplified by current attitudes toward drug use, abortion, and pornography. Few argue that these things are good. It is only said that where there is no victim the state or community has no business meddling in the peaceful behavior of its citizens, however morally suspect it may be.[16]

Furthermore, if the paradigm of punishment is in a "crisis period" it is as much because of its practical drawbacks as the uncertainty of its moral status. The infliction of suffering on a criminal tends to cause a general feeling of sympathy for him. There is no rational connection between a term of imprisonment and the harm caused the victim. Since the prison term is supposed to be unpleasant, at least a part of the public comes to see the criminal as a victim, and the lack of rationality also causes the offender to feel victimized. This reaction is magnified by the knowledge that most crimes go unpunished and that even if the offender is caught the judicial process is long, arduous, and far removed from the criminal act. While this is obvious to most, it is perhaps less obvious that the punishment paradigm is largely at fault. The slow, ponderous nature of our system of justice is largely due to a fear of an unjust infliction of punishment on the innocent (or even the guilty). The more awful the sanction, the more elaborate need be the safeguards. The more the system is perceived as arbitrary and unfair, the more incentive there is for defendants and their counsel to thwart the truth-finding process. Acquittal becomes desirable at all costs. As the punitive aspect of a sanction is diminished, so too would be the perceived need for the procedural protections.

A system of punishment, furthermore, offers no incentive for the victim to involve himself in the criminal justice process other than to satisfy his feelings of duty or revenge. The victim stands to gain little if at all by the conviction and punishment of the person who caused his loss. This is true even of those systems discussed below which dispense state compensation based on the victim's need. The system of justice itself imposes uncompensated costs by requiring a further loss of time and money by the victim and witnesses and by increasing the perceived risk of retaliation.

Finally, punishment which seeks to change an offender's moral outlook, or at least to scare him, can do nothing to provide him with the skills needed to survive in the outside world. In prison, he learns the advanced state of the criminal arts and vows not to repeat the mistake that led to his capture. The convict emerges better trained and highly motivated to continue a criminal career.

The crisis of the paradigm of punishment has at its roots the collapse of its twin pillars of support: its moral legitimacy and its practical efficacy. As Kaufmann concludes, "the faith in retributive justice is all but dead."[17]

Attempts to Salvage the Paradigm of Punishment

"All crises begin with the blurring of a paradigm and the consequent loosening of the rules for normal research."[18] And yet until a new paradigm is presented, authorities will cling to the old one, either ignoring the problem or salvaging the paradigm with ad hoc explanations and solutions. Why are paradigms never rejected outright? Why must there always be a new paradigm before the old one is abandoned?

Kuhn does not explicitly discuss this, but R.A. Childs hypothesizes "that, as such, paradigms may serve the function of increasing man's sense of control over some aspect of reality, or some aspect of his own life. If this is so, then we would expect that a straightforward abandonment of a paradigm would threaten that sense of control."[19]

This psychological need for an explanation may in turn explain the many efforts to shore up the paradigm of punishment. The three attempts to be examined next have at their roots a perception of its fundamental errors, and at the same time they highlight three goals of any new paradigm of criminal justice.

1. Proportionate punishment. The king abandoned the composition system[20] for the system of punishment because punishment struck terror in the hearts of the people, and this served to inspire awe for the power of the king and state. But there was no rational connection between the seriousness of the crime and the gravity of the punishment and, therefore, no limit to the severity of punishment. Hideous tortures came to be employed: "But some of the men of the Enlightenment sought to counter the inhumanity of their Christian predecessors with appeals to reason. They thought that retributive justice had a mathematical quality and that murder called for capital punishment in much the same way in which two plus two equals four."[21]

   The appeal to proportionality was one of the early attempts to come to grips with deficiencies in the paradigm of punishment. It was doomed to failure, for there is no objective standard by which punishments can be proportioned to fit the crime. Punishment is incommensurate with crime. This solution is purely ad hoc and intuitive. We shall, however, find the *goal* of proportionate sentencing useful in the formation of a new paradigm.

2. Rehabilitation. It was noted earlier that the infliction of punishment tends to focus attention on the plight of the criminal. Possibly for this reason, the next humanitarian trend was to explore the proper treatment of criminals. Punishment failed to reform the criminal, and this led observers to inquire how the situation might be improved. Some felt that the sole end of the penal system was rehabilitation, so attention was turned to modifying the criminal's behavior (an obviously manipulative end). Emphasis was placed on education, job training, and discipline.

Unfortunately, the paradigm of punishment and the political realities of penal administration have all but won out. There is simply no incentive for prison authorities to educate and train. Their job is essentially political. They are judged by their ability to keep the prisoners within the walls and to keep incidents of violence within the prison to a minimum; as a result, discipline is the main concern. Furthermore, since he is sentenced to a fixed number of years (less time off for good behavior—so-called good time), there is no institutional incentive for the prisoner to improve himself apart from sheer boredom. Productive labor in prison is virtually nonexistent, with only obsolete equipment, if any, available. Except perhaps for license plates and other state needs, the prisoners produce nothing of value; the prisons make no profit and the workers are paid, if at all, far below market wages. They are unable to support themselves or their families. The state, meaning the innocent taxpayer, supports the prisoner, and frequently the families as well via welfare.

Rehabilitation has been a long-time goal of the penal system, but the political nature of government-run prisons and the dominance of the paradigm of punishment has inevitably prevented its achievement. Prisons remain detention centers, all too temporarily preventing crime by physically confining the criminals.

3. Victim compensation. It is natural that the brutalities resulting from the paradigm of punishment would get first attention from humanitarians and that the persons subjected to those practices would be next. Until recently, the victim of crime was the forgotten party. Within the last few years a whole new field has opened up called victimology.[22] With it has come a variety of proposals, justifications, and statutes.[23]

   Certain features are common to virtually every compensation proposal: (*a*) Compensation for crimes would be dispensed by the state from tax revenue. (*b*) Compensation is "a matter of grace" rather than an assumption by the state of legal responsibility for the criminal loss suffered by the victim. (*c*) Most proposals allow for aid only on a "need" or "hardship" basis. (*d*) Most are limited to some sort of crime of violence or the threat of force or violence. (*e*) None questions the paradigm of punishment.

   The goal of these proposals and statutes is laudable. The victim *is* the forgotten man of crime. But the means proposed is the same tired formula: welfare to those in "need." In short, the innocent taxpayer repays the innocent victim (if the victim can prove he "needs" help) while the guilty offender is subjected to the sanction of punishment with all its failings. Like proportionate punishment and rehabilitation, the goal of victim compensation is a recognition of very real problems in our criminal justice system, and at the same time it ignores the source of these problems: our conception of crime as an offense against the state whose proper sanction is punishment. Until a viable, new paradigm is presented, *ad hoc* solutions like the ones discussed here are all that can be hoped for. And it is a vain hope indeed, for they attack the symptoms while neglecting the causes of the problem. What is needed is a new paradigm.

Outline of a New Paradigm

The idea of restitution is actually quite simple. It views crime as an offense by one individual against the rights of another. The victim has suffered a loss. Justice consists of the culpable offender making good the loss he has caused. It calls for a complete refocusing of our image of crime. Kuhn would call it a "shift of world-view." Where we once saw an offense against society, we now see an offense against an individual victim. In a way, it is a common sense view of crime. *The armed robber did not rob society; he robbed the victim*. His debt, therefore, is not to society; it is to the victim. There are really two types of restitution proposals: a system of "punitive" restitution and a "pure" restitutional system.

1. Punitive restitution. "Since rehabilitation was admitted to the aims of penal law two centuries ago, the number of penological aims has remained virtually constant. Restitution is waiting to come in."[24] Given this view, restitution should merely be added to the paradigm of punishment. Stephen Schafer outlines the proposal: "[Punitive] restitution, like punishment, must always be the subject of judicial consideration. Without exception it must be carried out by personal performance by the wrong-doer, and should even then be equally burdensome and just for all criminals, irrespective of their means, whether they be millionaires or labourers."[25]

   There are many ways by which such a goal might be reached. The offender might be forced to compensate the victim by his own work, either in prison or out. If it came out of his pocket or from the sale of his property this would compensate the victim, but it would not be sufficiently unpleasant for the offender. Another proposal would be that the fines be proportionate to the earning power of the criminal. Thus, "A poor man would pay in days of work, a rich man by an equal number of days' income or salary."[26] Herbert Spencer made a proposal along similar lines in his excellent "Prison-Ethics," which is well worth examining.[27] Murray N. Rothbard and others have proposed a system of "double payments" in cases of criminal behavior.[28] While closer to pure restitution than other proposals, the "double damages" concept preserves a punitive aspect.

   Punitive restitution is an attempt to gain the benefits of pure restitution, which will be considered shortly, while retaining the perceived advantages of the paradigm of punishment. Thus, the prisoner is still "sentenced" to some unpleasantness—prison labor or loss of X number of days' income. That the intention is to preserve the "hurt" is indicated by the hesitation to accept an out-of-pocket payment or sale of assets. This is considered too "easy" for the criminal and takes none of his time. The amount of payment is determined not by the *actual harm* but by the *ability of the offender to pay*. Of course, by retaining the paradigm of punishment this proposal involves many of the problems we raised earlier. In this sense it can be considered another attempt to salvage the old paradigm.

2. Pure restitution. "Recompense or restitution is scarcely a punishment as long as it is merely a matter of returning stolen goods or money. . . . The point is not that the offender deserves to suffer; it is rather that the offended party desires compensation."[29] This represents the complete overthrow of the paradigm of punishment. No longer would the deterrence, reformation, disablement, or rehabilitation of the criminal be the guiding principle of the judicial system. The attainment of these goals would be incidental to, and as a result of, reparations paid to the victim. No longer would the criminal deliberately be made to suffer for his mistake. Making good that mistake is all that would be required. What follows is a possible scenario of such a system.

   When a crime occurred and a suspect was apprehended, a trial court would attempt to determine his guilt or innocence. If found guilty, the criminal would be sentenced to make restitution to the victim.[30] If a criminal is able to make restitution immediately, he may do so. This would discharge his liability. If he were unable to make restitution, but were found by the court to be trustworthy, he would be permitted to remain at his job (or find a new one) while paying restitution out of his future wages. This would entail a legal claim against future wages. Failure to pay could result in garnishment or a new type of confinement.

If it is found that the criminal is not trustworthy, or that he is unable to gain employment, he would be confined to an employment project.[31] This would be an industrial enterprise, preferably run by a private concern, which would produce actual goods or services. The level of security at each employment project would vary according to the behavior of the offenders. Since the costs would be lower, inmates at a lower-security project would receive higher wages. There is no reason why many workers could not be permitted to live with their families inside or outside the facility, depending, again, on the trustworthiness of the offender. Room and board would be deducted from the wages first, then a certain amount for restitution. Anything over that amount the worker could keep or apply toward further restitution, thus hastening his release. If a worker refused to work, he would be unable to pay for his maintenance, and therefore would not in principle be entitled to it. If he did not make restitution he could not be released. The exact arrangement which would best provide for high productivity, minimal security, and maximum incentive to work and repay the victim cannot be determined in advance. Experience is bound to yield some plans superior to others. In fact, the experimentation has already begun.[32]

While this might be the basic system, all sorts of refinements are conceivable, and certainly many more will be invented as needs arise. A few examples might be illuminating. With such a system of repayment, victim *crime insurance* would be more economically feasible than at present and highly desirable. The cost of awards would be offset by the insurance company's right to restitution in place of the victim (right of subrogation). The insurance company would be better suited to supervise the offender and mark his progress than would the victim. To obtain an earlier recovery, it could be expected to innovate so as to enable the worker to repay more quickly (and, as a result, be released that much sooner). The insurance companies might even underwrite the employment projects themselves as well as related industries which would employ the skilled worker after his release.

Any successful effort on their part to reduce crime and recidivism would result in fewer claims and lower premiums. The benefit of this insurance scheme for the victim is immediate compensation, conditional on the victim's continued cooperation with the authorities for the arrest and conviction of the suspect. In addition, the centralization of victim claims would, arguably, lead to efficiencies which would permit the pooling of small claims against a common offender.

Another highly useful refinement would be *direct arbitration* between victim and criminal. This would serve as a sort of healthy substitute for plea bargaining. By allowing the guilty criminal to negotiate a reduced payment in return for a guilty plea, the victim (or his insurance company) would be saved the risk of an adverse finding at trial and any possible additional expense that might result. This would also allow an indigent criminal to substitute personal services for monetary payments if all parties agreed.

Arbitration is argued for by John M. Greacen, deputy director of the National Institute for Law Enforcement and Criminal Justice. He sees the possible advantages of such reform as the ". . . development of more creative dispositions for most criminal cases; for criminal victims the increased use of restitution, the knowledge that their interests were considered in the criminal process; and an increased satisfaction with the outcome; increased awareness in the part of the offender that his crime was committed against another human being, and not against society in general; increased possibility that the criminal process will cause the offender to acknowledge responsibility for his acts."[33] Greacen notes several places where such a system has been tried with great success, most notably Tucson, Arizona, and Columbus, Ohio.[34]

Something analogous to the medieval Irish system of *sureties* might be employed as well.[35] Such a system would allow a concerned person, group, or company to make restitution (provided the offender agrees to this). The worker might then be released in the custody of the surety. If the surety had made restitution, the offender would owe restitution to the surety who might enforce the whole claim or show mercy. Of course, the more violent and unreliable the offender, the more serious and costly the offense, the less likely it would be that anyone would take the risk. But for first offenders, good workers, or others that charitable interests found deserving (or perhaps unjustly convicted) this would provide an avenue of respite.

Restitution and Rights

These three possible refinements clearly illustrate the flexibility of a restitutional system. It may be less apparent that this flexibility is *inherent* to the restitutional paradigm. Restitution recognizes rights in the victim, and this is a principal source of its strength. The nature and limit of the victim's right to restitution at the same time defines the nature and limit of the criminal liability. In this way, the aggressive action of the criminal creates a *debt* to the victim. The recognition of rights and obligations make possible many innovative arrangements. Subrogation, arbitration, and suretyship are three examples mentioned above. They are possible because this right to compensation[36] is considered the property of the victim and can therefore be delegated, assigned, inherited, or bestowed. One could determine in advance who would acquire the right to any restitution which he himself might be unable to collect.

The natural owner of an unenforced death claim would be an insurance company that had insured the deceased. The suggestion has been made that a person might thus increase his personal safety by insuring with a company well known for tracking down those who injure its policy holders. In fact, the partial purpose of some insurance schemes might be to provide the funds with which to track down the malefactor. The insurance company, having paid the beneficiaries would "stand in their shoes." It would remain possible, of course, to simply assign or devise the right directly to the beneficiaries, but this would put the burden of enforcement on persons likely to be unsuited to the task.

If one accepts the Lockean trichotomy of property ownership,[37] that is, acquiring property via exchange, gifts, and *homesteading* (mixing one's labor with previously unowned land or objects), the possibility arises that upon a person's wrongful death, in the absence of any heirs or assignees, his right to compensation becomes unowned property. The right could then be claimed (homesteaded) by anyone willing to go to the trouble of catching and prosecuting the criminal. Firms might specialize in this sort of activity, or large insurance companies might make the effort as a kind of "loss leader" for public relations purposes.

This does, however, lead to a potentially serious problem with the restitutional paradigm: what exactly constitutes "restitution"? What is the *standard* by which compensation is to be made? Earlier we asserted that any such problem facing the restitutional paradigm faces civil damage suits as well. The method by which this problem is dealt with in civil cases could be applied to restitution cases. But while this is certainly true, it may be that this problem has not been adequately handled in civil damage suits either.

Restitution in cases of crimes against property is a manageable problem. Modern contract and tort doctrines of restitution are adequate. The difficulty lies in cases of personal injury or death. How can you put a price on life or limb, pain or suffering? Is not any attempt to do so of necessity arbitrary? It must be admitted that a fully satisfactory solution to this problem is lacking, but it should also be stressed that this dilemma, though serious, has little impact on the bulk of our case in favor of a restitutional paradigm. It is possible that no paradigm of criminal justice can solve every problem, yet the restitutional approach remains far superior to the paradigm of punishment or any other conceivable rival.

This difficulty arises because certain property is unique and irreplaceable. As a result, it is impossible to approximate a "market" or "exchange" value expressed in monetary terms. Just as there is no rational relationship between a wrongfully taken life and ten years in prison, there is little relationship between that same life and $20,000. Still, the nature of this possibly insoluble puzzle reveals a restitutional approach theoretically superior to punishment. For it must be acknowledged that a real, tangible loss *has* occurred. The problem is only one of incommensurability. Restitution provides *some* tangible, albeit inadequate, compensation for personal injury. Punishment provides none at all.[38]

It might be objected that to establish some "pay scale" for personal injury is not only somewhat arbitrary but also a disguised reimplementation of punishment. Unable to accept the inevitable consequences of restitutional punishment, the argument continues, I have retreated to a pseudorestitutional award. Such a criticism is unfair. The true test in this instance is one of primacy of intentions. Is the purpose of a system to compensate victims for their losses (and perhaps, as a consequence, punish the criminals), or is its purpose to punish the criminals (and perhaps, as a consequence, compensate the victims for their losses)? The true ends of a criminal justice system will determine its nature. In short, arbitrariness *alone* does not imply a retributive motive. And while arbitrariness remains to some extent a problem for the restitutional paradigm, it is less of a problem for restitution than for punishment, since compensation has *some* rational relationship to damages and costs.

Advantages of a Restitutional System

1. The first and most obvious advantage is the assistance provided to victims of crime. They may have suffered an emotional, physical, or financial loss. Restitution would not change the fact that a possibly traumatic crime has occurred (just as the award of damages does not undo tortious conduct). Restitution, however, would make the resulting loss easier to bear for both victims and their families. At the same time, restitution would avoid a major pitfall of victim compensation/welfare plans: Since it is the criminal who must pay, the possibility of collusion between victim and criminal to collect "damages" from the state would be all but eliminated.

2. The possibility of receiving compensation would encourage victims to report crimes and to appear at trial. This is particularly true if there were a crime insurance scheme which contractually committed the policyholder to testify as a condition for payment, thus rendering unnecessary oppressive and potentially tyrannical subpoenas and contempt citations. Even the actual reporting of the crime to police is likely to be a prerequisite for compensation. Such a requirement in auto theft insurance policies has made car thefts the most fully reported crime in the United States. Furthermore, insurance companies which paid the claim would have a strong incentive to see that the criminal was apprehended and convicted. Their pressure and assistance would make the proper functioning of law enforcement officials all the more likely.

3. Psychologist Albert Eglash has long argued that restitution would aid in the rehabilitation of criminals. "Restitution is something an inmate does, not something done for or to him. . . . Being reparative, restitution can alleviate guilt and anxiety, which can otherwise precipitate further offenses."[39] Restitution, says Eglash, is an active effortful role on the part of the offender. It is socially constructive, thereby contributing to the offender's self-esteem. It is related to the offense and may thereby redirect the thoughts which motivated the offense. It is reparative, restorative, and may actually leave the situation better than it was before the crime, both for the criminal and victim.[40]

4. This is a genuinely "self-determinative" sentence.[41] The worker would know that the length of his confinement was in his own hands. The harder he worked, the faster he would make restitution. He would be the master of his fate and would have to face that responsibility. This would encourage useful, productive activity and instill a conception of reward for good behavior and hard work. Compare this with the current probationary system and "indeterminate sentencing" where the decision for release is made by the prison bureaucracy, based only (if fairly administered) on "good behavior"; that is, passive acquiescence to prison discipline. Also, the fact that the worker would be acquiring *marketable* skills rather than more skillful methods of crime should help to reduce the shocking rate of recidivism.

5. The savings to taxpayers would be enormous. No longer would the innocent taxpayer pay for the apprehension and internment of the guilty. The cost of arrest, trial, and internment would be borne by the criminal himself. In addition, since now-idle inmates would become productive workers (able, perhaps, to support their families), the entire economy would benefit from the increase in overall production.[42]

6. Crime would no longer pay. Criminals, particularly shrewd white-collar criminals, would know that they could not dispose of the proceeds of their crime, and if caught, simply serve time. They would have to make full restitution plus enforcement and legal costs, thereby greatly increasing the incentive to prosecute. While this would not eliminate such crime it would make it rougher on certain types of criminals, like bank and corporation officials, who harm many by their acts with a virtual assurance of lenient legal sanctions.[43] It might also encourage such criminals to keep the money around for a while so that, if caught, they could repay more easily. This would make a full recovery more likely.

A restitutional system of justice would benefit the victim, the criminal, and the taxpayer. The humanitarian goals of proportionate punishment, rehabilitation, and victim compensation are dealt with on a *fundamental* level making their achievement more likely. In short, the paradigm of restitution would benefit all but the entrenched penal bureaucracy and enhance justice at the same time. What then is there to stop us from overthrowing the paradigm of punishment and its penal system and putting in its place this more efficient, more humane, and more just system? The proponents of punishment and others have a few powerful counterarguments. It is to these we now turn.

Objections to Restitution

1. Practical criticisms of restitution. It might be objected that "crimes disturb and offend not only those who are directly their victim, but also the whole social order."[44] Because of this, society, that is, individuals other than the victim, deserves some satisfaction from the offender. Restitution, it is argued, will not satisfy the lust for revenge felt by the victim or the "community's sense of justice." This criticism appears to be overdrawn. Today most members of the community are mere spectators of the criminal justice system, and this is largely true even of the victim.[45] One major reform being urged presently is more victim involvement in the criminal justice process.[46] The restitution proposal would necessitate this involvement. And while the public generally takes the view that officials should be tougher on criminals, with "tougher" taken by nearly everyone to mean more severe in punishing, one must view this "social fact" in light of the lack of a known alternative. The real test of public sympathies would be to see which sanction people would choose: incarceration of the criminal for a given number of years or the criminal's being compelled to make restitution to the victim: While the public's choice is not clearly predictable, neither can it be assumed that it would reject restitution. There is some evidence to the contrary.[47]

This brings us to a second practical objection: that monetary sanctions are insufficient deterrents to crime. Again, this is something to be discovered, not something to be assumed. There are a number of reasons to believe that our *current* system of punishment does not adequately deter, and for the reasons discussed earlier an increase in the level of punishment is unlikely. In fact, many have argued that the deterrent value of sanctions has less to do with *severity* than with *certainty*,[48] and the preceding considerations indicate that law enforcement would be more certain under a restitutional system. In the final analysis, however, it is irrelevant to argue that more crimes may be committed if our proposal leaves the victim better off. It must be remembered: *Our goal is not the suppression of crime: it is doing justice to victims.*

A practical consideration which merits considerable future attention is the feasibility of the employ- ment project proposal. A number of questions can be raised. At first blush, it seems naively optimistic to suppose that offenders will be able or willing to work at all, much less earn their keep and pay reparations as well. On the contrary, this argument continues, individuals turn to crime precisely because they lack the skills which the restitutional plan assumes they have. Even if these workers have the skills, but refuse to work, what could be done? Would not the use of force to compel compliance be tantamount to slavery? This criticism results in part from my attempt to sketch an "ideal" restitution system; that is, I have attempted to outline the type toward which every criminal justice system governed by the restitution paradigm should strive. This is not to say that every aspect of the hypothetical system would, upon implementation, function smoothly. Rather, such a system could only operate ideally once the paradigm had been fully accepted and substantially articulated.

With this in mind, one can advance several responses. First, the problem as usually posed assumes the offender to be highly irrational and possibly mentally unbalanced. There is no denying that some segment of the criminal population fits the former description.[49] What this approach neglects, however, is the possibility that many criminals are making rational choices within an irrational and unjust political system. Specifically I refer to the myriad laws and regulations which make it difficult for the unskilled or persons of transitory outlook[50] to find legal employment.[51] I refer also to the laws which deny legality to the types of services which are in particular demand in economically impoverished communities.[52] Is it "irrational" to choose to steal or rob when one is virtually foreclosed from the legal opportunity to do otherwise? Another possibility is that the criminal chooses crime not because of foreclosure, but because he enjoys and obtains satisfaction from a criminal way of life.[53] Though morally repugnant, this is hardly irrational.

Furthermore, it no longer can be denied that contact with the current criminal justice system is itself especially damaging among juveniles.[54] The offenders who are hopelessly committed to criminal behavior are not usually the newcomers to crime but those who have had repeated exposure to the penal system. In Kuhn's words, "Existing institutions have ceased to meet the problems posed by an environment *they have in part created.*"[55] While a restitutionary system might not change these hard-core offenders, it could, by the early implementation of sanctions perceived by the criminal to be just, break the vicious circle which in large part accounts for their existence.

Finally, if offenders could not or would not make restitution, then the logical and just result of their refusal would be confinement until they could or would. Such an outcome would be entirely in their hands. While this "solution" does not suggest who should justly pay for this confinement, the problem is not unique to a restitutionary system. In this and other areas of possible difficulty we must seek guidance from existing pilot programs as well as from the burgeoning research in this area and in victimology in general.

2. Distributionary criticisms of restitution. There remains one criticism of restitution which is the most obvious and the most difficult with which to deal. Simply stated, it takes the following form: "Doesn't this mean that rich people will be able to commit crimes with impunity if they can afford it? Isn't this unfair?" The *practical* aspect of this objection is that whatever deterrent effect restitution payments may have, they will be less for those most able to pay. The *moral* aspect is that whatever retributive or penal effect restitution payments may have they will be less for those who are well off. Some concept of equality of justice underlies both considerations.

Critics of restitution fail to realize that the "cost" of crime will be quite high. In addition to compensation for pain and suffering, the criminal must pay for the cost of his apprehension, the cost of the trial, and the legal expenditures of *both* sides. This should make even an unscrupulous wealthy person think twice about committing a crime. The response to this is that we cannot have it both ways. If the fines would be high enough to bother the rich, then they would be so high that a project worker would have no chance of earning that much and would, therefore, have no incentive to work at all. If, on the other hand, you lower the price of crime by ignoring all its costs, you fail to deter the rich or fully compensate the victim.

This is where the option of arbitration and victim crime insurance becomes of practical importance. If the victim is uninsured, he is unlikely to recover for all costs of a very severe crime from a poor, unskilled criminal, since even in an employment project the criminal might be unable to earn enough. If he had no hope of earning his release, he would have little incentive to work very hard beyond paying for his own maintenance. The victim would end up with less than if he had "settled" the case for the lesser amount which a project worker could reasonably be expected to earn. If, however, the victim had full-coverage criminal insurance, he would recover his damages in full, and the insurance company would absorb any dispar-

ity between full compensation and maximal employment project worker's output. This cost would be reflected in premium prices, enabling the insurance company which settled cases at an amount which increased the recovery from the criminal to offer the lowest rates. Eventually a "maximum" feasible fine for project workers would be determined based on these considerations. The "rich," on the other hand, would naturally have to pay in full. This arrangement would solve the practical problem, but it should not be thought of as an imperative of the restitutional paradigm.

The same procedure of varying the payments according to ability to pay would answer the moral considerations as well (that the rich are not hurt enough) and this is the prime motive behind *punitive* restitution proposals. However, we reject the moral consideration outright. The paradigm of restitution calls not for the (equal) hurting of criminals, but for restitution to victims. Any appeal to "inadequate suffering" is a reversion to the paradigm of punishment, and by varying the sanction for crimes of the same magnitude according to the economic status of the offender it reveals its own inequity. *Equality of justice means equal treatment of victims.* It should not matter to the victim if his attacker was rich or poor. His plight is the same regardless. Any reduction of criminal liability because of reduced earning power would be for practical, not moral, reasons.

Equality of justice derives from the fact that the rights of men should be equally enforced and respected. Restitution recognizes a victim's right to compensation for damages from the party responsible. Equality of justice, therefore, calls for equal enforcement of each victim's right to restitution. *Even if necessary or expedient, any lessening of payment to the victim because of the qualities of the criminal is a violation of that victim's rights and an inequality of justice.* Any such expedient settlement is only a recognition that an imperfect world may make possible only imperfect justice. As a practical matter, a restitutional standard gives victims an enormous incentive to pursue wealthy criminals since they can afford quick, full compensation. Contrast this with the present system where the preference given the wealthy is so prevalent that most victims simply assume that nothing will be done.

The paradigm of restitution, to reiterate, is neither a panacea for crime nor a blueprint for utopia. Panaceas and utopias are not for humankind. We must live in a less than perfect world with less than perfect people. Restitution opens the possibility of an improved and more just society. The old paradigm of punishment, even reformed, simply cannot offer this promise.

Other Considerations

Space does not permit a full examination of other less fundamental implications of such a system. I shall briefly consider five.

1. Civil versus criminal liability. If one accepts a restitutionary standard of justice, what sense does it make to distinguish between crime and tort, since both call for payment of damages? For most purposes I think the distinction collapses. Richard Epstein, in a series of brilliant articles, has articulated a theory of strict liability in tort.[56] His view is that since one party has caused another some harm and one of the parties must bear the loss, justice demands that it falls on the party who caused the harm. He argues that intention is only relevant as a "third-stage" argument; that notwithstanding some fault on the part of the plaintiff (a second-stage argument), the defendant intended the harm and is therefore liable.[57] With a restitutional system I see no reason why Epstein's theory of tort liability could not incorporate criminal liability into a single "system of corrective justice that looks to the conduct, broadly defined, of the parties to the case with a view toward the protection of individual liberty and private property."[58]

   There would, at least initially, be some differences, however. The calculation of damages under the restitutionary paradigm which includes cost of apprehension, cost of trial, and legal costs of both parties would be higher than tort law allows. A further distinction would be the power of enforcers to confine unreliable offenders to employment projects.[59]

2. Criminal responsibility and competency. Once a criminal sanction is based not on the offender's badness but on the nature and consequences of his acts, Thomas Szasz's proposal that the insanity plea be abolished makes a great deal of sense,[60] as does his argument that "all persons charged with offenses—except those grossly disabled—[are fit to stand trial and] should be tried."[61] On this view, Epstein's concept of fairness *as between the parties* is relevant. A restitution proceeding like a "lawsuit is always a comparative affair. The defendant's victory ensures the plaintiff's [or victim's] de-

feat. . . . Why should we prefer the injurer to his victim in a case where one may win and the other lose? . . . As a matter of fairness between the parties, the defendant should be required to treat the harms which he has inflicted upon another as though they were inflicted upon himself."[62]

3. Victimless crimes. The effect of restitutional standards on the legality of such crimes as prostitution, gambling, high interest loans, pornography, and drug use is intriguing. There has been no violation of individual rights, and consequently no damages and, therefore, no liability. While some may see this as a drawback, I believe it is a striking advantage of the restitutional standard of justice. So-called victimless crimes would in principle cease to be crimes. As a consequence, criminal elements would be denied a lucrative monopoly, and the price of these services would be drastically reduced. Without this enormous income, organized crime would be far less able to afford the "cost" of its nefarious activities than it is today.

4. Legal positivism. What is true for victimless crimes is true for the philosophy of legal positivism. On the positivist view, whatever the state (following all the correct political procedures) says is law, is law; hence, whatever the state makes a crime is a crime. A restitutional standard would hold the state to enforcing individual rights through the recovery of individual damages.

5. Legal process. Because the sanction for crime would no longer be punitive, the criminal process could explore less formal procedures for dispute settlement. Also, the voice of the victim would be added to the deliberations. One possible reform might be a three-tiered verdict: guilty, not proven, and not guilty. If found "guilty," the offender would pay all the costs mentioned above. If the charges are "not proven," then neither party would pay the other. If found "not guilty," the defendant would be reimbursed by the enforcement agency for his costs and inconvenience. This new interpretation of "not guilty" would reward those defendants who, after putting on a defense, convinced the trier of fact that they were innocent.

   These and many other fascinating implications of restitution deserve a more thorough examination. As any new paradigm becomes accepted, it experiences what Kuhn calls a period of "normal research," a period characterized by continuous expansion and perfection of the new paradigm as well as a testing of its limits. The experimentation with restitutionary justice will, however, differ from the trial and error of the recent past since we will be guided by the principle that the purpose of our legal system is not to harm the guilty but to help the innocent—a principle which will above all restore our belief that our overriding commitment is to do justice.

———————

1. *What immediately follows is a brief outline of Kuhn's theory. Those interested in the defense of that theory should refer to his book,* The Structure of Scientific Revolutions, *2d ed., enl. (Chicago: University of Chicago Press, 1970). A paradigm is an achievement in a particular discipline which defines the legitimate problems and methods of research within that discipline. This achievement is sufficiently unprecedented to attract new adherents away from rival approaches while providing many unsolved questions for these new practitioners to solve. As the paradigm develops and matures, it reveals occasional inabilities to solve new problems and explain new data. As attempts are made to make the facts fit the paradigm, the theoretical apparatus gradually becomes bulky and awkward, like Ptolemaic astronomy. Dissatisfaction with the paradigm begins to grow. Why not simply discard the paradigm and find another which better fits the facts? Unfortunately, this is an arduous process. All the great authorities and teachers were raised with the current paradigm and see the world through it. All the texts and institutions are committed to it. Radical alternatives hold promise but are so untested as to make wary all but the bold. The establishment is loath to abandon its broad and intricate theory in favor of a new and largely unknown hypothesis. Gradually, however, as the authorities die off and the problems with the old paradigm increase, the "young turks" get a better hearing in both the journals and the classroom. In a remarkably rapid fashion, the old paradigm is discarded for the new. Anyone who still clings to it is now considered to be antiquated or eccentric and is simply read out of the profession. All research centers on the application of the new paradigm. Kuhn characterizes this overthrow of one paradigm by another as a revolution.*

2. *Ibid., p. 92.*

3. *Stanley I. Benn, "Punishment," in* The Encyclopedia of Philosophy, *ed. Paul Edwards (New York: Macmillan Publishing Co., 1967), 7:29 (emphasis added).*

4. *Heinrich Oppenheimer,* The Rationale of Punishment *(London: University of London Press, 1913), p. 255.*

5. *Ibid.*

6. *See Thomas Szasz,* Law, Liberty and Psychiatry *(New York: Macmillan Co., 1963).*

7. *Giorgio del Vecchio, "The Struggle Against Crime," in* The Philosophy of Punishment, *ed. H. B. Acton (London: Macmillan Co., 1969), p. 199.*

8. *See, e.g., Samuel Yochelson and Stanton E. Samenow,* The Criminal Personality, *vol. 1, A Profile for Change (New York: Jason Aronson, Inc., 1976), pp. 411–16.*

9. *Del Vecchio, p. 199.*

10. *Robert Nozick,* Anarchy, State, and Utopia *(New York: Basic Books, 1974), p. 61.*

11. *Ibid., pp. 59–63.*

12. *For a concise summary, see Oppenheimer, p. 31.*

13. *Del Vecchio, p. 198.*

14. *See, e.g., Walter Kaufmann,* Without Guilt and Justice *(New York: Peter H. Wyden, Inc., 1973), esp. chap. 2.*

15. *See, e.g., "Crime: A Case for More Punishment,"* Business Week *(September 15, 1975), pp. 92–97.*

16. *This problem is examined, though not ultimately resolved, by Edwin M. Schur in his book* Crimes Without Victims—Deviant Behavior and Public Policy, Abortion, Homosexuality, and Drug Addiction *(Englewood Cliffs, N.J.: Prentice-Hall, Inc., 1965).*

17. *Kaufmann, p. 46.*

18. *Kuhn, p. 82.*

19. *R. A. Childs, "Liberty and the Paradigm of Statism," in* The Libertarian Alternative, *ed. Tibor Machan (Chicago: Nelson-Hall Co., 1974), p. 505.*

20. *Composition was the medieval version of a restitutionary system. For a fascinating outline of how such a system operated and how it came to be supplanted by state-authored punishment, see Stephen Schafer,* Compensation and Restitution to Victims of Crime, *2d ed., enl. (Montclair, N.J.: Patterson Smith Publishing Corp., 1970); Richard E. Laster, "Criminal Restitution: A Survey of Its Past History and an Analysis of Its Present Usefulness,"* University of Richmond Law Review *5 (1970): 71–80; L. T. Hobhouse,* Morals in Evolution *(London: Chapman & Hall, 1951).*

21. *Kaufmann, p. 45.*

22. *For a brief definition of "victimology," see Emilo C. Viano, "Victimology: The Study of the Victim,"* Victimology *1 (1976): 1–7. For an extensive collection of papers on various aspects of victimology, see Emilo C. Viano, ed.,* Victims and Society *(Washington, D.C.: Visage Press, 1976).*

23. *For a discussion and list of symposiums, journal articles, and statutes concerning victim compensation, see Steven Schafer, pp. 139–57, and appendix; see also Joe Hudson and Burt Galaway, eds.,* Considering the Victim: Readings in Restitution and Victim Compensation *(Springfield, Ill.: Charles C. Thomas, 1975), esp. pp. 361–436.*

24. *Gerhard O. W. Mueller, "Compensation for Victims of Crime: Thought Before Action,"* Minnesota Law Review *50 (1965): 221.*

25. *Schafer, p. 127.*

26. *Ibid.*

27. *Herbert Spencer, "Prison-Ethics," in* Essays: Scientific, Political and Speculative *(New York: D. Appleton & Co., 1907), 3: 152–91.*

28. *Murray N. Rothbard,* The Ethics of Liberty *(Atlantic Highlands, N.J.: Humanities Press, 1982) pp. 85–95.*

29. *Kaufmann, p. 55.*

30. *The nature of judicial procedure best designed to carry out this task must be determined. For a brief discussion of some relevant considerations, see Laster, pp. 80–98; Burt Galaway and Joe Hudson, "Issues in the Correctional Implementation of Restitution to Victims of Crime," in* Considering the Victim, *pp. 351–60. Also to be dealt with is the proper standard of compensation. At least initially, the problem of how much payment constitutes restitution would be no different than similar considerations in tort law. This will be considered at greater length below.*

31. *Such a plan (with some significant differences) has been suggested by Kathleen J. Smith in* A Cure for Crime: The Case for the Self-determinate Prison Sentence *(London: Gerald, Duckworth & Co., 1965), pp. 13–29; see also Morris and Linda Tannehill,* The Market for Liberty *(Lansing, Mich.: Privately printed, 1970), pp. 44–108.*

32. *For a recent summary report, see Burt Galaway, "Restitution as an Integrative Punishment," in Barnett and Hagel,* Assessing the Criminal, *pp. 331–347.*

33. *John M. Greacen, "Arbitration: A Tool for Criminal Cases?"* Barrister *(Winter 1975), p. 53; see also Galaway and Hudson, pp. 352–55; "Conclusions and Recommendations, International Study Institute on Victimology, Bellagio, Italy, July 1–12, 1975,"* Victimology *1 (1976): 150–51; Ronald Goldfarb,* Jails: The Ultimate Ghetto *(Garden City, N.Y.: Anchor Press/Doubleday, 1976), p. 480.*

34. *Greacen, p. 53.*

35. *For a description of the Irish system, see Joseph R. Peden, "Property Rights in Medieval Ireland: Celtic Law versus Church and State,"* Journal of Libertarian Studies *1 (1977): 86.*

36. *Or, perhaps more accurately, the compensation itself.*

37. *For a brief explanation of this concept and several of its possible applications, see Murray N. Rothbard, "Justice and Property Rights," in* Property in a Humane Economy, *ed. Samuel L. Blumenfeld (La Salle, Ill.: Open Court Publishing Co., 1974), pp. 101–22.*

38. *That the "spiritual" satisfaction which punishment may or may not provide is to be recognized as a legitimate form of "compensation" is a claim retributionists must defend.*

39. *Albert Eglash, "Creative Restitution: Some Suggestions for Prison Rehabilitation Programs,"* American Journal of Correction 10 *(November–December 1958): 20.*

40. *Ibid.; see also Eglash's "Creative Restitution: A Broader Meaning for an Old Term,"* Journal of Criminal Law and Criminology 48 *(1958): 619–22; Burt Galaway and Joe Hudson, "Restitution and Rehabilitation—Some Central Issues,"* Crime and Delinquency 18 *(1972): 403–10.*

41. *Smith, pp. 13–29.*

42. *An economist who favors restitution on efficiency grounds is Gary S. Becker, although he does not break with the paradigm of punishment. Those interested in a mathematical "cost-benefit" analysis see his "Crime and Punishment,"* Journal of Political Economy 76 *(1968): 169–217.*

43. *This point is also made by Minocher Jehangirji Sethna in his paper, "Treatment and Atonement for Crime," in* Victims and Society, *p. 538.*

44. *Del Vecchio, p. 198.*

45. *William F. McDonald, "Towards a Bicentennial Revolution in Criminal Justice: The Return of the Victim,"* American Criminal Law Review 13 *(1976): 659; see also his paper "Notes on the Victim's Role in the Prosecutional and Dispositional Stages of the Criminal Justice Process" (paper presented at the Second International Symposium on Victimology, Boston, September 1976), and "The Role of the Victim in America," in* Barnett and Hagel, Assessing the Criminal, *pp. 295–305; Jack M. Kress, "The Role of the Victim at Sentencing" (paper presented at the Second International Symposium on Victimology, Boston, September 1976).*

46. *McDonald, pp. 669–73; Kress, pp. 11–15. Kress specifically analyzes restitution as a means for achieving victim involvement.*

47. *In two types of studies conducted for the Ventura County Board of Supervisors, Ventura, California, support for a restitutional program was indicated: "Both the citizen attitude survey and the Delphi goal-setting exercise revealed a strong concern for the victim as the 'forgotten man' of criminal justice. The Delphi panelists, in particular, emphasized the need for new kinds of criminal penalties in which the offender would be required to make restitution to his victim(s)" (*Development of a Model Criminal Justice System *[Santa Barbara, Calif.: Public Safety Systems, 1973], p. 85). The report recommends the implementing of a system of restitution. In the two cities mentioned earlier (Columbus and Tucson), support, at least by the parties involved, appeared strong. In the thousands of cases arbitrated by trained law students in Columbus, only 4 percent proceeded further up in the criminal system. In Tucson after one year the program has been successful in all but nine of 204 cases (with the cost of handling each case at $304 compared with $1,566 required to process the average felony case). General approval of restitution in lieu of punishment was indirectly referred to in the Columbia Law Review's oft-cited study, "Restitution and the Criminal Law": "[E]ven where the complainant can be persuaded to continue the criminal case, after having received private satisfaction, his apathy is often so pronounced and his demeanor so listless that he becomes an extremely weak witness. . . . Also the knowledge of actual restitution seems to greatly assuage the jury. Even the knowledge of the existence of a civil suit can lead the jury to recommend leniency or acquittal" (39 [1939]: 1189; see also n. 31). Restitution, it seems, is accepted and preferred by the average person. Early studies indicate that, when properly administered, even offenders perceive a restitutionary sanction as fair (William Marsella and Burt Galaway, "Study of the Perceived Fairness of Restitution as a Sanction for Juvenile Offenders" [paper presented to the Second International Symposium on Victimology, Boston, September 1976]).*

48. *Yochelson and Samenow, pp. 453–57.*

49. *For a discussion rejecting the usefulness of the latter description, see Szasz, pp. 91–146; for a recent study verifying Szasz's thesis, see Yochelson and Samenow, esp. pp. 227–35.*

50. *Edward C. Banfield put forth his controversial theory of time horizon in his book* The Unheavenly City *(Boston: Little, Brown & Co., 1970) and amplified it in* The Unheavenly City Revisited *(Boston: Little, Brown & Co., 1974), and most recently, "Present-orientedness and Crime," in* Barnett and Hagel, Assessing the Criminal, *pp. 143–162. For a critical, but favorable analysis of this approach, see Gerald P. O'Driscoll, Jr., "Professor Banfield on Time Horizon: What Has He Taught Us about Crime?" in* Barnett and Hagel, Assessing the Criminal, *pp. 143–162. A contrary, but ultimately compatible view is presented by Yochelson and Samenow, pp. 369–72.*

51. *For example, minimum wage laws, and so-called closed-shop union protectionist legislation.*

52. *For example, laws prohibiting gambling, prostitution, sale of drugs, "jitney" cab services, etc.*

53. *"It is not the environment that turns a man into a criminal. Rather it is a series of choices that he makes at a very early age. . . . [T]he criminal is not a victim of circumstances" (Yochelson and Samenow, pp. 247, 249). This is in essence the main conclusion of their research. (For a concise summary of their provocative book, see Joseph Boorkin, "The Criminal Personality,"* Federal Bar Journal 35 *[1976]: 237–41.) In* The Criminal Personality, *vol. 2,* The Process of Change *(New York: Jason Aronson, Inc., 1977) they relate and examine the methods they have employed to change the criminal thought pattern. Of course, such an approach can itself be subject to abuse.*

54. *See, e.g., Edwin M. Schur,* Radical Noninterventionism, Rethinking the Delinquency Problem *(Englewood Cliffs, N.J.: Prentice-Hall, Inc., 1973).*

55. *Kuhn, p. 92 (emphasis added).*

56. *Richard A. Epstein, "A Theory of Strict Liability in Tort,"* Journal of Legal Studies 2 *(1973): 151–204.*

57. *Richard A. Epstein, "Intentional Harms,"* Journal of Legal Studies 3 *(1975): 402–8; see also his article "Defenses and Subsequent Pleas in a System of Strict Liability," ibid., 3 (1974): 174–85.*

58. *Epstein, "Intentional Harms," p. 441. Epstein himself would disagree. In a recent article, also notable for its well-reasoned rejection of victim compensation/welfare schemes, "Crime and Tort: Old Wine in Old Bottles," in* Barnett and Hagel, Assessing the Criminal, *pp. 231–257, he draws an emphatic distinction between tort and criminal law. He rests this distinction on two characteristics of the criminal law: (a) that its function is to punish (and therefore mens rea is required and more stringent procedural safeguards are appropriate), and (b) since the defendant is prosecuted by the state, fairness as between the parties is not relevant. From these assumptions, Epstein reasons quite correctly that the two systems are inherently different. It should be obvious that a restitutionary paradigm undermines both assumptions. Gilbert M. Cantor in his article, "An End to Crime and Punishment" (*Shingle 39 *[May 1976]: 99–114), takes precisely this view, arguing that "the time has come to abolish the game of crime and punishment and to substitute a paradigm of restitution and responsibility. I urge that we assign (reassign, actually) to the civil law our societal response to the acts or behaviors we now label and treat as criminal. The goal is the* civilization *of our treatment of offenders. I use the word, 'civilization' here in its specific meaning: to bring offenders under the civil, rather than the criminal law; and in its larger meaning: to move in this area of endeavor from barbarism toward greater enlightenment and humanity" (p. 107; emphasis in original).*

59. *It would seem that the only way to account for these differences would be an appeal to the mens rea or badness of the criminal as opposed to the unintentional tortfeasor. Yet such an approach, it might be argued, is not available to a restitutionary system which considers the moral outlook of an offender to be irrelevant to the determination of the proper criminal sanction. A possible response is that this overstates the restitutionist claim. That a criminal's mental state does not justify punishment does not imply that it is not relevant to any aspect of the criminal justice*

process. It may well be that it is relevant to the consideration of methods by which one is justified in extracting what, on other grounds, is shown to be a proper sanction, that is, restitution.
60. Szasz, pp. 228–30.
61. Ibid., pp. 228–29. "The emphasis here is on gross disability: it should be readily apparent or easily explicable to a group of lay persons, like a jury" (p. 229). But even the qualification of gross disablement might be unjustified (see Yochelson and Samenow, pp. 227–35).
62. Epstein, p. 398. In his article "Crime and Tort: Old Wine in Old Bottles," he takes exactly this approach with the insanity defense in tort law.

RETRIBUTION AND REVENGE*

Robert Nozick

A Framework for Retribution

How can someone be held responsible or deserve punishment for an action he was causally determined to do? Even if wrongful actions are freely chosen, in what sense is punishment deserved and what purpose does its infliction serve? Is not the notion of deserved punishment, of retribution, primitive—a disguise for vengeful passions? To answer these questions, I shall outline a theory of punishment, one I imagine is to be combined with a theory of compensation to victims. A wrongdoer deserves punishment for a wrongful act, and he must compensate the surviving victims of his act.

The punishment deserved depends on the magnitude H of the wrongness of the act, and the person's degree of responsibility r for the act, and is equal in magnitude to their product, $r \times H$. The degree of responsibility r varies between one (full responsibility) and zero (no responsibility), and may take intermediate numerical values corresponding to partial responsibility. Thus, the punishment deserved is equal to H when the person is fully responsible for the act, when r equals one, and he deserves no punishment when his degree of responsibility is zero; otherwise H is discounted by (because multiplied by) the person's intermediate degree of responsibility. The magnitude H is a measure of the wrongness or harm, done or intended, of the act.[1]

The details of the theory of compensation are not our concern here; but note that the compensation owed to victims will depend upon (the degree of) causation of the harmful consequences, not upon the r value of the act, the degree of responsibility for it. If someone nonnegligently and accidentally causes damage to your property, he owes you compensation, but since his r = 0 he does not deserve any punishment for this.

The punishment (deserved) is to affect the wrongdoer, but not simply as he finds himself after doing the wrongful act; his ill-gotten gains (including psychic ones) are removed or counterbalanced before the infliction of the deserved penalty. Thus, the punishment deserved, $r \times H$, is imposed relative to a baseline that marks the situation the wrongdoer would have been in had he not committed the wrong. However, the process of making compensation to victims (so that they are no worse off than they would have been had the wrong not been done to them) may itself lower the wrongdoer from his baseline situation by some amount c.[2] If so, then the punishment still to be inflicted will be equal in magnitude to $(r \times H) - c$; thereby the process of extracting compensation followed by punishment leaves the wrongdoer $r \times H$ below his baseline situation. Someone who by preference lives without much monetarily gainful employment, if he commits an assault, may find the process of doing what is necessary to provide monetary compensation to his victim so unpleasant as to be lowered by the full degree $r \times H$ from his baseline situation; no further punishment is appropriate since the (magnitude of the) deserved punishment has been visited upon him in the course of his paying compensation. (I leave aside issues about deserving a punishment that matches the wrong.) Providing compensation may even leave the person more than r × H below the baseline; however, in this case full compensation still is extracted—why should it be the victim who bears the undeserved cost?—but no further penalty is visited.*

Retributive matching penalties are penalties that not only fit the magnitude of r × H but, when r = 1, do to the wrongdoer the same H, to the extent this is feasible, as he has done.[3]

There are difficulties worth mentioning in understanding what the same or a comparable penalty would be, to equal the magnitude of the wrong or harm done. If a millionaire steals $100 from a poor person then, after restitution, the appropriate penalty is not $100 from the millionaire. Rather it is some deprivation as severe for the millionaire as a $100 loss is to the poor person he victimized. However, to set penalties at exactly the amount the victim's utility is lowered would set the penalty too low for theft from millionaires. Nor is it perfectly appropriate to set the penalty for a theft at the maximum of either how much utility the victim loses by the theft, or how much the thief would lose by a theft of that amount. In some special situation, losing that amount might have tremendous (but unforeseeable) disutility for the victim; this should not increase the punishment though it must be counted in the compensation stage. Rather, it seems appropriate to let the penalty be the maximum of the amount of disutility the victim reasonably could have been expected to undergo, and the amount of disutility the perpetrator would (reasonably be expected to?) undergo from that same act. . . .

---

*Here, some of r × H may be used up in the process of compensation. In *Anarchy, State, and Utopia* (pp. 62–63), I pointed out that (some of) r × H may be drawn upon and used up at the time of the crime, in self-defense against the criminal. For what is necessary for successful defense may go beyond what is allowed by the principle of proportionality, which holds that what may be inflicted in defense is some function of H, but not of *r*. Both types of "drawings" upon r × H that take place must be counted in fixing how great a penalty, by itself, still remains to be visited. There being two types of drawings raises issues about how they interact; how, if at all, do the future compensations that will occur affect what "drawings" upon r × H a person may make in self-defense?

Retribution and Revenge

The view that people deserve punishment for their wrongful acts in accordance with r × H, independently of the deterrent effect of such punishment,[4] strikes some people as a primitive view, expressive only of the thirst for revenge. Before pursuing the underlying rationale of retribution, punishment inflicted as deserved for a past wrong, we should consider some ways in which retribution differs from revenge.

1. Retribution is done for a wrong, while revenge may be done for an injury or harm or slight and need not be for a wrong.
2. Retribution sets an internal limit to the amount of the punishment, according to the seriousness of the wrong, whereas revenge internally need set no limit to what is inflicted. Revenge by its nature need set no limits, although the revenger may limit what he inflicts for external reasons.
3. Revenge is personal: "this is because of what you did to my _____" (self, father, group, and so on). Whereas the agent of retribution need have no special or personal tie to the victim of the wrong for which he exacts retribution.

Do not say he exacts the penalty because of the injury done to his own moral code; that overextends the notion of personal tie. Steps sometimes are taken to exclude the personal tie from intruding in a process of retribution and clouding the nature of what is happening by blurring the distinctness of retribution from revenge. Thus, under a system of capital punishment, if the sister of the official executioner is murdered and the killer is apprehended, someone else will be substituted to perform that execution.

This third point has two aspects: revenge can be desired only by someone with a personal tie (others can desire that some such person inflict revenge, but their desire is not a desire for revenge), and it can be inflicted only by (the agent of) someone with a personal tie.* Retribution, on the other hand, may be desired or inflicted by people without such a tie. This personal factor also enters into the revenger's desire, noted below, that his connection to the victim for whom revenge is being exacted be known to the recipient of revenge.

---

*Revenge may involve differing notions of linkage: (a) because of what you did to my _____; (b) because of what you did to me. If someone kills your father, under linkage *a* you kill him while under *b* you kill his father.

4. Revenge involves a particular emotional tone, pleasure in the suffering of another, while retribution either need involve no emotional tone, or involves another one, namely, pleasure at justice being done. Therefore, the thirster after revenge often will want to experience (see, be present at) the situation in which the revengee is suffering, whereas with retribution there is no special point in witnessing its infliction.

This connects with the previous point about the personal tie; one purpose of revenge may be to produce a psychological effect in the person who seeks revenge (that particular emotional tone, for example), while retribution has no such personal purpose.

5. There need be no generality in revenge. Not only is the revenger not committed to revenging any similar act done to anyone; he is not committed to avenging all done to himself. Whether he seeks vengeance, or thinks it appropriate to do so, will depend upon how he feels at the time about the act of injury. Whereas the imposer of retribution, inflicting deserved punishment for a wrong, is committed to (the existence of some) general principles (prima facie) mandating punishment in other similar circumstances. Furthermore, if possible these general standards will be made known and clear in the process of retribution; even those who act in retribution against the guilty agents of a torturing dictatorship, keeping their own identities secret, will make the principles known.

In drawing these contrasts between retribution and revenge, I do not deny that there can be mixed cases, or that people can be moved by mixed motives, partially a desire for retribution, partially a desire for revenge, or that a stated desire can mask another one that is operative. Usually, it is charged that those favoring retribution really crave revenge; but this will be especially implausible in the absence of a special tie to the victim. (The charge never is made in the other direction, that some who call for revenge really are seeking retribution but are embarrassed at appearing moralistic.) The charge itself, though, recognizes the distinction, even as it seeks to blur it. That retribution can be distinguished from revenge and is, on its surface at least, less primitive neither shows that, nor explains why, retribution is justified. Nor does it explain why retribution and revenge so often have been confused.

Retribution and revenge share a common structure: a penalty is inflicted for a reason (a wrong or injury) with the desire that the other person know why this is occurring and know that he was intended to know. (In the comic books of my youth, the villain seeking revenge always was thwarted by his desire that the hero not merely die but realize why he was dying and at whose hand, in prolonged agony—this gave the hero extended opportunity to escape.) I shall spell out that common structure as it is exemplified by retribution; this must be modified in accordance with the contrasts we have listed to obtain an account of revenge.

Under retributive punishment for S's act A (I speak here of the fullest and most satisfactory case):

1. Someone believes that S's act A has a certain degree of wrongness
2. and visits a penalty upon S
3. which is determined by the wrongness H of the act A, or by $r \times H$,
4. intending that the penalty be done because of the wrong act A
5. and in virtue of the wrongness of the act A,
6. intending that S know the penalty was visited upon him because he did A
7. and in virtue of the wrongness of A,
8. by someone who intended to have the penalty fit and be done because of the wrongness of A
9. and who intended that S would recognize (he was intended to recognize) that the penalty was visited upon him so that 1–8 are satisfied, indeed so that 1–9 are satisfied.

If S wrongfully shoots another in a canyon and the sound of the shot causes an avalanche that maims or kills S, then this happens to S because of his wrong act but not because of the wrongness of the act. Since an act's moral qualities, qua moral qualities, seem to lack causal power, if something is to happen to someone because of the moral quality of his act, this must occur through another's recognition of that moral quality and response to it. Not every such response, even to wrongness, will count as retribution. If, on the cliff above, a witness sees the wrongful act and scrambles off to get forces of the law, thereby kicking loose some stones that cause an avalanche, the ensuing crushing of the killer still does not occur in retribution for his act. The conditions about intention are not satisfied. (Also, a more careful account than I offer here might use the notion of tracking rather than "because of.")

"Poetic justice" involves the wrongdoer's undergoing a consequence that appropriately could be visited upon him in retribution but which was not produced in that way, usually owing to the failure of one of the first two conditions of retribution. A system of karma, whereby the moral quality of acts produces effects automatically in (this or) another lifetime, is not a system of poetic justice. It is crucial to poetic justice that the (penalty) effect is not a result of the moral quality of the act, even though it appropriately would fit that moral quality. Thus, although very many poetically just things could occur, there could not be a system of poetic justice. The generality a system involves (supporting subjunctives about what would occur) could stem only from the (appropriate) effects being due to the moral quality of the acts, qua moral quality, and so the justice done would not be merely "poetic."

The conditions demarcating retribution explain what otherwise appears to be a ludicrous phenomenon. If someone sentenced to death falls perilously ill or is accidentally injured or attempts suicide the day before the scheduled execution, then the execution is postponed and measures are taken to bring the condemned person back to health so that he then can be executed. Although due-process reasons might be conjured up for this, I believe the reason is that his punishment is to involve something's being visited upon him by others because of the wrongness of his act. His death by natural causes or by his own hand would avoid this, so measures are taken to restore him for punishment. . . .

1. Let us leave it ambiguous for now how the theory is to be filled in, whether with a measure of harm or of wrongness (apart from the r factor), whether of what is done or is intended.

This r × H framework, going alongside a framework of compensation, was presented in Anarchy, State, and Utopia, pp. 59–63. I have since learned from reading George Fletcher's probing book Rethinking Criminal Law (Little, Brown, Boston, 1978) that continental legal systems embody this (or a very similar) structure, terming "r" attribution and "H" wrongdoing. The reader should examine Fletcher's book for his different answers to many of the questions we discuss here. The positions presented here were formulated and lectured on before I encountered Fletcher's book, but I will draw the readers' attention in footnotes to some of its differing positions.

On measures of the (perceived) moral wrongness of crimes, see S. S. Stevens, "A Metric for the Social Consensus," Science, Vol. 151, 1966, pp. 530–541; and T. Sellin and M. E. Wolfgang, The Measurement of Delinquency (Wiley, New York, 1964).
2. This will not be so for thieves who immediately are apprehended, the stolen good returned, but it may well hold of assaulters, for example. Even for the victims of those thieves, does simply getting their goods back leave them no worse off, including psychologically, than if they had not been stolen from at all?
3. For the subtleties of the biblical lex talionis, and the degree to which, from the beginning, it indicated compensation, see David Daube, Studies in Biblical Law (Cambridge University Press, 1947), ch. III, pp. 102–153.
4. I raise some problems for deterrence theories in Anarchy, State, and Utopia, pp. 61–62.

RETRIBUTIVISM:
A Test Case for Ethical Objectivity*

J. L. Mackie

I

In my *Ethics: Inventing Right and Wrong* I have argued that there is a real issue about the objectivity or subjectivity of moral principles and values, and I have tried to clarify this issue, which is often treated in a confused way, and to say what I take the central problem to be. I have also argued that neither objectivism nor subjectivism can be dismissed as incoherent, and neither view can be established merely by conceptual or linguistic analysis, or indeed by any other sort of *a priori* argument. To decide whether moral principles and values are objective or subjective in the important sense, we have to consider which view can be developed so as to provide the best overall explanation of all the relevant phenomena or data, all the moral (or related) "appearances" with which we are confronted. I would relate this question to what Hume, for example, says in Book III of the *Treatise*. I do not think that he has *shown* in any conclusive way by the end of Book III Part i that moral distinctions are not derived from "reason" and that they are derived from a "moral sense" or from "sentiment." Hume's case for these theses is still incomplete at this point. It is completed only when he has shown, by the end of Book III Part iii, how on a "sentimentalist" foundation he can develop a sociological and psychological explanation of both the "artificial" and the "natural" virtues, that is, can explain why these various dispositions occur and why they are cultivated and approved of in human society, fairly uniformly though with some variations.

An examination of retributivism will, I suggest, contribute usefully to this discussion. Many people seem to have moral intuitions of a retributivist sort. But are these genuine intuitions which reveal objectively valid moral principles or requirements, or are they rather expressions of sentiments for which we should seek, and can find, psychological or sociological or even biological explanations? I shall argue that purportedly objective retributivist *principles* cannot be defended, but that retributivist *sentiments*—deeply ingrained, highly developed and organized—can be readily understood.

It is becoming more common for philosophers to declare their adherence to the retributive theory of punishment. This may be understood as an offshoot of the widespread tendency to reject utilitarianism in favor of some view which takes as central such concepts as those of justice and rights. However, this adherence may go along with a very broad or loose account of what the retributive theory is. Thus Jeffrie G. Murphy says that "A retributive theory of punishment is one which characterizes punishment primarily in terms of the concepts of justice, rights, and desert— i.e. is concerned with the just punishment, the punishment the criminal deserves, the punishment society has the right to inflict (and the criminal has the right to expect)."[1] J. G. Cottingham, in an admirable recent article, finds among views which have been called retributivist at least nine distinct approaches, and almost as many distinct strategies for justifying punishment, not all of which would fall under Murphy's description, broad though it is.[2]

Cottingham's headings are as follows: Repayment Theory (that by being punished the criminal repays a debt to society); Desert Theory (which seems to reduce to the bald assertion that crime deserves punishment, that it simply is just that the offender should be punished); Penalty Theory and Minimalism (I shall say more about these two later); Satisfaction Theory (that punishment is justified by the satisfaction that it gives to the victim of the crime or to others who have been injured or outraged by it); Fair Play Theory (that failure to punish would be unfair to those who, unlike the criminal, have obeyed the rules, and so have forgone satisfactions or advantages that the criminal has gained by breaking them); Placation Theory (that a god who has been angered by, say, a murder must be placated by the execution of the murderer, or else he will go on being angry with the whole nation); Annulment Theory (that the punishment somehow cancels or annuls the crime); and Denunciation Theory (that punishment is justified as an emphatic denunciation of a crime).

These are certainly a mixed bag. Cottingham takes the notion of repayment of a debt as what is central in retributivism, and rightly complains that several of the approaches he has listed have little to do with this. But let me suggest a way of bringing some sort of order into this mass of ideas.

It is true that *retribuo* in Latin means "I pay back." But surely the central notion is not that the criminal repays a debt, pays something back to society, but that someone else pays the criminal back for what he has done. Punitive retribution is the repaying of harm with harm, as reward is the repaying of benefit with benefit. We can class as an essentially retributivist approach any that sees at least some *prima facie* rightness in the repaying of evil with evil, especially a proportionate evil, but returning no evil where no evil has been done. This entails that justifications of punishment are retributive in so far as they are retrospective. On the other hand, suggestions (which Cottingham mentions under Penalty Theory and Minimalism) that a previous wrong act is a merely logical or definitional requirement for something to count as punishment, not in any way a moral justification, would be better not counted as retributivist.

Approaches that count as retributivist in this sense of involving retrospective justification must, however, be further subdivided. One important division is between what I would call *positive* and *neg-*

ative retributivism. Positive retributivism sees the previous wrong act as in itself a reason for inflicting a penalty. The crime at least tends positively to justify a penalty; but it may or may not be held that the wrong act is in itself morally *sufficient* for the penalty, or that it absolutely requires the penalty, irrespective of all other considerations. Negative retributivism (for which "minimalism" may be another name) holds that those who are not guilty must not (that is, morally must not, not *logically cannot*) be punished, that the absence of a crime morally requires the non-infliction of a penalty. There is also a quantitative variant of negative retributivism, that even if someone is guilty of a crime it is wrong to punish him more severely than is proportional to the crime. And of course there is an analogous quantitative variant of positive retributivism, that a crime of a certain degree of wrongness positively calls for a proportionate penalty.

This distinction is important for at least two reasons. One is that once they are distinguished negative retributivism will be found to have a greater measure of general acceptance than positive retributivism. Many thinking people who hold firmly that it is morally wrong in itself to punish the innocent—not merely definitionally impossible—and also wrong in itself to punish the guilty beyond the degree of their guilt, are far less confident that a previous wrong act in itself, if considerations of deterrence and the like are clearly set aside, even tends to provide a positive justification of a penalty. People are often negative but not positive retributivists. The other reason is that if we try to develop and explain these various retributivist theses, the positive and negative ones seem to call for or to fit in with quite different lines of thought. For example, very general and obviously attractive principles about the rights of individuals or human rights provide immediate backing for the thesis that it is wrong to punish the innocent; but these take us no distance at all towards a positive reason for punishing the guilty just because they are guilty.

Even negative retributivism, however, is not without its problems, particularly if it is taken to include permissive clauses: you must not punish the innocent, but *you may punish the guilty;* you must not punish excessively, but *you may punish up to a proportionate degree*. These permissive clauses still do not assert positive retributivism, they do not say that wrong acts are positively a reason *for* imposing penalties; but they do say that wrong acts somehow cancel the basic reason for not imposing penalties; the guilty person loses his immunity in proportion to his guilt. Strictly, then, we should recognize permissive

retributivism as a third variety, intermediate between negative and positive. The three principles can be stated briefly as follows:

Negative retributivism: One who is not guilty must not be punished.

Permissive retributivism: One who is guilty may be punished.

Positive retributivism: One who is guilty ought to be punished. (This "ought" may vary in strength between indicating only a weak *prima facie* reason and asserting an absolute requirement.)

The "must not," "may," and "ought" in each of these is moral. Also, these are to be considered as principles, morally valid in their own right. Obviously, the same statements could occur as derived rules in, for example, a utilitarian theory, where they would be explained and justified by their beneficial consequences, but they would not then constitute any sort of retributivism. For completeness, we should add quantitative variants of each of these three principles. Once these complications have been introduced, some further explanation is certainly needed both for the quantitative version of negative retributivism and for both versions of the permissive view. However, I leave these problems aside; they are as nothing compared with the difficulties in positive retributivism.

So far I have been drawing mainly formal distinctions, and have thus isolated the general form of a positive retributivist thesis, that a wrong act in itself positively calls for the imposition of a (proportionate) penalty. But this is a very dark saying. *Why* should it be so? Is there any way in which we can make sense of this curious principle, at least by relating it to some network of other moral ideas?

It is here, as developments or explanations or further justifications of the positive retributivist thesis, that several of the approaches listed by Cottingham come in: repayment, satisfaction, fair play, placation, annulment, denunciation. "Desert" is not such a further explanation, but is just the general, as yet unexplained, notion of positive retributivism itself. But these (and one or two more that have been suggested, which Cottingham does not list) are a remarkably unimpressive collection. They are, indeed, the philosophical analogues of the sort of opponents that a chessplayer would like to have if he were going to play, blindfold, a dozen or so opponents at once. Each of them can be despatched, with ease, in a very few moves.

Satisfaction: What this might justify, if it justified anything, would seldom be proportional to the wrongness of the crime. It would entail severer penalties where the surviving victims of the crime were of a vindictive nature, but lighter ones where the victims were forgiving or "Christian" in spirit. It would entail the punishment of any behavior in proportion to its unpopularity, whether it was criminal or not. In any case, this is obviously a consequentialist justification: the penalty is being justified by the satisfaction it is likely to produce. Its connection with retributivism is merely that widespread satisfaction, felt by others besides the surviving victims of the crime, will be produced by the punishment of criminals only if many members of the society are already retributivists. But that does not make this itself a retributivist justification, and it has no power to explain any strictly retributivist principle.

Placation: This, too, is obviously consequentialist. The reason it offers for punishing rests upon the supposed bad consequences of failing to punish—the god will still be angry. But these consequences themselves depend upon the supposed retributivist opinions of the god in question. Far from explaining retributivism, this account requires that there should be some *other* morally adequate explanation of retributivism, if it is to be ascribed to a morally respectable god.

Denunciation: This also seems to be consequentialist. It has sometimes been called the "educative" theory of punishment. It tries to justify punishment by way of its tendency to produce in the public an attitude of greater hostility to the crime. This also, therefore, has no tendency to explain the retributivist principle, though, like satisfaction and placation, it may presuppose retributivist views. A public which already sees punishment as being deserved by the wrongness of the previous act is more likely to interpret a punishment as a dramatic assertion that the act punished was wrong.

These three approaches, then, are not really retributivist, though in one way or another they ride on the back of retributivism. Three others of the approaches listed, repayment, annulment, and fair play, do a little better in that they are genuinely retributivist in our sense. They are retrospective, non-consequentialist, because in each case the alleged justification is complete once the penalty has been inflicted; no further results of this are relied upon. But otherwise these approaches are equally unsatisfactory.

Repayment: How does the criminal's suffering or deprivation pay anything to society? No doubt repaying a debt often hurts the person who pays it, but

it does not follow that anything that hurts someone amounts to his repaying a debt. If Jones owes Smith $10, it will hurt Jones just as much if he has to throw $10 away as if he has to give it to Smith, but throwing it away will not repay the debt. If the criminal's suffering or deprivation or incarceration doesn't do any good to society, it cannot be the payment of a debt to society. So this account is simply incoherent unless it is transformed into a theory of reparations, which are not punishment, or into the satisfaction theory which, as we saw, is consequentialist and will not explain retributivism.

Annulment: This notion, as Cottingham says, goes back at least to Hegel. But the remark he quotes (". . . das Aufheben des Verbrechens, das sonst gelten würde, und die Wiederherstellung des Rechts") would be better translated as referring to "the annulment of the crime, which would otherwise *remain in force,* and the restoration of right." Hegel's idea seems to be that as long as a criminal goes scot-free, the crime itself still exists, still flourishes, but when the criminal is adequately punished the crime itself is somehow wiped out. It is not, therefore, by any sort of repayment or restitution that "right is restored," but just by trampling on the previously flourishing crime. But this notion is simply incoherent: there is no comprehensible way in which a penalty wipes out an otherwise still-existing crime. What makes this suggestion plausible is a confusion with deterrence and prevention. A penalty may help, by deterrence, to wipe out, not the past crime, but other similar crimes which, but for the deterrence, would be committed either by this same criminal or by others; that is, it may help to wipe out a criminal tradition or practice. Similarly, the locking up or killing of a criminal will put a temporary or a permanent stop to his criminal career. But in neither case is it the past crime that is annulled or wiped out, and deterrence and prevention are plainly consequentialist justifications, not retributivist ones.

Kant's remark that if the "last murderer" is not executed blood-guilt will adhere to the people, which Cottingham takes as an appeal to the placation theory, might be better understood as something like an anticipation of Hegel's notion of annulment. The guilt, the badness, of the crime is still floating around as long as the criminal is unpunished, and by letting him go free the people would share in this guilt as accessories after the act. But to suppose that this guilt is extinguished by the carrying out of the penalty requires the incomprehensible Hegelian notion of annulment, and to say that the people would be accessories if they did not punish the criminal presupposes, and therefore cannot explain, the principle that the crime in itself morally requires the penalty.

Fair play: Here the suggestion is that the various members of society are all in competition with one another, a competition governed by rules. The criminal has gained an unfair advantage by breaking the rules; to restore fairness this advantage must be taken away from him. Unlike our last two approaches, this one is not incoherent; it makes perfectly good sense in certain contexts. It has its clearest exemplification in the award of a penalty in football (soccer) when there has been a foul in the penalty area, that is, when a player or his shot has been illegally stopped in the neighborhood of the other side's goal. It is also retributivist in our basic sense of being retrospective; the justification is complete when the penalty has been imposed; fairness has then (roughly at least) been restored, irrespective of whether there are or are not any further desirable consequences. The trouble with this approach, however, is that it has little relation to most cases of punishment. Any serious attempt to apply it would lead to bizarre results, not at all well correlated with what is thought of as desert or degree of wrongness or guilt. It implies that penalties should as far as possible be proportional to the advantage that the criminal has gained, in the social competition, by breaking the rules, just as a foul near the opponents' goal is penalized much more than one elsewhere. Thus if a businessman has secured a contract worth $100,000, but has exceeded the speed limit in order to get to the relevant appointment on time, he should presumably be fined $100,000, whereas a fine of $1 would be enough for someone who murders a blind cripple to rob him of $1. And so on. Unsuccessful attempts at murder (or anything else) should not be punished at all. There should be an advantage rule, as there is in football, where the referee will not penalize an infringement if the innocent side still has the advantage anyway. So while there are things that this fair play principle can plausibly be used to justify, it has little bearing on most legal penalties and will not serve as an expansion or explanation of the basic principle of retribution or desert, of the idea that a wrong act in itself calls for a penalty proportionate to its degree of wrongness.

But perhaps it will be said that what matters is not the loot but the self-indulgence. Someone who commits a crime, even if he gets very little out of it, has still let himself go in a way that law-abiding people do not, and his punishment only brings him back into balance with their self-restraint. But when we switch to this topic of self-indulgence the analogy of a competitive game becomes even less apt. The ideal of equality in self-indulgence is so remote that we hardly even think of it. If it were unusual self-indulgence that we objected to and wanted to counterbalance, it would be the rich, the owners of yachts and racehorses, and businessmen with elastic expense accounts, that we should be getting after, not thieves and murderers. Again many murders arise out of domestic conflicts, and most of these only from long-standing problems. When people eventually kill their husbands or wives or lovers, they have probably already shown far more self-restraint, in not having so earlier, than those who are more happily or more placidly situated, and on the score of equality in restraint and indulgence would be entitled to let their hair down and kill someone once in a while.

What is basically wrong with the fair play approach, as these rather fantastic examples bring out, is that it focuses on the advantage that may have been gained by the criminal in some sort of social competition, whereas the point of punishment surely lies not in this but in wrongness of his act and the harm that he has done or tried to do. We can agree that he has acted unfairly, and that this implies that he cannot say that it is unfair if he suffers some proportionate penalty, if someone acts against him in a way that would otherwise have been similarly wrong. But this takes us only to a defence of permissive retributivism. It is still quite unclear how fairness *to the law abiding* is secured by the punishing of the law-breaker in itself, that is, unless this punishment secures some benefit for the law-abiding. So the fair play theory still fails to yield any defence of the principle of positive retributivism.

A suggestion not on Cottingham's list, which is often used to support retributivism, is that it peculiarly respects the dignity of persons on whom penalties may or may not be imposed. We can see the force of this as a support for negative retributivism, though it is an understatement to say only that someone's dignity has been invaded if, while innocent, he is made to suffer for the sake of some benefit to others. Again, it may help to explain permissive retributivism: someone's dignity is perhaps being respected if it is his own choice that cancels his immunity. Penalties which accord with negative and permissive retributivism do not invade anyone's basic area of freedom. But these considerations give no support whatever to positive retributivism once it has been clearly distinguished from the other two views. It is quite incomprehensible how punishing a person because he has done wrong respects or enhances his dignity. Even as an argument against retributivism's traditional rivals as positive justifications of punishment, deterrence and utilitarianism generally, this has force. At most it shows that there should be restrictions on the deterrent (etc.) use of punishment, and this is commonly agreed by utilitarians although they hold that deterrence and the like are the only positive reasons for punishing. The utilitarian view can be and usually is developed in a way that introduces the negative and permissive theses as derived rules. Positive retributivism cannot gain even a comparative advantage by this appeal to dignity.

An even stranger suggestion on the retributivist side is that the criminal has a right to be punished. In general a right is something that the right-holder can either exercise or waive as he chooses, and most criminals would gladly waive this alleged right. If one of them would not, it could only be either because he actually wanted the penalty for itself, and then it would not be a punishment, or because he was himself a very keen retributivist—but then this, as a moral explanation of retributivism, would be circular, like the theories of satisfaction and placation we considered earlier. An associated view is that the criminal wills his own punishment. This may be just the point already noted, that it is by his own choice that he has lost his immunity; but this supports only the negative and permissive theses, not the positive one. Alternatively, what is invoked here may be Rousseau's general will: the criminal, *qua* citizen, subscribes to and helps to make the universal law by an application of which he is punished. Where this is true, it will help to justify punishment, and may indeed justify positive retributivist theses as derived rules about the imposition of penalties. Once the validity of the universal law attaching a penalty to a crime is established, the only further justification needed to provide *some* positive reason for imposing the penalty in a particular case is the retrospective one that a crime of the relevant sort has been committed. But this—which is, perhaps, the core of what Cottingham calls the penalty theory—explains positive retributivism only as a working rule, not as a justifying principle in its own right. Everything depends on the prior validity of the universal law, and this, on the present approach, depends on the two questions, whether the general will has actually made the universal law that is being applied and whether it was reasonable for it to do so. Since all the arguments for the positive retributivist *principle* are so weak, an affirmative answer to the second of these questions would have either to invoke non-retributivist considerations, or to move to some non-objectivist point of view, or both.

II

And that, it seems, is that. Every one of these approaches fails completely to supply any coherent expansion or explanation of the retributivist principle, and, as far as I know, there are no others on offer. On the other hand it is plain that a considerable number of people have what would be called an intuition that a wrong action in itself calls for the infliction of suffering or deprivation on the agent. In fact we might go further than this. Many people, perhaps most people, find unsatisfactory what I might call the standard compromise position about punishment.

What I mean by the compromise position is this. Negative retributivism is explained as a consequence of the rights of innocent persons, and permissive retributivism on the ground that a non-innocent person has to some extent lost those rights: rights make sense within a system of reciprocal rights, so that someone who has violated the rights of others cannot fairly claim the corresponding rights for himself. This system of reciprocal rights may in turn be explained within, say, some kind of utilitarian theory, or again it may be put forward on its own. In either case, this line of thought brings us to the point that someone who has done wrong *may* be punished, though someone who has done no wrong must not. But—the compromise runs—the positive decision to punish is justified, if at all, by the benefits that are likely to result from so doing, for example, by way of the deterrence of crime. So we combine negative and permissive retributivism (themselves explained immediately in terms of rights, though *perhaps* also, more indirectly, in terms of utility) with a positive justification of penalties that appeals directly to utility.

This compromise looks neat, and has therefore commended itself to some philosophers. But I think that most people will, on reflection, find it unsatisfactory. They will not feel happy about imposing a penalty on someone for the sake of benefits to others, even if he has lost his right to immunity, unless they can say further that he positively deserves this penalty. Strange though this may be, we want to be able to appeal to a positive retributivist principle as well as to whatever utilitarian or in general consequentialist justifications there may be. Also, positive retributivism is not a completely isolated moral principle: it has a counterpart in the view that gratitude and reward are morally appropriate. We feel that someone who has helped another person deserves gratitude, and that someone who has done good generally, especially something outstanding good, deserves some reward. And he deserves a reward simply because of what he has done, not because rewarding him will bring about this or that good further consequence.

Indeed, we could go further still: our basic moral concepts themselves of good and bad, right and wrong, cannot be adequately analyzed unless we include a retributive element, the notion of returning benefit for benefit and harm for harm. What is bad or wrong, for example, is not simply what is harmful or what is forbidden: it is thought of also as what deserves condemnation, where condemnation is some kind of hostile and unpleasant reaction. Equally, what is good or right is not simply what is beneficial or what is recommended: it is thought of also as what deserves praise and commendation, what calls for a friendly and pleasant response.

Have we, then, been engaged in a vain and unnecessary task of trying to explain and justify positive retributivism? It is rather true merely by definition that what is wrong or bad deserves punishment and that what is right or good deserves reward? Is it part of the very concepts of wrong, bad, right, and good that they carry such deserts with them?

It would be a mistake thus to dismiss the problem. For even if it is part of these concepts that good and bad deserve reward and punishment, there is still the question whether and how those concepts themselves are to be justified or explained. For example, if the concept of something's being bad combines the notions of its being *harmful* and *forbidden* and *deserving a hostile response,* we still have the question why these three notions should go together, in particular why what is harmful and forbidden deserves a hostile response. That these elements go together is a synthetic judgment, even though the combination of them emerges from the analysis of *bad.*

Now as allegedly objective moral principles, this combination, and the corresponding combination of being *beneficial, recommended,* and *deserving of a favorable response,* are still quite obscure, though they are undoubtedly deeply entrenched in our thought. But as soon as we make the Humean move of saying that moral distinctions are founded on sentiment, not

on reason, the obscurity disappears. If we ask, not, "Why do wrong actions deserve penalties and good actions deserve reward?" but rather "Why do we have an ingrained tendency to see wrong actions as calling for penalties and good actions as calling for reward?" then it is not difficult to outline an answer.

First let us consider the tendency to feel and show gratitude for benefits, and its hostile counterpart, the tendency to feel and express resentment of injuries. There is no doubt that these are very widespread human dispositions, and what look like the same or similar tendencies are not difficult to detect in some non-human animals. Nor is there the slightest difficulty in understanding how such instinctive patterns of behavior, and feelings that harmonize with that behavior, could have developed by an evolutionary process of biological natural selection. Since gratitude will reward the benefactor, and since tendencies that are rewarded are thereby psychologically reinforced, gratitude will tend to encourage further similar benefactions, and so will benefit the creature that feels and displays gratitude. We are not, of course, saying (as Hobbes did) that what looks like gratitude is really egoistically calculated behavior aimed at encouraging future benefits. The feeling of gratitude may be and normally is straightforward, sincere, and non-calculating; it is, so to speak, the natural selection process that does the calculating, not the grateful agent himself. Thus uncalculating gratitude will be produced *because* of the benefits it is likely to bring, but the agent himself does not act gratefully *for the sake of* or *in anticipation of* those benefits. Similarly resentment of injuries is likely to discourage similar injuries, and so again will benefit the creature that feels and displays resentment, and thus there will be natural selection in favor of resentment, though again the resentment in the agent himself will normally be spontaneous, not calculated.

Gratitude, however, is a favorable reaction by a particular agent to actions that have benefited *him,* and resentment similarly is a hostile reaction by a particular agent to actions that have harmed *him.* Reward and punishment are more generalized forms of retribution: they are responses to actions that are seen as good or bad in general, not as good or bad to some particular agent, and the retributive attitudes which we have to explain are those of seeing the good or bad actions as calling for reward or punishment as such, not as calling for favorable or hostile reactions *from* particular agents. The attitudes to be explained, therefore, are generalizations of gratitude and resentment in these two respects: specific reference to those to whom good or harm has been done is eliminated, and the attitudes arise in persons generally who know about the good or harm, not only in those who are themselves benefited or harmed.

However, once we have explained gratitude and resentment, it is easy to understand these generalizations of them. Hume would say that such generalization arises from sympathy; but a sociological explanation would be better than this purely psychological one. Within a social group, people tend to feel and show gratitude and resentment on behalf of one another, in some respects at least, because they are reciprocally benefited by doing so. Cooperation in resentment and gratitude grows up for the same reason that gratitude itself does, that it tends to be beneficial to each of the cooperators. This may be either an instinctive tendency, to be explained by biological natural selection, or a cultural trait or "meme," to be explained by a process of social evolution that is an analogue of biological selection. In saying this, we must guard against three errors. First, we are not saying that this cooperation is calculating from the point of view of the cooperators themselves: they feel genuine sympathy, righteous indignation, and the like. But they have come to feel in these ways as a result of some biological or social selective process in which the benefits of such cooperation has played a key role. But, secondly, we are not saying that this cooperation in gratitude and resentment has arisen because of its general utility, because the social group as a whole has been benefited by it. No doubt the group is benefited, but that would not in itself be a good explanation. A practice which *would* be socially useful may fail to arise; it is unlikely to arise unless it produces results which favor its own spreading and surviving, unless it works so as to propagate the genes or "memes" on which it depends; and in general this requires that it should benefit the individuals who engage in that practice. But cooperation in gratitude and resentment meets this requirement: it can grow up as a convention which in fact benefits all parties, even without being deliberately adopted for that purpose. However, thirdly, it is just not the case that all sorts of gratitude and resentment are generalized equally. Only some kinds of harm are socially, cooperatively, resented, and cooperation in gratitude is even more restricted. Again we must seek and can find sociological reasons for these differences: only with particular kinds of harm are the conditions favorable for the growth of a convention of cooperative hostility to them, so only some kinds of harm are seen as wrong and as calling for general resentment and punishment. For example, theft is cooperatively resented, but commercial competition is not.

In conclusion, therefore, I maintain that it is easy to understand why we have a deeply ingrained tendency to see wrong actions as calling for penalties and some sorts of good actions as calling for reward. Though retributive principles cannot be defended, with any plausibility, as allegedly objective moral truths, retributive attitudes can be readily understood and explained as sentiments that have grown up and are sustained partly through biological processes, and partly through analogous sociological ones.

That is why I have, in the title of this paper, called retributivism a test case for ethical objectivity. On objectivist assumptions, its force and its persistence are incomprehensible, but on a subjectivist or (in Hume's sense) sentimentalist approach they are easily understood.

---

1. *Jeffrie G. Murphy, in "Cruel and Unusual Punishments," to appear in the proceedings of the 1979 Conference of the Royal Institute of Philosophy on Law and Morality.*

2. *J. G. Cottingham, "Varieties of Retribution,"* Philosophical Quarterly, *July 1979.*

GETTING EVEN:
The Role of the Victim*

Jeffrie G. Murphy

*Not if his gifts outnumbered the sea sands
or all the dust grains in the world could
Agamemnon
ever appease me—not till he pays me back
full measure, pain for pain, dishonor for
dishonor.*

Iliad (IX. 383–386)

I. Introduction[1]

Achilles is vindictive; he wants to get even with Agamemnon. Being so disposed, he sounds rather like
many current crime victims who angrily complain that
the American system of criminal justice will not allow
them the satisfactions they rightfully seek. These victims often feel that their particular injuries are ignored
while the system addresses itself to some abstract injury to the state or to the rule of law itself—a focus
that appears to result in wrongdoers being treated
with much greater solicitation and respect than their
victims receive. If the actual victims are noticed at all
(other than to alert the state to a violation of *its* inter-
csts), they will likely be told that there is another
branch of law—tort law—that has the job of dealing
with private injuries and grievances and that, if they
pursue this route at their own expense, they might
ultimately get some financial compensation for the
wrongs done to them. However, just as Achilles felt
that mere compensation was inadequate to the kind
of injury done to him by Agamemnon, many of these
victims will often claim that the injuries they have suffered (brutal rape, perhaps) do not admit of financial
compensation. How, they might ask, can a dollar
value be set on the humiliation and degradation they
have experienced? They might also note that those

who injure them tend, unlike Agamemnon, to be judg-
ment-proof—so lacking in resources as to be unable
to make any meaningful contribution to any compensation package that the victim may win. From such a
perspective and from such feelings has the "victims'
rights movement" in part been born.[2]

In this essay I will address simply *one* of the
many issues raised by this movement—namely, the
issue of the legitimacy of hatred and desires for revenge as operative values in a system of criminal law.
It is widely assumed—as a part of liberal culture,
particularly Christian liberal culture—that such psychological states are either unambiguously evil or unambiguously sick and that, in either case, they deserve
no place in the moral and legal outlook of civilized
people. Thus opponents of the victims' rights movement will often characterize it as simply the institutionalization of vindictiveness—where such a
characterization is supposed to serve as a *reductio ad
absurdum* of the movement. Proponents of the movement will then generally take great pains attempting
to show that the movement is *not* based on these admittedly evil feelings but on something else—social
utility or justice, perhaps. Thus, both sides seem to
agree that if the movement is indeed based on these
feelings and the desire to institutionalize them, then
the movement is a mistake.

Since I am skeptical that this agreement is justified, I will in this essay attempt to do two things: (1) I
will suggest that the burden of proof should be placed
on those who in principle *oppose* hatred, vindictiveness and revenge—that someone other than the
champions of these responses should be put on the
defensive for a change; and (2) I will suggest that this
burden might not be as easy to bear as some might

*From Jeffrie G. Murphy, "Getting Even: The Role of the
Victim," in *Social Philosophy and Policy*, vol. 7, issue 2 (1990), pp. 209–225. Reprinted by permission of Blackwell
Publishers.

initially think. My purpose is neither to celebrate hatred and its close cousins nor to argue positively that this feeling and its associated practices should be built into the criminal law. I rather seek to expose some bad arguments against it and its institutionalization (but also to highlight some important arguments against it) in the hope that its possible role—and indeed the whole victims' rights movement—can be seen in a clearer and fairer light.

II. Who Has the Burden of Proof?

As a starting point in inquiry, I am inclined to accept what might be called a bias or presumption in favor of common sense—namely, that absent some good argument to make us withdraw our common-sense beliefs and attitudes, we should regard them as reasonable. We should not always feel obligated to defend our ordinary views, but should rather impose the burden of challenge on others—being honestly willing, of course, to abandon the comfort of the received wisdom if we are indeed provided with good arguments for so doing. The underlying assumption behind this bias or presumption can, I think, partly be understood in (loosely) evolutionary terms. Our ordinary views and attitudes must, at least at one time, have had *something* going for them—some useful and adaptive contact with our social world or with the world of nature. Otherwise, it would be hard to see why these beliefs and attitudes would survive and be so deeply entrenched in our psyches. Of course, some beliefs and attitudes that might have been adaptive at some distant time in our evolutionary history (e.g., racist beliefs and attitudes, perhaps) can properly be seen in present circumstances as maladaptive, irrational, and evil. But we come to see this, I assume, not because this was always obviously so (it clearly was *not*), but because we have listened to and been persuaded by overwhelming practical and moral arguments for a change in these beliefs and attitudes. Such an example, however, does not demonstrate the unreasonableness of a presumption in favor of common sense any more than the confident conviction of some guilty people demonstrates the unreasonableness of the presumption of innocence in criminal procedure.

In my role as armchair, anecdotal social scientist, I have come to the conclusion that most of us *do* accept, as a matter of common sense, the appropriateness of hatred and revenge in some circumstances—specifically, when these responses are exhibited by victims of serious wrongdoing and are directed against those who have wronged them. (In *Forgiveness and Mercy,* I call this "retributive hatred."[3]) Although most people pay a kind of general Sunday school lip service to the idea that even these hatreds are evil, their more casual conversations and practices will often fly in the face of these pious clichés. Give them the right criminal (e.g., John Mitchell for Watergate era liberals) and they will warm to shared fantasies of giving that criminal his "pain for pain, dishonor for dishonor." This also comes out rather clearly in people's entertainment preferences. For example, I recently resaw (with some equally civilized and equally liberal friends) the movie *Silverado*. In this classy Western, we are presented with four honest and decent men (and their friends and families) being subjected to unspeakable injuries by thugs of unspeakable evil. When, in the closing moments of the movie, these men take—and, indeed, *gleefully* take—their violent revenge on those who have wronged them, all who watched cheered them on and found this outcome not only aesthetically pleasing but morally satisfying. And I think that the vast majority of other normal people would have experienced a comparable reaction—otherwise, how could we explain the great popularity of revenge entertainment? We like to see the portrayal of evil people getting their painful but just deserts, and we particularly enjoy it when these deserts are administered by their victims. Portrayals are, of course, fiction and fantasy—and many of those who approve of the fictional portrayal of revenge might still have deep and even final objections to having it occur in the real world. (Perhaps, for example, they believe that we are never actually able to know that we confront the kind of genuine evil that is simply a given in the world of fiction—that, unlike The Shadow, we are unable to know what evil lurks in the hearts of men.) But this is a practical objection; it makes no contribution to establishing that all feelings of hatred and revenge are intrinsically, or inherently, or in principle irrational or immoral. Feelings that we genuinely regard as inherently depraved (e.g., racial hatred) we would not even welcome as fantasy or fiction; thus, I think, we would have great doubts about a person who applauded the fictionally portrayed successes of a Nazi deathcamp commandant— even if he followed up his entertainment by saying "But, of course, I would hate to see this happen in the real world." Thus I think that most typical, decent, mentally healthy people have a kind of commonsense approval of some righteous hatred and revenge (but not of simply unprovoked malicious hatred or racial hatred) and are in some sense willing publicly to admit this, at least symbolically—e.g., they will stand without shame in line to see such revenge movies as *Silverado,* but not to see a film that glorifies racial hatred.

So perhaps we can grant that those who are willing to take the trouble to present a case in favor of some hatreds and acts of revenge are really seeking not to challenge but simply to reinforce common sense—that most people, even if unwilling to provide verbal endorsement of such a view, do in fact find it acceptable in principle for victims to resent and hate those who wrong them and to seek revenge against those who victimize them.[4] (Perhaps Christianity's victory over pagan common sense here is largely verbal.) But, if this is so, then it looks as though we have the beginnings of an argument for the institutionalization of these feelings—an argument from *democracy.* For what is a democracy except a form of government in which the majority gets to have its dominant preferences enacted into law—even if those preferences are condemned by a refined and condescending elite? Thus, if most people want to create a system of criminal law that institutionalizes and expresses the hatreds and desires for revenge that crime victims feel toward those who have wronged them, what principle would allow anyone to say nay to the will of the people thus expressed?

This principle, perhaps: that the fundamental rights of citizens may not be abridged even when the majority so desires. Such a principle defines a *constitutionally constrained* democracy (as opposed to a pure democracy) and characterizes the kind of democracy at least theoretically present in the United States. Thus, since one of the presupposed principles of this society is that the government may not treat people (even criminals) in brutally inhuman ways, the United States Constitution imposes (in the Eighth Amendment) an absolute ban on such "cruel and unusual" punishments as torture.[5] This ban is not to be seen as an expression of the will of the people; it is rather a principled check, an absolute side-constraint, on what the people will be *allowed* to will.

I think that this constitutional excursion dramatically reinforces the point I want to make about burden of proof here. We may, I think, regard American society as one in which the majority may do whatever it jolly well feels like *unless* one can demonstrate that what it feels like doing is *fundamentally wrong in principle.* (I take it that the Bill of Rights seeks to provide an initial—but not a final—analysis of what it means to say that a governmental act is fundamentally

wrong in principle.) To use my earlier language: the presumption is that the will of the majority should determine policy, and thus the burden of proof lies upon those who—for any majoritarian outcome—would seek to prevent it. My question, then, is this: can it be shown to be fundamentally wrong in principle for the suffering that criminals receive from the state to be contingent to any degree on hatreds and desires for revenge felt by their victims? Do criminals have a fundamental right to be shielded from the consequences of such feelings? Since I think I have shown that it is not obvious that they do (and that, in fact, people, tend to believe quite the contrary), those who would argue for the irrelevance or injustice of those feelings and their institutionalization should do just that—namely, *argue.* They have the burden of proof. I will thus now begin to explore what these arguments might be and the degree to which, if at all, they are successful.

III. Making the Case Against Hatred and Revenge

Those who condemn hatred and revenge can avail themselves of two different strategies of argument. They can argue (1) that the emotions involved in these responses are inherently irrational (like phobias) or inherently evil (like sadism or unprovoked malice). Or they can argue (2) that, whatever the merits of the emotions themselves (even assuming they are intrinsically splendid), it would either be unwise or wrong in principle for these emotions to have any effect on the administration of criminal punishment. (Some—e.g., Kant—have reasoned this way about compassion and mercy—suggesting that compassion, though a splendid and admirable emotion in itself and often productive of wonderful results in other contexts, may produce excessive acts of mercy—and thus undermine justice—if too influential on judges or those with the power of pardon.[6]) While (1) is my primary interest in this paper, it is so frequently tied in with (2) that I think it will be worthwhile to discuss and evaluate them both in the present context.

IV. The Rational Case Against Hatred

Surely hatred cannot be regarded as irrational simply because it is an emotion. Emotions (e.g., guilt, shame, fear, envy, jealousy, hatred, love, and compassion) are not like mere sensations (e.g., headaches): one sign of this is that we can speak sensibly of irrational emotions but not of irrational headaches or other sensations. (What is a phobia except an irrational fear? And what would it mean to call some fears irrational unless it makes sense to refer to others as rational?) Of course we sometimes speak of people themselves as being irrational if they allow emotions to dominate their personalities to an excessive degree—e.g. Spinoza's point about a rational person being one who is not *led* by a fear of death.[7] But is there any good reason to assume that hatred and desires for revenge are uniquely able to dominate or lead in a way that other emotions are not? Consider the character of Michael Kohlhaas in von Kleist's famous story.[8] Why will so many people say of a character such as Kohlhaas that he was overcome, or dominated by, or in the thrall of vindictiveness—but would not tend to describe (for example) Mother Teresa as overcome, or dominated by, or in the thrall of compassion? (Is this anything more than a misleading way of noting that one likes compassion and does not like vindictiveness? Is a moral point masquerading as a psychological point and a question thereby being begged?) The literature of hatred and revenge does, of course, tend to portray these responses carried to a pathological extreme, but this may tell us more about what makes literature interesting than anything basic about human psychology. (What a boring story it would have been had Kohlhaas simply beaten up a couple of people and taken his horses back.) Surely *any* emotion can be carried to a pathological extreme; does not the fact that we can identify pathological extensions of retributive hatred (e.g., Michael Kohlhaas's) suggest that there must be non-pathological instances of this emotion? And must this emotion have an inevitable tendency to provoke excessive behavior—as it did for Kohlhaas? What if the person is provoked by this emotion to seek only a level of revenge that we, on other grounds (utility or justice), would find acceptable? Are there no such people? Are all people who seek revenge really after consequences so extreme and socially disruptive that we must regard them as crazed? (It is, of course, question-begging to say that these feelings are irrational simply because they often prompt people such as Kohlhaas to act outside the law. For perhaps these feelings prompt people to illegality only because we, not learning the lesson of Athena and the Furies, have refused to make a proper home for them and institutionalize them into the legal system.) And consider Nietzsche's famous argument

against *resentiment* (a kind of hatred)—namely, that it tends to poison a person from within.[9] But why, according to Nietzsche, does it so poison? It is because it is *repressed;* thus, Nietzsche's point argues equally for getting rid of the emotion *or for expressing it*—e.g., through getting even.

We might, of course, regard an emotion as irrational if it lacks any point or purpose that we can understand or with which we can sympathize. John Rawls argues in this way, for example, about the emotion of (malicious) envy. For what is the point, Rawls asks, of simply desiring that another lose some benefit when that benefit was not wrongfully acquired and when the benefit, when lost, will not transfer to the malicious envier?[10] Although I think that Rawls's position is not without problems, I will for present purposes grant it. Analogous arguments will not obviously condemn retributive hatred as irrational, however, since this emotion (with which, I have already argued, most of us sympathize) often has as its point the desire to annul (perceived) wrongful gains and to give people their (perceived) just deserts—in short, to "get even" through revenge. That, and not something further, is its point. Unless the desire to bring about these states of affairs is itself always wrong or irrational, then surely the emotion of retributive hatred—as a desire to bring them about—cannot be condemned as pointless and thus as irrational. (One would surely not want to give as one's argument against retributive hatred an appeal to some notion of pointlessness that would, if accepted, refute all deontological considerations in ethics.) But is revenge acceptable? I will explore this question in the final section of the paper, but it would, of course, beg the question simply to assume at this point that it is not.

The above considerations suggest to me that it is going to be very difficult to make a case that hatred (as a desire for revenge) is inherently irrational—the moral equivalent of a phobia. Though obviously (because by definition) pathological extensions of this emotion will not be present in a rational person, a lesser degree might well play some roles in the psyches of rational and healthy people—e.g., prompting them to seek restitution for injuries, liberating them from the bondage of resentment (through getting even), maintaining their self-respect, and even (by making themselves known as disposed to revenge) warding off some aggressors who might otherwise challenge their security and invade their "moral space." Thus if a case is to be made against the emotion of retributive hatred itself, the case will have to be *moral*—a case that the emotion, however rational it may be in some prudential or therapeutic sense for the person who experiences it, is still evil and would not be present in a truly virtuous person. It is to this moral case that I will now turn.

V. The Moral Case Against Hatred

The idea that hatred and desires for revenge are evil dispositions of character is linked, in our Christian culture, to the idea that these dispositions are *sinful*. God, through Jesus Christ, commands that we love and forgive our enemies rather than seek from them the "eye for an eye" that was characteristic of the older law.[11] If somebody embraces the Christian religion (so interpreted), then such a person does have—in my view—a sufficient moral reason to regard hatred as a vice and all acts based upon it as evils. All argument on the issue could thus stop here, as arguments have a way of doing when they collide with total faith.

My present inquiry, however, is this: does the moral case against retributive hatred essentially depend upon such faith or can a case that does not depend upon religious belief—a purely secular case—be made? I think that such a case may be possible and, indeed, that it might be possible even to draw a large part of the case from a secular interpretation of some Christian parables. This should not be surprising, since many Christians wish to regard their God as a supremely rational being. If so, He presumably did not command love and forgiveness of enemies capriciously (e.g., He did not flip a coin to get this command) but rather knew that such dispositions were of some benefit to us, His creatures. But if God had good reasons for issuing these commands, it is not impossible that we—with our reason—could discover at least part of the case that prompted Him and see its good moral sense for ourselves.

Consider, with this in mind, the story of Jesus at the stoning of the adulteress (there cautioning the crowd to "Let him who is without sin cast the first stone").[12] Think of this story in conjunction with the famous passage, *"Vengeance is mine; I will repay, saith the Lord."*[13] Consider also the parable of the unforgiving servant.[14]

The fact that God reserves vengeance for Himself suggests that, in His view, the desire for vengeance is not an inherently irrational (or even inherently evil) disposition of character. (Otherwise, God would be condemning Himself.) It is rather that He has reasons for claiming that the disposition to

vengeance is a uniquely divine prerogative. What might these reasons be? Presumably they are that only God *knows enough* and only God is *good enough* to seek vengeance reliably and without hypocrisy. His creatures lack these epistemological and moral qualifications; they must therefore wait and depend upon God to get the job done.[15] Thus these scriptural passages can be interpreted to mean that human beings, given their radical limitations, always manifest vices—specifically, the vices of *presumption* and *hypocrisy*—if they have and indulge feelings of retributive hatred.

Is this claim plausible? Are we too ignorant to be reliable retributive haters? Are we ourselves too morally flawed to hate, without hypocrisy, those who wrong us? Let us consider each of these questions separately.

What is it that we are unable to know about wrongdoers that poses no problem for God? We surely know what *acts* are unacceptable, and thus perhaps the problem is supposed to lie in some lack of ability we have in knowing the *mental states* and *dispositions of the will* present in wrongdoers. Kant, for example, claims that only God can "know the heart"; given his view that moral condemnation is addressed to the inner disposition of will, he argues (in his *Religion,* but not elsewhere) that human ignorance of such matters precludes the acceptability of the kind of harsh condemnation of others that legitimately hating them would involve.[16]

I think that this argument is important—one that should make us (as I stress in great detail in the book) *very cautious* of what we do in this area—but I am not convinced that it makes a fatal case against the moral legitimacy of all retributive hatred. For Kant is well known as being (to put it mildly) in favor of punishment; given his commitments to justice, he would want to condemn strenuously a system of punishment that employed only strict liability. This means, of course, that he would (like us) want a system of criminal liability that involves *mens rea,* excuse, and justification. But such a system can be administered only if, *in some sense,* we *can* "read the heart." Thus those who would make flip arguments against retributive hatred based upon some supposed inability to determine the appropriate inner dispositions should note the massive (and certainly unwelcome) reforms in the criminal law—and perhaps in our whole moral conception of personal responsibility—that would flow from the literal acceptance of such a slogan.

So too, I think, for those who would make an overly ambitious use of the important insight that each one of us is morally flawed ("Let him who is without sin. . .") and often stands in need of some gentle response, such as forgiveness from others (a point of the parable of the unforgiving servant). For such things are in fact, of course, matters of degree. That I have certain vices (a certain lack of generosity, perhaps) does not mean that I ever have or ever would even contemplate treating another human being in the way that Michael Kohlhaas was treated by those who wronged him, or in the way that some rape victims are brutalized by their attackers. Thus it seems that although I may not be utterly without sin, I may well be without sin *in the relevant sense* in some cases. And why may I not, without hypocrisy, indulge retributive hatred in these cases? John Rawls has taught us the useful device in ethics of imagining ourselves in all possible roles that will be affected by the moral rules we adopt. As one who may sometimes need the love and forgiveness of others, I will of course want a world where retributive hatred does not reign unchecked. But as someone who may sometimes want to get even for terrible wrongs done to me, I might not want to create a social world wherein desires for revenge are utterly condemned—regarded as, in themselves, signs of irrationality or vice.

Finally, there is the argument from moral equality. According to this argument (often appealed to by Christians), all human beings are of equal moral worth—perhaps even absolute moral worth—and are to be equally loved, because it is both irrational and immoral for any one of these creatures to rule any of his equals outside the domain of benevolent concern—as hatred certainly does. (In religious terms, this Kantian point might be made by saying that we are all children of God and equally beloved in His sight; that God's perspective should then be adopted in our own dealings with our fellow humans.) To this argument I have the following response: that all human beings (no matter how morally vile) are to be loved strikes me as a claim whose *intrinsic implausibility* is staggering. Thus, I can imagine no reason for taking such a claim seriously unless one views it as a command of God—i.e., one therefore has an *extrinsic* reason for taking it seriously. Here, then, we perhaps have a good example of an ethical issue where a secular world view leads us in one direction and the Christian world view leads us in quite another—perhaps dashing any hasty optimism (present, I think, in some strands of liberal Christianity) about the ultimate compatibility or reconciliation of the two.[17]

I conclude from the above that the case against the rationality and morality of the emotion I have labeled retributive hatred has not been made. Thus, I think that we may properly retain our common-sense belief that this feeling is sometimes acceptable—and sometimes even laudable. Those of us who want to retain the concept of genuine evil—in discussing the Holocaust perhaps—the perpetrators of which merit hatred are not yet defeated. As noted earlier, however, this does not establish that it is ever permissible for us to *act* on such feelings or that the law should ever assist us in so acting. Desires for revenge are one thing; acts of revenge are quite another. Thus I shall now move to a consideration of the permissibility of revenge itself.

VI. The General Case Against Revenge and Its Role in Criminal Law (Especially Sentencing)

By "revenge," I will mean any injury inflicted on a wrongdoer that satisfies the retributive hatred felt by that wrongdoer's victim and that is justified because of that satisfaction.[18] I here assume again (for the reasons earlier noted) that the burden of argument lies on those who would oppose the legitimacy of revenge, and I assume that the arguments given will (like all arguments in ethics) be either consequentialist arguments or arguments of principle.[19] I also believe that the really impressive and important arguments will be those of the latter sort.

Why might revenge be disutilitarian—wrong on consequentialist grounds? The most common thing said against it is that it is socially disruptive—it is likely to provoke an unpredictable and destabilizing level of conflict. But this argument, of course, seems most impressive as an argument against *private* revenge—vigilante activity—and, if this is the only argument, really supports rather than undermines the claim that revenge ought to be institutionalized by the state: that is, that the state, taking on the personae of crime victims, should elevate (at least some of) the private grievances of individuals to the status of public grievances. If revenge is not intrinsically evil or wrong in principle, why should its public expression not be justified by these two consequences: (1) the satisfaction given to victims and (2) the resulting tendency to defuse the potentiality for private revenge and its resulting social turmoil?[20] (This does not mean that the state should take on all desires for revenge—some are excessive—but it does suggest reasons why the state might take on some of them.) And consider the standard utilitarian value of deterrence: might not potential criminals be given an extra incentive to remain law-abiding if they know that they live in a system where victim outrage (or, in murder cases, survivor outrage) might have a bearing on their level of punishment?[21]

The above considerations suggest that the purely utilitarian or consequentialist case against the institutionalization of revenge is going to be fragile. Some utilitarian arguments will tell against the practice, and others will tell in its favor; an impartial observer might well conclude that the latter arguments, on balance, win the day. This is, of course, often the case with utilitarian arguments on complex issues; we often, after all, lack the kind of hard empirical evidence that would be needed really to establish the probability of the claimed consequences. We thus often run the risk of lapsing into anecdotes and hunches that are often tailored to the outcome we want to justify. For this reason, those who want a *fatal* argument to block the institutionalization of revenge had better attempt an argument from principle, for one great virtue of such arguments is that they are invulnerable to the shifting winds of empirical guesswork.

Are there good arguments that institutionalized revenge is wrong in principle? I think that there are two that must be taken very seriously:

1. *The argument from retributive justice.* "All criminals have a fundamental right not to be punished in excess of their just deserts. A person is punished in excess of his just deserts if he is punished with greater severity than the blameworthy character of his conduct would justify. A person cannot coherently be held blameworthy for the degree to which he is hated by those he wrongs (very blameworthy for injuring thin-skinned victims and minimally blameworthy for injuring stoic victims?), and thus any criminal sentencing that takes account of victim hatred (as any revenge system would have to do) violates a fundamental right, is unjust, and is thus wrong in principle."

2. *The argument from equal protection and due process.* "All criminals have a fundamental right to be protected against sentencing procedures that are inherently arbitrary and capricious. Sentencing systems based on victim hatred will inevitably have this feature and are thus wrong in principle."

These are very important arguments. (They were also the essential arguments at issue in the 1987 United States Supreme Court case of *Booth* v. *Maryland*—a case, regarded by many as a major setback to the victims' rights movement, holding that victim impact statements may not influence sentencing in capital cases.[22]) I take these arguments seriously, and I would like to consider them with some care. I will consider them in reverse order.

VII. The Argument from Equal Protection and Due Process

The best argument that revenge systems are inherently arbitrary and capricious lies in the fact that retributive hatred—the basis for such systems—is essentially a *subjective* response to being wronged; as such, it can vary enormously from one victim to the next. Thus, the very same injury that will be brushed off as trivial by those with a stoic disposition will generate anguish and deep hatred in the highly sensitive. Also, the level of hatred involved might well be a function of factors about the criminal that any reasonable person would regard as clearly irrelevant to culpability— e.g., the white rape victim who feels more deeply wronged if raped by a black person than if raped by a white person. If fairness requires that potential criminals receive accurate notice of the exact nature of the proscribed conduct and its attached penalties, it is hard to see how such notice could be given in a system where sentencing might actually depend upon factors that admit of such wide and subjective variation.[23] And if criminals have a right to be protected against mere prejudice (e.g., racial hatred), it might seem difficult if not impossible to give them this protection in a hate-based system, since hatreds often are a function of prejudices. I am by no means sure that it would not be possible to design procedures that would keep arbitrary and capricious sentencing at an acceptable level—i.e., at a level no greater than that already present and accepted at other points in the system—but we have at last found a principled objection to revenge that cannot simply be summarily dismissed. Those who look fondly upon revenge have an obligation to take this objection very seriously—i.e., seriously enough to recognize that the burden of argument may now have been properly shifted back to them and to take on the burden of formulating procedures to control these potential abuses. Of course, if it can be shown that criminals have a fundamental right to be sentenced in proportion to personal blameworthiness and that revenge is inconsistent with such a right, then we have the basis for an absolute ban on revenge (an absolute ban on its institutionalization) regardless of procedure. The procedural argument is thus secondary to what I have called "the argument from retributive justice," and it is to this most important argument that I shall now turn.[24]

VIII. The Argument from Retributive Justice

In *Booth* v. *Maryland* Justice Powell, writing for the majority, held that victim impact statements (VISs) are constitutionally impermissible in capital sentencing. Such statements—or actual testimony by victims if they are allowed to attend and speak at sentencing hearings—are very likely, according to Powell, to influence judges (or juries in states where juries have a sentencing role) to inflict cruel and unusual punishments. Their use and influence thus violates the Eighth Amendment.[25]

Powell essentially gives two arguments to support this view. One argument (a procedural one of the kind explored above) is that emotional appeals from attractive and articulate victims are likely to focus the judge's attention away from the legally relevant issues and produce arbitrary and capricious sentencing.[26] More fundamental than this procedural argument, however, is Powell's articulation of the principle that, in his view, defines what *is* legally relevant. Speaking essentially as a retributivist, Powell claims that criminal defendants in capital cases have a right that their sentence be solely a function of their personal *blameworthiness*—i.e., factors solely based on "the character of the individual and the circumstances of the crime" or on the defendant's "personal responsibility and moral guilt." Since VIS information may be, according to Powell, wholly unrelated to the blameworthiness of a particular defendant, and may cause the sentencing decision to turn on irrelevant factors such as the degree to which the victim's family is able to articulate grief and defend the victim's worth, such evidence will inevitably and improperly shift the focus away from the defendant and what he deserves. The essence of the argument, then, is this: sentencing should be based on what is morally blameworthy about the defendant; one is blameworthy only for that which is one's fault or which one brings about under one's own control; the degree to which a victim will be upset or outraged by what is done to him or will be

able to articulate feelings is subjective and variable; it is thus not within the defendant's control; therefore, it would be wrong in principle to let sentencing depend to any degree on such matters.

Given the wide variety of penal purposes that are often articulated by judges in sentencing (see, for example, Judge Frankel's well-known sentencing opinion in *U.S.* v. *Bergman*[27]), it is odd that Powell should only emphasize the one retributive purpose of making suffering proportional to blameworthiness. (I will, for present purposes, ignore the special problems posed by the fact that *Booth* is a capital case, since I am interested in victim revenge and VISs in general.) We know that judges—both in sentencing and in approving plea-bargain agreements—typically weigh such factors as jail crowding, likelihood of recidivism, impact on the defendant's family, the defendant's age and health, possible service the defendant might perform for the community, the need for special and general deterrence, the need for incapacitation, and the possibility of reform; none of these having any obvious connection with moral blameworthiness or any other valid retributive purpose. It is hard to see, if this long laundry list of (perhaps laudable) social and personal goals properly gets to play a role in sentencing, why it would be wrong in principle to find room for VISs as well.

Consider also the major (and, no doubt, quite unwelcome) reforms in the criminal law that a literal application of the moral blameworthiness principle would entail. As Justices Scalia and White noted in their dissents in *Booth,* we currently feel comfortable with making the penalty for successful murder more severe than that for an attempted murder that fails through a fortuity; yet it is obvious that the moral blameworthiness in the two cases is identical. We also punish reckless driving that kills much more severely than reckless driving *simpliciter;* yet, as Thomas Nagel would say, it is surely differences in "moral luck" rather than any differences in moral blameworthiness that distinguish the two cases.[28] Thus a decision to endorse some strong blameworthiness principle will not be cost-free; for it will force us to ignore other important factors—e.g., *harm* caused—that have typically been thought to be central to criminal liability. And with respect to the other factors, it is by no means obvious that VISs will be utterly irrelevant to them. For example: can the victim's personal response to the person who violated him tell us *nothing* about the degree of harm suffered? Is the revenge interest present in the victim worthy of no attention in a world where (for example) the community's supposed interest in service that the defendant might perform is regarded as relevant? All of this needs to be thought about much more deeply.[29]

But perhaps blameworthiness should be viewed simply as a *negative* retributive constraint on permissible punishment—a factor that sets an upper bound on the degree to which the state may legitimately pursue its other interests in punishing (e.g., crime deterrence). This might solve, for example, the puzzle about attempts. For even if attempters and succeeders have the same degree of blameworthiness, the state might have good reasons for punishing attempters less severely; no wrong will be done in such a system so long as the succeeders are not punished in excess of their just deserts understood as a function of their moral blameworthiness.

If we accept this weakened notion of retributivism, however, it is hard to see how this will form a principled objection to the institutionalization of victim revenge and the use of VISs. For, on this view, why not simply allow these factors to have influence—perhaps to counter sentimental tendencies to show mercy or make plans for community service—so long as their influence is capped off at the point when maximum just deserts for the offense is reached? This would, of course, simply be to restate Stephen's point: respect victim hatred and revenge, but institutionalize them so that their excesses can be constrained by other values equally worthy of respect in a system of criminal law.

IX. Conclusion

Let me close these ruminations on hatred and revenge by considering one final challenge to them. I can imagine a critic now arguing as follows: your case for hatred and revenge within the limits set by blameworthiness and desert has saved hatred and revenge at a very high price—namely, you have made them *redundant*. If these responses must operate within a context defined by retributive just deserts, then how does the account of punishment you call hatred-based revenge differ from what Kant, and Herbert Morris, your own previous self, and others have simply called retributivism?

My short response to this is the following: I have elsewhere argued that, given a traditional liberal-lib-

ertarian conception of the state (as modelled in social contract terms), it is hard to see why there is any important state interest served in securing retributive values—in seeing that wrongdoers get their just deserts—for the sake of these values themselves.[30] If rational contractors were forming a state, it is easy to see why they might give up some liberty and resources to protect themselves against assault (a basic human desire) by adopting a deterrence scheme of criminal law. It is very hard, however, to see why they would do this simply to achieve a state of affairs that seems of merely abstract worth—namely, one where wrongdoers get their just deserts. In short: given the rarity of an intense sense of abstract justice, classical retributivism seems unmotivated within liberal theory.

If desires for revenge are basic and important to many people, however, this would provide some motivational grounds—in victim hatred—for those schemes of criminal justice we tend to call retributive; securing the revenge interests involved might, even in traditional liberal terms, prompt social contractors to be willing to make the sacrifices necessary to maintain a (constrained) system of revenge. Abstract concern for justice might explain the blameworthiness cap on punishment, but garden variety desires for revenge may generate—and quite properly generate—some of the values that drive the system up to that point.[31]

I will not, however, press this argument. If a consequence of my view is that it will ultimately be impossible to draw a sharp distinction between the desire for retributive justice and the desire for revenge, then this in itself will put revenge in better philosophical company than it normally enjoys. Perhaps it will achieve the kind of impartial re-hearing for hatred and revenge that it has been the primary purpose of this essay to provoke.[32]

Let me now close by summarizing the main thrust of my argument. Crime victims often want to influence sentencing, and their motives for this are often vindictive. Perhaps such motives are dishonorable; perhaps giving a legal role to victims so motivated would indeed produce deep harm to our system of criminal justice. I have attempted to show that this has simply been assumed and not demonstrated, however, and that—in fairness to those victims—it should be demonstrated before the state simply dismisses as irrational or evil the passionate claims of those whom it has failed to protect from criminal violence.

1. *The present essay builds on some ideas initially developed in ch. 3 ("Hatred: A Qualified Defense") of* Forgiveness and Mercy, *by Jeffrie G. Murphy (Chapters 1, 3 and 5) and Jean Hampton (Chapters 2 and 4), (Cambridge: Cambridge University Press, 1988).*

2. *The phrase "victims' rights movement" refers to those who advocate changes in criminal law and procedure that will (at least in their view) make crime victims more satisfied with the system. Rules of evidence that make it harder for defense attorneys to probe a claimed rape victim's sexual past, finding ways to allow claimed victims of child abuse to testify with less embarrassment or fear (e.g., on video or behind a screen), and allowing crime victims to influence criminal sentencing (e.g., by presenting victim impact statements to the sentencing judge) are examples of developments that may be viewed as victories for the victims' rights movement. The 1987 United States Supreme Court case of* Booth v. Maryland, *where victim impact statements were ruled unconstitutional in capital cases, may be viewed as a setback for the victims' rights movement. (This case will be discussed below.) It should be noted that the phrase "victims' rights" is importantly misleading as a characterization of some of the practices noted above. Since the use of a victim impact statement occurs after a criminal conviction (though prior to sentencing), the word "victim" here is appropriate. Prior to a conviction, however, we do not know for sure that we actually have a victim; all we know for sure is that we have an* accuser. *Thus it would be better if those who favor such things as shield laws to prevent unnecessary probing of an alleged rape victim's sexual past would refer to these practices as a matter of "accusers' rights." Also, is it correct to refer to these practices as rights at all, or should they simply be characterized (by those who favor them) as good policy?*

3. *Although I tend to support the legitimacy of what I call retributive hatred, I am inclined to agree with Willard Gaylin's claim that much anger and hatred in contemporary culture is—though understandable—irrational and maladaptive. See his* The Rage Within: Anger in Modern Life *(New York: Penguin Books, 1989).*

4. *Those who have come out in support of some instances of hatred and revenge include God ("Vengeance is mine . . . etc."), Aristotle (*Nicomachean Ethics, *1125b ff.), Adam Smith (*The Theory of Moral Sentiments, *Indianapolis: Liberty Press, 1982, p. 38), James Fitzjames Stephen (*A History of the Criminal Law of England, *London, 1883, Vol. II, pp. 81 ff.), Ernest van den Haag ("In Defense of the Death Penalty,"* Criminal Law Bulletin, *Vol. 14, No. 1, Jan.–Feb. 1978), Walter Berns (*For Capital Punishment, *New York: Basic Books, 1979), and Robert Axelrod (indirectly—as an endorsement of the strategy of "tit for tat" in iterated prisoner's dilemmas—in his* The Evolution of Cooperation, *New York: Basic Books, 1984). I also present a supportive case for these responses in* Forgiveness and Mercy. *In this book I suggest that, in addition to the social usefulness of these responses in some contexts, some considerations of* vice *and* virtue *also offer relevant support— namely, that a person's failure to resent wrongs done to him and to manifest retributive hatred toward the wrongdoer may be a sign that he has the vice of* servility *(a lack of proper self-respect and a lack of proper tendencies for self-defense). I would hate to have readers unfamiliar with the book conclude from the present paper that I see no moral and social problems with retributive hatred, however, so let me note that the book contains numerous qualifications and cautions with respect to my defense of this emotion— qualifications and cautions that considerably constrain the domain of its legitimacy. No doubt the reader will want to check this out, and I recommend that he do so by purchasing—preferably in the hardcover edition—a copy of the book.*

5. *Amendment VIII of the United States Constitution reads as follows: "Excessive bail shall not be required, nor excessive fines imposed, nor cruel and unusual punishments inflicted." This has been interpreted by the United States Supreme Court to rule out such inherently barbaric punishments as torture, punishments that are radically disproportionate to the gravity of the offense, and the punishment of death when administered in an arbitrary and capricious fashion.*

6. *Might not hatred and compassion stand or fall together with respect to criminal punishment? If it is wrong to increase a criminal sentence out of hatred, will it not also be wrong to decrease a criminal sentence out of compassion? Can one consistently be meticulous and strict about justice only in one direction? Perhaps we tend to be more lax about mercy because we think that the compassion on which it is based is, unlike hatred, an acceptable or even admirable emotion. But this, of course, needs to be shown. For Kant's discussion, see his* The Metaphysical Elements of Justice *(Indianapolis: Bobbs-Merrill, 1965), p. 107.*

7. *Ethics,* Four, LXVII.

8. *Heinrich von Kleist's 1810 story* Michael Kohlhaas *portrays a man who, when he fails to receive legal justice over a comparatively small injury done to him (theft and abuse of his horses), takes matters into his own hands. In his pursuit of revenge, he forms an army, kills large numbers of people, and nearly topples the government under which he lives. This story was retold by E. L. Doctorow in his 1975 novel* Ragtime—*wherein Michael Kohlhaas becomes Coalhouse Walker.*

9. *On the Genealogy of Morals,* Essay I, Section 10.

10. *A Theory of Justice* (Cambridge: Harvard University Press, 1971, secs. 80 and 81).

11. *Matthew 5:38–48. The older law is well represented in Psalms 58:10–11: "The righteous shall rejoice when he seeth the vengeance: he shall wash his feet in the blood of the wicked. So that a man shall say, Verily there is a reward for the righteous." In Aeschylus's* Oresteia, *the Furies represent sentiments of this kind. Athena refuses to banish them, however, because she respects the impulses they represent and believes that, by institutionalizing them under due process of law, she can make them such valuable forces in support of community morality that they will become known as "the kindly ones."*

12. *John 8:7.*

13. *Romans 12:19.*

14. *Matthew 18:21–35.*

15. *God seems to promise that the job of vengeance will get done. Is this to reassure His creatures that their hated enemies may not go eternally unpunished? But why should He pander to His creatures' desires for vengeance, unless these desires are in some sense both rationally and morally legitimate on their part? May these creatures not even look forward with delight to the coming divine retribution on their enemies? May they not even have pleasing fantasies of it? When it happens, may they not look down from heaven with delight at the torments of their enemies below? Is God here in some sense promising (like Athena) to "institutionalize" (in His divine law) these legitimate feelings and thereby make their personal expression unnecessary? I raise these questions not to be impious, but simply to make the point that the "Vengeance is mine" passage can be read simply as a command that humans not act on retributive hatred—leaving open the possibility that feeling retributive hatred is neither an evil nor a vice. I do not believe that the simple command to love and forgive one's enemies is comparably ambiguous, however, for here feelings themselves are clearly the object of the command.*

16. *For a discussion of those aspects of Kant's moral philosophy that appear to be in tension with his commitments to retributivism, see my "Does Kant Have a Theory of Punishment?" in* Columbia Law Review, *Volume 87, No. 3 (April 1987).*

17. *Suppose I am willing to grant that hatred would properly be addressed toward me if I performed (with full responsibility) certain evil acts. Perhaps I would even resent it and regard it as an insult (because it would challenge my status as a responsible moral agent) if such hatred was not directed toward me in these circumstances. If I then address such hatred to others when they (with full responsibility) perform such acts, it is not clear that I violate any*

important equality demand. Saint Augustine tells us that we should "hate the sin but not the sinner." But if it is permissible to hate the act because it is bad, why is it wrong to hate the actor because he is bad? Of course, if the wrongdoer sincerely repents, this may block the legitimacy of hating or even resenting him—a theme I pursue in Ch. 1 of Forgiveness and Mercy.

18. Revenge is not to be identified with vigilante activity, and indeed I will assume for purposes of this paper that anyone who seeks revenge in ways that are illegal acts wrongly (not to mention uncreatively). The issue that I mainly want to explore, of course, is if the law itself should find a way of institutionalizing some of this revenge and thereby perhaps eliminate some temptations to self-help. I will also be assuming throughout that we are dealing with cases where the victims are not fantasizing the wrongdoing but have accurate beliefs that they have been wronged, accurate beliefs about the nature and degree of the wrong done to them, and accurate beliefs that the wrongdoer is as fully responsible for that wrongdoing as any human being ever is for any wrongdoing.

19. Some people might also suggest virtue arguments, but I am suspicious of their use in this context. For example: it is often suggested, as an argument against capital punishment, that it is wrong because of what it does to the characters of those who favor and inflict it—namely, it degrades and debases and dehumanizes them. But this is by no means obvious. In my view, a person is debased by the doing of X only if X is wrong (unjust, say), and thus—absent an independent showing that X is wrong—the character debasement argument will not get off the ground. Similarly, engaging in revenge will debase people only if it can be shown, on independent grounds, that revenge is wrong. So too for the common "two wrongs do not make a right" cliché that is often trotted out here. Obviously, those who regard revenge as justified will not see it as a wrong; they will thus quite properly fail to see the relevance of the cliché to their claim.

20. This, I take it, is the point of James Fitzjames Stephen's famous analogy between the criminal law and the law of marriage (see note 4). He argued that we deal in each case with a passion that is legitimate (the desire for revenge in the one case and sexual desire in the other), but we have also learned that the passion in question has high potential to provoke disruptive behavior. Thus, the way to honor the passion without risking serious social disruption is for the law to regulate that passion—to provide it with a proper channel for expression. Taking victim hatred seriously in this way (by building it into legal practice) may thus benefit both the community and the victims themselves, for the practice recognizes the validity of the hatred while placing important constraints on its excess. Such institutionalization might even help to educate persons on the legitimate bounds of hatred.

21. One might, of course, argue that such a deterrent system is unpredictable—an acceptable consequence from the point of view of deterrence, perhaps, but a disutilitarian consequence from many other points of view (e.g., liberty). I think that this is an important argument. However, since I think that unpredictability is an evil essentially because of its unfairness rather than because of its potentially disruptive social consequences, I will treat this as an objection of principle in the next section.

22. 482 U.S. 496 (1987). A victim impact statement is a statement from the crime victim or some representative of the victim that seeks to influence sentencing by stressing the impact of the crime on the victim and the victim's desires (or perhaps the survivor's desires in a murder case) with respect to the sentence.

23. Expressions of hatred might, of course, be evidence that something of assumed relevance to criminal liability—e.g., the existence of a certain level of harm—is present. I will explore this idea a bit later in the paper. As Ellen Paul has pointed out to me, one could argue that if criminals knew that they would face varying degrees of punishment based on the degree of hatred felt by their victims, they would factor this into their calculations of advantage/disadvantage before committing the crime. A rational criminal might then presume that his victim might be one with great capacity for hatred, and this might augment the deterrent value of the law.

The criminal, by committing an illegal act, puts himself willingly and knowingly (but within limits, of course) in a kind of punishment lottery with respect to the harm that actually results from what he does. So why not a comparable lottery (again within limits) with respect to hatred and desires for revenge that might be felt by his victim?

24. Had the United States Supreme Court held that capital punishment is, like torture, inherently cruel and unusual punishment, consideration of the procedural problems surrounding the administration of that punishment would never have achieved their current prominence. The reason why Furman v. Georgia (408 U.S. 238 (1972)) and most later death penalty cases have dealt primarily with procedural matters—the desire to avoid arbitrary and capricious capital sentences—is that the Court has held that the penalty of death is not inherently cruel and unusual—at least with respect to some crimes of murder. Thus, it is not surprising that, in America, most principled legal objections to the death penalty now take a procedural form.

25. The Court did not clearly indicate what it will rule on VISs in non-capital cases. In capital cases, of course, the VISs are not primary victim impact statements (the primary victim being dead) but rather statements from concerned survivors—e.g., family members considered as secondary victims.

26. It is not made clear why this poses any greater problem than that posed when the same victim appears as a witness during trial. Freedom from cross-examination, perhaps? Might it not be possible to allow such cross-examination at a sentencing hearing?

27. United States v. Bergman, United States District Court, S.D.N.Y., 416 F. Supp. 496 (1976). Rabbi Bergman, owner of several nursing homes, had been part of a scheme to defraud the United States government with respect to Medicaid payments. In his sentencing opinion, Judge Frankel explores a variety of punitive purposes that he believes must be weighed: retribution, community outrage, community support for the Rabbi because of his many philanthropic ventures, special and general deterrence, etc.

28. Thomas Nagel, "Moral Luck," in his Mortal Questions (Cambridge: Cambridge University Press, 1979).

29. The problem being noted here is that of the inconsistency of insisting on a blameworthiness basis for punishment in a system that gives the same weight to harm that most systems of criminal law currently do. This does not entail abandonment of a blameworthiness basis, of course, for one might instead avoid the inconsistency by arguing on retributivist grounds for the abandonment (or considerable qualification) of the relevance of harm. For an exploration of this issue, see Stephen J. Schulhofer, "Harm and Punishment: A Critique of Emphasis on the Results of Conduct in the Criminal Law," 122 University of Pennsylvania Law Review 1497 (1974).

30. See my "Retributivism, Moral Education, and the Liberal State" in Criminal Justice Ethics, Vol. 4, no. 1 (Winter/Spring, 1985). For a skeptical attack on the common idea that there is a sharp distinction in principle between criminal law (with the state as injured party) and tort law (with individual victims as injured parties), see my "Why Have the Criminal Law at All?" in ch. 3 of The Philosophy of Law: An Introduction to Jurisprudence, by Jeffrie G. Murphy (Chapters 1, 2 and 3) and Jules L. Coleman (Chapters 4 and 5) (Totowa: Rowman and Allanheld, 1984). (A revised edition of this book will appear from Westview Press in late 1989.)

31. Even Herbert Morris's very abstract notion of criminal punishment as annulment of wrongful gains or unfair advantages (in his "Persons and Punishment," The Monist, Volume 52, Number 4, October 1968) may ultimately depend not upon some abstract sense of justice (the desire to see justice done for its own sake) but on something very like victim revenge. What, on Morris's theory, motivates me to want the criminal (as free-rider) punished? That he has taken an unfair advantage of those who have been law-abiding. But that means, given that I am one of those who has been law-abiding, he has taken unfair advantage of me—he has derived a wrongful gain at my expense. If this is what is most vivid in my

mind (as it surely will be), then in what sense is my desire to see him punished impersonal and not a kind of victim revenge?
32. Most philosophical defenses of retributivism (including some of my own previous essays) take great pains to distinguish retribu-

tion (which is taken to be just) from vengeance (which is taken to be unjust or evil in some other way). Perhaps such attempts at drawing a sharp distinction have been misdirected.

PAYNE V. TENNESSEE*

United States Supreme Court, 1991

Chief Justice REHNQUIST delivered the opinion of the court.

In this case we reconsider our holdings in *Booth* v. *Maryland,* and *South Carolina* v. *Gathers,* that the Eighth Amendment bars the admission of victim impact evidence during the penalty phase of a capital trial.

The petitioner, Pervis Tyrone Payne, was convicted by a jury on two counts of first-degree murder and one count of assault with intent to commit murder in the first degree. He was sentenced to death for each of the murders, and to 30 years in prison for the assault.

The victims of Payne's offenses were 28-year-old Charisse Christopher, her 2-year-old daughter Lacie, and her 3-year-old son Nicholas. The three lived together in an apartment in Millington, Tennessee, across the hall from Payne's girlfriend, Bobbie Thomas. On Saturday, June 27, 1987, Payne visited Thomas' apartment several times in expectation of her return from her mother's house in Arkansas, but found no one at home. On one visit, he left his overnight bag, containing clothes and other items for his weekend stay, in the hallway outside Thomas' apartment. With the bag were three cans of malt liquor.

Payne passed the morning and early afternoon injecting cocaine and drinking beer. Later, he drove around the town with a friend in the friend's car, each of them taking turns reading a pornographic magazine. Sometime around 3 p.m., Payne returned to the apartment complex, entered the Christophers' apartment, and began making sexual advances towards Charisse. Charisse resisted and Payne became violent. A neighbor who resided in the apartment directly beneath the Christophers, heard Charisse screaming, "'Get out, get out,' as if she were telling the children to leave." The noise briefly subsided and then began, "'horribly loud.'" The neighbor called the police after she heard a "blood curdling scream" from the Christopher apartment. Brief for Respondent.

When the first police officer arrived at the scene, he immediately encountered Payne who was leaving the apartment building, so covered with blood that he appeared to be "'sweating blood.'" The officer confronted Payne, who responded, "'I'm the complainant.'" When the officer asked, "'What's going on up there?'" Payne struck the officer with the overnight bag, dropped his tennis shoes, and fled.

Inside the apartment, the police encountered a horrifying scene. Blood covered the walls and floor throughout the unit. Charisse and her children were lying on the floor in the kitchen. Nicholas, despite several wounds inflicted by a butcher knife that completely penetrated through his body from front to

---

*No. 90-5721. Argued April 24, 1991. Decided June 27, 1991. Not all deletions are noted in this edited text.

back, was still breathing. Miraculously, he survived, but not until after undergoing seven hours of surgery and a transfusion of 1700 cc's of blood—400 to 500 cc's more than his estimated normal blood volume. Charisse and Lacie were dead.

Charisse's body was found on the kitchen floor on her back, her legs fully extended. She had sustained 42 direct knife wounds and 42 defensive wounds on her arms and hands. The wounds were caused by 41 separate thrusts of a butcher knife. None of the 84 wounds inflicted by Payne were individually fatal; rather, the cause of death was most likely bleeding from all of the wounds.

Lacie's body was on the kitchen floor near her mother. She had suffered stab wounds to the chest, abdomen, back, and head. The murder weapon, a butcher knife, was found at her feet. Payne's baseball cap was snapped on her arm near her elbow. Three cans of malt liquor bearing Payne's fingerprints were found on a table near her body, and a fourth empty one was on the landing outside the apartment door.

Payne was apprehended later that day hiding in the attic of the home of a former girlfriend. As he descended the stairs of the attic, he stated to the arresting officers, "Man, I aint killed no woman." According to one of the officers, Payne had "a wild look about him. His pupils were contracted. He was foaming at the mouth, saliva. He appeared to be very nervous. He was breathing real rapid." He had blood on his body and clothes and several scratches across his chest. It was later determined that the blood stains matched the victims' blood types. A search of his pockets revealed a packet containing cocaine residue, a hypodermic syringe wrapper, and a cap from a hypodermic syringe. His overnight bag, containing a bloody white shirt, was found in a nearby dumpster.

At trial, Payne took the stand and, despite the overwhelming and relatively uncontroverted evidence against him, testified that he had not harmed any of the Christophers. Rather, he asserted that another man had raced by him as he was walking up the stairs to the floor where the Christophers lived. He stated that he had gotten blood on himself when, after hearing moans from the Christophers' apartment, he had tried to help the victims. According to his testimony, he panicked and fled when he heard police sirens and noticed the blood on his clothes. The jury returned guilty verdicts against Payne on all counts.

During the sentencing phase of the trial, Payne presented the testimony of four witnesses: his mother and father, Bobbie Thomas, and Dr. John T. Huston, a clinical psychologist specializing in criminal court evaluation work. Bobbie Thomas testified that she met Payne at church, during a time when she was being abused by her husband. She stated that Payne was a very caring person, and that he devoted much time and attention to her three children, who were being affected by her marital difficulties. She said that the children had come to love him very much and would miss him, and that he "behaved just like a father that loved his kids." She asserted that he did not drink, nor did he use drugs, and that it was generally inconsistent with Payne's character to have committed these crimes.

Dr. Huston testified that based on Payne's low score on an IQ test, Payne was "mentally handicapped." Huston also said that Payne was neither psychotic nor schizophrenic, and that Payne was the most polite prisoner he had ever met. Payne's parents testified that their son had no prior criminal record and had never been arrested. They also stated that Payne had no history of alcohol or drug abuse, he worked with his father as a painter, he was good with children, and that he was a good son.

The State presented the testimony of Charisse's mother, Mary Zvolanek. When asked how Nicholas had been affected by the murders of his mother and sister, she responded:

> "He cries for his mom. He doesn't seem to understand why she doesn't come home. And he cries for his sister Lacie. He comes to me many times during the week and asks me, Grandmama, do you miss my Lacie. And I tell him yes. He says, I'm worried about my Lacie."
> App. 30.

In arguing for the death penalty during closing argument, the prosecutor commented on the continuing effects of Nicholas' experience, stating:

> "But we do know that Nicholas was alive. And Nicholas was in the same room. Nicholas was still conscious. His eyes were open. He responded to the paramedics. He was able to follow their directions. He was able to hold his intestines in as he was carried to the ambulance. So he knew what happened to his mother and baby sister."
>
> "There is nothing you can do to ease the pain of any of the families involved in this case. There is nothing you can do to ease the pain of Bernice or Carl Payne, and that's a tragedy. There is nothing you can do basically to ease the pain of Mr. and Mrs. Zvolanek, and

that's a tragedy. They will have to live with it the rest of their lives. There is obviously nothing you can do for Charisse and Lacie Jo. But there is something that you can do for Nicholas.

"Somewhere down the road Nicholas is going to grow up, hopefully. He's going to want to know what happened. And he is going to know what happened to his baby sister and his mother. He is going to want to know what type of justice was done. He is going to want to know what happened. With your verdict, you will provide the answer."

In the rebuttal to Payne's closing argument, the prosecutor stated:

"You saw the videotape this morning. You saw what Nicholas Christopher will carry in his mind forever. When you talk about cruel, when you talk about atrocious, and when you talk about heinous, that picture will always come into your mind, probably throughout the rest of your lives.

". . . No one will ever know about Lacie Jo because she never had the chance to grow up. Her life was taken from her at the age of two years old. So, no there won't be a high school principal to talk about Lacie Jo Christopher, and there won't be anybody to take her to her high school prom. And there won't be anybody there—there won't be her mother there or Nicholas' mother there to kiss him at night. His mother will never kiss him good night or pat him as he goes off to bed, or hold him and sing him a lullaby. . . .

"[Petitioner's attorney] wants you to think about a good reputation, people who love the defendant and things about him. He doesn't want you to think about the people who love Charisse Christopher, her mother and daddy who loved her. The people who loved little Lacie Jo, the grandparents who are still here. The brother who mourns for her every single day and wants to know where his best little playmate is. He doesn't have anybody to watch cartoons with him, a little one. These are the things that go into why it is especially cruel, heinous, and atrocious, the burden that that child will carry forever."

The jury sentenced Payne to death on each of the murder counts.

The Supreme Court of Tennessee affirmed the conviction and sentence. The court rejected Payne's contention that the admission of the grandmother's testimony and the State's closing argument constituted prejudicial violations of his rights under the Eighth Amendment as applied in *Booth* v. *Maryland,* and *South Carolina* v. *Gathers.* The court characterized the grandmother's testimony as "technically irrelevant," but concluded that it "did not create a constitutionally unacceptable risk of an arbitrary imposition of the death penalty and was harmless beyond a reasonable doubt."

The court determined that the prosecutor's comments during closing argument were "relevant to [Payne's] personal responsibility and moral guilt." The court explained that "[w]hen a person deliberately picks a butcher knife out of a kitchen drawer and proceeds to stab to death a twenty-eight-year-old mother, her two and one-half year old daughter and her three and one-half year old son, in the same room, the physical and mental condition of the boy he left for dead is surely relevant in determining his 'blameworthiness.'" The court concluded that any violation of Payne's rights under *Booth* and *Gathers* "was harmless beyond a reasonable doubt."

We granted certiorari to reconsider our holdings in *Booth* and *Gathers* that the Eighth Amendment prohibits a capital sentencing jury from considering "victim impact" evidence relating to the personal characteristics of the victim and the emotional impact of the crimes on the victim's family.

In *Booth,* the defendant robbed and murdered an elderly couple. As required by a state statute, a victim impact statement was prepared based on interviews with the victims' son, daughter, son-in-law, and granddaughter. The statement, which described the personal characteristics of the victims, the emotional impact of the crimes on the family, and set forth the family members' opinions and characterizations of the crimes and the defendant, was submitted to the jury at sentencing. The jury imposed the death penalty. The conviction and sentence were affirmed on appeal by the State's highest court.

This Court held by a 5-to-4 vote that the Eighth Amendment prohibits a jury from considering a victim impact statement at the sentencing phase of a capital trial. The Court made clear that the admissibility of victim impact evidence was not to be determined on a case-by-case basis, but that such evidence was *per se* inadmissible in the sentencing phase of a capital case except to the extent that it "relate[d] directly to the circumstances of the crime." In *Gathers,* decided two years later, the Court extended the rule announced in *Booth* to statements made by a prosecutor to the sentencing jury regarding the personal qualities of the victim.

The *Booth* Court began its analysis with the observation that the capital defendant must be treated as a "'uniquely individual human bein[g],'" and therefore the Constitution requires the jury to make an individualized determination as to whether the defendant should be executed based on the "'character of the individual and the circumstances of the crime.'" The Court concluded that while no prior decision of this Court had mandated that only the defendant's character and immediate characteristics of the crime may constitutionally be considered, other factors are irrelevant to the capital sentencing decision unless they have "some bearing on the defendant's 'personal responsibility and moral guilt.'" To the extent that victim impact evidence presents "factors about which the defendant was unaware, and that were irrelevant to the decision to kill," the Court concluded, it has nothing to do with the "blameworthiness of a particular defendant." Evidence of the victim's character, the Court observed, "could well distract the sentencing jury from its constitutionally required task [of] determining whether the death penalty is appropriate in light of the background and record of the accused and the particular circumstances of the crime." The Court concluded that, except to the extent that victim impact evidence relates "directly to the circumstances of the crime," the prosecution may not introduce such evidence at a capital sentencing hearing because "it creates an impermissible risk that the capital sentencing decision will be made in an arbitrary manner."

Booth and *Gathers* were based on two premises: that evidence relating to a particular victim or to the harm that a capital defendant causes a victim's family do not in general reflect on the defendant's "blameworthiness," and that only evidence relating to "blameworthiness" is relevant to the capital sentencing decision. However, the assessment of harm caused by the defendant as a result of the crime charged has understandably been an important concern of the criminal law, both in determining the elements of the offense and in determining the appropriate punishment. Thus, two equally blameworthy criminal defendants may be guilty of different offenses solely because their acts cause differing amounts of harm. "If a bank robber aims his gun at a guard, pulls the trigger, and kills his target, he may be put to death. If the gun unexpectedly misfires, he may not. His moral guilt in both cases is identical, but his responsibility in the former is greater." The same is true with respect to two defendants, each of whom participates in a robbery, and each of whom acts with reckless disregard for human life; if the robbery in which the first defendant participated results in the death of a victim, he may be subjected to the death penalty, but if the robbery in which the second defendant participates does not result in the death of a victim, the death penalty may not be imposed.

The principles which have guided criminal sentencing—as opposed to criminal liability—have varied with the times. The book of Exodus prescribes the *Lex talionis,* "An eye for an eye, a tooth for a tooth." Exodus 21:22–23. In England and on the continent of Europe, as recently as the 18th century crimes which would be regarded as quite minor today were capital offenses. Writing in the 18th century, the Italian criminologist Cesare Beccaria advocated the idea that "the punishment should fit the crime." He said that "[w]e have seen that the true measure of crimes is the injury done to society."

Gradually the list of crimes punishable by death diminished, and legislatures began grading the severity of crimes in accordance with the harm done by the criminal. The sentence for a given offense, rather than being precisely fixed by the legislature, was prescribed in terms of a minimum and a maximum, with the actual sentence to be decided by the judge. With the increasing importance of probation, as opposed to imprisonment, as a part of the penological process, some States such as California developed the "indeterminate sentence," where the time of incarceration was left almost entirely to the penological authorities rather than to the courts. But more recently the pendulum has swung back. The Federal Sentencing Guidelines, which went into effect in 1987, provided for very precise calibration of sentences, depending upon a number of factors. These factors relate both to the subjective guilt of the defendant and to the harm caused by his acts.

Wherever judges in recent years have had discretion to impose sentence, the consideration of the harm caused by the crime has been an important factor in the exercise of that discretion:

> "*The first significance of harm in Anglo-American jurisprudence is, then, as a prerequisite to the criminal sanction. The second significance of harm—one no less important to judges—is as a measure of the seriousness of the offense and therefore as a standard for determining the severity of the sentence that will be meted out.*"

Whatever the prevailing sentencing philosophy, the sentencing authority has always been free to consider a wide range of relevant material. In the federal system, we observed that "a judge may appropriately conduct an inquiry broad in scope, largely unlimited as to the kind of information he may consider, or the source from which it may come." Even in the context of capital sentencing, prior to *Booth* the joint opinion of Justices Stewart, Powell, and STEVENS in *Gregg* v. *Georgia* had rejected petitioner's attack on the Georgia statute because of the "wide scope of evidence and argument allowed at presentence hearings." The joint opinion stated:

> "We think that the Georgia court wisely has chosen not to impose unnecessary restrictions on the evidence that can be offered at such a hearing and to approve open and far-ranging argument. . . . So long as the evidence introduced and the arguments made at the presentence hearing do not prejudice a defendant, it is preferable not to impose restrictions. We think it desirable for the jury to have as much information before it as possible when it makes the sentencing decision."

The Maryland statute involved in *Booth* required that the presentence report in all felony cases include a "victim impact statement" which would describe the effect of the crime on the victim and his family. Congress and most of the States have, in recent years, enacted similar legislation to enable the sentencing authority to consider information about the harm caused by the crime committed by the defendant. The evidence involved in the present case was not admitted pursuant to any such enactment, but its purpose and effect was much the same as if it had been. While the admission of this particular kind of evidence—designed to portray for the sentencing authority the actual harm caused by a particular crime—is of recent origin, this fact hardly renders it unconstitutional.

"We have held that a State cannot preclude the sentencer from considering 'any relevant mitigating evidence' that the defendant proffers in support of a sentence less than death." Thus we have, as the Court observed in *Booth,* required that the capital defendant be treated as a "'uniquely individual human bein[g].'" But it was never held or even suggested in any of our cases preceding *Booth* that the defendant, entitled as he was to individualized consideration, was to receive that consideration wholly apart from the crime which he had committed. The language quoted from

Woodson in the *Booth* opinion was not intended to describe a class of evidence that *could not* be received, but a class of evidence which *must* be received. Any doubt on the matter is dispelled by comparing the language in *Woodson* with the language from *Gregg* v. *Georgia,* quoted above, which was handed down the same day as *Woodson.* This misreading of precedent in *Booth* has, we think, unfairly weighted the scales in a capital trial; while virtually no limits are placed on the relevant mitigating evidence a capital defendant may introduce concerning his own circumstances, the State is barred from either offering "a glimpse of the life" which a defendant "chose to extinguish," or demonstrating the loss to the victim's family and to society which have resulted from the defendant's homicide.

Booth reasoned that victim impact evidence must be excluded because it would be difficult, if not impossible, for the defendant to rebut such evidence without shifting the focus of the sentencing hearing away from the defendant, thus creating a "'mini-trial' on the victim's character." In many cases the evidence relating to the victim is already before the jury at least in part because of its relevance at the guilt phase of the trial. But even as to additional evidence admitted at the sentencing phase, the mere fact that for tactical reasons it might not be prudent for the defense to rebut victim impact evidence makes the case no different than others in which a party is faced with this sort of a dilemma. As we explained in rejecting the contention that expert testimony on future dangerousness should be excluded from capital trials, "the rules of evidence generally extant at the federal and state levels anticipate that relevant, unprivileged evidence should be admitted and its weight left to the factfinder, who would have the benefit of cross examination and contrary evidence by the opposing party."

Payne echoes the concern voiced in *Booth*'s case that the admission of victim impact evidence permits a jury to find that defendants whose victims were assets to their community are more deserving of punishment than those whose victims are perceived to be less worthy. As a general matter, however, victim impact evidence is not offered to encourage comparative judgments of this kind—for instance, that the killer of a hardworking, devoted parent deserves the death penalty, but that the murderer of a reprobate does not. It is designed to show instead *each* victim's "uniqueness as an individual human being," whatever the jury might think the loss to the community resulting from his death might be. The facts of *Gathers* are an excellent illustration of this: the evidence showed that the victim was an out of work, mentally handicapped individual, perhaps not, in the eyes of most, a significant contributor to society, but nonetheless a murdered human being.

Under our constitutional system, the primary responsibility for defining crimes against state law, fixing punishments for the commission of these crimes, and establishing procedures for criminal trials rests with the States. The state laws respecting crimes, punishments, and criminal procedure are of course subject to the overriding provisions of the United States Constitution. Where the State imposes the death penalty for a particular crime, we have held that the Eighth Amendment imposes special limitations upon that process.

> "First, there is a required threshold below which the death penalty cannot be imposed. In this context, the State must establish rational criteria that narrow the decisionmaker's judgment as to whether the circumstances of a particular defendant's case meet the threshold. Moreover, a societal consensus that the death penalty is disproportionate to a particular offense prevents a State from imposing the death penalty for that offense. Second, States cannot limit the sentencer's consideration of any relevant circumstance that could cause it to decline to impose the penalty. In this respect, the State cannot challenge the sentencer's discretion, but must allow it to consider any relevant information offered by the defendant."

But, as we noted in *California* v. *Ramos,* "[b]eyond these limitations . . . the Court has deferred to the State's choice of substantive factors relevant to the penalty determination."

"Within the constitutional limitations defined by our cases, the States enjoy their traditional latitude to prescribe the method by which those who commit murder should be punished." The States remain free, in capital cases, as well as others, to devise new procedures and new remedies to meet felt needs. Victim impact evidence is simply another form or method of informing the sentencing authority about the specific harm caused by the crime in question, evidence of a general type long considered by sentencing authorities. We think the *Booth* Court was wrong in stating that this kind of evidence leads to the arbitrary imposition of the death penalty. In the majority of cases, and in this case, victim impact evidence serves entirely legitimate purposes. In the event that evidence is introduced that is so unduly prejudicial that it renders

the trial fundamentally unfair, the Due Process Clause of the Fourteenth Amendment provides a mechanism for relief. Courts have always taken into consideration the harm done by the defendant in imposing sentence, and the evidence adduced in this case was illustrative of the harm caused by Payne's double murder.

We are now of the view that a State may properly conclude that for the jury to assess meaningfully the defendant's moral culpability and blameworthiness, it should have before it at the sentencing phase evidence of the specific harm caused by the defendant. "[T]he State has a legitimate interest in counteracting the mitigating evidence which the defendant is entitled to put in, by reminding the sentencer that just as the murderer should be considered as an individual, so too the victim is an individual whose death represents a unique loss to society and in particular to his family." By turning the victim into a "faceless stranger at the penalty phase of a capital trial," *Gathers. Booth* deprives the State of the full moral force of its evidence and may prevent the jury from having before it all the information necessary to determine the proper punishment for a first-degree murder.

The present case is an example of the potential for such unfairness. The capital sentencing jury heard testimony from Payne's girlfriend that they met at church, that he was affectionate, caring, kind to her children, that he was not an abuser of drugs or alcohol, and that it was inconsistent with his character to have committed the murders. Payne's parents testified that he was a good son, and a clinical psychologist testified that Payne was an extremely polite prisoner and suffered from a low IQ. None of this testimony was related to the circumstances of Payne's brutal crimes. In contrast, the only evidence of the impact of Payne's offenses during the sentencing phase was Nicholas' grandmother's description—in response to a single question—that the child misses his mother and baby sister. Payne argues that the Eighth Amendment commands that the jury's death sentence must be set aside because the jury heard this testimony. But the testimony illustrated quite poignantly some of the harm that Payne's killing had caused; there is nothing unfair about allowing the jury to bear in mind that harm at the same time as it considers the mitigating evidence introduced by the defendant. The Supreme Court of Tennessee in this case obviously felt the unfairness of the rule pronounced by *Booth* when it said "[i]t is an affront to the civilized members of the human race to say that at sentencing in a capital case, a parade of witnesses may praise the background, character and good deeds of Defendant (as was done in this case), without limitation as to relevancy, but nothing may be said that bears upon the character of, or the harm imposed, upon the victims."

In *Gathers,* as indicated above, we extended the holding of *Booth* barring victim impact evidence to the prosecutor's argument to the jury. Human nature being what it is, capable lawyers trying cases to juries try to convey to the jurors that the people involved in the underlying events are, or were, living human beings, with something to be gained or lost from the jury's verdict. Under the aegis of the Eighth Amendment, we have given the broadest latitude to the defendant to introduce relevant mitigating evidence reflecting on his individual personality, and the defendant's attorney may argue that evidence to the jury. Petitioner's attorney in this case did just that. For the reasons discussed above, we now reject the view—expressed in *Gathers*—that a State may not permit the prosecutor to similarly argue to the jury the human cost of the crime of which the defendant stands convicted. We reaffirm the view expressed by Justice Cardozo in *Snyder* v. *Massachusetts:* "justice, though due to the accused, is due to the accuser also. The concept of fairness must not be strained till it is narrowed to a filament. We are to keep the balance true."

We thus hold that if the State chooses to permit the admission of victim impact evidence and prosecutorial argument on that subject, the Eighth Amendment erects no *per se* bar. A State may legitimately conclude that evidence about the victim and about the impact of the murder on the victim's family is relevant to the jury's decision as to whether or not the death penalty should be imposed. There is no reason to treat such evidence differently than other relevant evidence is treated.

Payne and his *amicus* argue that despite these numerous infirmities in the rule created by *Booth* and *Gathers,* we should adhere to the doctrine of *stare decisis* and stop short of overruling those cases. *Stare decisis* is the preferred course because it promotes the evenhanded, predictable, and consistent development of legal principles, fosters reliance on judicial decisions, and contributes to the actual and perceived integrity of the judicial process. Adhering to precedent "is usually the wise policy, because in most matters it is more important that the applicable rule of law be settled than it be settled right." Nevertheless, when governing decisions are unworkable or are badly reasoned, "this Court has never felt constrained to follow precedent." *Stare decisis* is not an inexorable command; rather, it "is a principle of policy and not a me-

chanical formula of adherence to the latest decision." This is particularly true in constitutional cases, because in such cases "correction through legislative action is practically impossible." Considerations in favor of *stare decisis* are at their acme in cases involving property and contract rights, where reliance interests are involved, the opposite is true in cases such as the present one involving procedural and evidentiary rules.

Applying these general principles, the Court has during the past 20 Terms overruled in whole or in part 33 of its previous constitutional decisions. *Booth* and *Gathers* were decided by the narrowest of margins, over spirited dissents challenging the basic underpinnings of those decisions. They have been questioned by members of the Court in later decisions, and have defied consistent application by the lower courts. Reconsidering these decisions now, we conclude for the reasons heretofore stated, that they were wrongly decided and should be, and now are, overruled. We accordingly affirm the judgment of the Supreme Court of Tennessee.

Affirmed.

Justice O'CONNOR, with whom Justice WHITE and Justice KENNEDY join, concurring.

In my view, a State may legitimately determine that victim impact evidence is relevant to a capital sentencing proceeding. A State may decide that the jury, before determining whether a convicted murderer should receive the death penalty, should know the full extent of the harm caused by the crime, including its impact on the victim's family and community. A State may decide also that the jury should see "a quick glimpse of the life petitioner chose to extinguish," to remind the jury that the person whose life was taken was a unique human being.

Given that victim impact evidence is potentially relevant, nothing in the Eighth Amendment commands that States treat it differently than other kinds of relevant evidence. "The Eighth Amendment stands as a shield against those practices and punishments which are either inherently cruel or which so offend the moral consensus of this society as to be deemed 'cruel and unusual.'" Certainly there is no strong societal consensus that a jury may not take into account the loss suffered by a victim's family or that a murder victim must remain a faceless stranger at the penalty phase of a capital trial. Just the opposite is true. Most States have enacted legislation enabling judges and juries to consider victim impact evidence. The possibility that this evidence may in some cases be unduly inflammatory does not justify a prophylactic, constitutionally based rule that this evidence may never be admitted. Trial courts routinely exclude evidence that is unduly inflammatory; where inflammatory evidence is improperly admitted, appellate courts carefully review the record to determine whether the error was prejudicial.

We do not hold today that victim impact evidence must be admitted, or even that it should be admitted. We hold merely that if a State decides to permit consideration of this evidence, "the Eighth Amendment erects no *per se* bar." If, in a particular case, a witness' testimony or a prosecutor's remark so infects the sentencing proceeding as to render it fundamentally unfair, the defendant may seek appropriate relief under the Due Process Clause of the Fourteenth Amendment.

That line was not crossed in this case. The State called as a witness Mary Zvolanek, Nicholas' grandmother. Her testimony was brief. She explained that Nicholas cried for his mother and baby sister and could not understand why they didn't come home. I do not doubt that the jurors were moved by this testimony—who would not have been? But surely this brief statement did not inflame their passions more than did the facts of the crime: Charisse Christopher was stabbed 41 times with a butcher knife and bled to death; her 2-year old daughter Lacie was killed by repeated thrusts of that same knife; and 3-year old Nicholas, despite stab wounds that penetrated completely through his body from front to back, survived—only to witness the brutal murders of his mother and baby sister. In light of the jury's unavoidable familiarity with the facts of Payne's vicious attack, I cannot conclude that the additional information provided by Mary Zvolanek's testimony deprived petitioner of due process.

Nor did the prosecutor's comments about Charisse and Lacie in the closing argument violate the Constitution. The jury had earlier seen a videotape of the murder scene that included the slashed and bloody corpses of Charisse and Lacie. In arguing that Payne deserved the death penalty, the prosecutor sought to remind the jury that Charisse and Lacie were more than just lifeless bodies on a videotape, that they were unique human beings. The prosecutor remarked that Charisse would never again sing a lullaby to her son and that Lacie would never attend a high school prom. In my view, these statements were permissible. "Murder is the ultimate act of depersonalization." It transforms a living person with hopes, dreams, and fears into a corpse, thereby taking away all that is special and unique about the person. The Constitution does

not preclude a State from deciding to give some of that back.

I agree with the Court that *Booth* v. *Maryland,* and *Gathers,* were wrongly decided. The Eighth Amendment does not prohibit a State from choosing to admit evidence concerning a murder victim's personal characteristics or the impact of the crime on the victim's family and community. *Booth* also addressed another kind of victim impact evidence—opinions of the victim's family about the crime, the defendant, and the appropriate sentence. As the Court notes in today's decision, we do not reach this issue as no evidence of this kind was introduced at petitioner's trial. Nor do we express an opinion as to other aspects of the prosecutor's conduct. As to the victim impact evidence that was introduced, its admission did not violate the Constitution. Accordingly, I join the Court's opinion.

Justice SCALIA, with whom Justice O'CONNOR and Justice KENNEDY join as to Part II, concurring.

I

The Court correctly observes the injustice of requiring the exclusion of relevant aggravating evidence during capital sentencing, while requiring the admission of all relevant mitigating evidence. I have previously expressed my belief that the latter requirement is both wrong and, when combined with the remainder of our capital sentencing jurisprudence, unworkable. Even if it were abandoned, however, I would still affirm the judgment here. True enough, the Eighth Amendment permits parity between mitigating and aggravating factors. But more broadly and fundamentally still, it permits the People to decide (within the limits of other constitutional guarantees) what is a crime and what constitutes aggravation and mitigation of a crime.

II

The response to Justice MARSHALL's strenuous defense of the virtues of *stare decisis* can be found in the writings of Justice MARSHALL himself. That doctrine, he has reminded us, "is not 'an imprisonment of reason.'" If there was ever a case that defied reason, it was *Booth* v. *Maryland,* imposing a constitutional rule that had absolutely no basis in constitutional text, in historical practice, or in logic. Justice MARSHALL has also explained that "'[t]he jurist concerned with public confidence in, and acceptance of the judicial system might well consider that, however admirable its resolute adherence to the law as it was, a decision contrary to the public sense of justice as it is, operates, so far as it is known, to diminish respect for the courts and for law itself.'" *Booth's* stunning *ipse dixit,* that a crime's unanticipated consequences must be deemed "irrelevant" to the sentence, conflicts with a public sense of justice keen enough that it has found voice in a nationwide "victim's rights" movement.

Today, however, Justice MARSHALL demands of us some "special justification"—*beyond* the mere conviction that the rule of *Booth* significantly harms our criminal justice system and is egregiously wrong—before we can be absolved of exercising "[p]ower, not reason." I do not think that is fair. In fact, quite to the contrary, what would enshrine power as the governing principle of this Court is the notion that an important constitutional decision with plainly inadequate rational support *must* be left in place for the sole reason that it once attracted five votes.

It seems to me difficult for those who were in the majority in *Booth* to hold themselves forth as ardent apostles of *stare decisis.* That doctrine, to the extent it rests upon anything more than administrative convenience, is merely the application to judicial precedents of a more general principle that the settled practices and expectations of a democratic society should generally not be disturbed by the courts. It is hard to have a genuine regard for *stare decisis* without honoring that more general principle as well. A decision of this Court which, while not overruling a prior holding, nonetheless announces a novel rule, contrary to long and unchallenged practice, and pronounces it to be the Law of the Land—such a decision, no less than an explicit overruling, should be approached with great caution. It was, I suggest, *Booth,* and not today's decision, that compromised the fundamental values underlying the doctrine of *stare decisis.*

Justice SOUTER, with whom Justice KENNEDY joins, concurring.

I join the Court's opinion addressing two categories of facts excluded from consideration at capital sentencing proceedings by *Booth* v. *Maryland* and *South Carolina* v. *Gathers,* information revealing the individuality of the victim and the impact of the crime on the victim's survivors. As to these two categories, I believe *Booth* and *Gathers* were wrongly decided.

To my knowledge, our legal tradition has never included a general rule that evidence of a crime's effects on the victim and others is, standing alone, irrelevant to a sentencing determination of the defendant's culpability. Indeed, as the Court's opinion today, and dissents in *Booth* and *Gathers* make clear, criminal conduct has traditionally been categorized and penalized differently according to consequences not specifically intended, but determined in part by conditions unknown to a defendant when he acted. The majority opinion in *Booth* nonetheless characterized the consideration in a capital sentencing proceeding of a victim's individuality and the consequences of his death on his survivors as "irrelevant" and productive of "arbitrary and capricious" results, insofar as that would allow the sentencing authority to take account of information not specifically contemplated by the defendant prior to his ultimate criminal decision. This condemnation comprehends two quite separate elements. As to one such element the condemnation is merited but insufficient to justify the rule in *Booth,* and as to the other it is mistaken.

Evidence about the victim and survivors, and any jury argument predicated on it, can of course be so inflammatory as to risk a verdict impermissibly based on passion, not deliberation. But this is just as true when the defendant knew of the specific facts as when he was ignorant of their details, and in each case there is a traditional guard against the inflammatory risk, in the trial judge's authority and responsibility to control the proceedings consistently with due process, on which ground defendants may object and, if necessary, appeal. With the command of due process before us, this Court and the other courts of the state and federal systems will perform the "duty to search for constitutional error with painstaking care," an obligation "never more exacting than it is in a capital case."

Booth, supra, nonetheless goes further and imposes a blanket prohibition on consideration of evidence of the victim's individuality and the consequential harm to survivors as irrelevant to the choice between imprisonment and execution, except when such evidence goes to the "circumstances of the crime," *id.,* 482 U.S., at 502, 107 S.Ct., at 2532, and probably then only when the facts in question were known to the defendant and relevant to his decision to kill, *id.,* at 505, 107 S.Ct., at 2534. This prohibition rests on the belief that consideration of such details about the victim and survivors as may have been outside the defendant's knowledge is inconsistent with the sentencing jury's Eighth Amendment duty "in the unique circumstance of a capital sentencing hearing . . . to focus on the defendant as a 'uniquely individual human bein[g].'" The assumption made is that the obligation to consider the defendant's uniqueness limits the data about a crime's impact, on which a defendant's moral guilt may be calculated, to the facts he specifically knew and presumably considered. His uniqueness, in other words, is defined by the specifics of his knowledge and the reasoning that is thought to follow from it.

To hold, however, that in setting the appropriate sentence a defendant must be considered in his uniqueness is not to require that only unique qualities be considered. While a defendant's anticipation of specific consequences to the victims of his intended act is relevant to sentencing, such detailed foreknowledge does not exhaust the category of morally relevant fact. One such fact that is known to all murderers and relevant to the blameworthiness of each one was identified by the *Booth* majority itself when it barred the sentencing authority in capital cases from considering "the full range of foreseeable consequences of a defendant's actions." Murder has foreseeable consequences. When it happens, it is always to distinct individuals, and after it happens other victims are left behind. Every defendant knows, if endowed with the mental competence for criminal responsibility, that the life he will take by his homicidal behavior is that of a unique person, like himself, and that the person to be killed probably has close associates, "survivors," who will suffer harms and deprivations from the victim's death. Just as defendants know that they are not faceless human ciphers, they know that their victims are not valueless fungibles, and just as defendants appreciate the web of relationships and dependencies in which they live, they know that their victims are not human islands, but individuals with parents or children, spouses or friends or dependents. Thus, when a defendant chooses to kill, or to raise the risk of a victim's death, this choice necessarily relates to a whole human being and threatens an association of others, who may be distinctly hurt. The fact that the defendant may not know the details of a victim's life and characteristics, or the exact identities and needs of those who may survive, should not in any way obscure the further facts that death is always to a "unique" individual, and harm to some group of survivors is a consequence of a successful homicidal act so foreseeable as to be virtually inevitable.

That foreseeability of the killing's consequences imbues them with direct moral relevance, cf. *Penry* v. *Lynaugh, supra,* 492 U.S., at 328, 109 S.Ct., at 2952

(death penalty should be "'reasoned moral response'"), and evidence of the specific harm caused when a homicidal risk is realized is nothing more than evidence of the risk that the defendant originally chose to run despite the kinds of consequences that were obviously foreseeable. It is morally both defensible and appropriate to consider such evidence when penalizing a murderer, like other criminals, in light of common knowledge and the moral responsibility that such knowledge entails. Any failure to take account of a victim's individuality and the effects of his death upon close survivors would thus more appropriately be called an act of lenity than their consideration an invitation to arbitrary sentencing. Indeed, given a defendant's option to introduce relevant evidence in mitigation, sentencing without such evidence of victim impact may be seen as a significantly imbalanced process.

I so view the relevance of the two categories of victim impact evidence at issue here, and I fully agree with the majority's conclusion, and the opinions expressed by the dissenters in *Booth* and *Gathers,* that nothing in the Eighth Amendment's condemnation of cruel and unusual punishment would require that evidence to be excluded.

I do not, however, rest my decision to overrule wholly on the constitutional error that I see in the cases in question. I must rely as well on my further view that *Booth* sets an unworkable standard of constitutional relevance that threatens, on its own terms, to produce such arbitrary consequences and uncertainty of application as virtually to guarantee a result far diminished from the case's promise of appropriately individualized sentencing for capital defendants. These conclusions will be seen to result from the interaction of three facts. First, although *Booth* was prompted by the introduction of a systematically prepared "victim impact statement" at the sentencing phase of the trial, *Booth's* restriction of relevant facts to what the defendant knew and considered in deciding to kill applies to any evidence, however derived or presented. Second, details of which the defendant was unaware, about the victim and survivors, will customarily be disclosed by the evidence introduced at the guilt phase of the trial. Third, the jury that determines guilt will usually determine, or make recommendations about, the imposition of capital punishment.

A hypothetical case will illustrate these facts and raise what I view as the serious practical problems with application of the *Booth* standard. Assume that a minister, unidentified as such and wearing no clerical collar, walks down a street to his church office on a brief errand, while his wife and adolescent daughter wait for him in a parked car. He is robbed and killed by a stranger, and his survivors witness his death. What are the circumstances of the crime that can be considered at the sentencing phase under *Booth?* The defendant did not know his victim was a minister, or that he had a wife and child, let alone that they were watching. Under *Booth,* these facts were irrelevant to his decision to kill, and they should be barred from consideration at sentencing. Yet evidence of them will surely be admitted at the guilt phase of the trial. The widow will testify to what she saw, and in so doing she will not be asked to pretend that she was a mere bystander. She could not succeed at that if she tried. The daughter may well testify too. The jury will not be kept from knowing that the victim was a minister, with a wife and child, on an errand to his church. This is so not only because the widow will not try to deceive the jury about her relationship, but also because the usual standards of trial relevance afford factfinders enough information about surrounding circumstances to let them make sense of the narrowly material facts of the crime itself. No one claims that jurors in a capital case should be deprived of such common contextual evidence, even though the defendant knew nothing about the errand, the victim's occupation or his family. And yet, if these facts are not kept from the jury at the guilt stage, they will be in the jurors' minds at the sentencing stage.

Booth thus raises a dilemma with very practical consequences. If we were to require the rules of guilt-phase evidence to be changed to guarantee the full effect of *Booth's* promise to exclude consideration of specific facts unknown to the defendant and thus supposedly without significance in morally evaluating his decision to kill, we would seriously reduce the comprehensibility of most trials by depriving jurors of those details of context that allow them to understand what is being described. If, on the other hand, we are to leave the rules of trial evidence alone, *Booth's* objective will not be attained without requiring a separate sentencing jury to be empaneled. This would be a major imposition on the States, however, and I suppose that no one would seriously consider adding such a further requirement.

But, even if *Booth* were extended one way or the other to exclude completely from the sentencing proceeding all facts about the crime's victims not known by the defendant, the case would be vulnerable to the further charge that it would lead to arbitrary sentencing results. In the preceding hypothetical, *Booth* would require that all evidence about the victim's family, including its very existence, be excluded from sentencing consideration because the defendant did not know of it when he killed the victim. Yet, if the victim's daughter had screamed "Daddy, look out," as the defendant approached the victim with drawn gun, then the evidence of at least the daughter's survivorship would be admissible even under a strict reading of *Booth,* because the defendant, prior to killing, had been made aware of the daughter's existence, which therefore became relevant in evaluating the defendant's decision to kill. Resting a decision about the admission of impact evidence on such a fortuity is arbitrary.

Thus, the status quo is unsatisfactory and the question is whether the case that has produced it should be overruled. In this instance, as in any other, overruling a precedent of this Court is a matter of no small import, for "the doctrine of *stare decisis* is of fundamental importance to the rule of law." But, even in constitutional cases, the doctrine carries such persuasive force that we have always required a departure from precedent to be supported by some "special justification."

The Court has a special justification in this case. *Booth* promises more than it can deliver, given the unresolved tension between common evidentiary standards at the guilt phase and *Booth's* promise of a sentencing determination free from the consideration of facts unknown to the defendant and irrelevant to his decision to kill. An extension of the case to guarantee a sentencing authority free from the influence of information extraneous under *Booth* would be either an unworkable or a costly extension of an erroneous principle and would itself create a risk of arbitrary results. There is only one other course open to us. We can recede from the erroneous holding that created the tension and extended the false promise, and there is precedent in our *stare decisis* jurisprudence for doing just this. In prior cases, when this Court has confronted a wrongly decided, unworkable precedent calling for some further action by the Court, we have chosen not to compound the original error, but to overrule the precedent. Following this course here not only has itself the support of precedent but of practical sense as well. Therefore, I join the Court in its partial overruling of *Booth* and *Gathers.*

Justice MARSHALL, with whom Justice BLACK-MUN joins, dissenting.

Power, not reason, is the new currency of this Court's decisionmaking. Four Terms ago, a five-Justice majority of this Court held that "victim impact" evidence of the type at issue in this case could not constitutionally be introduced during the penalty phase of a capital trial. By another 5-4 vote, a majority of this Court rebuffed an attack upon this ruling just two Terms ago. Nevertheless, having expressly invited respondent to renew the attack, today's majority overrules *Booth* and *Gathers* and credits the dissenting views expressed in those cases. Neither the law nor the facts supporting *Booth* and *Gathers* underwent any change in the last four years. Only the personnel of this Court did.

In dispatching *Booth* and *Gathers* to their graves, today's majority ominously suggests that an even more extensive upheaval of this Court's precedents may be in store. Renouncing this Court's historical commitment to a conception of "the judiciary as a source of impersonal and reasoned judgments," the majority declares itself free to discard any principle of constitutional liberty which was recognized or reaffirmed over the dissenting votes of four Justices and with which five or more Justices *now* disagree. The implications of this radical new exception to the doctrine of *stare decisis* are staggering. The majority today sends a clear signal that scores of established constitutional liberties are now ripe for reconsideration, thereby inviting the very type of open defiance of our precedents that the majority rewards in this case. Because I believe that this Court owes more to its constitutional precedents in general and to *Booth* and *Gathers* in particular, I dissent.

I

Speaking for the Court as then constituted, Justice Powell and Justice Brennan set out the rationale for excluding victim-impact evidence from the sentencing proceedings in a capital case. As the majorities in *Booth* and *Gathers* recognized, the core principle of this Court's capital jurisprudence is that the sentence of death must reflect an "'*individualized* determination'" of the defendant's "'personal responsibility and moral guilt'" and must be based upon factors that channel the jury's discretion "'so as to minimize the risk of wholly arbitrary and capricious action.'" The State's introduction of victim-impact evidence, Justice Powell and Justice Brennan explained, violates this fundamental principle. Where, as is ordinarily the case, the defendant was unaware of the personal circumstances of his victim, admitting evidence of the victim's character and the impact of the murder upon

the victim's family predicates the sentencing determination on "factors . . . wholly unrelated to the blameworthiness of [the] particular defendant." And even where the defendant *was* in a position to foresee the likely impact of his conduct, admission of victim-impact evidence creates an unacceptable risk of sentencing arbitrariness. As Justice Powell explained in *Booth,* the probative value of such evidence is always outweighed by its prejudicial effect because of its inherent capacity to draw the jury's attention away from the character of the defendant and the circumstances of the crime to such illicit considerations as the eloquence with which family members express their grief and the status of the victim in the community. I continue to find these considerations wholly persuasive, and I see no purpose in trying to improve upon Justice Powell's and Justice Brennan's exposition of them.

There is nothing new in the majority's discussion of the supposed deficiencies in *Booth* and *Gathers*. Every one of the arguments made by the majority can be found in the dissenting opinions filed in those two cases, and, as I show in the margin, each argument was convincingly answered by Justice Powell and Justice Brennan.

But contrary to the impression that one might receive from reading the majority's lengthy rehearsing of the issues addressed in *Booth* and *Gathers,* the outcome of this case does not turn simply on who— the *Booth* and *Gathers* majorities or the *Booth* and *Gathers* dissenters—had the better of the argument. Justice Powell and Justice Brennan's position carried the day in those cases and became the law of the land. The real question, then, is whether today's majority has come forward with the type of extraordinary showing that this Court has historically demanded before overruling one of its precedents. In my view, the majority clearly has not made any such showing. Indeed, the striking feature of the majority's opinion is its radical assertion that it need not even try.

II

The overruling of one of this Court's precedents ought to be a matter of great moment and consequence. Although the doctrine of *stare decisis* is not an "inexorable command," this Court has repeatedly stressed that fidelity to precedent is fundamental to "a society governed by the rule of law."

Consequently, this Court has never departed from precedent without "special justification." Such justifications include the advent of "subsequent changes or development in the law" that undermine a decision's rationale, *Patterson* v. *McLean Credit Union,* the need "to bring [a decision] into agreement with experience and with facts newly ascertained," and a showing that a particular precedent has become a "detriment to coherence and consistency in the law."

The majority cannot seriously claim that *any* of these traditional bases for overruling a precedent applies to *Booth* or *Gathers.* The majority does not suggest that the legal rationale of these decisions has been undercut by changes or developments in doctrine during the last two years. Nor does the majority claim that experience over that period of time has discredited the principle that "any decision to impose the death sentence be, and appear to be, based on reason rather than caprice or emotion."

The majority does assert that *Booth* and *Gathers* "have defied consistent application by the lower courts," *ante,* at 2610, but the evidence that the majority proffers is so feeble that the majority cannot sincerely expect anyone to believe this claim. To support its contention, the majority points to Justice O'CONNOR's dissent in *Gathers,* which noted a division among lower courts over whether *Booth* prohibited prosecutorial arguments relating to the victim's personal characteristics. That, of course, was the issue expressly considered and resolved in *Gathers.* The majority also cites THE CHIEF JUSTICE's dissent in *Mills* v. *Maryland.* That opinion does not contain a *single word* about any supposed "[in]consistent application" of *Booth* in the lower courts. Finally, the majority refers to a divided Ohio Supreme Court decision disposing of an issue concerning victim-impact evidence. Obviously, if a division among the members of a single lower court in a single case were sufficient to demonstrate that a particular precedent was a "detriment to coherence and consistency in the law," there would hardly be a decision in United States Reports that we would not be obliged to reconsider.

It takes little real detective work to discern just what *has* changed since this Court decided *Booth* and *Gathers:* this Court's own personnel. Indeed, the majority candidly explains why this particular contingency, which until now has been almost universally understood *not* to be sufficient to warrant overruling a precedent, *is* sufficient to justify overruling *Booth* and *Gathers.* "Considerations in favor of *stare decisis* are at their acme," the majority explains, "in cases involving property and contract rights, where reliance interests are involved[;] the opposite is true in cases such as the present one involving procedural and evi-

dentiary rules." In addition, the majority points out, "*Booth* and *Gathers* were decided by the narrowest of margins, over spirited dissents" and thereafter were "questioned by members of the Court." Taken together, these considerations make it legitimate, in the majority's view, to elevate the position of the *Booth* and *Gathers* dissenters into the law of the land.

This truncation of the Court's duty to stand by its own precedents is astonishing. By limiting full protection of the doctrine of *stare decisis* to "cases involving property and contract rights," the majority sends a clear signal that essentially *all* decisions implementing the personal liberties protected by the Bill of Rights and the Fourteenth Amendment are open to reexamination. Taking into account the majority's additional criterion for overruling—that a case either was decided or reaffirmed by a 5-4 margin "over spirited dissen[t]," the continued vitality of literally scores of decisions must be understood to depend on nothing more than the proclivities of the individuals who *now* comprise a majority of this Court.

In my view, this impoverished conception of *stare decisis* cannot possibly be reconciled with the values that inform the proper judicial function. Contrary to what the majority suggests, *stare decisis* is important not merely because individuals rely on precedent to structure their commercial activity but because fidelity to precedent is part and parcel of a conception of "the judiciary as a source of impersonal and reasoned judgments." Indeed, this function of *stare decisis* is in many respects even *more* critical in adjudication involving constitutional liberties than in adjudication involving commercial entitlements. Because enforcement of the Bill of Rights and the Fourteenth Amendment frequently requires this Court to rein in the forces of democratic politics, this Court can legitimately lay claim to compliance with its directives only if the public understands the Court to be implementing "principles . . . founded in the law rather than in the proclivities of individuals." Thus, as Justice STEVENS has explained, the "stron[g] presumption of validity" to which "recently decided cases" are entitled "is an essential thread in the mantle of protection that the law affords the individual. . . . It is the unpopular or beleaguered individual—not the man in power—who has the greatest stake in the integrity of the law."

Carried to its logical conclusion, the majority's debilitated conception of *stare decisis* would destroy the Court's very capacity to resolve authoritatively the abiding conflicts between those with power and those without. If this Court shows so little respect for its own precedents, it can hardly expect them to be treated more respectfully by the state actors whom these decisions are supposed to bind. By signaling its willingness to give fresh consideration to any constitutional liberty recognized by a 5-4 vote "over spirited dissen[t]," the majority invites state actors to renew the very policies deemed unconstitutional in the hope that this Court may now reverse course, even if it has only recently reaffirmed the constitutional liberty in question.

Indeed, the majority's disposition of this case nicely illustrates the rewards of such a strategy of defiance. The Tennessee Supreme Court did nothing in this case to disguise its contempt for this Court's decisions in *Booth* and *Gathers.* Summing up its reaction to those cases, it concluded:

> *"It is an affront to the civilized members of the human race to say that at sentencing in a capital case, a parade of witnesses may praise the background, character and good deeds of Defendant (as was done in this case), without limitation as to relevancy, but nothing may be said that bears upon the character of, or harm imposed, upon the victims."*

Offering no explanation for how this case could possibly be distinguished from *Booth* and *Gathers* —for obviously, there is none to offer—the court perfunctorily declared that the victim-impact evidence and the prosecutor's argument based on this evidence "did not violate either [of those decisions]." It cannot be clearer that the court simply declined to be bound by this Court's precedents.

Far from condemning this blatant disregard for the rule of law, the majority applauds it. In the Tennessee Supreme Court's denigration of *Booth* and *Gathers* as "an affront to the civilized members of the human race," the majority finds only confirmation of "the unfairness of the rule pronounced by" the majorities in those cases. It is hard to imagine a more complete abdication of this Court's historic commitment to defending the supremacy of its own pronouncements on issues of constitutional liberty. In light of the cost that such abdication exacts on the authoritativeness of *all* of this Court's pronouncements, it is also hard to imagine a more short-sighted strategy for effecting change in our constitutional order.

III

Today's decision charts an unmistakable course. If the majority's radical reconstruction of the rules for over-

turning this Court's decisions is to be taken at face value—and the majority offers us no reason why it should not—then the overruling of *Booth* and *Gathers* is but a preview of an even broader and more far-reaching assault upon this Court's precedents. Cast aside today are those condemned to face society's ultimate penalty. Tomorrow's victims may be minorities, women, or the indigent. Inevitably, this campaign to resurrect yesterday's "spirited dissents" will squander the authority and the legitimacy of this Court as a protector of the powerless.

I dissent.

Justice STEVENS, with whom Justice BLACKMUN joins, dissenting.

The novel rule that the Court announces today represents a dramatic departure from the principles that have governed our capital sentencing jurisprudence for decades. Justice MARSHALL is properly concerned about the majority's trivialization of the doctrine of *stare decisis.* But even if *Booth* and *Gathers* had not been decided, today's decision would represent a sharp break with past decisions. Our cases provide no support whatsoever for the majority's conclusion that the prosecutor may introduce evidence that sheds no light on the defendant's guilt or moral culpability, and thus serves no purpose other than to encourage jurors to decide in favor of death rather than life on the basis of their emotions rather than their reason.

Until today our capital punishment jurisprudence has required that any decision to impose the death penalty be based solely on evidence that tends to inform the jury about the character of the offense and the character of the defendant. Evidence that serves no purpose other than to appeal to the sympathies or emotions of the jurors has never been considered admissible. Thus, if a defendant, who had murdered a convenience store clerk in cold blood in the course of an armed robbery, offered evidence unknown to him at the time of the crime about the immoral character of his victim, all would recognize immediately that the evidence was irrelevant and inadmissible. Evenhanded justice requires that the same constraint be imposed on the advocate of the death penalty.

I

In *Williams* v. *New York,* this Court considered the scope of the inquiry that should precede the imposition of a death sentence. Relying on practices that had developed "both before and since the American colonies became a nation," Justice Black described the wide latitude that had been accorded judges in considering the source and type of evidence that is relevant to the sentencing determination. Notably, that opinion refers not only to the relevance of evidence establishing the defendant's guilt, but also to the relevance of "the fullest information possible concerning the defendant's life and characteristics." "Victim impact" evidence, however, was unheard of when *Williams* was decided. The relevant evidence of harm to society consisted of proof that the defendant was guilty of the offense charged in the indictment.

Almost 30 years after our decision in *Williams* the Court reviewed the scope of evidence relevant in capital sentencing. In his plurality opinion, Chief Justice Burger concluded that in a capital case, the sentencer must not be prevented "from considering, as a mitigating factor, any aspect of a defendant's character or record and any of the circumstances of the offense that the defendant proffers as a basis for a sentence less than death." As in *Williams,* the character of the offense and the character of the offender constituted the entire category of relevant evidence. "Victim impact" evidence was still unheard of when *Lockett* was decided.

As the Court acknowledges today, the use of victim impact evidence "is of recent origin." Insofar as the Court's jurisprudence is concerned, this type of evidence made its first appearance in 1987 in *Booth* v. *Maryland.* In his opinion for the Court, Justice Powell noted that our prior cases had stated that the question whether an individual defendant should be executed is to be determined on the basis of "'the character of the individual and the circumstances of the crime.'" Relying on those cases and on *Enmund* v. *Florida,* the Court concluded that unless evidence has some bearing on the defendant's personal responsibility and moral guilt, its admission would create a risk that a death sentence might be based on considerations that are constitutionally impermissible or totally irrelevant to the sentencing process. Evidence that served no purpose except to describe the personal characteristics of the victim and the emotional impact of the crime on the victim's family was therefore constitutionally irrelevant.

Our decision in *Booth* was entirely consistent with the practices that had been followed "both before and since the American colonies became a nation." Our holding was mandated by our capital punishment jurisprudence, which requires any decision to impose the death penalty to be based on reason rather than caprice or emotion. The dissenting opinions in *Booth* and in *Gathers* can be searched in vain for any judicial precedent sanctioning the use of evidence unrelated to the character of the offense or the character of the offender in the sentencing process. Today, however, relying on nothing more than those dissenting opinions, the Court abandons rules of relevance that are older than the Nation itself, and ventures into uncharted seas of irrelevance.

II

Today's majority has obviously been moved by an argument that has strong political appeal but no proper place in a reasoned judicial opinion. Because our decision in *Lockett* recognizes the defendant's right to introduce all mitigating evidence that may inform the jury about his character, the Court suggests that fairness requires that the State be allowed to respond with similar evidence about the *victim.* This argument is a classic *non sequitur.* The victim is not on trial; her character, whether good or bad, cannot therefore constitute either an aggravating or mitigating circumstance.

Even if introduction of evidence about the victim could be equated with introduction of evidence about the defendant, the argument would remain flawed in both its premise and its conclusion. The conclusion that exclusion of victim impact evidence results in a significantly imbalanced sentencing procedure is simply inaccurate. Just as the defendant is entitled to introduce any relevant mitigating evidence, so the State may rebut that evidence and may designate any relevant conduct to be an aggravating factor provided that the factor is sufficiently well defined and consistently applied to cabin the sentencer's discretion.

The premise that a criminal prosecution requires an even-handed balance between the State and the defendant is also incorrect. The Constitution grants certain rights to the criminal defendant and imposes special limitations on the State designed to protect the individual from overreaching by the disproportionately powerful State. Thus, the State must prove a defendant's guilt beyond a reasonable doubt. Rules of evidence are also weighted in the defendant's favor. For example, the prosecution generally cannot introduce evidence of the defendant's character to prove his propensity to commit a crime, but the defendant can introduce such reputation evidence to show his law-abiding nature. Even if balance were required or desirable, today's decision, by permitting both the defendant and the State to introduce irrelevant evidence for the sentencer's consideration without any guidance, surely does nothing to enhance parity in the sentencing process.

III

Victim impact evidence, as used in this case, has two flaws, both related to the Eighth Amendment's command that the punishment of death may not be meted out arbitrarily or capriciously. First, aspects of the character of the victim unforeseeable to the defendant at the time of his crime are irrelevant to the defendant's "personal responsibility and moral guilt" and therefore cannot justify a death sentence.

Second, the quantity and quality of victim impact evidence sufficient to turn a verdict of life in prison into a verdict of death is not defined until after the crime has been committed and therefore cannot possibly be applied consistently in different cases. The sentencer's unguided consideration of victim impact evidence thus conflicts with the principle central to our capital punishment jurisprudence that, "where discretion is afforded a sentencing body on a matter so grave as the determination of whether a human life should be taken or spared, that discretion must be suitably directed and limited so as to minimize the risk of wholly arbitrary and capricious action." Open-ended reliance by a capital sentencer on victim impact evidence simply does not provide a "principled way to distinguish [cases], in which the death penalty [i]s imposed, from the many cases in which it [i]s not."

The majority attempts to justify the admission of victim impact evidence by arguing that "consideration of the harm caused by the crime has been an important factor in the exercise of [sentencing] discretion." This statement is misleading and inaccurate. It is misleading because it is not limited to harm that is foreseeable. It is inaccurate because it fails to differentiate between legislative determinations and judicial sentencing. It is true that an evaluation of the harm caused by different kinds of wrongful conduct is a critical aspect in legislative definitions of offenses and determinations concerning sentencing guidelines. There is a rational correlation between moral culpability and the foreseeable harm caused by criminal conduct. Moreover, in the capital sentencing area, legislative identi-

fication of the special aggravating factors that may justify the imposition of the death penalty is entirely appropriate. But the majority cites no authority for the suggestion that unforeseeable and indirect harms to a victim's family are properly considered as aggravating evidence on a case-by-case basis.

The dissents in *Booth* and *Gathers* and the majority today offer only the recent decision in *Tison* v. *Arizona* and two legislative examples to support their contention that harm to the victim has traditionally influenced sentencing discretion. *Tison* held that the death penalty may be imposed on a felon who acts with reckless disregard for human life if a death occurs in the course of the felony, even though capital punishment cannot be imposed if no one dies as a result of the crime. The first legislative example is that attempted murder and murder are classified as two different offenses subject to different punishments. The second legislative example is that a person who drives while intoxicated is guilty of vehicular homicide if his actions result in a death but is not guilty of this offense if he has the good fortune to make it home without killing anyone.

These three scenarios, however, are fully consistent with the Eighth Amendment jurisprudence reflected in *Booth* and *Gathers* and do not demonstrate that harm to the victim may be considered by a capital sentencer in the ad hoc and post hoc manner authorized by today's majority. The majority's examples demonstrate only that harm to the victim may justify enhanced punishment if the harm is both foreseeable to the defendant and clearly identified in advance of the crime by the legislature as a class of harm that should in every case result in more severe punishment.

In each scenario, the defendants could reasonably foresee that their acts might result in loss of human life. In addition, in each, the decision that the defendants should be treated differently was made prior to the crime by the legislature, the decision of which is subject to scrutiny for basic rationality. Finally, in each scenario, every defendant who causes the well-defined harm of destroying a human life will be subject to the determination that his conduct should be punished more severely. The majority's scenarios therefore provide no support for its holding, which permits a jury to sentence a defendant to death because of harm to the victim and his family that the defendant could not foresee, which was not even identified until after the crime had been committed, and which may be deemed by the jury, without any rational explanation, to justify a death sentence in one case but not in another. Unlike the rule elucidated by the scenarios on which the majority relies, the majority's holding offends the Eighth Amendment because it permits the sentencer to rely on irrelevant evidence in an arbitrary and capricious manner.

The majority's argument that "the sentencing authority has always been free to consider a wide range of *relevant* material," thus cannot justify consideration of victim impact evidence that is *irrelevant* because it details harms that the defendant could not have foreseen. Nor does the majority's citation of *Gregg* v. *Georgia* concerning the "wide scope of evidence and argument allowed at presentence hearings," support today's holding. The *Gregg* plurality endorsed the sentencer's consideration of a wide range of evidence "[s]o long as the evidence introduced and the arguments made at the presentence hearing do not prejudice a defendant." Irrelevant victim impact evidence that distracts the sentencer from the proper focus of sentencing and encourages reliance on emotion and other arbitrary factors necessarily prejudices the defendant.

The majority's apparent inability to understand this fact is highlighted by its misunderstanding of Justice Powell's argument in *Booth* that admission of victim impact evidence is undesirable because it risks shifting the focus of the sentencing hearing away from the defendant and the circumstances of the crime and creating a "'mini-trial' on the victim's character." *Booth* found this risk insupportable not, as today's majority suggests, because it creates a "tactical" "dilemma" for the defendant, but because it allows the possibility that the jury will be so distracted by prejudicial and irrelevant considerations that it will base its life-or-death decision on whim or caprice.

IV

The majority thus does far more than validate a State's judgment that "the jury should see 'a quick glimpse of the life petitioner chose to extinguish.'" Instead, it allows a jury to hold a defendant responsible for a whole array of harms that he could not foresee and for which he is therefore not blameworthy. Justice SOUTER argues that these harms are sufficiently foreseeable to hold the defendant accountable because "[e]very defendant knows, if endowed with the mental competence for criminal responsibility, that the life he will take by his homicidal behavior is that of a unique person, like himself, and that the person who will be

killed probably has close associates, 'survivors,' who will suffer harms and deprivations from the victim's death." But every juror and trial judge knows this much as well. Evidence about who those survivors are and what harms and deprivations they have suffered is therefore not necessary to apprise the sentencer of any information that was actually foreseeable to the defendant. Its only function can be to "divert the jury's attention away from the defendant's background and record, and the circumstances of the crime."

Arguing in the alternative, Justice SOUTER correctly points out that victim impact evidence will sometimes come to the attention of the jury during the guilt phase of the trial. He reasons that the ideal of basing sentencing determinations entirely on the moral culpability of the defendant is therefore unattainable unless a different jury is empaneled for the sentencing hearing. Thus, to justify overruling *Booth,* he assumes that the decision must otherwise be extended far beyond its actual holding.

Justice SOUTER's assumption is entirely unwarranted. For as long as the contours of relevance at sentencing hearings have been limited to evidence concerning the character of the offense and the character of the offender, the law has also recognized that evidence that is admissible for a proper purpose may not be excluded because it is inadmissible for other purposes and may indirectly prejudice the jury. In the case before us today, much of what might be characterized as victim impact evidence was properly admitted during the guilt phase of the trial and, given the horrible character of this crime, may have been sufficient to justify the Tennessee Supreme Court's conclusion that the error was harmless because the jury would necessarily have imposed the death sentence even absent the error. The fact that a good deal of such evidence is routinely and properly brought to the attention of the jury merely indicates that the rule of *Booth* may not affect the outcome of many cases.

In reaching our decision today, however, we should not be concerned with the cases in which victim impact evidence will not make a difference. We should be concerned instead with the cases in which it will make a difference. In those cases, defendants will be sentenced arbitrarily to death on the basis of evidence that would not otherwise be admissible because it is irrelevant to the defendants' moral culpability. The Constitution's proscription against the arbitrary imposition of the death penalty must necessarily proscribe the admission of evidence that serves no purpose other than to result in such arbitrary sentences.

V

The notion that the inability to produce an ideal system of justice in which every punishment is precisely married to the defendant's blameworthiness somehow justifies a rule that completely divorces some capital sentencing determinations from moral culpability is incomprehensible to me. Also incomprehensible is the argument that such a rule is required for the jury to take into account that each murder victim is a "unique" human being. The fact that each of us is unique is a proposition so obvious that it surely requires no evidentiary support. What is not obvious, however, is the way in which the character or reputation in one case may differ from that of other possible victims. Evidence offered to prove such differences can only be intended to identify some victims as more worthy of protection than others. Such proof risks decisions based on the same invidious motives as a prosecutor's decision to seek the death penalty if a victim is white but to accept a plea bargain if the victim is black.

Given the current popularity of capital punishment in a crime-ridden society, the political appeal of arguments that assume that increasing the severity of sentences is the best cure for the cancer of crime, and the political strength of the "victims' rights" movement, I recognize that today's decision will be greeted with enthusiasm by a large number of concerned and thoughtful citizens. The great tragedy of the decision, however, is the danger that the "hydraulic pressure" of public opinion that Justice Holmes once described—and that properly influences the deliberations of democratic legislatures—has played a role not only in the Court's decision to hear this case, and in its decision to reach the constitutional question without pausing to consider affirming on the basis of the Tennessee Supreme Court's rationale, but even in its resolution of the constitutional issue involved. Today is a sad day for a great institution.

WHEN LAW BOWS TO POLITICS:
Explaining *Payne* v. *Tennessee**

David R. Dow

A stunning philosophical error lies at the heart of the Supreme Court's recent decision in Payne v. Tennessee.[1] *Although the root of the error is exposed in the majority opinion in* Payne, *neither the dissenting opinion in the case nor the academic criticism of the decision has focused on this flaw.[2] The error, however, is so egregious that it can mean but one thing: that in* Payne, *a majority of the Court bowed to politics, and in so doing abandoned principle and law.*

In Part I of this Essay, I describe the philosophical framework relevant to the question of why we punish certain conduct. In Part II, I review the decisions that Payne *overruled. Finally, in Part III, I argue that the Court's opinion in* Payne *is deeply flawed and that it reflects an obeisance to political forces at the expense of legal principle.*

---

*From David Dow, "When Law Bows to Politics: Explaining *Payne* v. *Tennessee*," in 26 *University of California, Davis* *Law Review* 157–76. Copyright 1992 by The Regents of the University of California. Reprinted with permission.

I. The Philosophical Framework

Consider three scenarios:

1. Harry comes home from work and discovers that his wife has left him. He drinks a few beers, loads his shotgun, goes out onto his back porch, and fires the gun over and over until his anger leaves him. He does damage to a bunch of trees, but nothing else.
2. At the same time that Harry is drinking his second beer, Harriet, who lives a mile or so down the road, gets home and discovers that her husband has left her. She skips the beer and heads straight out to her back porch, where she too fires her shotgun until her tears have stopped. The next day, the body of a homeless man, call him Darryl, is found in the trees behind Harriet's home. Her shooting spree has damaged a few trees, and it has killed someone.
3. The facts are the same as in scenario (2), but instead of killing Darryl, Harriet has killed Rabbi Ezra Cohen, an amateur entomologist who was searching in the wooded area for a rare beetle.

One of the central problems in the philosophy of punishment is why we distinguish between scenarios (1) and (2).[3] That is, why do we punish Harriet more severely than we punish Harry? There is a powerful sense in which their actions were identical, even though the consequences were different. Both behaved recklessly, but neither planned to kill, and neither expected that there would be a human being in the trees. We might also assume that neither Harry nor Harriet had ever known anyone to venture into the trees, and that no one would reasonably expect that human beings would be in the forest.

Nevertheless, the penal codes of most states would permit Harriet to be prosecuted for manslaughter. Notwithstanding the sense in which she and Harry "did" the same thing, Harriet will face substantially more serious penalties. Of course, a jury might well decide, in view of her state of mind, that Harriet should not be punished with especial severity. But it might also decide to punish her harshly; the important point is simply that it *may* so decide. In most jurisdictions, while Harriet may be held to answer for manslaughter, Harry will be charged, at most, with reckless conduct.

The criminal law literature and the philosophy of punishment generally have discussed this issue extensively.[4] My object in this brief Essay is not to rejoin the debate as to why we distinguish between Harry and Harriet for purposes of punishment. Rather, I propose to focus on Harriet. I assume, in other words, that the philosophical distinction between scenarios (1) and (2) is tenable. The question I examine is whether, having drawn this distinction, it is appropriate to draw a still more subtle distinction by focusing on the identity of the person whom Harriet has inadvertently killed. Or, put differently, does the tenability of the distinction between scenarios (1) and (2) also support a distinction between scenarios (2) and (3)? I will suggest that the answer is no. In so doing, I will focus on the Supreme Court's recent decision in *Payne* v. *Tennessee*,[5] in which the Court, overruling two earlier decisions (one that was barely four years old[6] and another that was barely two years old[7]), held that the answer is yes.

II. From *Booth* to *Payne*

The question in *Payne* concerned the relevance of the details of the murdered person's life to the punishment meted out to the murderer. That is, may Harriet be punished more severely if the person she accidentally kills turns out to be Rabbi Cohen rather than Darryl? *Payne* held "that if the State chooses to permit the admission of victim impact evidence and prosecutorial argument on that subject [during the sentencing phase of a capital trial], the Eighth Amendment erects no *per se* bar."[8] In other words, a state may distinguish between scenarios (2) and (3).[9] *Payne* overruled two recent decisions, *Booth* v. *Maryland*[10] and *South Carolina* v. *Gathers*.[11] Part of the reason that the *Payne* court embraced the distinction between scenarios (2) and (3) is that neither the *Booth* nor the *Gathers* majority opinions satisfactorily addressed the central contention of Justice Scalia's dissenting opinions in those cases.[12]

In *Booth,* the son, daughter, son-in-law, and granddaughter of a murdered couple were interviewed by a member of the Maryland Division of Parole and Probation. The resulting statement, called the Victim Impact Statement (VIS), was read to the jury during the sentencing phase of Booth's trial. The statement described, inter alia, the son's horror at finding his parents murdered; the daughter's and son-in-law's lasting depression, as well as the daughter's inability to eat; and, perhaps most poignantly, the pall cast over the granddaughter's wedding, which had been scheduled for the weekend following the murder and which, under Jewish law, proceeded in spite of the murder.[13] Justice Powell, writing for a majority of five,[14] attached the entire VIS as an appendix to his opinion.[15]

In *Gathers,* there was no victim impact evidence as such. Instead, during his closing argument, the prosecutor emphasized the murder victim's personal characteristics: specifically, the victim's deep religiosity (manifested by the fact that he always carried with him a bible, which the murderer had destroyed), and the victim's patriotism (manifested by the fact that he had with him his voter's registration card). Justice Brennan, writing for himself and four other Justices,[16] observed that the evidence deemed inadmissible under the Eighth Amendment by *Booth* included survivors' statements concerning the victim's personal characteristics.[17] He thus concluded that these descriptions were also barred from coming in, even by way of the prosecutor's closing argument.[18]

In *Booth,* upon which *Gathers* squarely rests, Justice Powell adduced two primary arguments against allowing victim impact evidence during the sentencing phase of a capital trial. One of these reasons is purely doctrinal; the other represents a blend of doctrinal and pragmatic concerns. The doctrinal basis for the holding has been further explicated by decisions rendered since *Booth* itself was decided.

With the benefit of these subsequent decisions, as well as those that *Booth* itself cites, the doctrinal strand of Justice Powell's argument can be summarized as follows: A sentence of death must be reliable.[19] Reliability means, at a minimum, that the sentence of death must be based on a "reasoned moral response" to the circumstances of the crime, as well as on the individuality of the defendant.[20] Hence, mandatory death penalty laws are unconstitutional because they do not permit the jury to analyze either of these variables.[21] Similarly, state statutes are unconstitutional as applied when they prevent the jury from giving effect to mitigating evidence, because it is precisely this evidence that helps define the criminal's individuality.[22] Survivors' statements, however, pertain to neither the individuality of the criminal defendant nor the individual circumstances of the defendant's crime. They are thus irrelevant to the reasoned moral response that the Eighth Amendment commands.[23]

In the second strand of the *Booth* opinion, Justice Powell argued that the practical ramifications of allowing victim impact evidence might transform the sentencing phase of a capital trial into a mini-trial on the victim's character.[24] The defendant would necessarily be permitted to cross-examine statements by survivors and would be permitted to call his own witnesses to rebut the characterizations proffered by the survivors.[25] One can imagine a daughter of a murder victim testifying as to her anguish, followed by the defendant's effort to discredit her by pointing out, for example, that she had been estranged from her murdered father for ten years. Of course, Justice Powell's attention to the enormous practical difficulties of managing this type of evidentiary ordeal was not altogether untethered to doctrinal concerns. He emphasized that because a rule allowing the daughter to testify would necessitate such a sideshow, it would undoubtedly divert the jury's attention from what it ought, under the Eighth Amendment, to be doing.[26]

Justice Brennan's opinion in *Gathers* stressed the doctrinal theme developed in *Booth.* He emphasized that personal characteristics of the murder victim of which the defendant was unaware before the crime do not bear on the murderer's personal culpability.[27] These characteristics are thus irrelevant to the sentencing decision.[28]

In both *Booth* and *Gathers,* Justice Scalia wrote acerbic dissenting opinions. His dissent in *Booth,* joined by Chief Justice Rehnquist and Justices White and O'Connor, argued that the survivors' testimony is relevant because it illuminates the nature of the harm that the defendant caused.[29] As Scalia put it: "It seems to me, however—and, I think, to most of mankind— that the *amount of harm* one causes does bear upon the extent of his 'personal responsibility.'"[30] That is, there is a tenable philosophical distinction between scenarios (1) and (2).

Justice Scalia's dissent in *Gathers,* which no other Justice joined, repeated the argument he put forward in *Booth* and concluded:

> Booth *has not even an arguable basis in the common-law background that led up to the Eighth Amendment, in any longstanding societal tradition, or in any evidence that present society, through its laws or the actions of its juries, has set its face against considering the harm caused by criminal acts in assessing responsibility.*[31]

After arguing that the doctrine of stare decisis did not support continued obedience to *Booth,* which he deemed unequivocally wrong, Justice Scalia added: "In any case, I would think it a violation of my oath to adhere to what I consider a plainly unjustified intrusion upon the democratic process in order that the Court might save face."[32]

In support of his understanding of the way in which society thinks that the magnitude of the harm bears on the defendant's personal responsibility, Justice Scalia in *Booth* offered two hypotheticals. Suppose, he mused, that a driver recklessly speeds down a residential street at sixty miles per hour. Society might punish him by taking away his driver's license. But if the same driver doing the same thing runs into a pedestrian and kills her, we put the driver in jail for manslaughter. The "moral guilt in both cases is identical,"[33] Scalia concluded, so the difference in punishment has to do with the fact that the driver who kills someone has greater responsibility.[34] According to Scalia, the same logic applies in the case of two bank robbers. Both aim their guns at a guard and pull the trigger, but one kills the guard while the other's gun misfires. Only the former may be put to death, even though their moral guilt is the same.[35]

In neither *Booth* nor *Gathers* did the majority respond to Justice Scalia's examples. Instead, the conclusions in *Booth* and *Gathers* at times appear to turn entirely on the distinctive nature of the death penalty itself, thus eliding Scalia's argument. This strategy was unfortunate, because once Justices Powell and Brennan—the authors of, respectively, *Booth* and *Gathers*—retired, Justice Scalia's unanswered argument captivated the new Court. The result was the *Payne* decision.

Writing for himself and five others,[36] Chief Justice Rehnquist explained that both the *Booth* and *Gathers* decisions rested on mistaken premises. Contrary to the view expressed in *Booth,* "the assessment of harm caused by the defendant as a result of the crime charged has understandably been an important concern of the criminal law."[37] Rehnquist then quoted Justice Scalia's example of the two "identical" bank robbers, adding that under the facts of *Tison* v. *Arizona,*[38] a bank robber who acts recklessly and kills someone can be put to death while a bank robber who acts recklessly and kills no one cannot.[39] Rehnquist asserted that *Booth* simply misread a large body of precedent, for "it was never held or even suggested in any of our cases preceding *Booth* that the defendant, entitled as he was to individualized consideration, was to receive that consideration wholly apart from the crime which he had committed."[40] Victim impact evidence was thus deemed relevant and admissible because it illuminates the particular harm that the defendant caused.[41]

III. Justice Scalia's Philosophical Mistake—And *Payne*'s

In 1972, in *Furman* v. *Georgia,*[42] the Supreme Court declared the then existing death penalty statutes unconstitutional. Since that time, the singular consistent strand of an otherwise arguably incoherent body of death penalty jurisprudence has been the proposition that "death is different."[43] As a doctrinal proposition, this statement rests on two distinct premises. The first is that death is irrevocable, and society therefore cannot recompense one who has been wrongfully punished.[44] The second is that the infliction of the death sentence is so awesome, so different in kind from all other punishments, that the procedures that surround it, as well as the normative and legal discourse used to analyze it, must be sui generis.[45] This important strand of Eighth Amendment law is a bedrock proposition; one accepts it or one does not.[46] It appears, however, that no member of the Supreme Court (including Justice Scalia) rejects it.[47]

When we ask, therefore, "why do we punish?" we are asking a question that is somewhat different from the question "why do we execute?" To be sure, reasons may overlap, but precisely because death is different, the answers that are generally satisfactory in philosophical analyses of punishment are of more limited value when we are talking with particularity about the death penalty.

To some extent, therefore, Justice Scalia's mistake in *Booth* is that he does not give proper weight to this central strand of death penalty doctrine and consequently does not account for the impact it has on his argument. In truth, however, Justice Scalia's mistake is far more basic. His position would thus remain vulnerable even if the "death is different" premise were formally jettisoned.

Justice Scalia notes that we punish the reckless driver who kills someone more severely than we punish the driver who luckily does not.[48] Similarly, we punish the bank robber whose gun happens not to misfire more severely than we punish the robber whose gun does not work.[49] Both of these observations are correct, of course, but they are neither helpful nor germane, for they are simply additional illustrations of the distinction between scenarios (1) and (2), which I do not challenge here.

Consider scenario (1). One might ask why we punish Harry at all. He, after all, caused no serious injury. We punish him nonetheless because he *might* have injured someone. It is not that what Harry did is so bad; it is that what he did might have been awful. We punish Harry to express to him and to the rest of society that our culture will not abide the creation of such risks. Our society metes out punishment partly because of the harm people do, but also partly because of the harm they might have done.[50] When we punish someone like Harry, retribution plays virtually no role in the motivation; instead, we punish him to deter others from doing what he did, and to express our culture's strong objection to creating the potential for injury that Harry's conduct created.

Justice Scalia's assertion that the moral guilt of the two actors is "identical" is therefore a bit peculiar.[51] As a subjective proposition it seems patently incorrect, for there is little doubt that the actor who causes the injury *feels* more guilty than the one who does not.[52] That is, Harriet feels much worse, more guilty, than Harry—and rightly so. Harry himself would feel much worse than he does if he had happened to kill someone. Further, and of critical importance, it is not at all clear that Harriet feels worse in scenario (3) than she does in scenario (2). She might, of course, but it is quite imaginable that she will not.

Perhaps, then, Justice Scalia has in mind some objective account of guilt. Obviously in the context of a theory that bases considerations of guilt solely on what the actor does, as distinguished from the consequences she causes, Justice Scalia's contention is tautologically true. But we do not live in such a context.[53] The very fact that we punish Harriet more severely than we do Harry suggests that our culture does not regard their guilt, their culpability, as identical.[54] This point becomes still more apparent when we ask exactly why it is that we punish Harriet so severely.

Whereas the reason we punish Harry is limited to our desire to deter similar conduct, when we punish Harriet under either scenario (2) or (3) our motivation is somewhat different. Needless to say, the impulses present in our decision to punish Harry remain in force, but now there is an additional, far more compelling, impetus: We punish Harriet because she *killed* someone. The retributive impulse not present in Harry's case is quite powerful in Harriet's. Indeed, the primary difference between our culture's desire to punish the conduct in scenarios (1) and (2) is that our culture's retributive impulse is triggered in one case but not in the other.

Two lessons can be gleaned from this observation. The first is that as an objective proposition,

Harry's and Harriet's guilt is arguably not identical. Second, and far more importantly, the distinction between Harry and Harriet, resting as it does on the fact that Harriet killed someone while Harry did not, does not support a further distinction between scenarios (2) and (3). When we ask why we punish Harriet severely, the answer is simple and straightforward: because she killed someone.[55] That is it.

Justice Scalia's own illustrations support this very analysis. It is thus appropriate to wonder how he has managed to think he has constructed an argument that supports a distinction between scenarios (2) and (3). The answer seems to be, as Justice Stevens pointed out in his *Payne* dissent, that Scalia's analysis has been distorted by his sensitivity to political concerns.[56] This sensitivity is evident in the following passage in which Justice Scalia, concurring separately in *Payne,* continued his rhetorical assault on the holdings of *Booth* and *Gathers:*

> *Booth's stunning* ipse dixit, *that a crime's unanticipated consequences must be deemed "irrelevant" to the sentence, . . . conflicts with a public sense of justice keen enough that it has found voice in a nationwide "victim's rights" movement.*[57]

Here, Justice Scalia's attentiveness to the political climate obviously extrudes itself; here, as well, his fundamental error shows. For notwithstanding Scalia's invective, *Booth* did *not* deny the relevance of the consequences of John Booth's actions. On the contrary, those consequences were indisputably relevant to the sentence, for it was precisely the consequences of his action that made Booth eligible for the death penalty; it was the consequences that made Booth more like Harriet than like Harry.

In short, what makes someone eligible for the death penalty in our culture is one simple fact: that the defendant killed someone, that he took a human life. The very core of this response is visceral, biblical even. A life for a life. We do not execute defendants because they took a *particular* life; we kill them simply because they killed.

Justice Scalia has confused the issue of why we punish at all with the different, and more specific, question of why we execute. Indeed, his vehemence apparently caused him to overlook two critical facts in his *Booth* dissent. First, Justice Powell's opinion in *Booth* was on its face limited to the capital context.[58] This limitation reflects the extent to which it relied on the "death is different" idea that has undergirded modern death penalty jurisprudence.[59]

Second, and more fundamentally, Justice Scalia's charge that *Booth* renders "consequences" irrelevant is absolutely incorrect, yet *Payne* rests intimately and inextricably on the accuracy of this characterization.[60] Because it is false, the logic of *Payne* unravels. We can discern the falsity once we distinguish between primary and secondary harm.

Criminal sentencing surely depends in part on the consequences of the defendant's actions. This is a difficult matter philosophically, but it is firmly established in law. Our culture deems consequences normatively relevant in assessing punishment.[61] *However, the consequences that are relevant in assessing punishment are precisely and exclusively those that are reflected in the laws that appertain to punishment.* These consequences we can call "primary harm." "Secondary harm" includes all other harm. Secondary harm is irrelevant (in both the capital and non-capital contexts)[62] to assessment of punishment. Penal statutes suggest that primary harm is the harm caused by the criminal to the direct object of his crime; secondary harm is all other harm. The direct object is what the law (i.e., the state's penal code), reflecting our culture's moral values, regards as the "victim."

This terminology is consistent with and informed by Hart and Honoré's observation concerning the equivocal meaning of "responsible." They write:

> Usually in discussion of the law and occasionally in morals, to say that someone is responsible for some harm means that in accordance with legal rules or moral principles it is at least permissible, if not mandatory, to blame or punish or exact compensation from him. . . . Very often, however, especially in discussion of morals, to say that someone is responsible for some harm is to assert (inter alia) that he *did* the harm or *caused* it. . . .[63]

In a moral sense, therefore, the distinction between primary and secondary harm may be illusory; in law, however, it is tenable and probably essential.

Thus, in the sentence, "Dick shot John," "Dick" is the subject (the defendant charged with committing the action), "shot" is the verb (the action the subject is accused of doing that *caused* the injury), and "John" is the direct object (the victim). The harm to the victim—that is, whether John is wounded or killed—is relevant to the very definition of Dick's crime, and hence to the range of punishment to which he may be subjected. Similarly, to use Justice Scalia's own illustration, when the bank robber points a gun at the bank guard and pulls the trigger, killing the guard, the primary harm is to the guard, who has been killed; when the robber's gun misfires, the primary harm is still to the guard, but now the injury is primarily psychological (i.e., the guard is scared; thus, the robber has committed assault). Criminal law might punish the first bank robber, but only the first bank robber, with death, owing to the variation in primary harm. In both cases, the secondary harm is irrelevant.

Put differently, the secondary harm is that which the law has disregarded for purposes of exacting punishment. Hence, if the bank guard's wife is present when the bank robber shoots and kills her husband, this neither enhances nor diminishes the bank robber's suitability for the death penalty.[64] On the other hand, if the bank guard's wife is present when the bank robber's gun misfires, it is not a germane argument in support of a harsher sentence that she believed that her husband was about to die.[65]

When we examine the harm that the criminal law deems primary, we learn what injuries the law seeks to prevent. More directly, we learn what actions that law forbids. Capital murder statutes—and the body of Supreme Court case law that has interpreted them—make clear beyond peradventure that the reason that society may execute the bank robber whose gun works is that he killed someone. It has nothing to do with whether the victim's wife witnessed the killing or whether it upset her. The reason that society may punish more severely the drunk driver who kills someone after running a red light is that the driver killed someone. The Court has time and again recognized this principle, and this recognition is epitomized by *Coker* v. *Georgia,*[66] in which the Court held that a state may not execute a rapist.[67] The reason is that the rapist did not kill.[68]

Actually, it is not precisely accurate to say that the reason we execute is because a human life has been taken, for some states do tend to distinguish among certain lives. These distinctions tend to be based on occupation. They are properly viewed as expressing the value to society of certain professions. Thus, a state may provide the death penalty only for those who kill a police officer, a judge, or an elected official.[69] Such distinctions, based on status rather than on the individual or personal characteristics of the murder victim, reflect society's normative judgments. That is, the salience of statutory distinctions that punish some murderers more harshly based on their victims' status is that these distinctions illuminate more clearly the normative basis upon which a certain sovereign society has based its decisions to execute.[70]

Justice Scalia's opinions in *Booth, Gathers,* and *Payne* rest on the conclusion that the distinction society recognizes by statute between scenarios (1) and (2) supports a further normative (but non-statutory) distinction between scenarios (2) and (3). This is an obvious non sequitur. Moreover, Justice Scalia's argument does not merely endorse the moral and legal legitimacy of statutory distinctions between scenarios (2) and (3); it implies, and seems to depend upon the idea, that our culture already utilizes such distinctions. As an empirical proposition, that contention seems dubious; and as a normative and legal proposition, it is as unwieldy as it is offensive.

For example, once the law permits a prosecutor to introduce evidence of secondary harm in the absence of a specific legislative classification (the result in *Payne*), there is no reason to limit such testimony to immediate family members.[71] One might be seriously traumatized by a murder even if one is not consanguineously related to the victim. If, say, Wallace Stevens had been murdered, would I, as a lover of Wallace Stevens' poetry, be permitted to testify against the murderer during the punishment phase of the trial? Would the impact of that crime on me be a factor that the state could permit the jury to consider? Suppose that I am severely traumatized by the murder of a complete stranger—for example, by the details of one of Jeffrey Dahmer's murders.[72] May I testify against Dahmer? These are rhetorical questions. Perhaps they would be hard constitutional questions if a state statute classified famous poets with police officers, or if it provided a harsher sentence for murderers who caused especial pain and anguish to members of society at large. But society has no such statutes, and there was none involved in *Payne*.

This illustrates the way in which politics, not sound legal thinking, is responsible for the result in *Payne*. The seeds of the problem were sowed in *Booth* itself, which addressed so-called "victim impact statements."[73] In truth, the *victim* in *Booth* was dead.[74] The statements at issue were not statements of the victim; they were statements of the survivors.[75] Justice Powell no less than Justice Scalia acquiesced in the improper characterization of distraught family members as victims.[76] There is a sense, no doubt, in which the loved ones of those whom Booth murdered

were victims too, just as there is a sense in which every member of society is victimized or harmed when a murder occurs. But that semantic sense—even that moral sense—is not the legal meaning of the term. The legal definition of victim is limited to the direct object of the crime; everyone else, regardless of proximity, is a mere bystander.[77]

This does not mean, contrary to Justice Scalia's nearly apoplectic protest, that the consequences of the criminal's conduct are deemed irrelevant. Quite the contrary: They remain pertinent to the very definition of the crime and to the determination of who is eligible for the death penalty. Thus, for example, the law differentiates—and properly so—among merely scaring someone, physically injuring that person, and killing her. Although each of these states can result from the same act (e.g., the pointing of a gun and the pulling of its trigger), the state exacts varying punishments because the same act results in different primary harm—different injuries to the direct object of the crime, the victim. Any other harm is irrelevant to the criminal sentence.[78] It matters that Harriet killed someone while Harry did not; it does not matter whom Harriet killed.

Conclusion

What murderers do is kill people. That is their crime. Further, the reason society chooses to execute them is that they have killed someone. They have killed a human being.[79] That is the offense for which we execute. The murderer's depravity is not less when he kills a homeless vagrant with no family rather than a mother whose children love her. What the murderer has done is the same irrespective of whether the murdered poet is Wallace Stevens, whose poems I cherish, or Ezra Pound, whose poems I refuse to read.

In arguing to the contrary, the Court in *Payne* adopted Justice Scalia's fallacious conception of the meaning of victim. Errors are always unfortunate in constitutional law. They are especially so when the stakes are so great—as they are when we execute—and more disturbing still when they are driven by politics rather than law.

---

1. *111 S. Ct. 2597 (1991).*
2. *See, e.g.,* Ranae Bartlett, Case Note, Payne *v.* Tennessee: Eviscerating the Doctrine of Stare Decisis in Constitutional Law

Cases, *45 Ark. L. Rev. 561 (1992);* Catherine Bendor, *Recent Development,* Defendants' Wrongs and Victims' Rights, *27 Harv. C.R.-C.L. L. Rev. 219 (1992);* Elizabeth A. Meek, *Note,* Victim Impact

Evidence and Capital Sentencing: A Casenote on Payne v. Tennessee, 52 La. L. Rev. 1299 (1992); K. Elizabeth Whitehead, Case Note, Mourning Becomes Electric: Payne v. Tennessee's Allowance of Victim Impact Statements During Capital Sentencing Proceedings, 45 Ark. L. Rev. 531 (1992); see also Richard S. Murphy, Comment, The Significance of Victim Harm: Booth v. Maryland and the Philosophy of Punishment in the Supreme Court, 55 U. Chi. L. Rev. 1303 (1988).

3. For a fine recent discussion that refers to much of the relevant literature and that utilizes the normative distinction between responsibility and blame, see Meir Dan-Cohen, Responsibility and the Boundaries of the Self, 105 Harv. L. Rev. 959 (1992). See also sources cited infra note 4.

4. The classic treatment of the broad issue is H.L.A. Hart & Tony Honoré, Causation in the Law 62–108, 325–405 (2d ed. 1985). See generally Andrew von Hirsch, Past or Future Crimes (1985); Michael Davis, Why Attempts Deserve Less Punishment than Complete Crimes, 5 Law & Phil. 1 (1986); Michael Davis, Harm and Retribution, 15 Phil. & Pub. Affairs 236 (1986); Joel Feinberg, The Expressive Function of Punishment, 49 The Monist 397 (1965); Symposium: Justice in Punishment, 25 Isr. L. Rev. 281 (1991).

5. 111 S. Ct. 2597 (1991).

6. Booth v. Maryland, 482 U.S. 496 (1987).

7. South Carolina v. Gathers, 490 U.S. 805 (1989).

8. Payne, 111 S. Ct. at 2609. In a tart dissent, Justice Stevens chastised the Court for abandoning such recent precedents, for betraying well-established Eighth Amendment values, and—most seriously—for succumbing to the political pressure exerted by the victims' rights movement. Id. at 2631 (Stevens, J., dissenting). Justice Stevens lamented: "Today is a sad day for a great institution." Id.

9. This conclusion follows from the holding in Payne because otherwise the evidence relating to the details of the murder victim's life would not be relevant, and would therefore be inadmissible. See id. at 2609.

10. 482 U.S. 496 (1987).

11. 490 U.S. 805 (1989).

12. See Payne, 111 S. Ct. at 2610–11.

13. Booth, 482 U.S. at 510–12.

14. Justices Powell, Brennan, Marshall, Blackmum, and Stevens. See id. at 497.

15. Id. at 509–15.

16. Justices White, Marshall, Blackmum, and Stevens. See Gathers, 490 U.S. at 805. Justice White dissented in Booth but joined the majority in Gathers on the basis of Booth. He wrote: "Unless Booth v. Maryland is to be overruled, the judgment below must be affirmed. Hence, I join JUSTICE BRENNAN'S opinion for the Court." Id. at 812 (White, J., concurring) (citation omitted). Despite Justice White's belief that Gathers was dictated by Booth, one might conclude that a salient fact distinguishes the cases: Whereas Booth concerned other people's feelings about the murder victim, Gathers concerned the personal characteristics of the victim himself.

17. Id. at 810–11.

18. Id. at 811.

19. See Booth, 482 U.S. at 502–09; see also Penry v. Lynaugh, 492 U.S. 302, 319 (1989); Lockett v. Ohio, 438 U.S. 586, 604 (1978) (plurality opinion); Woodson v. North Carolina, 428 U.S. 280, 305 (1976) (plurality opinion); cf. Franklin v. Lynaugh, 487 U.S. 164, 181 (1988) (stating that death penalty requires clear and objective standards providing specific and detailed guidance); California v. Ramos, 463 U.S. 992, 998–99 (1983) (stating that death penalty requires greater degree of scrutiny of capital sentencing procedures to minimize risk of arbitrary and capricious action); Enmund v. Florida, 458 U.S. 782, 798 (1982) (stating that focus in death penalty case must be on defendant's culpability, not on culpability of co-defendants).

20. See e.g., Blystone v. Pennsylvania, 494 U.S. 299, 304–05 (1990); Penry, 492 U.S. at 319; Franklin, 487 U.S. at 181–82. The "reasoned moral response" phrase appears to have originated in

Justice O'Connor's opinion in California v. Brown, 479 U.S. 538, 545 (1987) (O'Connor, J., concurring).

What we mean by "circumstances of the crime" is an issue I return to in Part III.

21. See Sumner v. Shuman, 483 U.S. 66, 75–76 (1987); Roberts v. Louisiana, 428 U.S. 325, 333–34 (1976) (plurality opinion); Woodson, 428 U.S. at 303.

22. See Penry, 492 U.S. at 319; Hitchcock v. Dugger, 481 U.S. 393, 399 (1987); McCleskey v. Kemp, 481 U.S. 279, 306 (1987); Skipper v. South Carolina, 476 U.S. 1, 4 (1986); Eddings v. Oklahoma, 455 U.S. 104, 113–14 (1982); Proffitt v. Florida, 428 U.S. 242, 251–52 (1976) (plurality opinion).

23. Writing in Payne, Chief Justice Rehnquist characterized Woodson, supra note 19, as describing "a class of evidence which must be received," as distinguished from Booth's ostensible conclusion that Woodson described "a class of evidence that could not be received." Payne v. Tennessee, 111 S. Ct. 2597, 2607 (1991). Here Chief Justice Rehnquist creates a straw man, as Woodson simply did not address what type of evidence must be excluded, but instead rested on the basic idea that the jury must be able to respond to the individuality of the defendant. See Woodson, 428 U.S. at 303. Booth says nothing to the contrary and, fairly read, construes Woodson no more broadly than does Rehnquist. See Booth, 482 U.S. at 504.

24. Booth, 482 U.S. at 506–07.

25. Id. at 506.

26. Id. at 506–07.

27. South Carolina v. Gathers, 490 U.S. 805, 811–12 (1989).

28. Id. What we mean by the murderer's "personal culpability" is an issue I return to in Part III.

29. Booth, 482 U.S. at 519–20 (Scalia, J., dissenting).

30. Id. at 519 (emphasis added).

31. Gathers, 490 U.S. at 825 (Scalia, J., dissenting).

32. Id. This sentence epitomizes Justice Scalia's hypersensitivity to the political process. See infra note 57 and accompanying text.

33. Booth, 482 U.S. at 519 (Scalia, J., dissenting). I must confess that I am somewhat baffled by Justice Scalia's peculiar usage of the term "moral guilt." Typically, when the law says that someone is guilty, that statement avers that the individual did an act proscribed by the law. When a philosopher describes an individual as morally guilty, however, the individual may or may not have done a legally proscribed act. It follows that to the extent that guilt is a moral notion at all, as distinct from a purely legal one, it is not at all clear that the moral guilt of Justice Scalia's two hypothetical figures is identical. Indeed, this is why some philosophers are persuaded that there is a tenable moral distinction between Harry and Harriet. Act-utilitarians, though perhaps not rule-utilitarians, would fall into this category. See e.g., John Austin, The Province of Jurisprudence Determined 38–40 (Isaiah Berlin et al. eds., 1954); Jeremy Bentham, Introduction to the Principles of Morals and Legislation 82–88 (Hafner Publishing Co. 1948); Charles Fried, Right and Wrong 30–53 (1978); G.E. Moore, Principia Ethica § 89 (1902); John Rawls, Two Concepts of Rules, 64 Phil. Rev. 3 (1955); see also Harry G. Frankfurt, The Importance of What We Care About 1–10, 95–103 (1988); David Gauthier, Morals by Agreement 157–89 (1986); see generally sources cited supra note 4 (discussing philosophy of punishment).

34. Booth, 482 U.S. at 519.

35. Id.; see supra note 33 and accompanying text (analyzing Justice Scalia's use of term "moral guilt").

36. Justices White, O'Connor, Scalia, Kennedy, and Souter. See Payne v. Tennessee, 111 S. Ct. 2597, 2601 (1991).

37. Id. at 2605.

38. 481 U.S. 137 (1987).

39. Payne, 111 S. Ct. at 2605. Ironically, Chief Justice Rehnquist's allusion to Tison provides an additional illustration of the argument I advance in the following section.

40. Id. at 2607.

41. Id. at 2608.

42. 408 U.S. 238 (1972).

43. See, e.g., id. at 286–91 (Brennan, J., concurring), 306 (Stewart, J., concurring); Lockett v. Ohio, 438 U.S. 586, 604 (1978) (plurality opinion); Woodson v. North Carolina, 428 U.S. 280, 304–05 (1976) (plurality opinion); Gregg v. Georgia, 428 U.S. 153, 187–88 (1976) (plurality opinion); see generally Ronald J. Mann, The Individualized-Consideration Principle and the Death Penalty as Cruel and Unusual Punishment, 29 Hous. L. Rev. (forthcoming 1992).

44. Furman, 408 U.S. at 290 (Brennan, J., concurring). It might be argued that society is also not able to give someone back the years that are lost serving an unjust prison sentence. But society might choose to compensate a wrongfully imprisoned person by paying some monetary stake. Even if it is true that neither injury—neither imprisonment nor death—can be fully remedied, it does seem that some repair is possible in one context but not the other.

45. See id. at 286–91.

46. See Ludwig Wittgenstein, Philosophical Investigations 85e (G.E.M. Anscombe trans., 2d ed. 1958).

47. But see William S. Geimer, Death at Any Cost: A Critique of the Supreme Court's Recent Retreat from Its Death Penalty Standards, 12 Fla. St. U. L. Rev. 737, 760–78 (1985); Daniel R. Harris, Note, Capital Sentencing After Walton v. Arizona: A Retreat from the "Death is Different" Doctrine, 40 Am. U. L. Rev. 1389, 1417–24 (1991). As I argue below, even if the Court has sub silentio rejected the "death is different" doctrine, Justice Scalia's argument remains vulnerable nonetheless.

48. Booth v. Maryland, 482 U.S. 496, 519 (1987) (Scalia, J., dissenting).

49. Id.

50. This too is why we punish offenses like speeding. Of course, the notion of causality is deeply problematic in criminal law as elsewhere, though the law attempts to deal with its infinitude by deploying the notion of proximate cause. Cf. Hart & Honoré, supra note 4, at 69 (analyzing concept of proximate cause); W.D. Ross, The Right and the Good 36 (1st ed. 1930) (describing philosophical difficulty of tracing an act's consequences).

51. See supra note 33 and accompanying text (discussing Justice Scalia's use of term "moral guilt").

52. For a helpful discussion of the concept of guilt, and the distinction between guilt and shame, see Herbert Morris, On Guilt and Innocence 59–63 (1976). Using Professor Morris's terminology, I would say that Harriet feels greater shame. One difficulty with Justice Scalia's argument is that he uses the vague and ambiguous concept of guilt without rigor or precision. See Booth, 482 U.S. at 519 (Scalia, J., dissenting).

53. See supra note 4 and accompanying text (discussing philosophical context of punishment).

54. See supra note 33 and accompanying text (discussing concept of moral guilt).

55. See e.g., Walter Berns, For Capital Punishment (1979); Ernest van den Haag, The Ultimate Punishment: A Defense, 99 Harv. L. Rev. 1662 (1986); see generally Immanuel Kant, The Philosophy of Law 198 (W. Hastie trans., 1887) (arguing that justice requires death penalty for murder).

56. Payne v. Tennessee, 111 S. Ct. 2597, 2627 (1991) (Stevens, J., dissenting).

57. Id. at 2613 (Scalia, J., concurring) (citation omitted).

58. See Booth v. Maryland, 482 U.S. 496, 509 (1987).

59. Id. at 504. The language of Booth cannot be read apart from this context; moreover, the language is purposefully narrow. Justice Powell wrote: "While the full range of foreseeable consequences of a defendant's actions may be relevant in other criminal and civil contexts, we cannot agree that it is relevant in the unique circumstance of a capital sentencing hearing." Id. (emphasis added). In not even acknowledging this limitation of Booth, Justice Scalia and the Payne majority would seem implicitly to have rejected this notion, which means that Scalia's argument is only as strong as his assault on this central pillar of death penalty law. See supra note 47 and accompanying text (arguing that no Supreme Court Justice rejects "death is different" doctrine).

For statements of the "death is different" doctrine, see, e.g., Fur-

man v. Georgia, 408 U.S. 238, 306 (1972) (Stewart, J., concurring); Lockett v. Ohio, 438 U.S. 586, 604 (1978) (plurality opinion); Gregg v. Georgia, 428 U.S. 153, 188 (1976) (plurality opinion). See generally Mann, supra note 43.

60. See Payne, 111 S. Ct. at 2604–05.

61. See supra note 4 and accompanying text (discussing philosophical context of punishment). It is also noteworthy that recent evidence attributes greater shaping force to culture than to gender in determining moral judgments. See B. Bower, Culture Puts Unique Spin on Moral Judgment, Sci. News, May 2, 1992, at 295.

62. Except insofar as the definition of the crime includes secondary harm. See infra note 63 and accompanying text.

63. Hart & Honoré, supra note 4, at 65.

64. It is also true, as I will elaborate upon momentarily, that the presence of the bank guard's wife is irrelevant for purposes of assessing punishment. Both of these conclusions assume that the bank robber does not know of the woman's presence. If we alter this assumption, then the bank robber's state of mind is changed, so that this variable might well become relevant.

I think that the distinction between primary and secondary harm also proves salutary in contexts other than homicide. For example, the victim in a robbery is the person from whom the property is taken. Where a bank is robbed, of course, it would be possible to define as the victim either the bank itself (i.e., its owners), the employees of the bank who were confronted by the robber, the depositors whose money was taken, or any combination of the above. But the law tends not to do this. Similarly, where an arsonist burns a building, the building itself might be thought of as the victim, or the victim might be the building's owner. But the criminal law (as distinguished from morals) makes clear that in no event would it be sensible to gauge the arsonist's punishment in terms of the trauma suffered by the owner.

65. Then there is the example of the bystander wife who is pregnant and miscarries as a consequence of the trauma. The frustrated robber may well be liable in tort for wrongful death, but, though criminal law may change, this harm is beyond the ken of that for which he is criminally liable.

66. 433 U.S. 584 (1977) (plurality opinion).

67. Id. at 598.

68. See id.

69. See Booth v. Maryland, 482 U.S. 496, 517 & n.2 (1987) (White, J., dissenting).

70. What is the difference between a statute that provides that murderers who kill police officers will be subject to the death penalty and one that provides that murderers who kill loving fathers will be? Perhaps nothing, for the existence of such a statute would cast doubt on the proposition that the reason we execute is that a human life has been taken. Nevertheless, there must surely be constitutional limits to the distinctions that may be drawn by a state legislature. Hence, a state could not punish those who kill whites, but not those who kill blacks, with death. Equally, a state could not statutorily distinguish between wealthy and destitute murder victims. This conclusion would remain true even if the number of poor people claiming entitlement program benefits seriously drained that state's treasury.

71. Of course, as suggested above, some immediate family members may be of little help. See supra text accompanying note 26 (providing example of estranged daughter testifying at trial of her father's murderer). If the murder victim's son is estranged, then it is hard to see how that son's testimony is relevant under Justice Scalia's approach in Payne.

In Payne itself, moreover, because the victim impact evidence came from one of the survivors of Payne's attack, Justice Scalia's approach makes it in Payne's interest to leave no survivors: no one who can testify as to her own anguish. Payne had stabbed a mother and her two children, killing the mother and her two-year-old daughter. The mother's three-year-old son survived. See Payne v. Tennessee, 111 S. Ct. 2597, 2601–02 (1991).

72. Jeffrey Dahmer is a serial killer accused of brutally murdering 17 people in Ohio and Wisconsin. In some cases, Dahmer cut up

his victims' bodies and cannibalized them. Dahmer pleaded guilty to 16 of the 17 murders in 1992; he was not charged in the remaining slaying. *See* Dahmer Pleads Guilty Again, and Receives 16th Life Sentence, *N.Y. Times,* May 2, 1992, § 1, at 5.

73. *See* Murphy, supra note 2, at 1304, 1316.

74. *Chief Justice Rehnquist also suggested in* Payne *that so-called victim impact statements help communicate to the jury that the victim, too, "is an individual whose death represents a unique loss to society and in particular to his family" rather than a "faceless stranger."* Payne, *111 S. Ct. at 2608 (quoting* Booth v. Maryland, *482 U.S. 496, 517 (1987) (White, J., dissenting) and* South Carolina v. Gathers, *490 U.S. 805, 821 (1989) (O'Connor, J., dissenting)). This concern is surely a red herring. There are many ways to communicate to the jury that the victim is not an amorphous, faceless stranger, and the state uses many of them. Data that I have collected elsewhere demonstrate that prosecutors, even in the aftermath of* Booth, *had no difficulty in portraying murder victims as unique individuals whose murders cried out for justice. See David R. Dow,* Teague and Death: The Impact of Current Retroactivity Doctrine on Capital Defendants, *19 Hastings Const. L.Q. 23, 54–72 (1991). Moreover, to the extent that Chief Justice Rehnquist's argument is persuasive, it argues in favor of the broad type of testimony to which I allude in the text.*

75. *See* Booth, *482 U.S. at 499.*

76. *See generally* id.

77. *This is not to say that bystanders are perforce legally of no moment. Some crimes, like reckless endangerment, might be de-fined in terms of the risk that they pose to people who turn out not to be injured at all. There are, then, crimes in which the presence of bystanders is pivotal.*

78. *A final irony. In* Teague v. Lane, *489 U.S. 288, 300–01 (1989) (plurality opinion), the Supreme Court determined that it would decide the retroactivity of so-called new rules as a threshold matter and articulate the new rule only after first determining that it would apply retroactively.* Payne *clearly represents a new rule in that it explicitly overruled two earlier decisions.* Payne, *111 S. Ct. at 2611 & n.2. Thus, the fact that the merits were reached in* Payne *suggests, under* Teague, *that the new rule it articulated will apply retroactively. This conclusion is important because one can easily imagine a scenario whereby the defendant would avail himself of the rule of* Payne. *Many murders are killings of unsavory victims. This is especially true when the murder is a by-product of a drug-related crime. A defendant might want to suggest, probably by indirection, that the victim of his crime was vermin.* Payne, *of course, seems to require that such a proffer be admissible, and the fact that the merits were reached in the case implies that defendants can raise the new rule in collateral proceedings. That is simply bizarre.*

79. *Justice O'Connor seems to have conceded precisely this point in* Gathers. *See* South Carolina v. Gathers, *490 U.S. 805, 819 (1989) (O'Connor, J., dissenting). The point has also been made by Justice Stevens. See* Spaziano v. Florida, *468 U.S. 447, 468–69 (1984) (Stevens, J., concurring in part and dissenting in part).*

The Death Penalty

*FURMAN V. GEORGIA**

United States Supreme Court, 1972

Mr. Justice Douglas, concurring.

In these three cases the death penalty was imposed, one of them for murder, and two for rape.[1] In each the determination of whether the penalty should be death or a lighter punishment was left by the State to the discretion of the judge or of the jury. In each of the three cases the trial was to a jury. They are here on petitions for certiorari which we granted limited to the question whether the imposition and execution of the death penalty constitutes "cruel and unusual punishment" within the meaning of the Eighth Amendment as applied to the States by the Fourteenth. I vote to vacate each judgment, believing that the exaction of the death penalty does violate the Eighth and Fourteenth Amendments.

. . . We cannot say from facts disclosed in these records that these defendants were sentenced to death because they were black. Yet our task is not restricted to an effort to divine what motives impelled these death penalties. Rather, we deal with a system of law and of justice that leaves to the uncontrolled discretion of judges or juries the determination whether defendants committing these crimes should die or be imprisoned. Under these laws no standards govern the selection of the penalty. People live or die, dependent on the whim of one man or of 12.

. . . In a Nation committed to equal protection of the laws there is no permissible "caste" aspect[2] of law enforcement. Yet we know that the discretion of judges and juries in imposing the death penalty enables the penalty to be selectively applied, feeding prejudices against the accused if he is poor and despised, and lacking political clout, or if he is a member of a suspect or unpopular minority, and saving those who by social position may be in a more protected position. In ancient Hindu law a Brahman was exempt from capital punishment,[3] and in those days, "[g]enerally, in the law books, punishment increased in severity as social status diminished."[4] We have, I fear, taken in practice the same position, partially as a result of making the death penalty discretionary and partially as a result of the ability of the rich to purchase the services of the most respected and most resourceful legal talent in the Nation.

The high service rendered by the "cruel and unusual" punishment clause of the Eighth Amendment is to require legislatures to write penal laws that are evenhanded, nonselective, and nonarbitrary, and to require judges to see to it that general laws are not applied sparsely, selectively, and spottily to unpopular groups.

A law that stated that anyone making more than $50,000 would be exempt from the death penalty would plainly fall, as would a law that in terms said that blacks, those who never went beyond the fifth grade in school, those who made less than $3,000 a year, or those who were unpopular or unstable should be the only people executed. A law which in the over-

---

*408 U.S. 238 (1972). Excerpts only. Footnotes numbered as in the original. Two cases from Georgia and one from Texas were considered and decided together by the Supreme Court. Endnotes have been renumbered.

all view reaches that result in practice[5] has no more sanctity than a law which in terms provides the same.

Thus, these discretionary statutes are unconstitutional in their operation. They are pregnant with discrimination and discrimination is an ingredient not compatible with the idea of equal protection of the laws that is implicit in the ban on "cruel and unusual" punishments.

Any law which is nondiscriminatory on its face may be applied in such a way as to violate the Equal Protection Clause of the Fourteenth Amendment. *Yick Wo* v. *Hopkins,* 118 U.S. 356. Such conceivably might be the fate of a mandatory death penalty, where equal or lesser sentences were imposed on the elite, a harsher one or the minorities or members of the lower castes. Whether a mandatory death penalty would otherwise be constitutional is a question I do not reach.

I concur in the judgments of the Court.

Mr. Justice Brennan, concurring.

. . . There are, then, four principles by which we may determine whether a particular punishment is "cruel and unusual." The primary principle, which I believe supplies the essential predicate for the application of the others, is that a punishment must not by its severity be degrading to human dignity. The paradigm violation of this principle would be the infliction of a torturous punishment of the type that the Clause has always prohibited. Yet "[i]t is unlikely that any State at this moment in history," *Robinson* v. *California,* 370 U.S., at 666, would pass a law providing for the infliction of such a punishment. Indeed, no such punishment has ever been before this Court. The same may be said of the other principles. It is unlikely that this Court will confront a severe punishment that is obviously inflicted in wholly arbitrary fashion; no State would engage in a reign of blind terror. Nor is it likely that this Court will be called upon to review a severe punishment that is clearly and totally rejected throughout society; no legislature would be able even to authorize the infliction of such a punishment. Nor, finally, is it likely that this Court will have to consider a severe punishment that is patently unnecessary; no State today would inflict a severe punishment knowing that there was no reason whatever for doing so. In short, we are unlikely to have occasion to determine that a punishment is fatally offensive under any one principle.

Since the Bill of Rights was adopted, this Court has adjudged only three punishments to be within the prohibition of the Clause. See *Weems* v. *United States,* 217 U.S. 349 (1910) (12 years in chains at hard and painful labor); *Trop* v. *Dulles,* 356 U.S. 86 (1958) (expatriation); *Robinson* v. *California,* 370 U.S. 660 (1962) (imprisonment for narcotics addiction). Each punishment, of course, was degrading to human dignity, but of none could it be said conclusively that it was fatally offensive under one or the other of the principles. Rather, these "cruel and unusual punishments" seriously implicated several of the principles, and it was the application of the principles in combination that supported the judgment. That, indeed, is not surprising. The function of these principles, after all, is simply to provide means by which a court can determine whether a challenged punishment comports with human dignity. They are, therefore, interrelated, and in most cases it will be their convergence that will justify the conclusion that a punishment is "cruel and unusual." The test, then, will ordinarily be a cumulative one: If a punishment is unusually severe, if there is a strong probability that it is inflicted arbitrarily, if it is substantially rejected by contemporary society, and if there is no reason to believe that it serves any penal purpose more effectively than some less severe punishment, then the continued infliction of that punishment violates the command of the Clause that the State may not inflict inhuman and uncivilized punishments upon those convicted of crimes.

. . . The question, then, is whether the deliberate infliction of death is today consistent with the command of the Clause that the State may not inflict punishments that do not comport with human dignity. I will analyze the punishment of death in terms of the principles set out above and the cumulative test to which they lead: It is a denial of human dignity for the State arbitrarily to subject a person to an unusually severe punishment that society has indicated it does not regard as acceptable, and that cannot be shown to serve any penal purpose more effectively than a significantly less drastic punishment. Under these principles and this test, death is today a "cruel and unusual" punishment.

Death is a unique punishment in the United States. In a society that so strongly affirms the sanctity of life, not surprisingly the common view is that death is the ultimate sanction. This natural human feeling appears all about us. There has been no national debate about punishment, in general or by imprisonment, comparable to the debate about the punishment of death. No other punishment has been so continuously restricted, see *infra,* at 296–298, nor has any State yet abolished prisons, as some have abolished this punishment. And those States that still inflict death reserve it for the most heinous crimes. Juries, of course, have always treated death cases differently, as have governors exercising their communication powers. Criminal defendants are of the same view. "As all practicing lawyers know, who have defended persons charged with capital offenses, often the only goal possible is to avoid the death penalty." *Griffin* v. *Illinois,* 351 U.S. 12, 28 (1956) (Burton and Minton, JJ., dissenting). Some legislatures have required particular procedures, such as two-stage trials and automatic appeals, applicable only in death cases. "It is the universal experience in the administration of criminal justice that those charged with capital offenses are granted special considerations." *Ibid.* See *Williams* v. *Florida,* 399 U.S. 78, 103 (1970) (all States require juries of 12 in death cases). This Court, too, almost always treats death cases as a class apart.[6] And the unfortunate effect of this punishment upon the functioning of the judicial process is well known; no other punishment has a similar effect.

The only explanation for the uniqueness of death is its extreme severity. Death is today an unusually severe punishment, unusual in its pain, in its finality, and in its enormity. No other existing punishment is comparable to death in terms of physical and mental suffering. Although our information is not conclusive, it appears that there is no method available that guarantees an immediate and painless death.[7] Since the discontinuance of flogging as a constitutionally permissible punishment, *Jackson* v. *Bishop,* 404 F. 2d 571 (CA8 1968), death remains as the only punishment that may involve the conscious infliction of physical pain. In addition, we know that mental pain is an inseparable part of our practice of punishing criminals by death for the prospect of pending execution exacts a frightful toll during the inevitable long wait between the imposition of sentence and the actual infliction of death. Cf *Ex parte Medley,* 134 U.S. 160, 172 (1890). As the California Supreme Court pointed out, "the process of carrying out a verdict of death is often so degrading and brutalizing to the human spirit as to constitute psychological torture." *People* v. *Anderson,* 6 Cal. 3d 628, 649, 493 P. 2d 880, 894 (1972).[8] Indeed, as Mr. Justice Frankfurter noted, "the onset of insanity while awaiting execution of a death sentence is not a rare phenomenon." *Solesbee* v. *Balkcom,* 339 U.S. 9, 14 (1950) (dissenting opinion). The "fate of ever-increasing fear and distress" to which the expatriate is subjected, *Trop* v. *Dulles,* 356 U.S., at 102, can only exist to a greater degree for a person confined in prison awaiting death.[9]

The unusual severity of death is manifested most clearly in its finality and enormity. Death, in these respects, is in a class by itself. Expatriation, for example, is a punishment that "destroys for the individual the political existence that was centuries in the development," that "strips the citizen of his status in the national and international political community," and that puts "[h]is very existence" in jeopardy. Expatriation thus inherently entails "the total destruction of the individual's status in organized society." *Id.,* at 101. "In short, the expatriate has lost the right to have rights." *Id.,* at 102. Yet, demonstrably, expatriation is not "a fate worse than death." *Id.,* at 125 (Frankfurther, J., dissenting).[10] Although death, like expatriation, destroys the individual's "political existence" and his "status in organized society," it does more, for, unlike expatriation, death also destroys "[h]is very existence." There is, too at least the possibility that the expatriate will in the future regain "the right to have rights." Death forecloses even that possibility.

Death is truly an awesome punishment. The calculated killing of a human being by the State involves, by its very nature, a denial of the executed person's humanity. The contrast with the plight of a person punished by imprisonment is evident. An individual in prison does not lose "the right to have rights." A prisoner retains, for example, the constitutional rights to the free exercise of religion, to be free of cruel and unusual punishments, and to treatment as a "person" for purposes of due process of law and the equal protection of the laws. A prisoner remains a member of the human family. Moreover, he retains the right of access to the courts. His punishment is not irrevocable. Apart from the common charge, grounded upon the recognition of human fallibility, that the punishment of death must inevitably be inflicted upon innocent men, we know that death has been the lot of men whose convictions were unconstitutionally secured in view of later, retroactively applied, holdings of this Court. The punishment itself may have been unconstitutionally inflicted, see *Witherspoon* v. *Illinois,* 391 U.S. 510 (1968), yet the finality of death precludes relief. An executed person has indeed "lost the right to have rights." As one 19th century proponent of punishing criminals by death declared, "When a man is hung, there is an end of our relations with him. His execution is a way of saying, 'You are not fit for this world, take your chance elsewhere.'"[11]

In comparison to all other punishments today, then, the deliberate extinguishment of human life by the State is uniquely degrading to human dignity. I would not hesitate to hold, on that ground alone, that death is today a "cruel and unusual" punishment, were it not that death is a punishment of longstanding usage and acceptance in this country. I therefore turn to the second principle—that the State may not arbitrarily inflict an unusually severe punishment.

. . . When the punishment of death is inflicted in a trivial number of the cases in which it is legally available, the conclusion is virtually inescapable that it is being inflicted arbitrarily. Indeed, it smacks of little more than a lottery system. The States claim, however, that this rarity is evidence not of arbitrariness, but of informed selectivity: Death is inflicted, they say, only in "extreme" cases.

Informed selectivity, of course, is a value not to be denigrated. Yet presumably the States could make precisely the same claim if there were 10 executions per year, or five, or even if there were but one. That there may be as many as 50 per year does not strengthen the claim. When the rate of infliction is at this low level, it is highly implausible that only the worst criminals or the criminals who commit the worst crimes are selected for this punishment. No one has yet suggested a rational basis that could differentiate in those terms the few who die from the many who go to prison. Crimes and criminals simply do not admit of a distinction that can be drawn so finely as to explain, on that ground, the execution of such a tiny sample of those eligible. Certainly the laws that provide for this punishment do not attempt to draw that distinction; all cases to which the laws apply are necessarily "extreme." Nor is the distinction credible in fact. If, for example, petitioner Furman or his crime illustrates the "extreme," then nearly all murderers and their murders are also "extreme."[12] Furthermore, our procedures in death cases, rather than resulting in the selection of "extreme" cases for this punishment, actually sanction an arbitrary selection. For this Court has held that juries may, as they do, make the decision whether to impose a death sentence wholly unguided by standards governing that decision. *McGautha* v. *California,* 402 U.S. 183, 196–208 (1971). In other words, our procedures are not constructed to guard against the totally capricious selection of criminals for the punishment of death.

Although it is difficult to imagine what further facts would be necessary in order to prove that death is, as my Brother Stewart puts it, "wantonly and . . . freakishly" inflicted, I need not conclude that arbitrary infliction is patently obvious. I am not considering this punishment by the isolated light of one principle. The probability of arbitrariness is sufficiently substantial that it can be relied upon, in combination with the other principles, in reaching a judgment on the constitutionality of this punishment.

When there is a strong probability that an unusually severe and degrading punishment is being inflicted arbitrarily, we may well expect that society will disapprove of its infliction. I turn, therefore, to the third principle. An examination of the history and present operation of the American practice of punishing criminals by death reveals that this punishment has been almost totally rejected by contemporary society.

. . . The progressive decline in, and the current rarity of, the infliction of death demonstrate that our society seriously questions the appropriateness of this punishment today. The States point out that many legislatures authorize death as the punishment for certain crimes and that substantial segments of the public, as reflected in opinion polls and referendum votes, continue to support it. Yet the availability of this punishment through statutory authorization, as well as the polls and referenda, which amount simply to approval of that authorization, simply underscores the extent to which our society has in fact rejected this punishment. When an unusually severe punishment is authorized for wide-scale application but not, because of society's refusal, inflicted save in a few instances, the inference is compelling that there is a deep-seated reluctance to inflict it. Indeed, the likelihood is great that the punishment is tolerated only because of its disuse. The objective indicator of society's view of an unusually severe punishment is what society does with it, and today society will inflict death upon only a small sample of the eligible criminals. Rejection could hardly be more complete without becoming absolute. At the very least, I must conclude that contemporary society views this punishment with substantial doubt.

The final principle to be considered is that an unusually severe and degrading punishment may not be excessive in view of the purposes for which it is inflicted. This principle, too, is related to the others. When there is a strong probability that the State is arbitrarily inflicting an unusually severe punishment that is subject to grave societal doubts, it is likely also that the punishment cannot be shown to be serving any penal purpose that could not be served equally well by some less severe punishment.

The States' primary claim is that death is a necessary punishment because it prevents the commission of capital crimes more effectively than any less severe punishment. The first part of this claim is that the infliction of death is necessary to stop the individuals executed from committing further crimes. The sufficient answer to this is that if a criminal convicted of a capital crime poses a danger to society, effective administration of the State's pardon and parole laws can delay or deny his release from prison, and techniques of isolation can eliminate or minimize the danger while he remains confined.

The more significant argument is that the threat of death prevents the commission of capital crimes because it deters potential criminals who would not be deterred by the threat of imprisonment. The argument is not based upon evidence that the threat of death is a superior deterrent. Indeed, as my Brother Marshall establishes, the available evidence uniformly indicates, although it does not conclusively prove, that the threat of death has no greater deterrent effect than the threat of imprisonment. The States argue, however, that they are entitled to rely upon common human experience, and that experience, they say, supports the conclusion that death must be a more effective deterrent than any less severe punishment. Because people fear death the most, the argument runs, the threat of death must be the greatest deterrent.

It is important to focus upon the precise import of this argument. It is not denied that many, and probably most, capital crimes cannot be deterred by the threat of punishment. Thus the argument can apply only to those who think rationally about the commission of capital crimes. Particularly is that true when the potential criminal, under this argument, must not only consider the risk of punishment, but also distinguish between two possible punishments. The concern, then, is with a particular type of potential criminal, the rational person who will commit a capital crime knowing that the punishment is long-term imprisonment, which may well be for the rest of his life, but will not commit the crime knowing that the punishment is death. On the face of it, the assumption that such persons exist is implausible.

In any event, this argument cannot be appraised in the abstract. We are not presented with the theoretical question whether under any imaginable circumstances the threat of death might be a greater deterrent to the commission of capital crimes than the threat of imprisonment. We are concerned with the practice of punishing criminals by death as it exists in the United States today. Proponents of this argument necessarily admit that its validity depends upon the existence of a system in which the punishment of

death is invariably and swiftly imposed. Our system, of course, satisfies neither condition. A rational person contemplating a murder or rape is confronted, not with the certainty of a speedy death, but with the slightest possibility that he will be executed in the distant future. The risk of death is remote and improbable; in contrast, the risk of long-term imprisonment is near and great. In short, whatever the speculative validity of the assumption that the threat of death is a superior deterrent, there is no reason to believe that as currently administered the punishment of death is necessary to deter the commission of capital crimes. Whatever might be the case were all or substantially all eligible criminals quickly put to death, unverifiable possibilities are an insufficient basis upon which to conclude that the threat of death today has any greater deterrent efficacy than the threat of imprisonment.[13]

There is, however, another aspect to the argument that the punishment of death is necessary for the protection of society. The infliction of death, the States urge, serves to manifest the community's outrage at the commission of the crime. It is, they say, a concrete public expression of moral indignation that inculcates respect for the law and helps assure a more peaceful community. Moreover, we are told, not only does the punishment of death exert this widespread moralizing influence upon community values, it also satisfies the popular demand for grievous condemnation of abhorrent crimes and thus prevents disorder, lynching, and attempts by private citizens to take the law into their own hands.

The question, however, is not whether death serves these supposed purposes of punishment, but whether death serves them more effectively than imprisonment. There is no evidence whatever that utilization of imprisonment rather than death encourages private blood feuds and other disorders. Surely if there were such a danger, the execution of a handful of criminals each year would not prevent it. The assertion that death alone is a sufficiently emphatic denunciation for capital crimes suffers from the same defect. If capital crimes require the punishment of death in order to provide moral reinforcement for the basic values of the community, those values can only be undermined when death is so rarely inflicted upon the criminals who commit the crimes. Furthermore, it is certainly doubtful that the infliction of death by the State does in fact strengthen the community's moral code; if the deliberate extinguishment of human life has any effect at all, it more likely tends to lower our respect for life and brutalize our values. That, after all, is why we no longer carry out public executions. In any event, this claim simply means that one purpose of punishment is to indicate social disapproval of crime. To serve that purpose our laws distribute punishments according to the gravity of crimes and punish more severely the crimes society regards as more serious. That purpose cannot justify any particular punishment as the upper limit of severity.

Mr. Justice White, concurring.

. . . Most important, a major goal of the criminal law—to deter others by punishing the convicted criminal—would not be substantially served where the penalty is so seldom invoked that it ceases to be the credible threat essential to influence the conduct of others. For present purposes I accept the morality and utility of punishing one person to influence another. I accept also the effectiveness of punishment generally and need not reject the death penalty as a more effective deterrent than a lesser punishment. But common sense and experience tell us that seldom-enforced laws become ineffective measures for controlling human conduct and that the death penalty, unless imposed with sufficient frequency, will make little contribution to deterring those crimes for which it may be exacted.

The imposition and execution of the death penalty are obviously cruel in the dictionary sense. But the penalty has not been considered cruel and unusual punishment in the constitutional sense because it was thought justified by the social ends it was deemed to serve. At the moment that it ceases realistically to further these purposes, however, the emerging question is whether its imposition in such circumstances would violate the Eighth Amendment. It is my view that it would, for its imposition would then be the pointless and needless extinction of life with only marginal contributions to any discernible social or public purposes. A penalty with such negligible returns to the State would be patently excessive and cruel and unusual punishment violative of the Eighth Amendment.

It is also my judgment that this point has been reached with respect to capital punishment as it is presently administered under the statutes involved in these cases. Concededly, it is difficult to prove as a general proposition that capital punishment, however administered, more effectively serves the ends of the criminal law than does imprisonment. But however that may be, I cannot avoid the conclusion that as the statutes before us are now administered, the penalty is so infrequently imposed that the threat of execution is too attenuated to be of substantial service to criminal justice.

I need not restate the facts and figures that appear in the opinions of my Brethren. Nor can I "prove" my conclusion from these data. But, like my Brethren, I must arrive at judgment; and I can do no more than state a conclusion based on 10 years of almost daily exposure to the facts and circumstances of hundreds and hundreds of federal and state criminal cases involving crimes for which death is the authorized penalty. That conclusion, as I have said, is that the death penalty is exacted with great infrequency even for the most atrocious crimes and that there is no meaningful basis for distinguishing the few cases in which it is imposed from the many cases in which it is not. The short of it is that the policy of vesting sentencing authority primarily in juries—a decision largely motivated by the desire to mitigate the harshness of the law and to bring community judgment to bear on the sentence as well as guilt or innocence—has so effectively achieved its aims that capital punishment within the confines of the statutes now before us has for all practical purposes run its course.

Mr. Chief Justice Burger, with whom Mr. Justice Blackmun, Mr. Justice Powell, and Mr. Justice Rehnquist join, dissenting.

. . . There are no obvious indications that capital punishment offends the conscience of society to such a degree that our traditional deference to the legislative judgment must be abandoned. It is not a punishment such as burning at the stake that everyone would ineffably find to be repugnant to all civilized standards. Nor is it a punishment so roundly condemned that only a few aberrant legislatures have retained it on the statute books. Capital punishment is authorized by statute in 40 States, the District of Columbia, and in the federal courts for the commission of certain crimes.[14] On four occasions in the last 11 years Congress has added to the list of federal crimes punishable by death.[15] In looking for reliable indicia of contemporary attitude, none more trustworthy has been advanced.

One conceivable source of evidence that legislatures have abdicated their essentially barometric role with respect to community values would be public opinion polls, of which there have been many in the past decade addressed to the question of capital punishment. Without assessing the reliability of such polls, or intimating that any judicial reliance could ever be placed on them, it need only be noted that the reported results have shown nothing approximating the universal condemnation of capital punishment that might lead us to suspect that the legislatures in general have lost touch with current social values.[16]

Counsel for petitioners rely on a different body of empirical evidence. They argue, in effect, that the number of cases in which the death penalty is imposed, as compared with the number of cases in which it is statutorily available, reflects a general revulsion toward the penalty that would lead to its repeal if only it were more generally and widely enforced. It cannot be gainsaid that by the choice of juries—and sometimes judges[17]—the death penalty is imposed in far fewer than half the cases in which it is available.[18] To go further and characterize the rate of imposition as "freakishly rare," as petitioners insist, is unwarranted hyperbole. And regardless of its characterization, the rate of imposition does not impel the conclusion that capital punishment is now regarded as intolerably cruel or uncivilized.

It is argued that in those capital cases where juries have recommended mercy, they have given expression to civilized values and effectively renounced the legislative authorization for capital punishment. At the same time it is argued that where juries have made the awesome decision to send men to their deaths, they have acted arbitrarily and without sensitivity to prevailing standards of decency. This explanation for the infrequency of imposition of capital punishment is unsupported by known facts, and is inconsistent in principle with everything this Court has ever said about the functioning of juries in capital cases.

In *McGautha* v. *California,* decided only one year ago, the Court held that there was no mandate in the Due Process Clause of the Fourteenth Amendment that juries be given instructions as to when the death penalty should be imposed. After reviewing the autonomy that juries have traditionally exercised in capital cases and noting the practical difficulties of framing manageable instructions, this Court concluded that judicially articulated standards were not needed to insure a responsible decision as to penalty. Nothing in *McGautha* licenses capital juries to act arbitrarily or assumes that they have so acted in the past. On the contrary, the assumption underlying the *McGautha* ruling is that juries "will act with due regard for the consequences of their decision." 402 U.S., at 208.

The responsibility of juries deciding capital cases in our system of justice was nowhere better described than in *Witherspoon* v. *Illinois, supra:*

"[A] jury that must choose between life imprisonment and capital punishment can do little

more—and must do nothing less—than express the conscience of the community on the ultimate question of life or death."

"And one of the most important functions any jury can perform in making such a selection is to maintain a link between contemporary community values and the penal system—a link without which the determination of punishment could hardly reflect 'the evolving standards of decency that mark the progress of a maturing society'" 391 U.S., at 519 and n. 15 (emphasis added).

The selectivity of juries in imposing the punishment of death is properly viewed as a refinement on rather than a repudiation of, the statutory authorization for that penalty. Legislatures prescribe the categories of crimes for which the death penalty should be available, and, acting as "the conscience of the community," juries are entrusted to determine in individual cases that the ultimate punishment is warranted. Juries are undoubtedly influenced in this judgment by myriad factors. The motive or lack of motive of the perpetrator, the degree of injury or suffering of the victim or victims, and the degree of brutality in the commission of the crime would seem to be prominent among these factors. Given the general awareness that death is no longer a routine punishment for the crimes for which it is made available, it is hardly surprising that juries have been increasingly meticulous in their imposition of the penalty. But to assume from the mere fact of relative infrequency that only a random assortment of pariahs are sentenced to death, is to cast grave doubt on the basic integrity of our jury system.

It would, of course, be unrealistic to assume that juries have been perfectly consistent in choosing the cases where the death penalty is to be imposed, for no human institution performs with perfect consistency. There are doubtless prisoners on death row who would not be there had they been tried before a different jury or in a different State. In this sense their fate has been controlled by a fortuitous circumstance. However, this element of fortuity does not stand as an indictment either of the general functioning of juries in capital cases or of the integrity of jury decisions in individual cases. There is no empirical basis for concluding that juries have generally failed to discharge in good faith the responsibility described in *Witherspoon*—that of choosing between life and death in individual cases according to the dictates of community values.[19]

. . . It seems remarkable to me that with our basic trust in lay jurors as the keystone in our system of criminal justice, it should now be suggested that we take the most sensitive and important of all decisions away from them. I could more easily be persuaded that mandatory sentences of death, without the intervening and ameliorating impact of lay jurors, are so arbitrary and doctrinaire that they violate the Constitution. The very infrequency of death penalties imposed by jurors attests their cautious and discriminating reservation of that penalty for the most extreme cases. I had thought that nothing was clearer in history, as we noted in *McGautha* one year ago, than the American abhorrence of "the common-law rule imposing a mandatory death sentence on all convicted murderers." 402 U.S., at 198. As the concurring opinion of Mr. Justice Marshall shows, *ante,* at 339, the 19th century movement away from mandatory death sentences marked an enlightened introduction of flexibility into the sentencing process. It recognized that individual culpability is not always measured by the category of the crime committed. This change in sentencing practice was greeted by the Court as a humanizing development. See *Winston* v. *United States,* 172 U.S. 303 (1899); cf. *Calton* v. *Utah,* 130 U.S. 83 (1889).

See also *Andres* v. *United States,* 333 U.S. 740, 753 (1948) (Frankfurter, J., concurring). I do not see how this history can be ignored and how it can be suggested that the Eighth Amendment demands the elimination of the most sensitive feature of the sentencing system.

As a general matter, the evolution of penal concepts in this country has not been marked by great progress, nor have the results up to now been crowned with significant success. If anywhere in the whole spectrum of criminal justice fresh ideas deserve sober analysis, the sentencing and correctional area ranks high on the list. But it has been widely accepted that mandatory sentences for crimes do not best serve the ends of the criminal justice system. Now, after the long process of drawing away from the blind imposition of uniform sentences for every person convicted of a particular offense, we are confronted with an argument perhaps implying that only the legislatures may determine that a sentence of death is appropriate, without the intervening evaluation of jurors or judges. This approach threatens to turn back the progress of penal reform, which has moved until recently at too slow a rate to absorb significant setbacks.

---

1. The opinion of the Supreme Court of Georgia affirming Furman's conviction of murder and sentence of death is reported in 225 Ga. 253, 167 S.E. 2d 628, and its opinion affirming Jackson's conviction of rape and sentence of death is reported in 225 Ga. 790, 171 S.E. 2d 501. The conviction of Branch of rape and the sentence of death were affirmed by the Court of Criminal Appeals of Texas and reported in 447 S.W. 2d 932.
2. See Johnson, The Negro and Crime, 217 Annals Amer. Acad. Pol. & Soc. Sci. 93 (1941).
3. See J. Spellman, Political Theory of Ancient India 112 (1964).
4. C. Drekmeier, Kingship and Community in Early India 233 (1962).
5. Cf. B. Prettyman, Jr., Death and The Supreme Court 296–297 (1961). "The disparity of representation in capital cases raises doubt about capital punishment itself, which has been abolished in only nine states. If a James Avery [345 U.S. 559] can be saved from electrocution because his attorney made timely objection to the selection of a jury by the use of yellow and white tickets, while an Aubry Williams [349 U.S. 375] can be sent to his death by a jury selected in precisely the same manner, we are imposing our most extreme penalty in an uneven fashion.

"The problem of proper representation is not a problem of money, as some have claimed, but of a lawyer's ability, and it is not true that only the rich have able lawyers. Both the rich and the poor usually are well represented—the poor because more often than not the best attorneys are appointed to defend them. It is the middle-class defendant, who can afford to hire an attorney but not a very good one, who is at a disadvantage. Certainly William Fikes [352 U.S. 191], despite the anomalous position in which he finds himself today, received as effective and intelligent a defense from his court-appointed attorneys as he would have received from an attorney his family had scraped together enough money to hire.

"And it is not only a matter of ability. An attorney must be found who is prepared to spend precious hours—the basic commodity he has to sell—on a case that seldom fully compensates him and often brings him no fee at all. The public has no conception of the time and effort devoted by attorneys to indigent cases. And in a first-degree case, the added responsibility of having a man's life depend upon the outcome exacts a heavy toll."
6. "That life is at stake is of course another important factor in creating the extraordinary situation. The difference between capital and non-capital offenses is the basis of differentiation in law in diverse ways in which the distinction becomes relevant." Williams v. Georgia, 349 U.S. 375, 391 (1955) (Frankfurter, J.). "When the penalty is death, we, like state court judges, are tempted to strain the evidence and even, in close cases, the law in order to give a doubtfully condemned man another chance." Stein v. New York, 346 U.S. 156 (1953) (Jackson, J.). "In death cases doubts such as those presented here should be resolved in favor of the accused." Andres v. United States, 333 U.S. 740, 752 (1948) (Reed, J.). Mr. Justice Harlan expressed the point strongly: "I do not concede that whatever process is 'due' an offender faced with a fine or a prison sentence necessarily satisfies the requirements of the Constitution in a capital case. The distinction is by no means novel, . . . nor is it negligible, being literally that between life and death." Reid v. Covert, 354 U.S. 1, 77 (1957) (concurring in result). And, of course, for many years this Court distinguished death cases from all others for purposes of the constitutional right to counsel. See Powell v. Alabama, 287 U.S. 45 (1932); Betts v. Brady, 316 U.S. 455 (1942); Bute v. Illinois, 333 U.S. 640 (1948).

7. *See Report of Royal Commission on Capital Punishment 1949–1953, ¶¶ 700–789, pp. 246–273 (1953); Hearings on S. 1760 before the Subcommittee on Criminal Laws and Procedures of the Senate Committee on the Judiciary, 90th Cong., 2d Sess., 19–21 (1968) (testimony of Clinton Duffy); H. Barnes & N. Teeters, New Horizons in Criminology 306–309 (3d ed. 1959); C. Chessman, Trial by Ordeal 195–202 (1955); M. DiSalle, The Power of Life and Death 84–85 (1965); C. Duffy, 88 Men and 2 Women 13–14 (1962); B. Eshelman, Death Row Chaplain 26–29, 101–104, 159–164 (1962); R. Hammer, Between Life and Death 208–212 (1969); K. Lamott, Chronicles of San Quentin 228–231 (1961); L. Lawes, Life and Death in Sing Sing 170–171 (1928); Rubin, The Supreme Court, Cruel and Unusual Punishment, and the Death Penalty, 15 Crime & Delin. 121, 128–129 (1969); Comment, The Death Penalty Cases, 56 Calif. L. Rev. 1268, 1338–1341 (1968); Brief amici curiae filed by James V. Bennett, Clinton T. Duffy, Robert G. Sarver, Harry C. Tinsley, and Lawrence E. Wilson 12–14.*

8. *See H. Barnes & N. Teeters, New Horizons in Criminology 309–311 (2d ed. 1959); Camus, Reflections on the Guillotine, in A. Camus, Resistance, Rebellion, and Death 131, 151–156 (1960); C. Duffy, 88 Men and 2 Women 68–70, 254 (1962); R. Hammer, Between Life and Death 222–235, 244–250, 269–272 (1969); S. Rubin, The Law of Criminal Correction 340 (1963); Bluestone & McGahee, Reaction to Extreme Stress: Impending Death by Execution, 119 Amer. J. Psychiatry 393 (1962); Gottlieb, Capital Punishment, 15 Crime & Delin. 1, 8–10 (1969); West, Medicine and Capital Punishment, in Hearings on S. 1760 before the Subcommittee on Criminal Laws and Procedures of the Senate Committee on the Judiciary, 90th Cong., 2d Sess., 124 (1968); Ziferstein, Crime and Punishment, The Center Magazine 84 (Jan. 1968); Comment, The Death Penalty Cases, 56 Calif. L. Rev. 1268, 1342 (1968); Note, Mental Suffering under Sentence of Death: A Cruel and Unusual Punishment, 57 Iowa L. Rev. 814 (1972).*

9. *The State, of course, does not purposely impose the lengthy waiting period in order to inflict further suffering. The impact upon the individual is not the less severe on that account. It is no answer to assert that long delays exist only because condemned criminals avail themselves of their full panoply of legal rights. The right not to be subjected to inhuman treatment cannot, of course, be played off against the right to pursue due process of law, but, apart from that, the plain truth is that it is society that demands, even against the wishes of the criminal, that all legal avenues be explored before the execution is finally carried out.*

10. *It was recognized in Trop itself that expatriation is a "punishment short of death." 356 U.S., at 99. Death, however, was distinguished on the ground that it was "still widely accepted." Ibid.*

11. *Stephen, Capital Punishments, 69 Fraser's Magazine 753, 763 (1864).*

12. *The victim surprised Furman in the act of burglarizing the victim's home in the middle of the night. While escaping, Furman killed the victim with one pistol shot fired through the closed kitchen door from the outside. At the trial, Furman gave his version of the killing:*

"They got me charged with murder and I admit, I admit going to these folks' home and they did caught me in there and I was coming back out, backing up and there was a wire down there on the floor. I was coming out backwards and fell back and I didn't intend to kill nobody. I didn't know they was behind the door. The gun went off and I didn't know nothing about no murder until they arrested me, and when the gun went off I was down on the floor and I got up and ran. That's all to it." *App. 54–55.*

The Georgia Supreme Court accepted that version:

"The admission in open court by the accused . . . that during the period in which he was involved in the commission of a criminal act at the home of the deceased, he accidentally tripped over a wire in leaving the premises causing the gun to go off, together with other facts and circumstances surrounding the death of the deceased by violent means, was sufficient to support the verdict of guilty of murder. . . ." *Furman v. State, 225 Ga. 253, 254, 167 S.E. 2d 628, 629 (1969).*

About Furman himself, the jury knew only that he was black and that, according to his statement at trial, he was 26 years old and worked at "Superior Upholstery." App. 54. It took the jury one hour and 35 minutes to return a verdict of guilt and a sentence of death. Id., *at 64–65.*

13. *There is also the more limited argument that death is a necessary punishment when criminals are already serving or subject to a sentence of life imprisonment. If the only punishment available is further imprisonment, it is said, those criminals will have nothing to lose by committing further crimes, and accordingly the threat of death is the sole deterrent. But "life" imprisonment is a misnomer today. Rarely, if ever, do crimes carry a mandatory life sentence without possibility of parole. That possibility ensures that criminals do not reach the point where further crimes are free of consequences. Moreover, if this argument is simply an assertion that the threat of death is a more effective deterrent than the threat of increased imprisonment by denial of release on parole, then, as noted above, there is simply no evidence to support it.*

14. *See Department of Justice, National Prisoner Statistics No. 46, Capital Punishment 1930–1970, p. 50 (Aug. 1971). Since the publication of the Department of Justice report, capital punishment has been judicially abolished in California, People v. Anderson, 6 Cal. 3d 628, 493 P. 2d 880, cert. denied, 406 U.S. 813 (1972). The States where capital punishment is no longer authorized are Alaska, California, Hawaii, Iowa, Maine, Michigan, Minnesota, Oregon, West Virginia, and Wisconsin.*

15. *See Act of Jan. 2, 1971, Pub. L. 91–644, Tit. IV, § 15, 84 Stat. 1891, 18 U.S.C. § 351; see Act of Oct. 15, 1970, Pub. L. 91–452, Tit. XI, § 1102 (a), 84 Stat. 956, 18 U.S.C. § 844 (f) (i); Act of Aug. 28, 1965, 79 Stat. 580, 18 U.S.C. § 1751; Act of Sept. 5, 1961, § 1, 75 Stat. 466, 49 U.S.C. § 1472 (i). See also opinion of Mr. Justice Blackmun, post, at 412–413.*

16. *A 1966 poll indicated that 42% of those polled favored capital punishment while 47% opposed it, and 11% had no opinion. A 1969 poll found 51% in favor, 40% opposed, and 9% with no opinion. See Erskine, The Polls: Capital Punishment, 34 Public Opinion Quarterly 290 (1970).*

17. *The jury plays the predominant role in sentencing in capital cases in this country. Available evidence indicates that where the judge determines the sentence, the death penalty is imposed with a slightly greater frequency than where the jury makes the determination. H. Kalven & H. Zeisel, The American Jury 436 (1966).*

18. *In the decade from 1961–1970, an average of 106 persons per year received the death sentence in the United States, ranging from a low of 85 in 1967 to a high of 140 in 1961; 127 persons received the death sentence in 1970. Department of Justice, National Prisoner Statistics No. 46, Capital Punishment 1930–1970, p. 9. See also Bedau, The Death Penalty in America, 35 Fed. Prob., No. 2, p. 32 (1971). Although accurate figures are difficult to obtain, it is thought that from 15% to 20% of those convicted of murder are sentenced to death in States where it is authorized. See, for example, McGee, Capital Punishment as Seen by a Correctional Administrator, 28 Fed. Prob., No. 2, pp. 11, 12 (1964); Bedau, Death Sentences in New Jersey 1907–1960, 19 Rutgers L. Rev. 1, 30 (1964); Florida Division of Corrections, Seventh Biennial Report (July 1, 1968, to June 30, 1970) 82 and the few other crimes made punishable by death in certain States is considerably lower. See, for example, Florida Division of Corrections, Seventh Biennial Report, supra, at 83; Partington, The Incidence of the Death Penalty for Rape in Virginia, 22 Wash. & Lee L. Rev. 43–44, 71–73 (1965).*

19. *Counsel for petitioners make the conclusory statement that "[t]hose who are selected to die are the poor and powerless, personally ugly and socially unacceptable." Brief for Petitioner in No. 68-5027, p. 51. However, the sources cited contain no empirical findings to undermine the general premise that juries impose the death penalty in the most extreme cases. One study has discerned a statistically noticeable difference between the rate of imposition on blue collar and white collar defendants; the study otherwise concludes that juries do follow rational patterns in imposing the sentence of death. Note, A Study of the California Penalty Jury in*

First-Degree-Murder Cases, 21 Stan. L. Rev. 1297 (1969). See also
H. Kalven & H. Zeisel, The American Jury 434–449 (1966).

Statistics are also cited to show that the death penalty has been
imposed in a racially discriminatory manner. Such statistics suggest, at least as a historical matter, that Negroes have been sentenced to death with greater frequency than whites in several
States, particularly for the crime of interracial rape. See, for example, Koeninger, Capital Punishment in Texas, 1924–1968, 15 Crime
& Delin. 132 (1969).

WOODSON V. NORTH CAROLINA*

United States Supreme Court, 1976

Judgment of the Court, and opinion of Mr. Justice
STEWART, Mr. Justice POWELL, and Mr. Justice STE-
VENS, announced by Mr. Justice STEWART.

The question in this case is whether the imposition of a death sentence for the crime of first-degree
murder under the law of North Carolina violates the
Eighth and Fourteenth Amendments.

I

The petitioners were convicted of first-degree murder
as the result of their participation in an armed robbery
of a convenience food store, in the course of which
the cashier was killed and a customer was seriously
wounded. There were four participants in the robbery: the petitioners James Tyrone Woodson and Luby
Waxton and two others, Leonard Tucker and Johnnie
Lee Carroll. At the petitioners' trial Tucker and Carroll
testified for the prosecution after having been permitted to plead guilty to lesser offenses; the petitioners
testified in their own defense.

The evidence for the prosecution established
that the four men had been discussing a possible robbery for some time. On the fatal day Woodson had
been drinking heavily. About 9:30 p.m., Waxton and
Tucker came to the trailer where Woodson was staying. When Woodson came out of the trailer, Waxton
struck him in the face and threatened to kill him in an
effort to make him sober up and come along on the
robbery. The three proceeded to Waxton's trailer
where they met Carroll. Waxton armed himself with a
nickel-plated derringer, and Tucker handed Woodson
a rifle. The four then set out by automobile to rob the
store. Upon arriving at their destination Tucker and
Waxton went into the store while Carroll and Woodson remained in the car as lookouts. Once inside the
store, Tucker purchased a package of cigarettes from
the woman cashier. Waxton then also asked for a
package of cigarettes, but as the cashier approached
him he pulled the derringer out of his hip pocket and
fatally shot her at point-blank range. Waxton then
took the money tray from the cash register and gave it
to Tucker, who carried it out of the store, pushing past
an entering customer as he reached the door. After he
was outside, Tucker heard a second shot from inside
the store, and shortly thereafter Waxton emerged, carrying a handful of paper money. Tucker and Waxton
got in the car and the four drove away.

*The petitioners' testimony agreed in large part
with this version of the circumstances of the
robbery. It differed diametrically in one important respect: Waxton claimed that he never
had a gun, and that Tucker had shot both the
cashier and the customer.*

During the trial Waxton asked to be allowed to
plead guilty to the same lesser offenses to which
Tucker had pleaded guilty, but the solicitor refused to

*428 U.S. 280, 49 L.Ed.2d 944. No. 75-5491. Argued March 31, 1976. Decided July 2, 1976.

accept the pleas. Woodson, by contrast, maintained throughout the trial that he had been coerced by Waxton, that he was therefore innocent, and that he would not consider pleading guilty to any offense.

The petitioners were found guilty on all charges, and, as was required by statute, sentenced to death. The Supreme Court of North Carolina affirmed. We granted certiorari, to consider whether the imposition of the death penalties in this case comports with the Eighth and Fourteenth Amendments to the United States Constitution.

II

The petitioners argue that the imposition of the death penalty under any circumstances is cruel and unusual punishment in violation of the Eighth and Fourteenth Amendments. We reject this argument for the reasons stated today in *Gregg* v. *Georgia*.

III

At the time of this Court's decision in *Furman* v. *Georgia,* North Carolina law provided that in cases of first-degree murder, the jury in its unbridled discretion could choose whether the convicted defendant should be sentenced to death or to life imprisonment. After the *Furman* decision the Supreme Court of North Carolina in *State* v. *Waddell,* held unconstitutional the provision of the death penalty statute that gave the jury the option of returning a verdict of guilty without capital punishment, but held further that this provision was severable so that the statute survived as a mandatory death penalty law.

The North Carolina General Assembly in 1974 followed the court's lead and enacted a new statute that was essentially unchanged from the old one except that it made the death penalty mandatory. The statute now reads as follows:

> "Murder in the first and second degree defined; punishment.—*A murder which shall be perpetrated by means of poison, lying in wait, imprisonment, starving, torture, or by any other kind of willful, deliberate and premeditated killing, or which shall be committed in the perpetration or attempt to perpetrate any arson, rape, robbery, kidnapping, burglary or other felony, shall be deemed to be murder in*

> *the first degree and shall be punished with death. All other kinds of murder shall be deemed murder in the second degree, and shall be punished by imprisonment for a term of not less than two years nor more than life imprisonment in the State's prison."*

It was under this statute that the petitioners, who committed their crime on June 3, 1974, were tried, convicted, and sentenced to death.

North Carolina, unlike Florida, Georgia, and Texas, has thus responded to the *Furman* decision by making death the mandatory sentence for all persons convicted of first-degree murder. In ruling on the constitutionality of the sentences imposed on the petitioners under this North Carolina statute, the Court now addresses for the first time the question whether a death sentence returned pursuant to a law imposing a mandatory death penalty for a broad category of homicidal offenses constitutes cruel and unusual punishment within the meaning of the Eighth and Fourteenth Amendments. The issue, like that explored in *Furman,* involves the procedure employed by the State to select persons for the unique and irreversible penalty of death.

A

The Eighth Amendment stands to assure that the State's power to punish is "exercised within the limits of civilized standards." Central to the application of the Amendment is a determination of contemporary standards regarding the infliction of punishment. As discussed in *Gregg* v. *Georgia,* indicia of societal values identified in prior opinions include history and traditional usage, legislative enactments, and jury determinations.

In order to provide a frame for assessing the relevancy of these factors in this case we begin by sketching the history of mandatory death penalty statutes in the United States. At the time the Eighth Amendment was adopted in 1791, the States uniformly followed the common-law practice of making death the exclusive and mandatory sentence for certain specified offenses. Although the range of capital offenses in the American Colonies was quite limited in comparison to the more than 200 offenses then punishable by death in England, the Colonies at the time of the Revolution imposed death sentences on all persons convicted of any of a considerable number of crimes, typically including at a minimum, murder, treason, piracy, arson, rape, robbery, burglary, and sodomy. As at common law, all homicides that were not involuntary, provoked, justified, or excused constituted murder and were automatically punished by death. Almost from the outset jurors reacted unfavorably to the harshness of mandatory death sentences. The States initially responded to this expression of public dissatisfaction with mandatory statutes by limiting the classes of capital offenses.

This reform, however, left unresolved the problem posed by the not infrequent refusal of juries to convict murderers rather than subject them to automatic death sentences. In 1794, Pennsylvania attempted to alleviate the undue severity of the law by confining the mandatory death penalty to "murder of the first degree" encompassing all "willful, deliberate and premeditated" killings. Other jurisdictions, including Virginia and Ohio, soon enacted similar measures, and within a generation the practice spread to most of the States.

Despite the broad acceptance of the division of murder into degrees, the reform proved to be an unsatisfactory means of identifying persons appropriately punishable by death. Although its failure was due in part to the amorphous nature of the controlling concepts of willfulness, deliberateness, and premeditation, a more fundamental weakness of the reform soon became apparent. Juries continued to find the death penalty inappropriate in a significant number of first-degree murder cases and refused to return guilty verdicts for that crime.

The inadequacy of distinguishing between murderers solely on the basis of legislative criteria narrowing the definition of the capital offense led the States to grant juries sentencing discretion in capital cases. Tennessee in 1838, followed by Alabama in 1841, and Louisiana in 1846, were the first States to abandon mandatory death sentences in favor of discretionary death penalty statutes. This flexibility remedied the harshness of mandatory statutes by permitting the jury to respond to mitigating factors by withholding the death penalty. By the turn of the century, 23 States and the Federal Government had made death sentences discretionary for first-degree murder and other capital offenses. During the next two decades 14 additional States replaced their mandatory death penalty statutes. Thus, by the end of World War I, all but eight States, Hawaii, and the District of Columbia either had adopted discretionary death penalty schemes or abolished the death penalty altogether. By 1963, all of these remaining jurisdictions had replaced their automatic death penalty statutes with discretionary jury sentencing.

The history of mandatory death penalty statutes in the United States thus reveals that the practice of sentencing to death all persons convicted of a particular offense has been rejected as unduly harsh and unworkably rigid. The two crucial indicators of evolving standards of decency respecting the imposition of punishment in our society—jury determinations and legislative enactments—both point conclusively to the repudiation of automatic death sentences. At least since the Revolution, American jurors have, with some regularity, disregarded their oaths and refused to convict defendants where a death sentence was the automatic consequence of a guilty verdict. As we have seen, the initial movement to reduce the number of capital offenses and to separate murder into degrees was prompted in part by the reaction of jurors as well as by reformers who objected to the imposition of death as the penalty for any crime. Nineteenth century journalists, statesmen, and jurists repeatedly observed that jurors were often deterred from convicting palpably guilty men of first-degree murder under mandatory statutes. Thereafter, continuing evidence of jury reluctance to convict persons of capital offenses in mandatory death penalty jurisdictions resulted in legislative authorization of discretionary jury sentencing—by Congress for federal crimes in 1897, by North Carolina in 1949, and by Congress for the District of Columbia in 1962.

As we have noted today in *Gregg* v. *Georgia,* legislative measures adopted by the people's chosen representatives weigh heavily in ascertaining contemporary standards of decency. The consistent course charted by the state legislatures and by Congress since the middle of the past century demonstrates that the aversion of jurors to mandatory death penalty statutes is shared by society at large.

Still further evidence of the incompatibility of mandatory death penalties with contemporary values is provided by the results of jury sentencing under discretionary statutes. In *Witherspoon* v. *Illinois,* the Court observed that "one of the most important functions any jury can perform" in exercising its discretion to choose "between life imprisonment and capital punishment" is "to maintain a link between contemporary community values and the penal system." Various studies indicate that even in first-degree murder cases juries with sentencing discretion do not impose the death penalty "with any great frequency." The actions of sentencing juries suggest that under contemporary standards of decency death is viewed as an inappropriate punishment for a substantial portion of convicted first-degree murderers.

Although the Court has never ruled on the constitutionality of mandatory death penalty statutes, on several occasions dating back to 1899 it has commented upon our society's aversion to automatic death sentences. In *Winston* v. *United States,* the Court noted that the "hardship of punishing with death every crime coming within the definition of murder at common law, and the reluctance of jurors to concur in a capital conviction, have induced American legislatures, in modern times, to allow some cases of murder to be punished by imprisonment, instead of by death." Fifty years after *Winston,* the Court underscored the marked transformation in our attitudes toward mandatory sentences: "The belief no longer prevails that every offense in a like legal category calls for an identical punishment without regard to the past life and habits of a particular offender. This whole country has traveled far from the period in which the death sentence was an automatic and commonplace result of convictions. . . ."

More recently, the Court in *McGautha* v. *California,* detailed the evolution of discretionary imposition of death sentences in this country, prompted by what it termed the American "rebellion against the common-law rule imposing a mandatory death sentence on all convicted murderers." Perhaps the one important factor about evolving social values regarding capital punishment upon which the Members of the *Furman* Court agreed was the accuracy of *McGautha*'s assessment of our Nation's rejection of mandatory death sentences. Mr. Justice Blackmun, for example, emphasized that legislation requiring an automatic death sentence for specified crimes would be "regressive and of an antique mold" and would mark a return to a "point in our criminology [passed beyond] long ago." The Chief Justice, speaking for the four dissenting Justices in *Furman,* discussed the question of mandatory death sentences at some length:

> "I had thought that nothing was clearer in history, as we noted in McGautha *one year ago, than the American abhorrence of 'the common-law rule imposing a mandatory death sentence on all convicted murderers.' As the concurring opinion of Mr. Justice Marshall shows, the 19th century movement away from mandatory death sentences marked an enlightened introduction of flexibility into the sentencing process. It recognized that individual culpability is not always measured by the category of the crime committed. This change*

> *in sentencing practice was greeted by the Court as a humanizing development."*

Although it seems beyond dispute that, at the time of the *Furman* decision in 1972, mandatory death penalty statutes had been renounced by American juries and legislatures, there remains the question whether the mandatory statutes adopted by North Carolina and a number of other States following *Furman* evince a sudden reversal of societal values regarding the imposition of capital punishment. In view of the persistent and unswerving legislative rejection of mandatory death penalty statutes beginning in 1838 and continuing for more than 130 years until *Furman,* it seems evident that the post-*Furman* enactments reflect attempts by the States to retain the death penalty in a form consistent with the Constitution, rather than a renewed societal acceptance of mandatory death sentencing. The fact that some States have adopted mandatory measures following *Furman* while others have legislated standards to guide jury discretion appears attributable to diverse readings of this Court's multi-opinioned decision in that case.

A brief examination of the background of the current North Carolina statute serves to reaffirm our assessment of its limited utility as an indicator of contemporary values regarding mandatory death sentences. Before 1949, North Carolina imposed a mandatory death sentence on any person convicted of rape or first-degree murder. That year, a study commission created by the state legislature recommended that juries be granted discretion to recommend life sentences in all capital cases:

> "We propose that a recommendation of mercy by the jury in capital cases automatically carry with it a life sentence. Only three other states now have the mandatory death penalty and we believe its retention will be definitely harmful. Quite frequently, juries refuse to convict for rape or first degree murder because, from all the circumstances, they do not believe the defendant, although guilty, should suffer death. The result is that verdicts are returned hardly in harmony with evidence. Our proposal is already in effect in respect to the crimes of burglary and arson. There is much testimony that it has proved beneficial in such cases. We think the law can now be broadened to include all capital crimes."

The 1949 session of the General Assembly of North Carolina adopted the proposed modifications of its rape and murder statutes. Although in subsequent years numerous bills were introduced in the legislature to limit further or abolish the death penalty in North Carolina, they were rejected as were two 1969 proposals to return to mandatory death sentences for all capital offenses.

As noted, when the Supreme Court of North Carolina analyzed the constitutionality of the State's death penalty statute following this Court's decision in *Furman,* it severed the 1949 proviso authorizing jury sentencing discretion and held that "the remainder of the statute with death as the mandatory punishment . . . remains in full force and effect." The North Carolina General Assembly then followed the course found constitutional in *Waddell* and enacted a first-degree murder provision identical to the mandatory statute in operation prior to the authorization of jury discretion. The State's brief in this case relates that the legislature sought to remove "*all* sentencing discretion [so that] there could be no successful *Furman* based attack on the North Carolina statute."

It is now well established that the Eighth Amendment draws much of its meaning from "the evolving standards of decency that mark the progress of a maturing society." As the above discussion makes clear, one of the most significant developments in our society's treatment of capital punishment has been the rejection of the common-law practice of inexorably imposing a death sentence upon every person convicted of a specified offense. North Carolina's mandatory death penalty statute for first-degree murder departs markedly from contemporary standards respecting the imposition of the punishment of death and thus cannot be applied consistently with the Eighth and Fourteenth Amendments' requirement that the State's power to punish "be exercised within the limits of civilized standards."

B

A separate deficiency of North Carolina's mandatory death sentence statute is its failure to provide a constitutionally tolerable response to *Furman's* rejection of unbridled jury discretion in the imposition of capital sentences. Central to the limited holding in *Furman* was the conviction that the vesting of standardless sentencing power in the jury violated the Eighth and Fourteenth Amendments. It is argued that North Carolina has remedied the inadequacies of the death penalty statutes held unconstitutional in *Furman* by withdrawing all sentencing discretion from juries in capital cases. But when one considers the long and consistent American experience with the death penalty in first-degree murder cases, it becomes evident that mandatory statutes enacted in response to *Furman* have simply papered over the problem of unguided and unchecked jury discretion.

As we have noted in Part III-A, *supra,* there is general agreement that American juries have persistently refused to convict a significant portion of persons charged with first-degree murder of that offense under mandatory death penalty statutes. The North Carolina study commission, reported that juries in that State "[q]uite frequently" were deterred from rendering guilty verdicts of first-degree murder because of the enormity of the sentence automatically imposed. Moreover, as a matter of historic fact, juries operating under discretionary sentencing statutes have consistently returned death sentences in only a minority of first-degree murder cases. In view of the historic record, it is only reasonable to assume that many juries under mandatory statutes will continue to consider the grave consequences of a conviction in reaching a verdict. North Carolina's mandatory death penalty statute provides no standards to guide the jury in its inevitable exercise of the power to determine which first-degree murderers shall live and which shall die. And there is no way under the North Carolina law for the judiciary to check arbitrary and capricious exercise of that power through a review of death sentences. Instead of rationalizing the sentencing process, a mandatory scheme may well exacerbate the problem identified in *Furman* by resting the penalty determination on the particular jury's willingness to act lawlessly. While a mandatory death penalty statute may reasonably be expected to increase the number of persons sentenced to death, it does not fulfill *Furman's* basic requirement by replacing arbitrary and wanton jury discretion with objective standards to guide, regularize, and make rationally reviewable the process for imposing a sentence of death.

C

A third constitutional shortcoming of the North Carolina statute is its failure to allow the particularized consideration of relevant aspects of the character and record of each convicted defendant before the imposition upon him of a sentence of death. In *Furman,* members of the Court acknowledge what cannot fairly be denied—that death is a punishment different from all other sanctions in kind rather than degree. A process that accords no significance to relevant facets of the character and record of the individual offender or the circumstances of the particular offense excludes from consideration in fixing the ultimate punishment of death the possibility of compassionate or mitigating factors stemming from the diverse frailties of humankind. It treats all persons convicted of a designated offense not as uniquely individual human beings, but as members of a faceless, undifferentiated mass to be subjected to the blind infliction of the penalty of death.

This Court has previously recognized that "[f]or the determination of sentences, justice generally requires consideration of more than the particular acts by which the crime was committed and that there be taken into account the circumstances of the offense together with the character and propensities of the offender." Consideration of both the offender and the offense in order to arrive at a just and appropriate sentence has been viewed as a progressive and humanizing development. While the prevailing practice of individualizing sentencing determinations generally reflects simply enlightened policy rather than a constitutional imperative, we believe that in capital cases the fundamental respect for humanity underlying the Eighth Amendment requires consideration of the character and record of the individual offender and the circumstances of the particular offense as a constitutionally indispensable part of the process of inflicting the penalty of death.

This conclusion rests squarely on the predicate that the penalty of death is qualitatively different from a sentence of imprisonment, however long. Death, in its finality, differs more from life imprisonment than a 100-year prison term differs from one of only a year or two. Because of that qualitative difference, there is a corresponding difference in the need for reliability in the determination that death is the appropriate punishment in a specific case.

For the reasons stated, we conclude that the death sentences imposed upon the petitioners under North Carolina's mandatory death sentence statute violated the Eighth and Fourteenth Amendments and therefore must be set aside. The judgment of the Supreme Court of North Carolina is reversed insofar as it upheld the death sentences imposed upon the petitioners, and the case is remanded for further proceedings not inconsistent with this opinion.

It is so ordered.

Mr. Justice BRENNAN, concurring in the judgment.

For the reasons stated in my dissenting opinion in *Gregg* v. *Georgia,* I concur in the judgment that sets aside the death sentences imposed under the North Carolina death sentence statute as violative of the Eighth and Fourteenth Amendments.

Mr. Justice MARSHALL, concurring in the judgment.

For the reasons stated in my dissenting opinion in *Gregg* v. *Georgia,* I am of the view that the death penalty is a cruel and unusual punishment forbidden by the Eighth and Fourteenth Amendments. I therefore concur in the Court's judgment.

Mr. Justice WHITE, with whom THE CHIEF JUSTICE and Mr. Justice REHNQUIST join, dissenting.

Following *Furman* v. *Georgia,* the North Carolina Supreme Court considered the effect of that case on the North Carolina criminal statutes which imposed the death penalty for first-degree murder and other crimes but which provided that "if at the time of rendering its verdict in open court, the jury shall so recommend, the punishment shall be imprisonment for life in the State's prison, and the court shall so instruct the jury." *State* v. *Waddell,* determined that *Furman* v. *Georgia* invalidated only the proviso giving the jury the power to limit the penalty to life imprisonment and that thenceforward death was the mandatory penalty for the specified capital crimes. Thereafter N.C.Gen.Stat. § 14–17 was amended to eliminate the express dispensing power of the jury and to add kidnapping to the underlying felonies for which death is the specified penalty. As amended in 1974, the section reads as follows:

> *"A murder which shall be perpetrated by means of poison, lying in wait, imprisonment, starving, torture, or by any other kind of willful, deliberate and premeditated killing, or which shall be committed in the perpetration or attempt to perpetrate any arson, rape, robbery, kidnapping, burglary or other felony, shall be deemed to be murder in the first degree and shall be punished with death. All other kinds of murder shall be deemed murder in the second degree, and shall be punished by imprisonment for a term of not less than two years nor more than life imprisonment in the State's prison."*

It was under this statute that the petitioners in this case were convicted of first-degree murder and the mandatory death sentences imposed.

The facts of record and the proceedings in this case leading to petitioners' convictions for first-degree murder and their death sentences appear in the opinion of Mr. Justice STEWART, Mr. Justice POWELL, and Mr. Justice STEVENS. The issues in the case are very similar, if not identical, to those in *Roberts* v. *Louisiana*. For the reasons stated in my dissenting opinion in that case, I reject petitioners' arguments that the death penalty in any circumstances is a violation of the Eighth Amendment and that the North Carolina statute, although making the imposition of the death penalty mandatory upon proof of guilt and a verdict of first-degree murder, will nevertheless result in the death penalty being imposed so seldom and arbitrarily that it is void under *Furman* v. *Georgia*. As is also apparent from my dissenting opinion in *Roberts* v. *Louisiana,* I also disagree with the two additional grounds which the plurality *sua sponte* offers for invalidating the North Carolina statute. I would affirm the judgment of the North Carolina Supreme Court.

Mr. Justice BLACKMUN, dissenting.

I dissent for the reasons set forth in my dissent in *Furman* v. *Georgia,* and in the other dissenting opinions I joined in that case.

Mr. Justice REHNQUIST, dissenting.

I

The difficulties which attend the plurality's explanation for the result it reaches tend at first to obscure difficulties at least as significant which inhere in the unarticulated premises necessarily underlying that explanation. I advert to the latter only briefly, in order to devote the major and following portion of this dissent to those issues which the plurality actually considers.

As an original proposition, it is by no means clear that the prohibition against cruel and unusual punishments embodied in the Eighth Amendment, and made applicable to the States by the Fourteenth Amendment, *Robinson* v. *California,* was not limited to those punishments deemed cruel and unusual at the time of the adoption of the Bill of Rights. *McGautha* v. *California.* If *Weems* v. *United States,* dealing not with the Eighth Amendment but with an identical provision contained in the Philippine Constitution, and the plurality opinion in *Trop* v. *Dulles,* are to be taken as indicating the contrary, they should surely be weighed against statements in cases such as *Wilkerson* v. *Utah, In re Kemmler, Louisiana ex rel. Francis* v. *Resweber,* and the plurality opinion in *Trop* itself, that the infliction of capital punishment is not in itself violative of the Cruel and Unusual Punishments Clause. Thus for the plurality to begin its analysis with the assumption that it need only demonstrate that

"evolving standards of decency" show that contemporary "society" has rejected such provisions is itself a somewhat shaky point of departure. But even if the assumption be conceded, the plurality opinion's analysis nonetheless founders.

The plurality relies first upon its conclusion that society has turned away from the mandatory imposition of death sentences, and second upon its conclusion that the North Carolina system has "simply papered over" the problem of unbridled jury discretion which two of the separate opinions in *Furman* v. *Georgia* identified as the basis for the judgment rendering the death sentences there reviewed unconstitutional. The third "constitutional shortcoming" of the North Carolina statute is said to be "its failure to allow the particularized consideration of relevant aspects of the character and record of each convicted defendant before the imposition upon him of a sentence of death."

I do not believe that any one of these reasons singly, or all of them together, can withstand careful analysis. Contrary to the plurality's assertions, they would import into the Cruel and Unusual Punishments Clause procedural requirements which find no support in our cases. Their application will result in the invalidation of a death sentence imposed upon a defendant convicted of first-degree murder under the North Carolina system, and the upholding of the same sentence imposed on an identical defendant convicted on identical evidence of first-degree murder under the Florida, Georgia, or Texas systems—a result surely as "freakish" as that condemned in the separate opinions in *Furman*.

II

The plurality is simply mistaken in its assertion that "[t]he history of mandatory death penalty statutes in the United States thus reveals that the practice of sentencing to death all persons convicted of a particular offense has been rejected as unduly harsh and unworkably rigid." This conclusion is purportedly based on two historic developments: the first a series of legislative decisions during the 19th century narrowing the class of offenses punishable by death; the second a series of legislative decisions during both the 19th and 20th centuries, through which mandatory imposition of the death penalty largely gave way to jury discretion in deciding whether or not to impose this ultimate sanction. The first development may have some relevance to the plurality's argument in general but has no bearing at all upon this case. The second development, properly analyzed, has virtually no relevance even to the plurality's argument.

There can be no question that the legislative and other materials discussed in the plurality's opinion show a widespread conclusion on the part of state legislatures during the 19th century that the penalty of death was being required for too broad a range of crimes, and that these legislatures proceeded to narrow the range of crimes for which such penalty could be imposed. If this case involved the imposition of the death penalty for an offense such as burglary or sodomy, the virtually unanimous trend in the legislatures of the States to exclude such offenders from liability for capital punishment might bear on the plurality's Eighth Amendment argument. But petitioners were convicted of first-degree murder, and there is not the slightest suggestion in the material relied upon by the plurality that there had been any turning away at all, much less any such unanimous turning away, from the death penalty as a punishment for those guilty of first-degree murder. The legislative narrowing of the spectrum of capital crimes, therefore, while very arguably representing a general societal judgment since the trend was so widespread, simply never reached far enough to exclude the sort of aggravated homicide of which petitioners stand convicted.

The second string to the plurality's analytical bow is that legislative change from mandatory to discretionary imposition of the death sentence likewise evidences societal rejection of mandatory death penalties. The plurality simply does not make out this part of its case, however, in large part because it treats as being of equal dignity with legislative judgments the judgments of particular juries and of individual jurors.

There was undoubted dissatisfaction, from more than one sector of 19th century society, with the operation of mandatory death sentences. One segment of that society was totally opposed to capital punishment, and was apparently willing to accept the substitution of discretionary imposition of that penalty for its mandatory imposition as a halfway house on the road to total abolition. Another segment was equally unhappy with the operation of the mandatory system, but for an entirely different reason. As the plurality recognizes, this second segment of society was unhappy with the operation of the mandatory system, not because of the death sentences imposed under it, but because people obviously guilty of criminal of-

fenses were *not* being convicted under it. Change to a discretionary system was accepted by these persons not because they thought mandatory imposition of the death penalty was cruel and unusual, but because they thought that if jurors were permitted to return a sentence other than death upon the conviction of a capital crime, fewer guilty defendants would be acquitted.

So far as the action of juries is concerned, the fact that in some cases juries operating under the mandatory system refused to convict obviously guilty defendants does not reflect any "turning away" from the death penalty, or the mandatory death penalty, supporting the proposition that it is "cruel and unusual." Given the requirement of unanimity with respect to jury verdicts in capital cases, a requirement which prevails today in States which accept a nonunanimous verdict in the case of other crimes, it is apparent that a single juror could prevent a jury from returning a verdict of conviction. Occasional refusals to convict, therefore, may just as easily have represented the intransigence of only a small minority of 12 jurors as well as the unanimous judgment of all 12. The fact that the presence of such jurors could prevent conviction in a given case, even though the majority of society, speaking through legislatures, had decreed that it should be imposed, certainly does not indicate that society as a whole rejected mandatory punishment for such offenders; it does not even indicate that those few members of society who serve on juries, as a whole, had done so.

The introduction of discretionary sentencing likewise creates no inference that contemporary society had rejected the mandatory system as unduly severe. Legislatures enacting discretionary sentencing statutes had no reason to think that there would not be roughly the same number of capital convictions under the new system as under the old. The same subjective juror responses which resulted in juror nullification under the old system were legitimized, but in the absence of those subjective responses to a particular set of facts, a capital sentence could as likely be anticipated under the discretionary system as under the mandatory. And at least some of those who would have been acquitted under the mandatory system would be subjected to at least *some* punishment under the discretionary system, rather than escaping altogether a penalty for the crime of which they were guilty. That society was unwilling to accept the paradox presented to it by the actions of some maverick juries or jurors—the acquittal of palpably guilty defendants—hardly reflects the sort of an "evolving standard of decency" to which the plurality professes obeisance.

Nor do the opinions in *Furman* which indicate a preference for discretionary sentencing in capital cases suggest in the slightest that a mandatory sentencing procedure would be cruel and unusual. The plurality concedes, as it must, that following *Furman* 10 States enacted laws providing for mandatory capital punishment. See State Capital Punishment Statutes Enacted Subsequent to *Furman* v. *Georgia*. These enactments the plurality seeks to explain as due to a wrong-headed reading of the holding in *Furman*. But this explanation simply does not wash. While those States may be presumed to have preferred their prior systems reposing sentencing discretion in juries or judges, they indisputably preferred mandatory capital punishment to no capital punishment at all. Their willingness to enact statutes providing that penalty is utterly inconsistent with the notion that they regarded mandatory capital sentencing as beyond "evolving standards of decency." The plurality's glib rejection of *these* legislative decisions as having little weight on the scale which it finds in the Eighth Amendment seems to me more an instance of its desire to save the people from themselves than a conscientious effort to ascertain the content of any "evolving standard of decency."

III

The second constitutional flaw which the plurality finds in North Carolina's mandatory system is that it has simply "papered over" the problem of unchecked jury discretion. The plurality states that "there is general agreement that American juries have persistently refused to convict a significant portion of persons charged with first-degree murder of that offense under mandatory death penalty statutes." The plurality also states that "as a matter of historic fact, juries operating under discretionary sentencing statutes have consistently returned death sentences in only a minority of first-degree murder cases." The basic factual assumption of the plurality seems to be that for any given number of first-degree murder defendants subject to capital punishment, there will be a certain number of jurors who will be unwilling to impose the death penalty even though they are entirely satisfied that the necessary elements of the substantive offense are made out.

In North Carolina jurors unwilling to impose the death penalty may simply hang a jury or they may so assert themselves that a verdict of not guilty is brought in; in Louisiana they will have a similar effect in causing some juries to bring in a verdict of guilty of a lesser included offense even though all the jurors are satisfied that the elements of the greater offense are made out. Such jurors, of course, are violating their oath, but such violation is not only consistent with the majority's hypothesis; the majority's hypothesis is bottomed on its occurrence.

For purposes of argument, I accept the plurality's hypothesis; but it seems to me impossible to conclude from it that a mandatory death sentence statute such as North Carolina enacted is any less sound constitutionally than are the systems enacted by Georgia, Florida, and Texas which the Court upholds.

In Georgia juries are entitled to return a sentence of life, rather than death, for no reason whatever, simply based upon their own subjective notions of what is right and what is wrong. In Florida the judge and jury are required to weigh legislatively enacted aggravating factors against legislatively enacted mitigating factors, and then base their choice between life or death on an estimate of the result of that weighing. Substantial discretion exists here, too, though it is somewhat more canalized than it is in Georgia. Why these types of discretion are regarded by the plurality as constitutionally permissible, while that which may occur in the North Carolina system is not, is not readily apparent. The freakish and arbitrary nature of the death penalty described in the separate concurring opinions of Justices Stewart, and White in *Furman* arose not from the perception that so *many* capital sentences were being imposed but from the perception that so *few* were bring imposed. To conclude that the North Carolina system is bad because juror nullification may permit jury discretion while concluding that the Georgia and Florida systems are sound because they *require* this same discretion, is, as the plurality opinion demonstrates, inexplicable.

The Texas system much more closely approximates the mandatory North Carolina system which is struck down today. The jury is required to answer three statutory questions. If the questions are unanimously answered in the affirmative, the death penalty *must* be imposed. It is extremely difficult to see how this system can be any less subject to the infirmities caused by juror nullification which the plurality concludes are fatal to North Carolina's statute. Justices STEWART, POWELL, and STEVENS apparently think they can sidestep this inconsistency because of their belief that one of the three questions will permit consideration of mitigating factors justifying imposition of a life sentence. It is, however, as those Justices recognize, far from clear that the statute is to be read in such a fashion. In any event, while the imposition of such unlimited consideration of mitigating factors may conform to the plurality's novel constitutional doctrine that "[a] jury must be allowed to consider on the basis of all relevant evidence not only why a death sentence should be imposed, but also why it should not be imposed," the resulting system seems as likely as any to produce the unbridled discretion which was condemned by the separate opinions in *Furman*.

The plurality seems to believe that provision for appellate review will afford a check upon the instances of juror arbitrariness in a discretionary system. But it is not at all apparent that appellate review of death sentences, through a process of comparing the facts of one case in which a death sentence was imposed with the facts of another in which such a sentence was imposed, will afford any meaningful protection against whatever arbitrariness results from jury discretion. All that such review of death sentences can provide is a comparison of fact situations which must in their nature be highly particularized if not unique, and the only relief which it can afford is to single out the occasional death sentence which in the view of the reviewing court does not conform to the standards established by the legislature.

It is established, of course, that there is no right to appellate review of a criminal sentence. *McKane* v. *Durston*. That question is not at issue here, since North Carolina, along with the other four States whose systems the petitioners are challenging in these cases, provides appellate review for a death sentence imposed in one of its trial courts.

By definition, of course, there can be no separate appellate review of the factual basis for the sentencing decision in a mandatory system. If it is once established in a fairly conducted trial that the defendant has in fact committed the crime in question, the only question as to the sentence which can be raised on appeal is whether a legislative determination that such a crime should be punished by death violates the Cruel and Unusual Punishments Clause of the Eighth Amendment. Here both petitioners were convicted of first-degree murder, and there is no serious question raised by the plurality that death is not a constitutionally permissible penalty for such a crime.

But the plurality sees another role for appellate review in its description of the reasons why the Georgia, Texas, and Florida systems are upheld, and the North Carolina system struck down. And it is doubtless true that Georgia in particular has made a substantial effort to respond to the concerns expressed in *Furman*, not an easy task considering the glossolalial manner in which those concerns were expressed. The Georgia Supreme Court has indicated that the Georgia death penalty statute requires it to review death sentences imposed by juries on the basis of rough "proportionality." It has announced that it will not sustain, at least at the present time, death penalties imposed for armed robbery because that penalty is so seldom imposed by juries for that offense. It has also indicated that it will not sustain death penalties imposed for rape in certain fact situations, because the death penalty has been so seldom imposed on facts similar to those situations.

But while the Georgia response may be an admirable one as a matter of policy, it has imperfections, if a failure to conform completely to the dictates of the separate opinions in *Furman* be deemed imperfections, which the opinion of Justices STEWART, POWELL, and STEVENS does not point out. Although there may be some disagreement between that opinion, and the opinion of my Brother White in *Gregg* v. *Georgia*, which I have joined, as to whether the proportionality review conducted by the Supreme Court of Georgia is based solely upon capital sentences imposed, or upon all sentences imposed in cases where a capital sentence could have been imposed by law, I shall assume for the purposes of this discussion that the system contemplates the latter. But this is still far from a guarantee of any equality in sentencing, and is likewise no guarantee against juror nullification. Under the Georgia system, the jury is free to recommend life imprisonment, as opposed to death, for no stated reason whatever. The Georgia Supreme Court cannot know, therefore, when it is reviewing jury sentences for life in capital cases, whether the jurors found aggravating circumstances present, but nonetheless decided to recommend mercy, or instead found no aggravating circumstances at all and opted for mercy. So the "proportionality" type of review, while it would perhaps achieve its objective if there were no possible factual lacunae in the jury verdicts, will not achieve its objective because there are necessarily such lacunae.

IN DEFENSE OF THE DEATH PENALTY:
A Practical and Moral Analysis*

Ernest van den Haag

Three questions about the death penalty so overlap that they must each be answered. I shall ask seriatim: Is the death penalty constitutional? Is it useful? Is the death penalty morally justifiable? . . .

Regardless of constitutional interpretation, the morality and legitimacy of the abolitionist argument regarding capriciousness, discretion, or discrimination, would be more persuasive if it were alleged that those selectively executed are not guilty. But the argument merely maintains that some guilty, but favored, persons or groups escape the death penalty. This is hardly sufficient for letting others escape it. On the contrary, that some guilty persons or groups elude it argues for *extending* the death penalty to them.[1]

Justice requires punishing the guilty—as many of the guilty as possible—even if only some can be punished, and sparing the innocent—as many of the innocent as possible, even if not all are spared. Morally, justice must always be preferred to equality. It would surely be wrong to treat everybody with equal injustice in preference to meting out justice to some. Justice cannot ever permit sparing some guilty persons, or punishing some innocent ones, for the sake of equality—because others have been unjustly spared or punished. In practice, penalties never could be applied if we insisted that they cannot be inflicted on any guilty persons unless we are able to make sure that they are equally applied to all other guilty persons. Anyone familiar with law enforcement knows that punishments can be inflicted only on an unavoidably capricious selection of the guilty.

Although it does not warrant serious discussion, the argument from capriciousness looms large in briefs and decisions. For the last seventy years, courts have tried—lamentably and unproductively—to pre-vent errors of procedure, or of evidence collection, or of decision-making, by the paradoxical method of letting defendants go free as a punishment, or warning, to errant law enforcers. Yet the strategy admittedly never has prevented the errors it was designed to prevent—although it has released countless guilty persons.[2] There is no more merit in the attempt to persuade the courts to let all capital crime defendants go free of capital punishment because some have wrongly escaped it, than in attempting to persuade the courts to let all burglars go, because some have wrongly escaped detection or imprisonment.

Is the death penalty morally just and/or useful? This is the essential moral, as distinguished from the constitutional, question. Discrimination is irrelevant to this moral question. If the death penalty were distributed equally and uncapriciously and with superhuman perfection to all the guilty, but were morally unjust, it would be unjust in each case. Contrariwise, if the death penalty is morally just, however discriminatorily applied to only some of the guilty, it remains just in each case in which it is applied.

The utilitarian (political) effects of unequal justice may well be detrimental to the social fabric because they outrage our passion for equality before the law. Unequal justice also is morally repellent. Nonetheless unequal justice is still justice. The guilty do not become innocent or less deserving of punishment because others escaped it. Nor does any innocent deserve punishment because others suffer it. Justice remains just, however unequal, while injustice remains unjust, however equal. While both are desired, justice and equality are not identical. Equality before the law should be extended and enforced—but not at the expense of justice.

*From Ernest Van Den Haag, "In Defense of the Death Penalty: A Political and Moral Analysis," in *Criminal Bulletin*, vol. 14, no. 1 (1978), pp. 51–68. Reprinted here by permission of Warren, Gorham and Lamont, Inc.

Capriciousness, at any rate, is used as a sham argument against capital punishment by abolitionists. They would oppose the death penalty if it could be meted out without any discretion. They would oppose the death penalty in a homogeneous country without racial discrimination. And they would oppose the death penalty if the incomes of those executed and of those spared were the same. Actually, abolitionists oppose the death penalty, not its possible maldistribution.

What about persons executed in error? The objection here is not that some of the guilty escape, but that some of the innocent do not—a matter far more serious than discrimination among the guilty. Yet, when urged by abolitionists, this, along with all distributional arguments, is a sham. Why? Abolitionists are opposed to the death penalty for the guilty as much as for the innocent. Hence, the question of guilt, if at all relevant to their position, cannot be decisive for them. Guilt is decisive only to those who urge the death penalty for the guilty. They must worry about distribution—part of the justice they seek.

The execution of innocents believed guilty is a miscarriage of justice that must be opposed whenever detected. But such miscarriages of justice do not warrant abolition of the death penalty. Unless the moral drawbacks of an activity or practice, which include the possible death of innocent bystanders, outweigh the moral advantages, which include the innocent lives that might be saved by it, the activity is warranted. Most human activities—medicine, manufacturing, automobile and air traffic, sports, not to speak of wars and revolutions—cause the death of innocent bystanders. Nevertheless, if the advantages sufficiently outweigh the disadvantages, human activities, including those of the penal system with all its punishments, are morally justified.

Is there evidence supporting the usefulness of the death penalty in securing the life of the citizens? Researchers in the past found no statistical evidence for the effects sought, marginal deterrent effects, or deterrent effects over and above those of alternative sanctions. However, in the last few years new and more sophisticated studies have led Professor Isaac Ehrlich to conclude that over the period 1933–1969, "an additional execution per year . . . may have resulted (on the average) in 7 or 8 fewer murders."[3] Other investigators have confirmed Ehrlich's tentative results. Not surprisingly, refutations have been attempted, and Professor Ehrlich has offered his rebuttals.[4] The matter will remain controversial for some time. However, two tentative conclusions can

be drawn with some confidence. First, Ehrlich has shown that previous investigations, that did not find deterrent effects of the death penalty, suffered from fatal defects. Second, there is now some likelihood—much more than hitherto—of statistically demonstrating marginal deterrent effects.

Thus, with respect to deterrence, we must now choose:

1. To trade the certain shortening of the life of a convicted murderer against the survival of between seven and eight innocent victims whose future murder by others becomes more probable, unless the convicted murderer is executed;
2. To trade the certain survival of the convicted murderer against the loss of the lives of between seven and eight innocent victims, who are more likely to be murdered by others if the convicted murderer is allowed to survive.

Prudence as well as morality command us to choose the first alternative.[5]

If executions had a zero marginal effect, they could not be justified in deterrent terms. But even the pre-Ehrlich investigations did not demonstrate this. They merely found that an above-zero effect could not be demonstrated statistically. While we do not know at present the degree of confidence with which we can assign an above marginal deterrent effect to executions, we can be more confident than in the past. I should now regard it as irresponsible not to shorten the lives of convicted murderers simply because we cannot be altogether sure that their execution will lengthen the lives of innocent victims: It seems immoral to let convicted murderers survive at the probable—or even at the merely possible—expense of the lives of innocent victims who might have been spared had the murderers been executed.

In principle, one could experiment to test the hypothesis of zero marginal effect. The most direct way would be to legislate the death penalty for certain kinds of murder if committed, say, on weekdays, but never on Sunday. Or, on Monday, Wednesday, and Friday, and not on other days. (The days could be changed around every few years to avoid possible bias.) I am convinced there would be fewer murders on death-penalty than on life-imprisonment days. Unfortunately, the experiment faces formidable obstacles.[6]

Our penal system rests on the proposition that more severe penalties are more deterrent than less severe penalties. We assume, rightly, I believe, that a $5 fine deters rape less than a $500 fine, and that the threat of five years in prison will deter more than either fine.[7] This assumption of the penal system rests on the common experience that, once aware of them, people learn to avoid natural dangers the more likely these are to be injurious and the more severe the likely injuries. People endowed with ordinary common sense (a class which includes some sociologists) have found no reason why behavior with respect to legal dangers should differ from behavior with respect to natural dangers. Indeed, it does not. Hence, the legal system proportions threatened penalties to the gravity of crimes, both to do justice and to achieve deterrence in proportion to that gravity.

Thus, if it is true that the more severe the penalty the greater the deterrent effect, then the most severe penalty—the death penalty—would have the greatest deterrent effect. Arguments to the contrary assume either that capital crimes never are deterrable (sometimes merely because not all capital crimes have been deterred), or that, beyond some point, the deterrent effect of added severity is necessarily zero. Perhaps. But the burden of proof must be borne by those who presume to have located the point of zero marginal returns before the death penalty.

As an additional commonsense observation, I should add that without the death penalty, we necessarily confer immunity on just those persons most likely to be in need of deterrent threats. Thus, prisoners serving life sentences can kill fellow prisoners or guards with impunity. Prison wardens are unlikely to prevent violence in prisons as long as they give humane treatment to inmates and have no threats of additional punishment available for the murderers among them who are already serving life sentences. I cannot see the moral or utilitarian reasons for giving permanent immunity to homicidal life prisoners, thereby endangering the other prisoners and the guards, and in effect preferring the life prisoners to their victims.

Outside the prison context, an offender who expects a life sentence for his offense may murder his victim, or witnesses, or the arresting officer, to improve his chances of escaping. He could not be threatened with an additional penalty for his additional crime—an open invitation. Only the death penalty could deter in such cases. If there is but a possibility—and I believe there is a probability—that it will, we should retain it.

However, deterrence requires that the threat of the ultimate penalty be reserved for the ultimate crime. It may be prevented by that threat. Hence, the extreme punishment should never be prescribed when the offender, because already threatened by it, might add to his crimes with impunity. Thus, rape, or kidnapping, should not incur the death penalty, while killing the victim of either crime should. This may not stop an Eichmann after his first murder, but it will stop most people before. The range of punishments is not infinite; it is necessarily more restricted than the range of crimes. Since death is the ultimate penalty, it must be reserved for the ultimate crime.

Consider now some popular arguments against capital punishment.

According to Beccaria, with the death penalty the "laws which punish homicide . . . themselves commit it," thus giving "an example of barbarity." Those who speak of "legalized murder" use an oxymoronic phrase to echo this allegation. Legally imposed punishments such as fines, incarcerations, or executions, although often physically identical to the crimes punished, are not crimes or their moral equivalent. The difference between crimes and lawful acts is not physical, but legal. Driving a stolen car is a crime, although not physically different from driving a car you own. Unlawful imprisonment and kidnapping need not differ physically from the lawful arrest and incarceration used to punish unlawful imprisonment and kidnapping. Finally, whether a lawful punishment gives an "example of barbarity" depends on how the moral difference between crime and punishment is perceived. To suggest that its physical quality, ipso facto, morally disqualifies the punishment, is to assume what is to be shown.

It is possible that all displays of violence, criminal or punitive, influence people to engage in unlawful imitations. This seems one good reason not to have public executions. But it does not argue against executions. Objections to displaying on television the process of violently subduing a resistant offender do not argue against actually engaging in the process.[8] Arguments against the public display of vivisections, or the painful medications, do not argue against either. Arguments against the public display of sexual activity do not argue against sexual activity. Arguments against public executions, then, do not argue against executions.[9] While the deterrent effect of punishments depends on their being known, the deterrent effect does not depend on punishments being carried out publicly. For example, the threat of imprisonment deters, but incarcerated persons are not on public display.

Abolitionists often maintain that most capital crimes are "acts of passion" that (1) could not be restrained by the threat of the death penalty, and (2) do not deserve it morally even if other crimes might. It is not clear to me why a crime motivated by, say, sexual passion, is morally less deserving of punishment than one motivated by passion for money. Is the sexual passion morally more respectable than others? More gripping? More popular? Generally, is violence in personal conflicts morally more excusable than violence among people who do not know each other? A precarious case might be made for such a view, but I shall not attempt to make it.

Perhaps it is true, however, that many murders are irrational "acts of passion" that cannot be deterred by the threat of the death penalty. Either for this reason or because "crimes of passion" are thought less blameworthy than other homicides, most "crimes of passion" are not punishable by death now.[10]

But if most murders are irrational acts, it would seem that the traditional threat of the death penalty has succeeded in deterring most rational people, or most people when rational, from committing the threatened act, and that the fear of the penalty continues to deter all but those who cannot be deterred by any penalty. Hardly a reason for abolishing the death penalty. Indeed, that capital crimes are committed mostly by irrational persons and only by some rational ones would suggest that more might commit these crimes if the penalty were lower. This hardly argues against capital punishment. Else, we would have to abolish penalties whenever they succeed in deterring people. Yet, abolitionists urge that capital punishment be abolished because capital crimes are often committed by the irrational—as though deterring the rational is not quite enough.

Finally, some observations on an anecdote reported by Boswell and repeated ad nauseam. Dr. Johnson found pickpockets active in a crowd assembled to see one of their number hanged. He concluded that executions do not deter. His conclusion does not follow from his observation.

1. Since the penalty Johnson witnessed was what pickpockets had expected all along, they had no reason to reduce their activities. Deterrence is expected to increase only when penalties do.

2. At most, a public execution could have had the deterrent effect Dr. Johnson expected because of its visibility. But it may have had a contrary effect: The spectacle of execution was probably more fascinating to the crowd than other spectacles; public executions thus might distract attention from the activities of pickpockets and thereby increase their opportunities more than other spectacles would.

Hence, an execution crowd might have been more inviting to pickpockets than other crowds. (As mentioned before, deterrence depends on knowledge, but does not require visibility.)

3. Even when the penalty is greatly increased, let alone when it is unchanged, the deterrent effect of penalties is usually slight with respect to those already committed to criminal activities.[11] Deterrence is effective by restraining people as yet not committed to criminal occupation from entering it.

The risk of a penalty is the cost of crime offenders must expect. When this cost is high enough, relative to the expected benefit, it will deter a considerable number of people who would have entered an occupation—criminal or otherwise—had the cost been lower. In this respect, the effects of the costs of crime are not different from the effects of the cost of automobiles or movie tickets, or from the effects of the cost of any occupation relative to its benefits. When (comparative) net benefits decrease because of cost increases, the flow of new entrants does. But those already in the occupation usually continue.

4. Finally, Dr. Johnson did not actually address the question of the deterrent effect of execution in any respect whatever. To do so, he would have had to compare the number of pocket-picking episodes in the crowd assembled to witness the execution with the number of such episodes in a similar crowd assembled for some other purpose. He did not do so, probably because he thought that a deterrent effect occurs only if the crime is altogether eliminated. That is a common misunderstanding. Crime can only be reduced, not eliminated. However harsh the penalties, there are always nondeterrables. Thus, most people can be deterred, but never all.

One popular moral objection to capital punishment is that it gratifies the desire for revenge, regarded as unworthy. The Bible quotes the Lord declaring: "Vengeance is mine" (Romans 12:19). He thus legitimized vengeance and reserved it to Himself. However, the Bible also enjoins, "the murderer shall surely be put to death" (Numbers 35:16–18), recognizing that the death penalty can be warranted—whatever the motive. Religious tradition certainly suggests no less.[12]

The motives for the death penalty may indeed include vengeance. Vengeance as a compensatory and psychologically reparatory satisfaction for an injured party, group, or society, may be a legitimate human motive—despite the biblical injunction. I do not see wherein that motive is morally blameworthy. When regulated and directed by law, vengeance also is socially useful: Legal vengeance solidifies social solidarity against lawbreakers and is the alternative to the private revenge of those who feel harmed.

However, vengeance is irrelevant to the death penalty, which must be justified by its purpose, whatever the motive. An action, or rule, or penalty, is neither justified nor discredited by the motive for it. No rule should be discarded or regarded as morally wrong because of the motive of those who support it. Actions, or rules, or penalties, are justified by their intent and by their effectiveness in achieving it, not by the motives of supporters.[13] Capital punishment is warranted if it achieves its purpose: doing justice and deterring crime, regardless of whether it gratifies vengeful feelings.

We must examine now the specific characteristics of capital punishment before turning to its purely moral aspects. Capital punishment is feared above all punishments because (1) it is not merely irreversible as most other penalties are, but also irrevocable; (2) it hastens an event, which unlike pain, deprivation, or injury, is unique in every life and never has been reported on by anyone. Death is an experience that cannot actually be experienced and ends all experience.[14] Because it is as unknown as it is certain, death is universally feared. The fear of death is often attached to the penalty that hastens it—as though, without the penalty, death would not come. (3) When death is imposed as a deliberate punishment by one's fellow men, it signifies a complete severing of human solidarity. The convict is rejected by human society, found unworthy of sharing life with it. This total rejection exacerbates the natural separation anxiety and fear of annihilation. The marginal deterrent effect of executions depends on these characteristics, and the moral justification of the death penalty, above and beyond the deterrent effect, does no less.

Hitherto I have relied on logic and fact. Without relinquishing either, I must appeal to plausibility as well, as I turn to questions of morality unalloyed to other issues. For, whatever ancillary service facts and logic can render, what one is persuaded to accept as morally right or wrong ultimately depends on what seems to be plausible.

If there is nothing for the sake of which one may be put to death, can there be anything worth dying for? If there is nothing worth dying for, is there any moral value worth living for? Is a life that cannot be transcended by anything beyond itself more valuable than one that can be transcended? Is existence,

life, itself a moral value never to be given up for the sake of anything? Does a value system in which any life, however it is lived, becomes the highest of goods, enhance the value of human life or cheapen it? I shall content myself here with raising the questions.[15]

"The life of each man should be sacred to each other man," the ancients tell us. They unflinchingly executed murderers.[16] They realized it is not enough to proclaim the sacredness and inviolability of human life. It must be secured as well, by threatening with the loss of their own life those who violate what has been proclaimed as inviolable—the right of innocents to live. Else, the inviolability of human life is neither credibly proclaimed nor actually protected. No society can profess that the lives of its members are secure if those who did not allow innocent others to continue living are themselves allowed to continue living—at the expense of the community. Does it not cheapen human life to punish the murderer by incarcerating him as one does a pickpocket? Murder differs in quality from other crimes and deserves, therefore, a punishment that differs in quality from other punishments.

If it were shown that no punishment is more deterrent than a trivial fine, capital punishment for murder would remain just, even if not useful. For murder is not a trifling offense. Punishment must be proportioned to the gravity of the crime, if only to denounce it and to vindicate the importance of the norm violated. Thus, all penal systems proportion punishments to crimes. The worse the crime the higher the penalty deserved. Why not the highest penalty—death—for the worst crime—wanton murder? Those rejecting the death penalty have the burden of showing that no crime deserves capital punishment[17]—a burden which they have not so far been willing to bear.

Abolitionists are wrong when they insist that we all have an equally inalienable right to live to our natural term—that if the victim deserved to live, so does the murderer. That takes egalitarianism too far for my taste: The crime sets victim and murderer apart; if the victim died, the murderer does not deserve to live. The thought that there are some who think that murderers have as much right to live as their victims oppresses me. So does the thought that a Stalin or a Hitler should have the right to go on living.

Never to execute a wrongdoer, regardless of how depraved his acts, is to proclaim that no act can be so irredeemably vicious as to deserve death—that no human being can be wicked enough to be deprived of life. Who actually believes that? I find it easier to believe that those who affect such a view do so because of a failure of nerve. They do not think themselves—and therefore anyone else—competent to decide questions of life and death. Aware of human frailty they shudder at the gravity of the decision and refuse to make it. The irrevocability of a verdict of death is contrary to the modern spirit that likes to pretend that nothing ever is definitive, that everything is open-ended, that doubts must always be entertained and revisions made. Such an attitude may be proper for inquiring philosophers and scientists. But not for courts. They can evade decisions on life and death only by giving up their paramount duties: to do justice, to secure the lives of the citizens, and to vindicate the norms society holds inviolable.

One may object that the death penalty either cannot actually achieve the vindication of violated norms, or is not needed for it. If so, failure to inflict death does not belittle the crime, nor imply that the life of the criminal is of greater importance than the moral value he violated, or the harm he did to his victim. But it is not so. In all societies, the degree of social disapproval of wicked acts is expressed in the degree of punishment threatened.[18] Thus, punishments both proclaim and enforce social values according to the importance given to them. There is no other way for society to affirm its value. To refuse to punish any crime with death, then, is to avow that the negative weight of a crime can never exceed the positive value of the life of the person who committed it. I find that proposition implausible.

---

1. *Nor do I read the Constitution to command us to prefer equality to justice. Surely, "due process of law" is meant to do justice: and "the equal protection of the law" is meant to extend justice equally to all.*

2. *It seems odd that the courts, which have been willing to take a managerial role to remedy discrimination in schooling, should find no better remedy for discrimination or other errors in the distribution of penalties by the courts than to abolish the penalty distributed.*

3. *Ehrlich, "The Deterrent Effect of Capital Punishment: A Question of Life and Death," Amer. Econ. Rev. (June 1975). In the period studied, capital punishment was already infrequent and uncertain. Its deterrent effect might be greater when more frequently imposed for capital crimes, so that a prospective offender would feel more certain of it.*

4. *See Journal of Legal Studies (Jan. 1977); Journal of Political Economy (June 1977); and American Economic Review (June 1977).*

5. *I thought so even when I believed that the probability of deterrent effects might remain unknown. (See van den Haag, "On Deterrence and the Death Penalty," J. Crim. I.C. & P.S. (June 1969).) That probability is now more likely to become known and to be greater than was apparent a few years ago.*

6. *It would, however, isolate deterrent effects of the punishment from incapacitating ones, and also from the effect of Durkheimian "normative validation" where it does not depend on threats.*

7. *As indicated before, demonstrations are not available for the exact addition to deterrence of each added degree of severity in various circumstances, and with respect to various acts. We have so far coasted on a sea of plausible assumptions.*

8. *There is a good argument against unnecessary public displays of violence here. (See van den Haag, "What to Do About TV Violence," The Alternative (Aug./Sept. 1976).)*

9. *It may be noted that in Beccaria's time, executions were regarded as public entertainments. Tempora mutantur, et nos mutamur in illis.*

10. *I have reservations on both these counts, being convinced that many crimes among relatives and friends are as blameworthy and as deterrable as crimes among strangers. Thus, major heroin dealers in New York are threatened with life imprisonment. In the absence of the death penalty, they find it advantageous to have witnesses killed. Such murders surely are not acts of passion in the classical sense, although they occur among associates. They are in practice encouraged by the penal law.*

11. *The high degree of uncertainty and arbitrariness of penalization in Johnson's time may also have weakened deterrent effects. Witnessing an execution cannot correct this defect.*

12. *Since religion expects both justice and vengeance in the world to come, the faithful may dispense with either in this world, and with any particular penalties, although they seldom have. But a secular state must do justice here and now, it cannot assume that another power, elsewhere, will do justice where its courts did not.*

For that matter, Romans 12:19 barely precedes Romans 13:4, which tells us [the ruler] "beareth not the sword in vain for he is the minister of God, a revenger to execute wrath upon him that doeth evil." It is not unreasonable to interpret Romans 12:19 to mean that revenge is to be delegated by the injured to the authorities.

13. *Different motives (the reasons why something is done) may generate the same action (what is done), purpose, or intent, just as the same motive may lead to different actions.*

14. *Actually, being dead is no different from not being born, a (non)experience we all had before being born. But death is not so perceived. The process of dying, a quite different matter, is confused with it. In turn, dying is feared mainly because death is anticipated, even though death is feared because it is confused with dying.*

15. *Insofar as these questions are psychological, empirical evidence would not be irrelevant. But it is likely to be evaluated in terms depending on moral views.*

16. *Not always. On the disastrous consequences of periodic failure to do so, Sir Henry Maine waxes with eloquent sorrow in his Ancient Law 408–09.*

17. *One may argue that some crimes deserve more than execution, and that on the above reasoning, torture may be justified. But penalties have already been reduced to a few kinds—fines, confinement, and execution—so the issue is academic. Unlike the death penalty, torture also have become repulsive to us. (Some reasons for this public revulsion are listed in Chapter X [of] van den Haag, Punishing Criminals: Concerning a Very Old and Painful Question (1975).)*

18. *Social approval is usually less unanimous, and the system of rewards reflects it less.*

SHOULD WE EXECUTE THOSE WHO DESERVE TO DIE?*

Stephen Nathanson

Many people believe that murderers deserve to die and therefore that the state ought to execute them. I will call this reasoning the "argument from desert."

The argument from desert has very broad appeal, and death penalty opponents need to show that it is mistaken if their position is to be taken seriously. In order to show this, death penalty opponents must make a convincing case for the truth of at least one of the following statements:

1. *People who commit murder do not deserve to die.*
2. *Even if people who commit murder deserve to die, it is wrong for the state to execute them.*

If either one of these statements can be established, then the argument from desert fails.

I will try to show that both of these statements are true and therefore that the argument from desert does not provide a morally sound justification for the death penalty.

Giving People What They Deserve

In beginning our consideration of the argument from desert, let us assume that death penalty advocates are correct in asserting that murderers deserve to die. While it may appear that if we assume this, then the argument for the death penalty is unstoppable, this impression is mistaken. There is no inconsistency in conceding that murderers deserve to die and still opposing the death penalty. These two beliefs are consistent because there may be quite good reasons in particular cases why people should not get what they deserve. This is especially true when the body that is to give someone his just deserts is the government.

One reason for not giving a person what he deserves is that doing so conflicts with other obligations that one has. In chapter 2, I mentioned the brutalization hypothesis, according to which executions actually cause homicides. If this hypothesis is true, it provides the government with a powerful reason not to execute convicted murderers, even if they deserve to die. The reason is that the government's policy of giving murderers their just deserts would be carried out at the cost of having innocent people lose their lives. Faced with a choice between giving murderers what they deserve and protecting innocent lives, the government ought to choose protection of the innocent over execution of the guilty. It is more important to save innocent lives than to terminate guilty ones, and it is a more central function of government that it protect people's well-being than that it carry out the distribution of just deserts.

This example is somewhat hypothetical because the brutalization effect remains controversial and has not yet influenced governmental policy. In any case, there are many ways in which our legal system currently departs from a policy of giving people what they deserve. One such case is the prohibition of double jeopardy. Our system does not permit a person to be tried more than once for a particular crime. If he is tried and acquitted, that is the end of it.

Now imagine a case of a person who has been accused of murder. He is tried and acquitted, and as he leaves the courthouse, he tells reporters, "I did it, and I got away with it." If this person did commit the murder and if murderers deserve to die, then he deserves to die. Nonetheless, the government may not prosecute him again for this charge and may not punish him, even though, from a moral point of view, he deserves to die. In this case, the prohibition on double jeopardy outweighs whatever obligation there might be to give this person what he deserves.

Considering this situation, one could claim, of course, that it shows that the legal system is defective and that we ought to abolish the double jeopardy rule. There are good reasons, however, for retaining the prohibition of double jeopardy. It protects all citizens from continued threats and harassment by government officials. If we could always be brought back for retrial even though we had been acquitted of the crime in question, then we would be continually exposed to threats by unscrupulous officials. The double jeopardy rule provides a significant protection for all citizens, and it is wise to keep the rule, even if this means sometimes failing to give the guilty what they deserve.

If giving people what they deserve were the only function of the legal system, these problems would not arise. The design of our legal system incorporates other aims, however. We have already seen this in discussing the costs of capital punishment and the necessity for procedural safeguards surrounding its use. The effect of these multiple aims is that we must sometimes sacrifice the goal of giving people what they deserve in order to satisfy other goals of greater importance. So, even if one concedes that murderers deserve to die, one need not grant that the government ought to execute them. This is because executing them may conflict with other important goals or ideals.

Death penalty supporters might concede this point in principle but deny that any such conflicts arise with respect to the death penalty. The question we must answer, then, is whether there are significant legal or moral goals and ideals which conflict with the imposition of the death penalty.

Furman v. *Georgia*

The Eighth Amendment to the United States Constitution prohibits the use of cruel and unusual punishments, and in 1972, the Supreme Court decided that the death penalty, *as it was then administered,* was cruel and unusual.

While each justice wrote a separate opinion in *Furman* v. *Georgia,* the most significant argument that emerged against the death penalty was based on the view that the death penalty was imposed in an arbitrary manner. In a widely accepted analysis of the Court's action, Charles Black has written:

> *The decisive ground of the 1972 Furman case anti-capital punishment ruling—the ground persuasive to the marginal justices needed for a majority—was that, out of a large number of persons "eligible" in law for the punishment, a few were selected as if at random, by no stated (or perhaps statable) criteria, while all the rest suffered the lesser penalty of imprisonment.*[1]

In focusing, then, on how the death penalty was administered, the Court was not concerned with whether the actual executions were performed in a cruel and unusual manner. Rather, the justices were concerned with the procedures under which death penalty sentences were being determined, and they judged the punishment to be unacceptable because life and death decisions were being made in an arbitrary way.

In understanding the Court's reasoning, it is important to recall that current laws do not embody the judgment that all people guilty of homicide deserve to die. Some killings are not even called "murder," but are classified as manslaughter, usually because there was no intention to kill. Even among murders, the laws of many states distinguish between first and second degrees of murder. Only those guilty of first degree murder are eligible for the death penalty, and even among these, judges or juries may decide that their crimes were not sufficiently terrible to merit death. The aim of this system of classifications is to select those killings which are the very worst and to impose the death penalty only in these cases. Underlying this system, then, is the judgment that only those guilty of the worst murders deserve to die. Some people who murder deserve a lesser punishment.

The Court's complaint with the administration of the death penalty was that this system of grading punishments according to the crime was not working. Decisions concerning executions were being made arbitrarily and not on the basis of facts about the crime. This was happening because the law contained no clear criteria that juries could apply when deciding which murderers ought to be executed and which ought to be imprisoned. In the absence of clear criteria, these judgments were determined by legally irrelevant factors.

In explaining their positions, different justices on the Court emphasized different forms of arbitrariness. Justice Stewart objected to the random aspects of the sentencing process, explaining his objection as follows:

> *These death sentences are cruel and unusual in the same way that being struck by lightning is cruel and unusual. For of all the people convicted of rapes and murders in 1967 and 1968,* many just as reprehensible as these, *the petitioners are among* a capriciously selected random handful *upon whom the sentence has in fact been imposed.*[2]

In other words, there was no reasonable basis for the execution of these people and the imprisonment of others. Many were equally reprehensible, and so it was "cruel and unusual" to single out only a few for the severest punishment.

Other justices stressed a fact that had long been emphasized by death penalty opponents, its discriminatory application. According to them, the application of the death penalty was arbitrary but not entirely random. Rather, racial bias created a situation in which blacks were more likely to be executed than whites. In fact, prejudice had a significant double effect on sentencing, since blacks who killed whites were among those most likely to be executed, while whites who killed blacks were the least likely to be sentenced to die.[3] Similarly, economic and social status influenced these judgments in illegitimate ways. These were the arbitrary features stressed by Justice Douglas. As he wrote,

> *In a Nation committed to equal protection of the laws there is no permissible "caste" aspect of law enforcement. Yet we know that the discretion of judges and juries in imposing the death penalty enables the penalty to be selectively applied, feeding prejudices against the accused if he is poor and despised, and lacking political clout, or if he is a member of a suspect or unpopular minority, and saving those who by social position may be in a more protected position.*[4]

Douglas argued, then, that the death penalty was cruel and unusual because it was applied to people (or not applied to them) for reasons that were legally irrelevant and impermissible. It would violate the Constitution to have a law that permitted the execution only of poor people or members of racial minorities. Since this was how the death penalty was operating in fact, its use under those conditions was unconstitutional.

The Moral Basis of the *Furman* Decision

In considering these issues, the Supreme Court was treating them as matters of constitutional law. The question facing the Court was whether the arbitrary imposition of the death penalty made it unconstitutional. Nonetheless, the issues involved in the *Furman* case are not solely matters of constitutional law. For opponents of the death penalty, the pattern of arbitrary and discriminatory sentencing is itself a deplorable moral injustice. Even if these practices were permissible under the Constitution, they would still be morally unjust.

I believe that this moral condemnation is appropriate and that the Court's reasoning has moral as well as legal force. The *Furman* argument illuminates the true but paradoxical judgment that it can be morally unjust to punish someone for a crime even if he morally deserves to be punished.

In order to see that it can actually be unjust to give someone what he deserves, imagine a group of fifty people, all of whom have committed dreadful murders. Suppose that each one's act is so horrible that we would have no trouble concluding that each one deserved to die. In spite of this, however, only those with red hair are sentenced to die, while all others are given lesser sentences. In this situation, the red-headed murderers would certainly feel that they were being treated unjustly, and I think that they would be correct.

Even if a person deserves to die, that is not enough to make his execution just. In addition, it is necessary that he be executed *because* he deserves to die. In the case I have described, we cannot explain why the red-headed murderers were sentenced to die by saying that they deserved it. This explanation is insufficient because others who were equally deserving were not sentenced to die. So, if we try to explain the decision to execute some but not others, the explanation would be that they were people with red hair who had committed heinous murders. Yet, it is surely unjust to execute someone *because* he is a red-headed murderer rather than a blond or black-haired murderer. This would be cruel and unusual in the sense stressed by Douglas, since it would involve basing the degree of punishment on features of a person which are irrelevant. It is especially unjust if the punishment is determined by features of a person over which he has little or no control.

Even if we grant, then, that only those who deserve to die are ever sentenced to die, we would be forced to see the death penalty as unjust if its actual imposition depended on such factors as race, economic status, ability to acquire adequate legal representation, or other facts which have nothing to do with a person's culpability. That is the underlying moral argument of the *Furman* decision, and it is a powerful, important moral argument, even apart from its constitutional significance.

Eliminating Arbitrariness

The problem of arbitrariness has been addressed by death penalty supporters in two ways. After the *Furman* decision, state legislatures passed new laws that were designed to eliminate the influence of arbitrary features from death penalty impositions. Two strategies were pursued. In some states, the death penalty was made mandatory for certain types of crimes. Anyone convicted of them would be executed so that both randomness and discrimination could play no role. This strategy was rejected by the Supreme Court. In *Woodson* v. *North Carolina,* it ruled that mandatory death sentences were unconstitutional, since they failed to permit consideration of individual differences among defendants.[5]

The second legislative strategy was to leave room for judgment but to eliminate arbitrariness by providing specific guidelines for juries to follow in deciding on the appropriate sentence. This is the strategy of "guided discretion," under which the law leaves the final judgment to juries but specifics what kinds of reasons may be used in determining whether a particular murderer ought to be executed or imprisoned. Typically, these guidelines consist of lists of aggravating and mitigating circumstances, features of the crimes or persons that may make the crime worse or less bad. The new laws also included other procedural safeguards, such as automatic appeals or reviews of death sentences and separate sentencing hearings, which allow defendants to present additional factors on their behalf.

In its 1976 decision in *Gregg* v. *Georgia,* the Supreme Court ruled that statutes incorporating "guided discretion" and other safeguards were constitutional because they made arbitrariness sufficiently unlikely. In making this ruling, the Court did not reject the *Furman* argument that arbitrarily imposed executions are cruel and unusual. Rather, it claimed that arbitrariness had been sufficiently eliminated so as to guarantee fair proceedings and controlled, unbiased sentencing.

The Gregg decision has prompted death penalty opponents to argue that "guided discretion" is an illusion and that even under the new laws, sentences in capital cases continue to be arbitrary and discriminatory. I do not at this point want to consider the evidence for these claims. Instead, I simply want to point out that if these claims are correct, then the Court would be bound to return to its earlier judgment that the death penalty was unconstitutional. This is because the Court did not reject the argument that *if* the death penalty is arbitrarily administered, then it violates the Constitution. Instead, it decided that under the new laws, the death penalty would no longer be administered arbitrarily.

Against the Argument from Arbitrariness

Although death penalty supporters have tried to make death sentencing less arbitrary, some of them explicitly reject the use of the argument from arbitrariness as a criticism of the death penalty. While favoring fairer sentencing, they think that the Court was wrong to accept the argument from arbitrariness in the first place. They think that the death penalty can be just even if it is administered in an arbitrary and discriminatory way. For those who hold this position, evidence showing the continued influence of arbitrary and discriminatory factors would have no force because, in their view, it never was legally or morally relevant to the question of whether death is a just punishment.

This rejection of the argument from arbitrariness has been stated forcefully by Ernest van den Haag, a longtime defender of the death penalty. According to van den Haag,

> *the abolitionist argument from capriciousness, or discretion, or discrimination, would be more persuasive if it were alleged that those selectively executed are not guilty. But the argument merely maintains that some other guilty but more favored persons, or groups, escape the death penalty. This is hardly sufficient for letting anyone else found guilty escape the penalty. On the contrary, that some guilty persons*

or groups elude it argues for extending the death penalty to them.[6]

For van den Haag, the only injustice that occurs here is that some people who deserve death are not executed. In his opinion, however, the failure to execute these fortunate people does not show that it is unjust to execute others who are no more deserving of death but are simply less fortunate.

From van den Haag's point of view, the justice of punishments is entirely a matter of individual desert. As he writes:

> *Justice requires punishing the guilty—as many of the guilty as possible, even if only some can be punished—and sparing the innocent—as many of the innocent as possible, even if not all are spared. It would surely be wrong to treat everybody with equal injustice in preference to meting out justice at least to some. . . . [If] the death penalty is morally just,* however discriminatorily applied to only some of the guilty, *it does remain just* in each case *in which it is applied.*[7]

According to van den Haag, then, the justice of individual punishments depends on individual guilt alone and not on whether punishments are equally distributed among the class of guilty people.

Van den Haag's argument is important because it threatens to undermine the moral basis of the *Furman* decision. It dismisses as irrelevant the abolitionist argument that the death penalty is unjust because its use in the United States has been inextricably bound up with patterns of racial discrimination. Even if we find this history abhorrent, we may yet think that van den Haag's argument is plausible. Its plausibility derives from the fact that we believe that it is often legitimate to punish or reward people, even though we know that others who are equally deserving will not be punished or rewarded. Here are two cases where common sense appears to support van den Haag's view about the requirements of justice.

> *A. A driver is caught speeding, ticketed, and required to pay a fine. Although we know that the percentage of speeders who are actually punished is extremely small, we would probably regard it as a joke if the driver protested that he was being treated unjustly or if someone argued that no one should be fined for speeding unless all speeders were fined.*

> *B. A person performs a heroic act and receives a substantial reward, in addition to the respect and admiration of his fellow citizens. Because he deserves the reward, we think it just that he receive it, even though many equally heroic persons are not treated similarly. That most heroes are unsung is no reason to avoid rewarding this particular heroic individual.*

Both of these cases appear to support van den Haag's view that we should do justice in individual cases whenever we can and that our failure to treat people as they deserve in all cases provides no reason to withhold deserved punishment or reward from particular individuals. If this is correct, then we must give up the argument from arbitrariness and accept van den Haag's view that "unequal justice is justice still."

Arbitrary Decisions About Who Deserves What

In order to evaluate this objection to the argument from arbitrariness, we need to look at the original argument more closely. What a closer look reveals is that there is in fact more than one problem of arbitrariness. Van den Haag fails to take note of this, and for this reason, his discussion leaves untouched many of the central issues raised by the argument.

We need to distinguish two different arguments, which I will call the argument from arbitrary judgment and the argument from arbitrary imposition. In making this distinction, I do not mean to contrast two stages in the actual legal process. Rather, the contrast is meant to help us focus on two different grounds for the claim that the death penalty is unjust because arbitrary.

Van den Haag assumes that judges and juries can and do make nonarbitrary judgments about what people deserve and that the problem of arbitrariness arises only in the imposition of punishments. For him, the arbitrariness arises when we try to determine who among those who deserve to die will actually be executed. This is what I want to call the argument from arbitrary imposition. It assumes that we know who deserves to die, and it objects to the fact that only some of those who deserve to die are executed. This version of the argument is expressed by Justice Stewart in the passage which I quoted earlier, and it is this argument which van den Haag addresses.

In doing so, however, he completely neglects the argument from arbitrary judgment. According to this argument, the determination of *who* deserves to die is itself arbitrary. It is not simply that arbitrary factors determine who among the deserving will be condemned to die. Rather, the problem is that the judgment concerning who deserves to die is itself a product of arbitrary factors. In other words, van den Haag assumes that we know who the deserving are, but this is just the assumption that the second form of the argument challenges.

Charles Black is clearly drawing our attention to the problem of arbitrary judgment when he writes that

> *the official choices—by prosecutors, judges, juries, and governors—that divide those who are to die from those who are to live are on the whole not made, and cannot be made, under standards that are consistently meaningful and clear, but . . . they are often made, and in the foreseeable future will continue to be made, under no standards at all or under pseudo-standards without discoverable meaning.*[8]

If Black is correct, judgments about who deserves a particular punishment are arbitrary because the law does not contain meaningful standards for distinguishing those who deserve death from those who deserve imprisonment. Given this lack of standards, factors that should have no influence will in fact be the primary bases of decision.

This important argument is completely neglected by van den Haag. In order to defend the death penalty against this criticism, he would have to show that our laws contain adequate criteria for deciding whether people deserve death or imprisonment and that judges and juries have made judgments of desert in a nonarbitrary way. Van den Haag makes no effort to do this. He simply assumes that the legal system does a good job of distinguishing those who deserve to die from those who do not. This, however, is just what the argument from arbitrary judgment challenges.

Van den Haag's assumption may gain plausibility from his tendency to oversimplify the kinds of judgments that need to be made. In contrast with Black, who stresses the complexity of the law of homicide and the many steps in the legal process leading toward punishment, van den Haag is content with the abstract maxim that "justice requires punishing the guilty . . . and sparing the innocent." This maxim makes it look as if officials and jurors are faced with the simple choice of dividing people into two neat categories, the guilty and the innocent. And if we think of these as *factual* rather than *legal* categories, it makes it look as if the only judgment that they must make is whether one person did or did not kill another.

In fact, of course, the judgments that must be made are much more complicated than this. To be guilty of a murder that merits the death penalty is not the same as having killed another person. While the basic factual judgment that one person has caused the death of another is itself not always easy to make, the legal judgments involved are more complex still. Of those who kill, some may have committed no crime at all if their action is judged to be justifiable homicide. For those guilty of some form of homicide, we need to decide how to classify their act within the degrees of homicide. What did the killer intend to do? Was he under duress? Was he provoked by the victim? Did he act with malice? Had the act been planned or was it spontaneous? These are among the factual issues that arise when juries try to determine the legal status of the action. Beyond these are legal questions. Was the act murder or manslaughter? And if it was murder, was it first or second degree murder? And if it was first degree murder, did any of the mitigating or aggravating circumstances characterize the act? These are the sorts of issues that actually confront prosecutors, juries, and judges, and they go well beyond the more familiar "whodunit" types of questions.[9]

If prosecutors, juries, and judges do not have clear criteria by which to sort out these issues or if the criteria can be neglected in practice, then judgments about who deserves to face death rather than imprisonment will be arbitrary. This would undermine van den Haag's optimistic assumption that it is only those who genuinely deserve execution who are sentenced to die.

In stressing the complexities of the judgments involved, I have tried to show why it is plausible to believe that the resulting judgments could well be influenced by arbitrary factors. Further, I assume that if we are not confident that the death penalty is imposed on those who truly deserve it, then we would reject the punishment as unjust. This is the moral force of the argument from arbitrary judgment. Even if those who deserve to die ought to be executed, we ought not to allow the state to execute them if the procedures adopted by the state are unlikely to separate the deserving from the undeserving in a rational and just manner. History supports the view that the death penalty has been imposed on those who are less favored for reasons which have nothing to do with their crimes. The judgment that they deserved to die has often been the result of prejudice, and their executions were unjust for this reason.[10]

Is the System Still Arbitrary?

One may wonder, however, whether this sort of arbitrary judgment is still occurring in the administration of the death penalty. Is there any evidence for the continued presence of this form of arbitrariness? Didn't the Supreme Court's Gregg decision show that this sort of arbitrariness is no longer a problem?

To decide whether the problem of arbitrariness remains, one could either examine the new laws themselves to see whether the criteria for selecting those who deserve death are clear and adequate, or one could study the actual legal process and its results to see what factors play a role in leading to actual sentences. Both types of investigations have been carried out, and the case for continuing arbitrariness and discrimination is quite strong. Since my primary purpose here is to show that the existence of arbitrariness is morally relevant to our assessment of the death penalty, I will mention only a few points that indicate that the system remains flawed by arbitrariness. Others have made the case for the persistence of arbitrariness with force and in great detail.[11]

In his book *Capital Punishment: The Inevitability of Caprice and Mistake,* Charles Black shows how unclear are the lists of mitigating and aggravating circumstances which are supposed to guide juries in their sentencing decisions. His purely legal analysis is strongly supported by evidence about the actual workings of the system. In a study of sentencing under the new post-*Furman* laws, William Bowers and Glen Pierce found strong evidence of continued and systematic racial discrimination in the process leading to a sentence of death. I will mention just a few items from their study.

Under the new laws, as they were applied between 1972 and 1977, the highest probability of a death sentence was found to occur in those cases where the killer was black and the victim white. The lowest probability of execution was found where the victim was black and the killer white. This same pattern emerged in a study by William Bowers and Glen Pierce of sentencing in Florida, Georgia, Texas, and Ohio. In Ohio and Florida during this period, there were 127 cases of whites killing blacks, and not one of these murderers was sentenced to death. At the same time, blacks who killed whites in these states had about a 25 percent chance of receiving a death sentence.[12]

The following chart, taken from the Bowers and Pierce study, shows the relationship between the races of victims and killers and the probability of a death sentence as this was exhibited in Ohio between 1974 and 1977.

RACIAL GROUPING	TOTAL	DEATH SENTENCES	DEATH SENTENCE PROBABILITY
Black kills white	173	44	.254
White kills white	803	37	.046
Black kills black	1170	20	.017
White kills black	47	0	.000

These findings strongly suggest that judgments about the seriousness of crimes and the amount of blameworthiness attaching to criminals are strongly influenced by deep-seated racial prejudices. It appears that judges and juries regard the killing of a white by a black as a more serious crime than the killing of a black by a white. Thus, they judge that blacks killing whites deserve more severe punishments than whites killing blacks. Given the bluntness of our ordinary moral judgments and the deep roots of racial prejudice in our society, it is perhaps not surprising that these results occur. But it is clear that no law which embodied these criteria, grading crimes by the race of victims and offenders, would be constitutional. Yet the administration of our laws reveals the de facto operation of just these discriminatory criteria.

Whatever role the criteria for assessing murders play, they do not effectively prevent the operation of discriminatory influences, and so they fail to eliminate the arbitrariness which the *Furman* ruling condemned. Rather than genuinely guiding judgments, the lists of mitigating and aggravating circumstances seem only to provide the language by which juries can justify judgments made on other grounds. This view is further supported by other data in the Bowers and Pierce study. If one compares the Florida and Georgia death penalty statutes, the following difference emerges. In Georgia, the law lists ten aggravating circumstances. If a jury finds one of these circumstances characterizing a particular murder, it can recommend death, and the judge *must* accept their recommendation. In Florida, eight aggravating circumstances are listed, and the jury must determine that aggravating circumstances outweigh mitigating ones. On this basis, they can recommend death, but the judge need not accept their judgment.

As a result of these differences, Florida juries must find more aggravating circumstances to support a recommendation of death than do Georgia juries. It is plausible to suppose that murders in Florida and Georgia do not themselves differ in systematic ways. If jury judgments about aggravating circumstances differ systematically, that would suggest that judgments about whether the defendant ought to be executed are made independently of the criteria and then fitted to the criteria in order to provide a legal rationalization for the decision. In particular, while it is implausible to suppose that murders committed in Florida are objectively worse than those committed in Georgia, we might expect to find that juries discover more aggravating circumstances in Florida so as to justify their independent conviction that a particular individual deserves to die.

This is just what Bowers and Pierce found. While juries in Georgia found 46 percent of the murders they considered to be especially vile or heinous, Florida juries found these features in 89 percent of the murders they judged. Likewise, while Georgia juries found the factor of "risk to others" in only 1 percent of the cases facing them, Florida juries found that 28 percent of their murders involved a risk to the lives of others beyond the victim. Similar results are found in all but one of the categories compared, further confirming the judgment that "guided discretion" remains a rather unguided and arbitrary process. The criteria function more as rationalizations of sentencing decisions than as determinants of them.

Finally, while there are many stages in the legal process leading to an execution, the Supreme Court's decision in Gregg focused only on the question of whether juries were provided with adequate guidelines in capital cases. It is important to recall, however, that important decisions are made by prosecutors, judges, governors, and clemency boards as well. The case of prosecutors is especially important and instructive. Prosecutors must decide what charges to file, whether to try to convict a person of manslaughter or murder and whether to press for the death penalty. In making these decisions, they often consider how good a chance they have of winning a case. This does not seem unreasonable, but it is easy to see how this could perpetuate and play upon racial and other prejudices. The black defendant or killer of a white victim may be more likely to be charged with first degree murder in the first place because the prosecutor expects to find a jury that is less sympathetic to these defendants.[13] In many cases, those who are already disadvantaged in society have a greater chance of being charged with more serious crimes, while others more fortunate never face a life or death judgment from a jury because their killing has been classified as manslaughter by the prosecutor. The process is unjustly discriminatory and is arbitrary as well because the judgment is not based on a notion of what the defendant deserves. It is based on a calculation of success or failure in court, which is itself influenced by factors which ought to play no role in the legal process.

Conclusions

In this chapter, we have seen that the system of capital punishment does not operate so as to execute people only on the basis of what they deserve. Other arbitrary factors play a significant role in determining who is to die for killing another human being. In *Furman* v. *Georgia*, the Supreme Court recognized that an injustice could occur even in cases where a person who is condemned to die actually deserves that punishment. I have tried to explain the moral basis for considering this an injustice.

I have also considered the objection that arbitrariness is irrelevant because justice requires only that those who are punished deserve it. How others are treated is irrelevant. In replying to this objection, I noted the importance of distinguishing two forms of the argument from arbitrariness—the argument from arbitrary judgment and the argument from arbitrary imposition. What I have tried to show is that van den Haag neglects the argument from arbitrary judgment and assumes that all those who are sentenced to die deserve this treatment. This optimistic assumption is unfounded, however, and I have cited some of the evidence that death sentences remain arbitrary and discriminatory in spite of the guided discretion system which the Supreme Court approved in *Gregg* v. *Georgia* and has upheld in subsequent decisions.

I should note that although much of the arbitrariness I have discussed arises from patterns of racial prejudice in the United States, this argument is not only relevant to the death penalty in our society. There is nothing unique about the situation in which societies contain both favored and unfavored groups. The groups may be identified by race, religion, class, political orientation, or other features. Wherever these divisions exist, arbitrariness and discrimination will be obstacles to the just administration of the law.

1. Capital Punishment: The Inevitability of Caprice and Mistake, 2d ed. (New York: Norton, 1981), 20.

2. From Furman v. Georgia, 408 U.S. 239 (1972); reprinted in H. Bedau, The Death Penalty in America, 3d ed. (New York: Oxford University Press, 1982), 263–64; emphasis added.

3. For extensive evidence of racial discrimination in the imposition of the death penalty, see W. Bowers, Legal Homicide (Boston: Northeastern University Press, 1984), chs. 3 and 7.

4. Reprinted in Bedau, 3d ed., 255.

5. 428 U.S. 280–324 (1976); excerpted in Bedau, 3d ed., 288–293.

6. "The Collapse of the Case Against Capital Punishment," National Review, March 31, 1978, 397. A briefer version of this paper appeared in the Criminal Law Bulletin 14 (1978): 51–68 and is reprinted in Bedau, 3d ed., 323–33.

7. Ibid., emphasis added.

8. Black, 29.

9. For an interesting account of a case in which classification problems emerge quite vividly, see Steven Phillips, No Heroes, No Villains (New York: Random House, 1977).

10. For historical material about the United States, see William Bowers, Legal Homicide, part I.

11. For this evidence, see Charles Black, Capital Punishment, passim; William Bowers and Glen Pierce, "Racial Discrimination and Criminal Homicide under Post-Furman Statutes," in W. Bowers, Legal Homicide, ch. 7, and reprinted in Bedau, 3d ed., 206–23; Ursula Bentele, "The Death Penalty in Georgia: Still Arbitrary," Washington University Law Quarterly 62 (1985): 573–646; and Samuel Gross and Robert Mauro, "Patterns of Death: An Analysis of Racial Disparities in Capital Sentencing and Homicide Victimization," Stanford Law Review 37 (1984): 27–153.

12. For a chart showing these figures in full, see Bowers, 225; reprinted in Bedau, 3d ed., 213.

13. On this point, see Bentele, 615.